Data Analysis Skills

We work with leading authors to develop the strongest educational materials bringing cutting-edge thinking and best learning practice to a global market.

Under a range of well-known imprints, including Financial Times/Prentice Hall, Addison Wesley and Longman, we craft high quality print and electronic publications which help readers to understand and apply their content, whether studying or at work.

Pearson Custom Publishing enables our customers to access a wide and expanding range of market-leading content from world-renowned authors and develop their own tailor-made book. You choose the content that meets your needs and Pearson Custom Publishing produces a high-quality printed book.

To find out more about custom publishing, visit www.pearsoncustom.co.uk

A Pearson Custom Publication

Data Analysis Skills

Compiled from:

Microsoft® Office Excel 2007 In Business, Comprehensive
by Joseph M. Manzo

Research Methods for Business Students
Fifth Edition
by Mark Saunders, Philip Lewis and Adrian Thornhill

Pearson Education Limited
Edinburgh Gate
Harlow
Essex CM20 2JE

And associated companies throughout the world

Visit us on the World Wide Web at:
www.pearsoned.co.uk

First published 2011

Compiled from:

Microsoft® Office Excel 2007 In Business, Comprehensive
by Joseph M. Manzo
ISBN 978 0 13 199171 2

Research Methods for Business Students Fifth Edition
by Mark Saunders, Philip Lewis and Adrian Thornhill
ISBN 978 0 273 71686 0

ISBN 978 0 85776 044 9

Printed and bound in Great Britain by Hobbs the Printers Limited, Totton, Hants.

Contents

Section One

Excel Labs

Introduction & Basic Operations

Chapter 1

Introduction

Chapter Goals

Few software programs have elevated the importance of desktop computers for business managers as much as Microsoft Excel. Similar to the way they use e-mail, business managers use Excel every day to accomplish their daily routines and objectives. This chapter provides a general overview of Excel and the reasons it is such a vital tool for business managers. The rest of the chapters in this text will illustrate how Excel is used to complete business objectives in fields that include, but are not limited to, marketing, transportation, finance, manufacturing, and accounting. It is important to note the basic terminology covered in this chapter because it will be referenced throughout the text.

Excel Skill Sets

What Is Excel?

- Why Are We Here?
- A Decision-Making Tool
- An Overview of Excel
- Ribbons, Tabs, and Icons
- The File Menu
- Excel 97–2003 File Format
- Right Click and Control Keys
- Settings and Status Bar
- Excel Help

Excel in Practice | Anecdote

Excel in Business

Over the course of my career, I have experienced how information systems have changed the ways in which business professionals manage data and make decisions. I am often amazed when I think back to the beginning of my career and remember the analytical projects I used to do on paper. Doing these same projects on paper today would be unthinkable. Excel played a significant role in this transformation. In fact, the ways in which I used Excel throughout my career seemed to grow every year. I initially used Excel once in a while to project the monthly sales of my department. However, it was not long before I was using Excel every day to complete objectives such as managing inventory, tracking orders, communicating production plans, or developing sales strategies.

Throughout this text I will be using this anecdote section to share my professional experiences and explain how I use Excel to make decisions, analyze data, or communicate information in business. I have used Excel to complete business objectives in industries such as fashion, grocery, food, toys, finance, and technology. At the beginning of each chapter, I will share an experience describing how I used Excel to manage or complete a specific business objective. At the end of each chapter, you will have an opportunity to use Excel to complete a similar business objective. These are all real business objectives and situations that actually happened in my career, and you may be faced with these same objectives at some point in your own career.

>> **Continued on page 19**

What Is Excel?

Skill Set

The focus of this text will be to illustrate how you can use Excel to complete a variety of business objectives. However, it is important to understand why Excel was created and the need it fulfills for business managers. In addition, you will need a basic understanding of the ways commands and features are accessed and activated. This section provides a fundamental definition of Excel and illustrates its basic functionality.

Why Are We Here?

In its most basic form, Excel is an electronic version of a paper ***spreadsheet***. The primary use of any spreadsheet is to record numeric and text ***data*** for the purposes of making calculations, analyzing results, or tracking and storing information. As mentioned in the anecdote, before the use of electronic spreadsheets such as Excel, spreadsheets were created by hand on paper. Figure 1.1 shows an example of a paper spreadsheet. Notice that it consists of numbered columns and rows. Each digit of a number is written in a separate rectangle on the spreadsheet. An Excel spreadsheet has a similar purpose and design.

Figure 1.1 | **Example of Paper Spreadsheet**

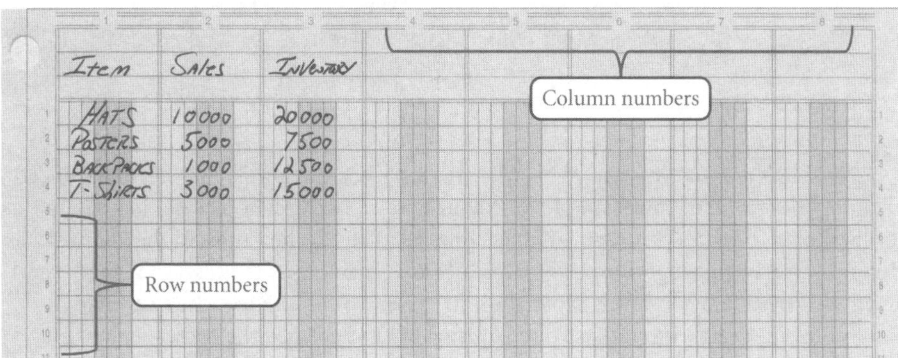

Figure 1.2 shows an example of a sales analysis project for 100 items sold in a small retail store. Because this project was done on a paper spreadsheet, the sales results for all 100 items are written by hand. In addition, a cumulative total is added in the second column to show the total after adding the sales results for each item. As a result, 100 calculations were performed using a calculator and added to the spreadsheet by hand. Just think how long it would take to write 100 numbers and make 100 calculations for this simple project.

Figure 1.2 | **Sales Project Done on Paper Spreadsheet**

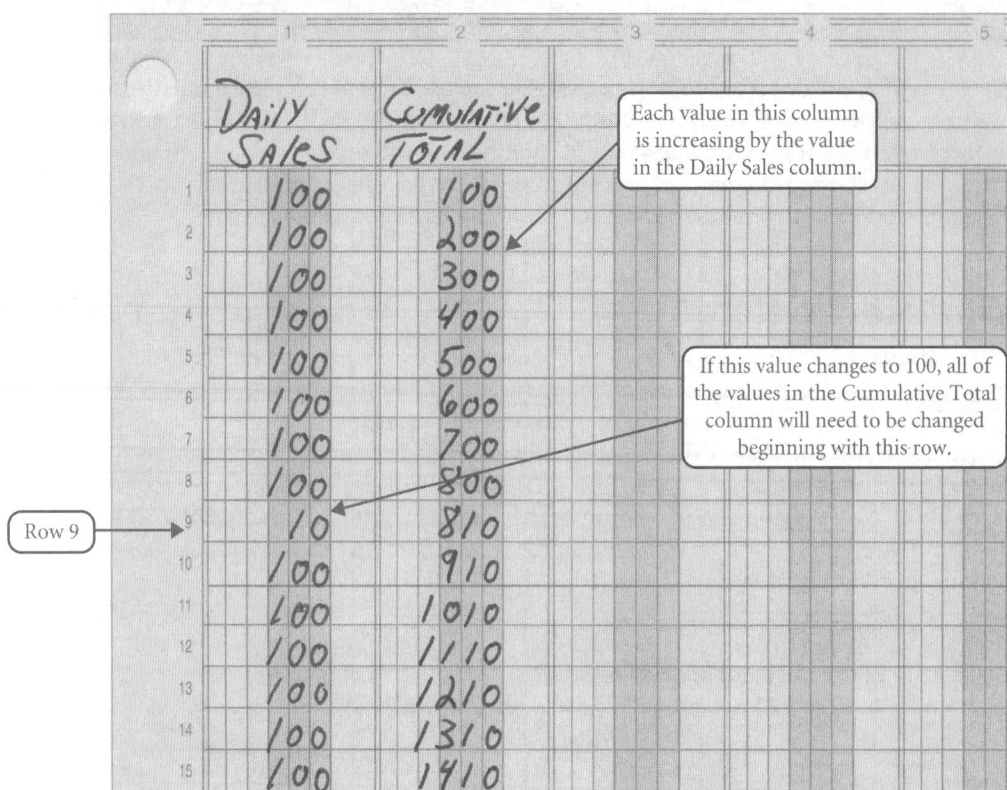

Now, let's assume you completed the spreadsheet shown in Figure 1.2 and noticed that the sales result in row 9 should be 100 instead of 10. After you erase this mistake and write the correct entry, you will have to recalculate all the values in the Cumulative Total column beginning with row 9. This means you will have to erase, recalculate, and rewrite 92 numbers. However, if you did this same project in Excel, the Cumulative Total column would automatically be adjusted after you typed the correct value into row 9. In fact, an Excel spreadsheet could be created such that if any of the numbers in your project are changed, all computations will automatically produce new outputs in a fraction of a second. This is what makes Excel extremely valuable for making business decisions and sets it apart from a paper spreadsheet.

Figure 1.3 shows how the project in Figure 1.2 appears in Excel. Notice that the column and row configuration are similar to the paper spreadsheet. However, letters are used to label each column instead of numbers.

Figure 1.3 | **Example of Project in an Excel Spreadsheet**

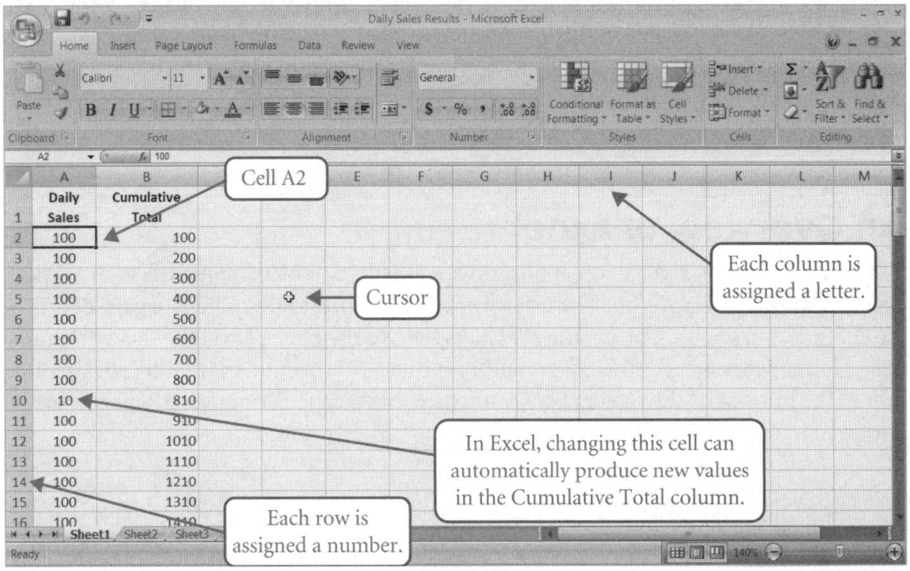

Another similarity between Figures 1.2 and 1.3 is that both spreadsheets are filled with small rectangles. In Excel, these rectangles are known as ***cells***, which is the intersection of a row and column. Data is typed into these cells as opposed to being handwritten, as shown in Figure 1.2. Each cell has a specific address called the ***cell location***, which is the column letter followed by the row number. In Figure 1.3, cell location A2 is activated. This is called cell *A2* because it is in column A and row 2.

Cell locations play a critical role when calculating data in Excel. If you were conducting mathematical computations using a calculator, you would enter numbers and mathematical operators to produce a result. With Excel, you will usually use cell locations, such as A2, instead of numbers when conducting the same mathematical computations. If the number in cell A2 is changed, Excel will automatically produce a new output. This is called ***cell referencing***, and it is this concept that gives Excel its power. You will learn more details about mathematical computations in Chapter 3.

A Decision-Making Tool

Business managers are often required to make numerous decisions in uncertain environments. These decisions can range from buying a publicly traded stock to calculating how many pairs of jeans to buy for a clothing store. In making these decisions, a business manager might ask questions such as "What if the stock market declines after buying a particular stock?" or "What if I don't buy enough jeans to satisfy the sales potential of a store?" These questions form the basis of ***what-if scenarios***. Business managers use what-if scenarios to understand how potential outcomes will impact the decisions they make. For example, a business manager who is buying a publicly traded stock might calculate how much he stands to lose if the stock declines 5%, 10%, or 20%. On the other hand, he could also calculate how much he could gain if the stock increases 5%, 10%, or 20%. Calculating these declines and increases equates to a total of six possible scenarios or outcomes to consider before making this decision. This manager could use Excel to calculate the results of each scenario by simply changing one number.

Most business executives would agree that information is power. Excel can be used to produce and evaluate far more information over a shorter period of time compared to paper spreadsheets. This fulfills a critical need for business managers to make informed decisions, which is usually a prerequisite for completing most business objectives. A variety of these objectives will be examined throughout this text as commands and applications are reviewed in each chapter.

An Overview of Excel

When you first launch the Excel application, you will see a blank spreadsheet or worksheet, as shown in Figure 1.4. The term ***worksheet*** is used to describe one page of an Excel file or workbook. The term ***workbook*** refers to the entire Excel file that contains a collection of worksheets. You can switch from one worksheet to another by clicking the tabs at the bottom of the screen. Each worksheet has a capacity of over 1 million rows and over 16,000 columns.

Figure 1.4 | **Blank Excel Worksheet**

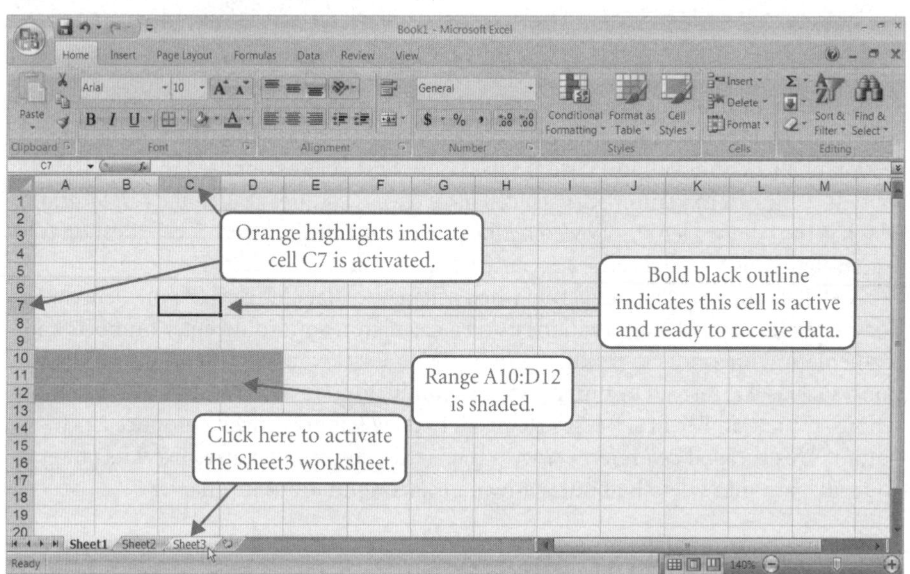

As shown in Figure 1.4, the highlighted column letter and row number indicate which cell is currently active. Notice that column letter C and row number 7 are highlighted in orange, indicating that cell C7 is active and ready to receive data. The cell is also outlined with a bold black line, which also indicates it is active. To activate other cells, use the arrow keys on your keyboard to move the black outline or move the cursor with the mouse and left click on a cell. You also can use your mouse to activate several cells or a range of cells at one time by left clicking and dragging. The term ***range*** refers to a group of cells on a worksheet and is noted by any two cell locations separated by a colon. For example, Figure 1.4 shows the range A10:D12 highlighted.

Ribbon, Tabs, and Icons

Excel commands and features are contained in the area at the top of the screen called the ***Ribbon***. As shown in Figure 1.5, the Ribbon consists of several ***icons*** arranged in related groups that are used to activate any Excel command. For example, the **Number** group of icons is used to format any numbers that are typed into the cells of a worksheet. If you are familiar with Microsoft Word, you already know how to use many of these icons. For example, Excel icons such as **Save**, **Copy**, **Paste**, and **Bold** are identical to Word's icons.

Along the top of the Ribbon are several ***tabs***. Each tab opens a separate page of the Ribbon that contains a different set of icons. Additional tabs will automatically be added to the Ribbon if you are working with special objects such as charts or text boxes. You will learn how to use the commands in each tab of the Ribbon throughout this text. The following is a brief description for each of the tabs shown in Figure 1.5:

- **Home**: Contains fundamental commands that are most frequently used when working in Excel. Commonly used icons such as **Copy** and **Paste** as well as formatting icons such as **Bold** and **Italics** are found in this tab.
- **Insert**: Contains commands used when inserting objects such as charts, circles, or arrows onto a worksheet.
- **Page Layout**: Provides access to commands used to prepare a worksheet for printing.
- **Formulas**: Provides access to mathematical functions and formula auditing tools.
- **Data**: Provides access to sorting commands. In addition, this tab contains features used to import data from external sources such as Microsoft Access.
- **Review**: Provides access to commands such as Spell Check and Track Changes.
- **View**: Contains commands used for adjusting the visual appearance of your Excel screen. For example, this tab contains the **Zoom** icon, which is identical to the **Zoom** icon in Microsoft Word.

Figure 1.5 shows icons that are contained in the **Home** tab of the Ribbon. Notice that when the cursor is placed over the **Copy** icon, a description of the command appears on the worksheet.

Figure 1.5 | **The Home Tab of the Ribbon**

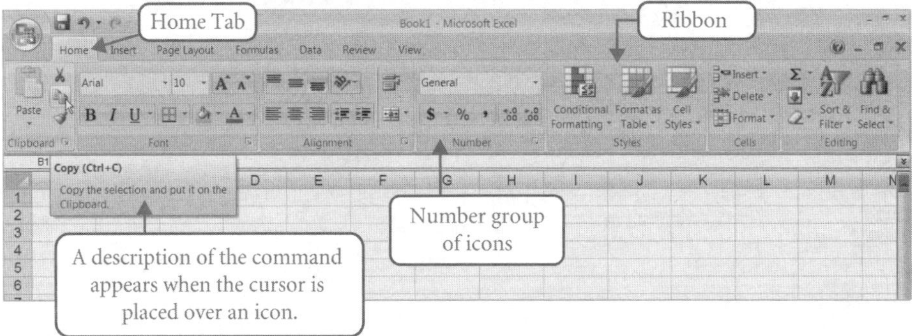

In addition to using the Ribbon, you can also access Excel commands through the ***Quick Access Toolbar***. The **Quick Access Toolbar** contains a few commonly used icons such as **Save** and **Undo**. As you can see in Figure 1.6, you can add additional icons by clicking the down arrow on the right side of the toolbar and selecting one of the commands listed in the menu or by clicking the **More Commands** option.

Figure 1.6 | **The Quick Access Toolbar**

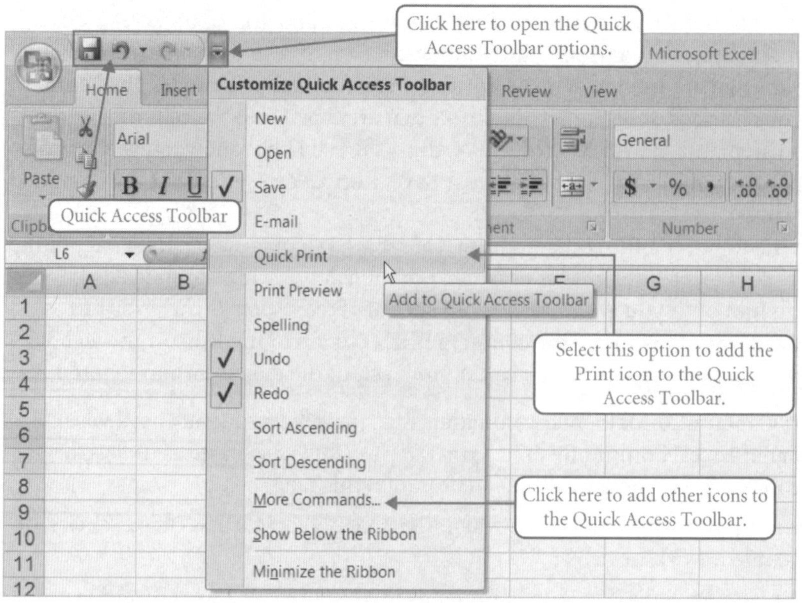

The File Menu

If you have worked with previous versions of Microsoft Excel, such as Microsoft Excel 2003, you may have noticed that something was missing when you first looked at Figure 1.3. There are no drop-down menus. The drop-down menus have been replaced with the Ribbon system, which provides faster access to the commands you need. However, one drop-down menu does exist in this version of Excel: The **File** menu. The file menu is opened by clicking the **Office Button** as shown in figure 1.7. Use the **File** menu for executing tasks such as opening existing Excel workbooks, creating new workbooks, or printing worksheets. Figure 1.7 shows the commands that are available in the **File** menu.

Figure 1.7 | **Commands in the File Menu**

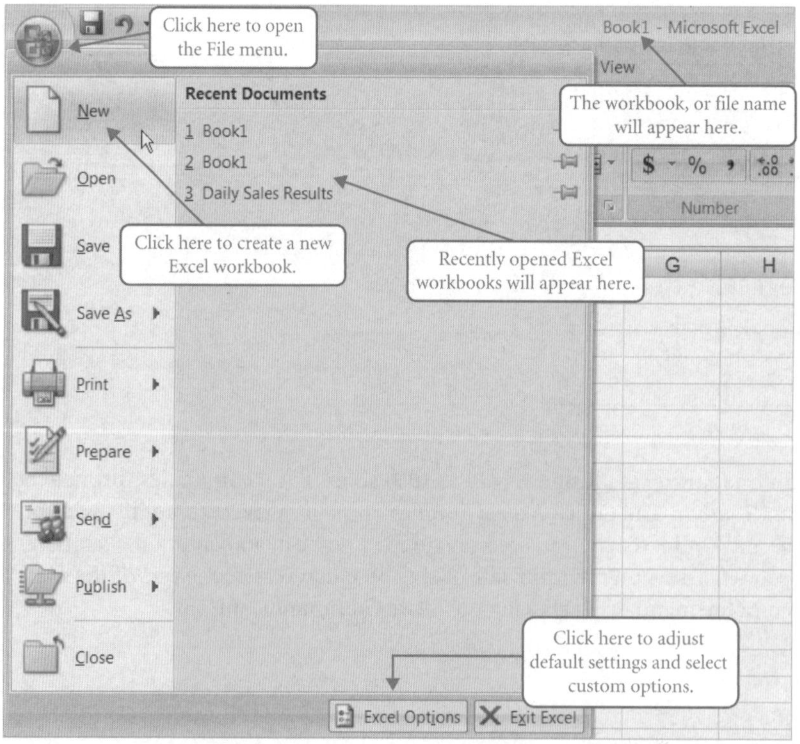

Excel 97-2003 File Format

It is important to note that the **Save As** command is found in the **File** menu. If you are working with people who are using older versions of Microsoft Excel, you will need to save your workbooks in the Excel 97–2003 format. Someone who is using Microsoft Office 2003 will not be able to open workbooks saved in the 2007 format. You save files in this format as follows:

- Open an existing Excel workbook or create a new one (see Figure 1.7).
- Click the **Office Button**.
- Click the arrow pointing to the right next to the **Save As** option.
- Select the **Excel 97-2003 Workbook** option on the right side of the **File** menu (see Figure 1.8).

Figure 1.8 shows an Excel workbook that has been saved in the Excel 97–2003 format. Notice at the top of the Excel screen the words **[Compatibility Mode]** appear next to the workbook name. This naming convention indicates that the workbook is compatible with older versions of Excel. In addition, notice that the **Convert** option appears in the **File** menu list of options. Select this option to convert a workbook saved in an older version of Excel to the 2007 version.

Figure 1.8 | **Saving a Workbook in Excel 97–2003 Format**

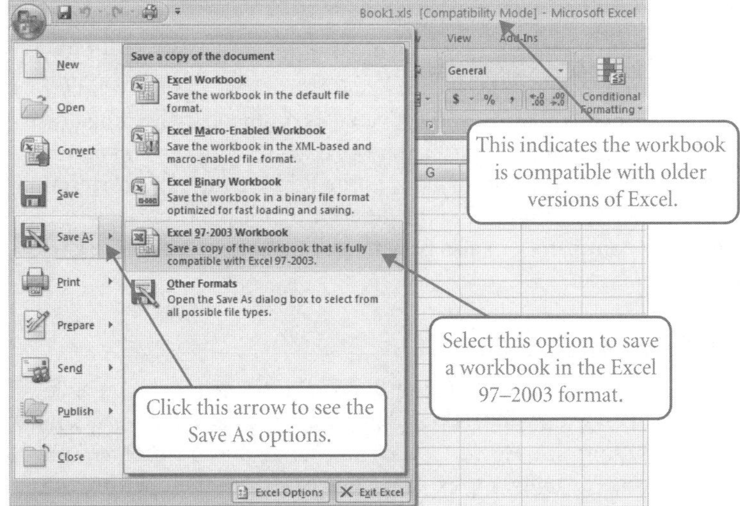

COMMON MISTAKES | Opening Excel 2007 Workbooks

You will not be able to open an Excel 2007 workbook using Excel 2003 or other prior versions of Excel. Excel workbooks with the .xlsx file extension can be opened only in the 2007 version of Microsoft Office. You must convert or save these workbooks using the Excel 97–2003 format to open them using an older version of Excel.

Right Click and Control Keys

If you have experience using older versions of Excel, you may be accustomed to accessing commands by right clicking or using Control keys. Both options are available in the 2007 version of Excel.

Right clicking provides you with the option of accessing a variety of commands without having to go to the Ribbon. As previously mentioned, older versions of Excel utilized a system of drop-down menus to access various Excel commands. Depending on the command you needed, you may have clicked through several drop-down menus

Quick Reference

Saving in Excel 97-2003 File Format

1. Open an existing Excel workbook or create a new one.
2. Click the **Office Button**.
3. Click the arrow to the right of the **Save As** option.
4. Click the **Excel 97-2003 Workbook** option on the right side of the **File** menu.
5. Select a location and type a file name in the **Save As** dialog box.

to complete a task. However, the Ribbon system in the 2007 version of Excel considerably reduces the amount of clicking you need to do before activating a command. Therefore, you may or may not find right clicking useful. Figure 1.9 shows the Excel commands and icons that appear after the right mouse button is clicked on a worksheet. These options will change when you are working with other objects on a worksheet such as charts or text boxes.

Figure 1.9 | **Options When Right Clicking**

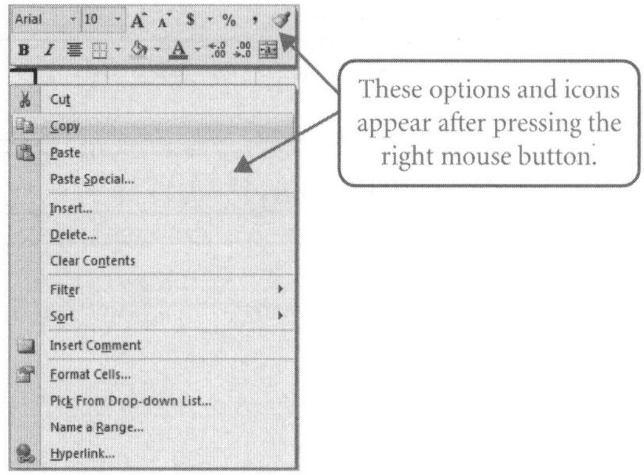

As mentioned, the other option for accessing Excel commands is through Control keys. In the earliest version of Microsoft Office, using Control keys was the primary method for accessing commands. That is, you activated a command by holding down the **Ctrl** key on your keyboard and pressing a letter or character. You can still use this system in Microsoft Office 2007. For several icons in the Ribbon, there is a corresponding **Ctrl** key combination. In fact, notice that the description for the **Copy** icon in Figure 1.5 shows that this command can also be activated by holding down the **Ctrl** key and pressing the letter C.

Settings and Status Bar

You have the ability to customize the settings and ***Status Bar*** of the Excel screen. For example, when you first open Excel, all data typed into a worksheet will have a Calibri font style with an 11-point font size. However, you can change this to whatever font style and font size you wish. The following explains how to change these settings:

- Click the **Office Button**.
- Click the **Excel Options** button at the bottom of the menu (see Figure 1.7). This will open the **Excel Options** dialog box.
- Click the **Popular** option on the left side of the **Excel Options** dialog box.
- Click the down arrow next to the **Use this font** option. This option can be found under the section heading **When creating new workbooks**.
- Select a new font style.
- Click the **OK** button at the bottom of the dialog box. For some settings, you may have to close and reopen Excel for any change to take place.

Figure 1.10 shows the options in the **Popular** section of the **Excel Options** dialog box. Notice that there are several other options you can adjust to customize the settings of your Excel screen such as the font size and your user name.

Figure 1.10 | **Excel Options Dialog Box**

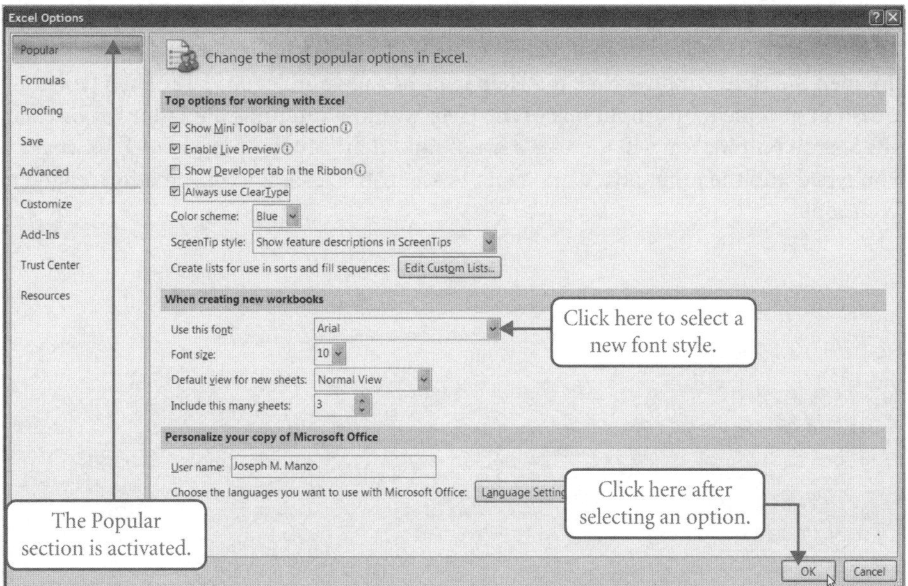

You can also customize the appearance of the Status bar at the bottom of the Excel screen. The Status bar in Figure 1.11 contains shortcuts for switching between various views as well as the Zoom Slider. To change what is displayed on the Status bar, place the cursor anywhere in the Status bar and right click. This will open the list of options shown in Figure 1.11.

Figure 1.11 | **Status Bar Options List**

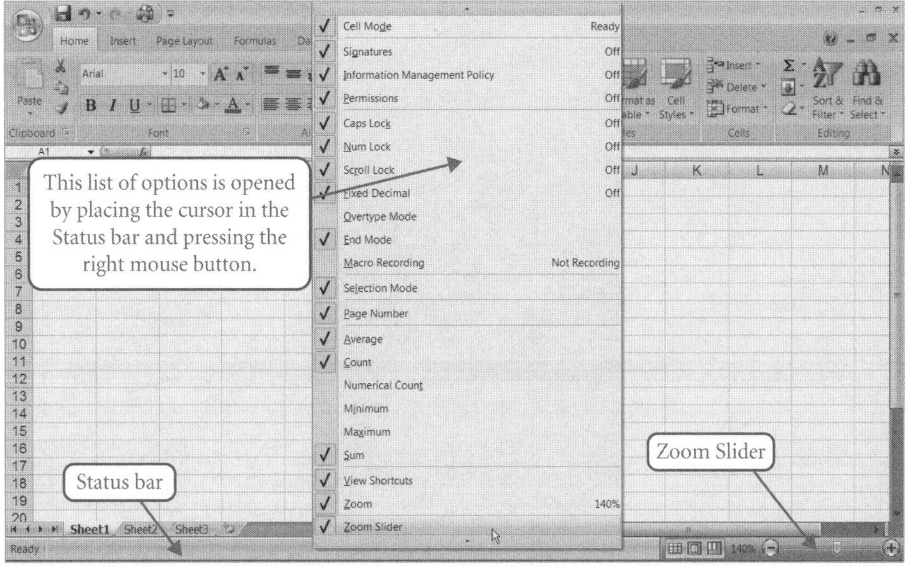

Quick Reference

Changing the Font Setting for New Workbooks

1. Open a blank Excel workbook.
2. Click the **Office Button**.
3. Click the **Excel Options** button.
4. Click the **Popular** section on the left side of the **Excel Options** dialog box.
5. Select a font style and size in the **When creating new workbooks** section of the **Excel Options** dialog box.
6. Click the **OK** button at the bottom of the dialog box.

Excel Help

The last area that will be covered in this introduction to Excel is the **Help** window. The **Help** window is a reference tool that you can use to research various Excel commands. To open the **Help** window, click the **Help** icon, as shown in Figure 1.12. Then type a question or topic in the input box of the **Help** window and press the **Enter** key or click the **Search** button. You will then see a list of links that contain topics related to what you typed into the input box. Click a link to see instructions and information related to your topic.

Figure 1.12 | **The Help Window**

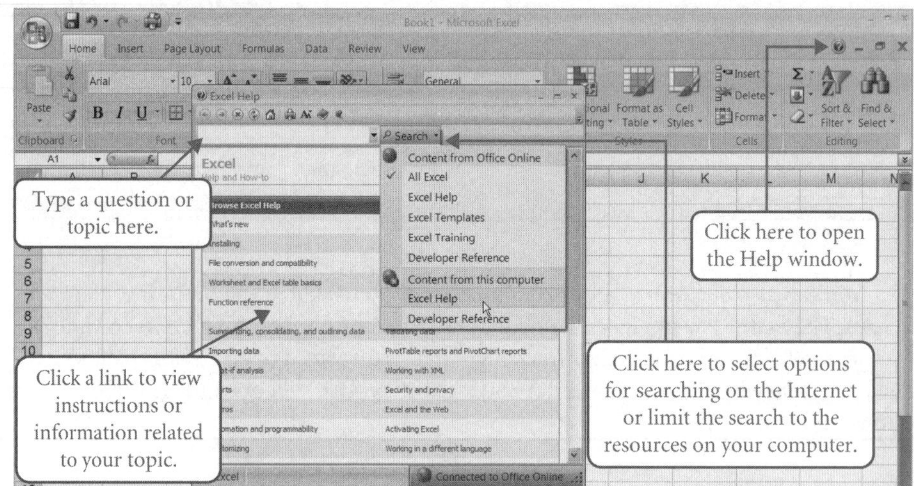

>> Introduction to Excel

VIDEO WORKSHOP

This workshop is the first of several that will be presented in this text. These workshops serve two purposes. The first is to give you an opportunity to practice the skills illustrated in each section of every chapter. The second is to watch the author demonstrate these skills. Many people have an easier time learning software skills after they see techniques and commands demonstrated. You can watch a video demonstration of each workshop by opening the related video file. Each workshop will usually require you to open an Excel file so that you can complete the tasks listed. However, there is no Excel file required for this workshop.
The purpose of this workshop is to open a blank Excel workbook and examine a few of the basic features that were described in this chapter. Try completing each task and then watch the video named **Introduction**.

1. **Open Excel (Video: Introduction)**
   a. Launch the Excel application.
   b. Use the up and down arrows to activate cell C7.
   c. Use the mouse to activate cell E3.
   d. Highlight the range B5:G10.
   e. Click each tab of the Ribbon and view the icons that are showing in each tab.
   f. Click the **Office Button** and save your workbook in Excel 97–2003 format. Save the workbook to any location on your computer and use any file name you wish.
   g. Activate **Sheet2** by clicking the worksheet tab.
   h. Use the Zoom Slider to increase the zoom to 140%.
   i. Open the **Help** window.
   j. Change the Search Option in the **Help** window to `Excel Help - Content from this computer`.
   k. Close the **Help** window.
   l. Close your workbook and then close Excel.

>> An Introduction to Cell Referencing

EXERCISE

Why Do I Need This?

This exercise is the first of several that are presented in each section of this text. The purpose of these exercises is to show how Excel skills are applied to typical business situations. These exercises will also illustrate how to use Excel's cell referencing capabilities to construct multiple scenarios or outcomes depending on the business objective. In addition to the exercise format that is presented here, you will also see an exercise that asks you to fix a spreadsheet that has errors. This exercise will come under the heading "What's Wrong with This Spreadsheet?"

Exercise

Cell referencing is Excel's most critical feature because it allows you to produce many mathematical outputs by changing just one or many inputs. The purpose of this exercise is to provide an introduction to Excel by looking at how cell referencing is used in the sales project example from the beginning of the chapter. You will need to open the file named ib_e01_dailysalesresults before completing the tasks in this exercise.

1. Activate cell A10. The number in this cell should be 10. Notice that the number in cell B10 is 810. This number is the result of a formula that takes the number in cell A10 and adds it to the value in cell B9. Each number in column B is calculated by similar formulas. Creating formulas in Excel will be covered in Chapter 3.

2. After activating cell A10, type the number `100`.

3. Press the **Enter** key. The number in cell B10 should change to 900, and every cell below B10 should also change. This is an example of how cell referencing is able to change many outputs by changing just one input.

4. Save and close your file.

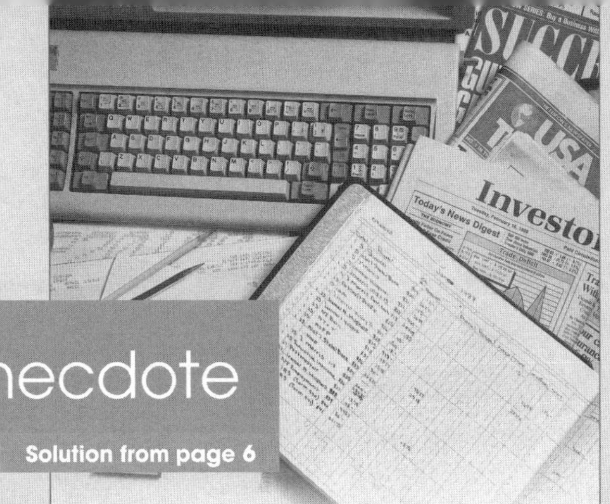

Excel in **Practice** | Anecdote

Solution from page 6

Few tools changed my job performance and decision-making abilities like Excel. With Excel, I was able to evaluate large amounts of information in a fraction of the time it took using a calculator and paper spreadsheet. I was not only more productive, but also more confident about the recommendations and decisions I made. Although the amount of time I spent ensuring that my results were accurate remained the same, once I started using Excel, there was no way I could ever consider going back to paper.

Questions for Discussion

1. Could a company gain a competitive advantage in its respective industry by having access to more information over its competitors? Why?
2. Does having more information automatically result in better business decisions?
3. The author mentioned that the amount of time ensuring the accuracy of results remained the same. Why wouldn't Excel automatically increase the accuracy of analytical projects?
4. The author mentions that after he started using electronic spreadsheets he could never consider going back to paper. Why do you think this is so?

Review Questions

This section features questions that will help you review the key concepts and skills that were presented in the chapter. There will always be a mix of Fill in the Blank, True or False, or Short Answer questions. For the True or False questions, if you think an answer is false, provide a short explanation as to why you think the phrase or comment is false.

1. Multiple outcomes or potential results are also known as__________.
2. What methods can you use to activate a cell?
3. True or False: An Excel file is made up of multiple workbooks.
4. A __________ is two cell locations separated by a colon.
5. Excel's capability to automatically produce new mathematical outputs when one or more inputs are changed is possible because of __________________.
6. Commands used to prepare a worksheet for printing can be found in the __________ tab of the Ribbon.
7. True or False: The **Quick Access Toolbar** can contain only four icons, and it must always appear at the top of the Ribbon.
8. You must click the__________ to activate various worksheets in a workbook.
9. Explain how you would open an existing workbook that is saved on your computer.
10. What could you do if you need to send an Excel workbook to someone who is using the 2003 version of Excel?

Skills Exam

The Skills Exam section will also be included at the end of each chapter and is used to test your knowledge of executing various skills presented in the text. As mentioned, the primary mission of this book is to explain and demonstrate how Excel is used to complete objectives in the field of business. However, knowing how to execute key skills that are required to operate Excel is also important. This section will present several skill-based questions that you will have to apply to an Excel workbook. Because this is an introductory chapter, the Skills Exams will begin at the end of Chapter 2.

Challenge Question

This section will follow the Skills Exam section and feature questions that require you to apply the skills you have learned to complete typical business objectives. There is usually no right or wrong method for completing the objectives presented in this section. However, the results you obtain must be accurate. This section might also include questions that ask you to identify how Excel or spreadsheets play a role in the success of a business or in the decision-making process of a business.

1. Identify three specific electronic devices or computer software programs that have changed the way you do things to such an extent that you cannot imagine living life without them? Explain the needs these devices or programs satisfy and the benefits they provide.

Chapter 2 Excel Basics

Chapter Goals

Chapter 1 provided an overview of Excel and its benefits. This chapter covers the following basic Excel skills you need to begin creating an Excel spreadsheet: data entry, copy and paste, formatting, editing, and printing. It also features two common types of spreadsheets used in business: Financial Plans and Merchandise Sales Reports. It is important to note that business terms such as Gross Sales, Cost of Goods Sold, Gross Profit, and Unit Sales will be mentioned but not explained in detail. These terms are commonly used in the business world and will be covered in depth in your core business courses.

Excel | Skill Sets

Data Management
- Data Entry
- Auto Fill
- Adjusting Columns and Rows
- Hiding Columns and Rows
- Copy and Paste
- Sorting Data (Single Level)
- Sorting Data (Multiple Levels)

Formatting
- Data Formats
- Data Alignment
- Number Formats
- Borders (Line Formats)
- Cell Color (Fill Color)

Editing
- Editing Data in a Cell
- Moving Data
- Deleting Columns and Rows
- Deleting Worksheets
- Inserting Columns and Rows
- Inserting, Moving, and Renaming Worksheet Tabs

Printing
- Page Setup
- Printing a Worksheet

Excel in Practice | Anecdote

The Role of a Production Planning Manager

You may think that in business, information is processed and communicated electronically. This is the 21st century, after all. Imagine my surprise when not all that long ago I started working as a production planning manager for a large apparel manufacturing company that produced thousands of garments every year. My role was to manage all of the production plans sent to our offices in China—a seemingly straightforward task, except for the fact that the production plans were handwritten on 17″ x 14″ paper spreadsheets, reduced in a copy machine, and mailed overnight to China. Each garment had a separate production plan that documented every detail: buttons, color, fabric, labels, zippers, and packaging. And guess what happened if a designer decided to use corduroy instead of denim at the last minute? Out came the correction fluid, followed by a trip to the mailroom for another costly overnight delivery. Communicating information in this cumbersome way was simply part of the company's culture, which I inherited. However, after gallons of correction fluid (and lots of noxious fumes), I decided there had to be a better way to track and communicate this information.

>> Continued on page 70

Data Management

Skill Set

The different ways Excel spreadsheets are used in business are too numerous to count. However, using spreadsheets to track the sales results of retail merchandise or to create a financial plan are probably the most common. With regards to tracking and planning financial data, business managers typically use spreadsheets to evaluate whether a company is achieving its financial goals in a current year or to plan its financial goals for future years. This section illustrates how you can use Excel's data management skills to begin constructing these spreadsheets. In fact, data management skills such as entering data, adjusting the widths of columns and rows, copying and pasting, and sorting are typically needed in the early stages of developing any spreadsheet.

Data Entry

Data entry is the most basic and fundamental Excel skill. The term ***data*** refers to any numbers or text items that will be analyzed or displayed on a spreadsheet. In a financial plan, the text items usually typed into an Excel worksheet include a title and the financial category labels, such as Gross Sales, Net Sales, Cost of Goods Sold, and so on. To type a title into a worksheet, do the following:

- Open a blank workbook.
- Activate cell A1 by left clicking it with the mouse, or use the keyboard arrow key to move the black outline to cell A1. The black outline indicates an active cell.
- Type the words Financial Plan.
- Enter the title into cell A1 by performing one of the following actions:
  - Press the **Enter** key.
  - Press one of the arrow keys.
  - Left click another cell location.

Figure 2.1 shows the title entered into cell A1 as well as the financial category labels entered into cells A3 through A7.

Figure 2.1 | **Building a Worksheet for Financial Planning**

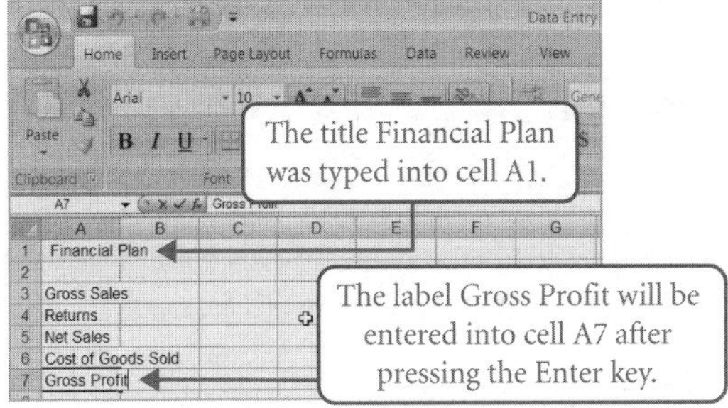

COMMON MISTAKES | Data Entry

The most common data entry mistake is forgetting to press the **Enter** key after typing an entry. *Data will not be entered into a cell unless you press the **Enter** or arrow keys.* Other data entry mistakes typically occur from typing the wrong number or transposing numbers. For example, the number 253 could be ***transposed*** as 235. Always proofread your spreadsheet for any data entry errors.

When you are entering numeric data, it is good practice to omit any symbols, such as commas. Future chapters will address the use of formulas and functions when you are developing an Excel spreadsheet. Typing commas to separate thousands (for example, 10,000) for numbers used in functions will prevent the function from working or produce erroneous results. The next section of this chapter reviews how to add symbols, such as commas, dollar signs, percent signs, and so on, to numbers typed into a worksheet.

Auto Fill

Commonly used in data entry tasks, ***Auto Fill*** automatically completes a set of data points that are in sequential order, such as numbers, years, months, or days of the week. With regards to the Financial Plan worksheet shown in Figure 2.1, the years 2008 through 2012 will be entered in cells B2 through F2. You can use the **Auto Fill** feature to complete this sequence of years by typing only the first two years in cells B2 and C2. The following points explain how this is accomplished.

- Type the year 2008 in cell B2 and 2009 in cell C2. Two sequential data points must be entered into two adjacent cells to use **Auto Fill**. For example, when completing a series of numbers in 100 unit increments, enter the number 100 into one cell and 200 in another. For creating a daily schedule, enter the word Monday in one cell and Tuesday in another.
- Highlight cells B2 and C2. To use the **Auto Fill** feature, you must have highlighted two cells containing sequential data.
- Place the cursor over the **Auto Fill Handle**. The **Auto Fill Handle** is the black square in the lower-right corner of a highlighted range.
- When you place the cursor over the **Auto Fill Handle**, it will change from a white plus sign to a black plus sign. When this occurs, left click and drag across to the right until the years increase to 2012 (see Figures 2.2 and 2.3).

COMMON MISTAKES | Auto Fill

Remember that to complete a sequence of data using the **Auto Fill** feature, you must highlight two or more adjacent cell locations. If you click and drag the **Auto Fill Handle** when only one cell is activated, you will duplicate the contents of this one cell to other cells without completing any sequence.

Figure 2.2 | **Typing Years into the Financial Plan Worksheet**

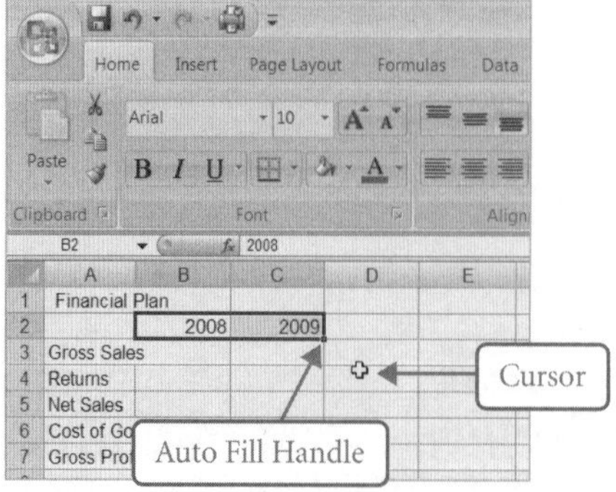

Quick Reference
Auto Fill

1. Enter sequential data into at least 2 adjacent cell locations.
2. Highlight all cell locations containing sequential data.
3. Drag the cursor over the **Auto Fill Handle**.
4. When the cursor changes from a white to a black plus sign, click and drag across or down to continue the sequence of data.

Figure 2.3 | **Using Auto Fill to Complete the Sequence of Years**

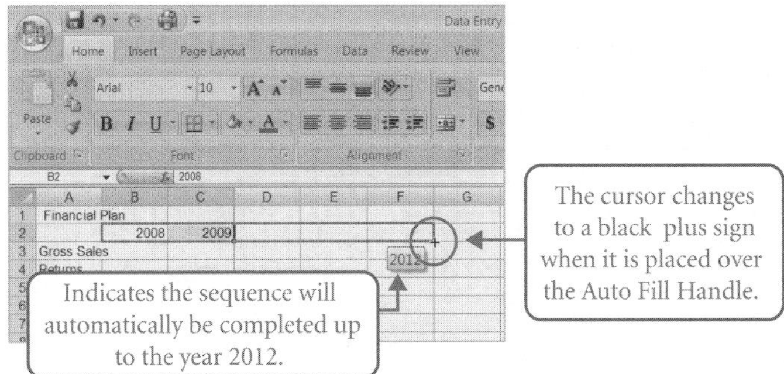

Adjusting Columns and Rows

When entering data into a spreadsheet, you may need to adjust the ***column width*** or ***row height,*** depending on the size of your entry. Entries too wide for a particular cell location may extend into one or more columns or appear truncated. For example, notice in Figure 2.1 that the Cost of Goods Sold entry in cell A6 extends into column B. However, when a number is typed into cell B6, the Cost of Goods Sold entry appears truncated, as shown in Figure 2.4.

Figure 2.4 | **Entries Too Long for a Cell Location Appear Truncated**

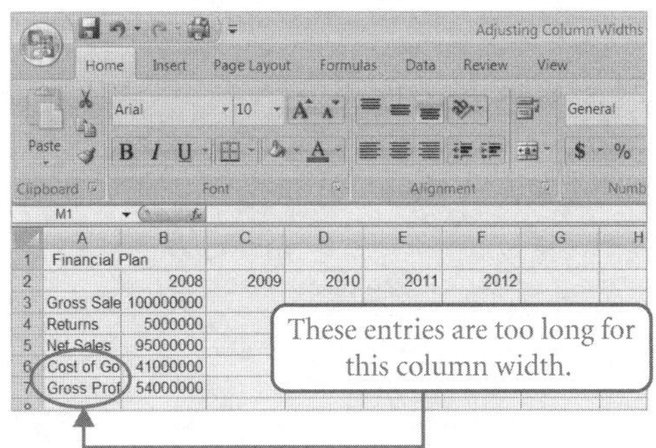

To prevent the entries shown in Figure 2.4 from being truncated, you will need to expand the width of column A. To accomplish this, do the following:

- Place the cursor between two columns.
- When the cursor changes from a white plus sign to a double black arrow, left click and drag to increase or decrease the column width (see Figure 2.5).
- Alternatively, when the cursor changes from a white plus sign to a double black arrow, double click with the left mouse button, and the column will automatically expand to fit the longest entry that has been typed. This method is especially helpful when you're working with large spreadsheets where you cannot see the largest entry on your screen.

Figure 2.5 | **Using the Cursor to Adjust Column Width**

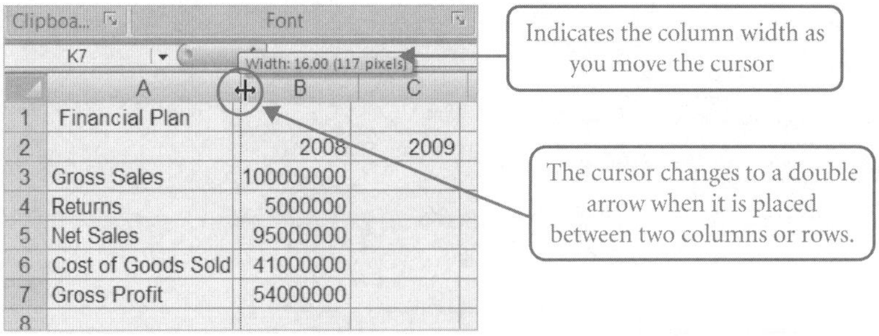

Clipboa...
Font
K7
Width: 16.00 (117 pixels)
A
B
C
1 Financial Plan
2 2008 2009
3 Gross Sales 100000000
4 Returns 5000000
5 Net Sales 95000000
6 Cost of Goods Sold 41000000
7 Gross Profit 54000000
8
Indicates the column width as you move the cursor
The cursor changes to a double arrow when it is placed between two columns or rows.

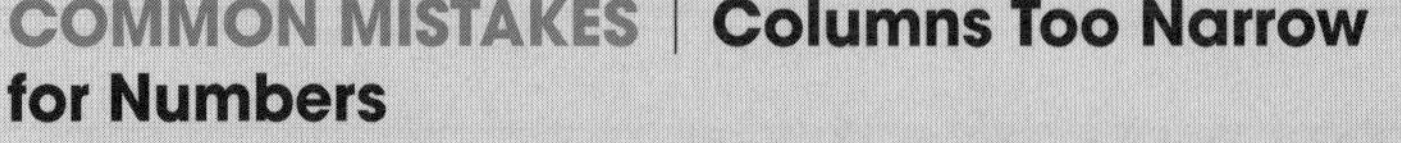

COMMON MISTAKES | Columns Too Narrow for Numbers

When entering numbers into a worksheet that is too long for the width of a column, you may see the symbols shown in Figures 2.6 and 2.7.

People often think these symbols are errors. However, they simply mean the column is too narrow to fit the number entered into the cell. Excel will not truncate numbers if a column is too narrow because you could be misled into thinking the number is a smaller value than reality. Therefore, increase the width of a column to remove scientific notation or "######" signs.

Figure 2.6 | **Scientific Notation When Number Is Too Wide for Column**

A
B
C
1 Financial Plan
2 2008 2009
3 Gross Sales 1E+08
4 Returns 5E+06
5 Net Sales 1E+08
6 Cost of Goods Sold 4E+07
7 Gross Profit 5E+07
Scientific notation appears when numbers are too long to fit in a cell.

Figure 2.7 | **"#####" Signs When Number Is Too Wide for Column**

A
B
C
1 Financial Plan
2 2008 2009
3 Gross Sales ######
4 Returns ######
5 Net Sales ######
6 Cost of Goods Sold ######
7 Gross Profit ######
These symbols indicate column B is too narrow for these numbers.

Similar to adjusting the width of a column, you may need to adjust the height of a row to show that cell's content. However, you can also use row height to highlight important information on a worksheet. For example, with regards to our example of a Financial Plan, the Gross Profit is an important financial result that can be highlighted by increasing the height of a row. The method for adjusting the height of rows is almost identical to adjusting the width of columns:

- Place the cursor between two rows.
- When the cursor changes from a white plus sign to a double black arrow, left click and drag up or down to increase or decrease the height of a row.
- Alternatively, when the cursor changes from a white plus sign to a double black arrow, double click with the left mouse button, and the row will automatically expand to fit the largest entry.

Figure 2.8 shows the Financial Plan worksheet with an expanded row 7. Notice that all of the numbers as well as the words *Gross Profit* automatically stay at the bot-

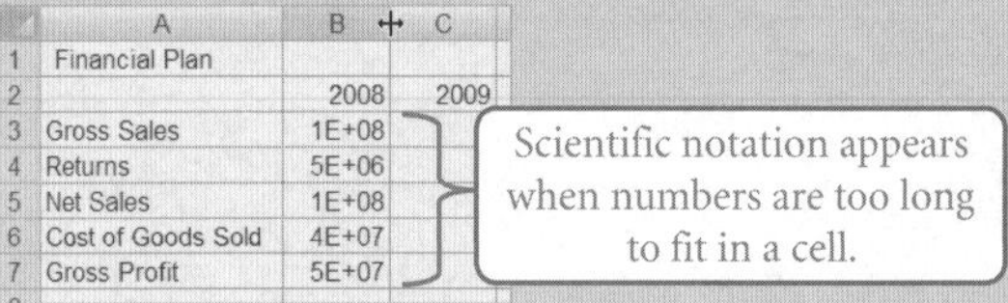

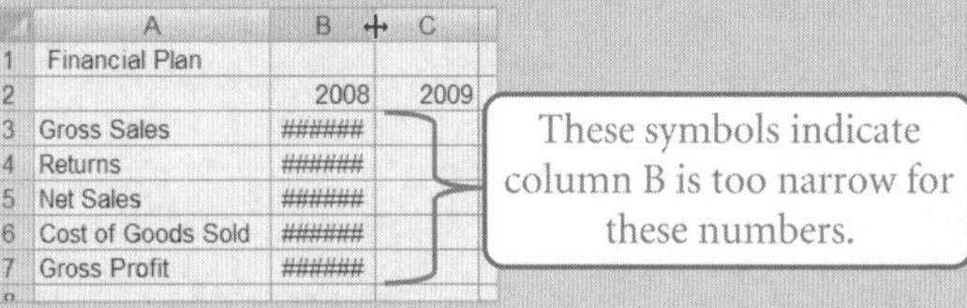

tom of the cells when the row height is increased. This creates space between the Cost of Goods Sold numbers and the Gross Profit numbers, which makes it easier for a business manager to evaluate the Gross Profit results of this plan. Adjusting the vertical position of data within a cell is covered in more detail in the next section.

Figure 2.8 | **Using the Cursor to Increase Row Height**

	A	B	C	D	E	F
1	Financial Plan					
2		2008	2009	2010	2011	2012
3	Gross Sales	100000000	110000000	120000000	14[illegible]	[illegible]
4	Returns	5000000	5500000	6000000	[illegible]	[illegible]
5	Net Sales	95000000	104500000	114000000	13[illegible]	[illegible]
6	Cost of Goods Sold	41000000	45100000	49200000	57400000	65600000
7	Gross Profit	54000000	59400000	64800000	75600000	86400000

An alternative way of changing the width of columns or the height of rows is to use the **Format** icon in the **Home** tab of the Ribbon (see Figure 2.9). Clicking the **Format** icon will open the following options.

- **Row Height:** Use to set a specific height for a row or group of rows. You must highlight at least one cell location in every row you intend to change *before* selecting this option. After you select this option, a dialog box will appear, asking you to enter a specific height number (the higher the number, the greater the height).
- **Auto Fit Row Height:** This option is identical to double clicking the cursor when it is placed between two rows. The height of rows containing cell locations that have been highlighted will automatically adjust to fit any data entries.
- **Column Width:** Use to set a specific column width. You must highlight at least one cell in every column you intend to change before selecting this option. After you select this option, a dialog box will appear, asking you to enter a specific width number (the higher the number, the wider the column).
- ***Auto Fit Column Width:*** This option automatically changes the width of a column to fit the width of the longest entered data. You must highlight at least one cell in each column to apply this option.
- **Default Width:** Use to set a specific width for every column in a spreadsheet. Since every column is being formatted, you don't need to highlight any cells to apply this option.

Figure 2.9 | **Using the Ribbon to Change Column Width and Row Height**

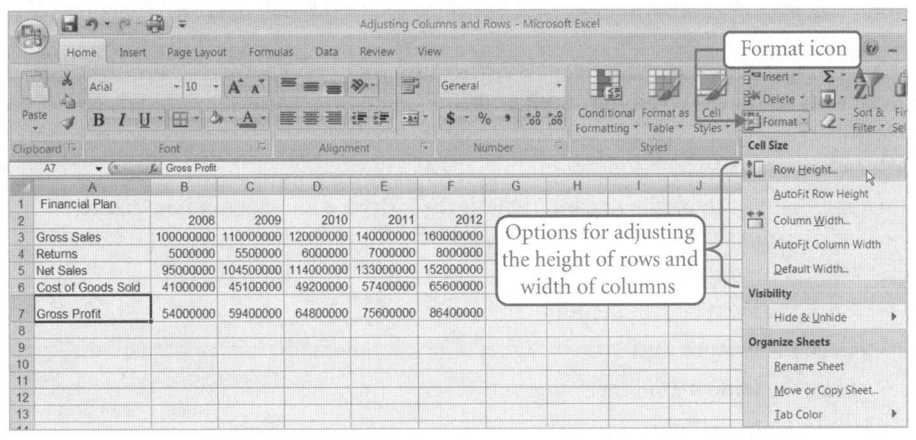

Quick Reference

Adjusting Column Widths

1. Place the cursor between 2 columns.
2. Click and drag to desired width or double click to automatically set to the widest data point.

Or

1. Highlight at least one cell in the columns you want to change.
2. Click the **Home** tab of the Ribbon.
3. Click the **Format** icon.
4. Select **Column Width**.
5. Enter a desired width number in the **Column Width** dialog box.
6. Click the **OK** button.

Quick Reference

Adjusting Row Heights

1. Place the cursor between 2 rows.
2. Click and drag to desired height or double click to automatically set to the largest data point.

Or

1. Highlight at least one cell in the rows you want to change.
2. Click the **Home** tab of the Ribbon.
3. Click the **Format** icon.
4. Select **Row Height**.
5. Enter a desired height number in the **Row Height** dialog box.
6. Click the **OK** button.

Hiding Columns and Rows

In some situations you may want to hide a column or row in a worksheet. Hiding certain columns or rows might make a worksheet easier to read, depending on its use. For example, if someone was interested only in using the Financial Plan worksheet (see Figure 2.8) to compare the years 2008 and 2012, columns containing data for the years 2009 through 2011 can be hidden from view. The following points explain how to hide these columns:

- Highlight the range C1:E1. At least one cell in each column you wish to hide must be highlighted. It does not matter which row number is highlighted.
- Click the **Home** tab of the Ribbon.
- Click the **Format** icon.
- Click the **Hide & Unhide** option. This will open a submenu of options showing items that you can hide or unhide.
- Select the **Hide Columns** option.

Figure 2.10 shows the Financial Plan worksheet with columns C, D, and E hidden from view. Notice that the column letters at the top of the worksheet grid are out of sequence.

Figure 2.10 | **Hiding Columns**

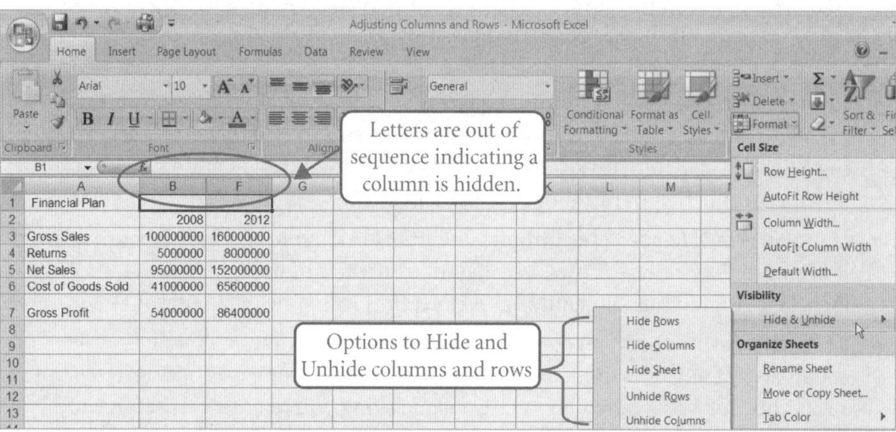

COMMON MISTAKES | Checking for Hidden Columns and Rows

Always check for hidden columns and rows when you're working with an Excel file that was created by someone else. People often spend time re-creating or adding data to a worksheet because it appears to be missing when in fact it is contained in a hidden column or row. Remember that the column letters at the top of a worksheet or row numbers along the left side of a worksheet will be out of sequence if a column or row is hidden.

>> Quick Reference

Hide Columns and Rows

1. Highlight at least one cell in each column or row you want to hide.
2. Click the **Home** tab of the Ribbon.
3. Click the **Format** icon.
4. Select the **Hide & Unhide** option.
5. Select one of the **Hide** options from the submenu.

>> Quick Reference

Unhide Columns and Rows

1. Click and drag over to a cell on either side of the hidden column or row.
2. Click the **Home** tab of the Ribbon.
3. Click the **Format** icon.
4. Select the **Hide & Unhide** option.
5. Select one of the **Unhide** options from the submenu.

Hiding columns is a valuable feature because you do not have to move or delete data from a worksheet you may need in the future. With regards to the Financial Plan worksheet in Figure 2.10, you can always unhide columns C through E when needed, which is accomplished as follows:

- Highlight a cell on the left and right of the hidden column. Notice in Figure 2.10, cell locations B1 and F1 are highlighted. The reason is that both cell locations border the columns that are hidden.
- Click the **Home** tab of the Ribbon.
- Click the **Format** icon.
- Click the **Hide & Unhide** option.
- Select **Unhide Columns**.

Copy and Paste

The ***Copy*** and ***Paste*** commands are perhaps the most convenient and commonly used Excel commands. This section demonstrates these commands using both a Merchandise Sales Report and the Financial Plan worksheet (created in Figures 2.1 through 2.10).

The purpose of the Merchandise Sales Report in this example is to show the sales results for products sold in an apparel retail store. The first few items in the report are from the Tops category. Here, we will use the **Copy** and **Paste** commands instead of typing the word "Tops" several times in the Category column:

- Activate cell A2 (see Figure 2.11). Before copying data, you must activate the cell or range of cells you need duplicated. In this example, the word *Tops* in cell A2 must be duplicated 4 times.
- Click the **Home** tab of the Ribbon.
- Click the **Copy** icon (see Figure 2.11).
- Highlight the range A3:A6. After clicking the **Copy** icon, highlight the cell, or range of cells, where the data needs to be duplicated.
- Click the **Paste** icon (see Figure 2.12). After you click the **Paste** icon, the word "Tops" will appear in cells A3 through A6.

Figure 2.11 | **Copying Data on the Merchandise Sales Report**

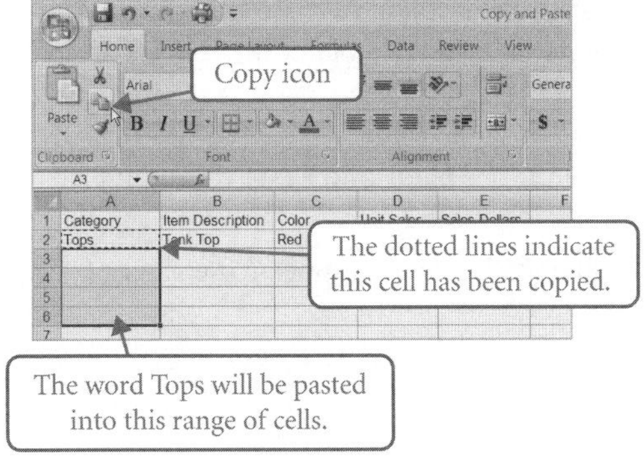

Figure 2.12 | **Pasting Data**

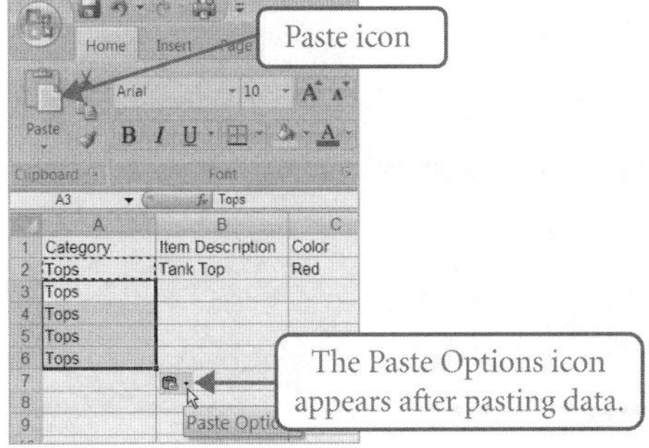

It is important to note that the **Paste** icon pastes all data and formats from the cell that was copied. However, you can choose various pasting options by clicking the smaller **Paste Options** icon, which appears on your worksheet each time you click the

Paste icon. These options are also referred to as **Paste Special** options and will be covered in the next chapter.

Data can also be duplicated using the **Auto Fill Handle**. As previously mentioned, **Auto Fill** is usually used to complete a sequence of data when two cells are highlighted. However, if you click and drag on the **Auto Fill Handle** when only one cell location is activated, the contents of that cell will be duplicated to other cell locations (see Figure 2.13).

Figure 2.13 | **Using Auto Fill to Duplicate Data**

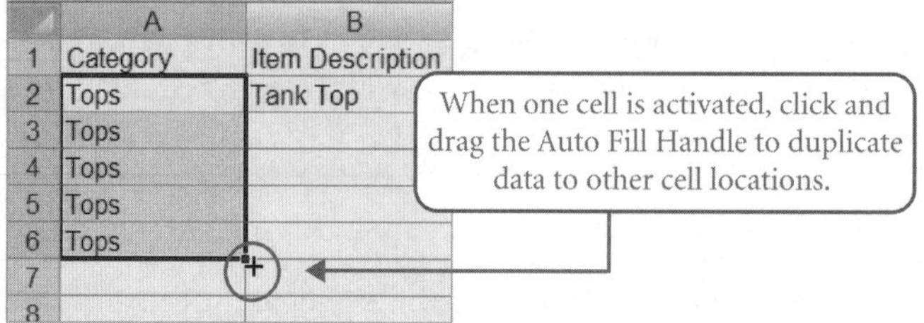

Another common use of the **Copy** and **Paste** commands is to create duplicate copies of an entire worksheet. Business managers can use this technique to create different scenarios for sales plans or business strategies. For example, a sales manager might need to develop three different scenarios showing the potential sales results for a region of retail stores. A financial planning manager might want to show a base case, worst case, or best case scenario for a company's profit plan. In these situations, a base worksheet is created and then copied and pasted into several blank worksheets. Once the worksheet is duplicated, the data can be changed to reflect the various scenarios for a particular business situation.

The following example explains how you use the **Copy** and **Paste** commands to create different versions for the example of the Financial Plan:

- Highlight the entire worksheet by clicking the box in the upper-left corner of Sheet1 (see Figure 2.14).

Figure 2.14 | **Copying an Entire Worksheet**

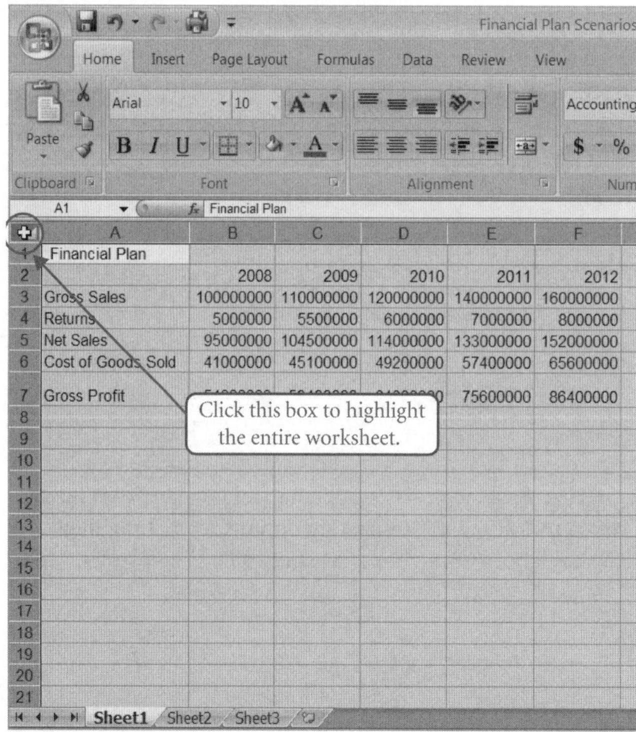

- Click the **Home** tab of the Ribbon.
- Click the **Copy** icon to copy the entire contents of the worksheet.
- Click the Sheet2 worksheet tab and activate cell A1. When pasting the contents of an entire worksheet, you must activate cell A1; otherwise, Excel will produce an error message.
- Click the **Paste** icon (see Figure 2.15).

Figure 2.15 | **Pasting an Entire Worksheet**

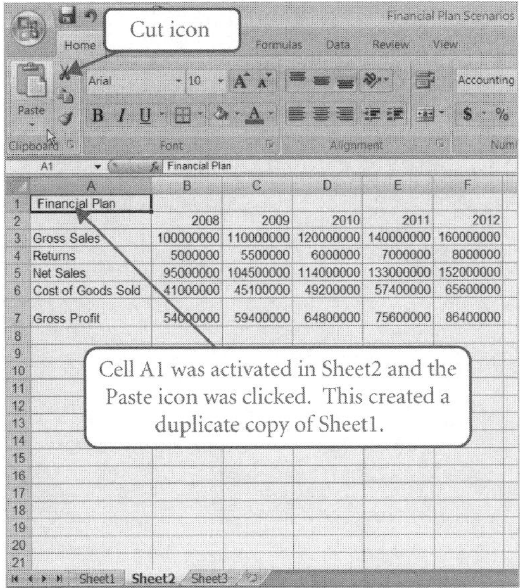

In some cases you may want to remove contents from one area of a worksheet and paste it to another. For these situations you can use the Cut command, which is activated by clicking the scissors icon in the **Home** tab of the Ribbon. After clicking the **Cut** icon, activate a cell or range of cells where the data should be replaced and click the **Paste** icon.

Sorting Data (Single Level)

After you construct a spreadsheet, you may need to sort the data. ***Sorting*** is one of the most critical Excel commands because it can rearrange data in a specific sequence or rank that enables business managers to assess information efficiently and make key decisions. For example, retail managers use sorting to rank merchandise based on sales results. This allows them to identify top-selling items that should be reordered as well as low-selling items that should be discontinued. Finance managers may rank a list of public companies with the highest shareholder return. This could help them identify stocks that should either be purchased or sold. Sorting data in Excel can be broken down into two broad categories: single level and multiple level. This segment will focus on single-level sorting, and the following segment will focus on multiple-level sorting.

Figure 2.16 shows the completed Merchandise Sales worksheet originally started in Figure 2.11. As previously mentioned, a retail manager might sort the items in this worksheet based on the Unit Sales column. If the manager wanted to identify the best-selling items, this data could be sorted so items with the highest unit sales appear at the top of the worksheet (***descending order***). If the manager wanted to identify the lowest-selling items, this data could be sorted so items with the lowest unit sales appear at the top of the worksheet (***ascending order***). These sorting options are considered single level because one column of data is used as the basis for ranking the items. The following explains how you sort the worksheet in Figure 2.16 in descending order:

- Activate any cell location that contains a number in column D. Since the goal is to sort this worksheet in descending order based on data in the Unit Sales column,

>> **Quick Reference**

Copy and Paste

1. Highlight a cell or range of cells to be copied.
2. Click the **Copy** icon in the Ribbon.
3. Highlight a cell or range of cells where copied data should appear.
4. Click the **Paste** icon in the Ribbon.

one cell in this column must be activated. Note that the cell you activate cannot be blank; otherwise, you will get an error message.

- Click the **Data** tab at the top of the Ribbon.
- Click the **Z to A** icon in the **Sort & Filter** group of the Ribbon (see Figure 2.17). After you click this icon, the Unit Sales column as well as all adjacent columns will be sorted in descending order. It is important to note that only adjacent columns are sorted when you use either the **Z to A** or **A to Z** icons (see Common Mistakes for this section).

Figure 2.16 | **Merchandise Sales Report Before Sorting**

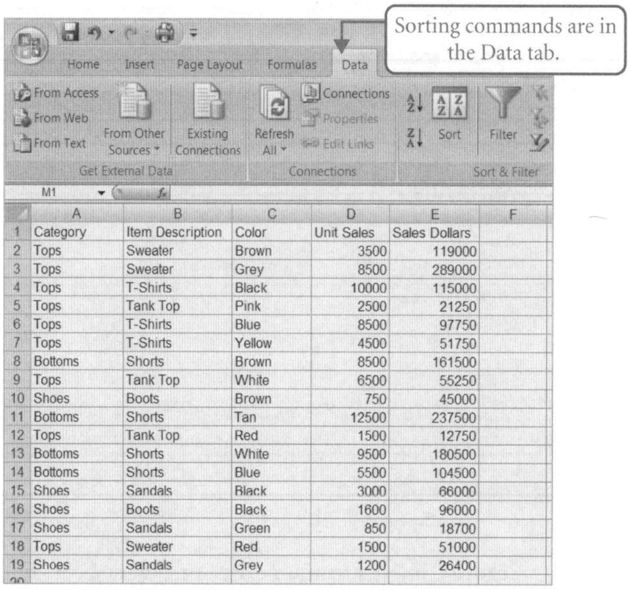

	A	B	C	D	E	F
1	Category	Item Description	Color	Unit Sales	Sales Dollars	
2	Tops	Sweater	Brown	3500	119000	
3	Tops	Sweater	Grey	8500	289000	
4	Tops	T-Shirts	Black	10000	115000	
5	Tops	Tank Top	Pink	2500	21250	
6	Tops	T-Shirts	Blue	8500	97750	
7	Tops	T-Shirts	Yellow	4500	51750	
8	Bottoms	Shorts	Brown	8500	161500	
9	Tops	Tank Top	White	6500	55250	
10	Shoes	Boots	Brown	750	45000	
11	Bottoms	Shorts	Tan	12500	237500	
12	Tops	Tank Top	Red	1500	12750	
13	Bottoms	Shorts	White	9500	180500	
14	Bottoms	Shorts	Blue	5500	104500	
15	Shoes	Sandals	Black	3000	66000	
16	Shoes	Boots	Black	1600	96000	
17	Shoes	Sandals	Green	850	18700	
18	Tops	Sweater	Red	1500	51000	
19	Shoes	Sandals	Grey	1200	26400	

Figure 2.17 shows the Merchandise Sales Report after the items are sorted in descending order based on the Unit Sales column. The manager of this business can quickly glance at the top of this report and see that the Tan Shorts and the Black T-Shirts are the two highest-selling items based on unit sales.

Figure 2.17 | **Merchandise Sales Report Sorted Based on the Unit Sales Column**

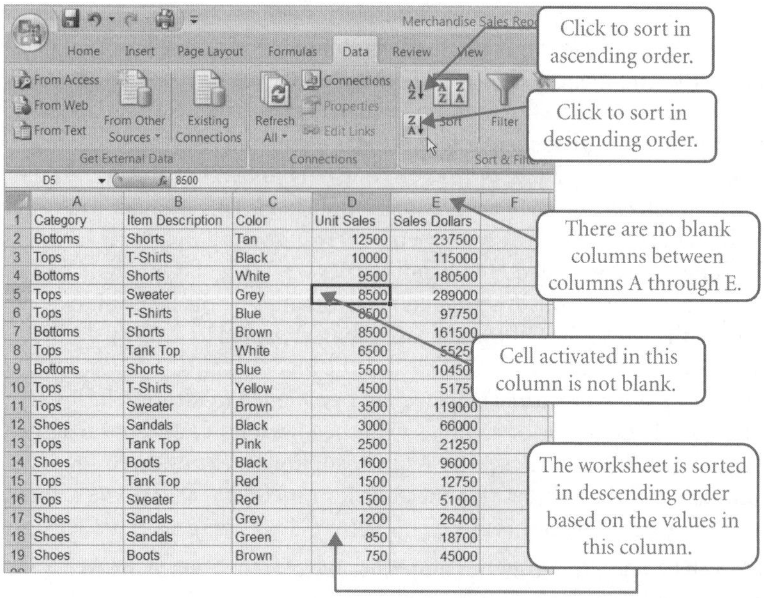

	A	B	C	D	E	F
1	Category	Item Description	Color	Unit Sales	Sales Dollars	
2	Bottoms	Shorts	Tan	12500	237500	
3	Tops	T-Shirts	Black	10000	115000	
4	Bottoms	Shorts	White	9500	180500	
5	Tops	Sweater	Grey	8500	289000	
6	Tops	T-Shirts	Blue	8500	97750	
7	Bottoms	Shorts	Brown	8500	161500	
8	Tops	Tank Top	White	6500	5525	
9	Bottoms	Shorts	Blue	5500	10450	
10	Tops	T-Shirts	Yellow	4500	5175	
11	Tops	Sweater	Brown	3500	119000	
12	Shoes	Sandals	Black	3000	66000	
13	Tops	Tank Top	Pink	2500	21250	
14	Shoes	Boots	Black	1600	96000	
15	Tops	Tank Top	Red	1500	12750	
16	Tops	Sweater	Red	1500	51000	
17	Shoes	Sandals	Grey	1200	26400	
18	Shoes	Sandals	Green	850	18700	
19	Shoes	Boots	Brown	750	45000	

>> ***Quick Reference***

Sorting Data (Single Level)

1. Activate a cell in the column you wish to use as the basis for sorting your data. The cell you activate must not be blank.
2. Make sure there are no blank columns separating data you wish to sort and the column containing the cell you activated in step 1.
3. Click the **Data** tab at the top of the Ribbon.
4. Click the **Z to A** (descending order) or **A to Z** (ascending order) icon in the **Sort & Filter** section of the Ribbon.

COMMON MISTAKES | Using the Z to A or A to Z Icons

When using the **Z to A** (descending) or **A to Z** (ascending) icons, make sure there are no blank columns in the data range you are sorting. These icons will sort data only in columns that are adjacent or connected to the column that contains the activated cell. For example, in Figure 2.18, the **A to Z** icon was used to sort the worksheet based on the Unit Sales column. Only columns A through D are sorted. Since a blank column separates columns D and F, column F is not sorted. As a result, it appears that the Brown Boots generated over 237,500 in sales dollars when these sales are actually associated with the Tan Shorts.

Figure 2.18 | **Example of a Sorting Error When Using the Ascending Icon**

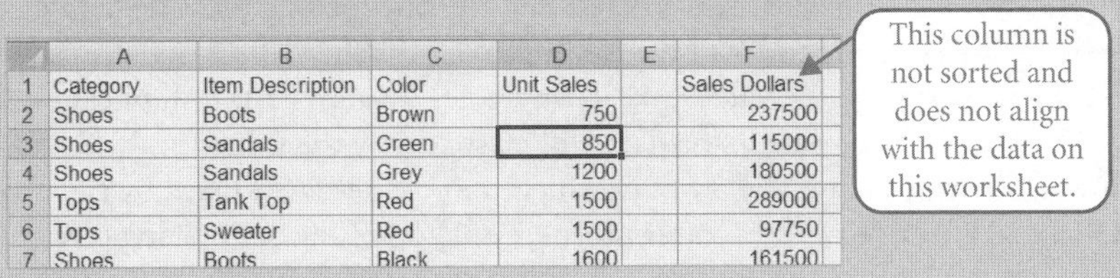

	A	B	C	D	E	F
1	Category	Item Description	Color	Unit Sales		Sales Dollars
2	Shoes	Boots	Brown	750		237500
3	Shoes	Sandals	Green	850		115000
4	Shoes	Sandals	Grey	1200		180500
5	Tops	Tank Top	Red	1500		289000
6	Tops	Sweater	Red	1500		97750
7	Shoes	Boots	Black	1600		161500

This column is not sorted and does not align with the data on this worksheet.

Sorting Data (Multiple Levels)

The focus of the preceding segment was single-level sorting. This segment will focus on multiple-level sorting. Use multiple-level sorting when duplicate values appear in the column that is used to sort the data in a worksheet. For example, notice in Figure 2.17 that 8500 units were sold for the Grey Sweater, Blue T-Shirt, and Brown Shorts. With multiple-level sorting, all items that sold 8500 units can be sorted by the values in the Sales Dollars column. This could help a manager prioritize the ordering of these items based on the number of sales dollars they generate for the business. The following explains how to accomplish this sort:

- Highlight the range A1:E19. Notice that this range includes the column headings in row 1. Also, when you are sorting data, it is important to note that all columns related to a single row of data must be highlighted. Leaving a column out of the highlighted range could distort the data, making it unusable.
- Click the **Data** tab on the Ribbon.
- Click the **Sort** icon in the Ribbon. This will open the **Sort** dialog box.
- Click the **Options** button and check to see that the **Sort top to bottom** option is selected. You can sort data from left to right in rows or top to bottom in columns. However, you will need to select the **Sort top to bottom** option when working with a list of items such as this example.
- Click the **OK** button in the **Sort Options** dialog box.
- Make sure a green check appears in the box next to the **My data has headers** option in the upper-right side of the **Sort** dialog box. Since column headings were included in the highlighted range before you opened the **Sort** dialog box, you must check this option.
- Click the drop-down arrow of the option box below the **Column** heading and select the Unit Sales column.
- Click the drop-down arrow of the option box below the **Sort On** heading and select the Values option. This drop-down box also contains options that allow you to sort data based on the font color or cell color in a column.
- Click the drop-down arrow of the option box below the **Order** heading and select **Largest to Smallest.** This box also contains an option called **Custom List.** This

option is helpful when you need to sort data by months of the year or days of the week.

- Click the **Add** button in the upper-left corner of the **Sort** window. This will add another set of option boxes to create a second sort level. You can add as many sort levels as needed.
- Make the following settings in the second sort level:
  - Column: **Sales Dollars**
  - Sort On: **Values**
  - Order: **Largest to Smallest**
- Click the **OK** button at the bottom of the **Sort** dialog box.

Figure 2.19 shows the final settings entered into the **Sort** dialog box. The data in a worksheet will be sorted in the order of the levels listed. Therefore, the Merchandise Sales Report will be sorted by the values in the Unit Sales column first. If duplicate values appear in the Unit Sales column, the data will be sorted by the values in the Sales Dollars column. You can change the order in which the sort levels are listed by clicking a level and then clicking one of the arrow buttons at the top of the **Sort** dialog box.

Figure 2.19 | **Settings in the Sort Dialog Box for the Merchandise Sales Report**

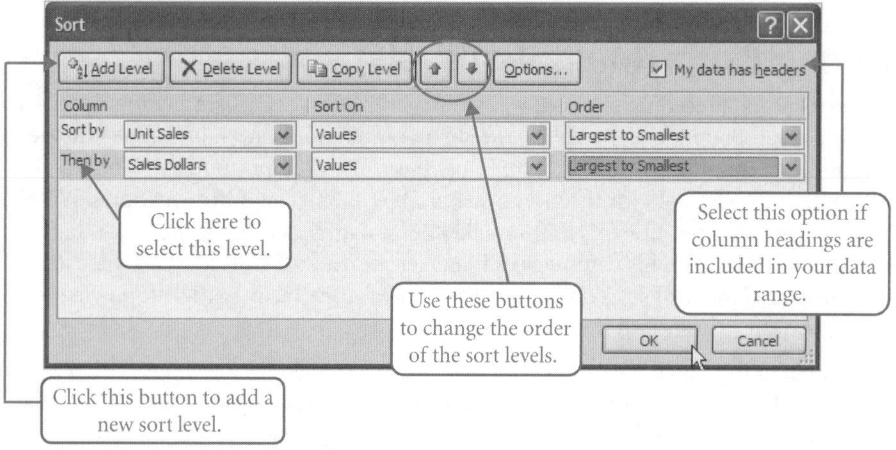

Figure 2.20 shows the final results of sorting the Merchandise Sales Report by the Unit Sales column and then by the Sales Dollars column. Notice that three items which sold 8500 units are now sorted in descending order based on the values in the Sales Dollars column.

COMMON MISTAKES | Missing Column Headings in the Sort Dialog Box

The column headings in your worksheet should appear in the drop-down box below the **Column** heading in the **Sort** dialog box. If you do not see the column heading names in these drop-down boxes, check to make sure you included them when you highlighted the range of cells to be sorted. If the column headings are included in your highlighted range but still do not appear in the drop-down boxes, check to see that the **My data has headers** option is selected in the upper-right corner of the **Sort** dialog box.

Quick Reference

Sorting Data (Multiple Levels)

1. Highlight *all* the data on your worksheet that will be sorted.
2. Click the **Data** tab of the Ribbon.
3. Click the **Sort** icon in the Ribbon.
4. Click the **Options** button in the **Sort** dialog box and select the **Sort top to bottom** option if you are sorting a list of items.
5. Click the **OK** button in the **Sort Options** dialog box.
6. Select the **My data has headers** option if column headings are included in the range you highlighted for step 1.
7. Set the **Column**, **Sort On**, and **Order** options for the first sort level.
8. Add other sort levels as needed by clicking the **Add Level** button.
9. Click the **OK** button.

Figure 2.20 | **Merchandise Sales Report Sorted Based on Unit Sales and Sales Dollars**

Click this icon when sorting by multiple levels.

Items with the same Unit Sales are sorted by Sales Dollars in descending order.

	A	B	C	D	E
1	Category	Item Description	Color	Unit Sales	Sales Dollars
2	Bottoms	Shorts	Tan	12500	237500
3	Tops	T-Shirts	Black	10000	115000
4	Bottoms	Shorts	White	9500	180500
5	Tops	Sweater	Grey	8500	289000
6	Bottoms	Shorts	Brown	8500	161500
7	Tops	T-Shirts	Blue	8500	97750
8	Tops	Tank Top	White	6500	55250
9	Bottoms	Shorts	Blue	5500	104500
10	Tops	T-Shirts	Yellow	4500	51750
11	Tops	Sweater	Brown	3500	119000
12	Shoes	Sandals	Black	3000	66000
13	Tops	Tank Top	Pink	2500	21250
14	Shoes	Boots	Black	1600	96000
15	Tops	Sweater	Red	1500	51000
16	Tops	Tank Top	Red	1500	12750
17	Shoes	Sandals	Grey	1200	26400
18	Shoes	Sandals	Green	850	18700
19	Shoes	Boots	Brown	750	45000

COMMON MISTAKES | Multiple-Level Sorting

When you are defining multiple levels to sort the data in a worksheet, it is important to highlight all data that is to be sorted first. *Any data that is not highlighted will not be sorted.* For example, if you forget to highlight a column that is related to your dataset, Excel will sort the highlighted columns creating an alignment problem with the column that was not highlighted. This will distort your data, and it may not be possible to correct this error. This problem is similar to the Common Mistake illustrated for the **Z to A** and **A to Z** icons in the previous segment.

>> Data Management Skills

VIDEO WORKSHOP

The purpose of this workshop is to demonstrate the data management skills presented in this section of the chapter. We will be creating a spreadsheet that tracks the sales results of a product line that could be sold at a university bookstore. I will be demonstrating the tasks in this workshop in the following four videos: **Data Entry**, **Adjusting Rows and Columns**, **Copy and Paste**, and **Sorting Data**. After completing each section of tasks, watch the related video in parentheses. Remember to try the tasks on your own first before watching the video.

1. **Open and Save a Workbook (Video: Data Entry)**
   a. Open a blank Excel workbook.
   b. Save the workbook as `ib_e02_videoworkshop`.
   c. Remember where you save this file. You will need this file to complete the three remaining video workshops in this chapter.

2. Data Entry (Video: Data Entry continued)

a. Activate Sheet1 by clicking the worksheet tab.

b. Type the following data into the cell locations listed:

Cell A1: `University Bookstore Sales Report`
Cell A2: `Season`
Cell A3: `Fall`
Cell A4: `Spring`
Cell A5: `Spring`
Cell A6: `Fall`
Cell A7: `Spring`
Cell A8: `Fall`
Cell A9: `Spring`
Cell A10: `Fall`
Cell A11: `Fall`
Cell A12: `Spring`
Cell B2: `Item Description`
Cell B3: `Sweatshirt`
Cell B4: `T-Shirts`
Cell B5: `Baseballs`
Cell B6: `Scarves`
Cell B7: `Sunglasses`
Cell B8: `Sweaters`
Cell B9: `Sandals`
Cell B10: `Blankets`
Cell B11: `Footballs`
Cell B12: `Sunscreen`
Cell D2: `Unit Sales`
Cell D3: `5000`
Cell D4: `8500`
Cell D5: `1200`
Cell D6: `2200`
Cell D7: `1800`
Cell D8: `3200`
Cell D9: `2200`
Cell D10: `900`
Cell D11: `500`
Cell D12: `1800`
Cell E2: `Average Price`
Cell E3: `49.99`
Cell E4: `18.99`
Cell E5: `12.99`
Cell E6: `9.99`
Cell E7: `22.99`
Cell E8: `69.99`
Cell E9: `29.99`
Cell E10: `32.99`
Cell E11: `59.99`
Cell E12: `5.99`
Cell F2: `Sales Dollars`
Cell F3: `249950`
Cell F4: `161415`
Cell F5: `15588`
Cell F6: `21978`
Cell F7: `41382`
Cell F8: `223968`
Cell F9: `65978`

Cell F10: `29691`
Cell F11: `29995`
Cell F12: `10782`

c. In cell C2, type `Item Number`.
d. In cell C3, type the number `70500`.
e. In cell C4, type the number `70501`.
f. Use **Auto Fill** to extend the series to cell C12. The number in Cell 12 should be 70509.

3. **Adjusting Rows and Columns (Video: Adjusting Rows and Columns)**
   a. Expand the height of row 1 to 27 points.
   b. Expand the height of row 2 to 31.5 points.
   c. Expand the width of column B to 12 points.

4. **Copy and Paste (Video: Copy and Paste)**
   a. Select all contents in Sheet1 by clicking the square in the upper-left corner next to column A.
   b. Click the **Copy** icon in the **Home** tab of the Ribbon to copy Sheet1.
   c. Activate Sheet2 by clicking the worksheet tab.
   d. Activate cell A1.
   e. Click the **Paste** icon in the **Home** tab of the Ribbon to paste Sheet1 into Sheet2.
   f. Activate Sheet3.
   g. Activate cell A1.
   h. Paste Sheet1 into Sheet3 by using the **Paste** icon.

5. **Sort (Video: Sorting Data)**
   a. Sort the data in Sheet1 as follows:
      i. Season: **A to Z**
      ii. Sales Dollars: **Largest to Smallest**
   b. Sort the data in Sheet2 as follows:
      i. Unit Sales: **Largest to Smallest**
      ii. Sales Dollars: **Largest to Smallest**
   c. Sort the data in Sheet3 as follows:
      i. Average Price: **Smallest to Largest**
      ii. Item Description: **A to Z**

6. **Save (Video: Sorting Data continued)**
   a. Save and close your workbook. Remember where you save this file as you will need it to do the next video workshop on formatting skills.

EXERCISE

Why Do I Need This?

>> Creating Merchandise Sales Reports

Knowing the skills covered in this section is essential for creating spreadsheets in Excel. For example, if you don't know how to adjust the width of columns, you may not be able to see the data that was entered onto a spreadsheet. Or, if you don't know how to use the copy and paste commands, you would always have to retype data when you wanted to create an identical or similar spreadsheet. Finally, knowing how to use a basic skill such as sorting can be critical in making business decisions.

Exercise

The purpose of this exercise is to create Merchandise Sales Reports for three different business managers. Each business manager will need a different arrangement of the merchandise report based on the decisions they are required to make. As a result, the spreadsheets you will create in this exercise will highlight information that is most important to the reader. Open the file named ib_e02_merchandise performancereport and complete the following tasks:

1. Copy the data in Sheet1 and paste it into Sheet2 and Sheet3.
2. Use Sheet1 to create a sales report for a buyer. The buyer will need to evaluate the sales performance of merchandise within each category. Sort the data in Sheet1 based on the columns listed below to show the buyer what item is generating the most sales dollars within each category:
   a. Category: Ascending order
   b. Total Sales Dollars: Descending order
3. Use Sheet2 to create a report for an inventory manager. An inventory manager will typically focus on the unit inventory and weeks of supply for each item. This information will be used to decide which orders to rush into the warehouse and which orders to postpone. Sort the data based on the columns listed below:
   a. Weeks of Supply: Ascending order
   b. Inventory Units: Descending order
4. Since the inventory manager is focusing only on the Weeks of Supply and Inventory Units column, hide the Units Sales, Price, and Total Sales Dollar columns.
5. Use Sheet3 to create a report for a pricing manager. The pricing manager will need to manage how items are priced and determine how many price tickets should be printed for each price point. Sort Sheet3 based on the columns listed below:
   a. Price: Ascending order
   b. Color: Ascending order
6. Since the pricing manager is focusing on the price for each item, hide the Unit Sales, Total Sales Dollars, Inventory Units, and Weeks of Supply columns.
7. Which item generates the most dollars for each category?
8. How many $19 price tickets will the pricing manager need to print?

>> What's Wrong with This Spreadsheet?

PROBLEM & EXERCISE

Problem

You are approached by a coworker who is having some difficulty with an Excel project. He sends you an Excel file with two spreadsheets in it. Sheet1 is the original spreadsheet that was given to him by an assistant buyer. Sheet2 is the spreadsheet he has been working on and is causing him trouble. The following is a list of problems the coworker has sent to you:

1. I don't know why these "####" errors appear on the spreadsheet. I was only entering numbers for the sales report, and these "####" errors keep popping up.
2. The data in Sheet1 was given to me by an assistant buyer. She told me that this worksheet would include the cost for each item. I don't see it! She keeps insisting the cost information is in there; however, I have a feeling I am going to have to enter this data myself.
3. I copied the data in Sheet1, pasted it into Sheet2, and sorted it by Sales Dollars. I had no problem sorting it except I did not see the name of each column in the Column drop-down boxes. I read somewhere that you should see the column names in those boxes, but I just saw Column A, Column B, and so on. I showed the report to one of the buyers in my department, and she said the department numbers don't seem to match the department name. I wonder if the assistant buyer did something wrong?

Exercise

The file this coworker sent you is named ib_e02_salesreporthelp. What's wrong with this spreadsheet? Consider the following points:

1. What would cause the "####" signs to appear on a spreadsheet? Is this really an error? How can this be fixed?
2. In point 2 of the Problem, the cost information is indeed in the spreadsheet. How can you tell if data exists on a spreadsheet if it cannot be seen?
3. Assume that the data in Sheet1 is accurate. What can you do to check the accuracy of the data your coworker sorted in Sheet2? Why is the coworker not seeing the column names in the Column drop-down boxes?

Write a short answer for each of these questions and fix the data in Sheet2. If a problem cannot be fixed, explain why.

>> Formatting

Skill Set

The previous section demonstrated how you can use Excel to construct a Financial Plan and a Merchandise Sales Report. This section will demonstrate how Excel's ***formatting*** commands can enhance the visual appearance of these spreadsheets. Excel's formatting features can transform the appearance of a basic spreadsheet into a professional-looking document. However, formatting also serves a more functional purpose in that it guides the reader's attention to the most critical information. This allows a business manager to scan a spreadsheet efficiently and identify the most important information required to make key decisions.

Excel's primary formatting features are found in the **Font**, **Alignment**, and **Number** groups of the **Home** tab in the Ribbon (shown in Figure 2.21). This section

Figure 2.21 | **Formatting Features Are Found in the Home Tab of the Ribbon**

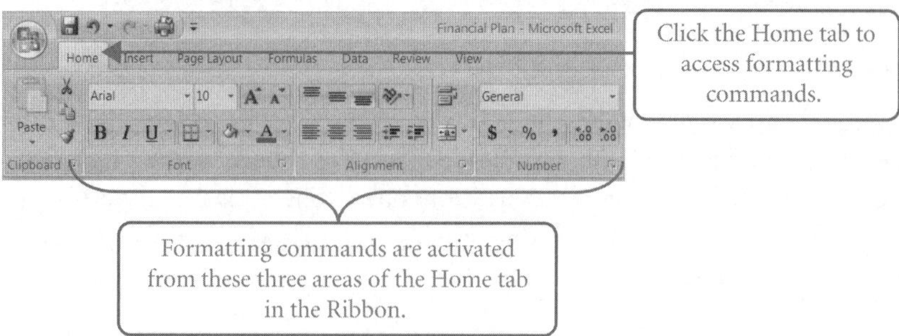

will illustrate the formatting commands that are available in each of these three groups and demonstrate how you apply them to the Financial Plan or Merchandise Sales Report spreadsheets, which were introduced previously in this chapter.

Data Formats

Commands you use to format the appearance of data are found in the Font group, as shown in Figure 2.22. Frequently used icons in this Group are the **Font Size**, **Font Color**, **Bold**, **Italic**, and **Underline**.

Figure 2.22 | **Format Icons in the Font Group**

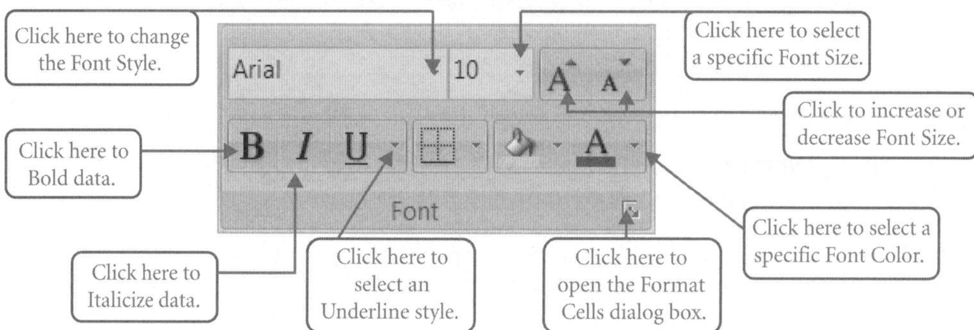

The icons highlighted in Figure 2.22 are valuable when you're making data stand out on a worksheet. For example, you can use them to enlarge the title of a worksheet, bold a critical row of data, or enhance the appearance of column headings. Formatting column headings can be particularly important because it separates the heading from the actual data, making it easier for the reader to locate specific types of data. The following points explain how to format the column headings for the Merchandise Sales Report shown in Figure 2.20:

- Highlight the range A1:E1. Before using any of the formatting icons in the **Home** tab of the Ribbon, you must first highlight a cell or range of cells that will be formatted.
- Click the **Home** tab of the Ribbon.
- Click the **Bold** icon.
- Click the **Italic** icon.
- Click the down arrow next to the **Font Color** icon and click the Dark Red square. When using icons such as the **Font Color**, **Font Size**, or **Font Style**, you will see the data in your highlighted range change as you move the cursor over the various options. This allows you to preview what your data will look like when it is formatted before making a choice (see Figure 2.23).

Figure 2.23 shows the Merchandise Sales Report with the column headings formatted. This simple enhancement makes it easy for the reader to separate the column headings from the actual data and identify what each column of data represents.

Figure 2.23 | **Formatted Column Headings for the Merchandise Sales Report**

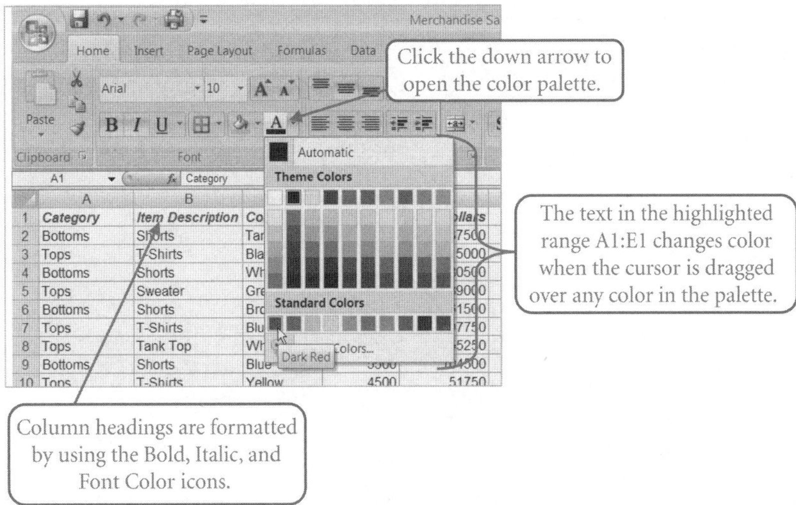

The icons shown in Figure 2.22 should satisfy almost all of your data format needs. However, you can find additional formatting options by opening the **Format Cells** dialog box. The **Format Cells** dialog box contains almost every available formatting option in Excel. You can open it by clicking the button in the lower-right corner of the **Font**, **Alignment**, and **Number** groups in the **Home** tab of the Ribbon (see Figure 2.22). Figure 2.24 shows the **Format Cells** dialog box and highlights options where an icon is not available in the Ribbon.

Figure 2.24 | **The Format Cells Dialog Box**

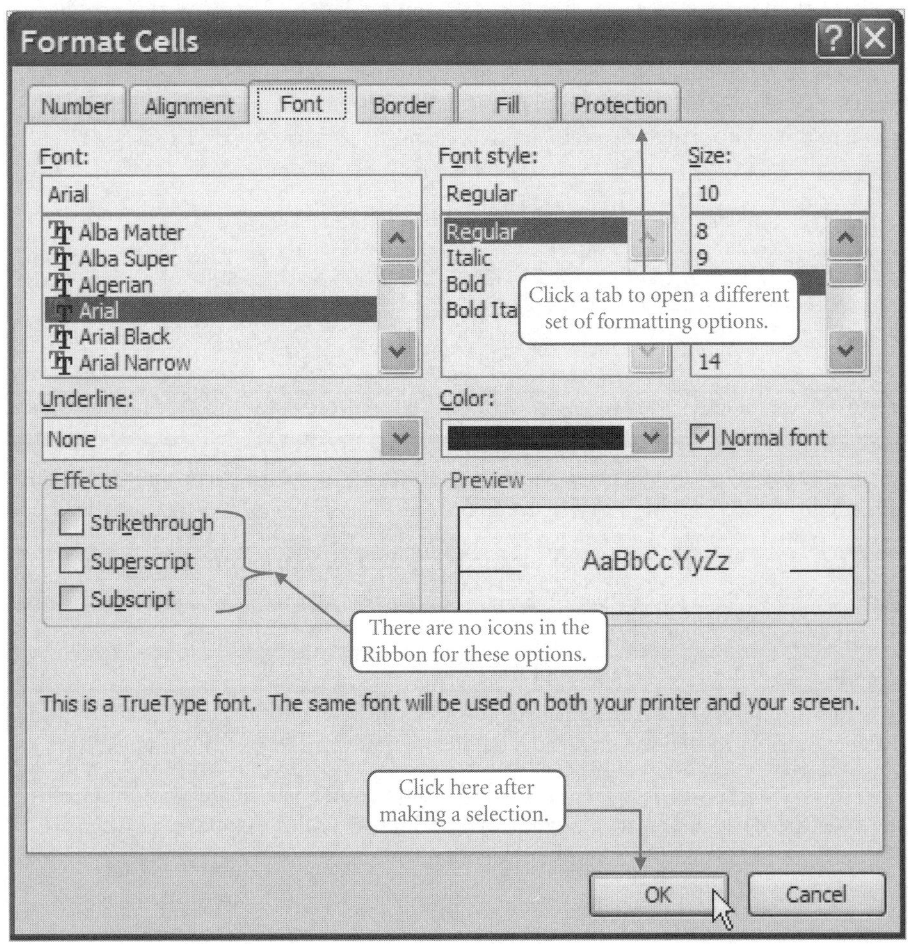

> **Quick Reference**
>
> **Formatting Data**
>
> 1. Highlight a range of cells to be formatted.
> 2. Click the **Home** tab of the Ribbon.
> 3. Click one of the icons in the **Font** group of the Ribbon or open the **Format Cells** dialog box by clicking the button in the lower-right corner of the **Font** group.
> 4. If using the **Format Cells** dialog box, click the **OK** button after making a selection.

Data Alignment

After applying data formatting techniques to a worksheet, you may need to adjust the ***alignment*** of data in a cell. For example, you may need to use the **Horizontal Alignment** icons to center or right justify data in a cell. If you are setting up accounting statements, you will need to use the **Indent** icons for certain financial headings. Figure 2.25 highlights the icons available in the **Alignment** group in the **Home** tab of the Ribbon.

Figure 2.25 | **Alignment Icons**

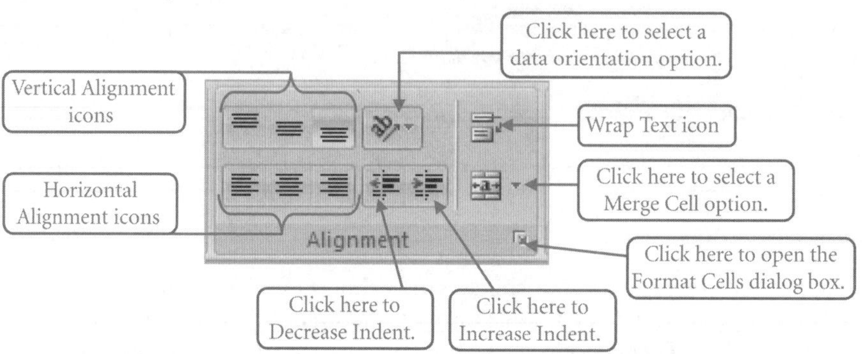

The ***Wrap Text*** icon is a commonly used feature because it will automatically expand the row height and create a second line to fit long entries. This reduces the need to expand the width of columns, which decreases the amount of information that can be seen on one screen or one page. For example, in Figure 2.26, the font size of the column headings in the Merchandise Sales Report was increased. These headings are now too large to fit in the space allocated for each column. You could resolve this problem by expanding the width of each column; however, doing so may reduce the amount of information a reader can see across one sheet of paper. This will make reading and evaluating the information on a report more difficult for a business manager who is trying to obtain information as efficiently as possible to make key decisions.

Figure 2.26 | **Column Headings Are Truncated When Font Size Is Increased**

	A	B	C	D	E	F
1	Category	Item Descrip	Color	Unit Sale	Sales Dollars	
2	Bottoms	Shorts	Tan	12500	237500	
3	Tops	T-Shirts	Black	10000	115000	
4	Bottoms	Shorts	White	9500	180500	

These column headings are truncated when the font size is increased.

The following explains how to use the **Wrap Text** feature to correct the column headings in the range A1:E1 in Figure 2.26:

- Highlight the range A1:E1.
- Click the **Home** tab at the top of the Ribbon.
- Click the **Wrap Text** icon. This will automatically expand the height of row 1 and place any word that was truncated below the first word in the column heading.

Figure 2.27 shows the appearance of the Merchandise Sales Report column headings after the **Wrap Text** feature is applied. In addition, notice that both the ***Vertical Alignment*** and ***Horizontal Alignment*** were set to center.

Figure 2.27 | **Columns Headings with Wrap Text Applied**

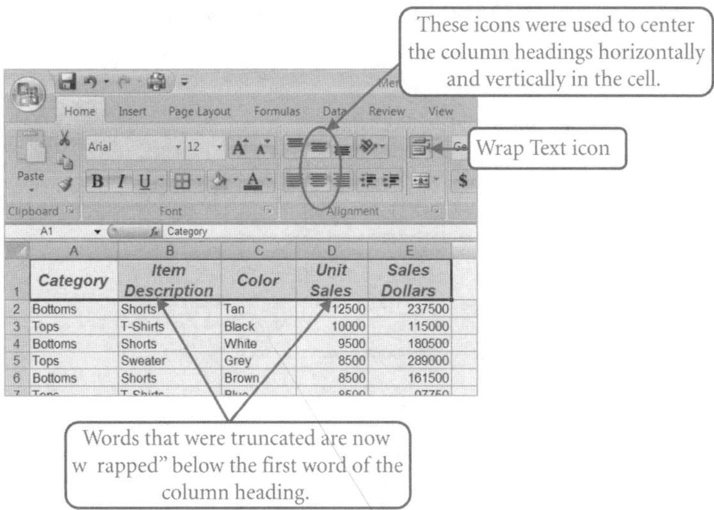

Another common feature used in the **Alignment** area is the **Merge & Center** icon. ***Merge & Center*** allows you to create one big cell out of several smaller cells and is commonly used to center a title at the top of a spreadsheet. For example, Figure 2.28 shows the Financial Plan spreadsheet. The **Merge & Center** icon will be used to center the title in cell A1 over the center of the worksheet. The following points explain how you accomplish this:

- Highlight the range A1:F1 (see Figure 2.28). When you are using the **Merge & Center** icon, cell locations within a highlighted range will be transformed into one cell.
- Click the **Home** tab of the Ribbon.
- Click the down arrow next to the **Merge & Center** icon and select the **Merge & Center** option. This will transform the cells in the range A1:F1 into one cell and horizontally center any data in the range. You could also use the **Merge Cells** option to just combine cells without centering the data.

Figure 2.28 | **Merge Cell Options**

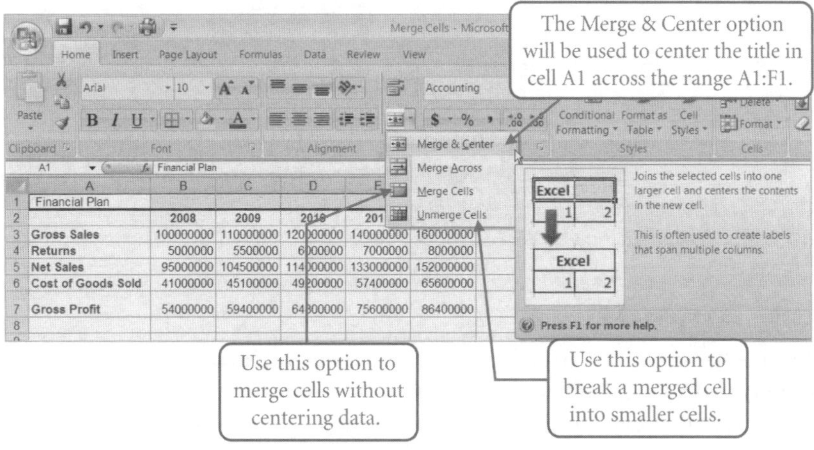

Quick Reference

Horizontal and Vertical Alignment

1. Highlight a range of cells to be formatted.
2. Click the **Home** tab of the Ribbon.
3. Click one of the **Vertical Alignment** icons , , to place data on the top, center, or bottom of a cell.
4. Click one of the **Horizontal Alignment** icons , , to left justify, center, or right justify data in a cell.

Quick Reference

Wrap Text

1. Highlight a range of cells to be formatted.
2. Click the **Home** tab of the Ribbon.
3. Click the **Wrap Text** icon .

Figure 2.29 shows the results of using the **Merge & Center** option to format the title of the Financial Plan. Notice that the font size was increased to 14 points, with bold and italic formats added.

Figure 2.29 | **Formatted Title in the Financial Plan Worksheet**

	A	B	C	D	E	F
1	***Financial Plan***					
2		**2008**	**2009**	**2010**	**2011**	**2012**
3	**Gross Sales**	100000000	110000000	120000000	140000000	160000000
4	**Returns**	5000000	5500000	6000000	7000000	8000000
5	**Net Sales**	95000000	104500000	114000000	1330000[illegible]	[illegible]
6	**Cost of Goods Sold**	41000000	45100000	49200000	57400[illegible]	[illegible]
7	**Gross Profit**	54000000	59400000	64800000	75600[illegible]	[illegible]

Cells in the range A1:F1 are merged and the title is centered horizontally.

As mentioned in the previous section, in some situations you may need to access additional formatting features through the **Format Cells** dialog box. The **Format Cells** dialog box will be opened to the **Alignment** tab when you click the button in the lower-right corner of the **Alignment** section of the Ribbon (see Figure 2.25). Figure 2.30 highlights a few useful features such as the indent and ***orientation*** settings. These options provide you with more detail when making specific indent settings or orienting data on a specific angle within a cell.

Figure 2.30 | **Alignment Tab of the Format Cells Dialog Box**

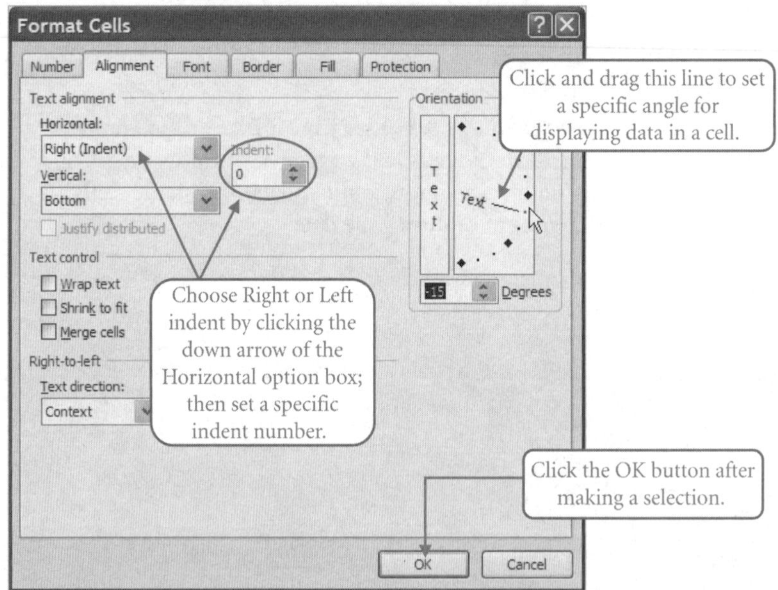

Number Formats

Commands used to format the appearance of numbers are found in the **Number** group, as shown in Figure 2.31. These options allow you to format numeric data such as currency, percentages, dates, or fractions.

> ***Quick Reference***
>
> **Merge Cells**
>
> 1. Highlight a range of cells to be merged.
> 2. Click the **Home** tab of the Ribbon.
> 3. Click the down arrow of the **Merge & Center** icon and select an option.

Figure 2.31 | **Icons for Number Formats**

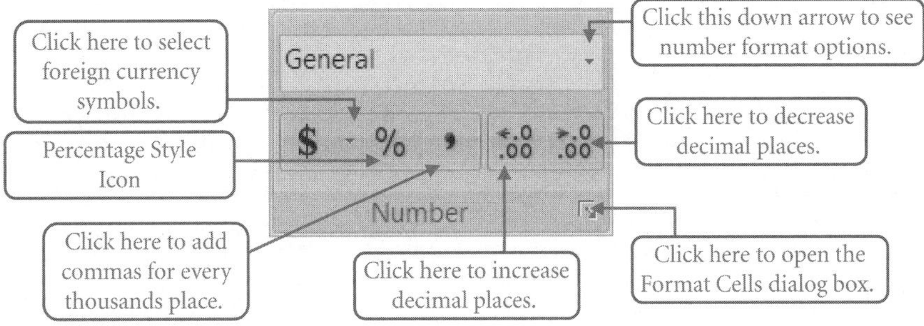

Figure 2.32 shows the options that are available when clicking the down arrow of the **Number Format** icon.

Figure 2.32 | **Number Format Icons Drop-Down Box**

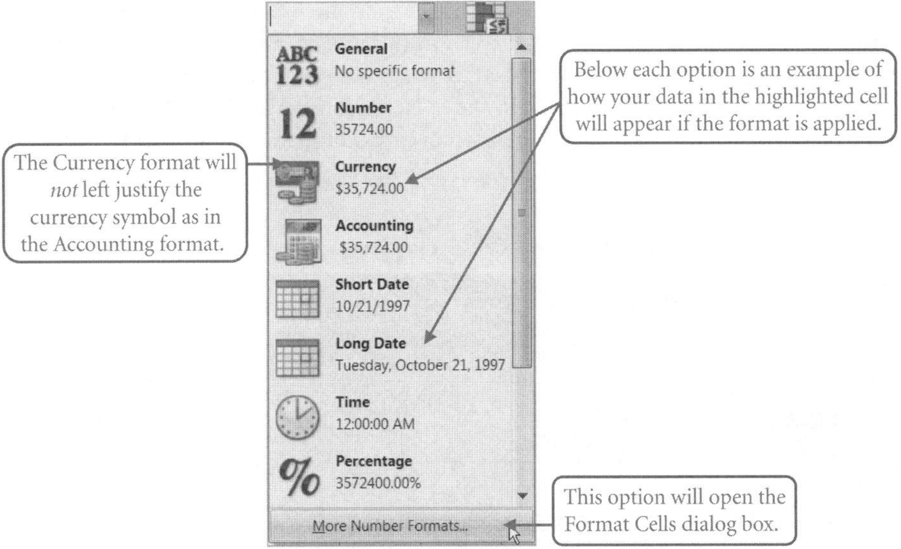

The following steps explain how you apply the Accounting format to the numbers in the Financial Plan worksheet. The Accounting format will left justify the currency symbol, add a comma for every thousands place, add two decimal places, and place negative numbers in parentheses.

- Highlight the range B3:F7. As with other formatting commands, you must highlight a range of cells first before selecting a number format.
- Click the **Home** tab on the Ribbon.
- Click the **Accounting Number Format** icon. If you are working with foreign currency, you can select a different currency symbol such as Euros or English Pounds by clicking the down arrow of this icon.
- Click the **Decrease Decimal** icon twice. As with most financial plans, carrying financial projections to two decimal places is not necessary. Therefore, you remove the decimal places by clicking the **Decrease Decimal** icon twice.

Quick Reference

Accounting Format

1. Highlight a range of cells to be formatted.
2. Click the **Home** tab of the Ribbon.
3. Click the **Accounting Number Format** icon [$ ▾]. Click the down arrow next to this icon to change the currency symbol.
4. Click the **Increase** or **Decrease Decimal** icons [.00] and [.0] as needed.

Figure 2.33 | **Accounting Format Applied to the Financial Plan Worksheet**

	A	B	C	D	E	F
1				*Financial Plan*		
2		2008	2009	2010	2011	2012
3	Gross Sales	$ 100,000,000	$ 110,000,000	$ 120,000,000	$ 140,000,000	$ 160,000,000
4	Returns	$ 5,000,000	$ 5,500,000	$ 6,000,000	$ 7,000,000	$ 8,000,000
5	Net Sales	$ 95,000,000	$ 104,500,000	$ 114,000,000	$ 133,000,000	$ 152,000,000
6	Cost of Goods Sold	$ 41,000,000	$ 45,100,000	$ 49,200,000	$ 57,400,000	$ 65,600,000
7	Gross Profit	$ 54,000,000	$ 59,400,000	$ 64,800,000	$ 75,600,000	$ 86,400,000

The Accounting format will left justify the dollar sign.

As you can see in Figure 2.32, you can open the **Format Cells** dialog box by selecting the **More Number Formats** option in the **Number Format** drop-down box. When you are applying number formats, the **Format Cells** dialog box provides several options that are not available in the Ribbon. For example, when applying the Currency format, you can choose an option that converts negative numbers to a red font color. This color is most helpful when you need to bring the reader's attention to negative results that are critical, such as Gross Profit or Net Income. The **Format Cells** dialog box also provides more options for formatting dates compared to the **Number Format** icon. These options are highlighted in Figure 2.34.

Figure 2.34 | **Number Tab of the Format Cells Dialog Box**

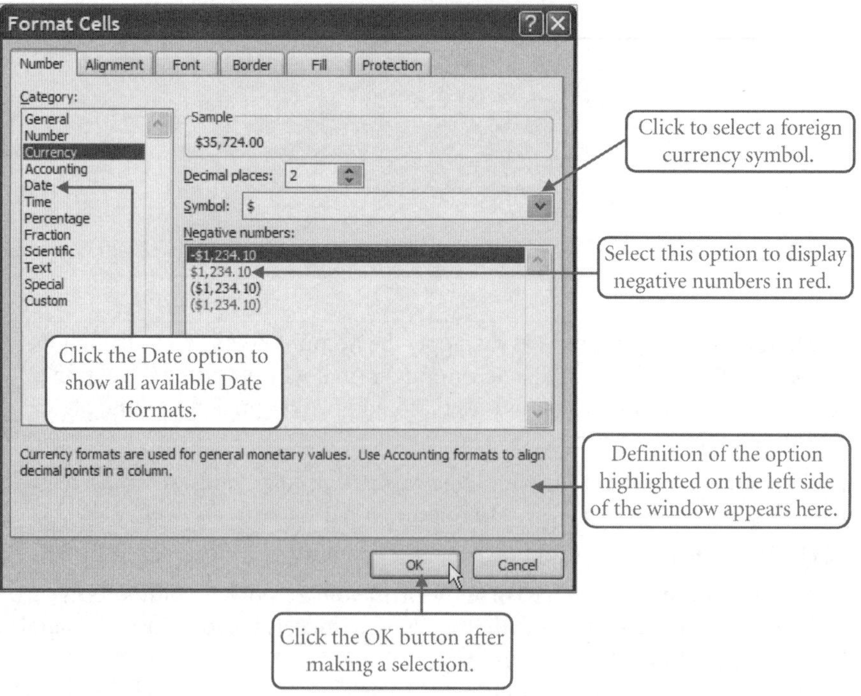

> **Quick Reference**
>
> **Formatting Numbers**
>
> 1. Highlight a range of cells containing numbers to be formatted.
> 2. Click the **Home** tab of the Ribbon.
> 3. Click one of the icons in the **Number** group of the Ribbon or open the **Format Cells** dialog box by clicking the button in the lower-right corner of the **Number** group.
> 4. If using the **Format Cells** dialog box, click the **OK** button after making a selection.

COMMON MISTAKES | Using the Currency Format

When selecting the Currency format from the **Format Cells** dialog box, check the **Symbol** setting. Occasionally, this box may be set to **none**. Also, if you are working on an accounting assignment and would like to left justify the dollar signs, use the Accounting format. Dollar signs will be placed in front of the value and will not align when using the Currency format.

Borders (Line Formats)

Use the ***Border*** command to place lines on an Excel worksheet. As previously mentioned, a key purpose for enhancing the appearance of a worksheet is to make it easy for a reader to find and analyze needed information. Adding lines to a worksheet advances this purpose because it helps the reader keep track of data associated with each row and also helps distinguish labels from data.

The **Borders** icon is found in the **Font** group in the **Home tab** of the Ribbon. Figure 2.35 illustrates the options that are available when you click the down arrow of the **Borders** icon. You add borders to a worksheet by first highlighting a range of cells and then selecting one of the line styles and placement options shown in the figure.

Figure 2.35 | **Line and Placement Options in the Borders Icon**

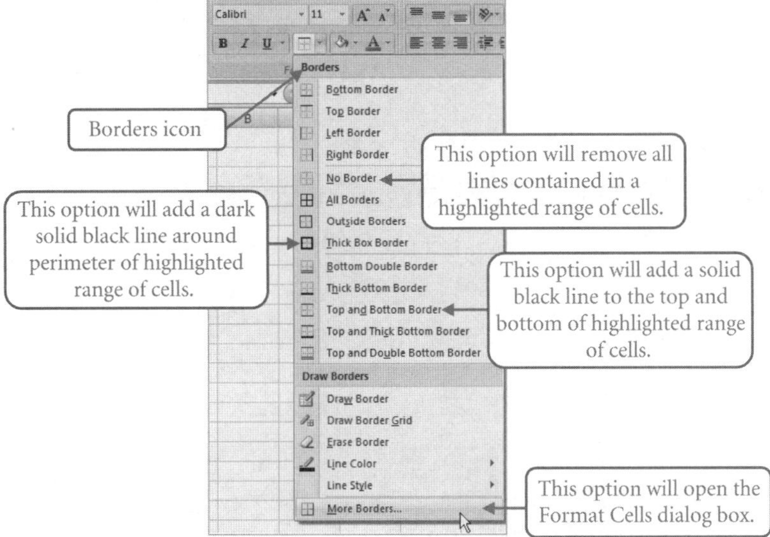

As illustrated in Figure 2.35, the **Borders** icon provides several options for adding lines to a worksheet. However, you may find these options limiting. For example, the options in the **Borders** icon will only provide black lines and contain only a few line styles. As a result, you may need to use the **Format Cells** dialog box when adding lines to a worksheet. The following steps explain how you use both the **Borders** icon and the **Format Cells** dialog box to add lines to the Merchandise Sales Report:

- Highlight the range A1:E19.
- Click the **Home** tab of the Ribbon.
- Click the down arrow in the **Borders** icon.
- Select the **Thick Box Border** option. A dark black line will appear around the perimeter of the highlighted range.
- Highlight the range A2:E19.
- Click the down arrow in the **Borders** icon and select the **More Borders** option. This will open the **Format Cells** dialog box to the **Border** tab. You can also click the button in the lower-right corner of the **Font** section in the Ribbon and click the **Border** tab when the **Format Cells** dialog box opens.
- Click the down arrow of the **Color** box and select the black square.
- Click the regular solid line style on the left side of the dialog box.
- Click the **Inside** icon at the upper-right side of the dialog box. You will see vertical and horizontal lines appear in the locator box. This option of placing lines only on

the inside of a range of cells and not the perimeter is not available in the **Borders** icon. This is why the **Format Cells** dialog box is needed in this case.

- Click the down arrow of the **Color** box and select the Dark Red square in the lower-left corner of the color palette.
- Click the dark solid line style on the left side of the dialog box.
- Click the top of the locator box on the right side of the dialog box. This will place a dark solid red line at the top of the highlighted range. Different line colors are not available in the **Borders** icon options. Therefore, you must use the **Format Cells** dialog box in these situations.

Figure 2.36 shows the final settings that were made in the **Border** tab of the **Format Cells** dialog box. Notice the red line that appears at the top of the locator box. This indicates that the line will be placed at the top of the highlighted range cells. If the middle of the locator box were selected, a red line would appear between every row in the middle of the highlighted range.

Figure 2.36 | **The Border Tab of the Format Cells Dialog Box**

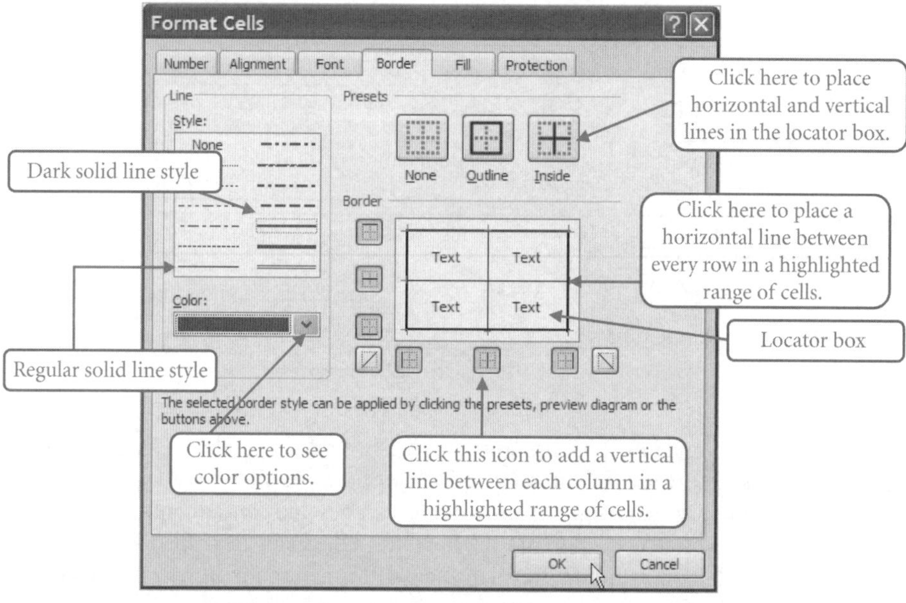

COMMON MISTAKES | Borders

Forgetting to select the color and line styles first are the most common mistakes people make when using the **Format Cells** dialog box to add borders to a worksheet. You must select the line color and style first before selecting a placement in the locator box.

Figure 2.37 shows the results of adding lines to the Merchandise Sales Report. The lines make it easier to read all the data pertaining to each row and also help to separate each column. Notice that the numbers in columns D and E are formatted.

Quick Reference

Borders

1. Highlight a range of cells where lines should appear.
2. Click the **Home** tab of the Ribbon.
3. Click the down arrow in the **Borders** icon.
4. Select a line style and placement option.

Or

1. Highlight a range of cells where lines should appear.
2. Click the **Home** tab of the Ribbon.
3. Click the down arrow in the **Borders** icon and select the **More Borders** option.
4. Select a color and line style on the right side of the window.
5. Select the placement of the line using the locator box or placement icons.
6. Click the **OK** button.

Figure 2.37 | **Results of Adding Lines to the Merchandise Sales Report**

	A	B	C	D	E
1	*Category*	*Item Description*	*Color*	*Unit Sales*	*Sales Dollars*
2	Bottoms	Shorts	Tan	12,500	$237,500
3	Tops	T-Shirts	Black	10,000	$11
4	Bottoms	Shorts	White	9,500	$18
5	Tops	Sweater	Grey	8,500	$28
6	Bottoms	Shorts	Brown	8,500	$161,
7	Tops	T-Shirts	Blue	8,500	$97,750
8	Tops	Tank Top	White	6,500	$55,250
9	Bottoms	Shorts	Blue	5,500	$104,500
10	Tops	T-Shirts	Yellow	4,500	$51,750
11	Tops	Sweater	Brown	3,500	$119,000
12	Shoes	Sandals	Black	3,000	$66,000
13	Tops	Tank Top	Pink	2,500	$21,250
14	Shoes	Boots	Black	1,600	$96,000
15	Tops	Sweater	Red	1,500	$51,000
16	Tops	Tank Top	Red	1,500	$12,750
17	Shoes	Sandals	Grey	1,200	$26,4
18	Shoes	Sandals	Green	850	$18,7
19	Shoes	Boots	Brown	750	$45,0

Vertical lines were added to the range A1:E1 using the Format Cells dialog box.

Numbers in these columns are formatted.

Cell Color (Fill Color)

Changing the color of the cells in a worksheet is another formatting technique that makes titles and column headings stand out. You change the cell colors in a worksheet by using the ***Fill Color*** icon shown in Figure 2.38.

Figure 2.38 | **Fill Color Icon**

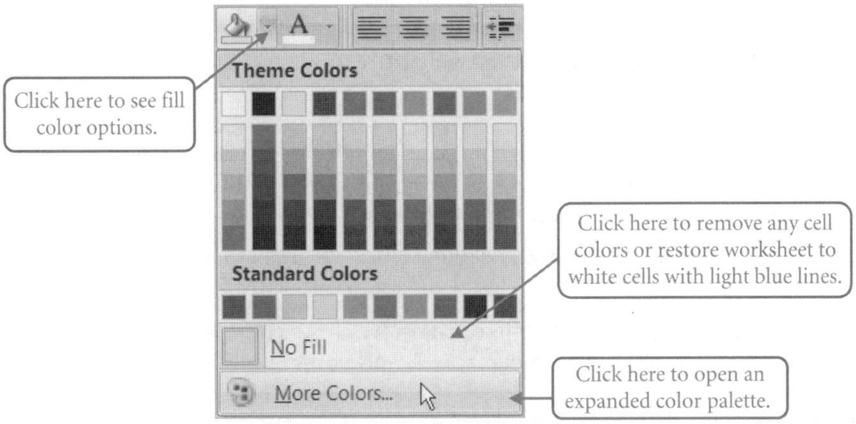

The following explains how you change the cell colors in the Financial Plan worksheet to make the title stand out:

- Highlight the range A1:F1.
- Click the **Home** tab of the Ribbon.
- Click the down arrow in the **Fill Color** icon.
- Click the Dark Blue box at the bottom of the color palette. You will notice the highlighted range changes as you move the cursor over the color palette. This allows you to see how your worksheet will appear before making a selection.
- Click the down arrow in the **Font Color** icon and select the white square. Since a dark cell color is being used, changing the color of the text to white will make the text stand out.

Figure 2.39 shows the results of the Financial Plan worksheet with cell colors added. In addition to the title, cells in the range B2:F2 and A3:A7 were changed to orange.

Quick Reference

Cell Color

1. Highlight range of cells to be colored.
2. Click the **Home** tab of the Ribbon.
3. Click the down arrow of the **Fill Color** icon.
4. Select a color from the palette.

Figure 2.39 | **Results of Adding Cell Color to the Financial Plan**

	A	B	C	D	E	F
1	Financial Plan					
2		2008	2009	2010	2011	2012
3	Gross Sales	$ 100,000,000	$ 110,000,000	$ 120,000,000	$ 140,000,000	$ 160,000,000
4	Returns	$ 5,000,000	$ 5,500,000	$ 6,000,000	$ 7,000,000	$ 8,000,000
5	Net Sales	$ 95,000,000	$ 104,500,000	$ 114,000,000	$ 133,000,000	$ 152,000,000
6	Cost of Goods Sold	$ 41,000,000	$ 45,100,000	$ 49,200,000	$ 57,400,000	$ 65,600,000
7	Gross Profit	$ 54,000,000	$ 59,400,000	$ 64,800,000	$ 75,600,000	$ 86,400,000
8						

>> Formatting

The purpose of this workshop is to demonstrate the formatting skills presented in this section of the chapter. We will continue to build the spreadsheet that was started in the Data Management Video Workshop. I will be demonstrating the tasks in this workshop in the following four videos: **Data Alignment**, **Number and Font Formats**, **Cell Color**, and **Borders**. After completing each section of tasks, watch the related video in parentheses. Remember to try the tasks on your own first before watching the video.

1. **Open File**
   a. Open the file named ib_e02_videoworkshop, which you completed for the Data Management Video Workshop previously in this chapter.

2. **Data Alignment (Video: Data Alignment)**
   a. Activate Sheet1 by clicking the worksheet tab.
   b. Highlight the range A1:F1.
   c. Merge the cells in the highlighted range without centering the text using the **Merge & Center** icon in the Ribbon.
   d. Set the horizontal and vertical alignment for the highlighted range to center.
   e. Highlight the range A2:F2.
   f. Wrap the text in the highlighted range by clicking the **Wrap Text** icon in the Ribbon. Then set the horizontal and vertical alignment to center.

3. **Adjusting Columns and Rows (Video: Data Alignment continued)**
   a. Change the width of column D to 7 points.
   b. Change the width of column F to 12 points.
   c. Change the height of row 8 to 23 points. Use the **Height** option in the **Format** icon, which is in the **Home** tab of the Ribbon.
   d. Repeat steps a and b for Sheet2 and Sheet3.

4. **Numbers and Fonts (Video: Number and Font Formats)**
   a. Activate Sheet1.
   b. For cell A1, make the following font settings: Type: Garamond; Style: Bold and Italic; Size: 14 points.
   c. Bold the text in the range A2:F3 and A8:F8
   d. Format the range D3:D12 with commas and 0 decimal places.
   e. Format the range E3:E12 to U.S. currency and 2 decimal places.

f. Format the range F3:F12 to U.S. currency and 0 decimal places.
g. Repeat steps d, e, and f for Sheet2 and Sheet3.

5. **Cell Color (Fill Color) (Video: Cell Color)**
   a. Activate Sheet1.
   b. For cell A1, change the cell color to brown and change the text color to white.
   c. Change the cell color to yellow for the range A2:F2.
   d. Change the text color to blue for the range A3:F3 and A8:F8.

6. **Borders (Video: Borders)**
   a. Highlight the range A1:F12 and add a thick bold black line around the perimeter of the range. Use the **Format Cells** dialog box to add this border.
   b. Highlight the range A1:F2 and add a horizontal bold black line in the middle and bottom of the range. Use the **Format Cells** dialog box to add these borders.
   c. Highlight the range A2:F2 and add a vertical regular black line to the middle of the range. Use the **Format Cells** dialog box to add this border.
   d. Highlight the range A3:F12 and add horizontal and vertical regular black lines to the middle of the range. Use the **Format Cells** dialog box to add these borders.
   e. Highlight the range A7:F7 and add a red double line to the bottom of the range. Use the **Format Cells** dialog box to add this border.
   f. Save and close your file. Remember where you saved this file because it will be used in the Editing Video Workshop.

>> Creating a Store Performance Report

EXERCISE

Why Do I Need This?

Formatting techniques are used to direct the reader to the most critical information on a spreadsheet and are often the difference between a mediocre and professional spreadsheet. It is important for you to be aware of the formatting commands available in Excel and how they can be applied to create an effective spreadsheet.

Exercise

Open the file named ib_e02_storeperformancereport. You will see a worksheet without any formatting techniques applied. Your goal will be to format this spreadsheet for the distribution manager of a retail store chain. Follow the directions and remember to save your work periodically.

1. Copy Sheet1 and paste it into Sheet2.

2. Make the title of the report stand out so that it can be easily distinguished from other reports this manager will be evaluating. Highlight the range A1:N1 in Sheet2 and apply the following formats:
   a. Merge the cells.
   b. Set the horizontal and vertical alignment to center.
   c. Change the font size to 14, the font style to bold, and change the font color to white.
   d. Change the cell color to green.

3. Your next task is to fix the column headings of the report. You will notice that in some instances you cannot see the entire column heading because it is too long to fit in a cell. Adjust the headings as follows:
   a. Highlight the range I2:N2. Merge the cells, set the horizontal alignment to center, and then bold and italicize the text.
   b. Highlight the range A3:N3. Instead of increasing the width of these columns to show the column headings, format the cells to wrap text, set the horizontal alignment to center, bold the text, and change the color of the cells to yellow.
   c. Since this spreadsheet has several columns, keep the width as narrow as possible. Make the following column width adjustments:
      i. Column A: `7.5`
      ii. Column B: `12`
      iii. Column C: `6`
      iv. Column E: `10`
      v. Column H: `10`
      vi. Column J: `9`
4. Format the numbers on the spreadsheet as follows:
   a. D4:E28: Number format with commas, 0 decimal places.
   b. F4:G28: U.S. Currency format, 0 decimal places. You may need to readjust the column widths.
   c. H4:H28: Number format with 0 decimal places.
   d. I4:N28: U.S. Currency format, 0 decimal places. You may need to readjust the column widths.
5. The information the distribution manager is most concerned about is the estimated annual truck deliveries. The distribution manager will need this information to calculate the shipping costs by store and for the entire retail chain. To make this column of data stand out, add the following format settings to the range H4:H28:
   a. Set the horizontal alignment to center.
   b. Bold and italicize the text.
   c. Italicize the text in cell H3.
   d. Change the color of the text in the range H3:H28 to dark blue.
6. The distribution manager will use the right side of this spreadsheet as a reference to get an idea of how the volume of deliveries might change from month to month. This section needs to be visually separated form the rest of the worksheet. Change the cell color to light green for the range I4:N28.
7. The last step in this formatting exercise is to add lines to the spreadsheet. Without lines, it will be very difficult to follow the data for each store across the spreadsheet. Add the following lines to the spreadsheet:
   a. Add regular black lines to the inside of the range A3:N28. Every cell in this range should have a regular black outline.
   b. Add a heavy dark bold line around the perimeter of the range A3:N28.
   c. Add a regular bold line around the perimeter of the range A3:N3.
   d. Add a regular bold line to the bottom of cell A1.
   e. Add a bold line to the left of range I2:I28.
8. Sort the worksheet based on the Estimated Annual Truck Deliveries column in descending order.

9. Compare Sheet1 and Sheet2. What formatting techniques make the biggest impact?

10. What stores are expected to receive 37 annual truck deliveries, and what is the size of these stores in square feet?

11. What information was necessary before adding format techniques to this spreadsheet?

12. Save and close your file.

>> What's Wrong with This Spreadsheet?

PROBLEM & EXERCISE

Problem

You are approached by a coworker who works in the price change division of a jewelry store. The company is having a sale and reducing the prices on several pieces of jewelry. Your coworker was asked to prepare a spreadsheet that lists all the items that will be included in the sale, the original price, and the new reduced price. She attaches an Excel file in an e-mail and asks for your help. Her e-mail includes the following points:

1. I set up a spreadsheet that shows all the sale items for this weekend. I listed each item with the current price, and I am trying to add a column to show the new reduced price. For some reason, no matter what I type into this column, nothing appears. Try it! I entered the first price which is $90. But nothing shows up in the cell. When I activate the cell (D3), I can see it says $90 in the formula bar, but I can't see it in the cell. I can't understand why this is happening. I didn't do anything but type in the price. Oh wait. . . I did try something. I tried to change the color of the cells by clicking on one of those icons at the top, but it didn't work. That still doesn't explain why nothing shows up in the cell.

2. The other problem I am having is with the border around the worksheet. I am simply trying to add a bold outline around the worksheet. I opened the Format Cells dialog box to the Border tab and clicked on all four sides of the locator box on the left. Then I clicked the dark bold line on the right and clicked the OK button. However, the regular thin line keeps appearing instead of the bold line. I must have clicked that bold line a hundred times, but I keep getting this stupid thin black line. At this point, I am beginning to think there is something seriously wrong with my computer! However, I heard you were really good with this stuff. Can you help?

Exercise

Open the file named ib_e02_pricechangeproblems. What's wrong with this spreadsheet? Consider the following points:

1. Try typing a number in any of the cells in the range D3:D12. Why can't you see the number?

2. Why is this coworker having trouble getting the bold line to appear on the worksheet? Follow the steps she explained in point 2 carefully. Is this right?

Write a short answer for each of these points and fix the spreadsheet for this coworker.

Skill Set

Editing

After creating a spreadsheet, you may need to make edits. Editing a spreadsheet may involve changing the data in a cell location, adding a new column of data, or deleting an existing column of data. The editing commands covered in this section can be found in the **Home** tab of the Ribbon. As in previous sections, we will again use the Financial Plan and Merchandise Sales Report spreadsheets to demonstrate the editing commands.

Editing Data in a Cell

After typing data into a cell location, you can change it by using the ***formula bar*** or by double clicking the cell. The formula bar, as shown in Figure 2.40, will always show the contents of an active cell. To change the data in an active cell, click the formula bar, type any adjustments, and press the **Enter** key. Figure 2.40 shows how the word "Description" was added to cell A1 using the formula bar. This edit can also be accomplished by double clicking cell A1.

Figure 2.40 | **Editing Data Using the Formula Bar**

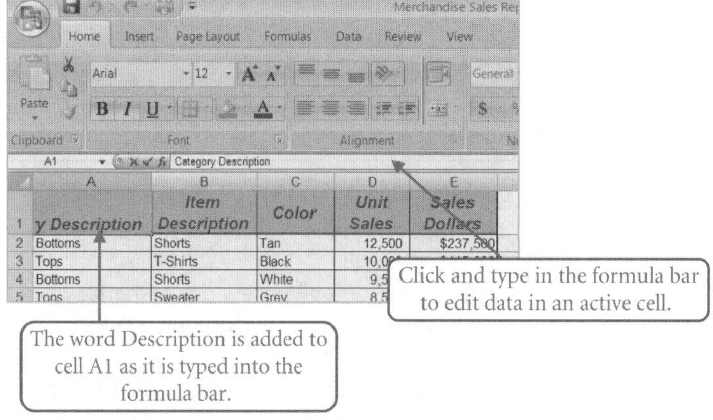

Quick Reference

Editing Data

1. Activate cell containing data.
2. Click in the formula bar.
3. Type edits in the formula bar.
4. Press the **Enter** key.

Or

1. Double click a cell with data.
2. Type edits.
3. Press the **Enter** key.

COMMON MISTAKES | Editing Data

Even though you are editing data, as opposed to entering data, you must still press the **Enter** key after completing your edits. Edits will not be finalized unless you press the **Enter** key, or you left click another cell. If you are using the formula bar to edit data in a cell, you can enter the change by clicking the check mark that appears on the left of the formula bar.

Moving Data

You can move data in Excel by clicking and dragging the edge of an active cell or a range of cells. Move the cursor to the edge of the active cell or range cells. When the cursor changes from a white plus sign to crossed arrows, click and drag the data to a new location on a spreadsheet (see Figure 2.41).

Quick Reference

Moving Data

1. Activate a cell or highlight a range of cells to be moved.
2. Move the cursor to the edge of the cell or range.
3. When the cursor changes to crossed arrows, click and drag.

Figure 2.41 | **Moving Data**

	A	B	C	D	E
1	Category	Item Description	Color	Unit Sales	Sales Dollars
2	Bottoms	Shorts	Tan	12,500	$237,500
3	Tops	T-Shirts	Black	10,000	$115,000
4	Bottoms	Shorts	White	9,500	$180,500
5	Tops	Sweater	Grey	8,500	$289,000
6	Bottoms	Shorts	Brown	8,500	$161,500
7	Tops	T-Shirts	Blue	8,500	$97,750
8	Tops	Tank Top	White	6,500	$55,250
9	Bottoms	Shorts	Blue	5,500	$104,500
10	Tops	T-Shirts	Yellow	4,500	$51,750
11	Tops	Sweater	Brown	3,500	$119,00
12	Shoes	Sandals	Black	3,000	$66,0
13	Tops	Tank Top	Pink	2,500	$21,2
14	Shoes	Boots	Black	1,600	$96,0
15	Tops	Sweater	Red	1,500	$51,0
16	Tops	Tank Top	Red	1,500	$12,7
17	Shoes	Sandals	Grey	1,200	$26,40
18	Shoes	Sandals	Green	850	$18,700
19	Shoes	Boots	Brown	750	$45,000

This range of cells can be moved by clicking and dragging to a new location when the cursor changes to crossed arrows.

Deleting Columns and Rows

A common Excel editing feature is deleting columns and rows, which is especially helpful when you are using a subset of data from a larger spreadsheet. For example, you may have received a large dataset from a classmate or coworker and want to reduce the spreadsheet to only the data you need. Or, you may need to remove rows of data that are no longer relevant to the purpose of a spreadsheet. The command to delete columns and rows is found in the **Cells** group of the **Home** tab in the Ribbon, as shown in Figure 2.42.

Figure 2.42 | **Icons in the Cells Group of the Ribbon**

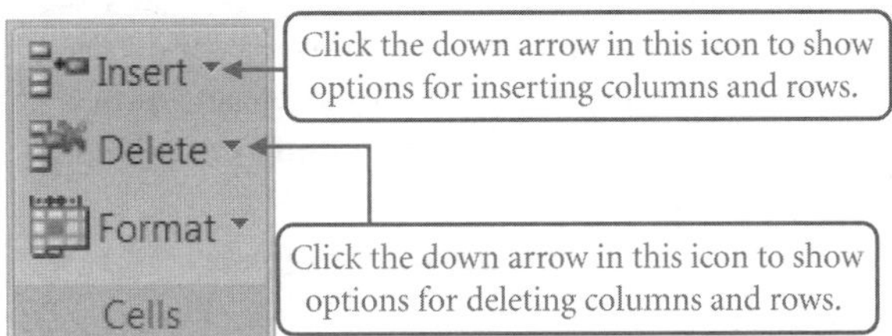

The following steps explain how you delete a row from the Merchandise Sales Report. This example assumes that the Green Sandals are being returned to the manufacturer and will no longer be sold in the store. Therefore, this row is being deleted from the sales report.

- Activate any cell in row 18. Since the Green Sandals are in row 18, you can activate any cell in this row to delete the entire row.
- Click the **Home** tab in the Ribbon.
- Click the drop-down arrow in the **Delete** icon in the **Cells** group.
- Select the **Delete Sheet Rows** option. This will remove row 18 and shift the data in row 19 up to row 18.

Figure 2.43 illustrates how row 18 is deleted from the Merchandise Sales Report. Note that the steps for deleting a column are identical to deleting a row; however, you need to activate one cell in the column that is being deleted. For example, notice that cell F18 in Figure 2.43 is activated. When the **Delete Sheet Rows** option is selected from the **Delete** icon, this row will be deleted. However, if the **Delete Sheet Columns** option is selected, *column* F will be deleted.

Quick Reference

Deleting Columns or Rows

1. Activate one cell in the row or column you want to delete.
2. Click the **Home** tab in the Ribbon.
3. Click the down arrow in the **Delete** icon in the **Cells** group.
4. Select the **Delete Sheet Columns** or **Delete Sheet Rows** options.

Figure 2.43 | **Deleting a Row from the Merchandise Sales Report**

	A	B	C	D	E
1	Category	Item Description	Color	Unit Sales	Sales Dollars
2	Bottoms	Shorts	Tan	12,500	$237,500
3	Tops	T-Shirts	Black	10,000	$115,000
4	Bottoms	Shorts	White	9,500	$180,500
5	Tops	Sweater	Grey	8,500	$289,000
6	Bottoms	Shorts	Brown	8,500	[illegible]
7	Tops	T-Shirts	Blue	8,500	[illegible]
8	Tops	Tank Top	White	6,500	[illegible]
9	Bottoms	Shorts	Blue	5,500	[illegible]
10	Tops	T-Shirts	Yellow	4,500	[illegible]
11	Tops	Sweater	Brown	3,500	$119,000
12	Shoes	Sandals	Black	3,000	$66,000
13	Tops	Tank Top	Pink	2,500	$21,250
14	Shoes	Boots	Black	1,600	$96,000
15	Tops	Sweater	Red	1,500	$51,000
16	Tops	Tank Top	Red	1,500	$12,750
17	Shoes	Sandals	Grey	1,200	$26,400
18	Shoes	Sandals	Green	850	$18,700
19	Shoes	Boots	Brown	750	$45,000

Row 18 will be deleted when this option is selected.

If this option is selected, column F will be deleted.

COMMON MISTAKES | Deleting Columns and Rows

You cannot delete a column or row by highlighting cells and pressing the **Delete** key. When you delete a column, the remaining columns should shift to the left. When you delete a row, the remaining rows should shift up.

Deleting Worksheets

Included in the **Delete** icon in the **Cells** group of the Ribbon is an option for deleting entire worksheets from a workbook. The reasons you may need to delete an entire worksheet are similar to the reasons explained for deleting columns and rows. The following steps explain how you delete a worksheet from a workbook:

- Activate a worksheet that will be deleted by clicking the worksheet tab.
- Click the **Home** tab of the Ribbon.
- Click the down arrow in the **Delete** icon in the **Cells** group.
- Select the **Delete Sheet** option (see Figure 2.44). When the **Delete Sheet** option is selected, a warning box will appear if there is data in the worksheet you are trying to delete.
- Click the **Delete** button on the warning box to delete the active worksheet (see Figure 2.45).

Quick Reference

Deleting Worksheets

1. Activate the worksheet you want to delete by clicking the worksheet tab.
2. Click the **Home** tab of the Ribbon.
3. Click the down arrow in the **Delete** icon in the **Cells** group.
4. Click the **Delete Sheet** option.
5. Check the worksheet carefully to make sure it is okay to delete.
6. Click the **Delete** button at the bottom of the warning box.

Figure 2.44 | **Deleting Worksheets**

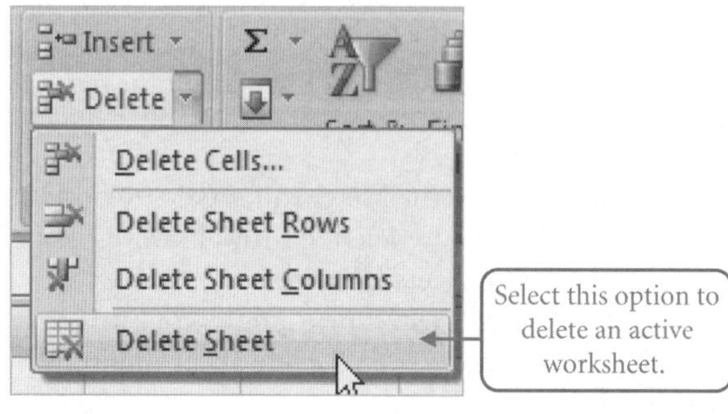

Figure 2.45 | **Warning Message When Deleting Worksheets**

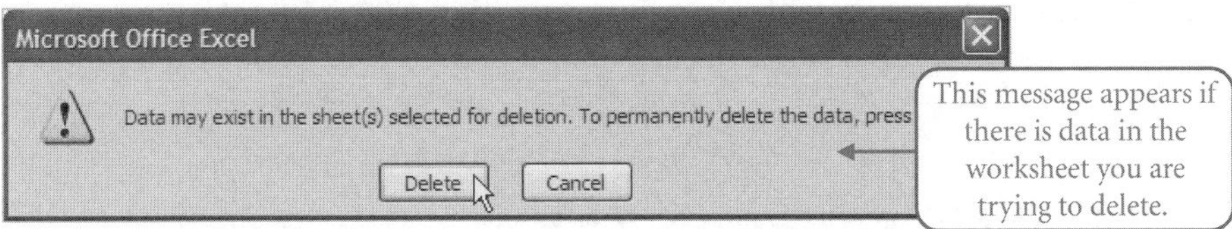

COMMON MISTAKES | Deleting Worksheets

You cannot use the **Undo** icon after a worksheet is deleted. Therefore, check the worksheet carefully before clicking the **Delete** button on the warning box shown in Figure 2.45. There is no way to retrieve a worksheet after it is deleted.

Inserting Columns and Rows

Another common Excel editing feature is inserting columns and rows. Often, you may need to add additional rows or columns of data to your own or other people's spreadsheets. For example, a noticeable omission in the Merchandise Sales Report (see Figure 2.43) is a title. If the report is without a title, it is impossible to know if the data in the Unit Sales column represents a week of sales, annual sales, or monthly sales. Therefore, a new row above the first row must be inserted for a title.

Similar to deleting columns and rows, the icon for inserting columns and rows also resides in the **Cells** group in the **Home** tab of the Ribbon (see Figure 2.42). The following steps explain how you add a row to the Merchandise Sales Report for the purpose of adding a title:

- Activate cell A1. Rows are always inserted above an active cell or range of cells. In this example, a row needs to be added above the first row in the worksheet. Therefore, cell A1 is activated.
- Click the **Home** tab in the Ribbon.
- Click the down arrow in the **Insert** icon in the **Cells** group.
- Click the **Insert Sheet Rows** option. After you select this option, a blank row will appear above row 1.

Figure 2.46 illustrates a row being inserted in the Merchandise Sales Report worksheet. Note the steps for inserting a column are identical to inserting a row; however, a column will always be inserted to the left of an active cell after you select the **Insert Sheet Columns** option from the **Insert** icon.

Figure 2.46 | **Inserting a Row in the Merchandise Sales Report**

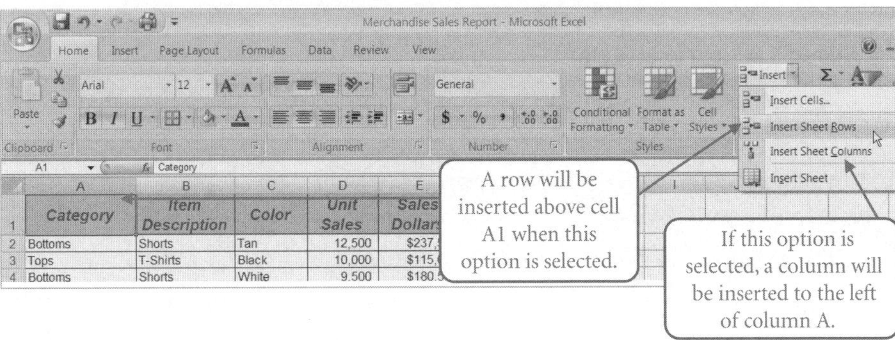

Figure 2.47 shows the results of adding a title to the Merchandise Sales Report. This figure reflects formatting enhancements that were added to make the title stand out. A reader can now see that the sales data shown in this worksheet are for the month of June.

Figure 2.47 | **Title Added to the Merchandise Sales Report**

	A	B	C	D	E
1	*Sales for the Month of June*				
2	*Category Description*	*Item Description*	*Color*	*Unit Sales*	*Sales Dollars*
3	Bottoms	Shorts	Tan	12,500	$237,500
4	Tops	T-Shirts	Black	10,000	$115,000
5	Bottoms	Shorts	White	9,500	$180,500
6	Tops	Sweater	Grey	8,500	$289,000
7	Bottoms	Shorts	Brown	8,500	$161,500

Inserting, Moving, and Renaming Worksheet Tabs

As mentioned earlier in this chapter, business managers will often create multiple versions or scenarios of a plan by copying an existing worksheet and pasting it into other worksheets in a workbook. This scenario was illustrated in Figure 2.14 for the Financial Plan spreadsheet. As a result, you may need to add additional worksheets to a workbook, arrange the order of those worksheets, and rename each worksheet tab. The following points explain how to accomplish each of these tasks:

- Click the **Insert Worksheet** tab at the bottom of a worksheet to add additional worksheets to a workbook (see Figure 2.48).
- Click and drag a worksheet tab to adjust the order it appears among the other worksheet tabs (see Figure 2.49).
- Double click a worksheet tab and type a new name. Press the **Enter** key after you type a desired name into the worksheet tab (see Figure 2.50).

Figure 2.48 | **Inserting New Worksheets**

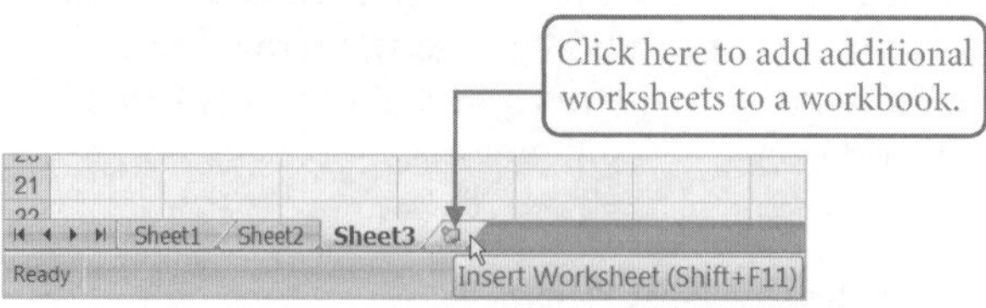

Figure 2.49 | **Moving Worksheets**

Sheet1 was moved to the right of Sheet2 by clicking and dragging the worksheet tab.

Sheet2 Sheet1 Sheet3 Sheet4

Ready

Quick Reference

Insert Columns or Rows

1. Activate a cell depending on where a blank column or row should be inserted. Rows are inserted above an active cell; columns are inserted to the left of an active cell.
2. Click the **Home** tab.
3. Click the down arrow in the **Insert** icon in the **Cells** group of the Ribbon.
4. Select **Insert Sheet Rows** or **Insert Sheet Columns**.

Figure 2.50 | **Renaming Worksheets**

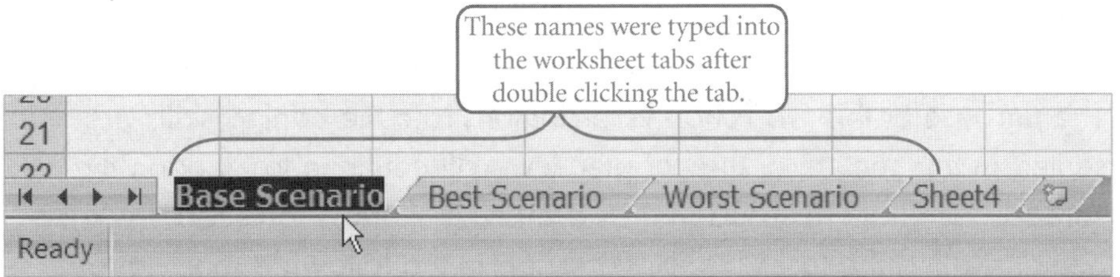

You can also rename worksheets by placing the cursor over a worksheet tab and clicking the right mouse button. This will open the set of worksheet commands shown in Figure 2.51. These commands are also contained in the **Format** icon in the **Cells** section of the Ribbon. The benefit of using this method is that it provides other options such as changing the color of the worksheet tab.

Figure 2.51 | **Changing the Worksheet Tab Color**

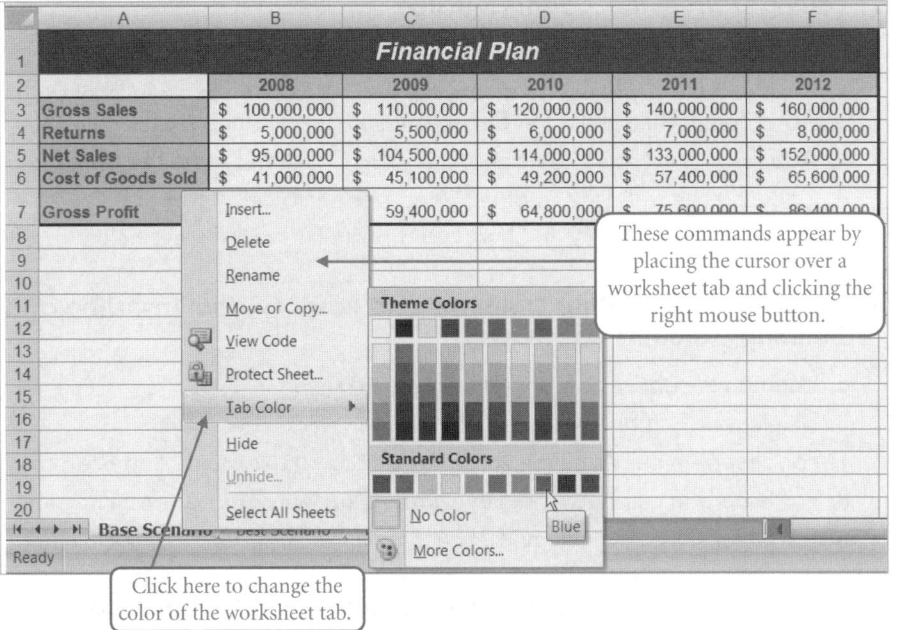

COMMON MISTAKES | Naming Worksheet Tabs

Excel will not let you use the same name for multiple worksheet tabs. Each tab must have a unique name. If you are getting a duplicate worksheet name error but do not see another worksheet with the same name, check to see whether any worksheets are hidden by selecting the **Unhide Sheet** option in the **Hide & Unhide** submenu of the **Format** icon.

Quick Reference

Inserting Worksheets

1. Click the **Insert Worksheet** tab at the bottom of the Excel screen.

Quick Reference

Moving Worksheets

1. Click and drag the worksheet tab.

Quick Reference

Renaming a Worksheet Tab

1. Double click the worksheet tab you wish to rename.
2. Type the new name.
3. Press the **Enter** key.

Quick Reference

Worksheet Tab Color

1. Click the worksheet tab where the color is to be changed.
2. Place the cursor over the worksheet tab.
3. Right click.
4. Select **Tab Color**.
5. Select a color from the color palette.

VIDEO WORKSHOP

>> Editing

The purpose of this workshop is to demonstrate the editing skills presented in this section of the chapter. We will continue to work on the spreadsheet that was used in the Formatting Video Workshop. I will be demonstrating the tasks in this workshop in the following four videos: **Editing Data**, **Inserting and Deleting Columns and Rows**, **Moving Data**, and **Renaming Worksheet Tabs**. After completing each section of tasks, watch the related video in parentheses. Remember to try the tasks on your own first before watching the video.

1. Open File

a. Open the file named ib_e02_videoworkshop, which you completed for the Formatting Video Workshop.

2. Editing Data (Video: Editing Data)

a. Activate cell A1 in Sheet1.
b. Click in the formula bar and type the word `Merchandise` in front of the word *Sales*. Then press the **Enter** key. In Sheet1, double click cell F2.
c. Add the word `Total` in front of the word *Sales* and press the **Enter** key.
d. Copy the range A1:F2 in Sheet1 and paste into cell A1 of Sheet2.
e. Copy the range A1:F2 in Sheet1 and paste into cell A1 of Sheet3.

3. Inserting and Deleting Columns and Rows (Video: Inserting and Deleting Columns and Rows)

a. Insert a row above row 1 in all three worksheets.
b. Delete row 1 in Sheet1.
c. For Sheet2 in cell A1, type `Arranged for Distribution Center`.
d. For Sheet3 in cell A1, type `Arranged for Merchandisers`.
e. For Sheet3, insert a column between columns A and B.

4. Moving Data and Adjusting Formats (Video: Moving Data)

a. In Sheet3, move the range D3:D13 to column B beginning in cell B3.
b. Move the range G3:G13 to column D beginning in cell D3.
c. Adjust the width of column D to 12 points.
d. Delete column G.
e. For cell D3, convert the bold line on the right side of the cell to a regular line.
f. Highlight the range A2:F13 and add a heavy bold line on the left, right, and bottom of the range.
g. Highlight the range A4:F13 and add regular horizontal and vertical lines inside the range.
h. Activate Sheet2.
i. Highlight the range A4:F13 and add a heavy bold line to the left, right, and bottom of the range and add regular horizontal and vertical lines inside the range.

5. **Worksheet Tabs (Video: Renaming Worksheet Tabs)**
   a. Change the tab name for Sheet1 to `Standard`.
   b. Change the tab name for Sheet2 to `DC Format`.
   c. Change the tab name for Sheet3 to `Merchant Format`.
   d. Save and close the file. Remember where this file is saved because you will use it in the next Video Workshop on Printing.

>> Editing Store Sales Reports

EXERCISE

Why Do I Need This?

In business, you will always need to adjust and format spreadsheets based on your reader's requirements. The editing skills covered in this section provide you with more tools to accomplish this task. Business managers are often very demanding when it comes to seeing information and reports that address their needs. This often results in your creating several spreadsheets that are different in appearance but display the same or similar data.

Exercise

Open the spreadsheet named ib_e02_monthlystoresalesreport. The goal of this exercise will be to edit this report for the manager of store 6214. We will assume that the primary concern of this manager is the change in sales year to date this year over last year. In addition, the manager would like to compare how his store is performing against other stores in his district. Make the following adjustments to create this report:

1. Copy the spreadsheet in the **Original Data** tab and paste it into Sheet2.
2. In Sheet2, sort the data based on the values in the District column in ascending order and the values in the Change in Sales to Date column in descending order.
3. Since this store manager wants to focus only on his store and the other stores in his district, delete any rows pertaining to districts 1 and 3.
4. Since the primary concern of this manager is the sales information for his store and other stores in his district, delete the following columns:
   a. Current Inventory Value
   b. Inventory pr Sqr Foot
   c. Total Deliveries
   d. Week 1
   e. Week 2
   f. Week 3
   g. Week 4
5. To place the Change in Sales to Date column next to the Size in Sqr Feet column, first insert a column between column C and D. Then move the Change in Sales to Date column next to the Size in Sqr Feet column.
6. Unmerge the range A1:G1 by clicking the **Merge & Center** and **Center Cells** icons and merge the cells in the range A1:F1.
7. Add a heavy bold border around the range A1:F13 and remove the line at the top of cell G1.

8. Change the name of the worksheet tab for Sheet2 to **`Store Manager Report`**.
9. Hide the Original Data worksheet.
10. Delete Sheet3.
11. How is store 6214 performing relative to other stores in this district?
12. What stores are experiencing a decrease in sales compared to last year?
13. Overall, how does the district appear to be performing? Are most stores seeing an increase in sales over last year, decrease, no change?
14. Save and close your file.

PROBLEM & EXERCISE

>> What's Wrong with This Spreadsheet?

Problem

You are the manager of an audio electronics store and have a meeting scheduled with your district manager. You have asked your assistant to make some changes to the annual Merchandise Sales Report since your conversation with the district manager will be focused on the change in sales this year verses last year. You have given your assistant the following instructions:

1. Copy the spreadsheet in the Original Report tab and paste it into Sheet2.
2. Rename the tab for Sheet2 as **`Sales Change`**.
3. Delete the following columns: Receipt Date, Next Order Date, and Inventory.
4. Sort the spreadsheet by the Sales Change column in descending order.

Your assistant completes everything except he keeps getting an error when trying to rename the tab for Sheet2 to Sales Change. He explains that everything else you requested has been done.

Exercise

Open the file named ib_e02_audiobreakdown and look at what the assistant completed on Sheet2. Are you comfortable presenting this spreadsheet to your district manager? Consider the following questions:

1. Did the assistant delete the columns you asked for? If not, what did he do? How could you fix this?
2. Why is your assistant getting an error when he tries to rename the tab for Sheet2 to Sales Change?
3. Do you have any other concerns with this spreadsheet?

Write a short answer to each of the following questions. Correct any problems you see on the spreadsheet. If you cannot correct a problem explain why.

Printing

Skill Set

After completing formatting and editing adjustments to a worksheet, you may want to print a hard copy or bring several copies to a business meeting. This section covers the features and commands used for printing Excel worksheets.

Page Setup

Before printing a worksheet, you will need to apply settings that manage how a document will appear when it is printed. These settings can be found in the **Page Layout** tab of the Ribbon. Commands related to printing a worksheet are found in the **Page Setup**, **Scale to Fit**, and **Sheet Options** groups, as shown in Figure 2.52.

Figure 2.52 | **Commands Used to Prepare a Worksheet for Printing**

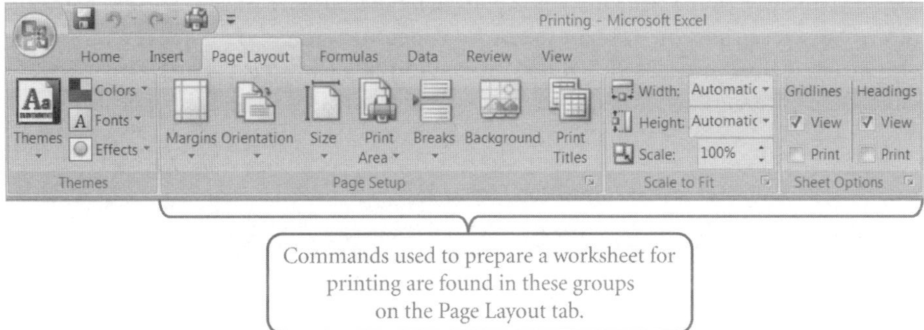

The commands needed to prepare a worksheet for printing will vary from project to project. If you are printing a small worksheet for your own reference, you may be able to print without using any of the commands shown in Figure 2.52. However, most worksheets will require some type of preparation. The following commands from the **Page Layout** tab are commonly used:

- ***Margins***: Click this icon to select one of three preset margin settings for a document. The **Custom Margins** option will open the **Page Setup** dialog box. Here, you can make your own settings for the margins of a document. The **Page Setup** dialog box is covered later in this section.
- **Orientation**: Click this icon to select either a ***Portrait*** or ***Landscape*** orientation for a document.
- **Size**: Click this icon to select from a list of different paper sizes. The **More Paper Sizes** option will open the **Page Setup** dialog box.
- ***Print Area***: Use this icon if you wish to print only a portion of a worksheet. Highlight the range of cells you wish to print, click this icon, and select the **Set Print Area** option.
- ***Print Titles***: This feature duplicates the column headings or row headings of a worksheet on each page that is printed. Clicking this icon opens the **Page Setup** dialog box, which is covered later in this section.
- **Width**: This icon allows you to determine how many pages are used to print the width of a worksheet. If you wish to print all the data contained in a worksheet on one piece of paper, you would set both the **Width** and **Height** icons to 1 page. The **More** option in this icon will open the **Page Setup** dialog box.
- **Height**: This icon is similar to the **Width** icon, but it allows you to determine how many pages are used to print the length of a worksheet.

- ***Scale***: Click this icon to manually reduce or enlarge the printed appearance of a worksheet.
- **Gridlines**: Click the box next to the **Print** option if you wish to print the ***gridlines*** that appear on the worksheet. Gridlines that appear on a worksheet when the Fill Color is set to No Fill will not appear in print unless this option is selected.
- **Headings**: Click the box next to the **Print** option if you wish to print the column letters and row numbers.

Similar to Excel's formatting commands, several of the features used to prepare a worksheet for printing are not available through the icons in the Ribbon. For these features, you will need to use the **Page Setup** dialog box. The descriptions of the icons in Figure 2.52 provided earlier indicate how you can open the **Page Setup** dialog box. In addition, you can open the **Page Setup** dialog box by clicking any of the buttons in the lower-right corner of the **Page Setup**, **Scale to Fit**, and **Sheet Options groups** sections of the Ribbon.

Figure 2.53 shows the **Page** tab of the **Page Setup** dialog box. The **Page Setup** dialog box will open to the **Page** tab when you click the button in the lower-right corner of the **Page Setup** section or select the **More Paper Sizes** option in the **Size** icon. Options in this tab include the printed orientation of a worksheet (Portrait or Landscape), the number of pages used to print the worksheet, and the paper size.

Figure 2.53 | **Page Tab of the Page Setup Dialog Box**

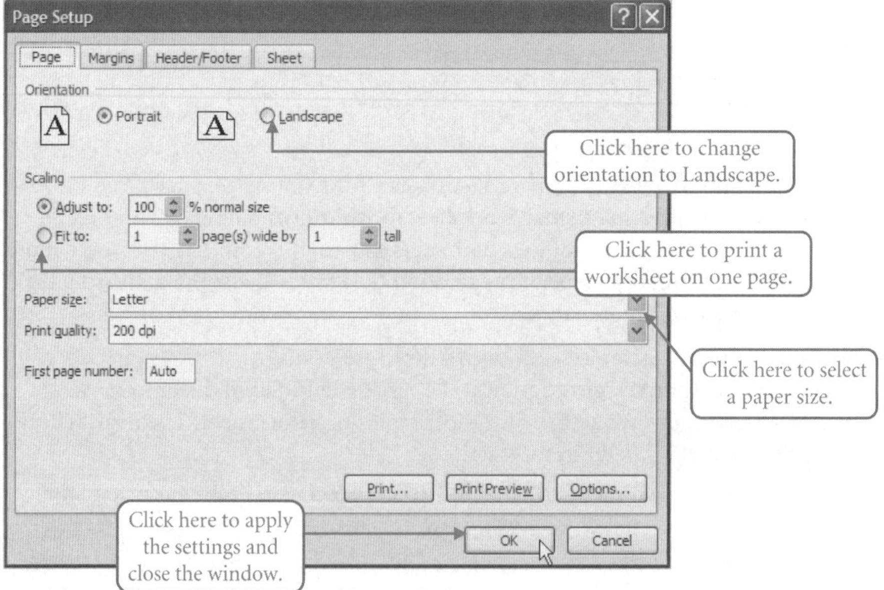

Figure 2.54 shows the **Margins** tab of the **Page Setup** dialog box. This tab allows you to make specific settings for the printed margins of a worksheet.

Figure 2.54 | **Margins Tab of the Page Setup Dialog Box**

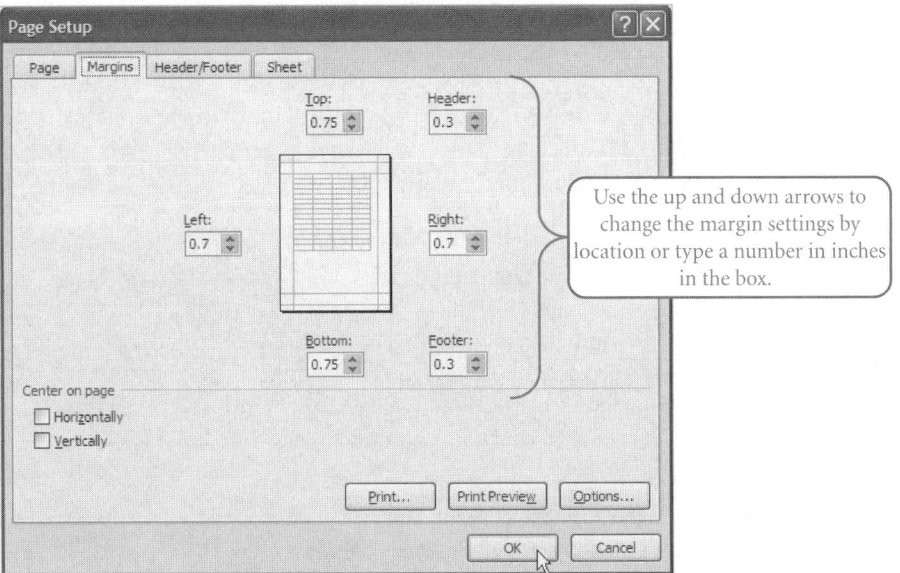

Figure 2.55 shows the **Header/Footer** tab of the **Page Setup** dialog box. This tab provides preset header and footer options that you can use to display items such as the page number, file name, or worksheet tab name at the top or bottom of a printed document. In addition, you can create your own header of footer by clicking either the **Custom Header** or **Custom Footer** buttons. Figure 2.56 shows the **Custom Header** dialog box, which opens after you click the **Custom Header** button. This is one of two options for creating custom ***headers*** and ***footers***. The second option is to type a header or footer directly on the worksheet when the workbook is in **Page Layout** view.

Figure 2.57 shows the **Sheet** tab of the **Page Setup** dialog box. Options in this tab allow you to set a specific print range, designate columns or rows to be printed on each page, or show gridlines in the printed output.

Figure 2.55 | **Header/Footer Tab of the Page Setup Dialog Box**

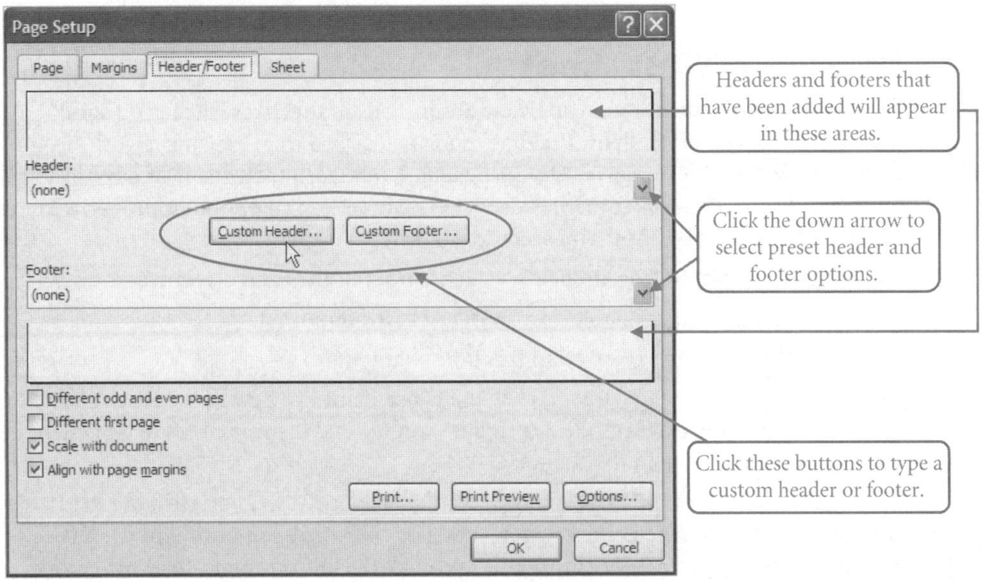

Figure 2.56 | **The Custom Header Dialog Box**

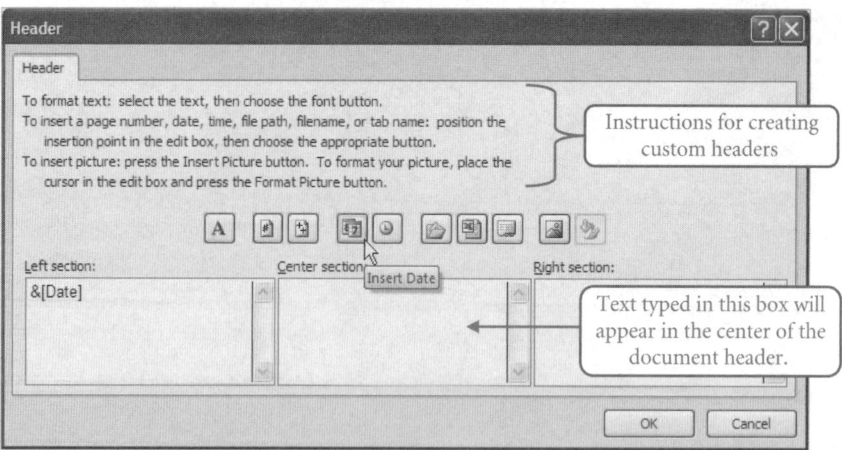

Figure 2.57 | **Sheet Tab of the Page Setup Dialog Box**

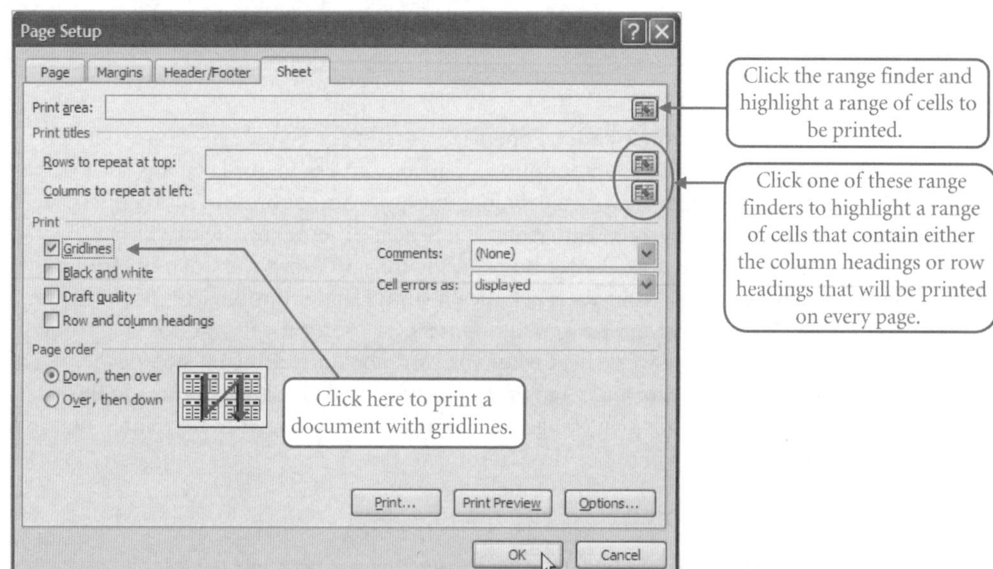

> **Quick Reference**
>
> **Printing Worksheets**
>
> 1. Activate a worksheet to be printed.
> 2. Click the **Page Layout** tab of the Ribbon.
> 3. Make any necessary Page Setup adjustments by using the icons in the Ribbon or by opening the **Page Setup** dialog box.
> 4. Click the **Office Button**.
> 5. Click the side arrow next to the **Print** option and select **Print Preview** to view the document.
> 6. Click the **Print** icon in the **Print Preview** mode Ribbon.
> 7. Make any necessary settings in the **Print** dialog box.
> 8. Click the **OK** button in the **Print** dialog box.

Printing a Worksheet

When you have finished setting any **Page Setup** options for a worksheet, you should ***preview*** the worksheet in **Print Preview** mode before printing. Viewing a worksheet before printing will reveal any additional changes that need to be made and could save you wasted paper if the document is distorted from setting an option improperly. The following points explain how you accomplish this:

- Click the **Office Button** in the upper-left corner of the Excel screen.
- Place the cursor over the side arrow of the **Print** option.
- Select the **Print Preview** option from the submenu.
- After reviewing the document, click the **Close Print Preview** icon in the Ribbon to exit the **Print Preview** mode. Or, if you want to send the worksheet to a printer, click the **Print** icon in the Ribbon.

Figure 2.58 shows the **Print** dialog box. This will open after you click the **Print** icon in the Ribbon of the **Print Preview** mode or click the **Print** option in the **Office Button**. Make any necessary adjustments and click the **OK** button to send your worksheet to a printer.

Figure 2.58 | **The Print Dialog Box**

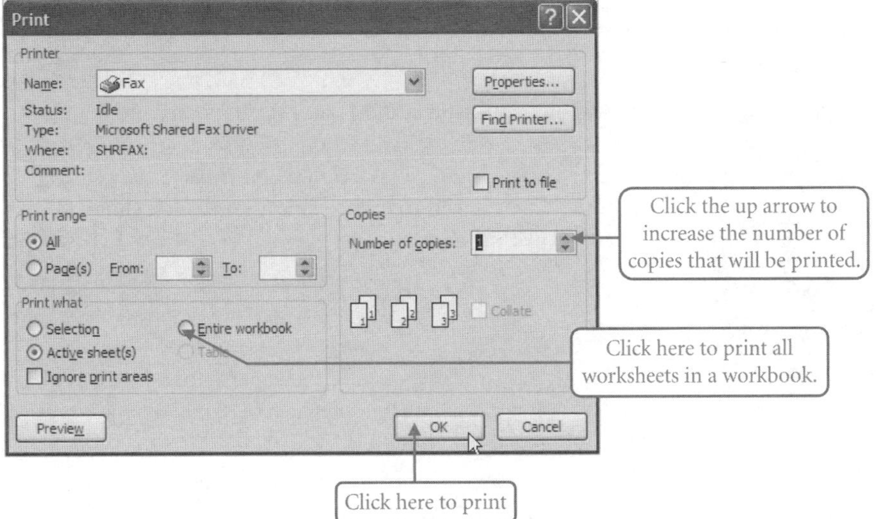

>> Printing

VIDEO WORKSHOP

The purpose of this workshop is to demonstrate the printing features and commands reviewed in this section. We will be printing the spreadsheet that was completed in the Editing Video Workshop. I will be demonstrating the tasks in this workshop in the video named **Printing**. Remember to try the tasks on your own first before watching the video.

1. Open the File

a. Open the file named, ib_e02_videoworkshop, which you completed for the Editing Video Workshop.

2. Page Setup (Video: Printing)

a. Make the following Page Setup adjustments for the Standard worksheet:
   i. Set the orientation to Landscape.
   ii. Set the scaling to fit on 1 page wide by 1 page tall.
   iii. Increase the left and right margins to 1 inch.
   iv. Add a header with the date left justified and the following title in the center: `Standard Report Format`. Format this title to a 12-point font and italicize.
   v. Click the drop-down arrow to show the list of preset footers. Select the option that shows the file name of your Excel workbook and the page number.

b. Make the same Page Setup adjustments for the DC Format worksheet and add the following title in the header: `Unit Volume Performance Report`.

c. Make the same Page Setup adjustments for the Merchant Format worksheet and add the following title in the header: `Sales Revenue by Item`.

3. Print (Video: Printing)

a. Preview each spreadsheet before printing.

b. Print the three spreadsheets in this workbook.

c. Save and close your file.

Excel in **Practice** | Anecdote

Solution from page 24

I was using electronic spreadsheets on a regular basis, and it seemed that the most basic skills would allow us to get rid of the paper spreadsheets and the correction fluid forever. If we had all our production data produced electronically, we could eliminate all paper and mailing charges.

Assignment

The following is a similar version of the paper spreadsheet used for our production plans. Using the skills covered in this chapter, create the same spreadsheet in Excel.

Production Spreadsheet							
Plan Number:	S143W	Season:	Fall 07		Division:	Men's Sportswear	
Style Number:	K44435		Description:		3 Button Rugby Long Sleeve Knit		
Packaging code:	PB			Button Style Code:	SRB.WT		
Production Details							
	Size						
Color	S	M	L	XL	XXL	Dozens	Ship Date
Solid Blue	10%	25%	30%	25%	10%	5.000	7/15/07
Solid Ivory	10%	25%	30%	25%	10%	2.500	7/15/07
Solid Green	10%	25%	30%	25%	10%	5.000	7/15/07
Navy / Ivory Stripe	10%	25%	30%	25%	10%	5.000	8/30/07
Green / Gold Stripe	10%	25%	30%	25%	10%	2.500	8/30/07
Green / Ivory Stripe	10%	25%	30%	25%	10%	2.500	8/30/07

Questions for Discussion

1. What other benefits, beyond those described in the anecdote, can you think of by converting the paper production plans into Excel spreadsheets?
2. What are some of the things that could go wrong with this project?
3. Identify solutions that could prevent any potential problems from occurring.

Review Questions

The following questions are related to the concepts addressed in this chapter. There are three types of questions: Short Answer, True or False, and Fill in the Blank. If your answer to a True or False question is False, write a short explanation as to why you think the statement is not true.

1. The following number was entered exactly as shown into a cell: 2,000. Is there anything wrong with this entry?

2. Besides pressing the **Enter** key, what else can you do to ensure data is entered into a cell?

3. What could typically go wrong with data entry tasks?

4. The following months were entered into two consecutive cells: January, June. Can **Auto Fill** be used to complete the rest of the months of the year? Why or why not?

5. What causes these symbols to appear in a cell: ####?

6. When using the **Format** icon to increase the height or width of a row or column, you must _________ in either the row or column you are adjusting.

7. The row numbers on the left side of a spreadsheet read 1,2,4,5,6,8,9,11. What does this mean?

8. What icon in the Ribbon can you use to hide a column?

9. In what Ribbon tab will you find the **Sort** command?

10. When you are using the **Sort** command, any column that is _________ will not be sorted.

11. True or False: Column headings should never be highlighted when sorting data.

12. True or False: If a column letter is missing at the top of a spreadsheet, it means that the column was deleted.

13. To center data over several cells, you would use the _________ command.

14. True or False: Selecting the **Currency** option when formatting numbers will always add a $ in front of the number.

15. True or False: There is no special accounting format for projects that require dollar signs and decimals to align.

16. True or False: Numbers and text entries will always be truncated if they are too large to fit into a cell. This is why you need the wrap text command.

17. You must select a _________ first when using the **Border** tab of the **Format Cells** dialog box.

18. The difference between a mediocre and professional-looking spreadsheet is often the result of _________ techniques.

19. List two options for changing data that has already been entered into a cell.

20. The cursor must change from a _________ sign to _________ before data can be dragged to a new location on a spreadsheet.

21. True or False: When you delete a column, the data disappears and an empty column remains.

22. Columns are inserted to the _________ of an active cell, and rows are inserted _________ an active cell.

23. Which icon in the Ribbon can you use to change the color of a worksheet tab?

24. True or False: To change the name of a worksheet tab, you can simply double click on the tab and type the new name.

25. How can you find out if there are any hidden spreadsheets in a workbook?

26. How can you change the order in which worksheet tabs are displayed in a workbook?

27. True or False: You cannot print all the spreadsheets in a workbook at one time. You have to activate each spreadsheet and print them one at a time.

28. True or False: Grid lines, besides the ones you may have added to a spreadsheet, will always appear on paper when a worksheet is printed.

29. How can you get column headings or row headings to print on every page when printing long or wide spreadsheets?

Skills Exam

The following exam is designed to test your ability to recognize and execute the Excel skills presented in this chapter. Read each question carefully and answer the questions in the order they are listed. You should be able to complete this exam in 60 minutes or less.

1. Open the ib_e02_skillsexam.
2. Copy the worksheet named "Original" and paste it into Sheet2.
3. For Sheet2, insert 2 rows above row 1.
4. Enter the title `Cost Analysis Report` in cell A1.
5. Merge the cells in the range A1:H1. Then color the cells Blue, change the color of the text to white, change the font size to 16, bold and italicize the text, and set both the horizontal and vertical alignment to center.
6. Increase the height of row 1 to 25 points.
7. For the range A3:H3, wrap the text, color the cells light yellow, bold the text, and set the horizontal alignment to center.
8. Adjust the column widths as follows:
   a. Column B: `11.5`
   b. Column C: `8`
   c. Column D: `8`
   d. Column E: `11`
   e. Column F: `9.5`
   f. Column G: `13`
   g. Column H: `14`
9. In Sheet2, use Auto Fill to add 18 more cost components to the list in column A. There should be a total of 20 cost components beginning in cell A4 and ending in cell A23.
10. Copy the range B4:B23 and paste it into column G beginning with cell G4.
11. Enter data into the following cells: H4: 5000, H5: 2500, H6: 8500, H7: -2000, H8: 3100, H9: 10000, H10: 1000, H11: -5000, H12: 4050, H13: 2925, H14: -150, H15: 1800, H16: -200, H17: 3800, H18: 5500, H19: -3000, H20: 250, H21: 16500, H22: 2000, H23: 35000.
12. Delete row 2.
13. Add a heavy bold border around the perimeter of the range A1:H24.
14. Add horizontal and vertical regular solid black lines to the range A1:H22.
15. Add a bold black line to the bottom of the range A2:H2.
16. Add a bold black line to the bottom of cells D22 and F22.
17. Bold and italicize the text in cells A24, D24, and F24.
18. Format the following ranges to a number with commas and 0 decimal places: B3:B22, E3:E22, and G3:G22.
19. Format the range C3:C22 to U.S. currency 2 decimal places.
20. Format the range D3:D22 and F3:F22 to U.S. currency 0 decimal places.
21. Format cells D24 and F24 to U.S. currency 2 decimal places.
22. Format the range H3:H22 as a number with commas, 0 decimal places, and show any negative numbers in parentheses and in red.
23. Eliminate any #### errors that may have appeared on the spreadsheet.
24. Rename the tab for Sheet2 to `All Cost Data`.
25. Make a copy of the All Cost Data spreadsheet and paste it into Sheet3.
26. Rename the tab for Sheet3 as `Total Cost Analysis`.

27. Add two new worksheets to the workbook. Paste a copy of the All Cost Data spreadsheet into these two worksheets.
28. Change the tab name for one of the two new worksheets to **`Inventory Cost Analysis`**. Change the tab name of the remaining worksheet to **`Purchasing Analysis`**.
29. Arrange the worksheet tabs in the following order and change the color of each tab as indicated:
    a. Original: Blue
    b. All Cost Data: Green
    c. Total Cost Analysis: Red
    d. Inventory Cost Analysis: Yellow
    e. Purchasing Analysis: Purple
30. Make the following adjustments to the Total Cost Analysis worksheet:
    a. Delete the following columns: Current Inventory Units, Inventory Cost, Future Consumption, and Current Inventory Less Future Consumption.
    b. Sort the spreadsheet based on the Total Cost column in descending order and for any duplicate entries sort by the Unit Cost column in descending order. Note: The Totals row (row 24) must remain at the bottom of the spreadsheet.
    c. Add a heavy bold line to the right side of the range D1:D24.
    d. Change the text in cell A1 to read **`Total Cost Analysis`**.
31. Make the following adjustment to the Inventory Cost Analysis spreadsheet:
    a. Delete the following columns: Total Cost, Future Consumption, and Current Inventory Less Future Consumption.
    b. Sort the spreadsheet based on the Inventory Cost column in descending order and for any duplicate entries sort by the Current Inventory Units column in ascending order. Note: The Totals row (row 24) must remain at the bottom of the spreadsheet.
    c. Add a heavy bold line to the right side of the range E1:E24.
    d. Change the text in cell A1 to read **`Inventory Cost Analysis`**.
32. Make the following adjustments to the Purchasing Analysis spreadsheet:
    a. Delete the following columns: Current Inventory Units, Unit Cost, Total Cost, and Inventory Cost.
    b. Sort the spreadsheet based on the Current Inventory Less Future Consumption column in ascending order and for any duplicate entries sort by the Item column in ascending order. Note: The Totals row (row 24) must remain at the bottom of the spreadsheet.
    c. Add a dark bold line to the right side of the range D1:D24.
    d. Change the text in cell A1 to read **`Purchasing Analysis`**.
33. What two components have both the highest Total cost and the highest Inventory cost?
34. If this company has a standard of not going below 1000 units when considering current inventory less future consumption, what components would have to be purchased?
35. Make the following adjustments so each worksheet will print as follows:
    a. Landscape
    b. Fits onto one page
    c. 1 inch margin for top, bottom, left, and right
    d. The date on the left side of the header and the worksheet name in center of the header
    e. The page number in the right side of the footer
    f. Print grid lines
36. Save and close your file.

Challenge Questions

The following questions are designed to test your ability to apply the Excel skills you have learned to complete a business objective. Use your knowledge of Excel as well as your creativity to answer these questions. For most questions, there are several possible ways to complete the objective.

1. What information will you need before starting an Excel project?

2. You are evaluating a long-term project for building several retail stores. The project will start on March 20 of this year and will take 35 months before the stores will be open for business. The months of January through April are very slow business periods. Historical sales suggest that it is best to open stores in May or August. Given the start date and the 35-month duration, are the stores opening at a good time? Using the skills in this chapter, how can you use Excel to help answer this question?

3. Open the file named ib_e02_purchasingmanagerdata. This file needs to be formatted and adjusted for the purchasing manager of a sports equipment store who is responsible for assessing the current unit inventory for each item and the weeks of supply for each item. From this information, the manager will determine which items need to be purchased or which items should be returned to the manufacturer. The purchasing manager will make this decision based on the weeks of supply data. Any item with a weeks of supply less than 4 will be purchased. Any item with a weeks of supply greater than 20 will be returned to the manufacturer. Use the skills covered in this chapter to format the spreadsheet based on the needs of this purchasing manager.

4. Open the file named ib_e02_furniturefiasco. How many mistakes can you find in this spreadsheet? Make a copy of the spreadsheet and correct as many mistakes as you can. If you cannot correct a mistake, explain why.

5. Open the file named ib_e02_merchandisedataforpresentation. Look at this spreadsheet carefully. Would you be comfortable presenting this information for a class project or to the executive managers of a company? Why or why not?

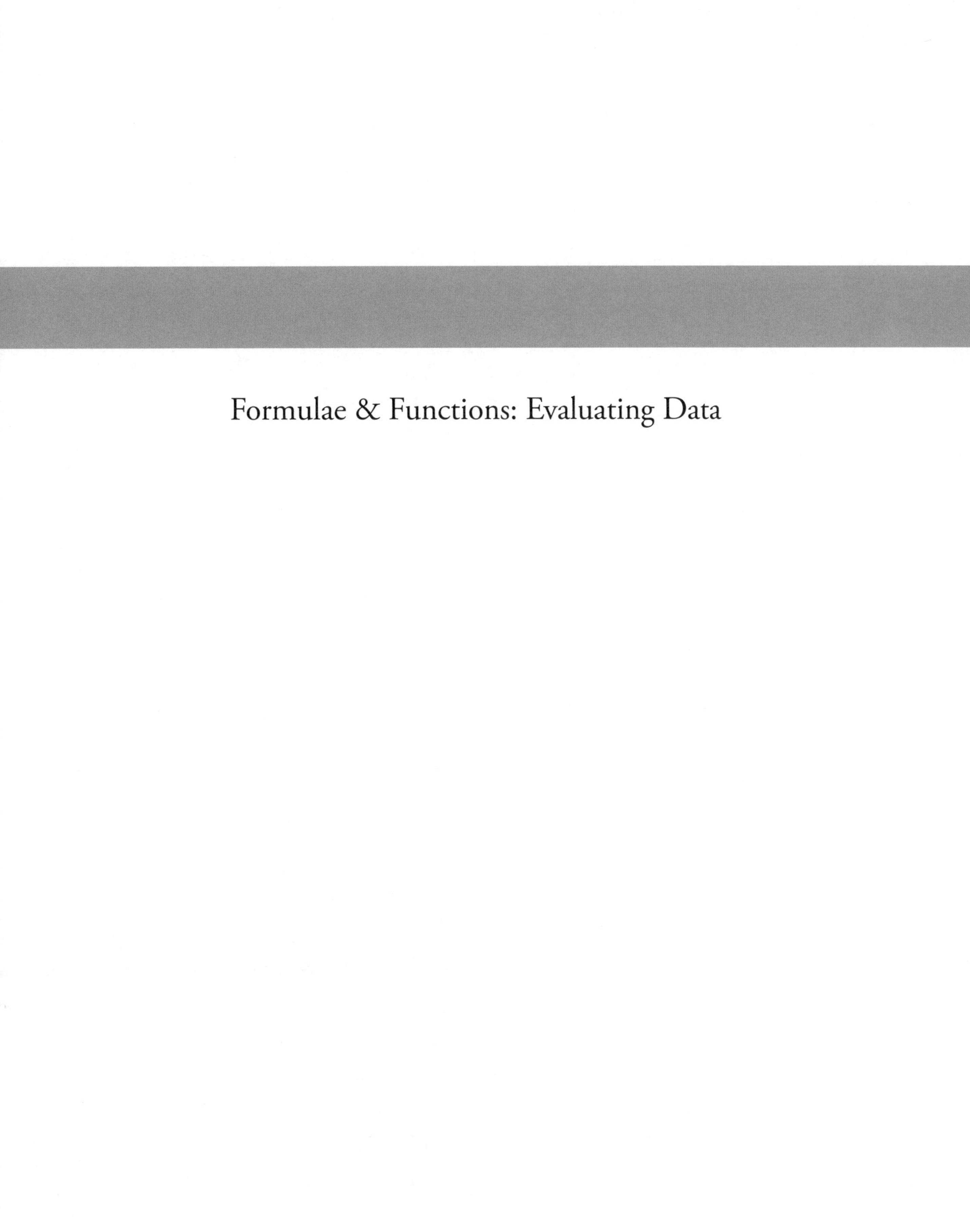

Formulae & Functions: Evaluating Data

Calculating Data

Formulas and Functions

Chapter Goals

This chapter introduces the calculating power of Excel through two main objectives. The first is to present the fundamental techniques of creating formulas and functions, which are the primary tools used to calculate data. The second is to show how cell referencing is used within formulas and functions to maximize the dynamic abilities of Excel. In other words, formulas and functions will automatically produce new outputs when the data in one or more cell locations is changed. In business, these dynamic abilities are critical when evaluating what-if scenarios. Chapter 2 introduced the concept of what-if scenarios by demonstrating how to create multiple versions of a worksheet within a workbook. This chapter develops this concept even further by demonstrating how to perform common business calculations and analyses using formulas and functions.

>> Excel | Skill Sets

Formulas

- Basic Formulas
- Copying and Pasting Formulas (Relative Reference and Paste Special)
- Complex Formulas
- Auditing Formulas.

Basic Functions

- Basic Statistical Functions
- AutoSum
- Absolute References (Turning Off Relative References)

Financial Functions

- The Future Value Function
- The Payment Function
- The Function Library

Excel in Practice | Anecdote

My Role as a Merchandise Analyst

If asked, could you predict how well printed skirts will sell this summer or say with certainty whether hip huggers are going out of style? Posing such what-if scenarios was my livelihood when I worked as a merchandise analyst for a women's fashion retail company where I projected the sales and profit for my department. Our goal each season was to sell all the clothes in the casual sportswear line with nothing left over. For example, every year we might purchase 25,000 pairs of shorts, which sold from the end of March to the end of July. If shorts still hung from the racks by the end of July, we were stuck with inventory, costing the department thousands of dollars in profit. To make matters worse, no one wanted last season's shorts, so reselling a previous season's inventory rarely worked.

Using a paper spreadsheet, I evaluated the sales of every item in my department, trying to determine what was hot and what was in danger of hitting the markdown table. While markdowns often increased the sales of an item, they also decreased our profits. Fortunately, sales in my department were booming, so I found myself working until midnight almost every day, recalculating sales and inventory data on my spreadsheets. While being part of a fast-growing business was a great experience, I had to find a better way of managing the sales and profit of my department; otherwise, I would burn out from exhaustion.

>> Continued on page 126

Formulas

Skill Set

The most basic method of calculating mathematical outputs in Excel is through formulas. In fact, several numeric values shown in the financial plan created in Chapter 2 (see Figure 2.39) can be created using formulas. For example, the Net Sales values in row 5 can be produced with a formula that subtracts the Returns in row 4 from the Gross Sales in row 3. The formula does the work of calculating the Net Sales values as opposed to your typing these values into each cell manually, which increases the risk of data-entry errors. As a result, formulas not only reduce the risk of data-entry errors by producing values electronically, but they also provide the ability to evaluate what-if scenarios. This section will highlight the analytical benefits of formulas and demonstrate the construction of several formulas typically used in business.

Basic Formulas

For the purposes of this text, ***basic formulas*** are defined as any equations that consist of two variables separated by a ***mathematical operator*** such as + (addition), - (subtraction), etc. Business managers use a variety of basic formulas to calculate key metrics such as Gross Profit, Net Sales, or Inventory Turn. The types of formulas used by business managers depend on their areas of responsibility. Typical basic formulas used in business include

- **Gross Profit**: Net Sales − Cost of Goods Sold
- **Net Sales**: Gross Sales − Returns
- **Average Price**: Sales Dollars ÷ Unit Sales
- **Inventory Turn:** Net Sales ÷ Average Inventory Value
- **Sales Dollars**: Price × Sales Units

It is important to note that the math operators you see on a calculator are not always the same in Excel. For example, the "×" symbol on a calculator is usually used for the multiplication operation. However, in Excel you would use the asterisk (*) for multiplication. Figure 3.1 shows a list of symbols used for constructing formulas in Excel.

Figure 3.1 | **Mathematical Operator Symbols Used in Excel**

Symbol	Operation
+	Addition
–	Subtraction
/	Division
*	Multiplication
^	Power/Exponent

As previously mentioned, you can use a basic formula to calculate the Net Sales for the Financial Plan created in Chapter 2. This formula is added to the worksheet as follows:

- Activate cell B5. This cell represents the Net Sales for the year 2008 (see Figure 3.2).
- Type an equal sign. An equal sign signifies that Excel will be calculating data instead of displaying what is typed into a cell.
- Type the cell location B3. As illustrated earlier, the formula for Net Sales is Gross Sales – Returns. Since cell B3 contains the Gross Sales for 2008, this cell is added to the formula first. You can also add this cell to the formula by clicking the cell location after typing the equal sign.
- Type a subtraction sign.

- Type cell location B4. The value in cell B4 represents the Returns for the year 2008. Since this cell location comes after the subtraction sign, it will be subtracted from the value that is contained in cell B3.
- Press the **Enter** key.

Figure 3.2 shows the setup of the formula calculating Net Sales in the Financial Plan worksheet. It is important to note that this formula is composed of ***cell references***. As a result, any value typed into cell B4 will be subtracted from any value typed into cell B3. If the value in either cell B3 or B4 is changed, the output of the formula will also change.

Figure 3.2 | **Basic Formula Calculating Net Sales**

SUM | =B3-B4

	A	B	C	D
1			Financial Plan	
2		2008	2009	2010
3	Gross Sales	$ 100,000,000	$ 110,000,000	$ 120,000,0
4	Returns	$ 5,000,000	$ 5,500,000	$ 6,000,0
5	Net Sales	=B3-B4		
6	Cost of Goods Sold	$ 41,000,000	$ 45,100,000	
7	Gross Profit			

Formula appears in the formula bar as you type.

Cell references used in the formula are outlined in color.

The equal sign must precede the formula to produce an output.

Figure 3.3 shows the result of the Net Sales formula in cell B5. Notice that when B5 is activated, you can see the formula `=B3 - B4` in the formula bar. This indicates that the value $95,000,000 is a formula output and that the number itself has not been entered into the cell. Excel is calculating this output because an equal sign precedes the formula. If the equal sign was omitted, you would see B3-B4 displayed in the cell.

Figure 3.3 | **Results of the Net Sales Formula**

B5 | =B3-B4

	A	B	C	
1			Financial Plan	
2		2008	2009	2010
3	Gross Sales	$ 100,000,000	$ 110,000,000	$ 120,000
4	Returns	$ 5,000,000	$ 5,500,000	$ 6,000
5	Net Sales	$ 95,000,000		
6	Cost of Goods Sold	$ 41,000,000	$ 45,100,000	$ 49,200
7	Gross Profit			

Formula appears in the formula bar when the cell is activated.

Formula output

COMMON MISTAKES | Formulas

When doing calculations in Excel, never use a calculator and type the result into a spreadsheet. Typing computed results into a spreadsheet completely eliminates Excel's cell referencing capabilities. Formulas created with cell references will automatically recalculate outputs when data is changed in any of the referenced cell locations. In addition, creating formulas with cell references provides a record of how outputs are being calculated.

As previously mentioned, the formula shown in Figure 3.2 utilizes cell references. If the values in cells B3 or B4 are changed, the formula will produce a new output. Therefore, what will happen to Net Sales if returns are $10 million higher than planned for the year 2008? Type 15000000 in cell B4, and the formula automatically calculates a new value, as shown in Figure 3.4.

Figure 3.4 | **Changing the Returns Value in Cell B4 Produces a New Value for Net Sales**

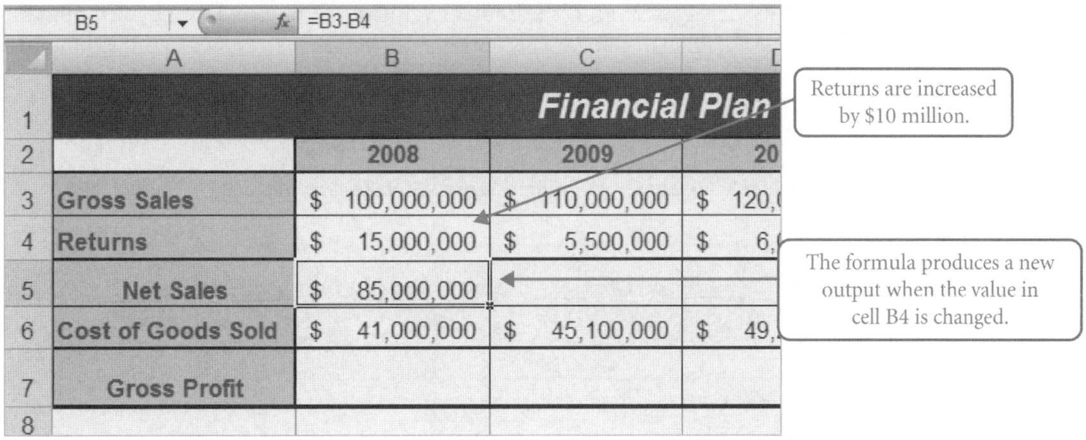

B5 =B3-B4

	A	B	C	D
1			Financial Plan	
2		2008	2009	20
3	Gross Sales	$ 100,000,000	$ 110,000,000	$ 120,
4	Returns	$ 15,000,000	$ 5,500,000	$ 6,
5	Net Sales	$ 85,000,000		
6	Cost of Goods Sold	$ 41,000,000	$ 45,100,000	$ 49,
7	Gross Profit			
8				

Returns are increased by $10 million.

The formula produces a new output when the value in cell B4 is changed.

Figures 3.5 and 3.6 show the setup and result of a basic formula calculating the Gross Profit in the Financial Plan worksheet. Notice that this formula references cell B5, which contains the formula for Net Sales. Therefore, if the output of the Net Sales formula is changed, the output of the Gross Profit formula will also change.

Figure 3.5 | **Basic Formula Calculating Gross Profit**

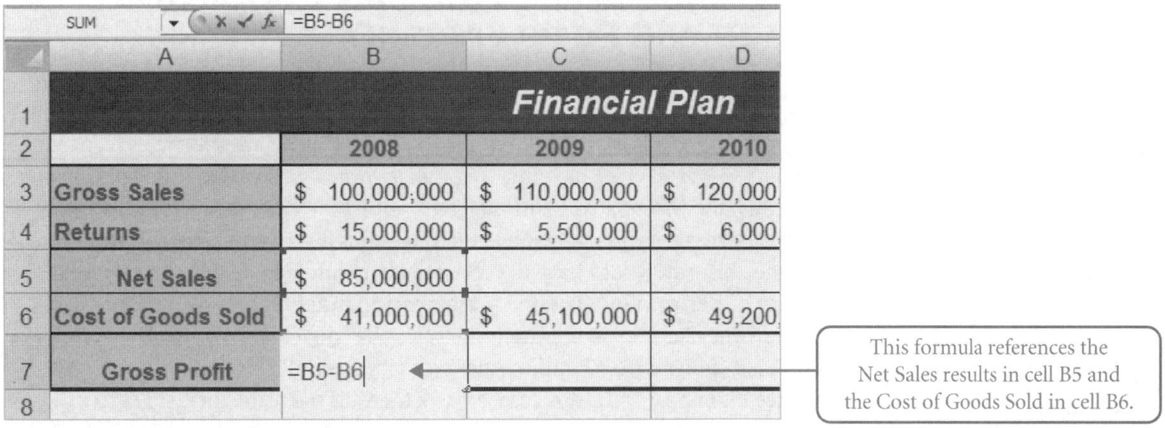

SUM =B5-B6

	A	B	C	D
1			Financial Plan	
2		2008	2009	2010
3	Gross Sales	$ 100,000,000	$ 110,000,000	$ 120,000
4	Returns	$ 15,000,000	$ 5,500,000	$ 6,000
5	Net Sales	$ 85,000,000		
6	Cost of Goods Sold	$ 41,000,000	$ 45,100,000	$ 49,200
7	Gross Profit	=B5-B6		
8				

This formula references the Net Sales results in cell B5 and the Cost of Goods Sold in cell B6.

Figure 3.6 | **Results of the Gross Profit Formula**

B7 | f_x =B5-B6

	A	B	C	D
1			Financial Plan	
2		2008	2009	2010
3	Gross Sales	$ 100,000,000	$ 110,000,000	$ 120,000,0(
4	Returns	$ 15,000,000	$ 5,500,000	$ 6,000,0(
5	Net Sales	$ 85,000,000		
6	Cost of Goods Sold	$ 41,000,000	$ 45,100,000	$ 49,200,0(
7	Gross Profit	$ 44,000,000		
8				

Gross Profit formula output

As mentioned, the formula calculating Gross Profit in the Financial Plan worksheet is referencing cell B5, which contains the formula for Net Sales. As a result, what will happen to the Gross Profit if the Returns value in cell B4 is reduced by $10 million? Type the value 5000000 in cell B4, and both the formula for Net Sales in cell B5 and the formula for Gross Profit in cell B7 produce new outputs, as shown in Figure 3.7.

Figure 3.7 | **Net Sales and Gross Profit Increase When Returns Decrease**

B7 | f_x =B5-B6

	A	B	C	D
1			Financial Plan	
2		2008	2009	
3	Gross Sales	$ 100,000,000	$ 110,000,	
4	Returns	$ 5,000,000	$ 5,500,	
5	Net Sales	$ 95,000,000		
6	Cost of Goods Sold	$ 41,000,000	$ 45,100,000	$ 49,20(
7	Gross Profit	$ 54,000,000		
8				

The output for Net Sales and Gross Profit automatically increases when Returns are decreased to $5 million.

> **Quick Reference**
>
> **Basic Formulas**
>
> 1. Activate the cell where formula output should appear.
> 2. Type an equal sign.
> 3. Type or click a cell location that contains a value that will be used to compute the formula output.
> 4. Type a math operator (see Figure 3.1).
> 5. Type or click a second cell location that contains a value that will be used to compute the formula output.
> 6. Press the **Enter** key.

Copying and Pasting Formulas (Relative Reference and Paste Special)

After constructing a formula in Excel, you can copy and paste it to other locations on a worksheet. When you paste a formula to a new location, Excel utilizes a process called ***relative referencing*** to adjust any cell references. For example, the Net Sales formula shown in Figure 3.2 is `=B3 - B4`. If this formula is copied and pasted into cell C5 (one cell to the right), the formula will automatically adjust to `=C3 - C4`. This adjustment is the result of relative referencing. Relative referencing is a very convenient feature because, without it, you would have to retype every formula in a worksheet even though it may be performing the same mathematical function.

The following example further demonstrates the convenience of relative references. Figure 3.8 shows a merchandise sales worksheet similar to the one created in Chapter 2 (see Figure 2.37). In this case, a basic formula is created in cell D2 to calculate the average price for the item in row 2. Notice that the forward slash symbol is used for division.

Figure 3.8 | **Average Price Formula**

SUM =B2/C2

	A	B	C	D
1	Item	Sales Dollars	Unit Sales	Average Price
2	T-Shirts	$ 150,000	12,000	=B2/C2
3	Notebooks	$ 85,000	32,500	
4	Sweatshirts	$ 225,000	5,000	
5	Hats	$ 125,000	8,200	
6	Scarves	$ 9,000	750	
7	Sweaters	$ 120,000	2,500	
8	Diploma Frames	$ 187,500	1,500	

Forward slash is used for division.

Figure 3.9 shows the results of copying and pasting the formula in cell D2 to cells D3 through D5. Notice that the formula in cell D5 reads `=B5/C5`, which accurately calculates the average price for the Hats in row 5. However, the formula that was typed into cell D2, as shown in Figure 3.8, was `=B2/C2`. Relative referencing increased the row numbers of the cell references by 3 because the formula was pasted 3 rows below its original location. Without relative referencing, this formula would calculate the average price of the T-Shirts in row 2 for every item in the worksheet.

Figure 3.9 | **Relative Referencing Adjusts Cell References in the Average Price Formula**

SUM =B5/C5

	A	B	C	D
1	Item	Sales Dollars	Unit Sales	Average Price
2	T-Shirts	$ 150,000	12,000	$12.50
3	Notebooks	$ 85,000	32,500	$2.62
4	Sweatshirts	$ 225,000	5,000	$45.00
5	Hats	$ 125,000	8,200	=B5/C5
6	Scarves	$ 9,000	750	
7	Sweaters	$ 120,000	2,500	
8	Diploma Frames	$ 187,500	1,500	

Row numbers in the cell references increase by 3 because the formula is pasted 3 rows below the original location.

While relative references provide a convenient way to copy and paste formulas, in some situations you may need to paste only the value of a formula and not the formula itself. For example, Figure 3.10 shows a worksheet used to calculate the sales plans for six retail stores. Column D contains basic formulas to add the Planned Growth values to the Last Year Sales values for each store.

Figure 3.10 | **Retail Store Sales Plans**

SUM =B2+C2

	A	B	C	D
1	Store Number	Last Year Sales	Planned Growth	Total Sales Plan
2	1	$5,750,000	$125,000	=B2+C2
3	2	$4,250,000	$400,000	$4,650,000
4	3	$6,500,000	$250,000	$6,750,000
5	4	$3,250,000	$750,000	$4,000,000
6	5	$5,250,000	$500,000	$5,750,000
7	6	$2,750,000	$1,000,000	$3,750,000
8				

This formula is calculating the Total Sales Plan by adding the Last Year Sales values to the Planned Growth values.

Figure 3.11 shows a new worksheet that will be used by a manager to monitor the Actual Sales for each store to see if the store is achieving its Total Sales Plan. Therefore, the Total Sales Plan numbers calculated in Figure 3.10 need to be pasted into this new worksheet.

Figure 3.11 | **Plan versus Actual Sales Worksheet**

B2

	A	B	C	D
1	Store Number	Total Sales Plan	Actual Sales	Difference
2	1			
3	2			
4	3			
5	4			
6	5			
7	6			
8				

The values from the formulas created in column D from Figure 3.10 will be placed in this column.

As mentioned, the Total Sales Plan numbers calculated in Figure 3.10 need to be pasted into the Plan versus Actual Sales worksheet in Figure 3.11. However, using the **Copy** and **Paste** icons in this situation will paste the formula that is used to calculate the Total Sales Plan values, not the result. To paste only the result of this formula, you will need to use a command called **Paste Values**. You accomplish this by doing the following:

- Highlight the range D2:D7 in the worksheet shown in Figure 3.10. This is the range of cells that contain the formulas which calculate the Total Sales Plan values.
- Click the **Copy** icon.
- Activate cell B2 in the worksheet shown in Figure 3.11.
- Click the down arrow below the **Paste** icon to open a list of paste options (see Figure 3.12). The paste options list allows you to access a few commonly used commands from the ***Paste Special*** dialog box.

Figure 3.12 | **Paste Options List**

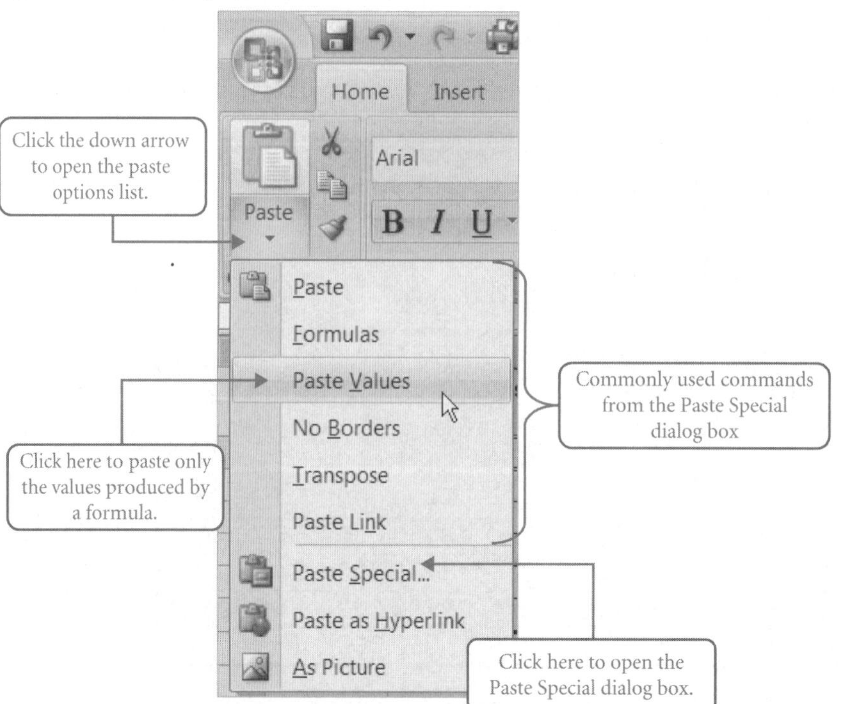

- Select the **Paste Values** option from the paste options list. This will paste only the values created by the Total Sales Plan formulas and not the formulas themselves (see Figure 3.13).

Figure 3.13 shows the results of pasting the values of the Total Sales Plan formulas from Figure 3.10. When cell B2 is activated, the formula bar shows that the content of the cell is a number. In addition, notice the **Paste Options** icon, which appears on the worksheet after selecting a paste command. You can use this icon to select a different paste option if the one you originally selected does not provide desirable results.

Figure 3.13 | **Pasting Formulas as Values**

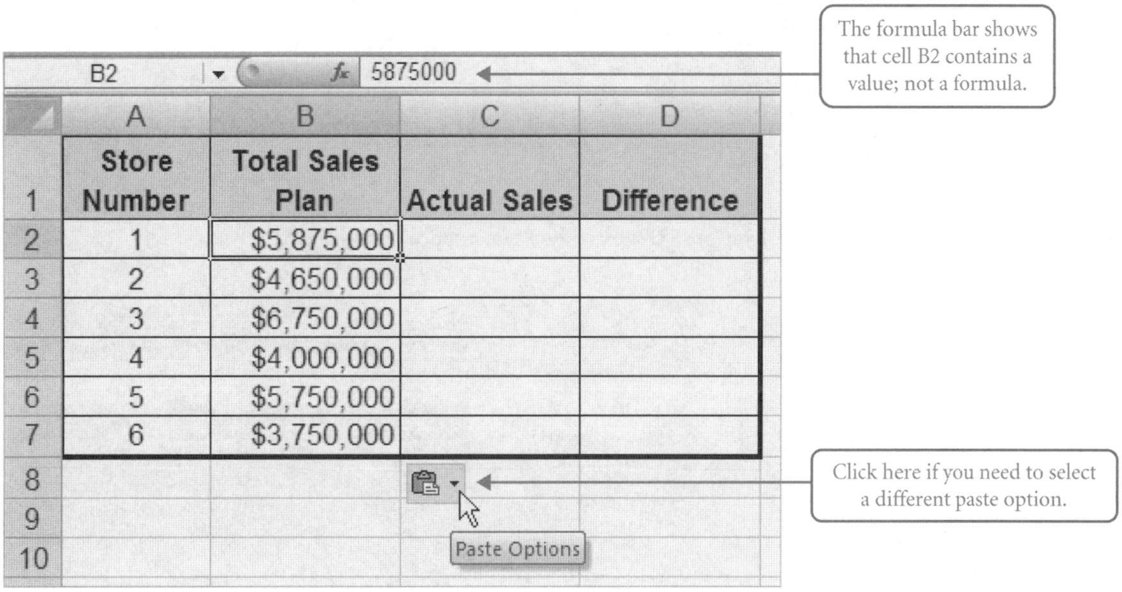

B2 | fx 5875000

The formula bar shows that cell B2 contains a value; not a formula.

	A	B	C	D
1	Store Number	Total Sales Plan	Actual Sales	Difference
2	1	$5,875,000		
3	2	$4,650,000		
4	3	$6,750,000		
5	4	$4,000,000		
6	5	$5,750,000		
7	6	$3,750,000		
8				
9				
10			Paste Options	

Click here if you need to select a different paste option.

The paste options list contains a few commonly used commands from the **Paste Special** dialog box shown in Figure 3.14. To open the **Paste Special** dialog box and view all the available commands, click the **Paste Special** option, as shown in Figure 3.12. The following are a few key options:

- **Formats**: This option allows you to paste only the formats from a range of cells that has been copied. As a result, you can paste a specific arrangement of borders, number formats, or cell colors from one area of a worksheet to another.
- **All except borders**: This option appears as **No Borders** in the paste options list. Use it in situations in which you need to paste all content and formats from a range of copied cells except for the borders.
- **Formulas**: Use this option when you want to paste only the formulas from a range of copied cells without any of the format settings.
- **Transpose**: This option, found at the bottom of the **Paste Special** dialog box, can be used in situations in which a range of cells copied in a column needs to be transposed to a row or vice versa. Figure 3.15 illustrates an example of this option.

>> Quick Reference

Paste Special

1. Copy a cell or range of cells.
2. Activate the cell where data is to be pasted.
3. Click the down arrow below the **Paste** icon to open the paste options list.
4. Select one of the paste options or select the **Paste Special** option to open the **Paste Special** dialog box.
5. If you are using the **Paste Special** dialog box, select an option and click the **OK** button.

Figure 3.14 | **Paste Special Dialog Box**

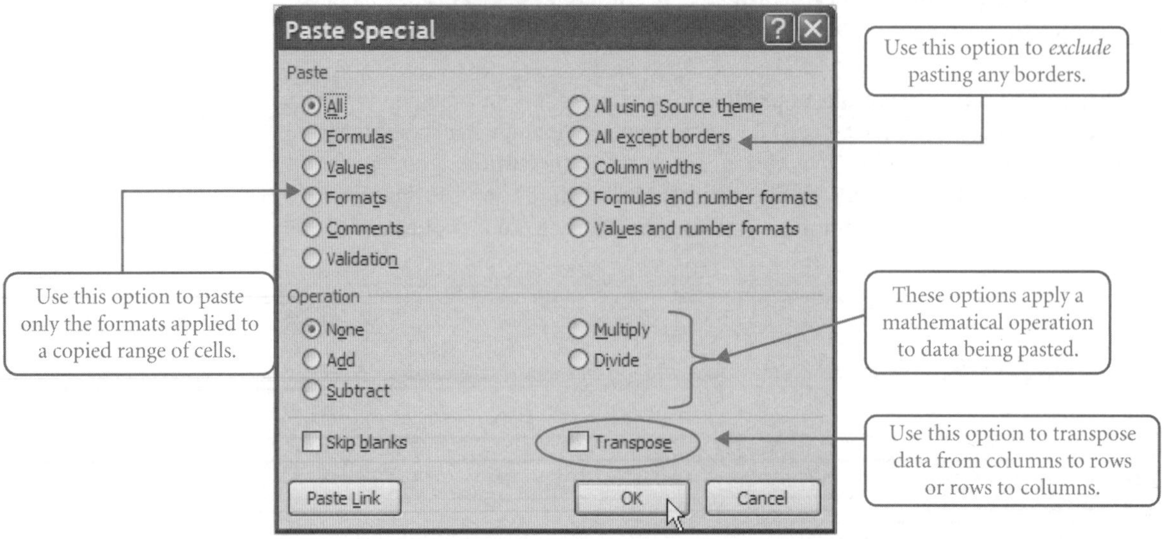

Figure 3.15 | **Transpose Option in the Paste Special Dialog Box**

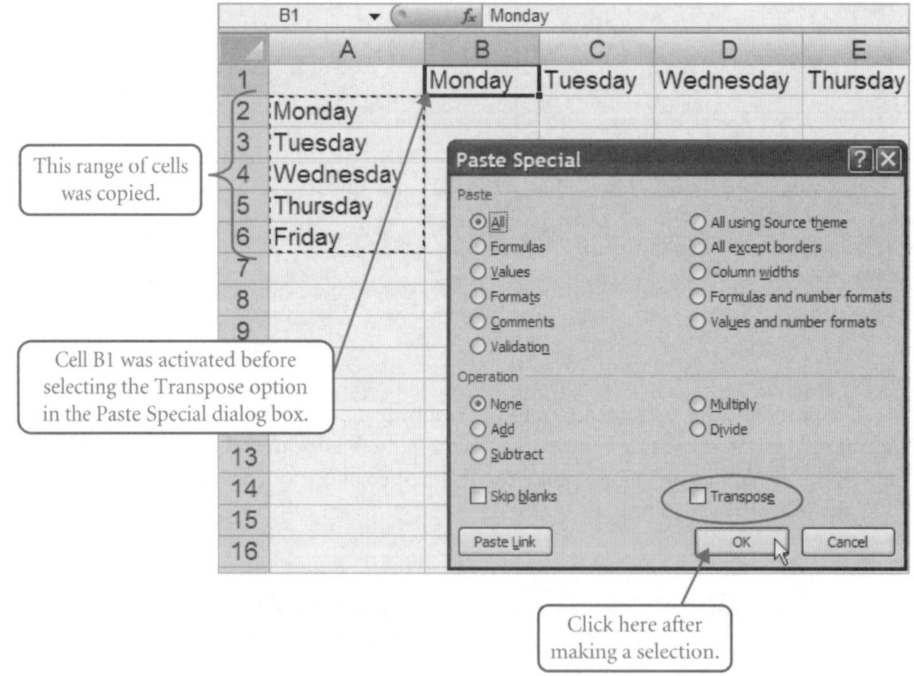

Complex Formulas

For the purposes of this text, ***complex formulas*** are defined as any equations that consist of more than two variables and require two or more mathematical operators. As previously illustrated, basic formulas are used to conduct several key calculations in business. However, business computations often require the use of formulas that consist of more than two variables. For example, you may need to add several components together to calculate the cost of a product. Or, you may need to estimate daily sales from weekly sales to calculate an annual inventory turn. These situations require more than two variables and may also require the use of constants or numeric values. In addition, parentheses may be necessary to change the standard order of mathematical operations.

Since a complex formula contains at least two or more mathematical operations, it is important to note the order in which Excel will execute each mathematical operation when calculating an output. Figure 3.16 lists the order in which Excel executes mathematical operations in a formula that does not contain parentheses. Note that the symbols shown in this figure were previously defined in Figure 3.1.

Figure 3.16 | **Order of Math Operations**

Symbol	Operation Order
^	First: Excel executes all exponential calculations.
* or /	Second: Excel executes multiplication and division after exponents. If both symbols are used in a formula, they are executed in order from left to right.
+ or -	Third: Excel executes addition and subtraction after multiplication and division. If both symbols are used in a formula, they are executed in order from left to right.

The complexity of formulas created in Excel is virtually limitless. As mentioned, when you are creating complex formulas involving several cell locations with several mathematical operators, Excel calculates the order of each operation as shown in Figure 3.16. However, in many situations you will need to change the order that each math operation is executed by adding parentheses. Math operations enclosed in parentheses are always executed first and override the order of operations shown in Figure 3.16. When several parentheses are used in a formula, Excel executes math operations by starting with the innermost parentheses and ends with the outermost parentheses.

Figure 3.17 illustrates an example in which parentheses are required in a complex formula. This worksheet shows an item from a merchandise worksheet similar to the example shown in Figure 3.9. The purpose of the formula in cell D2 is to estimate the inventory days on hand, which is calculated by dividing the inventory units by the number of units sold per day. However, notice that the sales results shown in column B are for last week. Therefore, assuming this store sells merchandise 7 days a week, the unit sales must first be divided by 7, and then the inventory units must be divided by this result to calculate the inventory days on hand.

Figure 3.17 | **Calculating Inventory Days on Hand**

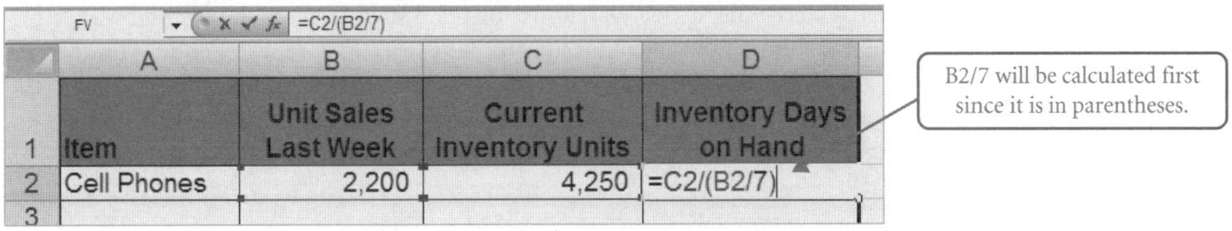

FV =C2/(B2/7)

	A	B	C	D
1	Item	Unit Sales Last Week	Current Inventory Units	Inventory Days on Hand
2	Cell Phones	2,200	4,250	=C2/(B2/7)
3				

B2/7 will be calculated first since it is in parentheses.

Figure 3.18 shows the results of the Inventory Days on Hand formula, which is 13.52. Thus, if no additional inventory is received, this company will sell out of cell phones in approximately two weeks. Retail buyers often use this type of calculation to determine when products should be reordered from suppliers.

Figure 3.18 | **Results of Calculating Days on Hand Inventory**

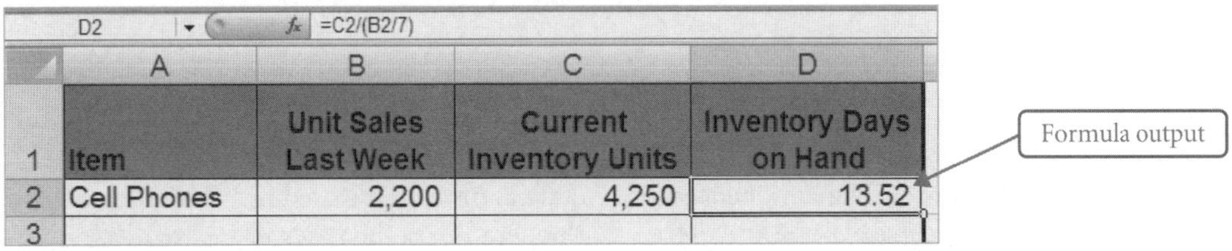

D2 =C2/(B2/7)

	A	B	C	D
1	Item	Unit Sales Last Week	Current Inventory Units	Inventory Days on Hand
2	Cell Phones	2,200	4,250	13.52
3				

Formula output

Figure 3.19 illustrates the importance of using parentheses when creating the Inventory Days on Hand formula from Figure 3.17. Notice that no parentheses are used in this formula (see formula bar). As a result, Excel will execute each division operation in the order it appears in the formula from left to right. Therefore, Excel will first divide B2 into C2, and this result will be divided by 7. This produces an erroneous result of .28.

Figure 3.19 | **Invalid Result When Removing Parentheses**

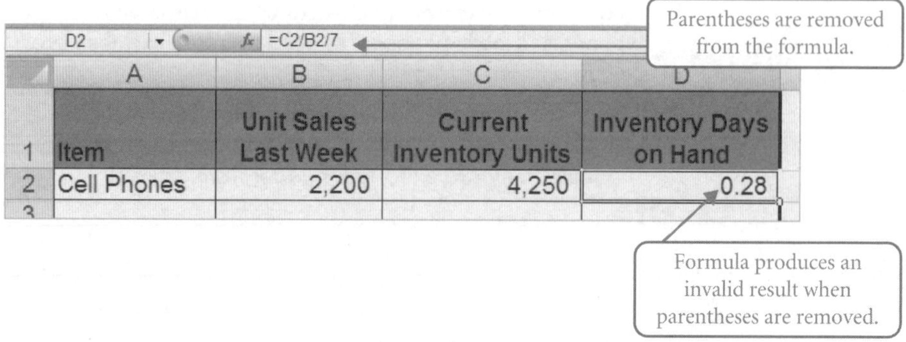

COMMON MISTAKES | Using Numeric Values in Formulas

Be careful when using numeric values in formulas, as shown in Figure 3.17. You should use numeric values when dealing with constant values that do not change, such as days of the week, months of the year, minutes in an hour, and so on. Do not type numeric values that exist in cell locations into a formula. Typing the numeric value instead of using the cell reference eliminates the ability to recalculate an output when data is changed in the referenced cell or cells. Whenever possible, always use cell references when creating formulas.

Figure 3.20 illustrates a second example requiring the use of parentheses to control the order of mathematical operations. The manager of a transportation company might use this worksheet to determine how much a customer should be charged for delivering merchandise to a warehouse or retail store. The method used by a transportation company to calculate a customer's price may vary depending on the company and the merchandise that is being delivered. This example assumes that a customer will be charged the company's total cost per mile plus a 25% markup for profit. The formula shown in cell F2 is calculating the price for a 750-mile trip.

Figure 3.20 | **Calculating the Price of a Merchandise Delivery**

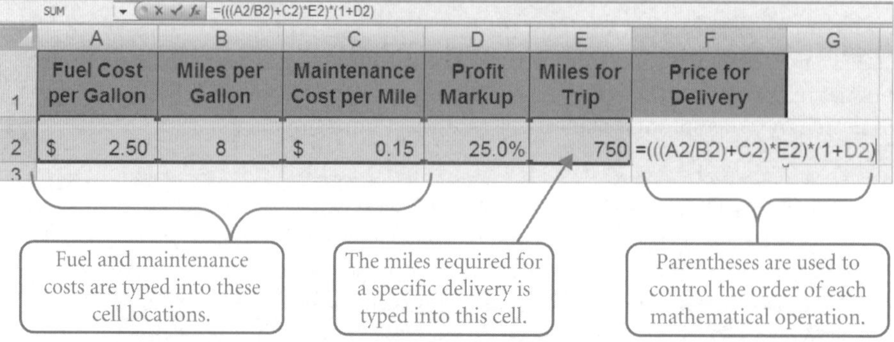

As previously mentioned, when several parentheses are used in a formula as shown in Figure 3.20, Excel will execute the math operation in the innermost parentheses first and continue toward the outermost parentheses. The order of each calculation for this example is as follows:

1. `(A2 / B2)`: This is the innermost set of parentheses, which is why this operation is being calculated first. This part of the formula is calculating the fuel cost per mile by dividing the Fuel Cost per Gallon in cell A2 by the Miles per Gallon in cell B2.
2. `((A2 / B2) + C2)`: After the fuel cost per mile is calculated, the Maintenance Cost per Mile is added. At this point, Excel has calculated one number that represents the fuel and maintenance cost per mile.
3. `(((A2 / B2) + C2) * E2)`: After Excel has calculated one number representing the transportation manager's cost per mile, it is multiplied by the number of miles typed into cell E2. The customer for this particular example has a delivery that requires a distance of 750 miles. At this point, Excel has calculated the total cost for a 750-mile trip.
4. `(((A2 / B2) + C2) * E2) * (1 + D2)`: This is the complete formula shown in Figure 3.20. The last operation to be performed is multiplying the cost of the trip by the markup. As previously mentioned, it is assumed that this company establishes a price based on a 25% profit markup. Excel will first add 1 to the markup percent typed into cell D2 because this operation is in its own set of parentheses. Then, this result is multiplied by the total cost of the trip established in step 3. Since .25 is typed into cell D2, the total cost of this trip will be increased by 1.25 or 25%.

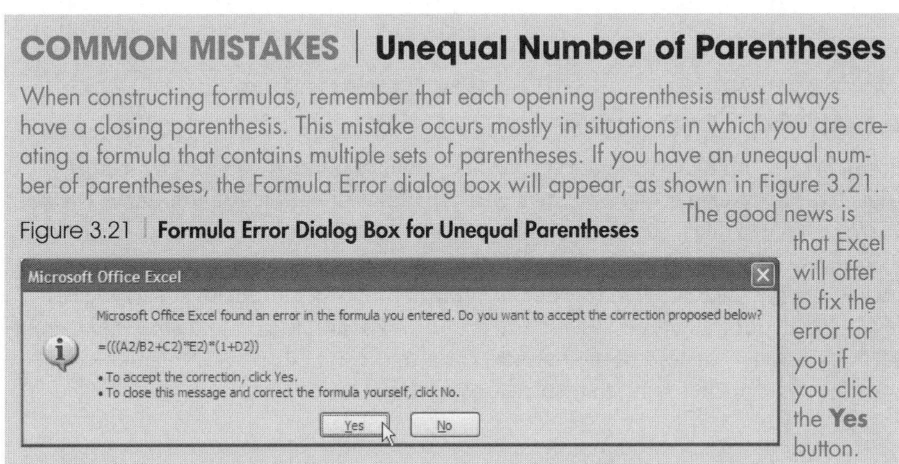

COMMON MISTAKES | Unequal Number of Parentheses

When constructing formulas, remember that each opening parenthesis must always have a closing parenthesis. This mistake occurs mostly in situations in which you are creating a formula that contains multiple sets of parentheses. If you have an unequal number of parentheses, the Formula Error dialog box will appear, as shown in Figure 3.21. The good news is that Excel will offer to fix the error for you if you click the **Yes** button.

Figure 3.21 | **Formula Error Dialog Box for Unequal Parentheses**

Figure 3.22 shows the final result of the formula calculating the price of a 750-mile trip. Because cell references were used in the construction of this formula, a new output can be calculated when any of the values in the yellow cells is changed. In fact, the cells in the range A2:E2 were intentionally colored yellow to indicate that these values can and should be changed when calculating a price for a new customer.

Figure 3.22 | **Results of Calculating the Price of a Merchandise Delivery**

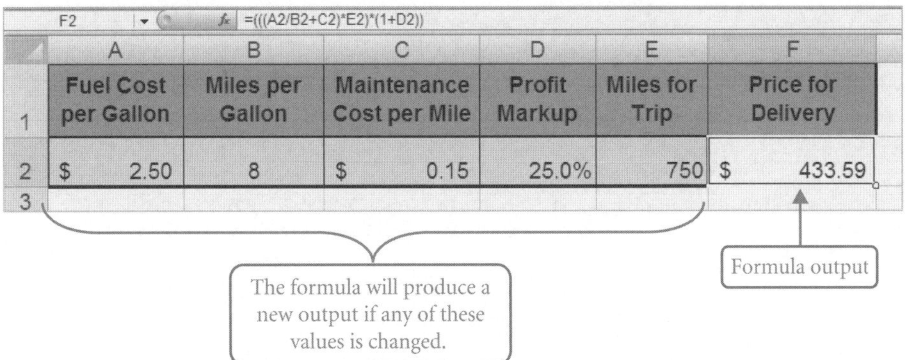

	A	B	C	D	E	F
1	Fuel Cost per Gallon	Miles per Gallon	Maintenance Cost per Mile	Profit Markup	Miles for Trip	Price for Delivery
2	$ 2.50	8	$ 0.15	25.0%	750	$ 433.59
3						

Because cell references are used in the formula shown in Figure 3.20, Excel calculates a new output when any of the values are changed in the range A2:E2. In fact, a transportation manager will most likely be changing these values on a daily basis. For example, the price of fuel might change, a new customer may request a price for a trip that is only 250 miles, or the company may need to lower its profit targets because of increased competition. How much will the company charge for the 750-mile trip shown in Figure 3.22 if the price of fuel increases to 2.75, and the profit markup is reduced to 20%? The answer is shown in Figure 3.23.

Figure 3.23 | **Formula Calculates a New Output When Data is Changed**

F2 =(((A2/B2+C2)*E2)*(1+D2))

	A	B	C	D	E	F
1	Fuel Cost per Gallon	Miles per Gallon	Maintenance Cost per Mile	Profit Markup	Miles for Trip	Price for Delivery
2	$ 2.75	8	$ 0.15	20.0%	750	$ 444.38
3						

These values were changed.

New output when the fuel cost and profit markup are changed.

Auditing Formulas

Formulas will not be visible on a spreadsheet unless a cell that contains a formula is activated. However, a group of icons in the **Formulas** tab of the Ribbon called ***Formula Auditing*** contains features that can be used for viewing and checking all formulas in a worksheet. This feature is most helpful when you are proofreading formulas for accuracy or tracing the cell references of a formula that may be producing an erroneous result. Figure 3.24 illustrates how to use the **Show Formulas** icon to display the formulas in a worksheet instead of the outputs. Click this icon to display all formulas in a worksheet and click it again to display formula outputs.

Figure 3.24 | **Show Formulas Instead of Outputs on a Worksheet**

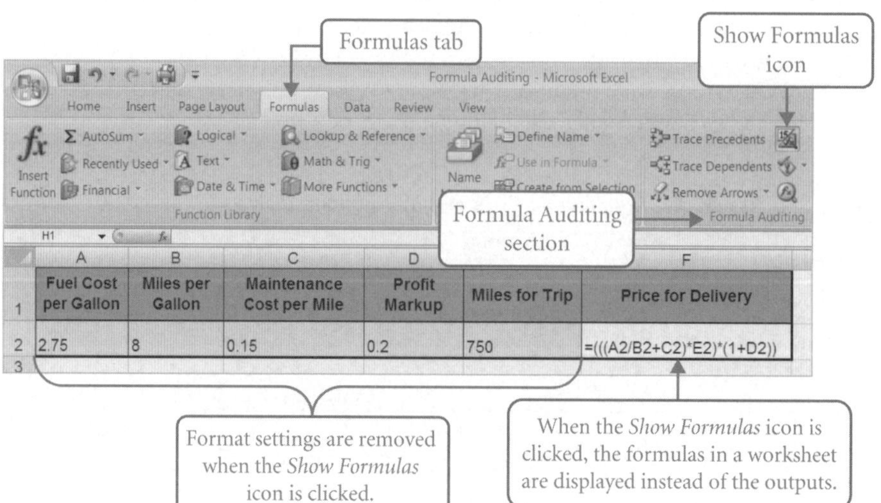

>> Quick Reference

Complex Formulas

1. Activate the cell where formula output should appear.
2. Type an equal sign.
3. Type or click cell locations or type numeric values if necessary.
4. Use parentheses and math operators where necessary.
5. Check that each opening parenthesis has a closing parenthesis.
6. Press the **Enter** key.

Another helpful proofreading option in the **Formula Auditing** section is the **Trace Precedents** icon. This feature will trace all cell references that are used in a formula. Activate a cell location that contains a formula and click the **Trace Precedents** icon. A blue arrow will appear on the worksheet indicating which cell locations are used in a formula, as shown in Figure 3.25. To remove the blue arrow, click the **Remove Arrows** icon, or click the down arrow next to this icon and select **Remove Precedent Arrows**.

Figure 3.25 | **Trace Precedents Arrow**

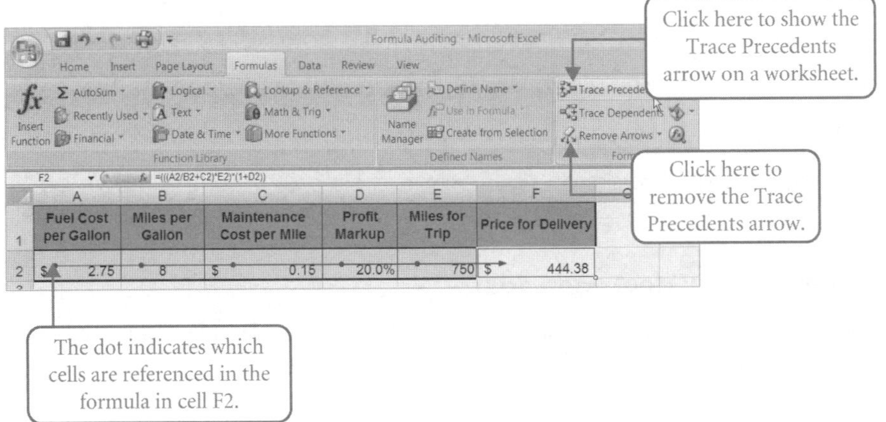

Use the **Trace Dependents** icon when you need to see where a particular cell is referenced in a formula. This capability is helpful if a cell has been improperly referenced in several formulas and you need to identify which formulas need to be edited. Activate a cell location and click the **Trace Dependents** icon. A blue arrow will point to the cell location that contains a formula where the cell is referenced, as shown in Figure 3.26. To remove the arrow, click the **Remove Arrows** icon, or click the down arrow next to this icon and select **Remove Dependent Arrows**.

Figure 3.26 | **Trace Dependents Arrow**

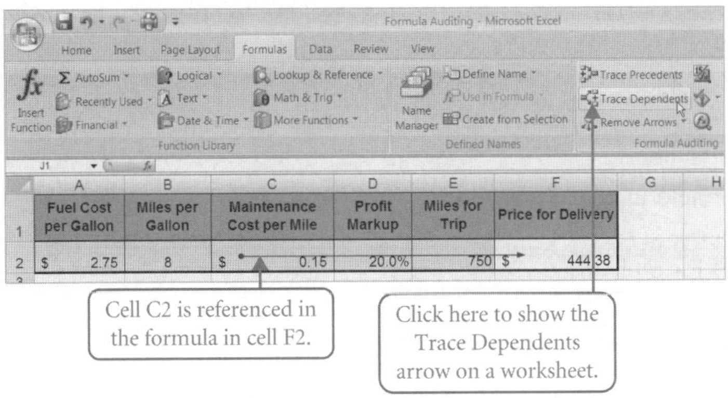

>> **Quick Reference**

Show Formulas

1. Click the **Formulas** tab of the Ribbon.
2. Click the **Show Formulas** icon.
3. Click the **Show Formulas** icon again to display the formula outputs.

>> **Quick Reference**

Trace Precedents

1. Activate a cell location that contains a formula.
2. Click the **Formulas** tab on the Ribbon.
3. Click the **Trace Precedents** icon.
4. Use the **Remove Arrows** icon to remove the **Trace Precedents** arrow.

>> **Quick Reference**

Trace Dependents

1. Activate a cell location that is referenced in a formula on a worksheet.
2. Click the **Formulas** tab on the Ribbon.
3. Click the **Trace Dependents** icon.
4. Use the **Remove Arrows** icon to remove the **Trace Dependents** arrow.

VIDEO WORKSHOP

>> Formulas

The purpose of this workshop is to demonstrate the use of basic and complex formulas presented in this section of the chapter. We will be using formulas to develop sales projections for items sold in a retail clothing store. I will be demonstrating the tasks in this workshop in the **Formulas** and **Paste Special** videos. After completing each section of tasks, watch the related video shown in parentheses. Open the file named ib_e03_salesprojections before starting this workshop. Remember to try the tasks on your own first before watching the video.

1. Data Entry (Video: Formulas)

a. Type the following data into the Sheet1 worksheet for the cell locations listed:

Cell C3: `10`
Cell C4: `-15`
Cell C5: `-50`
Cell C6: `20`
Cell C7: `0`

b. Type the formula `=B3+(B3*C3)` into cell D3 to calculate the Plan Unit Sales This Year.

c. Copy the formula in cell D3 and paste it into cells D4:D7.

d. Type the formula `=F3*D3` into cell G3 to calculate the Plan Sales Dollars for the first item.

e. Copy the formula in cell G3 and paste it into cells G4:G7.

f. Type the formula `=(G3-(D3*E3))/G3` into cell H3 to calculate the profit as a percent of sales for the first item.

g. Copy the formula in H3 and paste it into cells H4:H7.

h. Type the formula `=H3*G3` into cell I3 to calculate the estimated profit dollars for the first item.

i. Copy the formula in cell I3 and paste it into cells I4:I7.

j. Type the formula `=I3 + I4 + I5 + I6 + I7` in cell I9 to add up the plan profit dollars for all items.

2. Creating a New Scenario (Video: Formulas)

a. Rename the Sheet1 worksheet tab to `Profit Scenario 1`.

b. Insert a new worksheet.

c. Change the name of this new worksheet tab to `Profit Scenario 2`.

d. Copy the entire Profit Scenario 1 worksheet.

e. Activate cell A1 in the Profit Scenario 2 worksheet and click the **Paste** icon.

f. In the Profit Scenario 2 worksheet, type the following values in the cell locations listed:

   C4: 0
   C5: 0

3. **Paste Special (Video: Paste Special)**
   a. Copy the range D3:D7 in the Profit Scenario 2 spreadsheet.
   b. Activate cell C3 in the Sales Report spreadsheet.
   c. Click the down arrow below the **Paste** icon and select the **Paste Values** option.
   d. Click the **Paste Options** icon, which appears in cell D8 after completing step c.
   e. Select the **Values and Number Formatting** option.
   f. Save and close your workbook.

>> Startup Costs for a New Business

EXERCISE

Why Do I Need This?

Have you ever thought about starting your own business? One of the most significant challenges in starting a new business is determining how much sales are needed to pay for startup costs. Startup costs usually involve purchases such as machines, office equipment, or permanent marketing materials such as signs. In addition, certain statistics will either be fixed or inflexible. For example, the market price that customers are willing to pay for certain products and services may be fairly rigid. In these cases, raising the price of your product or service to cover startup costs will usually result in a losing proposition.

Exercise

The purpose of this exercise is to use Excel to determine how much sales are required to pay the startup costs of a landscaping business. Open the file named ib_e03_landscapingstartup and complete each of the following tasks:

1. Type the number 25 in cell B3 and change the color of the cell to yellow. You change the cell color to yellow to indicate where values need to be typed into the worksheet. The number 25 is simply a place holder for the number of customers this business might service in a year. This number will be adjusted in later steps of the exercise.

2. Indent the range A9:A11 by clicking the **Increase Indent** icon twice. Indenting will make the spreadsheet easier to read and is a common practice on most accounting and financial documents.

3. Indent cell A16 twice and then indent the range A21:A23 twice.

4. Type a formula in cell C12 that adds the values in cells C9, C10, and C11. This type of calculation is typically done with a function, which will be covered in the next section of this chapter. For now, use a formula to add these three values. This amount represents the total startup costs for this business. The primary focus of this business will be lawn care. Therefore, this exercise assumes that a lawnmower, trimmer, and blower are necessary startup purchases.
5. Type a formula that calculates the total cost of supplies in cell C16. The formula should multiply the value in cell B16 by the value in cell B3. This exercise assumes that supplies will cost $10 for every customer serviced. Costs such as fuel, garbage bags, and oil are usually consumed on every job. Therefore, the purpose of the formula is to multiply the cost per customer by the total number of customers planned for the business.
6. Type a formula in cell C18 that adds the value in cell C12 and C16. The output of this formula represents the total costs of the business.
7. Type a formula in cell B23 that calculates the Average Sales Revenue per Customer, which is Price per Acre multiplied by the Average Number of Acres per Lawn. This exercise assumes that the customer is willing to pay only $30 to service 1 acre of land. In addition, this case assumes that the average amount of land a customer will own in neighborhoods you service is 1.5 acres.
8. Type a formula in cell C25 that multiplies the Average Sales Revenue per Customer by the Number of Customers Serviced This Year.
9. Type a formula in cell B5 that takes the Total Sales in cell C25 and subtracts the Total Costs in cell C18. This is the Net Profit of the business. Is this business making any money if it services only 25 customers per year?
10. Change the value in cell B3 to `100`. Will this business be profitable if 100 customers are serviced per year?
11. How many customers must be serviced for the Net Profit to be approximately 0? How many customers for the profit to be approximately $5,000?
12. What if the price customers were willing to pay per acre dropped to $25, but the average number of acres per lawn increased to 1.75? How many customers will it take to achieve approximately $5,000 in Net Profit?
13. Save and close your file.

PROBLEM & EXERCISE

>> What's Wrong with This Spreadsheet?

Problem

You are directing a division of a major department store company. Your division is made up of four departments. At the beginning of each year, the directors from every division meet with the president of the company to discuss sales and profit targets. A colleague in another division gave you a spreadsheet with an assurance that it included all necessary formulas and that the only thing you had to do was enter numbers in the yellow cells that relate to your sales and profit targets.

Exercise

The spreadsheet that was given to you is named ib_e03_departmentstoreplanningmeeting. Open this file and examine the Sheet1 worksheet carefully. Would you be comfortable using this worksheet to plan the sales and profit targets for your division? Consider the following:

1. Look at the totals in cells B8, C8, and F8. Do the numbers add up?
2. Give the spreadsheet a test drive by changing the value in cell D4 to `.10`. The sales results in column C are calculated by multiplying the Sales Last Year in column B by the Sales Growth percentages in column D. Do you see a new sales plan number in cell C4 that makes sense?
3. Change the value in cell B4 to `8000000`. Do you see a new sales plan number in cell C4 when the value in cell B4 was changed?
4. The Profit Dollars in column F are calculated by multiplying the Profit Percent values in column E by the Sales values in column C. Change the value in cell E4 to `.20`. Does this change produce a new profit dollar value in cell F4?
5. Look at the totals in cells B8, C8, and F8. Do the numbers still add up?
6. What could you use to see and check all the formulas in this worksheet? What clues would tell you that something might be wrong with a formula?

What's wrong with this spreadsheet? Write a short answer for each of the points listed in the preceding problem. Then, fix any errors, adjust, or add formulas that you believe would make this spreadsheet more reliable.

Basic Functions

Skill Set

As previously mentioned, the two primary tools for conducting mathematical computations in Excel are formulas and functions. ***Functions*** are slightly different from formulas in that you do not have to define mathematical operators to produce an output. The mathematical operations are predefined depending on the function that is used. For example, the **AVERAGE** function can be used to calculate the average for a range of ten cells in a worksheet. Functions can produce exactly the same output as formulas. However, when a mathematical output requires the use of many cell locations, it is easier and faster to add a function to a worksheet as opposed to a formula. This section will review the use of basic statistical functions and illustrate why it is more efficient to use them for certain calculations instead of formulas.

Basic Statistical Functions

Using basic statistical methods to analyze data is a common practice in business. For example, a business manager may sum the sales results for a group of stores in a district, calculate the average trips per week for a fleet of trucks, or evaluate the most common number of items purchased when customers visit a store. In Excel, basic statistical functions can provide a convenient way to accomplish these computations, as opposed to using formulas. For example, the Merchandise Sales Report worksheet introduced in Chapter 2 (see Figure 3.28) contains sales information for 18 items. If you wanted to calculate the sum of the Unit Sales for all items in column D, you could add all 18 cell locations from D2 to D19 individually to a formula. Or, you could just add the range D2:D19 to the **SUM** function to produce the same result.

All Excel functions can be created using the following method:

- Type an equal sign. Similar to formulas, all functions begin with an equal sign in a cell location. The equal sign signifies that Excel will be performing some type of computation instead of displaying what is typed in a cell.
- Type the function name. After you type the first letter of a function, a list of possible function names beginning with the letter you typed will appear (see Figure 3.27). This feature is especially helpful if you forgot how to spell a particular function name. After you find the name of the function you would like to use, you can double click the name from the list or continue typing the function name manually.
- Type an open parenthesis. If you double click a function name from the function list as shown in Figure 3.27, Excel will insert the open parenthesis for you automatically.
- Type a cell range or define arguments. The information you type after the open parenthesis will depend on the type of function you are using. For the basic statistical functions covered in this section, you will need to type a cell range (two cell locations separated by a colon) after the open parenthesis. You can also type specific cell locations separated by commas if you are applying the function to cells that are not contained in a continuous range (for example, B2,H5,D10). Note that functions containing arguments are covered in the next section.
- Type a close parenthesis and press the **Enter** key. After you press the **Enter** key, the function output will be displayed in the cell.

As mentioned, when you begin typing the name of a function, a list of possible function names beginning with the first letter you typed will appear on the worksheet. For example, Figure 3.27 shows the function list after typing an equal sign and the letter S. In addition, if you click a function name one time, a definition of the function will appear.

Figure 3.27 | **The Function List**

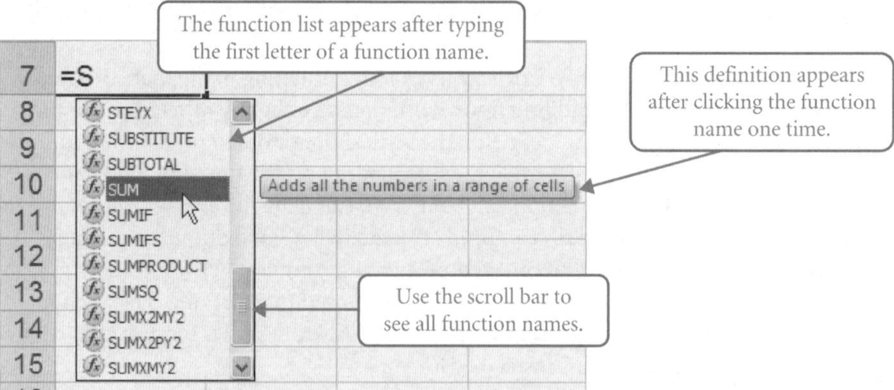

Figures 3.28 and 3.29 show the setup and results of adding a **SUM** function to the Merchandise Sales Report worksheet, which was constructed in Chapter 2. Here, the **SUM** function was added to calculate the total number of units sold for all items in the worksheet. As mentioned, it is more convenient to use the **SUM** function in this situation because a total is being computed from 18 cell locations. The following explains how to add this function to the worksheet:

- Activate cell D20. This is the last cell at the bottom of the Unit Sales column.
- Type an equal sign.
- Type the function name SUM. You can also double click the word **SUM** from the function list.
- Type an open parenthesis. If you double clicked the function name from the function list, the open parenthesis will already be added.

- Type the range D2:D19. You can also add this range to the function by clicking and dragging over cells D2 through D19.
- Type a close parenthesis.
- Press the **Enter** key.

Figure 3.28 | **Adding the SUM Function to the Merchandise Sales Report**

SUM | =SUM(D2:D19)

The function appears in the formula bar when cell D20 is activated.

	A	B	C	D	E
1	*Category Description*	*Item Description*	*Color*	*Unit Sales*	*Sales Dollars*
2	Bottoms	Shorts	Tan	12,500	$237,500
3	Tops	T-Shirts	Black	10,000	$115,000
4	Bottoms	Shorts	White	9,500	$180,500
5	Tops	Sweater	Grey	8,500	$289,000
6	Bottoms	Shorts	Brown	8,500	$161,500
7	Tops	T-Shirts	Blue	8,500	$97,750
8	Tops	Tank Top	White	6,500	$55,250
9	Bottoms	Shorts	Blue	5,500	$104,500
10	Tops	T-Shirts	Yellow	4,500	$51,750
11	Tops	Sweater	Brown	3,500	$119,000
12	Shoes	Sandals	Black	3,000	$66,000
13	Tops	Tank Top	Pink	2,500	$21,250
14	Shoes	Boots	Black	1,600	$96,000
15	Tops	Sweater	Red	1,500	$51,000
16	Tops	Tank Top	Red	1,500	$12,750
17	Shoes	Sandals	Grey	1,200	$26,400
18	Shoes	Sandals	Green	850	$18,700
19	Shoes	Boots	Brown	750	$45,000
20	***Total***			=SUM(D2:D19)	

This range can be added to the function by clicking and dragging over cells D2 through D19 after typing =SUM(.

Figure 3.29 | **Results of the SUM Function in the Merchandise Sales Report**

J1 |

	A	B	C	D	E
1	*Category Description*	*Item Description*	*Color*	*Unit Sales*	*Sales Dollars*
2	Bottoms	Shorts	Tan	12,500	$237,500
3	Tops	T-Shirts	Black	10,000	$115,000
4	Bottoms	Shorts	White	9,500	$180,500
5	Tops	Sweater	Grey	8,500	$289,000
6	Bottoms	Shorts	Brown	8,500	$161,500
7	Tops	T-Shirts	Blue	8,500	$97,750
8	Tops	Tank Top	White	6,500	$55,250
9	Bottoms	Shorts	Blue	5,500	$104,500
10	Tops	T-Shirts	Yellow	4,500	$51,750
11	Tops	Sweater	Brown	3,500	$119,000
12	Shoes	Sandals	Black	3,000	$66,000
13	Tops	Tank Top	Pink	2,500	$21,250
14	Shoes	Boots	Black	1,600	$96,000
15	Tops	Sweater	Red	1,500	$51,000
16	Tops	Tank Top	Red	1,500	$12,750
17	Shoes	Sandals	Grey	1,200	$26,400
18	Shoes	Sandals	Green	850	$18,700
19	Shoes	Boots	Brown	750	$45,000
20	***Total***			90,400	

Output produced by the SUM function.

The example in Figure 3.30 illustrates the **AVERAGE** function. This worksheet contains the sales and profit results for six stores in a district of a retail company. The **AVERAGE** function is used to calculate the average sales results that are achieved for each store in the district. Notice that the range in the **AVERAGE** function includes cell C7, which does not contain a numeric value. Statistical functions will ignore cells that are blank or do not contain numeric data. Therefore, the **AVERAGE** function will ignore this cell until a numeric value is typed into it.

Figure 3.30 | **The AVERAGE Function**

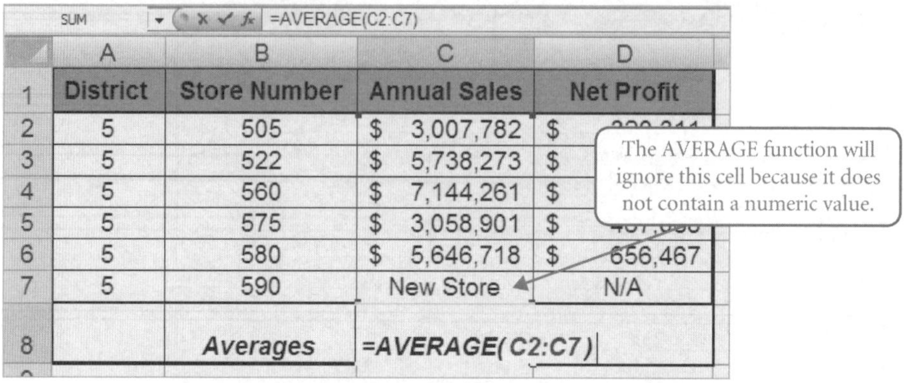

SUM =AVERAGE(C2:C7)

	A	B	C	D
1	District	Store Number	Annual Sales	Net Profit
2	5	505	$ 3,007,782	$ [illegible]
3	5	522	$ 5,738,273	$ [illegible]
4	5	560	$ 7,144,261	$ [illegible]
5	5	575	$ 3,058,901	$ [illegible]
6	5	580	$ 5,646,718	$ 656,467
7	5	590	New Store	N/A
8		*Averages*	*=AVERAGE(C2:C7)*	

The AVERAGE function will ignore this cell because it does not contain a numeric value.

Relative referencing (explained previously in the "Formulas" section) also applies to functions. Figure 3.31 shows the **AVERAGE** function after it was pasted into cell D8, which is one cell to the right of the cell location shown in Figure 3.30. Notice that the column letters of the range in the function changed from C to D. This function will show the average of the Net Profit results in column D and will ignore cell D7 because it does not contain a numeric value.

FIGURE 3.31 | **Relative Referencing Adjusts the Range in the AVERAGE Function**

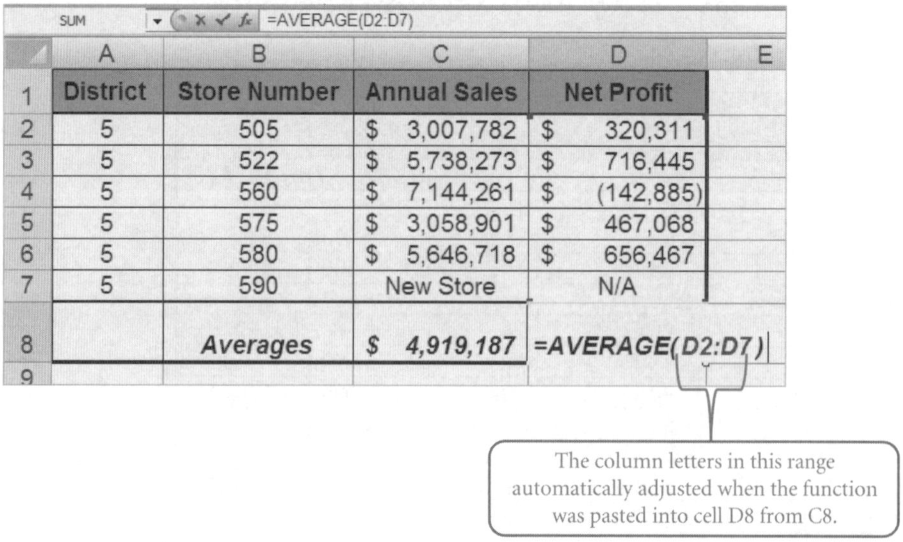

SUM =AVERAGE(D2:D7)

	A	B	C	D	E
1	District	Store Number	Annual Sales	Net Profit	
2	5	505	$ 3,007,782	$ 320,311	
3	5	522	$ 5,738,273	$ 716,445	
4	5	560	$ 7,144,261	$ (142,885)	
5	5	575	$ 3,058,901	$ 467,068	
6	5	580	$ 5,646,718	$ 656,467	
7	5	590	New Store	N/A	
8		*Averages*	*$ 4,919,187*	*=AVERAGE(D2:D7)*	
9					

The column letters in this range automatically adjusted when the function was pasted into cell D8 from C8.

Figure 3.32 shows how the **AVERAGE** function produces a new output when numeric data is typed into C7 and D7. As mentioned, these cells were previously ignored by the function because they did not contain numeric values. However, because of cell referencing, the functions automatically produce a new output when numeric values are typed into these cells.

Figure 3.32 | **The AVERAGE Function Produces a New Output When Data Is Changed**

	A	B	C	D
1	District	Store Number	Annual Sales	Net Profit
2	5	505	$ 3,007,782	$ 320,311
3	5	522	$ 5,738,273	$ 716,445
4	5	560	$ 7,144,261	$ (142,885)
5	5	575	$ 3,058,901	$ 467,068
6	5	580	$ 5,646,718	$ 656,467
7	5	590	$ 8,534,000	$ 775,640
8		*Averages*	***$ 5,521,656***	***$ 465,508***

Values are typed into cells C7 and D7.

This output changed when a value was typed into cell C7.

COMMON MISTAKES | Cell Ranges versus Specific Cells in Functions

Be careful when using a range of cells versus selected cells in basic statistical functions. If you want to apply a statistical function to a group of consecutive cells, you must use a range. A range is any two cells separated by a colon, NOT a comma. For example, the **SUM** function shown in Figure 3.33 will add only cells A2 and A6, providing an output of 3000. The reason is that a *comma* is separating the two cell locations. For this **SUM** function to add all of the values in cells A2 through A6, the range **A2:A6** must be typed between the parentheses of the function. Therefore, always check the outputs of all functions used in a worksheet. If you were expecting the **SUM** function to add all the values in column A in Figure 3.33 and saw an output of 3000, you would know something is wrong because one of the values in this column is 5000 (cell A4).

Figure 3.33 | **SUM Function Adding Values in Only Two Cell Locations**

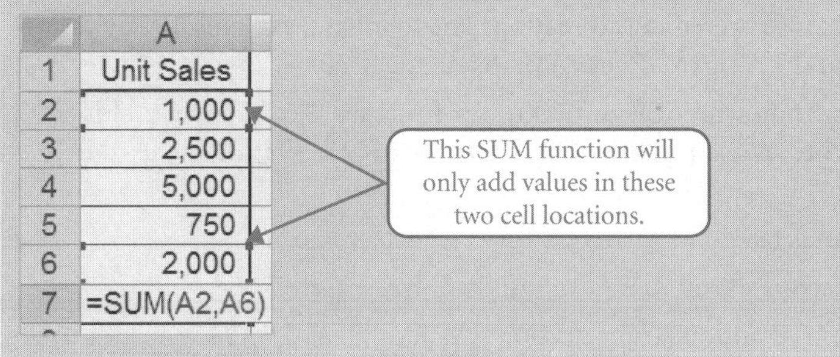

The **SUM** function and the **AVERAGE** function were used to demonstrate basic statistical functions in this section. However, this usage just scratches the surface of the 300+ functions in Excel. Figure 3.34 shows other commonly used statistical functions. The details of what these functions do and how they are applied in business situations will likely be covered in your business statistics or economics courses.

Quick Reference

Basic Functions

1. Activate a cell where the output of the function should appear.
2. Type an equal sign.
3. Type the name of the function or double click a function name from the function list.
4. Type an open parenthesis if you typed the function name manually.
5. Type a range or click and drag a range of cells (if you are using specific cells not in a continuous range, type or click each cell and separate with a comma).
6. Type a closing parenthesis.
7. Press the **Enter** key.

Figure 3.34 | **Table of Common Statistical Functions**

Function Name	Purpose
SUM	Calculates the total for numeric values in a range of cells or selected cells.
AVERAGE	Calculates the average for a series of numeric values.
MEDIAN	Returns the value that is in the middle of a *sorted* numeric series (the range of cells used with this function must be sorted in order for the function to produce an accurate result).
MODE	Identifies the value that occurs the most in a numeric series.
STDEV	Calculates the standard deviation for a range of cells.
VAR	Calculates the variance for a range of cells.
MIN	Returns the lowest value in a numeric series.
MAX	Returns the highest value in a numeric series.
COUNT	Counts the number of cells that contain a numeric value.
COUNTA	Counts the number of cells that contain either a numeric value or text value.
PRODUCT	Calculates the product of the values contained in a range of cells or selected cells.
SQRT	Returns the square root of a number.
ABS	Returns the absolute value of a number.

AutoSum

The **AutoSum** icon in the **Formulas** tab of the Ribbon provides quick access to a few basic statistical functions covered in this section. The following explains how to use the **AutoSum** icon to add the **AVERAGE** function to a worksheet:

- Activate a cell location where the output of the function should appear. This cell location should be below or to the right of a range of cells that will be used in the function.
- Click the **Formulas** tab.
- Click the down arrow next to the **AutoSum** icon (see Figure 3.35).
- Select the **AVERAGE** option. This selection will add the **AVERAGE** function to the worksheet and automatically select a range of cells immediately above the activated cell location (see Figure 3.36).
- Press the **Enter** key.

Quick Reference

AutoSum

1. Activate the cell where the output of the function should appear. The cell location should be below or to the right of a range of cells that will be used in the function.
2. Click the **Formulas** tab in the Ribbon.
3. Click the down arrow next to the **AutoSum** icon.
4. Select a function.
5. Press the **Enter** key.

Figure 3.35 | **Options in the AutoSum Icon**

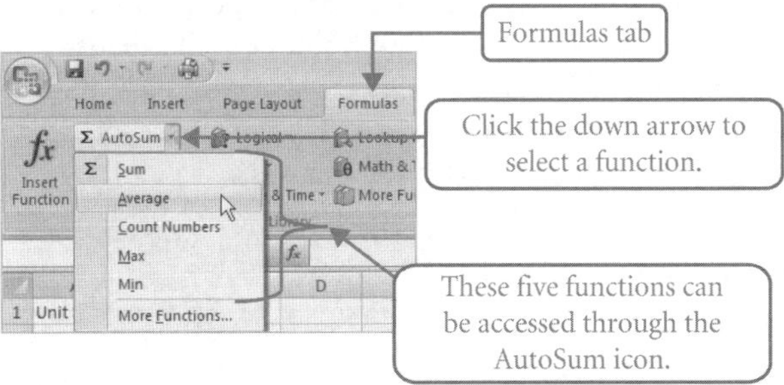

Figure 3.36 | **The Range Is Added to the AVERAGE Function Automatically**

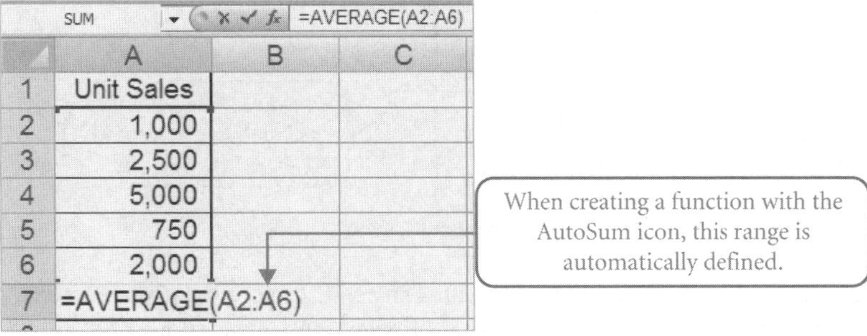

Absolute References (Turning Off Relative References)

As previously mentioned, because of relative referencing, Excel will automatically adjust the cell references used in formulas and functions when they are pasted into new cell locations. However, certain circumstances may require you to turn off this relative reference feature. In other words, you may need to paste a formula or function to a new cell location but do not want Excel to adjust the cell references. In these situations you will need to apply an ***absolute reference*** or a ***mixed reference*** to the cell references in a formula.

To place an absolute reference on a cell location, type a dollar sign in front of the column letter and row number. Placing the dollar sign here prevents relative referencing from adjusting the cell location when the formula is pasted to a new cell location. You can also create mixed references which is when a dollar sign is typed in front of the column letter *or* the row number. For example, if a dollar sign is typed only in front of the row number, the row number becomes an absolute reference, but the column letter remains a relative reference. If this cell was referenced in a formula, the column letter will change, but the row number will not when the formula is pasted into a new cell location. The following are examples of absolute and mixed references.

- `$C$10`: This is an absolute reference. This cell reference will not change when it is pasted to another cell location on a worksheet.
- `C$10`: This is a mixed reference. The row number will not change when this cell is pasted to a new location on a worksheet.
- `$C10`: This is another example of a mixed reference. The column letter will not change when this cell is pasted to a new location on a worksheet.

The example in Figure 3.37 illustrates when an absolute reference is used in a business situation. This worksheet shows a list of annual expenses for a hypothetical company. A **SUM** function was created in cell B8 to total the Cost Values for all expense items in column B. The goal for this example is to create a formula in column C that divides the Cost Value for each expense item by the total in cell B8. This will show what percentage each item contributes to the total expenses for the business.

Figure 3.37 | **Annual Expense Information for a Hypothetical Business**

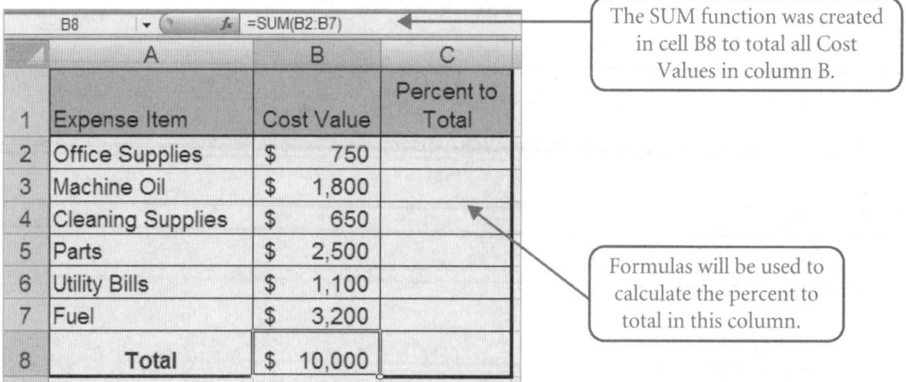

B8 =SUM(B2:B7)

	A	B	C
1	Expense Item	Cost Value	Percent to Total
2	Office Supplies	$ 750	
3	Machine Oil	$ 1,800	
4	Cleaning Supplies	$ 650	
5	Parts	$ 2,500	
6	Utility Bills	$ 1,100	
7	Fuel	$ 3,200	
8	Total	$ 10,000	

Figure 3.38 shows the formula that was created in cell C2 to compute the Percent to Total for Office Supplies. The result shows that Office Supplies makes up 7.5% of the total annual expenses for this business. This formula will be copied and pasted to cells C3 through C7 to calculate the Percent to Total for the rest of the Expense Items in column A.

Figure 3.38 | **Formula Used to Compute the Percent to Total**

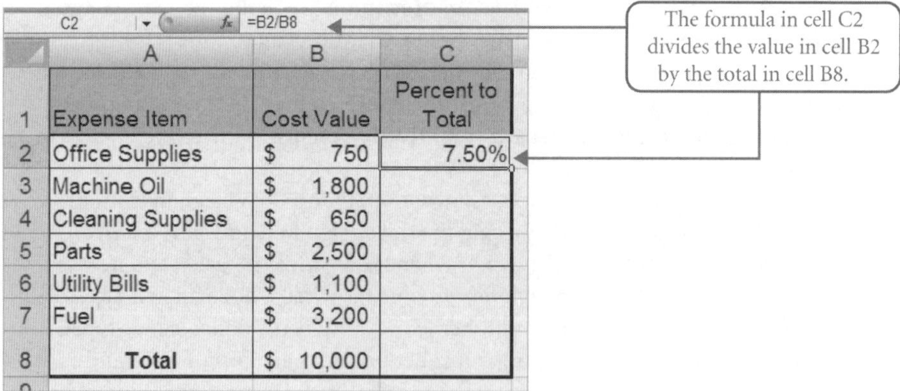

C2 =B2/B8

	A	B	C
1	Expense Item	Cost Value	Percent to Total
2	Office Supplies	$ 750	7.50%
3	Machine Oil	$ 1,800	
4	Cleaning Supplies	$ 650	
5	Parts	$ 2,500	
6	Utility Bills	$ 1,100	
7	Fuel	$ 3,200	
8	Total	$ 10,000	

Figure 3.39 shows that a divide by zero error (#DIV/0!) occurs when the formula created in cell C2 is pasted into cells C3 through C7. This error occurred because relative referencing is adjusting the cell that is being divided into the Cost Value for each Expense item.

Figure 3.39 | **Divide by Zero Error**

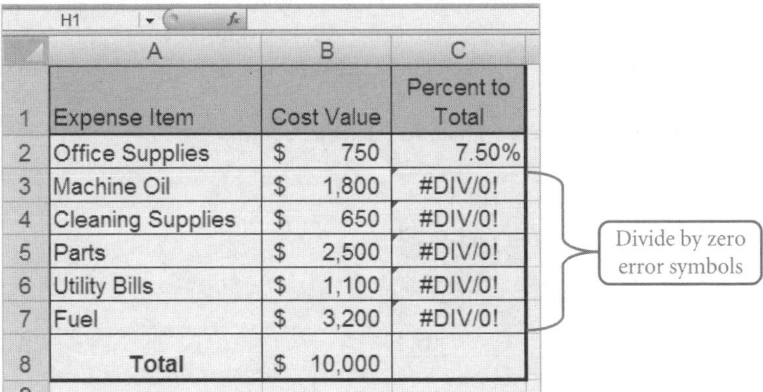

	A	B	C
1	Expense Item	Cost Value	Percent to Total
2	Office Supplies	$ 750	7.50%
3	Machine Oil	$ 1,800	#DIV/0!
4	Cleaning Supplies	$ 650	#DIV/0!
5	Parts	$ 2,500	#DIV/0!
6	Utility Bills	$ 1,100	#DIV/0!
7	Fuel	$ 3,200	#DIV/0!
8	Total	$ 10,000	

Figure 3.40 shows why the divide by zero error occurred in Figure 3.39. The goal of the formula created in cell C2 is to divide the Cost Value for the Office Supplies expense by the total annual expenses for the business. Therefore, the value in cell B2 is divided by the total in cell B8. However, notice how relative referencing adjusted the cell references in this formula when it was pasted into cell C3. The value in cell B3 is being divided by the value in cell B9. Since there is nothing in cell B9, the divide by zero error appears. Therefore, we need to prevent relative referencing from changing cell B8 when it is copied from cell C2 to other cell locations in the column. This is done by adding an absolute reference to cell B8 in the formula that was created in cell C2 (see Figure 3.38).

Figure 3.40 | **How Relative Referencing Causes the Divide by Zero Error**

SUM =B3/B9

	A	B	C
1	Expense Item	Cost Value	Percent to Total
2	Office Supplies	$ 750	7.50%
3	Machine Oil	$ 1,800	=B3/B9
4	Cleaning Supplies	$ 650	#DIV/0!
5	Parts	$ 2,500	#DIV/0!
6	Utility Bills	$ 1,100	#DIV/0!
7	Fuel	$ 3,200	#DIV/0!
8	Total	$ 10,000	
9			

Because of *relative* referencing, the second part of this formula is being divided by an empty cell.

As mentioned, to prevent relative referencing from adjusting cell B8 in the formula shown in Figure 3.38, we must use an absolute reference. This is accomplished by typing a dollar sign in front of the column letter and row number of cell B8, as shown in Figure 3.41.

Figure 3.41 | **Adding an Absolute Reference to Cell B8**

SUM =B2/$B$8

	A	B	C
1	Expense Item	Cost Value	Percent to Total
2	Office Supplies	$ 750	=B2/$B$8
3	Machine Oil	$ 1,800	
4	Cleaning Supplies	$ 650	
5	Parts	$ 2,500	
6	Utility Bills	$ 1,100	
7	Fuel	$ 3,200	
8	Total	$ 10,000	

Absolute reference is added to cell B8 with a dollar sign ($) in front of the column letter and row number.

> **Quick Reference**
>
> **Absolute Reference**
>
> 1. Identify a cell reference within a formula or function that requires an absolute reference or mixed reference.
> 2. Type a dollar sign in front of the column letter and row number of a cell reference to apply an absolute reference.
> 3. Type a dollar sign in front of the column letter or row number to apply a mixed reference.

Figure 3.42 shows the results of pasting the formula in Figure 3.41 to cell locations C3 through C7. As shown in the figure, there are no divide by zero errors. The reason is that cell B8 did not change when it was pasted to other cell locations in column C. Now all the Cost Values in column B are being divided by the total in cell B8.

Figure 3.42 | **Results of Pasting a Formula with an Absolute Reference**

SUM =B4/$B$8

	A	B	C
1	Expense Item	Cost Value	Percent to Total
2	Office Supplies	$ 750	7.50%
3	Machine Oil	$ 1,800	18.00%
4	Cleaning Supplies	$ 650	=B4/$B$8
5	Parts	$ 2,500	25.00%
6	Utility Bills	$ 1,100	11.00%
7	Fuel	$ 3,200	32.00%
8	Total	$ 10,000	

Cell B8 does not change when the formula is pasted to a new cell location.

VIDEO WORKSHOP

>> Statistical Functions

The purpose of this workshop is to demonstrate the use of statistical functions when conducting mathematical computations. We will be using statistical functions to summarize transaction data for a typical retail business. I will be demonstrating the tasks in this workshop in the **Statistical Functions** video. Open the file named ib_e03_retailtransactions before starting the following tasks:

1. **Statistical Functions (Video: Statistical Functions)**
   a. Type the **COUNT** function in cell G3 to count all the Transaction Numbers in the range A3:A50.
   b. Type a **SUM** function in cell G4 to add up the Amount Paid in the range C3:C50.
   c. Type an **AVERAGE** function in cell G5 to calculate the average Number of Items in the range B3:B50.
   d. Type an **AVERAGE** function in cell G6 to calculate the average of the range C3:C50.
   e. Calculate the average price per item purchased by using a **SUM** function to add up the values in the range C3:C50 and divide it by another **SUM** function adding up the values in the range B3:B50. The entry should be as follows: =Sum(C3:C50)/Sum(B3:B50).
   f. Type a **MAX** function in cell G8 to show the highest amount paid in the range C3:C50.
   g. Type a **MIN** function in cell G9 to show the lowest amount paid in the range C3:C50.
   h. Type a **MODE** function in cell G10 to calculate the most frequent number of items purchased in the range B3:B50.
   i. Save and close your file.

>> Absolute References

VIDEO WORKSHOP

The purpose of this workshop is to demonstrate how and why absolute references are used in business situations. We will be using an absolute reference to calculate the percent to total for items on a merchandise sales spreadsheet. I will be demonstrating the tasks in this workshop in the **Absolute Reference** video. Open the file named ib_e03_merchandisesales before starting the following tasks:

1. **Functions (Video: Absolute Reference)**
   a. Create a **SUM** function in cell E12 to add up the profit dollars in column E.

2. **Formulas (Video: Absolute Reference)**
   a. Type a formula in cell F3 that divides the profit dollars in cell E3 by the total profit dollars in cell E12.
   b. Format the output of the formula in cell F3 to a percentage with 2 decimal places.

3. **Absolute References (Video: Absolute Reference)**
   a. Edit the formula in cell F3 by placing an absolute reference on cell E12.
   b. Copy cell F3 and paste it into cells F4:F11.
   c. Save and close your file.

>> Evaluating a Transportation Business

EXERCISE

Why Do I Need This?

Summarizing data plays a critical role in making business decisions. The amount of data businesses store and analyze can be massive, especially in large corporations. Most business managers face the constant challenge of quickly summarizing large sets of data to assess business results. Knowing how to summarize data using the statistics functions covered in this section will enable you to quickly summarize and assess large sets of data relating to almost any business situation.

Exercise

The purpose of this exercise is to use statistical functions to evaluate the performance of a transportation company. Open the file named ib_e03_transportationperformance and complete the following tasks:

1. Using the **COUNT** function in cell C3, calculate the number of trips in the range A13:A52.
2. Use the **AVERAGE** function in cell G3 to calculate the average miles per trip in the range C13:C52.
3. Find the highest miles driven for a single trip in the range C13:C52 by using the **MAX** function in cell C4.

4. Find the lowest miles driven for a single trip in the range C13:C52 by using the **MIN** function in cell G4.

5. Using the **MODE** function in cell C6, determine which trailer size was used the most from the range B13:B52.

6. Calculate the average capacity per trip by typing an **AVERAGE** function in cell G6. The capacity for each trip is in the range D13:D52.

7. Use the **MAX** function in cell C7 to determine the highest capacity for a single trip in the range D13:D52.

8. Use the **MIN** function in cell G7 to determine the lowest capacity for a single trip in the range D13:D52.

9. Type the value `2.50` in cell G9 and `.25` in cell G10.

10. Calculate the total fuel cost in cell C9 by using a **SUM** function to add up all the fuel consumed in the range E13:E52 and multiplying it by the fuel cost in cell G9.

11. Calculate the dollars billed in cell C10 by using a **SUM** function to add up all the miles driven in the range C13:C52 and multiplying it by the current charge per mile in cell G10.

12. Compare the output of the formulas you created in cells C9 and C10. Is this company making enough money to cover its fuel cost?

13. If fuel prices are increased to $3.05 per gallon, how much will this company have to increase its charge per mile to cover the cost of fuel plus make approximately $1,000 in profit?

14. This company has a goal of maintaining an average capacity per trip of 90%. Is this company achieving its goal?

15. What could this company do to get closer to its capacity target of 90%? How else could you analyze the Trip Detail statistics in the range A12:E52 to answer this question? HINT: What size trailers are reaching the highest capacity levels on a consistent basis?

16. Save and close your file.

PROBLEM & EXERCISE

>> What's Wrong with This Spreadsheet?

Problem

Your classmate is having trouble with a project and has come to you for help. He is using Excel for an industry analysis project that is due for one of his business classes. He completed the spreadsheet but explains that for some reason a lot of the numbers do not look right. He e-mails the Excel file to you with the following explanation:

1. I am trying to calculate the market share for each company on the spreadsheet, which is nothing more than a percent to total. I used an absolute reference on one of the cell locations in the formula (you know, that dollar sign thing), but I still keep getting this error.

2. I'm wondering if my market share error in column C has something to do with the **SUM** function I used in cell B8. It worked fine, but before I e-mailed the file to you, I noticed that the number looked a little low.

3. The other thing that looks weird is the average I calculated in cell B9. The result is $43,750,000, but every company is below this number except for Company A. I used the **AVERAGE** function, so it must be right. I don't know; it just seems weird.

4. Finally, I used the **COUNT** function in cell C11 to count the number of companies in the spreadsheet, but it keeps giving me a result of 0. At this point I am wondering if this file got corrupted somehow. Can you take a look at this and let me know if I should just make another spreadsheet on a different computer?

Exercise

The file this classmate has sent to you is named ib_e03_industryanalysistrouble. Open the file and review each of the concerns listed in the Problem section. Is it the computer that's causing these problems? What's wrong with this spreadsheet? Write a short answer explaining what mistakes were made for each of the points your classmate listed. Then, correct any errors you find.

>> Financial Functions

Skill Set

The statistical functions demonstrated in the previous section were constructed by typing a range of cells or specific cell locations separated by commas between parentheses. However, other functions may require the definition of several inputs or ***arguments*** to produce an output. The purpose and number of arguments will vary depending on the function. This section reviews two such functions: Future Value and Payment. Both are related to the financial aspects of business with regard to evaluating investments and loans. This section will demonstrate how these functions are constructed and highlight how they can be used for making both professional and personal business decisions.

The Future Value Function

The ***Future Value***, or ***FV*** function, is used to calculate the value of investments over a specific period of time. To better understand how the **Future Value** function calculates the value of an investment, it is helpful to review an example relating to the time value of money.

Figure 3.43 illustrates the principles of the time value of money by showing how a bank account grows over three years. This example assumes that a bank is very generous and offers an interest rate of 8% for a traditional savings account. In reality, the interest rate that is usually offered for a traditional savings account is much less. The first row of the table, labeled Year 1, shows that an account is opened with $10. Assuming the interest rate does not change, the value of the account after one year will be $10.80 as shown in the End Balance column. The reason is that $.80 was paid in interest (see the Interest Earned column). The second row, labeled Year 2, assumes that another $10 is deposited into the account as shown in the Deposit column. Notice that the Interest Earned column increases from $.80 in Year 1 to $1.66 in Year 2. The value of the account at the end of Year 2 is $22.46, as shown in the End Balance column. At the end of the third year, the ending balance of the account is $35.06. However, if you add the values in the Deposits column, only $30 was added to this account. The additional money is the total amount of interest paid over the three-year period, which is $5.06. This is the sum of the values in the Interest Paid column.

Figure 3.43 **Time Value of Money Example**

	Begin Balance	Deposit	Interest Rate	Interest Paid	End Balance
Year 1	0	$10.00	8% × $10.00	$ .80	$10.80
Year 2	$10.80	$10.00	8% × $20.80	$1.66	$22.46
Year 3	$22.46	$10.00	8% × $32.46	$2.60	$35.06

The Future Value function will be used to calculate this result.

The **Future Value** function can be used to calculate the End Balance value, which is circled in Figure 3.43. You add the function to a worksheet by typing an equal sign (=), the function name FV, and an open parenthesis. You can also double click the function name FV from the function list after typing the equal sign and the letter F. To complete the function, you will need to define at least three of the five arguments shown in Figure 3.44. The arguments will appear in a hint box after you type an open parenthesis or double click the function name from the function list. The following is a definition for each of these arguments:

- **rate**: The interest rate applied to an investment.
- **nper**: The number of periods an investment is added to an account or the amount of time an investment is being measured. This argument must correspond to the interest rate entered in the **rate** argument. For example, if an annual interest rate is entered in the **rate** argument, the **nper** argument must be the number of years. If a monthly interest rate is entered in the **rate** argument, the **nper** argument must be the number of months. If a daily interest rate is used in the **rate** argument, the **nper** argument must be the number of days.
- **pmt**: The value of the payments that are added to an account. This argument is used when money is being added to an account over a period of time (such as $100 per month or $2,000 per year). The period of time will be the value that is entered in the **nper** argument. A negative sign must be placed in front of values or cell locations used to define this argument.
- ***[pv]: Present Value***: The argument used when a one-time investment is made to an account. It can be used with or without the **pmt** argument. You must place a negative sign in front of values or cell locations used to define this argument.
- **[type]**: The argument used to define when payments are made to an account; it can either be a 1 or 0. If this argument is not defined, Excel will assume the value is 0.
  - 1: Used for payments made at the beginning of a period (i.e., at the beginning of a month, year, etc.).
  - 0: Used for payments made at the end of a period.

Figure 3.44 | **Arguments of the Future Value Function**

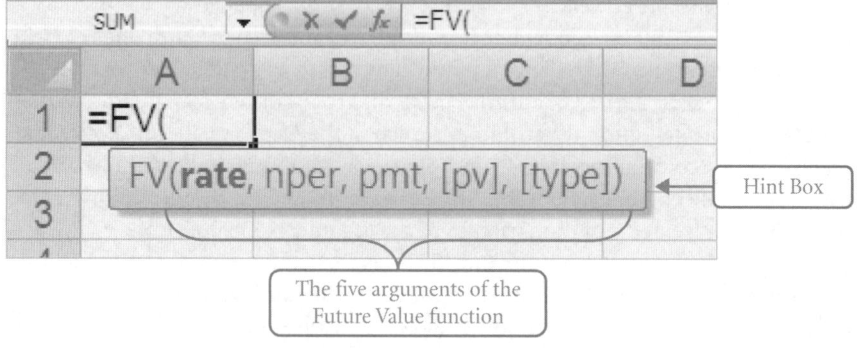

As mentioned, the **Future Value** function can be used to calculate the End Balance value circled in Figure 3.43. The following illustrates how each argument of the function would be defined based on the Time Value of Money Example (Figure 3.43). Remember, you must use a comma to separate each value that is used to define the arguments of the function.

- **rate**: `.08` This represents the annual interest rate shown in the Interest Rate column in Figure 3.43. When you are entering numbers into this function, it is best *not* to use any symbols except for decimal points. This is why the 8% interest rate is typed into the function as .08. If you are not sure how to convert a percentage to a decimal, simply divide the percent by 100 (i.e., `8 ÷ 100 = .08`).
- **nper**: `3` The Time Value of Money Example in Figure 3.43 shows that $10 is deposited into a bank account every year for three years. Therefore, the number 3 (representing 3 years) is entered for this argument. It is important to note that since an annual interest rate was entered in the **rate** argument, the time period entered for this argument must be in years.
- **pmt**: `-10` Since $10 is being deposited into a bank account over a three-year period, the number -10 is entered for this argument. *You must put a negative sign in front of any number or cell location used for this argument.*
- **[pv]**: This argument is used to evaluate a one-time lump sum investment. However, this example assumes that deposits are being made to the account annually. Therefore, this argument will be skipped by adding a comma with no spaces.
- **[type]**: For this example, we will assume that the $10 is being deposited into the account at the beginning of each year. Therefore, a value of 1 is entered for this argument.

Figure 3.45 shows how the arguments of the **Future Value** function are defined based on the Time Value of Money Example in Figure 3.43. Notice that each argument is separated with a comma. In addition, since the **[pv]** argument was skipped, a comma was typed with no spaces.

Figure 3.45 | **Setup of the Future Value Function Based on the Time Value of Money Example**

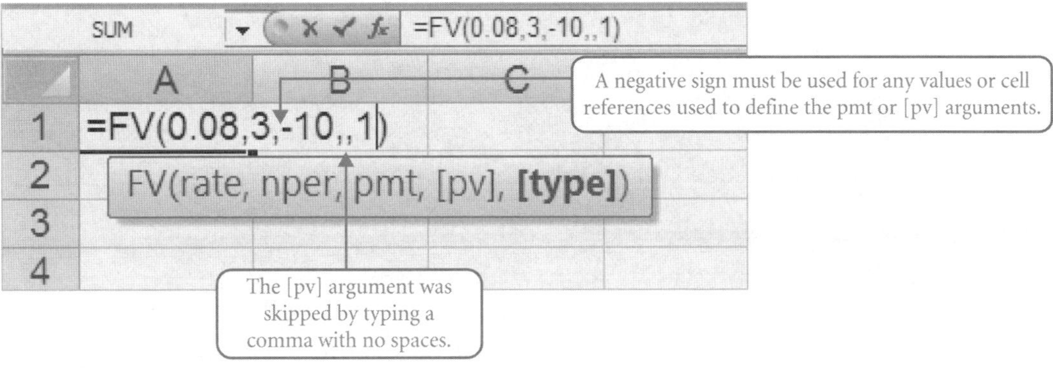

Figure 3.46 shows the results of the **Future Value** function after the **Enter** key was pressed. Notice that this output is identical to the End Balance number in Year 3 from the Time Value of Money Example in Figure 3.43.

Figure 3.46 | **Results of the Future Value Function**

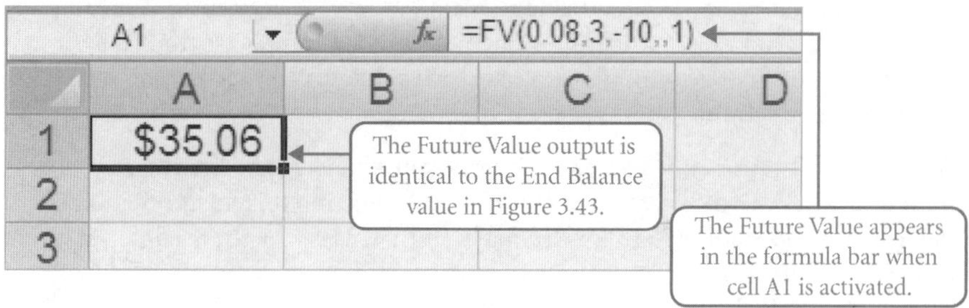

COMMON MISTAKES | Separate Arguments with Commas

You must type a comma after each argument of the **Future Value** function. If you are skipping an argument, as in Figure 3.45, type a comma with no spaces. If you are skipping both the **[pv]** and **[type]** arguments, you can type a closing parenthesis after the **pmt** argument. This is the reason these arguments are displayed in brackets [ ]. The function will produce an output if these arguments are not defined. Note that Excel assumes payments are made at the *end* of the year if the **[type]** argument is skipped.

As previously mentioned, the **Future Value** function can also evaluate an investment made in one lump sum. This would require the [**pv**] argument to be defined instead of the **pmt** argument. When using the [**pv**] argument, you must use a negative sign for all values or cell locations as in the **pmt** argument. Figure 3.47 shows how the arguments of the **Future Value** function are defined if $30 is deposited into a bank account at the beginning of Year 1 as opposed to making $10 deposits over a three-year period as shown in the Time Value of Money Example in Figure 3.43. It is assumed that the annual interest rate is 8% and that it will not change over the three-year period.

Figure 3.47 | **Setup of the Future Value Function for a One-Time Investment**

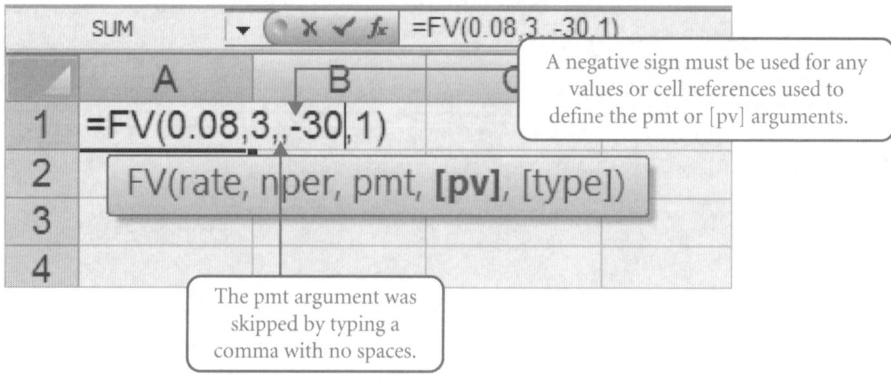

Figure 3.48 shows the output of the **Future Value** function which was set up in Figure 3.47. Notice that this output is higher than the output shown in Figure 3.46. The reason is that more interest is being paid into the account since $30 is deposited into the bank account on day 1 as opposed to being deposited over three years.

Figure 3.48 | **Results of the Future Value Function for a One-Time Investment**

A1 | fx =FV(0.08,3,,-30,1)

	A	B	C
1	$37.79		
2			

Figure 3.49 shows another example of the **Future Value** function. In this example, the information from the Time Value of Money Example (Figure 3.43) has been typed into a worksheet. Notice that the arguments of the function are defined using cell references (see the formula bar). As a result, the **Future Value** function will calculate a new output when any of the values are changed in the range B2:B5. Also, you will see that the output of the function is identical to the output shown in Figure 3.46. The reason is that the values that are typed into the cell references used to define the arguments of the function are identical to the values that were used to set up the **Future Value** function in Figure 3.45.

Figure 3.49 | **Future Value Function Using Cell References Instead of Numeric Values**

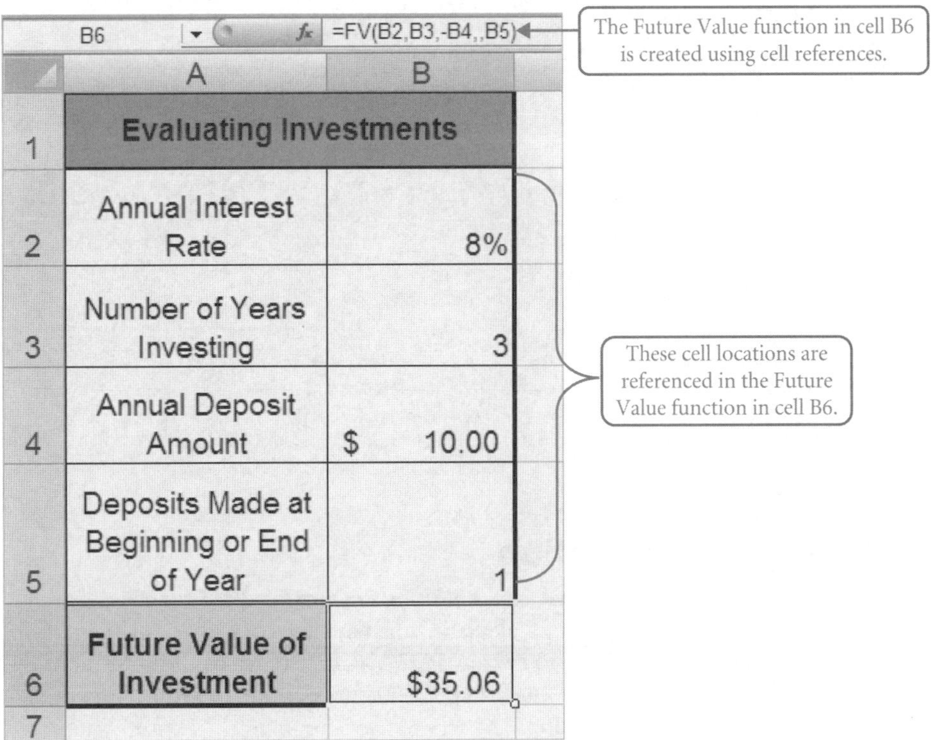

The benefit of using cell references to define the arguments of the **Future Value** function is that it allows you to conduct what-if scenarios with investments you may be evaluating professionally or personally. For example, what if you increased the Annual Deposit Amount in Figure 3.49 from $10 to $12, and what if you invested this money over a four-year period instead of a three-year period? Figure 3.50 shows how the output of the **Future Value** function changes when these values are changed in the worksheet.

Figure 3.50 | **Values in Cells Referenced by the Future Value Function Are Changed**

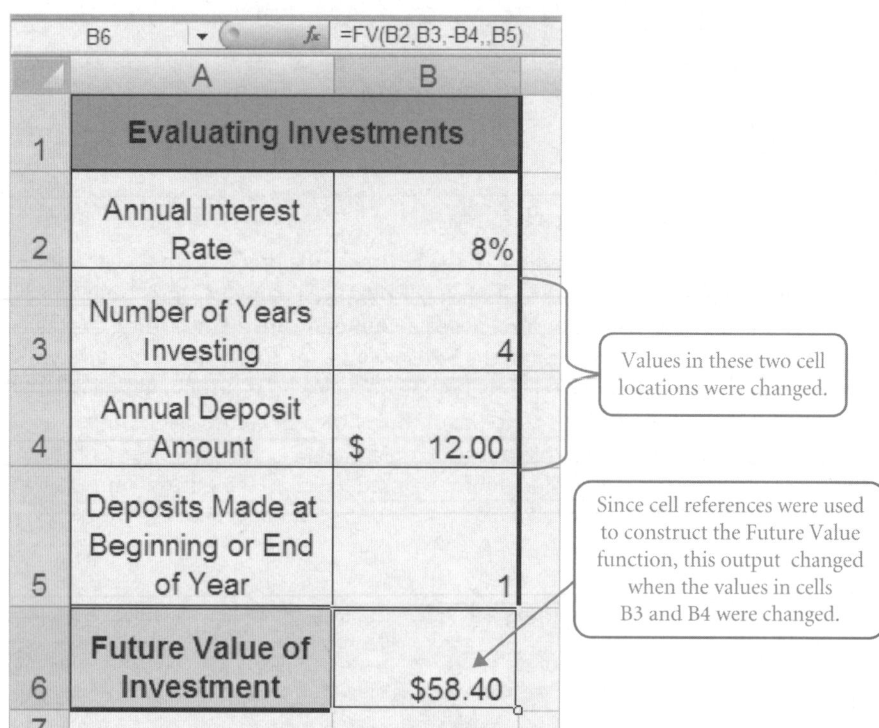

> **Quick Reference**
>
> **Future Value Function**
>
> 1. Activate the cell where output should appear.
> 2. Type an equal sign.
> 3. Type the function name FV or double click **FV** from the function list.
> 4. Type an open parenthesis (if you double clicked the function from the function list, this will already be added).
> 5. Define the following arguments:
>
>   **rate**: Interest Rate
>
>   **nper**: Number of Periods or Amount of time
>
>   **pmt**: Payments (must use a negative sign)
>
>   **[pv]**: Present Value
>
>   **[type]**: When payments are made (1 = beginning of year; 0 = end of year)
> 6. Close the parenthesis.
> 7. Press the **Enter** key.

> **COMMON MISTAKES | RATE, NPER, and PMT Arguments**
>
> Always check that the **rate**, **nper**, and **pmt** arguments of the **Future Value** function are expressed in equal terms. For example, investments might be made on a monthly basis, but the interest or return rate quoted by a bank or financial institution is expressed on an annual basis. In this case, you would have to define the **rate** argument by dividing the annual interest rate by 12 if the number of months is used to define the **nper** argument and the monthly investment value is used to define the **pmt** argument. The key is to make sure the **rate**, **nper**, and **pmt** arguments are all defined using equivalent terms.

The Payment Function

A close relative of the **Future Value** function is the ***Payment*** or ***PMT*** function. The **PMT** function is most helpful when calculating the payments of a loan. For example, if you were buying a home and had to borrow $225,000, how much would your monthly payment be if a bank charged 6% interest over a 30-year period? The **PMT** function can be used to answer this question.

Similar to the **Future Value** function, at least three of five arguments must be defined for the **Payment** function to produce an output. Figure 3.51 shows the five arguments of the **Payment** function, which are very similar to the arguments of the **Future Value** function. The following defines each of these arguments:

- **rate:** The interest charged by a lender.
- **nper:** The number of payments or, as in the **Future Value** function, a period of time (i.e., years, months, weeks, etc.).
- **pv:** Present Value; the argument used to define the amount of money being borrowed or the principal of the loan. As in the **Future Value** function, *you must use a negative sign for any values or cell references used for this argument.*
- **[fv]:** Future Value; the argument used when part of a loan is paid off with periodic payments and the balance of the loan is paid off in one lump sum at a future point

in time. This argument is especially helpful when evaluating the lease payments of a car. However, if a loan is structured such that there is no lump sum payoff at a future point in time, you can skip this argument by adding a comma with no spaces.

- **[type]**: A value that determines if payments are made at the beginning or end of a period and can either be a 1 or 0. If this argument is not defined, Excel will assume the value is 0.
  - 1: Used for payments made at the beginning of a period (i.e., at the beginning of a month, year, etc.).
  - 0: Used for payments made at the end of a period.

Figure 3.51 | **Arguments of the Payment Function**

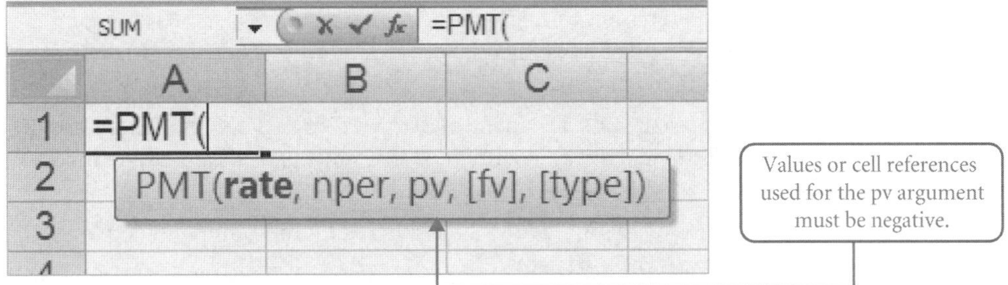

Figure 3.52 shows a worksheet that contains loan information for the purchase of a $250,000 home. The **Payment** function will be used in cell B6 to calculate the monthly mortgage payments for this loan. This example assumes that the bank will charge an interest rate of 6.5%, which is shown in cell B2. In addition, the repayment period for the loan is 30 years, as shown in cell B3. The amount of money that will be borrowed from the bank is $225,000. This example assumes a down payment of $25,000. Therefore, the remaining balance to pay for the house is $225,000, which is shown in cell B4. Finally, the number 1 is shown in cell B5, indicating that payments will be made at the beginning of each month.

FIGURE 3.52 | **Using the Payment Function to Determine the Monthly Payments of a Loan**

L1

	A	B
1	**Monthly Mortgage Payments**	
2	Annual Interest Rate	6.5%
3	Number of Years to Pay Loan	30
4	Amount Borrowed (Principal)	$ 225,000
5	Payments made at Beginning or End of Month	1
6	**Monthly Payments**	
7		

The Payment function will be added here to calculate the monthly mortgage payments for this loan.

As mentioned, the **Payment** function will be constructed in cell B6 of Figure 3.52 to determine the monthly mortgage payments for this loan. The following explains the setup of this function:

- Activate cell B6.
- Type an equal sign, the function name PMT, and an open parenthesis. This will open the hint box showing the arguments of the function (see Figure 3.51).
- Define the arguments of the **Payment** function as follows:
  - **rate**: `B2/12` The formula `B2/12` is used to define the **rate** argument of the function. The goal of this example is to calculate the monthly payments of the loan. However, cell B2 contains an annual interest rate. Therefore, this annual interest rate must be converted to a monthly interest rate so the payments can be expressed in terms of months instead of years.
  - **nper**: `B3*12` The formula `B3*12` is used to define the **nper** argument. Since the goal of this exercise is to calculate the monthly payments, the repayment period of the loan must be defined in terms of months. Therefore, the number of years in cell B3 is multiplied by 12.
  - **pv**: `-B4` The present value argument is defined using cell B4 which contains the principal of the loan. However, a negative sign must precede any value or cell reference used for this argument.
  - [**fv**]: , The future value argument will be skipped in this example. Therefore, a comma is typed with no spaces.
  - [**type**]: `B5` Cell B5 contains a value that indicates if payments are made at the beginning or end of the month. Therefore, it is referenced for this argument of the function.
- Type a closing parenthesis.
- Press the **Enter** key.

Figure 3.53 shows the results of the **Payment** function. Cell B6 is activated so you can see the setup of the function in the formula bar. Notice how formulas were used to define the **rate** and **nper** arguments. Similar to the **Future Value** function, the **rate**,

Figure 3.53 | **Results of the Payment Function**

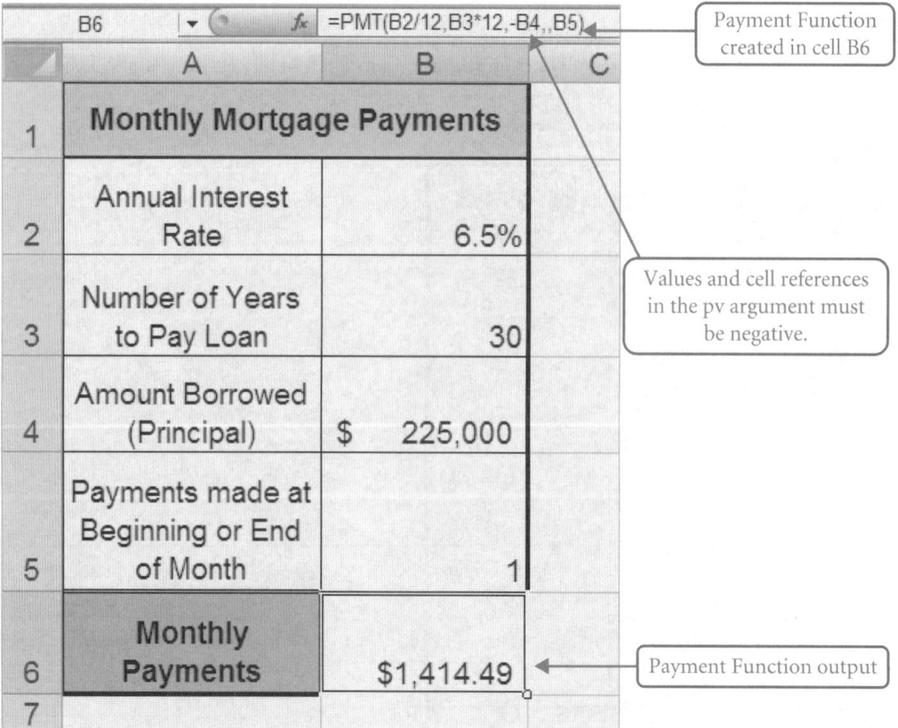

nper, and **[pv]** arguments of the **Payment** function must be expressed in equivalent terms. The formulas in the **rate** and **nper** arguments are converting the interest rate and repayment period to months. The results in this figure show that the monthly mortgage payment for this loan is $1,414.49.

COMMON MISTAKES | Negative Output for the FV or PMT Functions

If the output of a **Future Value** function or **Payment** function is negative, check the **pmt** and **[pv]** arguments of the **Future Value** function or the **pv** argument of the **Payment** function. Values and cell references used to define these arguments must be negative. If the negative sign is omitted for these arguments, the function will produce a negative number.

It is important to note that the **Payment** function constructed in Figure 3.53 uses cell references to define each of the arguments. As a result, if the values in cells B2 through B5 are changed, the function will produce a new output. Therefore, what if you decided that the loan payments shown in Figure 3.53 are too expensive for your budget? You can lower the principal in cell B4 and lower the interest rate in cell B2. Lowering these values will decrease the monthly mortgage payments. Figure 3.54 shows the results of the **Payment** function if the value in cell B4 is lowered to $205,000 and the interest rate in cell B2 is lowered to 6%.

FIGURE 3.54 | **New Output When Data Is Changed**

B6 =PMT(B2/12,B3*12,-B4,,B5)

	A	B	C
1	Monthly Mortgage Payments		
2	Annual Interest Rate	6.0%	
3	Number of Years to Pay Loan	30	
4	Amount Borrowed (Principal)	$ 205,000	
5	Payments made at Beginning or End of Month	1	
6	Monthly Payments	$1,222.96	
7			

The values in these cells were changed.

New output when data is changed in cells B2 and B4.

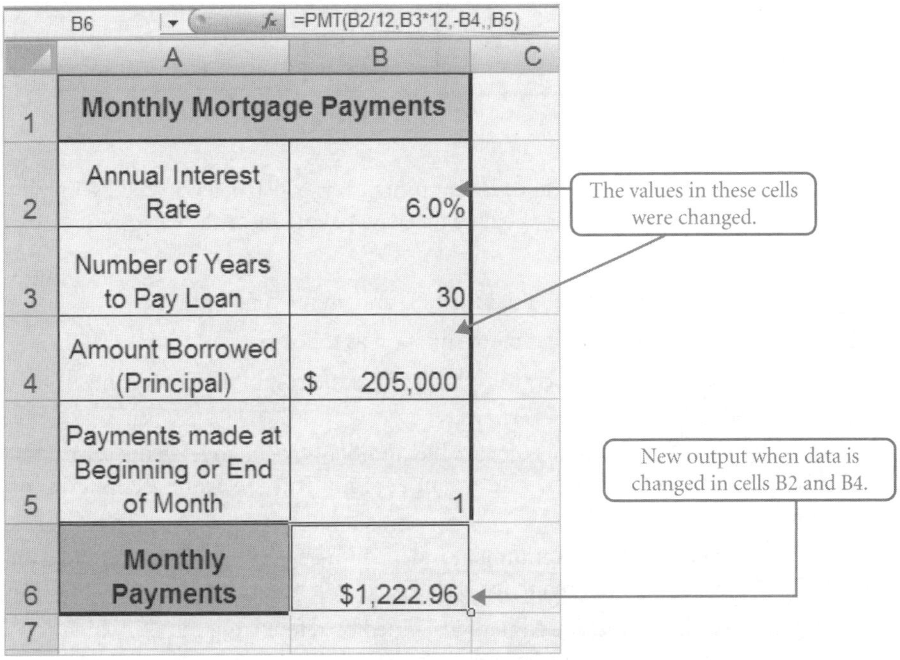

As previously mentioned, you can also use the **Payment** function to calculate the lease payments of a car. Leasing cars is often used as an alternative to buying. When leasing a car, a person pays only the value of the car that is used during a set period of time. The car dealer usually charges an interest rate for allowing the buyer to pay off the lease over several years.

The worksheet in Figure 3.55 contains data that will be used to calculate the monthly lease payments for a $23,000 car. The interest rate charged on the lease is 5% as shown in cell B2, and the car will be leased over a four-year period, as shown in cell B3. The residual value, or the future value, of the car is assumed to be $9,500 in four years (see cell B5). Therefore, if the car is worth $9,500 in four years, and the price of the car is $23,000, then the value of the car used during the four-year lease period is $13,500 ($23,000 - $9,500). The **Payment** function will automatically calculate this difference, factor in the interest rate, and determine the monthly payments.

Figure 3.55 | **Data Used to Calculate the Lease Payments of a Car**

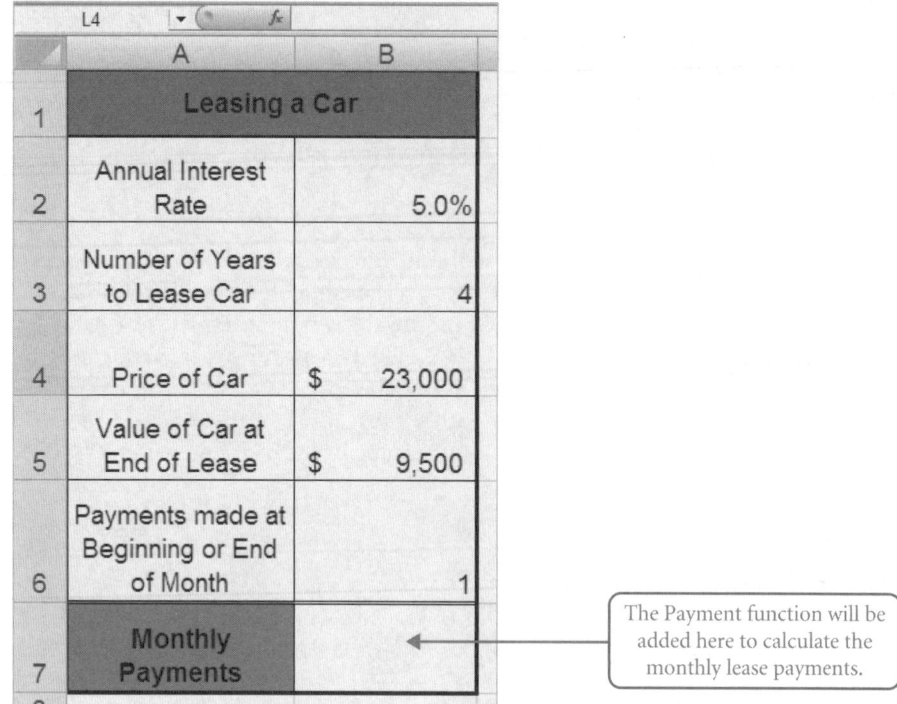

>> **Quick Reference**

Payment Function

1. Activate a cell where output should appear.
2. Type an equal sign.
3. Type the function name PMT or double click **PMT** from the function list.
4. Type an open parenthesis (if you double clicked the function from the function list, this will already be added).
5. Define the following arguments:

   rate: Interest rate

   nper: Number of payments or period of time

   pv: Present value

   [fv]: Future value

   [type]: When payments are made (1 = beginning of year, 0 = end of year)
6. Close the parenthesis.
7. Press the **Enter** key.

The following explains how the **Payment** function is constructed in cell B7 in the worksheet shown in Figure 3.55 to calculate the lease payments of the car:

- Activate cell B7.
- Type an equal sign, the function name PMT, and an open parenthesis.
- Define the arguments of the **Payment** function as follows:
  - **rate:** `B2/12` This formula converts the annual interest rate to a monthly interest rate.
  - **nper:** `B3*12` This formula converts the number of years to lease the car to months. As a result, both the **rate** and **nper** arguments are expressed in terms of months.
  - **pv:** `-B4` The present value argument is defined using cell B4, which contains the price of the car. This cell reference is preceded by a negative sign.
  - **[fv]:** `B5` The future value argument is defined by referencing cell B5, which contains the value of the car at the end of the lease.
  - **[type]:** `B6` Cell B6 contains a value indicating if payments are made at the beginning or end of the month.
- Type a closing parenthesis.
- Press the **Enter** key. The results of the function are shown in Figure 3.56.

Figure 3.56 | **Results Showing the Monthly Lease Payments**

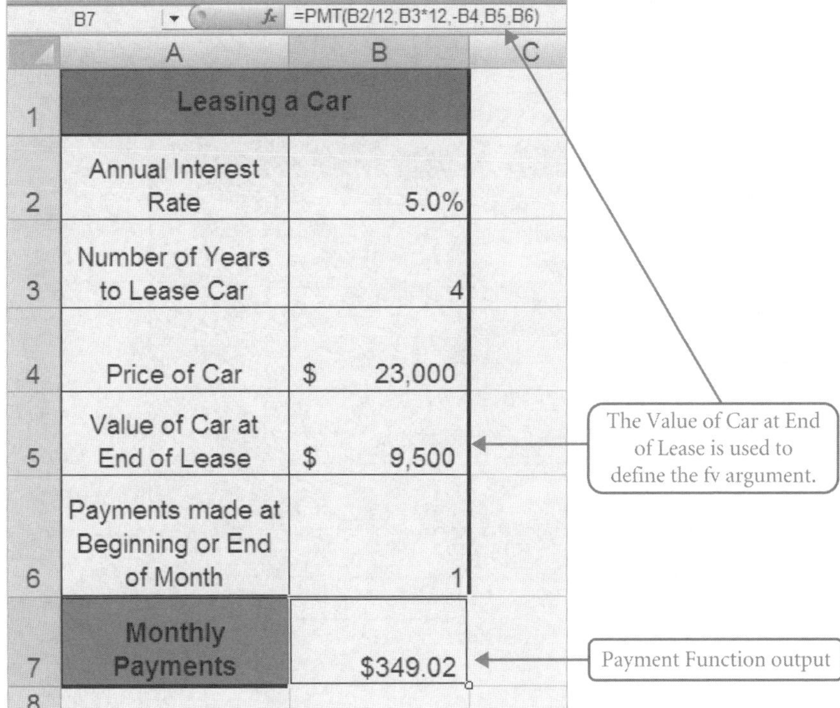

The Function Library

The Function Library is a resource that can be used to research and build any of the functions available in Excel. As shown in Figure 3.57, the Function Library is a group in the **Formulas** tab of the Ribbon. The icons in Function Library categorize all the functions in Excel by topic. For example, to see a list of all financial functions, click the **Financial** icon.

FIGURE 3.57 | **The Function Library**

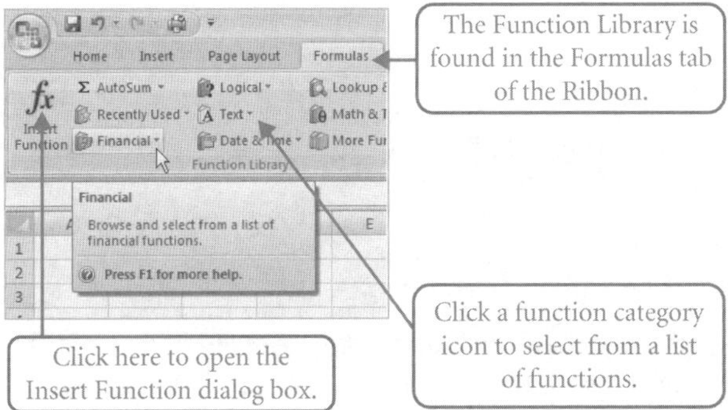

Use the Function Library to research detailed information regarding the purpose and arguments for all Excel functions. In addition, the Function Library can serve as an alternative way of building functions. After activating a cell location, select a function from one of the category icons in the Function Library. This will open the **Function Arguments** dialog box, which provides input boxes for each argument as well as a link to get detailed help in building the function. Figure 3.58 shows the **Function Arguments** dialog box for the **Future Value** function.

>> **Quick Reference**

Insert Function

1. Activate a cell where the output of a function should appear.
2. Click the **Formulas** tab in the Ribbon.
3. Select a function from one of the function category icons in the Function Library or click the **Insert Function** icon.
4. If using the **Insert Function** icon, select a function from the **Insert Function** dialog box and click the **OK** button.
5. Use the input boxes or range finders to define the arguments of the function in the **Function Arguments** dialog box.
6. Click **Help on this function** to see an expanded definition and instructions for building the function.
7. Click the **OK** button at the bottom of the **Function Arguments** dialog box.

Figure 3.58 | **The Function Arguments Dialog Box for the Future Value Function**

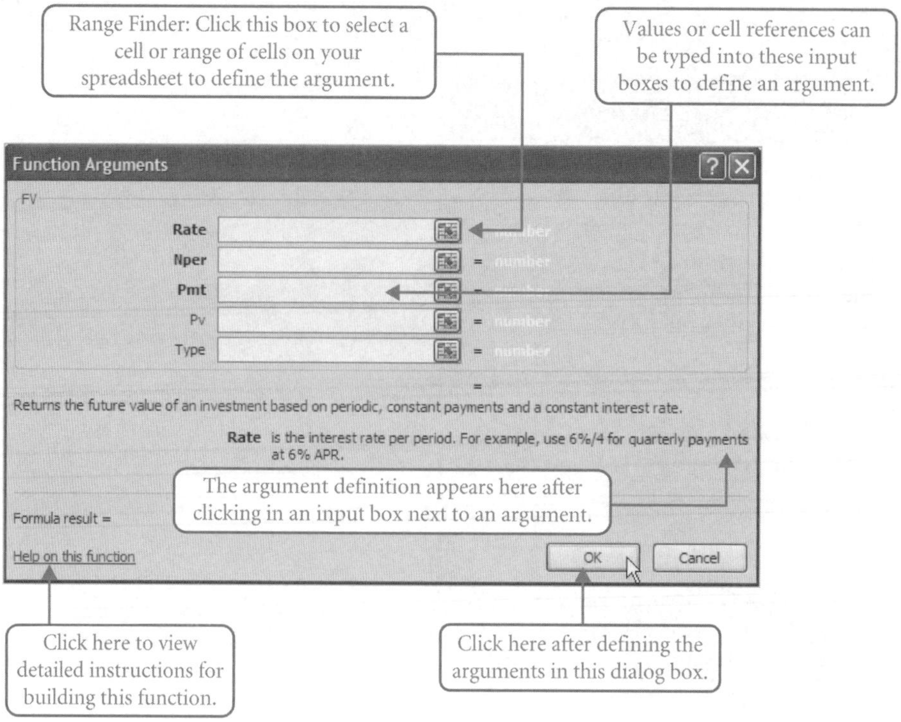

Excel functions can also be researched and built from the **Insert Function** icon. After activating a cell location where the output of the function should appear, click the **Insert Function** icon. This will open the **Insert Function** dialog box, as shown in Figure 3.59. Select a function from the middle of the dialog box and click the **OK** button. This will open the **Function Arguments** dialog box, as shown in Figure 3.58. Note that you can also open the **Insert Function** dialog box by clicking the **fx** symbol next to the formula bar.

Figure 3.59 | **The Insert Function Dialog Box**

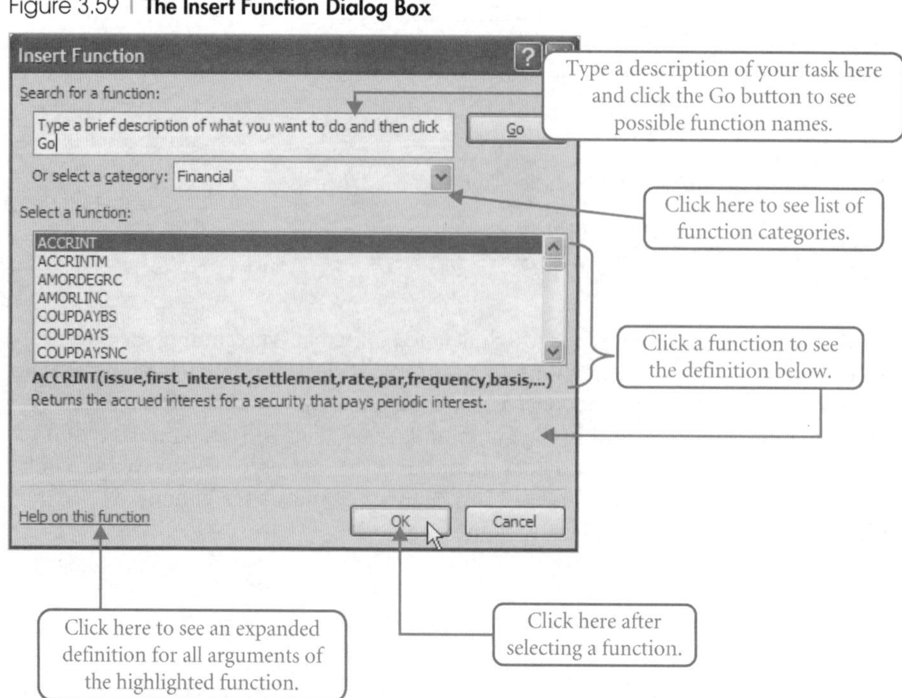

>> Future Value Function

VIDEO WORKSHOP

The purpose of this workshop is to review the use and construction of the **Future Value** function. I will be demonstrating the tasks in this workshop in the **Future Value Function** video. Open the file named ib_e03_thetimevalueofmoney before starting the following tasks.

1. **Data Entry (Video: Future Value Function)**
   a. Activate the Periodic Investment worksheet.
   b. Type the following values into the cell locations listed:
      Cell B2: `.08`
      Cell B3: `3`
      Cell B4: `10`
      Cell B5: `1`
   c. Format cell B2 to a percent with 1 decimal place and then format cell B4 to U.S. currency with 2 decimal places.

2. **Calculating the Future Value of a Periodic Investment (Video: Future Value Function)**
   a. Type an equal sign in cell B6, followed by the function name `FV` and an open parenthesis.
   b. Click cell B2 and type a comma.
   c. Click cell B3 and type a comma.
   d. Type a negative sign.
   e. Click cell B4 and type a comma.
   f. Type another comma.
   g. Click cell B5 and type a closing parenthesis.
   h. Press the **Enter** key.

3. **Calculating the Future Value of a One-Time Investment (Video: Future Value Function)**
   a. Activate the One Time Investment worksheet.
   b. Type an equal sign in cell B6, followed by the function name `FV` and an open parenthesis.
   c. Click cell B2 and type a comma.
   d. Click cell B3 and type a comma.
   e. Type another comma.
   f. Type a negative sign.
   g. Click cell B4 and type a comma.
   h. Click cell B5 and type a closing parenthesis.
   i. Press the **Enter** key.
   j. Save and close your file.

VIDEO WORKSHOP

Payment Function

This purpose of this workshop is to demonstrate how the **Payment** function is used to determine the mortgage payments for buying a home and the lease payments for a car. I will be demonstrating the tasks in this workshop on the video named **Payment Function**. Open the file named ib_e03_buyingahomeleasingacar before starting this workshop:

1. **Data Entry (Video: Payment Function)**
   a. Activate the Buying a Home worksheet.
   b. Type the following values into the cell locations listed:
      Cell B2: `.065`
      Cell B3: `30`
      Cell B4: `225000`
      Cell B5: `1`
   c. Format cell B2 to a percent with 1 decimal places and then format cell B4 to U.S. currency with 0 decimal places.

2. **Calculating the Monthly Payments for a Loan (Video: Payment Function)**
   a. Type an equal sign in cell B6, followed by the function name `PMT` and an open parenthesis.
   b. Click cell B2, type a forward slash (for division), type the number `12`, and type a comma.
   c. Click cell B3, type an asterisk (for multiplication), type the number `12`, and type a comma.
   d. Type a negative sign.
   e. Click cell B4 and type a comma.
   f. Type another comma.
   g. Click cell B5 and type a closing parenthesis.
   h. Press the **Enter** key.

3. **Data Entry (Video: Payment Function)**
   a. Activate the Leasing a Car worksheet.
   b. Type the following values into the cell locations listed:
      Cell B2: `.05`
      Cell B3: `4`
      Cell B4: `23000`
      Cell B5: `9500`
      Cell B6: `1`
   c. Format cell B2 to a percent with 1 decimal place and then format cells B4 and B5 to U.S. currency with 0 decimal places.

4. **Calculating the Lease Payment of a Car (Video: Payment Function)**
   a. Type an equal sign in cell B7, followed by the function name `PMT` and an open parenthesis.

b. Click cell B2, type a forward slash (for division), type the number `12`, and type a comma.
c. Click cell B3, type an asterisk (for multiplication), type the number `12`, and type a comma.
d. Type a negative sign.
e. Click cell B4 and type a comma.
f. Click cell B5 and type a comma.
g. Click cell B6 and type a closing parenthesis.
h. Press the **Enter** key.
i. Save and close your file.

>> The Function Library

VIDEO WORKSHOP

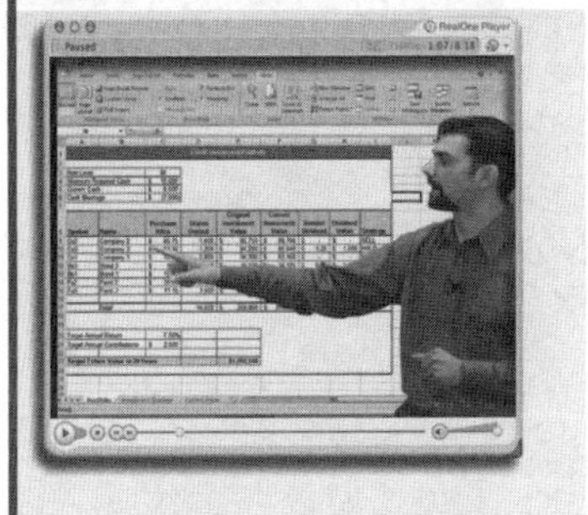

The purpose of this workshop is to demonstrate the Function Library. I will be demonstrating the tasks in this workshop on the video named **Function Library**. Open the file named ib_e03_propertyvalue before starting this workshop:

1. **Selecting a Function (Video: Function Library)**
   a. Activate cell D5 in the Commercial Property worksheet.
   b. Click the **Formulas** tab on the Ribbon.
   c. Click the **Financial** icon in the Function Library.
   d. Click the **FV** function.
   e. Click **Help on this function** in the lower left of the **Function Arguments** dialog box.
   f. Close the help window by clicking the X in the upper-right corner.

2. **Defining Arguments for the Future Value Function (Video: Function Library)**
   a. Click the range finder (box with the red arrow) to the right of the Rate argument.
   b. Click cell D2 on the worksheet and press the **Enter** key.
   c. Click the range finder next to the **nper** argument.
   d. Click cell D3 on the worksheet and press the **Enter** key.
   e. Type a negative sign in the box next to the **pv** argument.
   f. Click the range finder next to the **pv** argument.
   g. Click cell D4 on the worksheet and press the **Enter** key.
   h. Type the number 1 in the box next to the Type argument.
   i. Click the **OK** button at the bottom of the window.
   j. Save and close your file.

EXERCISE

Why Do I Need This?

>> Financial Planning for Retirement

A potential career goal for a person studying finance might be to work as a financial planner. One of the responsibilities a financial planner might have is to help people plan for retirement. This involves estimating how many years a person will work before they retire and how much money they can contribute to a retirement account. The financial planner's job is to evaluate various scenarios to see how clients can maximize the growth of a retirement account so they can live comfortably when they stop working. In this situation, the **Future Value** function can become a critical tool.

Exercise

Whether you have aspirations of being a financial planner or not, retirement is something everyone will eventually face. The purpose of this exercise is to construct a spreadsheet for a person who is planning to open a retirement account. Your job is to evaluate what interest rate and amount of contribution this person needs to achieve to make the account grow to $2 million. In addition, this person is age 25 and, for now, would like to plan on retiring at age 65. To do the tasks listed here, you will need to open the file named ib_e03_retirementplanning.

1. Type the value `.04` in cell B6 and type the word `Low` in cell C6. In this scenario, the money for this person's retirement will be invested in a conservative fashion. Therefore, the risk of losing money is low, but the potential growth is also low.

2. Type the value `.08` in cell B7 and the word `Medium` in cell C7. In this scenario, the risk is increased to Medium, but the potential return is increased to 8%.

3. For the final scenario, type the value `.15` in cell B8 and the word `High` in cell C8. In this scenario, both the risk and the potential return are high.

4. Type the number `40` in cell E2. Since this person is now 25 and is planning to retire at 65, she will be working and making contributions to her retirement account for 40 years.

5. Type the number `75` in cell E3. This person was thinking of putting $75 a month into this account but is not sure if this will get her to the goal of $2 million.

6. Calculate the future value of the conservative scenario. Use the **Future Value** function in cell D6 and define each argument of the function as follows:
   a. Use cell B6 to define the rate. This represents the Annual Potential Growth of the retirement investments.
   b. Use cell E2 to define the **nper** argument. Add an absolute reference to this cell reference. This function will be pasted into cells D7 and D8 to calculate the future value for the other two scenarios. Therefore, an absolute reference is used for cell E2 to prevent it from changing when the function is pasted.
   c. Type the formula `-E3 * 12` for the **pmt** argument and add an absolute reference to cell E3. This formula is used to convert the monthly payments to annual payments since both the **rate** and **nper** arguments are annual numbers. The absolute reference is used on cell E3 for the same reason explained in letter b.
   d. Type a closing parenthesis and press the **Enter** key. This person will not be making any lump sum investments to this account, and deposits will be made at the end of the month. Therefore, it is not necessary to define the **[pv]** or **[type]** arguments.

7. Copy the function created in cell D6 and use the **Paste Special** command to paste only the function into cells D7 and D8.

8. Given the current contribution of $75 per month, will this person reach her target through any of the scenarios?

9. How much money will she have to deposit in her account per month (approximately) to reach $2 million taking the Aggressive investment scenario?

10. How much money will she have to deposit in her account per month (approximately) to reach $2 million taking the Conservative investment scenario?

11. Save and close your file.

>> What's Wrong with This Spreadsheet?

PROBLEM & EXERCISE

Problem

You are the director of a real estate investment firm. An intern has just completed a project for you evaluating a potential investment. You are about to present the results to the president of the firm showing the potential return on property near a growing U.S. city. A recent assessment has shown that similar commercial properties in this area have been increasing in value 15% every six months. You will propose that the firm buy 10 acres of land at a total price of $1,750,000. You will recommend that the land be held for three years and then sold to developers.

You have asked the intern to

1. Evaluate the future value of the investment in three years given the 15% growth rate stated in the problem. The property will be purchased in one lump sum investment at the beginning of the first year.

2. Calculate the monthly payments of this loan considering the following: The company may opt to finance the price of the property through a bank instead of paying for the land in cash. A bank has offered a 15-year loan at a 3.5% interest rate if the company makes a $500,000 down payment. Payments will be made at the end of the month.

Open the file the intern has completed, named ib_e03_realestateresults. Look at the file carefully. Are you comfortable presenting these numbers to the president of the company? Consider the following:

1. Look at the results calculated on the spreadsheet. Do they make sense? What estimates can you quickly do to see if the results are in the "ballpark."

2. Were the arguments in the **PMT** and **FV** functions properly defined?

3. Are the statistics of the investment properly considered in the analysis?

Exercise

Write a short answer for each of the points in the Problem section. Then, make any adjustments or corrections that will improve the reliability of the spreadsheet.

Excel in **Practice** | Anecdote

Solution from page 80

I finally found relief after creating a spreadsheet that maintained and tracked all the items we were selling in the department. Projections that used to take 12 hours I could now do in minutes. I made the spreadsheet as flexible as possible so that if anyone asked "what if. . . " I would be able to give an answer in a few minutes. The only thing that took a lot of time was the preparation of the spreadsheet. At that time, our sales data was printed on paper, so I had to key the weekly sales results for every item. However, working late one night a week was better than working five nights.

Assignment

Open the file named ib_e03_casualappareldepartment. This file includes data for several items that are typically sold in a women's specialty retail store. Create a flexible spreadsheet that will evaluate the sales performance of each item and project the sales and profit for the department. You will have to add formulas, functions, and formatting to this spreadsheet. Following are formulas and information that will help in completing this assignment:

1. Current Weeks of Supply = Current Inventory Units ÷ Last Week Unit Sales
2. New Price = Current Price – (Markdown Percent x Current Price)
3. Projected Sales Dollars = Sales Dollars YTD + (Current Inventory x New Price)
4. Total Cost = Total Units Purchased x Item Cost
5. Projected Profit = Projected Sales Dollars – Total Cost
6. The price of any product that has a Current Weeks of Supply greater than 8 should be reduced through a markdown.
7. When the price of an item is reduced, unit sales for next week will generally increase as follows: a 50% price reduction will double sales; a 25% price reduction will increase unit sales by 50%; a 10% price reduction will increase sales by 25%.
8. If the price of an item is not reduced, assume unit sales remain constant.
9. Come up with a plan that reduces the overall weeks of supply for the department to 8.5, while maintaining at least 34% profit (Projected Profit ÷Projected Sales Dollars).

Questions for Discussion

1. When creating spreadsheets for business, why is it important to make them as flexible as possible?
2. What are some of the things that could go wrong with the spreadsheet solution described in the case?
3. Besides saving time, what other benefits could the spreadsheet solution described in the anecdote bring to the business?

Review Questions

The following questions are related to the concepts addressed in this chapter. There are three types of questions: Short Answer, True or False, and Fill in the Blank. If your answer to a True or False question is False, write a short explanation as to why you think the statement is not true.

1. The _______________ is used when creating formulas in Excel that require multiplication.
2. Hold the Shift key and press the number _______________ key when using exponents or raising a number to a certain power when creating formulas in Excel.
3. Explain why you should never do computations on a calculator and type the result into an Excel spreadsheet.
4. True or False: In cell referencing, the cell locations in a formula automatically change when you paste them to a new location.
5. When should you use numbers in Excel formulas?
6. True or False: You cannot use both numbers and cell locations in an Excel formula.
7. The_______________ _______________ command can be used to paste the value of a formula instead of the formula itself.
8. Why would you need to use parentheses in a formula?
9. True or False: Even if a formula contains only two cell references and one mathematical operator, you must still use parentheses.
10. In the following formula, what will be calculated second? `=((A4+B8)/C10)+A9+E6`.
11. True or False: This is a formula that will add the values in ten cell locations: `=SUM(A2:A10)`.
12. All functions start with an _______________, an _______________________, and a _______________.
13. What function could you use to count the names of people listed on a spreadsheet?
14. How would you type an **AVERAGE** function in a spreadsheet if you wanted to take the average of five cells in column C starting with cell location C1?
15. True or False: The following function will find the minimum value in cell locations B3 through and including B15: `=MIN(B3,B15)`.
16. A _________________ __________________ is used to apply an absolute reference to a cell location.
17. True or False: You cannot add two functions together like a formula; for example, `=SUM(C3:C10)+SUM(A4:A9)`.
18. True or False: Cell referencing will work with formulas but not with functions. Therefore, you must always retype functions and cannot copy and paste them to new cell locations.

19. True or False: If the following cell reference is used in a formula, the row number will change, but the column letter will remain the same when the formula is pasted to a new location: `C$10`.

20. What is the purpose of the **pmt** argument in the **Future Value** function?

21. What is the purpose of the **fv** argument in the **Payment** Function?

22. If you use the **Future Value** function to evaluate the growth of an investment over a 16-month period at a growth rate of 12% per year, what number would you enter in the **rate** argument?

23. When you use the **Future Value** function, you use the ______________ argument if you are making a one-time lump sum investment.

24. True or False: You cannot define both the **pmt** argument and the **pv** argument of the **Future Value** function. You must define one or the other; otherwise, Excel will give you an error message.

25. True or False: The following **Payment** function will return the monthly payments of a loan that charges a 6% annual interest rate over ten years with a principal of $25,000 and a down payment of $5,000. The payments will be made at the beginning of each month. `=PMT(.06,10,-25000,5000,1)`.

26. What should you do if you are skipping an argument in either the **PMT** or **FV** function?

27. What does Excel assume if you skip the **type** argument of either the **PMT** or **FV** function?

28. You must use a negative sign for numbers or cell locations entered for the ______________ argument and the ______________ argument when using the **Future Value** function.

29. True or False: You must always use a negative sign for both the **fv** and **pv** arguments of the **Payment** function.

30. What tab in the Ribbon would you click to find the Function Library?

Skills Exam

The following exam is designed to test your ability to recognize and execute the Excel skills presented in this chapter. Read each question carefully and answer the questions in the order they are listed. You should be able to complete this exam in 60 minutes or less.

1. Open the file named ib_e03_skillsexam.
2. Type a **SUM** function in cell B9 that adds the values in cells B3 through B8. Correct any #### signs if necessary.
3. Copy the **SUM** function in cell B9 and paste it into cell C9. Correct any #### signs if necessary.
4. Type a formula in cell D3 to calculate the growth rate. Your formula should subtract the Value Last Year in cell B3 from the Present Value in cell C3 and divide that result by the Value Last Year in cell B3: `(Present Value - Value Last Year) ÷ Value Last Year`.
5. Format the result in cell D3 to a percentage with 1 decimal place.
6. Copy cell D3 and paste it into cells D4:D9.
7. Type an **AVERAGE** function in cell B10 that calculates the average of cells B3 through B8.
8. Copy cell B10 and paste it into C10.
9. Calculate the average growth rate in cell D10 using the **SUM** and **COUNT** functions. Follow this example: `((Sum of Present Value C3:C8 ÷ Count of Present Value C3:C8)-(Sum of Value Last Year B3:B8 ÷ Count of Value Last Year B3:B8))/(Sum of Value Last Year B3:B8 ÷ Count of Value Last Year B3:B8)`.
10. Format the result in cell D10 to a percentage with 1 decimal place. The result in D10 should match the value in cell D9.
11. Type a formula in cell E3 that divides the present value in cell C3 by the total of the present values in cell C9. Place an absolute reference on cell C9.
12. Format the result in cell E3 to a percent with 2 decimals. Then, copy cell E3 and paste it to cells E4 through E8.
13. Use the **Payment** function in cell D14 to calculate the monthly mortgage payments. Your function should use cell A14 for the rate, B14 for the periods, and C14 for the present value. Assume that payments are made at the end of the month.
14. Use the **Payment** function in cell E18 to calculate the monthly lease payments. Your function should use cell A18 for the rate, B18 for the periods, C18 for the present value, and D18 for the future value. Assume payments made at the end of the month.
15. Use the **Future Value** function in cell E21 to calculate the future value of all the investments in two years. Your function should use cell D9 for the rate and the number 2 for the periods. The total present value for all investments in cell C9 should be treated as a one-time lump sum investment. Assume that this investment is made at the beginning of the year. Format the result to U.S. currency with 0 decimal places. Correct any #### signs if necessary.
16. Type a formula in cell E22 that subtracts the total present value of all investments in cell C9 from the future value of all investments in cell E21.
17. Type a formula in cell E23 that multiplies the monthly mortgage payments in cell D14 by 24. Format the result to U.S. currency with 0 decimal places.
18. Type a formula in cell E24 that multiplies the monthly lease payments in cell E18 by 24. Format the result to U.S. currency with 0 decimal places.
19. Type a formula in cell E25 that subtracts the result of adding cells E23 and E24 from cell E22. Format the result to U.S. currency with 0 decimal places. Fix any #### signs if necessary.
20. Sort the range A2:E8 in ascending order based on the values in the Present Value column.
21. Save and close your file.

Challenge Questions

The following questions are designed to test your ability to apply the Excel skills you have learned to complete a business objective. Use your knowledge of Excel as well as your creativity to answer these questions. For most questions, there are several possible ways to complete the objective.

1. *Without* using the **Future Value** function, create a worksheet that determines the value of an investment if a person deposits $1,500 into a mutual fund at the beginning of every year for 20 years. Assume that the mutual fund achieves a 6% annual growth rate every year. Your worksheet should show the value of this investment at the end of every year for 20 years. In addition, your worksheet should be flexible to show what the value of the account would be at different deposit amounts or annual growth rates. For example, be able to show the value of the account in 20 years if a person decides to deposit only $1,200 per year but achieves an annual growth rate of 7%. Then, show the value of the account if a person deposits $1,000 per year but achieves an annual growth rate of 8%.
2. Complete question 1 again using the **Future Value** function. However, your worksheet should show only one number indicating the value of the investment in 20 years. Remember to keep your worksheet flexible so a new output will be produced if the annual deposit amount or annual growth rate values are changed.
3. A person asks you for help on an investment she is thinking of making. She wants to invest $5,000 into a medium-term bond that earns 4.5% interest per year. In addition, she wants to add $100 at the beginning of every month into the account. She wants to know what the value of her investment will be after five years. Create a worksheet showing her the value of this investment.
4. If you were going to lease a car, but could afford to pay only *$175 a month*, what would be the maximum price you could pay for a car? Assume the lease will run for four years, the annual interest rate is 3%, and that the car will retain 40% of its value after four years. Create a worksheet that shows the maximum price of the car you can lease.
5. You have an opportunity to invest in residential property that will cost $325,000. A real estate survey has shown that the value of property in this town has been increasing at a rate of 25% per year. However, you will have to take out a loan to be able to purchase the property. You can secure a 30-year loan at an annual interest rate of 6.5%. You will also be making a down payment of $75,000. Your plan is to sell this property after three years. After selling the property, you will pay off the loan. Create a spreadsheet that will calculate how much money you will make on this investment.

Evaluating Data

Chapter Goals

Business managers are responsible for making numerous decisions every day based on various measures and statistics. For example, a retail buyer may decide to place orders, cancel future orders, issue returns, or do nothing depending on the ratio of current sales to current inventory. A finance manager may decide to sell, buy, or hold a particular stock based on a client's unrealized gain or loss. The challenge for these business managers is usually not the decision itself, but rather the volume of decisions they are required to make. For example, a retail buyer might be responsible for purchasing thousands of items. A finance manager might be managing portfolios for hundreds of clients. This chapter will review how business managers use Excel's logical and lookup functions to evaluate large volumes of data and produce decision outputs. As you will soon discover, logical and lookup functions can dramatically increase a business manager's decision-making power through Excel.

>> Excel | Skill Sets

Logical Functions (The IF Function)
- IF Function
- Nested IF Functions

Logical Functions (AND OR)
- AND Function
- OR Function
- Combining AND, OR, and IF Functions

Lookup Functions
- VLookup Function
- HLookup Function

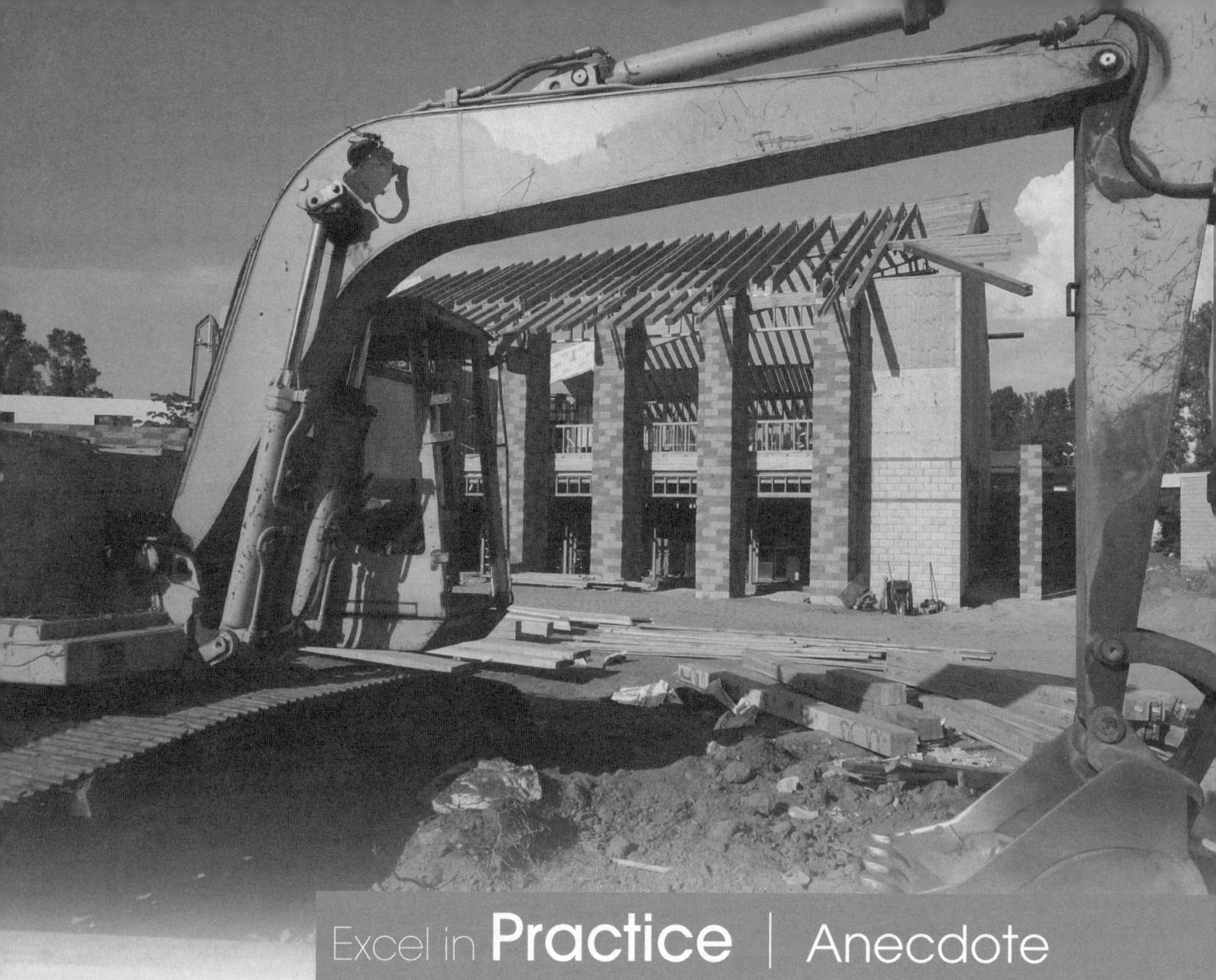

Excel in Practice | Anecdote

Managing Retail Store Expansion

Location is everything, especially in the retail industry. I learned this quickly while working on a consulting project for a major retail corporation. One of our biggest challenges was deciding where the company should build new stores as part of a growth strategy plan. Constructing a new store costs several million dollars and requires significant sales revenue to justify the investment. To support our recommendations, my team analyzed enormous amounts of data to determine the best locations for potential new stores. Our analysis began with a spreadsheet containing over 20,000 United States ZIP codes and associated population, population growth, number of households, household income, population by gender, and, most important, competitors. We finally limited the number of potential locations to 400 ZIP codes and set a meeting with the company's president to discuss our findings. However, at 7:00 PM the night before our meeting, my partner and I made a startling discovery. The real estate analyst who originally sent us the data did not include the state or city names in his file. We had no idea what state or city belonged to each ZIP code. To make matters worse, not only had the real estate analyst gone home for the day, but he was going to be on vacation for the next week. Needless to say, we were not thrilled with the idea of looking up 400 ZIP codes and manually typing the state and city names into our spreadsheet.

>> Continued on page 169

Logical Functions (The IF Function)

Skill Set

Chapter 3 demonstrated how functions are used to conduct statistical and financial calculations in business. However, functions can also be used to evaluate data and provide an output based on the results of a test. These are known as ***logical functions***. The most commonly used logical function in Excel is the **IF** function. The **IF** function can produce an output that you define based on the results of a ***logical test***. As with all logical functions, the results of a logical test will either be true or false. This section will demonstrate how business managers use **IF** functions to evaluate and highlight key statistics that require their attention for the purposes of making decisions.

IF Function

The **IF** function is used to evaluate data and provide an output based on the results of a logical test. Business managers often use the **IF** function to highlight key statistics related to their area of responsibility. For example, the inventory control manager of a candy company might be required to maintain at least 10,000 pounds of each ingredient used to produce a line of chocolate bars. Maintaining a specific inventory target is a common practice for companies that continually use the same components to produce a product, such as a candy manufacturer. Figure 4.1 shows a worksheet that contains ingredients that might be used to produce chocolate bars. An inventory control manager could use the **IF** function in the Status column (column C) to identify items in which the inventory in column B is less than 10,000 pounds.

Figure 4.1 | **Inventory Data for Chocolate Bar Production**

	A	B	C
1	Item Description	Inventory in Pounds	Status
2	Sugar	10,000	
3	Cocoa Beans	7,500	
4	Cocoa Butter	15,000	
5	Peanuts	8,000	
6	Almonds	5,000	
7	Starch	12,500	

Click here to see a list of Logical functions.

The IF function will be used to show a status message in this column.

To use the **IF** function, you will need to define three arguments, as shown in Figure 4.2. The definition for each of these arguments is as follows:

- **logical_test**: Used for evaluating the data in a cell location based on a test that you define. The results of this test will be either true or false. A basic logical test usually starts with a cell reference followed by a comparison operator (see Figure 4.3 for a list of comparison operators used in logical tests). The second part of the test can be a multitude of possibilities. For example, you may need to compare the value in a cell to a number, another cell location, a formula, a function, or a word. If you are using words, or text data, you must put them in quotation marks. Examples of logical tests are

- B9 > 25
- H7 < D12
- L8 = "Car"
- D17 < (A9 - 12) * 10

- **[value_if_true]**: Used for defining the output of the **IF** function if the results of the logical test are true. This argument can be defined with a cell reference, formula, function, number, or words. As in the **logical_test** argument, if you are going to use words, you must put them in quotation marks.
- **[value_if_false]**: Used to define the output of the function if the results of the logical test are false. The options for defining this argument are identical to the **[value_if_true]** argument.

Figure 4.2 | **Arguments of the IF Function**

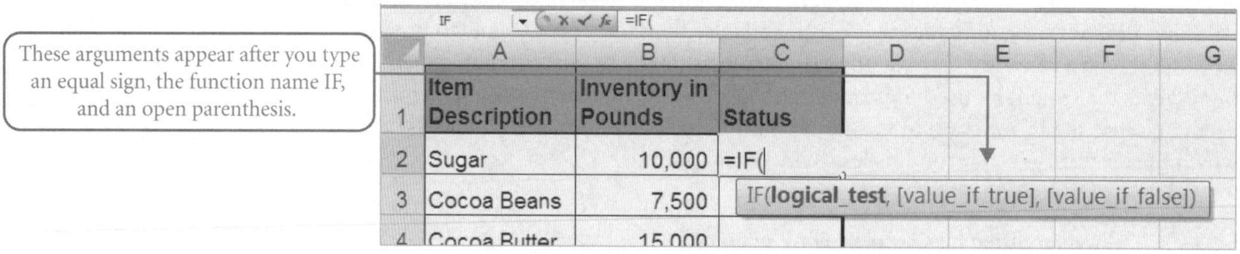

These arguments appear after you type an equal sign, the function name IF, and an open parenthesis.

	A	B	C
1	Item Description	Inventory in Pounds	Status
2	Sugar	10,000	=IF(
3	Cocoa Beans	7,500	IF(**logical_test**, [value_if_true], [value_if_false])
4	Cocoa Butter	15,000	

Figure 4.3 | **Comparison Operators Used in Logical Tests**

Symbol	Definition
=	Equal To
>	Greater Than
<	Less Than
<>	Not Equal To
>=	Greater Than or Equal To
<=	Less Than or Equal To

An inventory control manager could use the **IF** function in the worksheet shown in Figure 4.1 to identify items in which the inventory is less than 10,000 pounds. The following points explain how you add this to the worksheet:

- Activate cell C2.
- Type an equal sign, the function name IF, and an open parenthesis.
- Type B2<10000 to define the **logical_test** argument. This will test if the value in cell B2 is less than 10000. As noted previously, this example assumes that the inventory control manager is maintaining at least 10,000 pounds of inventory for each item. Type a comma after this argument.
- Type "LOW INV" to define the **[value_if_true]** argument. If the value in cell B2 is less than 10000, the message LOW INV will be displayed in cell C2. Notice that since this is a text message, it is put in quotation marks. Type a comma after this argument.

- Type "OK" to define the **[value_if_false]** argument. If the value in cell B2 is not less than 10000, the message OK will be displayed in cell C2. Again, notice that since this a text message, it is enclosed in quotation marks.
- Type a closing parenthesis and press the **Enter** key.
- Copy cell C2, which now contains the completed **IF** function, and paste it to cells C3 through C7. Since the cell reference B2 was used in the **logical_test** argument, it will automatically adjust to the appropriate row number because of relative referencing.

Figure 4.4 shows the arguments of the **IF** function that were typed into cell C2 of the worksheet shown in Figure 4.1. Notice that the text messages used to define the **[value_if_true]** and **[value_if_false]** arguments are enclosed in quotation marks. Also, notice that no commas were used in the value 10000 in the **logical_test** argument.

Figure 4.4 | **Setup of the IF Function to Evaluate Inventory Values in Column B**

IF =IF(B2<10000,"LOW INV","OK")

	A	B	C	D	E	F	G
1	Item Description	Inventory in Pounds	Status				
2	Sugar	10,000	=IF(B2<10000,"LOW INV","OK")				
3	Cocoa Beans	7,500	IF(logical_test, [value_if_true], [value_if_false])				
4	Cocoa Butter	15,000					
5	Peanuts	8,000					
6	Almonds	5,000					

Figure 4.5 shows the output of the **IF** functions in the range C2:C7. By glancing at the worksheet, the inventory control manager can easily see that three items—Cocoa Beans, Peanuts, and Almonds—are below the target of 10,000 pounds.

Figure 4.5 | **IF Function Outputs Based on the Values in Column B**

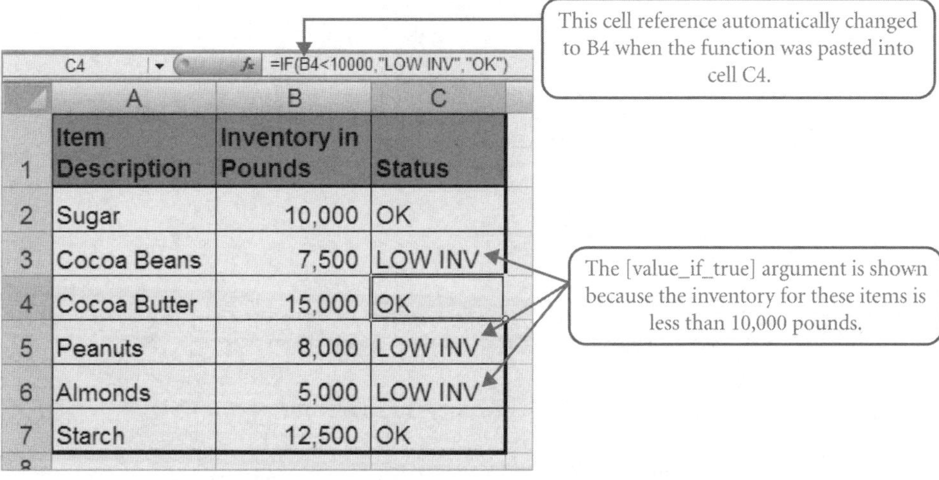

C4 =IF(B4<10000,"LOW INV","OK")

	A	B	C
1	Item Description	Inventory in Pounds	Status
2	Sugar	10,000	OK
3	Cocoa Beans	7,500	LOW INV
4	Cocoa Butter	15,000	OK
5	Peanuts	8,000	LOW INV
6	Almonds	5,000	LOW INV
7	Starch	12,500	OK

Figure 4.6 shows another way the **IF** function can be used to help an inventory control manager maintain a target of at least 10,000 pounds for each item shown in Figure 4.1. In this example, the **IF** function is used to calculate how much inventory needs to be purchased if an item is below the 10,000 pound target. As a result, notice that a formula is used to define the **[value_if_true]** argument. Each argument of the function is defined as follows:

- **logical_test:** `B2 < 10000` This is the same test that was used for the example shown in Figure 4.4.

- **[value_if_true]:** `10000 - B2` If the value in cell B2 is less than 10000, the function will calculate how many pounds need to be purchased to reach the 10,000 pound target.
- **[value_if_false]:** `0` If the value in cell B2 is at or above 10000, the function will display a value of 0, indicating there is no need to purchase additional inventory.

Figure 4.6 | **Using the IF Function to Calculate Order Quantities**

If the logical_test is true, the function will display the results of this formula.

IF =IF(B2<10000,10000-B2,0)

	A	B	C	D	E	F	G
1	Item Description	Inventory in Pounds	Order Quantity				
2	Sugar	10,000	=IF(B2<10000,10000-B2,0)				
3	Cocoa Beans	7,500	IF(logical_test, [value_if_true], **[value_if_false]**)				
4	Cocoa Butter	15,000					

Figure 4.7 shows the output of the **IF** function created in Figure 4.6. Similar to the example shown in Figure 4.5, this function was created in cell C2 and then copied to cells C3 through C7. In addition, the worksheet was sorted in descending order based on the order quantities produced by the **IF** function. As a result, the **IF** function not only identifies items that need to be ordered, but automatically calculates how much inventory needs to be purchased by item.

Figure 4.7 | **Results of Using the IF Function to Calculate Order Quantities**

I1

	A	B	C
1	Item Description	Inventory in Pounds	Order Quantity
2	Almonds	5,000	5,000
3	Cocoa Beans	7,500	2,500
4	Peanuts	8,000	2,000
5	Cocoa Butter	15,000	0
6	Starch	12,500	0
7	Sugar	10,000	0

The worksheet is sorted based on the outputs of the IF function in this column.

COMMON MISTAKES | Defining Arguments of the IF Function

People often make the mistake of using commas in values typed into the **logical_test** argument of the **IF** function. For example:

```
=IF(C2 < 10,000,"Low","High")
```

Excel will read the logical test for this function as C2 < 10, not C2 < 10000. The reason is that a comma signals the end of one argument and the start of another. For this example, Excel will display a warning stating too many arguments were entered because it assumes you are trying to define four arguments instead of three.

Nested IF Functions

By itself, the **IF** function provides the entry of one logical test and one output (value if true or value if false). However, a business project may require the function to display one of many possible outputs. For example, the items shown in Figure 4.1 may require a status rating based on five potential options: Very Low, Low, Good, High, or Very High. To produce one output from these five possibilities, you would need to create an **IF** function with four logical tests. You can accomplish this by using a nested **IF** function.

A nested **IF** function will be used to evaluate the inventory data shown in Figure 4.8, which contains revised data from Figure 4.1. For this example, we will assume the target inventory remains at 10,000 pounds. However, if the inventory level is too high for any item, it may spoil. On the other hand, if the inventory is significantly below 10,000 pounds, the company may fall short of its production goals. This example will use a nested **IF** function to display one of the following four outputs:

- Less than 5,000 pounds: Display the message "Prod Risk."
- Greater than 5,000 pounds but less than 10,000 pounds: Display the message "Low."
- Greater than 14,000 pounds: Display the message "Spoil Risk."
- Between 10,000 and 14,000 pounds: Display the message "OK."

Figure 4.8 | **Revised Inventory Data for Chocolate Bar Production**

G1 | fx

	A	B	C
1	Item Description	Inventory in Pounds	Status
2	Sugar	10,000	
3	Cocoa Beans	7,500	
4	Cocoa Butter	22,000	
5	Peanuts	5,200	
6	Almonds	1,200	
7	Starch	12,500	

A nested IF function will be created in column C to categorize each inventory value in column B as Prod Risk, Low, Spoil Risk, or OK.

The following points explain how to create a nested **IF** function in cell C2 of Figure 4.8 to display one of four outputs:

- Activate cell C2.
- Type an equal sign, the function name IF, and an open parenthesis.
- Type B2<5000 to define the **logical_test** argument. This will be the first of three logical tests that will be created in this function. Type a comma after this argument.
- Type "Prod Risk" to define the [**value_if_true**] argument. If the first logical test is true, the function will display this message. Type a comma after this argument.
- Type the function name **IF** followed by an open parenthesis to define the [**value_if_false**] argument. If the logical test is false, you will need to conduct a second logical test. You do this by starting a second **IF** function.
- Type B2 < 10000 to define the **logical_test** argument of the second **IF** function. If the first logical test, which is B2 < 5000, is false, then this logical test will evaluate if the value in cell B2 is less than 10000. Note that if the first logical test failed, and this logical test is true, then you can conclude that the value in cell B2 is greater

than 5,000 pounds but less than 10,000 pounds. Type a comma after this argument.

- Type "Low" to define the [**value_if_true**] argument of the second **IF** function. As previously mentioned, if the inventory quantity is greater than 5,000 pounds but less than 10,000 pounds, the status message should read "Low." Type a comma after this argument.
- Type the function name **IF** followed by an open parenthesis to define the [**value_if_false**] argument of the second **IF** function. As previously mentioned, to show one of four potential outputs, you will need to conduct three logical tests. To conduct a third logical test, you start a third **IF** function.
- Type B2 > 14000 to define the **logical_test** argument of the third **IF** function. If the previous two logical tests are false, then you can conclude that the value in cell B2 is greater than or equal to 10,000. Therefore, the third and final logical test will evaluate if the value in B2 is greater than 14,000 pounds. As mentioned, if any item has an inventory greater than 14,000 pounds, it will be at risk of spoiling. Type a comma after this argument.
- Type "Spoil Risk" to define the [**value_if_true**] argument of the third **IF** function. Type a comma after this argument.
- Type "OK" to define the [**value_if_false**] argument of the third **IF** function. If all logical tests are false, then you can conclude that the value in cell B2 is between 10,000 and 14,000 pounds.
- Type three closing parentheses. It is important to note that a closing parenthesis is required for every **IF** function you started. In this example, you started a total of three **IF** functions for the purpose of conducting three logical tests. Therefore, you must type three closing parentheses at the end of the function.
- Press the **Enter** key.
- Copy the cell C2, which now contains the nested **IF** function, and paste it into cells C3 through C7.

Figure 4.9 shows the setup of the nested **IF** function that was created in cell C2. In this example, a new **IF** function is started in the [**value_if_false**] argument for the purpose of conducting multiple logical tests. However, both the [**value_if_true**] and [**value_if_false**] arguments could be used to add multiple logical tests.

Figure 4.9 | **Setup of the Nested IF Function**

IF =IF(B2<5000,"Prod Risk",IF(B2<10000,"Low",IF(B2>14000,"Spoil Risk","OK")))

	A	B	C
1	Item Description	Inventory in Pounds	Status
2	Sugar	10,000	=IF(B2<5000,"Prod Risk",IF(B2<10000,"Low",IF(B2>14000,"Spoil Risk","OK")))
3	Cocoa Beans	7,500	
4	Cocoa Butter	22,000	
5	Peanuts	5,200	

Three closing parentheses

The logical tests are in a sequence from lowest to highest.

Figure 4.10 shows the outputs of the nested **IF** functions in column C. The inventory control manager can use this information to decide which items need to be purchased or which items may need to be monitored and tested for spoilage. In this case, the manager can easily see that purchasing additional inventory for Almonds is critical to support the production goals of the business. On the other hand, the Cocoa Butter needs to be monitored for possible spoilage. The inventory control manager might also inform the production manager to use containers of Cocoa Butter with the oldest receipt date first to reduce potential waste.

Figure 4.10 | **Outputs Produced by the Nested IF Function**

	A	B	C
1	Item Description	Inventory in Pounds	Status
2	Sugar	10,000	OK
3	Cocoa Beans	7,500	Low
4	Cocoa Butter	22,000	Spoil Risk
5	Peanuts	5,200	Low
6	Almonds	1,200	Prod Risk
7	Starch	12,500	OK

This nested IF function displays one of four potential outputs for each item.

COMMON MISTAKES | Nested IF Functions

You *cannot* enter a logical test directly into the **[value_if_false]** or **[value_if_true]** argument without typing the function name IF followed by an open parenthesis. For example, the following nested **IF** function will not work:

```
=IF(B2 < 5000,"Very Low",B2 < 10000,"Low","OK")
```

The logical test B2 < 10000 was entered directly into the **[value_if_false]** argument. This will produce an error stating too many arguments were defined. The following is the corrected version of this example:

```
=IF(B2 < 5000,"Very Low",IF(B2 < 10000,"Low","OK"))
```

It is important to note that Excel will execute the logical tests of a nested IF function from left to right. Therefore, the sequence of each logical test shown in Figure 4.9 makes the nested IF function work. Notice that each logical test is in a sequence that tests for the lowest possible value in cell B2 to the largest possible value. For example, the first logical test looks for the lowest possible values (B2 < 5000). The second test looks for any values below 10,000 (B2 < 10000), and the third test looks for the highest values (B2 > 14000). What would happen if the first logical test in this example was B2 < 10000 instead of B2 < 5000? It would be impossible to test if B2 contains a value less than 5000 because these values would immediately test true for B2 < 10000. Therefore, you must carefully plan the sequence of each logical test in a nested IF function so that a value cannot test true for two tests.

COMMON MISTAKES | Logical Test Sequence in a Nested IF Function

Excel will execute the logical tests in a nested **IF** function from left to right. If you are using the **[value_if_false]** argument only to add additional logical tests to a nested **IF** function, the function will immediately end when the results of a logical test are true. Therefore, you must check the sequence of each logical test to make sure a value cannot test true for two tests. The following points can help you create a valid logical test sequence:

1. Identify the lowest and highest values you are testing in your worksheet. The logical tests should be sequenced to look for the lowest values to highest values, or highest values to lowest values. This will prevent a value from testing true for two logical tests.
2. Talk through each logical test in sequence for a few data points on your spreadsheet and write down the result. In addition, try to consider various hypothetical data points that would trigger a true output for each test.

Quick Reference

IF Functions and Nested IF Functions

1. Activate a cell where the output of the function should appear.
2. Type an equal sign, the function name `IF`, and an open parenthesis.
3. Create a test for the **logical_test** argument.
4. Define an output for the **[value_if_true]** argument (text outputs must be in quotation marks).
5. Define an output for the **[value_if_false]** argument or enter another **IF** function by typing the function name `IF` and an open parenthesis.
6. Type a closing parenthesis. If creating a nested **IF** function, type a closing parenthesis for each **IF** function that you started.
7. Press the **Enter** key.

VIDEO WORKSHOP

>> IF Functions

The purpose of this workshop is to demonstrate the use of the **IF** and nested **IF** functions. I will be demonstrating the tasks in this workshop in the **IF Functions** and **Nested IF Functions** videos. After completing each section of tasks, watch the related video shown in parentheses. Open the file named ib_e04_markdownanalysis. Remember to try the tasks on your own first before watching the videos.

1. **Basic IF Function (Video: IF Functions)**
   a. Activate cell G3.
   b. Type an equal sign, the function name `IF`, and an open parenthesis.
   c. Define the **logical_test** argument by typing `B3 = C3` and then type a comma.
   d. Define the **[value_if_true]** argument by typing the word `"Regular"`. Be sure to include the quotation marks. Then type a comma.
   e. Define the **[value_if_false]** argument by typing the word `"Markdown"`.
   f. Type a closing parenthesis and press the **Enter** key.
   g. Copy cell G3 and paste it into cells G4:G7 using the **Paste Formulas** option.

2. **Nested IF Function (Video: Nested IF Functions)**
   a. Activate cell H3.
   b. Type an equal sign, the function name `IF`, and an open parenthesis.
   c. Define the **logical_test** argument by typing `F3 <= 8` and then type a comma.
   d. Define the **[value_if_true]** argument by typing the number `0` and then type a comma.
   e. Define the **[value_if_false]** argument by starting a second **IF** function. Type the function name `IF` followed by an open parenthesis.
   f. Define the **logical_test** argument of the second **IF** function by typing `F3 <= 12` and then type a comma.
   g. Define the **[value_if_true]** argument of the second **IF** function by typing the number `.15` and then type a comma.
   h. Define the **[value_if_false]** argument of the second **IF** function by adding a third **IF** function. Type the function name `IF` followed by an open parenthesis.
   i. Define the **logical_test** argument of the third **IF** function by typing `F3 <= 16` and then type a comma.
   j. Define the **[value_if_true]** argument of the third **IF** function by typing the number `.25` and then type a comma.
   k. Define the **[value_if_false]** argument of the third **IF** function by typing the number `.50`.
   l. Finish the function by typing three closing parentheses and then press the **Enter** key.
   m. Copy cell H3 and paste it to cells H4:H7 using the **Paste Formulas** option.
   n. Save and close your file.

>> Price Management

Price management is a common exercise for any business. As consumer demand changes, business managers must manage the price of their products and services to be able to maintain a company's sales goals and market share. Price management is especially critical for companies that need to sell large amounts of inventory. However, there are many questions to consider before changing the price of a product. For example, will sales increase for a given item if a price is decreased? If so, how much will sales increase? If the price of an item is decreased, its profitability will usually decrease. Therefore, how much can a price decrease before the company starts losing money on the item? A flexible spreadsheet that can evaluate product sales, inventory, and pricing is an extremely valuable tool in answering these questions.

EXERCISE

Why Do I Need This?

Exercise

This exercise demonstrates how **IF** functions can dramatically increase the calculating flexibility of Excel. Your goal is to build a price management tool that will not only calculate price changes, but enable a pricing manager to override these calculations if needed. To begin this exercise, open the Excel file named ib_e04_pricemanagementreport.

1. Enter a **SUM** function in cell D8 that adds the values in the range D3:D7.
2. Copy the **SUM** function in cell D8 and paste it into cells E8 and F8.
3. Type a formula in cell G3 that divides the Current Unit Inventory (cell F3) by the Sales Units LW (cell D3). Then copy the formula and paste it into cells G4:G8. This formula calculates the current weeks of supply, which will give the pricing manager an idea of how much the current inventory supply will last if sales remain constant.
4. Type a nested **IF** function in cell H3 that will calculate the suggested markdown. This type of calculation could be used by a company that sets target weeks of supply for the items it sells. If the weeks of supply get too high, the company may reduce, or mark down, the price to increase sales. Use the following criteria when creating the function. Also, make sure each logical test is entered into the function in the order listed here:
    a. If the Current Weeks of Supply <= 8, the suggested markdown should be 0.
    b. If the Current Weeks of Supply <= 14, the suggested markdown should be .15.
    c. If the Current Weeks of Supply <= 18, the suggested markdown should be .25.
    d. If the Current Weeks of Supply is greater than 18 (or not less than or equal to 18), the markdown should be .40.
5. Copy and paste the nested **IF** function in cell H3 to cells H4:H7.
6. Type a nested **IF** function into cell I3 to calculate the New Price. The goal of this worksheet is to allow the price change manager to override this calculation by entering a new price into one of the cells in column J. This **IF** function will see whether the price entered into column J is greater than 0. If it is, that number will become the new price. If the value in column J is less than or equal to 0, the nested **IF** function will calculate the new price based on the suggested markdown. The logical tests and outputs for this nested **IF** function are as follows. Be sure to enter each logical test in the sequence listed.
    a. If J3 > 0, the output of the function should be the value in cell J3. If J3 is greater than 0, the pricing manager has manually set a new price for this item.

b. If H3 = 0, the output of the function should be cell C3. If H3 is 0, then there is no suggested markdown. The output of the function should be whatever the current price is in cell C3.

c. If both logical tests (J3 > 0 and H3 = 0) are false, then the function should calculate the new price using the formula C3 - (C3 * H3).

7. Copy the function in cell I3 and paste it to cells I4:I7.

8. Type a regular **IF** statement in cell K3 to calculate the markdown in dollars. If the New Price (cell I3) is equal to the Current Price (cell C3), then the mark-down dollars are 0 because the price did not change. Otherwise, calculate the markdown dollars using the formula (C3 - I3) * F3.

9. Copy the function in cell K3 and paste it to cells K4:K7. Then enter a **SUM** function in cell K8 to add the markdown dollars in this column.

10. Type the formula `(D3 - E3) / E3` in cell L3 to calculate the change in sales. Copy this formula and paste it into cells L4:L8.

11. Even though the weeks of supply for T-shirts is below 8, the directors of the company are concerned that a major competitor will be having a T-shirt sale this weekend. Override the new price by typing `7.99` in cell J3.

12. Even though the weeks of supply for denim shirts is slightly higher than 8, sales are up compared to last year. Maintain the current price by typing `24.99` in cell J6.

13. The company did not want to go over 150,000 markdown dollars (cell K8). Is it achieving this goal? Override the price for the Polo and Twill shirts so the company does not go over its target.

14. Save and close your file.

PROBLEM & EXERCISE

>> What's Wrong with This Spreadsheet?

Problem

You just started a new job as a raw materials buyer for a manufacturing company. One of the analysts in your division has prepared a spreadsheet analyzing the firm's current inventory position. The goal of the spreadsheet is to help you decide which items need to be purchased because inventory is too low, or which items should be canceled or returned because inventory is too high. Your boss left a copy of the company's inventory policy on your desk. The inventory guidelines are as follows:

1. Weeks of Supply <= 4: Orders must be rushed in because the company may be at risk of losing production.

2. Weeks of Supply < 8: It's time to place new orders to keep up with the production schedule.

3. Weeks of Supply >10: Try to get suppliers to postpone the delivery date to keep inventory from accumulating too high.

4. Weeks of Supply > 15: Place a hold on all current and new orders. At this level the inventory is getting too high and will be at risk of spoiling.

5. Weeks of Supply > 20: Consumer demand must be declining for the product that uses this item for production. Return item to the supplier if possible.

6. The inventory status is normal for any item that does not fit into these categories.

The analyst e-mails the spreadsheet containing the inventory analysis to you. He states the following in his e-mail: "Sorry I could not discuss this with you in person. I have an Excel training seminar all morning. In any event, the inventory status for the department is in good shape. By looking at the Suggested Action column, you will see that a few items need to be purchased, and there are a few items for which we might need to push back the delivery date. Thankfully, there are no major things like rush orders or returns! I will stop by when I am finished with the training seminar."

Exercise

The spreadsheet this analyst sent to you is named ib_e04_inventorystatus. Are you comfortable making decisions based on the Suggested Action column? Consider the following:

1. Do the suggested actions make sense given the inventory guidelines listed in the Problem section?

2. How is the data for the Suggested Action column being calculated?

3. Follow the calculation method used for the Suggested Action column for a few data points in the Weeks of Supply column. Does the method make sense?

4. What else could you do to make this spreadsheet easier to read?

What's wrong with this spreadsheet? Write a short answer for each of the points listed and fix any errors you see on the spreadsheet that the analyst sent to you.

Logical Functions (AND OR)

Skill Set

The previous section identified how **IF** functions are used to evaluate data and produce various outputs based on a logical test. This section introduces two other logical functions that are also used to evaluate data based on logical tests. They are the **AND** and **OR** functions. These functions can be used independently but are often used in the logical test argument of an **IF** function. This section will first review how the **AND** and **OR** functions are used independently and then will demonstrate how they are used with the **IF** function to dramatically increase Excel's analytical capabilities.

AND Function

In many situations, business managers must decide if a group of conditions apply to a specific aspect of their business. This is especially relevant for companies that make specialized products for a specific target customer. For example, Figure 4.11 shows customer demographic data from a company that is seeking to sell a new product to people who are female, have children, and are less than 45 years old. The marketing manager of this firm would probably find it challenging to identify these people from a list of 100,000 potential customers. However, the **AND** function can automatically evaluate and highlight customers that meet all of the characteristics targeted by this product.

Figure 4.11 | **Customer Data**

The AND function will be used in this column to identify the target customers.

This worksheet continues down to row 22.

	A	B	C	D	E	F
1	Customer Detail Information					
2	Name	State of Residence	Gender	Age	Children	Target Customer
3	Customer 1	CA	F	22	No	
4	Customer 2	MO	M	44	Yes	
5	Customer 3	TX	F	65	Yes	
6	Customer 4	NJ	M	73	No	
7	Customer 5	FLA	M	29	Yes	
8	Customer 6	PA	F	26	Yes	
9	Customer 7	GA	F	34	No	
10	Customer 8	NH	F	54	Yes	
11	Customer 9	NY	M	36	No	
12	Customer 10	CO	F	41	Yes	
13	Customer 11	NJ	M	30	Yes	
14	Customer 12	NM	F	24	No	
15	Customer 13	NY	F	28	Yes	
16	Customer 14	VA	M	44	No	
17	Customer 15	PA	M	52	Yes	

The **AND** function evaluates data using the same logical test that was explained in the **IF** function section. However, with this function, you can enter up to 30 logical tests. Based on the results of all logical tests entered, the **AND** function will produce one of two possible outputs. If all logical tests are true, the function will display the word TRUE. If the results of any logical test are false, the function will display the word FALSE. The following points explain how to use the **AND** function to evaluate the customer data in Figure 4.11 to highlight any customers who are female, have children, and are younger than 45:

- Activate cell F3, which is the first cell location in the Target Customer column. Remember, the **AND** function will display either the word TRUE or FALSE based on the results of the logical tests. Therefore, the **AND** function will identify target customers by displaying the word TRUE.
- Type an equal sign, the function name AND, and an open parenthesis.
- Type C3 ="F" to define the first logical test. Since being female is one of the characteristics of the target customer, the first logical test will evaluate if the gender of the customer is female. Notice that since the logical test uses text data, it is placed in quotation marks. Just as in the logical test in the **IF** function, any words or text data must be placed in quotation marks. Type a comma after this argument.
- Type D3 < 45 to define the second logical test. This will evaluate if the age of the customer is less than 45. Type a comma after this argument.
- Type E3 ="Yes" to define the third logical test. This will evaluate if the customer has children. Similar to the first logical test, since text data is being used, it is enclosed in quotation marks.
- Type a closing parenthesis and press the **Enter** key.
- Copy the completed **AND** function in cell F3 and paste it into cells F4 through F22. Since cell references were used in each of the three logical tests, they will automatically adjust through relative referencing when the formula is pasted to the rest of the cells in this column.

Quick Reference

AND Function

1. Activate a cell location where the output of the function should appear.
2. Type an equal sign, the function name AND, and an open parenthesis.
3. Create at least one but no more than 30 logical tests. Separate each logical test with a comma. *All* tests must be true to produce a TRUE output.
4. Type a closing parenthesis.
5. Press the **Enter** key.

- Sort the worksheet based on the AND function outputs in the Target Customer column in descending order. This will place any customers showing a TRUE output in the Target Customer column at the top of the worksheet.

Figure 4.12 shows the setup of the **AND** function that will be used to identify target customers. Notice that each argument of the function is a complete logical test utilizing the comparison operators shown in Figure 4.3.

Figure 4.12 | **Setup of the AND Function**

AND =AND(C3="F",D3<45,E3="Yes")

	A	B	C	D	E	F
1	Customer Detail Information					
2	Name	State of Residence	Gender	Age	Children	Target Customer
3	Customer 1	CA	F	22	No	=AND(C3="F",D3<45,E3="Yes")
4	Customer 2	MO	M	44	Yes	AND(logical1, [logical2], **[logical3]**, [logical4], ...)
5	Customer 3	TX	F	65	Yes	
6	Customer 4	NJ	M	73	No	

Each argument of this function is a complete logical test.

Figure 4.13 shows the results of the **AND** function. The word TRUE is displayed in the Target Customer column for any customer that meets all three logical tests that were typed into the function. The word FALSE is displayed if the results are false for any of the three logical tests. Notice how all target customers are grouped together in the first rows of the worksheet. The marketing manager using this worksheet can easily identify the target customers since the data is sorted based on the results of the **AND** function.

Figure 4.13 | **Results of the AND Function**

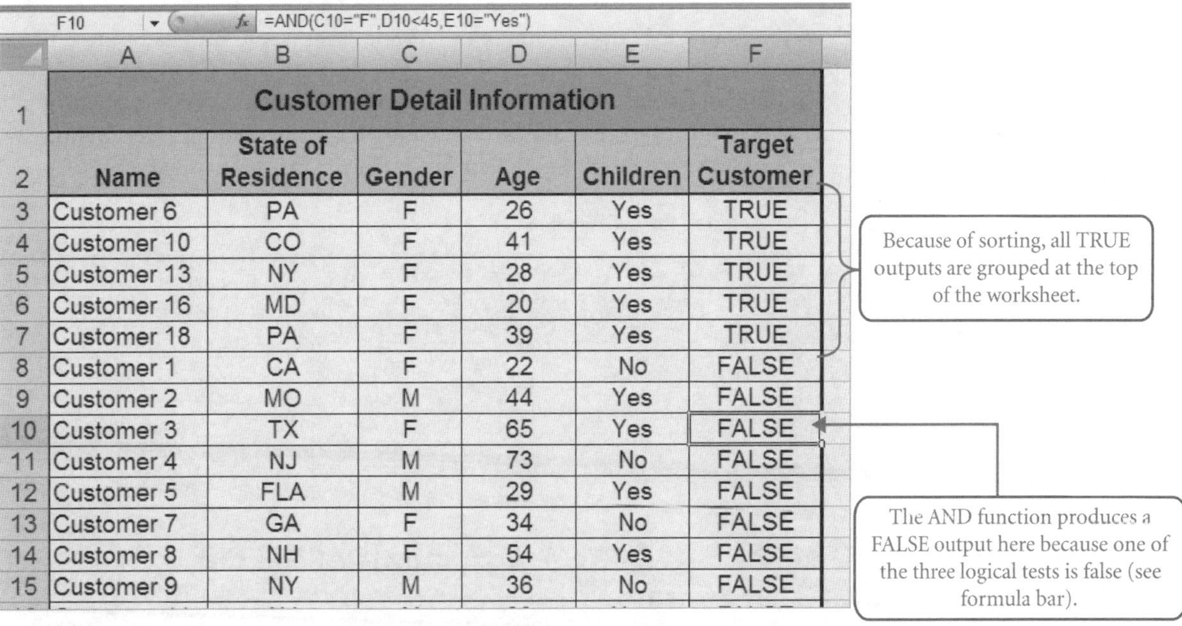

F10 =AND(C10="F",D10<45,E10="Yes")

	A	B	C	D	E	F
1	Customer Detail Information					
2	Name	State of Residence	Gender	Age	Children	Target Customer
3	Customer 6	PA	F	26	Yes	TRUE
4	Customer 10	CO	F	41	Yes	TRUE
5	Customer 13	NY	F	28	Yes	TRUE
6	Customer 16	MD	F	20	Yes	TRUE
7	Customer 18	PA	F	39	Yes	TRUE
8	Customer 1	CA	F	22	No	FALSE
9	Customer 2	MO	M	44	Yes	FALSE
10	Customer 3	TX	F	65	Yes	FALSE
11	Customer 4	NJ	M	73	No	FALSE
12	Customer 5	FLA	M	29	Yes	FALSE
13	Customer 7	GA	F	34	No	FALSE
14	Customer 8	NH	F	54	Yes	FALSE
15	Customer 9	NY	M	36	No	FALSE

COMMON MISTAKES | Outputs for the AND Function

You cannot define the output for the **AND** function. People often try to define the output for the **AND** function similar to the **[value_if_true]** or **[value_if_false]** arguments of the **IF** function. The only arguments you can define for the **AND** function are logical tests. The only output that will be produced by the **AND** function is the word TRUE or FALSE. This is also true for the **OR** function, which is covered in the next section.

OR Function

A close relative of the **AND** function is the **OR** function. The arguments of both functions are defined by logical tests. However, if *any* logical test is true, the **OR** function will display the word TRUE. The function displays the word FALSE if *all* logical tests are false. The **OR** function is used to evaluate data where the existence of just one criterion is required to trigger a decision or action. For example, a company may have a limited number of states where it can sell and distribute products. The **OR** function can be used to identify if a customer lives in one of the states within the company's territory. This information can then be used to distribute marketing information or promotional material relating to the company's product line.

The following demonstrates a variation for identifying target customers in Figure 4.11. In this example, a target customer is any person who lives in any of these three states: New York, Pennsylvania, or New Jersey. You use the **OR** function in this situation to produce a TRUE output if a person lives in *any* one of these three states. You add this function to the worksheet as follows:

- Activate cell F3.
- Type an equal sign, the function name OR, and an open parenthesis.
- Type B3="NJ" to define the first logical test. This will evaluate if the person lives in the state of New Jersey. Notice that quotation marks are placed around NJ because it is text data. Type a comma after this argument.
- Type B3="NY" to define the second logical test. This will evaluate if the customer lives in the state of New York. Type a comma after this argument.
- Type B3 ="PA" to define the third logical test. This will evaluate if the customer lives in the state of Pennsylvania.
- Type a closing parenthesis and press the **Enter** key.
- Copy the completed **OR** function in cell F3 and paste it into cells F4 through F22.

Figure 4.14 shows the setup of the **OR** function that is being used to evaluate if a customer lives in one of three states. Notice that each argument of the **OR** function, similar to the AND function, is a complete logical function.

Figure 4.14 | **Setup of the OR Function**

OR =OR(B3="NJ", B3="NY",B3="PA")

	A	B	C	D	E	F
1	Customer Detail Information					
2	Name	State of Residence	Gender	Age	Children	Target Customer
3	Customer 1	CA	F	22	No	=OR(B3="NJ", B3="NY",B3="PA")
4	Customer 2	MO	M	44	Yes	OR(logical1, [logical2], **[logical3]**, [logical4], ...)
5	Customer 3	TX	F	65	Yes	
6	Customer 4	NJ	M	73	No	

This function will display the word TRUE if *any* of these logical tests is true.

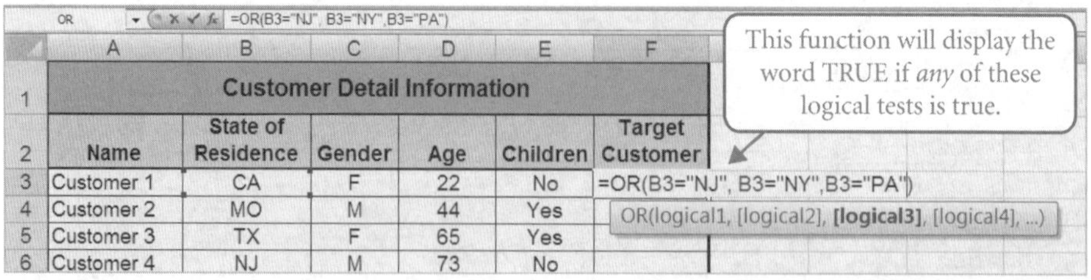

COMMON MISTAKES | Arguments of the OR and AND Functions

You must type complete logical tests when defining the arguments of both the **AND** and **OR** functions. People often try to enter multiple results separated by commas to test multiple values for one cell location as shown in the following example. This **OR** function will produce a TRUE output regardless of what value is contained in cell D10:

```
=OR(D10 = 14,25,33,55)
```

The following example illustrates how you should create the **OR** function if you are evaluating if *one* of four values (14, 25, 33, 55) is contained in cell D10.

```
=OR(D10 = 14,D10 = 25,D10 = 33,D10 = 55)
```

Figure 4.15 shows the results of the **OR** function. Similar to the output of the **AND** function in Figure 4.13, this worksheet was also sorted based on the function outputs in the Target Customer column. Notice that if NY or NJ or PA is shown in the State of Residence column for a customer, the output of the **OR** function is TRUE. A marketing manager can use this information to initiate a direct mail marketing campaign to the target customers identified in this worksheet.

Figure 4.15 | **Results of the OR Function**

F6 =OR(B6="NJ", B6="NY",B6="PA")

	A	B	C	D	E	F
1	Customer Detail Information					
2	Name	State of Residence	Gender	Age	Children	Target Customer
3	Customer 4	NJ	M	73	No	TRUE
4	Customer 6	PA	F	26	Yes	TRUE
5	Customer 9	NY	M	36	No	TRUE
6	Customer 11	NJ	M	30	Yes	TRUE
7	Customer 13	NY	F	28	Yes	TRUE
8	Customer 15	PA	M	52	Yes	TRUE
9	Customer 18	PA	F	39	Yes	TRUE
10	Customer 20	NJ	M	41	Yes	TRUE
11	Customer 1	CA	F	22	No	FALSE
12	Customer 2	MO	M	44	Yes	FALSE
13	Customer 3	TX	F	65	Yes	FALSE
14	Customer 5	FLA	M	29	Yes	FALSE
15	Customer 7	GA	F	34	No	FALSE
16	Customer 8	NH	F	54	Yes	FALSE

The function produces a TRUE output in these cells because at least one of the three logical tests is true (see formula bar).

This worksheet continues down to row 22.

Combining AND, OR, and IF Functions

The **OR** and **AND** functions can produce only one of two outputs: the word TRUE or the word FALSE. However, you can use these functions with the **IF** function to produce any output that is required for your project. This technique will be demonstrated using the worksheet shown in Figure 4.16, which contains customer buying data from a hypothetical retail company. Retailers typically offer a variety of reward promotions or discounts based on the buying history of their customers. For example, you may have signed up for a frequent shopper card at your favorite store or agreed to have a company contact you regarding future promotions when you purchased something online. These activities are usually indicative of a company that is running some type of customer loyalty program. A marketing manager will use the data collected from these programs to develop various discounts and promotional programs depending on a customer's buying history. The technique of combining the **AND**, **OR**, and **IF** functions can be used to tell the marketing manager what promotions should be sent to each customer.

The following points explain how you combine the **AND** and **IF** functions to show which promotion each customer should receive in Figure 4.16. This example assumes that a customer could receive one of two discount coupons. The first is a 50% off coupon for customers who have been purchasing products from the company for more than one year and have not made a purchase in the last 12 months. All other customers will receive a regular 10% off promotional coupon.

Quick Reference

OR Function

1. Activate a cell location where the output of the function should appear.
2. Type an equal sign, the function name OR, and an open parenthesis.
3. Create at least one but no more than 30 logical tests.
4. Separate each logical test with a comma. Only one test needs to be true to produce a TRUE output.
5. Type a closing parenthesis.
6. Press the **Enter** key.

Figure 4.16 | **Customer Rewards Program**

The AND, OR, and IF functions will be used in this column to show what promotion or discounts should be sent to each customer.

This worksheet continues down to row 17.

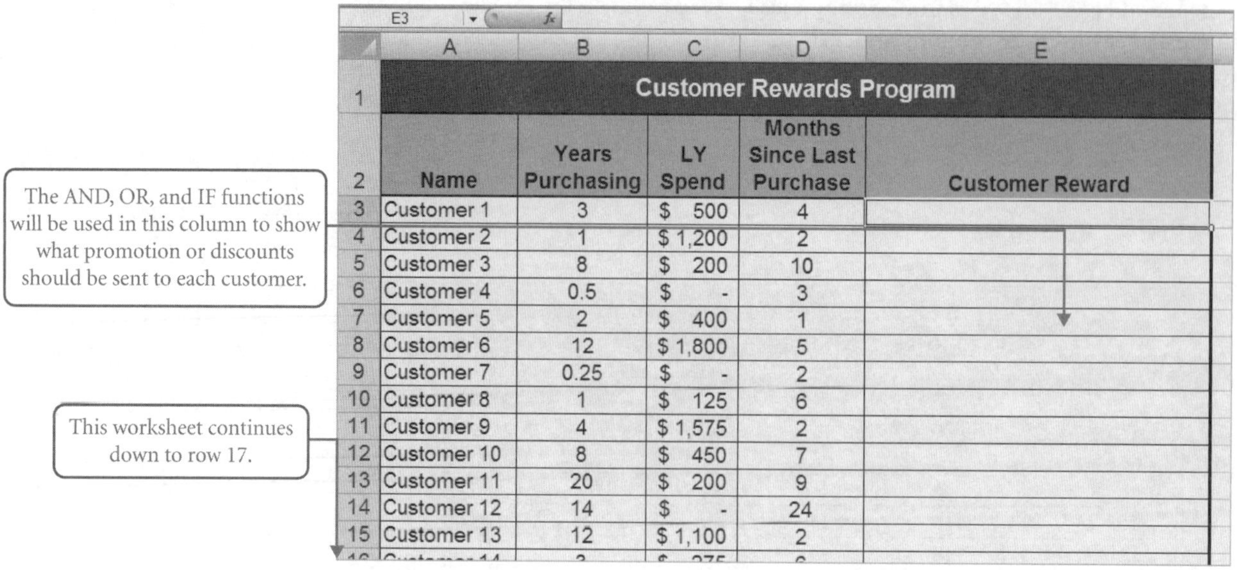

	A	B	C	D	E
1	Customer Rewards Program				
2	Name	Years Purchasing	LY Spend	Months Since Last Purchase	Customer Reward
3	Customer 1	3	$ 500	4	
4	Customer 2	1	$ 1,200	2	
5	Customer 3	8	$ 200	10	
6	Customer 4	0.5	$ -	3	
7	Customer 5	2	$ 400	1	
8	Customer 6	12	$ 1,800	5	
9	Customer 7	0.25	$ -	2	
10	Customer 8	1	$ 125	6	
11	Customer 9	4	$ 1,575	2	
12	Customer 10	8	$ 450	7	
13	Customer 11	20	$ 200	9	
14	Customer 12	14	$ -	24	
15	Customer 13	12	$ 1,100	2	

- Activate cell E3, which is the first cell location in the Customer Reward column.
- Type an equal sign, the function name IF, and an open parenthesis.
- Type the function name AND followed by an open parenthesis. The **AND** function will be used in defining the **logical_test** argument of the **IF** function.
- Type B3>1 to define the first logical test of the **AND** function. This test will evaluate if the value in the Years Purchasing column is greater than 1. Type a comma after defining this argument.
- Type D3>=12 to define the second logical test of the **AND** function. This test will evaluate if the value in the Months Since Last Purchase column is greater than or equal to 12.
- Type a closing parenthesis to complete the **AND** function.
- Type =TRUE followed by a comma to complete the **logical_test** argument of the **IF** function. The logical test of the **IF** function will now evaluate if the output of the **AND** function is TRUE. Notice that quotation marks are *not* placed on the word TRUE. The reason is that the word TRUE is an output of the **AND** function and not a text message or word that has been typed into a cell.
- Type "Please Come Back 50% Off" to define the [**value_if_true**] argument of the **IF** function. If the logical test of the **IF** function is true, then the output of the **AND** function is true. This indicates a person has been buying products from the company for more than one year *and* has not made a purchase in 12 or more months. Therefore, this message tells the marketing manager to send this customer a 50% off coupon. Type a comma after this argument.
- Type "Customer Appreciation 10% Off" to define the [**value_if_false**] argument of the **IF** function. Any customer that does not qualify for the 50% off coupon will be sent a 10% off coupon.
- Type a closing parenthesis and press the **Enter** key to complete the function.
- Copy the function in cell E3 and paste it into cells E4 through E17.
- Sort the worksheet based on the Customer Reward column in descending order.

Figure 4.17 shows the setup of the functions. Notice that the **AND** function defines the left side of the logical test. Also, note that the messages defining the value_if_true and value_if_false arguments are placed in quotation marks.

Figure 4.17 | **Setup for Combining the IF and AND Functions**

IF =IF(AND(B3>1,D3>=12)=TRUE,"Please Come Back 50% Off","Customer Appreciation 10% Off")

	B	C	D	E
1	Customer Rewards Program			
2	Years Purchasing	LY Spend	Months Since Last Purchase	Customer Reward
3	3	$ 500	4	=IF(AND(B3>1,D3>=12)=TRUE,"Please Come Back 50% Off","Customer Appreciation 10% Off")
4	1	$ 1,200	2	IF(**logical_test**, [value_if_true], [value_if_false])
5	8	$ 200	10	
6	0.5	$ -	3	
7	2	$ 400	1	

The AND function is used in the logical_test argument

Figure 4.18 shows the results of combing the **IF** function and **AND** function to determine the type of discount coupon that should be sent to each customer. Since the spreadsheet was sorted, the marketing manager can easily see that the first two customers listed on the worksheet should be sent the 50% off coupon.

Figure 4.18 | **Results of Combining the IF and AND Functions**

E4 =IF(AND(B4>1,D4>=12)=TRUE,"Please Come Back 50% Off","Customer Appreciation 10% Off")

	A	B	C	D	E
1	Customer Rewards Program				
2	Name	Years Purchasing	LY Spend	Months Since Last Purchase	Customer Reward
3	Customer 12	14	$ -	24	Please Come Back 50% Off
4	Customer 15	6	$ -	14	Please Come Back 50% Off
5	Customer 1	3	$ 500	4	Customer Appreciation 10% Off
6	Customer 2	1	$ 1,200	2	Customer Appreciation 10% Off
7	Customer 3	8	$ 200	10	Customer Appreciation 10% Off
8	Customer 4	0.5	$ -	3	Customer Appreciation 10% Off
9	Customer 5	2	$ 400	1	Customer Appreciation 10% Off
10	Customer 6	12	$ 1,800	5	Customer Appreciation 10% Off
11	Customer 7	0.25	$ -	2	Customer Appreciation 10% Off
12	Customer 8	1	$ 125	6	Customer Appreciation 10% Off
13	Customer 9	4	$ 1,575	2	Customer Appreciation 10% Off
14	Customer 10	8	$ 450	7	Customer Appreciation 10% Off

Since both logical tests of the AND function are true, the IF function displays the value_if_true output for this customer.

Figure 4.19 shows the setup of combining the **IF** and **OR** functions. This example assumes that the marketing manager will send a 25% off discount coupon to customers who have either been making purchases for more than two years or have spent more than $1,000 in the past year. Since customers will qualify for this coupon if they satisfy either criteria, the **OR** function will be used in defining the logical test of the **IF** function. The following points explain how you create this function using the worksheet shown in Figure 4.16:

- Activate cell E3.
- Type an equal sign, the function name IF, and an open parenthesis.
- Type the function name OR followed by an open parenthesis.
- Type B3>2 to define the first logical test of the **OR** function. This test will evaluate if the value in the Years Purchasing column is greater than 2. Type a comma after defining this argument.
- Type C3>1000 to define the second logical test of the **OR** function. This test will evaluate if the value in the LY Spend column is greater than 1000.
- Type a closing parenthesis to complete the **OR** function.
- Type =TRUE followed by a comma to complete the **logical_test** argument of the **IF** function. The logical test of the IF function is now evaluating if the output of the **OR** function is TRUE. Notice that quotation marks are *not* placed on the word TRUE.
- Type "Thanks for being loyal 25% Off" to define the [**value_if_true**] argument of the **IF** function. If the logical test of the **IF** function is true, then the output of the **OR** function is true. This indicates a person has been purchasing products from the company for more than two years *or* has spent more than $1,000 in the past year. Type a comma after defining this argument.
- Type "Customer Appreciation 10% Off" to define the [**value_if_false**] argument. Any customer who does not satisfy either criteria specified in the **OR** function will be sent a 10% off coupon.

- Type a closing parenthesis and press the **Enter** key to complete the function.
- Copy the completed function in cell E3 and paste it to cells E4 through E17.
- Sort the worksheet based on the Customer Reward column in descending order.

Figure 4.19 | **Combining the IF and OR Functions**

=IF(OR(B3>2,C3>1000)=TRUE,"Thanks for being loyal 25% Off", "Customer Appreciation 10% Off")

	C	D	E
1	Customer Rewards Program		
2	LY Spend	Months Since Last Purchase	Customer Reward
3	$ 500	4	=IF(OR(B3>2,C3>1000)=TRUE,"Thanks for being loyal 25% Off", "Customer Appreciation 10% Off")
4	$ 1,200	2	IF(**logical_test**, [value_if_true], [value_if_false])
5	$ 200	10	

The OR function is used in the logical_test argument.

Figure 4.20 shows the results of combining the **IF** and **OR** functions. Similar to the results shown in Figure 4.18, the marketing manager can easily see which discount coupon goes to each customer because the worksheet was sorted based on the output in the Customer Reward column.

Figure 4.20 | **Results of Combining the IF and OR Functions**

E5 =IF(OR(B5>2,C5>1000)=TRUE,"Thanks for being loyal 25% Off", "Customer Appreciation 10% Off")

	A	B	C	D	E
1	Customer Rewards Program				
2	Name	Years Purchasing	LY Spend	Months Since Last Purchase	Customer Reward
3	Customer 1	3	$ 500	4	Thanks for being loyal 25% Off
4	Customer 2	1	$ 1,200	2	Thanks for being loyal 25% Off
5	Customer 3	8	$ 200	10	Thanks for being loyal 25% Off
6	Customer 6	12	$ 1,800	5	Thanks for being loyal 25% Off
7	Customer 9	4	$ 1,575	2	Thanks for being loyal 25% Off
8	Customer 10	8	$ 450	7	Thanks for being loyal 25% Off
9	Customer 11	20	$ 200	9	Thanks for being loyal 25% Off
10	Customer 12	14	$ -	24	Thanks for being loyal 25% Off
11	Customer 13	12	$ 1,100	2	Thanks for being loyal 25% Off
12	Customer 14	3	$ 275	6	Thanks for being loyal 25% Off
13	Customer 15	6	$ -	14	Thanks for being loyal 25% Off
14	Customer 4	0.5	$ -	3	Customer Appreciation 10% Off
15	Customer 5	2	$ 400	1	Customer Appreciation 10% Off

Both logical tests in the OR function were false for this customer.

COMMON MISTAKES | Combining the AND, OR, and IF Functions

You cannot use the word **AND** or the word **OR** to combine multiple logical tests in an **IF** function. For example, the following **IF** function will produce an error:

```
=IF(B3 > 2 AND C3 > 500 AND D3 > 12,"Free Gift","Discount Coupon")
```

Based on the preceding example, if you wanted to show the words *Free Gift* in a cell if the value in cell B3 is greater than 2 *and* the value in C3 is greater than 500 *and* the value in D3 is greater than 12, then you need to use the **AND** function. The corrected **IF** function is as follows.

```
=IF(AND(B3 > 2,C3 > 500,D3 > 12) = TRUE, "Free Gift", "Discount Coupon")
```

Notice that the **AND** *function* is used in the **logical_test** argument of the **IF** function. If the **AND** function produces a TRUE output, the words *Free Gift* will appear in the cell. If the **AND** function produces a FALSE output, the function will show the words *Discount Coupon* in the cell.

»AND and OR Functions

VIDEO WORKSHOP

The purpose of this workshop is to demonstrate the use of the **AND** and **OR** functions. We will be using these functions to construct a merchandise allocation plan. I will be demonstrating the tasks in this workshop in the following three videos: **AND Function**; **OR Function**; and **Combining AND, OR, and IF Functions**. After completing each section of tasks, watch the related video shown in parentheses. Open the file named ib_e04_merchandiseallocations. Remember to try these tasks on your own first before watching the video.

1. **The AND Function (Video: AND Function)**
   a. Activate cell G3 in Sheet1.
   b. Type an equal sign, the function name `AND`, and an open parenthesis.
   c. Type `B3 = "Yes"` to define the first logical test and then type a comma.
   d. Type `F3 = "Yes"` to define a second logical test.
   e. Type a closing parenthesis and then press the **Enter** key.
   f. Copy cell G3 and paste it into cells G4:G13.

2. **The OR Function (Video: OR Function)**
   a. Activate cell H3.
   b. Type an equal sign, the function name `OR`, and an open parenthesis.
   c. Type `C3 = "Yes"` to define the first logical test and then type a comma.
   d. Type `D3 = "Yes"` to define a second logical test and then type a comma.
   e. Type `E3 >= 5000000` to define a third logical test.
   f. Type a closing parenthesis and press the **Enter** key.
   g. Copy cell H3 and paste it into cells H4:H13.

3. **OR, AND, and Nested IF Function (Video: Combining AND, OR, and IF Functions)**
   a. Activate cell I3.
   b. Type an equal sign, the function name `IF`, and an open parenthesis.
   c. Define the **logical_test** argument by typing the function name `AND` followed by an open parenthesis.
   d. Type the following logical tests for the **AND** function:
      `B3 = "Yes"`
      `F3 = "Yes"`
   e. Type a closing parenthesis to complete the **AND** function.
   f. Type an equal sign followed by the word `FALSE` and then type a comma to complete the **logical_test** argument of the **IF** function.
   g. Define the **[value_if_true]** argument by typing a `0` followed by a comma.
   h. Define the **[value_if_false]** argument by starting a new **IF** function. Type the function name `IF` followed by an open parenthesis.
   i. Define the **logical_test** argument of the second **IF** function by typing the function name `OR` followed by an open parenthesis.

j. Enter the following logical tests for the **OR** function:

```
C3 = "Yes"
D3 = "Yes"
E3 >= 5000000
```

k. Type a closing parenthesis to complete the **OR** function.

l. Type an equal sign followed by the word `TRUE` and then type a comma to complete the **logical_test** argument of the second **IF** function.

m. Define the **[value_if_true]** argument of the second **IF** function by typing the number `1` followed by a comma.

n. Define the **[value_if_false]** argument of the second **IF** function by typing `0`. Then complete the function by typing two closing parentheses and press the **Enter** key.

o. Copy cell I3 and paste it into cell I4:I13.

p. Save and close your file.

EXERCISE

Why Do I Need This?

>>Managing Product Shipments

When it comes to managing the process of shipping merchandise from a distribution center to a retail store, transportation managers often find themselves stuck between a rock and a hard place. On one hand they are under a lot of pressure to keep shipping costs as low as possible. To do this, transportation managers will try to maximize either the cubic capacity or weight capacity of every truck that leaves the distribution center. On the other hand, they need to ship products as frequently as possible so all stores have every item in stock all the time. As a result, if they wait too long to maximize the capacity of a truck, a store may run out of certain products, which could decrease sales.

Exercise

The goal of this exercise is to evaluate the shipping status for a fleet of trucks servicing a chain of retail stores. You will use the **AND**, **OR**, and **IF** functions to determine which trucks should ship and which trucks should be held at the distribution center. You will need to open the file named ib_e04_transportationstatus before completing the following tasks:

1. A truck must have fuel and not require any maintenance before it can be released to ship products. Use the **AND** function in cell J3 to determine if the first truck can be cleared for shipping. The function should show the word TRUE if cell H3 in the Fuel column is Yes and cell I3 in the Maintenance Required column is No.

2. Copy the **AND** function in cell J3 and paste it into cells J4:J20.

3. Use the **OR** function in cell K3 to determine if the first truck achieved the company capacity goal. The capacity goal is achieved when either the Current Cube (cell F3) or the Current Weight (cell G3) is greater than or equal to 90% of capacity. The logical tests to evaluate the current weight and cubic capacity are as follows:

   a. Current Cubic Capacity: `F3 >= D3 * .90`

   b. Current Weight Capacity: `G3 >= E3 * .90`

4. Copy the **OR** function in cell K3 and paste it to cells K4:K20.

5. Enter a nested **IF** function in cell L3 to determine if a truck should be held or shipped. The following logical tests should be used in this function in the order listed.
   a. If the output of the **AND** function in cell J3 is FALSE, then the output of this **IF** function should be the word *HOLD*. If the truck does not have fuel or requires maintenance, the transportation manager cannot allow it to leave the distribution center.
   b. If the output of the **OR** function in cell K3 is TRUE, then the output of this function should be SHIP.
   c. If the output of the **OR** function in cell K3 is FALSE and the value in cell C3 (Days Since Last Delivery) is greater than or equal to 3, the function should display the word *SHIP*. As mentioned, in order for the transportation manager to control shipping costs, the capacity of each truck must be maximized before shipping. However, a store needs to receive frequent deliveries to prevent merchandise from going out of stock. Therefore, even if a truck has not reached its capacity goal, it must be shipped.
   d. If all logical tests in this function fail, you can assume that a truck has not reached its capacity goal and it has been less than three days since the store received a delivery. Therefore, the output should be HOLD.
6. Copy the function in cell L3 and paste it to cells L4:L20.
7. Sort the spreadsheet based on the Ship or Hold column (column L) in ascending order and then based on the Fuel & Maintenance Ready column (column J) in ascending order.
8. How many trucks are being held?
9. How many trucks are being held only because of fuel and maintenance issues?
10. How many trucks had to be shipped without reaching their capacity goals?
11. Save and close your file.

>> What's Wrong with This Spreadsheet?

PROBLEM & EXERCISE

Problem

Your friend is working on a project for her finance class. She is having trouble putting together a spreadsheet in Excel and asks for your help. She attaches an Excel workbook to an e-mail and includes the following message:

Hi, I pulled together some data for a project I have to do for my finance class. I am trying to complete the Status column and the Investment Opportunity column. I thought these would be easy calculations; however, as you can see, something is going radically wrong here! Please help.

1. *For the Status column I'm trying to show the words Market Leader if the market share is greater than 20% or the sales growth is greater than 10%. I figured the **OR** function would be perfect for this, but as you can see, I keep getting errors.*
2. *For the Investment Opportunity column, I am just trying to identify public companies that have a 5-year sales growth rate greater than 10%. I am trying to use the **AND** function for this one, but as you can see, this is not working either.*

Exercise

The workbook your friend e-mailed to you is named ib_e04_companyanalysis. Take a look at the functions in the Status column and the Investment Opportunity column. What's wrong with this spreadsheet? Consider the following points:

1. Based on the criteria explained in your friend's e-mail, is she using the right functions to accomplish her goals?

2. Are the arguments for each function properly defined?

Write a short answer for each of the preceding points and fix the spreadsheet based on the facts stated from the message in the Problem section.

Skill Set

Lookup Functions

The previous sections in this chapter addressed how logical functions are used to evaluate the data in a worksheet. This section will review functions that can be used for assembling data in a worksheet. The data required for business projects rarely comes in one neat convenient spreadsheet. In many instances, you will have to pull data from several sources or pick specific points from larger datasets. The anecdote at the beginning of this chapter is an excellent example of having to pull pieces of information from one data source and insert them into a worksheet. Theses tasks can be accomplished through ***Lookup functions.*** Lookup functions are valuable assets when you are assembling data from several sources. The two lookup functions covered in this section are **VLookup** and **HLookup**.

VLookup Function

VLookup is a lookup function used mostly to display data from one worksheet or workbook into another. For example, you may have a worksheet filled with ZIP codes and need to insert the city and state, similar to the anecdote at the beginning of the chapter. Or, you may have a list of product codes and need to insert the product description. You can use the **VLookup** function to look for specific data values in a second worksheet or workbook and display the needed values in your primary worksheet.

The data in Figure 4.21 shows product sales and inventory data for a hypothetical retail store. The Sales Data worksheet contains several product numbers along with sales and inventory data. Notice that the Product Description column is blank. Therefore, we do not know which products are associated with each product number. However, the Product Data worksheet contains a list of the same product codes found on the Sales Data worksheet along with a variety of descriptive information.

Figure 4.21 | **Sales and Inventory Data by Product**

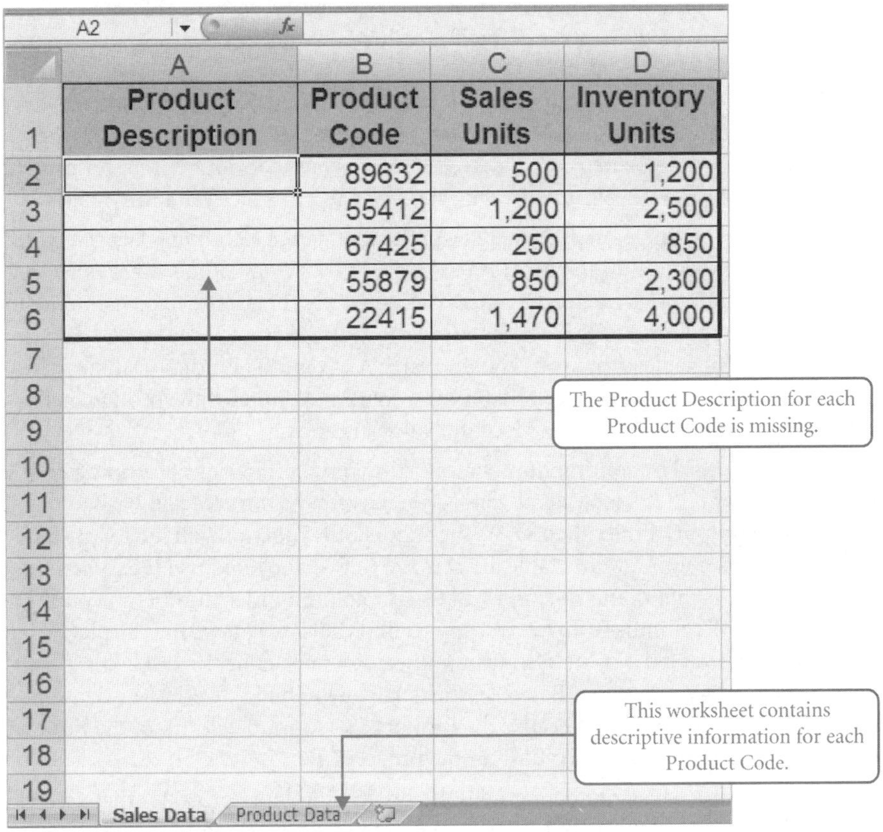

	A	B	C	D
1	Product Description	Product Code	Sales Units	Inventory Units
2		89632	500	1,200
3		55412	1,200	2,500
4		67425	250	850
5		55879	850	2,300
6		22415	1,470	4,000

Figure 4.22 shows the data contained in both worksheets from Figure 4.21 side by side. The goal of this example is to show how you can use the **VLookup** function to match the product codes in the Sales Data worksheet with the product codes in the Product Data worksheet. When a match is found, the function will show the Product Description from column C of the Product Data worksheet in column A of the Sales Data worksheet. There are two main reasons why you would want to accomplish this task using the **VLookup** function instead of typing these descriptions manually into the worksheet. The first is accuracy. As mentioned in Chapter 2, data entry errors are very common when information is manually typed into a worksheet. Using the **VLookup** function to bring data from one worksheet into another prevents data entry errors. The second reason is time. The data in Figure 4.22 represents a simplified example so it is easier for you to learn this function. However, imagine if you were faced with the situation that was described in the anecdote. It would probably take you a few hours to accurately type the state and city names for 400 ZIP codes into a worksheet. With the **VLookup** function, this task would take just a few minutes.

Figure 4.22 | **Sales Data and Product Data Worksheets Side by Side**

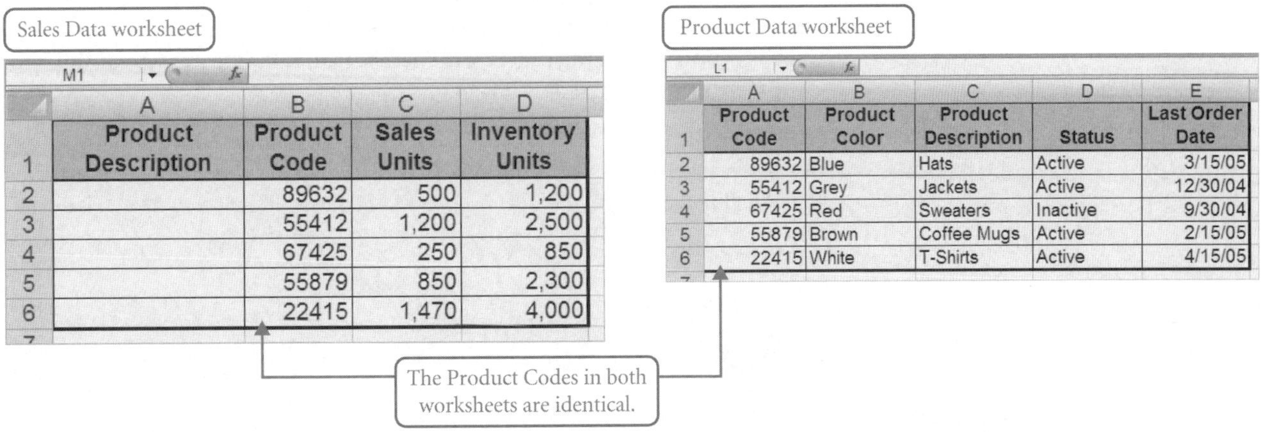

	A	B	C	D
1	Product Description	Product Code	Sales Units	Inventory Units
2		89632	500	1,200
3		55412	1,200	2,500
4		67425	250	850
5		55879	850	2,300
6		22415	1,470	4,000

	A	B	C	D	E
1	Product Code	Product Color	Product Description	Status	Last Order Date
2	89632	Blue	Hats	Active	3/15/05
3	55412	Grey	Jackets	Active	12/30/04
4	67425	Red	Sweaters	Inactive	9/30/04
5	55879	Brown	Coffee Mugs	Active	2/15/05
6	22415	White	T-Shirts	Active	4/15/05

As shown in Figure 4.23, the **VLookup** function contains four arguments that must be defined in order to display data from one worksheet or workbook into another. Each of these arguments is defined as follows:

- **lookup_value**: The common data point that exists in two different worksheets or in two parts of the same worksheet. Based on the data shown in Figure 4.22, the lookup value would be defined using cell locations in the Product Code column because these values exists in both the Sales Data and Product Data worksheets.
- **table_array**: The range of cells where both the lookup value and the data that will be used for the output of the function exist. *The first column of this range must contain the lookup value.* The function will look vertically (hence the name **Vlookup**) down the first column of this range to find the lookup value. Based on the data in Figure 4.22, the table array would be the range A2:E6 in the Product Data worksheet. This range starts with cell A2 because column A contains the product codes that would be used to define the **lookup_value** argument.
- **col_index_num**: The column number, counting from left to right beginning with the first column in the table array range, which contains the data you wish to display as the output of the function. As mentioned, the function will look vertically down the first column of the table array range to find the lookup value. When the lookup value is found, the function will use the column index number to count the number of columns from left to right to find the data you wish to display. When determining the column index number, you must consider the first column in the table array range as 1. Based on the data shown in Figure 4.22, the column index number would be 3, because the Product Description column in the Product Data worksheet is the third column in the range A2:E6.
- **[range_lookup]**: This argument guides the function to look for values that are either a close match or an approximate match to the lookup value. In most situations you will want the function to look for an exact match to the lookup value. However, you might want to look for close matches in situations such as survey scores. For example, a survey score of 90 to 100 might be given a description of "Excellent." The actual value on your primary worksheet might be the number 97. However, the worksheet containing the description of each score might have only the number 90. In this situation, setting the **range_lookup** argument to find an approximate match would be necessary. This argument is defined with one of two possible options:
  - **True**: Type the word True (no quotation marks) if you want the function to look for approximate matches to the lookup value. You must consider the following if you are using this option:
    - The range of cells used to define the **table_array** range *must be sorted in ascending order*; otherwise, the function may produce erroneous results.
    - The function will look for the next highest value that is *less than* the lookup value. For example, if the table array range contains the number 90, and the lookup value is 97, the function will match to the number 90. If the number 90 was the lowest value in the table array range, and the lookup value was 89, the function will produce an error. There reason is that there is no number in the table array range that is less than 89.
  - **False**: Type the word False (no quotation marks) if you want the function to look for exact matches to the lookup value. *It is important to note that if you do not define the [**range_lookup**] argument, the function will assume the True option.*

Figure 4.23 | **Arguments of the VLookup Function**

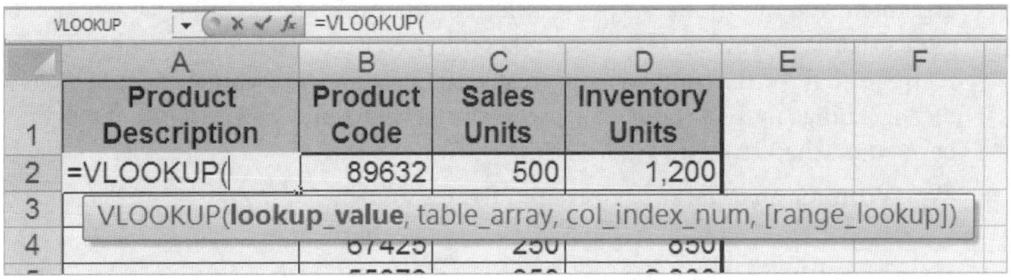

VLOOKUP =VLOOKUP(

	A	B	C	D	E	F
1	Product Description	Product Code	Sales Units	Inventory Units		
2	=VLOOKUP(	89632	500	1,200		

VLOOKUP(**lookup_value**, table_array, col_index_num, [range_lookup])

As mentioned, the **VLookup** function will be used to complete the Product Description column in the Sales Data worksheet shown in Figure 4.22. The following explains how you accomplish this:

- Activate cell A2 in the Sales Data worksheet shown in Figure 4.22.
- Type an equal sign, the function name VLOOKUP, and an open parenthesis.
- Type cell B2 to define the **lookup_value** argument. Cell B2 contains the product code for the first item in the Sales Data worksheet.
- Type a comma.
- Click the Product Data worksheet tab (see Figure 4.24).

Figure 4.24 | **Click the Product Data Worksheet Tab to Define the Table Array Range**

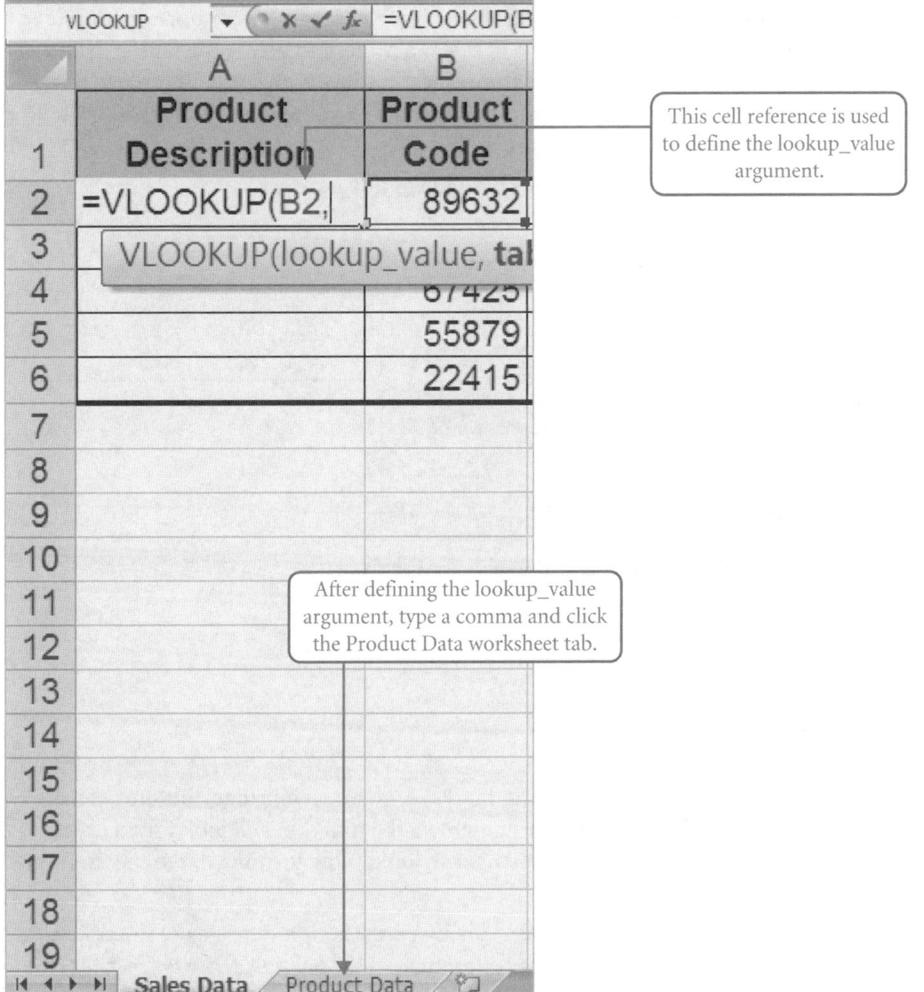

- Highlight the range A2:E6 in the Product Data worksheet to define the **table_array** argument. You may notice in the formula bar that this range is preceded by the worksheet name enclosed in apostrophes followed by an exclamation point. The reason is that the function is being created in the Sales Data worksheet but is referencing a range in the Product Data worksheet. This is known as a *link* and will be covered in Chapter 6 (see Figure 4.25).
- Type a comma after defining the **table_array** argument.

Figure 4.25 | **Defining the Table Array Range in the Product Data Worksheet**

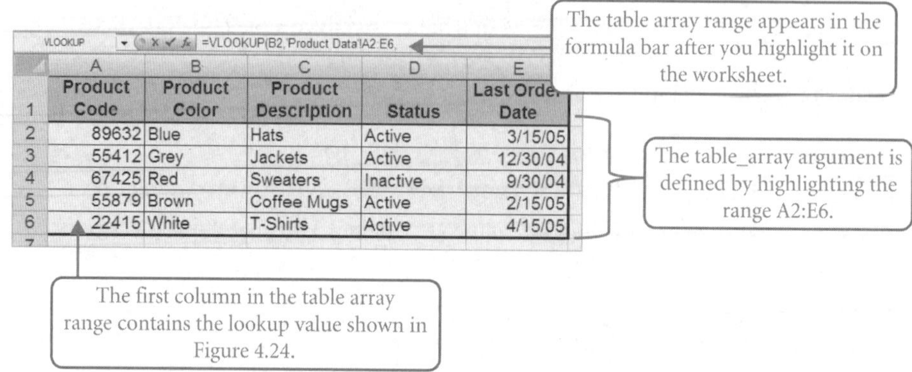

- Type the number 3 to define the **col_index_num** argument. The Product Description is the third column in the table array range. It is important to note that since the Product Data worksheet was activated to define the **table_array** argument, you will remain in this worksheet until you press the **Enter** key. Therefore, you will have to look in the formula bar to see the arguments of the function being defined (see Figure 4.26).
- Type a comma after defining the **col_index_num** argument.

Figure 4.26 | **Defining the Column Index Number**

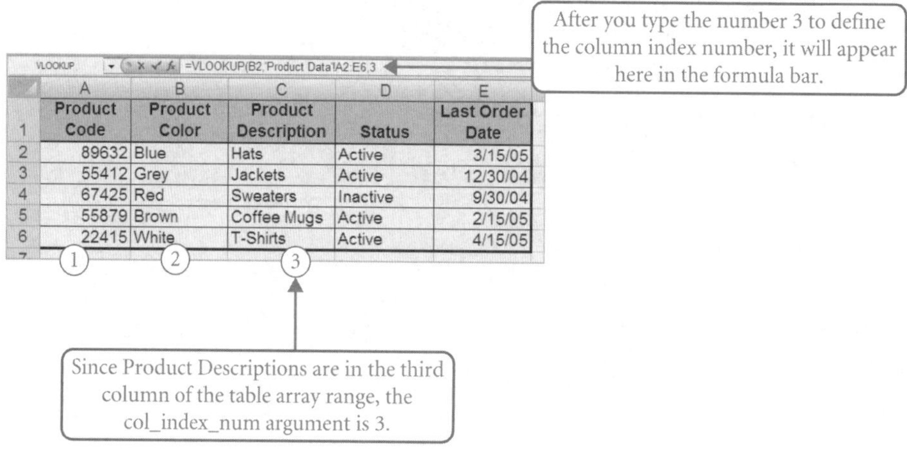

- Type the word False (no quotation marks) to define the **[range_lookup]** argument. You enter False into this argument so the function will look for an exact match for the lookup value. Remember to look in the formula bar to see this argument being defined as you type.
- Complete the function by typing a closing parenthesis and press the **Enter** key. After you press the **Enter** key, you will return to the Sales Data worksheet.
- Double click cell A2 in the Sales Data worksheet and add an absolute reference to both cell locations in the range used to define the **table_array** argument. You do

this so the range does not change from relative referencing when the function is pasted to the rest of the cell locations in column A. Remember that you add an absolute reference by typing a dollar sign in front of the column letter and row number of the cell reference.

- Copy the completed **VLookup** function in cell A2 and paste it into cells A3 through A6.

Figure 4.27 shows the final setup and results of the **VLookup** function. The function displays the word *Hats* in cell A2 of the Product Description column. The reason is that it found Product Code 89632 in the first column of the table array range, which is A2:E6 in the Product Data worksheet, and pulled the word *Hats* in the third column of this range (see Figure 4.26). In addition, notice that an absolute reference is placed on the range used to define the **table_array** argument.

Figure 4.27 | **Final Setup and Results of the VLookup Function**

A2 =VLOOKUP(B2,'Product Data'!$A$2:$E$6,3,FALSE)

	A	B	C	D	E
1	Product Description	Product Code	Sales Units	Inventory Units	
2	Hats	89632	500	1,200	
3	Jackets	55412	1,200	2,500	
4	Sweaters	67425	250	850	
5	Coffee Mugs	55879	850	2,300	
6	T-Shirts	22415	1,470	4,000	
7					

An absolute reference is placed on this range defining the table_array argument.

The VLookup function displays the product descriptions relating to all the product codes in column B.

COMMON MISTAKES | VLookup

The following mistakes are often made when using the **VLookup** function:

1. After defining the range for the **table_array** argument, immediately type a comma. People often click the original worksheet tab before typing a comma after defining the range for the **table_array** argument. This will distort the **table_array** argument and prevent the function from working.
2. Before pasting the **VLookup** function to other cells, do not forget to add an absolute reference on the table array range. The **#N/A** error codes in the worksheet shown in Figure 4.28 happened because the table array range was added without an absolute reference.

Figure 4.28 | **#N/A Errors After Pasting the VLookup Function**

K15

	A	B	C	D
1	Product Description	Product Code	Sales Units	Inventory Units
2	Hats	89632	500	1,200
3	Jackets	55412	1,200	2,500
4	#N/A	67425	250	850
5	#N/A	55879	850	2,300
6	T-Shirts	22415	1,470	4,000

3. When defining the column index number **(col_index_num)**, count the first column in table array range as 1. You will get an output that is one column to the left of what is intended if you forget to count the first column.

Quick Reference

VLookup

1. Activate the cell where the output should appear.
2. Type an equal sign, the function name VLookup, and an open parenthesis.
3. Define the following arguments:
   a. **lookup_value**: Cell location that contains the value to be searched and matched in a second worksheet.
   b. **table_array**: Range in a second worksheet or workbook that contains both the lookup value and data for the output of the function (first column in the range *must* contain the lookup value).
   c. **col_index_num**: Number of columns in the table array range counting from left to right that contains data for the output of the function (count the first column as 1).
   d. **range_lookup**: Type the word False to find an exact match to the lookup value. This argument will assume True and look for an approximate match for the lookup value if this argument is not defined.
4. Type a closing parenthesis and press the **Enter** key.
5. Use an absolute reference ($) on the range used to define the **table_array** argument if pasting the function to other cells.

HLookup Function

The previous section demonstrated how you use the **VLookup** function to search for a lookup value vertically down the first column of a range of cells. However, your data might be organized such that you have to look across a row instead of down a column to search for a lookup value. In these situations you will need to use an ***HLookup*** function. The **HLookup** function is identical to the **VLookup** function; however, it looks horizontally across the first row of a range of cells to find a lookup value instead of vertically down a column. For example, Figure 4.29 contains a workbook that a strategic planning manager might use to compare financial statistics between his company and other competitors in the industry. There are two worksheets in this workbook: Comparison and Competitor Data. The Competitor Data worksheet contains the financial statistics that need to be displayed in column C of the Comparison worksheet. However, the competitor names, as shown in cell C2 in the Comparison worksheet, are listed across row 2 in the Competitor Data worksheet. Therefore, the **HLookup** function would be needed to display the competitor data in Column C of the Comparison worksheet.

Figure 4.29 | **Data for Competitor Analysis**

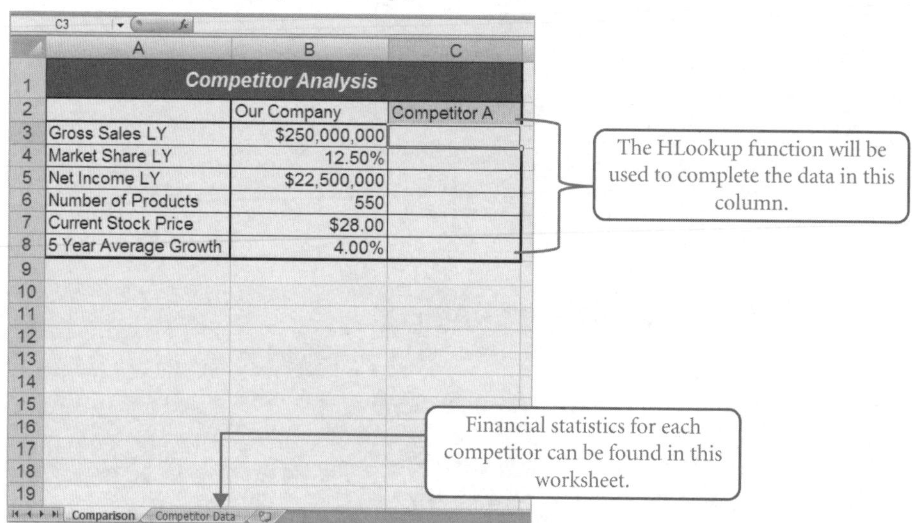

Figure 4.30 shows the two worksheets from Figure 4.29 side by side. Notice that the competitor names are listed across row 2, and the financial statistics relating to each competitor are listed in the column below each competitor's name. The **HLookup** function will be used to look for the competitor name typed into cell C2 of the Comparison worksheet in row 2 of the Competitor Data worksheet. When a match is found, the function will show the relevant financial statistic in the Comparison worksheet.

Figure 4.30 | **Comparison and Competitor Data Worksheets**

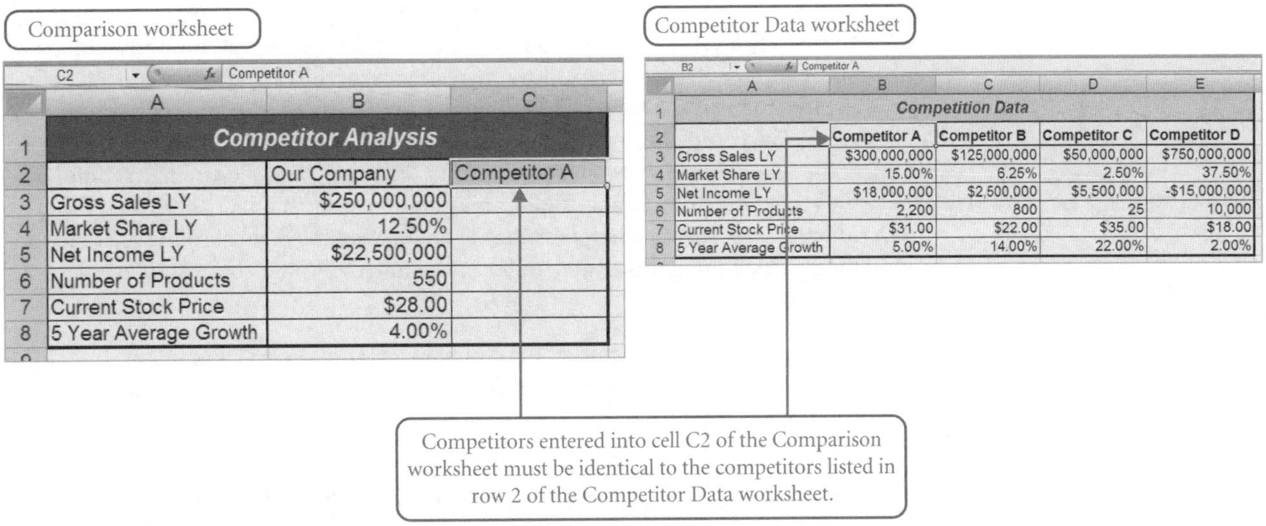

Comparison worksheet

C2 | Competitor A

	A	B	C
1	Competitor Analysis		
2		Our Company	Competitor A
3	Gross Sales LY	$250,000,000	
4	Market Share LY	12.50%	
5	Net Income LY	$22,500,000	
6	Number of Products	550	
7	Current Stock Price	$28.00	
8	5 Year Average Growth	4.00%	

Competitor Data worksheet

B2 | Competitor A

	A	B	C	D	E
1	Competition Data				
2		Competitor A	Competitor B	Competitor C	Competitor D
3	Gross Sales LY	$300,000,000	$125,000,000	$50,000,000	$750,000,000
4	Market Share LY	15.00%	6.25%	2.50%	37.50%
5	Net Income LY	$18,000,000	$2,500,000	$5,500,000	-$15,000,000
6	Number of Products	2,200	800	25	10,000
7	Current Stock Price	$31.00	$22.00	$35.00	$18.00
8	5 Year Average Growth	5.00%	14.00%	22.00%	2.00%

Competitors entered into cell C2 of the Comparison worksheet must be identical to the competitors listed in row 2 of the Competitor Data worksheet.

The arguments of the **HLookup** function are identical to the **VLookup** function with the exception of the **col_index_num** argument. Since the **HLookup** function looks horizontally across a row, it uses a row index number to count the number of rows from top to bottom in the range used to define the **table_array** argument. Similar to the column index number, the first row in the table array range must be counted as 1.

As mentioned, the **HLookup** function will be used to show the competitor information in column C of Figure 4.30. Here is how you accomplish this:

- Activate cell C3 in the Comparison worksheet. The **HLookup** function will be used to show the Gross Sales LY for the competitor typed into cell C2.
- Type an equal sign, the function name HLOOKUP, and an open parenthesis.
- Type cell C2 to define the **lookup_value** argument. The function will look for the competitor name that is typed into cell C2 of the Comparison worksheet.
- Type a comma.
- Click the Competitor Data worksheet tab.
- Highlight the range B2:B8 on the Competitor Data worksheet to define the **table_array** argument. When you are defining the **table_array** argument for the **HLookup** function, the first *row* in this range must contain the values used to define the **lookup_value** argument. This is similar to the **VLookup** function where the first *column* of the table array must contain the lookup values. The **HLookup** function will search horizontally (hence the name **HLookup**) across the first row in the range used to define the **table_array** range to find the lookup value.
- Type a comma.
- Type the number 2 to define the **row_index_num** argument. As previously mentioned, the purpose of this **HLookup** function is to show the Gross Sales LY for the competitor name typed into cell C2 of the Comparison worksheet. In the Competitor Data worksheet, the Gross Sales LY is in the second row of the range that was used to define the **table_array** argument (B2:E8). Remember to count the first row in the table array range as 1.
- Type a comma.
- Type the word False (no quotation marks) to define the **[range_lookup]** argument. For this example, you must search for an exact match to the lookup value. The rules applying to the **range_lookup** argument for the **HLookup** function are identical to the **VLookup** function. However, if you are using the **True** option for this function, the range used to define the **table_array** argument must be sorted in ascending order from left to right based on the values in the first row of the range.

- Type a closing parenthesis and press the **Enter** key to complete the function. This will bring you back to the Comparison worksheet.
- Double click cell C3 in the Comparison worksheet, which contains the complete **HLookup** function. Place an absolute reference on the cell reference used to define the **lookup_value** argument and the range used to define the **table_array** argument. The competitor name will always be entered into cell C2; therefore, this reference cannot change when the function is pasted to a new location. In addition, the range used to define the **table_array** argument must not change when the function is pasted to a new location. Therefore, you place an absolute reference on the range defining this argument. Press the **Enter** key after completing these adjustments.

Figure 4.31 shows the setup of the completed **HLookup** function in the Comparison worksheet. Notice that absolute references are used in the **lookup_value** and **table_array** arguments.

Figure 4.31 | **Setup for the HLookup Function in the Comparison Worksheet**

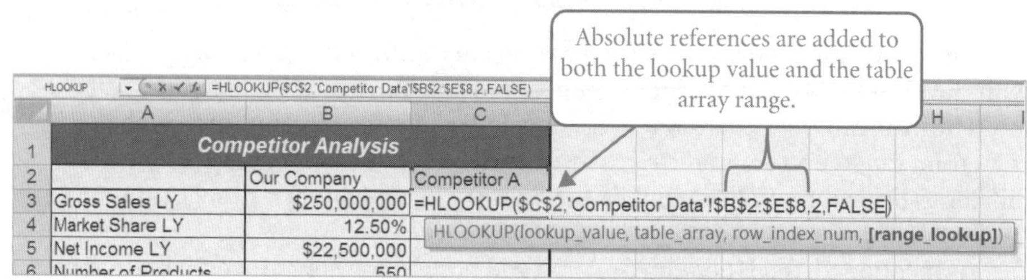

Figure 4.32 shows the output of the **HLookup** function. The function found Competitor A in the first row of the table array range in the Competitor Data worksheet, moved down two rows (counting the first row as 1), and displayed the value in this cell location. Following this path, you will find that two rows down from Competitor A (cell B2) in the Competitor Data worksheet is the number $300,000,000. Therefore, this number becomes the output of the function in cell C3 of the Comparison worksheet.

Figure 4.32 | **Results of the HLookup Function in the Comparison Worksheet**

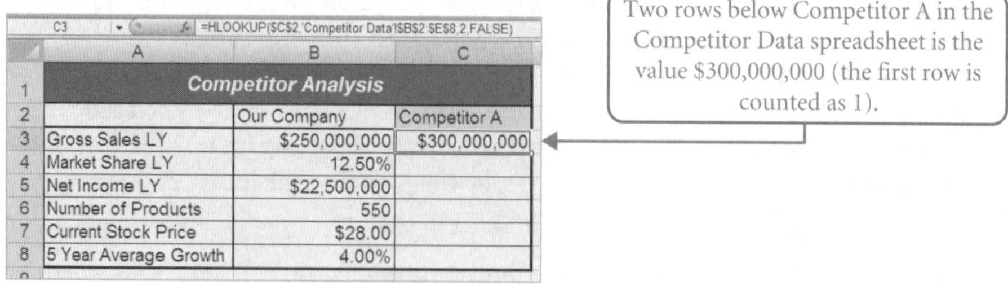

To complete the rest of the cell locations in column C of the Comparison spreadsheet, you cannot copy and paste the **HLookup** function without making additional adjustments. The reason is that each statistic in column C will require a different row index number. For example, cell location C5 in the Comparison worksheet is the Net Income LY statistic. This is four rows down from the first row in the table array range in the Competitor Data worksheet. The following points explain how to paste and adjust the **HLookup** function to complete cells C4 through C8 in Figure 4.32.

- Copy cell C3 in the Comparison worksheet, which contains the completed **HLookup** function.

- Highlight the range C4:C8 and select the **Formulas paste** option from the **Paste** icon.
- Double click cell C4, change the **row_index_num** to 3, and press the **Enter** key.
- Double click cell C5, change the **row_index_num** to 4, and press the **Enter** key.
- Double click cell C6, change the **row_index_num** to 5, and press the **Enter** key.
- Double click cell C7, change the **row_index_num** to 6, and press the **Enter** key.
- Double click cell C8, change the **row_index_num** to 7, and press the **Enter** key.

When the spreadsheet is complete, you can change the competitor name in cell C2 of the Comparison worksheet, and the data for column C will automatically change to reflect the financial statistics of the new competitor. Figure 4.33 shows a completed spreadsheet with the competitor changed to Competitor D.

Figure 4.33 | **Final Outputs of the HLookup Function**

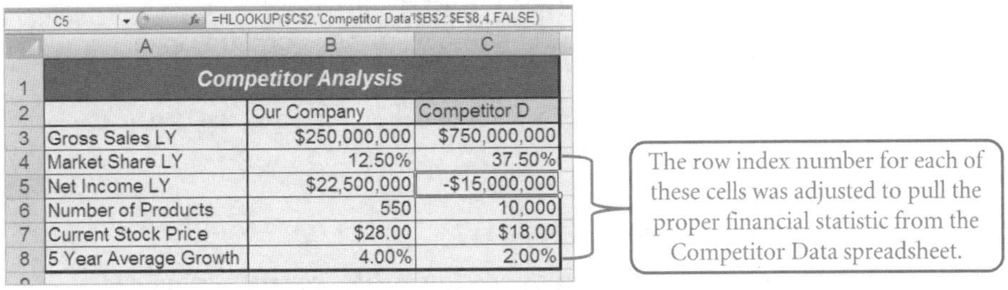

C5 =HLOOKUP($C$2,'Competitor Data'!$B$2:$E$8,4,FALSE)

	A	B	C
1	Competitor Analysis		
2		Our Company	Competitor D
3	Gross Sales LY	$250,000,000	$750,000,000
4	Market Share LY	12.50%	37.50%
5	Net Income LY	$22,500,000	-$15,000,000
6	Number of Products	550	10,000
7	Current Stock Price	$28.00	$18.00
8	5 Year Average Growth	4.00%	2.00%

The row index number for each of these cells was adjusted to pull the proper financial statistic from the Competitor Data spreadsheet.

COMMON MISTAKES | Error Codes for HLookup and VLookup

The following two error codes are common when using either the **VLookup** or **HLookup** functions.

#N/A: The Not Available error signifies that the function cannot find the lookup value in the table array range. Typical reasons this error occurs include

1. The first column of the table array range does not contain the lookup value. Check the range in the **table_array** argument and make sure the first column of the range contains the lookup value.
2. The lookup value does not exist at all in the second spreadsheet. Check the spreadsheet you are using for the table array range and make sure the lookup value is there.
3. The table array range or the lookup value was changed when the function was pasted to a new cell location. If you are copying and pasting the function, check both the **lookup_value** and **table_array** arguments. In most cases, you will need to use an absolute reference for these arguments to prevent cell references from changing when the function is pasted to a new location.

#REF!: The Reference error occurs because either the column index number or row index number is too high given the range that was used to define the **table_array** argument. For example, if the table array range contains four rows for an **HLookup** function and the row index number is 8, the Reference error will appear.

Quick Reference

HLookup

1. Activate the cell where output should appear.
2. Type an equal sign, the function name HLookup, and an open parenthesis.
3. Define the following arguments:
   a. **lookup_value**: Cell location that contains the value to be searched in a second worksheet.
   b. **table_array**: Range in a second worksheet or workbook that contains both the lookup value and data for the output of the function (the first row in this range *must* contain the lookup value).
   c. **row_index_num**: Number of rows in the table array range counting from top to bottom that contains data for the output of the function (count the first row as 1).
   d. **range_lookup**: Type the word False to find the exact match to the lookup value. This argument will assume True and look for an approximate match for the lookup value if this argument is not defined.
4. Type a closing parenthesis and press the **Enter** key.
5. Use an absolute reference ($) on the range of the table array segment if copying and pasting the function to other cells. You may also need an absolute reference on the lookup value depending on your project.
6. Check the row index number after pasting to see if any adjustments are necessary.

VIDEO WORKSHOP

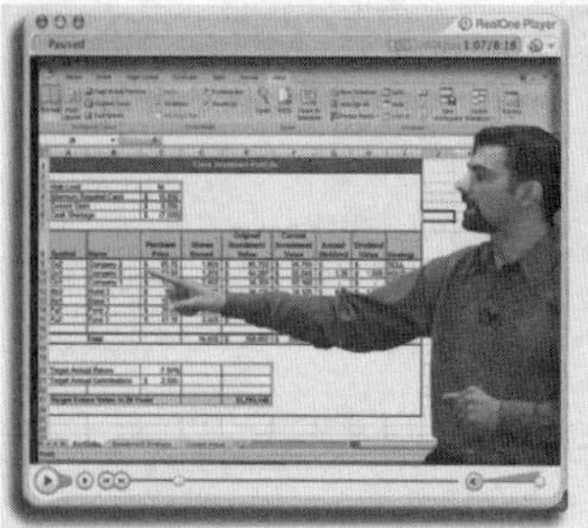

>> The VLookup Function

The purpose of this workshop is to demonstrate the use of the **VLookup** function. We will be reviewing the same example that was presented earlier in this section. I will be demonstrating the tasks in this workshop in the video named **VLookup Function**. Watch this video after completing the tasks in this workshop. Open the file named ib_e04_vlookuppractice before starting the following tasks:

1. Defining the VLookup Arguments (Video: VLookup Function)

a. Activate cell A2 on the Sales Data worksheet.
b. Type an equal sign, the function name `VLOOKUP`, and an open parenthesis.
c. Type `B2` or click on cell location B2 to define the **lookup_value** argument.
d. Type a comma.
e. Click the **Product Data** worksheet tab.
f. Highlight the range A2:E6 to define the **table_array** argument.
g. Type a comma.
h. Counting column A as number 1, count the number of columns to go from column A to column C. Column C should be the third column, which is the Product Description column.
i. Type the number `3` to define the **col_index_num** argument.
j. Type a comma.
k. Type the word `False` with no quotation marks.
l. Type a closing parenthesis and press the **Enter** key.

2. Absolute Reference (Video: VLookup Function)

a. Double click cell A2 on the Sales Data worksheet.
b. Add an absolute reference to the range A2:E6 in the **table_array** argument.
c. Press the **Enter** key.

3. Copy and Paste Formulas (Video: VLookup Function)

a. Copy cell A2 on the Sales Data worksheet.
b. Highlight the range A3:A6.
c. Click the **Home** tab of the Ribbon.
d. Click the down arrow on the **Paste** icon.
e. Select the **Formulas** option.
f. Save and close your file.

>> The HLookup Function

VIDEO WORKSHOP

The purpose of this workshop is to demonstrate the use of the **HLookup** function. We will be reviewing the same example that was presented earlier in this section. I will be demonstrating the tasks in this workshop in the video named **HLookup Function**. Watch this video after completing the tasks in this workshop. Open the file named ib_e04_hlookuppractice before starting the following tasks:

1. **Defining the HLookup Arguments (Video: HLookup Function)**
   a. Activate cell C3 on the Comparison worksheet.
   b. Type an equal sign, the function name **HLOOKUP**, and an open parenthesis.
   c. Type `C2` or click cell location C2 to define the **lookup_value** argument.
   d. Type a comma.
   e. Click the **Competitor Data** worksheet tab.
   f. Highlight the range B2:E8 to define the **table_array** argument.
   g. Type a comma.
   h. Counting row 2 as number 1, count the number of rows to go from row 2 to row 3. This should be the second row, which is Gross Sales LY.
   i. Type the number `2` to define the **row_index_num** argument.
   j. Type a comma.
   k. Type the word `False` with no quotation marks.
   l. Type a closing parenthesis and press the **Enter** key.

2. **Absolute Reference (Video: HLookup Function)**
   a. Double click cell C3 on the Comparison worksheet.
   b. Add an absolute reference to cell location C2 in the **lookup_value** argument. Then add an absolute reference to the range B2:E8 in the **table_array** argument.
   c. Press the **Enter** key.

3. **Copy and Paste Formulas (Video: HLookup Function)**
   a. Copy cell C3 on the Comparison worksheet.
   b. Highlight the range C4:C8.
   c. Click the **Home** tab of the Ribbon.
   d. Click the down arrow on the **Paste** icon.
   e. Select the **Formulas** option.

4. **Editing the Row Index Numbers (Video: HLookup Function)**
   a. Double click cell C4 on the Comparison worksheet.
   b. Change the row index number from 2 to `3` and press the **Enter** key.
   c. Repeat step **b** for each cell in the range C5:C8 increasing the row index number from 2 to `4`, then 2 to `5`, then 2 to `6`, and 2 to `7` for the last cell.

5. **Evaluate the Competition (Video: HLookup Function)**
   a. Change the competitor in cell C2 on the Comparison worksheet to read `Competitor D`.
   b. Change the competitor again to `Competitor B`.
   c. Save and close your file.

EXERCISE

Why Do I Need This?

>>Personal Investment Strategies

A professional financial planner will develop investment strategies for people based on their risk preference. That is, some people prefer to make low risk investments, whereas others will take on higher risk strategies with the hopes of higher returns. The lookup functions covered in this chapter can provide significant value to a financial planner who is managing investments for several clients.

Exercise

The purpose of this exercise is to develop a spreadsheet for a financial planner who is deciding how to invest money for several clients. Open the file named ib_e04_investmentstrategies before starting this exercise.

1. Use a **VLookup** function in cell C3 of the Investment Plan worksheet to find the Risk Preference of the customer showing in cell C2. You can find the data in the Customers worksheet. Define the arguments of the function as follows:
   a. **lookup_value**: Cell location C2. The function will look for the customer name that is typed into this cell in the Customers worksheet.
   b. **table_array**: The range A2:C11 in the Customers worksheet. Once the **lookup_value** argument is defined, you can click the Customers worksheet tab and highlight this range.
   c. **col_index_num**: The number 3. The reason is that the Risk Preference column is the third column in the range defined for the **table_array** argument.
   d. **range_lookup**: The word `False`.
2. Use a **VLookup** function in cell C4 of the Investment Plan worksheet to find the number of dollars being invested for the customer name showing in cell C2. Each argument will be defined identically to the **VLookup** function that was created in number 1. However, the **col_index_num** argument should be 2 instead of 3.
3. Use the **HLookup** function in cell C7 of the Investment Plan worksheet to calculate the customer's proposed investment for Bonds. Use the function to find the investment percentage for Bonds in the Risk Levels worksheet based on the customer's risk preference showing in cell C3 on the Investment Plan worksheet. The arguments of this function should be defined as follows:
   a. **lookup_value**: Cell location C3. The function will look for the risk preference that appears in cell C3 of the Investment Plan worksheet in the Risk Levels worksheet.
   b. **table_array**: The range B2:D5 in the Risk Levels worksheet. Once the **lookup_value** argument is defined, you can click the Risk Levels worksheet and then highlight this range.

c. **row_index_num**: The number 2. The reason is that the percentage for the Bonds category is in the second row of the range defined for the **table_array** argument.

d. **range_lookup**: The word `False`.

4. Edit the **HLookup** function you created in step 3 by typing an asterisk after the function and cell location C4. This will multiply the Dollars Investing in cell C4 of the Investment Plan worksheet by the percentage for Bonds in the Risk Levels worksheet.

5. Use the **HLookup** function in cell D8 of the Investment Plan worksheet to calculate the customer's investment plan for Mutual Funds. This function will be identical to the function created in steps 3 and 4. However, the row index number should be 3 instead of 2.

6. Use the **HLookup** function in cell D9 of the Investment Plan worksheet to calculate the customer's investment plan for Stocks. This function will be identical to the function created in steps 3 and 4. However, the row index number should be 4 instead of 2.

7. Change the customer name in cell C2 of the Investment Plan worksheet to Customer 2. Is this customer investing more money or less money compared to Customer 1?

8. How much money is Customer 8 planning to invest in Stocks?

9. On the Risk Levels worksheet, change the Moderate investment strategy to 30% Bonds, 30% Mutual Funds, and 40% Stocks.

10. How did the change you made to the Risk Levels worksheet in number 9 change the investment strategy for Customer 8?

11. Save and close your file.

>> What's Wrong with This Spreadsheet?

PROBLEM & EXERCISE

Problem

In one of your business classes, you are working on a project that involves researching historical data for Company D. You must compare the current stock price of Company D with other firms in the industry. One of your teammates volunteers to compile everyone's research and create a spreadsheet. He explains that by simply typing the year into a cell, you will be able to use the spreadsheet to pull the historical data for Company D. In addition, he explains that by typing a ticker symbol into another cell, you can compare Company D's current stock price with other firms in the industry. Impressed with his plan, the team agrees to let him build the spreadsheet to complete the analysis required for the project.

Exercise

The spreadsheet your teammate created is named ib_e04_groupproject. Look at the data in this spreadsheet. Would you be comfortable submitting this file to your professor for your team grade? Consider the following points.

1. Look at the data on the Company D Analysis worksheet. Does the data appear to make sense?

2. Test-drive the spreadsheet. Your teammate explained that the Year in cell C3 and the Stock Symbol in cell C9 can be changed. In addition, you will see the values that are available to enter on the right of these cell locations. When you change the Year and Stock Symbol, does the data still make sense?

3. What method is your teammate using to show the data in cells C4:C6 and C10:C11? Do these methods appear to be entered correctly?

4. How many worksheets does this workbook contain? What will you need to do to check the accuracy of the data appearing in the Company D Analysis worksheet?

What's wrong with this spreadsheet? Write a short answer to each of the questions listed here. Then fix any errors you discover in the Company D Analysis worksheet.

Excel in **Practice** | Anecdote

Solution from page 132

Excel's lookup functions provided a much better solution for us compared to typing the state and city names manually into the spreadsheet. The first step was to find all ZIP codes in the United States with city names and states. After some searching on the Internet, we found a way to download over 20,000 ZIP codes with state and town names included. Once we had this data in a separate worksheet, our problem was essentially solved. A few seconds later we had the states and city names in our worksheet for every ZIP code.

Assignment

1. Open the file named ib_e04_newstorestrategy. This is a small subset of data similar to what was described in the anecdote.
2. Use this data to create a spreadsheet that will evaluate potential locations for new stores. You will need to add formulas, functions, and formats.
3. Your spreadsheet should include the following:
    a. Add the city and state for each ZIP code listed on the Potential Locations worksheet. You can find a master list of several ZIP codes, states, and cities on the Zip Codes worksheet.
    b. Add a column that shows if a ZIP code has a high population of children and a low number of competitors. High child population is anything greater than or equal to 30% of children population over total population. Low competitors is if a ZIP code has less than or equal to two competitors.
    c. Add a column that shows what ZIP codes would qualify as being potential locations for a new store. A potential location is any ZIP code that has high children and low competition, or an average household income greater than $50,000. However, a ZIP code cannot be considered for a new store if it has more than five competitors.
4. Show ZIP codes that qualify as potential locations for new stores on a separate worksheet. Assume this will be presented to the president of the company. Create a way to summarize this data on another worksheet so you can start off the presentation with highlights of your analysis.

Questions for Discussion

1. Why is it important to know alternative ways of calculating and manipulating data?
2. The anecdote mentioned that ZIP codes were downloaded from the Internet. What other sources are available on the Internet that could be used for the project described in the anecdote (i.e., population statistics, household income, number of household)?

Review Questions

The following questions are related to the concepts addressed in this chapter. There are three types of questions: Short Answer, True or False, and Fill in the Blank. If your answer to a True or False question is False, write a short explanation as to why you think the statement is not true.

1. Words or text data must be put in _______ when defining the output of the _______ function as well as the logical tests of the _______ and _______ functions.
2. Explain why commas should not be used when entering numbers for the logical test argument of the **IF** function.
3. When you are using text data for either the **value_if_true** or **value_if_false** arguments of the **IF** function, the comma separating the arguments goes _______ the quotation marks.
4. What are the differences and similarities between financial functions and logical functions?
5. True or False: A spreadsheet cannot be sorted based on the output of an **IF** function.
6. True or False: The sequence of the logical tests in a nested **IF** function does not matter because the function will always evaluate all logical tests.
7. True or False: When you are creating a nested **IF** function, you can add logical tests without typing the function name IF and an open parenthesis.
8. Explain what you can do to make sure the logical tests of a nested **IF** function are in the appropriate sequence.
9. True or False: A nested **IF** function will not work if the logical tests are in the wrong sequence. An error code will appear telling you that something is wrong with the function.
10. What are the arguments of the **AND** function?
11. Briefly explain how the **AND** function works.
12. True or False: You do not need to use quotation marks when using text data with either an **OR** or **AND** function.
13. If only one of five logical tests in an **OR** function is False, the function will display the word __________.
14. True or False: This function will test whether D7 is equal to the value in either C7, A7, or H7: =OR(D7 = C7,A7,H7).
15. What would you do to try to fix an #N/A error when using either the **VLookup** or **HLookup** functions?
16. What does the #REF! error mean?
17. When you are defining the column index number of the **VLookup** function, it is important to always count the first column as number _______.
18. Before pasting either a **VLookup** or an **HLookup** function, always check to see whether _______ are needed.

19. The range of cells used to define the table array of either a **VLookup** or an **HLookup** function must contain both the _______ and the _______ that is needed for the output.

20. True or False: You cannot use a **VLookup** function or an **HLookup** function to calculate data.

21. True or False: Lookup functions cannot be combined with logical functions.

22. True or False: When defining the **table_array** argument of either the **VLookup** or **HLookup** functions, you can just click another worksheet tab and highlight the range of cells needed.

23. True or False: Excel will always assume you need to find an exact match for the lookup value when using either a **VLookup** or an **HLookup** function.

24. What is the Range lookup argument used for in the either the **VLookup** or **HLookup** functions?

Skills Exam

The following exam is designed to test your ability to recognize and execute the Excel skills presented in this chapter. Read each question carefully and answer the questions in the order they are listed. You should be able to complete this exam in 60 minutes or less.

1. Open the ib_e04_skillsexam file. All of the tasks listed in this exam should be executed in the Portfolio worksheet.
2. Use the **HLookup** function in cell C4 to display the minimum cash requirement. The function should look for the Risk Level code showing in cell C3 on the Portfolio worksheet in row 3 of the Investment Strategy worksheet. The minimum cash requirements are listed for each risk level in row 8.
3. Enter a formula in cell C6 that subtracts the minimum cash requirement in cell C4 from the current cash value in cell C5.
4. Use an **IF** function in cell A6 to determine if there is a shortage or surplus of cash. The function should display the message *Cash Surplus* if the value in cell C6 is greater than or equal to 0. Otherwise, the function should display the message *Cash Shortage.*
5. Enter a formula in cell E9 that calculates the value of the original investment. The formula should multiply the Shares Owned by the Purchase Price. Copy and paste this formula to cells E10:E15.
6. Use a **VLookup** function to calculate the Current Investment Value in cell F9. The function should look for the symbol in cell A9 of the Portfolio worksheet in column A of the Current Prices worksheet and determine what Current Price relates to that symbol. The result of the **VLookup** function should be multiplied by the Shares Owned in cell D9.
7. Copy the function in cell F9 and paste it into cells F10:F15.
8. Use an **IF** function to calculate the Dividend Value in cell H9. The function should check to see if cell G9 is greater than 0. If it is, then multiply cell G9 by D9. Otherwise, display the number 0.
9. Determine the Strategy in cell I9 by entering a nested **IF** function. The function should display the following outputs based on the criteria listed.

   If the dividend in cell G9 is greater than 0 *and* the Current Investment in cell F9 is greater than or equal to the Original Investment in cell E9, display the word *HOLD.*

   If the Current Investment in cell F9 is less than the Original Investment in cell E9 *or* the Current Investment is less than the Original Investment multiplied by 1.035, then display the word *SELL.*

   Otherwise, display the word *HOLD.*
10. Copy the function in cell I9 and paste it to cells I10:I15.
11. Enter a **SUM** function in cell D17 to add the values in the range D9:D15.
12. Copy the **SUM** function in cell D17 and paste it to cells E17 and F17.
13. Use the **Future Value** function in cell E23 to calculate the Target value of the portfolio in 20 years. This function should use cell C20 as the rate of return, C21 as the target payments to be made every year for the next 20 years, and F17 as the one-time lump sum payment. The function should calculate payments being made at the beginning of the period. Correct any ### signs if they appear.
14. Use your judgment in adding any formatting features that will enhance the visual appearance and readability of the spreadsheet.
15. Save and close your file.

Challenge Questions

The following questions are designed to test your ability to apply the Excel skills you have learned to complete a business objective. Use your knowledge of Excel as well as your creativity to answer these questions. For most questions, there are several possible ways to complete the objective.

1. Open the spreadsheet named ib_e04_frequentshopper. Use a nested **IF** function to complete the Customer Reward column. The output and criteria of the function are listed below.

   - **Welcome & Thanks 30% Off:** This reward is given to customers who spent $0 last year and the number of years purchasing is less than one.
   - **Please Come Back 50% Off:** This reward is given to customers who have been purchasing from the store for more than one year but have not made a purchase in the past 12 months.
   - **Thanks for Being Loyal 25% Off:** This reward is given to customers who have been making purchases for more than two years or spent more than $1,000 last year.
   - **Customer Appreciation 10% Off:** This reward is given to any customer who does not meet the criteria of the other three rewards.

2. Open the spreadsheet named ib_e04_competitoranalysis. This is the same spreadsheet that was used for the video workshop. Edit this spreadsheet so that the **HLookup** function can be created in cell C3 and then copied and pasted to cells C4:C8. Your revised spreadsheet should have the same appearance as the original. Hint: Cell locations should be used for every argument of the function except for the range lookup.

3. Open the file named ib_e04_investmentstrategy. This file was used for the exercise in the **VLookup** function section. How would you modify this file such that the financial planner can override any of the proposed investments in cells C7:C9?

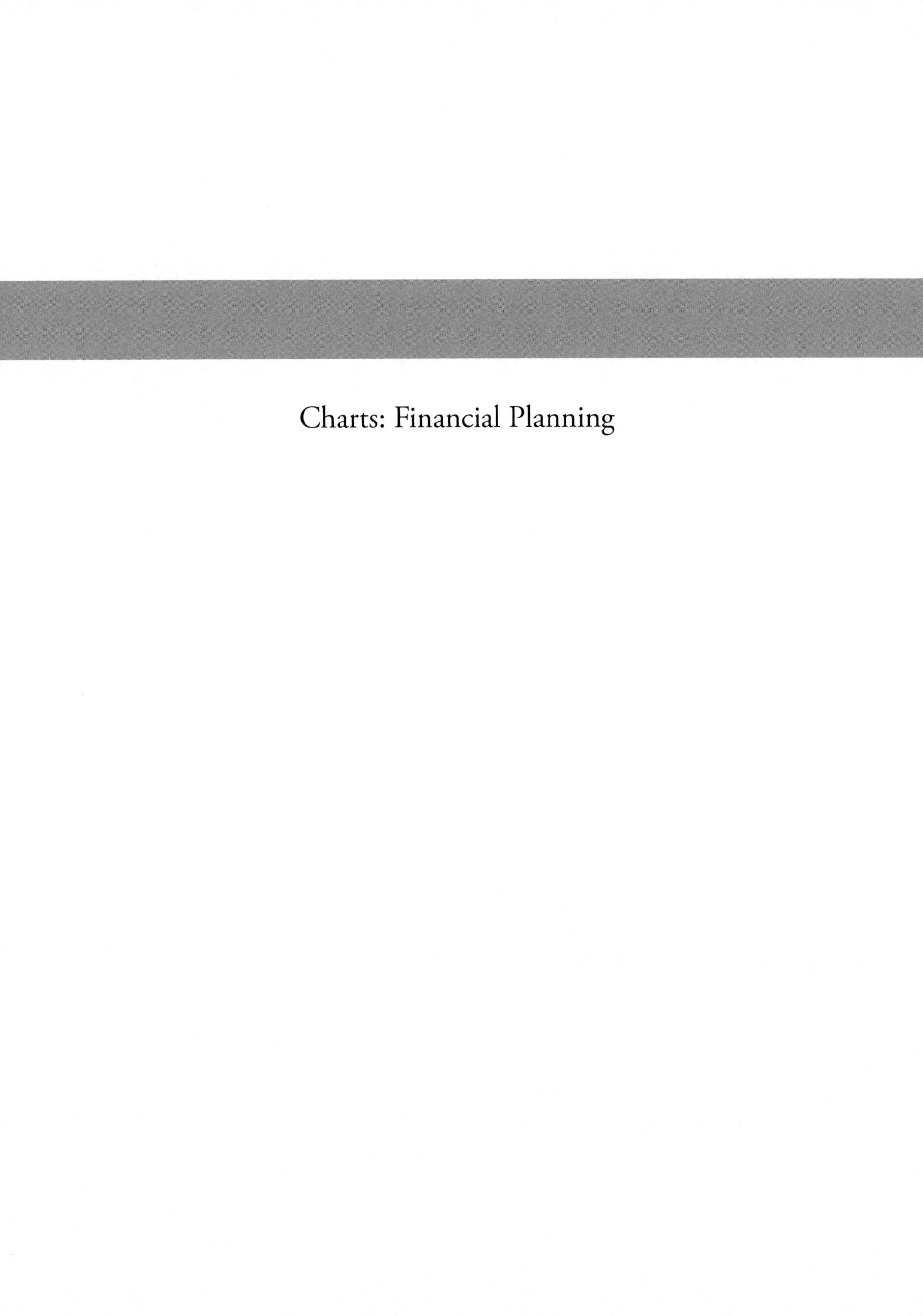

Charts: Financial Planning

Presenting Information with Charts

Chapter Goals

Presenting data and information is a common and often critical routine for most business managers. So far, this text has demonstrated how you can use Excel as a flexible analytical tool to accomplish a variety of business objectives. Although Excel worksheets are useful for tracking, reporting, calculating, and analyzing data, they are typically ineffective for presenting business data and information to an audience. As a result, most business managers rely on charts when preparing and delivering presentations. This chapter illustrates a variety of charts available in Excel and demonstrates how business managers use them to study and communicate key information and trends.

Excel | Skill Sets

Creating Charts

- Column Charts (Data Comparisons)
- Stacked Column Charts (Percent to Total Over Time)
- Line Charts (Trends Over Time)
- Pie Charts (Percent to Total)

Formatting Charts

- Titles and Legends
- Plot Area and Data Series
- X- and Y-Axes Labels
- Adding Annotations and Objects

Advanced Chart Options

- Defining the X- and Y-Axes Manually
- The Scatter Plot Chart
- Pasting Charts into PowerPoint and Word

Excel in **Practice** | Anecdote

My Role as a Consultant

You may *think* that, after you've completed hours of intense research and analysis related to a project, the hard work is over. However, in reality, how you present your findings is just as critical as the quality of the information you present. I learned this lesson quickly when I first began working as a consultant. My primary responsibility was to analyze the performance of a client's business and compare it with other companies within that industry. My results then served as a basis for developing recommendations on ways my clients could improve or grow their business. Although I had piles of written documents to support my findings, my main forum for sharing this information was in front of an audience of business owners or head managers at meetings called progress reviews. These people had busy schedules and little time. The pressure to deliver an accurate, appropriate, and efficient presentation was always an intense challenge.

>> **Continued on page 229**

Creating Charts

Skill Set

This section will illustrate one of two methods for creating charts in Excel. If you are working with data that is arranged in adjacent columns or rows, you can use Excel to automatically assign values to the X- and Y-axes of a chart. In these situations, you can simply highlight a range of cells before selecting the chart you wish to create. This section will use this method to illustrate four basic charts commonly used by business managers: column charts, stacked column charts, line charts, and pie charts.

Column Charts (Data Comparisons)

The ***column chart*** is the most common chart type used to present business data and is most useful when making comparisons. For example, it can compare the earnings of companies within an industry, sales projections for a new business, or the sales growth of product categories. The column chart can compare data at a specific point in time or show how this comparison changes over a period of time. Figure 5.1 shows four years' worth of data for a hypothetical car manufacturer. The example demonstrates the construction of a column chart that compares the sales for each automobile class in the year 2006. Then a second column chart will show how the sales for each auto class changes over a four-year period.

Figure 5.1 | **Automobile Sales Data**

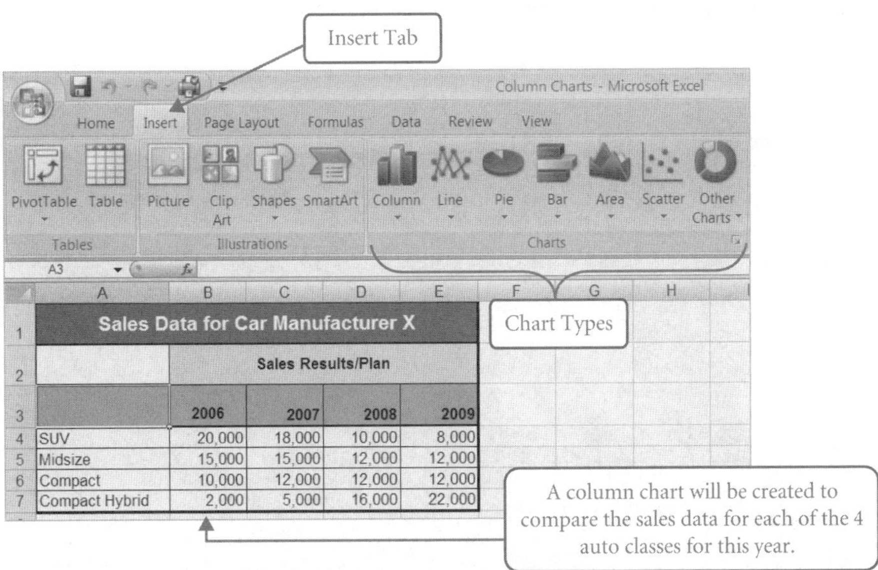

Creating a chart in Excel typically involves the following five steps:

- *Identify the data that will be used to define the X- and Y-axes values.* This section will demonstrate examples in which the data used to define the X- and Y-axes are in a contiguous range. Therefore, you can highlight a range of cells before selecting a chart type.
- *Select a chart type.* Figure 5.1 shows the chart types available in the **Insert** tab on the Ribbon.
- *Select a chart format.* For each chart type, Excel provides a variety of format options. These options establish the arrangement of data and visual appearance of a chart.
- *Specify a location.* When a chart is initially created, it will be embedded in the worksheet that is currently activated. You can then move the chart to another

worksheet or create a new worksheet that is dedicated for the chart, which is known as a ***chart sheet***.

- *Add or adjust the chart and axis titles.* A chart will not contain proper titles for the X- and Y-axes when it is initially created. You must add or adjust them after creating the chart.

This example creates a column chart to compare the 2006 sales by automobile class from Figure 5.1. The following points explain how to create this chart:

- Highlight the range A3:B7 on the worksheet shown in Figure 5.1. The data in this range will define the values for the X- and Y-axes of the chart.
- Click the **Insert** tab on the Ribbon.
- Select a chart type by clicking the **Column** icon on the Ribbon (see Figure 5.2).
- Select a chart format by clicking the **Clustered Column** option under the **2-D Column** heading (see Figure 5.2). After you select this option, the column chart will appear in the worksheet that is currently active.

Figure 5.2 shows the selections that were made to create a two-dimensional column chart. Excel provides a variety of format options for creating a column chart. Some options give the chart a three-dimensional appearance, and others change the shape of the columns to cylinders, cones, or pyramids. In addition, selecting an option called **All Chart Types** at the bottom of the format list opens the **Create Chart** dialog box, which provides access to every chart type and format available in Excel. Use this as an alternative method for selecting a chart type and format. After you select the chart format from either the list shown in Figure 5.2 or the dialog box shown in Figure 5.3, the chart will appear in the worksheet that is currently active.

Figure 5.2 | **Selecting a Chart Type and Format**

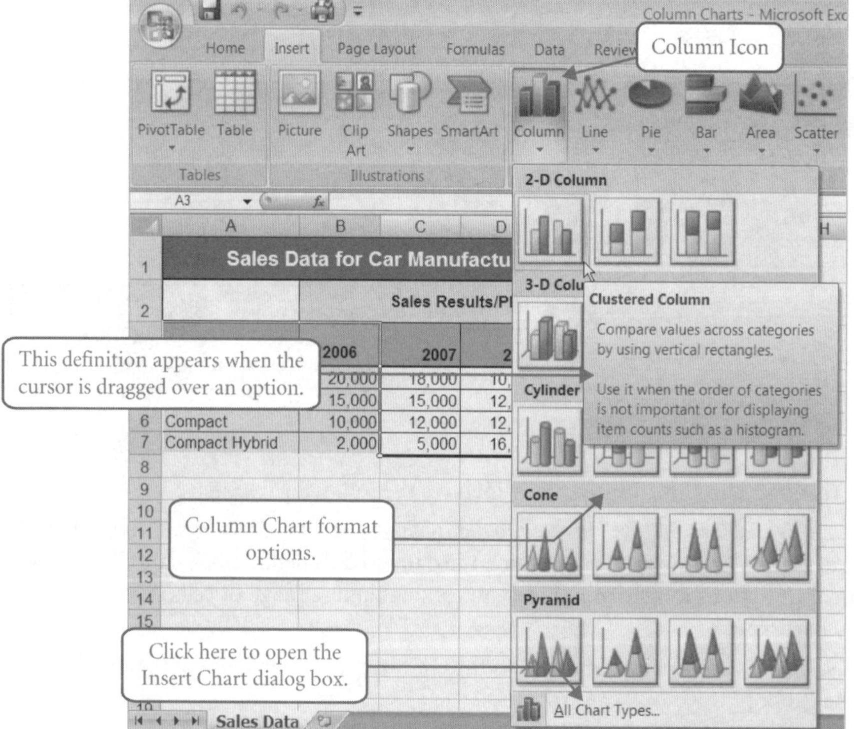

Figure 5.3 | **Create Chart Dialog Box**

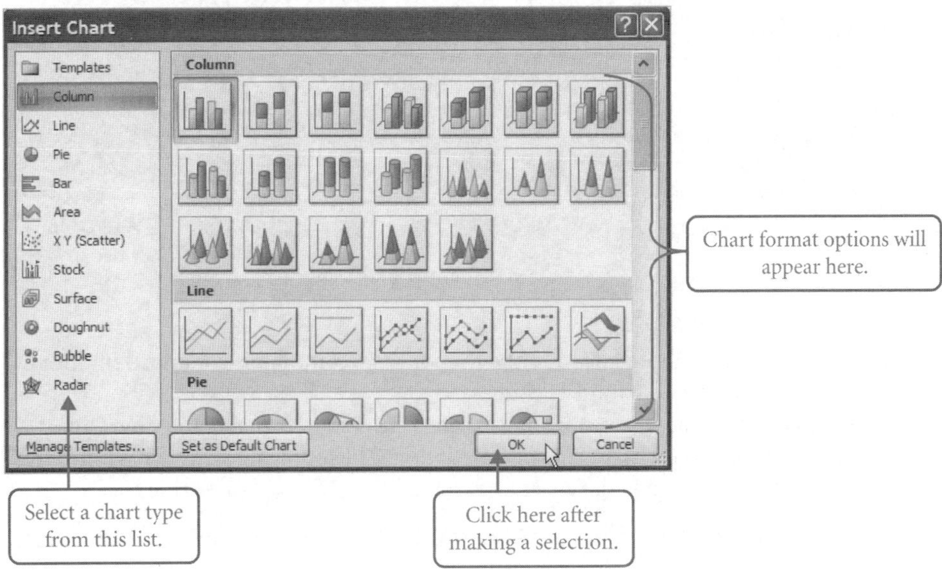

Figure 5.4 shows the column chart created to display the sales of each automobile class from Figure 5.1. This is known as an ***embedded chart*** because it appears within a worksheet that could also contain other data. After embedding the chart in a worksheet, you can move it on that worksheet by clicking and dragging the chart frame. You then can adjust the size of the chart by clicking and dragging on any of the dotted areas on the frame, which are also known as ***sizing handles***. Notice that a new set of tabs

Figure 5.4 | **Embedded Column Chart**

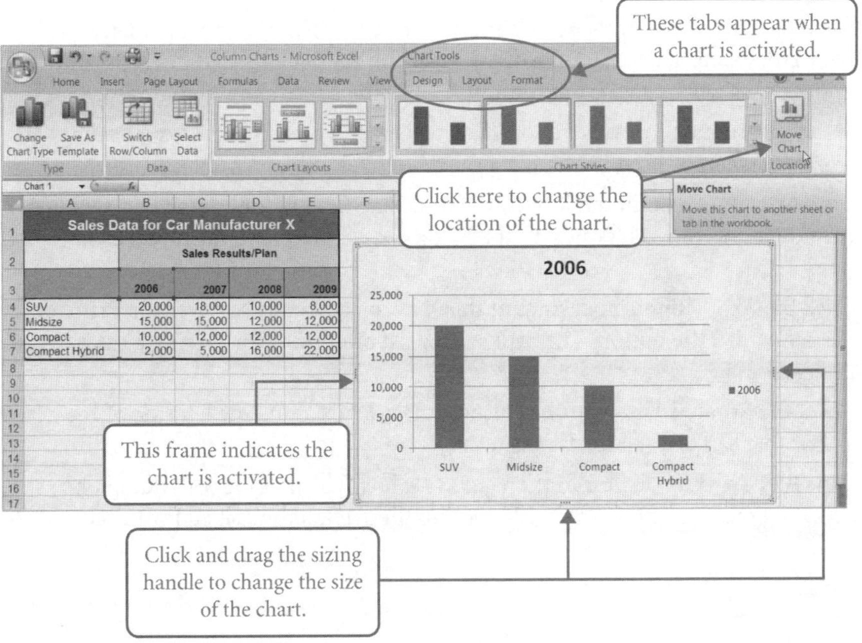

COMMON MISTAKES | Activating a Chart to Use Chart Tools

You must activate a chart to be able to see the **Chart Tools** tabs on the Ribbon. People often make the mistake of going back to the **Insert** tab on the Ribbon to find the **Chart Tools** commands. However, the commands in the **Insert** tab are used only to create a chart. The **Chart Tools** tabs will appear on the upper-right side of the Ribbon only when a chart is active. To activate a chart, click anywhere inside its border. A frame will appear around the chart when it is active, as shown in Figure 5.4.

called *Chart Tools* has been added to the Ribbon. The commands contained in this new set of tabs will be used to complete this chart.

After creating charts, you can adjust them as necessary by using the **Chart Tools** tabs that are added to the right side of the Ribbon. The following steps explain how to change the location, change the chart title, and add the X- and Y-axes titles:

- Activate the chart by clicking it. A chart is activated when a frame appears around its perimeter, as shown in Figure 5.4.
- Click the **Move Chart** icon in the **Design** tab of the **Chart Tools** set of tabs on the Ribbon (see Figure 5.4). This will open the **Move Chart** dialog box.
- Click the **New Sheet** option in the **Move Chart** dialog box and type the name **`Auto Sales 2006`** in the box next to this option (see Figure 5.5). Then click the **OK** button at the bottom of the dialog box. This will place the chart in a dedicated worksheet called a chart sheet with the tab name Auto Sales 2006.
- Activate the chart title at the top of the chart by clicking it once. Then click a second time at the beginning of the title to place the cursor in front of the first number of the year 2006 (see Figure 5.6). This will allow you to change or type a new chart title. For this example, the title is changed to Unit Sales by Auto Class 2006.
- Click the **Layout** tab in the **Chart Tools** set of tabs on the Ribbon and click the **Axis Titles** icon. Then place the cursor over the **Primary Horizontal Axis Title** option. This will open a set of options for placing a title along the X-axis.
- Select the **Title Below Axis** option. This will place a box at the bottom of the *X-axis* that can be used for typing a title.
- Type **`Auto Class`** in the X-axis title box. The method for adding or adjusting the title in this box is identical to the method described for adjusting the chart title.
- Click the **Axis Titles** icon again, but this time, place the cursor over the **Primary Vertical Axis Title** option. This will show a list of options for placing a title along the Y-axis.
- Select the **Rotated Title** option. This will place a box along the left side of the *Y-axis* that can be used for typing a title.
- Type **`Sales in Units`** in the Y-axis title box. The method for adding or adjusting the title in this box is identical to the method described for the chart title.

Figure 5.5 | **Move Chart Dialog Box**

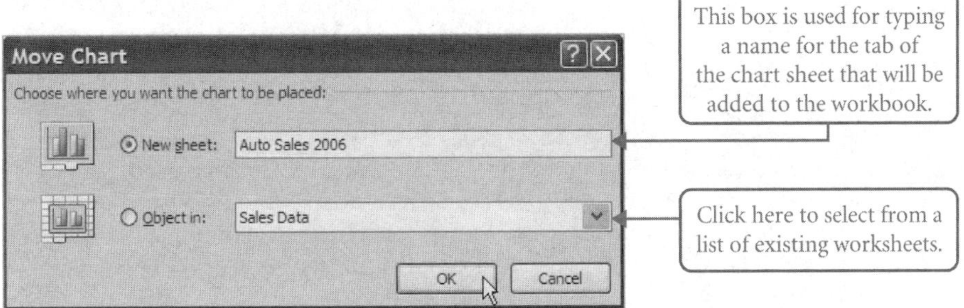

Figure 5.6 shows the adjustment that was made to the chart title. Notice the dots that appear on each corner of the chart title box. They indicate that the title box is activated. Also, notice that the cursor was placed in front of the year 2006 by clicking a second time. This method is also used for adjusting the X- and Y-axes titles.

Figure 5.6 | **Adjusting the Title of a Chart**

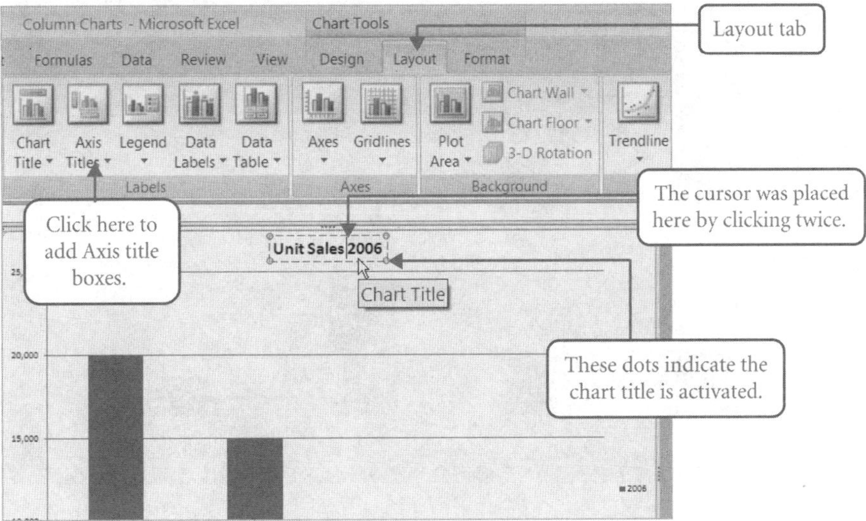

Figure 5.7 shows the completed column chart using the automobile sales data from Figure 5.1. The reader of this chart can immediately see that SUVs generated the most unit sales compared to the other three auto classes in the year 2006. Notice that the bars appear on the chart in order from tallest to shortest. The reason is that the values in column B of Figure 5.1 are sorted in descending order.

COMMON MISTAKES | Sorting Data for a Column Chart

The order of the bars on a column chart will be based on the order of the values on the worksheet used to create the chart. If you wish to see the bars on a column chart in height sequence (tallest to shortest or shortest to tallest) you must sort the range of cells that contain values defining the X- and Y-axes. In addition, *you can sort this data after the chart is created.* People often make the mistake of deleting the chart and re-creating it if the bars are not in a desirable sequence. However, the sequence of the bars will change if the data is sorted after the chart is created.

Figure 5.7 | **Final Column Chart for the Car Manufacturer Sales Data**

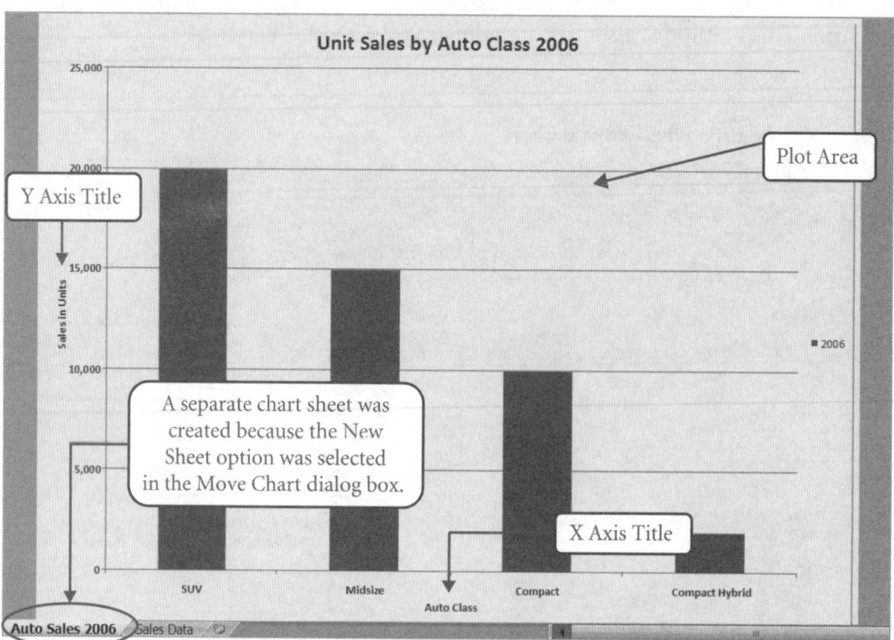

Figure 5.8 shows the second chart created using the worksheet shown in Figure 5.1. The purpose of this chart is to show how the sales comparison of each auto class changes over time. The method used to create this chart is identical to the first column chart shown in Figure 5.4. However, the range A3:E7 was highlighted before creating the chart. This range includes all the values for each auto class for the years 2006 through 2009. Notice how Excel automatically adjusted the X-axis and the ***chart legend***. Instead of placing each auto class on the X-axis (see Figure 5.7), Excel shows each year. As a result, each bar on the chart represents a different auto class. The legend shows which color corresponds to the appropriate auto class. In addition, an alternate chart style was selected from the **Design** tab on the Ribbon to enhance the colors of each bar in the chart. The next section covers some additional formatting features that can be used to enhance the appearance of a chart.

Figure 5.8 | **Second Column Chart Showing a Four-Year Sales Comparison**

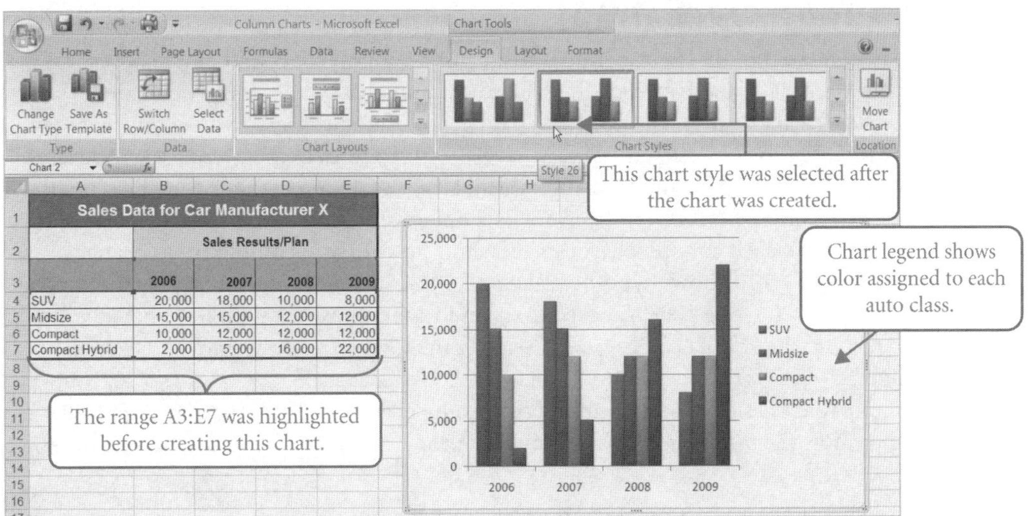

Figure 5.9 shows the final version of the second column chart. The method used to place this chart in a separate worksheet, or chart sheet, along with the addition of axis titles, is identical to that used for the first column chart shown in Figure 5.7. The chart title was added by selecting **Centered Overlay Title** from the **Chart Title** icon in the **Layout** tab of the **Chart Tools** section on the Ribbon. This places the title over the ***plot area*** of the chart. The reader of this chart can quickly see a shift in the projected sales of the car manufacturer's product line. In the year 2006, the SUV class dominates the other three auto classes in unit sales. However, by the year 2009 the Compact Hybrid is expected to become the dominant class in unit sales. The chart also shows a small decrease in the Midsize line of cars, while the Compact line of cars remains mostly consistent over the four-year period. A business manager can use this chart to visually show how the product sales of the company are expected to change over time.

Figure 5.9 | **Final Column Chart Showing Four-Year Automobile Sales Comparison**

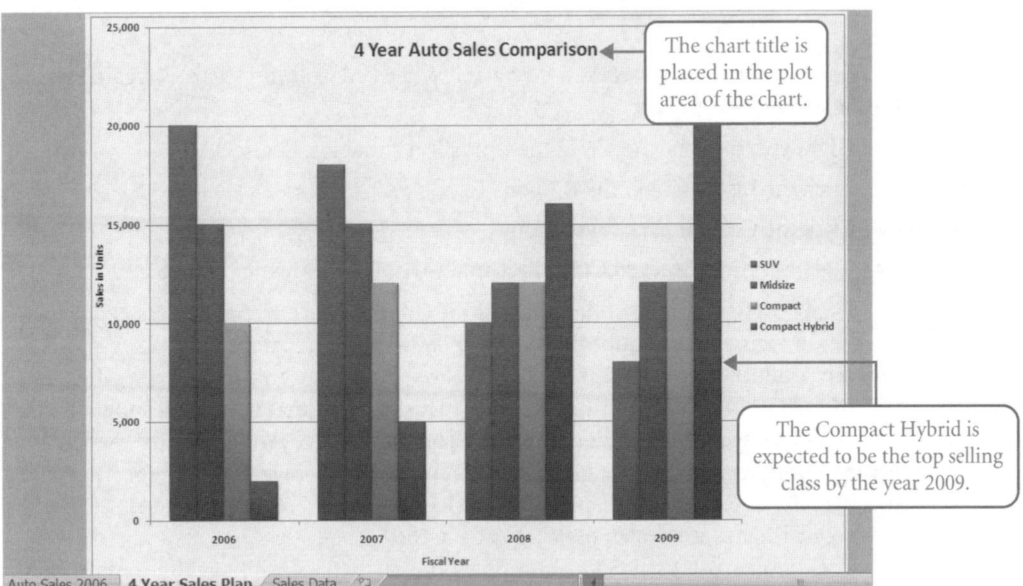

Stacked Column Charts (Percent to Total Over Time)

The *stacked column chart* is similar to a regular column chart in that it uses vertical bars to display data. However, the stacked column chart shows the proportion or percentage each category contributes to a total. For example, a stacked column chart can be used to show the percentage each division contributes to the overall sales of a large corporation, the percentage each product category represents to the total sales of an industry, or the market share percent by company for an industry. In each of these cases, the stacked column chart can also show how these percent to totals change over time. Figure 5.10 shows hypothetical data for the Sporting Goods Industry for the years 1990 and 2000. The 100% Stacked Column format option is selected to show the percentage each product category represents to the total sales of the Sporting Goods industry between the years 1990 and 2000. Looking at the data in Figure 5.10, you will notice that sales have increased for each product category. However, this chart will show how the *rate* of sales growth for each product category has changed over time.

Figure 5.10 | **Hypothetical Sales Data for the Sporting Goods Industry**

Select this option to create a 100% Stacked Column chart.

Sporting Goods Industry Sales (in Billions)		
	1990	2000
Equipment	$14.2	$26.3
Footwear	$10.9	$14.8
Clothing	$10.1	$11.2

Product categories for the Sporting Goods Industry

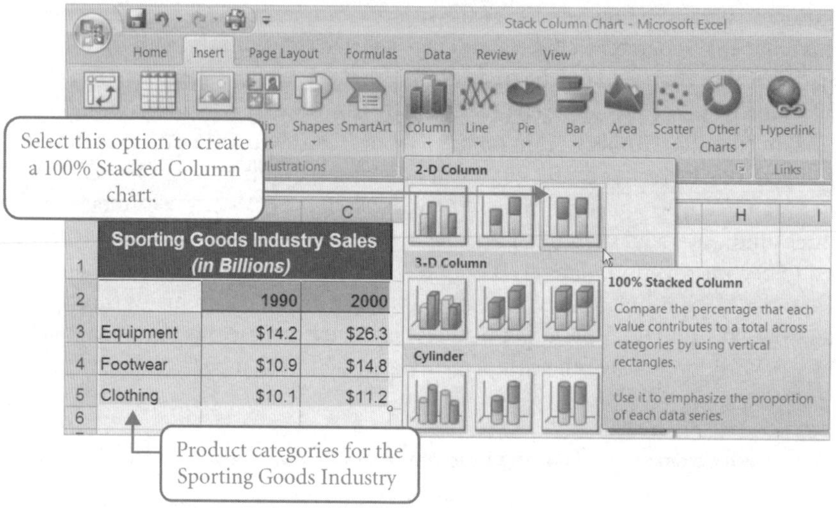

The following points explain how a 100% Stacked Column Chart is created using the data from Figure 5.10:

- Highlight the range A2:C5 in the worksheet shown in Figure 5.10.
- Click the **Insert** tab on the Ribbon.
- Click the **Column** chart type icon.
- Click the **100% Stacked Column** format option, as shown in Figure 5.10.

Figure 5.11 shows the initial result of the column chart, which was created using the data in Figure 5.10. Notice that each bar shows the percentage each year represents for each product category. However, the goal of this chart is to compare the sales percent of each product category for each year. This requires that the year is shown on the X-axis as opposed to the product category. Therefore, you need to click the **Switch Row/Column** icon in the **Design** tab of the **Chart Tools** area on the Ribbon. This places the years that are currently displayed in the legend on the X-axis and places the product categories that are shown on the X-axis in the legend.

The following steps explain additional options used to complete the column chart that was started in Figure 5.11:

- Click the **Layout** tab of the **Chart Tools** section on the Ribbon.
- Click the **Data Table** icon (see Figure 5.12) and select the **Show Data Table with Legend Keys** option. This will place a table at the bottom of the chart showing the

Figure 5.11 | **Initial Result of the 100% Stacked Column Chart**

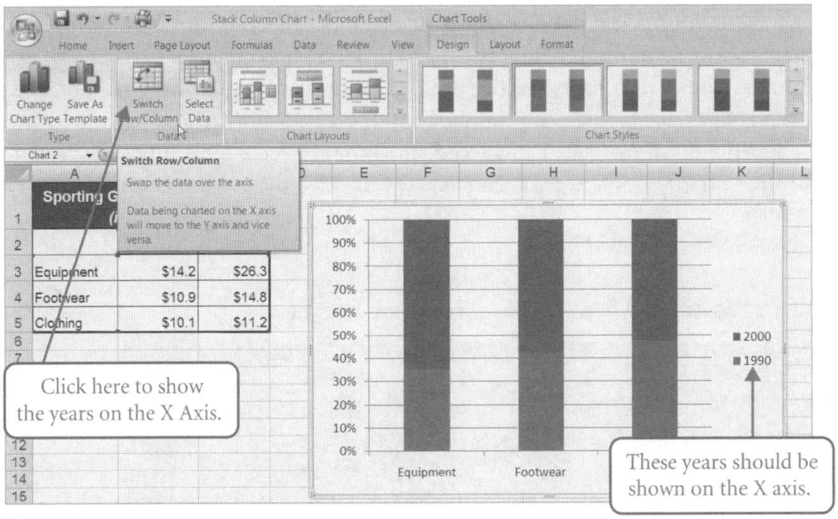

dollar values for each product category. In addition, the legend showing which color corresponds to each product category will be included in the table.

- Click the **Legend** icon.
- Select the **None** option. This will remove the legend that is shown on the right side of the chart in Figure 5.11. As shown in Figure 5.12, the data table that was added to the bottom of the chart shows which color corresponds to each product category. Therefore, the legend on the right side of the chart is not needed.

Figure 5.12 shows the final 100% Stacked Column chart. By looking at the Y-axis, you can see how the percentage each product represents to the total sales of the industry changes from 1990 to the year 2000. Notice that the "Equipment" category represents 40% of the industry's sales in 1990 and grows to 50% in the year 2000. The "Footwear" category is approximately the same at 30% in 1990 and 2000. However, the "Clothing" category declines from approximately 30% of the industry's sales in 1990 to 20% in 2000. Product and/or marketing managers typically conduct this type of analysis to identify what areas of an industry present the best opportunities for growth.

Figure 5.12 | **Final 100% Stacked Column Chart**

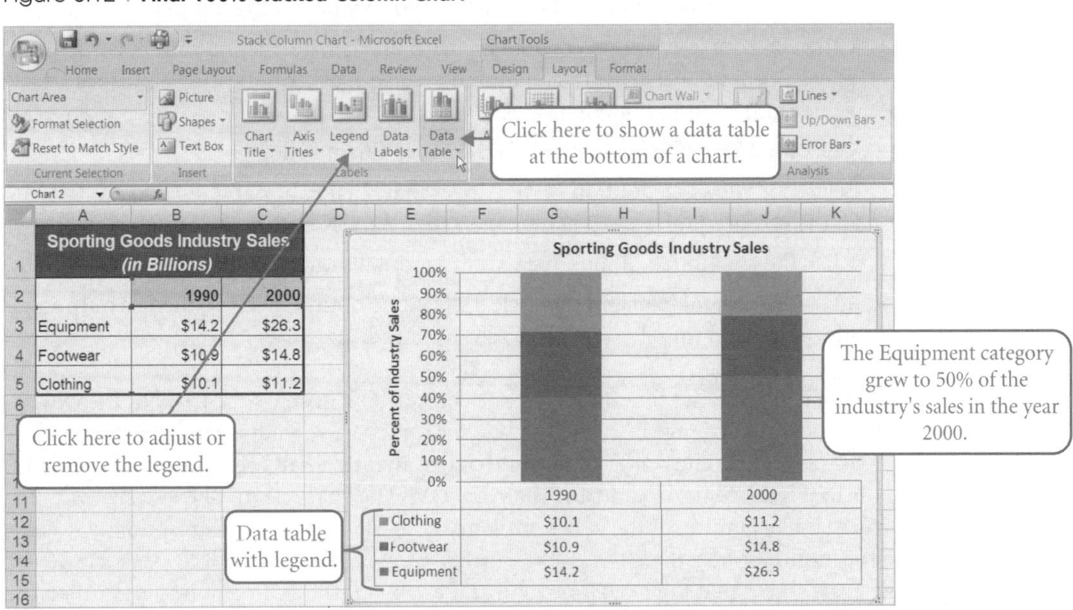

Line Charts (Trends Over Time)

Business managers commonly use ***line charts*** in a number of situations. For example, they effectively show data trends over a period of time, such as changes in stocks or stock market averages. Line charts are also great tools to compare trends. For example, the 12-month trend of a stock can be compared to the 12-month trend of an index like the Dow Jones Industrial Average. Figure 5.13 shows data for the Dow Jones Industrial Average for the year 2004. A line chart will be used to show the adjusted closing price for each month.

Figure 5.13 | **2004 Adjusted Average Close of the Dow Jones**

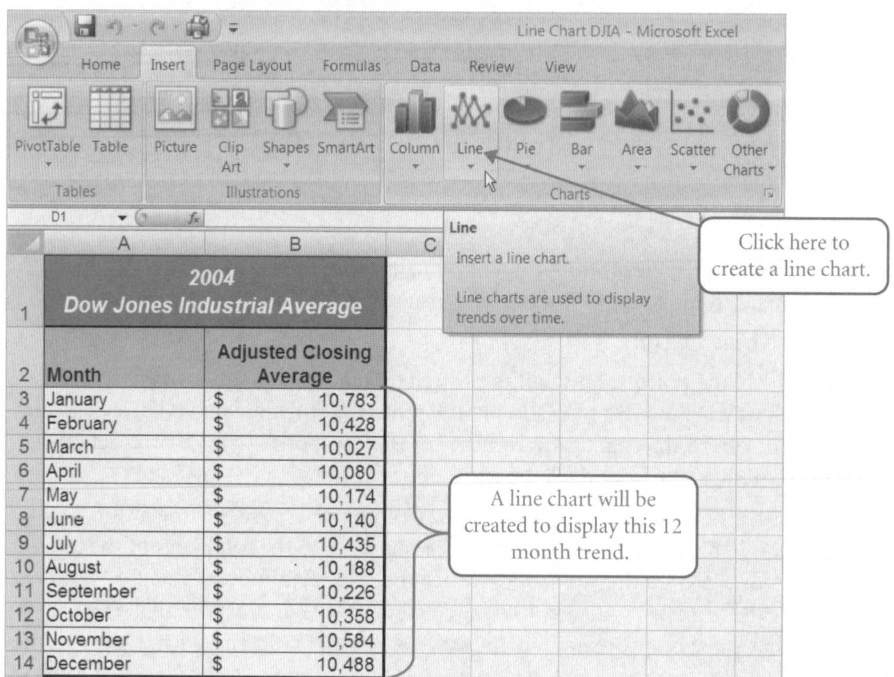

2004 Dow Jones Industrial Average	
Month	**Adjusted Closing Average**
January	$ 10,783
February	$ 10,428
March	$ 10,027
April	$ 10,080
May	$ 10,174
June	$ 10,140
July	$ 10,435
August	$ 10,188
September	$ 10,226
October	$ 10,358
November	$ 10,584
December	$ 10,488

The following points explain how to create a line chart using the data in Figure 5.13:

- Highlight the range A2:B14. Then click the **Insert** tab on the Ribbon.
- Click the **Line** icon and select the **Line with Markers** format option. This will display a line on the chart with a diamond-shaped marker indicating each specific value from column B in Figure 5.13.
- Click the **Move Chart** icon to open the **Move Chart** dialog box.
- Select the **New sheet** option in the **Move Chart** dialog box and type **`DJIA 2004`** in the box used for the tab name. Then click the **OK** button.
- Click the **Layout** tab in the **Chart Tools** set of tabs on the Ribbon.
- Click the **Legend** icon and then select the **None** option. Because there is only one line of data on this chart, the legend is not needed.

Figure 5.14 shows the completed line chart, which displays the trend of the Dow Jones Industrial Average in 2004. The title for this chart was adjusted and a title for the Y-axis was added. The reader of this line chart can immediately see how the Dow Jones Industrial Average trended during the year 2004. The chart clearly shows a significant drop in the beginning of the year from January to March. With the exception of a spike in the month of July, there is a gradual increase for the remainder of the year. However, the chart shows that the Dow Jones ended the year a few hundred points lower than the beginning.

Figure 5.14 | **Line Chart Showing the Adjusted Average Close of the Dow Jones in 2004**

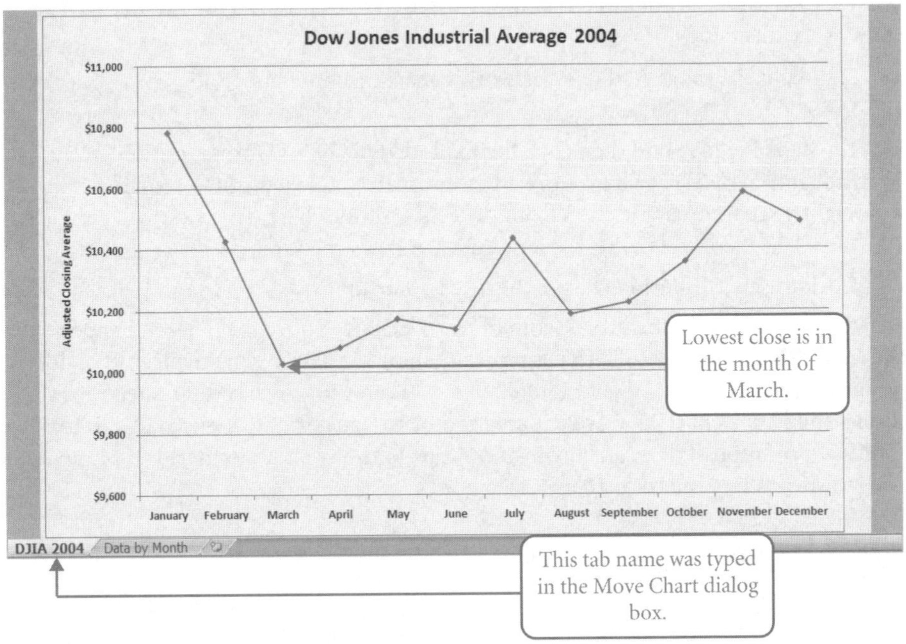

Dow Jones Industrial Average 2004

Lowest close is in the month of March.

This tab name was typed in the Move Chart dialog box.

Pie Charts (Percent to Total)

The ***pie chart*** is the last chart demonstrated in this section. Similar to the stacked column chart, the pie chart shows a percent to total comparison for various data categories. However, unlike the stacked column chart, the pie chart is not effective in showing a percent to total change over time. It is mostly used to show how several components make up a total for one specific point in time. For example, a business manager might use a pie chart to show the percentage each asset category contributes to the total startup costs for a business. Examples of asset categories are Land, Machines, Office Supplies, Automobiles, and so on. An example of this data is shown in Figure 5.15.

Figure 5.15 | **Startup Costs for a Business**

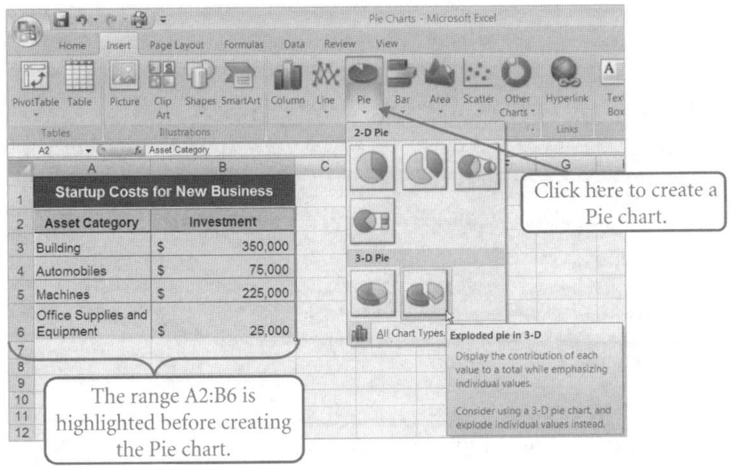

Startup Costs for New Business	
Asset Category	Investment
Building	$ 350,000
Automobiles	$ 75,000
Machines	$ 225,000
Office Supplies and Equipment	$ 25,000

The following points explain how to create a pie chart to visually show the percentage each asset category in column A in Figure 5.15 represents to the total startup costs of the business:

- Highlight the range A2:B6 in the worksheet shown in Figure 5.15. Then click the **Insert** tab on the Ribbon.
- Click the **Pie** icon and then click the **Exploded pie in 3-D** format option, as shown in Figure 5.15. This will produce a three-dimensional view of the pie chart and slightly separate each section from the center of the chart. This view will enhance the visual display showing the amount each investment represents to the total.
- Click the chart title and change the title to Startup Costs.

Figure 5.16 shows the initial setup of the pie chart. Notice that a legend appears on the right side of the chart. Pie charts typically show the category name next to each wedge of the pie chart. A legend could be used in cases in which several categories are displayed in a pie chart. However, adding too many categories to a pie chart can make it difficult or impossible to see any relationships to the total. A pie chart is typically used to show a maximum of 10 to 12 categories.

Figure 5.16 | **Initial Setup of the Pie Chart**

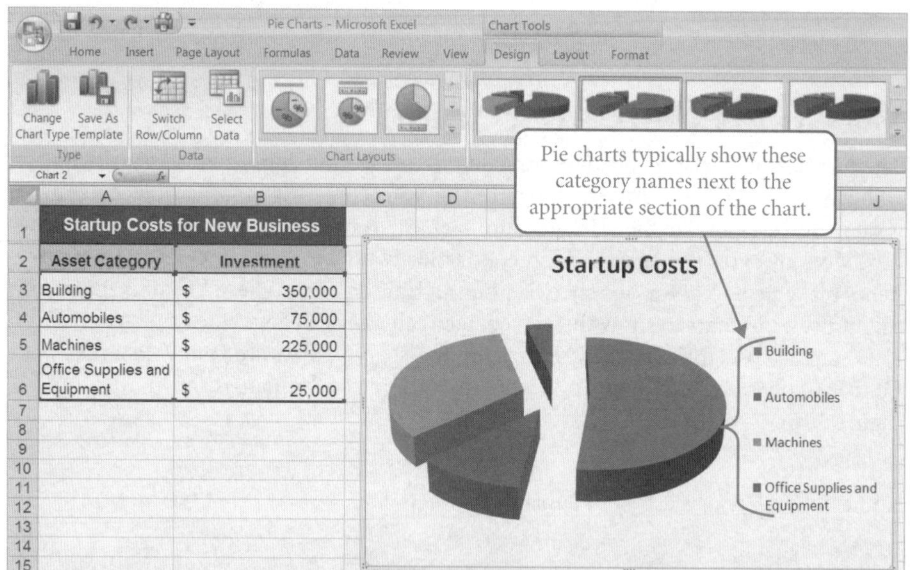

COMMON MISTAKES | Too Many Categories for a Pie Chart

The most common mistake people make when creating pie charts is trying to add too many categories. A pie chart can typically show a maximum of 10 to 12 categories. As the number of categories added to a pie chart exceeds 12, it becomes increasingly difficult to determine what each category represents to the total. If you need to create a chart with more than 12 categories, consider using a column chart or create subgroups that represent multiple categories.

The following points explain how to show each Asset Category shown in the legend of Figure 5.16 next to each section of the pie chart:

- Click the **Layout** tab in the **Chart Tools** set of tabs on the Ribbon.
- Click the **Legend** icon and select the **None** option. Because the category name will be placed next to each section of the chart, the legend is not needed.
- Click the **Data Labels** icon and select the **More Data Label Options** (see Figure 5.17). This will open the **Format Data Labels** dialog box.

- In the **Format Data Labels** dialog box, click the box next to the **Value** option to remove the green check. Then click the box next to the **Category name** option to add a green check (see Figure 5.18).
- Click the **Outside End** option and then click the **Close** button at the bottom of the **Format Data Labels** dialog box. This will add the category labels next to each section of the pie chart. You can adjust the position of these labels by clicking and dragging.

Figures 5.17 and 5.18 show how to open the **Format Data Labels** dialog box. Notice the settings in the **Format Data Labels** dialog box in Figure 5.18.

Figure 5.17 | **Opening the Format Data Labels Dialog Box**

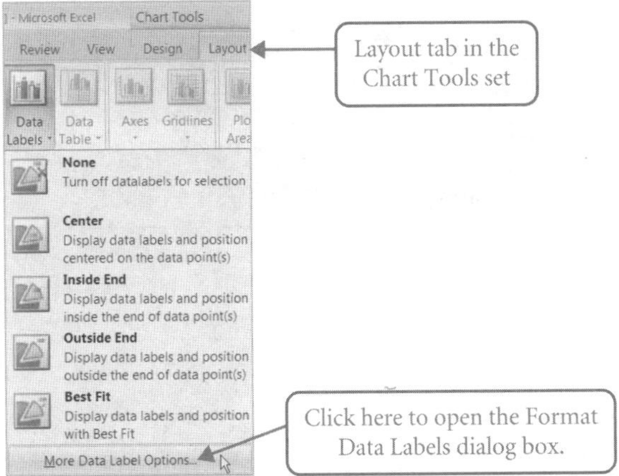

Figure 5.18 | **Settings in the Format Data Labels Dialog Box**

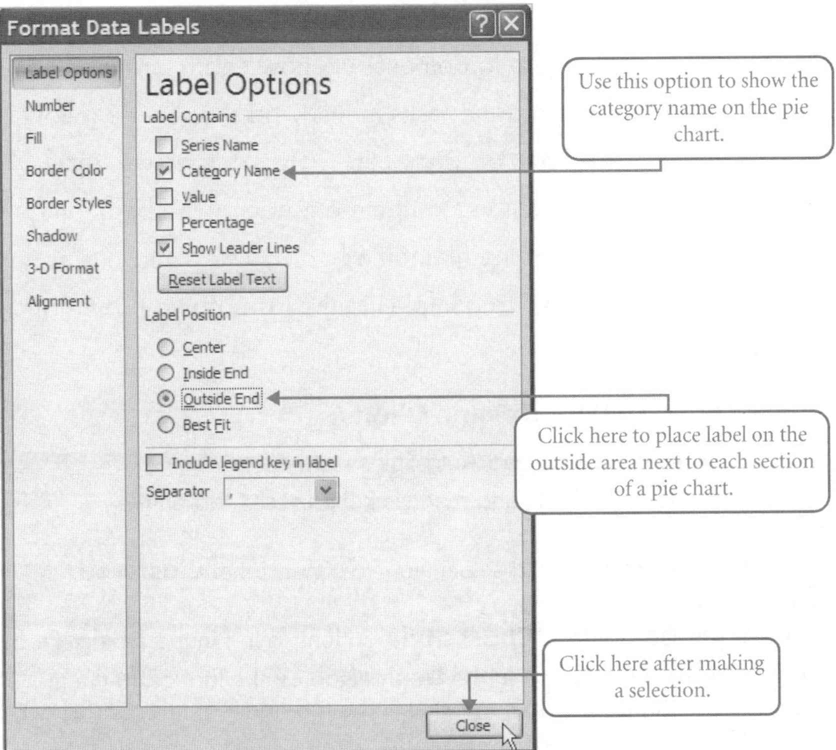

Figures 5.19 shows the final pie chart, which is embedded in a worksheet. A business manager can use this chart to demonstrate that most of the startup costs for this business will be dedicated to the Building and Machines asset categories. Notice how each section of the pie chart is separated or pulled away from the center. This makes it easier to see the proportion each section represents to the total. The reader of this chart can easily see that the cost of the Building represents a little over 50% of the total startup costs for this business.

>> **Quick Reference**

Creating Charts

1. Highlight a range of cells that contain values that will be used to define the X- and Y-axes of the chart.
2. Click the **Insert** tab on the Ribbon.
3. Click one of the **Chart Type** icons in the **Charts** group on the Ribbon.
4. Select a chart format option based on the needs of your project and the desired visual appearance.
5. Click the **Switch Row/Column** icon (in the **Design** tab) if the data on the X- and Y-axes needs to be reversed.
6. Click the **Move Chart** icon (in the **Design** tab) to move the chart to another existing worksheet or place the chart in a separate chart sheet.
7. Click the **Layout** tab in the **Chart Tools** section on the Ribbon and click the **Chart Title** and/or **Axis Titles** icons to add or adjust boxes for the chart title or axis titles.
8. After adding a title box to the chart, click it twice to type a new title or description.

Figure 5.19 | **Final Pie Chart**

Startup Costs for New Business	
Asset Category	Investment
Building	$ 350,000
Automobiles	$ 75,000
Machines	$ 225,000
Office Supplies and Equipment	$ 25,000

Startup Costs

Office Supplies and Equipment

Machines

Building

Automobiles

Category labels are displayed next to each section based on the settings in Figure 5.18.

This section represents a little more than 50% of the total.

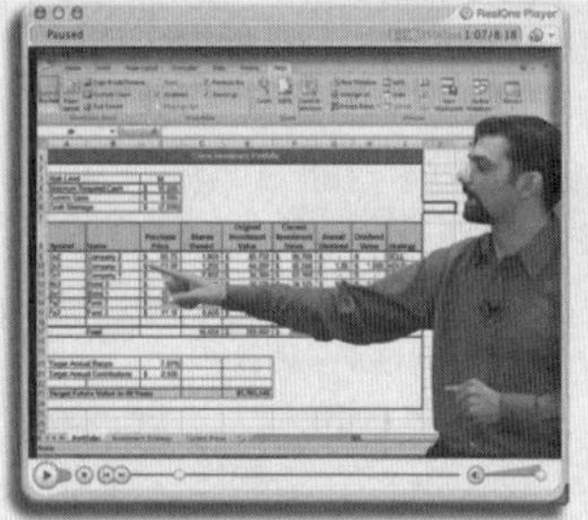

>> Creating Charts

The purpose of this workshop is to demonstrate how charts are created in Excel. I will be demonstrating the tasks in this workshop in the following four videos: **Column Charts**, **Stacked Column Charts**, **Line Charts**, and **Pie Charts**. Each video name appears at the beginning of each section of tasks. Open the file named ib_e05_chartsforbusiness before starting this workshop. Try completing the tasks on your own and then watch the video.

1. **Column Charts (Video: Column Charts)**
   a. Activate the worksheet named Auto Sales Data.
   b. Highlight the range A3:E7 and then click the **Insert** tab on the Ribbon.
   c. Click the **Column** icon and select the two-dimensional **Clustered Column** format option.
   d. Select **Style 34** from the **Chart Style** options found in the **Design** tab.
   e. Use the **Move Chart** icon in the **Design** tab on the Ribbon to the move the column chart to its own chart sheet. The tab name of this chart sheet should be `4 Year Sales Plan`.
   f. Click the **Chart Title** icon in the **Layout** tab on the Ribbon to add a title box to the chart. Select the **Above Chart** option.
   g. Click the chart title box and change the title to `4 Year Auto Sales Comparison`.
   h. Using the **Axis Titles** icon, add a title box to the X- and Y-axes. For the Y-, or vertical, axis, select the **Rotated Title** option.

i. Click the X-axis title box twice and change the title to `Fiscal Year`.
j. Click the Y-axis title box twice and change the title to `Sales in Units`.

2. Stacked Column Charts (Video: Stacked Column Charts)

a. Activate the worksheet named Industry Sales.
b. Highlight the range A2:C5 and then click the **Insert** tab on the Ribbon.
c. Click the **Column** icon and select the **100% Stacked Column** format option.
d. Click the **Switch Row/Column** icon in the **Design** tab on the Ribbon to show the years on the X-axis instead of the product categories.
e. Select **Style 10** from the **Chart Style** options found in the **Design** tab.
f. Remove the legend on the chart by clicking the **Legend** icon in the **Layout** tab on the Ribbon and select the **None** option.
g. Move the chart so the upper-left corner is in cell E2 by clicking and dragging the frame.
h. Place a data table at the bottom of the chart by clicking the **Data Table** icon and selecting the **Show Data Table with Legend Keys** option.
i. Increase the size of the chart by clicking and dragging the bottom sizing handle to the bottom of row 20. Then click and drag the right sizing handle to the right side of column N.
j. Add a chart title `Sporting Goods Industry Sales`. Use the **Above Chart** option in the **Chart Title** icon.
k. Add a title to the Y-axis `Percent of Industry Sales`. Use the **Rotated Title** option from the **Axis Title** icon.

3. Line Charts (Video: Line Charts)

a. Activate the worksheet named Dow Jones Data.
b. Highlight the range A2:B14 and click the **Insert** tab on the Ribbon.
c. Click the **Line** icon and select the **Line with Markers** format option.
d. Use the **Move Chart** icon in the **Design** tab on the Ribbon to move the line chart to its own chart sheet. The tab name of this chart sheet should be `DJIA 2004`.
e. Use the **Legend** icon in the **Layout** tab to remove the legend.
f. Change the chart title to `Dow Jones Industrial Average 2004`.
g. Add a Y-axis title `Adjusted Closing Average`.

4. Pie Charts (Video: Pie Charts)

a. Activate the worksheet named Startup Cost.
b. Highlight the range A2:B6 and click the **Insert** tab on the Ribbon.
c. Click the **Pie** icon and select the **Exploded pie in 3-D** format option.
d. Select the **Style 26** chart style.
e. Remove the legend.
f. Change the title of the chart to `Startup Costs`.
g. Open the **Format Data Labels** dialog box. Select the **More Data Label Options** in the **Data Labels** icon in the **Layout** tab on the Ribbon.

h. In the **Format Data Labels** dialog box, click the **Value** option to remove the green check. Then click the **Category Name** option to add a green check. Then click the **Outside End** option and click the **Close** button.

i. Save and close your file.

EXERCISE

Why Do I Need This?

>> Analyzing Industry Statistics

Analyzing an industry is a critical exercise when developing business strategies. Understanding whether an industry is growing or declining and identifying the top-performing companies are critical when making strategic decisions. The outcome of this analysis could support decisions such as entering a market, exiting a market, or making an acquisition. The chart techniques covered in this section are valuable for presenting industry statistics, but they can also be used as analytical tools.

Exercise

The purpose of this exercise is to construct two charts for the purpose of analyzing and presenting statistics that have been collected for a hypothetical industry. To begin the exercise, open the file named ib_e05_industryx.

1. Activate the worksheet named Sales Growth.
2. Highlight the range A3:H7 and create a line chart. Use a chart format that shows markers at each data point. The purpose of this chart is to show the seven-year sales trend for each of the companies listed in the Sales Growth worksheet. Notice that the averages located in row 7 are included in the highlighted range. This will enable the reader of the chart to compare the growth trends for each company with the overall average of the industry.
3. Select a chart style that assigns a different color for each of the lines on the chart. Select a style that keeps the plot area white or light grey.
4. Move the line chart to a separate chart sheet. The tab name for this chart sheet should be `Industry Sales by Company`.
5. Move the legend to the bottom of the chart.
6. Add the title `Industry X Sales Analysis` to the chart. The title should appear above the chart.
7. Add a title `Change in Sales` to the Y-axis. Use the **Vertical Title** option.
8. What company is showing a sales growth trend from the year 2000 to 2006 that is most similar the overall average of the industry?
9. Activate the worksheet named Competitors.
10. Highlight the range A2:B6 and create a pie chart. Use a chart format that will show each section of the chart separated from the center and have a three-dimensional appearance. The purpose of this chart is to show the total net sales for all the companies in Industry X. When placed in a pie chart, this data will show how much market share or percentage of sales each company

obtained in the industry last year. This chart will show if the industry is dominated by a few companies or if the sales are divided among several small firms.

11. Select a chart style that assigns a different color for each section of the pie chart. Select a style that keeps the plot area white or light grey.
12. Change the title of the chart to `LY Market Share`.
13. Remove the chart legend.
14. Add data labels outside each section in the chart. The data labels should show both the category name and the value. As a result, the chart should show the company name as well as the total net sales.
15. Which company has the highest market share in the industry?
16. Does the company with the highest market share also have the highest sales growth rate relative to the industry average?
17. Which company—A, B, or C—has the lowest market share?
18. Reports in this industry claim Company A is "stealing" market share away from Company C. Does this claim make sense when looking at the line chart you created? Why?
19. Save and close your file.

>> What's Wrong with This Spreadsheet?

PROBLEM & EXERCISE

Problem

You are a business analyst working in the product development division of a large products manufacturing company. Your boss, the director of product development, is preparing for a meeting with the president of the company to explain potential sales opportunities based on three years' worth of historical sales data. He is having difficulty creating a chart that visually displays the sales trends for five product categories and asks for your help. He explains his goal for this chart as follows:

1. I am trying to create a basic column chart that shows how the product sales mix of the company has changed over the past three years. Our sales are increasing every year; however, the sales of some product categories have increased dramatically, whereas others have actually declined. Therefore, I am trying to create a chart that shows the three years at the bottom of the chart with bars representing the sales for each of the five product categories. However, the column chart I created shows the exact opposite configuration. I was wondering if I should re-create my data so the column headings in row 2 show the product categories instead of the years.

2. If possible, I would like to show the bars for the year 2004 in order, starting with the tallest bar down to the shortest. I know the height of the bars will change for the following two years; however, it is so much easier to see these trends when the bars for the first year are in order.

3. Is there any way to create this chart without having all the bars green? It would be nice if each bar is a different color. Someone told me that there is a **Design** tab on the Ribbon that would allow me to select a new color scheme. However, I must have a different version of Excel because I don't see this tab.

Exercise

The chart your boss created is in the Excel file named ib_e05_productmixpresentation. Open the file and consider the following points:

1. Your boss mentioned that he might have to re-create the data in his worksheet to display the years on the bottom of the chart. Is this necessary?
2. In the second point, your boss mentioned that he would like to change the order in which the bars are displayed for the year 2004. Is this possible? How?
3. With regards to the third point, why is your boss not seeing the **Design** tab?
4. Is anything missing from the chart your boss attempted to create in this file?
5. Read the first point carefully. Your boss mentioned that he would like to create a basic column chart. Would you recommend that your boss use another chart in this situation? Why?

Write a short answer for each of the points listed here. Then fix the chart based on the points your boss mentioned and add anything you think is missing. In addition, create an alternate version of this chart that might improve your boss's presentation to the president.

Skill Set

Formatting Charts

The previous section demonstrated how charts are created and used in a variety of business situations. However, formatting can significantly enhance the appearance of these charts. In Chapter 2, you saw how appropriate formatting can often make the difference between a mediocre and professional-looking spreadsheet. The same rule applies to charts. Formatting can direct the reader to the most critical data points on a chart and bring the appearance of charts to a professional level. This section will demonstrate various formatting techniques using the charts created in the previous section.

Titles and Legends

After creating a chart, you might need to make formatting adjustments to the legend and titles. For example, you may have noticed that the axis titles as well as the legend in the column chart shown in Figure 5.9 are hard to read because the font size is so small. Formatting adjustments can solve this problem.

There are many ways to apply formatting commands to any area of a chart. The best method to use ultimately depends on your preference and needs. The following points demonstrate these methods using the chart title from Figure 5.9:

- Activate the chart title and select one of the formatting icons on the **Home** tab on the Ribbon. When an area on the chart is activated, you can click the **Home** tab and use any of the formatting icons such as **Font Size**, **Bold**, **Italics**, and so on.
- Activate the chart title and right click on it. Right clicking will provide access to the formatting icons in the **Home** tab on the Ribbon as well as other commands. The benefit of using this method is that you can access icons on the **Home** tab while another tab on the Ribbon is active (see Figure 5.20).
- Activate the chart title and use the commands in the **Format** tab in the **Chart Tools** area on the Ribbon (see Figure 5.21).
- Activate the chart title and open the **Format Chart Title** dialog box (see Figure 5.22). A formatting dialog box can be opened for every area of a chart. For example, there is a **Format Plot Area** dialog box, **Format Axis** dialog box, **Format Legend** dialog box, and so on. You can open these format dialog boxes by clicking

the **Format Selection** icon in the **Format** tab after activating the area of the chart you wish to format (see Figure 5.21). The benefit of this method is that it provides access to more detailed formatting controls in addition to the commands found in the **Format** tab.

Figure 5.20 through 5.22 illustrate the various methods for accessing and implementing formatting commands for charts. As previously mentioned, the method you choose depends on your preference and project needs.

Figure 5.20 | **Right-Click Method to Access Formatting Commands**

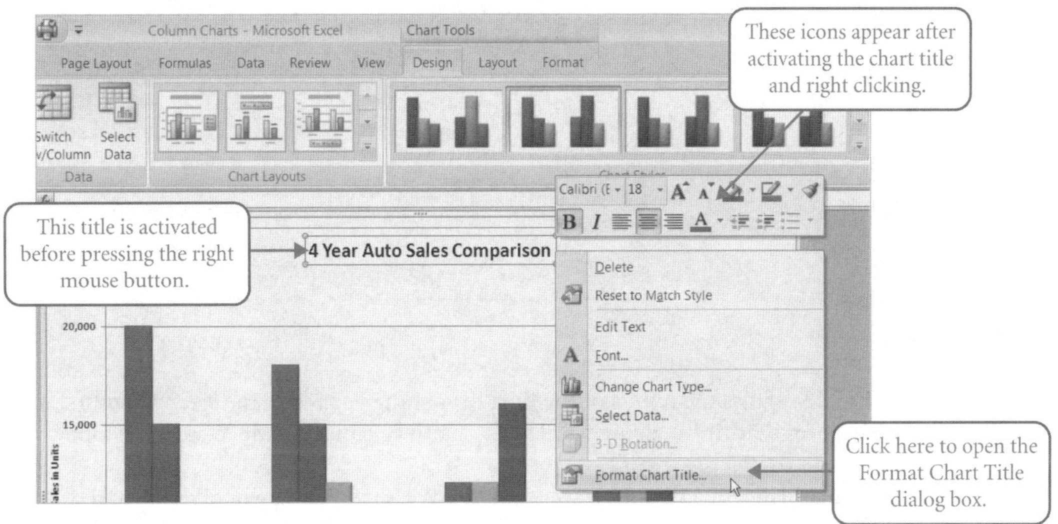

Figure 5.21 | **Chart Formatting Commands in the Format Tab**

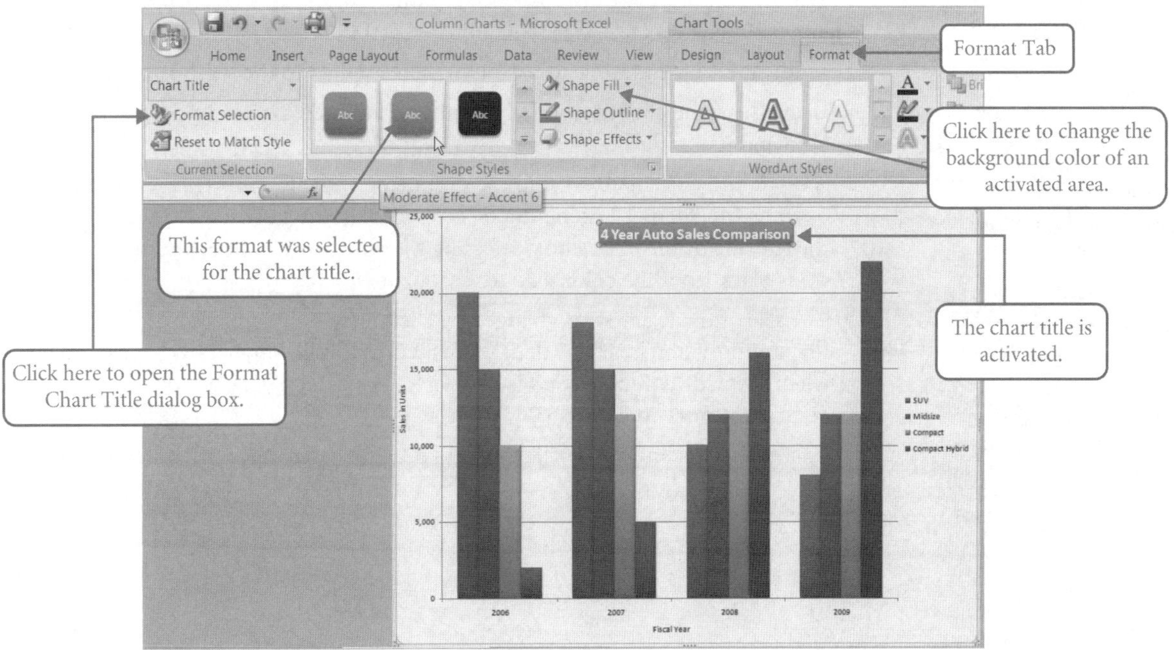

Figure 5.22 | **Format Chart Title Dialog Box**

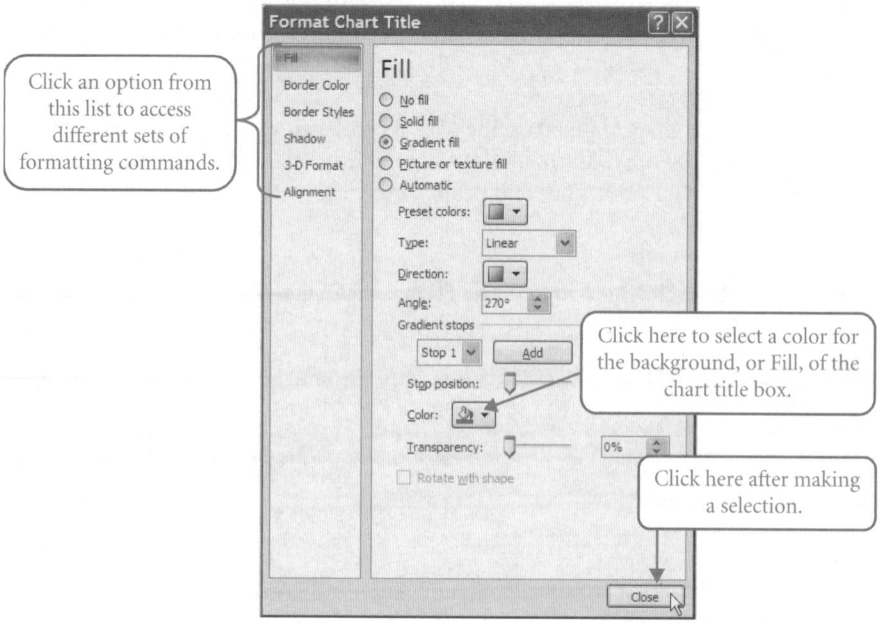

Figure 5.24 shows the results of the final formatting applied to the legend and titles on the column chart from Figure 5.9. The formatting changes made include the following:

- **Chart Title**: In addition to applying the style that was shown in Figure 5.21, the font size was increased to 20 points and italicized. The title was also repositioned above the chart by selecting the **Above Chart** option in the **Chart Title** icon of the **Layout** tab.
- **X- and Y-Axes Titles**: The font size was increased to 14 points. This was done by selecting the axis title box and clicking the right mouse button, as shown in Figure 5.20. The font size was then adjusted to 14 points.
- **Legend**: Several formatting adjustments were applied to the legend:
  - Using the right-click method, the font size was increased to 16 points, and the bold and italics formats were added.
  - A black line was added around the perimeter of the legend. This was done by opening the **Format Legend** dialog box, clicking the Border Color category on the left side of the dialog box, selecting the **Solid Line** option, and selecting the color black from the color palette (see Figure 5.23).
  - The size of the legend was changed by clicking and dragging the sizing handles that appear when it is activated. Words will automatically wrap to a second line when the width of the legend is decreased. For example, notice the Compact Hybrid category in Figure 5.24.
  - The legend was moved by clicking and dragging after it was activated.

>> ***Quick Reference***

Formatting Titles and Legends

1. Activate the legend or title by clicking it once.
2. Select any of the format icons in the **Home** tab on the Ribbon and/or the icons in the **Format** tab of the **Chart Tools** area on the Ribbon.
3. To access more detailed formatting controls, click the **Format Selection** icon in the **Format** tab to open the **Format Legend** or **Format Title** dialog box.
4. To edit the wording of a title, click it twice and type any adjustments.
5. To move the legend or titles, click and drag it.
6. To change the size of the legend or titles, click and drag on one of the sizing handles.

Figure 5.23 | **Format Legend Dialog Box**

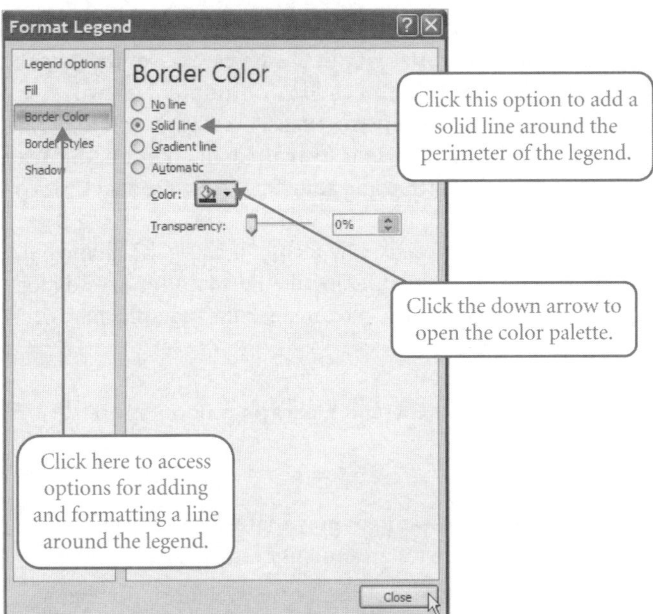

Figure 5.24 | **Formatting Changes Applied to the Legend and Titles**

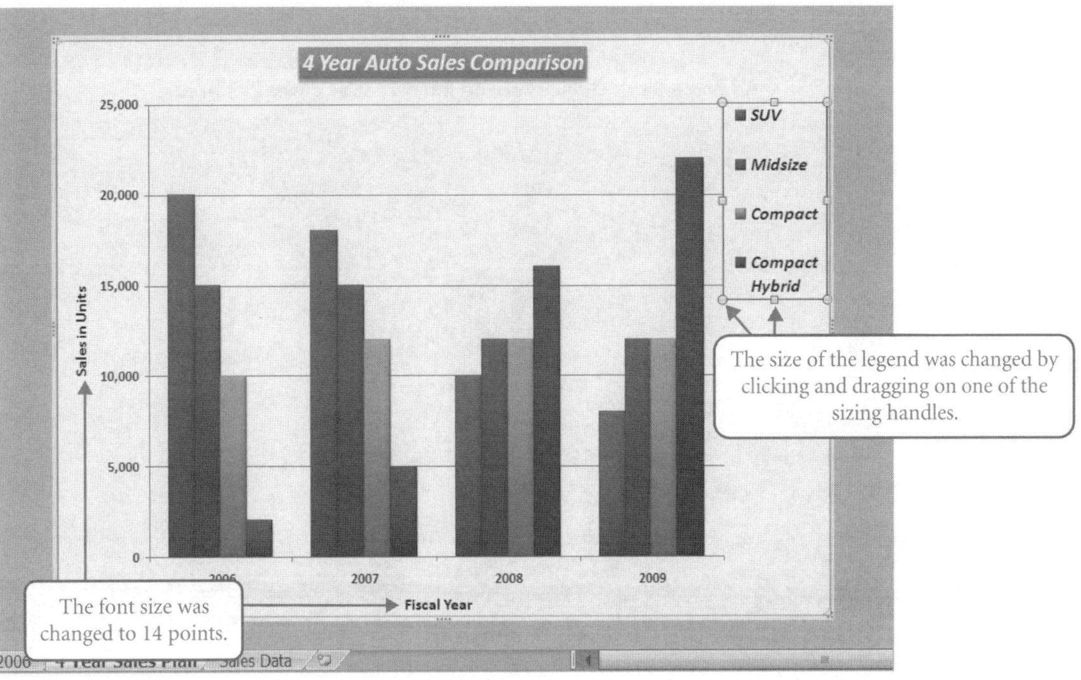

Plot Area and Data Series

The plot area is an area of a chart that frequently requires formatting adjustments. The color of the plot area can make a significant difference in the appearance of the data that is being displayed. The color or background you choose for the plot area will depend on the colors and type of chart you are constructing. This section will illustrate how the plot area of the column chart in Figure 5.24 is formatted. In addition, this segment will also illustrate how you can apply formatting adjustments to the data series of a chart.

After activating the plot area of a chart, you usually format it using the **Shape Fill** and **Shape Outline** icons in the **Format** tab or by opening the **Format Plot Area** dialog box. The following steps explain how to format the plot area for the column chart in Figure 5.24 using the icons in the **Format** tab:

- Activate the plot area by clicking inside the X-and Y-axes but not on one of the grid lines.
- Click the **Format** tab.
- Click the **Shape Fill** icon and select the color light grey (darker 15%) from the palette. This will change the color of the plot area to light grey.
- Click the **Shape Outline** icon and place the cursor over the **Weight** option below the color palette (see Figure 5.25). Then select the **1 ½ pt** option. This will place a black outline around the perimeter of the plot area.

Figure 5.25 | **Adding a Black Outline Around the Perimeter of the Plot Area**

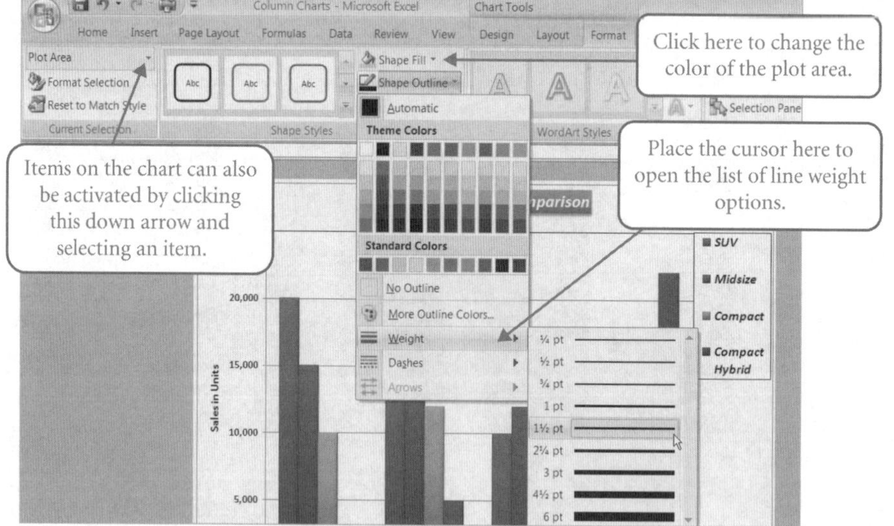

Figure 5.26 shows the results of the final formatting adjustments made to the plot area of the column chart. In addition, space was created on the bottom, left, and right sides of the plot area by clicking and dragging on the sizing handles, which appear when the plot area is activated. Notice how the axis labels and values appear more prominent when the color of the plot area is changed to light grey. This makes it easy for the reader to see the magnitude of the bars in the plot area.

Figure 5.26 | **Formatted Plot Area**

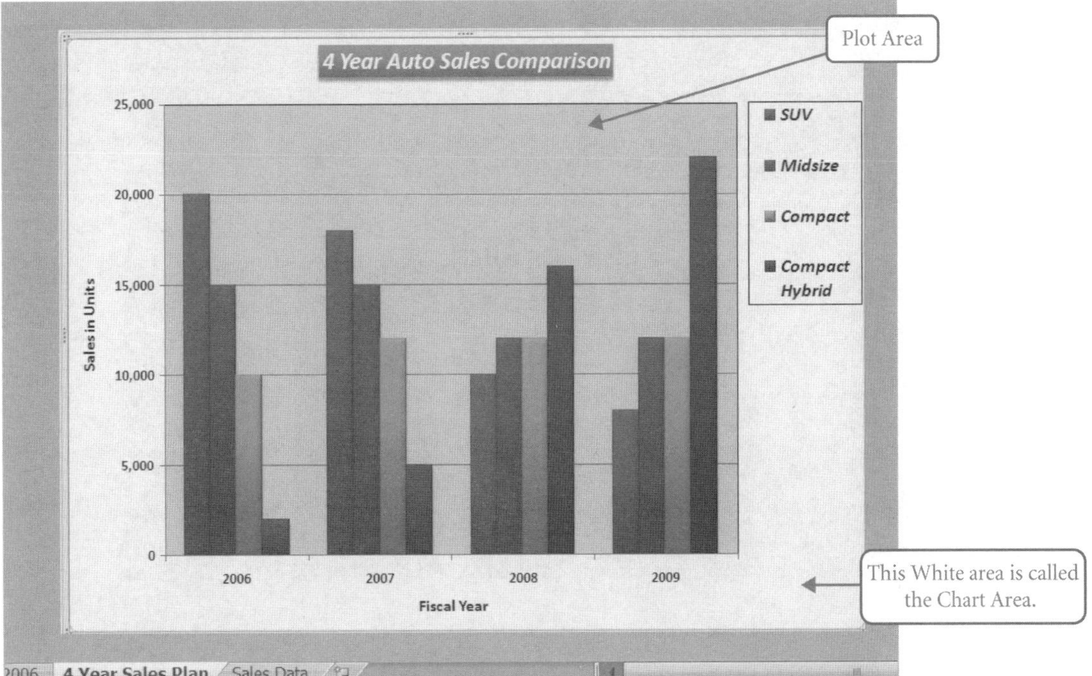

As previously mentioned, you can also format the data series displayed on a chart. A ***data series*** refers to the image that appears on the chart that is representing a category of values. For example, the blue bars in the column chart shown in Figure 5.26 represent the SUV data series. On a line chart, markers could be used to represent a data series. For this formatting example, the color of the bars representing the Compact and Compact Hybrid categories will be changed. You may recall that the color of these bars was determined by selecting one of the chart styles in the **Design** tab when the chart was initially created (see Figure 5.8). However, what if you wanted the bars for the Compact Hybrid category to be green because this car is environmentally friendly? You can change this color to green by applying formatting techniques to the data series.

The method used to format the data series of a chart is similar to formatting the plot area. When one element of a data series is clicked one time, images related to the data series will be activated. For example, when one of the bars representing the Compact Hybrid category is clicked, all the Compact Hybrid bars will be activated. If one of the bars representing the Compact Hybrid category is clicked a second time, that specific bar, or ***series point***, will be activated. This gives you the option of formatting all the bars or images related to a data series or just one. After activating a data series or series point, you can use the **Shape Fill** and **Shape Outline** icons in the **Format** tab to change the color and the line around its perimeter. The following points explain how to format both the Compact and Compact Hybrid data series:

- Click one of the green bars representing the Compact car category on the column chart shown in Figure 5.26. This will activate all the green bars on the chart.
- Click the **Format** tab and then click the **Shape Fill** icon. Select the color yellow at the bottom of the palette (see Figure 5.27). You should see the color of the bars change as you drag the cursor over a color in the palette. In addition, the **Shape Fill** icon also contains an option called **Picture**. This option enables you to import a digital picture you have saved on your computer into the area that is activated on the chart.
- Click one of the purple bars representing the Compact Hybrid car category on the column chart. This will activate all the purple bars on the chart.
- Click the **Format** tab and then click the **Shape Fill** icon. Select the color light green at the bottom of the palette.

>> **Quick Reference**

Formatting the Plot Area

1. Activate the plot area by clicking it once.
2. Click the **Format** tab in the **Chart Tools** set of tabs.
3. Click the **Shape Fill** icon and select a color from the palette to change the plot area color.
4. Click the **Shape Outline** icon and select a color from the palette, one of the **Weight** options, or one of the **Dashes** options.

Figure 5.27 | **Using the Shape Fill Icon to Format a Data Series**

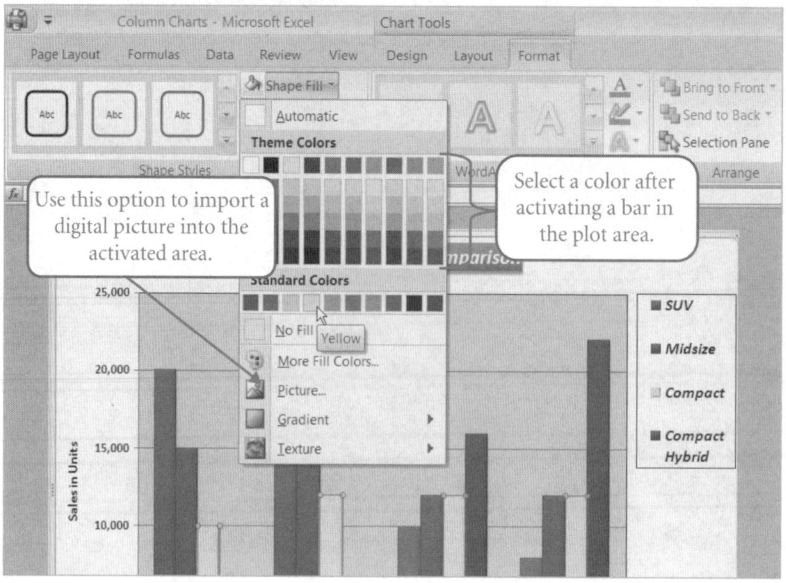

Figure 5.28 shows the final changes made to the Compact and Compact Hybrid data series. Notice that the legend adjusts automatically after the color of the data series is changed. Remember that you can access other formatting features by opening the **Format Data Series** dialog box using the **Format Selection** icon. For example, you can adjust the size of the gap between each set of bars. This capability is helpful when you want to show more or less space between each category on the X-axis of a column chart.

Figure 5.28 | **Completed Formatting Adjustments to the Data Series**

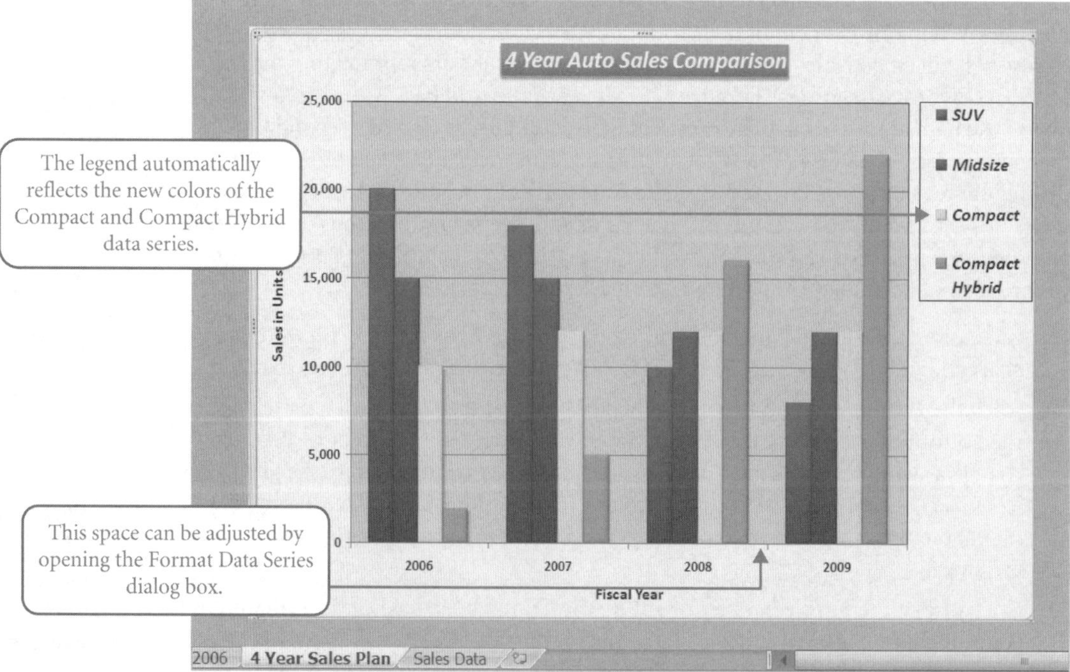

X- and Y-Axes Labels

The last areas that will be formatted on the column chart shown in Figure 5.28 are the X- and Y-axes. Similar to the Axis titles, the values or labels along the X- and Y-axes frequently require formatting so they are easy to see and read.

As with other chart formatting features, you can change the appearance of either the X- or Y-axis by clicking it once and using the icons in the **Home** and **Format** tabs. However, you can access other important features such as controlling the scale of an axis, tick marks, position of the axis labels, or grid lines through the **Format Axis** dialog box. You open it by clicking the axis one time and selecting the **Format Selection** icon in the **Format** tab. Figure 5.29 shows the **Format Axis** dialog box for the Y-axis of the column chart in Figure 5.28.

Figure 5.29 | **Format Axis Dialog Box**

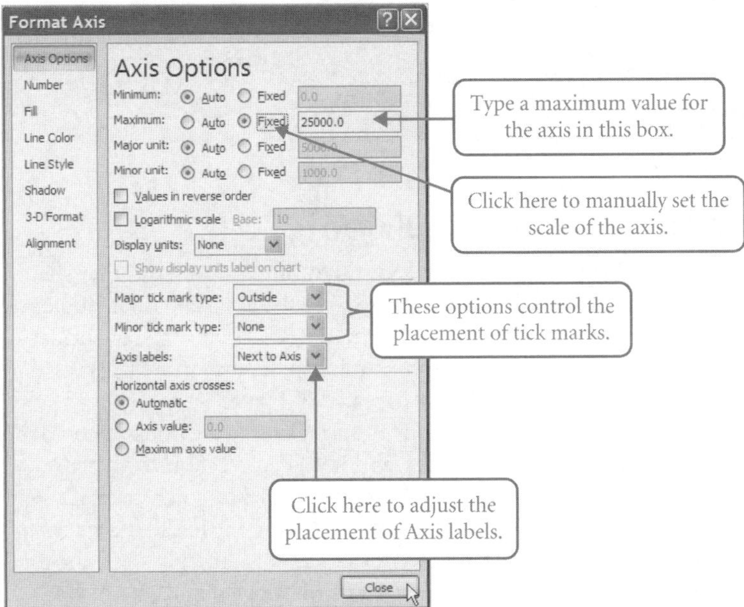

Figure 5.30 shows the final column chart that was started in Figure 5.9. The font size for the sales values and years along the X- and Y-axes was increased to 14 points. Notice how formatting features were used to make all the key elements of the chart easier to see and read such as the titles, legend, and bars.

> **Quick Reference**
>
> **Formatting a Data Series**
>
> 1. Activate a data series by clicking an image (i.e., bar, marker, pie section) one time. Or click an image a second time to activate a series point.
> 2. Click the **Format** tab in the **Chart Tools** set of tabs.
> 3. Click the **Shape Fill** icon and select a color from the palette to change the data series or series point color.
> 4. Click the **Shape Outline** icon and select a color from the palette, one of the **Weight** options, or one of the **Dashes** options.

Figure 5.30 | **Final Automobile Sales Chart with the X- and Y-Axes Formatted**

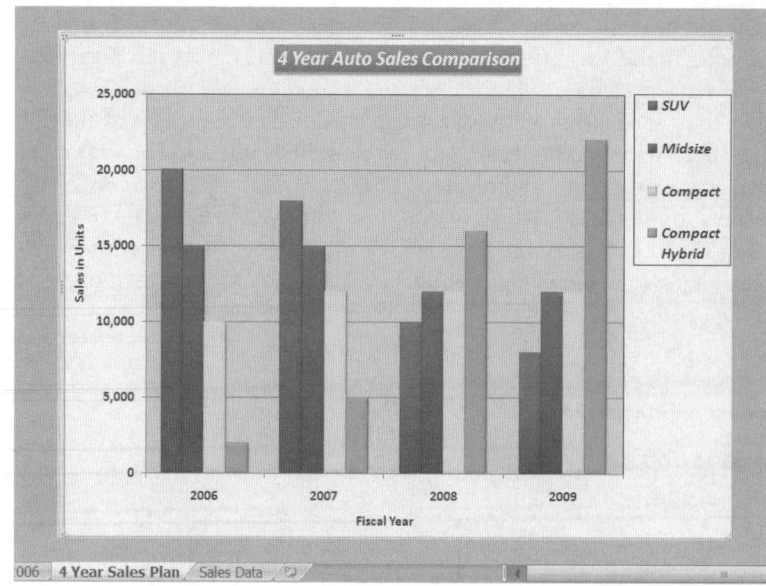

Adding Annotations and Objects

Depending on your project, you may need to add annotations, callouts, or other shapes to a chart. These items can be especially helpful in guiding the attention of an audience during a presentation or for adding additional information that helps the reader identify key facts and trends. The next example demonstrates these formatting features using the 100% Stacked Column chart originally created in Figure 5.12.

As shown in Figure 5.31, the Sporting Goods Industry chart (previously shown in Figure 5.12) includes several formatting features, and it was moved to its own chart sheet. Two formatting enhancements are typically added to stacked column charts such as the one shown in this Figure 5.31. The first shows the total value for all the stacks in each bar. Because the Y-axis shows only the percent to total, it is difficult to see the total sales that were generated in the industry. The second formatting enhancement connects the top of each stack with a line. This feature will make it easier for the reader to see how the percent to total changes over time for each stack in the bar.

Formatting X- and Y-Axes Labels

1. Activate the X- or Y-axis by clicking once anywhere along the axis.
2. Select any of the format icons in the **Home** tab on the Ribbon and/or the icons in the **Format** tab of the **Chart Tools** area on the Ribbon.
3. To access more detailed formatting controls such the axis scale, tick marks, or label position, click the **Format Selection** icon in the **Format** tab to open the **Format Axis** dialog box.

Figure 5.31 | **Sports Industry 100% Stacked Chart with Formatting Enhancements**

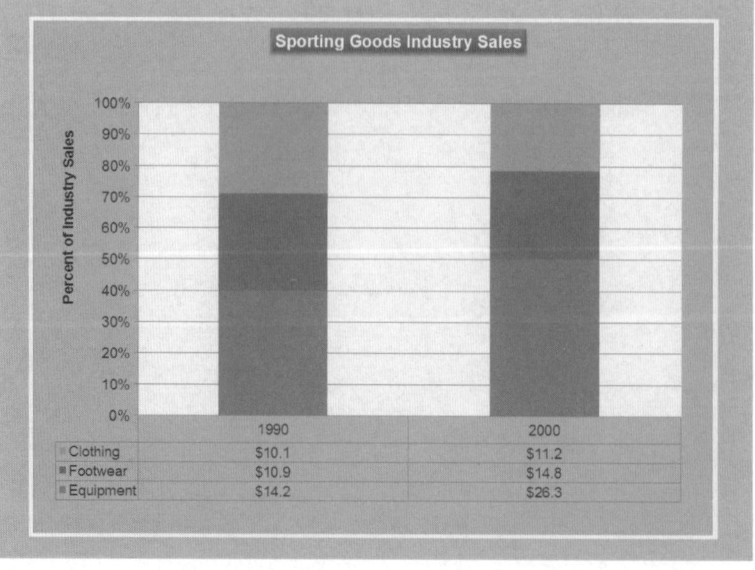

The following steps explain how to add annotations to the chart in Figure 5.31 to show the total industry sales at the top of each bar:

- Activate the chart.
- Click the **Layout** tab in the **Chart Tools** section on the Ribbon.
- Click the **Text Box** icon. Then click and drag a rectangle box over the top of the Y-axis, as shown in Figure 5.32. This text box can be used for typing annotations or information onto the chart.
- Place the cursor over one of the sizing handles of the text box and click the right mouse button. This will open a menu of options used for adding and formatting the data or message typed into the text box (see Figure 5.33). Select the **Edit Text** option and type `100% of Sales =`. This tells the reader that sales figures showing at the top of each bar represent the total sales results for the industry. Additional text boxes will be added to show these sales figures on the chart.
- Highlight the message you typed into the text box and click the right mouse button. Use the formatting icons as shown in Figure 5.33 to change the font size to 12 and then bold and italicize the text.
- Click and drag the right sizing handle to the right so the message does not wrap to two lines.

Figure 5.32 | **Adding a Text Box to a Chart**

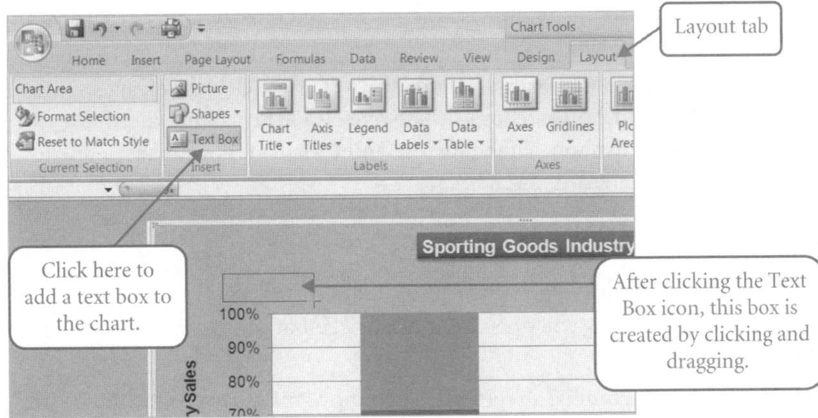

Figure 5.33 | **Right-Click Options for a Text Box**

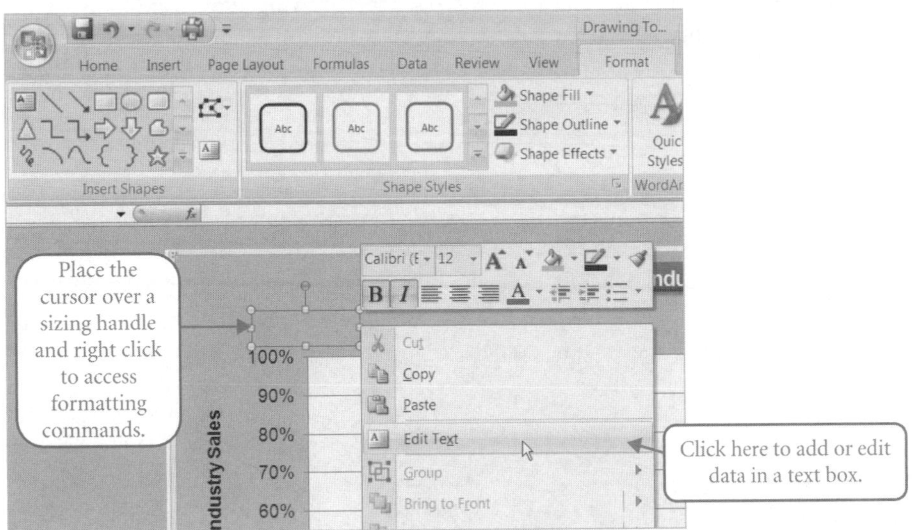

Figure 5.34 shows the completed text box. Notice that after the text box is added to the chart, a **Format** tab is added to the Ribbon under the heading **Drawing Tools**. The commands in this tab are used for applying formatting features to any added object that is activated on a chart or worksheet. Similar to the **Chart Tools Format** tab, the benefit of using icons in this tab is that you can see how a particular formatting command appears before selecting it.

Figure 5.34 | **Completed Text Box**

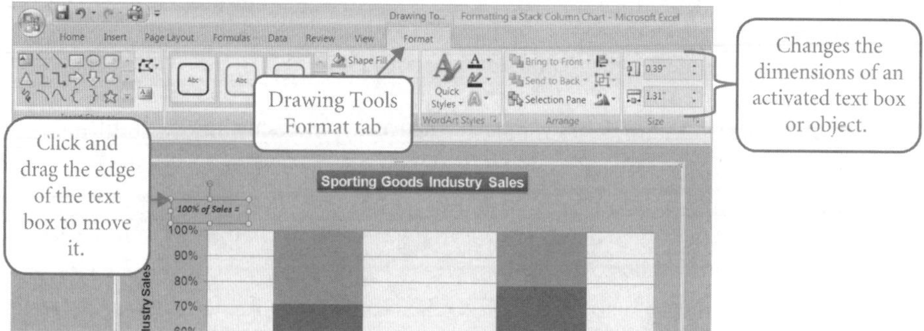

As mentioned earlier, the second formatting enhancement usually applied to a 100% Stacked Column chart is a line connecting the top of each stacked section of the bar. Besides text boxes, other objects can also be added to a chart, such as lines, arrows, circles, callout boxes, and so on. You can access these objects in the **Layout** tab of the **Chart Tools** section on the Ribbon. The following points explain how to add a line to the 100% Stacked Column chart in Figure 5.31:

- Activate the chart.
- Click the **Layout** tab in the **Chart Tools** section on the Ribbon.
- Click the **Shapes** icon. This will open a list of objects that can be added to the chart (see Figure 5.35).
- Click the **Line** option from the shapes list. Then move the cursor to the top of the blue stack of the bar for 1990 and click and drag over to the top of the blue stack for the year 2000 (see Figure 5.36).
- Click the **Shape Outline** icon in the **Format** tab of the **Drawing Tools** section on the Ribbon. The line must be activated to see the **Drawing Tools** section on the Ribbon. Select black from the palette; then click the icon again and select the **1 ½ pt** weight option.

Figure 5.35 | **Options for Adding Shapes to a Chart**

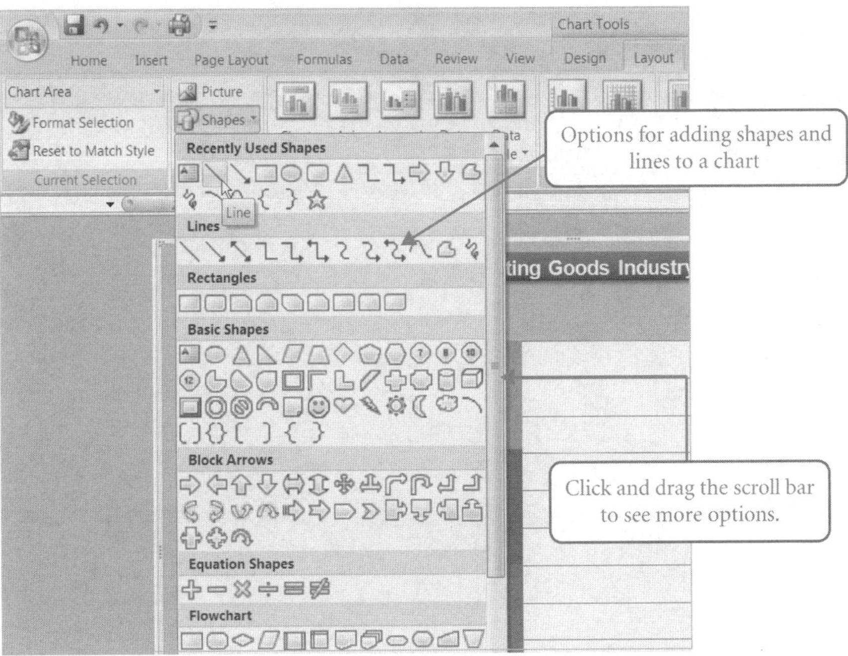

Figure 5.36 shows the line that was added to the 100% Stacked Column chart. Notice that because the line is moving in an upward direction, the reader can easily see that the percent to total sales for Equipment increased from 1990 to 2000.

Figure 5.36 | **Adding a Line to a 100% Stacked Column Chart**

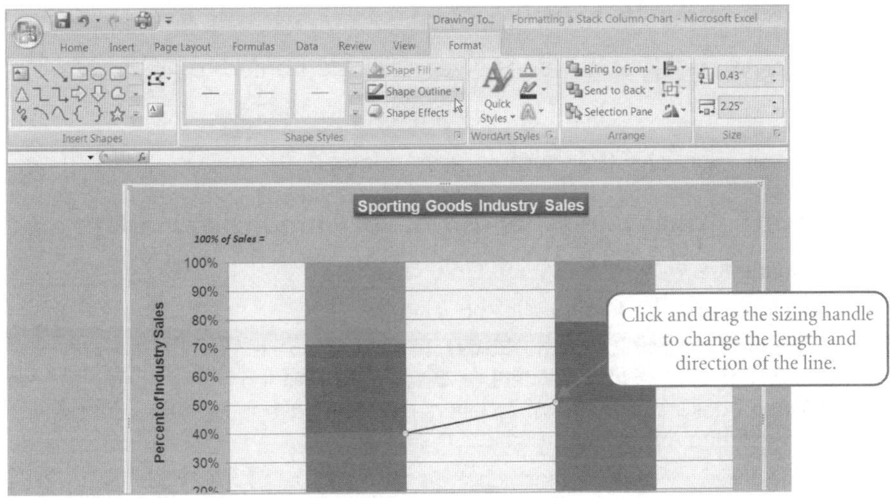

Figure 5.37 shows the final 100% Stacked Column chart showing the sales trend for the Sporting Goods Industry. Notice that text boxes were added to the top of each bar showing the total industry sales for the year. In addition, a second line was added connecting the "Footwear" category between the 1990 and 2000 bars.

>> **Quick Reference**

Adding Annotations and Objects

1. Activate the chart.
2. Click the **Layout** tab of the **Chart Tools** area on the Ribbon.
3. Click the **Text Box** icon to add an annotation or the **Shapes** icon to add an object. If adding an object, select an option after clicking the **Shapes** icon.
4. Click and drag on the chart to place and set the desired size of the text box or object.
5. Format the text box or object by activating it and right clicking, or using the icons in the **Format** tab of the **Drawing Tools** area on the Ribbon.

Figure 5.37 | **Final 100% Stacked Column with Lines and Annotations Added**

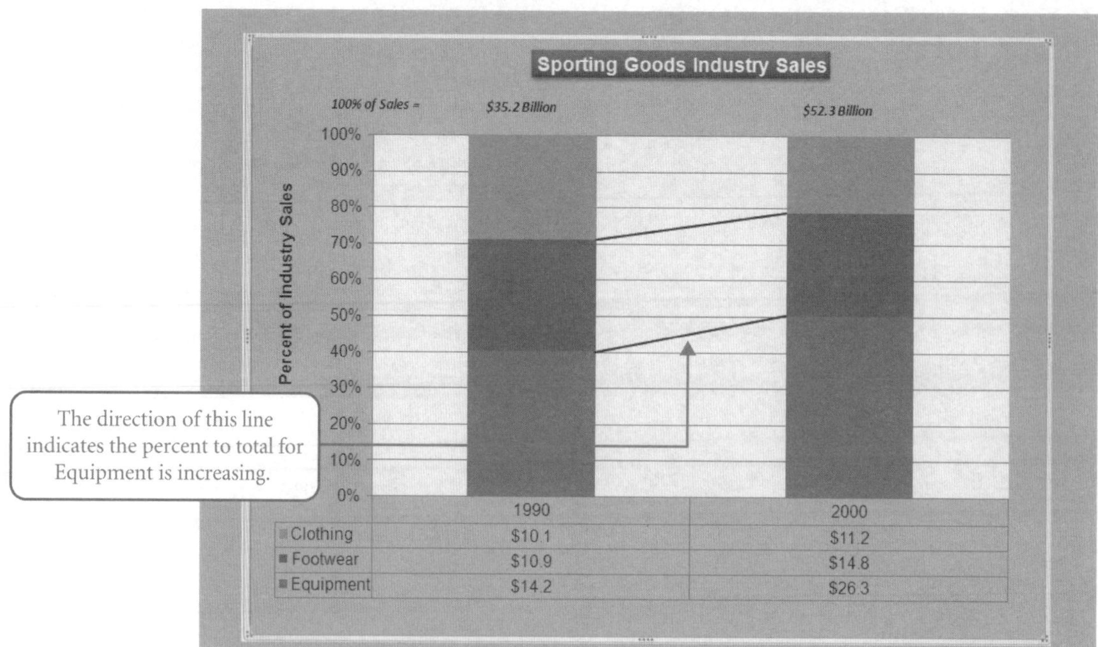

>> Formatting Charts

The purpose of this workshop is to review the techniques used to format the appearance of charts. I will be demonstrating the tasks in this workshop in the **Formatting Charts** and **Adding Annotations and Objects to Charts** videos. Open the file named ib_e05_formattingcharts before starting the following tasks. Try completing these tasks on your own and then watch both videos.

1. **Formatting Titles and Legends (Video: Formatting Charts)**
   a. Activate the worksheet named Column Chart.
   b. Activate the chart title by clicking it once.
   c. Click the **Format** tab in the **Chart Tools** section on the Ribbon. Then select the "Intense Effect-Accent 6" **Shape Styles** icon. This option has an orange background with white letters. You will have to click the scroll down arrow to find this option.
   d. Using the right-click method, change the font size of the chart title to 20 points and italicize the text.
   e. Activate the Legend. Using either the right-click method or the format icons in the **Home** tab on the Ribbon, increase the font size to 14 points; then bold and italicize the text.
   f. Click the **Shape Outline** icon in the **Format** tab on the Ribbon. Place the cursor over the **Weight** option and select the **1 pt** line weight. Then click the **Shape Outline** icon again and select the color black.
   g. Click the top edge of the legend and move it up so the top of the legend is aligned with the 35,000 grid line. Make sure you do not click and drag on a sizing handle to move the legend.

h. Click the X-axis title and increase the font size to 14 points.
i. Click the Y-axis title and increase the font size to 14 points.

2. Formatting the Plot Area and Data Series (Video: Formatting Charts)

a. Activate the plot area of the column chart.
b. Click the **Format** tab on the Ribbon.
c. Click the **Shape Fill** icon and select the white color in the upper-left side of the palette.
d. Click the **Shape Outline** icon, place the cursor over the **Weight** option, and click the **1 ½ pt** line weight. Then click the **Shape Outline** icon again and select the color black.
e. Activate the Compact data series by clicking one of the green bars.
f. Click the **Shape Fill** icon in the **Format** tab and select the color yellow.
g. Activate the Compact Hybrid data series by clicking one of the purple bars.
h. Click the **Shape Fill** icon in the **Format** tab and select the color light green.

3. Formatting the X- and Y-Axes Labels (Video: Formatting Charts)

a. Click any of the years on the X-axis.
b. Change the font size to 12 points.
c. Click any sales value on the Y-axis.
d. Change the font size to 12 points.

4. Annotations and Objects (Video: Adding Annotations and Objects to Charts)

a. Activate the worksheet named Stacked Column Chart.
b. Activate the chart.
c. Click the **Layout** tab and then click the **Text Box** icon.
d. Click and drag the shape of a rectangle above the Y-axis.
e. Place the cursor over one of the sizing handles on the text box and click the right mouse button. Then select the **Edit Text** option.
f. Type the description `100% of Sales =`. Then highlight this description, right click, and change the font size to 12. Then bold and italicize the text.
g. Click anywhere in the chart area to deactivate the text box.
h. Click the **Layout** tab and then click the **Text Box** icon to add a second text box.
i. Click and drag the shape of a rectangle above the 1990 bar.
j. Place the cursor over one of the sizing handles on the text box and click the right mouse button. Then select the **Edit Text** option.
k. Type the description `$35.2 Billion`. Then highlight this description, right click, and change the font size to 12. Then bold and italicize the text.
l. Click anywhere in the chart area to deactivate the text box.
m. Click the **Layout** tab and then click the **Text Box** icon.
n. Click and drag the shape of a rectangle above the year 2000 bar.
o. Place the cursor over one of the sizing handles on the text box and click the right mouse button. Then select the **Edit Text** option.

p. Type the description `$52.3 Billion`. Then highlight this description, right click, and change the font size to 12. Then bold and italicize the text.

q. Click anywhere in the chart area to deactivate the text box.

r. Click the **Layout** tab and then click the **Shapes** icon.

s. Click the first **Line** option in the Lines category of shapes.

t. Place the cursor at the top right of the blue stack of the 1990 bar. Then click and drag to the top left of the blue stack in the year 2000 bar.

u. Click the **Shape Outline** icon and select the color black. Then click the **Shape Outline** icon again and select the **1 ½ pt** line weight.

v. Click anywhere in the chart area to deactivate the line.

w. Click the **Layout** tab and then click the **Shapes** icon. Select the first **Line** option in the Lines category of shapes.

x. Place the cursor at the top right of the red stack of the 1990 bar. Then click and drag to the top left of the red stack in the year 2000 bar.

y. Click the **Shape Outline** icon and select the color black. Then click the **Shape Outline** icon again and select the **1 ½ pt** line weight.

z. Click anywhere in the chart area to deactivate the line.

aa. Save and close the file.

EXERCISE

Why Do I Need This?

>> Charting Stocks versus the Dow Jones Industrial Average

Formatting enhancements are often needed when a chart is initially created. In fields such as consulting, adding formatting enhancements to charts can be a critical component to running a successful client meeting. In addition, the formatting enhancements made to a chart are often a sign of a consulting firm's professionalism and attention to detail.

Exercise

The purpose of this exercise is to enhance the appearance of a chart that has been created for a business presentation. The purpose of the chart is to compare the change in a company's stock price to the change in the adjusted closing average of the Dow Jones Industrial Average. Open the file named ib_e05_stockpricecomparison. The following tasks will require you to add several formatting features to this chart:

1. Add the title `Change in Market Value by Month` to the chart. Add the following formatting enhancements:
   a. Font size should be 18 points, bold, and italic.
   b. Add a white fill by selecting the color white from the **Shape Fill** icon.
   c. Add a black line around the title with a 1-point weight.
   d. Add a shadow. You do this by clicking the **Shape Effects** icon, placing the cursor over the **Shadow** option, and selecting the **Offset Diagonal Bottom Right** option, which is the first option in the Outer set of options.
2. Add the title `Change in Value Year to Date` for the Y-axis. Apply the same formatting features that are listed in number 1 except make the font size 14 points instead of 18. Move the title to the left to create space between the title and the percentages along the Y-axis.

3. Format the Legend by applying the same formatting features listed in step 1. Then adjust the size of the legend so all the text is visible and move it so it is centered at the bottom of the chart.
4. Activate the Chart Area and change the color to light green by clicking the **Shape Fill** icon. Then click the **Shape Fill** icon again and place the cursor over the **Gradient** option. Select the **From Corner** option. This is the fourth option in the first row of the Dark Variations set of gradients.
5. Format the percentages along the Y-axis to a 12-point font size and change the color to white. Because this side of the chart is dark green, a white font will make the percentages easier to read.
6. Format the months along the X-axis to a 12-point font size.
7. Add a 2 ¼ point black line around the perimeter of the plot area.
8. Activate the "DJIA" data series. Change the color of the line to dark red and increase the weight of the line to 2 ¼ points. You can apply both formatting features by using the **Shape Outline** icon. This will make it easier to see the Dow Jones Industrial Average trend against the white background of the plot area.
9. Activate the "Our Company" data series. Change the color of the line to dark blue and increase the weight of the line to 2 ¼ points. This will make it easier to see the trend of the stock price for the managers of this company.
10. Add a text box named `Fed Rate Increase in March` to the plot area of the chart. Notice that the DJIA trend drops significantly from February to March. This text box will tell the reader that this was a key factor contributing to the decline in the market. Therefore, place this text box by the month of March at the 2% grid line and apply the following formats:
    a. The text should have a font size of 12 points, bold, and italic.
    b. The fill color should be orange.
    c. The perimeter should have a black line with a 1-point weight.
    d. Adjust the size of the text box so all the text is visible.
11. Add a second text box named `Earnings Decrease Announced in Sept` to the plot area of the chart. Notice that the trend for the company's stock drops significantly from September to December. This text box will explain why this decline occurred. Therefore, place this text box by the month of September at the 6% grid line and apply the same formats listed in step 10.
12. Save and close your file.

>> What's Wrong with This Spreadsheet?

PROBLEM & EXERCISE

Problem

You just finished creating a chart for a strategy meeting and have asked one of the interns in the department to make a few formatting enhancements to help highlight the product trends. After several hours, the intern comes to you in a panic asking for help. He explains that he tried to make several of the formatting enhancements you requested but is afraid he may have ruined the chart. He admits he was rushing to get this job done and thinks the entire chart will have to be deleted and re-created. The intern mentions the following points in his discussion with you:

1. I'm not sure what happened, but one of the bars seems to have disappeared. I was trying to change the color of the bars for the Casual Knits category to purple. I though this might look better. However, the bar for 2007 has mysteriously disappeared.

2. The other thing that happened was a bunch of the bars got cut off. I was using the dialog box to format the Y-axis, and then the phone rang. I went to pick up the phone and dropped it on my keyboard. I looked at the screen and a bunch of the bars were cut off.

3. Finally, I added the data labels to each bar like you asked, but they look terrible. A lot of the numbers are running into each other, and you really can't see them that well.

Exercise

The chart the intern was working on is named ib_e05_chartchaos. Open this file and look at the Product Chart. Consider the following points:

1. Did the Casual Knits bar in the year 2007 really disappear? Can an individual bar be formatted on a column chart?
2. Why are some of the bars cut off at the top of the chart? Look at the worksheet named Sales Data. What is the highest unit sales value? Compare this to the highest sales value along the Y-axis. How could the values or scale for the Y-axis change?
3. In the years 2007 and 2008, several data labels merged together. Can an individual data label be formatted or moved?

What's wrong with this chart? Write a short answer for each of the points listed here. Then fix the formatting problems for the Product Chart. In addition, add any other formatting enhancements that you think will make the chart easier to read.

Skill Set >> Advanced Chart Options

This section will illustrate techniques that utilize Excel's dynamic capabilities. As long as you use cell locations to define the source data, a chart will adjust itself automatically when the source data changes. Therefore, charts are useful for visually studying data trends when certain inputs are changed. This capability is helpful in economic fields that study changes in consumer demand or market supplies. This section will also illustrate how charts are created when data is not contained in adjacent columns and rows. Finally, this section will close with an illustration on how you can paste Excel charts into Word documents when writing reports or PowerPoint slides for presentations.

Defining the X- and Y-Axes Manually

Throughout this chapter so far, all the examples and exercises have utilized the method in which Excel automatically assigns values and labels to the X- and Y-axes. This method is used when the data you are displaying on a chart exists in a contiguous range of cells. However, in business, you will frequently be working with data that is not in a continuous range. For example, look at the column chart displayed in Figure 5.38. The purpose of this chart is to show the sales values in column C for each item listed in column A. However, notice that column B contains descriptive information that is not related to the sales of each item. When the range A2:C8 is highlighted to create the column chart, the data in column B distorts the labels along the X-axis.

Figure 5.38 | **Distorted Column Chart**

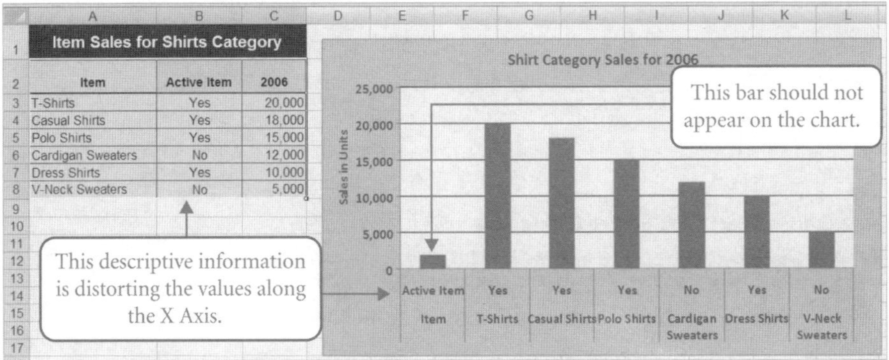

To create a basic column chart using the data in Figure 5.38, you will manually define the labels shown on the X-axis and the values shown on the Y-axis. As a result, instead of highlighting a range of cells and selecting a chart type in the **Insert** tab, you will activate a blank cell. This will produce a blank chart where the data series, as well as the values and labels assigned to the X- and Y-axes, can be defined manually. You accomplish this method as follows:

- Activate any blank cell that is at least two columns to the right or two rows below the data shown in Figure 5.38. You must leave at least one blank column or one blank row between the activated cell and the data on your worksheet. For this example, cell F2 is activated.
- Click the **Insert** tab, click the **Column** icon, and select the **Clustered Column** chart format. This will add a blank column chart to the worksheet, as shown in Figure 5.39.
- In the **Design** tab of the **Chart Tools** section on the Ribbon, click the **Select Data** icon. This will open the **Select Data Source** dialog box, as shown in Figure 5.40.

Figure 5.39 shows the appearance of a blank column chart and the **Select Data** icon, which is used to open the **Select Data Source** dialog box shown in Figure 5.40. Using the **Select Data Source** dialog box, you can define data series and the values and labels that are assigned to the X- and Y-axes. For a column chart, you use the left side of the **Select Data Source** dialog box to add data series or bars to the chart, which also adds values to the Y-axes and creates the legend. On the right side of the **Select Data Source** dialog box, you can define the range of cells that will be used to display the labels along the X-, or horizontal, axis.

Figure 5.39 | **Inserting a Blank Column Chart**

	A	B	C
1	Item Sales for Shirts Category		
2	Item	Active Item	2006
3	T-Shirts	Yes	20,00
4	Casual Shirts	Yes	18,00
5	Polo Shirts	Yes	15,00
6	Cardigan Sweaters	No	12,000
7	Dress Shirts	Yes	10,000
8	V-Neck Sweaters	No	5,000

Click here to open the Select Data Source dialog box.

Blank Column Chart

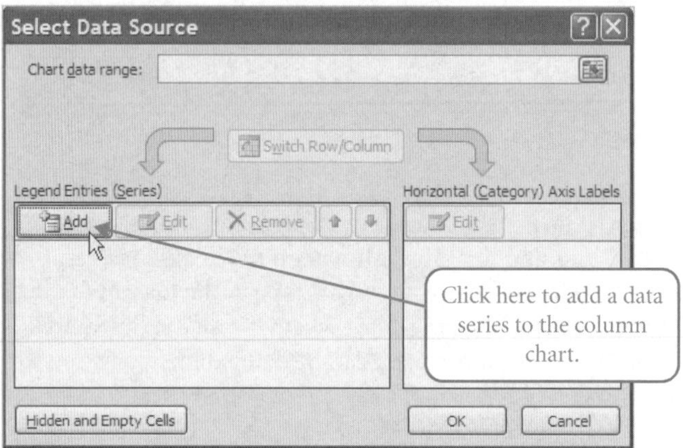

Figure 5.40 | **Select Data Source Dialog Box**

To complete the blank chart shown in Figure 5.39, you must define the data series and the labels for the X-, or horizontal, axis. You accomplish this as follows:

- Click the **Add** button on the left side of the **Select Data Source** dialog box under the **Legend Entries (Series)** heading. This will open the **Edit Series** dialog box (see Figure 5.41). For a column chart, a data series represents the bars that appear in the plot area of the chart. Therefore, the settings in the **Edit Series** dialog box will define how the bars are classified in the legend and assign values to the Y-, or vertical, axis.
- Click the range finder next to the **Series name** input box, highlight cell C2, and press the **Enter** key. This will add one data series to the column chart with the name "2006" in the legend.
- Click the range finder next to the **Series values** input box, highlight the range C3:C8, and press the **Enter** key. This will define the values for the 2006 data series. It is important to note that a bar will appear on the chart for every cell in the range C3:C8. As a result, six bars will appear on the column chart—one for each item in column A of the worksheet.
- Click the **OK** button at the bottom of the **Edit Series** dialog box after defining the Series values.
- Click the **Edit** button on the right side of the **Edit Data Source** dialog box. This will open the **Axis Labels** dialog box (see Figure 5.42).

- Click the range finder next to the **Axis Label Range** input box, highlight the range A3:A8, and press the **Enter** key. As previously mentioned, six bars will be added to the chart for each item in column A. Therefore, the X-, or horizontal, axis labels are defined using the descriptions in the range A3:A8.
- Click the **OK** button on the **Axis Labels** dialog box and then click the **OK** button on the **Select Data Source** dialog box.

Figure 5.41 shows the settings in the **Edit Series** dialog box. Notice that the description in the cell location used to define the Series name appears in the legend. Figure 5.42 shows the **Axis Labels** dialog box. The descriptions in the range of cells that appear in the input box will appear on the X-axis.

Figure 5.41 | **Edit Series Dialog Box**

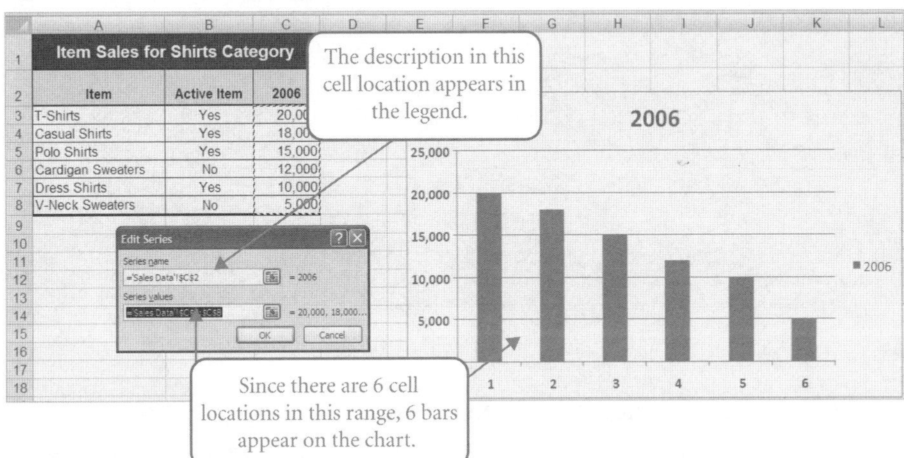

COMMON MISTAKES | Defining a Series Name

When using the **Edit Series** dialog box to add a data series to a chart, be sure to use only one cell location for the **Series name** input box. Highlighting a range of cells for this input box will distort your chart. You can also define the Series name by typing a description; however, you must place your description in quotation marks.

Figure 5.42 | **Axis Labels Dialog Box**

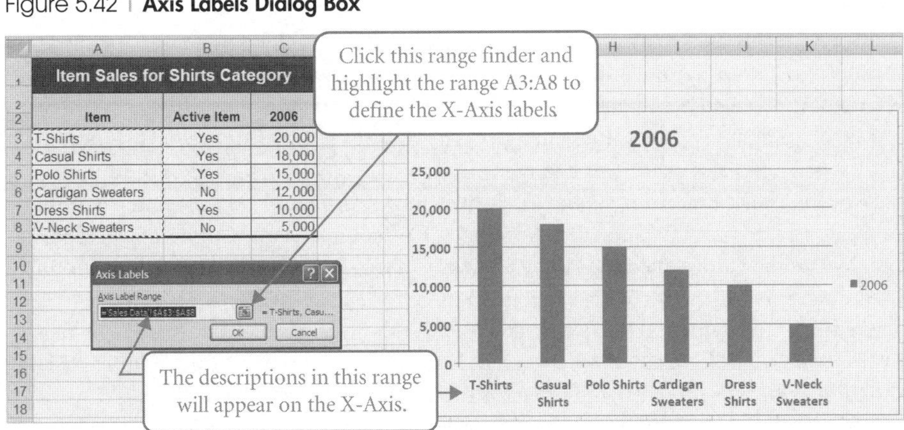

>> **Quick Reference**

Manually Defining a Column Chart

1. Activate a blank cell on a worksheet. A blank column or a blank row must appear between the data on a worksheet and the blank cell that is activated.
2. Select a chart type from the **Insert** tab on the Ribbon.
3. Select a chart format.
4. With the blank chart activated, click the **Select Data** icon in the **Design** tab on the Ribbon.
5. Click the **Add** button on the left side of the **Select Data Source** dialog box to add a data series.
6. Define the Series name in the **Edit Series** dialog box with one cell location or type a name in quotation marks.
7. Define the Series values with a range of cells.
8. Click the **OK** button to close the **Edit Series** dialog box.
9. Repeat steps 5–8 to add additional data series if needed.
10. Click the **Edit** button on the right side of the **Select Data Source** dialog box.
11. Use a range of cells to define the Axis Label Range. The descriptions in this cell range will be used for the X-axis labels.
12. Click the **OK** button on the **Axis Labels** dialog box.
13. Click the **OK** button on the **Select Data Source** dialog box.

Figure 5.43 shows the final settings in the **Select Data Source** dialog box. Figure 5.44 shows the final column chart that was created by manually defining the data series, and the values and labels along the X- and Y-axes. In addition, several formatting enhancements were added to the chart. Notice that the legend was removed because the chart represents only one year's worth of data. If this chart displayed several years' worth of data, such as the chart shown in Figure 5.30, a data series would be added for each item in column A, and the years would be used as labels for the X-axis. This would require you to click the **Add** button in Figure 5.43 six times and set the **Edit Series** dialog box for each of the six items in column A in Figure 5.44.

Figure 5.43 | **Final Settings in the Select Data Source Dialog Box**

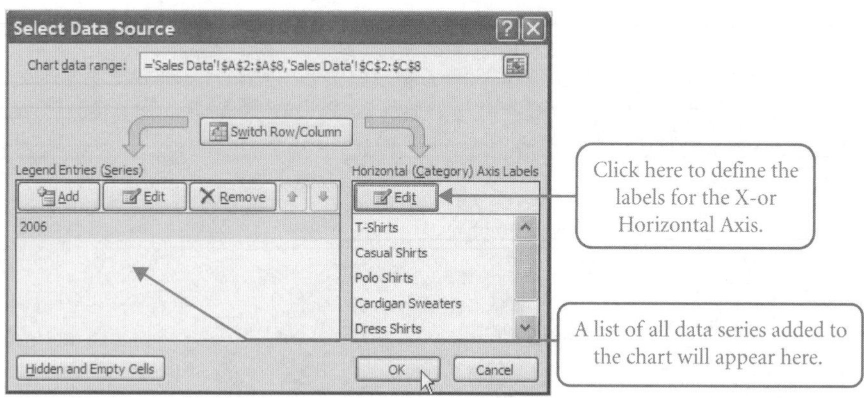

Figure 5.44 | **Final Column Chart Including Format Enhancements**

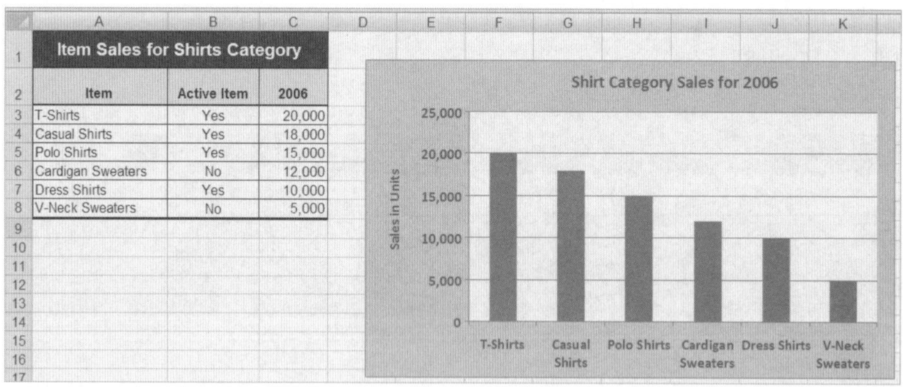

Item Sales for Shirts Category		
Item	Active Item	2006
T-Shirts	Yes	20,000
Casual Shirts	Yes	18,000
Polo Shirts	Yes	15,000
Cardigan Sweaters	No	12,000
Dress Shirts	Yes	10,000
V-Neck Sweaters	No	5,000

The Scatter Plot Chart

Throughout this text you have seen the benefits of Excel's cell referencing capabilities through the use of formulas and functions to complete various business objectives. Cell referencing can also play a valuable role when using charts to analyze business or economic data. That is, if the values change in the cells used to define the data series, X-axis, or Y-axis of a chart, this change will automatically be reflected in the appearance of the chart. For example, the worksheet shown in Figure 5.45 contains hypothetical price and demand data for four beverages: Coffee, Tea, Decaf Coffee, and Herbal Tea. Notice the value called the "Price Change Driver" in cell D15. This cell location is used in formulas that calculate a change in price for each week for each beverage. Therefore, if the value in D15 is changed to 5%, the price of all beverages will increase by 5% every week for each of the 10 weeks listed on the worksheet (see Figure 5.46). If the value is changed to –5%, the price for each beverage will decrease 5% every week for the 10 weeks listed on the worksheet. As the price changes for each beverage in columns B through E, another set of formulas calculates the sales demand in columns F through I. As a result, when this data is used to create a chart, if the value is changed in cell D15, all the values in the worksheet will change, which will automatically be reflected in the appearance of the chart.

Figure 5.45 | **Beverage Demand Data Worksheet**

	A	B	C	D	E	F	G	H	I
1	Beverage Demand Data								
2		Price per Cup				Sales in Cups			
3	Week	Coffee	Tea	Decaf Coffee	Herbal Tea	Coffee	Tea	Decaf Coffee	Herbal Tea
4	1	$0.50	$0.65	$0.75	$0.95	1,000	1,000	1,000	1,000
5	2	$0.50	$0.65	$0.75	$0.95	1,000	1,000	1,000	1,000
6	3	$0.50	$0.65	$0.75	$0.95	1,000	1,000	1,000	1,000
7	4	$0.50	$0.65	$0.75	$0.95	1,000	1,000	1,000	1,000
8	5	$0.50	$0.65	$0.75	$0.95	1,000	1,000	1,000	1,000
9	6	$0.50	$0.65	$0.75	$0.95	1,000	1,000	1,000	1,000
10	7	$0.50	$0.65	$0.75	$0.95	1,000	1,000	1,000	1,000
11	8	$0.50	$0.65	$0.75	$0.95	1,000	1,000	1,000	1,000
12	9	$0.50	$0.65	$0.75	$0.95	1,000	1,000	1,000	1,000
13	10	$0.50	$0.65	$0.75	$0.95	1,000	1,000	1,000	1,000
14									
15	Price Change Driver			0.00%					

Hypothetical data shows 1,000 cups sold at the current price for each beverage.

Values entered in this cell will change the Price and Sales data.

Figure 5.46 | **Beverage Demand Data Worksheet with 5% Price Increase per Week**

	A	B	C	D	E	F	G	H	I
1	Beverage Demand Data								
2		Price per Cup				Sales in Cups			
3	Week	Coffee	Tea	Decaf Coffee	Herbal Tea	Coffee	Tea	Decaf Coffee	Herbal Tea
4	1	$0.50	$0.65	$0.75	$0.95	1,000	1,000	1,000	1,000
5	2	$0.53	$0.68	$0.79	$1.00	988	975	950	900
6	3	$0.55	$0.72	$0.83	$1.05	975	951	903	810
7	4	$0.58	$0.75	$0.87	$1.10	963	927	857	729
8	5	$0.61	$0.79	$0.91	$1.15	951	904	815	656
9	6	$0.64	$0.83	$0.96	$1.21	939	881	774	590
10	7	$0.67	$0.87	$1.01	$1.27	927	859	735	531
11	8	$0.70	$0.91	$1.06	$1.34	916	838	698	478
12	9	$0.74	$0.96	$1.11	$1.40	904	817	663	430
13	10	$0.78	$1.01	$1.16	$1.47	893	796	630	387
14									
15	Price Change Driver			5.00%					

The demand for each beverage is decreasing at different rates when the price is increased.

Entering the number 5 in this cell increased the price 5% each week in columns B, C, D, and E.

Looking at Figure 5.46, you can see that the formulas calculating the Sales in Cups for each beverage are based on fundamental economic principles. That is, as the Price per Cup for each beverage increases in columns B through E, the Sales in Cups, or quantity demanded, decrease in columns F through I. However, a key question that most business managers try to answer is how much will demand increase or decrease when the price of a product is changed? To help answer this question, the next example constructs a scatter plot chart using the data from Figure 5.45. A scatter plot chart will place a marker for each beverage in the plot area based on its price and quantity demanded. Therefore, for each data series, or each beverage, the value for both the Y-axis and X-axis must be defined. This example is different from the charts that were demonstrated in the first two sections of this chapter; in those examples, values were assigned only to the Y-axis and labels were assigned to the X-axis (i.e., months, product category). Furthermore, the values for the X- and Y-axes in Figure 5.45 are not in a continuous range. Therefore, you must use the method of manually defining the data series, X-axis and Y-axis, that was demonstrated in the preceding section. The following points explain how this is accomplished:

- Activate cell K5, which is a blank cell. This will create a blank chart on the worksheet.
- Click the **Scatter** icon in the **Insert** tab on the Ribbon.
- Select the **Scatter with Straight Lines and Markers** format option. This will create a chart that has the visual appearance of a line chart with markers.
- Click the **Select Data** icon in the **Design** tab to open the **Select Data Source** dialog box.
- Click the **Add** button in the **Select Data Source** dialog box to add the first data series, which is Coffee. Notice that when the **Edit Series** dialog box opens, it has input boxes for both the X-axis and Y-axis values (see Figure 5.47).
- Click the range finder next to **Series name**, highlight cell B3, and press the **Enter** key. Cell B3 contains the word *Coffee*, which will appear in the legend to describe this data series.
- Click the range finder next to **Series X values**, highlight the range F4:F13, and press the **Enter** key. As mentioned, the goal of this chart is to show the quantity demanded, or Sales in Cups on the X-axis and the Price per Cup on the Y-axis. The range F4:F13 contains the quantity demanded for Coffee.
- Click the range finder next to **Series Y values**, highlight the range B4:B13, and press the **Enter** key. This range contains the price of Coffee for each of the 10 weeks listed in column B.
- Click the **OK** button to close the **Edit Series** dialog box. Then click the **Add** button in the **Select Data Source** dialog box to add the next data series, which is "Tea."
- Add the "Tea, Decaf Coffee, and Herbal Tea" data series using the same method described for Coffee. For each data series, use "Sales in Cups" to define the Series X values and Price per Cup to define the Series Y values.
- Click the **OK** button at the bottom of the **Select Data Source** dialog box to complete the chart.

Figure 5.47 shows the completed **Edit Series** dialog box for the Coffee data series. Notice that it has input boxes for defining both the X- and Y-axes values. In addition, as you define a data series, you will see a sample of the values appear on the right side of the **Edit Series** dialog box as well as on the chart itself.

Figure 5.47 | **Edit Series Dialog Box for Scatter Plot Chart**

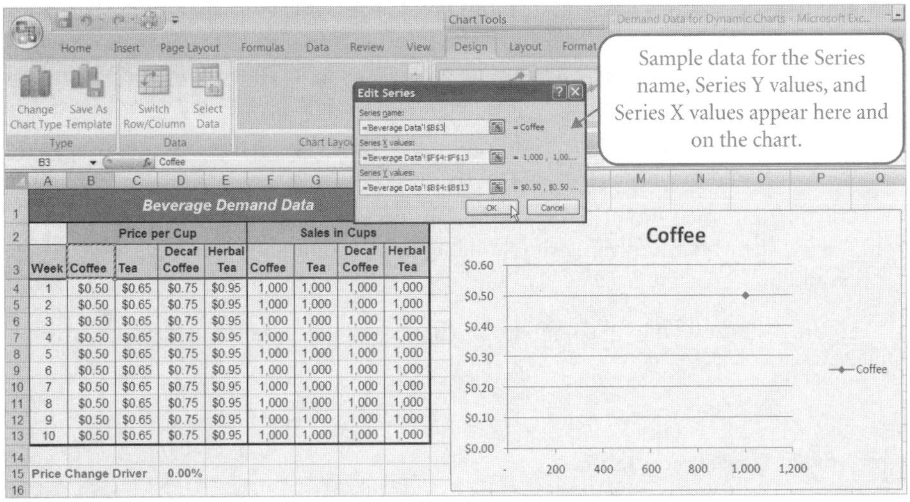

Figure 5.48 shows the completed **Select Data Source** dialog box after adding and defining each data series as shown in Figure 5.47. The name of each data series is listed on the left side of the **Select Data Source** dialog box. Notice that a unique marker is displayed for each data series, or beverage, in the plot area of the chart.

Figure 5.48 | **Final Settings in the Edit Data Source Dialog Box**

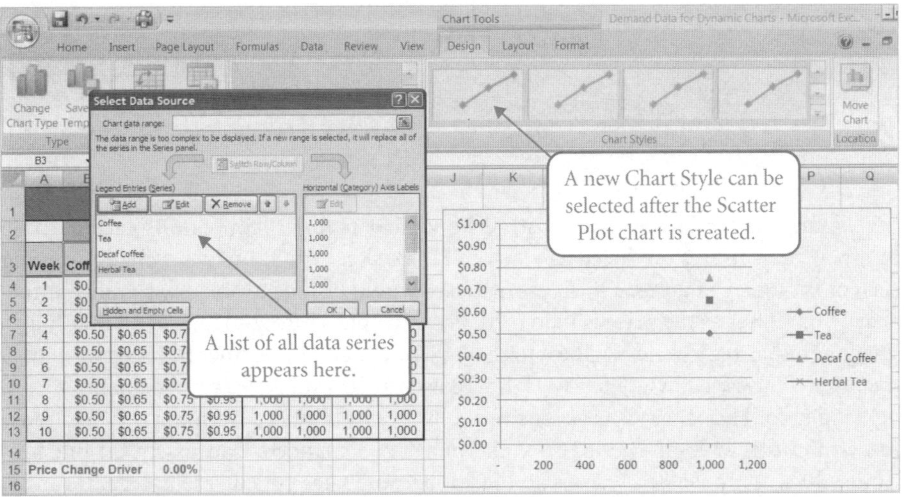

To complete the chart in Figure 5.48, several formatting techniques are applied such as adding titles, adjusting font sizes, and changing the color of the chart area. However, the most important formatting adjustment is fixing the scale of both the X- and Y-axes. The goal of this example is to show how the appearance of the chart changes when the formulas in the worksheet produce new outputs. Seeing how the data series changes, or moves, on the chart will provide insights as to how significant the Sales per Cup will change when the price is changed. However, the scale of the X- and Y-axes will constantly readjust when the data is changed, making it impossible to accurately read any data movements. Therefore, the scale of the X- and Y-axes must be fixed. You accomplish this as follows:

- Activate the Y-axis.
- Click the **Format** tab and then click the **Format Selection** icon. This will open the **Format Axis** dialog box, which was originally shown in Figure 5.29.

- In the **Axis Options** section, click the **Fixed** option next to the **Minimum** setting and type the number **`.40`** in the input box to the right. This will fix the **Minimum** value on the Y-axis at .40. Then click the **Fixed** option next to the **Maximum** setting and type the number **`1.80`** in the box to the right. This will fix the **Maximum** value of the Y-axis at 1.80.
- Click the **Close** button at the bottom of the **Format Axis** dialog box. Then activate the X-axis and open the **Format Axis** dialog box again.
- Use the same method for fixing the **Maximum** and **Minimum** values for the X-axis. The **Maximum** value should be set to 1,100 and the **Minimum** value should be set to 200.

Figure 5.49 shows the final scatter plot chart with all formatting enhancements added.

Figure 5.49 | **Final Scatter Plot Chart**

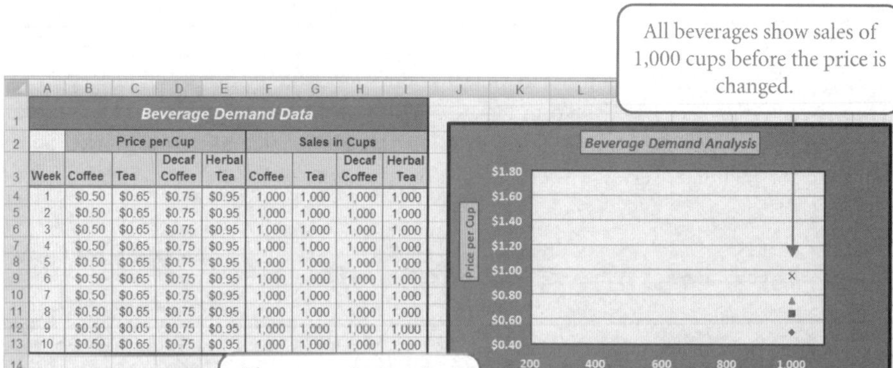

Beverage Demand Data								
	Price per Cup				Sales in Cups			
Week	Coffee	Tea	Decaf Coffee	Herbal Tea	Coffee	Tea	Decaf Coffee	Herbal Tea
1	$0.50	$0.65	$0.75	$0.95	1,000	1,000	1,000	1,000
2	$0.50	$0.65	$0.75	$0.95	1,000	1,000	1,000	1,000
3	$0.50	$0.65	$0.75	$0.95	1,000	1,000	1,000	1,000
4	$0.50	$0.65	$0.75	$0.95	1,000	1,000	1,000	1,000
5	$0.50	$0.65	$0.75	$0.95	1,000	1,000	1,000	1,000
6	$0.50	$0.65	$0.75	$0.95	1,000	1,000	1,000	1,000
7	$0.50	$0.65	$0.75	$0.95	1,000	1,000	1,000	1,000
8	$0.50	$0.65	$0.75	$0.95	1,000	1,000	1,000	1,000
9	$0.50	$0.05	$0.75	$0.95	1,000	1,000	1,000	1,000
10	$0.50	$0.65	$0.75	$0.95	1,000	1,000	1,000	1,000

Price Change Driver 0.00%

Figures 5.50, 5.51, and 5.52 illustrate how the data series representing each of the four beverages moves on the chart when cell D15 is set to 1, 3, and 5%. After examining each of these three figures, a business manager would be able to see how significant the change in sales is as the price is increased. For example, notice in Figure 5.50 that the line for Herbal Tea extends farthest to the left compared to the other beverages when the price is increased by 1% per week for 10 weeks. This suggests that the quantity demanded for Herbal Tea is very sensitive to increases in price, assuming this data represents industrywide changes in price and quantity demanded. Conversely, the line for Coffee does not move nearly as far to the left because sales per cup are not significantly declining when the price is increased.

Figure 5.50 | **Sales in Cups When Price Is Increased 1%**

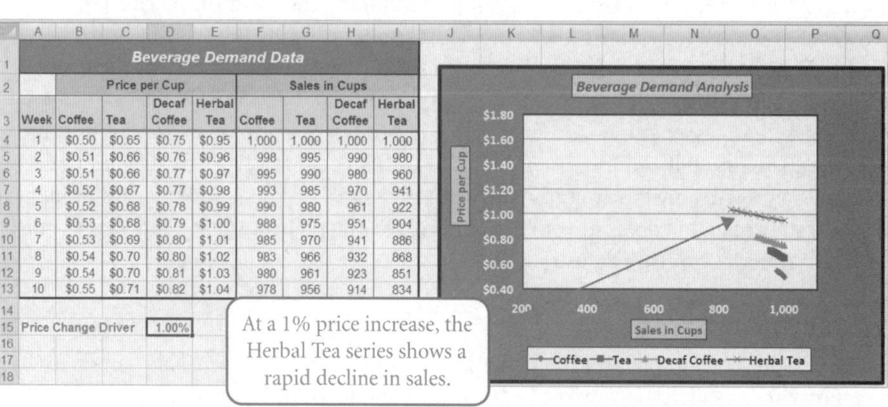

Beverage Demand Data								
	Price per Cup				Sales in Cups			
Week	Coffee	Tea	Decaf Coffee	Herbal Tea	Coffee	Tea	Decaf Coffee	Herbal Tea
1	$0.50	$0.65	$0.75	$0.95	1,000	1,000	1,000	1,000
2	$0.51	$0.66	$0.76	$0.96	998	995	990	980
3	$0.51	$0.66	$0.77	$0.97	995	990	980	960
4	$0.52	$0.67	$0.77	$0.98	993	985	970	941
5	$0.52	$0.68	$0.78	$0.99	990	980	961	922
6	$0.53	$0.68	$0.79	$1.00	988	975	951	904
7	$0.53	$0.69	$0.80	$1.01	985	970	941	886
8	$0.54	$0.70	$0.80	$1.02	983	966	932	868
9	$0.54	$0.70	$0.81	$1.03	980	961	923	851
10	$0.55	$0.71	$0.82	$1.04	978	956	914	834

Price Change Driver 1.00%

Figure 5.51 | **Sales in Cups When Price Is Increased 3%**

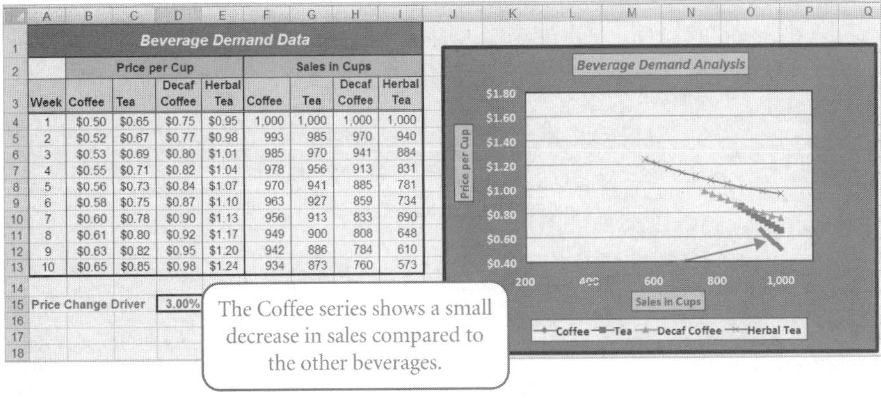

Beverage Demand Data								
	Price per Cup				Sales in Cups			
Week	Coffee	Tea	Decaf Coffee	Herbal Tea	Coffee	Tea	Decaf Coffee	Herbal Tea
1	$0.50	$0.65	$0.75	$0.95	1,000	1,000	1,000	1,000
2	$0.52	$0.67	$0.77	$0.98	993	985	970	940
3	$0.53	$0.69	$0.80	$1.01	985	970	941	884
4	$0.55	$0.71	$0.82	$1.04	978	956	913	831
5	$0.56	$0.73	$0.84	$1.07	970	941	885	781
6	$0.58	$0.75	$0.87	$1.10	963	927	859	734
7	$0.60	$0.78	$0.90	$1.13	956	913	833	690
8	$0.61	$0.80	$0.92	$1.17	949	900	808	648
9	$0.63	$0.82	$0.95	$1.20	942	886	784	610
10	$0.65	$0.85	$0.98	$1.24	934	873	760	573

Price Change Driver 3.00%

Figure 5.52 | **Sales in Cups When Price Is Increased 5%**

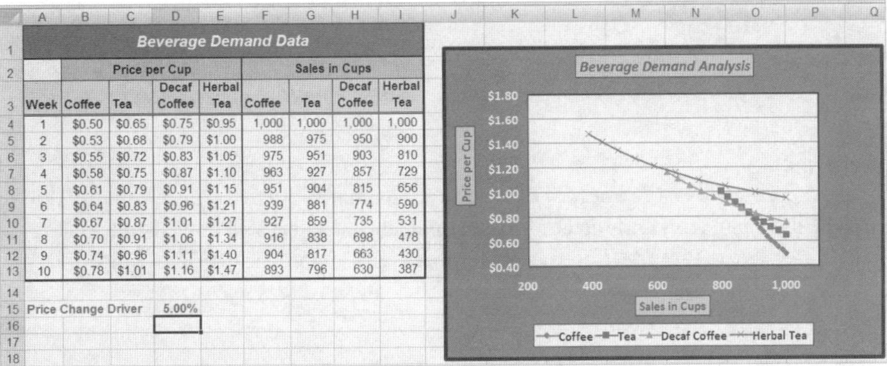

Beverage Demand Data								
	Price per Cup				Sales in Cups			
Week	Coffee	Tea	Decaf Coffee	Herbal Tea	Coffee	Tea	Decaf Coffee	Herbal Tea
1	$0.50	$0.65	$0.75	$0.95	1,000	1,000	1,000	1,000
2	$0.53	$0.68	$0.79	$1.00	988	975	950	900
3	$0.55	$0.72	$0.83	$1.05	975	951	903	810
4	$0.58	$0.75	$0.87	$1.10	963	927	857	729
5	$0.61	$0.79	$0.91	$1.15	951	904	815	656
6	$0.64	$0.83	$0.96	$1.21	939	881	774	590
7	$0.67	$0.87	$1.01	$1.27	927	859	735	531
8	$0.70	$0.91	$1.06	$1.34	916	838	698	478
9	$0.74	$0.96	$1.11	$1.40	904	817	663	430
10	$0.78	$1.01	$1.16	$1.47	893	796	630	387

Price Change Driver 5.00%

Pasting Charts into PowerPoint and Word

Excel charts are frequently added to PowerPoint slides or Word documents for business presentations and reports. This section will demonstrate how you can copy and paste Excel charts into either a PowerPoint slide or Word document.

Figure 5.53 shows a PowerPoint slide that could be used by a business manager who is presenting the results of the column chart shown in Figure 5.30. The following steps explain how to copy and paste this chart into this slide:

- Open both the PowerPoint file and the Excel file containing the column chart.
- Activate the Excel file by clicking it in the taskbar at the bottom of the screen (see Figure 5.54).
- Activate the column chart and click the **Copy** icon.
- Activate the PowerPoint file by clicking it in the taskbar at the bottom of the screen.
- Select the **Paste Special** option in the **Paste** icon in **Home** tab on the Ribbon in the PowerPoint file. This will open the **Paste Special** dialog box.
- Select the **Picture (Enhanced Metafile)** option in the **Paste Special** dialog box and click the **OK** button. The chart will appear in the slide.
- Use the sizing handles on the chart to change the size of the chart and click and drag the chart to reposition on the slide if necessary.

» Quick Reference

Scatter Plot Charts

1. Activate a blank cell on a worksheet. A blank column or a blank row must appear between the data on a worksheet and the blank cell that is activated.
2. Click the **Scatter** icon in the **Insert** tab on the Ribbon.
3. Select a chart format.
4. With the blank chart activated, click the **Select Data** icon in the **Design** tab on the Ribbon.
5. Click the **Add** button on the left side of the **Select Data Source** dialog box to add a data series.
6. Define the Series name in the **Edit Series** dialog box with one cell location or type a name in quotation marks.
7. Define the X Series values with a range of cells.
8. Define the Y Series values with a range of cells.
9. Click the **OK** button to close the **Edit Series** dialog box.
10. Repeat steps 5–9 to add additional data series if needed.
11. Click the **OK** button on the **Select Data Source** dialog box.

Figure 5.53 | **View of a PowerPoint Slide**

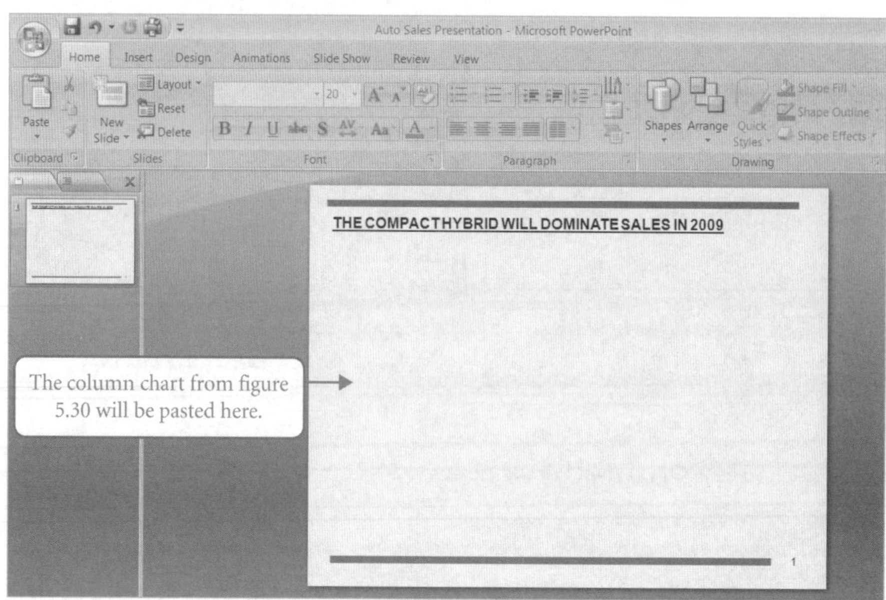

Figure 5.54 shows the **Paste Special** dialog box that is opened by clicking the down arrow of the **Paste** icon and selecting **Paste Special.** The chart will appear in the slide after you select the **Picture (Enhanced Metafile)** option and click the **OK** button.

Figure 5.54 | **Paste Special Dialog Box for Pasting a Chart**

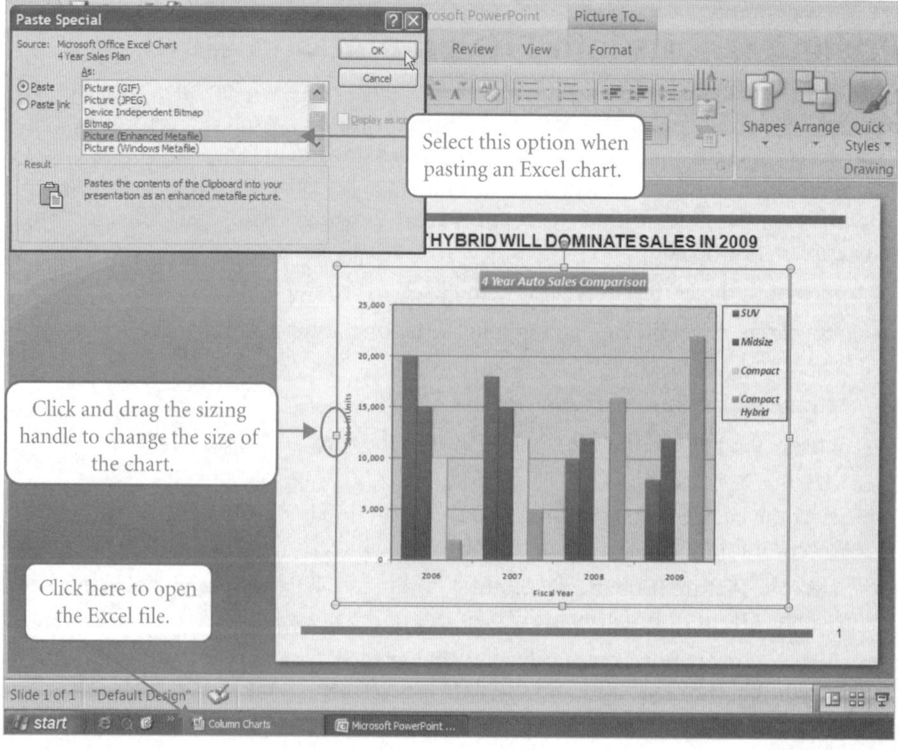

Figure 5.55 shows the final PowerPoint slide with the Excel chart. Notice that the chart was repositioned on the slide to make room for the triangle and text box.

Figure 5.55 | **Final PowerPoint Slide**

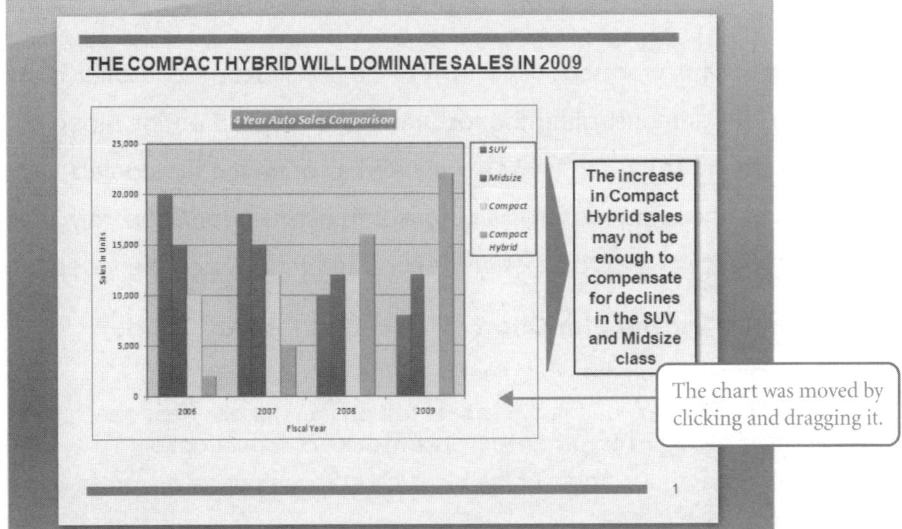

Figure 5.56 shows an example of pasting the 100% Stacked Column chart shown in Figure 5.37 into a Word document. This business research paper example demonstrates the trends in the Sporting Goods industry. The method for pasting this chart into the Word document is identical to the method illustrated for pasting a chart into a PowerPoint slide. After copying the chart in an Excel file, place the cursor in your Word document where you want the chart to appear. Then open the **Paste Special** dialog box and select the **Picture** (**Enhanced Metafile**) option.

Figure 5.56 | **Excel Chart Pasted into a Word Document**

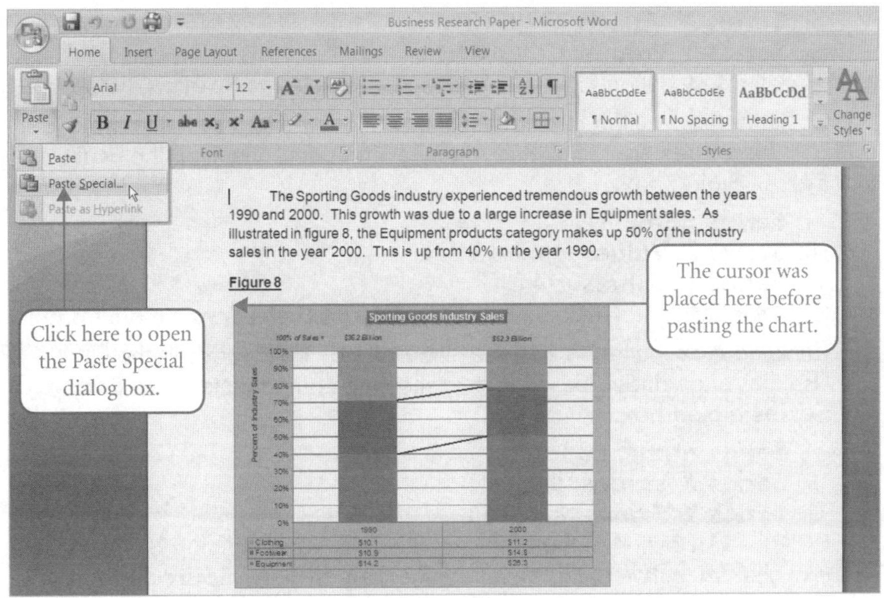

>> Quick Reference

Pasting Charts into PowerPoint and Word

1. Activate a chart in an Excel file and click the **Copy** icon.
2. Open a PowerPoint file to a slide where the chart should appear. For a Word document, place the cursor where the chart should appear.
3. Click the **Home** tab in the Ribbon.
4. Click the down arrow below the **Paste** icon.
5. Select the **Paste Special** option to open the **Paste Special** dialog box.
6. Select the **Picture (Enhanced Metafile)** option and click the **OK** button in the **Paste Special** dialog box.
7. Adjust the size of the chart by clicking and dragging the sizing handles as needed.

VIDEO WORKSHOP

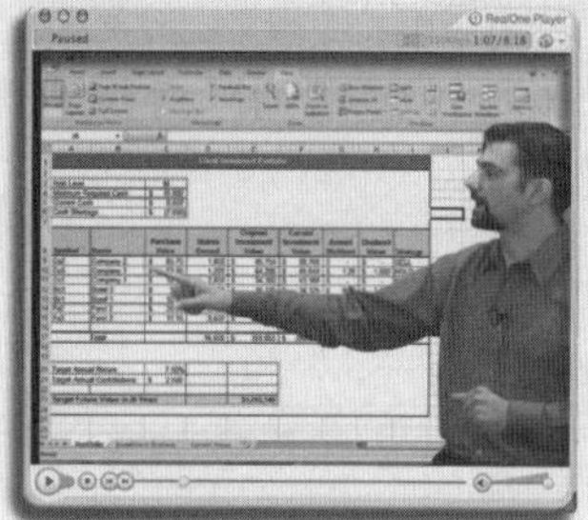

>>Scatter Plot Charts

The purpose of this workshop is to review the construction of scatter plot charts. I will be demonstrating the tasks in this workshop on the video named **Scatter Plot Charts**. You will need to open the file named ib_e05_beveragedemandanalysis before starting this workshop. Try completing the following tasks on your own and then watch the video.

1. **Creating a Scatter Plot Chart (Video: Scatter Plot Charts)**
   a. Activate cell L1 on the worksheet named Beverage Data.
   b. Click the **Scatter** icon in the **Insert** tab on the Ribbon. Then select the **Scatter with Straight Lines and Markers** format option.
   c. Click and drag the frame of the blank chart so the upper-left corner is in cell J1.
   d. Click the **Select Data** icon in the **Design** tab on the Ribbon.
   e. Click the **Add** button to add the "Coffee" data series to the chart. Use the range finder to define the following components of the **Edit Series** dialog box:
      i. **Series name**: B3
      ii. **Series X Values**: F4:F13
      iii. **Series Y Values**: B4:B13
   f. Click the **OK** button to go back to the **Select Data Source** dialog box.
   g. Click the **Add** button to add the "Tea" data series to the chart. Use the range finder to define the following components of the **Edit Series** dialog box:
      i. **Series name**: C3
      ii. **Series X Values**: G4:G13
      iii. **Series Y Values**: C4:C13
   h. Click the **OK** button to go back to the **Select Data Source** dialog box.
   i. Click the **Add** button to add the "Decaf Coffee" data series to the chart. Use the range finder to define the following components of the **Edit Series** dialog box:
      i. **Series name**: D3
      ii. **Series X Values**: H4:H13
      iii. **Series Y Values**: D4:D13
   j. Click the **OK** button to go back to the **Select Data Source** dialog box.
   k. Click the **Add** button to add the "Herbal Tea" data series to the chart. Use the range finder to define the following components of the **Edit Series** dialog box:
      i. **Series name**: E3
      ii. **Series X Values**: I4:I13
      iii. **Series Y Values**: E4:E13
   l. Click the **OK** button at the bottom of the **Edit Series** dialog box and then click the **OK** button at the bottom of the **Select Data Source** dialog box.
   m. Select the **Style 18 Chart Styles** icon in the **Design** tab on the Ribbon.
   n. Click the **Legend** icon in the **Layout** tab and select the **Show Legend at Bottom** option.

o. Add the chart title `Beverage Demand Analysis`. Use the **Above chart** option.
p. Add the title `Price per Cup` to the Y-axis.
q. Add the title `Sales in Cups` to the X-axis.

2. **Formatting (Video: Scatter Plot Charts)**
   a. Center the title over the middle of the chart and then center the legend at the bottom of the chart.
   b. Format the chart title with a 12-point font, bold, italics, orange background, and black outline with a 1-point weight.
   c. Format the legend with a 10-point font, bold, white background, and black outline with a 1-point weight.
   d. Create space between the left side of the plot area and the Y-axis title. Decrease the plot area to the right and move the Y-axis title to the left.
   e. Make the same formatting enhancements to the X- and Y-axes titles as the chart title, except keep the font size at 10 points.
   f. Change the color of the chart area to green.
   g. Change the color of the Y-axis and X-axis values to white.

3. **Fixing the Scale for the X- and Y-Axes (Video: Scatter Plot Charts)**
   a. Click anywhere on the Y-axis and click the **Format Selection** icon in the **Format** tab on the Ribbon.
   b. Set the **Minimum** and **Maximum** options to **Fixed**. Then type the following values in the input box next to each option:
      i. **Minimum**: `.40`
      ii. **Maximum**: `1.80`
   c. Click the **Close** button at the bottom of the **Format Axis** dialog box.
   d. Click anywhere on the X-axis and click the **Format Selection** icon in the **Format** tab on the Ribbon.
   e. Set the **Minimum** and **Maximum** options to **Fixed**. Then type the following values in the input box next to each option:
      i. **Minimum**: `200`
      ii. **Maximum**: `1100`
   f. Click the **Close** button at the bottom of the **Format Axis** dialog box.
   g. Change the value in cell D15 to `1`. Then change it to `3`.
   h. Save and close your file.

>> Pasting Charts into Word

The purpose of this workshop is to demonstrate the method of pasting Excel charts into a Word document. I will be demonstrating the tasks in this workshop in the video named **Pasting Charts into Word**. You will need to open the Word file named ib_e05_businessplanpaper and the Excel file named ib_e05_costschart before starting this workshop. Try completing the following tasks on your own and then watch the video.

1. **Inserting Charts into Word Documents (Video: Pasting Charts into Word)**
   a. Activate the Excel file named ib_e05_costschart.
   b. Activate the pie chart named Startup Costs and copy it.
   c. Activate the Word document named ib_e05_businessplanpaper and place the cursor below the **Figure 2** heading along the left margin.
   d. Open the **Paste Special** dialog box by clicking the down arrow below the **Paste** icon.
   e. Select the **Picture (Enhanced Metafile)** option in the **Paste Special** dialog box and click the **OK** button.
   f. Select the chart and reduce the height of the pie chart to 2.5 inches using the **Height** icon in the **Format** tab on the Ribbon. This will automatically reduce the width to 4.06 inches.
   g. Save and close your file.

EXERCISE

Why Do I Need This?

>> Analyzing Supply and Demand

Studying changes in supply and demand is a common area of research for professional economists and business analysts. Changes in supply and demand can impact decisions such as product pricing, entry into new markets, exiting existing markets, increasing product lines, or decreasing product lines. Having the ability to visually display these trends can not only serve as a powerful presentation tool, but can also serve as a powerful analytical tool.

Exercise

The purpose of this exercise is to create a supply and demand chart using a scatter plot chart. In addition, this exercise will demonstrate how a change in price impacts the quantity supplied and the quantity demanded for a hypothetical industry. Your goal will be to change the price to identify where the demand and supply lines intersect, which is also known as *reaching equilibrium*. This data can be found in the file named ib_e05_supplyanddemand. Open this file before working on the following tasks:

1. Type the number `10` into cell C15. Note the price in cell B12 by typing it into a blank cell on the worksheet or jot it down on a piece of paper. You will need to know this number later in the exercise.

2. Type the number `-10` into cell C15. Note the quantity value in cell D12 by typing it into another blank cell on the worksheet or jot it down on a piece of paper. You will need to know this number later in the exercise.

3. Type the number `0` into cell C15. Then activate a blank cell for the purposes of creating a blank chart.

4. Create a blank **Scatter** chart using the **Scatter with Straight Lines and Markers** format option. After creating the blank chart, move it so the upper-left corner is in cell E1.

5. Open the **Select Data Source** dialog box and add the Supply data series to the chart. The settings in the **Edit Series** dialog box should be as follows:
   a. **Series name**: Cell C2, which contains the word *Supply*.
   b. **Series X values**: The range C3:C12, which contains the quantity supplied values.
   c. **Series Y values**: The range B3:B12, which contains the price.

6. Add the Demand data series to the chart using the following details in the **Edit Series** dialog box:
   a. **Series name**: Cell D2, which contains the word *Demand*.
   b. **Series X values**: The range D3:D12, which contains the quantity demand values.
   c. **Series Y values**: The range B3:B12, which contains the price.
7. Change the **Chart Style** of the chart to **Style 34**. This will change the color of the Demand data series to red and the Supply data series to blue.
8. Add the following titles to the chart:
   a. **Chart Title**: `Supply and Demand for Product A`
   b. **X-Axis Title**: `Quantity`
   c. **Y-Axis Title**: `Price`
9. Change the font size of the chart title to 14 points and change the font size of the X- and Y-axes titles to 12 points. Then move the Y-axis title to the left to create space between the title and Y-axis values.
10. Fix the scale of the Y-axis using the **Format Axis** dialog box. Use the number you identified in step 1 rounded *up* to the nearest dollar to set the **Maximum** value for the axis. Set the **Minimum** value of the axis to `0`.
11. Fix the scale of the X-axis using the **Format Axis** dialog box. Use the number you identified in step 2 to set the **Maximum** value for the axis. Set the **Minimum** value to `0`.
12. Type the number `3`, then `5`, and then `10` into cell C15. At what price (approximately) does the demand line intersect the supply line?
13. Enter the number `0`, then `-3`, then `-5`, and then `-10` into cell C15. Can the quantity supplied satisfy the quantity demanded at these prices?
14. Save and close your file.

>> What's Wrong with This Spreadsheet?

PROBLEM & EXERCISE

Problem

A coworker in your department is trying to create a chart for a strategy presentation being held tomorrow morning. She is having difficulty creating a column chart based on the sales results contained in an Excel file and has come to you for help. Her goal is to show the change in Net Sales from the year 2006 to 2007 for each company in her worksheet. Her conversation with you includes the following points:

1. I am trying to create a basic column chart that shows the Net Sales values along the Y-axis and the name of each company on the X-axis. Because I have two years' worth of data, I thought I would use the legend to show what bar pertains to what year.
2. A friend of mine showed me this trick in which you just highlight everything on the worksheet; click that chart icon in the Ribbon, and bingo, the chart appears. I did the same exact thing as my friend, but my chart is horrible!
3. The other thing I noticed is the Public Company indicator (Column B) keeps popping up in the chart. I just want the sales data in a simple column chart. However, I guess this is more complicated than I thought!

Exercise

The chart your coworker tried to create is on the file named ib_e05_charttrouble. Open this file and take a look at the Chart1 chart sheet. Consider the following points:

1. What method is your coworker using to create the chart? Will this enable her to achieve her goals?
2. Why is the Public Company indicator (column B) appearing in the chart?
3. Your coworker is trying to create a column chart. Is that apparent in the chart that was attempted on the file?
4. Your coworker wants the year to be in the legend of the chart. How can this be accomplished?

What's wrong with this chart? Write a short answer to each of the points listed here. Then create a second chart in the ib_e05_charttrouble Excel file based on the requirements stated here. Apply any formatting features that you think will make the chart easier to read. The chart you create should appear in its own chart sheet.

Excel in **Practice** | Anecdote

Solution from page 178

Using charts is the key to conducting an effective progress review meeting. A well-constructed chart can explain trends, relationships, and results in a very short period time. Therefore, I converted the data calculated and evaluated in numerous Excel files to a few charts, pasted them into PowerPoint slides, and presented them at progress review meetings. Constructing charts this way not only increased the efficiency of the meetings, but also demonstrated a professional standard that my clients often appreciated.

Assignment

1. The file named ib_e05_clientresearchdata contains data for a meeting with the executives of a major corporation.
2. Create a chart that will best display the sales trend by region in the Regional Sales worksheet. This chart should demonstrate how the overall sales of the company have shifted between the regions.
3. Use any annotations, objects, and formatting techniques to highlight changes in the company's sales by region. Note that the total sales for the company by year are in row 8 of the worksheet. Your chart must show these total sales results.
4. Create a PowerPoint slide with the title `Region 4 Provides Future Growth`. Display the chart you created in this slide. This PowerPoint slide as well as the chart should have a professional appearance.

Questions for Discussion

1. Why are charts better to use in presentations as opposed to worksheets?
2. Is it possible to have too much formatting on a chart?
3. What do you need to know to create an effective chart?

Review Questions

The following questions are related to the concepts addressed in this chapter. There are three types of questions: Short Answer, True or False, and Fill in the Blank. If your answer to a True or False question is False, write a short explanation as to why you think the statement is not true.

1. Excel charts are usually used for displaying and analyzing ____________ data.
2. How are charts used in business?
3. The ____________ tab on the Ribbon is used for creating charts.
4. True or False: You must *always* highlight data on a worksheet before creating a chart.
5. What three tabs are added to the Ribbon after you create a chart?
6. After you create a chart, if the data you wanted on the X-axis appears on the Y-axis, you can use the ____________ icon in the ____________ tab on the Ribbon.
7. Explain when you would use a 100% Stacked Column chart instead of a pie chart.
8. What is the purpose of adding lines to a 100% Stacked Column chart?
9. A ____________ chart is commonly used to display trends over time, such as stock prices or market indices.
10. A data table can be added to the bottom of a chart using the ____________ icon in the ____________ tab on the Ribbon.
11. Specific data values can be added to a chart by using the ____________ icon in the ____________ tab on the Ribbon.
12. True or False: The formatting icons in the **Home** tab cannot be used when formatting an area of a chart.
13. True or False: The data values or data table added to a chart cannot be formatted.
14. Explain when you would need to use the **Format Axis** dialog box when formatting either the X- or Y-axis.
15. How would you change the color of one individual bar on a column chart?
16. The ____________ icon in the ____________ tab is used for adding annotations to a chart.
17. Lines and arrows can be added to a chart by clicking the ____________ icon in the ____________ tab on the Ribbon.
18. True or False: A **Format** dialog box can be opened for any area of the chart by activating that area, right clicking, and selecting the appropriate command.
19. Explain why you would want to manually define the data series, X-axis values, and Y-axis values for a chart.
20. True or False: For a column chart, both the X and Y series values can be defined for each data series added to the chart.

21. True or False: Once a chart is created, it will never change even if the data used to create it changes.

22. What chart would you need to use if you wanted to define X-axis and Y-axis values for each data series.

23. For you to see data moving on a chart, it is best to use the ____________ of the X- and Y-axes.

24. What option in the **Paste Special** dialog box should you use when pasting charts into a Word or PowerPoint file?

25. True or False: When you are pasting a chart into a Word file, the chart will always appear in the upper-left corner of the page that is currently visible on the screen.

Skills Exam

The following exam is designed to test your ability to recognize and execute the Excel skills presented in this chapter. Read each question carefully and answer the questions in the order they are listed. You should be able to complete this exam in 60 minutes or less.

1. Open the ib_e05_skillsexam.
2. For the Global Sales worksheet, create a 100% Stacked Column chart that can be used to evaluate the sales growth of this company by country/region. The chart should include the following details:
   a. The X-axis should display the years in the range B3:E3.
   b. The Legend should display the name of the country or region from column A.
   c. The chart title above the chart should be `Global Net Sales`.
   d. The title for the Y-axis should be `Percent of Total Net Sales`.
   e. Data labels showing the sales value for each country should appear on the inside end of the bars.
   f. The chart should appear in its own chart sheet with the tab name `Global Sales Chart`.
3. Change the font size for the percentages along the Y-axis to 12 points.
4. Change the font size for the years along the X-axis to 14 points.
5. Make the following format adjustments to the Y-axis title:
   a. Add a black outline with a 1-point weight.
   b. Change the background color to blue.
   c. Change the font size to 12 and change the text color to white.
6. Make the following format adjustments to the chart title:
   a. Add a black outline with a 1-point weight.
   b. Change the background color to blue.
   c. Change the font size to 18 and change the text color to white.
7. Decrease the height of the plot area so there is approximately ½ inch of space between the top of the plot area and the chart title.
8. Make the following format adjustments to the chart legend:
   a. Add a black outline with a 1-point weight.
   b. Change the font size to 16 and bold the text.
   c. Move the legend next to the plot area.
   d. Increase the height of the legend so it is the same height as the plot area.
9. Change the color of the Europe data series to red, the Canada data series to orange, and the Asia Pacific data series to light green.
10. For all the data labels on the bars of the chart, increase the font size to 12 points.
11. Add the following annotation to the chart: `Dollars in U.S. Billions`. This annotation should appear in the upper-left corner of the chart area. Change the font size to 10 points and add italics.
12. Add the following annotation to the chart: `100% Net Sales =`. This annotation should appear next to the left border of the chart area above the Y-axis. The font size should be 10 points, bold, and italic.
13. Add an annotation to the top of each bar of the chart showing the total Net Sales for each year. The total sales for each year can be found in row 8 of the Global Sales worksheet. A dollar sign should appear in front of each number, and the font should be 12 points, bold, and italic. Make sure the number is completely visible.

14. Connect the top of each bar for the USA data series with a *black* line. Do the same for the Europe and Canada data series. Use a 1-point weight for all lines.
15. Create a line chart based on the data in the Income Summary worksheet. The chart should include the following details:
    a. The X-axis should display the years in the range B2:J2.
    b. The Legend should display the name of the income categories in column A.
    c. The chart title shouldbe `Income Summary`.
    d. The title for the Y-axis should be `Percent Change at Year End`.
    e. The legend should appear at the bottom of the chart.
    f. The chart should appear in its own chart sheet with the tab name `Income Summary Chart`.
    g. The Style of the chart should be set to the **Style 2** option.
16. Change the font size of the percentages and years on the Y- and X-axes to 12 points.
17. Make the following format adjustments to the chart legend:
    a. Add a black outline with a 1-point weight.
    b. Change the font size to 12 points and bold the text.
    c. Move the legend so that it is centered under the plot area.
18. Change the line weight for each data series to 2¼ points. Do not change the colors.
19. Fix the scale of the Y-axis as follows:
    a. Minimum: `-.08`
    b. Maximum: `.16`
    c. Major Unit: `04`
20. Open the Word document named ib_e05_internationalsalesreport.
21. Paste the **Global Sales Chart** from the Excel file into this Word document. The chart must appear below the words *Figure 1* in bold text. Leave one space between the chart and this heading.
22. Save and close both the Word file and the Excel file.

Challenge Questions

The following questions are designed to test your ability to apply the Excel skills you have learned to complete a business objective. Use your knowledge of Excel as well as your creativity to answer these questions. For most questions, there are several possible ways to complete the objective.

1. If you are presenting data for an international company, what chart would you use to show the percent of sales generated by country for one year? Assume this company is operating in five countries. Create a spreadsheet showing one year of sales data for an international company by country. You can make up the countries and the sales numbers. Create a chart to present this data.

2. Pick two public companies and research the historical closing price of the stock for every month last year. In addition, research the historical adjusted closing price of the Dow Jones Industrial Average for every month last year. Record your data onto an Excel worksheet and create an appropriate chart to present this information. Your chart should have a professional appearance and should clearly highlight any significant trends displayed.

3. What chart would you use to show a two-year divisional sales trend of a corporation? The divisions of the corporation could be three different retail store chains such as clothing stores, jewelry stores, and sports equipment. Another example can be a corporation that sells different brands of candy such as a chocolate brand, a marshmallow brand, and a hard candy brand. Research the financial statement of a public company that operates several divisions such as these. Find and record two years' worth of sales data for each division on an Excel worksheet. Then create an appropriate chart to present this data and place it in a PowerPoint slide. Your chart, as well as the PowerPoint slide, should have a professional appearance.

4. The following formula is used to calculate the quantity supplied for a given market:

   $Q = P \times 27 - 5$, where Q = quantity supplied and P = price

   Create a spreadsheet with three columns of data. The first column should be labeled **`Data Points`** and should contain a list of numbers from 1 to 10. The second column should be labeled **`Price`**. The first value in the Price column should be **`$3`**. The third column should be **`Quantity`**. Use the supply formula shown here to calculate the data in this column. Create a formula for the remainder of the values in the Price column so that you can control how much the price increases for each of the remaining nine data points. You should be able to enter a percentage into another cell on the spreadsheet and have the Price column calculate a price each week based on the value you enter. A positive number will increase the price for every data point; a negative number will decrease the price for every data point. After constructing the spreadsheet, create an appropriate chart that can be used to study the data as the price is changed.

Chapter 6

Applying Core Competency Skills

Financial Planning and Accounting

Chapter Goals

The purpose of this chapter is to show how the skills covered in this text can be applied to two common business practices. The first is financial planning. Business managers often use Excel to develop financial strategies for improving the performance and growth of existing businesses or for starting new ones. The second is constructing a full set of financial accounting statements. Excel is a great tool for building basic accounting spreadsheets, especially when you are working on assignments for accounting courses. You can accomplish both of these critical business exercises in Excel utilizing the core competency skills you have learned in previous chapters of this text. This chapter begins by demonstrating the technique of linking data between worksheets or workbooks. Worksheets are often linked when spreadsheets for financial planning or accounting are constructed, which is why they are covered in the first section of this chapter.

Excel | Skill Sets

Linking Data
- Linking Worksheets and Workbooks
- Updating Workbook Links
- SUMIF Function

Financial Planning
- Financial Assumptions
- Freeze Panes
- Financial Data
- Cash Analysis (The NPV Function)

Financial Accounting
- T-Accounts
- Journals
- Ledgers
- Trial Balance and Work Sheets
- Statements

Excel in **Practice** | Anecdote

My Role as a Strategic Planning Manager

When I worked as a strategic planning manager, I was responsible for developing business plans that demonstrated the financial potential of new businesses ideas and corporate initiatives. These plans were constructed from several assumptions related to almost every aspect of the business. Assumptions could include the cost of shipping goods, expected growth in sales, change in the cost of goods sold, the number of full-time employees, the wage per employee, and so on. The decision to invest in a new business or initiative depended on the result of a net present value analysis, which showed whether an investment could provide an adequate return. I would then present the completed business plans with net present value results to the directing officers of the company, which often included both the CEO and CFO. One of the biggest challenges in preparing for these meetings was to show different scenarios regarding the potential performance of a business idea. For example, the executives would often ask questions such as "What if the business requires more employees? What if the cost of construction goes over budget? What if sales come in lower than planned?" A negative change in any of these assumptions could reduce or eliminate any potential profits. Therefore, I had to construct and present several different plans showing a worst, best, and target case scenario. Constructing so many plans and being prepared to answer any question from the directing officers appeared to be in impossible task at first.

>> **Continued on page 285**

Linking Data

Skill Set

Linking data between multiple worksheets or workbooks is a common technique used in financial planning and financial accounting spreadsheets. This section will demonstrate how you can use the technique of linking data to construct a sales and gross profit plan for a division of a hypothetical manufacturing company. This plan will be very similar to the one introduced in Chapter 2 (see Figure 2.39). Linking data is also commonly used with the **SUMIF** function, which will also be introduced in this section.

Linking Worksheets and Workbooks

Chapter 4 demonstrated the concept of cell referencing when working with formulas and functions on a specific worksheet. However, you can also use cell referencing to link data between two worksheets or workbooks. This is also referred to as a ***3-D reference*** and was first introduced in Chapter 4 in the VLookup section. You may recall that to define the **table_array** argument of the **VLookup** function you highlighted a range of cells in a second worksheet. This is essentially how data is linked from one worksheet to another. Linking data is especially valuable when constructing financial plans because business managers are typically required to show various scenarios when planning the financial goals for their area of responsibility. Since linking data uses cell references, the business manager can change values in key cell locations to produce new outputs for the formulas and functions used to create the plan.

This example demonstrates the technique of linking data by creating a sales and gross profit plan for a division in a hypothetical manufacturing company (Division B). Large companies will typically require the managing director of each division to create a comprehensive financial plan which outlines all expenses, sales, and profits that will be generated by their product line or service. For example, a large electronics manufacturer might consist of four divisions: Personal Computers, Cameras, Corporate Services, and Copy Machines. The directors for each of these divisions would be required to develop and present a financial plan to the executive officers of the company. This demonstration will focus on the sales and gross profit portion of these financial plans. Figures 6.1 through 6.3 show the data that will be used for this example. The worksheet shown in Figure 6.3 is the blank financial plan that will be completed by creating links to the worksheets shown Figure 6.1 and 6.2.

Figure 6.1 | **Financial Results LY Workbook: Results for 2006 Worksheet**

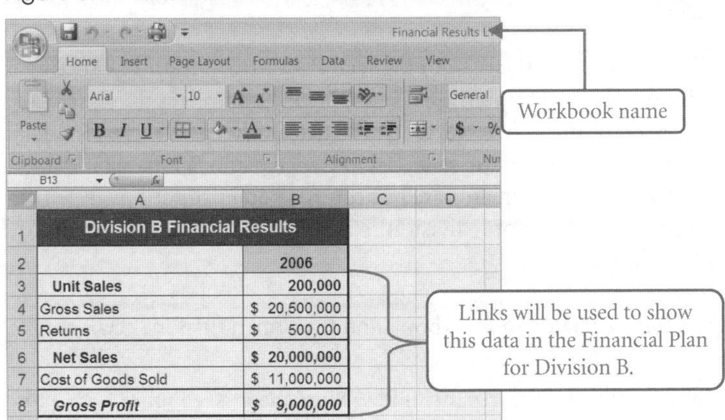

Figure 6.2 | **Division B Financial Plan Workbook: Plan Assumptions Worksheet**

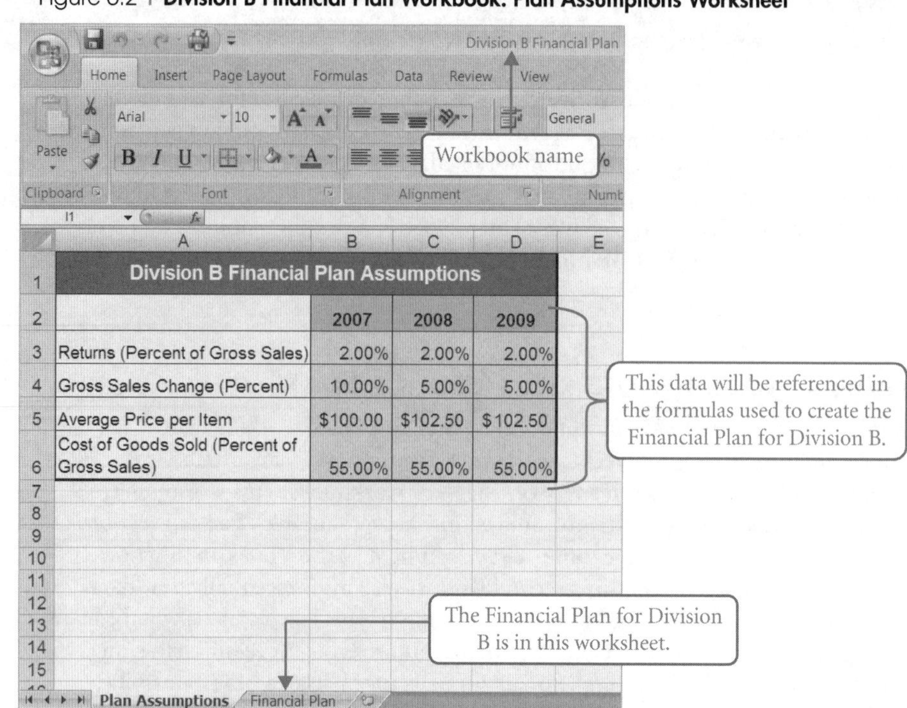

Figure 6.3 | **Division B Financial Plan Workbook: Financial Plan Worksheet**

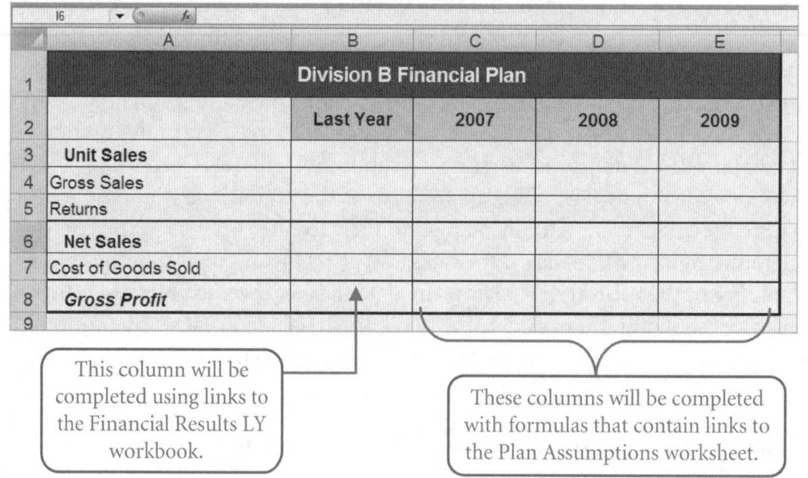

As mentioned, Figure 6.3 shows the blank Financial Plan for Division B. Creating a link to the Financial Results LY workbook shown in Figure 6.1 completes the Last Year column in this worksheet. Once the link is created, if the data is changed in the Financial Results LY workbook, those changes will be reflected in the Division B Financial Plan workbook. Adjustments to last year data are rare but can happen in situations in which a company moves a product line from one division to another. The following points explain how to create this link:

- Open the Division B Financial Plan workbook and then open the Financial Results LY workbook.
- Type an equal sign in cell B3 of the Financial Plan worksheet (see Figure 6.3). This cell represents the Unit Sales for Division B last year.
- Activate the Financial Results LY workbook by clicking the workbook name in the task bar (see Figure 6.4).

- Activate cell B3 in the Results for 2006 worksheet in the Financial Results LY workbook.
- Press the **Enter** key.

Figures 6.4 and 6.5 show the setup and results of creating a link between the Division B Financial Plan and Financial Results LY workbooks. Notice in Figure 6.5 that the workbook and worksheet name precede the cell location that was used to create the link in cell B3 to show the Unit Sales for Last Year.

Figure 6.4 | **Creating a Link in the Financial Plan Worksheet**

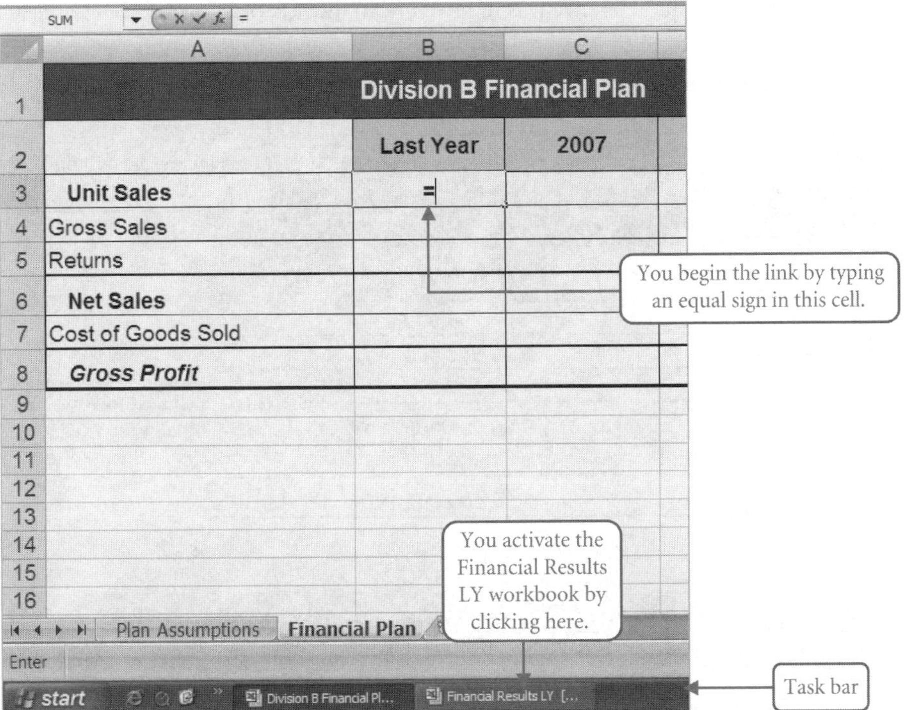

Figure 6.5 | **Results of Creating a Link in the Financial Plan Worksheet**

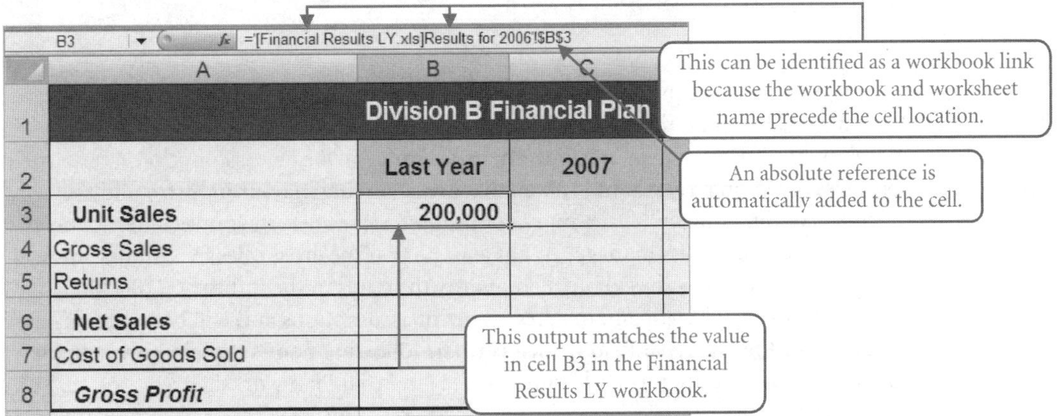

Copying the link that was created in cell B3 and pasting it to cells B4 through B8 completes the Last Year column in Figure 6.5. This example can use relative referencing to adjust the link because the financial items listed in the Financial Plan worksheet in Figure 6.5 are in the same sequence as the financial items listed in the Financial Results LY workbook in Figure 6.1. However, notice that the cell reference in the link shown in the formula bar of Figure 6.5 contains an absolute reference that must be removed before copying and pasting the link. You accomplish this by doing the following:

- Edit cell B3 in the Financial Plan worksheet to remove the absolute reference on cell B3 in the link.
- Copy cell B3 in the Financial Plan worksheet and then highlight the range B4:B8.
- Select the **Formulas** option from the **Paste** icon in the Ribbon. Using the **Formulas** option will paste the link without changing any of the formats in the worksheet.

Figure 6.6 shows the completed Last Year column in the Financial Plan worksheet. Notice that the absolute reference was removed from the link (see formula bar).

Figure 6.6 | **Completed Last Year Column in the Financial Plan Worksheet**

B3 | fx ='[Financial Results LY.xls]Results for 2006'!B3

	A	B	C
1	Division B Financial Plan		
2		Last Year	2007
3	Unit Sales	200,000	
4	Gross Sales	$ 20,500,000	
5	Returns	$ 500,000	
6	Net Sales	$ 20,000,000	
7	Cost of Goods Sold	$ 11,000,000	
8	Gross Profit	$ 9,000,000	
9			

The absolute reference was removed from this cell before copying.

Relative referencing automatically adjusts the link that was pasted into these cell locations.

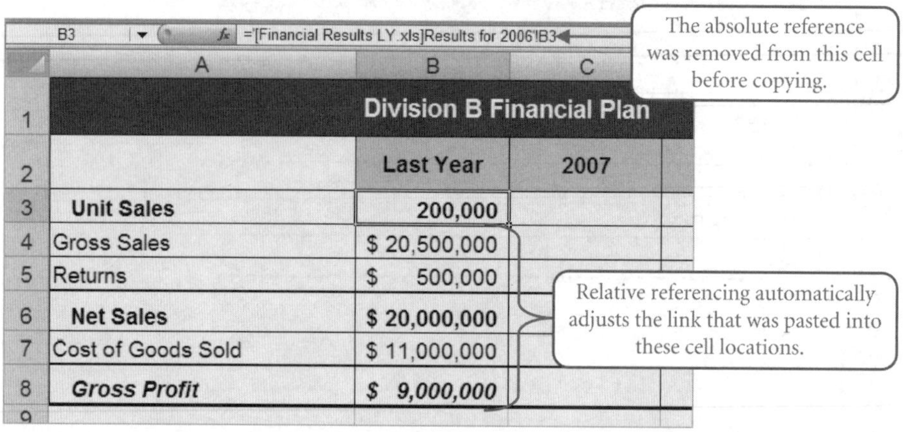

COMMON MISTAKES | Copying and Pasting Workbook Links

Excel will automatically place an absolute reference on cell references used to link data between two workbooks. Therefore, you must remove the absolute reference after creating the link if you intend to use relative referencing to automatically adjust the link when it is pasted to a new location on the worksheet.

The remaining columns in the Financial Plan worksheet will be completed using formulas that contain links to the Plan Assumptions worksheet in Figure 6.2. When developing a financial plan, business managers must make key assumptions about their business based on research and trends that are occurring in their industry and the overall economy. You will learn more about these techniques in your business courses. For example, a business manager might assume that the gross sales for his division will increase 10% next year based on current growth trends in the industry. The Plan Assumptions worksheet contains these types of assumptions and will be used to calculate data for the Financial Plan worksheet. The following points explain how data for the year 2007 (column C) is calculated in the Financial Plan worksheet:

- Activate cell C4 in the Financial Plan worksheet. Skip the Unit Sales formula for now because the Net Sales has not been calculated. That said, skipping this formula is not a requirement. You could still type the formula for Unit Sales, and a result will be produced once the Net Sales is calculated.
- Type an equal sign and the beginning of the formula B4 + B4*.
- Activate the Plan Assumptions worksheet and then activate cell B4, which contains the percent change for Gross Sales. This will place a link in the formula that will

reference the value in cell B4 in the Plan Assumptions worksheet. The formula will take the Gross Sales for Last Year (cell B4) in the Financial Plan worksheet and add to it the Gross Sales from Last Year multiplied by the percent change in Gross Sales on the Plan Assumptions worksheet (this formula was covered in the Formulas workshop in Chapter 3).

- Press the **Enter** key.

Figure 6.7 shows the result of the formula calculating the Gross Sales for 2007. Notice in the formula bar that the worksheet name Plan Assumptions is enclosed in apostrophes and is followed by an exclamation point. This indicates that the formula will use the value in cell B4 in the Plan Assumptions worksheet. The first two cell references in the formula, which are also B4, are from the Financial Plan worksheet. Since these cell references are not preceded by a worksheet name, they relate to the current worksheet that contains this formula.

Figure 6.7 | **Calculating Gross Sales for 2007 in the Financial Plan Worksheet**

C4 =B4+B4*'Plan Assumptions'!B4

	A	B	C
1		Division B Finar	
2		Last Year	
3	Unit Sales	200,000	
4	Gross Sales	$ 20,500,000	$ 22,550,000
5	Returns	$ 500,000	
6	Net Sales	$ 20,000,000	
7	Cost of Goods Sold	$ 11,000,000	
8	*Gross Profit*	*$ 9,000,000*	

This cell can be identified as a link because it is preceded by the worksheet name Plan Assumptions.

This output will change if the value in cell B4 in the Plan Assumptions worksheet is changed.

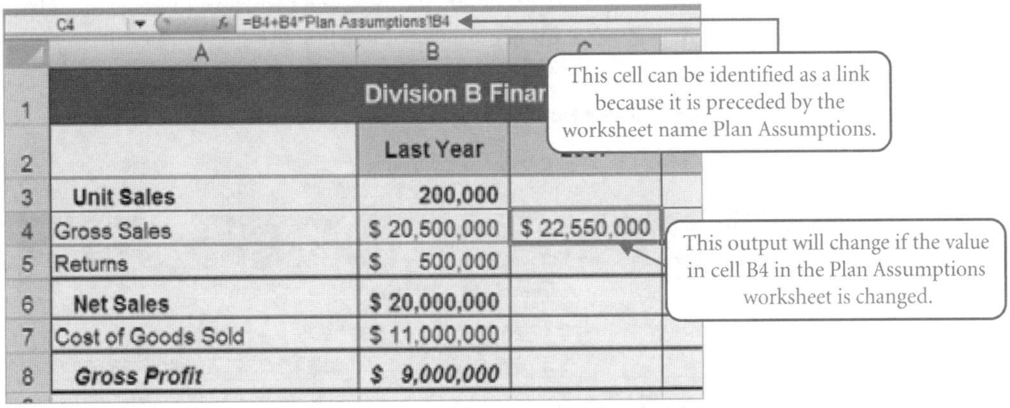

The following steps explain how to create formulas to complete the data for 2007 in the Financial Plan worksheet:

- Activate cell C5. This cell will contain the planned Returns for 2007.
- Type an equal sign and the beginning of the formula `C4 *`.
- Activate the Plan Assumptions worksheet and then activate cell B3. This formula will multiply the Gross Sales, which was calculated in cell C4 of the Financial Plan worksheet, by the percentage in cell B3 of the Plan Assumptions worksheet.
- Press the **Enter** key.
- Activate cell C6.
- Type an equal sign, type the formula `C4-C5`, and then press the **Enter** key. This formula will calculate the Net Sales by subtracting the Returns from the Gross Sales (this formula was covered in the first section of Chapter 3).
- Activate cell C3. Since the Net Sales are calculated, you can now calculate the Unit Sales.
- Type an equal sign and the beginning of the formula `C6/`(cell C6 divided by).
- Activate the Plan Assumptions worksheet and activate cell B5. This formula will take the Average Price per Item and divide it into the Net Sales to calculate the planned Unit Sales for the division.
- Press the **Enter** key.
- Activate cell C7.
- Type an equal sign and the beginning of the formula `C4 *`.
- Activate the Plan Assumptions worksheet and then activate cell B6. This formula will calculate the Cost of Goods Sold by multiplying the percentage in cell B6 of

>> **Quick Reference**

Linking Data between Worksheets

1. Activate a cell location where the data or output of a formula or functions should appear.
2. Type an equal sign, or type an equal sign and the beginning of a formula or function.
3. Click a **Worksheet** tab that contains the data you wish to display in the first worksheet or use in a formula or function.
4. Activate a cell location that contains the data you wish to display or use in a formula or function.
5. Press the **Enter** key, or complete the formula or function and then press the **Enter** key.

the Plan Assumptions worksheet by the Gross Sales in cell C4 of the Financial Plan worksheet.

- Press the **Enter** key.
- Activate cell C8.
- Type an equal sign, type the formula `C6-C7`, and then press the **Enter** key. This formula will calculate the Gross Profit by subtracting the Cost of Goods Sold from the Net Sales (this formula was also covered in the first section of Chapter 3).
- Copy the range C3:C8. Then highlight cells D3 and E3 and select the **Formulas** option from the **Paste** icon. This will paste the formulas created for the year 2007 into the years 2008 and 2009 to complete the Financial Plan worksheet. Relative referencing will automatically adjust the cell references for the links and formulas to make the appropriate calculations for the years 2008 and 2009.

Figure 6.8 shows the completed Financial Plan worksheet. As previously mentioned, this represents part of a financial plan that the directing manager of a division in a large company would typically create. In addition, the formats and items included in a financial plan will vary depending on the business that is being managed.

Figure 6.8 | **Completed Financial Plan Worksheet**

This formula was originally created in cell C4 but was adjusted through relative referencing.

E4 =D4+D4*'Plan Assumptions'!D4

	A	B	C	D	E
1	Division B Financial Plan				
2		Last Year	2007	2008	2009
3	Unit Sales	200,000	220,990	226,380	237,699
4	Gross Sales	$ 20,500,000	$ 22,550,000	$ 23,677,500	$ 24,861,375
5	Returns	$ 500,000	$ 451,000	$ 473,550	$ 497,228
6	Net Sales	$ 20,000,000	$ 22,099,000	$ 23,203,950	$ 24,364,148
7	Cost of Goods Sold	$ 11,000,000	$ 12,402,500	$ 13,022,625	$ 13,673,756
8	*Gross Profit*	*$ 9,000,000*	*$ 9,696,500*	*$ 10,181,325*	*$ 10,690,391*
9					

Business managers will most likely be required to present their financial plans to the executive officers of the company. During this presentation, the business manager might be asked questions such as "What if our sales only increase 5% in 2007?" or "What if our cost of goods sold increases to 60%?" Simply typing new assumptions into the Plan Assumptions worksheet in Figure 6.2 easily answers these questions. Because of cell referencing, the outputs of the financial plan shown in Figure 6.8 will automatically change when the data in the Plan Assumptions worksheet is changed.

>> **Quick Reference**

Linking Data between Workbooks

1. Open two workbooks.
2. Activate a cell location in the workbook where the data or output of a formula or functions should appear.
3. Type an equal sign, or type an equal sign and the beginning of a formula or function.
4. Click the name of the second workbook in the task bar.
5. Click a **Worksheet** tab that contains the data you wish to display or use in a formula or function.
6. Activate a cell location that contains the data you wish to display or use in a formula or function.
7. Press the **Enter** key, or complete the formula or function and then press the **Enter** key.

Updating Workbook Links

When an Excel file contains workbook links, a ***Security Alert*** prompt will appear just below the Ribbon of the Excel screen, as shown in Figure 6.9, when the file is opened. The purpose of this prompt is to inform you that data is being linked to an external workbook and to give you the option of updating these links. Workbook links must be updated to show any changes that might have occurred in the external workbook. You can use two methods for updating workbook links. The first is to click the **Options** button in the Security Alert prompt, as shown in Figure 6.9. After you click this button, a dialog box will open giving you the option to automatically update all workbook links. To update any workbook links, you click the *Enable this content* option and click the **OK** button in the dialog box. Once the workbook links are updated, or ***refreshed***, any changes that might have occurred in the external workbook will appear in the current workbook.

Figure 6.9 | **Updating Workbook Links Using the Security Alert Prompt**

Data tab

Click here to open the Edit Links dialog box.

Security Alert prompt

Security Warning Automatic update of links has been disabled Options...

	A	B	C	D	E
1	Division B Financial Plan				
2		Last Year	2007	2008	2009
3	Unit Sales	200,000	220,990	226,380	237,699
4	Gross Sales	$ 20,500,000	$ 22,550,000	$ 23,677,500	$ 24,861,375
5	Returns	$ 500,000	$ 451,000	$ 473,550	$ 497,228
6	Net Sales	$ 20,000,000	$ 22,099,000	$ 23,203,950	$ 24,364,148
7	Cost of Goods Sold	$ 11,000,000	$ 12,402,500	$ 13,022,625	$ 13,673,756
8	*Gross Profit*	*$ 9,000,000*	*$ 9,696,500*	*$ 10,181,325*	*$ 10,690,391*

Click here to view options for updating any workbook links.

The second method for updating workbook links is through the **Edit Links** dialog box. You can open the **Edit Links** dialog box by clicking the **Edit Links** icon in the **Data** tab of the Ribbon (see Figure 6.9). As shown in Figure 6.10, this dialog box allows you to select and manually update any workbook links that are in your Excel file. In addition, it provides options for checking a selected workbook link to see if it needs to be updated, changing the source file for a selected workbook link, or breaking a workbook link.

Figure 6.10 | **Edit Links Dialog Box**

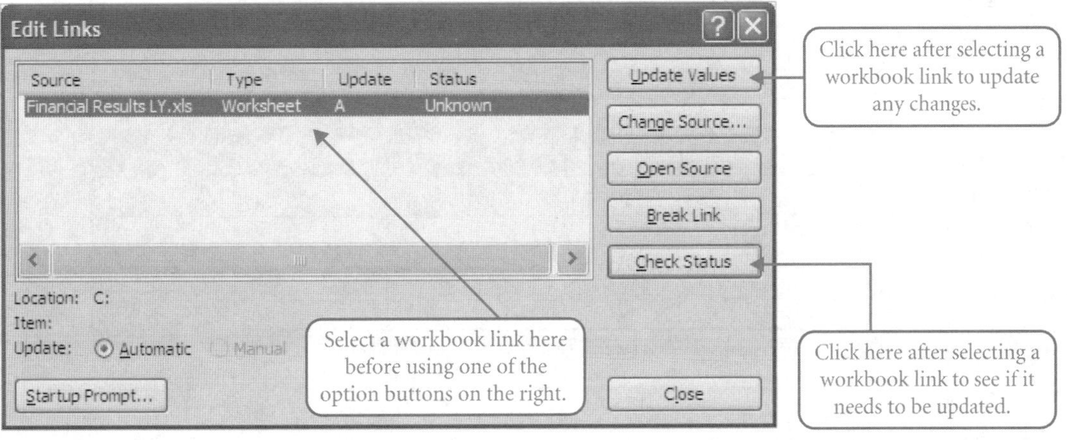

SUMIF Function

The **SUMIF** function allows you to add specific values in a worksheet based on the results of a logical test. In business, this function is often used to summarize financial or statistical data. For example, Figure 6.11 shows a worksheet that contains gross sales projections for the departments of a hypothetical electronics retail company. Notice that several departments are assigned to each division. The **SUMIF** function will be used to total the gross sales projections for each division in the Sales Summary worksheet.

Figure 6.11 | **Gross Sales Projections by Division/Department**

	A	B	C	D	E	F
1	Gross Sales Projections by Division / Department					
2	Division	Department	2007	2008	2009	3 Year Total
3	Electronics	PDA	$2,100,000	$2,750,000	$3,750,000	$8,600,000
4	Electronics	Video	$1,750,000	$2,500,000	$3,250,000	$7,500,000
5	Computers	Laptop	$1,500,000	$2,100,000	$2,850,000	$6,450,000
6	Electronics	Home Audio	$1,500,000	$1,750,000	$2,250,000	$5,500,000
7	Appliances	Kitchen	$1,450,000	$1,880,000	$2,005,000	$5,335,000
8	Computers	Desktop	$1,750,000	$1,500,000	$1,500,000	$4,750,000
9	Furniture	Family Room	$1,230,000	$1,500,000	$1,700,000	$4,430,000
10	Computers	Video Game	$1,230,000	$1,260,000	$1,300,000	$3,790,000
11	Computers	Accessories	$750,000	$900,000	$1,100,000	$2,750,000
12	Appliances	Laundry	$650,000	$700,000	$700,000	$2,050,000
13	Furniture	Office	$250,000	$300,000	$300,000	$850,000
14	Furniture	Bedroom	$125,000	$200,000	$225,000	$550,000

Sales Detail / Sales Summary

The gross sales for each division will be summarized in this worksheet.

Figure 6.12 shows the worksheet that will be used to summarize the gross sales projections for each division. Since this is a different worksheet, a link will be used in the **SUMIF** function to reference the data in the Sales Detail worksheet shown in Figure 6.11. Using links in the **SUMIF** function is a common technique, especially when you are creating summary reports such as the one shown in Figure 6.12. The **SUMIF** function will be used to search for the division listed in column A from the Sales Summary worksheet in the Sales Detail worksheet and calculate a total for each division for each year.

Figure 6.12 | **Sales Summary Worksheet**

	A	B	C	D	E
1	Gross Sales Projections by Division				
2	Division	2007	2008	2009	3 Year Total
3	Appliances				$0
4	Computers				$0
5	Electronics				$0
6	Furniture				$0

The SUMIF function will be used to complete these columns.

A SUM function has been added to this column.

As shown in Figure 6.13, the **SUMIF** function contains three arguments. Each of these arguments is defined as follows:

- **range**: The range of cells that will be evaluated by the logical test or data used to define the **criteria** argument. In some cases, this argument may be identical to the range of data that is being summed.
- **criteria**: The logical test or data that will be used to determine which values are summed. This is similar to the **logical_test** argument of the **IF** function. However, this argument can be defined by a particular value, cell location, text, and so on, without entering a complete logical test.

>> **Quick Reference**

Updating Workbook Links

1. Click the **Options** button in the Security Alert prompt.
2. Select the **Enable this content** option in the **Security Options** dialog box and click the **OK** button.

Or

1. Click the **Data** tab of the Ribbon.
2. Click the **Edit Links** icon.
3. Select the workbook link you wish to update from the **Edit Links** dialog box.
4. Click the **Update Values** button on the right side of the **Edit Links** dialog box.
5. Click the **Close** button at the bottom of the **Edit Links** dialog box.

- **[sum_range]**: The range of cells that contain data that will be summed if the data in the **criteria** argument is found in the **range** argument. This argument is needed only if the range of cells used for the **range** argument does not contain the values that need to be summed. Otherwise, it can be omitted.

Figure 6.13 | **Arguments of the SUMIF Function**

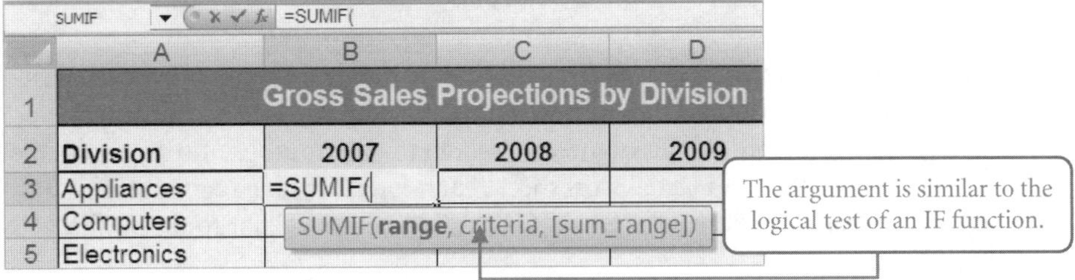

As mentioned, the Sales Summary worksheet in Figure 6.12 summarizes by division the gross sales projections by department (from Figure 6.11). The following steps explains how you accomplish this:

- Activate cell B3 in the Sales Summary worksheet. This cell will show the gross sales projections for the Appliances division for the year 2007.
- Type an equal sign, the function name SUMIF, and an open parenthesis.
- Define the **range** argument by clicking the Sales Detail worksheet and highlighting the range A3:A14. This will create a link to the Sales Detail worksheet. Type a comma after defining this argument.
- Type the cell location A3 to define the **criteria** argument. The function will search for the division name in cell A3 in the Sales Summary worksheet by looking in the range A3:A14 in the Sales Detail worksheet. Note that you will still be in the Sales Detail worksheet when you define this argument; therefore, you must type cell A3 instead of clicking it. Type a comma after defining this argument.
- Define the [**sum_range**] argument by highlighting the range C3:C14 in the Sales Detail worksheet, which contains the gross sales projections for the year 2007. You will still be in the Sales Detail worksheet, so you can simply click and drag over this range. This will create a second link in the function. When a match is found in the **criteria** argument, the function will add whatever value is in the same row in the range of cells used to define this argument.
- Type a closing parenthesis and press the **Enter** key. This will bring you back to the Sales Summary worksheet.

Figure 6.14 shows the results of the **SUMIF** function. The function found the word *Appliances* in column A of the Sales Detail worksheet and summed whatever value is in the same row in the range C3:C14, which contains the gross sales projections for 2007. Notice the links that are created in the **range** and [**sum_range**] arguments.

Figure 6.14 | **Results of the SUMIF Function**

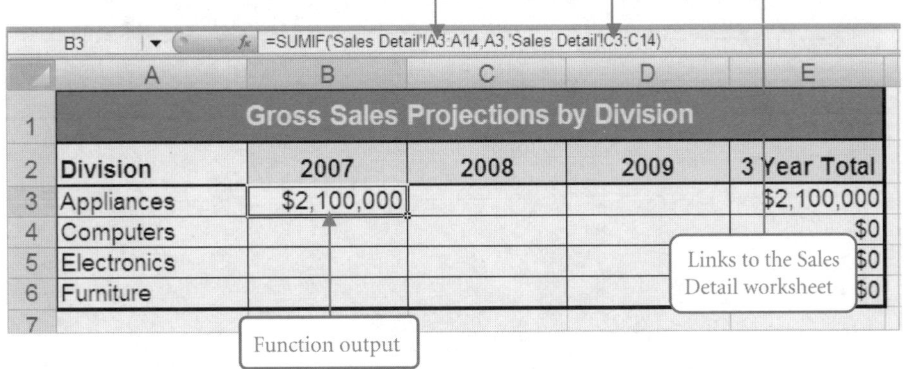

You can copy and paste the **SUMIF** function to calculate the gross sales projections for the rest of the divisions and years in Figure 6.14. However, you would need to add absolute references to the function to prevent relative referencing from making unwanted adjustments to the cell locations in each argument. You accomplish this as follows:

- Double click cell B3 in the Sales Summary worksheet to edit the function, or activate cell B3 and click in the formula bar.
- Place an absolute reference on the link used to define the **range** argument. Type a dollar sign in front of both the column letters and row numbers of the range A3:A14. The function will always need to search for the appropriate division name in column A of the Sales Detail worksheet. Therefore, this range cannot be adjusted by relative referencing when it is pasted to other cell locations on the worksheet.
- Type a dollar sign *only* in front of the column letter of cell A3 in the **criteria** argument. This argument requires a mixed reference because a different division is in each row in column A of the Sales Summary worksheet (see Figure 6.14). Therefore, it is important for relative referencing to adjust the row number when the function is pasted to a new location. However, the column letter must not change.
- Type a dollar sign *only* in front of the two row numbers in the link used to define the **[sum_range]** argument. This argument also requires a mixed reference because each year of sales projections is in a different column in the Sales Detail worksheet. Therefore, it is important for relative referencing to adjust the column letters when the function is pasted to columns C and D of the Sales Summary worksheet. However, the row numbers must not change. Press the **Enter** key after making this adjustment.
- Copy cell B3 and paste it down to cells B4 through B6. Then copy the range B3:B6 and paste it into the range C3:C6 and D3:D6.

Figure 6.15 shows the completed Sales Summary worksheet. Notice the mixed references that were placed on the **criteria** and **[sum_range]** arguments.

> **Quick Reference**
>
> **SUMIF Functions**
>
> 1. Activate the cell where output should appear.
> 2. Type an equal sign, the function name **SUMIF**, and an open parenthesis.
> 3. Define the following arguments:
>   a) **range**: A range of cells that will be evaluated by data used to define the **criteria** argument.
>   b) **criteria**: A logical test, cell location, value, and so on, that will be searched in the range used to define the **range** argument.
>   c) **[sum_range]**: A range of cells containing values that will be summed if the data in the **criteria** argument is found in the range used to define the **range** argument. Define this argument only if the **range** argument does not contain the values that need to be summed.
> 4. Type a closing parenthesis and press the **Enter** key.

Figure 6.15 | **Completed Sales Summary Worksheet**

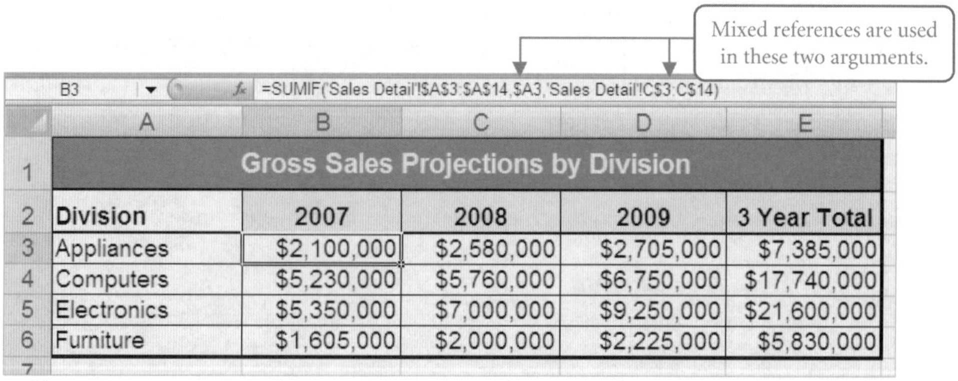

Mixed references are used in these two arguments.

B3 =SUMIF('Sales Detail'!$A$3:$A$14,$A3,'Sales Detail'!C$3:C$14)

	A	B	C	D	E
1	Gross Sales Projections by Division				
2	Division	2007	2008	2009	3 Year Total
3	Appliances	$2,100,000	$2,580,000	$2,705,000	$7,385,000
4	Computers	$5,230,000	$5,760,000	$6,750,000	$17,740,000
5	Electronics	$5,350,000	$7,000,000	$9,250,000	$21,600,000
6	Furniture	$1,605,000	$2,000,000	$2,225,000	$5,830,000
7					

COMMON MISTAKES | SUMIF Function

When you are using both the **range** and the **[sum_range]** argument, make sure each range of cells used to define these arguments contains the same number of cells. Excel will automatically adjust the range in the **[sum_range]** argument to match the number of cells in the range used to define the `range` argument. If there are fewer cells in the range argument compared to the **[sum_range]** argument, Excel will add only the number of cells in the range used to define the **range** argument. For example, the following **SUMIF** function will add only values in the range C3:C7. The reason is that the range of cells used to define the **range** argument is smaller than the range of cells used to define the **[sum_range]** argument.

```
=SUMIF('Sales Detail'!A3:A7,A4,'Sales Detail'!C3:C14)
```

>> Linking Data

VIDEO WORKSHOP

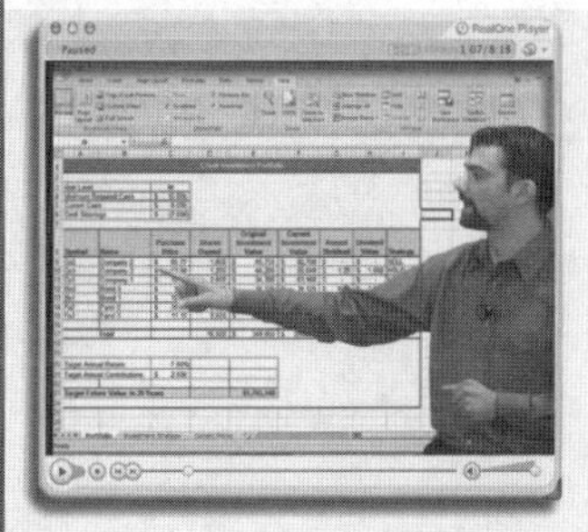

The purpose of this workshop is to review the techniques of linking data between workbooks and worksheets. I will be demonstrating the tasks in this workshop on the **Workbook Links** and **Worksheet Links** videos. After completing each section of tasks, watch the related video shown in parentheses. You will need to open the following two Excel files before starting this workshop: ib_e06_financialplan and ib_e06_lastyeardata. Both are identical to the example demonstrated earlier in this section. You must open both files before completing the tasks in this workshop.

1. **Linking Data between Two Workbooks (Video: Workbook Links)**
   a. Activate the Financial Plan workbook.
   b. Activate cell B3 in the Plan worksheet and type an equal sign.
   c. Activate the Last Year Data workbook, activate cell B3, and press the **Enter** key.
   d. Edit the workbook link that was created in cell B3 in the Plan worksheet to remove the absolute reference.
   e. Copy the workbook link in cell B3 of the Plan worksheet and paste it into cells B4 through B8 using the **Formulas** option in the **Paste** icon.
   f. Activate the Last Year Data workbook and close it.

2. **Linking Data between Two Worksheets (Video: Worksheet Links)**
   a. In cell C4 of the Plan worksheet, type the beginning of the formula `=B4 + B4 *`.
   b. Activate cell B4 in the Plan Assumptions worksheet and press the **Enter** key.
   c. In cell C5 of the Plan worksheet, type the beginning of the formula `=C4*`.
   d. Activate cell B3 in the Plan Assumptions worksheet and press the **Enter** key.
   e. Type the formula `=C4-C5` in cell C6 of the Plan worksheet.
   f. In cell C3 of the Plan worksheet, type the beginning of the formula `=C6/`.
   g. Activate cell B5 in the Plan Assumptions worksheet and press the **Enter** key.

h. In cell C7 of the Plan worksheet, type the beginning of the formula `=C4 *`.
i. Activate cell B6 in the Plan Assumptions worksheet and press the **Enter** key.
j. Type the formula `=C6 - C7` into cell C8 of the Plan worksheet.
k. Copy the range C3:C8 in the Plan worksheet. Using the **Paste Formulas** option, paste this range into cells D3 through D8 and cells E3 through E8.
l. Save and close your file.

>> SUMIF Function

The purpose of this workshop is to demonstrate the **SUMIF** function. I will be demonstrating the tasks in this workshop in the video named **SUMIF Function**. Open the file named ib_e06_divisionsalessummary and then complete the tasks in this workshop.

SUMIF (Video: SUMIF Function)

a. Activate cell B3 in the Sales Summary worksheet.
b. Type an equal sign, the function name **SUMIF**, and an open parenthesis.
c. Activate the Sales Detail worksheet and highlight the range A3:A14. Then type a comma.
d. Type the cell location A3 and then type a comma.
e. Highlight the range C3:C14 in the Sales Detail worksheet, type a closing parenthesis, and press the **Enter** key.
f. Add the following absolute and mixed references to the **SUMIF** function in cell B3 in the Sales Summary worksheet:
   i. Add an absolute reference to the worksheet link used to define the **range** argument. You will need to add four dollar signs to the range A3:A14 in this argument.
   ii. Add an absolute reference to the column letter only in the **criteria** argument (cell A3). The row number should remain a relative reference.
   iii. Add an absolute reference to the row numbers only in the worksheet link used to define the **[sum_range]** argument. You will need to add two dollar signs to the range C3:C14. The column letters for this range should remain a relative reference.
g. Copy cell B3 and paste it to cells B4:B6. Then copy the range B3:B6 and paste it into the range C3:D6.
h. Type a **SUM** function in cell E3 in the Sales Summary worksheet that totals the values in the range B3:D3. Then copy and paste this function into the range E4:E6.
i. Save and close your file.

>> Store Construction Plans

EXERCISE

Why Do I Need This?

This section demonstrated how linking data can be used to develop a financial plan for the division of a corporation. However, linking data can also be useful when planning other aspects of business such as the construction of stores, the distribution of merchandise, or the capacity of a distribution center. These exercises involve separate components or assumptions that have to be planned and then utilized to calculate a final output.

Exercise

The goal of this exercise is to develop a store construction plan for a hypothetical retail company. You will use the technique of linking data to calculate the construction cost of each store and also to produce a summary report. The summary report will use the **SUMIF** function to show how much total retail space is constructed or planned by state. To begin this exercise, open the file named ib_e06_storeconstruction.

1. Calculate the Construction Cost in cell G3 on the Construction Plan worksheet. You calculate this cost by multiplying the "Size (square feet)" column in the Construction Plan worksheet by the "Cost per Square Foot" column in the Cost by State worksheet. You will need to create this formula using the **VLookup** function to find the cost per square foot for each state listed in column C of the Construction Plan worksheet in column B of the Cost by State worksheet. The arguments of the **VLookup** function should be defined as followed:
   a. **lookup_value**: `C3`
   b. **table_array**: The range `A2:B12` in the Cost by State worksheet
   c. **col_index_num:** `2`
   d. **[range_lookup]**: `False`
2. Add an absolute reference to the range used to define the **table_array** argument of the VLookup portion of the formula you created in number 1. Then copy the formula and paste it into cells G4 through G25.
3. Type a formula into cell H3 in the Construction Plan worksheet that calculates the Total Cost to Open. Your formula should add the Construction Cost calculated in number 1 to the Inventory Value. Copy your formula and paste it into cells H4 through H25.
4. Create a link in cell A3 of the Store Summary worksheet to cell A2 in the Cost by State worksheet. Then copy this link and paste it into cells A4 through A12.
5. Type a **SUMIF** function in cell B3 of the Store Summary worksheet to calculate the total square feet of store space in the state of Massachusetts. The arguments of the function should be defined as follows:
   a. **range**: `C3:C30` in the Construction Plan worksheet
   b. **criteria**: `A3`
   c. **[sum_range]**: `E3:E30` in the Construction Plan worksheet
6. Add an absolute value to the link used to define the **range** and **[sum_range]** arguments of the **SUMIF** function created in step 5. Then copy the function and paste it into cells B4 through B12.
7. Type a **SUMIF** function in cell E33 of the Construction Plan worksheet. The purpose of this function is to add the total square footage of retail space that

exists for each size category of store. The definitions for each argument are listed here. Notice that only two of the three arguments are listed because the range that is used to define the **range** argument contains the values that are being summed.

a. **range** = `E3:E30`

b. **criteria** = `D33`

8. Place an absolute reference on the range E3:E30 in the **SUMIF** function that you created in step 7. Then copy the function and paste it into cells E34 through E36.

9. Which size category has the highest square footage of retail space for this company?

10. You may have noticed that the range used to define the **range** argument of the **SUMIF** function created in step 7 included blank cells. This is so the summary report will automatically include new stores when they are added. For example, type `VA` in cell A10 in the Cost by State worksheet and add a Cost per Square Foot of **32** in cell B10.

11. In row 26 of the Construction Plan spreadsheet, type open date: `3/23/2008`; store number: `2801`; state: `VA`; city: `Reston`; size: `15000`; and inventory value: `3700500`.

12. Copy cells G25 and H25 in the Construction Plan worksheet and paste them into cells G26 and H26.

13. Which size category has the highest total square footage?

14. Look at the Store Summary worksheet. Is Virginia (VA) added to the list? Sort this worksheet based on the values in the Total Space (sqr feet) column in descending order. Which state has the highest square footage of retail space?

15. Save and close your file.

PROBLEM & EXERCISE

>> What's Wrong with This Spreadsheet?

Problem

You are managing a department in a large public corporation. Each year the company holds a planning meeting to determine what sales targets will be announced to the stockholders. You receive an e-mail from a coworker who created an Excel spreadsheet to help you plan the sales of your department. He explains how the spreadsheet works as follows:

1. The spreadsheet shows two years of history (2005 and 2006) and three years of projections. The history is linked to another workbook named Sales History, which is attached to this e-mail. You do not have to enter any history data for your sales plan. The history workbooks for each department are maintained by the accounting department. As a result, if they make any adjustments to the results of your department (mostly returns), the changes will automatically show up on the Department Sales Plan workbook I attached to this e-mail.

2. The only things you have to enter in the Department Sales Plan workbook are the Growth of Gross Sales, percent of Returns, and the Average Price. These

items are in the Assumptions worksheet. When you change any of the numbers on this worksheet, it will automatically update the Sales Plan.

3. The Sales Plan worksheet contains all the plan data for the department. Just print this worksheet and bring it to the meeting. It's that easy!

Exercise

Your coworker e-mailed you the Sales History and Department Sales Plan workbooks. Open the file named ib_e06_departmentsalesplan. Would you be comfortable printing the Sales Plan worksheet and presenting this data at the sales meeting? Consider the following points:

1. Do the numbers appear to make sense? For example, the formula to calculate Net Sales is `Gross Sales - Returns`. The Unit sales are calculated by dividing the Net Sales by the Average Price entered onto the Assumptions worksheet.

2. Give the spreadsheet a test drive. The coworker explained that changing the data in the Assumptions worksheet will produce new outputs on the Sales Plan worksheet. Change the data in the Assumptions worksheet one item at a time and check the Sales Plan worksheet. For example, change the Growth of Gross Sales percentages and check the Gross Sales results on the Sales Plan worksheet.

3. Does the historical data for 2005 and 2006 look suspicious?

4. Do the Net Sales results still make sense?

Write a short answer for each of the points listed here. Then fix any errors you find in the Department Sales Plan workbook.

Financial Planning

Skill Set

The previous section demonstrated how the sales and gross profit portion of a financial plan is constructed in Excel using the technique of linking data. This section will provide an illustrative review of how you can use the core competency skills in this text to construct a comprehensive financial plan for starting a new business. A total of three worksheets will be used to construct this plan, as opposed to the two worksheets that were used in the previous section: Financial Assumptions, Financial Data, and Cash Analysis. In addition, this section introduces the **NPV** function, which you use to compute the net present value of an investment. It is important to note that this section will mention and work with several terms and rules that apply to the disciplines of finance, but they will not be explained in detail. You will receive more detailed instruction regarding these concepts in your financial accounting courses and reference material.

Financial Assumptions

Figures 6.16 and 6.17 show the first component that will be demonstrated for the comprehensive financial plan: the Financial Assumptions worksheet. The purpose of this worksheet is identical to the Plan Assumptions worksheet that was shown in Figure 6.2.

All of the assumptions related to the financial plan will be entered into this worksheet. In addition, this will be the only worksheet in the plan that is used for any data entry needs. The other two worksheets, Financial Data and Cash Analysis, will be constructed using formulas and functions. A business manager would use the Financial Assumptions worksheet to enter all critical decisions required to develop the comprehensive financial plan such as startup investments, first-year sales estimates, sales growth rates, cost of goods sold, and so on.

The Financial Assumptions worksheet, shown in Figures 6.16 and 6.17, is designed to enter plan data for five financial categories. The number and types of categories that are used to create a financial plan will change depending on the business and purpose of the plan. As previously mentioned, this financial plan will be used for starting a new business. In addition, this example will assume that the business will be manufacturing a product that will be sold to retail stores. Therefore, items such as Cost of Goods Sold and Inventory are included on the Financial Assumptions spreadsheet. If you were planning a service business, these items would not be included in the design of the plan. The following five categories are used for the design of this plan:

- Startup Investments
- Sales Information
- Cost and Expense Information
- Asset Information
- Liability Information

Figure 6.16 | **Financial Assumptions Worksheet (Rows 1 – 25)**

	A	B	C	D
1	**Financial Assumptions**			
2	***Startup Investments***			
3	**Total Initial Investment**	**$ 400,000**		
4	*Amount Funded by Loans*	$ 325,000	Interest Rate	6.50%
5	*Amount Invested by Owner 1*	$ 25,000		
6	*Amount Invested by Owner 2*	$ 25,000		
7	*Amount Invested by Owner 3*	$ 25,000		
8	***Sales Information***	Year 1	Year 2	Year 3
9	Inflation		2.00%	2.00%
10	First Year Gross Sales Estimate (Dollars)	$ 175,000		
11	Gross Sales Growth (Percent)		150.00%	90.00%
12	Price Charged to Retailers	$ 22.00	$ 22.00	$ 22.00
13	Returns (Percent of Gross Sales)	3.50%	2.00%	1.75%
14	***Cost & Expense Information***	Year 1	Year 2	Year 3
15	Cost of Goods Sold (Percent of Gross Sales)	48.00%	46.00%	44.00%
16	Average Life of Assets (Years Depreciating)	10	10	10
17	Employee Salary and Benefits	$ 90,000	$ 140,000	$ 200,000
18	*Number of Employees*	3	4	5
19	*Average Annual Salary with Benefits*	$ 30,000	$ 35,000	$ 40,000
20	Shipping Expense (as a percent of Sales)	1.50%	1.50%	1.50%
21	Annual Rent	$ 15,000	$ 16,000	$ 17,000
22	Utilities (Dollars)	$ 5,000	$ 6,500	$ 10,000
23	Advertising Expense (Dollars)	$ 25,000	$ 40,000	$ 60,000
24	Office Expenses	$ 4,000	$ 6,000	$ 10,000
25	Taxes (percent)	38.00%	38.00%	38.00%

Figure 6.17 | **Financial Assumptions Worksheet (Rows 26 – 39)**

	A	B	C	D
1	**Financial Assumptions**			
26	***Asset Information***	Year 1	Year 2	Year 3
27	Accounts Receivable (Turn)	12	12	12
28	Inventory (Turn)	5	5	6
29	Other Assets	$ 75,000	$ 75,000	$ 75,000
30	*Property*	$ -	$ -	$ -
31	*Equipment*	$ 75,000	$ 75,000	$ 75,000
32	***Liability Information***	Year 1	Year 2	Year 3
33	Accounts Payable (Cost of Goods Sold Turn)	6	6	6
34				
35	NOTES:			
36	Loan has a 15 year repayment period from National Good Bank.			
37	Loan Payments are made annually at the beginning of the year.			
38				
39				

Row 1 remains at the top of the worksheet when the Freeze Panes command is activated.

SUM functions in this row calculate the total Property and Equipment.

The following list highlights how a few of the core competency skills were used in the construction of the Financial Assumptions worksheet in Figures 6.16 and 6.17:

- **Formatting (Chapter 2)**: Besides the obvious use of formatting techniques such as borders, alignment, number formats, and so on, the use of cell color (also known as fill color) is used as a way of communicating how to use this worksheet. For example, the yellow cells indicate that a business manager must enter key financial data. The white cells indicate labels or calculations that should not be changed. The color grey identifies unused cells.
- **Formulas (Chapter 3)**: Basic formulas are used to calculate the cost of Employee Salary and Benefits in row 17. The formula multiplies the Number of Employees entered in row 18 by the Average Annual Salary with Benefits in row 19 for each year. If your project requires, you could add another worksheet to this workbook that is dedicated to calculating the employee costs for this business. The results of that worksheet would then be linked into the Financial Assumptions worksheet.
- **Functions (Chapter 3)**: Two **SUM** functions are used in this worksheet. The first is in cell B3, which calculates the total investments planned to start the business in the range B4:B7. Similar to the way you calculate employee costs, you could add another worksheet to this workbook that is dedicated for creating a more detailed plan of how investments are being obtained. This worksheet can include various types of loans and other investment arrangements. The results of this worksheet can then be linked into the Financial Assumptions worksheet. The second **SUM** function is used in row 29 to total the Other Assets in rows 30 and 31.

Freeze Panes

You may have noticed in Figure 6.17 that the first row number showing on the left side of the figure is 1, but the second number is 26. Although it appears as if rows 2 through 25 are hidden, this is not the case. Since the Financial Assumptions spreadsheet is very long, a feature called **Freeze Panes** was used to prevent row 1 from moving off the screen when scrolling down the worksheet. Commonly used when working with long or wide worksheets, this feature allows you lock a specific row and column when

Quick Reference

Freeze Panes

1. Activate a cell that is below the row and to the right of the column you wish to lock in place when scrolling (except cell A1).
2. Click the **View** tab in the Ribbon.
3. Click the **Freeze Panes** icon.
4. Select the **Freeze Panes** option (select the **Unfreeze Panes** option to remove any locked rows and columns).
5. Use the **Freeze Top Row** or **Freeze First Column** options to lock the first column or row.

scrolling up and down or left and right. The following steps explain how to apply **Freeze Panes** to the Financial Assumptions worksheet in Figure 6.17:

- Click the **View** tab of the Ribbon.
- Click the **Freeze Panes** icon.
- Select the **Freeze Top Row** option. Select the **Unfreeze Panes** option to remove any locked columns and rows on the worksheet.

Financial Data

Figures 6.18 and 6.19 show the next component of the comprehensive financial plan: the Financial Data worksheet. The purpose of this worksheet is to show the financial results of the plan based on the data that is entered into Financial Assumptions spreadsheet. Most of the data shown in this worksheet is produced by formulas and functions that are linked to the Financial Assumptions worksheet. A business manager will most likely focus on the Net Income in row 14 to see if the data that was entered in the Financial Assumptions worksheet results in a profit. Notice that in year 1, the Net Income shows a loss of ($75,038), a small loss of ($1,432) in year 2, and a profit in year 3 of $87,365. This trend is typical for new businesses.

Figure 6.18 | **Financial Data Worksheet Rows 1 – 15**

Changes made to the data in the Financial Assumptions worksheet will produce new outputs in this worksheet.

The Net Income trend shown in this row is typical for new businesses.

	A	B	C	D
1	Financial Data for Business Strategy			
2	*Sales and Income*	Year 1	Year 2	Year 3
3	**Unit Sales**	**7,676**	**19,878**	**38,623**
4	Gross Sales	$ 175,000	$ 446,250	$ 864,833
5	Returns	$ 6,125	$ 8,925	$ 15,135
6	**Net Sales**	**$ 168,875**	**$ 437,325**	**$ 849,698**
7	Cost of Goods Sold	$ 84,000	$ 205,275	$ 380,526
8	**Gross Profit**	**$ 84,875**	**$ 232,050**	**$ 469,172**
9	Depreciation	$ 7,500	$ 7,500	$ 7,500
10	Selling, General & Admin. Expenses	$ 141,625	$ 215,194	$ 309,972
11	Interest	$ 10,788	$ 10,788	$ 10,788
12	**Income Before Taxes**	**$ (75,038)**	**$ (1,432)**	**$ 140,911**
13	Taxes	$ -	$ -	$ 53,546
14	**Net Income**	**$ (75,038)**	**$ (1,432)**	**$ 87,365**
15	*Percent of Net Sales*	*-44.4%*	*-0.3%*	*10.3%*

Figure 6.19 | **Financial Data Worksheet Rows 16 – 23**

The Freeze Panes command is locking this row at the top of the worksheet.

This row contains links to the Cash Analysis worksheet.

	A	B	C	D
1	Financial Data for Business Strategy			
16	*Assets*	Year 1	Year 2	Year 3
17	Cash	$ 189,423	$ 106,394	$ 108,242
18	Accounts Receivable	$ 14,583	$ 37,188	$ 72,069
19	Inventory	$ 35,000	$ 89,250	$ 144,139
20	Other Assets	$ 75,000	$ 75,000	$ 75,000
21	Total Assets	$ 314,007	$ 307,832	$ 399,450
22	*Liabilities*	Year 1	Year 2	Year 3
23	Accounts Payable	$ 14,000	$ 34,213	$ 63,421

As previously mentioned, the numbers shown on the Financial Data worksheet (Figures 6.18 and 6.19) are produced by formulas and functions, most of which contain links to the Financial Assumptions worksheet. With the exception of linking data, which was covered previously in this chapter, the core competency skills that were applied to this worksheet were covered in Chapters 2 through 4. The appearance of the worksheet is a result of the formatting and data management techniques covered in Chapter 2. The formulas and the **Payment** function were covered in Chapter 3, and the **IF** function was covered in Chapter 4. The following lists each formula or function that was created for Year 1. These formulas and functions are copied and pasted to produce the results for Year 2 and Year 3 unless otherwise noted:

- **Unit Sales**: `B6/'Financial Assumptions'!B12` This formula takes the Net Sales value calculated in cell B6 of the Financial Data worksheet and divides it by the Price Charged to Retailers in cell B12 of the Financial Assumptions worksheet.
- **Gross Sales Year 1**: `'Financial Assumptions'!B10` Since this is a new business, the first year of sales is typed into cell B10 of the Financial Assumptions worksheet. Therefore, the Gross Sales for Year 1 on the Financial Data worksheet is simply a link to cell B10 on the Financial Assumptions worksheet.
- **Gross Sales Year 2 and 3**: `(B4 + B4*'Financial Assumptions'!C11)* (1 + 'Financial Assumptions'!C9)` The first part of this formula is identical to the one used in Figure 6.7 in the previous section, which calculates the Gross Sales based on a percentage change. However, in this example an adjustment is made for inflation. The percentage change in inflation, which is entered into cell C9 in the Financial Assumptions worksheet, is added to 1 and then multiplied by the result of calculating the Gross Sales. This formula is copied and pasted into to cell D4 to calculate the Gross Sales for Year 3.
- **Returns**: `B4*'Financial Assumptions'!B13` The returns are calculated by multiplying the percentage entered into cell B13 on the Financial Assumptions worksheet by the Gross Sales calculated in cell B4.
- **Net Sales**: `B4 - B5` This basic formula takes the Gross Sales calculated in cell B4 and subtracts the Returns calculated in cell B5.
- **Cost of Goods Sold**: `B4*'Financial Assumptions'!B15` The Cost of Goods Sold percentage in the Financial Assumptions worksheet is multiplied by the Gross Sales in cell B4.
- **Gross Profit**: `B6-B7` This basic formula subtracts the Cost of Goods Sold from the Net Sales.
- **Depreciation**: `'Financial Assumptions'!B29/'Financial Assumptions'!B16` This formula takes a straight-line depreciation method approach (depreciation methods will be covered in your accounting courses). The Other Assets calculated in cell B29 in the Financial Assumptions worksheet is simply divided by the number of years entered into cell B16 of the Financial Assumptions worksheet.
- **Selling, General & Admin. Expenses**: `'Financial Assumptions'!B17+ ('Financial Assumptions'!B20*B4)+SUM('Financial Assumptions'!B21:B24)` The first part of this formula is simply a link to the total Employee Salary and Benefits cost in cell B17 in the Financial Assumptions worksheet. This is added to the Shipping Expenses, which are calculated by multiplying the percentage in cell B20 of the Financial Assumptions worksheet by the Gross Sales in cell B4. This result is then added to the summation of all expenses in the range B21:B24 in the Financial Assumptions worksheet.
- **Interest**: `PMT('Financial Assumptions'!D4,15,-'Financial Assumptions'!B4)-('Financial Assumptions'!B4/15)` This formula estimates the interest expense paid on a loan entered into cell B4 in the Financial Assumptions worksheet. The annual payments calculated by the **PMT** function include the principal *and interest* of the loan. When the principal divided

by the number of periods is subtracted from this result, what is left is an estimate of the interest that is paid each year. Years 2 and 3 for the interest expense simply reference the output of this formula in cell B11.

- **Income Before Taxes:** `B8 – SUM(B9:B11)` The **SUM** function adds the expenses in the range B9:B11 and subtracts it from the Gross Profit calculated in cell B8.
- **Taxes:** `IF(B12 > 0,B12 * 'Financial Assumptions'!B25,0)` An **IF** function is used to calculate the projected tax expense. This function checks to see if the Income Before Taxes, which is calculated in cell B12, is greater than zero. If the Income Before Taxes is greater than 0, it is multiplied by the tax percentage entered into cell B25 in the Financial Assumptions worksheet. If the Income Before Taxes is not greater than 0, the tax expense is assumed to be 0. This is a rather simple approach to projecting tax expenses. Depending on your project, you may be required to apply other tax accounting methodologies.
- **Net Income:** `B12 - B13` The Net Income is calculated by taking the Income Before Taxes and subtracting any taxes calculated in cell B13.
- **Percent of Net Sales:** `B14 / B6` This formula calculates Net Income as a percentage of Net Sales.
- **Cash:** `'Cash Analysis'!B11` This is a link to cell B11 in the Cash Analysis worksheet. The methods of data calculation in the Cash Analysis worksheet will be covered in the next section.
- **Accounts Receivable:** `B4 / 'Financial Assumptions'!B27` This formula estimates the accounts receivable by dividing the Accounts Receivable Turn in cell B27 in the Financial Assumptions worksheet into the Gross Sales in cell B4.
- **Inventory:** `B4 / 'Financial Assumptions'!B28` This formula divides the Inventory Turn in cell B28 in the Financial Assumptions worksheet into the Gross Sales in cell B4.
- **Other Assets:** `'Financial Assumptions'!B29` This is simply a link to cell B29 in the Financial Assumptions worksheet.
- **Account Payable:** `B7 / 'Financial Assumptions'!B33` The accounts payable is calculated by dividing the Accounts Payable Turn in cell B33 in the Financial Assumptions worksheet into the Cost of Goods Sold calculated in cell B7.

Cash Analysis (The NPV Function)

The third and final component of the comprehensive financial plan is the Cash Analysis worksheet, which is shown in Figure 6.20. The purpose of this worksheet is to show how much cash is used or accumulated as a result of the assumptions entered into the Financial Assumptions worksheet. Similar to the Financial Data worksheet, the Cash Analysis worksheet is created entirely of formulas and functions. In fact, most of the formulas and functions created in the Cash Analysis worksheet are linked to the Financial Data worksheet. Therefore, when the outputs of the formulas and functions change in the Financial Data worksheet, the outputs of the Cash Analysis worksheet will also change. The results of the Cash Analysis worksheet enable you to conduct a net present value analysis, which is a method used to determine the value of an investment or business. This will be calculated through the **NPV** function, which is covered in this section.

FIGURE 6.20 | **Cash Analysis Worksheet**

	A	B	C	D
1	Cash Analysis			
2		Year 1	Year 2	Year 3
3	Beginning Cash	$ 400,000	$ 189,423	$ 106,394
4	Net Income	$ (75,038)	$ (1,432)	$ 87,365
5	Depreciation	$ 7,500	$ 7,500	$ 7,500
6	Change in Inventory	$ (35,000)	$ (54,250)	$ (54,889)
7	Change in Accounts Receivable	$ (14,583)	$ (22,604)	$ (34,882)
8	Change in Accounts Payable	$ 14,000	$ 20,213	$ 29,209
9	Capital Expenditures	$ (75,000)	$ -	$ -
10	Repayment of Debt	$ (32,455)	$ (32,455)	$ (32,455)
11	*Ending Cash*	*$ 189,423*	*$ 106,394*	*$ 108,242*
12				
13				
14	*Net Present Value of Plan for Three Years*		$ (36,363)	
15				
16	Net Present Value Assuming Ending Cash in Year 3 is Sustained 3 More Years		$ 186,477	

The data in this area of the worksheet is produced by formulas and functions that contain links to the Financial Data worksheet.

The NPV function has been entered into these two cells.

With the exception of linking data and the **NPV** function, the skills used to create the Cash Analysis worksheet in Figure 6.20 were covered in Chapters 2 and 3. The appearance of the worksheet is a result of the formatting and data management techniques covered in Chapter 2. The formulas and **Payment** function were covered in Chapter 3. The following is a list of the formulas and functions that were created for Year 2. In several cases, a different calculation method is required for Year 1 and is noted accordingly:

- **Beginning Cash**: `B11` The Beginning Cash for Year 2 references the Ending Cash from Year 1. The Beginning Cash for Year 1 is a link to cell B3 in the Financial Assumptions worksheet, which contains the Total Initial Investment to start the business.
- **Net Income**: `'Financial Data'!C14` The Net Income is a link to the Financial Data worksheet.
- **Depreciation**: `'Financial Data'!C9` This is also a link to the Financial Data worksheet.
- **Change in Inventory**: `'Financial Data'!B19 - 'Financial Data'!C19` This formula takes the inventory value in Year 2 from the Financial Data worksheet and subtracts it from the inventory value in Year 1. As inventory increases from one year to the next, the formula produces a negative number, which shows that more cash is absorbed from the business. For Year 1 the inventory value in cell B18 in the Financial Data worksheet is subtracted from 0. As a result, the entire inventory required to start the business in Year 1 absorbs cash from the business.
- **Change in Accounts Receivable**: `'Financial Data'!B18 - 'Financial Data'!C18` Similar to the Change in Inventory calculation, the Change in Accounts Receivable is calculated by subtracting the Accounts Receivable value in Year 2 in the Financial Data worksheet from Year 1. Year 1 is calculated by subtracting the Accounts Receivable value from 0.
- **Change in Accounts Payable**: `'Financial Data'!C23 - 'Financial Data'!B23` This formula subtracts the Accounts Payable value in Year 1 from Year 2 in the Financial Data worksheet. This calculation is the opposite of the calculations used for Change in Inventory and Change in Accounts Receivable because, as Accounts Payable increases, cash is added to the business. The value for

Year 1 is a link to the Accounts Payable value in Year 1 on the Financial Data worksheet.

- **Capital Expenditures**: `'Financial Data'!B20 - 'Financial Data'!C20` This formula subtracts the Other Assets value in Year 2 from Year 1 in the Financial Data worksheet. If the value of Other Assets increases in Year 2 over Year 1, a negative number will be produced, indicating cash was used. The value for Year 1 subtracts the Other Assets value in cell B20 in the Financial Data worksheet from 0.
- **Repayment of Debt**: `PMT('Financial Assumptions'!D4,15,-'Financial Assumptions'!B4,,1) * -1` The **Payment** function calculates the annual payments of the loan based on the details listed in the Financial Assumptions worksheet. The result of the function is multiplied by –1 because it reduces the cash available to the business.
- **Ending Cash**: `C3 + SUM(C4:C10)` The Ending Cash is calculated by adding all of the items that add or reduce the cash of the business and adding that number to the beginning cash value.

The final calculation shown on the Cash Analysis worksheet in Figure 6.20 is the net present value of the comprehensive financial plan. This value is calculated using the **NPV** function. Details regarding the concepts of a net present value analysis will be covered in your finance courses. However, the following definitions for the arguments of the **NPV** function will provide a few insights as to what a net present value analysis can tell a business manager:

- **rate**: This is the interest rate or cost of borrowing money for the business. The goal of the **NPV** function is to calculate the present value of cash that is generated by a business in the future. It might be best to think of this concept as the **Future Value** function in reverse. That is, the **Future Value** function calculates how much money will be worth in the future when interest is added to a principal value over a period of time. The **NPV** function takes cash that is expected to be generated in the future and calculates how much that money is worth today. A new business is often considered a worthy investment if the NPV is a positive number.
- **value1**: This is the initial investment required to start, rebuild, or enhance a business. A negative sign must be used when entering values or cell locations for this argument.
- [**value(n)**]: Each value entered into the function after the **value1** argument is the cash flow that is expected for the year. Therefore, if you are using the **NPV** function to calculate the net present value for a ten-year financial plan, you will have ten cash values after you input the initial investment for the **value1** argument.

The arguments for the **NPV** function entered into cell C14 in the Cash Analysis worksheet are defined as follows:

- **rate**: `'Financial Assumptions'!D4` This is the interest rate from the loan details on the Financial Assumptions spreadsheet. This rate is used as the cost of borrowing money for this business.
- **value1**: `'Financial Assumptions'!B3` This is the principal of the loan from the Financial Assumptions worksheet. Notice that a negative sign is placed in front of this link.
- [**value2**]: `B11` This is the Ending Cash value in Year 1 on the Cash Analysis worksheet.
- [**value3**]: `C11` This is the Ending Cash value in Year 2 on the Cash Analysis worksheet.
- [**value4**]: `D11` This is the Ending Cash value in Year 3 on the Cash Analysis worksheet.

>> **Quick Reference**

NPV Function

1. Activate cell where the output should appear.
2. Type an equal sign, the function name **NPV**, and an open parenthesis.
3. Define the following arguments:
   a. **rate**: The interest rate that is charged for a loan or a firm's cost to borrow money.
   b. **value1**: The initial investment for starting a new business or in an existing business. You must precede values or cell locations with a negative sign.
   c. **[value(n)]**: Cash generated by the end of the year for a new business or incremental cash generated by an existing business. Use a separate argument to add cash value for each year.
4. Type a closing parenthesis and press the **Enter** key.

The Cash Analysis worksheet also shows a second **NPV** function that was entered into cell C16. The purpose of this function is to show the net present value of the comprehensive financial plan if the Ending Cash in Year 3 were produced for another three years. As a result, the cell reference D11 is simply repeated for the [**value5**] through [**value7**] arguments. Notice that the output of the **NPV** function in cell C14 is negative. This suggests that the financial plan for this new business does not generate a substantial return if it were in operation only for three years. However, the second **NPV** function in cell C16 shows a substantial return if the business operates for six years and continues to generate the same Ending Cash in Year 3 for an additional three years.

One of the key benefits of setting up a comprehensive financial plan through the methods described in this section is that the outputs in the Financial Data worksheet and Cash Analysis worksheet will automatically change when you change the inputs in the Financial Assumptions worksheet. This feature allows you to evaluate multiple scenarios to determine what would happen to the profitability or net present value of the business when certain assumptions are changed. The importance of this concept was demonstrated in a variety of situations throughout this text. It is this process of evaluating several scenarios that helps business managers make key financial decisions, such as how much money can be spent on advertising, how many people should be hired, or how much equipment should be purchased. There is no way to say for certain what will happen in business. However, business managers will use Excel to construct plans similar to what was described in this section to determine what is possible with respect to various business initiatives and ultimately decide which initiatives to execute and which initiatives to drop.

>> NPV Function

The purpose of this workshop is to demonstrate how the **NPV** function is used to evaluate an investment. I will be demonstrating the tasks in this workshop in the video named **NPV Function**. Open the file named ib_e06_investmentvalue and complete the tasks in this workshop.

1. **NPV Function (Video: NPV Function)**
   a. Activate cell E8 on the NPV Analysis worksheet.
   b. Type an equal sign, the function name **NPV**, and an open parenthesis.
   c. Click cell D3 to define the rate segment and type a comma.
   d. Type a negative sign and click cell D2. Then type a comma.
   e. Click cell A6 and type a comma.
   f. Click cell B6 and type a comma.
   g. Click cell C6 and type a comma.
   h. Click cell D6 and type a comma.
   i. Click cell E6 and type a closing parenthesis.
   j. Press the **Enter** key.
   k. Change the value in cell D2 to **975000**.
   l. Save and close your file.

VIDEO WORKSHOP

>> Financial Plans

The purpose of this workshop is to construct the comprehensive financial plan that was presented in this section. I will be demonstrating the tasks in this workshop in the following three videos: **Financial Assumptions**, **Financial Data**, and **Cash Analysis**. These video names appear at the beginning of each section of tasks. Open the file named ib_e06_newbusinessfinancialplan. Complete each section of tasks and then watch the related video.

1. **Financial Assumptions (Video: Financial Assumptions)**
   a. Activate the Financial Assumptions worksheet.
   b. Type a **SUM** function in cell B3 that adds the values in the range B4:B7.
   c. Type the formula `B18 * B19` in cell B17.
   d. Copy the formula in cell B17 and paste it into cells C17 and D17 using the **Formulas** option.
   e. Type a **SUM** function in cell B29 that adds the values in the range B30:B31.
   f. Copy the **SUM** function in cell B29 and paste it into cells C29 and D29 using the **Formulas** option.
   g. Type the following text in cell A38: **Target Scenario for New Business**.
   h. Bold and italicize the text in cell A38 and change the text color to red.

2. **Financial Data (Video: Financial Data)**
   a. Activate the Financial Data worksheet.
   b. Type a link in cell B4 that displays the Gross Sales value in cell B10 in the Financial Assumptions worksheet.
   c. Type a formula in cell C4 that calculates the Gross Sales for Year 2. Your formula should add to the Gross Sales value in cell B4 the result of multiplying the Gross Sales value in cell B4 by the Gross Sales Growth in cell C11 in the Financial Assumptions worksheet.
   d. Edit the formula that was created in cell C4 to account for inflation. Place parentheses around the formula and then multiply it by the result of adding 1 to the inflation percentage in cell C9 of the Financial Assumptions worksheet.
   e. Copy the formula in cell C4 and paste it into cell D4 using the **Formulas** option.
   f. Type a formula in cell B5 that calculates the Returns for Year 1. Your formula should multiply the Gross Sales value in cell B4 by the Returns percent in cell B13 in the Financial Assumptions worksheet.
   g. Copy the formula in cell B5 and paste it into cell C5 and D5 using the **Formulas** option.
   h. Type a formula in cell B6 that calculates the Net Sales. Your formula should subtract the Returns from the Gross Sales. Then copy this formula and paste it into cells C6 and D6 using the **Formulas** option.
   i. Type a formula in cell B3 that calculates the Unit Sales. Your formula should divide the Net Sales value in cell B6 by the Price Charged to Retailers in cell B12 in the Financial Assumptions worksheet.

j. Copy the formula in cell B3 and paste it into cells C3 and D3 using the **Formulas** option.
k. Type a formula in cell B7 that calculates the Cost of Goods Sold for Year 1. Your formula should multiply the Gross Sales value in cell B4 by the percentage in cell B15 in the Financial Assumptions worksheet.
l. Copy the formula in cell B7 and paste it into cells C7 and D7 using the **Formulas** option.
m. Type a formula in cell B8 that calculates the Gross Profit. Your formula should subtract the Cost of Goods Sold value in cell B7 from the Net Sales value in cell B6. Then copy this formula and paste it into cells C8 and D8 using the **Formulas** option.
n. Type a formula in cell B9 that calculates the Depreciation for Year 1. Your formula should divide the Other Assets value in cell B29 in the Financial Assumptions worksheet by the Average Life of Assets in cell B16, which is also in the Financial Assumptions worksheet.
o. Copy the formula in cell B9 and paste it into cells C9 and D9 using the **Formulas** option.
p. Type a formula in cell B10 that calculates the Selling, General & Admin. Expenses for Year 1. Your formula should add the Employee Salary and Benefits, the Shipping Expense, and all expenses in the range B21:B24 from the Financial Assumptions worksheet. Note that the Shipping Expense is calculated by multiplying the percentage in cell B20 in the Financial Assumptions worksheet by the Gross Sales value in cell B4 in the Financial Data worksheet.
q. Copy the formula in cell B10 and paste it into cells C10 and D10 using the **Formulas** option.
r. Type a formula in cell B11 that estimates the Interest Expense for Year 1. Your formula should first calculate the payments on the loan value in cell B4 in the Financial Assumptions worksheet using the **Payment** function. Use the Interest Rate in cell D4 of the Financial Assumptions worksheet to define the rate argument, use the number `15` to define the **nper** argument, and assume that payments are made at the beginning of the period. Then subtract from the output of this **Payment** function the result of dividing the loan value in cell B4 in the Financial Assumptions worksheet by 15.
s. Type the cell reference **B11** in cells C11 and D11 to display the output of the formula showing the Interest Expense in Year 1.
t. Type a formula in cell B12 to calculate the Income Before Taxes in Year 1. Your formula should subtract the sum of the expenses in the range B9:B11 from the Gross Profit value in cell B8. Then copy this formula and paste it into cells C12 and D12 using the **Formulas** option.
u. Type an **IF** function in cell B13 to calculate the Taxes for Year 1. If the Income Before Taxes is greater than 0, the function should multiply the Tax percent in cell B25 in the Financial Assumptions worksheet by the Income Before Taxes value in cell B12. Otherwise, the function should display a value of 0.
v. Copy the **IF** function in cell B13 and paste it into cells C13 and D13 using the **Formulas** option.
w. Type a formula in cell B14 to calculate the Net Income for Year 1. Your formula should subtract the Taxes value in cell B13 from the Income Before Taxes in cell B12. Then copy this formula and paste it into cells C14 and D14 using the **Formulas** option.
x. Type a formula in cell B15 to calculate the Percent of Net Sales for Year 1. Your formula should divide the Net Income value in cell B14 by the Net

Sales value in cell B6. Then copy this formula and paste it into cells C15 and D15 using the **Formulas** option.

y. Show the value of the Cash Assets in cell B17 by creating a link to cell B11 in the Cash Analysis worksheet. Then copy this link and paste it into cells C17 and D17 using the **Formulas** option.

z. Type a formula in cell B18 to calculate the Accounts Receivable for Year 1. Your formula should divide the Gross Sales value in cell B4 by the Accounts Receivable Turn in cell B27 in the Financial Assumptions worksheet.

aa. Copy the formula in cell B18 and paste it into cells C18 and D18 using the **Formulas** option.

bb. Type a formula in cell B19 to calculate the Inventory value for Year 1. Your formula should divide the Gross Sales in cell B4 by the Inventory Turn value in cell B28 in the Financial Assumptions worksheet.

cc. Copy the formula in cell B19 and paste it into cells C19 and D19 using the **Formulas** option.

dd. In cell B20, create a link to cell B29 in the Financial Assumptions worksheet. Then copy this link and paste it into cells C20 and D20 using the **Formulas** option.

ee. Type a **SUM** function in cell B21 that totals the values in the range B17:B20. Then copy the function and paste it into cells C21 and D21 using the **Formulas** option.

ff. Type a formula in cell B23 to calculate the Accounts Payable for Year 1. Your formula should divide the Cost of Goods Sold value in cell B7 by the Accounts Payable value in cell B33 in the Financial Assumptions worksheet.

gg. Copy the formula in cell B23 and paste it into cells C23 and D23 using the **Formulas** option.

3. Cash Analysis (Video: Cash Analysis)

a. Activate the Cash Analysis worksheet.

b. Create a link in cell B3 in the Cash Analysis worksheet that shows the value in cell B3 in the Financial Assumptions worksheet.

c. Type the cell reference `B11` in cell C3 to show the Ending Cash for Year 1. Then copy this cell reference and paste it into cell D3 using the **Formulas** option.

d. Create a link in cell B4 that shows the Net Income value in cell B14 in the Financial Data worksheet. Then copy this link and paste it into cells C4 and D4 using the **Formulas** option.

e. Create a link in cell B5 that shows the Depreciation value in cell B9 in the Financial Data worksheet. Then copy this link and paste it into cells C5 and D5 using the **Formulas** option.

f. Type a formula in cell B6 that calculates the Change in Inventory for Year 1. Your formula should subtract the value in cell B19 in the Financial Data worksheet from 0.

g. Type a formula in cell C6 that calculates the Change in Inventory for Year 2. Your formula should subtract the value in cell C19 in the Financial Data worksheet from the value in cell B19 in the Financial Data worksheet.

h. Copy the formula in cell C6 and paste it into cell D6 using the **Formulas** option.

i. Type a formula in cell B7 that calculates the Change in Accounts Receivable for Year 1. Your formula should subtract the value in cell B18 in the Financial Data worksheet from 0.

j. Type a formula in cell C7 that calculates the Change in Accounts Receivable for Year 2. Your formula should subtract the value in cell C18 in the Financial Data worksheet from the value in cell B18 in the Financial Data worksheet.
k. Copy the formula in cell C7 and paste it into cell D7 using the **Formulas** option.
l. Create a link in cell B8 that displays the value in cell B23 in the Financial Data worksheet.
m. Type a formula in cell C8 that calculates the Change in Accounts Payable for Year 2. Your formula should subtract the value in cell B23 in the Financial Data worksheet from the value in cell C23 in the Financial Data worksheet.
n. Copy the formula in cell C8 and paste it into cell D8 using the **Formulas** option.
o. Type a formula in cell B9 that calculates the Capital Expenditures for Year 1. Your formula should subtract the value in cell B20 in the Financial Data worksheet from 0.
p. Type a formula in cell C9 that calculates the Capital Expenditures for Year 2. Your formula should subtract the value in cell C20 in the Financial Data worksheet from the value in cell B20 in the Financial Data worksheet.
q. Copy the formula in cell C9 and paste it into cell D9 using the **Formulas** option.
r. Use the **Payment** function in cell B10 to calculate the Repayment of Debt in Year 1. Use the Interest Rate in cell D4 of the Financial Assumptions worksheet to define the **rate** argument, use the number `15` to define the **nper** argument, use the value in cell B4 in the Financial Assumptions worksheet to define the **pv** argument, and assume that payments are made at the beginning of the period. Multiply this function by −1 to show a negative number in cell B10.
s. Type the cell reference `B10` in cell C10 and D10.
t. Type a formula in cell B11 that adds the sum of the range B4:B10 to the value in cell B3. Then copy this formula and paste it into cells C11 and D11 using the **Formulas** option.
u. Type an **NPV** function into cell C14 to determine the net present value of the plan. Use the value in cell D4 in the Financial Assumptions worksheet to define the **rate** argument, the value in cell B3 in the Financial Assumptions worksheet to define the **[value1]** argument, and the Ending Cash values in the Cash Analysis worksheet to define the **[value2]**, **[value3]**, and **[value4]** arguments.
v. Save and close your file.

>> Evaluating Business Initiatives Using Net Present Value

EXERCISE

Why Do I Need This?

Business managers frequently evaluate how various financial assumptions change the profitability and cash flow of a business. This information is vital before making critical investment or operational decisions. These decisions include areas such as acquiring new businesses, starting new businesses, or improving existing businesses. In addition, many businesses evaluate the quality of an investment through a net present value analysis.

Exercise

The purpose of this exercise is to evaluate a decision to invest money in a new computer system that is expected to increase the productivity of a division within a major corporation. You will use a net present value analysis to evaluate the investment and its expected return. Open the file named ib_e06_systemimprovements.

1. Examine the formulas used to produce the data in the Revised Plan worksheet. What will happen if any value in the yellow cells of the Assumptions worksheet is changed?

2. Type a formula in cell B3 on the Change in Plan worksheet that subtracts cell B3 in the Current Plan worksheet from cell B3 in the Revised Plan worksheet. This will calculate the change in Gross Sales from the current to the revised plan. Copy this formula and paste it into the cells C3 through E3.

3. Type a formula in cell B4 in the Change in Plan worksheet to calculate the change in Returns by subtracting cell B4 in the Current Plan from cell B4 in the Revised Plan. Copy this formula and paste it into cells C4 through E4. What impact is the new system expected to have on returns?

4. Type a formula in cell B5 in the Change in Plan worksheet that shows the Change in Returns as a percent of Gross Sales. Your formula should subtract cell B5 in the Current Plan worksheet from cell B5 in the Revised Plan worksheet. Copy this formula and paste it into cells C5 through E5.

5. Copy the range B3:E3 and paste it into the range B6:E15. This will show the difference between the Current Plan and Revised Plan for each financial item listed in column A. You will want to use the Formulas option when pasting to maintain the formatting of the worksheet.

6. Type a **SUM** function in cell G3 on the Change in Plan worksheet that totals the values in the range B3:E3. What is the total increase in sales over four years the new system is expected to generate for the business?

7. Copy the **SUM** function in cell G3 and paste it in to cells G4, G6, G7, G9, and the range G11:G14. How much additional Net Income is the new system expected to generate for the business over a four-year period? Compare this number to the Total Initial Investment value in cell B2 in the Assumptions worksheet. Does this system seem be a good investment?

8. As previously mentioned, many business managers measure the quality of an investment based on the results of a net present value analysis. This will tell the business manager if the profits generated from an investment make sense given the time value of money. Therefore, type an **NPV** function in cell C18 on the Change in Plan worksheet. Define each argument of the function as follows:

   a. **Rate**: Cell B3 in the Assumptions worksheet. This is the division's cost to borrow money to pay for the initial cost of the new computer system.

   b. **value1**: Cell B2 in the Assumptions worksheet. This is the investment that is required to purchase and install the system.

   c. **[value2]**: The range B14:E14 in the Change in Plan worksheet. We will assume that the entire increase in Net Income will be incremental, or extra, cash added to the business as a result of the computer system.

9. Assume that this company has a policy that states all investments must prove that a minimum net present value of $5,000 is achievable over a four-year period. Should the manager of this division buy the computer system? Why?

10. In the Assumptions spreadsheet, change the values in the range B7:E7 to `15%`. This will assume that Gross Sales will increase 15% over the current

financial plan of the division. What is the total increase in Gross Sales (cell G3 in the Change in Plan worksheet) after making this change? Is the NPV of this investment positive or negative after making this change? Is it at least $5,000?

11. Change the Gross Sales percent values in the range B7:E7 on the Assumptions worksheet back to **10%**. Then change the values in the range B8:E8 to **2%**. This assumes that the new system will decrease the amount of Returns as a Percent of Gross Sales by 2% instead of 1%. Check the NPV on the Change in Plan worksheet. Is it positive or negative? Is it positive by at least $5,000?

12. Go back to the Assumptions worksheet and change the Gross Sales percent values in the range B7:E7 to **5%**. This assumes that the new system will increase Gross Sales over the current plan by only 5%. However, it will still assume that Returns as a Percent of Gross Sales will be reduced by 2%. Check the NPV of the investment. Is it positive or negative? Is it at least $5,000?

13. What does your assessment of step 12 tell you about the value of business initiatives that increase quality or reduce costs versus increasing sales?

14. Save and close your file.

>> What's Wrong with This Spreadsheet?

PROBLEM & EXERCISE

Problem

You are the CEO of a corporation. Your directors of Strategic Planning are presenting the results of a financial plan for starting a new business. This business will operate as a separate division and will add a new brand of merchandise to the current portfolio of the corporation. You have set the following NPV standard for evaluating investments made by the company:

1. For new businesses, the NPV must be positive by at least $10,000 considering three years of cash flow.

2. For existing businesses, the NPV must be positive by at least $5,000 considering four years of cash flow.

With these standards in mind, the directors of Strategic Planning are very excited to present this new business idea. They explain that a $2,500,000 investment will be required to start the business. In addition, the results of the plan show that the NPV is positive and well over $100,000. They explain that this business will generate Net Sales of over $3.3 million over a three-year period and will produce over $2 million in gross profit over the same time period. However, the directors point out that the business will lose a considerable amount of money in the first year and show that the Net Income is negative by over $600,000 in Year 1. That said, they also show that the Net Income makes a dramatic improvement in Year 2 and that the company is expected to show a profit in Year 3.

You look carefully at the spreadsheets the team has printed out for you, and they appear to be well constructed. As you glance at the numbers, they all appear to make sense. You congratulate the Strategic Planning team for a job well done and tell them that you would like to look at the plan one more time before approving the $2,500,000 investment. In addition, you ask the team to e-mail you the Excel file that was used to produce the spreadsheets in the meeting.

Exercise

The Excel file that the Strategic Planning department e-mailed to you is named ib_e06_agreatbusinessidea. Would you let the team spend the $2,500,000? Consider the following points:

1. Look at the numbers in the Financial Data worksheet. This information was presented to you at the meeting. Do the numbers make sense?
2. The formulas in the Financial Data worksheet are based on the numbers entered on the Assumptions worksheet. Do the outputs on the Financial Data worksheet change when the assumptions are changed?
3. Is the NPV really positive and over $100,000?

What's wrong with this spreadsheet? Write a short answer for each of the points listed here and explain why you would or would not approve this investment? Then fix any errors you find in the workbook.

Skill Set

Financial Accounting

The previous section illustrated how you can use the core competency skills in this text to construct a comprehensive financial plan. This section will provide an illustrative review of how you can use the core competency skills to construct spreadsheets used for financial accounting. Business professionals will typically use specialized software for managing the accounting needs of their business. However, for business students, Excel can be a very convenient and valuable tool for completing assignments typically required in accounting courses. As a result, several financial accounting concepts and rules will be mentioned but not explained in detail. You will receive more detailed instruction regarding these concepts in your financial accounting courses and reference material.

T-Accounts

Many financial accounting courses include assignments related to T-accounts. T-accounts are often considered a teaching tool when you are learning how certain transactions are treated according to the rules of accounting. Figure 6.21 shows an example of a blank T-account that was created in Excel. The layout of the T-account utilizes formatting techniques that were covered in Chapter 2. You use the **Borders** command to create the "T," and cells at the top of the T-account are merged so the name of the account can be centered over the "T."

Figure 6.21 | **Blank T-Account**

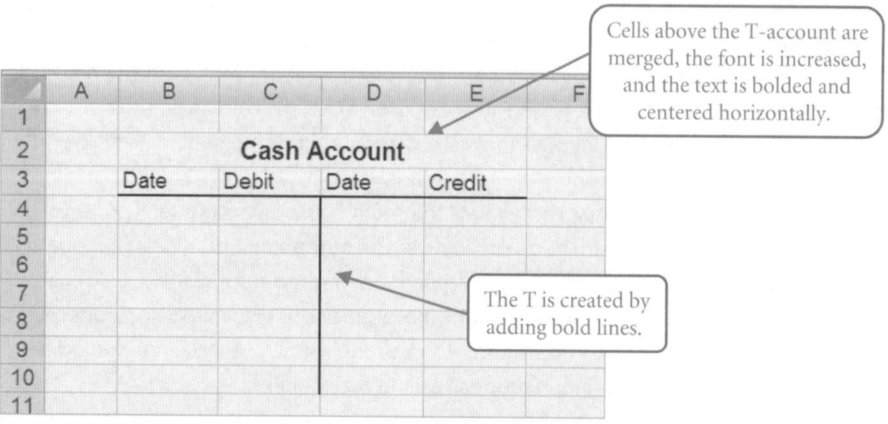

Figure 6.22 shows the T-account with dates and numbers entered into the debits and credits columns. A standard rule in accounting is that debits are always shown on the left and credits are always shown on the right. The **SUM** function is used at the bottom of the T-account to total the Debit and Credit columns.

Figure 6.22 | **T-Account with Dates and Dollar Entries**

	A	B	C	D	E	F
1						
2			Cash Account			
3			Date	Debit	Date	Credit
4			14-Aug	4,150	1-Sep	1,200
5			28-Sep	825	19-Sep	450
6			1-Oct	855	5-Oct	618
7			13-Oct	1,550	28-Oct	3,145
8			21-Oct	2,200		
9						
10				9,580		5,413

Debits are always shown on the left and Credits on the right.

The SUM function is used to total the Debit and Credit columns.

These blank cells are included in the range of the SUM function for additional entries.

Figure 6.23 shows a completed T-account which includes a formula that calculates the balance of the Cash Account (see cell B10). It is important to remember that the formula for calculating the balance of an account will change depending on the account. For example, Cash is an asset account, which means debits will increase the account and credits will decrease the account. For liability accounts, debits decrease the account and credits increase the account. These rules will be covered in your accounting courses.

Figure 6.23 | **Completed T-Account with Formula Calculating the Balance**

B10 =D10-F10

	A	B	C	D	E	F
2			Cash Account			
3			Date	Debit	Date	Credit
4			14-Aug	4,150	1-Sep	1,200
5			28-Sep	825	19-Sep	450
6			1-Oct	855	5-Oct	618
7			13-Oct	1,550	28-Oct	3,145
8			21-Oct	2,200		
9						
10	***Balance***	***4,167***		9,580		5,413

For asset accounts, the balance is calculated by subtracting the total credits from the total debits.

A big benefit of doing T-accounts in Excel is that you can easily copy and paste them for other accounts. If you were assigned to do a T-account for another asset account, such as Accounts Receivables, you could copy the Cash Account, paste it to another location, delete the dates and numbers, and enter new dates and numbers. As shown in Figure 6.24, the **SUM** function totaling the debits and credits and the formula calculating the balance of the account produce new outputs when new data is entered. However, you must be careful when pasting a T-account from one account class to another. *The formula calculating the balance for an asset account will be different for a Liability account.* Therefore, if you are creating a Liability T-account from an asset account, you must delete the formula and re-create it to properly account for debits and credits.

Figure 6.24 | **Creating a New T-Account Using the Copy and Paste Commands**

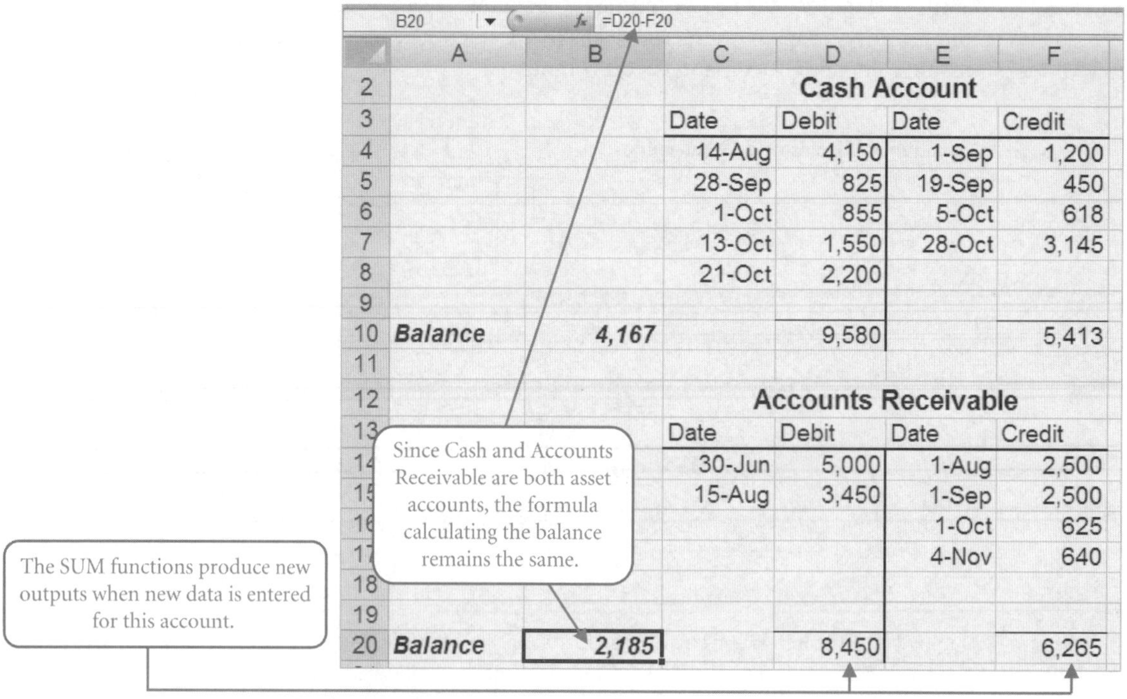

	A	B	C	D	E	F
2			Cash Account			
3			Date	Debit	Date	Credit
4			14-Aug	4,150	1-Sep	1,200
5			28-Sep	825	19-Sep	450
6			1-Oct	855	5-Oct	618
7			13-Oct	1,550	28-Oct	3,145
8			21-Oct	2,200		
9						
10	*Balance*	*4,167*		9,580		5,413
11						
12			Accounts Receivable			
13			Date	Debit	Date	Credit
14			30-Jun	5,000	1-Aug	2,500
15			15-Aug	3,450	1-Sep	2,500
16					1-Oct	625
17					4-Nov	640
18						
19						
20	*Balance*	*2,185*		8,450		6,265

COMMON MISTAKES | T-Accounts

The most common mistake made when creating T-accounts in Excel is copying old T-accounts into different account classes. When you copy an old T-account to create a new one, *always check the formula that is calculating the balance of the account.* You may need to adjust the formula to properly account for debits and credits in order to calculate an accurate balance.

Journals

Creating a journal is another common exercise that is required in accounting courses. A journal is used to keep track of all transactions that occur in a business and consists of the transaction date, the account description, and a monetary entry in either a Debit or Credit column. Formatting skills covered in Chapter 2 are used to create the appearance of the journal, similar to T-accounts. Figure 6.25 shows an example of a journal with several entries. Notice that each entry consists of at least two accounts (at least one debit and one credit), debit entries are listed before credit entries, and accounts with credit entries are indented (also see Figure 2.25, which shows the indent icons).

Figure 6.26 shows the Accounting journal with the **SUM** function added to total the Debit and Credit columns. The amount of debits entered in a journal must equal the amount of credits. If the outputs of the two **SUM** functions are not identical, then there was most likely an error with one of the entries in the journal.

Figure 6.25 | **Accounting Journal**

	A	B	C	D	E
1	JOURNAL				
2	Date	Description	Post. Ref.	Debit	Credit
3	10-Nov	Supplies	14	$ 1,350.00	
4	10-Nov	Accounts Payable	21		$ 1,350.00
5		*Purchased supplies on account*			
6					
7	18-Nov	Cash	11	$ 7,500.00	
8	18-Nov	Fees Earned	41		$ 7,500.00
9		*Received fees from customers*			
10					
11	30-Nov	Wages Expense	51	$ 2,125.00	
12	30-Nov	Rent Expense	52	$ 800.00	
13	30-Nov	Utilities Expense	54	$ 450.00	
14	30-Nov	Miscellaneous Expense	59	$ 275.00	
15	30-Nov	Cash	11		$ 3,650.00
16		*Paid Expenses*			
17					
18	30-Nov	Accounts Payable	21	$ 950.00	
19	30-Nov	Cash	11		$ 950.00
20		*Paid creditors on account*			

Accounts with a credit entry along with the transaction description are indented.

The Accounting number format is used for the dollar values in these columns.

Figure 6.26 | **The SUM Function Is Used to Total the Debit and Credit Entries**

D22 =SUM(D3:D18)

	A	B	C	D	E
1	JOURNAL				
2	Date	Description	Post. Ref.	Debit	Credit
9		*Received fees from customers*			
10					
11	30-Nov	Wages Expense	51	$ 2,125.00	
12	30-Nov	Rent Expense	52	$ 800.00	
13	30-Nov	Utilities Expense	54	$ 450.00	
14	30-Nov	Miscellaneous Expense	59	$ 275.00	
15	30-Nov	Cash	11		$ 3,650.00
16		*Paid Expenses*			
17					
18	30-Nov	Accounts Payable	21	$ 950.00	
19	30-Nov	Cash	11		$ 950.00
20		*Paid creditors on account*			
21					
22				$ 13,450.00	$ 13,450.00

The Freeze Panes command was used to lock these two rows.

SUM functions are used to total all debit and credit entries.

Ledgers

This section will illustrate how you use Excel to create an Accounting Ledger. A ledger is used to record all transactions for one specific account such as Cash, Accounts Payable, Inventory, and so on. Figure 6.27 shows an example of a blank ledger for the Cash account. As in the previous examples, formatting techniques from Chapter 2 were used to create the appearance of this ledger.

Figure 6.27 | **Blank Ledger for the Cash Account**

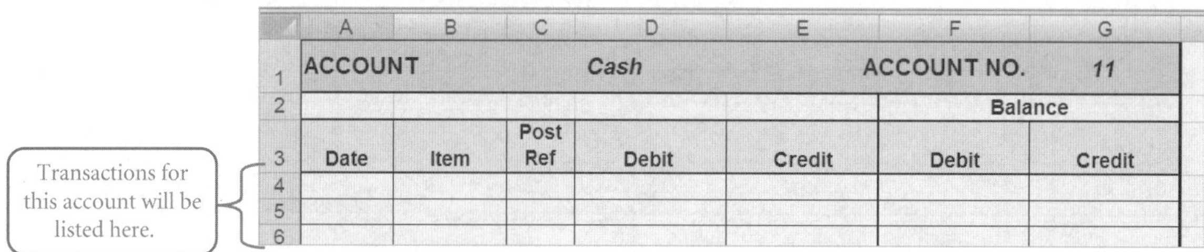

	A	B	C	D	E	F	G
1	ACCOUNT			*Cash*		ACCOUNT NO.	*11*
2						Balance	
3	Date	Item	Post Ref	Debit	Credit	Debit	Credit
4							
5							
6							

To complete the ledger shown in Figure 6.27, entries for the Cash Account are taken directly from the journal as shown in Figure 6.28. As demonstrated in the Data Management section of Chapter 2, a copy of the journal is pasted into a new worksheet (see Figure 2.14) and then sorted by the Description and Date columns in ascending order (see Figure 2.19). After the data is sorted, the Cash Account entries can be copied and pasted into the ledger. This eliminates the need to manually type the data into the ledger, which opens the possibility for data entry errors.

Figure 6.28 | **Journal Entries Sorted for Pasting Data into the Ledger**

	A	B	C	D	E
1		**JOURNAL**			
2	**Date**	**Description**	**Post. Ref.**	**Debit**	**Credit**
3	10-Nov	Accounts Payable	21		$ 1,350.00
4	30-Nov	Accounts Payable	21	$ 950.00	
5	18-Nov	Cash	11	$ 7,500.00	
6	30-Nov	Cash	11		$ 3,650.00
7	30-Nov	Cash	11		$ 950.00
8	18-Nov	Fees Earned	41		$ 7,500.00
9	30-Nov	Miscellaneous Expense	59	$ 275.00	
10		*Paid creditiors on account*			

These cash entries are grouped together after sorting the worksheet.

Figure 6.29 shows the entries that were pasted into the Cash account ledger from the journal in Figure 6.28. The next step will be to calculate the balance for the account. As previously mentioned, since Cash is an asset account, debits will increase the account and credits will decrease the account. Therefore, an **IF** function will be used to determine if the balance of the account should be increased or decreased based on the entry.

Figure 6.29 | **Cash Account Ledger with Entries Added**

	A	B	C	D	E	F	G
1	ACCOUNT			*Cash*		ACCOUNT NO.	*11*
2						Balance	
3	Date	Item	Post Ref	Debit	Credit	Debit	Credit
4	1-Nov	Balance				$ -	
5	18-Nov		1	$ 7,500.00			
6	30-Nov		2		$ 3,650.00		
7	30-Nov		2		$ 950.00		
8							

The first entry reflects a beginning balance of 0.

An IF function will be created in this cell to calculate the balance.

The **IF** function is used to calculate the balance of the Cash ledger shown in Figure 6.29. The technique of using the **IF** function when making calculations was introduced in Chapter 4 (see Figure 4.6). The function will be created in cell F5 under the Debit column because asset accounts have a normal debit balance. Your accounting course will provide instruction on what the normal balance is for each type of account. The arguments of this **IF** function are defined as follows:

- **logical_test:** `D5 > 0` The logical test of the **IF** function will be used to determine if there is a value entered in the Debit column.
- **[value_if_true]:** `F4 + D5` If the logical test is true, it can be assumed that there is no entry in the Credit column. An entry *cannot* have a value in both the Debit and Credit columns. As a result, if the logical test is true, then this is a debit entry, which increases the balance of an asset account. Therefore, the value in cell D5 is added to the prior balance of the account, which is in cell F4.
- **[value_if_false]:** `F4 - E5` If the logical test is false, then it is assumed that there is a value in the Credit column. For asset accounts, credits decrease the balance. Therefore, the value in cell E5 is subtracted from cell F4, which is the prior balance of the account.

After the **IF** function is created in cell F5, it can be copied and pasted to the rest of the rows in the ledger. Figure 6.30 shows the completed ledger for the Cash account with the balance being calculated by the **IF** function.

Figure 6.30 | **Complete Ledger for the Cash Account**

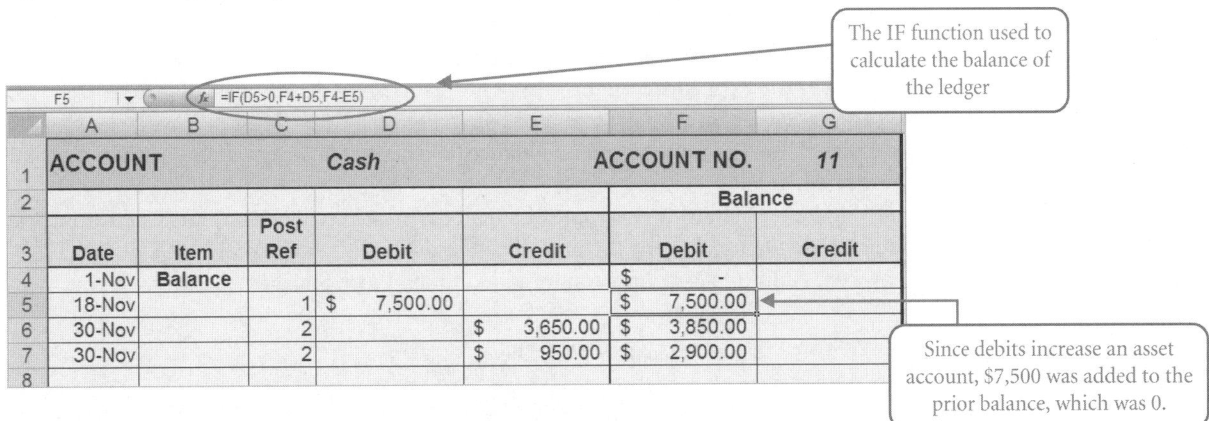

	A	B	C	D	E	F	G
1	ACCOUNT		Cash		ACCOUNT NO.		11
2						Balance	
3	Date	Item	Post Ref	Debit	Credit	Debit	Credit
4	1-Nov	Balance				$ -	
5	18-Nov		1	$ 7,500.00		$ 7,500.00	
6	30-Nov		2		$ 3,650.00	$ 3,850.00	
7	30-Nov		2		$ 950.00	$ 2,900.00	
8							

Trial Balance and Work Sheets

This section will illustrate two key components of the financial accounting system. The first is a Trial Balance. A Trial Balance is a list showing the current balance of all accounts for a particular business. The second is an accounting Work Sheet. Work Sheets are used to make any necessary adjustments and finalize the balance of all accounts for a business.

As previously mentioned, each account type has either a normal debit or credit balance. The purpose of the Trial Balance is to assess whether the total for all accounts that carry a debit balance are equal to the total for all accounts that carry a credit balance. Figure 6.31 shows an example of a completed Trial Balance. If a ledger was created in Excel for each account listed in column A, the balance can either be pasted, or preferably linked, into the Trial Balance. A **SUM** function is used to add both columns of the Trial Balance in row 20 to see whether they are equal. The double underline at the bottom of each result signifies that the accounts are balanced, meaning the sum of all debit balances is equal to the sum of all credit balances. You can access the double underline through the **Underline** icon (see Figure 2.22).

Figure 6.31 | **Example of a Completed Trial Balance**

	A	B	C
1	Company A		
2	Trial Balance		
3	December 31, 2006		
4	Cash	$ 3,000.00	
5	Accounts Receivable	$ 2,500.00	
6	Supplies	$ 2,000.00	
7	Prepaid Insurance	$ 2,500.00	
8	Land	$ 20,000.00	
9	Office Equipment	$ 2,000.00	
10	Accounts Payable		$ 1,000.00
11	Unearned Rent		$ 500.00
12	Owner A, Capital		$ 25,000.00
13	Owner A, Drawing	$ 4,000.00	
14	Fees Earned		$ 18,000.00
15	Wages Expense	$ 4,500.00	
16	Rent Expense	$ 1,500.00	
17	Utilities Expense	$ 1,000.00	
18	Supplies Expense	$ 1,000.00	
19	Miscellaneous Expense	$ 500.00	
20		$ 44,500.00	$ 44,500.00
21			

The balance for each account can be pasted or linked to the ledger.

SUM functions are used to total the debit and credit columns.

An accounting Work Sheet is used to make adjusting entries to the Trial Balance of each account and calculate a new balance if necessary. Not all accounts will have an adjusting entry; therefore, the calculated balance on the worksheet may be identical to the trial balance. In addition, the Work Sheet is used to identify the balance of each account as either income statement or balance sheet values. Once the Work Sheet is completed, the Income Statement, Balance Sheet, and Statement of Owners Equity can be created.

Figure 6.32 shows an example of a blank Work Sheet. The accounts listed along the left side are identical to the accounts listed in the Trial Balance shown in Figure 6.31; however, additional accounts can be added to the Work Sheet if necessary. The balance

Figure 6.32 | **Blank Accounting Work Sheet**

	A	B	C	D	E	F	G	H	I	J	K
1	Company A										
2	Work Sheet										
3	For Year End December 31, 2006										
4		Trial Balance		Adjustments		Adjusted Trial Balance		Income Statement		Balance Sheet	
5	Account Title	Dr	Cr	Dr	Cr	Dr	Cr	Dr	Cr	Dr	Cr
6	Cash										
7	Accounts Receivable										
8	Supplies										
9	Prepaid Insurance										
10	Land										
11	Office Equipment										
12	Accounts Payable										
13	Unearned Rent										
14	Owner A, Capital										
15	Owner A, Drawing										
16	Fees Earned										
17	Wages Expense										
18	Rent Expense										
19	Utilities Expense										
20	Supplies Expense										
21	Miscellaneous Expense										
22											
23											
24											
25											
26											
27											

Trial Balance | Work Sheet

The abbreviation for Debit or Dr and for Credit is Cr.

The Trial Balance is in this worksheet.

The accounts in this column are identical to the Trial Balance.

for each account in the first two columns of the Work Sheet should be identical to the Trial Balance. The next set of columns is for adding any necessary adjustments. Columns F and G are used for calculating a new balance for each account to include any adjusting entries. The Income Statement and Balance Sheet columns are for categorizing the adjusted balance for each account in its respective financial statement. Therefore, the balance for each account used to construct an income statement will be shown in the Income Statement columns, and the balance for each account used to construct a balance sheet will be shown in the Balance Sheet columns.

As previously mentioned, the balance that appears in the first two columns of the Work Sheet must match the Trial Balance. Therefore, links are created in the Work Sheet to show the debit and credit values under the Trial Balance heading. If the order of the accounts in the Work Sheet is identical to the Trial Balance, the first link can be copied and pasted for the other accounts. Linking data in this situation ensures that the balance for each account in the Trial Balance matches the Work Sheet. If any changes are made to the Trial Balance, it will automatically be reflected in the Work Sheet. Figure 6.33 shows the links that were created in the Work Sheet.

Figure 6.33 | **Work Sheet with Links to the Trial Balance**

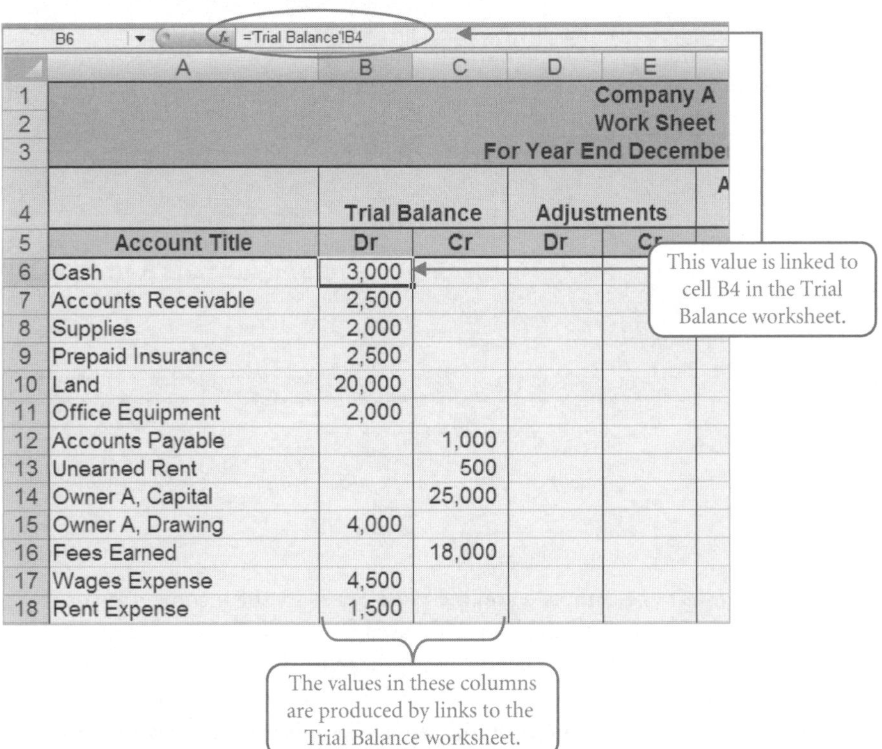

	A	B	C	D	E
1					Company A
2					Work Sheet
3					For Year End Decembe
4		Trial Balance		Adjustments	
5	Account Title	Dr	Cr	Dr	Cr
6	Cash	3,000			
7	Accounts Receivable	2,500			
8	Supplies	2,000			
9	Prepaid Insurance	2,500			
10	Land	20,000			
11	Office Equipment	2,000			
12	Accounts Payable		1,000		
13	Unearned Rent		500		
14	Owner A, Capital		25,000		
15	Owner A, Drawing	4,000			
16	Fees Earned		18,000		
17	Wages Expense	4,500			
18	Rent Expense	1,500			

The next set of columns in the Work Sheet is used for adding any adjusting entries for each account. Once the adjustments are added into the Work Sheet, an adjusted balance is calculated. Similar to calculating the balance on a ledger, the **IF** function will be used to calculate the adjusted balance on the Work Sheet by determining if the adjustments in columns D and E should be added or subtracted from the balance in the Trial Balance columns (columns B and C). To do this, you must first determine how debits and credits change the balance of an account. For the accounts on this Work Sheet, *debits will increase the balance of an account except for* Accounts Payable; Unearned Rent; Owner A, Capital; and Fees earned. For these accounts, the formula in the **IF** function must be adjusted so that any value in the Debit column is subtracted from the trial balance. Figure 6.34 shows an example of two **IF** functions that are used to calculate the Adjusted Trial Balance columns in the Work Sheet.

Figure 6.34 | **Using the IF Function to Calculate the Adjusted Trial Balance in the Work Sheet**

Account	Trial Balance Cell Location	Adjusting Entry Cell Locations	Account Type	IF Function
Cash	**B6**	Debits = **D6** Credits = **E6**	**Asset:** Debits increase the balance.	**=IF(D6 > 0,B6 + D6,B6 - E6)**
Accounts Payable	**C12**	Debits = **D12** Credits = **E12**	**Liability:** Debits decrease the balance.	**=IF(D12 > 0,C12 - D12,C12 + E12)**

Figure 6.35 shows the Work Sheet with adjusting entries added to columns D and E and the adjusted trial balance calculated by **IF** functions in columns F and G. In addition, **SUM** functions were added to row 22 to show the total debits and credits for each set of columns. Notice that the debits match the credits for each set of columns.

Figure 6.35 | **Work Sheet with Adjustments and Adjusted Trial Balance Added**

	A	B	C	D	E	F	G	H	I	J	K
1	Company A										
2	Work Sheet										
3	For Year End December 31, 2006										
4		Trial Balance		Adjustments		Adjusted Trial Balance		Income Statement		Balance Sheet	
5	Account Title	Dr	Cr	Dr	Cr	Dr	Cr	Dr	Cr	Dr	Cr
6	Cash	3,000			500	2,500					
7	Accounts Receivable	2,500		500		3,000					
8	Supplies	2,000			500	1,500					
9	Prepaid Insurance	2,500				2,500					
10	Land	20,000				20,000					
11	Office Equipment	2,000		500		2,500					
12	Accounts Payable		1,000	250			750				
13	Unearned Rent		500				500				
14	Owner A, Capital		25,000				25,000				
15	Owner A, Drawing	4,000				4,000					
16	Fees Earned		18,000		500		18,500				
17	Wages Expense	4,500				4,500					
18	Rent Expense	1,500				1,500					
19	Utilities Expense	1,000				1,000					
20	Supplies Expense	1,000		250		1,250					
21	Miscellaneous Expense	500				500					
22		44,500	44,500	1,500	1,500	44,750	44,750				

The IF function calculating the balance of this account is =IF(D12 > 0, C12 - D12,C12 + E 12).

The IF function calculating the balance of this account is =IF(D6 > 0,B6 + D6,B6 - E6).

SUM functions are used to add the total debits and credits for each set of columns.

The last columns to be completed on the Work Sheet are the Income Statement and Balance Sheet columns. These columns are used to classify the adjusted trial balances as either income statement or balance sheet accounts. This is accomplished by referencing the appropriate cell location in the Debit or Credit column of either the Income Statement or Balance Sheet headings. Your accounting course will provide details on which accounts are income statement or balance sheet accounts.

Figure 6.36 shows how each account in the Work Sheet is classified with respect to the Income Statement or Balance Sheet columns. For the first account, which is Cash, the cell reference =F6 is used to display the Adjusted Trial Balance in the Debit column under the Balance Sheet heading. As a result, any changes to the Adjusted Trial Balance for each account will be reflected in either the Income Statement or Balance Sheet columns.

COMMON MISTAKES | Accounting Work Sheets

Make sure cell references are typed into the appropriate Debit or Credit column for the Income Statement or Balance Sheet columns of the Work Sheet. If an account shows a debit balance in the Adjusted Trial Balance column, then it must also have a debit balance in either the Income Statement or Balance Sheet columns. The same is true for accounts that have credit balances.

Figure 6.36 | **Work Sheet with Income Statement and Balance Sheet Columns Completed**

	A	B	C	D	E	F	G	H	I	J	K
1					Company A						
2					Work Sheet						
3					For Year End December 31, 2006						
4		Trial Balance		Adjustments		Adjusted Trial Balance		Income Statement		Balance Sheet	
5	Account Title	Dr	Cr	Dr	Cr	Dr	Cr	Dr	Cr	Dr	Cr
6	Cash	3,000			500	2,500				2,500	
7	Accounts Receivable	2,500		500		3,000				3,000	
8	Supplies	2,000			500	1,500				1,500	
9	Prepaid Insurance	2,500				2,500				2,500	
10	Land	20,000				20,000				20,000	
11	Office Equipment	2,000		500		2,500				2,500	
12	Accounts Payable		1,000	250			750				750
13	Unearned Rent		500				500				500
14	Owner A, Capital		25,000				25,000				25,000
15	Owner A, Drawing	4,000				4,000				4,000	
16	Fees Earned		18,000		500		18,500		18,500		
17	Wages Expense	4,500				4,500		4,500			
18	Rent Expense	1,500				1,500		1,500			
19	Utilities Expense	1,000				1,000		1,000			
20	Supplies Expense	1,000		250		1,250		1,250			
21	Miscellaneous Expense	500				500		500			
22		44,500	44,500	1,500	1,500	44,750	44,750	8,750	18,500	36,000	26,250

The cell reference =F6 is entered here.

SUM functions are used to total the debit and credit columns.

The final step in completing the Work Sheet is entering a formula to calculate the Net Income. You may have noticed in Figure 6.36 that the total debits and credits for the Income Statement and Balance Sheet columns do not match. This is why a double underline was not added to these results. For the Debit and Credit columns to match, the Net Income must be calculated and added to the Debit column of the Income Statement and to the Credit column of the Balance Sheet. This is done using basic formulas. For the Income Statement column, you calculate the Net Income by subtracting the total debits from the total credits. For the Balance Sheet column, you subtract the total credits from the total debits. You enter this formula in the Debit column for the Income Statement and in the Credit column for the Balance Sheet. When the net income is added to the total debits in the Income Statement column, the total debits will match the total credits. When the net income is added to the total credits of the Balance Sheet column, the total credits will match the total debits. The final Work Sheet is shown in Figure 6.37.

Figure 6.37 | **Final Work Sheet**

	A	B	C	D	E	F	G	H	I	J	K
1					Company A						
2					Work Sheet						
3					For Year End December 31, 2006						
4		Trial Balance		Adjustments		Adjusted Trial Balance		Income Statement		Balance Sheet	
5	Account Title	Dr	Cr	Dr	Cr	Dr	Cr	Dr	Cr	Dr	Cr
6	Cash	3,000			500	2,500				2,500	
7	Accounts Receivable	2,500		500		3,000				3,000	
8	Supplies	2,000			500	1,500				1,500	
9	Prepaid Insurance	2,500				2,500				2,500	
10	Land	20,000				20,000				20,000	
11	Office Equipment	2,000		500		2,500				2,500	
12	Accounts Payable		1,000	250			750				750
13	Unearned Rent		500				500				500
14	Owner A, Capital		25,000				25,000				25,000
15	Owner A, Drawing	4,000				4,000				4,000	
16	Fees Earned		18,000		500		18,500		18,500		
17	Wages Expense	4,500				4,500		4,500			
18	Rent Expense	1,500				1,500		1,500			
19	Utilities Expense	1,000				1,000		1,000			
20	Supplies Expense	1,000		250		1,250		1,250			
21	Miscellaneous Expense	500				500		500			
22		44,500	44,500	1,500	1,500	44,750	44,750	8,750	18,500	36,000	26,250
23								9,750			9,750
24								18,500	18,500	36,000	36,000
25											

The formula entered into this cell is =I22 - H22.

This is the output of a formula adding cells H22 and H23.

The formula entered into this cell is =J22 - K22.

Statements

Once the Work Sheet is completed, you can create a set of financial statements. The data used to create these statements will be linked to the Work Sheet. As a result, when the data is changed in the Work Sheet, it will adjust the outputs of the financial statements. Three statements will be created from the Work Sheet shown in Figure 6.37: an Income Statement, a Balance Sheet, and a Statement of Owners Equity.

The purpose of an Income Statement is to report the profitability of a business by showing all sales and expenses incurred by a company. Figure 6.38 shows an example of a blank Income Statement. The first item listed in column A (cell A4) is Fees earned, which is typically used to represent the sales of a service business. The items listed in the range A7:A11 represent various expenses for this service business. The total expenses in row 12 will be subtracted from the Fees earned to calculate the Net Income.

Figure 6.38 | **Blank Income Statement**

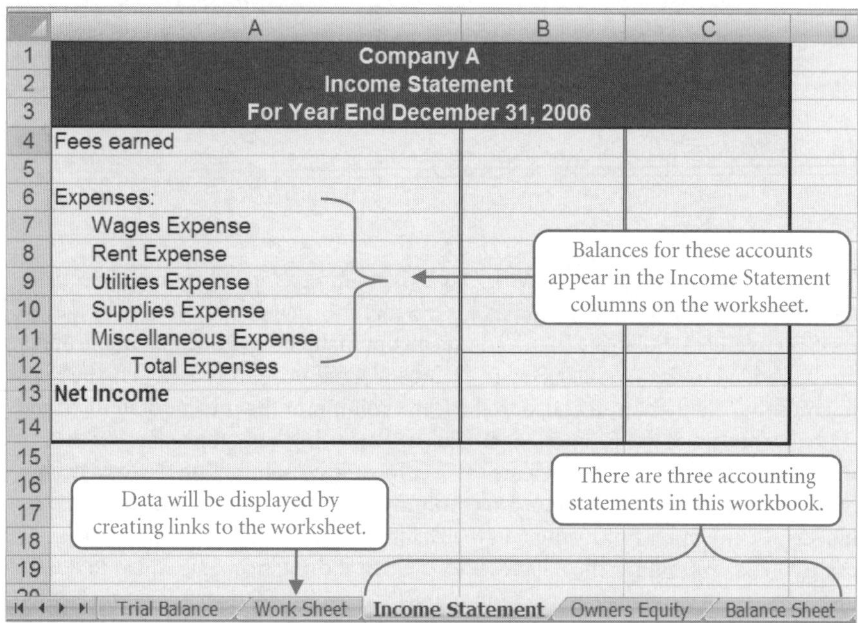

Figure 6.39 shows the completed Income Statement. The value for the Fees earned is the result of a link to cell I16 in the Work Sheet shown in Figure 6.37. Links are also created for each expense account listed in column A. A **SUM** function is used in cell C12 to calculate a total for all expenses. Then a formula is entered in cell C13 to calculate the Net Income; this formula subtracts the Total Expenses from the Fees earned.

Figure 6.39 | **Complete Income Statement**

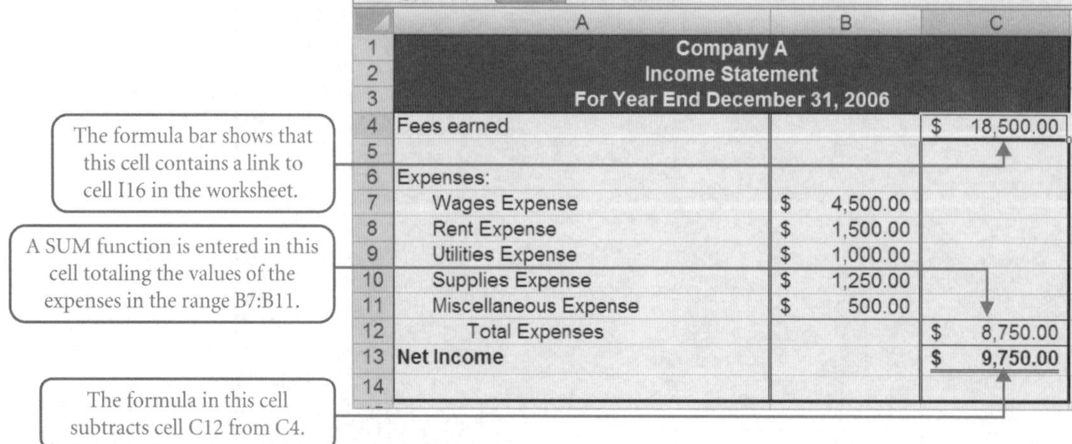

In your accounting classes, you will learn that the assets of a company are entitled to either owners or creditors. The Statement of Owners Equity presents the value of a company's assets that is entitled to the owners. Figure 6.40 shows a blank Statement of Owners Equity.

Figure 6.40 | **Blank Statement of Owners Equity**

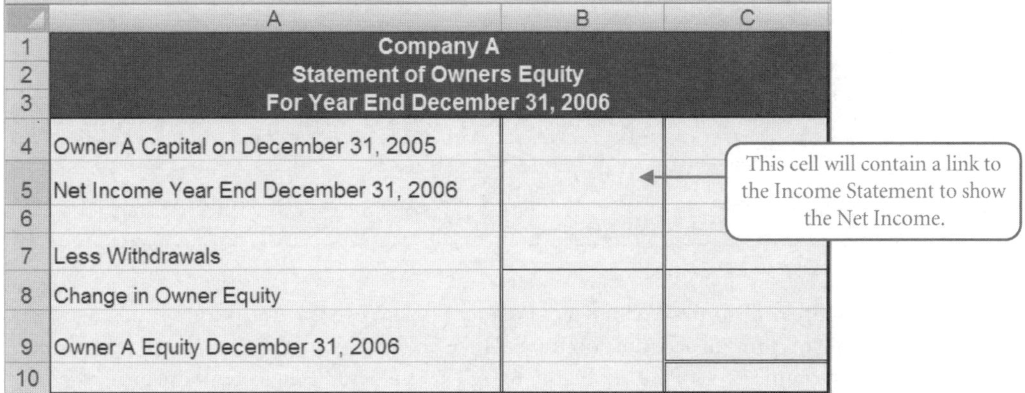

Figure 6.41 shows a completed Statement of Owners Equity. The value for the first item—Owner A Capital on December 31, 2005—is the result of link to cell K14 on the Work Sheet in Figure 6.37. This is the Owners Equity balance in the Balance Sheet column. The Withdrawals value in row 7 is linked to the Owner A Drawing account balance in cell J15 of the Work Sheet. The Net Income value in row 5 is linked to the Net Income that was calculated in cell C13 on the Income Statement in Figure 6.39. The Change in Owner Equity is calculated with a formula that subtracts the Withdrawals in row 7 from the Net Income in row 5. The Owners Equity for this period is calculated using a formula in cell C9 that adds the Change in Owner Equity in cell C8 from Owner's Capital in cell C4.

Figure 6.41 | **Completed Statement of Owners Equity**

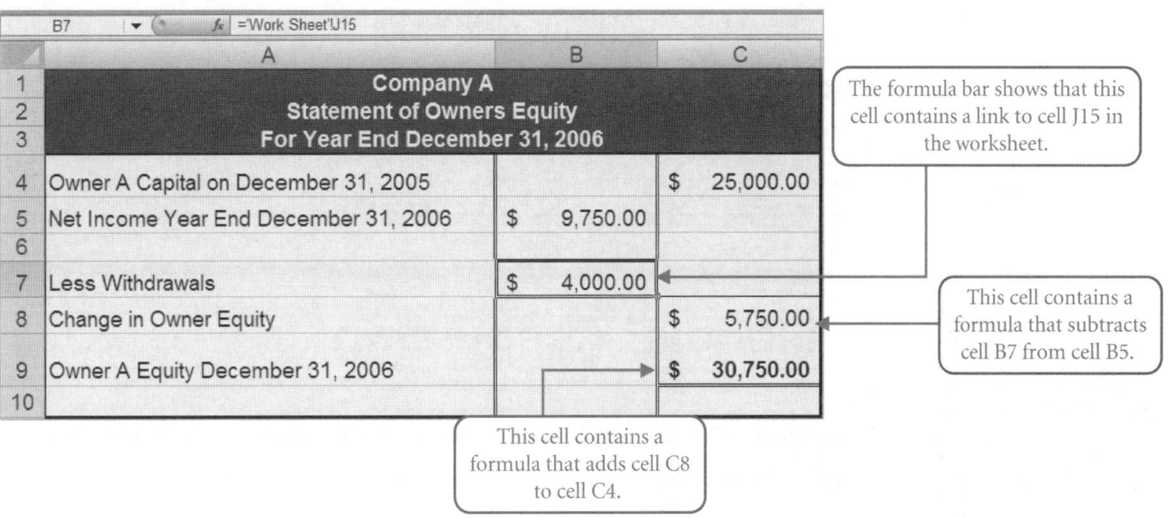

Figure 6.42 shows an example of a blank Balance Sheet. The Balance Sheet contains current account balance information for all Asset accounts, Liability accounts, and Owners Equity. The Balance Sheet follows the accounting equation `Assets = Liabilities + Owners Equity`. Details regarding this equation will be covered in your accounting courses. However, a cursory knowledge of this equation is required when constructing a Balance Sheet. The data used for the Balance Sheet will come from links to the worksheet in Figure 6.37 and the Statement of Owners Equity in Figure 6.41.

Figure 6.42 | **Blank Balance Sheet**

	A	B	C	D	E	F
1	Company A					
2	Balance Sheet					
3	December 31, 2006					
4	Assets			Liabilities		
5	**Current assets:**			**Current liabilities:**		
6	Cash			Accounts payable		
7	Accounts receivable			Unearned Rent		
8	Supplies			Total liabilities		
9	Prepaid insurance					
10	Total current assets					
11	**Property, Plant, & Equipment** *(net of Accumulated Depreciation):*					
12	Land					
13	Office equipment			Owners Equity		
14	Total PP&E			Owner A, Capital		
15						
16	*Total assets*			*Total Liabilities and OE*		
17						

Figure 6.43 shows a completed Balance Sheet. With the exception of the Owner A Capital, links for all accounts on the Balance Sheet can be found in the Balance Sheet column on the Work Sheet in Figure 6.37. The links for each account are created in columns B and E in Figure 6.43. The **SUM** function is used in column C to total each category of accounts such as Current assets and Property, Plant, & Equipment. At the bottom of the Balance Sheet, formulas are used to add the Total assets and the Total Liabilities and OE. The results of these formulas will match if the Balance Sheet, Work Sheet, Income Statement, and Statement of Owners Equity were properly constructed.

Figure 6.43 | **Completed Balance Sheet**

	A	B	C	D	E	F
1	Company A					
2	Balance Sheet					
3	December 31, 2006					
4	Assets			Liabilities		
5	**Current assets:**			**Current liabilities:**		
6	Cash	$ 2,500.00		Accounts payable	$ 750.00	
7	Accounts receivable	$ 3,000.00		Unearned Rent	$ 500.00	
8	Supplies	$ 1,500.00		Total liabilities		$ 1,250.00
9	Prepaid insurance	$ 2,500.00				
10	Total current assets		$ 9,500.00			
11	**Property, Plant, & Equipment** *(net of Accumulated Depreciation):*					
12	Land	$ 20,000.00				
13	Office equipment	$ 2,500.00		Owners Equity		
14	Total PP&E		$ 22,500.00	Owner A, Capital		$ 30,750.00
15						
16	*Total assets*		$ 32,000.00	*Total Liabilities and OE*		$ 32,000.00
17						

VIDEO WORKSHOP

>> Financial Accounting

The purpose of this workshop is to demonstrate how to use Excel to construct the financial accounting spreadsheets and statements illustrated in this section. I will be demonstrating the tasks in this workshop in the following seven videos: **T-Accounts**, **Journals**, **Ledgers**, **Trial Balance and Work Sheet**, **Income Statement**, **Owners Equity**, and **Balance Sheet**. The name of the video appears at the beginning of each section. At the beginning of each section, you will be instructed to open the Excel file that is required to complete the tasks. Complete each section and then watch the related video.

1. **T-Accounts (Video: T-Accounts)**
   a. Open the file named ib_e06_t-accounts.
   b. Type a **SUM** function in cell D12 that sums the values in the range D5:D11.
   c. Type a **SUM** function in cell F12 that sums the values in the range F5:F11.
   d. Type a formula in cell B12 that subtracts cell F12 from D12.
   e. Bold and italicize cell B12.
   f. Copy the range A3:F12 and paste it after activating cell A15.
   g. Type `Accounts Receivable` in cell C15.
   h. Delete the contents in the range C17:D21 and E17:F20.
   i. Type the data listed for the following cell locations:
      i. C17: `June 30`
      ii. C18: `August 15`
      iii. D17: `5000`
      iv. D18: `3000`
      v. E17: `August 1`
      vi. F17: `2500`
   j. Copy the range A15:F24 and paste it after activating cell H3.
   k. Delete the contents in J5:K6, L5:M5, and cell I12.
   l. Type `Accounts Payable` in cell J3.
   m. Type the data listed for the following cell locations:
      i. L5: `June 1`
      ii. L6: `June 30`
      iii. M5: `3000`
      iv. M6: `3000`
      v. J5: `August 1`
      vi. K5: `1000`
   n. Type a formula into cell I2 that subtracts cell K12 from M12.
   o. Save and close your file.

2. **Journals (Video: Journals)**
   a. Open the file named ib_e06_journals.
   b. Type the date `November 30` in cells A18 and A19.
   c. Type the data listed for the following cell locations:
      i. B18: `Accounts Payable`
      ii. C18: `21`
      iii. D18: `950`
      iv. B19: `Cash`
      v. C19: `11`
      vi. E19: `950`
      vii. B20: `Paid creditors on account`
   d. Indent cell B19 once and cell B20 twice. Then italicize the text in cell B20.
   e. Type a **SUM** function into cell D22 that totals the values in the range D3:D20.
   f. Copy the **SUM** function in cell D22 and paste it into cell E22 using the **Formulas** option.
   g. Save and close your file.

3. Ledgers (Video: Ledgers)

a. Open the file named ib_e06_ledger.

b. Type the word `Cash` in cell C1 in the Ledger worksheet.

c. Add a new worksheet to the workbook.

d. Copy the Journal worksheet and paste it into the new worksheet.

e. Sort the Journal pasted in the new worksheet by the Description and Date column in ascending order.

f. Copy cells A5:A7 in the copy of the Journal. Activate cell A5 on the Ledger worksheet and paste.

g. Copy cells D5:E7 on the copy of the Journal. Activate cell D5 on the Ledger worksheet and paste.

h. Type an **IF** function into cell F5 of the Ledger worksheet that tests whether the value in cell D5 is greater than 0. If the test is true, then have the function add the value in cell D5 to the value in cell F4. If the test is false, have the function subtract the value in cell E5 from the value in cell F4.

i. Copy cell F5 in the Ledger worksheet and paste it to cells F6 through F8.

j. Type the date `October 1` into cell A8 and the number 100 into cell E8. Then format cell E8 with the Accounting number format.

k. Save and close your file.

4. Trial Balance and Work Sheet (Video: Trial Balance and Work Sheet)

a. Open the file named ib_e06_trialbalanceandworksheet.

b. Type a **SUM** function into cell B20 in the Trial Balance worksheet that totals the values in the range B4:B19. Then copy this function and paste it into cell C20 using the **Formulas** option.

c. Add a double underline to cells B20 and C20.

d. Activate the Work Sheet worksheet.

e. Create a link in cell B6 that shows the value in cell B4 in the Trial Balance worksheet.

f. Copy cell B6 and paste it into the range B7:C21 using the **Formulas** option. Then delete any links in the range B7:C21 that display a value of 0.

g. Type a **SUM** function in cell B22 that totals the values in the range B6:B21. Then copy this function and paste it into the range C22:E22.

h. Add a double underline to cells B22:E22.

i. Type an **IF** function into cell F6. If the value in cell D6 is greater than 0, the function should add the value in cell B6 to the value in cell D6. Otherwise, the function should subtract the value in cell E6 from the value in cell B6.

j. Copy the **IF** function in cell F6 and paste it into the range F7:F11, cell F15, and cells F17:F21.

k. Type an **IF** function into cell G12. If the value in cell D12 is greater than 0, the function should subtract the value in cell D12 from the value in cell C12. Otherwise, the function should add the value in cell C12 to the value in cell E12.

l. Copy cell G12 and paste it into G13, G14, and G16.

m. Type the cell reference `=F6` into cell J6.

n. Copy cell J6 and paste into the range J7:J11 and J15.

o. Type the cell reference `=G12` into cell K12.

p. Copy cell K12 and paste it into cells K13 and K14.
q. Type the cell reference `=G16` into cell I16.
r. Type the cell reference `=F17` into cell H17. Then copy cell H17 and paste it into the range H18:H21.
s. Type a **SUM** function into cell F22 that totals the values in the range F6:F21.
t. Copy the **SUM** function in cell F22 and paste it into cells G22:K22.
u. Add a double accounting underline to cells F22 and G22.
v. Type a formula in cell H23 that subtracts H22 from I22.
w. Type a formula in cell K23 that subtracts K22 from J22.
x. Type a formula in cell H24 that adds cells H22 and H23. Then copy this formula and paste it into cell K24.
y. Type the cell reference `=I22` into cell I24. Then copy this cell reference and paste it into cell J24.
z. Add a double underline to the range H24:K24.
aa. Save and close your file.

5. Income Statement (Video: Income Statement)

a. Open the file named ib_e06_accountingstatements. Use this file for sections 5–7.
b. Activate the Income Statement worksheet.
c. Create a link in cell C4 that displays the value in cell I16 in the Work Sheet worksheet.
d. Create a link in cell B7 that displays the value in cell H17 in the Work Sheet worksheet. Then copy this link and paste it into the range B8:B11.
e. Type a **SUM** function in cell C12 that totals the values in the range B7:B11.
f. Type a formula in cell C13 that subtracts the value in cell C12 from the value in cell C4.

6. Owners Equity (Video: Owners Equity)

a. Activate the Owners Equity worksheet.
b. Create a link in cell C4 that displays the value in cell K14 in the Work Sheet worksheet.
c. Create a link in cell B5 that displays the value in cell C13 in the Income Statement worksheet.
d. Create a link in cell B7 that displays the value in cell J15 in the Work Sheet worksheet.
e. Type a formula in cell C8 that subtracts the value in cell B7 from the value in cell B5.
f. Type a formula in cell C9 that adds cells C4 and C8.

7. Balance Sheet (Video: Balance Sheet)

a. Activate the Balance Sheet worksheet.
b. Create a link in cell B6 that displays the value in cell J6 in the Work Sheet worksheet. Then copy this link and paste it into the range B7:B9.
c. Type a **SUM** function into cell C10 that totals the values in the range B6:B9.

d. Create a link in cell B12 that displays the value in cell J10 in the Work Sheet worksheet. Then copy this link and paste it into cell B13.

e. Type a **SUM** function into cell C14 that totals the values in the range B12:B13.

f. Type a formula into cell C16 that adds the value in cell C10 to the value in cell C14.

g. Create a link in cell E6 that displays the value in cell K12 in the Work Sheet worksheet. Then copy this link and paste it into cell E7.

h. Type a **SUM** function into cell F8 that totals the values in the range E6:E7.

i. Create a link in cell F14 that displays the value in cell C9 in the Owners Equity worksheet.

j. Type a formula in cell F16 that adds the value in cell F8 to the value in cell F14.

k. Add double underlines to cells C16 and F16.

l. Save and close your file.

EXERCISE

Why Do I Need This?

>> Analyzing Adjusting Entries and Net Income

The benefits of Excel's cell referencing features are very apparent in the construction of financial accounting spreadsheets and statements. A change in the value of just one account can impact every accounting statement. As a result, this section demonstrated how to use linking techniques so that when the value of one account changes in the Trial Balance, or when adjustments are made on the Work Sheet, every statement will automatically calculate new outputs. Imagine doing these spreadsheets with paper and pencil! A change in one account would require you to erase, recalculate, and rewrite the outcome of every statement.

Exercise

The purpose of this exercise is to show how to use cell referencing and linking techniques to analyze how adjustments to certain accounts impact the Net Income of a company. As a result, this exercise will focus on the construction of an accounting Work Sheet and the adjustment of various accounts. Open the file named ib_e06_accountinganalysis before starting this exercise.

1. Type an **IF** function in cell F6 of the Work Sheet to calculate the Adjusted Trial Balance of the Cash account. The arguments of the **IF** function should be defined as follows:

   a. **logical_test**: `D6 > 0`

   b. **[value_if_true]**: `B6 + D6`

   c. **[value_if_false]**: `B6 - E6`

2. The **IF** function you created in number 1 will add any debits in the Adjustment column to the Trial Balance for Cash (cell B6). If there are any credits in the Adjustment column, it will subtract them from the balance. This is because Cash is an Asset account and debits increase the value of the account and credits decrease the value of the account. Every account on the Work Sheet follows this rule except for Accounts Payable, Unearned Rent, Owner A Capital, and Fees earned. Therefore, copy cell F6 and paste it into the range F7:F11, cell F15, and the range F17:F21.

3. Type an **IF** function in cell G12 to calculate the Adjusted Trial Balance of the Accounts Payable account. The segments of the function should be defined as follows:
   a. **[logical_test]**: `D12 > 0`
   b. **[value_if_true]**: `C12 - D12`
   c. **[value_if_false]**: `C12 + E12`
4. Copy the **IF** function in cell G12 and paste it into cells G13, G14, and G16.
5. Create a **SUM** function in cell F22 that sums the values in the range F6:F21. Copy the function and paste it to cell G22. Add a double underline to cells F22 and G22.
6. Type a cell reference in cell J6 to show the Adjusted Trial balance for the Cash account in cell F6. Copy this cell reference and paste it into the range J7:J11 and into cell J15. These are all Balance Sheet accounts that carry a normal debit balance.
7. The Accounts Payable account is also a Balance Sheet account; however, it carries a normal credit balance. Therefore, type a cell reference into cell K12 that displays the value in cell G12. Copy this link to cells K13 and K14.
8. Fees earned is an Income Statement account, which carries a normal credit balance. Type a cell reference into cell I16 that shows the value in cell G16. The rest of the accounts on the Work Sheet from Wages Expense down to Selling Expense are also Income Statement accounts. Type a cell reference into cell H17 that shows the value in cell F17. Then copy this cell reference and paste it into the range H18:H21.
9. Create a **SUM** function in cell H22 that adds the values in the range H6:H21. Copy this function and paste it into the range I22:K22.
10. Calculate the Net Income in cell H23 using a formula that subtracts cell H22 from cell I22. Create another formula in cell K23 that subtracts cell K22 from J22.
11. Type a formula in cell H24 that adds cells H22 and H23. Copy this formula and paste it into cell K24.
12. Type a cell reference into cell I24 that displays the value in cell I22. Then type a cell reference into cell J24 that displays the value in cell J22. Add a double underline to the range H24:K24.
13. Assume that a customer was not satisfied with the service this company provided and demanded a refund. Type a `5000` debit adjustment for Fees earned in cell D16 and a `5000` credit to Accounts Receivable in cell E7. What was the change in Net Income?
14. Assume this company was issued a rent rebate from the landlord. Type a `3000` credit adjustment to Rent Expense in cell E18 and a `3000` debit adjustment to Cash in cell D6. What happened to the Net Income?
15. The CEO of this company promised its shareholders that it would achieve a target of $78,000 in Net Income. As you can see, this company is falling significantly short of this goal. An unethical accountant proposes an idea of reclassifying $50,000 in sales training expenses as Other Assets. Activate the Trial Balance worksheet and reduce the balance of selling expenses in cell B19 to `120000`. Then increase the balance of Other Assets in cell B7 to `52000`. Check to make sure the values in cell B20 and C20 match. What happened to the Net Income in cells H23 and K23 on the Work Sheet?
16. Save and close your file.

PROBLEM & EXERCISE

>> What's Wrong with This Spreadsheet?

Problem

You and two other classmates are working on a group project for a Financial Accounting class. The assignment includes a Trial Balance, T-accounts, and Ledgers. Your professor mentions the following list of key accounting rules for each of the three requirements of the project:

1. Trial Balance: The sum of the debits must equal the sum of the credits.
2. T-accounts and Ledgers: For Asset accounts (i.e., Cash and Accounts Receivable), the balance is calculated by subtracting total credits from total debits. For Liability accounts (i.e., Accounts Payable), the balance is calculated by subtracting the sum of all debits from the sum of all credits.

Exercise

One of your teammates says that this project will be easy and offers to do the assignment for the team in Excel. She completes the project and e-mails a completed file to each team member to review before printing and handing in at class the next day. The file your teammate e-mailed is named ib_e06_accountingproject. Would you be comfortable printing each worksheet and handing them in for a grade? Consider the following points:

1. Compare the requirements listed in the Problems section to the data in each worksheet. Does the data in this file comply with these rules?
2. Your teammate thought this assignment would be easy to do in Excel. Why?

What's wrong with this spreadsheet? Write a short answer for each of the points listed here. Then correct any mistakes you find in the workbook.

Excel in **Practice** | Anecdote

Solution from page 236

Using Excel to prepare and manage business plans made my job so much easier and fun. In fact, when presenting business plans at executive meetings, I would bring my laptop to the meeting, pull up my business plan workbook, and type changes in my assumptions spreadsheet to answer any questions the directing officers asked. However, I had to make sure that all possible assumptions that were related to the business I was presenting were included in the spreadsheet. As a result, the details of every business plan I constructed were different, but the techniques I used to construct them in Excel were always the same.

Assignment

1. Open the file named ib_e06_financialprojectionsfornewbusiness.
2. This file includes a worksheet showing five years' worth of financial assumptions for a new business. Construct a financial data and a cash analysis worksheet showing the five-year financial performance of this new business based on the assumptions included in this file.
3. The format of the financial data and cash analysis worksheets should be modeled after the example that was illustrated in the Financial Planning section of this chapter. This section also includes extensive details on how each financial statistic was calculated for each worksheet.
4. Adjust the assumptions in this file such that the NPV of this business achieves at least a positive $10,000 result.

Questions for Discussion

1. This anecdote mentions that researching the assumptions for a business plan was one of the key factors for creating a successful business plan. What else is required to build a successful and accurate business plan?
2. How would you present a business plan to a group of executive officers? What Excel techniques can you use to build an effective and dynamic presentation?

Review Questions

The following questions are related to the concepts addressed in this chapter. There are three types of questions: Short Answer, True or False, and Fill in the Blank. If your answer to a True or False question is False, write a short explanation as to why you think the statement is not true.

1. Cell referencing can be used to _______ data between worksheets or workbooks.
2. Explain how a link is created between two workbooks.
3. Data can be identified as a link to a workbook because the _______ and _______ names precede the cell location.
4. True or False: Data linked to another workbook will always be automatically updated.
5. True or False: Excel will automatically add an absolute value to any cell location that is linked to another workbook.
6. Explain how you can check the Status of data that is linked to other workbooks.
7. The three arguments of the **SUMIF** function are _______, _______, and _______.
8. What range of cells will be added in the following **SUMIF** function: `=SUMIF(A3:A6,D18,C3:C10)`
9. True or False: You must always complete all three arguments of the **SUMIF** function.
10. True or False: Creating ledgers in Excel is easy because after you create the first ledger, you can simply copy and paste it to another worksheet, delete all the entries and dates, enter new dates and entries, and the formulas and functions will automatically calculate a new output.
11. Why should you minimize the need to enter data manually into a worksheet when constructing financial plans?
12. What function can be used to calculate the balance on either a ledger or Work Sheet?
13. Explain the value in using links between the Trial Balance, Work Sheet, and Accounting Statements.
14. The _______ command in the _______ tab of the Ribbon is used to lock specific rows and columns when scrolling a worksheet.
15. What is the **value1** argument used for in the **NPV** function?
16. Why is it important to add a Notes section to the Assumptions worksheet of a financial plan?
17. True or False: The data-linking techniques used to construct financial plans do not work well with other business planning exercises.
18. True or False: An **NPV** function will always give you a positive number if you forget to add a negative sign in front of the **value1** argument.

Skills Exam

The following exam is designed to test your ability to recognize and execute the Excel skills presented in this chapter. Read each question carefully and answer the questions in the order they are listed. You should be able to complete this exam in 60 minutes or less.

1. Open the ib_e06_skillsexam.
2. Calculate the construction cost for restaurant 11, which is cell D3 in the Restaurant Detail worksheet. Use a formula that multiplies the size of the restaurant in cell C3 by the cost listed for its appropriate state in the Cost by State worksheet. Use the **VLookup** function to find the cost for the appropriate state for restaurant 11 in the Cost by State worksheet and multiply it by the restaurant size in the Restaurant Detail Worksheet.
3. Copy the formula you created in cell D3 of the Restaurant Detail worksheet and paste it into the range D4:D12 using the **Formulas** option. Be sure to add absolute references where needed.
4. Use **SUMIF** functions to calculate the Total Profit per Square Foot for MD, which is cell F16 of the Restaurant Detail worksheet. This will require two **SUMIF** functions. The first **SUMIF** function will look for the state entered in cell E16 in the range B3:B12 and sum the corresponding values in the range F3:F12. This should be divided by a second **SUMIF** function that will look for the state entered in cell E16 in the range B3:B12 and sum the corresponding values in the range C3:C12.
5. Copy the formula created in cell F16 and paste it into cells F17 and F18 using the Formulas option. Add absolute references where needed.
6. Type a **SUM** function in cell B3 of the Assumptions worksheet that adds the values in the range D3:D12 in the Restaurant Detail worksheet.
7. Type a **SUM** function in cell B2 of the Sales and Profit Plan worksheet that adds the values in the range E3:E12 in the Restaurant Detail worksheet.
8. Type a formula in cell C2 of the Sales and Profit Plan worksheet that uses the percentage in cell B8 in the Assumptions worksheet to calculate the projected sales for Year 1. Copy this formula and paste it to cells D2 and E2.
9. Type a **SUM** function into cell B3 of the Sales and Profit Plan worksheet that adds the values in the range F3:F12 in the Restaurant Detail worksheet.
10. Type a formula into cell B4 of the Sales and Profit Plan worksheet that divides the value in cell B3 by the value in cell B2.
11. Create a formula into cell C3 that multiplies the sales value in cell C2 by the value in cell B4. Place an absolute reference on cell B4 in this formula. Then copy the formula and paste it into cells D3 and E3.
12. Copy cell B4 and paste it into the range C4:E4.
13. Type a formula into cell C5 of the Sales and Profit Plan worksheet that multiplies cell C2 by cell B9 in the Assumptions worksheet. Copy the formula and paste it into the range D5:E5.
14. Type a formula in cell B7 of the Sales and Profit Plan worksheet that subtracts the sum of the range B5:B6 from the value in cell B3.
15. Copy cell B7 and paste it into the range C7:E7.
16. Type an **IF** function into cell C8 of the Sales and Profit Plan worksheet that evaluates whether cell C7 is greater than 0. If it is, then multiply cell C7 by the value in cell B10 on the Assumptions worksheet. If the value in cell C7 is not greater than 0, then show 0. Copy this function and paste it into cells D8 and E8.
17. Type a formula into cell B9 of the Sales and Profit Plan worksheet that subtracts the value in cell B8 from the value in cell B7. Copy this formula and paste it into the range C9:E9.

18. Calculate the loan payments in cell B11 on the Sales and Profit Plan worksheet using the **PMT** function. You should use Cell B4 in the Assumptions worksheet for the rate, cell B5 in the Assumptions worksheet for the periods, and cell B3 for the principal of the loan. Assume that these loan payments are made annually at the beginning of each year.
19. For cells C11, D11, and E11 on the Sales and Profit plan worksheet, type a cell reference that shows the value in cell B11.
20. Type a formula into cell B13 that subtracts the value in cell B11 from the value in cell B9.
21. Type a formula into cell C13 that adds the value in cell B13 to the result of subtracting the value in cell C11 from cell C9.
22. Copy the formula in cell C13 and paste it into cells D13 and E13.
23. Type an **NPV** function in cell E16. The rate of the function should be cell B4 in the Assumptions worksheet, the initial investment value should be cell B3 in the Assumptions worksheet, the cash flow values should be the range B13:E13 in the Sales and Profit Plan worksheet.
24. Add any appropriate formats to the values in the Sales and Profit Plan worksheet. In addition, add formatting features that you think will enhance the appearance of the spreadsheet and make it easier to read.
25. Save and close your file.

Challenge Questions

1. Open the file named ib_e06_companye. This is a completed Trial Balance. Use this Trial Balance to construct a worksheet and set of three financial statements (Income Statement, Statement of Owners Equity, and Balance Sheet). Model the worksheet and statements from the example that was illustrated in the Financial Accounting section of this chapter. After completing the Work Sheet, note the net income. Then add the following adjustments to the Work Sheet and note how the net income changes.
   a. **Fees earned**: Debit $500,000
   b. **Accounts Receivable**: Credit $500,000
   c. **Accounts Payable**: Debit $25,000
   d. **Office Equipment**: Credit $25,000
2. You are considering the purchase of a company that was offered to you at a price of $1,200,000. Your cost to borrow money to buy this firm, or the interest rate charged by a bank, will be 6.0%. Would you buy this company? Develop a spreadsheet to analyze this offer and explain why you would or would not buy this company from a purely five-year financial point of view. What other considerations might you make beyond this financial perspective when considering the purchase of a company? The company has been generating the following cash flows for the past five years:
   a. Year 1 = $150,000
   b. Year 2 = $175,000
   c. Year 3 = $250,000
   d. Year 4 = $350,000
   e. Year 5 = $550,000
3. This chapter illustrated that the balance of a ledger can be calculated using an **IF** function. In addition, you learned that there should never be a number entered for both a debit and credit for a single entry in a ledger. How would you calculate the balance of a ledger and show an error message if a person makes a mistake and enters both a debit and credit for a single entry on the ledger. Create a hypothetical ledger in Excel and type your solution in the balance column.
4. Get a financial statement from any public company. In an Excel spreadsheet, type the financial statistics for the current reporting year and the prior reporting year from the firm's Income Statement. Then create a second spreadsheet with assumptions estimating how you think this company will perform over the next three years. For example, do you think Gross Sales will increase 5% per year over the next three years, do you think the company will maintain its current cost of goods sold percentage of gross sales, and so on? Then create a third spreadsheet showing your projected financial statistics for each item on the firm's income statement.

Date, Text & IS Functions: Managing Large Volumes of Data

Date Text and IS Functions

Chapter Goals

This chapter demonstrates how you can use advanced functions to develop sophisticated spreadsheets for making business decisions. The first section presents Date functions, which are used to calculate a person's age or determine the timing of certain events. The second section reviews various Text functions, which are used to isolate and extract specific parts of data that has been entered into a cell. The last section demonstrates IS functions, which are used to evaluate the type of data that is typed into a cell or the result produced by a function or formula.

A common theme for all of the functions in this chapter is that they are rarely used independently. That is to say, these functions are usually integrated with other functions such as the IF and VLOOKUP functions, which are covered in Chapter 4. Therefore, it will be important for you to review these functions before continuing.

Advanced Excel | Skill Sets

Date Functions
- TODAY Function
- YEAR Function
- MONTH Function
- DATE and DAY Functions

Text Functions
- CONCATENATE Function
- SEARCH, LEFT, LEN, and MID Functions

IS Functions
- ISNUMBER and ISTEXT Functions
- ISERROR Function

Excel in Practice | Anecdote

My Role as a Retirement Analyst

Imagine using a calculator and a calendar to figure out when thousands of your customers would each turn 70.5 years old. That is the situation I encountered in one of my most challenging projects as a consultant.

I was hired by a firm that managed the distribution of IRA investments. IRA accounts are a popular way to save money for retirement because you do not have to pay taxes on the money you invest, and companies will usually invest money into an IRA account for their employees before taxes are deducted from employees' paychecks. Federal law mandates that after you reach the age of 70.5, you must withdraw money out of your IRA account the following year. And the amount of this withdrawal depends on your age. Over the years, the firm that hired me had calculated these withdrawal amounts manually (as described above). However, as the company grew larger and supported thousands of customers, this manual process became cumbersome. And even worse, customers would have to pay a tax penalty if they did not make their mandatory withdrawal on time. The company hired me to automate this manual process to improve accuracy and efficiency.

So there I was, trying to come up with a way to figure out which customers, out of several thousand, had reached 70.5 years of age the previous year. Then, out of these customers, I had to figure out how much money they needed to withdraw from their accounts. To do this, I had to calculate their exact age the previous year so I could determine how much money they needed to withdraw from their account this year. This was definitely a challenging problem to solve.

>> Continued on page 340

Date Functions

Skill Set

Date functions are commonly used in business situations that are related to the management of human resources. This is because companies usually provide certain benefits to their employees based on years of service or age. For example, some companies offer employees additional vacation time the longer they remain employed by the firm. A human resource manager can use Date functions to calculate the number of years each employee has been working for the company to determine who is eligible for additional vacation time. This section will demonstrate how a human resource manager could use Date functions to administer the employee benefits of a company. The functions demonstrated in this section will be used to calculate the results for columns D through F in Figure 7.1.

Figure 7.1 | **HR Benefits Worksheet**

	A	B	C	D	E	F	G
1	*Employee Benefits Analysis*						
2	*Today's Date*						
3	Employee Name	Birthdate	Date Employed	Years of Service	Early Retirement Year	Vacation Effective Year	401K Vesting Date
4	Employee 1	6/29/1968	1/31/1986				
5	Employee 2	8/14/1977	11/17/2003				
6	Employee 3	12/5/1941	5/12/1993				
7	Employee 4	4/18/1964	9/21/2000				
8	Employee 5	7/22/1978	10/25/2002				
9	Employee 6	9/26/1983	12/29/2004				
10	Employee 7	3/16/1951	9/22/2000				
11	Employee 8	3/13/1961	7/17/1996				
12	Employee 9	6/21/1971	10/25/2002				
13	Employee 10	6/24/1957	12/30/2005				
14	Employee 11	1/3/1965	3/6/1989				
15	Employee 12	5/15/1952	11/21/2002				
16	Employee 13	3/10/1973	6/13/1994				
17	Employee 14	5/14/1977	7/16/1996				
18	Employee 15	8/5/1942	1/2/1986				

Date functions will be used to complete these columns.

TODAY Function

The purpose of the **TODAY** function is to display the current date on a worksheet. This is especially useful when you need to compare a historical date to the current date. For example, the first column we will complete in the HR Benefits Worksheet (Figure 7.1) is the Years of Service column. To do this, the employed dates in column C will be compared to today's date. The following explains how today's date is added to cell B2 using the **TODAY** function.

- Type an equal sign into cell B2 to begin the function.
- Type the function name TODAY.
- Type an open parenthesis and then a closing parenthesis. This function is unique because it does not require anything to be typed between the parentheses.
- Press the **Enter** key.

Figure 7.2 | **The TODAY Function**

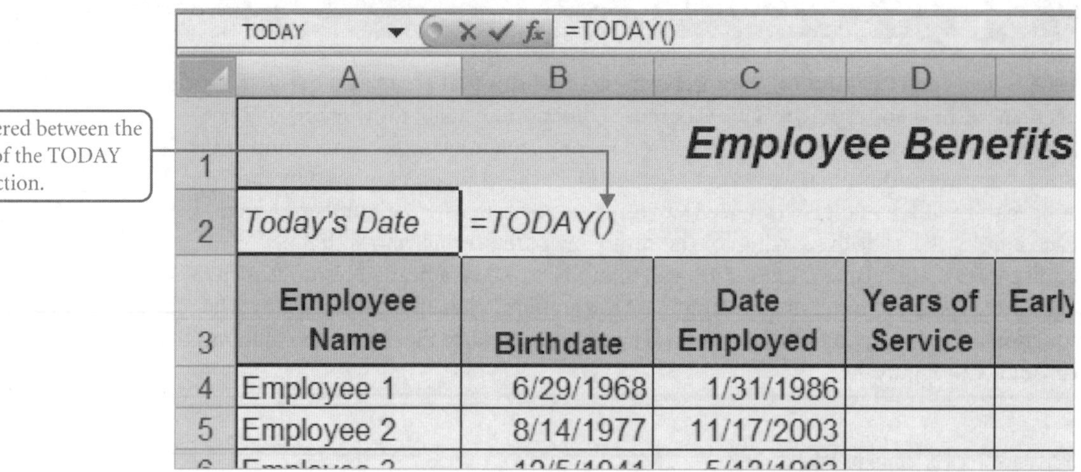

Figure 7.3 shows the results of the **TODAY** function after pressing the **Enter** key. The date displayed is the current date at the time this text was written. If you open this Excel file today, the function will show today's date.

Figure 7.3 | **Results of the TODAY Function**

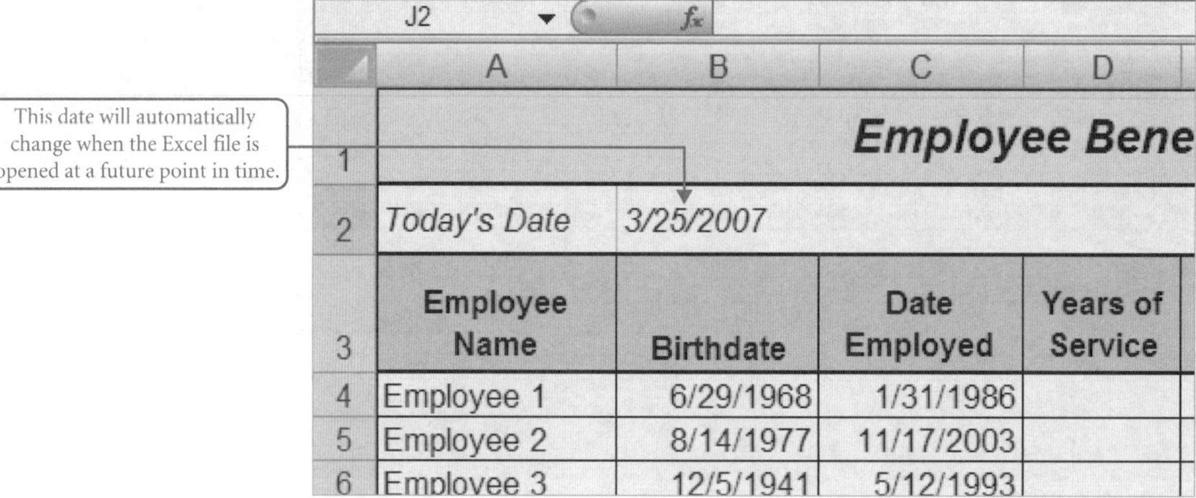

The addition of the **TODAY** function to the HR Benefits Worksheet makes it possible to calculate the Years of Service for each employee in column D. These values are calculated by subtracting the dates in the Date Employed column (column C) from today's date in cell B2. A formula can be used to calculate these values because Excel stores every date as a unique ***Serial Number***. For example, Figure 7.4 shows the results of the **TODAY** function when the cell formatting is changed to a standard number with 0 decimal places. Notice that the Serial Number for 3/25/2007 is 39166. An increase in the Serial Number represents a date in the future, and a decrease in the Serial Number represents a date in the past. For example, Serial Number 39167 represents the date 3/26/2007, and Serial Number 39165 represents the date 3/24/2007. To change the Serial Number back to a date, select one of the **Date** options from the **Number Format** drop-down box in the **Home** tab of the Ribbon.

>> Quick Reference

TODAY Function

1. Activate a cell.
2. Type an equal sign.
3. Type the function name TODAY.
4. Type an open and then a closing parenthesis.
5. Press the **Enter** key.

Figure 7.4 | **Date Serial Number**

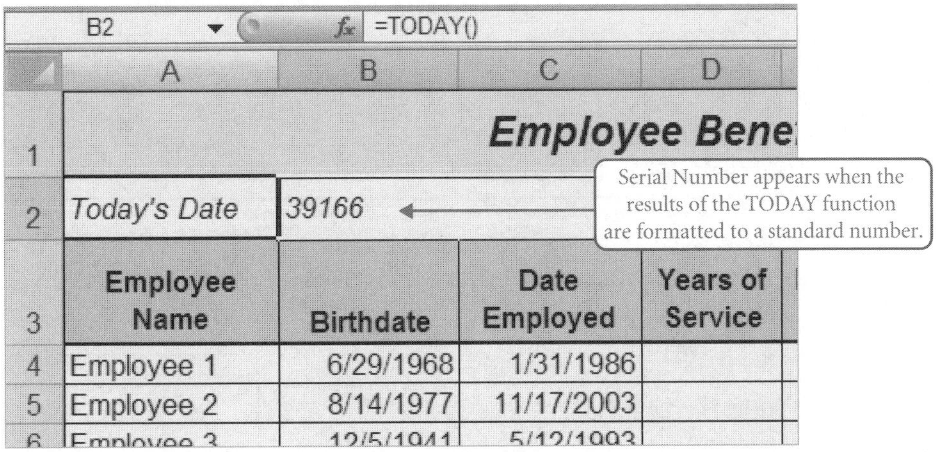

B2 =TODAY()

	A	B	C	D
1			*Employee Bene*	
2	*Today's Date*	*39166*		
3	Employee Name	Birthdate	Date Employed	Years of Service
4	Employee 1	6/29/1968	1/31/1986	
5	Employee 2	8/14/1977	11/17/2003	
6	Employee 3	12/5/1941	5/12/1993	

Serial Number appears when the results of the TODAY function are formatted to a standard number.

COMMON MISTAKES | Dates and Formatting

People often mistake the date Serial Number as some type of error. However, this simply means that a cell containing a date has been formatted to a number. To convert the Serial Number to a date, choose one of the Date formats from the **Number Format** drop-down box in the **Home** tab of the Ribbon.

Figure 7.5 shows the results of subtracting the dates in the Date Employed column from today's date in cell B2 to calculate the Year of Service for each employee. Because the **TODAY** function always shows the current date, the formula will produce a new output each day the workbook is opened. The following explains how this formula was created.

- Type an equal sign in cell D4.
- Type the formula `($B$2 - C4)/365`. Because the date Serial Number represents a single day, subtracting C4 from B2 will provide the number of days each employee has worked for the company. To convert the days to years, this result is divided by 365. Also, notice that an absolute reference was placed on cell B2. This is because every date in the Date Employed column must be subtracted from B2. Therefore, an absolute reference is used to prevent cell B2 from changing because of relative referencing when the formula is pasted to the rest of the cells in the column.
- Format the results of the formula in cell B2 to a standard number with 2 decimal places.
- Copy cell D4 and paste it to the rest of the cells in the column.

Figure 7.5 | **Completed Years of Service Column**

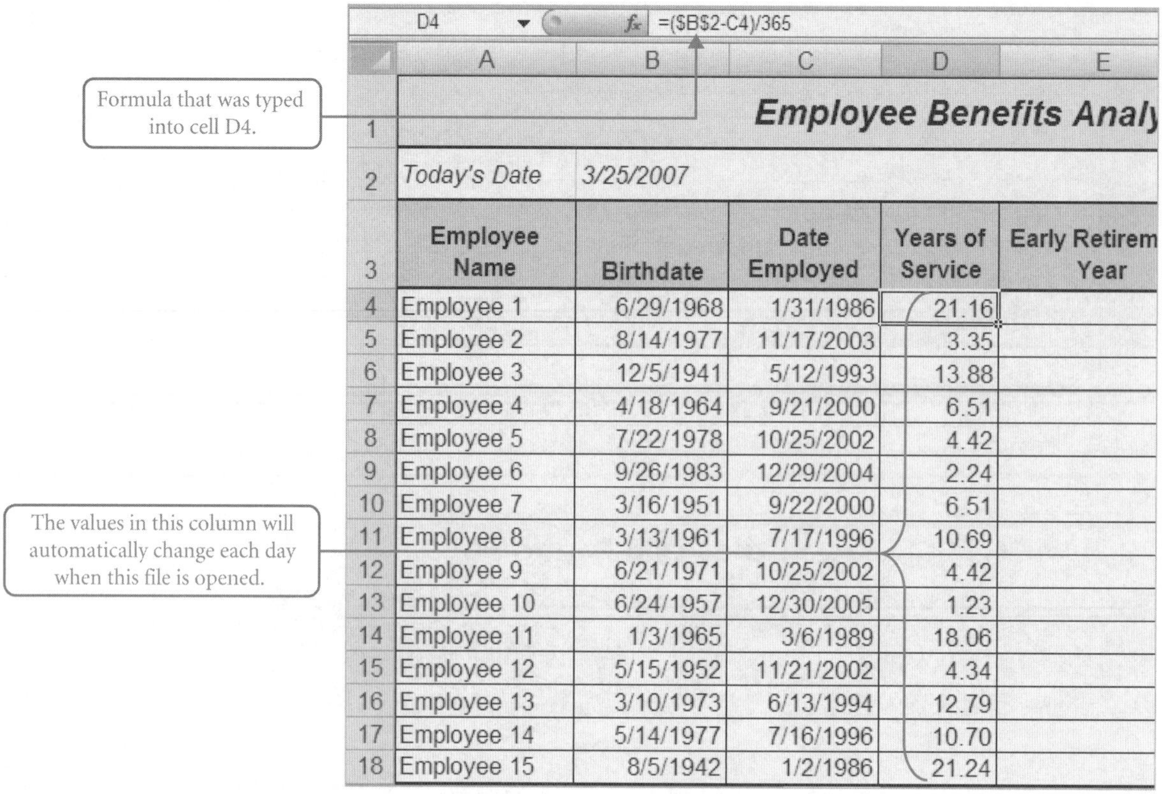

Formula that was typed into cell D4.

D4 =($B$2-C4)/365

	A	B	C	D	E
1			***Employee Benefits Analy***		
2	*Today's Date*	*3/25/2007*			
3	Employee Name	Birthdate	Date Employed	Years of Service	Early Retirem Year
4	Employee 1	6/29/1968	1/31/1986	21.16	
5	Employee 2	8/14/1977	11/17/2003	3.35	
6	Employee 3	12/5/1941	5/12/1993	13.88	
7	Employee 4	4/18/1964	9/21/2000	6.51	
8	Employee 5	7/22/1978	10/25/2002	4.42	
9	Employee 6	9/26/1983	12/29/2004	2.24	
10	Employee 7	3/16/1951	9/22/2000	6.51	
11	Employee 8	3/13/1961	7/17/1996	10.69	
12	Employee 9	6/21/1971	10/25/2002	4.42	
13	Employee 10	6/24/1957	12/30/2005	1.23	
14	Employee 11	1/3/1965	3/6/1989	18.06	
15	Employee 12	5/15/1952	11/21/2002	4.34	
16	Employee 13	3/10/1973	6/13/1994	12.79	
17	Employee 14	5/14/1977	7/16/1996	10.70	
18	Employee 15	8/5/1942	1/2/1986	21.24	

The values in this column will automatically change each day when this file is opened.

COMMON MISTAKES | Date Related Calculations

If you are calculating data that relies on the current date, *do not* type the date into a cell and use that cell in a formula. The results that are produced by your formula will be valid for only one day. In addition, this forces you to type in a new date manually each time you open the file. For this type of calculation it is good practice to use the **TODAY** function. Using the **TODAY** function instead of typing the date will produce current results when the file is opened at a future point in time.

>> Quick Reference

YEAR Function

1. Activate a cell.
2. Type an equal sign.
3. Type the function name YEAR.
4. Type an open parenthesis.
5. Enter a cell location that contains a valid date Serial Number or type a valid date Serial Number.
6. Type a closing parenthesis. You can also type a date enclosed in quotations, i.e. "10/21/2006".
7. Press the **Enter** key.

YEAR Function

The next column that will be completed in the HR Benefits Worksheet (see Figure 7.1) is the Early Retirement Year column. Some companies offer their employees the option to take an early retirement or to stop working and receive payments from their retirement pension before reaching the official retirement age of 65. The amount of income an employee receives from a pension usually depends on salary and years of service to the company. The purpose of column E in the HR Benefits Worksheet is to show what year each employee will qualify for early retirement. The age at which an employee qualifies for early retirement varies, depending on the plan offered by the company. For this example, we will assume an employee must be at least 55 years old.

The **YEAR** function isolates the year that is associated with a date Serial Number and displays it as a number. In this example, the **YEAR** function will be used in column E of the HR Benefits Worksheet to show the year each employee qualifies for early retirement. The following explains how the **YEAR** function is used to determine the year each employee becomes eligible for early retirement.

- Type an equal sign in cell E4.
- Type the function name YEAR and an open parenthesis.

- Type cell B4, and then type a closing parenthesis. Cell B4 contains the birth date of the first employee, which is required to determine the year of early retirement eligibility.
- Type a plus sign (+) after the **YEAR** function, and then type the number 55. As previously mentioned, we will assume that employees are eligible for early retirement when they reach the age of 55. To determine the year in which they become eligible, 55 is added to the year of their birth date (see Figure 7.6).
- Press the **Enter** key. The formula will calculate the year Employee 1 will turn 55. This formula can now be copied and pasted to show the early retirement year for the rest of the employees listed on the worksheet (see Figure 7.7).

Figure 7.6 | **YEAR Function Setup**

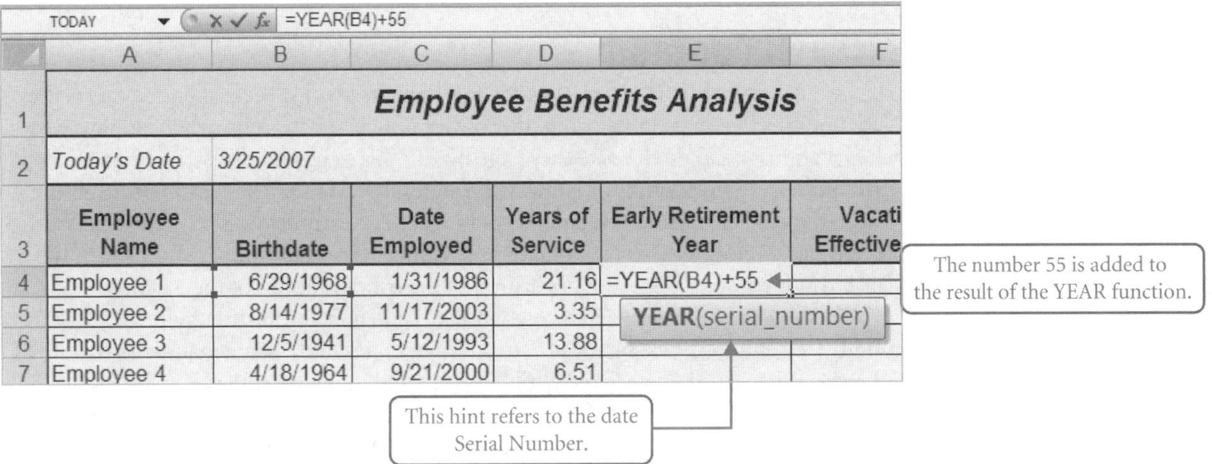

	A	B	C	D	E	F
1	Employee Benefits Analysis					
2	Today's Date	3/25/2007				
3	Employee Name	Birthdate	Date Employed	Years of Service	Early Retirement Year	Vacati Effective
4	Employee 1	6/29/1968	1/31/1986	21.16	=YEAR(B4)+55	
5	Employee 2	8/14/1977	11/17/2003	3.35		
6	Employee 3	12/5/1941	5/12/1993	13.88		
7	Employee 4	4/18/1964	9/21/2000	6.51		

Figure 7.7 | **Results of the YEAR Function**

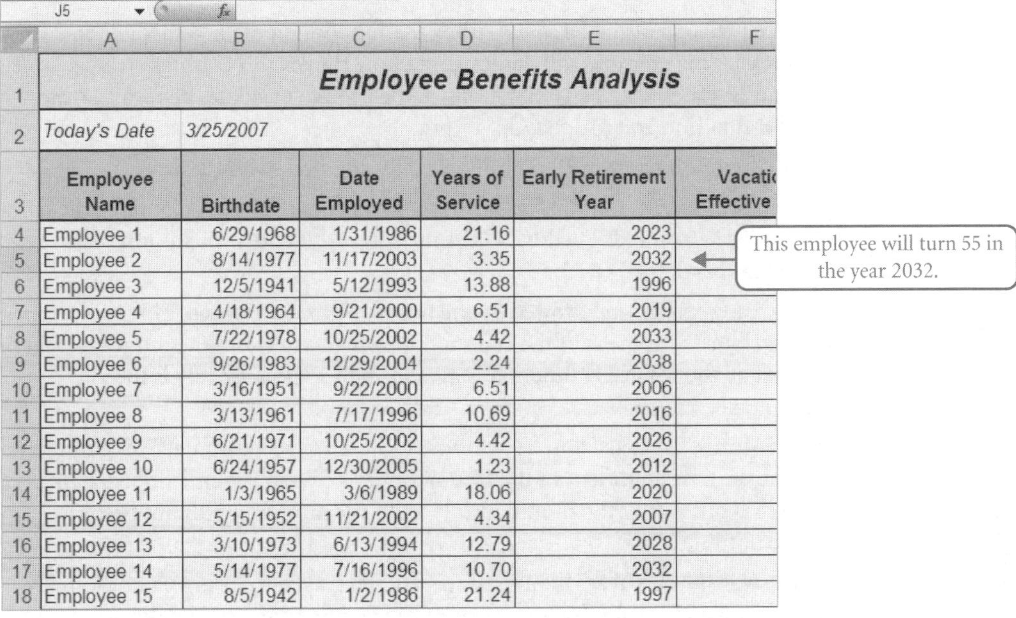

	A	B	C	D	E	F
1	Employee Benefits Analysis					
2	Today's Date	3/25/2007				
3	Employee Name	Birthdate	Date Employed	Years of Service	Early Retirement Year	Vacatic Effective
4	Employee 1	6/29/1968	1/31/1986	21.16	2023	
5	Employee 2	8/14/1977	11/17/2003	3.35	2032	
6	Employee 3	12/5/1941	5/12/1993	13.88	1996	
7	Employee 4	4/18/1964	9/21/2000	6.51	2019	
8	Employee 5	7/22/1978	10/25/2002	4.42	2033	
9	Employee 6	9/26/1983	12/29/2004	2.24	2038	
10	Employee 7	3/16/1951	9/22/2000	6.51	2006	
11	Employee 8	3/13/1961	7/17/1996	10.69	2016	
12	Employee 9	6/21/1971	10/25/2002	4.42	2026	
13	Employee 10	6/24/1957	12/30/2005	1.23	2012	
14	Employee 11	1/3/1965	3/6/1989	18.06	2020	
15	Employee 12	5/15/1952	11/21/2002	4.34	2007	
16	Employee 13	3/10/1973	6/13/1994	12.79	2028	
17	Employee 14	5/14/1977	7/16/1996	10.70	2032	
18	Employee 15	8/5/1942	1/2/1986	21.24	1997	

COMMON MISTAKES | The #Value! Error and Date Functions

If the cell location or value you use in the parentheses of the **YEAR** function is not a valid date Serial Number, you will see the #Value! error. This error commonly occurs when the date on a spreadsheet is a text entry. For example, typing a space in front of a date will convert it to a text value. A date could also become a text value if it is produced from a text function. You can convert a text date to a valid Serial Number date by typing the appropriate cell location in the parentheses of the **DATEVALUE** function. This error will also occur when using date functions that are similar to the **YEAR** function, such as the **MONTH** and **DAY** functions.

MONTH Function

The next column we will complete in the HR Benefits Worksheet (see Figure 7.1) is the Vacation Effective Year. Some companies have a policy to determine when employees can take vacations based on the date they were hired. This example will assume that employees hired during the months of January through July can use their vacation time in the year they were hired. However, employees hired after July must wait until the next year to use any vacation time. This type of policy is common in retail companies in which the Fall and Winter holiday seasons are critical to the overall success of the business.

The **MONTH** function will be used in the HR Benefits worksheet to identify the month each employee was hired. This function operates in the same manner as the **YEAR** function. When a valid date Serial Number is entered in the parentheses of the **MONTH** function, the month number of the date will be isolated and displayed in a cell. For example, if you entered the Serial Number representing the date 10/21/2006 (39011) in the parentheses of the **MONTH** function, the number 10 would be displayed in the cell.

The following explains how the **MONTH** function is used within an **IF** function to complete the Vacation Effective Year column on the HR Benefits Spreadsheet.

- Type an equal sign in cell F4, followed by the function name IF and an open parenthesis. This example will demonstrate how the **MONTH** function is used within an **IF** function. The **IF** function will be used to evaluate the result of the **MONTH** function and produce an output.
- Type the function name MONTH followed by an open parenthesis.
- Type cell location C4, followed by a closing parenthesis. This cell contains the date the employee was hired. The **MONTH** function will identify the month that is represented in this date.
- Type a greater-than sign followed by the number 7 and a comma. This completes the **logical_test** argument of the **IF** function, which assesses if the month number produced by the **MONTH** function is greater than 7 (because July is the 7th month).
- Type the words "Next Year" in quotations, and then type a comma. This completes the **value_if_true** argument of the **IF** function. As previously mentioned, if an employee is hired after the month of July, then vacation time will not become effective until next year.
- Type the words "This Year" in quotations, and then type a closing parenthesis. This completes the **value_if_false** argument of the **IF** function (see Figure 7.8). If the number produced by the **MONTH** function is not greater than 7, then the employee must have been hired in or before the month of July.
- Press the **Enter** key to complete the function. Then, copy cell F4 and paste it to the remaining cell locations in the column.

>> Quick Reference

MONTH Function

1. Activate a cell.
2. Type an equal sign and the function name MONTH.
3. Type an open parenthesis.
4. Enter a cell location that contains a valid date Serial Number or type a valid date Serial Number.
5. Type a closing parenthesis. You can also type a date enclosed in quotations, i.e. "10/21/2006".
6. Press the **Enter** key.

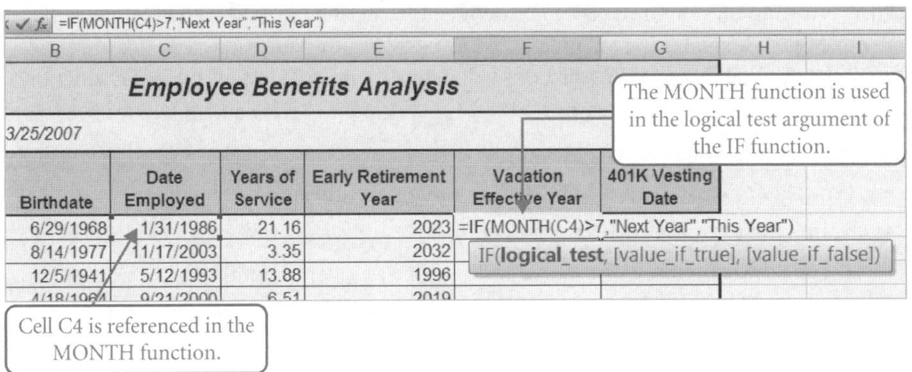

Figure 7.8 | **Setup of the MONTH Function within an IF Function**

Figure 7.9 shows the results of the **MONTH / IF** function illustrated in Figure 7.8. Because Employee 1 was hired in the month of January (see cell C4), the **IF** function displays the words This Year. Therefore, this employee was entitled to use vacation time the same year he was hired. Conversely, Employee 2 was hired in the month of November and, therefore, unable to take any vacation time until the year after he was hired.

Figure 7.9 | **Results of the MONTH Function within an IF Function**

	A	B	C	D	E	F	G
1	*Employee Benefits Analysis*						
2	*Today's Date*	*3/25/2007*					
3	Employee Name	Birthdate	Date Employed	Years of Service	Early Retirement Year	Vacation Effective Year	401K Vesting Date
4	Employee 1	6/29/1968	1/31/1986	21.16	2023	This Year	
5	Employee 2	8/14/1977	11/17/2003	3.35	2032	Next Year	
6	Employee 3	12/5/1941	5/12/1993	13.88	1996	This Year	
7	Employee 4	4/18/1964	9/21/2000	6.51	2019	Next Year	
8	Employee 5	7/22/1978	10/25/2002	4.42	2033	Next Year	
9	Employee 6	9/26/1983	12/29/2004	2.24	2038	Next Year	
10	Employee 7	3/16/1951	9/22/2000	6.51	2006	Next Year	
11	Employee 8	3/13/1961	7/17/1996	10.69	2016	This Year	
12	Employee 9	6/21/1971	10/25/2002	4.42	2026	Next Year	
13	Employee 10	6/24/1957	12/30/2005	1.23	2012	Next Year	
14	Employee 11	1/3/1965	3/6/1989	18.06	2020	This Year	
15	Employee 12	5/15/1952	11/21/2002	4.34	2007	Next Year	
16	Employee 13	3/10/1973	6/13/1994	12.79	2028	This Year	
17	Employee 14	5/14/1977	7/16/1996	10.70	2032	This Year	
18	Employee 15	8/5/1942	1/2/1986	21.24	1997	This Year	

Output of the IF function based on the month number in the Date Employed column

DATE and DAY Functions

The last column to complete in the HR Benefits Worksheet (see Figure 7.1) is the 401K Vesting Date column. Employees invest a certain percentage of their salary into a 401K account to save money for their retirement. This is similar to the IRA accounts explained in the anecdote at the beginning of this chapter. In addition, many companies will add money to their employees' retirement accounts as an added form of compensation. For example, a company might contribute fifty cents for every dollar an employee invests in her 401K account. However, companies usually set a vesting period before an employee can actually own this money. For example, a 5-year vesting period means employees must stay with the company for at least 5 years in order to take ownership of any money that is contributed to their 401K account by the firm.

The **DATE** function will be used to calculate the dates for the 401K Vesting Date column in the HR Benefits worksheet. For this example, we will assume that employees will become vested if they work in the firm for 5 years. The **DATE** function converts numbers into a date Serial Number. The function has three arguments: **year**, **month**, and **day**. Like all other functions, these arguments can be defined by entering numeric values. However, they are most often defined using formulas, cell locations, or other functions. For this example, the **YEAR**, **MONTH**, and **DAY** functions will define each argument of the **DATE** function. The following explains how to construct this function for the HR Benefits Worksheet.

- Type an equal sign in cell G4.
- Type the function name DATE and an open parenthesis.
- Define the **year** argument as follows:
  - Type the function name YEAR followed by an open parenthesis.
  - Type the cell location C4 followed by a closing parenthesis. Cell C4 contains the date the employee was hired.
  - Type a plus sign (+) followed by the number 5. The goal for this column is to show the date exactly 5 years from the day the employee was hired. Therefore, the first argument of the **DATE** function is being defined by adding 5 years to the result of the **YEAR** function.
  - Type a comma.
- Define the **month** argument as follows:
  - Type the function name MONTH followed by an open parenthesis.
  - Type the cell location C4 followed by a closing parenthesis. This will add the exact month that is in the Date Employed column for each employee.
  - Type a comma.
- Define the **day** argument as follows:
  - Type the function name DAY followed by an open parenthesis. The **DAY** function operates exactly like the **MONTH** and **YEAR** functions. It will isolate the day that is contained in a date and display it as a number in a cell.
  - Type the cell location C4 followed by a closing parenthesis. This will add the exact day that is in the Date Employed column for each employee.
  - Type a comma.
- Type a closing parenthesis to complete the **DATE** function and press the **Enter** key.

Figure 7.10 shows the final setup of the **DATE** function. It is important to note that it is coincidental that the functions used to define the arguments of the **DATE** function have the same name as the arguments. You could define the arguments of the DATE using any function, formula, cell location, or numbers that satisfy the needs of your project.

Figure 7.10 | **Setup of the DATE Function**

=DATE(YEAR(C4)+5,MONTH(C4),DAY(C4))

Employee Benefits Analysis

3/25/2007

Birthdate	Date Employed	Years of Service	Early Retirement Year	Vacation Effective Year	401K Vesting Date
6/29/1968	1/31/1986	21.16	2023	This Year	=DATE(YEAR(C4)+5,MONTH(C4),DAY(C4))
8/14/1977	11/17/2003	3.35	2032	Next Year	DATE(year, month, day)
12/5/1941	5/12/1993	13.88	1996	This Year	

The YEAR function is used to define the Year argument of the DATE function.

Arguments of the DATE function

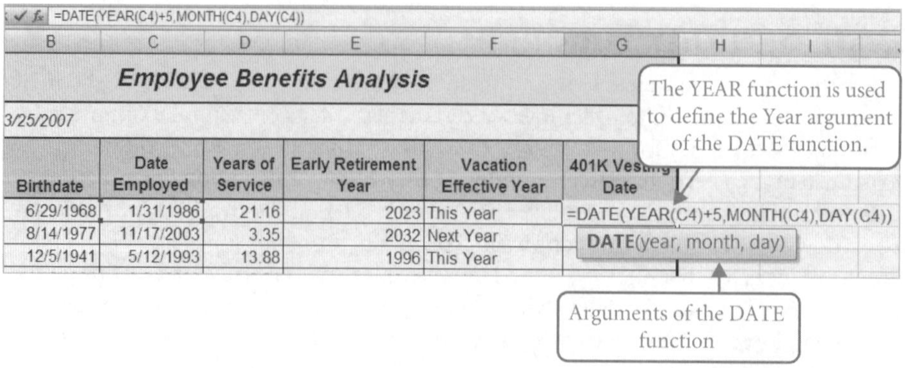

Figure 7.11 shows the results of the **DATE** function illustrated in Figure 7.10. Notice that the 401K Vesting Date for Employee 1 is exactly 5 years later than the Date Employed. This is because the number 5 was added to the result of the **YEAR** function in the **year** argument of the **DATE** function.

Figure 7.11 | **Results of the DATE Function for Calculating the 401K Vesting Dates**

G4 =DATE(YEAR(C4)+5,MONTH(C4),DAY(C4))

	A	B	C	D	E	F	G
1	*Employee Benefits Analysis*						
2	*Today's Date*	*3/25/2007*					
3	Employee Name	Birthdate	Date Employed	Years of Service	Early Retirement Year	Vacation Effective Year	401K Vesting Date
4	Employee 1	6/29/1968	1/31/1986	21.16	2023	This Year	1/31/1991
5	Employee 2	8/14/1977	11/17/2003	3.35	2032	Next Year	11/17/2008
6	Employee 3	12/5/1941	5/12/1993	13.88	1996	This Year	5/12/1998
7	Employee 4	4/18/1964	9/21/2000	6.51	2019	Next Year	9/21/2005
8	Employee 5	7/22/1978	10/25/2002	4.42	2033	Next Year	10/25/2007
9	Employee 6	9/26/1983	12/29/2004	2.24	2038	Next Year	12/29/2009
10	Employee 7	3/16/1951	9/22/2000	6.51	2006	Next Year	9/22/2005
11	Employee 8	3/13/1961	7/17/1996	10.69	2016	This Year	7/17/2001
12	Employee 9	6/21/1971	10/25/2002	4.42	2026	Next Year	10/25/2007
13	Employee 10	6/24/1957	12/30/2005	1.23	2012	Next Year	12/30/2010
14	Employee 11	1/3/1965	3/6/1989	18.06	2020	This Year	3/6/1994
15	Employee 12	5/15/1952	11/21/2002	4.34	2007	Next Year	11/21/2007
16	Employee 13	3/10/1973	6/13/1994	12.79	2028	This Year	6/13/1999
17	Employee 14	5/14/1977	7/16/1996	10.70	2032	This Year	7/16/2001
18	Employee 15	8/5/1942	1/2/1986	21.24	1997	This Year	1/2/1991

The dates in the 401K Vesting column are exactly 5 years later than the dates in the Date Employed column.

COMMON MISTAKES | Converting Years to Days and Adding to Date Serial Number

It might seem that a simple approach to calculating the dates for the 401K Vesting Date column in Figure 7.11 is to add 1825 days (365 × 5 years) to the date Serial Number in the Date Employed column. However, you will not get a date that is exactly 5 years from the Date Employed because of leap year. For example, notice that the 401K Vesting Date in Figure 7.12 is off by 1 day. You can increase a date Serial Number by converting and adding several years to days, but you will have to make adjustments to account for leap years. The **DATE** function method illustrated in Figure 7.10 does not require this type of adjustment.

Figure 7.12 | **Example of Adding Days to Date Serial Number**

	Employee Name	Birthdate	Date Employed	401K Vesting Date	
4	Employee 1	6/29/1968	1/31/1986	1/30/1991	1/31/1991
5	Employee 2	8/14/1977	11/17/2003		
6	Employee 3	12/5/1941	5/12/1993		

Result of adding 1825 days to the Date Employed

Result using DATE function method from Figure 7.10

Quick Reference

DAY Function

1. Activate a cell.
2. Type an equal sign and the function name DAY.
3. Type an open parenthesis.
4. Enter a cell location that contains a valid date Serial Number or type a valid date Serial Number.
5. Type a closing parenthesis. You can also type a date enclosed in quotations, i.e. "10/21/2006".
6. Press the **Enter** key.

Quick Reference

DATE Function

1. Activate a cell.
2. Type an equal sign, the function name DATE, and an open parenthesis.
3. Define the **year**, **month**, and **day** arguments using numbers, cell locations, formulas, or functions.
4. Type a closing parenthesis.
5. Press the **Enter** key.

VIDEO WORKSHOP

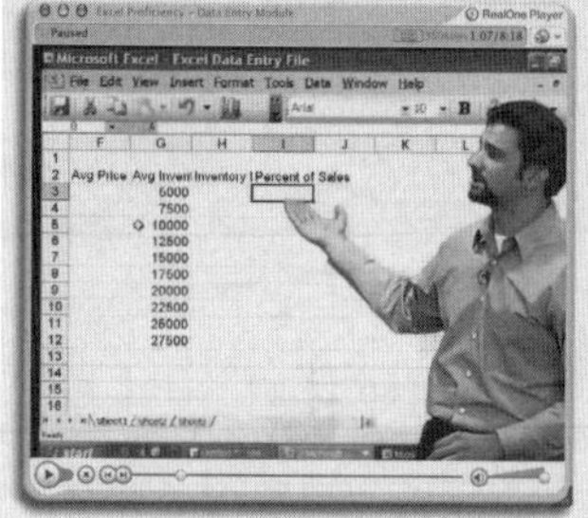

>> DATE Functions

The purpose of this workshop is to demonstrate the use of **DATE** functions. The Excel workbook that will be used in this workshop is identical to the one shown in Figure 7.1. I will be demonstrating the tasks in this workshop in the following four videos named **TODAY Function**, **YEAR Function**, **MONTH Function**, and **DATE Function**. The name of the video appears in parentheses next to the relevant section heading. Open the Excel workbook named ib_e07_datefunctions. Complete each section of tasks first, and then watch the video pertaining to that section.

1. **TODAY Function (Video: TODAY Function)**
   a. Activate cell B2. Note that the cells in range B2:G2 are merged.
   b. Type an equal sign followed by the function name `TODAY`.
   c. Type an open then a closing parenthesis and press the **Enter** key.
   d. Format cell B2 to a number with 0 decimal places. Then, switch the format back to the Short Date format.
   e. Type an equal sign in cell D4 followed by the formula `($B$2 - C4) / 365`.
   f. Copy the formula in cell D4 and paste it into the range D5:D18 using the **Formulas** option in the **Paste** icon.

2. **YEAR Function (Video: YEAR Function)**
   a. Type an equal sign in cell E4 followed by the function name `YEAR`.
   b. Type an open parenthesis, cell location `B4`, and a closing parenthesis.
   c. Type a plus sign and the number `55`.
   d. Press the **Enter** key. Then, copy and paste the function in cell E4 to the range E5:E18 using the **Formulas** option in the **Paste** icon.

3. **MONTH Function (Video: MONTH Function)**
   a. Type an equal sign in cell F4 followed by the function name `IF` and an open parenthesis.
   b. For the **logical_test** argument, type the function name **MONTH** followed by an open parenthesis. Then, type `C4` followed by a closing parenthesis.
   c. Complete the **logical_test** argument by typing a greater-than sign `(>)` followed by the number `7` and a comma.
   d. Define the **value_if_true** argument with the words `"Next Year"`. Remember to use the quotations.
   e. Define the **value_if_false** argument with the words `"This Year"`.
   f. Complete the function by typing a closing parenthesis and press the **Enter** key.
   g. Copy cell F4 and paste it into the range F5:F18 using the **Formulas** option in the **Paste** icon.

4. **DATE Function (Video: DATE Function)**
   a. Type an equal sign in cell G4 followed by the function name `DATE` and an open parenthesis.

b. Define the **year** argument by typing the function name `YEAR` followed by an open parenthesis.
c. Type `C4` followed by a closing parenthesis. Then, type a plus sign followed by the number `5`. Complete the **year** argument by typing a comma.
d. Define the **month** argument by typing the function name `MONTH` followed by an open parenthesis. Then, type `C4` followed by a closing parenthesis and a comma.
e. Define the **day** argument by typing the function name `DAY` followed by an open parenthesis. Then, type `C4` followed by a closing parenthesis.
f. Complete the DATE function by typing a closing parenthesis and press the **Enter** key.
g. Copy cell G4 and paste it into the range G5:G18 using the **Formulas** option in the **Paste** icon.
h. Save and close the workbook.

>> Project Management for a New Store

EXERCISE

Why Do I Need This?

Most executives agree that timing is one of the most critical success factors in business. Whether a company is launching a new product or opening a new store, the timing of when these events occur could mean the difference between making and losing money. As a result, business projects must be planned carefully. A project plan is a business manager's guide for making decisions, such as ordering supplies, hiring people, or buying inventory. This plan is critical to a business manager's decision process because a change in the completion date for just one component could change the execution of every task in the plan. Most business managers use project-planning software for large business projects. However, Excel is a great tool for planning small-to-medium projects.

Exercise

The purpose of this exercise is to use Excel to plan the opening of a new retail store. In order for a store to open on a specific target date, several activities and events must take place. Planning these events is the focus of this exercise. To begin, open the Excel workbook named ib_e07_openinganewstore and continue with the tasks listed below.

1. The first event listed is Renovations in cell A3. Most retail stores require some type of construction renovations to suit the needs of the business. Cell B3 contains the target date of when these renovations will begin, which is March 1, 2007. Cell C3 shows how long it will take to complete the renovations, which is 90 days. Calculate the completion date of the renovations in cell D3 by adding cell C3 to cell B3.

2. The next event listed is Order Fixtures in cell A4. The fixtures include the shelves that will hold the products, the check-out counter, signs, etc. The goal is to have the fixtures delivered to the store the day the renovations are completed. Considering that it takes 45 days to receive the fixtures, calculate the order date in cell B4 by subtracting cell C4 from cell D3.

3. Calculate the delivery date for the fixtures in cell D4 by adding cell B4 to cell C4. The delivery date for the fixtures should match the completion date for renovations.

4. The next event listed is Assemble Fixtures in cell A5. The fixtures must first be received before they can be assembled. Therefore, the begin date in

cell B5 must be equal to the delivered date in cell D4. Use a link to show the completion date in D4 in cell B5.

5. Calculate the completion date for assembling the fixtures in cell D5 by adding cell B5 to cell C5.

6. The next event listed is Order Inventory in cell A6. The inventory must not be received before the fixtures are assembled. Therefore, calculate the order date by subtracting cell C6 from cell D5. Notice that inventory must be ordered before renovations begin.

7. Calculate the delivery date for the inventory in cell D6 by adding cell C6 to cell B6. The delivery date for the inventory should match the completion date for assembling the fixtures.

8. The next event listed is Order Cash Registers in cell A7. The cash registers should arrive at the same time as the inventory so they can be tested. Calculate the order date for the cash registers in cell B7 by subtracting cell C7 from cell D6.

9. Calculate the delivery date for the cash registers in cell D7 by adding cell B7 to cell C7. This date should match the delivery date of the inventory.

10. The final event listed is Assemble and Test Registers in cell A8. The registers must first be received before they can be assembled and tested. Therefore, link cell B8 to cell D7.

11. Calculate the completion date for assembling and testing the registers in cell D8 by adding cell C8 to cell B8.

12. Calculate the date the store will be open for business in cell C11. The store can open the day after the registers have been assembled and tested. Therefore, add 1 to cell D8.

13. You just received a call from the renovation contractor telling you that renovations cannot be started until March 14. Change the date in cell B3 to 3/14/2007. Given this date, when should you order inventory? When should you order fixtures? When will the store be open for business?

14. You find out that the inventory can be delivered in 110 days instead of 120. Will this allow you to open the store 10 days sooner? Why or why not?

15. For which events could you decrease the process time to compensate for the delay in renovations so the store could be opened sooner?

16. Save and close the workbook.

PROBLEM & EXERCISE

>> What's Wrong with This Spreadsheet?

Problem

You are managing a human resources department for a large company. Your department is currently in the process of constructing a benefits statement for each employee that includes information such as salary, vacation time, and health insurance plan. This statement also includes the date on which the employee will qualify for early retirement benefits. An employee is eligible for early retirement benefits on they day he reaches the age of 60. An intern working in your department constructs an Excel spreadsheet that calculates the early retirement date for each employee.

The information from this spreadsheet will be used to produce the final benefits statement, which will be mailed to each employee's home.

Exercise

The Excel file created by the intern in your department is named ib_e07_earlyretirement. Open the file and examine the retirement dates that were calculated by the intern. Would you be comfortable using this information to produce each employee's benefit statement? Consider the following:

1. Look at the birth dates for the first few employees. Does the early retirement date fall on the employee's 60th birthday?
2. Explain how the early retirement dates in column C are being calculated for each employee.
3. Why would the method you identified in point 2 not produce an employee's exact 60th birthday?

What's wrong with this spreadsheet? Write a short answer for each of the points listed above. Create an alternate method in column D for calculating the date on which each employee will reach the age of 60.

>> Text Functions

Skill Set

The previous section demonstrated how you can use Excel Date functions to manipulate dates and use them in calculations. Similarly, you can use Text functions to extract specific parts of data within a cell or combine data from multiple cells to match the data configuration you are currently using in a workbook. The commands and calculations executed in Excel are always applied to an entire cell or range of cells in a worksheet. However, there may be situations when you need to isolate a specific portion of data within a cell or combine data from multiple cells into one. These situations require the use of Text functions. This section will illustrate a variety of situations showing why and when text functions are useful when using Excel in business.

CONCATENATE Function

You can use the **CONCATENATE** function to combine data from two or more cell locations into one. This function is often used when you require a unique value to reference data in a second worksheet using a **VLOOKUP** or **HLOOKUP** function. For example, let us assume you are a human resources manager and you receive a data file from your company's IT department listing all new employees hired in the past month. You open the file in Excel and realize that the name of every employee is separated into two columns (see Figure 7.13). The first column contains the employees' last names and the second column contains the employees' first names. You intend to add this data to an Excel file you created previously that contains a list of current employees (see Figure 7.14). However, this file has each employee's full name in one cell location. This is because there are several employees with the same last name and you frequently use the employee's name as the lookup value in a **VLOOKUP** function to reference data in other Excel files. Therefore, to make the data you received match the data in your current Excel file, you must combine each employee's first and last name together in one cell. This task is done using the **CONCATENATE** function.

Figure 7.13 | **New Employee List**

The first and last names of each employee are separated into two columns.

	A	B	C	D
1	*New Employee List*			
2	**Last Name**	**First Name**	**Department**	**Title**
3	Bee	Beth	Planning	Vice President
4	Dee	Ed	Transportation	Vice President
5	Henry	Gladys	Production	Manager
6	James	William	Planning	Assistant
7	James	Gloria	Production	Coordinator
8	Johnson	Hal	Marketing	Manager
9	Johnson	Julie	Planning	Manager
10	Johnson	Beth	Purchasing	Buyer
11	Jolly	Bernice	Transportation	Manager
12	Lu	Gloria	Marketing	Vice President

FIGURE 7.14 | **Previously Created List of Current Employees**

Each employee's name is combined into one column, last name followed by first name.

	A	B	C
1	*Current Employees*		
2	**Full Name**	**Department**	**Title**
3	Angello, Salvatore	Transportation	Manager
4	Ball, Gloria	Warehousing	Director
5	Bee, Bernice	Production	Vice President
6	Best, Jennifer	IT	Vice President
7	Blu, Natalie	Warehousing	Manager
8	Charles, Hale	Transportation	Assistant
9	Cowlins, John	Accounting	Director
10	Frank, Bill	Sales	Regional Director
11	Gil, Anthony	Production	President
12	Henry, Keith	IT	Programmer
13	Jay, Mary	Human Resources	Vice President
14	Keey, Mary	Accounting	Manager

The new list of employees shown in Figure 7.13 cannot be added to the current list of employees in Figure 7.14 unless the first and last name of each employee is combined into one column. The following explains how the **CONCATENATE** function is used to accomplish this goal.

- Insert a new column between columns B and C in the New Employee List worksheet (Figure 7.13). This will create a new column C, which is blank.
- Type the column heading Full Name in cell C2.
- Type an equal sign in cell C3 followed by the function name CONCATENATE.
- Type an open parenthesis.
- Type cell location A3 followed by a comma.
- Type an open quotation mark followed by a comma, a space, and a closing quotation mark. This will add a comma and a space between the last and first names,

which is how the names are configured in column A of Figure 7.14. As with most other functions, in addition to using cell locations you can use numeric or text data to define each argument. However, if you are using text data or symbols, you must put them in quotations.

- Type a comma.
- Type cell location B3 followed by a closing parenthesis.
- Press the **Enter** key. Then, copy cell C3 and paste it to the rest of the cells in the list.

Figure 7.15 shows the setup of the **CONCATENATE** function that was added to the New Employee List worksheet in Figure 7.13. The comma and space enclosed in quotations in the middle of the function will separate the last and first names as shown in Figure 7.14.

Figure 7.15 | **Setup of the CONCATENATE Function**

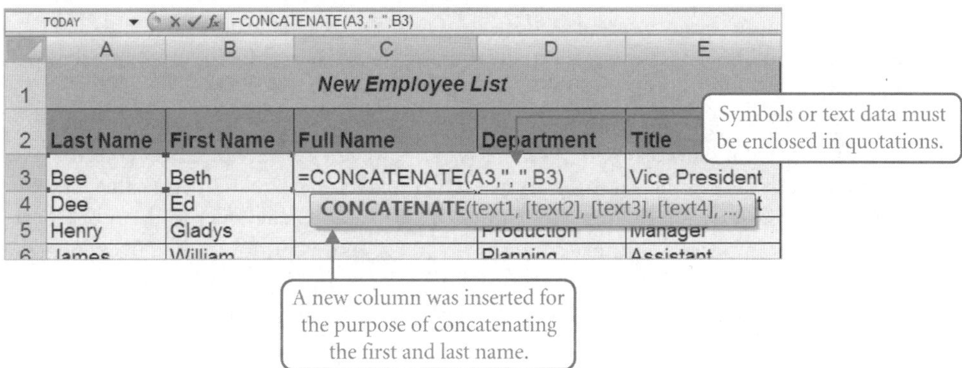

Figure 7.16 shows the results of the **CONCATENATE** function from Figure 7.15. Each employee's last and first names from columns A and B have been combined in column C. A comma and a space were added between the last and first names to match the configuration of the names in column A of Figure 7.14. The data in Figure 7.16 can now be copied and pasted into the Excel file shown in Figure 7.14. However, remember to use the **Paste Values** option in the **Paste** icon. If you use the regular paste command, you will be pasting the **CONCATENATE** function and not the names that were produced as a result of the function output.

Figure 7.16 | **Results of the CONCATENATE Function**

C3 =CONCATENATE(A3,", ",B3)

Concatenate function entered in cell C3.

	A	B	C	D	E
1	New Employee List				
2	Last Name	First Name	Full Name	Department	Title
3	Bee	Beth	Bee, Beth	Planning	Vice President
4	Dee	Ed	Dee, Ed	Transportation	Vice President
5	Henry	Gladys	Henry, Gladys	Production	Manager
6	James	William	James, William	Planning	Assistant
7	James	Gloria	James, Gloria	Production	Coordinator
8	Johnson	Hal	Johnson, Hal	Marketing	Manager
9	Johnson	Julie	Johnson, Julie	Planning	Manager
10	Johnson	Beth	Johnson, Beth	Purchasing	Buyer
11	Jolly	Bernice	Jolly, Bernice	Transportation	Manager
12	Lu	Gloria	Lu, Gloria	Marketing	Vice President

Last and first names in columns A and B are now combined.

COMMON MISTAKES | The #Name? Error and CONCATENATE Function

If you see the #Name? error when using the **CONCATENATE** function, check to see that any text data is enclosed in quotations. Cell locations and numbers can be typed directly into the arguments of the function. However, you will see the #Name? error if you typed any symbols, words, or letters into one of the arguments without using quotations.

SEARCH, LEFT, LEN, and MID Functions

In the previous segment, you saw how the **CONCATENATE** function enables you to combine a list of employee names from two columns into one. You will now learn how to use the **LEN**, **SEARCH**, **LEFT**, and **MID** functions to separate a list of employee names from one column into two. These four functions are being demonstrated together because they are rarely used individually. The results produced by the **SEARCH** and **LEN** functions are usually used by the **MID** and **LEFT** functions to separate data from one column into two or more columns.

Figure 7.17 shows an Excel worksheet containing a list of new employees that is similar to the worksheet shown in Figure 7.13. However, in this worksheet column A contains both the first and last names of each employee. The goal is to add this data to the worksheet shown in Figure 7.18. Notice that the employee names in this worksheet are separated into two columns (columns B and C). In this example, the HR manager uses an ID number (column A) to identify each employee. This eliminates the need to combine the first and last names of each employee into one column. As a result, the employee names in Figure 7.17 need to be separated into two columns before they can be pasted into the worksheet shown in Figure 7.18.

Figure 7.17 | **Worksheet with Employee Names in One Column**

F1

	A	B	C
1	*New Employee List*		
2	Name	Department	Title
3	Bee, Beth	Planning	Vice President
4	Dee, Ed	Transportation	Vice President
5	Henry, Gladys	Production	Manager
6	James, William	Planning	Assistant
7	James, Gloria	Production	Coordinator
8	Johnson, Hal	Marketing	Manager
9	Johnson, Julie	Planning	Manager
10	Johnson, Beth	Purchasing	Buyer
11	Jolly, Bernice	Transportation	Manager
12	Lu, Gloria	Marketing	Vice President

Employee names are combined into one column.

>> Quick Reference

CONCATENATE Function

1. Activate a cell.
2. Type an equal sign followed by the function name CONCATENATE and an open parenthesis.
3. Identify data that you wish to combine and enter it into each argument of the function, followed by commas. Remember to use quotation marks if you are typing words or text into an argument.
4. Type a closing parenthesis.
5. Press the **Enter** key.

Figure 7.18 | **Worksheet with Employee Names in Two Columns**

	A	B	C	D	E
1	*Current Employees*				
2	**ID Number**	**Last Name**	**First Name**	**Department**	**Title**
3	101401	Angello	Salvatore	Transportation	Manager
4	592889	Ball	Gloria	Warehousing	Director
5	845966	Bee	Bernice	Production	Vice President
6	110602	Best	Jennifer	IT	Vice President
7	576409	Blu	Natalie	Warehousing	Manager
8	855442	Charles	Hale	Transportation	Assistant
9	671718	Cowlins	John	Accounting	Director
10	665153	Frank	Bill	Sales	Regional Director
11	401034	Gil	Anthony	Production	President
12	265349	Henry	Keith	IT	Programmer
13	244502	Jay	Mary	Human Resources	Vice President
14	876674	Keey	Mary	Accounting	Manager
15	763649	Lite	Bruce	Human Resources	Recruiting Manager
16	125544	Love	Bill	Planning	Manager

Employee names are separated into two columns.

As mentioned previously, the **SEARCH**, **LEN**, **LEFT**, and **MID** functions will be used to separate the employee names in column A of Figure 7.17 into two columns. The following provides a brief definition of these four functions and explains how they are used together to separate data contained in one column into two or more columns.

- **LEN:** The **LEN** function is used to count the total number of characters of data that is entered into a cell location. The function has one argument, which is usually defined by a cell location that contains text data. The number of characters produced by this function can be used in the **LEFT** or **MID** function to select specific characters from data that is entered into a target cell location.
- **SEARCH:** The **SEARCH** function is used to count the number of characters up to and including a target symbol for data contained in a cell. The function counts the number of characters up to the target symbol from left to right. For example, column A in Figure 7.17 contains each employee's last and first names separated by a comma. The letters preceding the comma make up the employee's last name. The **SEARCH** function can be used to count the number of characters that precede and include the comma. This number can then be used in one of the arguments of the **LEFT** function to separate the employee's last name and place it into another cell location. The following are the three arguments of the **SEARCH** function.
    - **find_text:** Type the symbol or character you are searching for and enclose it in quotation marks. For example, if you wanted to count the number of characters up to and including a comma, you would type a comma enclosed in quotation marks. You can also type a cell location that contains a character or symbol into this argument. However, quotation marks are not required if you are using cell locations.
    - **within_text:** Type the cell location that contains the text entry you are searching. You can also type a word into this segment, but it must be enclosed in quotation marks.
    - **[start_num]:** The **SEARCH** function will automatically look for the character used to define the **find_text** argument beginning with the first character. Use this argument if you want to begin searching after the first character of a text string, or when the character used to define the **find_text** argument appears multiple times in a text string.

- **LEFT:** The **LEFT** function is used to select a specific number of characters from a text entry beginning from left to right. The number of characters this function selects is usually determined by using a function such as the **SEARCH** function. For example, to select only the last name from column A in Figure 7.17, you can use the **SEARCH** function to determine how many letters appear before the comma. The number produced by the **SEARCH** function can then be used in the **LEFT** function to select only the last name from each name listed in column A. This function contains the following two arguments.
  - **text:** Type the cell location containing text data from which the function will select characters. You can also type a text entry directly into this argument, but it must be enclosed in quotation marks.
  - **[num_chars]:** Type the cell location, formula, or number that contains the number of characters the **LEFT** function will select from a text entry. The function will select the first character of a text entry and continue selecting, from left to right, the number of characters defined by this argument.
- **MID:** The **MID** function serves the same purpose as the **LEFT** function. However, the **LEFT** function will always select the *first character of a text entry* and continue selecting characters from left to right. The **MID** function allows you to start selecting characters at a specific point in a text entry. For example, after the last name is selected from column A in Figure 7.17, characters after the comma must be selected to separate the first name. The **MID** function can be used to start selecting characters after the comma so that only the first name is selected and placed into a separate cell location. The following are the three arguments of this function.
  - **text:** Identical to the **text** argument in the **LEFT** function.
  - **start_num:** Type the cell location, formula, or number that defines where the function should begin selecting characters from the data used to define the **text** argument. The function will use the number in this argument to select the starting character by counting from left to right. For example, if the number 3 is typed into this argument, the function will begin selecting characters from left to right beginning with the third character.
  - **[num_chars]:** Identical to the **num_chars** argument in the **LEFT** function.

As mentioned previously, the **SEARCH**, **LEN**, **LEFT**, and **MID** functions will be used to separate the names listed in column A in Figure 7.17 into two columns. This is necessary in order to paste the data shown in Figure 7.17 into the worksheet shown in Figure 7.18. The following explains how these four functions are used to accomplish this task.

- Insert 4 columns between columns A and B in the New Employee List worksheet (see Figure 7.17).
- Type the column heading Last Name in cell D2 and the column heading First Name in cell E2.
- Type an equal sign followed by the function name **LEN** and an open parenthesis in cell B3.
- Type the cell location A3 followed by a closing parenthesis. This will count the number of characters in the first employee's name (see Figure 7.19).
- Copy the function in cell B3 and paste it to the rest of the cells in the list.

>> Quick Reference

LEN Function

1. Activate a cell.
2. Type an equal sign followed by the function name LEN.
3. Type an open parenthesis followed by a cell location containing text data, or type a text entry enclosed in quotation marks.
4. Type a closing parenthesis and press the **Enter** key.

Figure 7.19 | **Setup of the LEN Function**

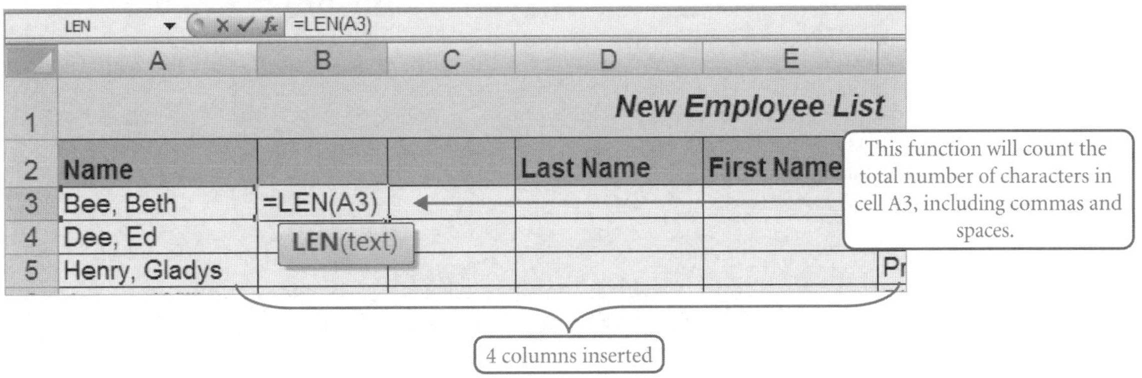

The following explains how the **SEARCH** function is added to the New Employee List worksheet:

- Type an equal sign in cell C3, followed by the function name SEARCH and an open parenthesis. This function will be used to count the number of characters preceding and including the comma in the first employee's name in cell A3. Define the three arguments of this function as follows.
  - **find_text:** Type an open quotation mark followed by a comma and then a closing quotation mark. The function will stop counting characters from left to right when it encounters a comma. Type a comma to complete this argument.
  - **within_text:** Type cell location A3 followed by a closing parenthesis.
  - **[start_num]:** Because a comma appears only one time in the names listed in column A, there is no need to define this argument. The function will begin searching for a comma after the first letter of the employee's name. This is why a closing parenthesis was typed after the **within_text** argument (see Figure 7.20).
- Copy the **SEARCH** function in cell C3 and paste it to the rest of the cells in the list.

Figure 7.20 | **SEARCH Function Setup and LEN Function Results**

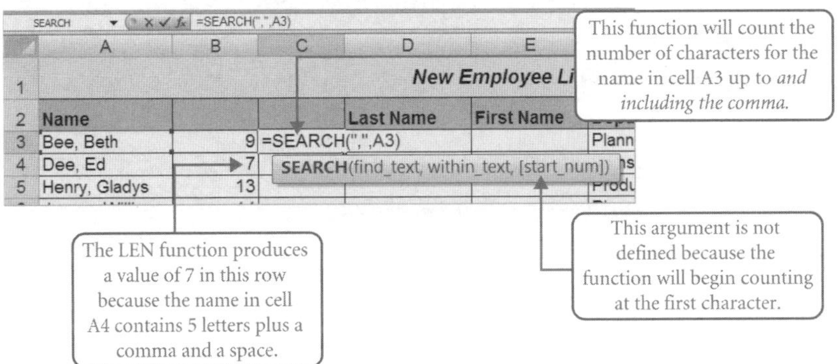

» Quick Reference

SEARCH Function

1. Activate a cell.
2. Type an equal sign followed by the function name SEARCH.
3. Type an open parenthesis and define the following three arguments:
   a. **find_text:** The character the function will search for in a text entry. Characters typed into this argument must be enclosed in quotation marks.
   b. **within_text:** The characters of the text data used to define this argument will be counted.
   c. **[start_num]:** Position in a text entry at which the function will begin searching for the character in the **find_text** argument. The function assumes 1 if not defined.
4. Type a closing parenthesis and press the **Enter** key.

COMMON MISTAKES | (start_num) Argument in the SEARCH function

Most people confuse the result of the **SEARCH** function when using the **[start_num]** argument. The **SEARCH** function will *always* count the number of characters in a text string beginning with the first character. The **[start_num]** argument changes only the point at which the function will begin looking for the character used to define the **find_text** argument. For example, the function listed below will return the number 9. This is because there are 9 characters preceding the *second comma* in the **within_text** argument. Because the number 6 is entered in the **[start_num]** argument, the function will begin looking for a comma starting with the letter T in the word Two.

```
=SEARCH(",","One, Two, Three",6)
```

The following explains how the **LEFT** function is added and used in the New Employee List worksheet:

- Type an equal sign in cell D3 followed by the function name LEFT and an open parenthesis. Define the two arguments of this function as follows (see Figure 7.21).
  - **text:** Type cell location A3 followed by a comma. This function will be used to select only the last name of the employee entered in cell A3.
  - **[num_chars]:** Type cell location C3 followed by a subtraction sign and the number 1. The **SEARCH** function in C3 is providing the number of characters that precedes the comma for the first employee, which is the employee's last name. However, this number also includes the comma. Therefore, the number 1 is subtracted from cell C3 so that the **LEFT** function does not include the comma when selecting the employee's last name.
- Type a closing parenthesis to complete the **LEFT** function and press the **Enter** key.
- Copy the **LEFT** function in cell D3 to the rest of the cells in the list.

Figure 7.21 | **LEFT Function Setup and SEARCH Function Results**

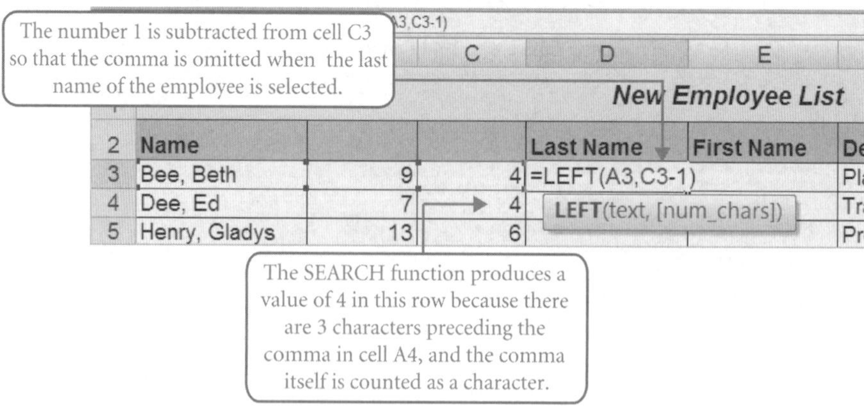

> **Quick Reference**
>
> **LEFT Function**
>
> 1. Activate a cell.
> 2. Type an equal sign followed by the function name LEFT.
> 3. Type an open parenthesis and define the following two arguments:
>   a. **text:** Cell location containing text data or typed text in quotation marks.
>   b. **[num_chars]:** Number of characters the function will select from the text data in the **text** argument beginning from left to right.
> 4. Type a closing parenthesis and press the **Enter** key.

The following explains how the **MID** function is added and used in the New Employee List worksheet:

- Type an equal sign in cell E3 followed by the function name MID and an open parenthesis. Define the three arguments of this function as follows (see Figure 7.22).
  - **text:** Type cell location A3 followed by a comma. This function will be used to select the first name of the employee entered in cell A3.
  - **[start_num]:** Type cell location C3, a plus sign, and the number 2. The goal for this function is to begin selecting the letters of the employee's first name. Cell

C3 contains the results of the **SEARCH** function, which is counting the letters of the employee's last name plus the comma. After the comma there is a space, and the next letter begins the employee's first name. Therefore, the number 2 is added to the result of the **SEARCH** function so that this function can select characters beginning with the first letter of the employee's first name. Complete this argument by typing a comma.

- **[num_chars]:** Type cell location B3-C3 enclosed in parentheses. Then, type a subtraction sign and the number 1. Cell B3 contains the result of the LEN function, which is counting all of the characters for the employee's name in cell A3. The result of the **SEARCH** function in cell C3 is counting all of the characters in the employee's last name including the comma. Therefore, the number of characters calculated by subtracting the **SEARCH** function in cell C3 from the **LEN** function in cell B3 is the employee's first name. However, to account for the space after the comma, the number 1 is subtracted from this result.

- Type a closing parenthesis to complete the **MID** function and press the **Enter** key.
- Copy the **MID** function in cell E3 and paste it to the rest of the cell locations in the list.

Figure 7.22 | **MID Function Setup and LEFT Function Results**

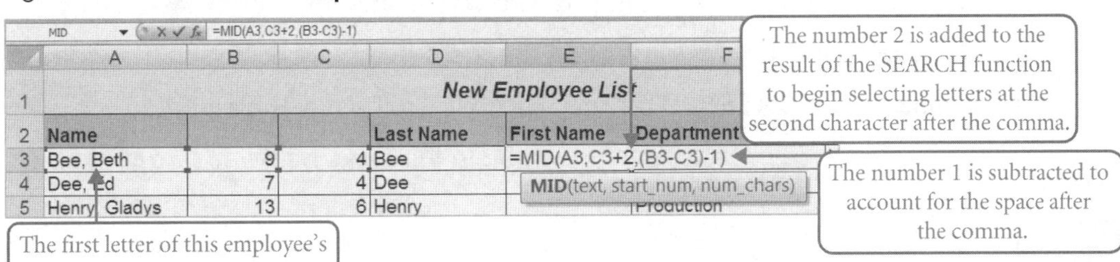

COMMON MISTAKES | Each Space Is Counted as a Character

It is important to remember that when working with text functions, each space counts as one character. Many people make the mistake of using a number in the **[num_chars]** argument of the **MID** or **LEFT** function that is too high. In order to select the exact number of characters in a text entry, you must account for any spaces in the data that is used to define the **text** argument.

Figure 7.23 shows the final results of using the **LEN**, **SEARCH**, **LEFT**, and **MID** functions to separate each of the employee names in column A into columns D and E. Columns D, E, F, and G can now be pasted into the worksheet shown in Figure 7.18. However, these columns must be pasted using the **Paste Values** option in the **Paste** icon because the names in columns D and E are being produced by functions.

>> Quick Reference

MID Function

1. Type an equal sign followed by the function name MID.
2. Type an open parenthesis and define the following three arguments:
   a. **text:** Cell location containing text data or typed text in quotation marks.
   b. **[start_num]:** Number of the first character that will be selected counting from left to right.
   c. **[num_chars]:** Number of characters that will be selected from the text data in the **text** argument beginning from the character number in the **[start_num]** argument from left to right.
3. Type a closing parenthesis and press the **Enter** key.

Figure 7.23 | **Final Results of Separating Names with the LEN, SEARCH, LEFT, and MID Functions**

Each name in column A is separated into two columns.

	A	B	C	D	E	F	G
1	New Employee List						
2	Name			Last Name	First Name	Department	Title
3	Bee, Beth	9	4	Bee	Beth	Planning	Vice President
4	Dee, Ed	7	4	Dee	Ed	Transportation	Vice President
5	Henry, Gladys	13	6	Henry	Gladys	Production	Manager
6	James, William	14	6	James	William	Planning	Assistant
7	James, Gloria	13	6	James	Gloria	Production	Coordinator
8	Johnson, Hal	12	8	Johnson	Hal	Marketing	Manager
9	Johnson, Julie	14	8	Johnson	Julie	Planning	Manager
10	Johnson, Beth	13	8	Johnson	Beth	Purchasing	Buyer
11	Jolly, Bernice	14	6	Jolly	Bernice	Transportation	Manager
12	Lu, Gloria	10	3	Lu	Gloria	Marketing	Vice President

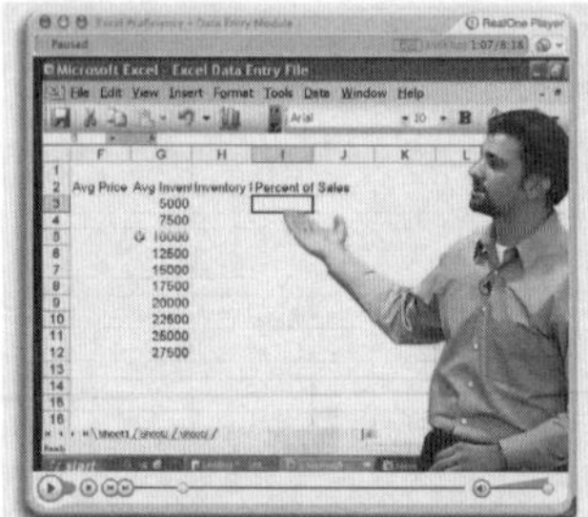

»CONCATENATE Function

The purpose of this workshop is to demonstrate the **CONCATENATE** function. I will be demonstrating the tasks in this workshop in the video named **CONCATENATE Function.** Open the Excel file named ib_e07_concatenatefunction. Complete the tasks below first, and then watch the video.

1. **Concatenating Data (Video: CONCATENATE Function)**
   a. Activate the New Employees List worksheet.
   b. Activate cell C2 and Insert a column.
   c. Type the column heading `Full Name` in cell C2.
   d. Type an equal sign in cell C3 followed by the function name `CONCATENATE` and an open parenthesis.
   e. Type cell `A3` followed by a comma.
   f. Type an opening quotation mark, a comma, a space, and a closing quotation mark.
   g. Type a comma.
   h. Type cell `B3` followed by a closing parenthesis. Then press the **Enter** key.
   i. Copy cell C3 and paste it into the range C4:C12.
   j. Copy the range C3:E12.
   k. Activate the Current Employees worksheet and activate cell A22.
   l. Paste the data using the **Paste Values** option in the **Paste** icon on the **Home** tab of the Ribbon.
   m. Highlight the range A22:C31. Then, add a dark line to the right side, left side, and bottom of the range and a regular line on the inside of the range.
   n. Sort the data in the Current Employees worksheet based on the Full Name column in ascending order.
   o. Save and close your file.

>>LEN, SEARCH, LEFT and MID Functions

VIDEO WORKSHOP

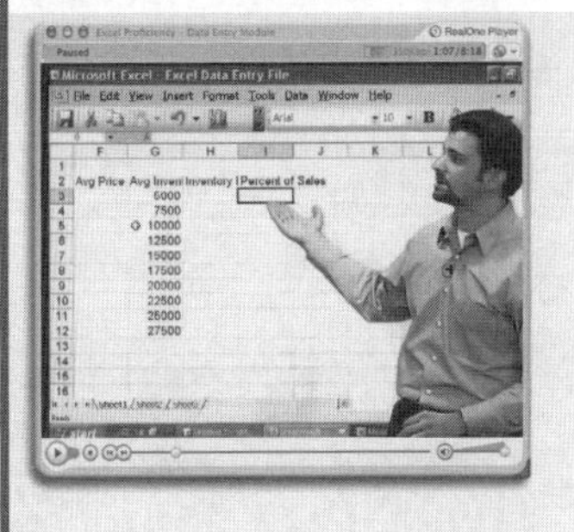

The purpose of this workshop is to demonstrate the use of the **LEN**, **SEARCH**, **LEFT**, and **MID** functions. I will be demonstrating the tasks in this workshop in the four videos named **LEN Function**, **SEARCH Function**, **LEFT Function**, and **MID Function**. The name of the video will appear in parentheses next to the relevant section heading. Open the Excel workbook named ib_e07_separatingdata. Complete each section of tasks first, and then watch the video pertaining to that section.

1. **Counting All Characters in a Cell (Video: LEN Function)**
   a. Activate the New Employees worksheet and activate cell B3.
   b. Insert 4 columns.
   c. Type the column heading `Last Name` in cell D2 and type the column heading `First Name` in cell E2.
   d. Type an equal sign in cell B3 followed by the function name `LEN` and an open parenthesis.
   e. Type cell `A3` followed by a closing parenthesis and press the **Enter** key.
   f. Copy cell B3 and paste it into the range B4:B12.

2. **Counting Target Characters in a Cell (Video: SEARCH Function)**
   a. Type an equal sign in cell C3 followed by the function name `SEARCH` and an open parenthesis.
   b. Define the **find_text** argument by typing an opening quotation mark, a comma, and a closing quotation mark. Complete the argument by typing a comma.
   c. Define the **within_text** argument by typing cell `A3`.
   d. Complete the function by typing a closing parenthesis and press the **Enter** key.
   e. Copy cell C3 and paste it into the range C4:C12.

3. **Selecting Characters from the Beginning of Text (Video: LEFT Function)**
   a. Type an equal sign in cell D3 followed by the function name `LEFT` and an open parenthesis.
   b. Define the text argument by typing cell `A3` followed by a comma.
   c. Define the **[num_chars]** argument by typing the formula `C3-1`.
   d. Complete the function by typing a closing parenthesis and press the **Enter** key.
   e. Copy cell D3 and paste it into the range D4:D12.

4. **Selecting Characters from the Middle of Text (Video: MID Function)**
   a. Type an equal sign in cell E3 followed by the function name `MID` and an open parenthesis.
   b. Define the text argument by typing cell `A3` followed by a comma.
   c. Define the **[start_num]** argument by typing the formula `C3+2` followed by a comma.

d. Define the **[num_chars]** argument by typing the formula `(B3 - C3) -1`.
e. Complete the function by typing a closing parenthesis and press the **Enter** key.
f. Copy cell E3 and paste it into the range E4:E12.
g. Save and close the workbook.

EXERCISE

Why Do I Need This?

>> Calculating Cubic Capacity

The data that business managers use in Excel spreadsheets can come from a variety of sources. In some cases data might be manually typed into a spreadsheet. However, manually typing large amounts of data into an Excel spreadsheet increases the risk of data entry errors. Therefore, many business managers receive data from other sources such as the Internet or from their company's database system. This eliminates the risk of data entry errors. However, a potential challenge with this data is that it may not be in a format that is usable in mathematical formulas and functions. For example, the term 9′ is usually used to indicate a dimension of 9 feet. Excel will read 9′ as a text value that would not be usable in any mathematical formulas or functions. In these situations, text functions can transform a term such as 9′ into just the number 9.

Exercise

The purpose of this exercise is to calculate the cubic capacity for a fleet of trucks. Open the Excel workbook named ib_e07_trailercapacity. The data in this worksheet is similar to what a transportation manager might receive from a database system. The following tasks will feature the use of text functions to convert data in this worksheet into numeric values to calculate the cubic capacities in column E.

1. Column A contains the ID number for each trailer. Each ID number ends in a 3-digit number. The first two digits of this number is the length of the trailer. Use the MID function in cell B3 to select the trailer length from the ID number in cell A3. Define each argument of the MID function as follows:
   a. **text**: `A3`
   b. **start_num:** `SEARCH(" ",A3) + 1` Notice that the **find_text** argument of the **SEARCH** function is a space enclosed in parentheses. This is because the trailer length begins after the space in the trailer ID number. The **MID** function will begin selecting numbers one character after the space of the trailer ID number in cell A3.
   c. **num_chars:** `2` The first two digits of the ending 3-digit number in cell A3 is the length of the trailer.
2. Copy cell B3 and paste it into the range B4:B26.
3. Calculate the cubic capacity in cell E3 by multiplying the trailer length in cell B3 by the trailer height in cell C3 by the trailer width in cell D3. However, use the **LEFT** function to select only the first character in cells C3 and D3 because the apostrophe sign cannot be used in formulas (i.e., B3 * LEFT(C3,1) * LEFT(D3,1)).
4. Copy your formula in cell E3 and paste it into the range E4:E26.
5. What is the total cubic capacity of the entire fleet?
6. Save and close your file.

>> What's Wrong with This Spreadsheet?

PROBLEM & EXERCISE

Problem

You are directing the strategic planning department for a large textile manufacturing corporation that produces a variety of fabrics used in the production of clothes. Your department was asked to evaluate the capacity of a textile dying and finishing factory that might be acquired as part of a growth strategy. You receive a file listing the dyeing machines in the factory and the number of batches each machine is capable of producing per day. Given the cost to maintain and operate the factory, the machines must be able to process at least 50,000 pounds of fabric per day. You ask one of the analysts in your department to calculate the total capacity of the factory to see if the machines can produce this minimum target. He completes his analysis and mentions the following points in an e-mail message.

1. Unfortunately, the results of my analysis show that this factory is falling significantly short of our minimum capacity target. Looks like we should probably pass on buying this factory.
2. I calculated the daily production per machine by multiplying the machine capacity by the batches per day as per your instructions. I had a slight problem with the machine capacity because the data you gave me had only a listing of the machine ID numbers. However, I spoke to a manager at the factory and he told me that the machine capacity is the number after the space in the Machine ID number.
3. I attached the Excel file containing my analysis to this e-mail. Let me know if you have any questions.

Exercise

The Excel file your analyst attached to his e-mail in named ib_e07_textileincapacity. Do you agree with your analyst's assessment that this factory is incapable of producing the minimum 50,000 pounds of fabric per day? Consider the following points:

1. The analyst stated that the capacity for each machine is the number that follows the space in the Machine ID number (column A). Calculate the daily capacity of the first machine by multiplying this number by the batch number in column B. Does your calculation match the number the analyst calculated?
2. Look at the formula in cell C3. Explain how this formula is producing the number that is being multiplied by cell B3.
3. Is the calculation you analyzed in point 2 producing an accurate result of each machine's daily capacity?

What's wrong with this spreadsheet? Write a short answer for each of the points listed above. Then, fix the calculation in cell C3 and paste it into the range C4:C38. What is the total capacity of the factory?

>> IS Functions

Skill Set

The previous section demonstrated how you can use text functions to manipulate data within a cell. **IS** functions (pronounced like the word "is") are used to determine the type of data within a cell or establish whether the result of a formula or function is an error. These functions are often used with the **IF**, **AND**, and **OR** functions to develop advanced spreadsheets in which different outputs are produced based on the type of data that is entered into a cell. Combining these functions allows you to build flexible spreadsheets in which users are required to type data into one or more cell locations to produce calculated results. This section illustrates how **IS** functions are used in various business situations and demonstrates how they are used to handle errors that might be produced by formulas and functions based on what the user types into a cell location.

ISNUMBER and ISTEXT Functions

You can use the **ISNUMBER** and **ISTEXT** functions to determine if the data typed into a cell is either numeric data or text data. The output of both functions is either TRUE or FALSE depending on the data contained in a cell. These functions are frequently used together and will be demonstrated in a spreadsheet that might be used by a human resources manager to discuss a company's retirement plan with an employee. As mentioned earlier in the chapter, many companies offer some type of retirement plan for their employees. This example assumes that a company will contribute fifty cents for every dollar the employee contributes to his retirement plan. The worksheet shown in Figure 7.24 could be used by a human resources manger to show an employee the total annual investment that would be made into his retirement account. The **ISNUMBER** and **ISTEXT** functions will be used to display a message in cell B6 depending on the data that is entered into the spreadsheet.

Figure 7.24 | **Retirement Investment Worksheet**

	A	B	C	D	E	F
1	*Retirement Plan*					
2	Salary	Percent of Salary	Your Annual Investment	Company Annual Contribution	Total Annual Investment	Monthly Investment
3			$0	$0	$0	$0
4						
5						
6	Message:					
7						

The ISNUMBER and ISTEXT functions will be used in an IF function to produce instructions for using this worksheet here.

Formulas have been created in these cells to calculate an employee's retirement investment based on the salary and percent that is entered in cells A3 and B3.

Again, the output of the **ISNUMBER** or **ISTEXT** function is the word TRUE or the word FALSE. Figures 7.25 and 7.26 show the setup and results of these functions using a basic example. Notice that Figure 7.25 demonstrates only one argument for each function, which is usually defined by typing a cell location.

Figure 7.25 | **Setup of Basic ISNUMBER and ISTEXT Example**

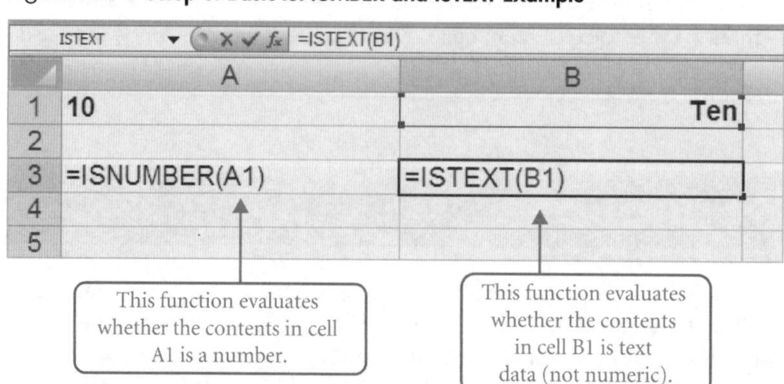

Figure 7.26 | **Results of Basic ISNUMBER and ISTEXT Example**

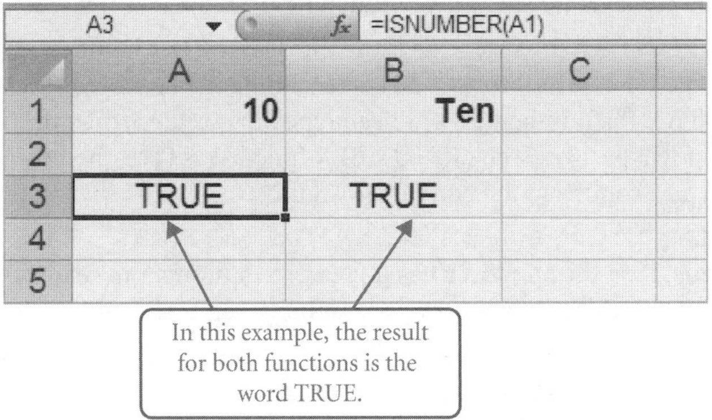

Figures 7.25 and 7.26 demonstrate the results of the **ISNUMBER** and **ISTEXT** functions when they are used independently. However, these functions are often used with an **IF** function to produce various outputs based on what is typed into a cell. The following explains how the **ISNUMBER** and **ISTEXT** functions are used with the **IF**, **AND**, and **OR** functions to produce instructions in cell B6 of the worksheet shown in Figure 7.24. The purpose of these instructions is to inform the employee what to type into cells A3 and B3 to calculate the amount of money that will be invested into a retirement account. A secondary goal is to inform the employee if the wrong information has been typed into a cell.

- Type an equal sign in cell B6 followed by the function name IF and an open parenthesis. The instructions displayed on this worksheet will be the output of a three-part nested **IF** function. The following is the **logical_test** and **value_if_true** arguments for the first **IF** function.
  - **logical_test:** `OR(ISTEXT(A3),ISTEXT(B3))=TRUE` This logical test is using a combination of the **OR** function and the **ISTEXT** function. The **OR** function is evaluating if *either* of the **ISTEXT** functions produces an output of TRUE. If either **ISTEXT** function is true, then the result of the **OR** function will be TRUE. If the result of the **OR** function is TRUE, the output of the function will be the instruction in the **value_if_true** argument. Type a comma at the end of this argument.
  - **value_if_true:** "You can only enter numeric values in cells A3 and B3." If the first logical test is true, then the function will tell the employee that only numbers can be entered into cells A3 and B3. As illustrated later in this segment, typing words into either cell A3 or cell B3 will produce errors in the formulas that were created in the worksheet. The **ISTEXT** function is being used to determine whether the employee inadvertently typed words or symbols into these cells. Type a comma to complete this argument.
- Define the **value_if_false** argument for the first **IF** function by starting a second **IF** function. The following is how the **logical_test** and **value_if_true** arguments should be defined for this second **IF** function.
  - **logical_test:** `AND (ISNUMBER(A3),ISNUMBER(B3))=TRUE` This is the second logical test in the nested IF function. The **AND** function is evaluating whether a number has been typed into both cells A3 and B3. If both **ISNUMBER** functions are true, then the **AND** function and this logical test are true. Type a comma to complete this argument.
  - **value_if_true:** `" "` If the second logical test is true, then the output of the function will be a blank cell. This is why this argument is defined using two quotation marks. Once numbers are typed into both cells A3 and B3, there are no required instructions or messages. Type a comma to complete this argument.

- Define the **value_if_false** argument for the second **IF** function by starting a third **IF** function. The three arguments for the third IF function are defined as follows.
    - **logical_test:** `ISNUMBER(A3)=FALSE` This is the third logical test in the nested **IF** function. The ISNUMBER function is determining if a number has been entered into cell A3. If a number has not been typed into cell A3, then the **ISNUMBER** function will be false. If the **ISNUMBER** function is false, then the logical test is *true*. Type a comma at the end of this argument.
    - **value_if_true:** `"Enter your annual salary in cell A3."` If the third logical test is true, then the employee has not entered a number in cell A3. Therefore, the instructions will tell the employee to enter an annual salary into cell A3.
    - **value_if_false:** `"Enter the percentage of your salary you wish to invest in cell B3."` If all three logical tests are false, then we can assume that a number has not been entered into cell B3, which is the percentage of the employee's salary that will be invested.
- Type three closing parentheses to complete the nested **IF** function and press the **Enter** key.

COMMON MISTAKES | Evaluating the Result of ISNUMBER/ISTEXT

When evaluating the result of an **ISNUMBER** or **ISTEXT** function in the logical test argument of an **IF** function, *do not use quotation marks.* Quotation marks are used to evaluate text data that is entered in a cell except when it is a TRUE or FALSE output from a function or formula.

Figure 7.27 shows the setup of the nested **IF** function in the Retirement Plan worksheet. Figures 7.28 through 7.30 show the results of the nested **IF** function as data is typed into cells A3 and B3.

Figure 7.27 | **Setup of Nested IF Function with ISNUMBER and ISTEXT Functions**

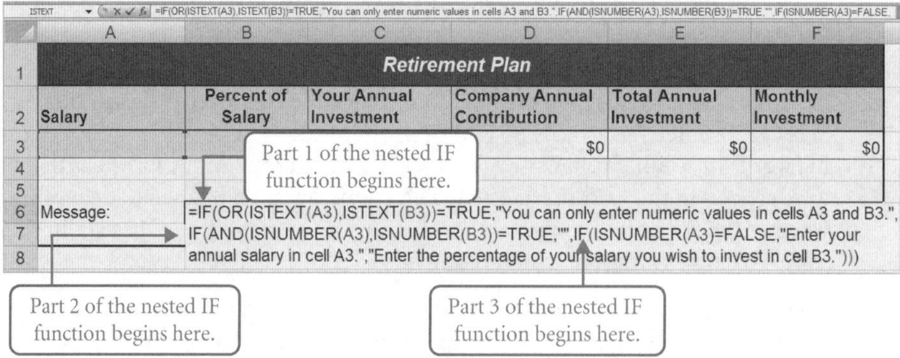

Figure 7.28 | **Results of Nested IF Function with ISNUMBER and ISTEXT Functions, Part 1**

	A	B	C	D	E	F
1	Retirement Plan					
2	Salary	Percent of Salary	Your Annual Investment	Company Annual Contribution	Total Annual Investment	Monthly Investment
3			$0	$0	$0	$0
4						
5						
6	Message:	Enter your annual salary in cell A3.				
7						

The function shows the third value_if_true argument because cell A3 is empty.

Figure 7.29 | **Results of Nested IF Function with ISNUMBER and ISTEXT Functions, Part 2**

	A	B	C	D	E	F
1	Retirement Plan					
2	Salary	Percent of Salary	Your Annual Investment	Company Annual Contribution	Total Annual Investment	Monthly Investment
3	$50,000		$0	$0		
4						
5						
6	Message:	Enter the percentage of your salary you wish to invest in cell B3.				
7						

The nested IF function shows this message because all logical tests are false.

Salary is typed into this cell.

Figure 7.30 | **Results of Nested IF Function with ISNUMBER and ISTEXT Functions, Part 3**

	A	B	C	D	E	F
1	Retirement Plan					
2	Salary	Percent of Salary	Your Annual Investment	Company Annual Contribution	Total Annual Investment	Monthly Investment
3	$50,000	10.00%	$5,000	$2,500	$7,500	$625
4						
5						
6	Message:					
7						

The output of the function is a blank cell since both cells A3 and B3 contain a number.

Figures 7.28 through 7.30 show the output of the nested **IF** function as numbers are being typed into cells A3 and B3. Figure 7.31 shows what will happen if the employee makes a mistake and types text data into cell B3. Notice that instead of typing a number, the employee typed 10 Percent. Notice that this causes an error in the formulas in the range C3:F3.

Figure 7.31 | **Results When Text Is Typed into Cell B3**

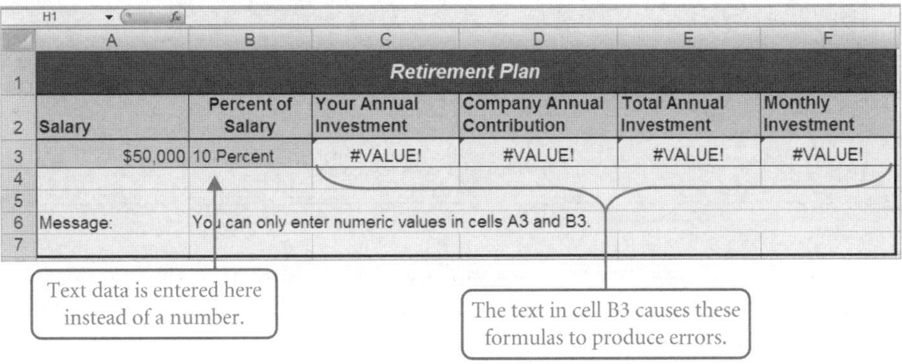

	A	B	C	D	E	F
1	Retirement Plan					
2	Salary	Percent of Salary	Your Annual Investment	Company Annual Contribution	Total Annual Investment	Monthly Investment
3	$50,000	10 Percent	#VALUE!	#VALUE!	#VALUE!	#VALUE!
4						
5						
6	Message:	You can only enter numeric values in cells A3 and B3.				
7						

You can use the **ISTEXT** function to prevent the #VALUE! error codes from being displayed in the range C3:F3 in Figure 7.31. These errors appear in the figure because text data was typed into cell B3 instead of a number. The following explains how the **ISTEXT** function is used along with the **OR** and **IF** functions to recreate the formulas in the range C3:F3 in Figure 7.31.

- Type an equal sign in cell C3 followed by the function name IF and an open parenthesis. The following text explains how each of the arguments in the **IF** function is defined.
  - **logical_test:** `OR(ISTEXT(A3),ISTEXT(B3))=TRUE` The **OR** function in this logical test is evaluating if either ISTEXT function is true. If text has been

typed into either cell A3 or cell B3, the **OR** function and the logical test will be true. Type a comma after this argument.

- **value_if_true:** `""` Typing text data into either cell A3 or cell B3 will cause an error to occur in the formula that calculates the amount of money the employee will be investing into the retirement account. Therefore, if the logical test is true, instead of executing a formula (which will produce an error), the function displays nothing in the cell. Type a comma after this argument.
- **value_if_false:** `B3 * A3` If the logical test for this function is false, either numbers or nothing has been typed into cell B3 or cell A3. Therefore, the formula for calculating how much money the employee is investing into a retirement account can be executed. This formula is taking the percent typed into cell B3 and multiplying it by the salary typed into cell A3.

- Type a closing parenthesis and press the **Enter** key to complete this **IF** function.

Figure 7.32 and 7.33 show the setup and results of the **IF** function used to calculate the amount of money the employee is investing into the retirement account. Notice that cell C3 in Figure 7.33 is blank. This is because text data is typed into cell B3.

Figure 7.32 | **Setup of the IF and ISTEXT Functions**

The cell will be blank if the logical test of this function is true.

=IF(OR(ISTEXT(A3),ISTEXT(B3))=TRUE,"",B3*A3)

	A	B	C	D	E	F
1	Retirement Plan					
2	Salary	Percent of Salary	Your Annual Investment	Company Annual Contribution	Total Annual Investment	Monthly Investment
3	$50,000	10 Percent	=IF(OR(ISTEXT(A3),ISTEXT(B3))=TRUE,"",B3*A3)			#VALUE!
4			IF(logical_test, [value_if_true], [value_if_false])			
5						
6	Message:	You can only enter numeric values in cells A3 and B3.				
7						

Figure 7.33 | **Results of the IF and ISTEXT Functions**

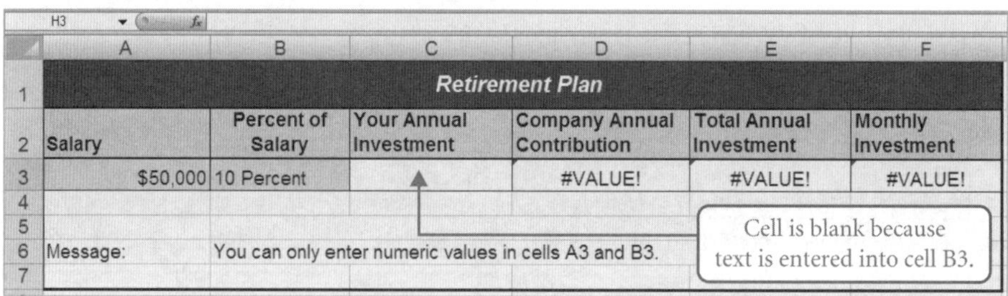

Figure 7.34 shows the final adjustments that were made to all of the formulas in the range C3:F3 in the Retirement Plan worksheet. Because text is entered into cell B3, these cells are now blank instead of displaying the #Value! error code. The following lists the IF functions that are used for cells D3, E3, and F3.

- **Cell D3:** `IF(OR(ISTEXT(A3),ISTEXT(B3))=TRUE,"",(A3 * B3) / 2)` This function will calculate the amount of money the company will contribute to the employee's retirement account if the logical test is not true. It was mentioned at the beginning of this section that the company will contribute fifty cents for every dollar invested by the employee. The formula takes the result of the employee's investment, which is the salary in cell A3 multiplied by the percent in cell B3, and divides it by 2.
- **Cell E3:** `IF(OR(ISTEXT(A3),ISTEXT(B3))=TRUE,"",C3+D3)` This function will calculate the total investment that will be made into the employee's retirement account if the logical test is false. The formula is adding the employee's investment in cell C3 to the Company's contribution in cell D3.

- **Cell F3:** `IF(OR(ISTEXT(A3),ISTEXT(B3))=TRUE,"",E3/12)` This function will calculate the monthly investment that will be made into the employees retirement account if the logical test is false. The formula is taking the total annual investment in cell E3 and dividing it by 12.

Figure 7.34 | **Final Results of the Retirement Plan Spreadsheet**

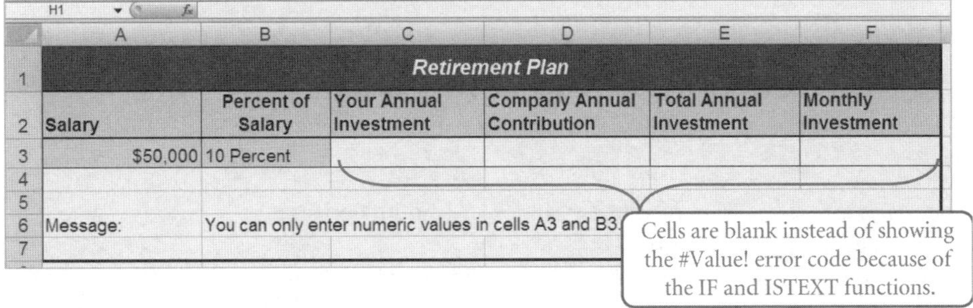

ISERROR Function

The **ISERROR** function is used to identify if the result of a formula or function produces an error. In Figure 7.32 the **ISTEXT** function was used in an **IF** function to prevent the formula from calculating the result of the employee's retirement investment if cells A3 and B3 contained text. The **ISERROR** function could have been used in this situation to serve the same purpose. However, in the case of Figure 7.32, the error occurs only if text data is typed into either cell A3 or B3. The **ISERROR** function is used in situations in which you may not know when or what will cause a formula or function to produce an error. As with the **ISTEXT** and **ISNUMBER** functions, the output of the **ISERROR** function is either TRUE or FALSE. Like most IS functions, the **ISERROR** function is rarely used independently and is usually used with an **IF** function.

Figure 7.35 shows a worksheet that will be used to demonstrate the **ISERROR** function. A human resources manager might use this worksheet to show an employee the current value of a retirement account. The worksheet also shows an employee how funds in her retirement account are invested. Companies often work with financial firms to offer their employees a variety of investment options for their retirement accounts. For example, one option could be a mutual fund that is a medium-risk investment with slow and steady growth. Another option could be a high-risk fund with the potential for either large gains or large losses.

>> **Quick Reference**

ISNUMBER Function

1. Activate a cell.
2. Type an equal sign.
3. Type the function name ISNUMBER and open parenthesis.
4. Type a cell location.
5. Type a closing parenthesis.
6. Press the **Enter** key.

Figure 7.35 | **Retirement Investment Details Worksheet**

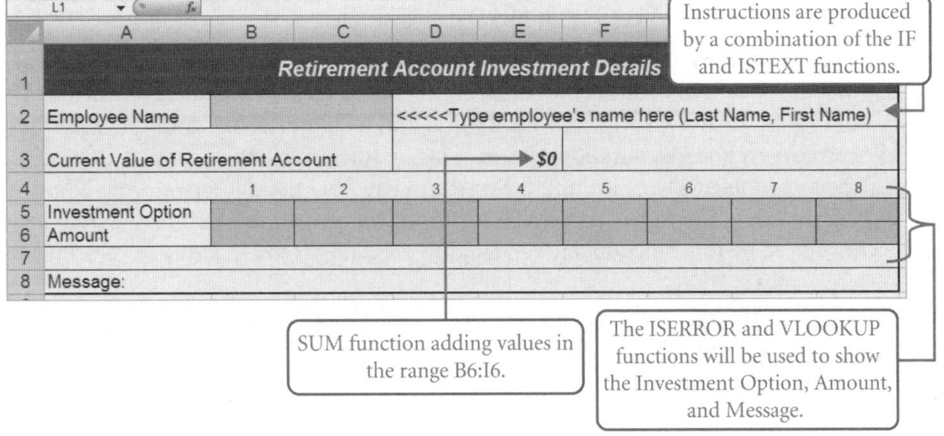

>> **Quick Reference**

ISTEXT Function

1. Activate a cell.
2. Type an equal sign.
3. Type the function name ISTEXT and an open parenthesis.
4. Type a cell location.
5. Type a closing parenthesis.
6. Press the **Enter** key.

Figure 7.36 shows the data that will be used to populate the worksheet in Figure 7.35. Notice that the investment options for each employee are listed vertically in column B. However, these options are listed horizontally in row 5 in Figure 7.35. This example will demonstrate how to display data that is listed in vertical columns in rows. This is a common problem in business because mangers typically receive data from a database system arranged in columns. However, they frequently work with spreadsheets that require the same data to be arranged in rows.

Figure 7.36 | **Data Worksheet with Investment Details by Employee**

F1

	A	B	C
1	Name	Investment Option	Amount Invested
2	Charles, Louis	Blue Chip Fund	$3,300
3	Jay, Jackie	Blue Chip Fund	$1,500
4	Ray, David	Blue Chip Fund	$4,400
5	Bee, Bernice	Company Stock	$4,500
6	Dee, Ed	Company Stock	$10,000
7	Charles, Louis	High Risk Fund	$1,800
8	Jay, Jackie	High Risk Fund	$2,500
9	Dee, Ed	Low Risk Fund	$5,000
10	Dee, Ed	Med Risk Fund	$5,000
11	Jay, Jackie	Money Market	$5,000
12	Bee, Bernice	Over Seas Fund	$3,200
13	Jay, Jackie	Over Seas Fund	$2,200
14			

The data in these two columns is displayed horizontally in rows 5 and 6 in Figure 7.35.

The following explains how the **ISERROR**, **VLOOKUP**, **CONCATENATE,** and **IF** functions are used to display data from the worksheet shown in Figure 7.36 to the worksheet shown in Figure 7.35. The data displayed in the Retirement Investment Details worksheet (Figure 7.35) will be based on the name that is typed into cell B2. The purpose of the first several points for this example is to prepare the Data worksheet in Figure 7.36. Then, the use of the **ISERROR** function combined with the **IF** and **VLOOKUP** functions are explained in the next part of this example.

- Sort the Data worksheet (Figure 7.36) based on the Name column in ascending order and the Amount Invested column in descending order. After sorting the worksheet, you will see the name of each employee appear several times. This is because an employee can invest their retirement money into eight different investment options.
- Type the number 1 in cell D2 in the Data worksheet.
- Type the following IF function in cell D3: `IF(A3=A2,1+D2,1)` The purpose of this function is to count the number of times each employee name appears in column A of the Data worksheet. The IF function will increase the count by 1 if the employee name in column A repeats. When a different name appears in column A, the logical test will be false and the function will start the count over from 1 (see Figure 7.37). The **CONCATENATE** function will be used to combine the numbers produced by this function and the employee's name to create a unique value in every row.
- Copy the **IF** function in cell D3 and paste it to the rest of the cells in the worksheet (see Figure 7.38).

Figure 7.37 | **Setup of IF Function to Count Duplicate Employee Names**

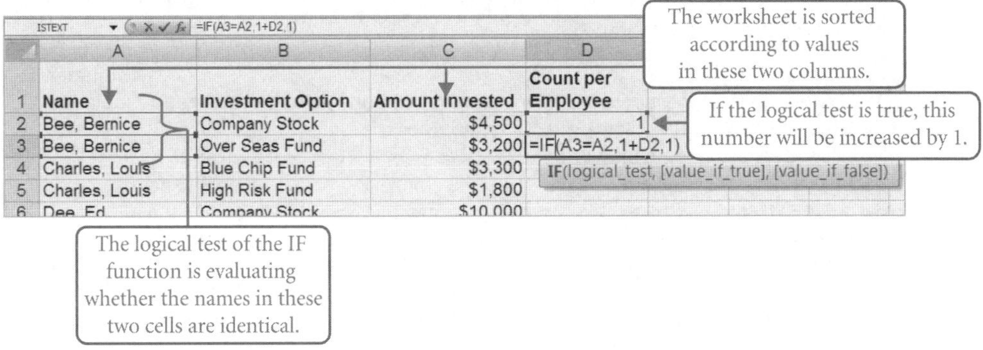

Figure 7.38 | **Results of IF Function to Count Duplicate Employee Names**

	A	B	C	D
1	Name	Investment Option	Amount Invested	Count per Employee
2	Bee, Bernice	Company Stock	$4,500	1
3	Bee, Bernice	Over Seas Fund	$3,200	2
4	Charles, Louis	Blue Chip Fund	$3,300	1
5	Charles, Louis	High Risk Fund	$1,800	2
6	Dee, Ed	Company Stock	$10,000	1
7	Dee, Ed	Low Risk Fund	$5,000	2
8	Dee, Ed	Med Risk Fund	$5,000	3
9	Jay, Jackie	Blue Chip Fund	$1,500	1
10	Jay, Jackie	High Risk Fund	$2,500	2
11	Jay, Jackie	Money Market	$5,000	3
12	Jay, Jackie	Over Seas Fund	$2,200	4
13	Ray, David	Blue Chip Fund	$4,400	1

This number is the result of the formula 1+D2, which is the value_if_true argument of the IF function.

Because the name in cell A9 does not equal the name in A8, the number 1 appears here, which is the value_if_false argument.

The following explains how the **CONCATENATE** function is used for this example:

- Insert a column to the left of column A in the Data worksheet (Figure 7.38).
- Type the following **CONCATENATE** function in cell A2: `CONCATENATE(E2,B2)` The purpose of this function is to combine the number produced by the IF function in cell E2 with the employee's name in cell B2. This creates a unique value in each row of the Data worksheet (see Figure 7.39). The reason for creating this unique value will become evident when the **VLOOKUP** function is used later in this example.
- Copy the **CONCATENATE** function in cell A2 and paste it to the rest of the cells in the worksheet (see Figure 7.40).

Figure 7.39 | **Setup of CONCATENATE Function Combining Count and Employee Name**

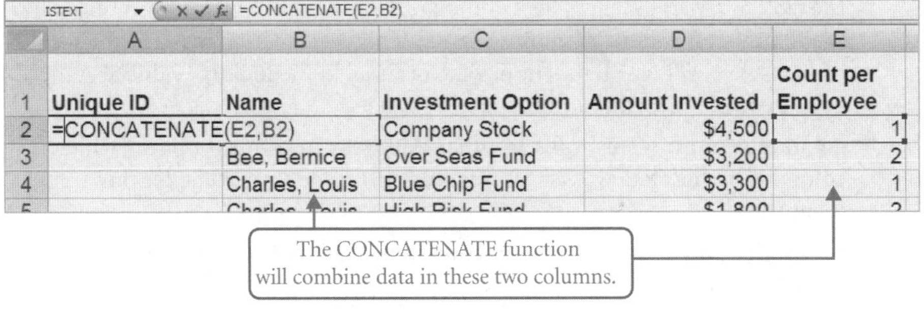

Figure 7.40 | **Results of CONCATENATE Function Combining Count and Employee Name**

The data in this column makes every row in the worksheet unique.

	A	B	C	D	E
1	Unique ID	Name	Investment Option	Amount Invested	Count per Employee
2	1Bee, Bernice	Bee, Bernice	Company Stock	$4,500	1
3	2Bee, Bernice	Bee, Bernice	Over Seas Fund	$3,200	2
4	1Charles, Louis	Charles, Louis	Blue Chip Fund	$3,300	1
5	2Charles, Louis	Charles, Louis	High Risk Fund	$1,800	2
6	1Dee, Ed	Dee, Ed	Company Stock	$10,000	1
7	2Dee, Ed	Dee, Ed	Low Risk Fund	$5,000	2
8	3Dee, Ed	Dee, Ed	Med Risk Fund	$5,000	3
9	1Jay, Jackie	Jay, Jackie	Money Market	$5,000	1
10	2Jay, Jackie	Jay, Jackie	High Risk Fund	$2,500	2
11	3Jay, Jackie	Jay, Jackie	Over Seas Fund	$2,200	3
12	4Jay, Jackie	Jay, Jackie	Blue Chip Fund	$1,500	4
13	1Ray, David	Ray, David	Blue Chip Fund	$4,400	1

COMMON MISTAKES | Sorting Duplicate Data in a Worksheet

Figure 7.40 shows the results of counting duplicate data entries in a column for the purposes of creating a unique ID value for each row. The most critical step in this process is sorting the data. You must remember to sort the worksheet using the column that contains duplicate values. Forgetting this step makes it impossible to accurately count the number of times an entry is duplicated in a column.

The following points explain why and how the **ISERROR** function is used for this example. The first set of points is designed to show you what happens if the ISERROR function is not used. The second set of points will then integrate the **ISERROR** function to complete this example.

- Type an equal sign in cell B5 of the Retirement Investment Details worksheet (see Figure 7.35) followed by the function name VLOOKUP and an open parenthesis. The following shows how each argument of the **VLOOKUP** function is defined.
  - **lookup_value:** `CONCATENATE(B4,$B$2)` The **CONCATENATE** function is defining the lookup value by combining the number in cell B4 with the employee's name in cell B2. Because this example assumes that employees can choose up to eight different options for investing their retirement money, row 4 contains cell locations numbered 1 through 8. The absolute reference used in cell B2 allows the function to be copied and pasted to the rest of the cells in row 5. Type a comma after this argument.
  - **table_array:** `Data!$A$2:$D$13` The table array is the range A2:D13 in the Data worksheet (Figure 7.40). Both the Data worksheet and the Retirement Investment Details worksheet are in the same workbook. The first column in the table array argument is the combination of the count number produced by the IF function and the employee's name. This combination matches the result of the CONCATENATE function, which is used in the **lookup_value** argument. Type a comma after this argument.
  - **col_index_num:** `3` This will select the employee's investment option, which is column C in the Data worksheet (Figure 7.40). Type a comma after this argument.
  - **[range_lookup]:** `False` This forces the function to search for exact matches to the lookup value.

- Complete the **VLOOKUP** function by typing a closing parenthesis (see Figure 7.41) and then press the **Enter** key.
- Copy the **VLOOKUP** function in cell B5 and paste it into the range C5:I5 (see Figure 7.42).

Figure 7.41 | **Setup of VLOOKUP Function in Retirement Investment Details Worksheet**

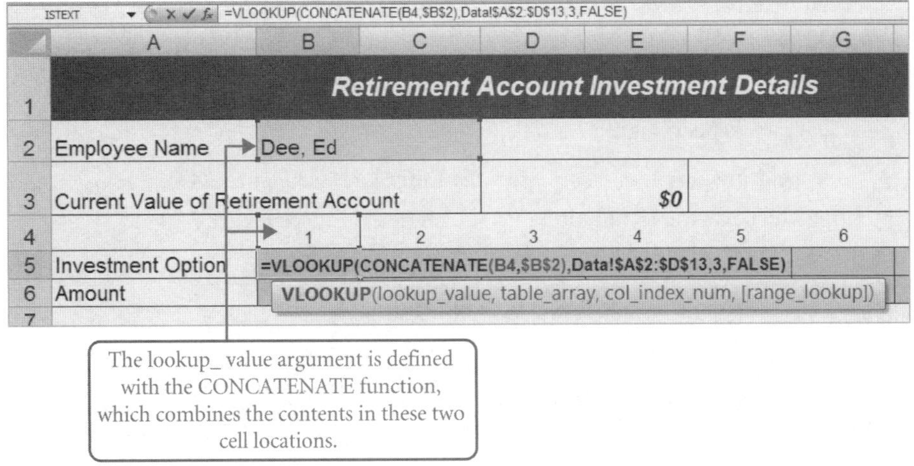

Figure 7.42 shows the results of the **VLOOKUP** function when it is pasted into the range C5:I5. A different investment option appears in each cell in row 5 because the **CONCATENATE** function is combining a different number with the employee name as the **VLOOKUP** function is pasted to the rest of the cells in the row. However, notice that in the range E5:I5, the error #N/A is displayed. This is because the employee entered into cell B5 is investing his retirement money in only three of the eight available options. In cell 5, the **VLOOKUP** function is looking for 4Dee, Ed in column A of the Data worksheet (see Figure 7.40), but it does not exist. This produces the #N/A error.

Figure 7.42 | **Results of VLOOKUP Function in Retirement Investment Details Worksheet**

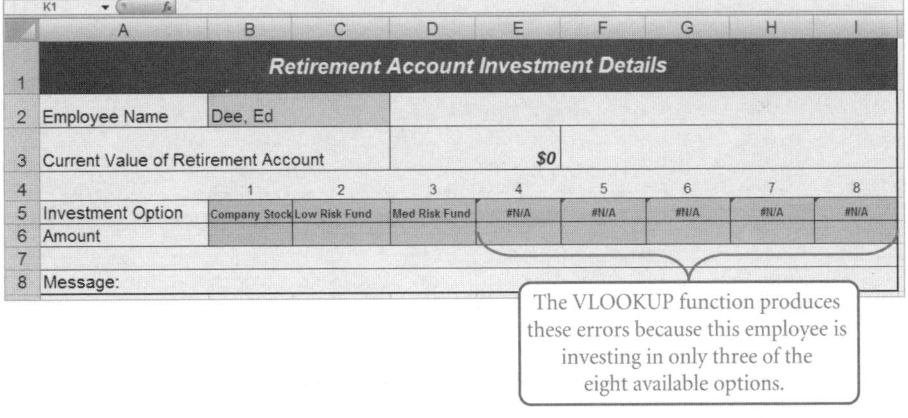

The errors displayed in Figure 7.42 can be removed by using the **VLOOKUP** function with the **ISERROR** and **IF** functions. The following explains how to recreate the function in cell B5 to display either the employee's investment option or a blank cell.

- Type an equal sign in cell B5 followed by the function name IF and an open parenthesis. The following explains how each argument of the function is defined.
  - **logical_test:** `ISERROR(VLOOKUP(CONCATENATE(B4,$B$2), Data!$A$2:$D$13,3,FALSE))=TRUE` The logical test is evaluating

whether the result of the **ISERROR** function is true. The **ISERROR** function is evaluating the **VLOOKUP** function that was illustrated in Figure 7.41. If the **VLOOKUP** function produces a #N/A error, the result of the **ISERROR** function will be true, which makes the logical test true. Type a comma after this argument.

- **value_if_true:** " " If the logical test is true, then the IF function will leave the cell blank. Type a comma after this argument.
- **value_if_false:** `VLOOKUP(CONCATENATE(B4,$B$2),Data!$A$2:$D$13,3,FALSE)` If the logical test is false then the **VLOOKUP** function is not producing an error. Therefore, the **VLOOKUP** function will be executed to pull the employee's investment option from the Data worksheet (Figure 7.40).

- Type a closing parenthesis and press the **Enter** key (see Figure 7.43).
- Copy and paste the **IF** function into the range C5:I5 (see Figure 7.44).

Figure 7.43 | **Setup of IF, ISERROR, and VLOOKUP Functions**

	A	B	C	D	E	F	G	H	I
1	Retirement Account Investment Details								
2	Employee Name	Dee, Ed							
3	Current Value of Retirement Account				$0				
4		1	2	3	4	5	6	7	8
5	Investment Option	=IF(ISERROR(VLOOKUP(CONCATENATE(B4,$B$2),Data!$A$2:$D$13,3,FALSE))=TRUE,"",VLOOKUP(							
6	Amount	CONCATENATE(B4,$B$2),Data!$A$2:$E$13,3,FALSE))							
7		IF(logical_test, [value_if_true], [value_if_false])							
8	Message:								

value_if_true argument

value_ if_false argument begins here.

Figure 7.44 | **Results of the IF, ISERROR, and VLOOKUP Functions**

	A	B	C	D	E	F	G	H	I
1	Retirement Account Investment Details								
2	Employee Name	Dee, Ed							
3	Current Value of Retirement Account				$0				
4		1	2	3	4	5	6	7	8
5	Investment Option	Company Stock	Low Risk Fund	Med Risk Fund					
6	Amount								
7									
8	Message:								

Cells are blank because the ISERROR function is making the logical test of the IF function true.

To complete the Retirement Account Investment Details worksheet, functions must be added for the Amount row and the Message. The function used to complete the Amount row, which begins in cell B6, is identical to the function used for the Investment Option row. However, the column index argument for the **VLOOKUP** function will be 4 instead of 3. The purpose of the Message row is to tell the user if a name that was typed into cell B2 does not exist in the Data worksheet (see Figure 7.40). The following explains these functions and the functions that were created in cells D2 and D3.

- **Amount Row** (begins with cell B6): `IF(ISERROR(VLOOKUP(CONCATENATE(B4,$B$2),Data!$A$2:$D$13,4,FALSE))=TRUE,"",VLOOKUP(CONCATENATE(B4,$B$2),Data!$A$2:$E$13,4,FALSE))` As previously mentioned, this function is identical to the one illustrated in Figure 7.43. However, the column index number is changed from 3 to 4. This will pull the dollar amount for each employee's investment.

- **Message** (cell B8): IF(ISTEXT(B2)=FALSE,"",IF(ISERROR (VLOOKUP(CONCATENATE(B4,B2),Data!A2:A13,1,FALSE))=TRUE, "There is no match for the name you entered. Check the spelling or type a new name.","")) The purpose of this function is to check if the name typed into cell B2 is listed at least one time in the Data worksheet. However, the function must first check if anything has been typed into cell B2. If the **ISTEXT** function in the first logical test is false, the cell will be left blank. If the **ISERROR** function in the second logical test is true, the message will tell the user that the name typed into the worksheet could not be found. If the result of the **ISERROR** function is false, the cell will be left blank.
- **Current Value of Retirement Account** (cell D3): Sum(B6:I6) The **SUM** function is totaling all of the values in the Amount row.
- **Initial Instructions** (cell D2): IF(ISTEXT(B2)=TRUE,"","<<<<<Type employee's name here (Last Name, First Name)") This function is evaluating if text data has been typed into cell B2. If cell B2 contains text data, cell D2 will be blank. If there is no text typed into cell B2, instructions will be provided in cell D2 telling the user to type an employee's name. Notice that the greater-than sign is used at the beginning of the message to create an arrow (see Figure 7.35).

Figure 7.45 shows the completed Retirement Account Investment Details worksheet. Figure 7.46 shows how the worksheet appears if a name typed into cell B2 does not match the name from the Data worksheet.

Figure 7.45 | **Completed Retirement Investment Details Worksheet**

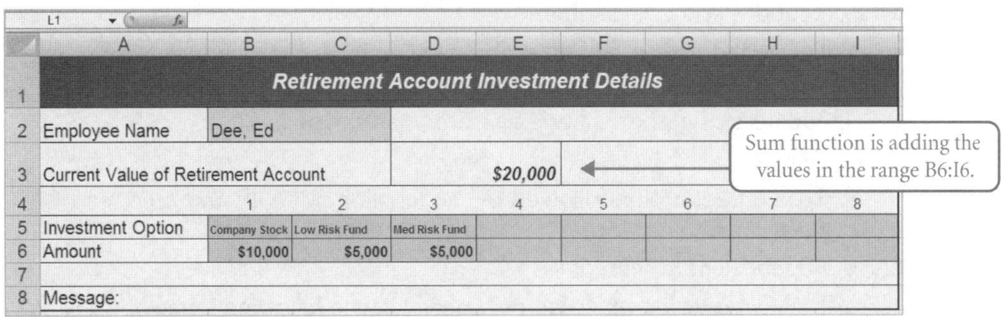

Figure 7.46 | **Retirement Investment Details Worksheet with Unknown Name**

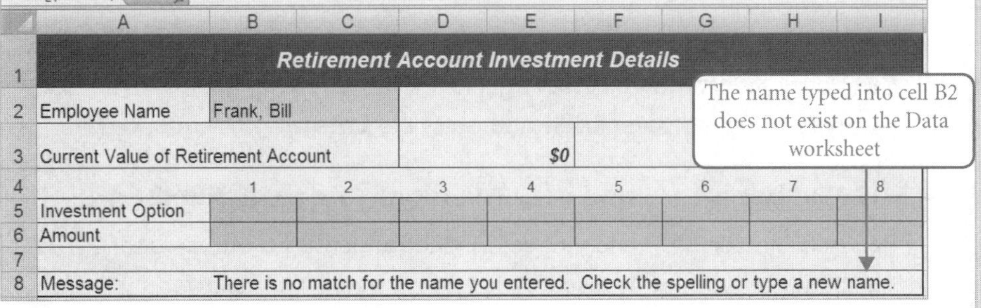

>> **Quick Reference**

ISERROR Function

1. Activate a cell.
2. Type an equal sign.
3. Type the function name ISERROR and open parenthesis.
4. Type a cell location that contains a formula or function or type a formula or function.
5. Type a closing parenthesis.
6. Press the **Enter** key.

VIDEO WORKSHOP

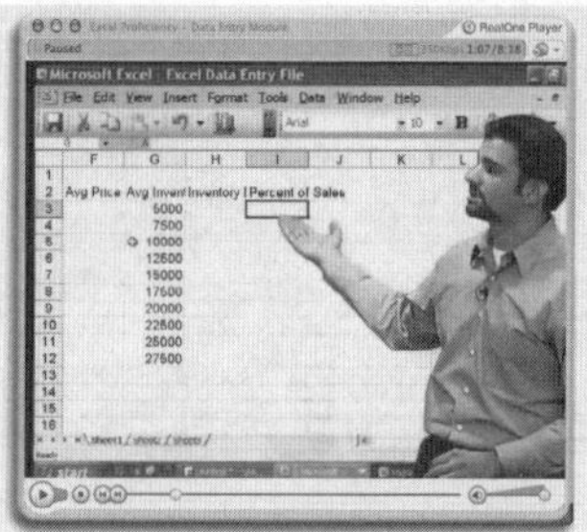

>> IS Text/IS Number Functions

The purpose of this workshop is to demonstrate the **IS TEXT** and **ISNUMBER** functions. I will be demonstrating the tasks in this workshop on the **IS Text** and **IS Number** videos. The name of the video will appear in parentheses next to the relevant section heading. Open the Excel workbook named ib_e07_istextisnumber. Complete each section of tasks first, and then watch the video pertaining to that section.

1. IS Text with IF and OR Functions (Video: IS Text)

a. Activate cell C3.
b. Type an equal sign followed by the function name `IF` and an open parenthesis.
c. Define the logical test of the IF function by typing the following **OR** function: `OR(ISTEXT(A3),ISTEXT(B3))`.
d. Complete the logical test by typing an equal sign and the word `TRUE`. Then, type a comma.
e. Define the **value_if_true** argument by typing two quotation marks followed by a comma.
f. Define the **value_if_false** argument with the following formula: `B3 * A3`.
g. Type a closing parenthesis and press the **Enter** key.
h. Activate cell D3.
i. Type an equal sign followed by the function name **IF** and an open parenthesis.
j. Repeat steps c. through e.
k. Define the **value_if_false** argument with the following formula: `(A3 * B3) / 2`.
l. Type a closing parenthesis and press the **Enter** key.
m. Activate cell E3.
n. Type an equal sign followed by the function name **IF** and an open parenthesis.
o. Repeat steps c. through e.
p. Define the **value_if_false** argument with the following formula: `C3 + D3`.
q. Type a closing parenthesis and press the **Enter** key.
r. Activate cell F3
s. Type an equal sign followed by the function name `IF` and an open parenthesis.
t. Repeat steps c. through e.
u. Define the **value_if_false** argument with the following formula: `E3/12`.
v. Type a closing parenthesis and press the **Enter** key.

2. IS Number with IF and AND Functions (Video: IS Number)

a. Activate cell B6. Note that cells in the range B6:F6 are merged.
b. Begin a nested **IF** function by typing an equal sign followed by the function name **IF** and an open parenthesis.
c. Define the first **logical_test** argument as follows: `OR(ISTEXT(A3),ISTEXT(B3))=TRUE,`

d. Type the following phrase in the first **value_if_true** argument: `"You can only enter numeric values in cells A3 and B3."` Complete the argument by typing a comma.
e. For the **value_if_false** argument, begin a second **IF** function by typing the function name `IF` followed by an open parenthesis.
f. Define the **logical_test** of the second **IF** function as follows: `AND(ISNUMBER(A3),ISNUMBER(B3))=TRUE,`
g. Define the **value_if_true** argument of the second **IF** function by typing two quotation marks followed by a comma.
h. For the **value_if_false** argument of the second **IF** function, begin a third **IF** function by typing the function name `IF` followed by an open parenthesis.
i. Define the **logical_test** argument of the third **IF** function by typing the following: `ISNUMBER(A3)=FALSE,`
j. Type the following phrase in the **value_if_true** argument for the third **IF** function: `"Enter your annual salary in cell A3."` Complete the argument by typing a comma.
k. Type the following phrase in the **value_if_false** argument: `"Enter the percentage of your salary you wish to invest in cell B3."`.
l. Complete the nested **IF** function by typing three closing parentheses.
m. Type the number `50000` in cell A3.
n. Type the number `10` in cell B3.
o. Type `10 Percent` in cell B3.
p. Save and close the workbook.

>> IS Error Function

VIDEO WORKSHOP

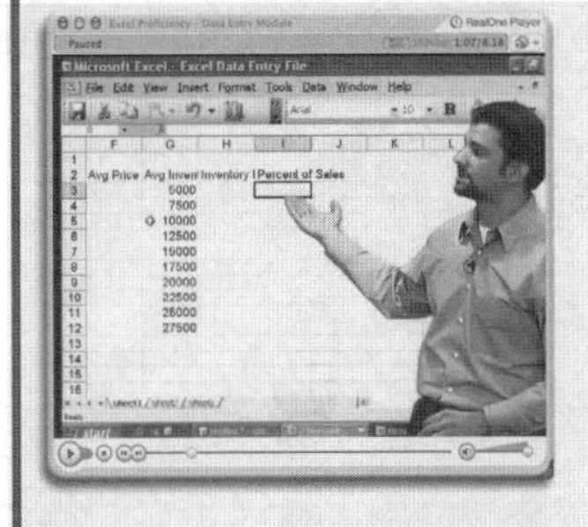

The purpose of this workshop is to demonstrate the IS Error function. I will be demonstrating the tasks in this workshop in the three videos named: **Unique Sequencing**, **IS Error**, and **IS Error and IS Text**. The name of the video will appear in parentheses next to the relevant section heading. Open the Excel file named ib_e07_iserror. Complete each section of tasks first, and then watch the video pertaining to that section.

1. Creating a Unique Sequence (Video: Unique Sequencing)

a. Activate the Data worksheet and highlight the range A1:C13.
b. Sort the data based on the Name column in ascending order and the Amount Invested column in descending order.
c. Type the column heading `Count per Employee` in cell D1.
d. Type the number `1` in cell D2.
e. Type an equal sign in cell D3 followed by the function name `IF` and an open parenthesis.
f. Define the logical test of the function with the formula `A3=A2` and type a comma.
g. Define the **value_if_true** argument with the formula `1 + D2` and type a comma.

h. Define the **value_if_false** by typing the number `1`. Complete the function by typing a closing parenthesis and press the **Enter** key.
i. Copy cell D3 and paste it into the range D4:D13.
j. Activate cell A2 and insert a column.
k. Type the column heading `Unique ID` in cell A1.
l. Type an equal sign in cell A2 followed by the function name `CONCATENATE` and an open parenthesis.
m. Type cell `E2` followed by a comma and then cell `B2`.
n. Complete the function by typing a closing parenthesis and press the **Enter** key.
o. Copy cell A2 and paste it into cell A3:A13.

2. Displaying Vertical Data Horizontally (Video: IS Error)

a. Activate the Investment Detail worksheet.
b. Activate cell B5 and type an equal sign followed by the function name `IF` and an open parenthesis.
c. Define the logical test of the **IF** function by typing the function name `ISERROR` followed by an open parenthesis.
d. Type the following **VLOOKUP** function after the open parenthesis of the `ISERROR` function: `VLOOKUP(CONCATENATE(B4,$B$2),Data!$A$2:$D$13,3,FALSE)`
e. Complete the **ISERROR** function by typing a closing parenthesis.
f. Complete the logical test of the **IF** function by typing an equal sign followed by the word `TRUE` and a comma.
g. Define the **value_if_true** argument by typing two quotation marks followed by a comma.
h. Define the **value_if_false** argument by typing the same **VLOOKUP** function listed in step d.
i. Complete the **IF** function by typing a closing parenthesis and press the **Enter** key.
j. Copy cell B5 and paste it into the range C5:I5 using the **Formulas** option from the **Paste** icon.
k. Activate cell B6 and type an equal sign followed by the function name `IF` and an open parenthesis.
l. Define the logical test of the **IF** function by typing the function name `ISERROR` followed by an open parenthesis.
m. Type the following **VLOOKUP** function after the open parenthesis of the ISERROR function: `VLOOKUP(CONCATENATE(B4,$B$2),Data!$A$2:$D$13,4,FALSE)`
n. Complete the **ISERROR** function by typing a closing parenthesis.
o. Complete the logical test of the **IF** function by typing an equal sign followed by the word `TRUE` and a comma.
p. Define the **value_if_true** argument by typing two quotation marks followed by a comma.
q. Define the **value_if_false** argument by typing the same **VLOOKUP** function listed in step m.
r. Complete the **IF** function by typing a closing parenthesis and press the **Enter** key.
s. Copy cell B6 and paste it into the range C6:I6 using the **Formulas** option from the **Paste** icon.

3. Instructions and Messages (Video: IS Error and IS Text)

a. Activate the Investment Detail worksheet.

b. Activate cell D3 and use the **SUM** function to total the values in the range B6:I6.

c. Activate cell D2 and type an equal sign followed by the function name `IF` and an open parenthesis.

d. Define the **logical_test** argument by typing the following function: `ISTEXT(B2)`.

e. Complete the logical test by typing an equal sign followed by the word `TRUE` and a comma.

f. Define the **value_if_true** argument by typing two quotation marks and a comma.

g. Define the **value_if_false** argument by typing the following phrase: `"<<<<<Type employee's name here (Last Name, First Name)"`

h. Complete the **IF** function by typing a closing parenthesis and press the **Enter** key.

i. Activate cell B8 and begin a nested **IF** function by typing an equal sign, the word `IF`, and an open parenthesis.

j. Define the first **logical_test** argument by typing the following function: `ISTEXT(B2)`

k. Complete the first **logical_test** argument by typing an equal sign followed by the word `FALSE` and a comma.

l. Define the first **value_if_true** argument by typing two quotation marks and a comma.

m. Start the second **IF** function by typing the function name `IF` followed by an open parenthesis.

n. Define the second **logical_test** argument by typing the function name `ISERROR` followed by an open parenthesis.

o. Type the following **VLOOKUP** function after the open parenthesis of the ISERROR function: `VLOOKUP(CONCATENATE(B4,B2),Data!A2:A13,1,FALSE)`

p. Complete the **ISERROR** function by typing a closing parenthesis.

q. Complete the second **logical_test** argument by typing an equal sign followed by the word `TRUE` and a comma.

r. Define the second **value_if_true** argument by typing the following phrase: `"There is no match for the name you entered. Check the spelling or type a new name."`

s. Type a comma and define the **value_if_false** argument by typing two quotation marks.

t. Complete the nested **IF** function by typing two closing parentheses and press the **Enter** key.

u. Type the name `Dee, Ed` in cell B2.

v. Type the name `Charles, Louis` in cell B2.

w. Type your name in cell B2 (Last Name, First Name).

x. Save and close the workbook.

EXERCISE

Why Do I Need This?

>> Sales and Profit Plans

One of the key benefits of using Excel to make business decisions is that one spreadsheet design can be used by all managers in a department. This makes it possible for a department or company to execute consistent standards for calculating certain business metrics. For example, a business might have a specific profit requirement for every product it sells. You can design an Excel spreadsheet that includes the calculations for this profit requirement that can be used by every manager making product decisions in the company. However, the challenge of designing a spreadsheet that will be used by other people is that it must provide some direction as to the type of data that needs to be typed into certain cells, and it must notify the user if any data has been typed incorrectly. Without these instructions, you may be looking into many false claims that your spreadsheet does not work. Many instructions and messages can be added to a spreadsheet using the **ISNUMBER**, **ISTEXT**, and **ISERROR** functions.

Exercise

The purpose of this exercise is to develop a spreadsheet that might be used by the buyers of a small retail company. This spreadsheet will help the buyers plan the price and unit sales for items that will be sold in their company's retail stores. Open the Excel workbook named ib_e07_salesandprofittargets before completing the tasks listed below.

1. Enter the first set of instructions in cell C3 (cells C3:E3 are merged). Use an **IF** function to instruct the user to enter the Item Cost into cell B3. Define each of the arguments for this function as follows:
   a. **logical_test:** `ISNUMBER(B3)=TRUE` Use the **ISNUMBER** function to determine if a number has been typed into cell B3.
   b. **value_if_true:** `""` If a number has been typed into cell B3, then the function should leave the cell blank.
   c. **value_if_false: "<<<Enter the item cost here."** If a number has not been typed into cell B3, then the function should display the instructions. The less-than signs are used to point to cell B3.
2. Use the same **IF** function you created in step 1 to display instructions for the Retail Price in cell C4 (cells C4:E4 are merged). **The logical_test** argument should determine if a number has been typed into cell B4. The **value_if_false** argument should read `"<<<Enter the planned retail price here."`
3. Calculate the Gross Profit in cell B5 using the **ISERROR** and **IF** functions. The formula for calculating the Gross Profit is `B4-B3`. However, if the user types text data in cells B3 or B4, the formula will produce an error. Therefore, use the **ISERROR** function in the **logical_test** argument to determine if the formula B4-B3 produces an error. If the formula produces an error, then leave the cell blank. Otherwise, calculate the Gross Profit.
4. Calculate the Net Profit in cell B6 using the same method described in step 3. The formula for calculating the Net Profit is `B5 - (B4 * 0.1)`. This formula is taking 10% of the retail price and subtracting it from the Gross Profit. The 10% is accounting for any freight, warehousing, and stocking costs. As stated in step 3, use the **ISERROR** function in the **logical_test** argument to check if the formula produces an error. If so, then leave the cell blank.
5. Use an **IF** function to provide instructions in cell D7 (cells D7:E7 are merged). This **IF** function is identical to the one described in step 1. However, the

ISNUMBER function in the **logical_test** argument will be evaluating cell C7. The **value_if_false** argument should read `"<<Override unit sales here."` The purpose of cell C7 is to allow the buyer to overwrite the calculated Planned Unit Sales number in cell B7 (see next step).

6. Create a three-part nested IF function in cell B7 to calculate the Planned Unit Sales. The purpose of cell B7 is to show the buyer the minimum number of units that must be sold to reach the company's minimum profit target of $10,000 per item. However, as stated in step 5, the buyer can override this number by typing a new sales plan number in cell C7. The following shows how each argument of this nested **IF** function should be defined.
   a. **logical_test:** `B6<=0` This test is evaluating if the value in cell B6, which is the Net Profit, is less than or equal to 0. If the net profit is not greater than 0, then the item should not be sold.
   b. **value_if_true:** `""` If the first logical test is true, then the function will leave the cell blank. This will prevent the buyer from planning any unit sales because the item is losing money for the company.
   c. **logical_test 2:** `ISNUMBER(C7)=TRUE` This is the second **logical_test** of the nested IF function. This logical test is evaluating whether the buyer typed a number into C7. If the buyer wants to overwrite the calculated Planned Unit Sales, a number can be typed into cell C7, which will be displayed in this cell.
   d. **value_if_true 2:** `C7` This is the second **value_if_true** argument for the nested IF function. If the buyer typed a number in cell C7, then it will be displayed in this cell.
   e. **logical_test 3:** `ISERROR(10000/B6)` This is the third **logical_test** of the **nested IF** function. This logical test will evaluate whether the formula for calculating the Planned Unit Sales produces an error.
   f. **value_if_true 3:** `""` This is the third **value_if_true** argument of the nested IF function. If the third logical test is true, then the function will leave the cell blank.
   g. **value_if_false:** `10000/B6` This is the **value_if_false** argument for the third IF function. This is the formula for calculating the number of units that must be sold to reach the company's minimum profit target of $10,000. Therefore, the number 10000 is divided by the value in cell B6, which is the Net Profit for the item.

7. Create an **IF** function in cell B8 to calculate the Planned Profit. This **IF** function serves the same purpose as the one created in step 3. Use the **ISERROR** function in the **logical_test** argument to determine if the formula produces an error. If the logical test is true, leave the cell blank. The Planned Profit is calculated by multiplying the Net Profit in cell B6 by the Planned Unit Sales in cell B7 (B6 * B7).

8. Create a four-part nested **IF** function to display a message in cell B10 based on what the buyer types into cells B3, B4, and C7 (cells B10:E10 are merged). Define each argument of the function as follows.
   a. **logical_test:** `OR(ISTEXT(B3),ISTEXT(B4))=TRUE` This test is determining whether the buyer typed text data into either cell B3 or cell B4.
   b. **value_if_true:** `"This spreadsheet will accept only numeric values."` If the first logical test is true, then the function will display this message telling the buyer that only numeric values can be typed into the spreadsheet.
   c. **logical_test 2:** `AND(ISNUMBER(B3),ISNUMBER(B4))=FALSE` This is the second logical test of the **nested IF** function. This is determining if a number has been typed into *both* cells B3 and B4.

d. **value_if_true 2:** `""` This is the second **value_if_true** argument for the **nested IF** function. If the second logical test is true, it is assumed that the buyer has not finished typing the cost and retail price information into cells B3 and B4. Therefore, the cell will be left blank.

e. **logical_test 3:** `B6 <= 0` This is the third logical test for the **nested IF** function. This test is determining if the Net Profit is less than or equal to 0. This is the same logical test that was used in step 6a.

f. **value_if_true 3:** `"Net Profit is negative—Do not purchase this item at the current plan."` This is the third **value_if_true** argument for the **nested IF** function. If the third logical test is true, then the function will notify the buyer that the company will lose money if this item is sold.

g. **logical_test 4:** `B8 < 10000` This is the fourth logical test of the **nested IF** function. This test will determine if the Planned Profit in cell B8 is less than the company's minimum profit target of $10,000. The reason for this test is to ensure that any sales number the buyer types into cell C7 achieves the company's minimum profit target of $10,000.

h. **value_if_true 4:** `"Item is currently planned below the company's minimum profit standard of $10,000."` This is the fourth value_if_true argument of the **nested IF** function. If the fourth logical test is true, then the function will notify the buyer that the current plan is not sufficient to achieve the company's minimum profit target.

i. **value_if_false:** `""` This is the **value_if_false** argument for the fourth **IF** function. If all logical tests in the function are false, then there is no need to display a message. Therefore, the cell will be left blank.

9. Type an Item Cost of `12.35` in cell B3 and a Retail Price of `15.99` in cell B4. What is the minimum number of units that must be sold to reach the company's minimum profit target of $10,000?

10. Type the number `2500` in cell C7. Notice the message in cell B10 stating that the current plan is below the company's minimum profit target.

11. Determine how much the buyer can pay a supplier for this item by decreasing the item cost in cell B3. At what cost will the item achieve the minimum profit target of $10,000?

12. Type a retail price of `9.99` in cell B4. Notice the message informing the buyer that the Net Profit is negative. In addition, notice that the Planned Unit Sales in cell B7 is blank.

13. Type the word `"Ten"` in cell B3. Notice the message in cell B10.

14. Type an item cost of `11.39` in cell B3. What retail price should the buyer charge if he is trying to generate $25,000 of profit on planned unit sales of 2,500?

15. Delete the values in cells B3, B4, and C7.

16. Save and close the workbook.

>> What's Wrong with This Spreadsheet?

PROBLEM & EXERCISE

Problem

You are working as a director for a small finance company that manages investments for approximately 100 customers. These customers trust your firm to invest money they will need for future events such as retirement, children's college tuition, or a new home purchase. One of the analysts in the firm creates an Excel spreadsheet to help the company manage these investments more efficiently. He explains that a customer's investments will automatically be grouped and displayed into six investment categories. He attaches the Excel file to an e-mail and includes the following points in his message.

1. I developed this Excel spreadsheet using data for only a few customers so you can see how it works. I added the investment information for the following customers to the Data worksheet: Bill Frank, Louis Charles, Olivia Angelo, Bernice Blu, and Albert Henry.
2. Type a customer's name in cell B2 and you will see his investments displayed in rows 5 and 6. Row 7 shows the percentage each investment category contributes to the customer's total account value. You must type the customer's last name first followed by a comma and then the first name.
3. Thanks for looking at this file! I really think this Excel spreadsheet will help us stay on top of the market by evaluating more investments over a shorter period of time.

Exercise

The Excel file the analyst attached to the e-mail is named ib_e07_customerinvestments. Would you be comfortable using this file to make investment decisions for your customers? Consider the following points:

1. Test the spreadsheet by typing a few names listed at the end of point 1 above into cell B2 in the Investment Detail worksheet. Follow the directions the analyst provides in point 2. Does the spreadsheet work? Do you see the customer's investments in rows 5 and 6?
2. Does the spreadsheet accurately display and total a customer's investments?
3. Does the spreadsheet show any error codes? Why?
4. Try typing your own name in cell B2. What happens?
5. Did the spreadsheet provide any instructions or messages as you typed names into B2? What messages or instructions would you add?

What's wrong with this spreadsheet? Write a short answer for each of the questions listed above. Then, fix any errors you find. In addition, add any instructions or messages to the Investment Detail worksheet that you identified in question 5.

Excel in **Practice** | Anecdote

Solution from page 294

Excel's Date functions played a key role in solving the problem of identifying the age of my client's customers to determine their mandatory IRA distributions. In addition, a key technique to completing this project was combining other functions such as the **IF**, **ISNUMBER**, **ISERROR**, and **VLOOKUP** functions to create a spreadsheet that would be easy to use by other analysts working in the firm. After completing the project, we ran several tests to ensure that the spreadsheet was accurately calculating each customer's age and the required withdrawal amounts from the IRA accounts.

Assignment

1. Open the file named ib_e07_iraproject. This file contains data similar to that used in the project that was explained in the anecdote.
2. The purpose of this assignment is to complete the IRA Analysis worksheet. This worksheet contains four items in column A that need to be displayed when a customer's name is typed into cell B2. The following is a list of formulas and features that must be designed into this worksheet:
   a. Cell B3 should display the date the customer will reach the age of 70.5.
   b. Cell B4 should indicate (Yes or No) if the customer is required to withdraw money from her IRA. Customers must make a withdrawal if they reached the age of 70.5 on or before December 31 last year.
   c. Cell B5 should calculate the required withdrawal amount if cell B4 indicates Yes. This is calculated by dividing the current value of the IRA account (column C in the Customer Data worksheet) by one of the distribution factors in column B of the Distribution Factor worksheet. The formula is `Current Value of IRA Account / Distribution Factor`. You will need to determine the customer's age *on his birthday last year* to identify the distribution factor that should be used in this calculation.
   d. Cell C5 in the IRA Analysis worksheet should allow the user to type an alternate IRA Distribution Amount. If a number is typed into cell C5, it should appear in cell B5.
   e. Cell B7 should be used to notify the user if the customer name typed into cell B2 does not exist, or if the alternate distribution amount typed into cell C5 is less than the required distribution that is calculated in item 2c.
3. Add any instructions you think are appropriate to the worksheet.
4. Format the spreadsheet so that it has a professional appearance and is easy to read.

Questions for Discussion

1. The anecdote discussed freeing up the analysts' time through the use of Excel. What other benefits can electronic spreadsheets bring to a company like an investment firm?

2. The author mentions in the anecdote that the spreadsheet was tested. Explain why it is important to test a spreadsheet such as the one described in this anecdote. What are some key points you would hope to learn or validate from testing a spreadsheet?

3. The anecdote mentioned that several functions were used together to produce a spreadsheet that could be used by any analyst in the firm. What are the benefits of creating a spreadsheet that can be used by several people? What techniques can you apply that will make a spreadsheet flexible and easy to use?

Review Questions

The following questions are related to the concepts addressed in this chapter. There are three types of questions: Short Answer, True or False, and Fill in the Blank. If your answer to a True or False question is False, write a short explanation as to why you think the statement is not true.

1. The ______________ function will always display the current date in a cell.
2. Explain why it is best not type the current date into a cell when calculating data such as a person's age or the amount of time a machine has been in use at a factory.
3. The date Serial Number for September 15, 2007, is 39340. What is the date Serial Number for October 15, 2007?
4. True or False: If a number appears in a cell after typing a date, the date was typed incorrectly. For example, 4/12/2007 will appear as a number instead of a date.
5. True or False: The **YEAR, MONTH,** and **DAY** functions are used only to define the three arguments of the **DATE** function.
6. If you wanted to add 10 years to the date 10/21/2007, explain why adding 3650 days would not give you a result of 10/21/2017.
7. What would be the result of the following **CONCATENATE** function if it were typed into a cell: =CONCATENATE("A3"," ","B3")
8. True or False: If the **#Name?** error appears in a cell when using the **CONCATENATE** function, there is an error in one of the cells that is used in the arguments of the function.
9. The number ______________ will appear in a cell as a result of the following **LEN** function: `=LEN("Vice President")`
10. The number ______________ will appear in a cell as a result of the following **SEARCH** function: `=SEARCH(",","Birds, And, Trees",9)`
11. True or False: Spaces cannot be used in the **find_text** argument of a **SEARCH** function because spaces are not recognized as characters in Text functions.
12. The letter ______________ will appear in a cell as a result of the following **MID** function: `=MID("Outstanding",5,1)`
13. True or False: The following **IF** function can be used to evaluate if a number was typed into cell A3: `=IF(ISNUMBER(A3)="True","Yes","No")`
14. Explain how the **ISERROR** function can be used to prevent an error code from appearing in a cell.
15. To create a column of unique values in a worksheet that contains data that is duplicated several times, the worksheet must be ______________ based on the column that contains ______________ data.

Skills Exam

The following exam is designed to test your ability to recognize and execute the Excel skills presented in this chapter. Read each question carefully and answer the questions in the order they are listed. You should be able to complete this exam in 60 minutes or less.

1. Open the file named ib_e07_chapter7skillsexam.
2. Activate the Color Detail worksheet and use the **CONCATENATE** function in cell A2 to combine the data in cells B2 and D2. The data in cell B2 must appear first.
3. Copy cell A2 and paste it into the range A3:A23.
4. Activate the Order Worksheet and enter the **TODAY** function in cell B6.
5. Calculate the Delivery Date in cell B8 by adding cell B7 to today's date in cell B6. Format the date in cell B8 to the Short Date format.
6. Use the **DATE** function to calculate the In Store Date in cell B9. The In Store Date will be exactly 3 months after the Received Date in cell B8. Use the **YEAR**, **MONTH**, and **DAY** functions to define the **year**, **month**, and **day** arguments of the **DATE** function.
7. In cell D11, enter the **LEN** function to count the characters in cell B5.
8. In cell C11, use the **SEARCH** function to count the number of characters in cell B5 up to and including the space. The function should begin counting from the first character in the cell. Note that there is only one space in the Manufacturer Model Number entered in cell B5.
9. In cell B11, use the **MID** function to select only the last two digits of the Manufacturer Model Number entered in cell B5. You must use cells C11 and D11 when defining the arguments of this function.
10. Use an **IF** function in cell B13 to calculate the Order Quantity in Cartons. Use the **ISNUMBER** function in the **logical_test** argument to determine if a number has been typed into cell C13. If the logical test is true, then display whatever number had been typed into cell C13. If the logical test is false, calculate the Order Quantity in Cartons by dividing B11 into B10.
11. Create a two-part nested **IF** function in cell B17 to display one of three different outputs. Use the **ISTEXT** function in the first logical test to determine if text data has been typed into cell C13. If the first logical test is true, display the message **"You can type only numeric data into cell C13."** The second logical test should evaluate whether cell B14 is equal to cell B10. If cell B14 does not equal B10, display the message **"Order quantity does not match unit sales plan."** If both logical tests are false, leave cell B17 blank.
12. Use an **IF** function to display instructions in cell A2. Use the **OR** function in the **logical_test** argument to determine if a number or text data has been typed into cell B4. If the logical test is true, leave cell A2 blank. If the logical test is false, display the instruction **"Enter an item description or number in cell B4."**
13. Use the **VLOOKUP**, **ISERROR**, and **IF** functions in cell C4 to display the colors of the item typed into cell B4. Use an **ISERROR** function in the **logical_test** argument of an **IF** function to determine whether the **VLOOKUP** function produces an error. If the logical test is true, then leave cell C4 blank. If the logical test is false, then execute the **VLOOKUP** function. The following explains how each argument of the **VLOOKUP** function should be defined.
    a. **lookup_value:** Use the **CONCATENATE** function to combine the data in cells B4 and C3. Cell B4 must be added to the function first followed by cell C3. Add an absolute reference to cell B4.
    b. **table_array:** The range A2:D23 in the Color Detail worksheet. You must use an absolute reference on this range.
    c. **col_index_num:** 3
    d. **[range_lookup]:** FALSE
14. Copy cell C4 and paste it into the range D4:I4 using the **Formulas** option.
15. Save and close your workbook.

Challenge Questions

The following questions are designed to test your ability to apply the Excel skills you have learned to complete a business objective. Use your knowledge of Excel and your creativity to answer these questions. For most questions, there are several possible ways to complete the objective.

1. Open the Excel workbook named ib_e07_challengea. This file contains a list of machine serial numbers in column A. The serial number is divided into four parts separated by one space. The first part is the model number of the machine. The second part is the capacity of the machine in pounds. The third part is the year the machine was manufactured. The fourth part is the processing time of the machine in hours. Use the information contained in these serial numbers to create a spreadsheet with the following information and features:

a. Show the model number for each machine in a separate column.

b. Show the age of the machine based on today's date in a separate column.

c. Calculate the number of batches *each* machine can produce depending on the operating hours of the factory. A batch is calculated by dividing the processing time of the machine in hours into the factory operating hours. Create the spreadsheet so that a user can enter the factory operating hours in one cell that will be used to calculate the batches for all machines.

d. Calculate the total capacity for each machine by multiplying the capacity of each machine in pounds by the number of batches you calculated in step 1c.

e. Show the total capacity of the factory by summing the total capacity for all machines.

f. Include any formatting and instructions that would make your spreadsheet easy to read and use.

2. Open the Excel workbook named ib_e07_challengeb. The DJIA Trend worksheet shows the adjusted average close of the Dow Jones Industrial Average every month for the past 4 years. Create a spreadsheet using this data that contains the following information and features:

a. Allow the user to type a year into a cell that will be used to display the data in step b.

b. Display the adjusted closing price of the DJIA *horizontally in a row* for 12 months based on the year that was typed into a cell by a user in step a.

c. Calculate the percent change of the DJIA for all 12 months in a row below the adjusted closing price that was constructed in step b.

d. Construct your spreadsheet so that no error codes appear in any cell displaying data.

e. Include any formatting and instructions that would make your spreadsheet easy to read and use.

3. Research the *monthly* adjusted closing stock price for any three public companies for the years 2004 and 2005. Place your data into an Excel worksheet (you can download this data from the Internet for free from a site such as Yahoo Finance). Construct a spreadsheet that allows the user to type a stock symbol in one cell and the year in another. Display the adjusted closing price for the stock and the year typed by the user. Your spreadsheet should include the same information and features listed in steps b through e in question 2.

Chapter 8

Managing Large Volumes of Data

Chapter Goals

The purpose of this chapter is to review tools that you can use to manage large volumes of data in Excel. Excel can store over 1 million rows of data in a single worksheet; however, summarizing and analyzing this volume of data can be challenging. Although Microsoft Access is usually the tool of choice to manage and analyze large volumes of data, Excel includes several tools you can use to perform this task. In the first section of this chapter, you will learn how PivotTables summarize large amounts of data into a two dimensional grid using various mathematical computations such as Sum, Average, Count, and so on. The second section of this chapter will then review three additional tools that are used to apply specific functions to analyze large volumes of data: Filters, Subtotals, and List Boxes.

Excel | Skill Sets

PivotTables

- Creating a New PivotTable
- Adding Fields and Changing Field Settings
- Applying Filters to Fields
- Adding and Removing Report Totals
- Adding Formulas (Calculated Fields)
- Sorting Data
- PivotCharts

Tools for Selecting and Summarizing Data

- Filters
- Subtotals
- Adding the Developer Tab
- List Boxes

Excel in Practice | Anecdote

Managing Data for a Strategy Team

When I worked in the Strategic Planning department for a large retail corporation, we frequently worked with large volumes of data. The company managed almost 2,000 stores and collected customer transaction data from every cash register in every store. This amounted to almost 10,000 cash registers transmitting sales transactions to the company's database everyday. As a result, most analytical projects that I managed usually involved thousands of rows of data. To analyze this volume of data, I usually used tools such as Microsoft Access. For one project in particular, however, the team asked me to use Excel to analyze over 7,500 rows of data. This was a large project that was managed by a team of 20 people, and involved the financial and physical evaluation of over 1,500 stores across the U.S. The data assembled for this project included five years of key statistics for every store in the company, such as population growth, sales, number of competitor stores, and the average distance customers traveled to get to the store. Most members on the team were not familiar with Access, but they all used Excel. In addition, the type of analysis that a team member needed to conduct would vary depending on the district of stores that was being evaluated. For example, some team members needed to focus on statistics such as population growth; others needed to focus on the growth in the number of competitors. I knew how to do this type of analysis in Access, but was not sure if I could accomplish the same results using Excel.

>> **Continued on page 392**

PivotTables

Skill Set

PivotTables are a valuable Excel feature used for summarizing and analyzing large volumes of data. This section demonstrates how a PivotTable is used to evaluate customer shopping patterns for a large retail corporation. Most business executives would agree that the level of success you achieve in any industry depends on how well you listen to and stay in touch with your customers. This usually requires the collection and evaluation of large amounts of data. For example, Figure 8.1 shows a worksheet containing customer shopping patterns for stores in three regions of a hypothetical retail corporation (East, West, and South). The worksheet contains five years of data for each region, and 750 rows of data. It can be a challenge to evaluate this data and identify any significant trends in customer buying patterns; however, a PivotTable can quickly turn this large volume of data into valuable trend information.

Figure 8.1 | **Retail Customer Data**

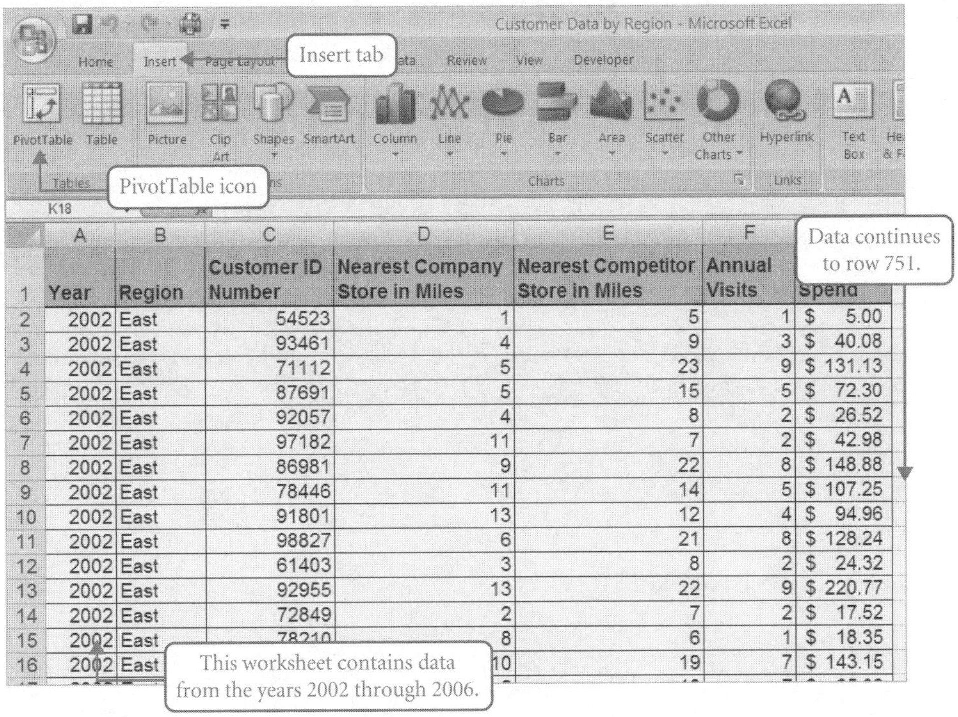

	A	B	C	D	E	F	G
1	Year	Region	Customer ID Number	Nearest Company Store in Miles	Nearest Competitor Store in Miles	Annual Visits	Spend
2	2002	East	54523	1	5	1	$ 5.00
3	2002	East	93461	4	9	3	$ 40.08
4	2002	East	71112	5	23	9	$ 131.13
5	2002	East	87691	5	15	5	$ 72.30
6	2002	East	92057	4	8	2	$ 26.52
7	2002	East	97182	11	7	2	$ 42.98
8	2002	East	86981	9	22	8	$ 148.88
9	2002	East	78446	11	14	5	$ 107.25
10	2002	East	91801	13	12	4	$ 94.96
11	2002	East	98827	6	21	8	$ 128.24
12	2002	East	61403	3	8	2	$ 24.32
13	2002	East	92955	13	22	9	$ 220.77
14	2002	East	72849	2	7	2	$ 17.52
15	2002	East	78210	8	6	1	$ 18.35
16	2002	East		10	19	7	$ 143.15

Creating a New PivotTable

This example shows the construction of a PivotTable using the data in Figure 8.1 to summarize the five-year trend in Annual Visits (column F) and Annual Spend (column G) for each region. In addition, the distance the customers live from the company's stores is compared to the distance they live to a competitor's store (column D vs. E). The results of this analysis could be used by a marketing manager to develop specialized advertising and promotional strategies for each region to maintain and grow a company's business. The following explains how the PivotTable is initially created.

- Click the down arrow of the **PivotTable** icon in the **Insert** tab of the Ribbon and then select the **PivotTable** option. This will open the **Create PivotTable** dialog box.
- Click the range finder next to the **Table/Range** box. Highlight all of the data on the worksheet including the column headings and then press the **Enter** key. If you activated any cell location in your data range prior to opening the **PivotTable** dialog box, Excel will come up with a suggested cell range. Check this range to ensure it covers all the data you need to create your PivotTable.

- Select the New Worksheet option near the bottom of the **Create PivotTable** dialog box (see Figure 8.2). This will place the PivotTable in a new worksheet in the workbook.
- Click the **OK** button at the bottom of the **Create PivotTable** dialog box. This will add a new worksheet that contains the tools you need to build the PivotTable (see Figure 8.3).

Figure 8.2 | **Settings in the Create PivotTable Dialog Box**

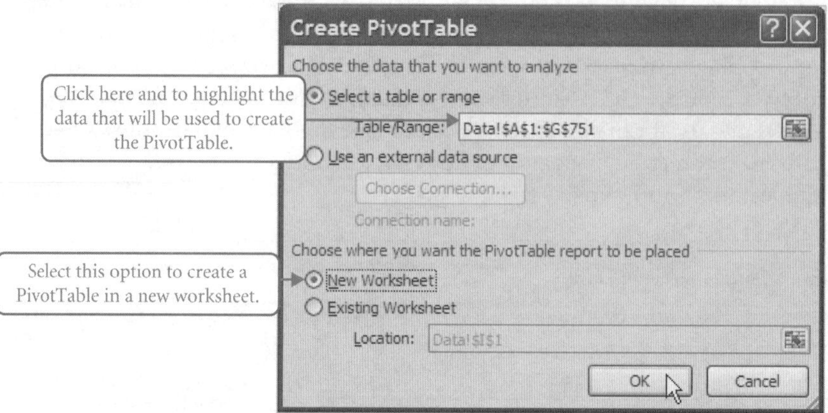

COMMON MISTAKES | Defining the Data Range for a PivotTable

When defining the Table/Range in the **Create PivotTable** dialog box, be sure to include the column headings in the first row of the range. These column headings will become the field names in the PivotTable Field List. If there are no column headings included in your data range, the PivotTable Field List will show the value that is typed into the first cell of each column. This will make it difficult to identify what data you are placing into the PivotTable Report.

Figure 8.3 | **Tools for Creating a PivotTable**

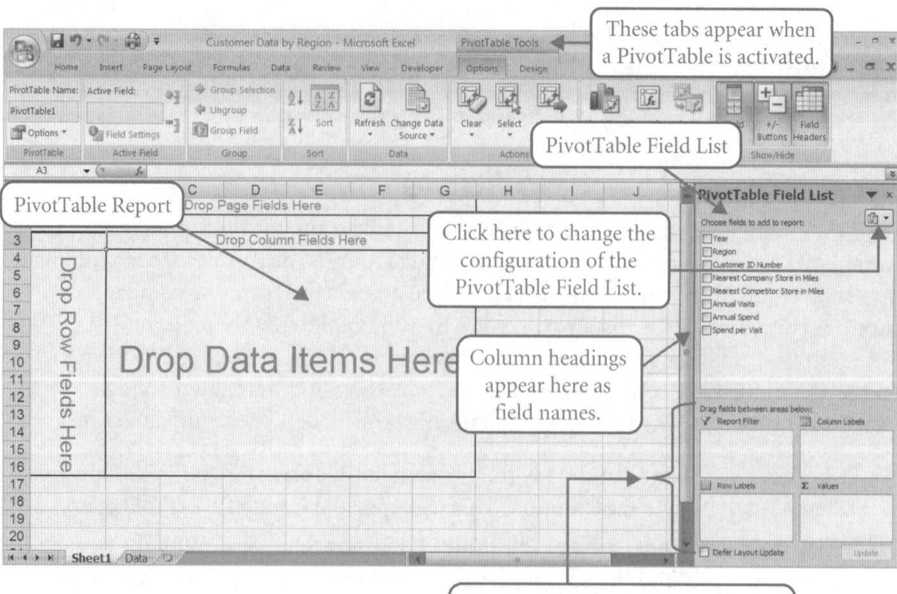

COMMON MISTAKES | You Can't Drag Fields onto This PivotTable

If your PivotTable looks similar the following figure, you will not be able to click and drag fields onto it from the PivotTable Field List. You must first change the settings in the **PivotTable Options** dialog box. To do this, click anywhere in the blank PivotTable and then click the **Options** icon in the **Options** tab of the Ribbon. This will open the **PivotTable Options** dialog box. Click the **Display** tab at the top of the **PivotTable Options** dialog box, and select the **Classic PivotTable layout (enables dragging of fields in the grid)** option; then, click the **OK** button at the bottom of the dialog box to apply this setting to your PivotTable.

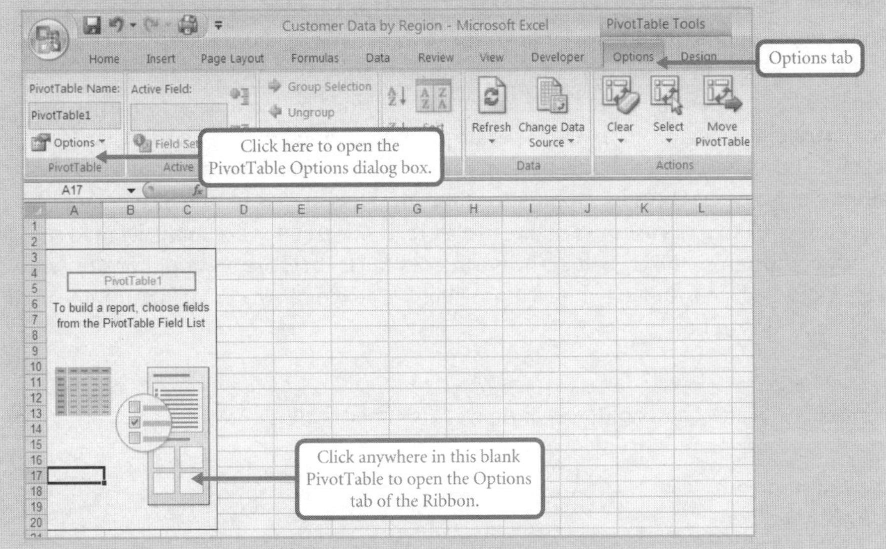

Figure 8.3 shows the tools that are used to construct a PivotTable. The following is a brief definition of each one:

- **PivotTable Field List:** This is a list of the column headings that are contained in the first row of the Table/Range in the **Create PivotTable** dialog box (see Figure 8.2). When building PivotTables, each column of data is referred to as a *field.* For example, the column heading Annual Visits in cell F1 in Figure 8.1 is considered the Annual Visits field when constructing a PivotTable. Fields from the upper area of the PivotTable Field List can be dragged down to one of the four locations in the lower section to place data onto the PivotTable Report.
- **PivotTable Report:** This area is used to construct and analyze the final results of the PivotTable. Fields can be dragged from the PivotTable Field List over to the PivotTable Report to place data in specific locations.
- **PivotTable Tools:** When a PivotTable is created or activated, the **Options** and **Design** tabs get added to the Ribbon (see Figure 8.3). These tabs contain commands that are used to adjust the settings and appearance of the PivotTable.

Quick Reference

Creating a New PivotTable

1. Click the drop-down arrow of the **PivotTable** icon in the **Insert** tab of the Ribbon and then select the **PivotTable** option.
2. Define the Table/Range in the **Create PivotTable** dialog box. If a range is provided, check it to ensure it contains all the data that is required for your PivotTable. To create a new range, click the range finder, highlight the range of cells that contain data for the PivotTable, and press the **Enter** key.
3. Select either New Worksheet or Existing Worksheet near the bottom of the **Create PivotTable** dialog box.
4. Click the **OK** button at the bottom of the **Create PivotTable** dialog box.

COMMON MISTAKES | Data Consistency Within a Column

Each column of data that is used for a PivotTable must contain only numeric or text data and not a combination of both. If a column contains a mix of both types of data, the PivotTable will not be able to conduct mathematical calculations and summaries. This problem occurs mostly in situations where the letters NA are used for a numeric value that is not available for specific row of data. Instead of using the letters NA, it is better to leave the cell blank or use the number zero.

Adding Fields and Changing Field Settings

The purpose of creating a PivotTable for the Retail Customer Data worksheet (Figure 8.1) in this example is to evaluate trends in the Annual Visits, Distance to Company Store, and Distance to Competitor Store. The information provided by this analysis could be used by a marketing manager to develop specific promotion and advertising strategies by region. The first analysis that will be demonstrated is the average number of times a customer visits a store. The opportunity of selling products in a retail store is measured by the number of visits a customer makes to a store. If this trend is declining, it could significantly compromise the growth of the business because there are fewer opportunities to sell products to a customer. Figure 8.4 provides a sketch of how a PivotTable can be used to evaluate this trend.

Figure 8.4 | **Sketch Showing Design of Annual Visit Trend Table**

	2002	2003	2004	2005	2006
East					
West	Average store visits per customer will be displayed here				
South					
Total Company					

Each row will show the five-year store visit trend for each region and for the entire company.

The following explains how the sketch in Figure 8.4 is produced by using the PivotTable tools shown in Figure 8.3.

- Click anywhere in the PivotTable Report section. This will show the PivotTable Field List, and activate the **Options** and **Design** tabs on the Ribbon.
- Click the Year field in the PivotTable Field List and then drag it over to the Column Fields section of the PivotTable report. This will show the years 2002 through 2006 across the top of the PivotTable report (see Figure 8.8). You can also click and drag the Year field into the Column Labels section in the lower area of the PivotTable Field List. This will place the years 2002 through 2006 across the top of the PivotTable report.
- Click the Region field in the PivotTable Field List, and drag it over to the Row Fields section of the PivotTable Report. This will list the three regions down the left side of the report. You can also click and drag this field into the Row Labels section in the lower area of the PivotTable Field list.
- Click the Annual Visits field in the PivotTable Field List, and drag it to the Data section of the PivotTable Report. As soon as this field is dragged into the PivotTable Report, all 750 rows of data are immediately summed for each region for every year. This data will be changed to *average* visits per customer by adjusting the field properties, which is covered next. You can also click and drag this field into the Values section in the lower area of the PivotTable Field list.

Figure 8.5 shows the process of dragging fields from the PivotTable Field List to the PivotTable Report. Notice that an icon appears when a field is dragged over to the PivotTable Report indicating where a field is being placed.

Figure 8.5 | **Dragging Fields into the PivotTable Report**

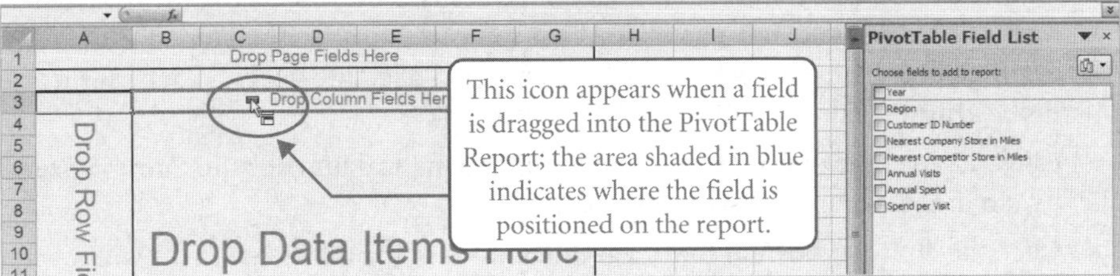

Figure 8.6 shows the results of adding the Year field to the Column Fields section of the PivotTable report. Notice that this field also appears in the Column Labels section in the lower area of the PivotTable Field List.

Figure 8.6 | **Column Fields Section of the PivotTable Report**

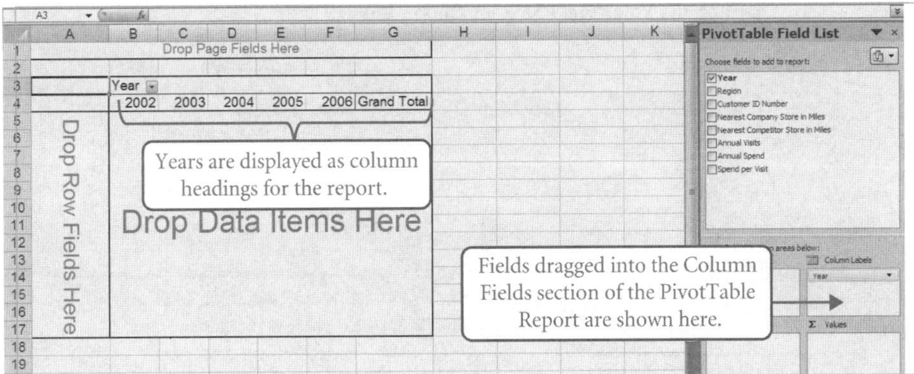

Figure 8.7 shows the completed PivotTable designed to match the sketch shown in Figure 8.4. Notice that the Annual Visits field, which was dragged into the Data section of the PivotTable Report, is shown in the Values section in the lower area of the PivotTable Field List. The words *Sum of* precede the field name because the PivotTable is showing the sum of all the Annual visits.

Figure 8.7 | **Region and Annual Visits Fields Added to the PivotTable Report**

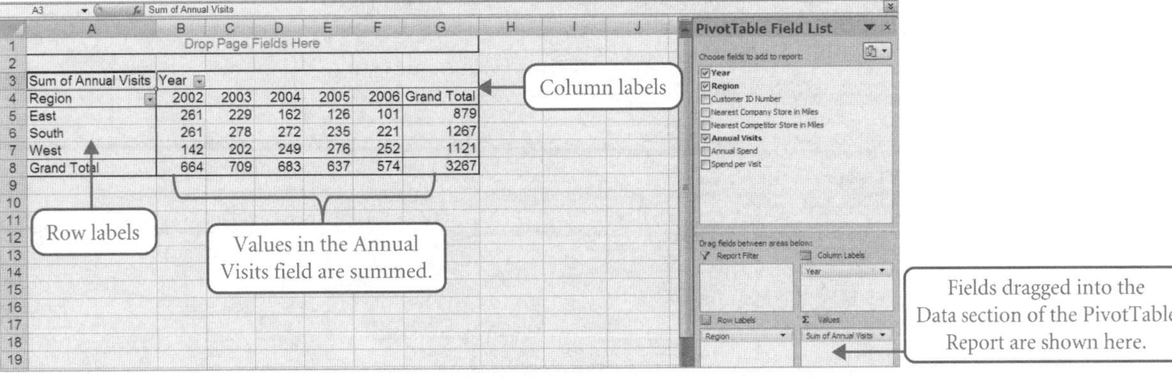

The goal for the PivotTable sketch shown in Figure 8.4 is to show the average customer visits per store. The sum of the Annual Visits field in Figure 8.7 will be changed to an average by adjusting the field settings. The following explains how this is accomplished.

- Double-click the Annual Visits field in the PivotTable Report (see cell A3 in Figure 8.7). Because the annual visits are being summed for all customers by region by year, Excel renames the field Sum of Annual Visits. Double-clicking the field will open the **Value Field Settings** dialog box. You can also open the **Value Field Settings** dialog box by clicking the field and then selecting the **Field Settings** icon in the **Options** tab of the Ribbon (see Figure 8.8).
- Click the **Average** option from the list of mathematical functions in **Summarize by** tab in the dialog box (see Figure 8.9).
- Click the **Number Format** button at the bottom of the dialog box. This will open the **Number** tab of the **Format Cells** dialog box. Select the **Number** option and set the decimal places to 1.
- Click the **OK** button at the bottom of the **Value Field Settings** dialog box. This will change the results in the PivotTable to show an average of the values in the Annual Visits field.

Figure 8.8 | **Opening the Value Field Settings Dialog Box**

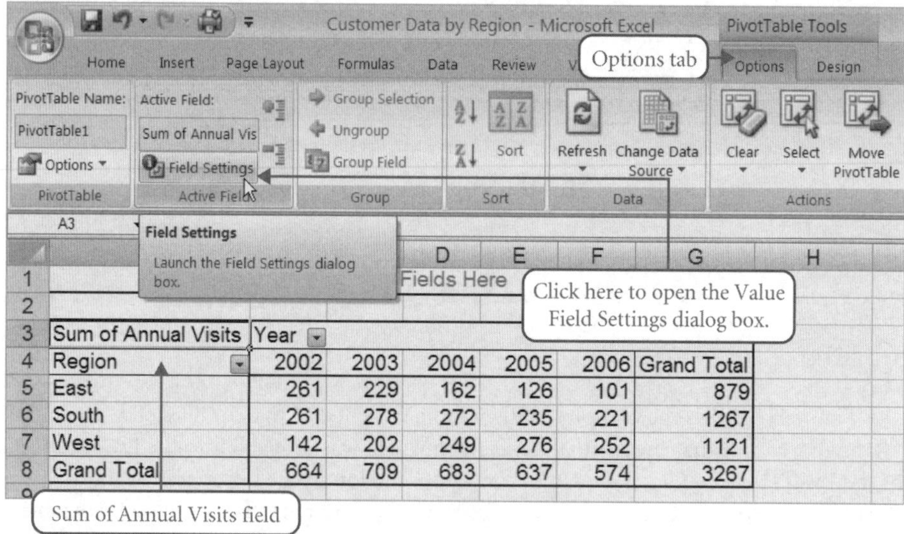

Sum of Annual Visits	Year					
Region	2002	2003	2004	2005	2006	Grand Total
East	261	229	162	126	101	879
South	261	278	272	235	221	1267
West	142	202	249	276	252	1121
Grand Total	664	709	683	637	574	3267

Figure 8.9 | **Value Field Settings Dialog Box**

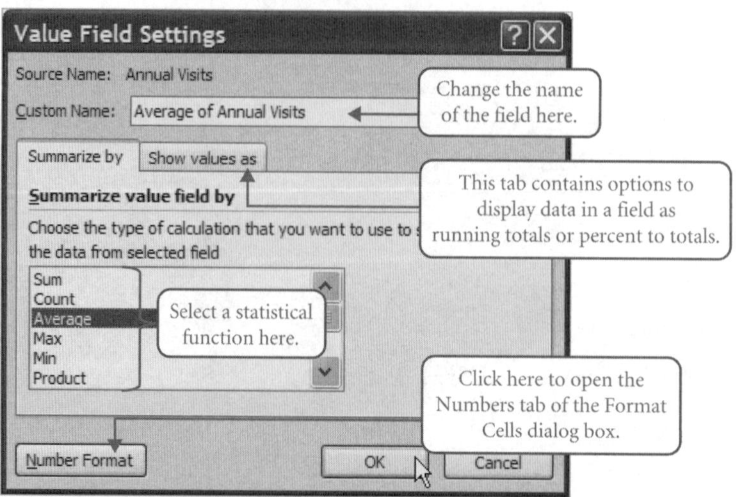

Figure 8.10 shows the results of computing the average number of times a customer visits a company store per region. A marketing manager can immediately see that the East region is experiencing a significant decline in customer visits. In the year 2002, a customer visited a company store in the East region an average of 5.2 times per year. By the year 2006, however, this number drops to 2.0. A marketing manager for this company will need to analyze additional data for this region to understand why customers are not visiting the company's stores as often as they did in 2002.

Figure 8.10 | **Results of Changing the Annual Visits Field Properties**

A3 — Average of Annual Visits

	A	B	C	D	E	F	G
1		Drop Page Fields Here					
2							
3	Average of Annual Visits	Year					
4	Region	2002	2003	2004	2005	2006	Grand Total
5	East	5.2	4.6	3.2	2.5	2.0	3.5
6	South	5.2	5.6	5.4	4.7	4.4	5.1
7	West	2.8	4.0	5.0	5.5	5.0	4.5
8	Grand Total	4.4	4.7	4.6	4.2	3.8	4.4
9							
10							

The trend for the East region shows a significant decline in customer visits.

The arrangement of the PivotTable in Figure 8.10 assumed that a marketing manager could easily evaluate the annual visit trends by placing the years across the top and listing the region names down the left side. However, after the PivotTable is constructed, the data can be manipulated into a few different configurations depending on your preference. For example, the PivotTable shown in Figure 8.11 was created by clicking the Year field in the Column Fields section and then dragging it over to the Row Fields section. This adjustment is also known as *pivoting*, which is why this is called a PivotTable. This can also be accomplished from the lower area of the PivotTable Field List. You can click and drag the Year field from the Column Labels section to the Row Labels section.

Figure 8.11 | **Results of Pivoting the Year Field**

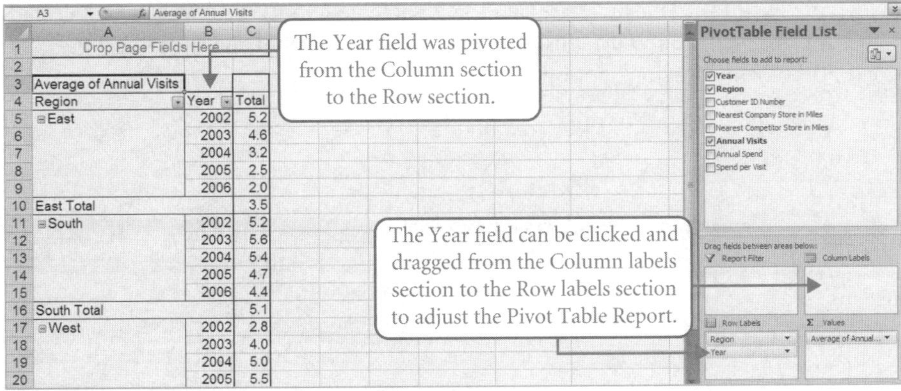

	A	B	C
3	Average of Annual Visits		
4	Region	Year	Total
5	East	2002	5.2
6		2003	4.6
7		2004	3.2
8		2005	2.5
9		2006	2.0
10	East Total		3.5
11	South	2002	5.2
12		2003	5.6
13		2004	5.4
14		2005	4.7
15		2006	4.4
16	South Total		5.1
17	West	2002	2.8
18		2003	4.0
19		2004	5.0
20		2005	5.5

Applying Filters to Fields

As previously mentioned, the PivotTable in Figure 8.10 reveals a significant decline in the number of visits a customer makes to stores in the East region. A marketing manager can apply a filter to the Region field in the PivotTable to isolate the East region and add more fields to determine why this decline is taking place. The following explains how this filter is applied.

- Click the drop-down arrow next to the Region field in the PivotTable Report area. This will open a list of filter options for this field (see Figure 8.12).

>> **Quick Reference**

Adding Data to a PivotTable

1. Click anywhere in the PivotTable Report to open the PivotTable Field. List and activate the **PivotTable Tools** tabs of the Ribbon.
2. Click a field in the PivotTable Field List, and drag it over to one of the sections of the PivotTable Report. You can also click and drag a field to one of the sections in the lower area of the PivotTable Field List.

>> **Quick Reference**

Changing Field Settings

1. Click a field name in one of the sections of the PivotTable Report.
2. Click the **Field Settings** icon in the **Options** tab of the Ribbon.
3. Select a statistical function in the **Summarize by** tab in the **Value Field Settings** dialog box.
4. Click the **Number Format** button to open the **Number** tab of the **Format Cells** dialog box to format the values in a field.
5. Click the **OK** button in the **Format Cell** dialog box (if opened).
6. Click the **OK** button in the **Value Field Settings** dialog box.

- Click the box next to the **(Select All)** option. This will remove the check marks next to each region.
- Click the box next to the East region. A black check mark will appear.
- Click the **OK** button. The PivotTable will be reduced to only the East region (see Figure 8.13).

Figure 8.12 | **Applying a Filter to the Region Field**

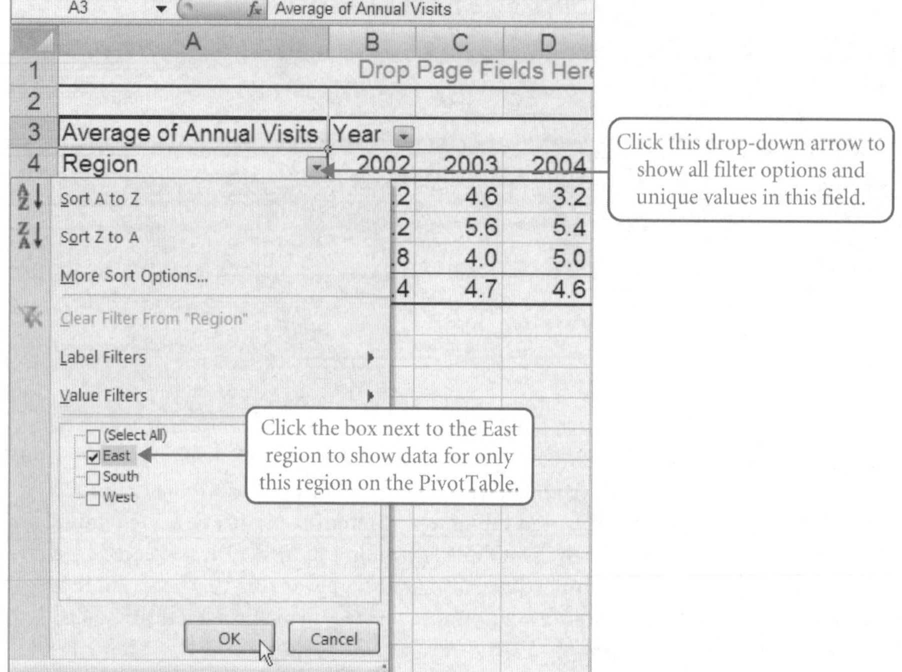

Figure 8.13 shows the results of applying a filter to the Region field. Notice the symbol that appears next to the Region field on the PivotTable Report and in the PivotTable Field List. This indicates that the PivotTable Report is showing only selected values for this field. To remove this filter, click the filter symbol and then select the **Clear Filter From "Region"** option.

Figure 8.13 | **Results of Isolating the East Region**

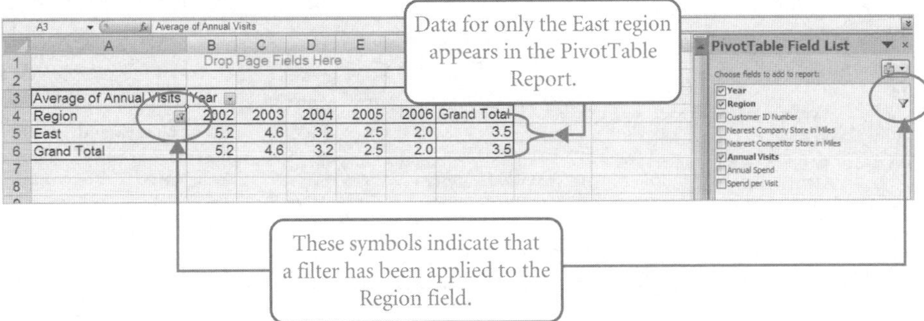

After you have isolated the East region on the PivotTable Report, you can add more fields to determine why the annual visits are declining. For example, fields that a marketing manager might want to add are the Nearest Company Store in Miles and Nearest Competitor Store in Miles. Store location is especially critical in the retail industry. The purpose of this analysis is to compare data for two years: 2002 and 2006. This trend will indicate if competitors have built stores in more valuable locations compared to the company stores. The following explains how this analysis is constructed.

- Click and drag the Nearest Company Store in Miles field from the PivotTable Field List to the Data section of the PivotTable Report.
- Change the field settings for the Nearest Company Store in Miles by double-clicking the field name on the PivotTable Report. This will open the **Value Field Settings** dialog box.
- Select the Average option from the **Value Field Settings** dialog box; then, click the **Number Format** button and select the Number format with 1 decimal place.
- Click the **OK** button on the **Format Cells** dialog box and then click the **OK** button on the **Value Field Settings** dialog box. This will calculate the average distance each customer needs to travel to get to the nearest company store.
- Add the Nearest Competitor Store in Miles field to the Data section of the PivotTable Report; then, open the **Value Field Settings** dialog box, select the average mathematical function, and format the values using the Number format with 1 decimal place. This will show the average distance a customer must travel to get to a competitor's store.
- Click the drop-down arrow next to the Year field, and click the box next to the (**Select All**) option. Click the box next to the years 2002 and 2006 and then click the **OK** button. This will apply a filter to the Year field so the PivotTable Report shows values only for the years 2002 and 2006.

Figure 8.14 shows the results of adding two more fields to the PivotTable Report shown in Figure 8.13. Data is shown only for the years 2002 and 2006 for the East region. The trend shows that when customers were visiting stores in the East region 5.2 times per year in 2002, the average distance they traveled to get to the store was 8.1 miles. If they wanted to visit the competitor's store, they had to drive 14.4 miles. However, this distance to a competitor's store declines to 8.3 miles by the year 2006. In addition, the average distance a customer must travel to get to a company store increases to 10.6 miles in the year 2006. This suggests that the competition might be building stores in better locations, and could partially explain why the average number of visits a customer makes to the company store declines to 2.0 in the year 2006.

>> **Quick Reference**

Filters

1. Click the down arrow next to a field added to the PivotTable Report.
2. Select a filter option or specific value by clicking a check box.
3. Click the **OK** button.
4. Click the filter symbol next to a field and select the **Clear Filter** option to remove a filter.

Figure 8.14 | **Results of Adding Additional Fields to Evaluate the East Region**

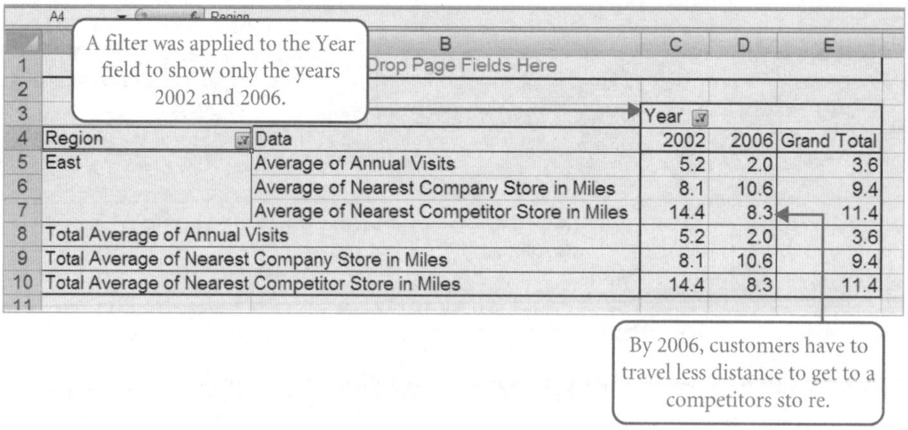

A filter was applied to the Year field to show only the years 2002 and 2006.

	A	B	C	D	E
1		Drop Page Fields Here			
2					
3			Year		
4	Region	Data	2002	2006	Grand Total
5	East	Average of Annual Visits	5.2	2.0	3.6
6		Average of Nearest Company Store in Miles	8.1	10.6	9.4
7		Average of Nearest Competitor Store in Miles	14.4	8.3	11.4
8	Total Average of Annual Visits		5.2	2.0	3.6
9	Total Average of Nearest Company Store in Miles		8.1	10.6	9.4
10	Total Average of Nearest Competitor Store in Miles		14.4	8.3	11.4

By 2006, customers have to travel less distance to get to a competitors sto re.

Adding and Removing Report Totals

Looking at Figure 8.14, you may have noticed that the three totals beginning in row 8 are merely duplicating the data in rows 5, 6, and 7. When multiple items are listed in the Row Fields section, these totals are very helpful. However, in this example they are not necessary because we are isolating only one item in the row fields section, which is the East region. You can adjust the totals in the PivotTable Report by using the **PivotTable Options** dialog box. The following explains how this is used to remove the totals listed in rows 8, 9, and 10 in Figure 8.14.

- Click anywhere in the PivotTable Report to activate the **PivotTable Tools** tabs of the Ribbon.
- Click the **Options** icon in the **Options** tab of the Ribbon. This will open the **PivotTable Options** dialog box.
- Click the **Totals & Filters** tab near the top of the dialog box.
- Click in the box next to the **Show grand totals for columns** option (see Figure 8.15). This will remove the green check that appears when the dialog box is opened.
- Click the **OK** button at the bottom of the dialog box. This will remove the totals at the bottom of the PivotTable Report which is shown in Figure 8.16.

Figure 8.15 | **PivotTable Options Dialog Box**

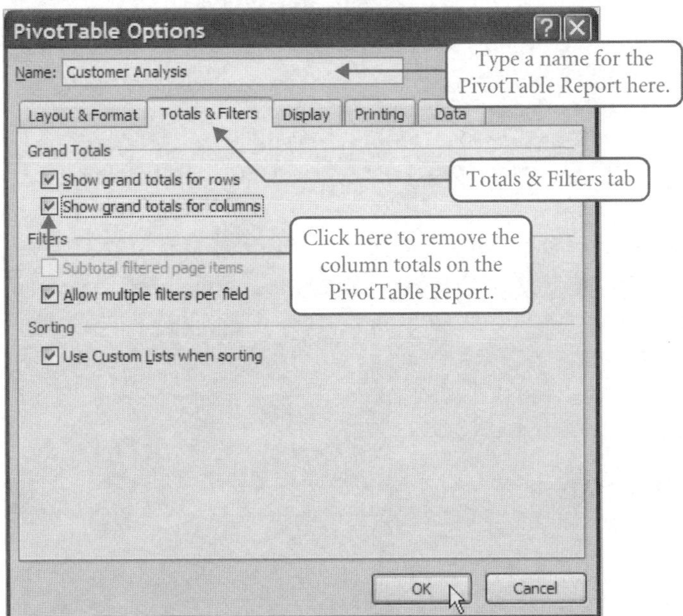

Figure 8.16 | **PivotTable Report Without Column Totals**

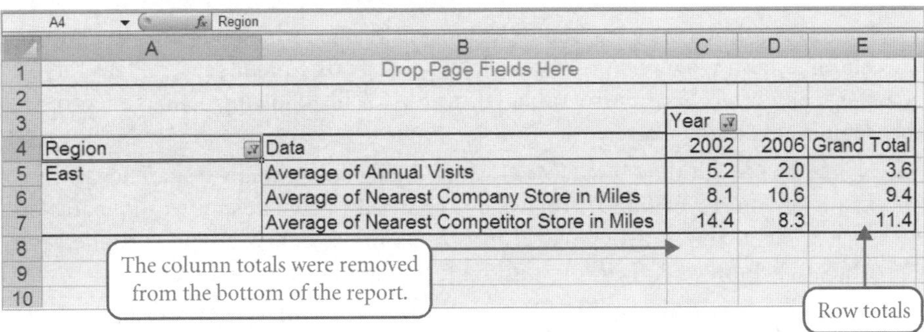

	A	B	C	D	E
1	Drop Page Fields Here				
2					
3			Year		
4	Region	Data	2002	2006	Grand Total
5	East	Average of Annual Visits	5.2	2.0	3.6
6		Average of Nearest Company Store in Miles	8.1	10.6	9.4
7		Average of Nearest Competitor Store in Miles	14.4	8.3	11.4
8					
9					
10					

COMMON MISTAKES | Report Totals versus Subtotals

You can not add or remove subtotals on the PivotTable Report through the **PivotTable Options** dialog box. Subtotals are usually used when multiple fields are added to the Row Labels section of the PivotTable Report and are controlled through the Field Settings dialog box. When adjusting the field settings for a field in the Row Label section of the PivotTable, the dialog box is named Field Settings instead of Value Field Settings. Figure 8.17 shows an example of this dialog box.

Figure 8.17 | **Field Settings Dialog Box**

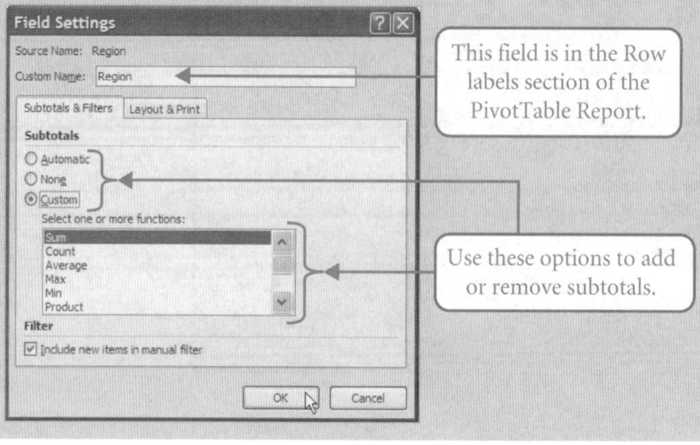

>> **Quick Reference**

Adding and Removing Report Totals

1. Click anywhere in the PivotTable Report to activate the **PivotTable Tools** tabs on the Ribbon.
2. Click the **Options** icon in the **Options** tab of the Ribbon.
3. Click the **Totals & Filters** tab near the top of the dialog box.
4. Click the box next to the **Show grand totals for columns** or **Show grand totals for rows** to add or remove the check mark. When the check mark appears in the box, totals will be added to the PivotTable Report.
5. Click the **OK** button at the bottom of the **PivotTable Options** dialog box.

Figure 8.15 shows the **PivotTable Options** dialog box, which was used to remove the column totals in Figure 8.16. However, this dialog box contains several tabs for accessing commands that control other key features. The following defines a few of these commonly used features.

- **Name:** The top of the **PivotTable Options** dialog box provides a space to type a name for your PivotTable. Excel will automatically assign a name to a PivotTable such as PivotTable1, PivotTable2, and so on; however, you can type a unique name, which is helpful when working with multiple tables in a workbook.
- **Show grand totals for rows:** This command is in the **Totals & Filters** tab of the dialog box and is used to add or remove totals for all rows in the PivotTable Report.
- **Refresh data when opening the file:** This command is in the **Data** tab of the dialog box, and will automatically update a PivotTable when the Excel workbook is opened. If you change data in the range of cells that is used to create a PivotTable, the changes *will not* appear in the PivotTable unless you click the **Refresh** icon in the **Data** group in the **Options** tab of the Ribbon.
- **Sort A to Z** (Field List): This option is in the **Display** tab of the **PivotTable Options** dialog box in the Field List section. This is used to show the fields in the PivotTable Field List window in alphabetical order. Excel will automatically show fields in the PivotTable Field List in the order in which they appear in the source range of cells. If your project uses many fields, however, it may be easier to find what you need if the fields are shown in alphabetical order.
- **Classic PivotTable layout (enables dragging of fields in the grid)**: This option is also in the **Display** tab of the PivotTable options dialog box. This option must be selected if you want to click and drag fields from the PivotTable Field List into the PivotTable Report.

COMMON MISTAKES | Refresh the PivotTable Report

You must click the **Refresh** icon in the **Options** tab of the Ribbon to show any data revisions in the PivotTable Report. People often make revisions in the range of cells that is used to supply data for a PivotTable and expect to see changes in the PivotTable Report; however, the PivotTable Report will not change unless the data is refreshed. In addition, if you select the **Refresh data when opening the file** option in the **Data** tab of the **PivotTable Options** dialog box, the data will refresh only when you open the workbook, but not immediately when the data is changed.

Adding Formulas (Calculated Fields)

The PivotTable shown in Figure 8.16 reveals that a customer needed to travel less distance to get to a competitor's store compared to the company's store in the year 2006. This might explain why the customer visits to a company store in the East region declined significantly from the year 2002 to 2006. Another key statistic that might also explain this decline is the amount of money customers spend per visit. This is calculated by taking the Annual Spend field and dividing it by the Annual Visits field; however, creating a formula in the PivotTable Report is *not* the same as typing a formula into the cell of a worksheet. To produce mathematical results on the PivotTable Report, a calculated field must be created. The following explains how a calculated field is added to the PivotTable Report shown in Figure 8.16 to calculate the average spend per visit.

- Click anywhere in the PivotTable Report to activate the **PivotTable Tools** tabs on the Ribbon.
- Click the **Formulas** icon in the **Options** tab of the Ribbon and then select the **Calculated Field** option to open the **Insert Calculated Field** dialog box.
- Type the name Spend per Visit in the **Name** input box at the top of the **Insert Calculated Field** dialog box.
- Double-click the Annual Spend field from the list of fields in the lower area of the **Insert Calculated Field** dialog box.
- Type the slash symbol for division in the formula input box. Double-click the Annual visits field from the list in the lower area of the **Insert Calculated Field** dialog box.
- Click the **OK** button at the bottom of the dialog box. This will add the new field to the PivotTable Field List.
- Click and drag the Spend per Visit calculated field from the PivotTable Field List into the Data section of the PivotTable Report.

Figure 8.18 | **Opening the Insert Calculated Field Dialog Box**

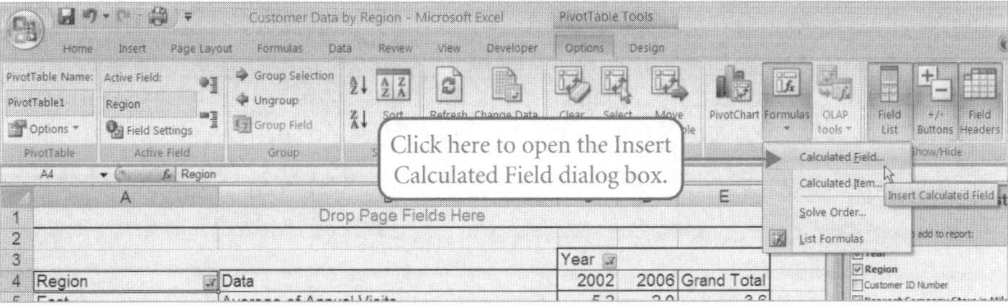

Figure 8.19 | **The Insert Calculated Field Dialog Box**

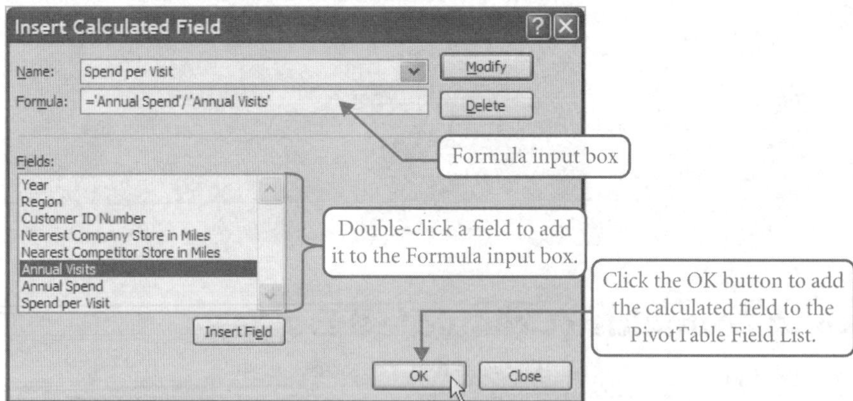

Figure 8.20 shows the appearance of the PivotTable Report after adding the Spend per Visit calculated field to the Data section. Notice the PivotTable renames the field **Sum of Spend per Visit**. This is because all fields, including calculated fields, are automatically summed when they are added to the PivotTable Report; however, this calculated field is actually producing an *average* for the amount of money a customer spends when they visit the store, even though Excel is summing the results. In other words, the sum of the Annual Spend divided by the sum of the Annual Visits is still an average. Therefore, the name of this field is changed in the **Value Field Settings** dialog box after double-clicking the field.

>> **Quick Reference**

Adding Formulas (Calculated Fields)

1. Click anywhere in the PivotTable Report to activate the **PivotTable Tools** tabs on the Ribbon.
2. Click the **Formulas** icon in the **Options** tab of the Ribbon.
3. Select the **Calculated Field** option.
4. Type a name for the calculated field at the top of the **Insert Calculated Field** dialog box.
5. Build a formula by double-clicking the fields in the field list and typing mathematical operators in the formula input box.
6. Click the **OK** button to add the calculated field to the PivotTable Field List.
7. Click and drag the calculated field from the PivotTable Field List into the Data section of the PivotTable Report.

Figure 8.20 | **Adding the Spend per Visit Calculated Field to the PivotTable Report**

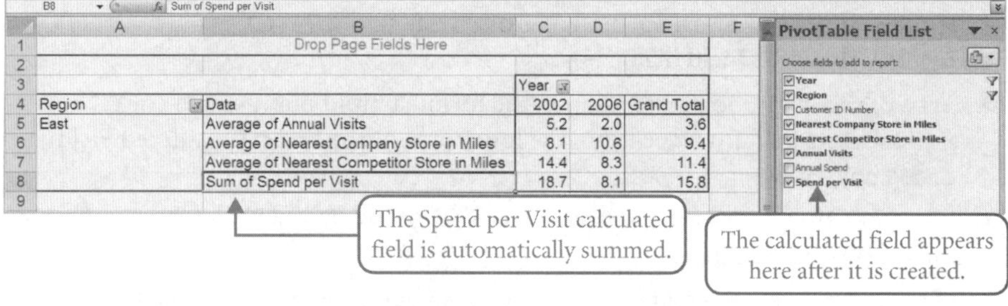

The final result of adding the Spend per Visit calculated field to the PivotTable Report is shown in Figure 8.21. Notice that in the year 2002, customers were spending on average $18.70 per visit; however, this is reduced by over 50 percent in the year 2006 to $8.10. The trend in this statistic suggests that the company is not selling products that customers want, or the competition might be selling the same products at lower prices. Therefore, a marketing manager might develop a more aggressive promotional strategy compared to other regions in the company based on these results.

Figure 8.21 | **Final Results of the Spend per Visit Calculated Field**

A4 | Region

	A	B	C	D	E
1	Drop Page Fields Here				
2					
3			Year		
4	Region	Data	2002	2006	Grand Total
5	East	Average of Annual Visits	5.2	2.0	3.6
6		Average of Nearest Company Store in Miles	8.1	10.6	9.4
7		Average of Nearest Competitor Store in Miles	14.4	8.3	11.4
8		Average Spend per Visit	18.7	8.1	15.8
9					

Customers are spending less money per visit in 2006 compared to 2002.

Sorting Data

PivotTables provide the option of sorting fields in either the Row Fields section or the Column Fields section based on values in the Data section. The sorting commands will be demonstrated using the configuration of the PivotTable shown in Figure 8.11. The following explains how the Year field is sorted based on the data in the Annual Visits field.

- Click the Year field in cell B4.
- Click the **Sort** icon in the **Options** tab of the Ribbon. This will open the **Sort (Year)** dialog box. The field you are sorting will appear in the parentheses of the dialog box title.
- Click the circle next to the **Descending (Z to A) by** option, which is near the center of the dialog box.
- Click the drop-down arrow next to the box below the **Descending (Z to A) by** option and then select the **Average of Annual Visits** option. This will sort the years for each region based on the average values in the Annual Visits field.
- Click the **OK** button at the bottom of the **Sort (Year)** dialog box.

Figures 8.22 and 8.23 show the setup and results of sorting the PivotTable shown in Figure 8.11. Notice in Figure 8.22, the Summary section near the bottom of the **Sort (Year)** dialog box describes how your data will be sorted based on the options selected. In Figure 8.23 you will see that the years for each region are sorted based on the values for the Average of Annual Visits field in descending order.

> **Quick Reference**
> **Sorting Data**
> 1. Click a field in either the Row Fields or Column Fields section on the PivotTable Report.
> 2. Click the **Sort** icon in the **Options** tab of the Ribbon.
> 3. Select one of the sort options in the **Sort** dialog box.
> 4. If you selected the **Ascending or Descending** option in Step 3, click the down arrow next to the box below these options and then select a field that will be used to set the sort sequence.
> 5. Click the **OK** button.

Figure 8.22 | **Sort (Year) Dialog Box**

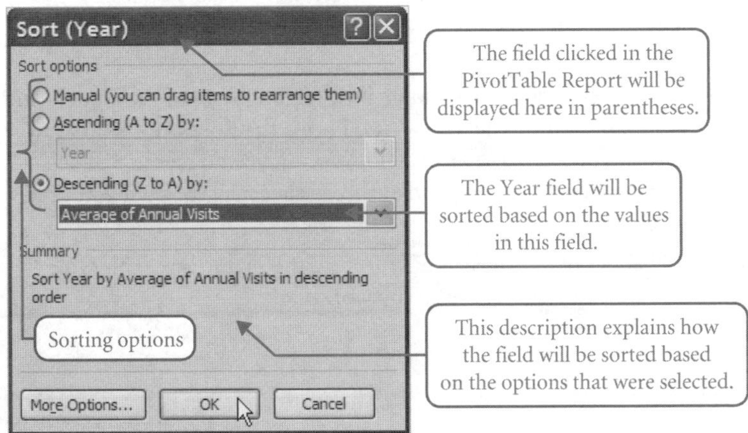

Figure 8.23 | **Results of Sorting the Year Field Based on Values in the Average Annual Visits Field**

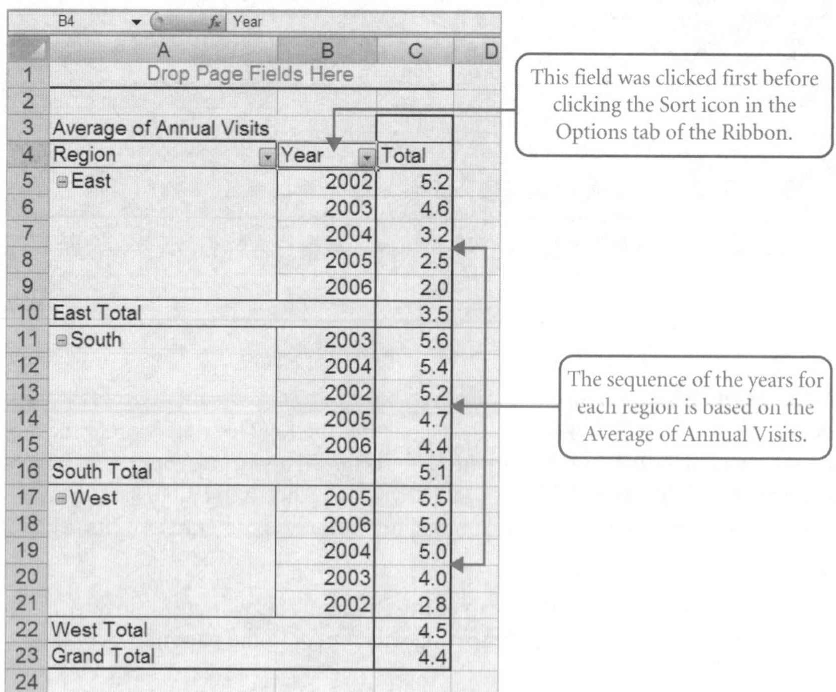

Average of Annual Visits		
Region	Year	Total
East	2002	5.2
	2003	4.6
	2004	3.2
	2005	2.5
	2006	2.0
East Total		3.5
South	2003	5.6
	2004	5.4
	2002	5.2
	2005	4.7
	2006	4.4
South Total		5.1
West	2005	5.5
	2006	5.0
	2004	5.0
	2003	4.0
	2002	2.8
West Total		4.5
Grand Total		4.4

PivotCharts

The **PivotTable** icon in the **Insert** tab of the Ribbon contains an option for creating a PivotChart as well as a PivotTable. The mechanics and features of a PivotChart are similar to a PivotTable; however, instead of summarizing data in the form of a grid, the PivotChart displays data graphically in the form of a chart. You can use these charts for comparing data across multiple categories and for business presentations. This segment will demonstrate how to construct a PivotChart using the Retail Customer Data shown in Figure 8.1. The following explains how the PivotChart is initially created.

- Click the down arrow of the **PivotTable** icon in the **Insert** tab of the Ribbon, and select the **PivotChart** option. This will open the Create PivotTable with **PivotChart** dialog box, which is identical to the **Create PivotTable** dialog box (see Figure 8.2).
- Click the range finder next to the **Table/Range** box. Highlight all of the data on the worksheet—including the column headings—and press the **Enter** key. Similar to creating a PivotTable, if you activated any cell location in your data range, Excel will suggest a cell range. Check this range to ensure it covers all the data you need to create your PivotChart.
- Select the **New Worksheet** option near the bottom of the dialog box. This will place the PivotChart in a new worksheet in the workbook.

- Click the **OK** button at the bottom of the dialog box. This will add a new worksheet to the workbook that contains the tools you need to build the PivotChart (see Figure 8.24).
- Figure 8.24 shows the tools that are displayed for constructing a PivotChart after clicking the **OK** button in the Create PivotTable with **PivotChart** dialog box. These tools appear on a separate worksheet that is added to the workbook. In addition, a blank PivotTable will appear on the left side of the worksheet because a PivotChart is always associated with a PivotTable. In fact, the PivotTable will be used during the process of constructing the PivotChart for this example.

COMMON MISTAKES | PivotCharts are Linked to a PivotTable

Any change you make to a PivotTable that is associated to a PivotChart will change the PivotChart. If you intend to use a PivotChart and a PivotTable to show different statistics for the same project, you will need to add a separate and independent PivotTable. This means your workbook will have two PivotTables: one which is independent and a second which is associated to the PivotChart.

Figure 8.24 | **Tools for Building a PivotChart**

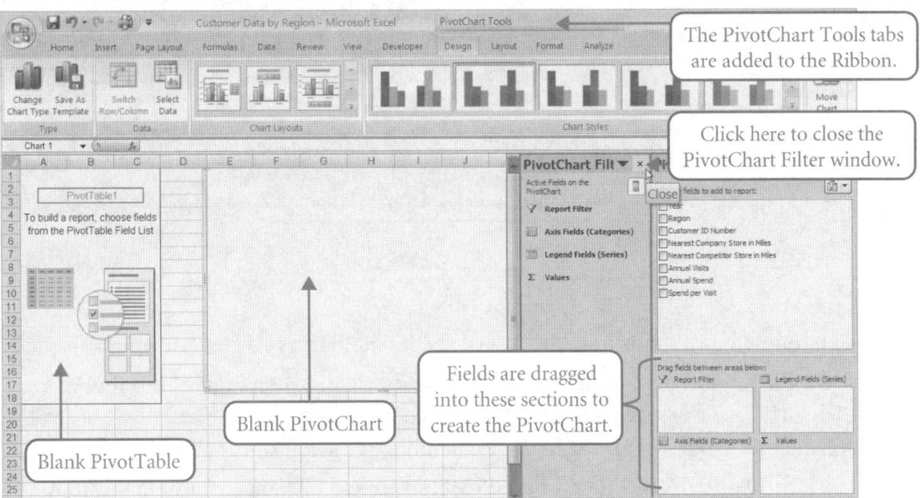

As shown in Figure 8.24, the **PivotChart Filter** window will be opened when the PivotChart is initially created. To see the PivotChart as it is being constructed, close this window by clicking the X in the upper-right corner.

Looking at Figure 8.24, you may have noticed the instructions in the blank PivotTable that state you can simply select fields in the PivotTable Field List to build a chart. Although this is true, there is no guarantee Excel will build the chart that you need for your project. The following method will provide you with the most control for placing data exactly where you want to see it on a chart. The goal for this example is to construct a PivotChart that compares the average number of visits per store by region for a selected year.

- Click the Year field in the PivotTable Field List, and drag it into the Report Filter section in the lower area of the PivotTable Field List. Placing fields in this section will allow you to focus the data displayed on the chart for one specific item or category, or for this example, a specific year. When creating a PivotTable, you can click and drag fields from the PivotTable Field List directly onto the PivotTable Report; however, you cannot drag fields directly onto a PivotChart. When building a PivotChart you will click and drag fields into the sections in the lower area of the PivotTable Field List.
- Click the down arrow next to the Year field on the *PivotTable* and then select the year 2002 (see Figure 8.25). This will show data only for the year 2002 on the PivotChart. Other years of data can be viewed on the chart by changing the filter to a different year.

Figure 8.25 shows the appearance of the PivotTable and PivotChart when the Year field is dragged into the Report Filter section of the PivotTable Field List. Notice that the PivotChart is still blank. Objects on the chart will not be visible until fields are added to the Values section of the PivotTable Field List.

Figure 8.25 | **Adding Fields to the Report Filter Section**

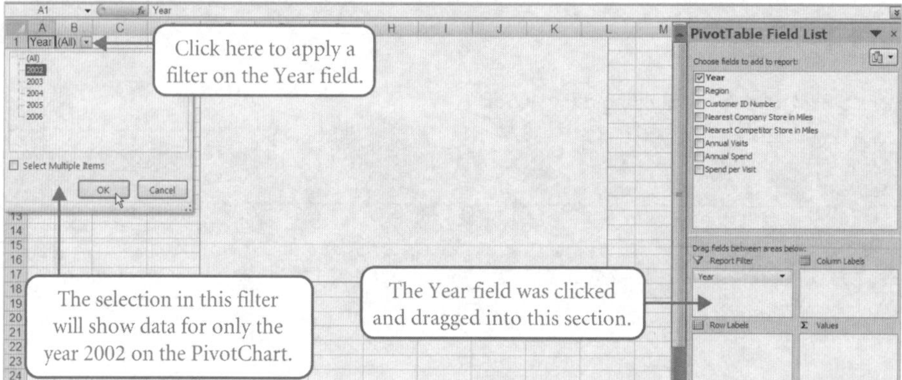

The following explains how the rest of the PivotChart is created for this example.

- Click the Region field in the PivotTable Field List and then drag it into the Axis Fields (Categories) section in the lower area of the PivotTable Field List. You will see the three regions appear in the PivotTable to the left of the PivotChart.
- Click the Annual Visits field in the PivotTable Field List and then drag it into the Values section in the lower area of the PivotTable Field List. The PivotChart will automatically sum the total number of customer visits for each region, and bars for each region will appear on the chart.
- Double-click the Sum of Annual Visits field in the PivotTable to open the **Value Field Settings** dialog box. Select the Average option in the **Summarize by** tab, and click the **OK** button at the bottom of the dialog box. Because the objective for this chart is to compare the *average* number of times a customer visits the company's stores, the field settings are changed to Average.
- Click and drag the chart down and to the left until it is full view. To view the entire chart after it is created, you will have to move it or close the PivotTable Field List so it is fully visible.

COMMON MISTAKES | Opening the PivotTable Field List

If you close the PivotTable Field List, you must activate either the PivotTable or PivotChart and then click the **Field List** icon in either the **Options** or **Analyze** tabs of the Ribbon to open it again. People often find it difficult to open the PivotTable Field List after closing it. If you close the PivotTable Field List by clicking the X in the upper-right corner, it will not appear when you activate the PivotTable Report or PivotChart unless you click the **Field List** icon.

Figure 8.26 shows the results of PivotChart comparing the average annual visits by region for the year 2002. The chart can be changed to a different year by clicking the filter icon next to the Year field in the PivotTable and selecting a different year. In addition, a filter can be placed on the Region field by clicking the down arrow next to the Row Labels heading in the PivotTable. Notice that the **PivotChart Tools** tabs are added to the Ribbon when the PivotChart is activated. The **Design**, **Layout**, and **Format** tabs contain commands that are identical to the ones covered in Chapter 5. These commands can be used to adjust the design or select a different chart type. The PivotChart will automatically use the Clustered Column chart type when it is created.

Figure 8.26 | **Results of the PivotChart**

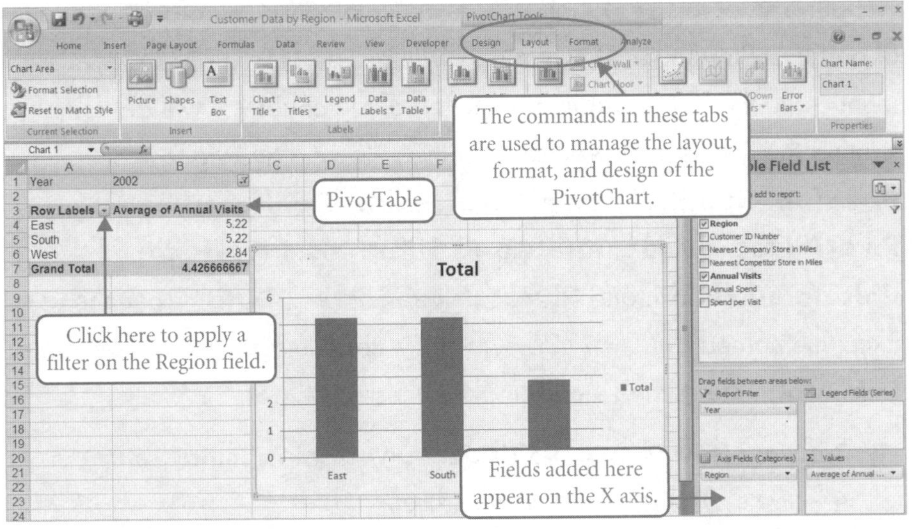

Figure 8.27 shows a variation of the PivotChart shown in Figure 8.26, and includes formatting adjustments. In this chart the Year field was clicked and dragged from the Report Filter section into the Legend Fields (Series) section in the lower area of the PivotTable Field List. This creates a bar on the PivotChart for each year by region, and the legend shows the color associated with each year. The formatting adjustments applied to this chart were accomplished using the same techniques covered in Chapter 5.

>> **Quick Reference**

Creating a New PivotChart

1. Click the drop-down arrow of the **PivotTable** icon in the Insert tab of the Ribbon, and select the **PivotChart** option.
2. Define the Table/Range in the **Create PivotTable with PivotChart** dialog box. If a range is provided, check it to ensure it contains all the data that is required for your PivotChart. To create a new range, click the range finder, highlight the range of cells that contain data for the PivotChart, and press the **Enter** key.
3. Select either New Worksheet or Existing Worksheet near the bottom of the **Create PivotTable with PivotChart** dialog box and then click the **OK** button.
4. Click and drag fields from the upper area of the PivotTable Field List into one of the sections in the lower area.
5. Make any formatting adjustments to the PivotChart using the same commands and techniques that would be used for any Excel chart.

Figure 8.27 | **PivotChart Variation with Formatting**

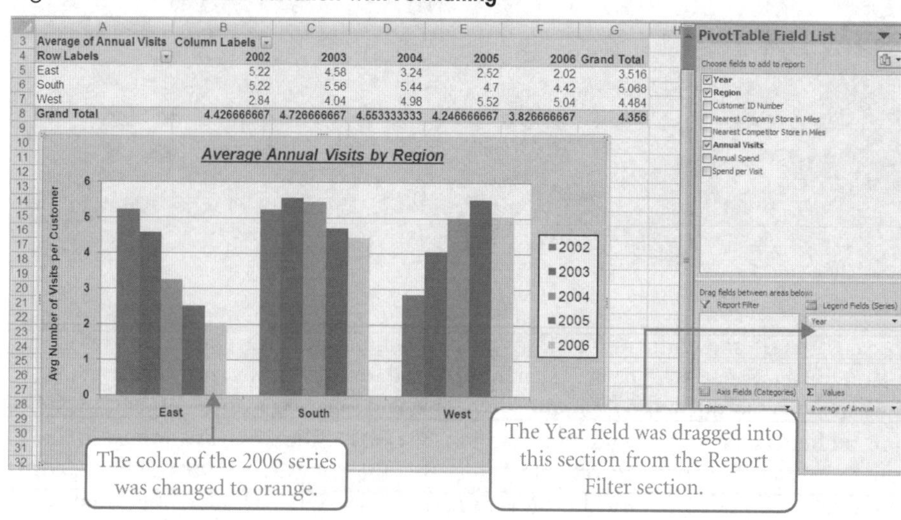

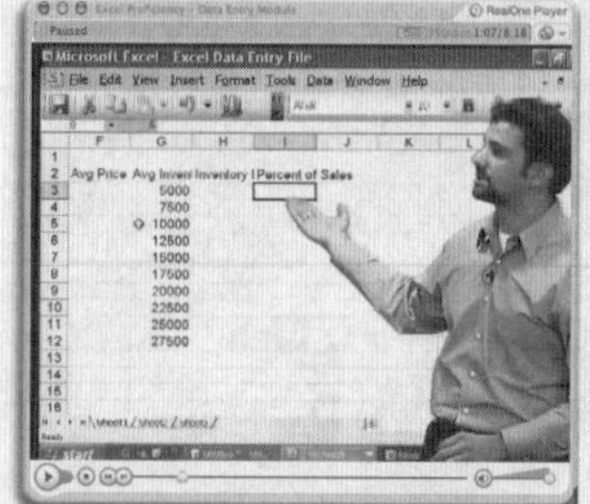

PivotTables

The purpose of this workshop is to review the construction and features of an Excel PivotTable. The data that will be used for this workshop is identical to the data used in this section of the chapter. I will be demonstrating the tasks in this workshop in the following five videos: **PivotTables: Initial Setup**; **PivotTables: Fields and Settings**; **PivotTables: Report Totals and Subtotals**; **PivotTables: Calculated Fields**; and **PivotTables: Sorting Data**. Open the Excel file named ib_e08_customerdata. After completing each section of tasks, watch the related video in parentheses.

1. **Create a New PivotTable (Video: PivotTables: Initial Setup)**
   a. Activate cell A1 in the Data worksheet.
   b. Click the down arrow on the **PivotTable** icon in the **Insert** tab of the Ribbon, and select the **PivotTable** option.
   c. In the Create **PivotTable** dialog box, check that the range in the **Table/Range** box is Data!$A$1:$G$751. Select the New Worksheet option near the bottom of the dialog box and then click the **OK** button.
   d. Click the **Options** icon in the **Options** tab of the Ribbon.
   e. Click the **Display** tab near the top of the **PivotTable Options** dialog box. A check mark should appear next to the Classic PivotTable layout (enables dragging of fields in the grid) option. If you do not see a check mark, click the box next to this option.
   f. Click the **OK** button at the bottom of the **PivotTable Options** dialog box.

2. **Adding Fields (Video: PivotTables: Fields and Settings)**
   a. Click anywhere in the PivotTable Report area in the Sheet1 worksheet.
   b. Click the Year field in the PivotTable Field List and drag it into the Column Fields section of the PivotTable Report.

c. Click the Region field in the PivotTable Field List and drag it into the Row Fields section of the PivotTable Report.
d. Click the Annual Visits field in the PivotTable Field List and drag it into the Data section of the PivotTable Report.
e. Double-click the Sum of Annual Visits field name in cell A3 on the PivotTable Report
f. Select the Average option in the **Summarize by** tab in the **Value Field Settings** dialog box.
g. Click the **Number Format** button at the bottom of the **Value Field Settings** dialog box; then, select the **Number** option and set the decimal places to 1 in the **Format Cells** dialog box.
h. Click the **OK** button in the **Format Cells** dialog box and then on the **Value Field Settings** dialog box.
i. Click the drop down arrow next to the Region field name on the PivotTable Report, and set the filter for the East region.
j. Click and drag the Nearest Company Store in Miles field from the PivotTable Field List into the Data section of the PivotTable Report.
k. Look in the Column Labels section in the lower area of the PivotTable Field List. If the Values field appears in this section below the Year field, click and drag it into the Row Labels section below the Region field.
l. Change the field settings for the Nearest Company Store in Miles from Sum to Average, and format the values in this field using the Number format with 1 decimal place.
m. Click and drag the Nearest Competitor Store in Miles field from the PivotTable Field List into the Data section of the PivotTable Report.
n. Change the field settings for the Nearest Competitor Store in Miles from Sum to Average, and format the values in this field using the Number format with 1 decimal place.

3. Report Totals (Video: PivotTables: Report Totals and Subtotals)

a. Click anywhere on the PivotTable Report in the Sheet1 worksheet.
b. Click the **Options** icon in the **Options** tab of the Ribbon.
c. At the top of the **PivotTable Options** dialog box, change the name of the PivotTable in the Name: input box to `Customer Analysis`.
d. Click the **Totals & Filters** tab in the **PivotTable Options** dialog box, and then click the box next to the Show grand totals for columns option to remove the check mark. Click the **OK** button at the bottom of the **PivotTable Options** dialog box.
e. Click the filter symbol next to the Region field on the PivotTable Report, and remove the filter by selecting the **Clear Filter From "Region"** option.
f. In the lower area of the PivotTable Field List, click the Year field in the Column Labels section. Drag it between the Region and Values fields in the Row Labels section.
g. In the lower area of the PivotTable Field List, click the Values field in the Row Labels section and then drag it into the Column Labels section
h. Double-click the Region field name in the PivotTable Report (cell A4).
i. In the Subtotals & Filters tab of the **Field Settings** dialog box, click the Custom option and then select the Average function. Click the **OK** button at the bottom of the dialog box.

4. Adding Formulas (Video: PivotTables: Calculated Fields)

a. Click anywhere on the PivotTable Report in the Sheet1 worksheet.

b. In the lower area of the PivotTable Field List, click and drag the Year field into the Column Labels section, and then click and drag the Values field into the Row Labels section below the Region field.

c. Click the **Formulas** icon in the **Options** tab of the Ribbon, and select the **Calculated Field** option.

d. Type the name `Spend per Visit` in the Name: input box at the top of the **Insert Calculated Field** dialog box. Delete the name Field1 before typing the field name.

e. Double-click the Annual Spend field from the field list, type a slash symbol, and double-click the Annual Visits field.

f. Click the **OK** button at the bottom of the **Insert Calculated Field** dialog box.

g. Double-click the Sum of Spend per Visit field name in the PivotTable Report (cell B8). Change the name of the field to `Average Spend per Visit`; then, click the **Number Format** button, select the **Currency** option, and set the decimal places to 2.

h. Click the **OK** button on the **Format Cells** dialog box and again on the **Value Field Settings** dialog box.

5. Sorting (Video: PivotTables: Sorting Data)

a. Click anywhere on the PivotTable Report in the Sheet1 worksheet.

b. In the PivotTable Field List, click the box next to the Nearest Company Store in Miles, Nearest Competitor Store in Miles, and Spend per Visit fields to remove the check mark.

c. Click the Year field name in the PivotTable Report (cell B3), and drag it over to the Row Fields section next to the regions.

d. Click the Year field name in the PivotTable report (cell B4) and then click the Sort icon in the **Options** tab of the Ribbon.

e. Click the Descending (Z to A) option in the center of the Sort (Year) dialog box. Click the drop-down arrow next to the box below this option, and select the Average of Annual Visits field.

f. Click the **OK** button on the **Sort (Year)** dialog box.

g. Save and close your file.

VIDEO WORKSHOP

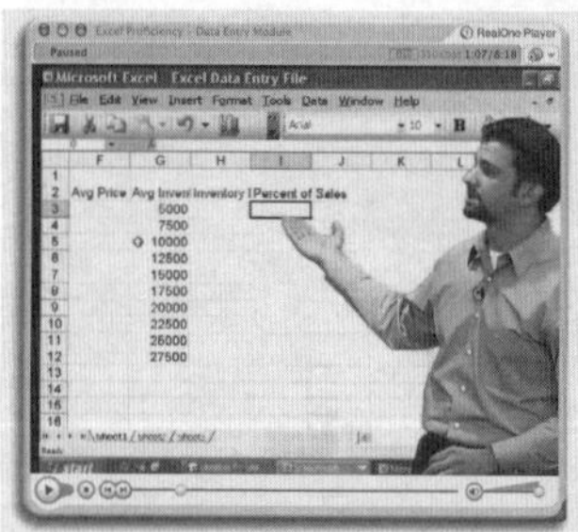

>> PivotCharts

The purpose of this workshop is to review the construction and features of a PivotChart. This workshop will use the same Excel file that was used for the PivotTable workshop. I will be demonstrating the tasks in this workshop in the video named **PivotCharts**. Open the ib_e08_customerdata file, and begin the workshop.

1. PivotCharts (Video: PivotCharts)

a. Activate cell A1 in the Data worksheet.

b. Click the down arrow on the **PivotTable** icon in the **Insert** tab of the Ribbon, and select the **PivotChart** option.

c. In the **Create PivotTable** dialog box, check that the range in the **Table/Range** box is Data!$A$1:$G$751. Select the New Worksheet option near the bottom of the dialog box and then click the **OK** button.

d. Close the **PivotChart Filter** window by clicking the X in the upper-right corner of the window.
e. Click the Year field in the PivotTable Field List and drag it into the Report Filter section in the lower area of the PivotTable Field List.
f. Click the drop-down arrow next to the Year field on the PivotTable, and set the filter for the year 2002.
g. Click anywhere in the blank PivotChart and then click the Region field in the PivotTable Field List. Drag it into the Axis Fields (Categories) section in the lower area of the PivotTable Field List.
h. Click the Annual Visits field in the PivotTable Field List, and drag it into the Values section in the lower area of the PivotTable Field List.
i. Double-click the Sum of Annual Visits field in cell B3. Change the field settings to Average, and format the values using the Number format with 1 decimal place.
j. Change the filter on the Year field in the PivotTable to the year 2006.
k. Save and close your file.

>> Analyzing Customer Survey Data

EXERCISE

Why Do I Need This?

Data plays a critical role in the decision making process of most businesses; however, most business managers struggle to turn large volumes of data into information they can use for making decisions. The amount and type of data business managers evaluate depends on the function they serve within a company. For example, marketing mangers might work with large volumes of data, especially if they are conducting and evaluating consumer surveys. These surveys are sometimes administered over the Internet, mailed to consumers' homes, or conducted in person as customers leave a retail store. Companies can use these survey methods to collect data from thousands of customers. Business managers can then use tools such as Excel PivotTables to convert this data into valuable information.

Exercise

The purpose of this exercise is to use a PivotTable to evaluate the results of a survey that was conducted as customers were leaving the stores of a home furnishings retail company. The data collected from this survey is contained in the Excel file named ib_e08_customersurveyresults. Open the file and complete the following tasks.

1. Create a new PivotTable using the range A1:G751 on the Data worksheet. This PivotTable should appear in a new worksheet in the workbook. Note: If you do not see the layout of the PivotTable Report that allows you to click and drag fields into it, check the **Classic PivotTable layout (enables dragging of fields in the grid)** option in the **Display** tab of the **PivotTable Options** dialog box.

2. The fields in the PivotTable Field List contain data pertaining to the sales growth of each store in the company as well as the scores from the customer survey. The goal of this analysis is to determine if the results of the survey can explain the sales growth trends of the stores. Therefore, the first step of this exercise will be to analyze the sales growth trends of the stores. To accomplish this, arrange the PivotTable Report as follows.
   a. Use the Store field to establish the Row Labels.
   b. Use the Year field to establish the Column Labels.
   c. Use the Sales Growth field for the values of the report.

3. Change the field settings of the Sales Growth field to Average, and format the numbers in this field to Currency with 0 decimal places.

4. Sort the stores in the Row Labels section of the PivotTable in Descending order based on the values in the Sales Growth field. Remember to click the Store field name first in the PivotTable Report. This will enable a business manager to quickly identify stores with the highest and lowest sales growth results.

5. Store 2 should be the last store listed in the PivotTable Report because it had the largest sales decrease over the years 2004 through 2006. Set a filter on the Store field so only this store appears in the PivotTable report.

6. Add the In Stock, Price, and Associates fields to the Values section of the PivotTable Report. Move the Values field from the Column Labels section in the lower area of the PivotTable Field List to the Row Labels section. Change the field settings for these fields to Average, and format the numbers to a regular Number format with 1 decimal place. The data in these three fields will now show the average score that was surveyed for this store by its customers. Customers rated the store on a 10 point scale (1=Poor, 10=Superior). The In Stock score is the customers' response to the question: "Did you find the product you wanted?" The Price score is in response to the question: "Do you think products in the store are fairly priced?" The Associates score is in response to the question "Do think the associates are friendly and helpful?" Given the results of these scores, does it make sense that this store experienced the most significant sales decline compared to the other stores?

7. Remove the report totals at the bottom of the PivotTable Report. Because there is only one store in the PivotTable report, these totals are not necessary.

8. Adjust the filter on the Store field to show Stores 2 and 7 on the PivotTable Report. Store 7 has also experienced a significant decline in sales. Compare the data for the In Stock, Price, and Associates fields for both stores. Based on this comparison, explain why you think sales in Store 7 are declining.

9. Adjust the Store field filter to add Store 5 to the PivotTable Report. The PivotTable Report should now show three stores (5, 7, and 2). Based on the Price field scores, which store did customers rate as having the best prices? Why do you think the sales growth for Store 5 is much higher than store 7?

10. Adjust the Store field filter to add Store 6 to the PivotTable Report. If you are the president of this company and can invest money to improve either the Price score or the Associates score for this store, which would you choose? Why?

11. If you could only invest money to improve two scores to improve the sales of Store 2, which would you choose? Why?

12. Save and close your file.

PROBLEM & EXERCISE

>> What's Wrong with This Spreadsheet?

Problem

You are working in the marketing and sales division of a large retail corporation and receive an e-mail from your boss who needs help putting together a presentation for the firm's executive officers. The purpose of the presentation is to show the three-year trend in customer survey scores and change in sales for the company's stores. Your boss explains the following in an e-mail.

1. Please take a look at the Excel file attached to this e-mail. I am trying to use a PivotTable and a PivotChart to show the results of the customer survey results in the Data worksheet.

2. The first problem is that there are few fields in the PivotTable Field List that do not match the column headings in the Data worksheet. I can't figure out why some fields match the column headings, and some don't.

3. The second problem is that the PivotChart keeps changing on me! I want to show the executives an overview of the *Average* sales results by store for all three years on a basic column chart. Then I want to use the PivotTable to show the Average sales and the *Average* survey scores for the *three stores that had the biggest decrease* in sales for each year. However, every time I change the PivotTable, the PivotChart changes.

4. You will see the PivotChart that I attempted to create in Sheet2 of the workbook. Is there any way to make this look better and move it to separate worksheet so I can use it for a presentation?

Exercise

The Excel file that was attached to the e-mail sent by your boss in named ib_e08_pivotcharttroubles. Open this file and look at the PivotChart in the Sheet2 worksheet. What's wrong with this PivotChart? Consider the following points.

1. Your boss mentioned that some of the field names in the PivotTable Field List do not match the column headings in the Data worksheet. Why is this happening?

2. Why is the PivotChart changing when your boss tries to show the average sales and survey score results on the PivotTable in Sheet2?

3. Is it possible to move a PivotChart to a separate worksheet or chart sheet and apply formatting enhancements as you would any other Excel chart?

Write a short answer for each of these points; then, help your boss complete this presentation by fixing any errors you find. The PivotChart should show the average sales results for each year for all stores *sorted in descending order.* Also, make any formatting enhancements to this chart so it has a professional appearance (for example, add a title, adjust font sizes, color, and so on) and place it in a separate chart sheet. Finally, the workbook should include a PivotTable that shows the average sales and survey scores *by year* for the three stores with the lowest sales results.

>> Tools for Selecting and Summarizing Data

Skill Set

The previous section demonstrated how you can use PivotTables to execute a variety of mathematical functions and data processes when analyzing large volumes of data. The purpose of this section is to demonstrate three other tools that can also be used for this purpose. Each tool covered in this section is used to apply one specific function or process to a large data set. The section begins with the **Filter** tool, which is designed to select a specific number of rows from a large data set based on criteria that you define. The next tool is Subtotals, which is designed to provide a mathematical summary for specified columns within a large dataset. The last tool that will be demonstrated is the List Box, which allows you to select specific values from a large column of data.

Filters

Excel's **Filter** tool is a way to identify and select key data points from large volumes of data contained in a worksheet. Similar to the example demonstrated in the PivotTable section, this tool is also helpful when analyzing data that might be used by a marketing manager. One of the most important goals of a marketing manager is to determine where a company's products should be promoted and sold; however, finding the best markets to sell products is sometimes like finding a needle in a haystack. Marketing managers might collect and analyze thousands of rows of data to decide which markets best represent a firm's target customer. For example, Figure 8.28 shows age of population and household income statistics for 500 hypothetical markets or locations. A marketing manager would analyze this data to determine which markets might provide a company with the best potential for promoting and selling its products. This example assumes that the marketing manager's goal is to promote products to consumers between the ages of 25 to 35 with a household income of at least $70,000.

Figure 8.28 | **Hypothetical Market Data**

	A	B	C	D	E
1	Market	Total Population	Percent of Population Age 25-35	Growth in Population Age 25-35	Household Income
2	Market 441	215,036	16.10%	4.00%	44,327
3	Market 156	66,587	27.32%	22.00%	96,089
4	Market 378	101,452	10.57%	13.00%	70,156
5	Market 464	94,184	20.41%	6.00%	50,932
6	Market 450	100,144	8.47%	14.00%	72,494
7	Market 197	70,463	11.79%	-2.00%	29,066
8	Market 483	100,615	27.80%	23.00%	98,375
9	Market 291	101,875	21.77%	10.00%	63,770
10	Market 91	81,710	12.45%	-3.00%	26,706
11	Market 239	141,594	26.90%	1.00%	35,819
12	Market 374	100,820	23.47%	20.00%	92,027

Filter icon

Data continues to row 501.

The following explains how a marketing manger could use the **Filter** tool to decide which of the 500 markets shown in Figure 8.28 best represent the firm's target customer.

- Click any cell that contains data. If you are using a worksheet that contains several adjacent columns of data as shown in Figure 8.28, you can click any cell that contains data and Excel will automatically configure the **Filter** tool.
- Click the **Filter** icon in the **Data** tab of the Ribbon (see Figure 8.28).

Figure 8.29 shows the Market Data worksheet after applying the **Filter** tool. Notice that drop-down arrows appear next to each column heading in row 1 of the worksheet. This figure also shows the list of options that appear when an arrow is clicked.

Figure 8.29 | **Filter Options**

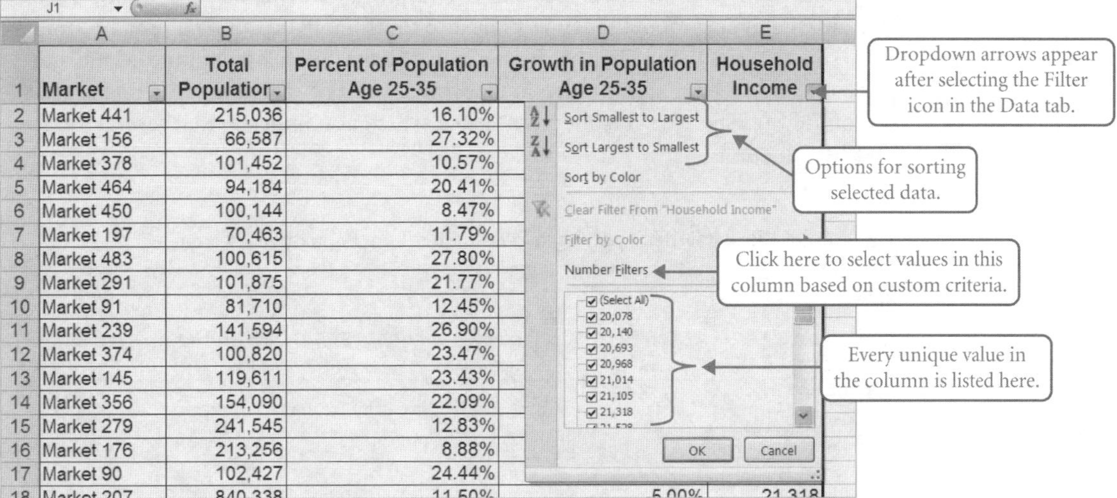

As shown in Figure 8.29, the **Filter** tool provides several options for selecting values in a column of data. Notice that when the drop-down arrow is clicked, every unique value in the column is displayed. The **Number Filters** option is used to select multiple values that meet the conditions of a logical test that you define. The following explains how this option is used to select markets that represent the best opportunities to sell products based on a target customer that is between the age of 25 to 35 with a household income of at least $70,000.

- Click the down arrow next to the Total Population column heading in cell B1 and then place the cursor over the **Number Filters** option.
- Select the **Custom Filter** from the list of options. This will open the **Custom AutoFilter** dialog box (see Figure 8.30).
- Click the drop-down arrow to the left of the box in the upper-left area of the **Custom AutoFilter** dialog box. Select the **greater than or equal to** comparison criterion.
- Click the drop-down arrow next to the box to the right of the comparison criterion, and select the value 100,002. This will reduce the data shown in Figure 8.28 to those rows where the total population is greater than or equal to the 100,002 people. A marketing manager might use this type of criterion to set an overall minimum market size standard.
- Click the **OK** button at the bottom of the **Custom AutoFilter** dialog box.

Figure 8.30 | **Custom AutoFilter Window for the Total Population Column**

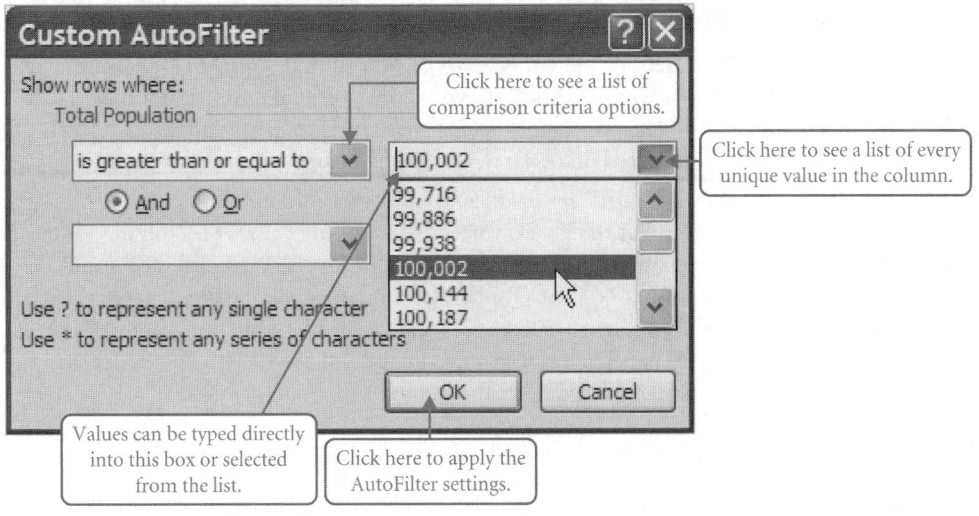

Figure 8.31 shows the results of the Hypothetical Market data after applying the AutoFilter settings to the Total Population column. Notice that the row numbers are blue and the filter symbol that appears next to the Total Population column heading is blue. This signifies that a filter has been applied to the Total Population column, and that rows of data have been hidden in the worksheet. The row numbers along the left side of the worksheet will be out of sequence, which also indicates that several rows have been hidden.

Figure 8.31 | **Results After Applying a Filter on the Total Population Column**

	A	B	C	D	E
1	Market	Total Population	Percent of Population Age 25-35	Growth in Population Age 25-35	Household Income
2	Market 441	215,036	16.10%	4.00%	44,327
4	Market 378	101,452	10.57%	13.00%	70,156
6	Market 450	100,144	8.47%	14.00%	72,494
8	Market 483	100,615	27.80%	23.00%	98,375
9	Market 291	101,875	21.77%	10.00%	63,770
11	Market 239	141,594	26.90%	1.00%	35,819
12	Market 374	100,820	23.47%	20.00%	92,027
13	Market 145	119,611	23.43%	-4.00%	21,528
14	Market 356	154,090	22.09%	2.00%	40,444

Row numbers are out of sequence.

Data is reduced to only rows where the total population is greater than or equal to 100,002.

This symbol indicates a filter is applied to this column.

The following explains how filters are applied to three more columns to further reduce the data shown in Figure 8.31 to markets that best represent the company's target customer.

- **Percent of Population Age 25-35:** The filter was set to **greater than or equal to** .20. This will select rows of data where at least 20 percent of the population is between the ages of 25 and 35. Notice that 20 percent in decimal form is used to set this filter. Based on the filter that was applied to the Total Population field, this ensures the company is selecting markets where there are at least 20,000 potential customers. Marketing managers will usually calculate what the minimum number of potential customers must be to enter a market based on factors such as number of competitors, industry growth trends, and their company's past performance in new markets.
- **Growth in Population Age 25-35:** The filter was set to **greater than** .05. The purpose of this filter is to ensure that the number of people age 25 to 35 is growing within a particular market. This filter will select markets where the number of people age 25 to 35 has grown by more than 5 percent in the past year.
- **Household Income:** The filter was set to **greater than or equal to** 70000, and will select only markets where the household income is equal to or greater than $70,000. Marketing managers may sometimes target markets with certain levels of household income based on research and the price of their firm's product.

Figure 8.32 shows the final results of setting filters on four columns in the Market Data worksheet. Notice that the data is sorted in ascending order based on the values in the Total Population column. This is because the Sort Smallest to Largest option was selected from the list of filter options for this column. Overall, the filters have reduced the 500 markets shown in Figure 8.28 to 63. You can see this by looking in the lower-left corner of the status bar. The results of this analysis allow a company to focus marketing investments in markets that have the highest potential for success.

>> ***Quick Reference***

Applying Filters

1. Click any cell containing data in a worksheet with several adjacent columns.
2. Click the **Filter** icon in the **Data** tab of the Ribbon.
3. Click the drop-down arrow next to any of the column headings and select a filter option.

Figure 8.32 | **Final Results After Applying Filters on Four Columns of Data**

	A	B	C	D	E
1	Market	Total Population	Percent of Population Age 25-35	Growth in Population Age 25-35	Household Income
8	Market 483	100,615	27.80%	23.00%	98,375
12	Market 374	100,820	23.47%	20.00%	92,027
17	Market 90	102,427	24.44%	18.00%	83,978
24	Market 131	104,713	24.80%	17.00%	83,677
41	Market 440	109,007	24.67%	14.00%	73,780
54	Market 163	113,004	25.11%	18.00%	85,124
65	Market 421	113,516	24.97%	15.00%	75,350
66	Market 234	113,742	20.64%	13.00%	72,400
94	Market 407	116,768	28.61%	19.00%	87,477
95	Market 165	116,801	24.71%	23.00%	98,152
96	Market 146	122,404	28.63%	14.00%	72,559
100	Market 476	132,641	28.67%	24.00%	102,562
101	Market 424	135,367	23.22%	13.00%	72,302
107	Market 231	141,057	22.04%	22.00%	97,511
113	Market 437	142,136	20.00%	18.00%	84,976

Sheet1 Sheet2 Sheet3

Ready 63 of 500 records found

A total of 63 markets are listed in the worksheet.

Data is sorted by values in this column.

COMMON MISTAKES | Identifying Number of Rows Using the Filter Tool

It is sometimes difficult to determine how many rows of data you have after applying the Filter to data in a worksheet. Because the **Filter** tool hides rows of data, you cannot use the row number next to your last row of data to determine the size of a filtered set of data. Instead, you need to look in the lower-left corner of the status bar, or you can copy and paste the data into a new worksheet. When you copy and paste filtered data to a new worksheet, Excel will only paste the data from rows that are not hidden. This allows you to use either the row numbers or use a count function to determine how many rows of data you have.

Subtotals

One of the key challenges when working with large volumes of data in Excel is summarizing totals and subtotals for multiple categories. This is one of the key benefits of using a PivotTable to analyze large sets of data; however, subtotals can be added directly to a large data set contained in a worksheet. This might be a better option compared to a PivotTable if you need to analyze the details that make up the total result for a particular category in your data set. For example, Figure 8.33 contains category sales data for the stores of a hypothetical electronics retail company. The company sells three categories of merchandise in every store, and there are 80 stores in the company. Every store is assigned to a district and each district is assigned to a region. Overall, there are 241 rows of data in this example. The **Subtotal** tool will be used to analyze the sales performance of this company by summing the sales results in columns E, F, and G by region, district, and store.

Figure 8.33 | **Merchandise Sales for a Hypothetical Electronics Retail Store**

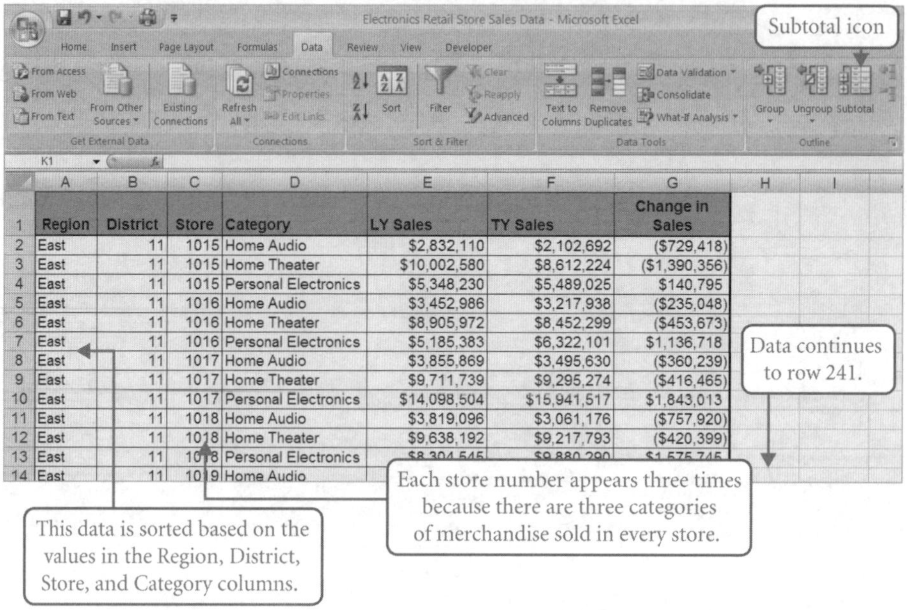

	A	B	C	D	E	F	G
1	Region	District	Store	Category	LY Sales	TY Sales	Change in Sales
2	East	11	1015	Home Audio	$2,832,110	$2,102,692	($729,418)
3	East	11	1015	Home Theater	$10,002,580	$8,612,224	($1,390,356)
4	East	11	1015	Personal Electronics	$5,348,230	$5,489,025	$140,795
5	East	11	1016	Home Audio	$3,452,986	$3,217,938	($235,048)
6	East	11	1016	Home Theater	$8,905,972	$8,452,299	($453,673)
7	East	11	1016	Personal Electronics	$5,185,383	$6,322,101	$1,136,718
8	East	11	1017	Home Audio	$3,855,869	$3,495,630	($360,239)
9	East	11	1017	Home Theater	$9,711,739	$9,295,274	($416,465)
10	East	11	1017	Personal Electronics	$14,098,504	$15,941,517	$1,843,013
11	East	11	1018	Home Audio	$3,819,096	$3,061,176	($757,920)
12	East	11	1018	Home Theater	$9,638,192	$9,217,793	($420,399)
13	East	11	1018	Personal Electronics	$8,304,545	$9,880,290	$1,575,745
14	East	11	1019	Home Audio			

The first step in analyzing the sales data from Figure 8.33 is to add subtotals to the Region column. This will provide an overall view of the sales performance of the company by summarizing 241 rows of data into 5. The following explains how this is accomplished.

- Sort the data in the worksheet in ascending order based on values in the following columns: Region, District, Store, and Category. The data in a worksheet must be sorted for the **Subtotal** tool to work properly. The sort order should be based on the subtotals you need to analyze for your project.
- Click any cell that contains data. If you are using a worksheet that contains several adjacent columns of data as shown in Figure 8.33, you can click any cell that contains data and Excel will automatically configure the **Subtotal** tool.
- Click the **Subtotal** icon in the **Data** tab of the Ribbon. This will open the **Subtotal** dialog box (see Figure 8.34).
- Click the drop-down arrow next to the first box labeled **At each change in:** and select Region. This will add a subtotal after the last row of each region.
- Click the drop-down arrow next to the second box labeled **Use function:** and select Sum. The drop-down arrow for this box will list several different mathematical functions that can be processed through the Subtotal tool.
- The third box in this window lists all the column headings from the worksheet in Figure 8.33. The check mark next to a column heading shows what data Excel will be subtotaling. The checks can be added or removed by clicking in the box next to the column heading. For this example, the LY Sales, TY Sales, and Change in Sales columns are selected.
- Click the **OK** button at the bottom of the **Subtotal** dialog box.

Figure 8.34 | **Subtotal Dialog Box**

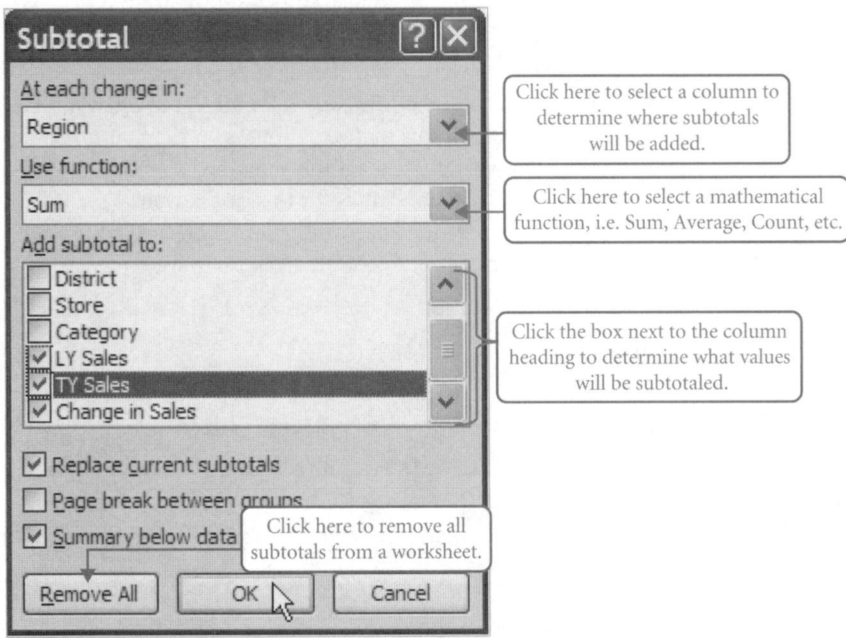

COMMON MISTAKES | Sorting Data Before Using Subtotals

The data in a worksheet must be sorted in a logical sequence before using the **Subtotal** tool. The **Subtotal** tool will subtotal data based on the way data is sorted. Therefore, before adding subtotals make sure the data in your worksheet is sorted based on the columns that will be used for adding subtotals.

Figure 8.35 shows the results of adding subtotals to the data shown in Figure 8.33. Notice that a button with a minus sign appears to the left of the subtotal. This is one of two types of buttons that are used to control the rows of detail that are displayed on the worksheet. These buttons are as follows:

- **Hide/Show Detail Buttons:** These buttons appear next to each subtotal that is added to the worksheet. They are used to hide or show all the values that make up the subtotal for a particular category.
- **Level Buttons:** These buttons appear at the top-left side of the worksheet. They are used to hide or show details for an entire level of subtotals. For example, these buttons can be used to hide or show details for the subtotals of every region in Figure 8.35.

Figure 8.35 | **Results of Adding Subtotals to the Region Column**

A1

	A	B	C	D	E	F	G
55	East	15	1053	Personal Electronics	$4,775,719	$5,574,833	$799,114
56	East	15	1054	Home Audio	$3,707,581	$3,386,653	($320,928)
57	East	15	1054	Home Theater	$9,415,161	$8,983,491	($431,670)
58	East	15	1054	Personal Electronics	$7,760,663	$8,771,225	$1,010,562
59	East	15	1055	Home Audio	$5,515,831	$5,019,364	($496,467)
60	East	15	1055	Home Theater	$13,031,663	$12,905,473	($126,190)
61	East	15	1055	Personal Electronics	$11,267,806	$11,754,828	$487,022
62	**East Total**				$468,024,133	$478,695,003	$10,670,870
63	Midwest	21	2015	Home Audio	$5,964,933	$5,093,927	($871,006)
64	Midwest	21	2015	Home Theater	$13,929,866	$13,920,096	($9,770)
5	Midwest	21	2015	Personal Electronics	$10,956,086	$12,402,137	$1,446,051
6	Midwest	21	2016	Home Audio	$4,444,362	$3,700,878	($743,484)
7	Midwest	21	2016	Home Theater	$10,88		78)
68	Midwest	21	2016	Personal Electronics	$11,98		12

Level buttons

Hide/Show Detail button

A row has been added showing subtotals for the East region.

Figure 8.36 shows a variation of the results shown in Figure 8.35. The Level 2 button was clicked to hide all of the details in the worksheet so the only rows showing are the subtotals for each region and the grand total results for the entire company. Removing the detail allows a manager to evaluate the overall sales results of the company and identify any key trends. Notice that the company sales increased by over $65 million dollars and that almost 50 percent of this increase came from the South region. All regions showed an increase in sales with the East region showing the smallest increase. A manager might want to look at more details for the East region to see if there is any one district that is lowering sales for the entire region; however, additional subtotals will need to be added to the worksheet to conduct this analysis.

Figure 8.36 | **Hiding Details for All Subtotals**

	A	B	C	D	E	F	G
1	Region	District	Store	Category	LY Sales	TY Sales	Change in Sales
62	East Total				$468,024,133	$478,695,003	$10,670,870
123	Midwest Total				$524,869,458	$536,578,141	$11,708,683
184	South Total				$532,194,145	$562,214,853	$30,020,708
245	West Total				$474,813,509	$488,065,175	$13,251,666
					$1,999,901,245	$2,065,553,172	$65,651,927

Click the Level 2 button to hide all details.

The company increased sales by over $65 million.

The South region had the highest increase in sales over last year.

As previously mentioned, to evaluate the sales results by region, additional subtotals need to be added to the worksheet in Figure 8.36. The following explains how subtotals are added for the District and Store columns.

- Click any cell that contains data in the worksheet.
- Click the **Subtotal** icon in the **Data** tab of the Ribbon.
- Select the District column in the first drop-down box of the **Subtotal** dialog box.
- Set the function to Sum in the second drop-down box.
- Check to see that a check mark appears next to the LY Sales, TY Sales, and Change in Sales fields in the **Add subtotal to** box. You can add a check mark by clicking the box next to the field.
- Click the box next to the **Replace Current Subtotals** option to *remove* the check mark. This option must *not* be selected or the subtotals for the Region column will be removed.
- Click the **OK** button at the bottom of the **Subtotal** dialog box.
- Add a subtotal for the Store column by opening the **Subtotal** dialog box again, and repeat the same process that was explained for the District column.

Figures 8.37 through 8.40 show how sales for the East region can be analyzed by examining different levels of subtotals. The Level 5, 4, 3, and 2 buttons were clicked to show just the region totals in Figure 8.37.

Figure 8.37 | **Subtotals Added for Three Additional Columns**

	Region	District	Store	Category	LY Sales	TY Sales	Change in Sales
87	East Total				$468,024,133	$478,695,003	$10,670,870
173	Midwest Total				$524,869,458	$536,578,141	$11,708,683
259	South Total				$532,194,145	$562,214,853	$30,020,708
345	West Total				$474,813,509	$488,065,175	$13,251,666
346	Grand Total				$1,999,901,245	$2,065,553,172	$65,651,927

Additional Level Buttons are added to the worksheet.

Click here to view details for the East region.

Notice in Figure 8.38 that District 14 is showing a significant decline in sales. Sales declined over 1.7 million dollars from last year.

Figure 8.38 | **Details for the East Region**

	Region	District	Store	Category	LY Sales	TY Sales	Change in Sales
22		11 Total			$101,915,039	$102,033,116	$118,077
35		12 Total			$81,628,605	$84,361,667	$2,733,062
52		13 Total			$108,623,073	$117,419,182	$8,796,109
73		14 Total			$103,547,560	$101,823,067	($1,724,493)
86		15 Total			$72,309,856	$73,057,971	$748,115
87	East Total				$468,024,133	$478,695,003	$10,670,870
173	Midwest Total				$524,869,458	$536,578,141	$11,708,683
					$532,194,145	$562,214,853	$30,020,708
					$474,813,509	$488,065,175	$13,251,666
					$1,999,901,245	$2,065,553,172	$65,651,927

Click here to hide details for the East region.

Subtotals for all districts in the East region.

District 14 shows the largest decrease in sales compared to other districts in the East region.

Figure 8.39 shows that Store 1044 had the largest decrease in sales for District 14. Sales declined in this store over $900,000.

Figure 8.39 | **Details for District 14**

	Region	District	Store	Category	LY Sales	TY Sales	Change in Sales
22		11 Total			$101,915,039	$102,033,116	$118,077
35		12 Total			$81,628,605	$84,361,667	$2,733,062
52		13 Total			$108,623,073	$117,419,182	$8,796,109
56			1040 Total		$10,860,900	$10,862,649	$1,749
60			1041 Total		$18,769,919	$18,447,657	($322,262)
64			1042 Total		$29,937,133	$29,298,804	($638,329)
68			1043 Total		$18,442,508	$18,578,249	$135,741
72			1044 Total		$25,537,100	$24,635,708	($901,392)
73		14 Total			3,547,560	$101,823,067	($1,724,493)
86		15 Total			2,309,856	$73,057,971	$748,115
					8,024,133	$478,695,003	$10,670,870

Click here to hide details for district 14.

Subtotals for all stores in district 14

Store 1044 shows the largest sales decrease in the district.

Figure 8.40 shows that all of the sales decrease for Store 1044 is coming from the Home Audio merchandise category. This decrease might be the result of a strong competitor opening one or several stores in this market. A marketing manager might use this information to create an aggressive promotional campaign for Home Audio merchandise to regain this business.

>> Quick Reference

Applying Subtotals

1. Sort your data based on columns where subtotals will be applied.
2. Click any cell containing data in a worksheet with several adjacent columns.
3. Click the **Subtotal** icon in the **Data** tab of the Ribbon.
4. Select a column where a subtotal will be added in the first drop-down box of the **Subtotal** dialog box.
5. Select a mathematical function in the second drop-down box.
6. Select columns that contain data to be subtotaled in the third box.
7. If you are adding multiple subtotals to a worksheet, make sure the Replace Current Subtotals is not selected.
8. Click the **OK** button in the **Subtotal** dialog box.
9. Use the +/– buttons to show or hide details for a specific subtotal.

Figure 8.40 | **Details for Store 1044**

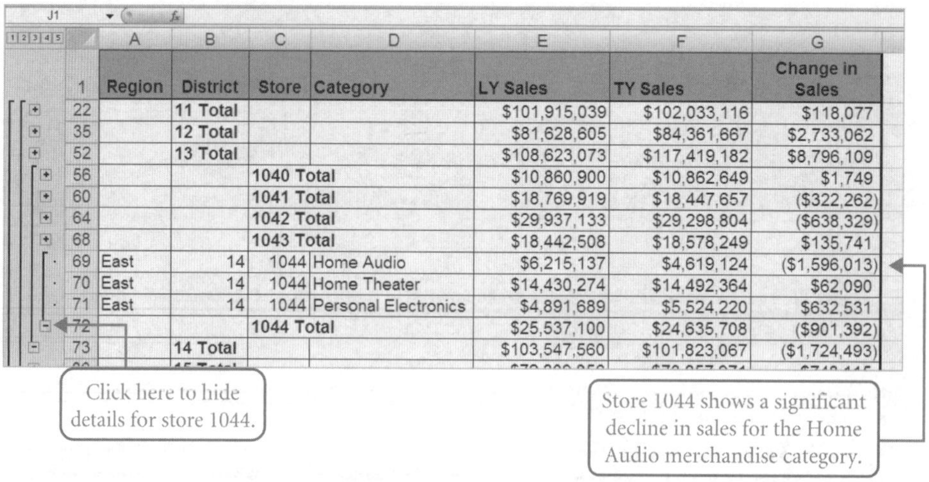

1	Region	District	Store	Category	LY Sales	TY Sales	Change in Sales
22		11 Total			$101,915,039	$102,033,116	$118,077
35		12 Total			$81,628,605	$84,361,667	$2,733,062
52		13 Total			$108,623,073	$117,419,182	$8,796,109
56			1040 Total		$10,860,900	$10,862,649	$1,749
60			1041 Total		$18,769,919	$18,447,657	($322,262)
64			1042 Total		$29,937,133	$29,298,804	($638,329)
68			1043 Total		$18,442,508	$18,578,249	$135,741
69	East	14	1044	Home Audio	$6,215,137	$4,619,124	($1,596,013)
70	East	14	1044	Home Theater	$14,430,274	$14,492,364	$62,090
71	East	14	1044	Personal Electronics	$4,891,689	$5,524,220	$632,531
72			1044 Total		$25,537,100	$24,635,708	($901,392)
73		14 Total			$103,547,560	$101,823,067	($1,724,493)

Adding the Developer Tab

You will need to add the **Developer** tab to the Ribbon before reviewing the next tool in this section. The Developer tab contains advanced features for creating macros and adding controls to a worksheet. The following explains how this tab is added to the Ribbon.

- Click the **Office Button**.
- Click the **Excel Options** button to open the **Excel Options** dialog box.
- Click the Popular option on the left side of the **Excel Options** dialog box.
- Click the box next to the **Show Developer tab in the Ribbon** option to add a check mark (see Figure 8.41).
- Click the **OK** button at the bottom of the **Excel Options** dialog box.

Figure 8.41 shows the Developer tab option in the **Excel Options** dialog box. After the **OK** button is clicked, the **Developer** tab will be added to the Ribbon.

Figure 8.41 | **The Excel Options Dialog Box**

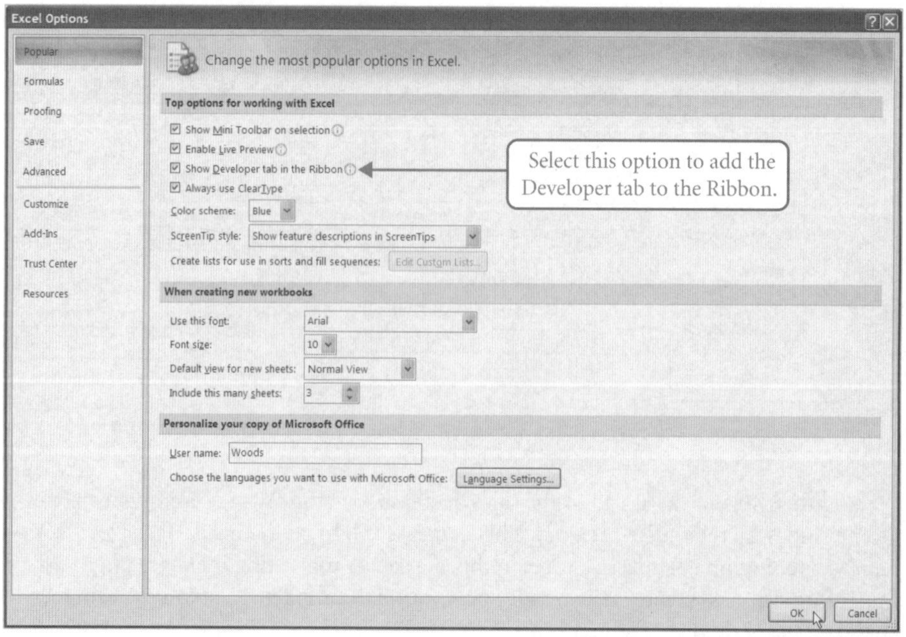

List Boxes

The last tool that will be demonstrated in this section is the List Box. The List Box is used to select specific values from a column of data. Similar to the other tools covered in this chapter, this demonstration shows how a business manager can evaluate specific trend information from a large dataset. The List Box is often used with the **Vlookup** function because values can be selected by pointing and clicking from a list of options instead of typing them into a cell. This eliminates spelling error problems or typing wrong data into the lookup cell of a **Vlookup** function. This feature will be demonstrated using a variation of the Electronics Retail Store Sales data shown in Figure 8.33. Figure 8.42 shows the same data; however, sales for each store is shown for each month of the year and there is no merchandise category detail. The purpose of this demonstration is to evaluate the monthly and overall sales trend for specific stores.

Figure 8.42 | **Electronics Retail Store Data by Month**

	A	B	C	D	E	F	G
1	Store/Month	Region	District	Store	Month	LY Sales	TY Sales
2	1015January	1	11	1015	January	$1,876,167	$824,674
3	1015February	1	11	1015	February	$632,782	$625,750
4	1015March	1	11	1015	March	$900,681	$1,001,241
5	1015April	1	11	1015	April	$1,026,778	$1,020,506
6	1015May	1	11	1015	May	$1,171,174	$1,059,090
7	1015June	1	11	1015	June	$1,165,468	$1,043,707
8	1015July	1	11	1015	July	$1,214,917	$1,296,513
9	1015August	1	11	1015	August	$1,992,039	$2,095,867
10	1015September	1	11	1015	September	$2,503,066	$2,152,621
11	1015October	1	11	1015	October	$1,866,679	$1,635,170
12	1015November	1	11	1015	November	$1,772,117	$1,663,390
13	1015December	1	11	1015	December	$2,061,052	$1,785,413
14	1016January	1	11	1016	January	$1,810,277	$915,691
15	1016February	1	11	1016	February	$610,559	$694,813
16	1016March	1	11	1016	March	$869,049	$1,111,746
17	1016April	1	11	1016	April	$990,718	$1,133,137

Store List | Store Sales | Store Analysis

Data continues to row 961.

Concatenate function was used to combine the store and month.

Each unique store number is listed in this worksheet.

This worksheet will be used to display store sales data by month.

Figure 8.42 shows the *Store Sales* worksheet from the workbook that will be used to demonstrate the List Box. Notice that the Store Number and Month columns are concatenated together in column A. This will enable a Vlookup function to select sales for a specific month for each store. This example will utilize two other worksheets in this workbook. The Store List worksheet contains a list of every unique store in the company, which will be used to populate the window of the List Box. The stores in this column will be used to populate the window of the List Box. The *Store Analysis* worksheet is shown in Figure 8.43. This worksheet will be the focus of this demonstration and will be used to display the monthly sales results for a selected store by using a combination of the List Box and the **Vookup** function.

Figure 8.43 | **Store Analysis Worksheet**

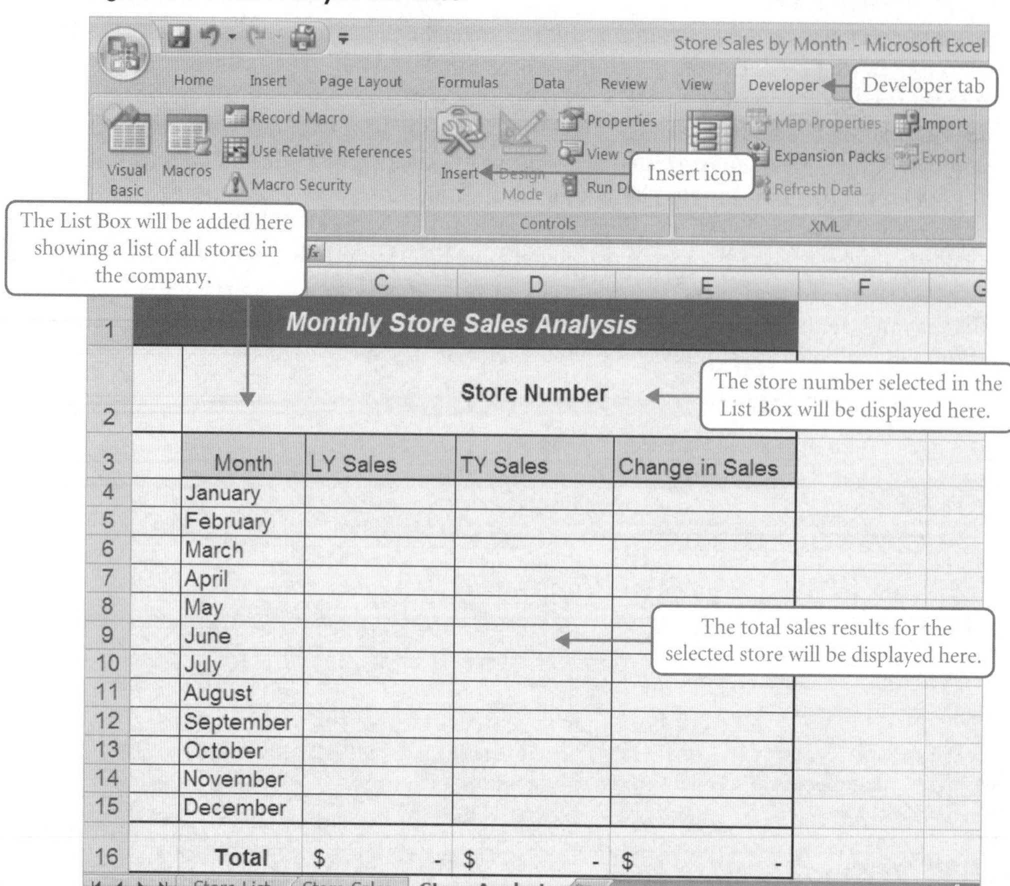

Figure 8.43 shows the worksheet that will be used to show the monthly sales results for a store that is selected using the List Box. The following explains how the List Box is added to this worksheet in the area of cells B2 and C2.

- Click the **Insert** icon in the **Developer** tab of the Ribbon.
- Click the **List Box** icon from the **Form Controls** options.
- Click and drag a square over cells B2 and C2 in the Store Analysis worksheet. The List Box will appear after releasing the mouse button. White circles will appear around the perimeter of the List Box indicating it is ready to be configured (see Figure 8.44).

Figure 8.44 | **Adding a List Box to the Store Analysis Worksheet**

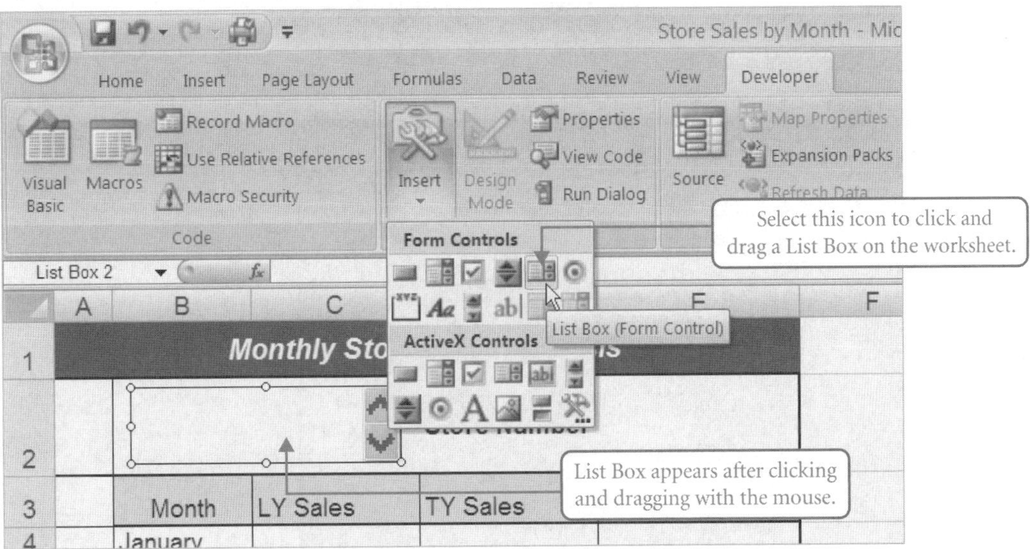

Figure 8.44 shows the results of adding an empty List Box to the Store Analysis worksheet. The List Box must be configured for store numbers to appear in the List Box window. The following explains how this is accomplished.

- Make sure the List Box is not active. If white circles appear around the perimeter of the List Box, the box is not active and can be configured. If the List Box *is* active (no white circles around the perimeter) hold down the **Ctrl** key and click the box.
- Click the **Properties** icon in the **Developer** tab of the Ribbon. This will open the **Format Control** dialog box (see Figure 8.45).
- Click the **Control** tab at the top of the **Format Control** dialog box.
- Click the range finder next to the **Input Range** box, highlight the range B2:B81 on the Store List worksheet, and press the **Enter** key. The stores contained in this range will appear in the window of the List Box when it is activated.
- Click the range finder next to the **Cell Link** box, activate cell A2 on the Store Analysis worksheet, and press the **Enter** key. When a store is selected in the List Box, the sequence number of where that store appears in the list in the Store List worksheet will be displayed in cell A2 of the Store Analysis worksheet. This number will be used in a **Vlookup** function to display the store number that was selected in the List Box in cell E2 of the Store Analysis worksheet.
- Select the Single option in the Selection Type options area of the **Format Control** dialog box. This will allow only one store to be selected at a time.
- Click the **OK** button at the bottom of the **Format Control** dialog box and then click anywhere on the Store Analysis worksheet to activate the List Box.

Figure 8.45 shows the settings that were made in the **Format Control** dialog box for this example.

Figure 8.45 | **Format Control Dialog Box for a List Box**

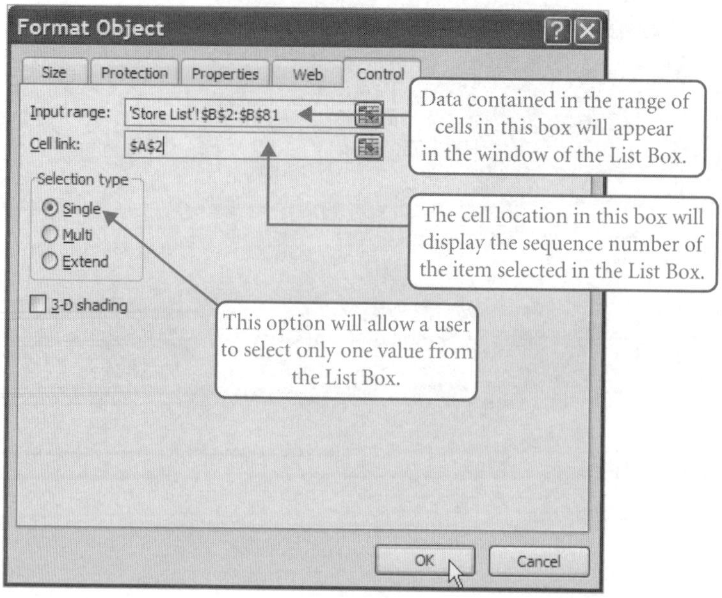

Figure 8.46 shows the List Box activated in the Store Analysis worksheet. Store 1015 has been selected from the List Box. Notice that the number 1 appears in cell A2. This is because store 1015 is listed first in the list of stores contained in the range B2:B81 in the Store List worksheet (see Figure 8.47).

Figure 8.46 | **Active List Box in the Store Analysis Worksheet**

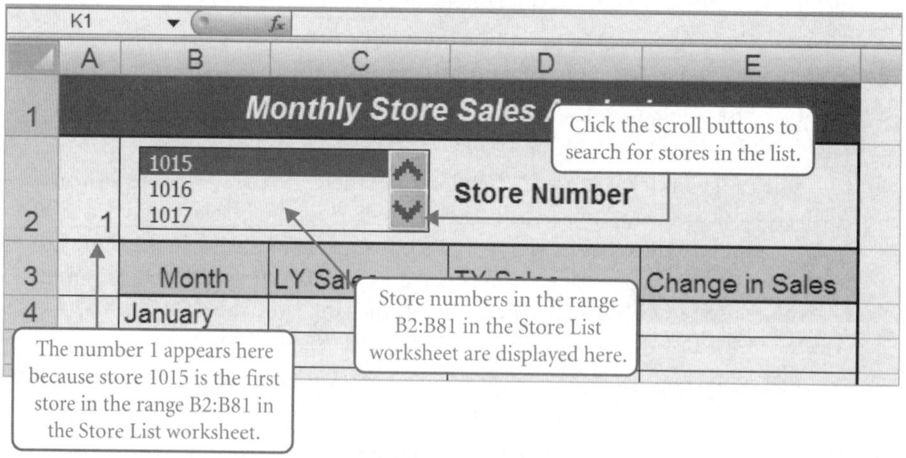

Figure 8.47 | **Data from the Store List Worksheet**

	A	B
1	Sequence	Store
2	1	1015
3	2	1016
4	3	1017
5	4	1018
6	5	1019
7	6	1020

This column was added so a Vlookup function can use the Cell Link number displayed in cell A2 of the Store Analysis worksheet as a lookup value.

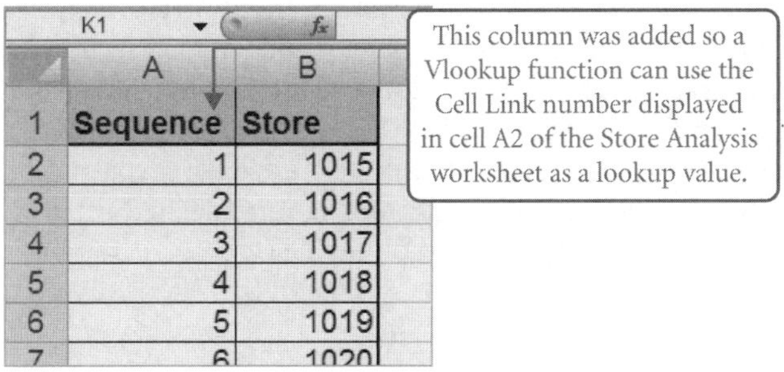

After the List Box is configured and activated, the Store Analysis worksheet can be completed by using **Vlookup** functions to find and display sales data for the store that is selected. The **Vlookup** functions that will be added to the Store Analysis worksheet will serve two purposes. The first purpose is to display the store number that was selected in the List Box in cell location E2. This is done to display the store prominently on the spreadsheet so it can be easily identified when the worksheet is printed. The following is how each argument of this **Vlookup** function is defined.

- **lookup_value:** `A2` Cell A2 contains the sequence number that is displayed in the Store Analysis worksheet (see Figure 8.46). The function will look for the number that is displayed in this cell in Column A of the Store List worksheet (see Figure 8.47).
- **table_array:** `'Store List'!A2:B81` This is the range of data that contains the sequence number and the store numbers in the Store List worksheet.
- **col_index_num:** `2` The store numbers are in the second column to the right of the first column in the table array range.
- **[range_lookup]:** `False` The function will only look for exact values.

The second purpose the **Vlookup** functions will serve is to display the sales data that pertains to each month for the store selected in the List Box. The lookup value for these **Vlookup** functions will be created by concatenating the store number displayed in cell E2 with the month displayed in Column B of the Sales Analysis worksheet (see Figure 8.48). The following is how each of the arguments of this function is constructed for the LY Sales column. The **Vlookup** function that is used for the TY Sales column is identical to the LY Sales column except the column index number is 7 instead of 6.

- **lookup_value:** `CONCATENATE($E$2,B4)` The function will look for the combination of the store number displayed in cell E2 and the month displayed in cell B4, which is January. Notice that an absolute reference is placed on cell E2 but not B4. This is because when the function is pasted to the rest of the cells in the LY Sales column, a different month will be concatenated with the store number.
- **table_array:** `'Store Sales'!$A$2:$G$961` The function will search for the lookup value in Column A of the Store Sales worksheet (see Figure 8.42). As previously mentioned, this column was added to the worksheet by concatenating the values in the Store Number column with the Month column. This makes it possible for sales data to be matched up with the store number selected in the Store Analysis worksheet for each month of the year.
- **col_index_num:** `6` The sales data for Last Year in the Store Sales worksheet is six columns to the right of Column A which is the first column in the table array range.
- **[range_lookup]:** `False` The function will only look for exact values.

>> Quick Reference

List Box

1. Click the **Insert** icon in the **Developer** tab of the Ribbon.
2. Click the **List Box** icon from the **Form Controls** options.
3. Click and drag the desired size of the List Box on your worksheet.
4. Click the **Properties** icon in the **Developer** tab of the Ribbon.
5. Click the **Control** tab at the top of the **Format Control** dialog box.
6. Click the range finder next to the **Input Range** box and then highlight a range of cells in one column that contains data displayed in the **List Box** window.
7. Click the range finder next to the **Cell Link** box and then activate a cell location that will be used to display the sequence number of the item selected in the List Box.
8. Choose a Selection Type.
9. Click the **OK** button in the **Format Control** dialog box.
10. Click any cell location on your worksheet to activate the List Box.

Figure 8.48 shows the completed Sales Analysis worksheet. Noticed that Column A is hidden. The only value in this column is the Cell Link number from the List Box, which is not necessary for the reader to see. It was mentioned in the Subtotal section that Store 1044 showed a considerable decrease in sales for the East region. Figure 8.48 shows this store selected in the List Box. Notice that most of the sales decline for this store occurred in the month of January. In fact, March, July, and August were particularly strong months for this store; however, sales for this store declined again during September through December. This might suggest that competing stores had an aggressive Fall/Holiday promotional marketing strategy.

Figure 8.48 | **Completed Store Analysis Worksheet**

K1

	B	C	D	E
1	Monthly Store Sales Analysis			
2	1042 1043 1044		Store Number	1044
3	Month	LY Sales	TY Sales	Change in Sales
4	January	$ 2,634,993	$ 1,253,795	$ (1,381,198)
5	February	$ 888,714	$ 951,361	$ 62,647
6	March	$ 1,264,966	$ 1,522,240	$ 257,274
7	April	$ 1,442,063	$ 1,551,529	$ 109,466
8	May	$ 1,644,862	$ 1,610,190	$ (34,672)
9	June	$ 1,636,848	$ 1,586,803	$ (50,045)
10	July	$ 1,706,297	$ 1,971,157	$ 264,860
11	August	$ 2,797,730	$ 3,186,457	$ 388,727
12	September	$ 3,515,445	$ 3,272,743	$ (242,702)
13	October	$ 2,621,667	$ 2,486,036	$ (135,631)
14	November	$ 2,488,860	$ 2,528,940	$ 40,080
15	December	$ 2,894,655	$ 2,714,458	$ (180,197)
16	Total	$25,537,100	$ 24,635,709	$ (901,391)

Store List | Store Sales | Store Analysis

Formulas subtracting LY Sales from TY Sales are used in this column.

Sum functions are used in these cells.

Most of the sales decline for this store occurred in January.

VIDEO WORKSHOP

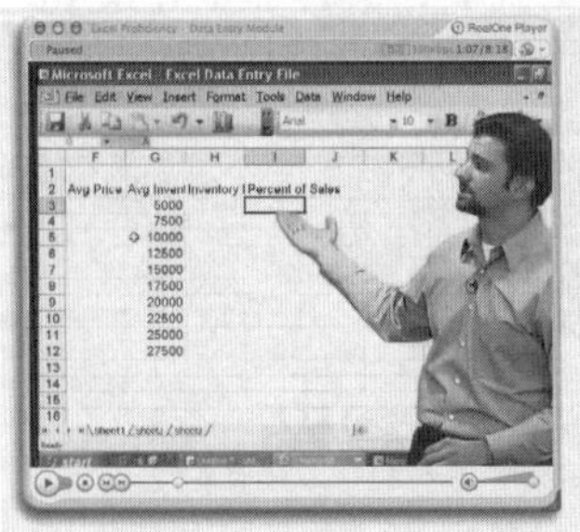

>> Filters

The purpose of this workshop is to review the setup and use of the **Filter** tool. This workshop will use the same data that was shown in the Filters segment. I will be demonstrating the tasks in this workshop in the video named **Filters**. Open the Excel file named ib_e08_marketanalysis and then complete the tasks in the workshop.

1. **Applying Filters (Video: Filters)**
   a. Activate cell location A1 on the Data worksheet.
   b. Click the **Filter** icon in the **Data** tab of the Ribbon.
   c. Click the drop-down arrow next to the Total Population column heading, place the cursor over the **Number Filters** option, and select the **Custom Filter** option.
   d. Click the drop-down arrow next to the first box in the **Custom AutoFilter** dialog box, and select the is greater than or equal to option.
   e. Click the drop-down arrow next to the second box in the **Custom AutoFilter** dialog box, and select the value 100,002; then click the **OK** button.
   f. Open the **Custom AutoFilter** dialog box for the Percent of Population Age 25-35 column. Set the filter for any values greater than or equal to .20.
   g. Open the **Custom AutoFilter** dialog box for the Growth in Population Age 25-35 column. Set the filter for any values greater than .05
   h. Open the **Custom AutoFilter** dialog box for the Household Income column. Set the filter for any values greater than or equal to 70000.
   i. Insert a new worksheet in the workbook. Copy the range A1:A501 in the Data worksheet and paste it into cell A1 of the new worksheet.
   j. Save and close your workbook.

>> Subtotals

VIDEO WORKSHOP

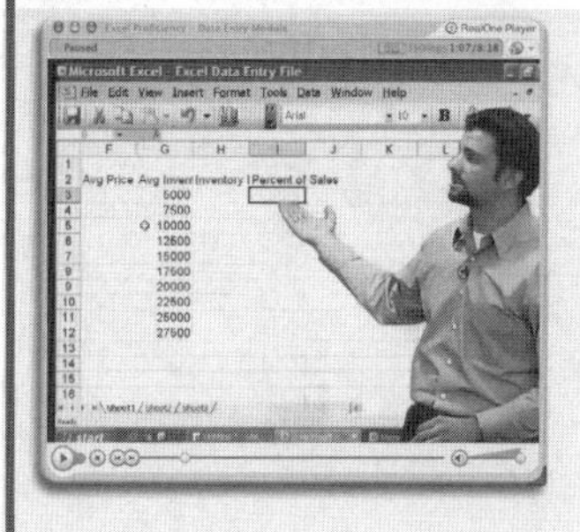

The purpose of this workshop is to review the setup and use of Subtotals. This workshop will use the same data that was shown in the Subtotals segment. I will be demonstrating the tasks in this workshop in the video named **Subtotals.** Open the Excel file named ib_e08_electronicsstoreanalysis and then complete the tasks in the workshop.

1. **Applying Subtotals to Data (Video: Subtotals)**
   a. Sort the range A1:G241 based on values in the Region, District, and Stores columns. Set the sort option for each column to ascending or smallest to largest.
   b. Activate cell A1 in the Data worksheet.
   c. Click the **Subtotals** icon in the **Data** tab of the Ribbon.
   d. Select the Region column for the first drop-down box in the **Subtotal** dialog box.
   e. Select the **Sum** function in the second drop-down box in the **Subtotal** dialog box.
   f. In the **Add subtotal to** box, check marks should appear next to the LY Sales, TY Sales, and Change in Sales columns. Click the box next to the column name to add a check mark, if necessary.
   g. Click the **OK** button at the bottom of the **Subtotal** dialog box.
   h. Click the **Level 2** button in the upper-left margin of the worksheet.
   i. Activate cell A1 and then open the **Subtotal** dialog box.
   j. Select the District column for the first drop-down box in the **Subtotal** dialog box and repeat Steps e and f

k. Click the box next to the Replace current subtotals option to remove the check mark and then click the **OK** button.
l. Click the **Level 2** button and then activate cell A1.
m. Open the **Subtotal** dialog box, select the Store column, and repeat Steps e and f; then click the **OK** button.
n. In this order, click the **Level 4, 3**, and **2** buttons.
o. Click the **Show Details** button next to the East region.
p. Click the **Show Details** button next to District 14.
q. Click the **Show Details** button next to Store 1044.
r. Save and close your workbook.

VIDEO WORKSHOP

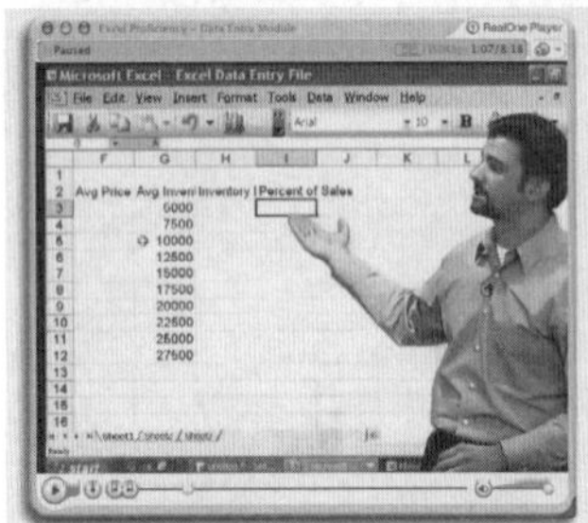

>> List Boxes

The purpose of this workshop is to review the setup and use of List Boxes. This workshop will use the same data that was shown in the List Boxes segment. I will be demonstrating the tasks in this workshop in the video named **List Boxes**. Open the Excel file named ib_e08_storesalesbymonth and complete the tasks in the workshop.

1. List Boxes (Video: List Boxes)

a. Activate the Store Analysis worksheet.
b. Click the **Insert** icon in the **Developer** tab of the Ribbon.
c. Click the **List Box** icon from the **Form Controls** set of options.
d. Click and drag a rectangle in the space between cells B2 and C2.
e. Click the **Properties** icon in the **Developer** tab of the Ribbon.
f. In the **Control** tab of the **Format Control** dialog box, click the range finder next to the Input range box, highlight the range B2:B81 in the Store List worksheet, and press the **Enter** key.
g. Click the range finder next to the **Cell link** box, activate cell A2 in the Store Analysis worksheet, and press the **Enter** key.
h. Click the **OK** button in the **Format Objects** dialog box, and then activate cell F1 in the Store Analysis worksheet.
i. Select Store 1015 in the List Box.
j. Type a **VLOOKUP** function in cell E2 on the Store Analysis worksheet, defining each argument as follows:
    i. lookup_value: Cell A2 in the Store Analysis worksheet
    ii. table_array: A2:B81 in the Store List worksheet
    iii. col_index_num: 2
    iv. [range_lookup]: False
k. Type a **VLOOKUP** function in cell C4 on the Store Analysis worksheet defining each argument as follows (use absolute references as shown):
    i. lookup_value: Concatenate($E$2,B4)
    ii. table_array: $A$2:$G$961 in the Store Sales worksheet
    iii. col_index_num: 6
    iv. [range_lookup]: False
l. Copy the **VLOOKUP** function in cell C4 and paste it into the range C5:C15 in the Store Analysis worksheet.
m. Type a **VLOOKUP** function in cell D4 on the Store Analysis worksheet defining each argument as follows:

i. lookup_value: Concatenate($E$2,B4)
ii. table_array: $A$2:$G$961 in the Store Sales worksheet
iii. col_index_num: 7
iv. [range_lookup]: False

n. Copy the **VLOOKUP** function in cell D4 and paste it into the range D5:D15 in the Store Analysis worksheet.
o. Type the formula `D4-C4` in cell E4 of the Store Analysis worksheet; then copy and paste this formula into the range E5:E15.
p. Type a sum function in cells C16, D16, and E16 to add the values in rows 4 through 15 for each column.
q. Hide column A in the Store Analysis worksheet.
r. Select Store 1044 in the List Box.
s. Save and close your workbook.

>> Summarizing the Sales Performance of a Business

EXERCISE

Why Do I Need This?

Attention to detail is often the difference between success and failure in any business. Business mangers working in today's corporations have access to enormous amounts of data. However, it is impossible for a person to evaluate every row of data that is collected for their business or industry every day. As a result, business managers must determine what details they need to evaluate to improve their firm's business. This usually begins with some type of general performance report for the business they are managing, which then directs them to areas where more detailed information is needed. For example, if a business manger is running a division of company that sells five categories of products, a general performance report might show the overall sales results of the division by category. If one of the categories is showing a significant decline in sales, the manager will research more details for that category. This type of analysis can be conducted using Excel's AutoFilter and Subtotal tools.

Exercise

The purpose of this exercise is to use Excel's **Subtotal** and **Filter** tools to evaluate the sales performance of a clothing business. Open the Excel file named ib_e08_salesbyitem before completing the following tasks.

1. Activate cell A1 in the Data for Subtotals worksheet. This worksheet contains almost 500 rows of data showing the sales results for this year and last year for every item sold by this clothing business for each month of the year. The data is sorted in month order and then by the Category and Item columns in ascending order. The first goal of this analysis is to use the Subtotal tool to evaluate the overall sales performance of the business by month.
2. Open the **Subtotal** dialog box. Create a subtotal for each month of sales data. Sum the values in the LY Sales, TY Sales, and Change in Sales columns.
3. Click the **Level 2** button to hide all the details in the worksheet except for the subtotals by month. Are the overall sales for this business increasing or decreasing? Which month is showing a decrease in sales?
4. Add a second subtotal to this worksheet for the Category column. Make sure the **Replace Current Subtotals** is *not* checked. Click the box next to this option to remove the check.

5. Add a third subtotal for the Item column. There should be a total of three subtotals on this worksheet.
6. In this order, click the **Level 5, 4, 3**, and **2** buttons. The worksheet should be back to showing just the overall sales result of the business by month.
7. Click the **Show Details** button for the month you identified in number 3. Are all categories showing a decrease in sales? Which category is showing the biggest decrease in sales?
8. Click the **Show Details** button for the category you identified in number 7. Are all items in this category showing a decrease in sales? Which item is showing the largest decrease in sales?
9. Click the **Show Details** button for the item you identified in number 8. Which colors for this item are showing a decrease in sales?
10. Activate cell A1 in the Data for AutoFilter worksheet.
11. Click the **Filter** icon in the **Data** tab of the Ribbon.
12. Click the drop-down arrow next to the Change in Sales column heading. Place the cursor over the **Number Filters** option and select the **Top 10** option. The goal of this task is to identify items in the business with largest decline in sales compared to last year. Select the **Bottom** option in the first drop-down box in the **Top 10 AutoFilter** dialog box and then click the **OK** button.
13. Sort the items selected by the filter based on the values in the Change in Sales column in ascending order—smallest to largest. Which item/color appears most frequently in this list? Based on these sales results, do you think this item should be discontinued?
14. Remove the filter on the Change in Sales column.
15. Set a filter on the Sales TY column to show the top ten highest sales results. Sort the values in this column in descending order—largest to smallest. Are all the items showing an increase in sales over last year? Would you still consider discontinuing the item you identified in number 13?
16. Set a filter on the Change in Sales column to show any item where the sales increased by more than $100,000 (you will need to remove the filter from the Sales TY column). Which category appears to have the best potential for increasing sales for the company?
17. Save and close your file.

PROBLEM & EXERCISE

>> What's Wrong with This Spreadsheet?

Problem

You are working as a business analyst in the buying division of a large retail company. Your coworker sends you an e-mail asking for help on a report he is trying to put together for a purchasing meeting. He is trying to use the **Subtotal** tool to summarize the sales results of the division by month. The following points are included in his e-mail.

- Can you do me a huge favor and take a look at the Excel file I attached to this e-mail? Someone told me that I would be able to summarize the total sales results by month for each category by using this **Subtotal** tool, but I can't figure out why this is not working.

- I am trying to show the total sales results for the company by month. I would also like to click on a month and see a summary of the sales results by category just for that month. Then, I want to see a summary of the sales results by item within the category.

- I set up the **Subtotal** tool on the attached file. I thought this was working fine because the total results for the divisions are correct. However, when I clicked on the box with the plus sign, the spreadsheet grew to almost 1900 rows. I thought this was odd because I started with less than 500 rows of data. Please help!

Exercise

The Excel file your coworker attached to the e-mail is named ib_e08_suspicioussubtotals. Open this file and examine the subtotals that were added in the Data worksheet. What's wrong with this spreadsheet? Consider the following points.

1. Test the worksheet by clicking the **Show Details** button. What happens? Does the worksheet show a summary of the total sales results by month?

2. Continue to test the worksheet by clicking the show details button for the first month, then the category, and then the item. What do you notice about the sales results as you show more details?

3. Why would the number of rows increase by such a large amount after applying the subtotals?

Write a short answer for each of these points; then fix the spreadsheet so the subtotals provide the proper sales summaries as described in the second point of your coworker's e-mail.

Excel in **Practice** | Anecdote

Solution from page 346

After investigating Excel's features for managing large datasets, I found a few tools that were perfect for this project. Everyone on the team found these tools easy to use, and they were flexible enough to solve each team member's unique analytical needs. I took the original worksheet which contained the 7,500 rows of data and copied it to two other worksheets. I then set up a different tool in each worksheet so each team member had a choice of using any of these tools to analyze the data based on their needs and preferences.

Assignment

1. Open the Excel file named ib_e08_storeevaluations. The data contained in this file is similar to the data that was explained in the anecdote.
2. Use any of the tools covered in this chapter to analyze the data in the Sheet1 worksheet to answer the follow questions and tasks.
   a. Analyze the overall sales performance of the business. Are sales increasing every year? Which year is showing the greatest increase in sales?
   b. Analyze the population statistics for the overall business. The products sold in the stores of this business are targeted for children between the ages of 4 and 11. Overall, are these stores located in areas where the Total Population and the Population Age 4-11 is increasing every year?
   c. Analyze the sales performance of this business by Region. Which region is showing the strongest sales growth from 2004 to 2006? Which region is showing the largest sales decline?
   d. Compare the population and competition trends between the region with the largest sales increase and the region with the largest sales decrease. Explain the difference in the trends between these two regions and explain why you think sales are increasing or decreasing for these regions.
   e. Add a new worksheet to the Store Evaluations workbook. Create a list of stores in this worksheet where the Population Age 4-11 is equal to or less than 15 percent of the Total Population in the year 2006. In addition, these stores should be in areas were the competition has less than or equal to two stores. Sort this list based on values in the Population Age 4-11 column. How many stores are on your list?
   f. Save and close your file.

Questions for Discussion

1. The anecdote suggests that both Access and Excel can be used to analyze large volumes of data. What are the benefits of being able to analyze data and get the same results using different tools and methods?

2. The main theme of this chapter is managing and analyzing large volumes of data. Why do companies collect so much data? What purpose does this data serve in a business?

3. Can companies achieve a competitive advantage if they collect and store more data than their competitors?

Review Questions

The following questions are related to the concepts addressed in this chapter. There are three types of questions: Short Answer, True or False, and Fill in the Blank. If your answer to a True or False question is False, write a short explanation as to why you think the statement is not true.

1. The ________ icon in the ________ tab of the Ribbon is used to create a PivotChart.
2. You must click anywhere in the ________ ________ to see the PivotTable Field List as well as the ________ and ________ tabs of the Ribbon.
3. True or False: The PivotTable Field names must be typed into the **Field Settings** dialog box before they appear in the PivotTable Field List.
4. How can you count the values in a field that is added to the Data section of the PivotTable Report instead of summing them?
5. The ________ button in the ________ dialog box can be used to format numbers to currency in the Data section of the PivotTable Report.
6. How can you reduce the data on a PivotTable to a specific item from a field that is dragged into the Row Fields section?
7. True or False: To adjust the subtotals shown on a PivotTable Report, double-click the field name that was added to the Data or Values section to open the **Value Field Settings** dialog box.
8. True or False: Similar to most other Excel operations, a key benefit of PivotTables is that if the source data is changed, the change will immediately be seen in the values and calculations on the PivotTable Report.
9. Explain how you would use two fields in the Data section of a PivotTable Report to create a formula.
10. The grand totals on a PivotTable can be added or removed by selecting the appropriate options in the ________ tab in the ________ dialog box.
11. True or False: A PivotTable is always added to your workbook when you create a PivotChart, and the PivotChart can be created by adding and manipulating fields in this PivotTable.
12. True or False: When using the **Filter** tool, you must highlight the first row containing column headings in your worksheet for the drop-down arrows to appear in the proper place.
13. How can you sort the results that are displayed using the **Filter** tool?
14. True or False: When using Filters, after you apply a filter rule to a specific column, you can *not* sort the data based on values in that column.
15. Before using the **Subtotals** tool, you must ________ all the data in your worksheet.
16. True or False: You can only set subtotals for one column at a time in **Subtotals** dialog box; therefore, you will need to open the **Subtotals** dialog box multiple times to create subtotals for multiple columns.

17. The ________ ________ are used to either hide or show all details from a column that has been subtotaled using the **Subtotals** tool.

18. If store number 6215 is the 12th store in a list of 100 stores, what number will appear in the Cell Link cell when this store is selected from a List Box?

19. How do you know if a List Box is inactive, which means the controls for the List Box can be set or modified?

20. You must hold down the ________ ________ before clicking a List Box to deactivate it.

Skills Exam

The following exam is designed to test your ability to recognize and execute the Excel skills presented in this chapter. Read each question carefully and answer the questions in the order they are listed. You should be able to complete this exam in 60 minutes or less.

1. Open the ib_e08_chapter8skillsexam Excel file.
2. Apply the **Filter** tool to the data in the Filter worksheet.
3. Apply the following filters to these columns:
   a. Year: equal to 2002
   b. Gross Sales: less than 1000000000
4. Sort results from number 3 in ascending order based on the values in the Gross Sales column.
5. Sort the data in the Subtotal worksheet so subtotals can be calculated for the Industry and Company columns.
6. Use the **Subtotals** tool to subtotal the values in the Gross Sales column for each industry.
7. Add a *second* subtotal to the data in the Subtotal worksheet for the Company column. Subtotal the values in the Gross Sales column for each company.
8. Use the **Level** buttons to hide all details for the Industry column in the Subtotals worksheet. The worksheet should show the subtotals for only the four industries and the Grand Totals.
9. Show the details for the Specialty Retail Industry.
10. Show the details for Sp Retail Company 1.
11. Use the data in the PivotTable worksheet to create a blank PivotTable Report in a new worksheet that is added to the workbook.
12. Add the following fields to the PivotTable Report in the locations specified:
    a. Year field: Column Labels section
    b. Industry field: Row Labels section
    c. Gross Sales field: Values section
13. Change the field settings for the Gross Sales field so the values are averaged instead of summed. Format the values in this field to a Currency format with 0 decimal places.
14. Add the Company field to the Values section of the PivotTable Report.
15. Change the name of the Company field to Number of Companies and make sure the field settings are set to Count.
16. Add a calculated field to the Values section of the PivotTable Report that divides the Gross Sales field by 52. Name this calculated field `Industry Weekly Sales`.
17. Show only the Computer Hardware industry on the PivotTable Report.
18. Remove the report totals for the columns on the PivotTable Report.
19. Adjust the PivotTable Report so the years are shown as row labels instead of column labels.
20. Sort the Year field based on the values in the Gross Sales field in Ascending order.
21. Add a Format Control List Box to the Company Analysis worksheet over cell locations B2 and C2.
22. Set the controls of the List Box you added in number 21 to show the list of companies in the range B3:B35 in the Company List worksheet. Use cell location A2 in the Company Analysis worksheet to define the Cell Link of the control. Set the Selection Type to Single.

23. Use a **VLOOKUP** function to display the company that is selected in the List Box in cell D2 of the Company Analysis worksheet.
24. Use a **VLOOKUP** function to display the industry sales for the appropriate year in cells C4 through C7 based on the company that is selected in the List Box. Industry sales data for each company can be found in the List Box Data worksheet.
25. Use the **VLOOKUP** function to show the Gross Sales for the company selected in the List Box for the appropriate year in cells D4 through D7. Gross sales data for each company can be found in the List Box data worksheet.
26. Use a formula to calculate the market share in cells E4 through E7 in the Company Analysis worksheet. Your formula should divide the industry sales into the gross sales for each year. Format the results to a percentage with 1 decimal place.
27. Hide Column A on the Company Analysis worksheet; then select the Restaurant 6 company from the List Box.
28. Save and close your file.

Challenge Questions

The following questions are designed to test your ability to apply the Excel skills you have learned to complete a business objective. Use your knowledge of Excel as well as your creativity to answer these questions. For most questions, there are several possible ways to complete the objective.

1. Open the Excel file named ib_e08_challengea. This is the same data that was used in the subtotals workshop. Analyze the sales performance of this business by category through the following points:

   a. Identify the total change in sales *by category* for the entire company.

   b. Identify the category that experienced the largest decrease in sales and show the change in sales for each region just for this category.

   c. Identify the region from letter b that experienced the largest decrease in sales and show the change in sales for every district in this region. Are the sales decreasing for all districts in this region?

2. Open the Excel file named ib_e08_challengeb. The data in this file is identical to the ib_e08_challengea file. Design a worksheet where a business manager can select a store number from a List Box to analyze sales data by category. Each unique store number in Column C should appear in the List Box only one time. After the store is selected, the following information should be displayed on the worksheet:

   a. The region number and district number for the store.

   b. The store's TY Sales and Change in Sales by category.

   c. The TY Sales for the store's region by category.

   d. The percentage of TY Sales the store contributes to the region (store TY Sales/region TY Sales) by category.

   e. Total Change in Sales and TY Sales for the store and region as well as the total percentage of TY Sales the store contributes to the region.

Scenario Tools & Statistics: Practice for Test

Chapter 9

Scenario Tools and Advanced Statistics

Chapter Goals

This chapter will demonstrate tools designed for conducting "What if" scenarios and advanced statistical computations. Excel's cell-referencing abilities have been used throughout this text to conduct a variety of business scenarios. The first section of this chapter also presents business scenarios, but through the use of tools that can provide greater flexibility and speed. The second section will introduce data analysis tools that can provide an entire range of descriptive statistics outputs at one time or execute other statistical methods such as regression and histograms. Finally, the third section will demonstrate the Solver tool, which is used to calculate minimum or maximum outputs given certain constraints or conditions that exist for a specific business situation.

This chapter will touch on fundamental concepts used in Cost Accounting and Economics. Although mastering these disciplines is *not* a prerequisite for learning the content in this chapter, you should have a working knowledge of each from your Accounting, Economics, and/or Statistics courses. This text will not provide in-depth explanations or instructions regarding the practice and theory of these disciplines.

Excel | Skill Sets

Scenario Tools
- Scroll Bar
- Conditional Formatting
- Data Tables
- Goal Seek
- Scenario Manager

Data Analysis Tools
- Add-Ins
- Descriptive Statistics
- Histogram
- Regression

Solver
- Defining Constraints
- Defining Solver Parameters

Excel in Practice | Anecdote

My Role as a Profit Analyst

One of the most intense jobs I have had in my career was working as a profit analyst in the women's fashion industry. The company I worked for manufactured and sold women's fashion clothes in specialty stores across the United States. I was responsible for planning the sales and profits for all merchandise purchased in my department. I worked closely with the designers and production coordinators to develop a financial plan for merchandise that was purchased at the beginning of each season. This plan, along with the merchandise line, was presented to the executive officers of the company. It was at these meetings that I was constantly asked several "What if" questions. For example, "What if you have to sell 50% of this item at a 40% markdown." In other words, if an item we purchased, such as a printed skirt, did not meet our sales expectations, we would reduce the price to sell as much of the remaining inventory as possible. Depending on how much inventory we sold at full price, the amount of remaining inventory sold at the reduced price could decrease or eliminate any planned profits. As a result, the executive officers frequently wanted to know "the worst-case scenario." Therefore, I had to prepare almost every possible profit scenario for each item in the line and for the overall department. The kicker was that for some meetings, I would prepare what seemed to be hundreds of scenarios, and the executive officers would not ask one question. However, I was sure that if I came to a meeting without my "What if" scenarios, I would get questions on every item in the line.

>> Continued on page 454

Scenario Tools

Skill Set

Excel provides several tools that can use cell referencing to enhance your ability to evaluate multiple "What if" scenarios when making business decisions. This section will demonstrate four of these tools and explain how business managers use them to set prices, manage profits, and evaluate the return on investments. You will need to add the **Developer** tab to the Ribbon to access the tools covered in this section. To do this, click the **Office Button**, click the **Excel Options** button, and select the **Show Developer** tab in the Ribbon option in the Popular section of the **Excel Options** dialog box (see Chapter 8 for more details).

Scroll Bar

You learned about adding the **Developer** tab to the Ribbon to access the Form Controls in the last segment of Chapter 8 during the demonstration of the List Box. The Form Controls also contains an option called Scroll Bar, which can be used as a scenario tool. You can use the Scroll Bar to change a number in a target cell location in single-unit increments. This allows you to produce various outputs in other cells that are referencing the target cell in formulas and functions. This tool can be especially helpful when conducting a break-even analysis for a new business or product line. The goal of a break-even analysis is to determine the product price and unit sales required to meet or exceed the costs of production. For example, Figure 9.1 shows the sales and costs of a new hypothetical shirt company. Based on the cost of producing a shirt, a business manager will need to know how many shirts need to be sold and at what price for the company to produce a profit. However, determining the price of the shirt can be tricky, because as the price increases, the total number of shirts that can be sold will decrease. Therefore, this example uses the Scroll Bar to change the price in cell B2 of Figure 9.1 gradually to determine when the business will meet and exceed its costs.

Figure 9.1 | **Sales and Costs for a Shirt-Manufacturing Company**

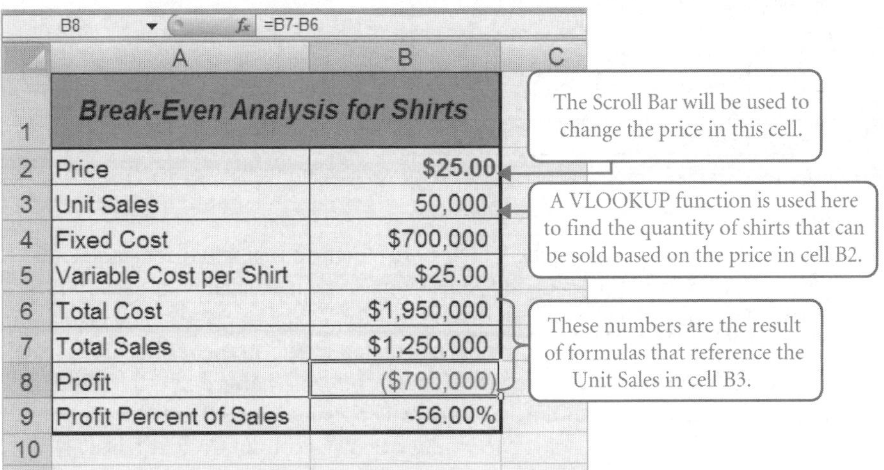

The Scroll Bar will be used to change the price in cell B2 in the worksheet shown in Figure 9.1. A second worksheet in this workbook shows how many shirts can be sold based on the price that is entered in cell B2 (see Figure 9.2). Following basic economic principles, as the price of the shirt increases, the quantity demanded for the shirt decreases. As a result, a VLOOKUP function is used in cell B3 to show the unit sales based on the price that is entered in cell B2 (see Figure 9.3).

Figure 9.2 | **Price and Sales Units Worksheet**

	A	B
1	Price & Unit Sales	
2	Price	Unit Sales
3	$25.00	50,000
4	$26.00	49,500
5	$27.00	49,000
6	$28.00	48,500
7	$29.00	48,000
8	$30.00	47,500
9	$31.00	47,000
10	$32.00	46,500
11	$33.00	46,000
12	$34.00	45,500
13	$35.00	45,000
14	$36.00	44,500

Unit Sales are decreasing as Price is increasing.

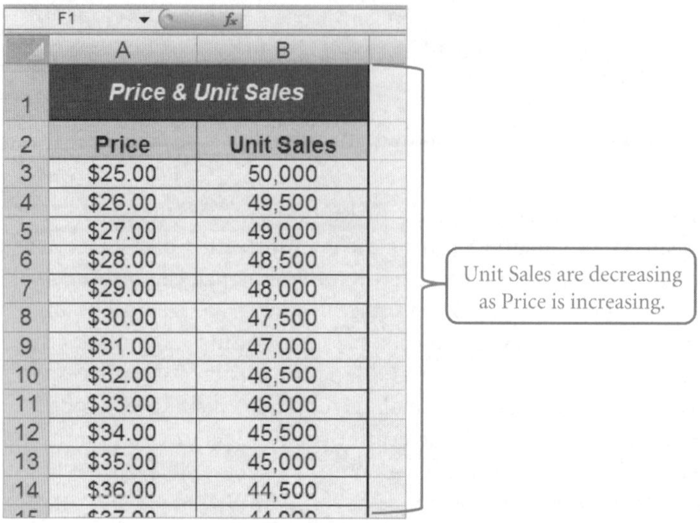

Figure 9.3 | **VLOOKUP Referencing Unit Sales from the Price and Sales Units Worksheet**

=VLOOKUP(B2,'Price and Sales Units'!A3:B53,2,TRUE)

	A	B
1	Break-Even Analysis for Shirts	
2	Price	$25.00
3	Unit Sales	=VLOOKUP(B2,'Price and Sales Units'!A3:B53,2,TRUE)
4	Fixed Cost	$700,000
5	Variable Cost per Shirt	$25.00
6	Total Cost	$1,950,000
7	Total Sales	$1,250,000
8	Profit	($700,000)
9	Profit Percent of Sales	-56.00%
10		

The lookup value is the price that is entered into cell B2.

The function will search for the lookup value in the Price and Sales Units worksheet (Figure 9.2).

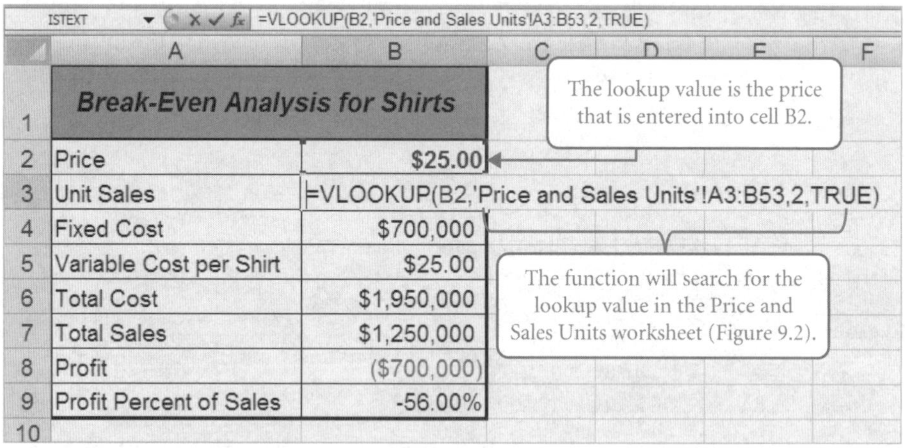

Figure 9.3 shows the setup of the **VLOOKUP** function that will display the Unit Sales value in cell B3 from the Price and Sales Units worksheet. Cell B3 is used in formulas to calculate the Total Cost in cell B6 and the Total Sales in cell B7. The Profit and Profit Percent of Sales in cells B8 and B9 are calculated based on the results of the Total Cost and Total Sales formulas. As a result, when the price is changed in cell B2, the **VLOOKUP** function will display a new value for Unit Sales in cell B3. When the value in cell B3 is changed, the results of the formulas calculating Total Cost, Total Sales, Profit, and Profit Percent of Sales will also change. Therefore, a business manager can keep typing different prices into cell B2 to see when the company produces a profit. However, instead of typing different prices, the Scroll Bar will be used to change the price gradually to see when profits become positive. The following explains how this is accomplished.

- Click the **Insert** icon in the **Controls** group on the **Developer** tab of the Ribbon.
- Click the **Scroll Bar** icon in the Form Controls set of options. Then, click and drag the shape of a vertical rectangle in the area of cells C2 through C9 (see Figure 9.4).

Figure 9.4 | **Adding a Scroll Bar to the Sales and Costs Worksheet**

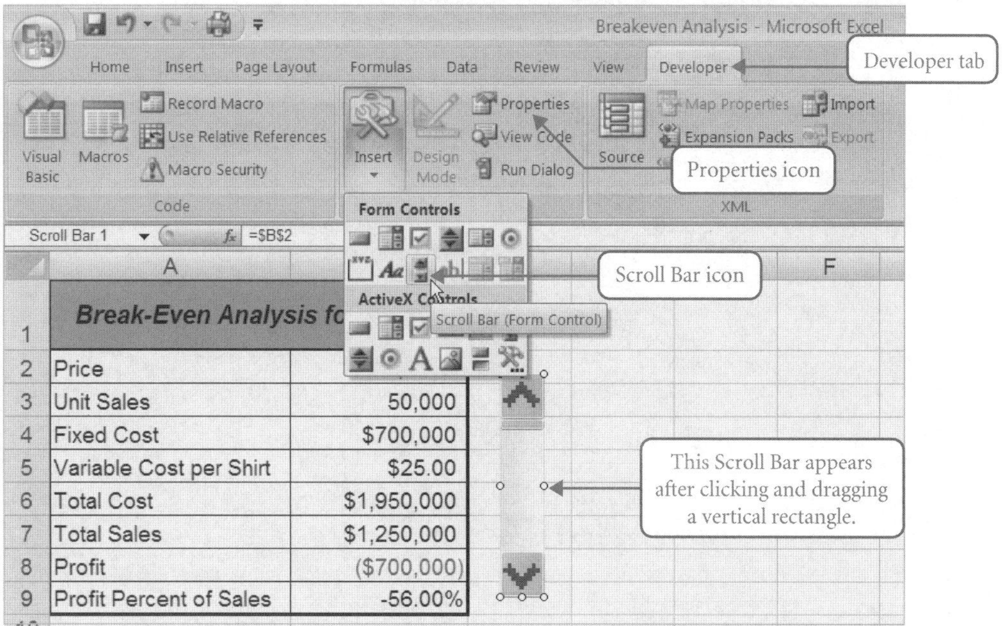

Figure 9.4 shows the results of adding a Scroll Bar to the worksheet that is calculating the profitability of a shirt manufacturing company. The white dots around the perimeter of the Scroll Bar signify that it is deactivated. Before the Scroll Bar is activated, it must be configured to change the price in cell B2 when either the Up or the Down arrow is clicked or the slide is dragged. The following explains how the Scroll Bar is configured for this example.

- Make sure the Scroll Bar is deactivated. White dots will appear around the perimeter of the Scroll Bar if it is deactivated. If the Scroll Bar is active, click it while holding the **Ctrl** key.
- Click the **Properties** icon in the **Developer** tab of the Ribbon (see Figure 9.4). This will open the **Format Control** dialog box.
- Click the **Control** tab at the top of the **Format Control** dialog box. Then, type the number 25 in the box labeled Current Value. The number 25 is typed into this box because it is the value that is currently entered into cell B2 (see Figure 9.3).
- Type the number 25 in the box labeled Minimum Value. As shown in Figure 9.3, at a price of $25 the company is losing a substantial amount of money. Therefore, there is no need to go below $25.
- Type the number 75 in the box labeled Maximum Value. For this example we will assume that there is very little demand for shirts priced more than $75.
- Type the number 1 in the box labeled Incremental Change. This will increase or decrease the price by $1 when either the Up arrow or the Down arrow is clicked.
- Type the number 5 in the box labeled Page Change. This will increase or decrease the price by $5 when the space above or below the slide in the Scroll Bar is clicked.
- Click the range finder next to the box labeled Cell Link, click cell B2, and press the **Enter** key. This connects the Scroll Bar to cell B2, which contains the price of the shirt.

- Click the **OK** button on the **Format Control** dialog box and then click anywhere on the worksheet to activate the Scroll Bar. Figure 9.5 shows the final setup of the **Format Control** dialog box for the Scroll Bar.

Figure 9.5 | **Format Control Settings for the Scroll Bar**

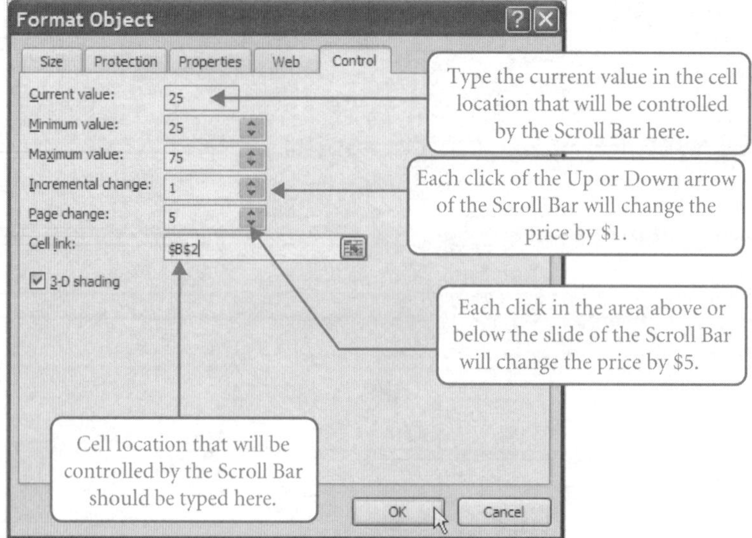

COMMON MISTAKES | Setting Increment Values for the Scroll Bar

The Scroll Bar can increase or decrease the value in a target cell location only by whole-number increments. Therefore, you cannot type a number with a decimal point in either the **Incremental Change** box or the **Page Change** box in the Format Control dialog box for a Scroll Bar. Excel will automatically round numbers with decimal places to the nearest whole unit. In addition, if you enter a number such as .25 in either the Incremental **Change** box or the **Page Change** box, Excel will round this number to 0 and the Scroll Bar will not work. Finally, only positive numbers can be used in the Scroll bar control settings, and the settings must be in the range of 0 to 30,000.

Figure 9.6 shows the results of using the Scroll Bar to change the price in cell B2 to determine at what price the shirt company produces a profit. The slide in the middle of the Scroll Bar was clicked and dragged to gradually change the price to determine when the profit value in cell B8 becomes positive. As shown in the figure, the company begins to produce a profit when a price of $43 is charged for the shirt.

Figure 9.6 | **Using the Scroll Bar to Set the Prices**

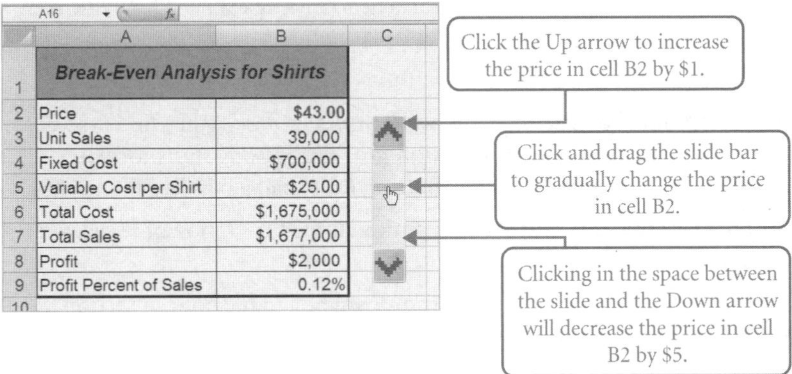

	A	B
1	Break-Even Analysis for Shirts	
2	Price	$43.00
3	Unit Sales	39,000
4	Fixed Cost	$700,000
5	Variable Cost per Shirt	$25.00
6	Total Cost	$1,675,000
7	Total Sales	$1,677,000
8	Profit	$2,000
9	Profit Percent of Sales	0.12%

Conditional Formatting

Looking at Figure 9.4 in the previous segment, you might have noticed that the profit value in cell B8 is in parentheses with a red font color. However, when the profit becomes positive in Figure 9.6, the value in cell B8 is no longer in parentheses and the font color changes to black. This is because the Currency category in the **Format Cells** dialog box provides an option to show negative values in parentheses with a red font color (see Figure 9.7). Managers frequently use this format option in business reporting because it helps draw the reader's attention to negative numbers that probably need to be addressed. However, this option is not available for all types of numbers. For example, in Figure 9.4 the profit value in cell B8 is red, but the percentage is still black. To change the percentage to a red font color to match the profit value, the **Conditional Formatting** features will need to be used.

Figure 9.7 | **Negative Currency Option in the Format Cells Dialog Box**

This option will show negative currency values in parentheses and will change the font color to red.

The Conditional Formatting feature will be used to set any negative percentage values in cell B9 in Figure 9.4 to a red font color. The following explains how this is accomplished.

- Activate cell B9 (see Figure 9.4).
- Click the **Conditional Formatting** icon in the **Styles** group on the **Home** tab of the Ribbon. Then, click the **New Rule** option near the bottom of the format options list. This will open the **New Formatting Rule** dialog box (see Figure 9.8).
- Select the **Format only cells that contain** option in the top section of the **New Formatting Rule** dialog box.
- Select the **Cell Value** option in the first drop-down box in the bottom section of the **New Formatting Rule** dialog box.
- Select the **Less Than** option in the second drop-down box at the bottom of the dialog box.
- Type the number 0 in the third box. This will complete the criteria that will be used to apply a format to the value in cell B9. Excel will apply a designated format when the value in cell B9 is less than 0.
- Click the **Format** button near the bottom of the **New Formatting Rule** dialog box. This will open the **Format Cells** dialog box. Change the color to red in the **Font** tab of the dialog box.
- Click the **OK** button in the **Format Cells** dialog box and then the **OK** button at the bottom of the **New Formatting Rule** dialog box. The text color will be changed to red for any value in cell B9 that is less than 0.

Figure 9.8 shows the options that appear after the **Conditional Formatting** icon is selected. Click the **New Rule** option to set criteria that will be used to apply a designated format to a cell or range of cells.

>> **Quick Reference**

Scroll Bar

1. Click the **Insert** icon in the **Developer** tab of the Ribbon.
2. Click the **Scroll Bar** icon from the **Form Controls** options.
3. Click and drag a vertical rectangle on your worksheet to define the size and placement of the Scroll Bar.
4. With the Scroll Bar deactivated, click the **Properties** icon in the **Developer** tab of the Ribbon to open the **Format Control** dialog box.
5. Set the Current Value, Minimum Value, and Maximum Value based on the needs of your project (must be between 0 and 30,000).
6. Type a whole number in the **Incremental Change** box.
7. Type a whole number in the **Page Change** box.
8. Type the target cell location in the **Cell Link** box or use the range finder.
9. Click the **OK** button on the **Format Control** dialog box.
10. Click anywhere on your worksheet to activate the Scroll Bar.

Figure 9.8 | **Creating a New Conditional Formatting Rule**

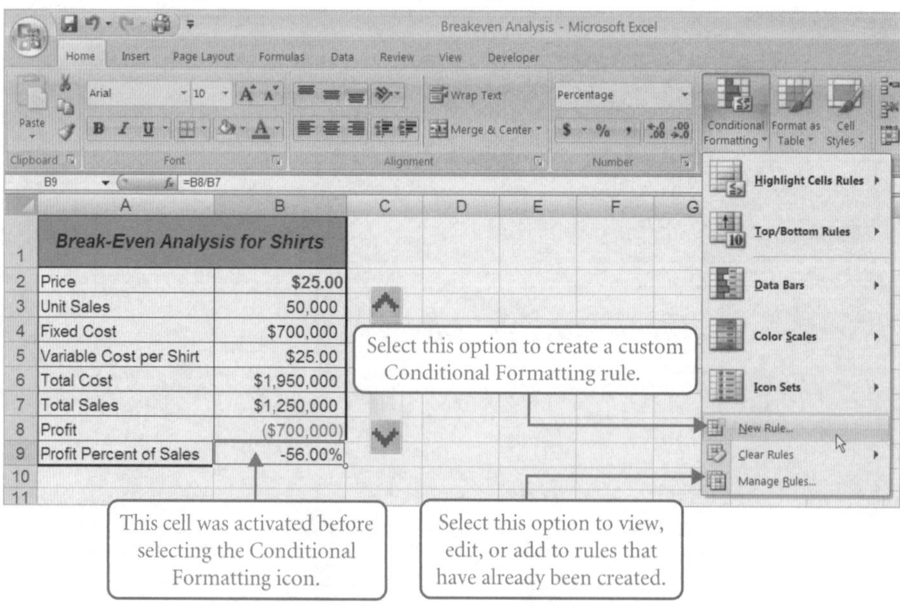

Figure 9.9 shows the final settings in the **New Formatting Rule** dialog box. If the criteria at the bottom of this dialog box are true, the formats selected in the **Format Cells** dialog box will be applied to cell B9.

Figure 9.9 | **New Formatting Rule Dialog Box**

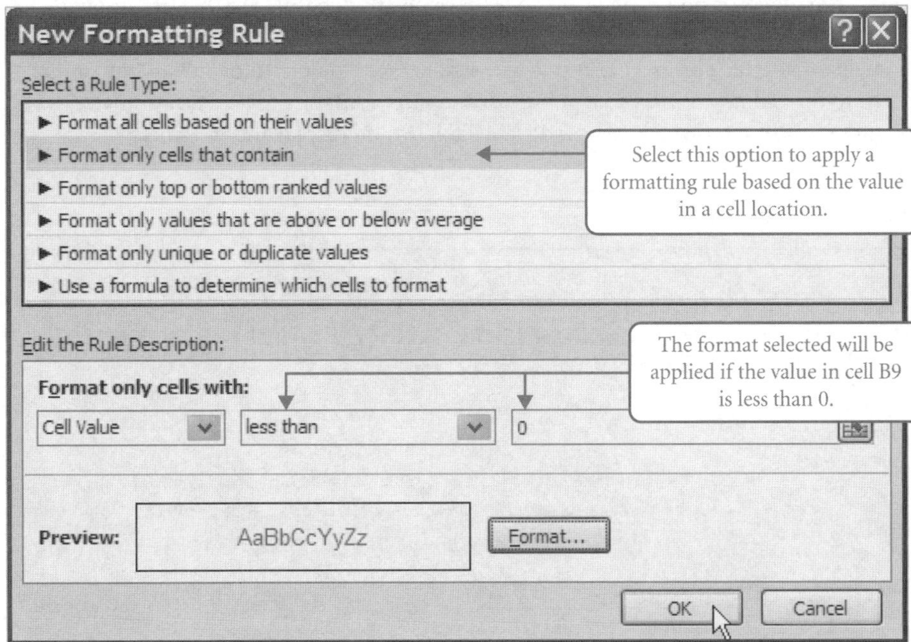

Figure 9.10 shows the final results of the break-even analysis worksheet with the conditional formatting rule applied. Because the value in cell B9 is less than 0, the font color was changed to red. To view or edit any conditional formatting rules that have been applied to a worksheet, click the **Manage Rules** option after clicking the **Conditional Formatting** icon in the **Home** tab of the Ribbon (see Figure 9.8).

Figure 9.10 | **Break-Even Worksheet with Conditional Formats**

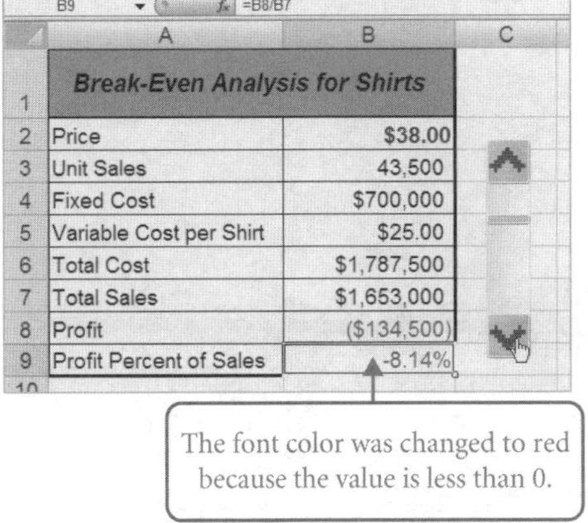

Data Tables

The previous segment demonstrated how the Scroll Bar can be used to assess the profitability of a shirt company by changing the selling price of the product. This example assumed that a specific number of units could be sold based on the price that was charged. As a result, the **VLOOKUP** function was used in a second worksheet to find the exact number of units that could be sold based on the price that was entered in the first worksheet. However, what if you were not sure how many shirts you could sell at

> **Quick Reference**
>
> **Conditional Formatting**
>
> 1. Activate the cell location where the conditional format will be applied.
> 2. Click the **Conditional Formatting** icon in the **Styles** group on **Home** tab of the Ribbon.
> 3. Select the **New Rule** option near the bottom of the **Conditional Format** list.
> 4. Select the **Format only cells that contain** option in the top section of the **New Formatting Rule** dialog box if your criteria are based on the value in a cell location.
> 5. Set the first drop-down box to **Cell Value**.
> 6. Select a comparison operator in the second drop-down box.
> 7. Type a value in the third box or use the range finder to select a cell location on your worksheet.
> 8. Click the **Format** button to open the **Format Cells** dialog box.
> 9. Set the formatting options that will be applied to the cell activated in step 1 if the conditions defined in steps 6 and 7 are true.
> 10. Click the **OK** button on the **Format Cells** dialog box.
> 11. Click the **OK** button on the **New Formatting Rule** dialog box.
> 12. Click the **Conditional Formatting** icon and select the **Manage Rules** option to edit or add additional rules to the same cell location.

different prices? In this case, you might need to ask the question, "If I charge a price of X, how many units do I need to sell to achieve positive profits?" In this situation you would need to use a data table. Data tables show multiple results of a formula in a two-dimensional grid. This next example uses a data table to determine how many units need to be sold at various price points for the shirt company to achieve positive profits. Figure 9.11 shows a sketch of how a Data Table would display these results.

Figure 9.11 | **Data-Table Sketch**

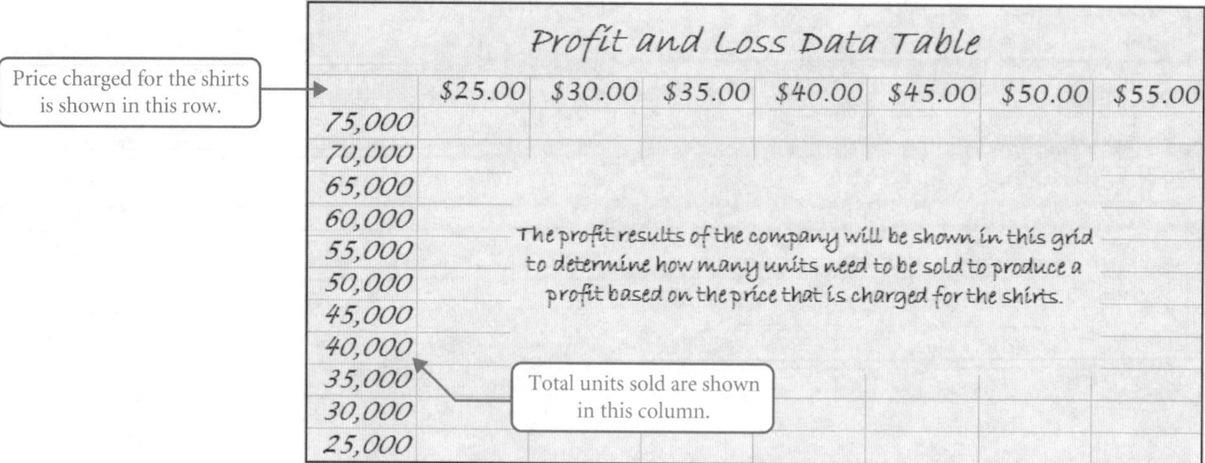

Figure 9.12 shows the setup of the worksheet that will be used to construct the data table that is sketched in Figure 9.11. As mentioned, the data table will be used to show the profit results of the company when a certain price is charged and a certain number of units are sold. For this example we will assume that the company cannot produce more than 75,000 shirts a year and will need to produce a minimum of 25,000 shirts to operate the factory for at least one shift throughout the year. This is why the numbers along the left side of the sketch in Figure 9.11 are between 75,000 and 25,000.

Figure 9.12 | **Worksheet for Profit and Loss Table**

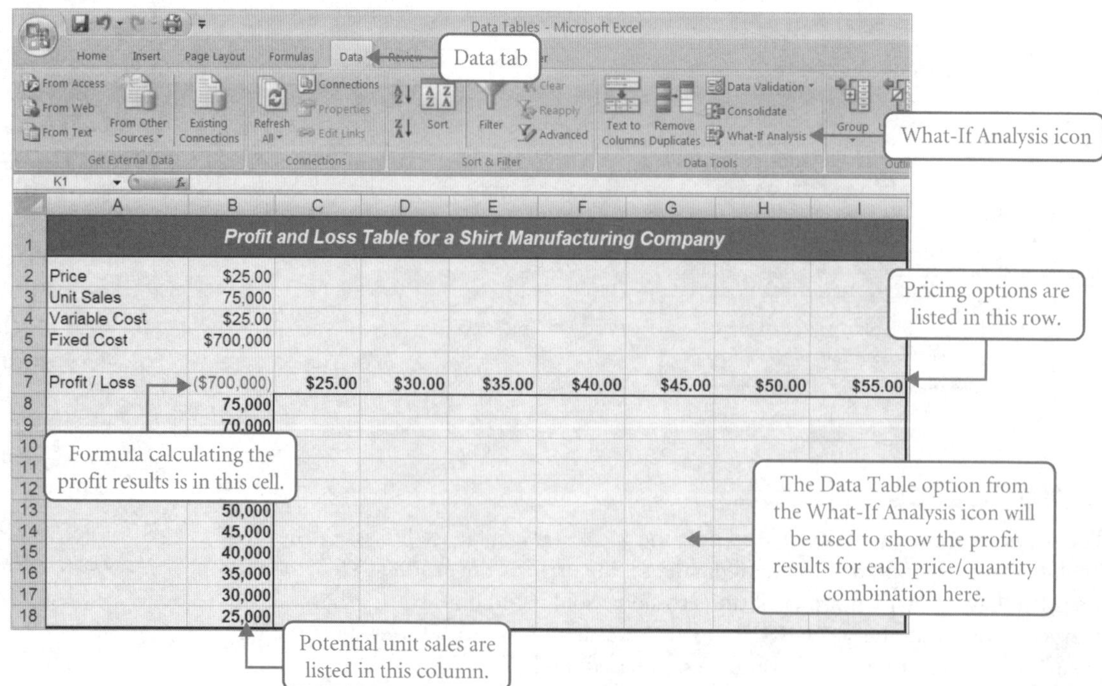

The **Data Table** option from the **What-If Analysis** icon will be used to calculate the profit of the shirt company for each combination of price and quantity in the range C8:I18 in Figure 9.12. These calculations will be made using the formula `=(B2 * B3) - ((B4 * B3) + B5)` in cell B7. To calculate the total sales of the business, the shirt price is multiplied by the unit sales, which are in cells B2 and B3: `(B2 * B3)`. The total cost of manufacturing the shirts is subtracted from the total sales to calculate the profit or loss for the business. The costs are calculated by multiplying the unit sales by the variable cost of producing each shirt (cell B4) and then adding the fixed costs in cell B5: `(B4 * B3) + B5`. The variable cost for manufacturing each shirt includes items such as fabric, thread, and buttons. The fixed cost includes items such as cutting and sewing machines. Your Managerial Accounting or Cost Accounting courses will provide more details on the nature of these costs. For now it is important to understand that the profit or loss for the business is calculated by subtracting these costs from the total sales. The following explains how you can use the **Data Table** feature to complete the profit calculations in the range C8:I18 in Figure 9.12.

- Define the table range by highlighting cells B7 through I18. Notice that this range includes the formula in cell B7 and the price and quantity options in the ranges B8:B18 and C7:I7.
- Click the **What-If Analysis** icon in the **Data** tab of the Ribbon and select the **Data Table** option. This will open the **Data Table** dialog box.
- Click the range finder next to the **Row Input Cell** box, click cell B2 on the worksheet, and press the **Enter** key. Excel will substitute any values in the first row of the table range (C7:I7) into cell B2 when using the formula in cell B7 to calculate the profit or loss.
- Click the range finder next to the **Column Input Cell** box, click cell B3, and press the **Enter** key. Excel will substitute any values in the left column of the table range (B8:B18) into cell B3 when using the formula in cell B7 to calculate the profit or loss. As a result, Excel will be substituting price values in cell B2 and unit sales values in cell B3 simultaneously when calculating the profit or loss of the business (see Figure 9.13).
- Click the **OK** button on the **Data Table** dialog box.

Figure 9.13 | **The Data Table Window**

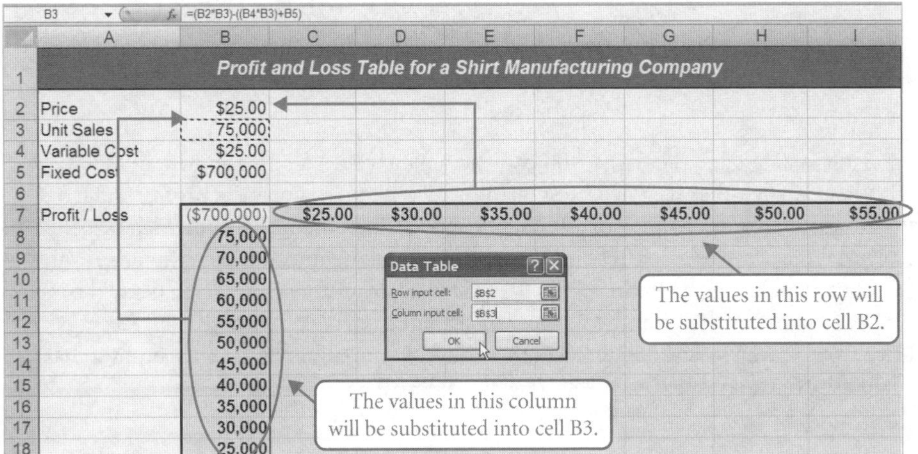

COMMON MISTAKES | Defining the Cell Range for a Data Table

The cell range highlighted before selecting the **Data Table** option from the **What-If Analysis** icon must include the formula that will produce the results of the table. People often make the mistake of highlighting only the range of cells in which the results of the table should appear. However, the Data Table feature will not produce any results if the cell range does not begin with a formula.

Figure 9.14 shows the results of the Data Table. Negative values are shown in red because the parentheses/red font option was selected for negative values in the numbers tab of the **Format Cells** dialog box. Notice that when the company charges $25, the profit is negative for all quantities sold. This makes sense considering that the variable cost to produce each shirt is $25. Therefore, the company is not able to recover any of the $700,000 in fixed costs. According to this table, the company does not cover both the variable and fixed costs until a price of $35 is charged. At this price, the company must sell at least 70,000 shirts to meet all costs, and 75,000 shirts to produce a profit of $50,000. As the company increases the price, it needs to sell fewer shirts to produce a profit.

Figure 9.14 | **Data Table Results**

B7 =(B2*B3)-((B4*B3)+B5)

	A	B	C	D	E	F	G	H	I
1	Profit and Loss Table for a Shirt Manufacturing Company								
2	Price	$25.00							
3	Unit Sales	75,000							
4	Variable Cost	$25.00							
5	Fixed Cost	$700,000							
6									
7	Profit / Loss	($700,000)	$25.00	$30.00	$35.00	$40.00	$45.00	$50.00	$55.00
8		75,000	($700,000)	($325,000)	$50,000	$425,000	$800,000	$1,175,000	$1,550,000
9		70,000	($700,000)	($350,000)	$0	$350,000	$700,000	$1,050,000	$1,400,000
10		65,000	($700,000)	($375,000)	($50,000)	$275,000	$600,000	$925,000	$1,250,000
11		60,000	($700,000)	($400,000)	($100,000)	$200,000	$500,000	$800,000	$1,100,000
12		55,000	($700,000)	($425,000)	($150,000)	$125,000	$400,000	$675,000	$950,000
13		50,000	($700,000)	($450,000)	($200,000)	$50,000	$300,000	$550,000	$800,000
14		45,000	($700,000)	($475,000)	($250,000)	($25,000)	$200,000	$425,000	$650,000
15		40,000	($700,000)	($500,000)	($300,000)	($100,000)	$100,000	$300,000	$500,000
16		35,000	($700,000)	($525,000)	($350,000)	($175,000)	$0	$175,000	$350,000
17		30,000	($700,000)	($550,000)	($400,000)	($250,000)	($100,000)	$50,000	$200,000
18		25,000	($700,000)	($575,000)	($450,000)	($325,000)	($200,000)	($75,000)	$50,000

The company cannot cover both fixed and variable costs at a price of $30 or less.

After a data table is created, you can change the values in the top row and left column to evaluate other scenarios. For example, Figure 9.14 shows the profit results of the company in a price range of $25 to $55 with $5 increments between each price. However, these prices can be changed to smaller increments to evaluate more specific pricing strategies, as shown in Figure 9.15. The results of this table were changed by simply typing new prices in the top row of the table (C7:I7). Notice that increasing the price from $34.25 to $34.85 increases the profit by more than $40,000, assuming that 75,000 shirts are sold.

>> Quick Reference

Data Tables

1. Create a formula that will be used to produce the results of the table. Your formula *must* use cell references.
2. Type one set of alternate values, which will be substituted into one of the cell locations referenced by the formula in step 1. These values must be typed in a *row* to the right and *adjacent to* the formula created in step 1.
3. Type a second set of alternate values, which will be substituted into a second cell location that is referenced by the formula created in step 1. These values must be typed in the *column* directly below and *adjacent to* the formula created in step 1.
4. Highlight a range of cells that begins with the formula created in step 1 and covers all of the values typed for steps 2 and 3.
5. Click the **What-If Analysis** icon in the **Data** tab of the Ribbon and select the **Data Table** option.
6. In the **Data Table** dialog box, define the Row Input Cell with a cell location that will be used to substitute the values you typed for step 2.
7. Define the Column Input Cell with a cell location that will be used to substitute the values typed for step 3.
8. Click the **OK** button on the **Data Table** dialog box.

Figure 9.15 | **Data Table Results with New Prices**

	A	B	C	D	E	F	G	H	I
1	Profit and Loss Table for a Shirt Manufacturing Company								
2	Price	$25.00							
3	Unit Sales	75,000							
4	Variable Cost	$25.00							
5	Fixed Cost	$700,000							
6									
7	Profit / Loss	($700,000)	$34.25	$34.35	$34.45	$34.55	$34.65	$34.75	$34.85
8		75,000	($6,250)	$1,250	$8,750	$16,250	$23,750	$31,250	$38,750
9		70,000	($52,500)	($45,500)	($38,500)	($31,500)	($24,500)	($17,500)	($10,500)
10		65,000	($98,750)	($92,250)	($85,750)	($79,250)	($72,750)	($66,250)	($59,750)
11		60,000	($145,000)	($139,000)	($133,000)	($127,000)	($121,000)	($115,000)	($109,000)
12		55,000	($191,250)	($185,750)	($180,250)	($174,750)	($169,250)	($163,750)	($158,250)
13		50,000	($237,500)	($232,500)	($227,500)	($222,500)	($217,500)	($212,500)	($207,500)
14		45,000	($283,750)	($279,250)	($274,750)	($270,250)	($265,750)	($261,250)	($256,750)
15		40,000	($330,000)	($326,000)	($322,000)	($318,000)	($314,000)	($310,000)	($306,000)
16		35,000	($376,250)	($372,750)	($369,250)	($365,750)	($362,250)	($358,750)	($355,250)
17		30,000	($422,500)	($419,500)	($416,500)	($413,500)	($410,500)	($407,500)	($404,500)
18		25,000	($468,750)	($466,250)	($463,750)	($461,250)	($458,750)	($456,250)	($453,750)

Typing new prices in this row will automatically change the results of the table.

Goal Seek

Similar to the Scroll Bar and the Data Table tools, Goal Seek is another valuable scenario tool that maximizes Excel's cell-referencing capabilities. Goal Seek allows a business manager to target a specific outcome by changing the value in a cell location that is used in a formula or function. For example, Figure 9.16 shows a worksheet that uses the Future Value function to calculate the value of a person's monthly retirement investments. The example assumes that the person is 25 years old and will retire at the age of 65. Therefore, the monthly investment in cell B3 will be made over a 40-year period. This is calculated using a formula that subtracts the person's age in cell B2 from 65.

Figure 9.16 | **Investing for Retirement Worksheet**

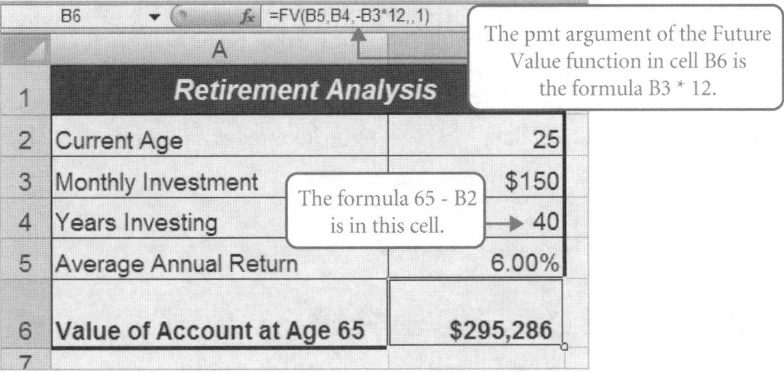

The result of the **Future Value** function displayed in cell B6 of Figure 9.16 shows that the value of this person's investments will be more than $295,000 at the age of 65. However, what if this person has a goal of reaching $1 million by the age of 65? How much money will need to be invested each month? What if this person could invest money in a mutual fund that provides a higher rate of return? What would the rate of return have to be to reach $1 million? All of these questions can be answered using the **Goal Seek** tool.

Using the data in Figure 9.16, the following explains how you can use the **Goal Seek** tool to determine how much money a person should invest per month assuming that the annual rate of return and the number of years investing cannot change.

- Select the **Goal Seek** option after clicking the **What-If Analysis** icon in the **Data** tab of the Ribbon. This will open the **Goal Seek** dialog box.

>> ***Quick Reference***

Goal Seek

1. Create a formula or function that uses cell references to produce a mathematical result.
2. Select the **Goal Seek** option from the **What-If Analysis** icon in the **Data** tab of the Ribbon.
3. Type a cell location into the **Set Cell** box or use the range finder to click a cell on your worksheet. This cell location should contain the formula or function you created in step 1.
4. Type a number in the **To Value** box that you want the formula or function you created in step 1 to produce.
5. Type a cell location into the **By Changing Cell** box or use the range finder to click a cell on your worksheet. The cell location in this box must be a cell that is referenced in the formula or function created in step 1.
6. Click the **OK** button on the **Goal Seek** dialog box.
7. Click the **OK** button on the **Goal Seek Status** dialog box.

- Click the range finder next to the **Set Cell** box, click cell B6 on the worksheet, and press the **Enter** key. This will set cell B6 to the value that will be typed into the To Value box.
- Type 1000000 in the **To Value** box. This will set cell B6 to $1,000,000 by changing the value in the cell location that is entered into the **By Changing Cell** box.
- Click the range finder next to the **By Changing Cell** box, click cell B3 on the worksheet, and press the **Enter** key. The Goal Seek tool will change cell B6 to $1,000,000 by changing the value in cell B3, which is the monthly investment.
- Click the **OK** button on the **Goal Seek** dialog box.
- Click the **OK** button on the **Goal Seek Status** dialog box. This notifies you if a solution was found for the value that was typed into the **To Value** box of the **Goal Seek** dialog box.

Figure 9.17 shows the setup of the **Goal Seek** dialog box. Goal Seek will determine the value that should appear in cell B3 so that the output of the **Future Value** function in cell B6 is equal to 1,000,000.

Figure 9.17 | **Setup of the Goal Seek Window**

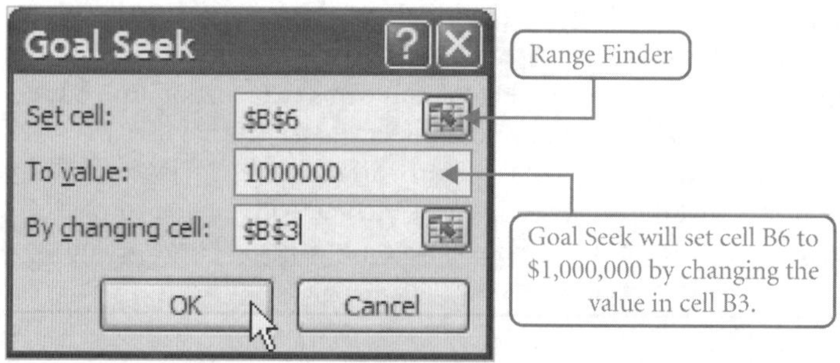

Figure 9.18 shows the results of the Retirement Analysis worksheet after clicking the **OK** button on the **Goal Seek Status** dialog box. Notice that the value in cell B6 is $1,000,000. This is because the monthly investment in cell B3 was changed to $508. Therefore, if this person wants to grow his retirement investments to $1 million over 40 years at a 6% rate of return, $508 dollars will need to be invested each month.

Figure 9.18 | **Monthly Investments Calculated by Goal Seek**

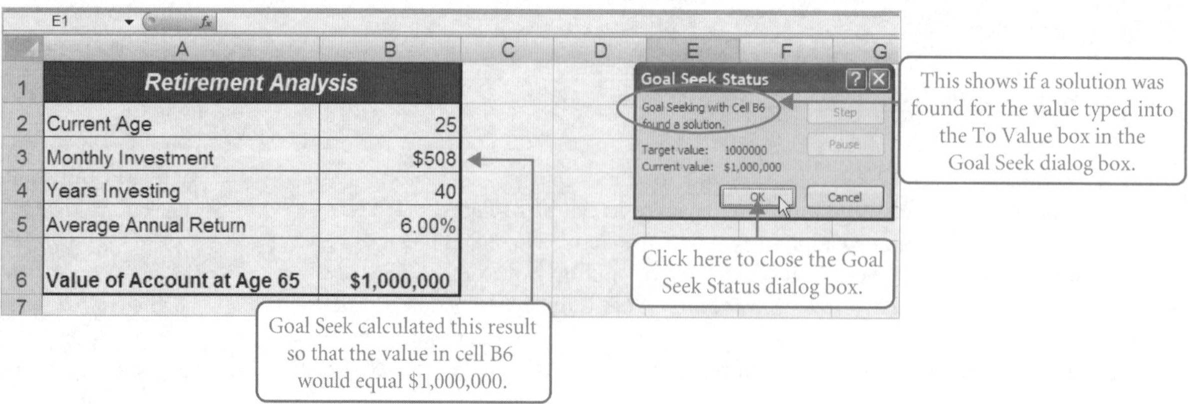

As previously mentioned, you can also use the **Goal Seek** tool to determine what rate would grow the retirement investments in Figure 9.16 to $1 million if the monthly investment is $150 and the years investing remains at 40. Figure 9.19 shows the settings in the Goal Seek dialog box and the results in the Retirement Analysis worksheet. Notice that the settings in the Goal Seek dialog box are identical to those in Figure 9.17 except the **By Changing Cell** box, which is set to cell B5. Goal Seek will change the rate of return in cell B5 so that the output of the Future Value function in cell B6 is $1,000,000. The results in the worksheet show that a 10.47% growth rate is required to achieve an investment value of $1 million by investing $150 a month over 40 years.

Figure 9.19 | **Annual Rate of Return Calculated by Goal Seek**

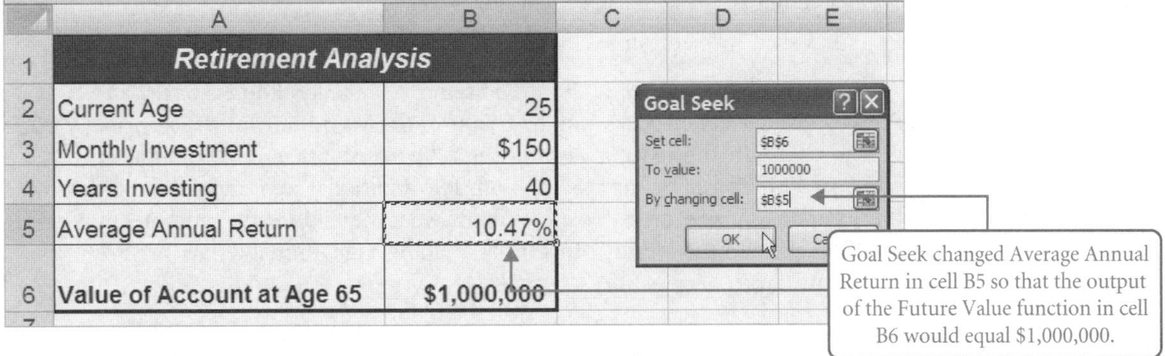

Scenario Manager

The **Goal Seek** tool allows you to change one of the cell locations or variables in a formula to produce the results of a "What if" scenario. However, you may need to change more than one variable when conducting these scenarios. With the Scenario Manager, you can assign numbers to several variables or cell locations that are referenced in a formula or function. You can also assign several different numbers to a single variable or cell location. For example, suppose you wanted to use the investment data in Figure 9.16 to create three different scenarios for your retirement. The first scenario could calculate the future value of investing $200 per month at a 12% return over 40 years. The second scenario could show the results of investing $175 per month at a 9% return over 40 years, and the third scenario could show the results of investing $150 per month at a 6% return over 40 years. Each of these scenarios requires you to assign several different numbers to two variables or cell locations that are referenced by the Future Value function in cell B7 of Figure 9.16. In addition, the results of these scenarios can show you how much money you could make by looking at three different monthly investment and rate-of-return options.

The following explains how you can use the Scenario Manager to build three distinct retirement scenarios for the data in Figure 9.16. The first scenario will assume a monthly investment of $200 per month at a 12% average annual return.

- Select the **Scenario Manager** option from the **What-If Analysis** icon in the **Data** tab of the Ribbon. This will open the **Scenario Manager** dialog box (see Figure 9.20).
- Click the Add button on the right side of the **Scenario Manager** dialog box. This will open the **Add Scenario** dialog box.
- Type Maximum Target in the box labeled Scenario Name at the top of the **Add Scenario** dialog box. As mentioned, you can assign several different numbers to a single variable or cell reference used in a formula or function. However, a separately named scenario must be added in the **Add Scenario** dialog box for each number that is assigned to the same cell location. In this first scenario, we will assume that $200 per month is the maximum investment this person can afford and 12% is the highest estimated growth rate based on this person's investment decisions. Therefore, this scenario is named "Maximum Target."
- Click the range finder next to the box labeled Changing Cells. Click cell B3, hold the **Ctrl** key down, click cell B5, and press the **Enter** key. This will allow values to be defined for each of these cell locations in the Scenario Values dialog box. Once cell locations are added to the **Changing Cells** box, the name of the dialog box will change to Edit Scenario (see Figure 9.21).

- Click the **OK** button at the bottom of the **Edit Scenario** dialog box. This will open the **Scenario Values** dialog box.
- Type the number 200 in the box labeled $B$3 and .12 in the box labeled $B$5.
- Click the **OK** button in the **Scenario Values** dialog box. This will bring you back to the **Scenario Manager** dialog box.
- Click the **Show** button at the bottom of the **Scenario Manager** dialog box to show the results of the scenario on the worksheet.
- Click the **Close** button to close the **Scenario Manager** dialog box.

Figures 9.20 through 9.23 show the **Scenario Manager**, **Edit Scenario**, and **Scenario Values** dialog boxes and the results of the Maximum Target scenario. Notice in Figure 9.23 the future value of investing $200 per month at a 12% annual growth rate over 40 years is more than $2 million. Two additional scenarios will be added to the Scenario Manager dialog box to evaluate what the value of the retirement investments might be if the Monthly Investment and Average Annual Return are below the Maximum Target.

Figure 9.20 | **The Scenario Manager Dialog Box**

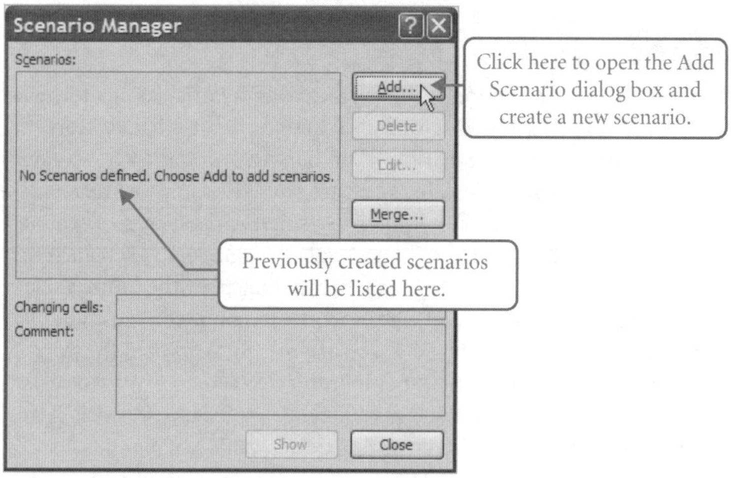

Figure 9.21 | **The Add/Edit Scenario Dialog Box**

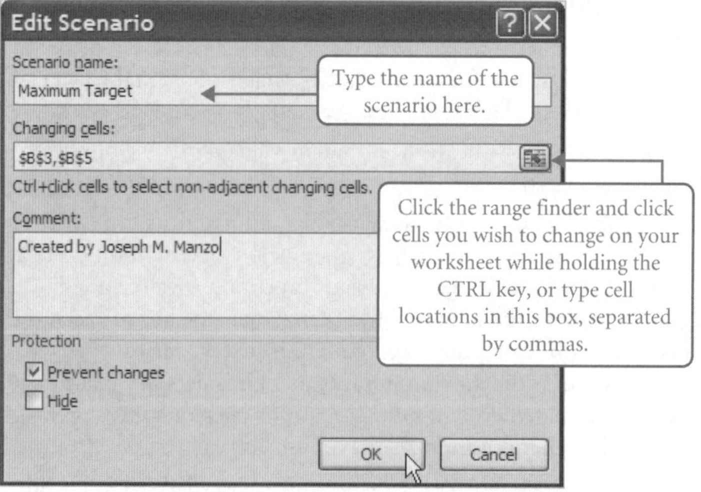

Figure 9.22 | **The Scenario Values Dialog Box**

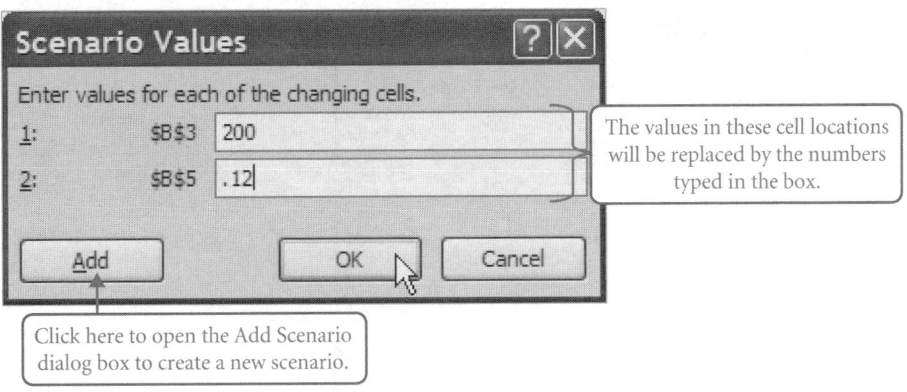

Figure 9.23 | **Results of the Maximum Target Scenario**

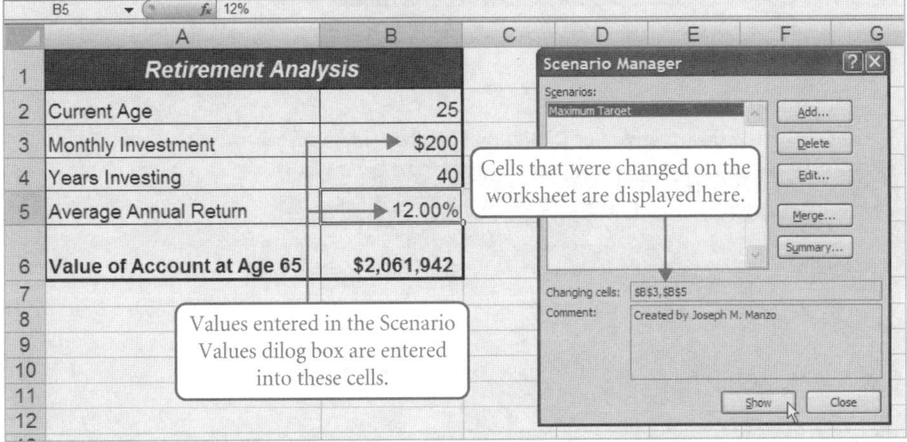

Figures 9.24 through 9.26 show the setup and results of a second scenario that was added to the **Scenario Manager** dialog box. This scenario calculates the future value of an investment if a person can invest only $175 per month and is expecting a lower annual growth rate of 9%. Notice in Figure 9.26 that the **Scenario Manager** dialog box shows both scenarios that have been created for this example. To show the results of a scenario on a worksheet, click the scenario name and then click the **Show** button on the right side of the **Scenario Manager** dialog box.

>> ***Quick Reference***

Scenario Manager

1. Create a formula or function that uses cell references to produce a mathematical result.
2. Select the **Scenario Manager** option from the **What-If Analysis** icon in the **Data** tab of the Ribbon.
3. Click the **Add** button in the **Scenario Manager** dialog box.
4. Type a name for the scenario in the **Scenario Name** box.

(Continued)

Scenario Manager (*Continued*)

5. Select cells that are referenced by the formula or function in step 1 by using the range finder, or type cells into the **Changing Cells** box, separating each cell location with a comma.
6. Click the **OK** button at the bottom of the **Edit Scenarios** dialog box.
7. Type values in the box next to each cell location that appears in the **Scenario Values** dialog box, then click the **OK** button.
8. Click the name of the Scenario you wish to apply to your worksheet in the **Scenario Manager** dialog box.
9. Click the **Show** button to apply the scenario selected in step 8 to your worksheet.
10. Click the **Close** button to close the Scenario Manager.

Figure 9.24 | **Add/Edit Scenario Dialog Box for the Middle Target**

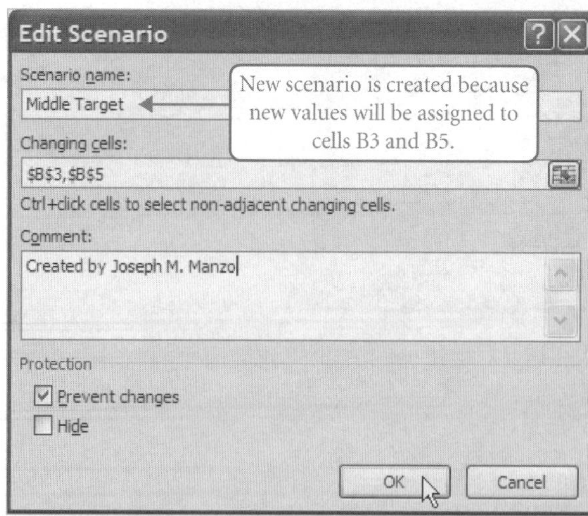

Figure 9.25 | **The Scenario Values Dialog Box for the Middle Target**

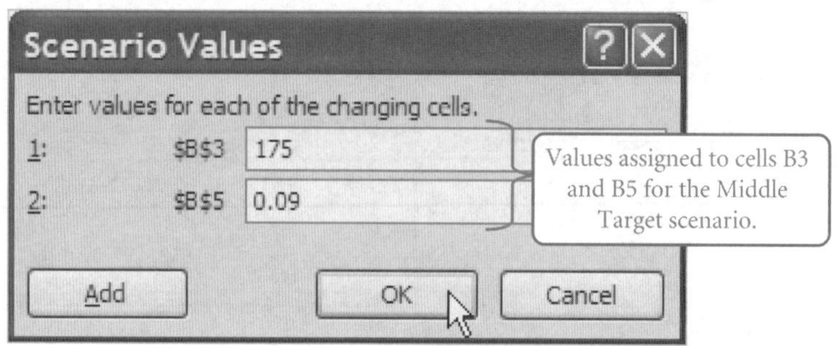

Figure 9.26 | **Results of the Middle Target Scenario**

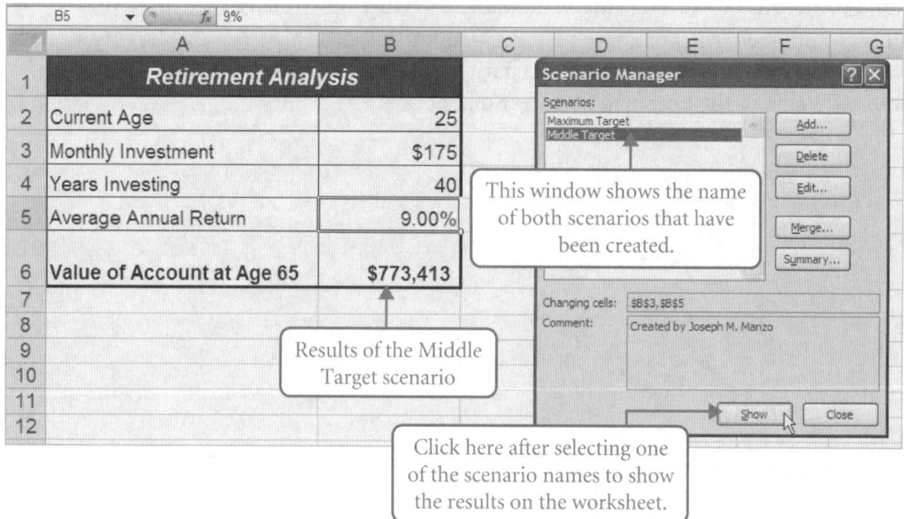

Next, we will add a third scenario to the **Scenario Manager** dialog box that will calculate the value of the retirement investments assuming that $150 is invested every month at an annual growth rate of 6% over 40 years. These are the original Monthly Investment and Average Annual Return values that were used in Figure 9.16, and they represent the minimum expectations for this person's retirement investments. Therefore, Figure 9.27 shows a third scenario in the **Scenario Manager** dialog box labeled Minimum Target. A report showing the results of all three scenarios can be created by clicking the **Summary** button on the right side of the **Scenario Manager** dialog box.

Figure 9.27 | **Results of the Minimum Target Scenario**

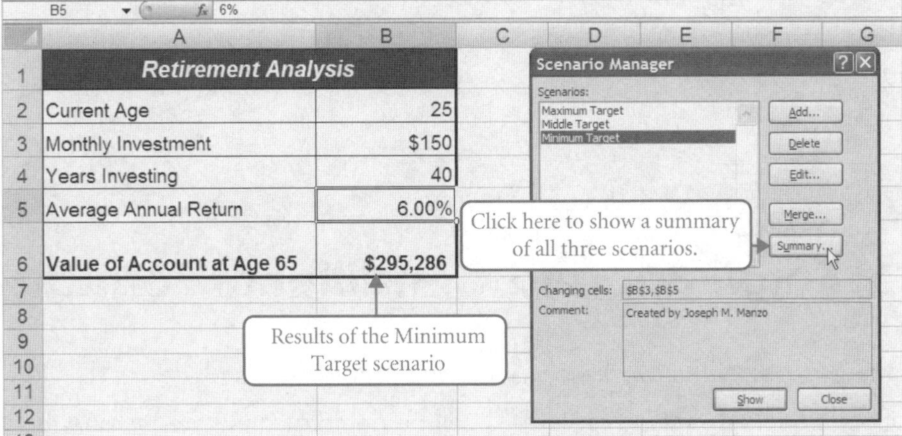

The Scenario Manager will automatically create a report showing the results of all scenarios that have been created when you click the **Summary** button. The **Summary** button will open the **Scenario Summary** dialog box, which gives you the option of creating a PivotTable or a worksheet with subtotals showing the results of the scenarios. Figures 9.28 and 9.29 show the **Scenario Summary** dialog box and the Summary Report for the three scenarios shown in Figure 9.27.

Figure 9.28 | **Scenario Summary Dialog Box**

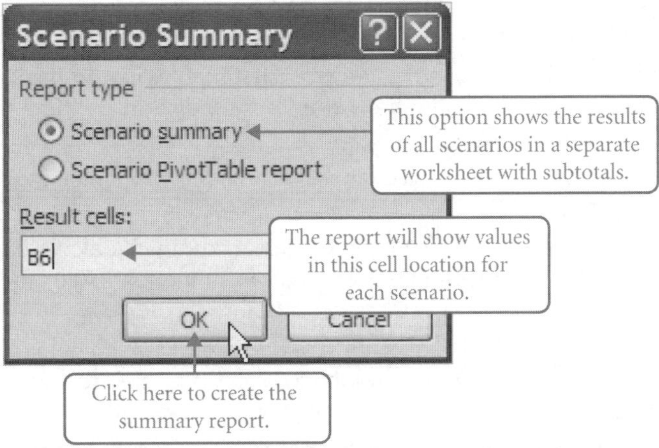

Figure 9.29 | **Scenario Summary Report**

Scenario Summary	Current Values:	Maximum Target	Middle Target	Minimum Target
Changing Cells:				
$B$3	$150	$200	$175	$150
$B$5	6.00%	12.00%	9.00%	6.00%
	$295,286	$2,061,942	$773,413	$295,286

…column represents values of changing cells at time Scenario Summary Report was created. Changing cells for each scenario are highlighted in gray.

Click here to show comments for each scenario.

Values that were assigned to each cell location are displayed here.

Click buttons to show or hide details.

>>Scroll Bar and Conditional Formats

The purpose of this workshop is to demonstrate the Scroll Bar and Conditional Formatting features. I will be demonstrating the tasks in this workshop in the **Scroll Bar** and **Conditional Formatting** videos. After completing each section of tasks, watch the related video shown in parentheses. Open the Excel file named ib_e09_profitanalysis before starting this workshop.

1. **Scroll Bar (Video: Scroll Bar)**
   a. Enter a **VLOOKUP** function in cell B3 of the Break-Even worksheet that will find the value in cell B2 in the Price and Sales Units worksheet. The function should return the exact value in the Unit Sales column from the Price and Sales Units worksheet.
   b. Enter a formula in cell B6 of the Break-Even worksheet that will add the fixed costs to the result of multiplying the variable cost per shirt by the unit sales.
   c. Enter a formula in cell B7 of the Break-Even worksheet that will calculate the total sales in dollars.
   d. Enter a formula in cell B8 of the Break-Even worksheet that will calculate the total profit dollars by subtracting the total costs from the total sales in dollars.
   e. Enter a formula in cell B9 of the Break-Even worksheet that will calculate the profit as a percent of sales by dividing the total sales in dollars into the total profit dollars.
   f. Select the Scroll Bar form control from the **Insert** icon in the **Developer** tab of the Ribbon.
   g. Click and drag a vertical rectangle between cells C2 and C8.
   h. Click the **Properties** icon in the **Developer** tab of the Ribbon.
   i. Click the **Control** tab at the top of the **Format Control** dialog box.
   j. Type the number `25` in the **Current Value** box.
   k. Use the arrows or type the number `25` in the **Minimum Value** box.

l. Use the arrows or type the number `75` in the **Maximum Value** box.
m. Use the arrows or type the number `5` in the **Page Change** box.
n. Use the range finder or type cell location `B2` in the **Cell Link** box.
o. Click the **OK** button, and then click on any cell on the worksheet.
p. Click the Down arrow of the Scroll Bar until the profit in cell B8 reads $2,000.
q. Use the Scroll Bar slide to increase the price in cell B2 to any value greater than $65. Notice the profit value in cell B8.

2. Conditional Formatting (Video: Conditional Formatting)

a. Activate cell B9 in the Break-Even worksheet.
b. Select the **New Rule** option from the **Conditional Formatting** icon in the **Home** tab of the Ribbon.
c. Select the **Format only cells that contain** option in the top section of the **New Formatting Rule** dialog box.
d. Set the first drop-down box in the bottom section of the **New Formatting Rule** dialog box to Cell Value.
e. Set the second drop-down box to Less Than, and then type `0` in the third box.
f. Click the **Format** button, set the font color to red, and then click the **OK** button in the **Format Cells** dialog box.
g. Click the **OK** button in the **New Formatting Rule** dialog box.
h. Save and close your file.

>> Data Tables

VIDEO WORKSHOP

The purpose of this workshop is to demonstrate how data tables are used to assess the profitability of a business. I will be demonstrating the tasks in this workshop in the video named **Data Table**. Open the Excel file named ib_e09_profitandloss before starting this workshop. Complete the tasks below first, and then watch the video.

1. Data Tables (Video: Data Table)

a. Enter the following formula in cell B7 in the Profit Table worksheet: `(B2 * B3) - (B5 + (B4 * B3)).`
b. Type the following values in cells C7 through I7: `25, 30, 35, 40, 45, 50, 55.`
c. Type the following values in cells B8 through B18: `75000, 70000, 65000, 60000, 55000, 50000, 45000, 40000, 35000, 30000, 25000.`
d. Highlight the range C8:I18 and place a bold line on the top and left side of the range.
e. Highlight the range B7:I18.
f. Select the **Data Table** option from the **What-If Analysis** icon in the **Data** tab of the Ribbon.
g. Use the range finder or type cell location `B2` in the **Row Input Cell** box of the **Data Table** dialog box.

h. Use the range finder or type cell location `B3` in the **Column Input Cell** box of the **Data Table** dialog box.
i. Click the **OK** button on the **Data Table** dialog box.
j. Change the value in cell F7 to `35.50`, G7 to `36.00`, H7 to `36.50`, and I7 to `37.00`.
k. Save and close your file.

VIDEO WORKSHOP

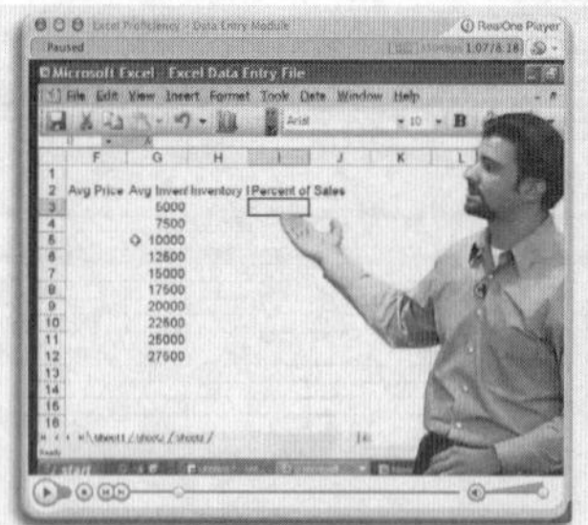

>> Goal Seek

The purpose of this workshop is to demonstrate how the Goal Seek tool is used to assess the future value of investments. I will be demonstrating the tasks in this workshop in the video named **Goal Seek**. Open the Excel file named ib_e09_retirementanalysis. Complete the tasks below first, and then watch the video.

1. **Goal Seek (Video: Goal Seek)**
   a. Use the **FV** function in cell B6 of the Retirement Value worksheet to calculate the future value of the investment given the values in cells B3, B4, and B5. Note that the value in cell B3 represents monthly investments. Assume that investments are made at the beginning of each month.
   b. Select the **Goal Seek** option from the **What-If Analysis** icon in the **Data** tab of the Ribbon.
   c. Use the range finder or type cell location `B6` in the **Set Cell** box of the **Goal Seek** dialog box.
   d. Type the number `1000000` in the **To Value** box in the **Goal Seek** dialog box.
   e. Use the range finder or type cell location `B3` in the **By Changing Cell** box of the **Goal Seek** window.
   f. Click the **OK** button in the **Goal Seek** dialog box.
   g. Click the **OK** button in the **Goal Seek Status** dialog box.
   h. Type the number `150` in cell B3.
   i. Use Goal Seek to determine what annual growth rate would be required to achieve a future value of $1 million given a $150-a-month investment for 40 years.
   j. Save and close your file.

VIDEO WORKSHOP

>> Scenario Manager

The purpose of this workshop is to demonstrate how the Scenario Manager is used to establish a variety of investment scenarios. I will be demonstrating the tasks in this workshop in the video named **Scenario Manager**. Open the Excel file named ib_e09_investmentscenarios. Complete the tasks below first, and then watch the video.

1. **Scenario Manager (Video: Scenario Manager)**
   a. Select the **Scenario Manager** option from the **What-If Analysis** icon in the **Data** tab of the Ribbon.
   b. Click the **Add** button on the **Scenario Manager** dialog box.
   c. Type `Maximum Target` in the **Scenario Name** box of the **Add Scenario** dialog box.
   d. Use the range finder or type cell locations `B3` and `B5` in the **Changing Cells** box of the **Add Scenario** dialog box. Use a comma to separate each cell location if you are typing them into the box.
   e. Click the **OK** button on the **Edit Scenario** dialog box.
   f. Type `200` in the box next to cell $B$3 and `.12` in the box next to cell $B$5 in the **Scenario Values** dialog box. Delete any numbers that appear in the boxes before typing these values.
   g. Click the **OK** button in the **Scenario Values** dialog box.
   h. Click the **Show** button in the **Scenario Manager** dialog box.
   i. Click the **Add** button in the **Scenario Manager** dialog box.
   j. Type `Middle Target` in the **Scenario Name** box of the **Add Scenario** dialog box.
   k. Click the **OK** button on the **Add Scenario** dialog box.
   l. Type `175` in the box next tko cell $B$3 and `.09` in the box next to cell $B$5 in the **Scenario Values** dialog box. Delete any numbers that appear in the boxes before typing these values.
   m. Click the **OK** button in the **Scenario Values** dialog box.
   n. Click the **Show** button in the **Scenario Manager** window.
   o. Create a third scenario called `Minimum Target`. This scenario should assign the value `150` to cell B3 and `.06` to cell B5. Show the results of this scenario on the worksheet.
   p. Click the **Summary** button in the **Scenario Manager** dialog box.
   q. Select the **Scenario Summary** option in the **Scenario Summary** dialog box and click the **OK** button.
   r. Save and close your file.

>> Sales Scenarios for Grocery Merchandise

EXERCISE

Why Do I Need This?

Uncertainty is one of the biggest challenges business managers face when launching new products or developing new businesses. A great business idea does not automatically produce great profits when it is executed by a company. As a result, most prudent business executives will test new ideas before launching them on a grand scale. A well-designed test can provide valuable information about a new business and can also help produce substantial growth in sales and profit for a company. The results of a test might tell a business manager whether the company should launch or abandon a new idea. However, in most instances managers use these results to determine *how* to execute a new business to maximize its profit potential. For example, the sales from a test might show a business manager which products in a new line of merchandise should be dropped. Or, the test results could indicate whether the amount of space allotted for a product line in a retail store should be increased or decreased. Consequently, business managers will analyze several "What if" scenarios before a test ever takes place, then compare these results with the results of the test, before making decisions about either implementing the business idea or determining how it should be implemented to produce a profit. Excel's scenario tools are valuable when developing the criteria that support a variety of decisions that are made on the basis of the results of a business test.

Exercise

The purpose of this exercise is to develop scenarios for a new line of merchandise that will be launched in a grocery store. The results of these scenarios can be compared with the results of a test to determine if this new line of merchandise can be sold successfully and how the company should purchase and display the line to maximize its profit potential. Open the file named ib_e09_grocerymerchandisetest before starting this exercise.

1. Activate the Sales Mix worksheet. The line of merchandise to be tested involves two main categories: Cookware and Utensils. The results of this business will change dramatically depending on how much Cookware sells versus Utensils because the profit margins for these two categories are different. Therefore, the next several tasks of this exercise will focus on setting up the formulas for the Sales Mix worksheet so you can better understand how the sales combination of the two categories impact the overall results of the business.
2. Type a formula in cell C5 of the Sales Mix worksheet that calculates the Unit Sales of the Utensils category. This formula should subtract the sales of the Cookware category in cell C4 from the overall unit sales of both categories in cell B2. As a result, when the Unit Sales of the Cookware category is changed, the sales for the Utensils category will also change.
3. Type a formula in cell B5 that calculates the total percent of sales for the Utensils category. This formula should divide the sales results in cell C5 by the total sales in cell B2.
4. Type a formula in cell F4 that calculates the Sales Dollars for the Cookware category. This formula should multiply the Average Price in cell D4 by the Unit Sales in cell C4. Then, copy this formula and paste it into cell F5.
5. Type a formula in cell G4 that calculates the Profit Dollars for the Cookware category. This formula should first subtract the Average Cost in cell E4 from the Average Price in cell D4, and then this result should be multiplied by the Unit Sales in cell C4. Copy this formula and paste it into cell G5.
6. Type a formula in cell H4 that calculates the Profit Percent of Sales for the Cookware category. This formula should divide the Profit Dollars in cell G4 by the Sales Dollars in cell F4. Copy this formula and paste it into cell H5. Notice that the profit percent for the Cookware category is lower than for the Utensils category.
7. Type a **SUM** function in cells F6 and G6 to calculate the total Sales Dollars and Profit Dollars.
8. Type a formula in cell H6 that calculates the total Profit Percent of Sales by dividing the value in cell G6 by the value in cell F6.
9. Type a formula in cell D6 that calculates the total Average Price. This formula should divide the total Sales Dollars in cell F6 by the total Unit Sales in cell C6.
10. Type a formula in cell E6 that calculates the total Average Cost. This formula should first subtract the total Profit Dollars in cell G6 from the total Sales Dollars in cell F6, and then divide this result by the total Unit Sales in cell C6.

11. The total profit as a percent of sales in cell H6 should be 49.3%. However, this profit rate will decrease as sales in the Cookware category increases. The next several tasks will focus on adding a Scroll Bar to determine the maximum percent of Cookware sales needed to achieve at least a 40% profit rate for both categories. Begin by selecting the Scroll Bar format control from the **Insert** icon in the **Developer** tab of the Ribbon.

12. Add the Scroll Bar in the area of B8:B15.

13. Open the **Format Control** dialog box for the Scroll Bar and enter the following settings in the **Control** tab.

    a. Current Value: `100`

    b. Minimum Value: `100`

    c. Maximum Value: `14900`

    d. Incremental Change: `100`

    e. Page Change: `500`

    f. Cell Link: `C4`

14. Click the **OK** button of the **Format Control** dialog box and then click a cell location to activate the Scroll Bar.

15. Use the Scroll Bar to get the percentage in cell H6 as close as possible to 40%. What sales mix must the grocery store achieve (percent of total sales for Cookware and Utensils) if the company is targeting an overall profit rate of 40% or higher?

16. What is the profit rate in cell H6 if the grocery store achieves a sales mix of approximately 50% Cookware and 50% Utensils?

17. If this company has a profit rate target of 41.5% for all general-merchandise sales, what sales mix must be achieved to reach this goal? You may notice that getting the profit rate in cell H6 to read exactly 41.5% is difficult using the Scroll Bar. In these situations, Goal Seek is a better tool. Therefore, use the **Goal Seek** tool to answer this question by entering the following criteria in the **Goal Seek** dialog box.

    a. Set Cell: `H6`

    b. To Value: `.415`

    c. By Changing Cell: `C4`

18. The Average Price values showing in cells D4 and D5 are an important assumption made in this analysis. However, these prices could change depending on the mix of items that are sold within each category. If customers buy more of the lower-priced merchandise, the average price could decline. If customers buy more of the higher priced merchandise in the assortment, the average price could increase. As a result, the following tasks will focus on using the Scenario Manager to analyze the impact a change in the average price might have on the overall sales and profit of the business.

19. Create three different scenarios that will change the values in cell locations D4 and D5. Use the following scenario names and values for these cell locations.

    a. `Maximum Price:` `D4:45, D5:15`

    b. `Base Scenario:` `D4:35, D5:10`

    c. `Worst Case:` `D4:30, D5:8`

20. Select the Maximum Price scenario in the **Scenario Manager** dialog box and click the **Show** button. Then, close the **Scenario Manager** dialog box and use the Scroll Bar to set the sales mix to `40%` Cookware and `60%` Utensils. What is the overall profit rate of the business?

21. Activate the Sales per Square Foot worksheet. A key metric that many grocers use to measure the productivity of a product line is the sales per square foot. Maintaining space in any retail store is a significant cost. As a result, retailers usually set sales-per-square-foot targets to ensure that the appropriate amount of space is given to a line of products. A data table will be constructed in this worksheet to evaluate how much space should be allocated for the Cookware and Utensils product line.

22. Use a link to show the total average price in cell D6 of the Sales Mix worksheet in cell B3 of the Sales per Square Foot worksheet.

23. Type a formula in cell B4 of the Sales per Square Foot worksheet that calculates the Total Sales. This formula should multiply the Average Price in cell B3 by the Total Unit Sales in cell B2.

24. Type a formula in cell B7 of the Sales per Square Foot worksheet that calculates the Sales per Square Foot. This formula should divide the Space in Square Feet in cell B5 into the total sales in cell B4.

25. Highlight the range B7:H16 and use a Data Table to produce a sales-per-square-foot grid. Use cell B2 for the Row Input Cell and cell B5 for the Column Input Cell.

26. This company has a goal of maintaining at least $500 per square foot for the Cookware and Utensils merchandise. Use Conditional Formatting to color any value less than $500 in red within the data table results (C8:H16).

27. Based on the scenario that was selected in the Price Mix worksheet (should be the Maximum Price scenario, Cookware 40% of sales, and Utensils 60% of sales), will the company achieve at least $500 per square foot if it uses 1200 square feet of space to display this merchandise, assuming unit sales are 15,000? If sales are 15,000 units, what is the maximum amount of space the company should use to achieve at least $500 per square foot? What if sales drop to 10,000 units?

28. Go back to the Sales Mix worksheet and open the **Scenario Manager** dialog box. Select the Worst Case scenario and click the **Show** button. Then, close the **Scenario Manager** dialog box.

29. Use the Scroll Bar to change the sales mix to 25% Cookware and 75% Utensils. Then, activate the Sales per Square Foot worksheet. What is the maximum amount of space the company could dedicate to this product line if total unit sales are 15,000? What would the minimum percent of Cookware sales have to be to achieve at least $500 per square foot should sales drop to 10,000 units?

30. Save and close your file.

>> What's Wrong with This Spreadsheet?

PROBLEM & EXERCISE

Problem

You are the director of a product development division for a large retail corporation. You are about to give the president of the company an overview of a test your division will be conducting to determine if a new line of products has the potential of increasing the company's overall sales and profit. You have worked with this president for a few years and know that he is notorious for asking "What if" questions and wanting the "worst-case scenario." You give one of the analysts in your division instructions to assemble financial scenarios regarding this test. You inform the analyst that the president will be interested in seeing how the new product lines will reach the company standard of $600 per square foot and an overall profit margin of 47.5%. The analyst e-mails an Excel workbook to you and mentions the following points in his message.

1. The workbook attached to this e-mail contains two worksheets. The Sales Mix worksheet shows the sales and profit estimates for the two product lines. You need to change only the sales in cell C4 (shaded yellow) to change the overall Sales Mix.
2. The average price can be changed by typing new values in cells D4 and D5 (also shaded yellow) in the Sales Mix worksheet. I spoke to marketing and they expect the average price to be $42 for Line A and said that should be accurate within plus or minus $5. They expect the average price for Line B to be $18 and that should be accurate within plus or minus $3.
3. All of the data that is calculated in the Sales Mix worksheet is linked to the second worksheet (cells B2:B4). Therefore, any changes you make in the Sales Mix worksheet will automatically carry over into the Sales per Square Foot worksheet. I created a data table showing the sales per square foot at different unit sales and space allocations.
4. I think the profit target is a slam dunk. My estimates show us at 50%. However, I am concerned about the space. The good news is that it looks like the sales per square foot data is consistent no matter how many units we sell. However, I think the space will have to be reduced to 1,000 square feet.

Exercise

The Excel file the analyst attached to your e-mail is named ib_e09_producttest. Would you be comfortable presenting this information to the president of the company? Review the file and consider the following points:

1. Look at the Sales Mix worksheet. Do the calculations and data in this worksheet make sense?
2. Look at the data table in the Sales per Square Foot worksheet. The analyst mentioned that the sales per square foot results do not change when the unit sales change. Does this make sense? Why or why not?
3. Can the current results in this workbook be used to explain a "worst-case scenario" to the president? Why or why not?

Write a short answer for each of the points above. Fix any errors you find in the workbook and prepare what you think would be a worst-case scenario. Write a short justification explaining why you think your adjustments better address a worst-case scenario. Make any other enhancements or adjustments you think would improve your meeting with the president.

Skill Set

Data Analysis Tools

As you have learned in previous chapters, Excel provides several functions for conducting statistical calculations. However, Excel also provides an entire suite of tools for conducting statistical analyses called **Data Analysis Tools**. The **Data Analysis Tools** provide 19 options for conducting statistical calculations using data that is contained in a worksheet. This section will focus on three of these options: Descriptive Statistics, Histogram, and Regression.

Add-Ins

You may need to activate the **Data Analysis Tools** and **Solver** features on your computer before continuing with this section. Figure 9.30 shows how the **Data** tab of the Ribbon will appear if these tools are currently activated on your computer. You should see both the **Data Analysis** and **Solver** options in the **Analysis** group of icons.

Figure 9.30 | **Data Tab after the Data Analysis Tools and Solver Are Activated**

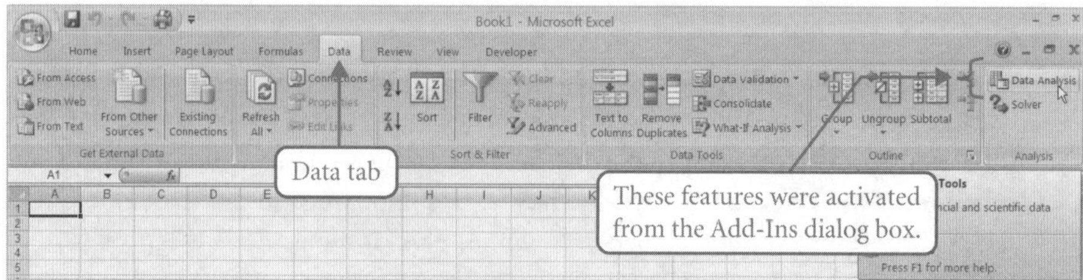

If you do not see the **Analysis** group of icons on your computer, you must activate the **Data Analysis Tools** and **Solver**. The following points explain how this is done:

- Click the **Office** icon and then the **Excel Options** button.
- Click the Add-Ins category on the left side of the **Excel Options** dialog box (see Figure 9.31).
- Make sure the **Manage** drop-down box at the bottom of the **Excel Options** dialog box is set to **Excel Add-Ins,** and then click the **Go** button. This will open the **Add-Ins** dialog box (see Figure 9.32).
- Click the **Analysis Toolpak** and **Solver Add-in** options in the **Add-Ins** dialog box.
- Click the **OK** button in the **Add-Ins** dialog box. This will add both features to your computer as shown in Figure 9.30.

Quick Reference

Add-Ins

1. Click the **Office** icon.
2. Click the **Excel Options** button.
3. Click the **Add-Ins** category on the left side of the **Excel Options** dialog box.
4. Set the **Manage** drop-down box to **Excel Add-Ins**.
5. Click the **Go** button.
6. Select the desired feature(s) in the **Add-Ins** dialog box and click the **OK** button.

Figure 9.31 | **Excel Options Dialog Box**

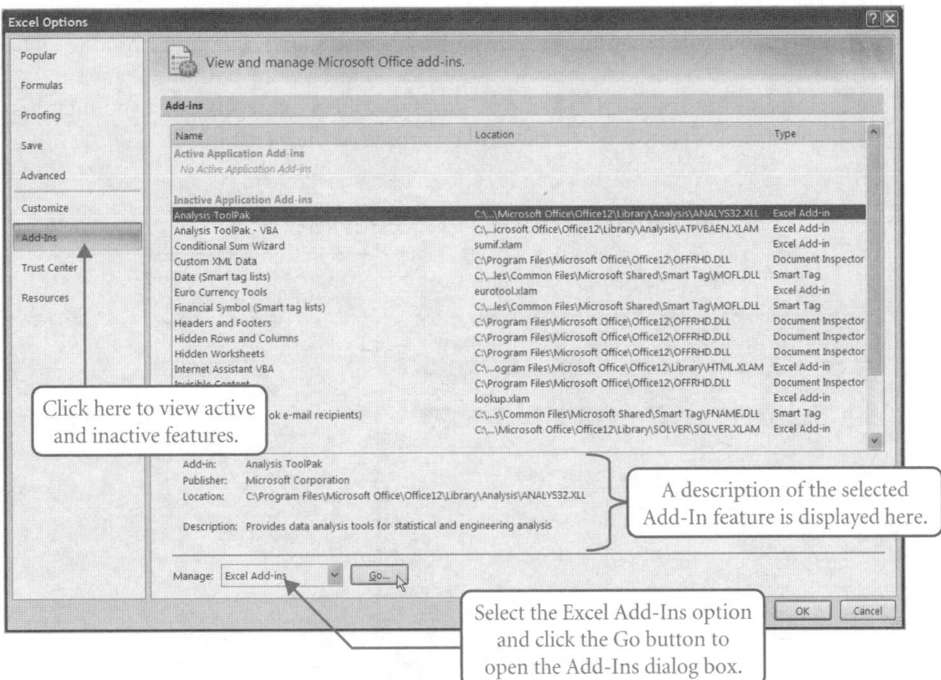

Figure 9.32 | **Add-Ins Dialog Box**

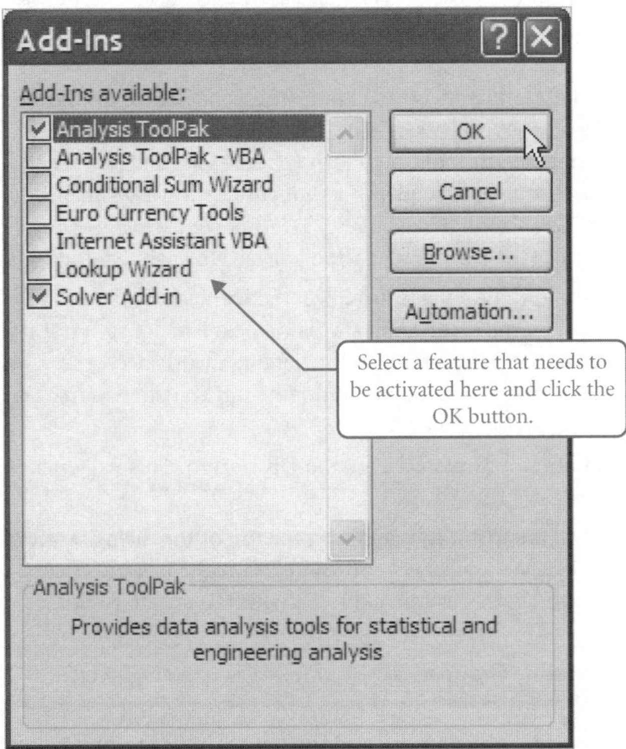

Descriptive Statistics

Statistical calculations can be conducted using functions such as SUM, AVERAGE, MAX, MIN, etc. However, these functions must be added to a worksheet one at a time. You can use the **Descriptive Statistics** option from the **Data Analysis Tools** to conduct more than 13 different statistical calculations at the same time. In addition, this option also makes it easier to apply statistical calculations to a large data set. For example, Figure 9.33 shows 200 transactions from a general-merchandise retail company. Each transaction represents a customer's cash-register receipt. For each transaction number, the worksheet shows the number of items purchased (Items per Transaction) and the total dollars spent (Transaction Value). The Descriptive statistics option from the **Data Analysis Tools** will be used to provide a statistical summary for both the Items per Transaction and the Transaction Value columns. Business managers often conduct this type of analysis to establish an overall buying profile of their customers.

Figure 9.33 | **Transaction Data for a General-Merchandise Retailer**

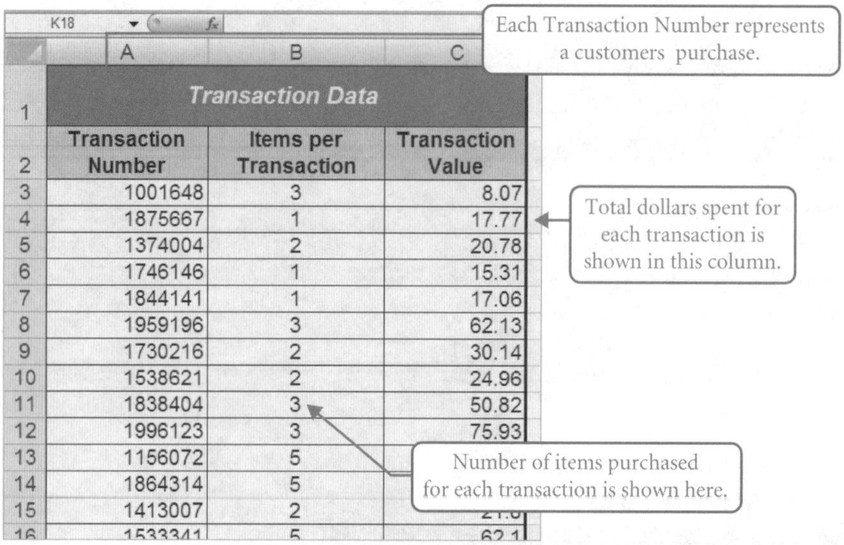

	A	B	C
1	Transaction Data		
2	Transaction Number	Items per Transaction	Transaction Value
3	1001648	3	8.07
4	1875667	1	17.77
5	1374004	2	20.78
6	1746146	1	15.31
7	1844141	1	17.06
8	1959196	3	62.13
9	1730216	2	30.14
10	1538621	2	24.96
11	1838404	3	50.82
12	1996123	3	75.93
13	1156072	5	[illegible]
14	1864314	5	[illegible]
15	1413007	2	[illegible]
16	1533341	5	[illegible]

Each Transaction Number represents a customers purchase.

Total dollars spent for each transaction is shown in this column.

Number of items purchased for each transaction is shown here.

A common goal for most retail companies is to sell more than one item to a customer each time she visits the store. For a large retailer servicing millions of customers per year, an increase of just one item per transaction could significantly boost sales and profits. As a result, business managers in these companies frequently conduct statistical assessments of transaction data similar to what is displayed in Figure 9.33. The following explains how the Descriptive Statistics option from the Data Analysis Tools is used to analyze this data.

- Click the **Data Analysis** icon in the **Analysis** group on the **Data** tab of the Ribbon (see Figure 9.30). This will open the **Data Analysis** dialog box, which lists a number of options for applying statistical methods to the data in a worksheet (see Figure 9.34). Most concepts that are covered in a fundamental Statistics course are listed in this dialog box.
- Select the **Descriptive Statistics** options and click the **OK** button. This will open the **Descriptive Statistics** dialog box.
- Click the range finder next to the **Input Range** box at the top of the dialog box and highlight the range B2:C202 in the worksheet shown in Figure 9.33. Notice that the column headings are included in this range. Press the **Enter** key after highlighting this range.
- Select the **Columns** option in the Grouped By section, which appears directly below the **Input Range** box.
- Make sure a green check appears in the box next to the **Labels in First Row** option. Click the box to add or remove a check. Because the column headings were highlighted when the Input Range was defined, this option must be checked.
- Select the **New Worksheet Ply** option in the Output Options section. This will add a new worksheet to the workbook showing the results of the statistical analysis. You can also enter a worksheet tab name in the box next to this option.
- Click the box next to the **Summary Statistics** option. A green check should appear in this box. You must select this box to produce a statistical summary of the data you are analyzing.

- Below the Summary Statistics check box are options for adjusting the confidence level for the Mean and for displaying the largest and smallest values in your data set. The confidence level for the mean will automatically be set to 95%. In addition, the summary will automatically show the largest and smallest values from the data set you are analyzing. However, by checking the box next to these options, you can type a value in the input box to show any number from the top and bottom of the dataset (i.e., 3rd largest value, 4th largest value, 5th smallest value, etc.).
- Click the **OK** button. This will add a new worksheet to the workbook and display several statistical outputs for the data in the range entered in the **Input Range** box.

Figure 9.34 | **Data Analysis Dialog Box**

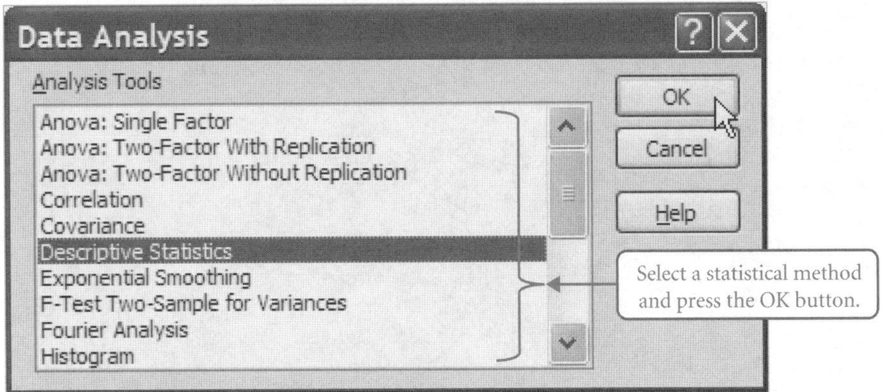

Figure 9.35 | **Descriptive Statistics Dialog Box**

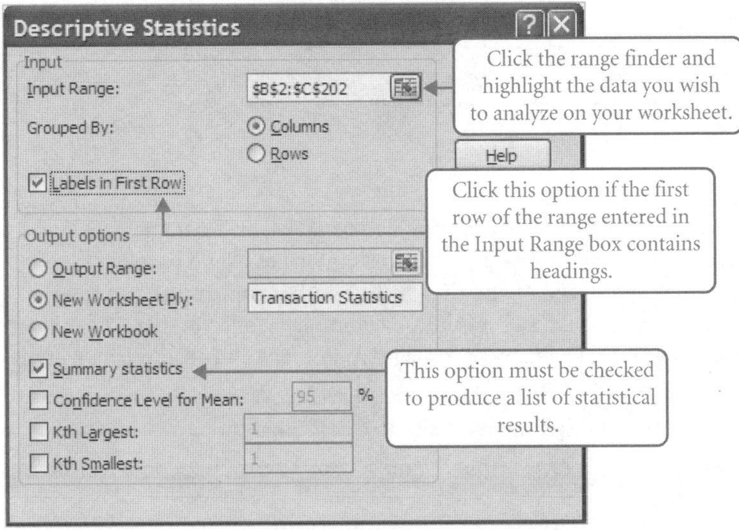

Figure 9.36 shows the Descriptive Statistics output for the transaction data in Figure 9.33. These results are automatically placed into a new worksheet if the New Worksheet Ply is selected in the **Descriptive Statistics** dialog box. In addition, adjustments can be made to the number formats and to the visual appearance (i.e., borders, font color, cell shading, etc.) as needed. Notice that there are two sets of statistics showing in this worksheet. This is because two columns of data were highlighted when the **Input Range** box was defined in the **Descriptive Statistics** dialog box.

COMMON MISTAKES | Descriptive Statistics Window Settings

A green check must appear next to the **Summary Statistics** option in the **Descriptive Statistics** dialog box to produce the comprehensive output of statistical results. If you wish to see only the Confidence Level for Mean, the Kth Largest value, or the Kth Smallest value, then select these options without selecting the Summary Statistics. You can also select all four options if needed.

Figure 9.36 | **Descriptive Statistics Output**

	A	B	C	D
1	*Items per Transaction*		*Transaction Value*	
2				
3	Mean	4.61	Mean	56.6133
4	Standard Error	0.268795	Standard Error	3.777009
5	Median	3	Median	42.29
6	Mode	1	Mode	11.66
7	Standard Deviation	3.8013354	Standard Deviation	53.41498
8	Sample Variance	14.450151	Sample Variance	2853.16
9	Kurtosis	2.8387259	Kurtosis	4.505986
10	Skewness	1.6071632	Skewness	1.923072
11	Range	19	Range	313.96
12	Minimum	1	Minimum	0.87
13	Maximum	20	Maximum	314.83
14	Sum	922	Sum	11322.66
15	Count	200	Count	200

Column heading pertaining to each set of statistics is shown in this row.

Separate results are calculated for each column of data highlighted in the dialog box.

The statistics shown in Figure 9.36 can provide several key insights for a business manager in this retail company. Ultimately, a business manager would have to compare these results with the company's goals and the results of other companies operating in the same industry to determine if these results are favorable or unfavorable. The following are some key highlights that a business manager might take away from this analysis.

- **Mean (Row 3):** The Mean statistics show that on average, customers are buying between 4 and 5 items and spending almost $57 per transaction.
- **Mode (Cell B6):** The Mode reveals that the most common transaction is a customer buying only one item.
- **Standard Deviation (Cell D7) and Range (Cell D11):** The Standard Deviation and Range for the Transaction Value data is fairly high. This indicates a wide disparity in the amount of money customers spend when they visit the store.
- **Sum (Row 14):** The transactions analyzed in this example represent total sales of 922 items at $11,322.66. Depending on the size of this company, these transactions may or may not provide sufficient representation of this business.

COMMON MISTAKES | Using the Currency Format

You will most likely need to expand the column width of the Descriptive Statistics output to see all the data. If the results appear distorted after clicking the **OK** button on the **Descriptive Statistics** window, expand the column widths on the output worksheet. You can also apply any of Excel's formatting features to enhance the appearance of a Descriptive Statistics output.

Histogram

Business managers use histograms to calculate the frequency or number of occurrences within certain categories of data. For example, a retail business manager will often measure how many items are purchased by price point. As with the example illustrated in the previous segment, this type of analysis will give a business manager an understanding of how customers are buying products in the company's stores. In addition, this analysis can also provide valuable insights into a company's strength in selling certain products or categories of merchandise.

Figure 9.37 shows transaction data that is similar to the data shown in Figure 9.33. However, in this worksheet the transaction number is duplicated for each item the customer purchased. For example, if a customer purchased three items, the transaction number will be listed three times. As a result, there are 650 rows of data in this worksheet. Next to each transaction number is the price the customer paid for the item purchased. You will also see seven price categories listed in column D. With the exception of the first two price categories, each category is in $10 increments. The **Histogram** option from the **Data Analysis Tools** will be used to calculate how many items were purchased in each of these price categories.

Figure 9.37 | **Transactions and Price Points**

	A	B	C	D
1	Transaction Details			
2	Transaction Number	Price		Price Categories
3	101483	$2.00		$4.99
4	107334	$9.29		$9.99
5	110245	$7.82		$19.99
6	110245	$8.28		$29.99
7	110245	$8.95		$39.99
8	110245	$12.76		$49.99
9	110245	$19.68		$59.99
10	110245	$3.30		
11	110245	$25.30		
12	110245	$31.08		
13	110245	$38.29		
14	110739	$9.14		
15	111701	$3.17		
16	111701	$7.62		

The Histogram will count the number of transactions with a price between $0 and $4.99 and assign the number to this group.

This transaction is listed 9 times because the customer purchased 9 different items.

>> Quick Reference

Data Analysis Tools: Descriptive Statistics

1. Click the **Data Analysis** icon from the **Analysis** group on the **Data** tab of the Ribbon.
2. Select **Descriptive Statistics** from the **Data Analysis** dialog box and click the **OK** button.
3. Click the range finder next to the **Input Range** box and highlight the range of data you wish to analyze on your worksheet or type the range in the box.
4. Select either Columns or Rows based on the orientation of your data.
5. If you highlighted labels in step 3, click the box next to the **Labels in First Row** option.
6. Select an option designating where the output calculations will appear.
7. Select **Summary Statistics** to produce a comprehensive output of statistical calculations.
8. Select any or all of the three remaining output options if necessary.
9. Click the **OK** button.
10. Apply formatting adjustments to the output as needed.

The Histogram feature will be used to count the price frequency for each of the categories listed in column D using the prices in column B of Figure 9.37. The following explains how this is accomplished.

- Click the **Data Analysis** icon in the **Data** tab of the Ribbon.
- Select the **Histogram** option from the **Data Analysis** dialog box. This will open the **Histogram** dialog box shown in Figure 9.38.
- Click the range finder next to the **Input Range** box and highlight the range B2:B652. Notice that this range includes data in only the Price column (see Figure 9.37).
- Click the range finder next to the **Bin Range** box and highlight the range D2:D9. This is the range of price categories listed in column D. The Histogram will count the frequency of prices in the range of cells used to define the Input Range box based on the values that are contained in the range of cells entered for the Bin Range box.
- Select the **Labels** option, which is directly below the **Bin Range** box. Because the column headings were included in the range of cells used to define both the **Input Range** and **Bin Range** boxes, this option is selected.
- Select the **New Worksheet Ply** option in the center of the **Histogram** options window. The box next to this option is used for naming the worksheet that will be added to the workbook.
- Select the **Cumulative Percentage** and **Chart Output** options at the bottom of the **Histogram** dialog box. The Cumulative Percentage will display the price frequency for each of the groups in the Bin Range and show the cumulative percentage for each group.
- Click the **OK** button in the **Histogram** dialog box. This will add a new worksheet to the workbook showing the frequency results along with a histogram chart.

Figure 9.38 | **Settings in the Histogram Dialog Box**

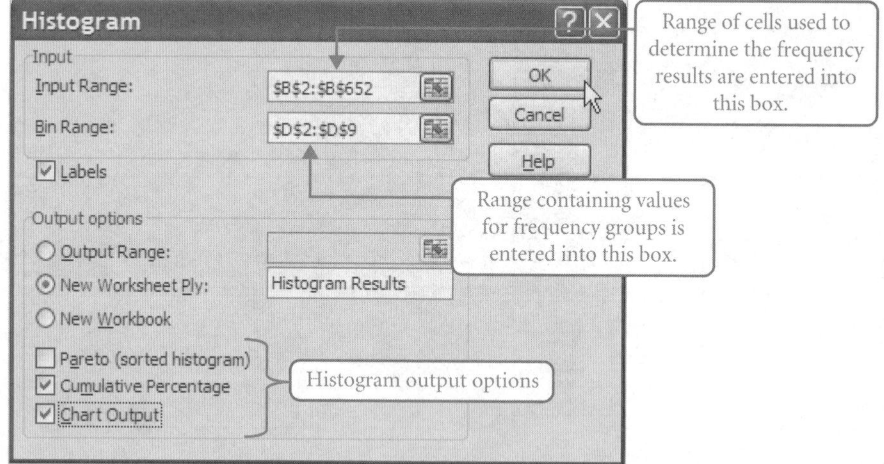

Figure 9.39 shows the Histogram output. Because of the options selected at the bottom of the **Histogram** dialog box shown in Figure 9.38, the price frequency is shown in category order (i.e., 4.99, 9.99, 19.99, etc.). In addition, a chart displaying the frequency data is also included. Note that both the data output and the histogram chart in Figure 9.39 have been formatted. You will most likely need to expand the column widths of the histogram data output to see the results. You will also need to resize and format the chart. Chart formatting techniques are covered in Chapter 5.

Figure 9.39 | **Histogram Output**

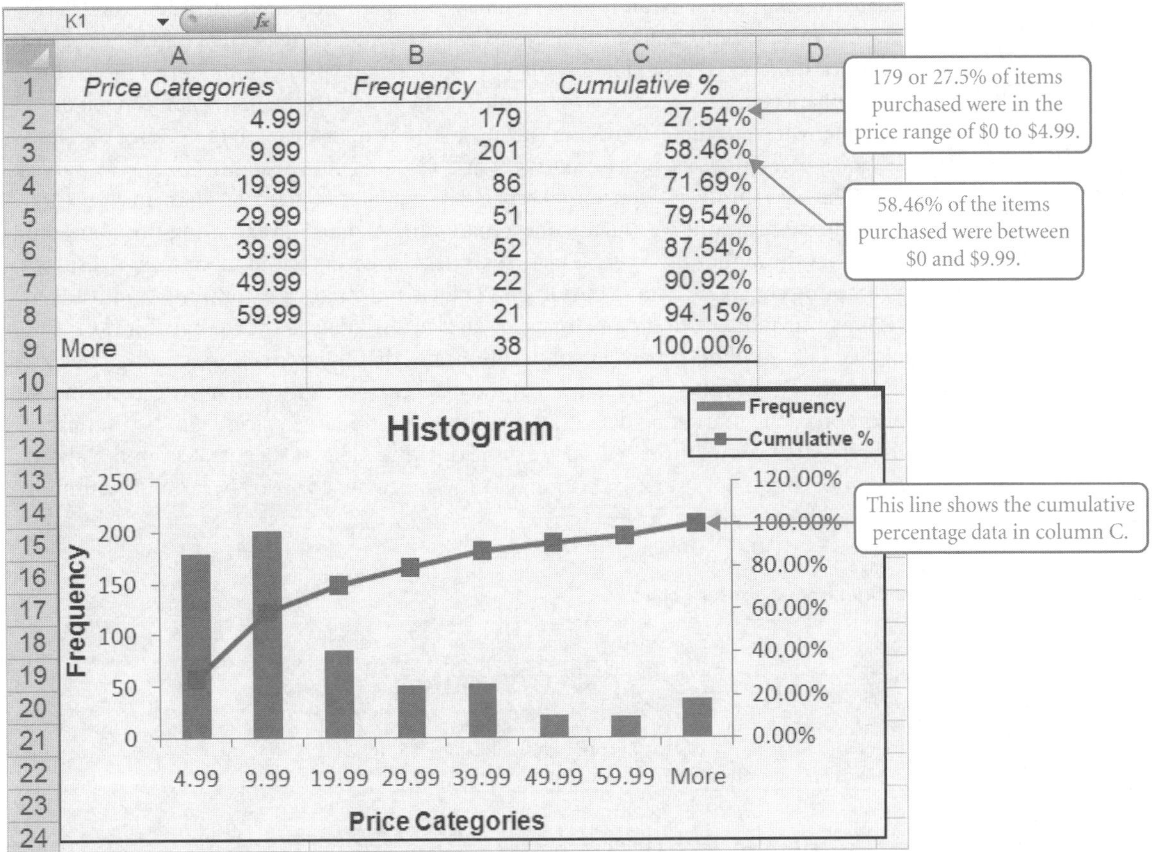

Price Categories	Frequency	Cumulative %
4.99	179	27.54%
9.99	201	58.46%
19.99	86	71.69%
29.99	51	79.54%
39.99	52	87.54%
49.99	22	90.92%
59.99	21	94.15%
More	38	100.00%

COMMON MISTAKES | Setting the Histogram Bin Range Values

Most mistakes with histograms occur when setting the category values that will be used for defining the **Bin Range** box in the **Histogram** dialog box. The category values should be the highest value in a group range. For example, if you wish to count the frequency of prices in a range of $0 to $4.99, the Bin Range value would be 4.99. If you wish to add a second category that counts the number of prices in the range $5.00 to $9.99, the Bin Range value would be 9.99. You can create any number of categories that suit the needs of your project. Any values that exceed the category values that are used to define the Bin Range will automatically be placed into a group called "More."

The results in Figure 9.39 show that 58.46% of all the items purchased are within the price range of $0 to $9.99. This result is also displayed visually in the histogram chart. Notice that the chart bars for price categories $19.99 and greater are considerably lower than in the $4.99 and $9.99 categories. A business manager might be concerned that customers are reluctant to purchase more-expensive products from the store. However, this depends on how much inventory the company owns at prices greater than $9.99. If more than 50% of this company's inventory is priced higher than $9.99, then a business manager will need to investigate why almost 60% of the company's sales are coming from products priced below $9.99. This analysis may ultimately change the way this company buys its inventory.

Regression

Business managers use regression analysis in situations that require the measurement of how much the change in one performance metric, such as Unit Sales, can be explained by other events related to the business. For example, a marketing manager might want

>> Quick Reference

Data Analysis Tools: Histograms

1. Click the **Data Analysis** icon from the **Analysis** group on the **Data** tab of the Ribbon.
2. Select **Histogram** from the **Data Analysis** dialog box and click the **OK** button.
3. Click the range finder next to the **Input Range** box and highlight the range of data for which you wish to calculate the frequency on your worksheet.
4. Click the range finder next to the **Bin Range** box and highlight the range of data that contains values that will be used for grouping the frequency results.
5. If you highlighted labels in step 3 and 4, click the box next to the **Labels** option.

(Continued)

Histograms (*Continued*)

6. Select a placement option for the Histogram results.
7. Select any combination of output options. You must select at least one option.
8. Click the **OK** button.
9. Apply formatting adjustments to the data output and/or chart as needed.

to know if certain advertising strategies have a statistically significant impact on the change of Unit Sales. In addition, a business manager will usually include several variables in this process because many events could be impacting the demand for a specific product at the same time. These variables could include price, competitor's prices, display enhancements, or changes in inventory. The results of the regression can tell the manager which of these events has the most significant impact on the change of sales when changes in all the other events, or variables, are held constant.

The data shown in Figure 9.40 represents the sales of chocolate bars in a grocery store. In this example we will assume a marketing manager is executing two marketing strategies throughout the year. The first strategy is setting up an in-store sign display promoting chocolate bars to customers. The second strategy is running a radio advertisement in addition to the in-store sign display. This data is shown in columns F and G. The number 0 in either column indicates that the marketing activity is not executed and the number 1 indicates that the marketing activity is being executed. In addition to the marketing data, the worksheet also contains prices from two similar grocery store competitors selling the same or similar chocolate bars. Column C shows the price the grocery store is charging for the chocolate bars each week and column B shows the unit sales each week.

Figure 9.40 | **Chocolate-Bar-Demand Data from a Grocery Store**

	A	B	C	D	E	F	G
1	One Year Demand for Chocolate Bars						
2	Week	Unit Sales	Price	Price of Competitor 1	Price of Competitor 2	Display for Chocolate	Display and Ad for Chocolate
3	1	3,000	$0.95	$0.80	$2.29	0	0
4	2	3,329	$0.95	$0.80	$2.29	0	0
5	3	2,500	$0.95	$0.75	$2.29	0	0
6	4	2,000	$0.95	$0.75	$2.29	0	0
7	5	1,650	$0.95	$0.50	$2.29	1	0
8	6	3,773	$0.85	$0.75	$2.29	1	0
9	7	7,500	$0.85	$0.75	$2.29	1	1
10	8	5,000	$0.85	$0.65	$2.29	1	0
11	9	3,500	$0.85	$0.65	$2.29	1	0
12	10	7,550	$0.65	$0.75	$2.29	1	0
13	11	10,500	$0.65	$0.75	$2.29	1	1
14	12	8,339	$0.75	$0.70	$2.29	1	0
15	13	8,500	$0.75	$0.70	$2.29	1	0
16	14	2,416	$0.80	$0.50	$2.29	1	0

The number 1 in this column indicates the grocer has an in-store sign display and is also running radio advertisements.

Data continues for all 52 weeks of the year.

Chocolate bar prices from two competing grocery stores

The following explains how the Regression option from the **Data Analysis Tools** is used to determine which of the five variables, or columns, in Figure 9.40 are statistically significant in explaining the change in Unit Sales shown in column B. As a result, the dependent variable in this example is Units Sales, and the five independent variables are Price, Price of Competitor 1, Price of Competitor 2, Display for Chocolate, and Display and Ad for Chocolate. It is important to note that this example will briefly discuss the regression results but will not provide in-depth interpretations. It is assumed that you have some knowledge of the terms and principles of regression.

- Click the **Data Analysis** icon in the **Data** tab of the Ribbon. Then, select the **Regression** option from the **Data Analysis** dialog box. This will open the **Regression** dialog box.
- Click the range finder next to the **Input Y Range** box and highlight the range B2:B54. This range contains the data for the dependent variable of the regression. Press the **Enter** key after highlighting this range.

- Click the range finder next to the **Input X Range** box, highlight the range C2:G54, and press the **Enter** key. This range contains the data for all five independent variables of the regression.
- Click the box next to the **Labels** option so that a green check appears. Because column headings were included in the range defining the dependent and independent variables, this option must be selected.
- Click the New Worksheet Ply in the Output Options area.
- Click the **OK** button in the **Regression** dialog box.

Figure 9.41 shows the settings that we made in the **Regression** dialog box for this example. Although they are not used for this example, there are options at the bottom of the dialog box for producing plot charts as part of the regression output. **Chart** options include line fit plots, residual plots, and normal probability plots.

COMMON MISTAKES | Configuring Data Columns for Regression

When regressions are conducted in Excel, columns of data used for the independent variables must be adjacent. People often make the mistake of highlighting non-adjacent columns of data while holding the **CTRL** key when defining the independent variables, or Input X Range. However, this will produce the error shown below. Therefore, make sure the columns of data used to define the Input X Range are all adjacent.

Figure 9.41 | **Settings in the Regression Options Window**

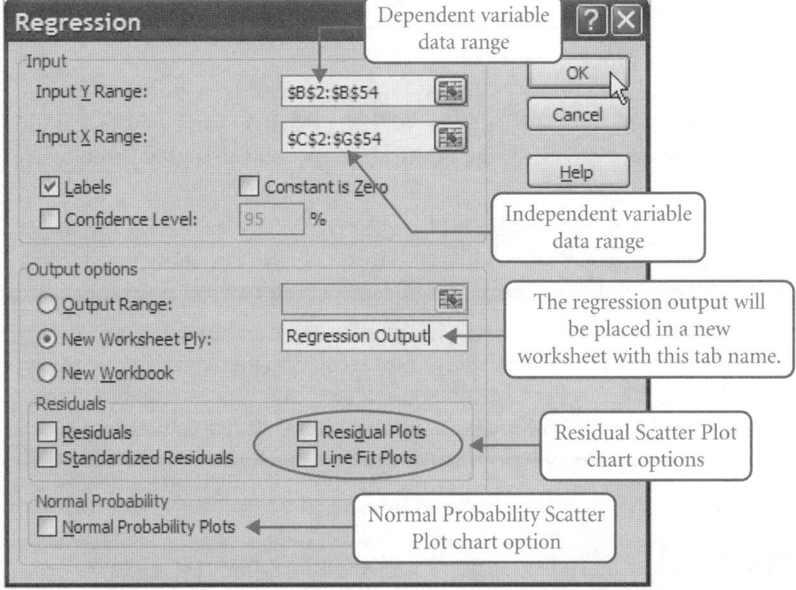

Figure 9.42 shows the regression output. As with the output for Descriptive Statistics and Histograms, the Regression output will most likely need to be formatted, especially with regard to column widths. Figure 9.42 shows the regression output after several formatting adjustments are made.

Figure 9.42 | **Regression Output**

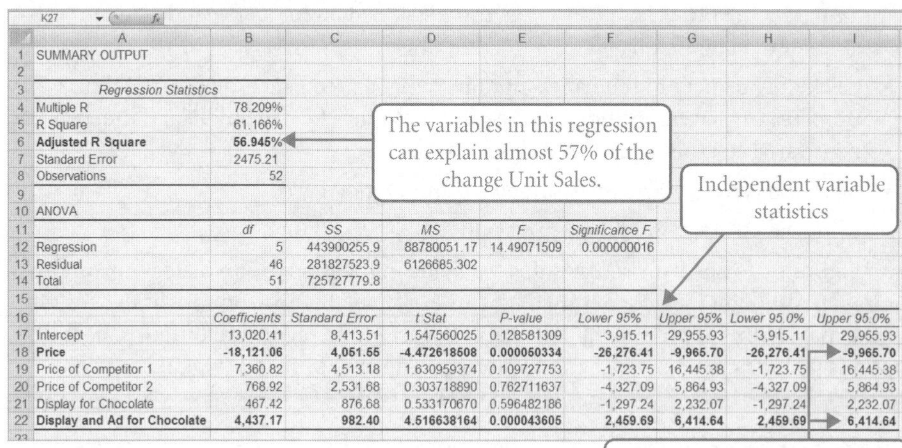

	A	B	C	D	E	F	G	H	I
1	SUMMARY OUTPUT								
2									
3	*Regression Statistics*								
4	Multiple R	78.209%							
5	R Square	61.166%							
6	**Adjusted R Square**	**56.945%**							
7	Standard Error	2475.21							
8	Observations	52							
9									
10	ANOVA								
11		*df*	*SS*	*MS*	*F*	*Significance F*			
12	Regression	5	443900255.9	88780051.17	14.49071509	0.000000016			
13	Residual	46	281827523.9	6126685.302					
14	Total	51	725727779.8						
15									
16		*Coefficients*	*Standard Error*	*t Stat*	*P-value*	*Lower 95%*	*Upper 95%*	*Lower 95.0%*	*Upper 95.0%*
17	Intercept	13,020.41	8,413.51	1.547560025	0.128581309	-3,915.11	29,955.93	-3,915.11	29,955.93
18	**Price**	**-18,121.06**	**4,051.55**	**-4.472618508**	**0.000050334**	**-26,276.41**	**-9,965.70**	**-26,276.41**	**-9,965.70**
19	Price of Competitor 1	7,360.82	4,513.18	1.630959374	0.109727753	-1,723.75	16,445.38	-1,723.75	16,445.38
20	Price of Competitor 2	768.92	2,531.68	0.303718890	0.762711637	-4,327.09	5,864.93	-4,327.09	5,864.93
21	Display for Chocolate	467.42	876.68	0.533170670	0.596482186	-1,297.24	2,232.07	-1,297.24	2,232.07
22	**Display and Ad for Chocolate**	**4,437.17**	**982.40**	**4.516638164**	**0.000043605**	**2,459.69**	**6,414.64**	**2,459.69**	**6,414.64**

>> **Quick Reference**

Data Analysis: Regression

1. Click the **Data Analysis** icon in the **Analysis** group on the **Data** tab of the Ribbon.
2. Select **Regression** from the **Data Analysis** dialog box and click the **OK** button.
3. Click the range finder next to the **Input Y Range** box and highlight the range of cells that contain data for the dependent variable on your worksheet.
4. Click the range finder next to the **Input X Range** box and highlight the range of cells that contain data for up to 16 independent variables on your worksheet.
5. If you highlighted column headings in steps 3 and 4, click the box next to the **Labels** option.
6. Select a placement option for the Regression output.
7. Select any of the **Residual** and/or **Normal Probability** chart options at the bottom of the **Regression** dialog box.
8. Click the **OK** button.
9. Apply formatting adjustments to the data output and/or charts as needed.

COMMON MISTAKES | Independent Variable Limit

You can define only 16 independent variables when using the **Regression** option from the Data Analysis Tool Pack. Excel will give you an error message and will not provide an output if you try to add more than 16 columns in the range of cells defining the Input X Range.

The regression output shown in Figure 9.42 provides many valuable insights with regard to marketing initiatives of this business. The following are a few key findings a marketing manager might take away from this analysis.

- The **Adjusted R Square** shows that the variables in this regression can explain almost 57% percent of the variation, or change in Unit Sales. Considering all of the factors that can influence a customer's decision to buy products, a marketing manager might be fairly satisfied that more than half of the variation in Unit Sales can be explained by these five variables.
- The statistical significance of the **Price** and **Display and Ad for Chocolate** variables are very high. Given these results, a marketing manager can be fairly certain that these variables have a statistically significant impact on changing the unit sales for chocolate.
- Notice that the t Stat and the Coefficient for the **Price** variable are negative. This indicates that Unit Sales decrease with an increase in Price. The statistical significance and negative correlation of this variable make perfect sense given fundamental economic principles.
- The statistical significance of the **Display and Ad for Chocolate** variable is much greater than for the **Display for Chocolate** variable. This gives a marketing manager a valuable insight as to how to execute promotional strategies that provide the greatest potential for increasing the sales of chocolate bars.

COMMON MISTAKES | Dialog Box Settings for Data Analysis Tools

The settings you enter into the **Regression**, **Histogram**, **Descriptive Statistics**, or any **Data Analysis** tools dialog boxes will remain in the dialog box until you close Excel. Therefore, you must check these dialog boxes carefully before starting a new project.

>> Descriptive Statistics

VIDEO WORKSHOP

The purpose of this workshop is to demonstrate how the Descriptive Statistics option from the Data Analysis Tools is used to analyze transactions from a retail company. I will be demonstrating the tasks in this workshop in the video named **Descriptive Statistics**. Open the Excel file named ib_e09_transactionanalysis. Complete the tasks below first, and then watch the video.

1. **Descriptive Statistics (Video: Descriptive Statistics)**
   a. Click the **Data Analysis** icon from the **Data** tab of the Ribbon.
   b. Select the **Descriptive Statistics** option from the **Data Analysis** dialog box and click the **OK** button.
   c. Click the range finder next to the **Input Range** box in the **Descriptive Statistics** dialog box. Highlight the range B2:C202 in the Data worksheet and press the **Enter** key.
   d. Check that the **Columns** option is selected in the Grouped By section.
   e. Click the box next to the Labels in **First Row** option to place a checkmark in the box.
   f. Select the **New Worksheet Ply** option in the Output Options section. Type the name `Transaction Stats` in the box next to the **New Worksheet Ply** option.
   g. Select the **Summary Statistics** option at the bottom of the **Descriptive Statistics** dialog box.
   h. Select the **Kth Largest** option and type the number 2 in the box next to this option.
   i. Select the **Kth Smallest** option and type the number 2 in the box next to this option.
   j. Click the **OK** button on the **Descriptive Statistics** dialog box.
   k. Increase the width of the columns in the Transaction Stats worksheet so that all the data is visible.
   l. Save and close your worksheet.

>> Histograms

VIDEO WORKSHOP

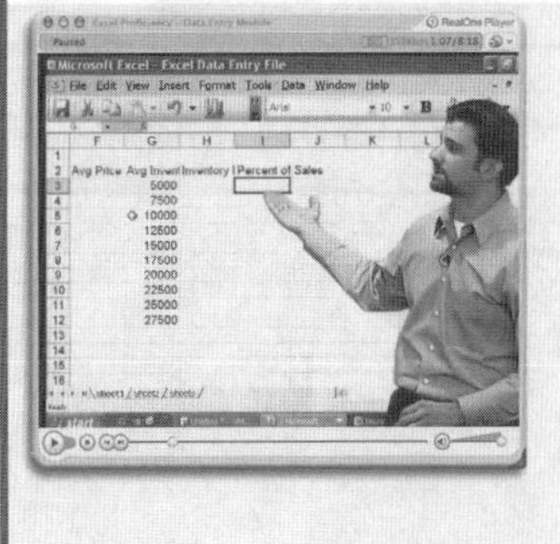

The purpose of this workshop is to demonstrate how the **Histograms** option from the Data Analysis Tools is used to determine the purchase frequency of retail items by price point. I will be demonstrating the tasks in this workshop in the video named **Histograms**. Open the Excel file named ib_e09_pricefrequency before starting this workshop. Complete the tasks below first, and then watch the video.

1. **Histograms (Video: Histograms)**
   a. Click the **Data Analysis** icon from the **Data** tab of the Ribbon.
   b. Select the **Histogram** option from the **Data Analysis** dialog box and click the **OK** button.
   c. Click the range finder next to the **Input Range** box in the **Histogram** dialog box. Then, highlight the range B2:B652 on the Data worksheet and press the **Enter** key.
   d. Click the range finder next to the **Bin Range** box in the **Histogram** dialog box. Then, highlight the range E2:E9 on the Data worksheet and press the **Enter** key.
   e. Click the box next the **Labels** options so that a green check appears.
   f. Select the **New Worksheet Ply** option in the Output Options section and type the name `Price Frequency` in the box next to the right.
   g. Select the **Cumulative Percentage** and **Chart Output** options at the bottom of the dialog box and click the **OK** button.
   h. In the Price Frequency worksheet, move the chart under the data to row 12. Then, increase the width of columns A, B, and C so that all the data is visible.
   i. Increase the overall height and width of the chart and change the position of the legend to the bottom. Then, increase the height and width of the plot area so that all the bars are clearly visible. Make any additional formatting adjustments to the chart so that it is easy to see and read.
   j. Save and close your file.

VIDEO WORKSHOP

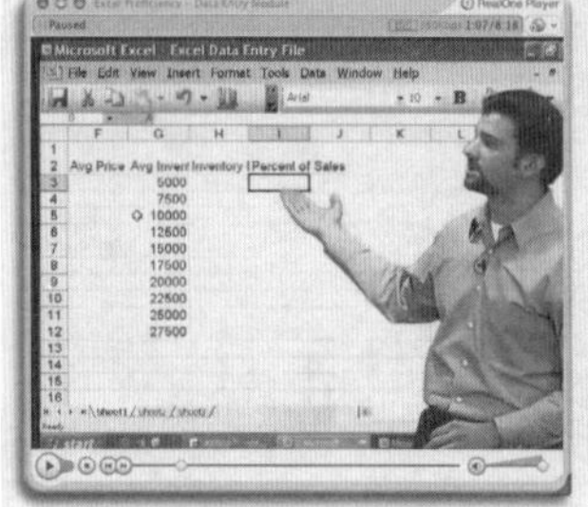

>> Regression

The purpose of this workshop is to demonstrate how the **Regression** option from the Data Analysis Tools is used to measure the statistical significance of various marketing tactics. I will be demonstrating the tasks in this workshop in the video named **Regression**. Open the Excel file named ib_e09_marketinganalysis. Complete the tasks below first, and then watch the video.

1. **Regression (Video: Regression)**
   a. Click the **Data Analysis** icon from the **Data** tab of the Ribbon.
   b. Select the **Regression** option from the **Data Analysis** dialog box and click the **OK** button.
   c. Click the range finder next to the **Input Y Range** box in the **Regression** dialog box. Then, highlight the range B2:B54 on the Data worksheet and press the **Enter** key.
   d. Click the range finder next to the **Input X Range** box in the **Regression** dialog box. Then, highlight the range C2:G54 on the Data worksheet and press the **Enter** key.
   e. Click the box next the **Labels** options so that a green check appears.
   f. Select the **New Worksheet Ply** option in the Output Options section of the **Regression** dialog box. Then, type the name `Regression Results` in the box next to the **New Worksheet Ply** option.
   g. Click the **OK** button in the **Regression** dialog box.

h. Increase the width of columns of A through I in the Regression Results worksheet so that all the data is visible.

i. Change the font to bold for the rows containing the two variables in the regression output that have the highest t Stat score.

j. Save and close your file.

>> Evaluating Historical Performance and Strategic Decisions

EXERCISE

Why Do I Need This?

Rebuilding or turning around a failing business can be a formidable challenge for any business executive. First, it might not always be clear why a business is failing. Many businesses suddenly fail after enjoying years of profitable success. Factors that might contribute to this decline include a drastic change in consumer demand, increased competition, or technological innovations that make a firm's product obsolete. In some cases, the reason for a company's decline is more tactical. For example, strategies that are executed to boost a firm's profits in the short term might cripple its long-term sales growth. As a result, executives might decide to hire a consulting firm to evaluate their company and determine why their business is declining. A common approach most consulting firms take when evaluating a company's business is to collect and analyze historical data to identify key trends and relationships. An analyst working on a consulting team could use many of Excel's statistical tools to conduct this type of analysis.

Exercise

The purpose of this exercise is to evaluate 3 years of sales and cost data for a hypothetical home-audio manufacturing company. This company experienced rapid sales growth up to the year 2004. In 2004, the company's profit fell short of Wall Street's expectations, and the executive officers took action to increase the firm's profit for 2005. However, although the profit rate increased in 2005, sales declined. As a result, you will be taking on the role of an analyst in a consulting firm to determine why this company's sales are declining. To begin this exercise, open the file named ib_e09_businessevaluation.

1. Activate the Cost Demand Data worksheet. This worksheet contains 3 years of Unit Sales by month along with data for three key cost categories: Advertising, Human Resources, and Warehousing. The first tasks of this exercise will focus on using the **Descriptive Statistics** option from the **Data Analysis Tools** to summarize the data in this worksheet for each year. The data produced by this tool can be used to identify key trends that have occurred over the past 3 years.

2. Use the **Descriptive Statistics** option from the **Data Analysis Tools** to produce a statistical summary output for the cell range C2:C14 in the Cost Demand Data worksheet. This represents the Unit Sales history for the year 2004. Note that this range includes the column heading. The output should appear in the Sales Summary worksheet beginning in cell A2. This can be accomplished using the **Output Range** option (click the range finder and selected cell A2 in the Sales Summary worksheet).

3. Format the statistics in the range B4:B16 in the Sales Summary worksheet to a standard number with commas, and 0 decimal places.

4. Type a formula in cell B18 that multiples the sum of the sales units in cell B15 by 150, which is the average selling price this company charges per unit.

5. Type a formula in cell B19 that divides the result in cell B18 by 12. This will show on average how much revenue the company generates per month.

6. Activate the Cost Demand Data worksheet. Repeat steps 2, 3, and 4 to produce and format a statistical summary for the unit sales in the years 2005 (C15:C26) and 2006 (C27:C38). Note that these ranges *do not* include column headings. The output for the year 2005 should begin in cell C2 in the Sales Summary worksheet, and the output for the year 2006 should begin in cell E2.

7. Delete the descriptions in cells C2 and E2 in the Sales Summary worksheet. These descriptions are automatically created by the Descriptive Statistics output and are not needed.

8. Copy the formulas in cells B18 and B19 in the Sales Summary worksheet and paste them into cells D18 and D19, and F18 and F19.

9. Type formulas in cells D20 and F20 to calculate the percent change in sales revenue from the year 2004 to the year 2006. How much have sales declined from the year 2004 to 2006 in dollars? Compare the average (Mean) Unit Sales per month in the year 2004 and 2006. How much has the average monthly Unit Sales declined between these years?

10. Activate the Cost Summary worksheet. The **Descriptive Statistics** tool was used to create a 3-year summary for each of the cost categories in the Cost Demand Data worksheet. Type a formula in cell D18 to compare the percent change in Advertising Costs from the year 2004 to 2005. Copy this formula and paste it to cell F18. When did Advertising Costs increase, and by how much?

11. Copy the formula you created in step 10 and paste it to cells D36, F36, D54, and F54 to analyze the change in Human Resource and Warehousing costs. Explain the trend that has occurred in these two cost categories from 2004 to 2006. State the specific percent change and dollar change for both categories.

12. Activate the Receiving Data worksheet. From your analysis in step 11, you should have found that Warehousing costs of have increased from 2004 to 2006. The managers of this company were surprised at this statistic because the warehouse has an abundance of surplus space and the company pays for this space whether they use it or not. However, one of the key cost drivers in warehousing operations is the number of unique items the warehouse receives per inbound shipment. As a result, the **Histogram** tool will be used to analyze the inbound shipment data in this worksheet. Begin by opening the **Histogram** dialog box.

13. Define the Input Range in the **Histogram** dialog box using cells B2:B102 on the Receiving Data worksheet. This range contains the number of unique items received for a sample of 100 manifests taken from the years 2005 and 2006.

14. Define the Bin Range in the **Histogram** dialog box using cells E2:E7 on the Receiving Data worksheet. The frequency of the data in the Input Range will be categorized into the groups in this range. Other analysts on your consulting team have concluded that labor costs increase significantly when a shipment contains more than 15 unique items.

15. Select the Labels option in the **Histogram** dialog box and place the output in a new worksheet with a tab named `Item Frequency`. The Histogram output should include a cumulative percentage for each category as well as a chart. Produce this output by clicking the **OK** button on the dialog box.

16. Move the chart in the Item Frequency worksheet to row 10 beginning in column A. Then, increase the widths of columns A, B, and C so that all the frequency data in rows 1 through 7 are visible.

17. Increase the height of the Histogram chart and reposition the legend to the bottom of the chart. Apply any necessary formatting features so that the bars and trend lines are clear and easy to read. On the basis of the Histogram output and the information explained in step 14, what might be contributing to the increase in warehousing costs?

18. Activate the Cost Demand Data worksheet. The last goal of this analysis is to determine which of the three cost categories in this worksheet are statistically significant in explaining changes in unit sales. This will require the use of the Regression tool from the Data Analysis Tools. The results of this analysis will tell management the impact a change in one of the three costs categories has on the sales performance of the company. Begin by opening the **Regression** dialog box.

19. Define the Input Y Range (dependent variable) in the **Regression** dialog box using the range C2:C38 on the Cost Demand Data worksheet.

20. Define the Input X Range (independent variables) using the range D2:F38 on the Cost Demand Data worksheet.

21. Finish the Regression by selecting the **Labels** option and place the output in a new worksheet with the tab name `Regression Output`. Produce the output by clicking the **OK** button in the dialog box.

22. Expand the columns in the Regression Output worksheet so that all the data is visible. What are the t Stat results for each of the three cost variables (Advertising, Human Resources, and Warehousing)? Notice that Advertising has the lowest t Stat or statistical significance to Unit Sales. What does this suggest about the impact the company's advertising investments have on sales?

23. The t-Stat results for the Warehouse variable should be a negative number, suggesting that as warehousing costs increase, unit sales decrease. Why do you think this is so?

24. Which of the three independent variables has the highest t Stat?

25. The executive officers of this company are optimistic about sales and profit in the year 2007. They believe the primary reason for the company's sales decline is that advertising investments were too low. They plan to increase the amount of money invested in advertising and intend to fund this investment by reducing costs in Human Resource benefits and Warehousing. Considering the data you analyzed in this exercise, do you agree with management that this strategy will increase sales? Why or why not?

26. Save and close your file.

>> What's Wrong with This Spreadsheet?

PROBLEM & EXERCISE

Problem

You are working as a business analyst in the marketing department of retail company that sells kitchen and bathroom furnishings. One of your coworkers is analyzing data regarding the annual spending of customers enrolled in the company's frequent shopper program. She is having trouble using Excel to put together a project for the vice president of your division and asks for your help. She sends you an e-mail with an Excel file attached and mentions the following points.

- Thank you so much for helping me with this project! The vice president of our division asked for a report showing the number of customers that fit into seven different annual spend categories. He gave me a list of these categories, which I typed into the Excel file attached to this e-mail.
- The data I am analyzing is a sample of 100 customers from our Frequent Shopper database. I found this Histogram feature in Excel and thought this would be a great way to put the annual-spend data into groups. However, I cannot get this thing to work. I keep getting this error message that says something like "bin range cannot have non-numeric data." What does that mean? If this is too much trouble I'll do this manually, but I figured I would ask anyway.
- By the way, he also asked for a statistical summary of the annual-spend data for the customers in my sample. Do you know what he is talking about? He was in a rush when he asked me to do this so I didn't have time to ask. He wants this done before noon and the only thing I can think of is adding an AVERAGE function.

Exercise

The Excel file that was attached to your coworker's e-mail is named ib_e09_annualcustomerspendfrequency. What's wrong with this spreadsheet? Consider the following points:

1. Take a look at the annual-spend categories that were typed into the Excel worksheet. Why is a bin error occurring?

2. Your coworker mentioned that she would count the annual-spend frequency manually if she could not get the Histogram feature to work. What are the downsides of doing this type of project manually?

3. With regard to your coworker's last point, what could you recommend as an alternative to merely calculating the average of the annual customer spend?

Write a short answer for each of the points listed above. Then, fix any errors in the worksheet that are causing the bin range error. In addition, include the alternative you identified in point 3 above in the workbook.

Skill Set >> Solver

The **Solver** tool is very similar to the scenario tools demonstrated in the first section of this chapter. Business managers use Solver in situations that require an output to be maximized or minimized given various constraints. For example, a finance manager might use Solver to determine an investment strategy that maximizes the potential return given certain investment requirements and risks. Solver could also be used by a production manager to determine which combination of raw materials minimizes the cost of producing a product. This section will show how a financial planning manager might use Solver to create a basic investment strategy that maximizes the potential return given a specific level of risk.

Defining Constraints

This example of the Solver tool involves a basic investment strategy that maximizes potential returns given a target level of risk. Financial planning managers usually plan investments on the basis of their clients' risk preference. In other words, some people might be averse to risk and concerned about losing money during market downturns. Therefore, these people might prefer slow-growing investments that will not be severely impacted by market fluctuations. Other people might prefer high-risk investments in hopes of achieving higher-than-average returns during market upswings. As a result, an investment manager will develop a strategy that suits the preferences of their clients. How does a financial planner know if an investment strategy is maximizing the potential return for a person's portfolio? Solver is one of several tools that a financial planner might use to answer this question.

Figure 9.43 shows hypothetical data of a basic personal-investment strategy. This example assumes that a financial planner will invest a person's money in four main categories: Bonds, Balanced Funds, Growth Funds, and Common Stocks. The column next to each investment category is a risk level based on a 10-point scale. Each investment category is assigned a value based on a person's potential risk of losing money. For example, Bonds are given a low-risk rating of 2 because they provide a fixed rate of return. Common Stocks are given a high-risk rating of 10 because these investments are focused on specific companies. If for some reason a company experiences any operational hardships, a person could lose a significant percentage of his investment. The remaining columns of data show the amount of money invested in each category, the percent each investment represents to the entire portfolio, the Estimated Annual Return, the Estimated Future Value in 3 Years, and the overall Portfolio Risk. The Estimated Future Value in 3 Years is calculated using the **future value (FV)** function. The overall Portfolio Risk (column G) is calculated by multiplying the Percent of Portfolio (column D) by the Risk Level (column B). Each of the values in column G is then summed to determine an overall risk level for the portfolio.

Figure 9.43 | **Personal Investment Strategy**

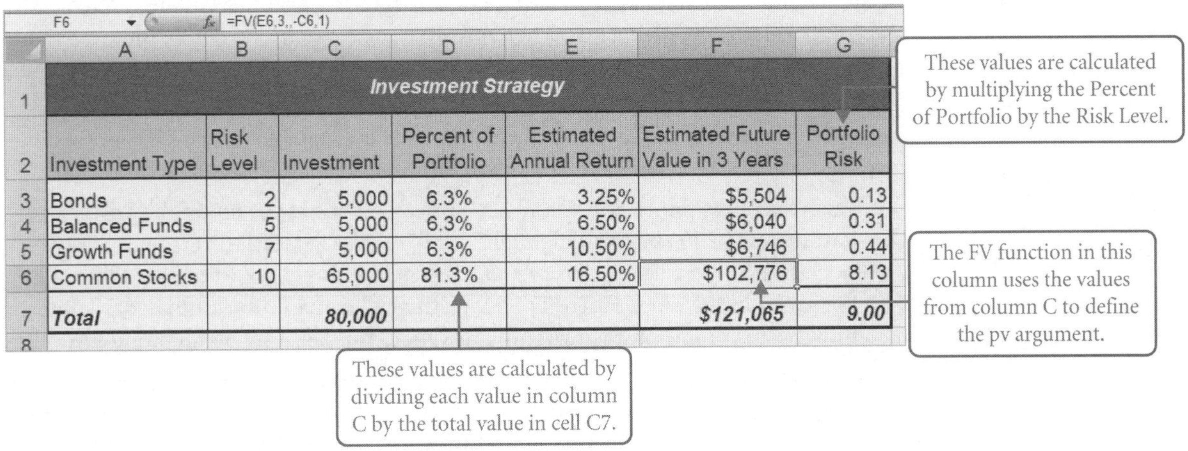

F6 =FV(E6,3,,-C6,1)

	A	B	C	D	E	F	G
1	*Investment Strategy*						
2	Investment Type	Risk Level	Investment	Percent of Portfolio	Estimated Annual Return	Estimated Future Value in 3 Years	Portfolio Risk
3	Bonds	2	5,000	6.3%	3.25%	$5,504	0.13
4	Balanced Funds	5	5,000	6.3%	6.50%	$6,040	0.31
5	Growth Funds	7	5,000	6.3%	10.50%	$6,746	0.44
6	Common Stocks	10	65,000	81.3%	16.50%	$102,776	8.13
7	***Total***		***80,000***			***$121,065***	***9.00***
8							

These values are calculated by multiplying the Percent of Portfolio by the Risk Level.

The FV function in this column uses the values from column C to define the pv argument.

These values are calculated by dividing each value in column C by the total value in cell C7.

The investment strategy in Figure 9.43 shows that a person's investment of $80,000 (cell C7) could potentially grow to $121,065 (cell F7) in 3 years. However, notice that the overall Portfolio Risk of this strategy is 9 (cell G7). As a result, whereas this strategy seems like it could provide significant growth, it could also result in a significant loss given the high level of risk. What if a person wanted to cut the overall risk of the portfolio in half to 4.5? What combination of investments would maximize the potential return at this target risk level? Solver can be used to answer this question; however, the constraints of this problem should be defined first.

The constraints of a Solver problem are any rules that *cannot* be broken in order to produce a result. For example, the following rules or constraints must be followed when determining an investment strategy that satisfies an overall portfolio risk level of 4.5 while maximizing the potential future value.

- The total dollars invested in the four categories listed in column A of Figure 9.43 must equal $80,000. This example will assume that the person has only $80,000 that can be invested. Therefore, the **SUM** function in cell C7 that is totaling the values in cells C3 through C6 must equal 80000.
- A minimum investment of $5,000 must be made in each category. This example assumes that a diversified investment strategy is desired. Therefore, the goal is to make a minimum investment of $5,000 in each of the four categories listed in column A.
- Investments must not exceed $40,000, or 50% of the portfolio in any category. For the purposes of moderating risk, this example will assume that 50% of the portfolio cannot be invested in any one category.
- The risk value in cell G7 must equal 4.5.

COMMON MISTAKES | Cell References for Solver Problems

You must use formulas and/or functions with cell references in order to use the **Solver** tool. The **Solver** tool works by changing the values in cells referenced by a formula or function until the result is minimized, is maximized, or reaches a target value.

Defining Solver Parameters

Once you have defined the constraints or the rules that must be followed when determining the optimal solution for a problem, you are ready to open the Solver tool. Each of the constraints defined in the previous segment of this example will be entered into the Solver Parameters dialog box. Therefore, it is good practice to define the constraints of the problem *before* opening the tool. The following explains how to open and set up the **Solver** tool.

- Click the **Solver** icon in the Analysis group on the **Data** tab of the Ribbon (see Figure 9.30). This will open the **Solver Parameters** dialog box.
- Click the range finder next to the **Set Target Cell** box at the top of the **Solver Parameters** dialog box and highlight cell F7 on the Personal Investment Strategy worksheet (Figure 9.43). This cell contains a SUM function, which is adding all of the values in the range F3:F6. Therefore, this cell contains the estimated 3-year future value of the entire portfolio. Press the **Enter** key after highlighting this cell.
- Click the **Max** option, which is one of the **Equal To** options listed below the **Set Target Cell** box. The goal is to maximize the value of the portfolio given a specific risk value. Therefore, the **Max** option is selected for this example. There are also options for minimizing the value of a target cell or setting a specific value for a target cell.
- Click the range finder next to the **By Changing Cells** box, highlight the range C3:C6, and press the **Enter** key. Solver will change the values in these cells, which contain the amount of money invested in each category, to maximize the future value of the portfolio given at a specific target risk value.

Figure 9.44 shows the initial setup of the **Solver Parameters** dialog box before adding any constraints. The settings in this window show that Solver will maximize the output in cell F7 by changing the values in cells C3 through C6 in Figure 9.43. Changing the values in these cells will directly impact the outputs in the Estimated Future Value in 3 Years column, and indirectly impact the values in the Portfolio Risk column. As previously mentioned, the values in the Portfolio Risk column are calculated by multiplying the values in the Percent of Portfolio column by the values in the Risk Level column.

Figure 9.44 | **Solver Parameters before Adding Constraints**

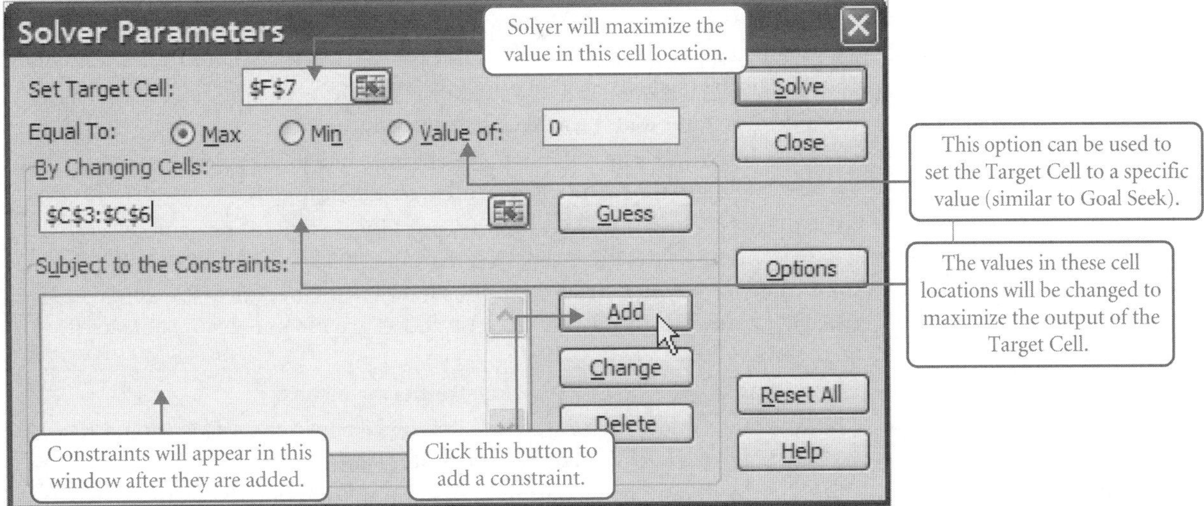

After making the initial settings in the **Solver Parameters** dialog box as shown in Figure 9.44, you are ready to begin adding constraints. The constraints for this example were defined in the previous segment. The following explains how the first constraint is added to the **Solver Parameters** dialog box.

- Click the **Add** button next to the **Subject to Constraints** box. This will open the **Add Constraint** dialog box.
- Click the range finder next to the **Cell Reference** box, highlight cell C7, and press the **Enter** key. Cell C7 is the output of the **SUM** function totaling the amount of money invested in all four investment categories.
- Click the drop-down arrow next to the conditional operator box and select the equal sign. Then, type the value 80000 in the **Constraint** box. As previously mentioned, the amount of money invested in all four categories must equal $80,000. Therefore, this constraint will ensure Solver provides a solution in which the total money invested is equal to $80,000.
- Click the Add button in the **Add Constraint** dialog box. This will add the first constraint to the **Solver Parameters** dialog box and clear the **Add Constraint** dialog box so that a second constraint can be added (see Figure 9.45).

Figure 9.45 shows the settings in the **Add Constraint** dialog box for the first constraint. Additional constraints can be added by clicking the **Add** button in this dialog box.

Figure 9.45 | **Add Constraint Dialog Box**

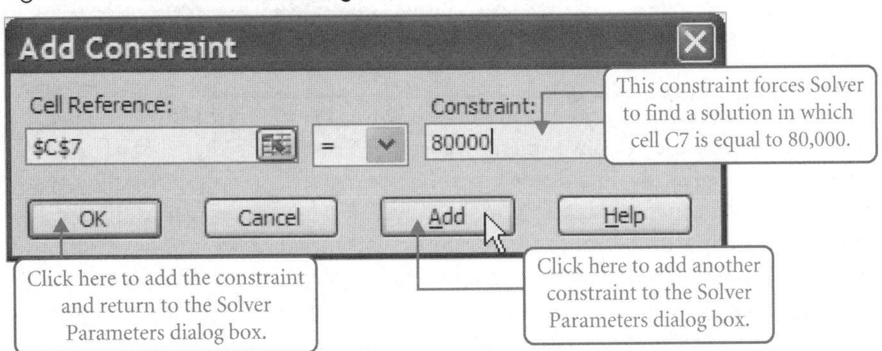

The following points explain how the remaining three constraints for this example are added to the **Solver Parameters** dialog box.

- Click the range finder next to the **Cell Reference** box in the **Add Constraints** dialog box. Highlight the range C3:C6, and press the **Enter** key. The range C3:C6 contains the investment values for the portfolio.
- Click the drop-down arrow next to the conditional operator box and select the greater-than-or-equal-to sign. Then, type the value 5000 in the **Constraint** box. The second constraint listed for this example states that a minimum investment of $5,000 must be made in each investment category.
- Click the Add button in the **Add Constraints** dialog box.
- Click the range finder next to the **Cell Reference** box in the **Add Constraints** dialog box. Highlight the range C3:C6, and press the **Enter** key.
- Click the drop-down arrow next to the conditional operator box and select the less-than-or-equal-to sign. Then, type the value 40000 in the **Constraint** box. The third constraint listed for this example states that an investment cannot exceed $40,000 for any category. Notice that we added two separate constraints to the same range of cells.
- Click the Add button in the **Add Constraints** dialog box.
- Click the range finder next to the **Cell Reference** box in the **Add Constraints** dialog box, highlight cell G7, and press the **Enter** key.
- Click the drop-down arrow next to the conditional operator box and select the equal sign. Then, type the value 4.5 in the **Constraint** box. The fourth constraint listed for this example states that the overall risk target for the portfolio is 4.5.
- Click the **OK** button in the **Add Constraint** dialog box. This will bring you back to the **Solver Parameters** dialog box.

Figure 9.46 shows the final settings in the **Solver Parameters** dialog box. Notice that all four constraints are listed in the **Subject to the Constraints** box. These constraints can be changed or deleted by highlighting a constraint and clicking either the **Change** or **Delete** button.

Figure 9.46 | **Final Solver Parameters Settings**

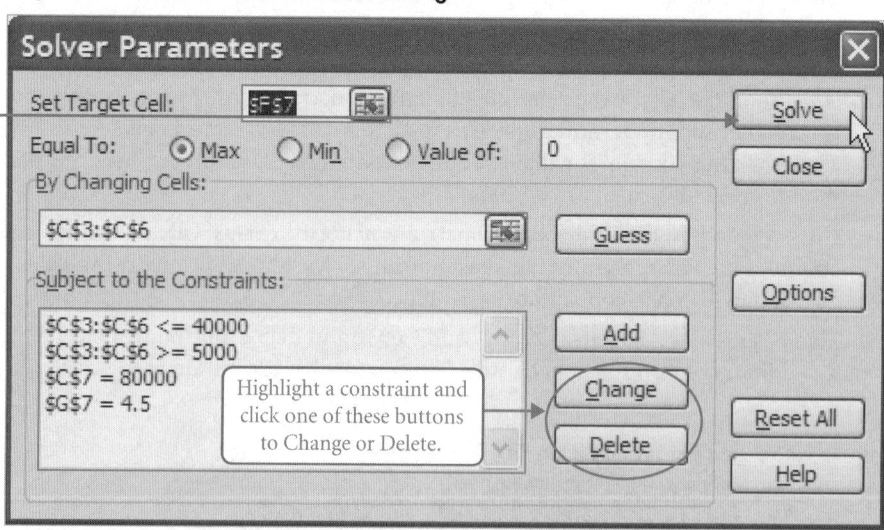

Once all the parameters are entered into the **Solver Parameters** dialog box, click the Solve button to show the new investment strategy for Figure 9.43. After clicking the **Solve** button, the **Solver Results** dialog box will appear, notifying you if a solution was found based on the constraints entered in the **Solver Parameters** dialog box. In this dialog box, you can apply the Solver solution to your worksheet or restore your worksheet to its original values. In addition, you can also create reports showing the mathematical details of how Solver arrived at the solution. As shown in Figure 9.47, Solver found a solution for the problem, and the **Keep Solver Solution** option has been selected.

Figure 9.47 | **Solver Results Dialog Box**

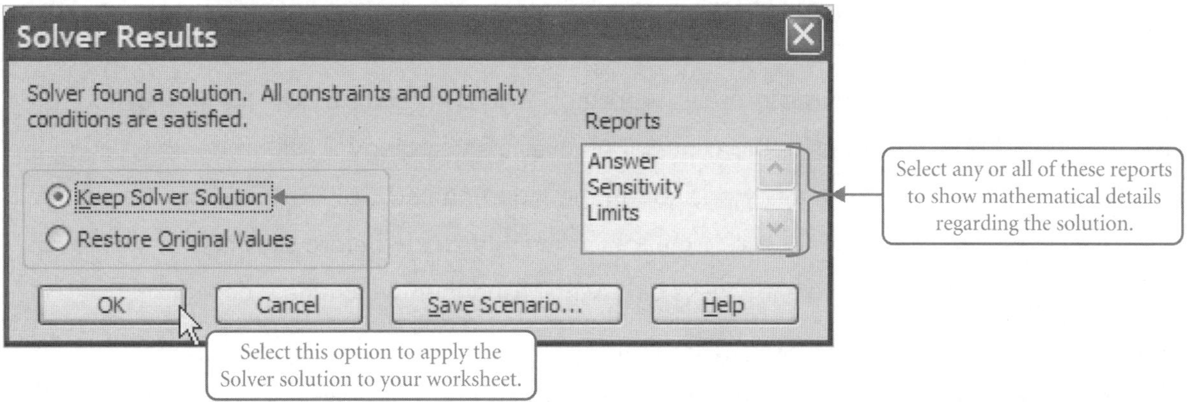

Figure 9.48 shows the values Solver applied to the range C3:C6 in Figure 9.43. Notice that more than 75% of the portfolio is invested in the Bonds and Balanced Funds categories. This strategy maximizes this person's portfolio return while achieving a risk level of 4.5. As a result, the future value of the portfolio in cell F7 is lower than what was originally shown in Figure 9.43. However, the risk level of this investment strategy is lowered to the target of 4.5, which is 50% less than the original risk level. A financial planning analyst could use Solver to run other scenarios showing a client how the future value of the portfolio changes at different risk levels.

COMMON MISTAKES | Solver Iterations and Time Limits

After clicking the **Solve** button in the **Solver Parameters** dialog box, the dialog box shown below may appear. This is because Solver will automatically run through 100 solution iterations and/or calculate solutions for 100 seconds. However, your problem might require more than 100 iterations or 100 seconds to calculate an optimal solution. Solver will continue to calculate the optimal solution for your problem if you click the Continue button in this dialog box. However, Solver will not stop calculating iterations until an optimal solution is found, which might take a long period of time. To increase the number of iterations or seconds to calculate a solution, click the Options button in the Solver Parameters dialog box.

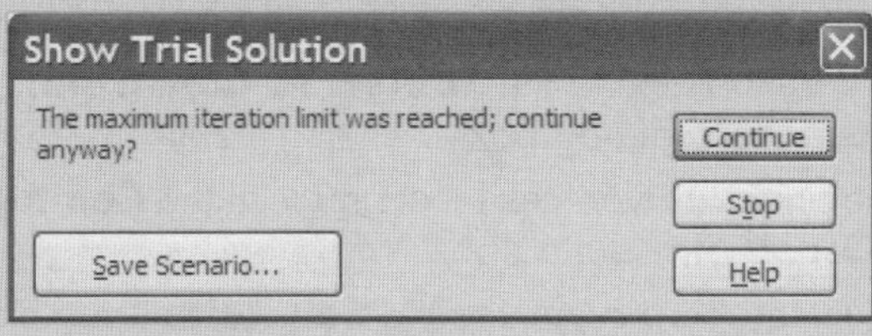

Figure 9.48 | **Solver Results**

A15

	A	B	C	D	E	F	G
1	Investment Strategy						
2	Investment Type	Risk Level	Investment	Percent of Portfolio	Estimated Annual Return	Estimated Future Value in 3 Years	Portfolio Risk
3	Bonds	2	40,000	50.0%	3.25%	$44,028	1.00
4	Balanced Funds	5	21,000	26.2%	6.50%	$25,367	1.31
5	Growth Funds	7	5,000	6.3%	10.50%	$6,746	0.44
6	Common Stocks	10	14,000	17.5%	16.50%	$22,136	1.75
7	*Total*		*80,000*			*$98,278*	*4.50*
8							

Target risk level which was one of the constraints

Maximum and minimum constraints were used for these cell locations.

Maximum return value given the constraints entered for this problem

» Quick Reference

Solver

1. Create a formula or function that uses cell references to produce a mathematical result.
2. Click the **Solver** icon in the **Analysis** group on the **Data** tab of the Ribbon to open the **Solver Parameters** dialog box.
3. Click the range finder next to the **Set Target Cell** box and highlight a cell location on your worksheet. This cell location should contain the formula or function you created in step 1.
4. Select one of the **Equal To** options based on the goals of your project. If you select the **Value Of** option, type a value in the box.
5. Click the range finder next to the **By Changing Cells** box and highlight cell locations that are directly or indirectly referenced by the formula you created in step 1.
6. Click the **Add** button in the **Solver Parameters** dialog box to enter any required constraints for your project.
7. Click the **Solve** button to calculate a solution.
8. Select either the **Keep Solver Solution** or **Restore Original Values** options in the **Solver Results** dialog box.
9. Click the **OK** button in the **Solver Results** dialog box.

VIDEO WORKSHOP

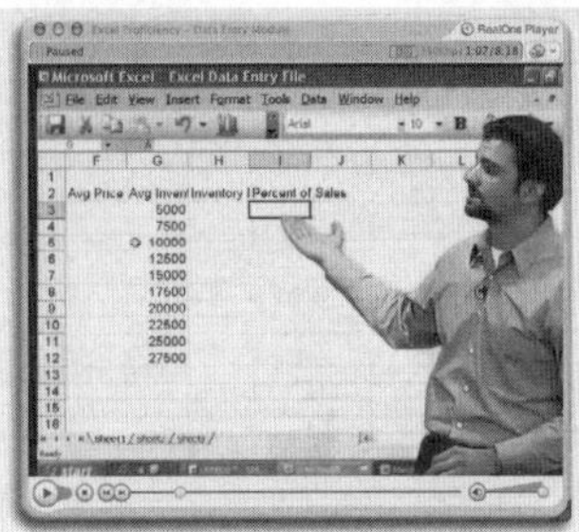

>> Solver

The purpose of this workshop is to demonstrate how the **Solver** tool is used to create a personal investment strategy. I will be demonstrating the tasks in this workshop in the video named **Solver**. Open the Excel file named ib_e09_optimalinvestmentstrategy before starting this workshop. Complete the tasks below first, and then watch the video.

1. **Solver (Video: Solver)**
   a. Type a **SUM** function in cell C7 of the Investments worksheet that adds the values in the range C3:C6.
   b. Type a formula in cell D3 that divides the value in cell C3 by the output of the **SUM** function in cell C7. Place an absolute reference on cell C7 in this formula. Then, copy the formula and paste it into the range D4:D6 using the **Formulas paste** option.
   c. Enter a Future Value function in cell F3 that will determine the value of the investment in column C in 3 years. There are no periodic investments. Assume that the investment will be made at one time at the beginning of the period. Copy and paste this function into cells F4:F6.
   d. Type a **SUM** function in cell F7 that adds the values in cell F3:F6.
   e. Type a formula in cell G3 that multiplies the value in cell D3 by the value in cell B3. Copy this formula and paste it into the range G4:G6.
   f. Type a **SUM** function in cell G7 that adds the values in the range G3:G6.
   g. Click the **Solver** icon in the **Data** tab of the Ribbon.
   h. Use the range finder or type cell location `F7` in the **Set Target Cell** box of the **Solver Parameters** dialog box.
   i. Check to see that the **Max** option is selected in the **Equal To** options of the **Solver Parameters** dialog box.
   j. Use the range finder or type the range `C3:C6` in the **By Changing Cells** box of the **Solver Parameters** dialog box.
   k. Click the **Add** button next to the **Subject to Constraints** box in the **Solver Parameters** dialog box.
   l. Use the range finder or type cell location `C7` in the **Cell Reference** box of the **Add Constraint** dialog box.
   m. Select the equal-to operator next to the **Cell Reference** box of the **Add Constraint** dialog box.
   n. Type `80000` in the **Constraint** box and click the **Add** button in the **Add Constraint** dialog box.
   o. Use the range finder or type the range `C3:C6` in the **Cell Reference** box of the **Add Constraint** dialog box.
   p. Select the greater-than-or-equal-to operator next to the **Cell Reference** Box in the **Add Constraint** dialog box.
   q. Type `5000` in the **Constraint** box and click the **Add** button in the **Add Constraint** dialog box.
   r. Use the range finder or type the range `C3:C6` in the **Cell Reference** box of the **Add Constraint** dialog box.
   s. Select the less-than-or-equal-to operator next to the **Cell Reference** box in the **Add Constraint** dialog box.
   t. Type `40000` in the **Constraint** box and click the **Add** button in the **Add Constraint** dialog box.

u. Use the range finder or type cell location `G7` in the **Cell Reference** box of the **Add Constraint** dialog box.
v. Select the equal-to operator next to the **Cell Reference** box of the **Add Constraint** dialog box.
w. Type `4.5` in the **Constraint** box and click the **OK** button in the **Add Constraint** dialog box.
x. Click the **Solve** button on the **Solver Parameters** dialog box.
y. Click the **OK** button on the **Solver Results** dialog box.
z. Save and close your file.

>> Optimizing Pick Costs in a Distribution Center

EXERCISE

Why Do I Need This?

Managing the efficiency and costs of a merchandise warehouse can be a challenging task. In some cases, a warehouse, commonly referred to as a distribution center (DC), can encompass more than 1 million square feet and extend several stories in height. The size of a distribution center usually depends on the amount of merchandise shipped as well as the type of merchandise sold by a company. Initially, many people think that the operations of a DC are very simple. Cartons come off a truck, are put on a shelf, and then are taken off a shelf when whatever is inside the carton is sold or shipped to a store. In theory, this is correct. However, decisions such as where cartons are stored in a DC can drastically change the costs and efficiency of the entire operation. For example, there is a significant cost difference between storing an item on the floor of the DC and on a shelf four stories high. When a carton is stored on the floor of the DC, a person can literally walk to that location, place the carton on a hand truck, and wheel it over to an outbound truck. However, the same carton stored on a shelf four stories high requires a special machine that must be operated by a skilled and licensed operator. Therefore, the cost of the machine, skilled operator, and added time increases the cost of picking a carton in the DC. As a result, the decision of where cartons are stored in a DC can have huge cost implications. A tool such as Solver can give DC managers valuable insights in developing a storage plan that minimizes the cost of picking cartons.

Exercise

The purpose of this exercise is to use Solver to create a storage plan that minimizes carton picking costs for a DC. This DC is operated by a relatively small manufacturing company that sells 20 products. To begin this exercise, open the file named ib_e09_storageoptions.

1. Activate the Storage and Pick Data worksheet. This worksheet is divided into two parts. The top part (rows 1–24) shows the location and the number of cartons stored for each of the 20 products sold by this company, which are listed in column A. Row 2 shows the cost of picking cartons from each location listed in row 3. **SUM** functions are used in column F (F4:F23) to add the total number of cartons stored in all locations for each product. This number must match the Inventory in Cartons values in column G. Column H shows the weekly sales for each product in cartons. This is how many cartons of each product the DC will need to pick and ship out each week.

2. Scroll down the worksheet so that rows 26 through 48 are visible. This is the second part of the worksheet, which shows the number of cartons picked by location based on the product sales listed in the range H4:H23. The cells in range B28:E47 contain IF functions that compare the number of cartons stored in each location with the sales for each product in column H. The range F28:F47

contains formulas that calculate the Total Pick Cost for each product. Cell F48 shows the total cost of picking all required cartons to satisfy 1 week of sales. Notice that it costs this company more than $37,000 to pick and ship cartons for 1 week of sales. Multiplied by 52, this amounts to almost $2 million per year.

3. Notice that the Total Pick Cost for product 1 in cell F28 is $150. This is because all cartons for this product are stored on the Ground Level, which has a pick cost of $1.50 per carton. Change the value in cell B4 to `0` and type `300` in cell E4. Notice that the Total Pick Cost for product 1 is now $1,200. This is because the cost of picking a carton out of level 3 is $12.00 per carton. The next tasks of this exercise will use Solver to determine how cartons should be stored in cells B4:E23 to minimize the total cost calculated in cell F48.
4. Insert a new worksheet in this workbook. Rename the worksheet tab `Original Cost`. Copy all of the data in the Storage and Pick Data worksheet and paste it into the Original Cost worksheet.
5. Activate the Storage and Pick Data worksheet. Then, open the **Solver Parameters** dialog box.
6. Use the range finder or type cell location `F48` in the **Set Target Cell** box in the **Solver Parameters** dialog box.
7. Select Min in the set of **Equal To** options in the **Solver Parameters** dialog box.
8. Click the range finder next to the **By Changing Cells** box in the **Solver Parameters** dialog box and highlight the range B4:E23 in the Storage and Pick Data worksheet. Based on the settings you entered in the **Solver Parameters** dialog box to this point, Solver will minimize the output of the formula in cell F48 by changing the values in the range B4:E23, which contain the number of cartons stored for each location. However, there are several rules or constraints Solver will have to consider when calculating this solution. These constraints will be entered into the **Solver Parameters** dialog box next.
9. Click the **Add** button in the **Solver Parameters** dialog box. Then, click the range finder next to the **Cell Reference** box in the **Add Constraint** dialog box. Highlight the range B4:E23 on the Storage and Pick Data worksheet. Click the Down arrow next the comparison operator box and select **int**. Notice that the word "integer" automatically appears in the constraint box. This constraint will ensure that Solver does not place any partial cartons in a location (e.g., 1.4). Click the **Add** button in the **Add Constraint** dialog box.
10. Add a second constraint that requires Solver to use only positive numbers when assigning values to the range B4:E23. Therefore, any values Solver assigns to this range must be greater than or equal to 0.
11. As mentioned in step 1, the values in the range F4:F23 must match the values in the range G4:G23. Add a constraint to Solver that ensures that the values in these two cell ranges are equal to each other.
12. Each location in this DC can hold a maximum of 5000 cartons. As a result, each of the SUM functions in the range B24:E24 must be less than or equal to 5000. Add these constraints to Solver and then return to the **Solver Parameters** dialog box.
13. Click the **Options** button on the **Solver Parameters** dialog box. Type the number `300` in the **Max Time** box of the **Solver Options** dialog box and click the **OK** button. Given the complexity of this problem, it may take Solver several minutes to calculate a final solution.
14. Click the **Solve** button in the **Solver Parameters** dialog box. When the **Show Trial Solution** dialog box appears notifying you that the maximum *iterations* was reached, click the **Continue** button.

15. If the **Show Trial Solution** window appears again notifying you that the time limit has expired, click the **Continue** button. Solver should come up with a solution after a few more minutes. Processing times will vary depending on the type of computer you are using. The Branch number in the lower left corner of the Excel screen will reach 156 before Solver completes the solution.

16. Click the **Keep Solver Solution** option when the **Solver Results** dialog box appears and click the **OK** button.

17. Compare the Total Pick Cost in cell F48 between the Storage and Pick Data worksheet and the Original Cost worksheet. How much did the cost decrease? Compare the difference in cost between these two worksheets on an annual basis assuming cell F48 represents the weekly cost of the DC's picking operation. How much was the cost reduced on an annualized basis.

18. Save and close your file.

>> What's Wrong with This Spreadsheet

PROBLEM & EXERCISE

Problem

You are the director of a small hardware store. You asked one of your assistant managers to develop a purchasing plan for several items that will maximize the potential profits of the business. You give the assistant a list showing the cost and retail price of 16 different items in 4 different merchandise categories. In addition, you tell the assistant not to buy more than 1500 units of any one item and that the total units purchased for all items combined should not be greater than 10,000. Finally, you mention that most suppliers require a minimum purchase of 250 units per item. Your assistant works on developing a purchasing plan for the 16 items in Excel and attaches the file in an e-mail. He mentions the following points in his message.

- Thank you for giving me this assignment. I just learned how to use this cool tool in Excel called Solver and it can tell me exactly how many units we should be buying for each item.
- I typed all the items along with the cost and retail price information into an Excel spreadsheet. I calculated the profit dollars and profit rate for each item. Then, I calculated the profit rate for each category and for the entire purchase. You will notice that the last row of the spreadsheet labeled Grand Total shows the total sales and profit potential of this purchasing strategy.
- It's interesting how this math works. The Solver calculations are basically saying we can maximize our profits if we buy 1500 units of everything. Overall, it makes sense because if we sell everything we buy, we will maximize the profits of the store.

Exercise

The Excel file your assistant attached to the e-mail is named ib_e09_purchaseplan. What's wrong with this spreadsheet? Consider the following points.

1. Take a look at the assistant's plan. Does the data make sense?
2. The settings the assistant used for the **Solver Parameters** window should still be visible. Open the **Solver** tool and look at these settings. Do they make sense?
3. Are there any flaws in the overall logic of this plan? Why or why not?

Write a short answer for each of the points listed above. Then, make any necessary adjustments to the Solver settings and come up with a new solution for this plan.

Excel in **Practice** | Anecdotes

Solution from page 402

Excel's scenario tools were amazing in helping me put together all the information I needed for my merchandise plans. These tools were great for putting together reports that were reviewed by the executive officers at the merchandise planning meetings. However, what I liked most about these tools is that I could bring my laptop to the meeting and use the Excel tools to answer any questions that were raised by the executives. I would create spreadsheets with tools such as the Scroll Bar or Scenario Manager setup and be ready to go if someone asked the infamous question "What if. . . ?"

Assignment

1. Open the file named ib_e09_merchandiseplanningmeeting. The data in this workbook is very similar to what appeared in the merchandise financial plans that were mentioned in the anecdote. The purpose of this assignment is to prepare various financial scenarios as if you were presenting this plan to the executive officers of an apparel retail company.
2. Add the necessary formulas and functions to complete the Item List worksheet including the Department Grand Totals (row 23). The following are a few formulas used for this type of analysis:
   a. `Units Sold at Full Price = Percent Sold at Full Price × Units Purchased`
   b. `Units Sold at Markdown Price = Units Purchased - Units Sold at Full Price`
   c. `Markdown Price = Retail Price × (1-Percent Markdown)`
3. Every year the executives are concerned about all velvet products in the line. Prepare the following three scenarios for all velvet items. Assume all other products in the department are sold at 65% of the full price with the remainder being sold at 30% off the original retail price. What is the *department profit rate* for each scenario?
   a. Best Case: 75% Full Price Sales selling remaining inventory at 25% off.
   b. Average Case: 60% Full Price Sales selling remainder at 40% off.
   c. Worst Case: 40% Full Price Sales selling remainder at 55% off.
4. The profit rate for the Printed Rayon Skirts is fairly strong; however, 15,000 units were purchased. Assuming the average markdown rate for this item is 50% off, what will the full price sales units need to be to achieve at least a 43.5% overall profit rate for this item?
5. The executives usually ask questions regarding the overall profit rate for the department when the average Percent Sold at Full Price and the average Percent Markdown *for the department* changes. For example, a typical question might be, "What if the department sells 60% of all merchandise at full price and sells the remaining inventory at an average of 40% off the original retail price?" They are most concerned about what combination of Percent Sold at Full Price and Percent of Markdown for the department will drive the profit rate of the entire department below 45%. Prepare a scenario that can answer these types of questions.

Questions for Discussion

1. The anecdote mentions that several scenarios were created before money was spent to purchase a line of merchandise. Why would business managers need to evaluate so many scenarios before making inventory investments? What questions are they trying to answer?

2. Most business executives would agree that the process of evaluating scenarios can potentially improve the decisions a company makes. However, what key issues could undermine the integrity and value of scenario analysis?

Review Questions

The following questions are related to the concepts addressed in this chapter. There are three types of questions: Short Answer, True or False, and Fill in the Blank. If your answer to a True or False question is False, write a short explanation as to why you think the statement is not true.

1. You must use ________ ________ in formulas or functions in order to use any of Excel's scenario tools.
2. The Scroll Bar is accessed from the ________ tab of the Ribbon.
3. List three limitations of which you must be aware when setting up the controls of a Scroll Bar.
4. True or False: Once a Scroll Bar is activated, you cannot go back and change any of the controls. If the controls need to be changed, you must delete the Scroll Bar and create a new one.
5. Explain how you can delete a Scroll Bar without deleting any columns or rows.
6. True or False: The use of the Conditional Formatting feature is somewhat limited because you can set only one condition for any given cell.
7. When creating a two-dimensional data table, if the formula used to create the output or results of the table is located in cell D5, the values that make up the top row and left column of the table must begin in cells ________ and ________.
8. When highlighting a range of cells before creating a two-dimensional data table, the first cell in the range must contain either a ________ or a ________.
9. True or False: After creating a Data Table, you cannot change any of the values along the top row or left column. Changing these values could create an error in the table results.
10. True or False: You can use both Solver and Goal Seek to set a specific value for a target cell location. Therefore, both of these tools can be used to accomplish the same tasks.
11. What is the difference between Scenario Manager and Goal Seek?
12. Tools for analyzing data using various statistical methods can be accessed by selecting the ________ ________ icon from the ________ tab of the Ribbon.
13. True or False: When using any option from the Data Analysis Tools, the output will automatically be formatted based on the results that are produced.
14. If you are using the **Histogram** tool, what bin range value should be entered into a cell location if the following is one of the groups you are using to count the frequency of purchases by price point: 15.99 and 19.99?
15. True or False: When defining the input X range of a regression, you can highlight a range of cells extending over continuous columns or hold down the Control key and highlight specific columns.
16. What is the maximum independent variable limit when running a regression in Excel?

Skills Exam

The following exam is designed to test your ability to recognize and execute the Excel skills presented in this chapter. Read each question carefully and answer the questions in the order they are listed. You should be able to complete this exam in 60 minutes or less.

1. Open the file named ib_e09_chapter9skillsexam.
2. Activate the Fleet Details worksheet. Use Solver to maximize the Total Cartons in cell E27 by changing the Trips per Year in the range D3:D26. The solution must include the following constraints:
   a. Each trailer must make at least 24 trips per year.
   b. The maximum number of trips a trailer can make per year is 100.
   c. The total number of trips per year for all trailers must equal 1500.
   d. There cannot be any partial trips (e.g., 1.5).
3. Activate the Capacity worksheet. Type a formula in cell B6 that calculates the total cubic feet of freight capacity. This formula should first multiply the Average Capacity in cell B2 by the Number of Trucks in cell B3, and then multiply this result by the Number of Trips per Year in cell B4.
4. Create a Data Table that shows the total cubic feet of freight capacity when the values in the range D6:I6 are substituted for the number of trucks in cell B3 and the values in the range B7:B18 are substituted for the Total Trips per Year in cell B4.
5. Activate the Break-Even worksheet. Use Conditional Formatting to change the color of the value in cell B8 to red for any output that is less than 0.
6. Add a Scroll Bar to the Break-Even worksheet.
7. Set the controls of the Scroll Bar added in question 6 to change the value in cell B5. The value in cell B5 should not be less than 10,000 and should not be greater than 30,000. For each click of the arrow on the Scroll Bar, the value in cell B5 should increase 100 miles. For each page click of the Scroll Bar (space between the arrows), the value in cell B5 should change by 500 miles.
8. Use the Scroll Bar or type the value **20000** in cell B5.
9. Open the Scenario Manager and enter the following three scenarios, which assign different values to the Cost per Mile and Cost per Truck variables in the Break-Even worksheet. Use the scenario names listed below in the Scenario Manager.
   a. Target Scenario: Cost per Mile = **.40**; Cost per Truck = **40000**
   b. Best Scenario: Cost per Mile = **.25**; Cost per Truck = **30000**
   c. Worst Scenario: Cost per Mile = **.55**; Cost per Truck = **50000**
10. Create a Scenario Summary report showing the results of cell B7 for the three scenarios created in question 9.
11. Activate the Break-Even worksheet and show the results of the Worst Scenario that you created in question 9.
12. Use the Goal Seek tool to set the value in cell B8 of the Break-Even worksheet to 14.34% by changing the value in cell B4.
13. Activate the Store Sales Data worksheet. Use the Descriptive Statistics option from the Data Analysis Tools to provide a statistical summary for the Total Population and Population Age 4-11 data. The statistics output should appear in a new worksheet with the tab name **Population Stats**. Format the output so that all data is visible and numbers are formatted.
14. Activate the Store Sales Data worksheet. Create a Histogram for the Sales data in column B. Your histogram should count the number of stores in the sales groups listed below. The Histogram output should include the Cumulative Percentage as well as a Histogram chart. The output should appear in a new worksheet with the tab name **Sales Frequency**.

a. $0 - $3,000,000

b. $3,000,001 – $6,000,000

c. $6,000,001 - $9,000,000

d. Greater than $9,000,000

15. Format the Histogram data output that was created in question 14 so that all data is visible and easy to read. Then, format the Histogram chart. Expand the chart and add any formatting enhancements so that all the data is visible and easy to read.

16. Use the **Regression** option from the Data Analysis Tools to evaluate if Total Population, Population Age 4-11, and Competitor within 5 Miles can explain variations in the Sales data found in the Store Sales Data worksheet. The Sales data should be the dependent variable (Y Range) and the Total Population, Population Age 4-11, and Competitor within 5 Miles should be the independent variables (X Range). The regression output should appear in a new worksheet with the tab name `Regression Output`.

17. Format the data produced by the regression output in question 16. All data should be visible and numbers formatted with no more than 4 decimal places.

18. Save and close your file.

Challenge Questions

The following questions are designed to test your ability to apply the Excel skills you have learned to complete a business objective. Use your knowledge of Excel and your creativity to answer these questions. For most questions, there are several possible ways to complete the objective.

1. The example shown in the Data Table segment suggested that, based on the price that was charged for a shirt, a business manager could determine how many units need to be sold to achieve a positive profit. The example also shows that the price of the shirt must exceed the variable cost to generate a profit. What other factors do you think need to be taken into consideration when setting the price of a product? Explain why a company might sell a product at a price that only meets its variable cost. Create an Excel spreadsheet with examples that support your answer.

2. As mentioned in the Scenario Tools segment of this chapter, the controls for the Scroll Bar can be set to change a value only in whole-number increments. However, with some creative thinking, you can use the Scroll Bar to increment the value in a target cell in fractional units. Open the file named ib_e09_challengea. The data in this file shows a simple investment analysis for a common stock. As the future price of the stock increases in cell B3, a formula in cell B7 calculates the Investment Gain/Loss. Add a Scroll Bar to increase the Future Price in cell B3 in $.10 increments. Set up the controls of the Scroll Bar so that the price can decrease as low as $5.00 and increase as high as $75.00.

3. It was mentioned in the Descriptive Statistics segment that the results shown in Figure 9.36 would have to be compared with company goals and statistics of other firms operating in the same industry. Research the annual reports of any two general-merchandise retail firms or a report on the General Merchandise industry published by a financial institution. Compare the results of your research with the results in Figure 9.36. If you were the president of a general-merchandise retail company, would you consider these results desirable? Why or why not? Assume that the transactions analyzed in Figure 9.36 provide sufficient representation of this company's business.

4. Open the Excel file named ib_e09_challengeb. This is the same data that was used in the Histogram workshop. Show the following statistics for this data in the Transaction Summary worksheet:

    - Total number of unique transactions.
    - The average dollars spent for each transaction.
    - The average number of items purchased per transaction. Assume that the transaction number is repeated for each item purchased.

Section Two

Research Labs

Introduction to Business Research and Data

Chapter 1

The nature of business and management research and structure of this book

Learning outcomes

By the end of this chapter you should:

- be able to outline the purpose and distinct focus of management research;
- be able to place your research project on a basic-applied research continuum according to its purpose and context;
- understand the stages you will need to complete (and revisit) as part of your research process;
- have an overview of this book's purpose, structure and features;
- be aware of some of the ways you can use this book.

1.1 Introduction

This book is designed to help you to undertake your research project, whether you are an undergraduate or postgraduate student of business and management or a manager. It provides a clear guide on how to undertake research as well as highlighting the realities of undertaking research, including the more common pitfalls. The book is written as an introductory text to provide you with a guide to the research process and with the necessary knowledge and skills to undertake a piece of research from thinking of a research topic to writing your project report. As such, you will find it useful as a manual or handbook on how to tackle your research project.

After reading the book you will have been introduced to and explored a range of approaches, strategies and methods with which you could tackle your research project. Of equal importance, you will know that there is no one best way for undertaking all research. Rather you will be aware of the choices you will have to make and how these choices will impact upon what you can find out. This means you will be able to make an informed choice about the approaches, strategies and methods that are most suitable to your own research project and be able to justify this choice. In reading the book you will have been introduced to the more frequently used techniques and procedures for collecting and analysing different types of data, have had a chance to practise them, and be able to make a reasoned choice regarding which to use. When selecting and using these techniques you will be aware of the contribution that the appropriate use of information technology can make to your research.

However, before you continue, a word of caution. In your study, you will inevitably read a wide range of books and articles. In many of these the terms 'research method' and 'research methodology' will be used interchangeably, perhaps just using methodology as a more verbose way of saying method. In this book we have been more precise in our use of these terms. Throughout the book we use the term **methods** to refer to techniques and procedures used to obtain and analyse data. This, therefore, includes questionnaires, observation and interviews as well as both quantitative (statistical) and qualitative (non-statistical) analysis techniques and, as you have probably gathered from the title, is the main focus of this book. In contrast, the term **methodology** refers to the theory of how research should be undertaken. We believe that it is important that you have some understanding of this so that you can make an informed choice about your research. For this reason, we also discuss a range of philosophical assumptions upon which research can be based and the implications of these for the method or methods adopted.

The Post-it® note is one of the best known and most widely used office products in the world. Yet, despite the discovery of the repositionable adhesive that made the Post-it® note possible in 1968, it was not until 1980 that the product was introduced to the market (Lemelson-MIT Program 2007). In the 1960s 3M research scientist, Spence Silver, was looking for ways to improve the adhesive used in tapes. However, he discovered something quite different from what he was looking for, an adhesive that did not stick strongly when coated onto the back of tapes! What was unclear was how it might be used. Over the next five years he demonstrated and talked about his new adhesive to people working within the company.

Most people working for 3M know the story of what happened next and how the Post-it® note concept came about. A new product development researcher working for 3M, Art Fry, was frustrated by how the scraps of paper he used as bookmarks kept falling out of his church choir hymn book. He realised that Silver's adhesive would mean his bookmarks would not fall out. Soon afterwards the Post-it® note concept was developed and market research undertaken. This was extremely difficult as the product was revolutionary and was, in effect, designed to replace pieces of torn scrap paper! However, despite some initial scepticism within the company, Post-it® notes were launched in 1980. One year after their launch, they were named 3M's outstanding new product.

Post-it® notes in use
Source: © Mark Saunders 2006

Whilst your research project will be within the business and management discipline rather than natural science (such as developing a new adhesive), our introductory example still offers a number of insights into the nature of research and in particular the business and management research you will be undertaking. In particular, it highlights that when undertaking research we should be open to finding the unexpected and how sometimes the applicability of our research findings may not be immediately obvious. It also emphasises the importance of discussing your ideas with other people.

1.2 The nature of research

When listening to the radio, watching the television or reading a daily newspaper it is difficult to avoid the term 'research'. The results of 'research' are all around us. A debate about the findings of a recent poll of people's opinions inevitably includes a discussion of 'research', normally referring to the way in which the data were collected. Politicians often justify their policy decisions on the basis of 'research'. Newspapers report the findings of research companies' surveys (Box 1.1). Documentary programmes tell us about 'research findings', and advertisers may highlight the 'results of research' to encourage you to buy a particular product or brand. However, we believe that what these examples really emphasise is the wide range of meanings given to the term 'research' in everyday speech.

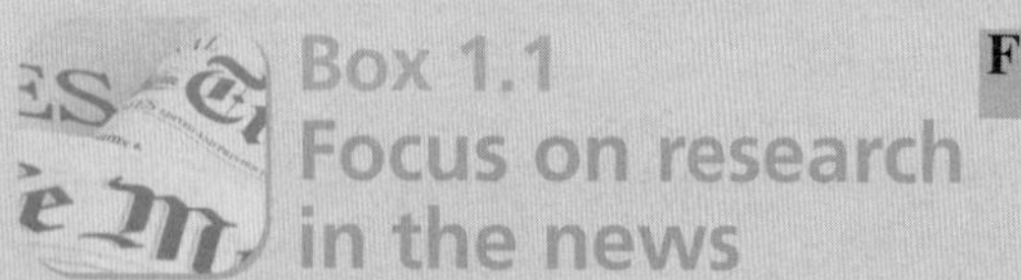

FT

Research that aids publicists but not the public

This is the age of the bogus survey. I woke up recently to the news that 95 per cent of children in Britain had been victims of crime. Of course they had. From a legal perspective, pushing a classmate or taking a pencil without the intention of returning it is a crime. School playgrounds are hotbeds of crime and always have been.

The difference between the bogus survey and real research is that real research has the objective of yielding new information, while bogus surveys are designed to generate publicity. The organisation that had undertaken this bogus survey – I forbear from mentioning its name – did not disguise that it had done so in order to draw attention to the problem of abuse of children.

Statistics about the incidence of real criminal activity against and among children are hard to come by and hard to interpret. We do not really know whether things are getting better or worse, or by how much – at least not without careful research and analysis, which would be hard to explain on television. Programme producers will not ask you to appear to spell out these complexities, but will allow you to horrify viewers and listeners with alarming news.

Public relations professionals understand these triggers, to such an extent that commissioning a bogus survey is now a standard element in the pitch they present to potential clients and conducting these surveys is an increasingly large part of the activity of market research organisations.

There is even a term for this kind of activity. It is called 'thought leadership'. That term illustrates the problem. It probably does not matter much that the bogus survey is used to generate spurious news. The danger is that opinion polls designed to produce eye-catching answers displace serious thought and analysis. The organisation that announced that 95 cent of children had been victims of crime judged, correctly, that its survey better served its needs than serious research into the problems with which it was concerned, that had not been done.

The study of business is afflicted by confusion between the results of a survey of what people think about the world and a survey of what the world is really like. At another recent meeting I heard a platform speaker announce that 40 per cent of books would be electronically published by 2020. A pesky academic asked exactly what this number meant and what evidence it was based on. The speaker assured the audience that the number had been obtained in a survey by eminent consultants of the opinions of the industry's thought leaders.

Newspapers, broadcasters and consultants will start to distinguish bogus surveys from substantive knowledge only when their audience demonstrates that it knows the difference. When you are asked for your opinion in your role as thought leader, put the phone down. You will be serving the public interest as well as saving your time.

Source: article by John Kay, *Financial Times*, FT.Com site. 30 Oct. 2007.

Walliman (2005) argues that many of these everyday uses of the term 'research' are not research in the true meaning of the word. As part of this, he highlights ways in which the term is used wrongly:

- just collecting facts or information with no clear purpose;
- reassembling and reordering facts or information without interpretation;
- as a term to get your product or idea noticed and respected.

The first of these highlights the fact that, although research often involves the collection of information, it is more than just reading a few books or articles, talking to a few people or asking people questions. While collecting data may be part of the research process, if it is not undertaken in a systematic way, on its own and, in particular, with a clear purpose, it will not be seen as research. The second of these is commonplace in many reports. Data are collected, perhaps from a variety of different sources, and then assembled in a single document with the sources of these data listed. However, there is no interpretation of the data collected. Again, while the assembly of data from a variety of sources may be part of the process of research, without interpretation it is not research. Finally, the term 'research' can be used to get an idea or product noticed by people and to suggest that people should have confidence in it. In such instances, when you ask for details of the research process, these are either unclear or not forthcoming.

Based upon this brief discussion we can already see that research has a number of characteristics:

- Data are collected systematically.
- Data are interpreted systematically.
- There is a clear purpose: to find things out.

We can therefore define **research** as something that people undertake in order to find out things in a systematic way, thereby increasing their knowledge. Two phrases are important in this definition: 'systematic way' and 'to find out things'. 'Systematic' suggests that research is based on logical relationships and not just beliefs (Ghauri and Grønhaug 2005). As part of this, your research will involve an explanation of the methods used to collect the data, will argue why the results obtained are meaningful, and will explain any limitations that are associated with them. 'To find out things' suggests there are a multiplicity of possible purposes for your research. These may include describing, explaining, understanding, criticising and analysing (Ghauri and Grønhaug 2005). However, it also suggests that you have a clear purpose or set of 'things' that you want to find out, such as the answer to a question or number of questions.

1.3 The nature of business and management research

Using our earlier definition of research it would seem sensible to define business and management research as undertaking systematic research to find out things about business and management.

Easterby-Smith *et al.* (2008) argue that four things combine to make business and management a distinctive focus for research:

- the way in which managers (and researchers) draw on knowledge developed by other disciplines;

- the fact that managers tend to be powerful and busy people. Therefore, they are unlikely to allow research access unless they can see personal or commercial advantages.
- The fact that managers are educated. Many now have undergraduate and postgraduate degrees and, as such, tend often to be as well educated as those conducting research about them.
- The requirement for the research to have some practical consequence. This means it either needs to contain the potential for taking some form of action or needs to take account of the practical consequences of the findings.

Ongoing debate within the British Academy of Management has explored the status of management research. One feature, which has gained considerable support, is the *trans-disciplinary* nature of such research. While this has similarities to Easterby-Smith *et al.*'s (2008) point regarding the use of knowledge from other disciplines, it also emphasises that the research 'cannot be reduced to any sum of parts framed in terms of contributions to associated disciplines' (Tranfield and Starkey 1998:352). In other words, using knowledge from a range of disciplines enables management research to gain new insights that cannot be obtained through all of these disciplines separately. Another feature of management research highlighted in the debate is a belief that it should be able to develop ideas and to relate them to practice. In particular, that research should complete a virtuous circle of theory and practice (Tranfield and Starkey 1998) through which research on managerial practice informs practically derived theory. This in turn becomes a blueprint for managerial practice, thereby increasing the stock of relevant and practical management knowledge. Thus, business and management research needs to engage with both the world of theory and the world of practice. Consequently, the problems addressed should grow out of interaction between these two worlds rather than either on their own.

In the past decade debate about the nature of management research has focused on how it can meet the *double hurdle* of being both theoretically and methodologically rigorous, while at the same time embracing the world of practice and being of practical relevance (Hodgkinson *et al.* 2001). Much of this debate has centred around the work by Gibbons *et al.* (1994) on the production of knowledge and, in particular, the concepts of Mode 1 and Mode 2 knowledge creation. **Mode 1** knowledge creation emphasises research in which the questions are set and solved by academic interests, emphasising a fundamental rather than applied nature, where there is little if any focus on utilisation of the research by practitioners. In contrast, **Mode 2** emphasises a context for research governed by the world of practice, highlighting the importance of collaboration both with and between practitioners (Starkey and Madan 2001) and the need for the production of practical relevant knowledge. Based upon this, Starkey and Madan (2001) observe that research within the Mode 2 approach offers a way of bringing the supply side of knowledge represented by universities together with the demand side represented by businesses and overcoming the double hurdle.

Drawing from these debates, it could be argued that business and management research not only needs to provide findings that advance knowledge and understanding, it also needs to address business issues and practical managerial problems. However, this would negate the observation that Mode 2 practices develop from Mode 1. It might also result in business and management research that did not have obvious commercial benefit not being pursued. This, Huff and Huff (2001) argue, could jeopardise future knowledge creation as research that is currently not valued commercially might have value in the future. Building upon these ideas Huff and Huff, rather like Fukami (2007) who found a third road in addition to the two academic career roads of research and teaching, highlight a further form of knowledge production: Mode 3. **Mode 3** knowledge production focuses on an appreciation of the human condition as it is and as it might become, its purpose being to 'assure survival and promote the common good at various levels of social aggregation' (Huff and Huff 2001:53). This emphasises the importance of broader issues of human relevance of research. Consequently, in addition to research that satisfies your intellectual curiosity for its own sake, the findings of business and management research might also contain practical implications, and these findings may have societal consequences far broader and complex than perhaps envisaged by Mode 2.

Tranfield and Denyer (2004) draw attention to concerns resulting from the separation of knowledge producers from knowledge users. This had the effect of introducing a schism, or what (Starkey and Madan 2001) call the 'relevance gap' which, they argue, has become more marked over recent years. More encouragingly, academic management research can be seen as a design science (Huff *et al.* 2006), its mission being to develop valid knowledge to support thoughtful, designing practitioners. From the design science perspective, the main purpose of academic management research is to develop valid knowledge to support organisational problem solving in the field. That support can be direct, instrumental or more indirect – giving general enlightenment on the type of problem at hand.

Rousseau (2006) has drawn attention to ways of closing what she terms the prevailing 'research-practice gap' – the failure of organisations and managers to base practices on best available evidence. She extols the virtues of 'evidence-based management', which derives principles from research evidence and translates them into practices that solve organisational problems. Rousseau's argument is that research findings do not appear to have transferred well to the workplace. Instead of a scientific understanding of human behaviour and organisations, managers, including those with MBAs, continue to rely largely on personal experience, to the exclusion of more systematic knowledge.

However, perhaps the most telling comment on the so-called 'relevance gap' is from Tranfield and Denyer (2004:13) who assert that ignoring such a gap would be 'unthinkable in other professional fields, such as medicine or engineering, where a national scandal would ensue if science base and practice were not inextricably and necessarily interlinked'. The article by Hodgkinson *et al.* (2001) offers a useful four-fold taxonomy for considering this in relation to managerial knowledge. Using the dimensions of theoretical and methodological rigour and of practical relevance they identify four quadrants (see Table 1.1).

Hodgkinson *et al.* argue that pedantic science is characterised by a focus on increasing methodological rigour at the expense of results that are relevant and can sometimes be found in refereed academic journals. In contrast, popularist science is characterised by a focus on relevance and usefulness whilst neglecting theoretical and methodological rigour, examples being found in some books targeted at practising managers. Consequently, whilst findings might be useful to managers, the research upon which they are based is unlikely to be valid or reliable. Puerile science both lacks methodological rigour and is of limited practical relevance and, although unlikely to be found in refereed

Table 1.1 A taxonomy for considering the 'relevance gap' in relation to managerial knowledge

Theoretical and methodological rigour	Practical relevance	Quadrant
Higher	Lower	Pedantic science
Lower	Higher	Popularist science
Lower	Lower	Puerile science
Higher	Higher	Pragmatic science

Source: developed from Hodgkinson *et al.* (2001).

Box 1.2 Focus on management research

In an *Academy of Management Review* article Van De Ven and Johnson (2006) examine three related ways in which the gap between theory and practice has been framed. One approach views it as a knowledge transfer problem. Practitioners fail to adopt the findings of research in fields, such as management because the knowledge is produced in a form that cannot be readily applied in practical contexts.

A second approach views knowledge of theory and practice as distinct kinds of knowledge. Each reflects a different fundamental approach for addressing different questions. To say that the knowledge of theory and practice are different is not to say that they are in conflict, or that they substitute for each other; rather, they complement one another.

This leads to a third view – namely, that the gap between theory and practice is a knowledge-production problem which questions the traditional mode of research practised in business and professional schools and has led to the proposal that a key defining characteristic of management research is its applied nature.

Having reviewed the problems and assumptions of the first two approaches, Van De Ven and Johnson propose a method of *engaged scholarship* in which researchers and practitioners coproduce knowledge that can advance theory and practice in a given domain.

academic journals, can be found in other media. Finally, pragmatic science is both theoretically and methodologically rigorous and relevant.

Within these boundaries of advancing knowledge, addressing business issues, solving managerial problems and promoting the common good, the purpose and the context of your research project can differ considerably. For some research projects your purpose may be to understand and explain the impact of something, such as a particular policy. You may undertake this research within an individual organisation and suggest appropriate action on the basis of your findings. For other research projects you may wish to explore the ways in which various organisations do things differently. In such projects your purpose may be to discover and understand better the underlying processes in a wider context, thereby providing greater understanding for practitioners. For yet other research projects you may wish to place an in-depth investigation of an organisation within the context of a wider understanding of the processes that are operating.

Despite this variety, we believe that all business and management research projects can be placed on a continuum (Figure 1.1) according to their purpose and context. At one extreme of the continuum is research that is undertaken purely to understand the processes of business and management and their outcomes. Such research is undertaken largely in universities and largely as the result of an academic agenda. Its key consumer is the academic community, with relatively little attention being given to its practical applications. This is often termed **basic, fundamental** or **pure research**. Given our earlier discussion it is unlikely that Mode 2 and Mode 3 business and management research would fulfil these criteria due to at least some consideration being made of the practical consequences. Through doing this, the research would start to move towards the other end of the continuum (Figure 1.1). At this end is research that is of direct and immediate relevance to managers, addresses issues that they see as important, and is presented in ways that they understand and can act on. This is termed **applied research**. In our view applied research is very similar to consultancy in many cases, particularly when the latter is conducted in a thorough manner.

Basic research ←→	Applied research
Purpose:	***Purpose:***
• Expand knowledge of processes of business and management	• Improve understanding of particular business or management problem
• Results in universal principles relating to the process and its relationship to outcomes	• Results in solution to problem
	• New knowledge limited to problem
• Findings of significance and value to society in general	• Findings of practical relevance and value to manager(s) in organisation(s)
Context:	***Context:***
• Undertaken by people based in universities	• Undertaken by people based in a variety of settings including organisations and universities
• Choice of topic and objectives determined by the researcher	• Objectives negotiated with originator
• Flexible time scales	• Tight time scales

Figure 1.1
Basic and applied research
Sources: authors' experience; Easterby-Smith *et al.* 2008; Hedrick *et al.* 1993.

Research by Shapiro *et al.* (2007) indicates that many managers and academics do perceive a problem with a gap between basic, fundamental or pure research and applied research. Clearly this has implications for the take up of research findings. Echoing the work of Van De Ven and Johnson (2006) (see Box 1.1 above), Shapiro *et al.* (2007:250) argue that if managers and academics believe that there is problem in which management research is 'lost in translation', then proposed solutions might focus on changes in the way research findings are disseminated. Alternatively, if the belief is that there is a knowledge production problem, so that any chance for impact on practice is 'lost before translation' (Shapiro *et al.* 2007:250), then proposed solutions might focus on ways to foster more researcher practitioner collaboration as research programs are developed and carried out.

Wherever your research project lies on this basic–applied continuum, we believe that you should undertake your research with rigour. To do this you will need to pay careful attention to the entire research process.

Inevitably, your own beliefs and feelings will impact upon your research. Although you might feel that your research will be value neutral (we will discuss this in greater detail later, particularly in Chapter 4), it is unlikely that you will stop your own beliefs and feelings influencing your research. Your choice of what to research is also likely to be influenced by topics that excite you, and the way you collect and analyse your data by the skills you have or are able to develop. Similarly, as we discuss in Chapter 2, practical considerations such as access to data and the time and resources you have available will also impact upon your research process.

1.4 The research process

Most research textbooks represent research as a multi-stage process that you must follow in order to undertake and complete your research project. The precise number of stages varies, but they usually include formulating and clarifying a topic, reviewing the literature, designing the research, collecting data, analysing data and writing up. In the majority of these the research process, although presented with rationalised examples, is described as a series of stages through which you must pass. Articles you have read may also suggest that the research process is rational and straightforward. Unfortunately, this is very rarely true, and the reality is considerably messier, with what initially appear as great ideas sometimes having little or no relevance (Saunders and Lewis 1997). While research is often depicted as moving through each of the stages outlined above, one after the other, this is unlikely to be the case. In reality you will probably revisit each stage more than once. Each time you revisit a stage you will need to reflect on the associated issues and refine your ideas. In addition, as highlighted by some textbooks, you will need to consider ethical and access issues during the process.

This textbook also presents the research process as a series of linked stages and gives the appearance of being organised in a linear manner. However, as you use the book you will see from the text, extensive use of cross-referencing, examples of research by well-known researchers and how research is reported in the news, examples of student research and case studies that we have recognised the iterative nature of the process you will follow. As part of this process, we believe that it is vital that you spend time formulating and clarifying your research topic. This we believe should be expressed as one or more research questions that your research must answer, accompanied by a set of objectives that your research must address. However, we would also stress the need to reflect on your ideas continually and revise both these and the way in which you intend to progress your research. Often this will involve revisiting stages (including your research question(s) and objectives) and working through them again. There is also a need to plan ahead, thereby ensuring that the necessary preliminary work for later stages has been undertaken. This is emphasised by Figure 1.2, which also provides a schematic index to the remaining chapters of the book. Within this flow chart (Figure 1.2) the stages you will need to complete as part of your research project are emphasised in the centre of the chart. However, be warned: the process is far messier than a brief glance at Figure 1.2 suggests!

1.5 The purpose and structure of this book

The purpose

As we stated earlier (Section 1.1), the overriding purpose of this book is to help you to undertake research. This means that early on in your research project you will need to be clear about what you are doing, why you are doing it, and the associated implications of what you are seeking to do. You will also need to ensure that you can show how your ideas relate to research that has already been undertaken in your topic area and that you have a clear research design and have thought about how you will collect and analyse your data. As part of this you will need to consider the validity and reliability of the data you intend to use, along with associated ethical and access issues. The appropriateness and suitability of the analytical techniques you choose to use will be of equal importance. Finally, you will need to write and present your research project report as clearly and precisely as possible.

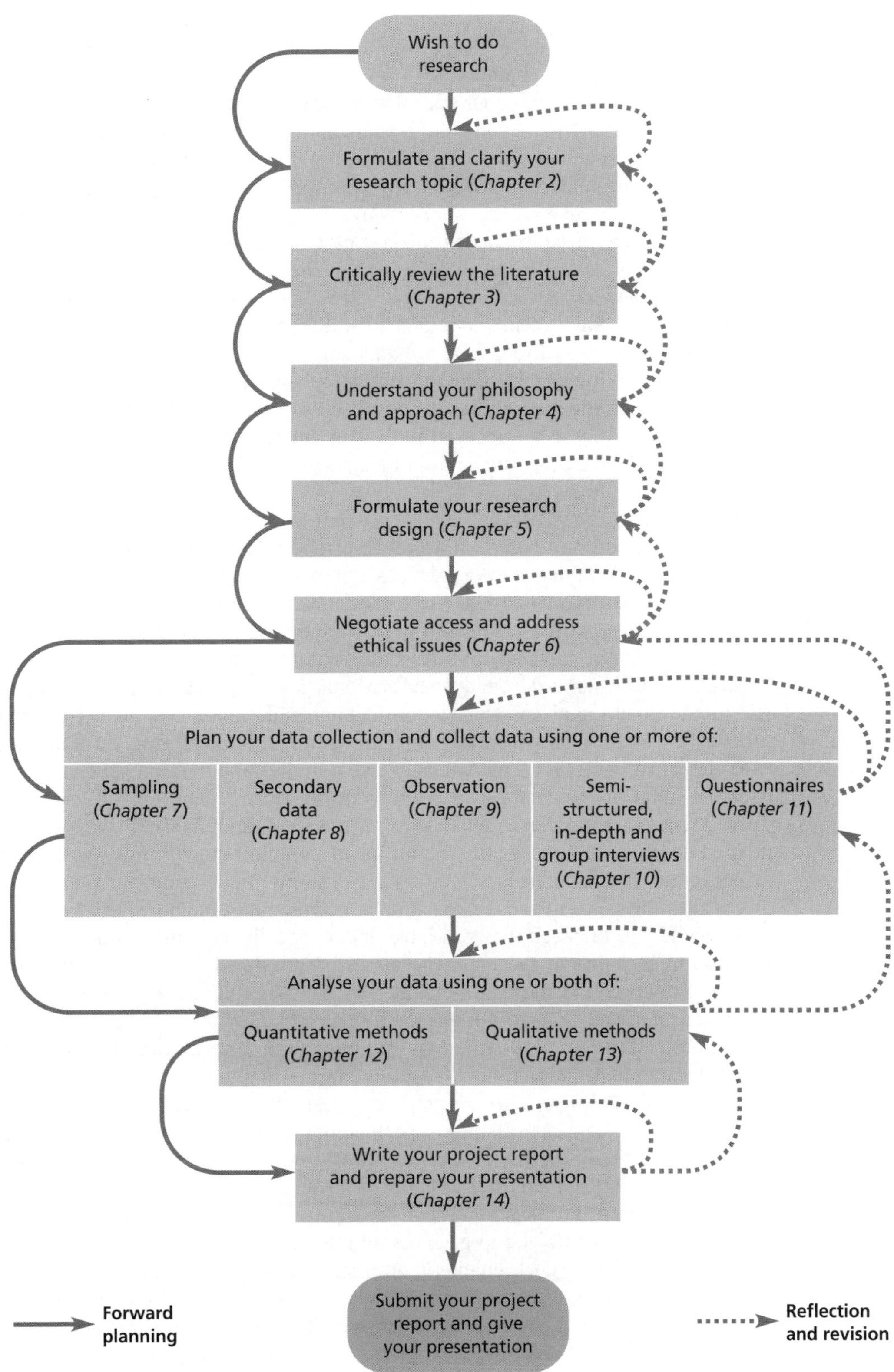

Figure 1.2
The research process
Source: © Mark Saunders, Philip Lewis and Adrian Thornhill 2009.

The structure of each chapter

Each of the subsequent chapters deals with part of the research process outlined in Figure 1.2. The ideas, techniques and methods are discussed using as little jargon as is possible. Where appropriate you will find summaries of these, using tables, checklists or diagrams. When new terms are introduced for the first time they are shown in **bold**, and a definition or explanation follows shortly afterwards. They are also listed with a brief definition in the glossary. The application of appropriate information technology is considered in most instances as an integral part of the text. Discussion of information technology is not software specific but is concerned with general principles. However, we recognise that you may wish to find out more about how to use data analysis software packages and so have included tutorials for the quantitative data analysis software SPSS™, the spread sheet Excel™ and the qualitative data analysis software NVivo™ (with practice data sets) on this book's Companion Website. These will enable you to utilise whatever software you have available most effectively. We have also included the Smarter Online Searching Guide to help you with your Internet searches. Chapters have been cross-referenced as appropriate, and an index is provided to help you to find your way around the book.

Included within the text of each chapter is a series of boxes which are called *Focus on student research*. These are based on actual research projects, undertaken by students, in which points made in the text are illustrated. In many instances these examples illustrate possible pitfalls you may come across while undertaking your research. Further illustrations are provided by *Focus on management research* and *Focus on research in the news* boxes. *Focus on management research* boxes discuss recent research in business and management. These are normally derived from refereed academic journal articles and you are likely to be able to download the actual articles from online databases at your university. *Focus on research in the news* boxes provide topical newspaper articles that illustrate pertinent research-related issues. All these will help you to understand the technique or idea and to assess its suitability or appropriateness to your research. Where a pitfall has been illustrated, it will, it is hoped, help you to avoid making the same mistake. There is also a series of boxed *Checklists* to provide you with further focused guidance for your own research. At the end of each chapter there is a *Summary* of key points, which you may look at before and after reading the chapter to ensure that you have digested the main points.

To enable you to check that you have understood the chapter a series of *Self-check questions* is included at the end. These can be answered without recourse to other (external) resources. *Answers* are provided to all these self-check questions at the end of each chapter. Self-check questions are followed by *Review and discussion questions*. These suggest a variety of activities you can undertake to help you further develop your knowledge and understanding of the material in the chapter, often involving discussion with a friend. Self-test multiple choice questions are available on this book's Companion Website. Each chapter also includes a section towards the end headed *Progressing your research project*. This contains a series of questions that will help you to consider the implications of the material covered by the chapter for your research project. Answering the questions in the section *Progressing your research project* for each chapter will enable you to generate all the material that you will need to include in your project report. Each chapter's questions involve you in undertaking activities that are more complex than self-check questions, such as a library-based literature search or designing and piloting a questionnaire. They are designed to help you to focus on the techniques that are most appropriate to your research. However, as emphasised by Figure 1.2, you will almost certainly need to revisit and revise your answers as your research progresses.

Each chapter is also accompanied by *References*, *Further reading* and a *Case study*. Further reading is included for two distinct reasons:

- to direct you to other work on the ideas contained within the chapter;
- to direct you to further examples of research where the ideas contained in the chapter have been used.

The main reasons for our choice of further reading are therefore indicated.

The new case studies at the end of each chapter are drawn from a variety of business and management research scenarios and have been based on the case study's authors' and students' experiences when undertaking a research project. They have been written to highlight real issues that occur when undertaking business and management research. To help to focus your thoughts or discussion on some of the pertinent issues, each case is followed by evaluative questions. Additional case studies relating to each chapter are available from the book's companion website. A case study follows every chapter.

An outline of the chapters

The book is organised in the following way.

Chapter 2 is written to assist you in the generation of ideas, which will help you to choose a suitable research topic, and offers advice on what makes a good research topic. If you have already been given a research topic, perhaps by an organisation or tutor, you will need to refine it into one that is feasible, and should still therefore read this chapter. After your idea has been generated and refined, the chapter discusses how to turn this idea into clear research question(s) and objectives. (Research questions and objectives are referred to throughout the book.) Finally, the chapter provides advice on how to write your research proposal.

The importance of the critical literature review to your research is discussed in Chapter 3. This chapter outlines what a critical review needs to include and the range of primary, secondary and tertiary literature sources available. The chapter explains the purpose of reviewing the literature, discusses a range of search strategies, and contains advice on how to plan and undertake your search and to write your review. The processes of identifying key words and searching using online databases and the Internet are outlined. It also offers advice on how to record items and to evaluate their relevance.

Chapter 4 addresses the issue of understanding different research philosophies, including positivism, realism, interpretivism, objectivism, subjectivism and pragmatism. Within this the functionalist, interpretive, radical humanist and radical structuralist paradigms are discussed. Deductive and inductive approaches to research are also considered. In this chapter we challenge you to think about your own values and how you view the world and the impact this will have on the way you undertake your research.

These ideas are developed further in Chapter 5 which explores formulating your research design. As part of this, a range of research strategies are discussed and the difference between quantitative and qualitative methods explained. The use of multiple methods is explored and consideration given to the implications of design choices for the credibility of your research findings and conclusions.

Chapter 6 explores issues related to gaining access and to research ethics. It offers advice on how to gain access both to organisations and to individuals. Potential ethical issues are discussed in relation to each stage of the research process and different data collection methods. Issues of data protection are also introduced.

A range of the probability and non-probability sampling techniques available for use in your research is explained in Chapter 7. The chapter considers why sampling is necessary, and looks at issues of sample size and response rates. Advice on how to relate your choice of sampling techniques to your research topic is given, and techniques for assessing the representativeness of those who respond are discussed.

Chapters 8, 9, 10 and 11 are concerned with different methods of obtaining data. The use of secondary data is discussed in Chapter 8, which introduces the variety of data that are likely to be available and suggests ways in which they can be used. Advantages and disadvantages of secondary data are discussed, and a range of techniques for locating these data, including using the Internet, is suggested. Chapter 8 also offers advice on how to evaluate the suitability of secondary data for your research.

In contrast, Chapter 9 is concerned with collecting primary data through observation. The chapter examines two types of observation: participant observation and structured observation. Practical advice on using each is offered, and particular attention is given to ensuring that the data you obtain are both valid and reliable.

Chapter 10 is also concerned with collecting primary data, this time using semi-structured, in-depth and group interviews. The appropriateness of using these interviews in relation to your research strategy is discussed. Advice on how to undertake such interviews is offered, including the conduct of focus groups, Internet-mediated (including online) and telephone interviews. Particular attention is given to ensuring that the data collected are both reliable and valid.

Chapter 11 is the final chapter concerned with collecting data. It introduces you to the use of both self-administered and interviewer-administered questionnaires, and explores their advantages and disadvantages. Practical advice is offered on the process of designing, piloting and administering Internet-mediated, postal, delivery and collection, and telephone questionnaires to enhance their response rates. Particular attention is again given to ensuring that the data collected are both reliable and valid.

Analysis of data is covered in Chapters 12 and 13. Chapter 12 outlines and illustrates the main issues that you need to consider when preparing data for quantitative analysis and when analysing these data by computer. Different types of data are defined, and advice is given on how to create a data matrix and to code data. Practical advice is also offered on the analysis of these data using computer based analysis software. The most appropriate diagrams to explore and illustrate data are discussed, and suggestions are made about the most appropriate statistics to use to describe data, to explore relationships and to examine trends.

Chapter 13 outlines and discusses the main approaches available to you to analyse data qualitatively both manually and using computer aided qualitative data analysis software (**CAQDAS**). The nature of qualitative data and issues associated with transcription are discussed. Following an overview of the analysis process, the use of deductively based and inductively based analytical procedures is discussed. These include pattern matching, explanation building, data display and analysis, template analysis, analytic induction, grounded theory, discourse analysis and narrative analysis.

Chapter 14 helps you with the structure, content and style of your final project report and any associated oral presentations. Above all, it encourages you to see writing as an intrinsic part of the research process that should not be left until everything else is completed.

Appendices and glossary

This book contains four appendices designed to support you at different stages of your research project. In the early stages, as you begin to read, you will need to keep a reference of what you have read using a recognised system, the most frequently used of which are detailed in Appendix 1. When selecting your sample you may need to calculate the minimum sample size required and use random sampling numbers (Appendices 2 and 3). Finally, when designing your data collection tools and writing your project report you will need to ensure that the language you use is non-discriminatory. Guidelines for these are given in Appendix 4. A separate glossary of over 400 research-methods-related terms is also included for quick reference.

1.6 Summary

- This book is designed to help you to undertake a research project whether you are an undergraduate or postgraduate student of business and management or a manager. It is designed as an introductory text and will guide you through the entire research process.
- Business and management research involves undertaking systematic research to find out things. It is transdisciplinary, and engages with both theory and practice.
- All business and management research projects can be placed on a basic–applied continuum according to their purpose and context.
- Wherever your research project lies on this continuum, you should undertake your research with rigour. To do this you will need to pay careful attention to the entire research process.
- In this book, research is represented as a multi-stage process; however, this process is rarely straightforward and will involve both reflecting on and revising stages already undertaken and forward planning.
- The text of each chapter is supported through a series of boxed examples. These include, focus on student research and focus on research in the news. In addition, there are checklists, self-check questions and review and discussion questions, an assignment and a case study with questions. Answers to all self-check questions are at the end of the appropriate chapter.
- Answering the questions in the section 'Progressing your research project' for Chapters 2–13 will enable you to generate all the material that you will need to include in your project report. When you have also answered the questions in this section for Chapter 14, you will have written your research report.

Self-check questions

Help with these questions is available at the end of the chapter.

1.1 Outline the features that can make business and management research distinctive from research in other disciplines.

1.2 What are the key differences between basic and applied research (and consultancy)?

1.3 Examine Figure 1.2. What does this suggest about the need to plan and to reflect on and revise your ideas?

Review and discussion questions

1.4 Agree with a friend to each read a different quality newspaper. Make a note of at least 10 articles in your newspaper that mention the word 'research'. Now examine the articles one at a time. As you examine each article, does the reference to research . . .

- . . . refer to the collection of facts or information with no clear purpose?
- . . . refer to the reassembling and reordering of facts or information without interpretation?
- . . . provide a means of getting the reader to respect what is being written?
- . . . refer to the systematic collection and interpretation of data with a clear purpose?

Discuss your answers with your friend.

1.5 Obtain a copy of one or two of the articles referred to in Section 1.3. Read the article carefully. To what extent do you believe that business and management research should always meet the twin requirements of rigour and relevance? Give reasons for your answer.

References

Easterby-Smith, M., Thorpe, R. Jackson, P. and Lowe, A. (2008) *Management Research* (3rd edn). London: Sage.

Fukami, C. (2007) 'The third road', *Journal of Management Education,* Vol. 31, pp. 358–64.

Ghauri, P. and Grønhaug, K. (2005) *Research Methods in Business Studies: A Practical Guide* (3rd edn). Harlow: Financial Times Prentice Hall.

Gibbons, M.L., Limoges, H., Nowotny, S., Schwartman, P., Scott, P. and Trow, M. (1994) *The New Production of Knowledge: The Dynamics of Science and Research in Contemporary Societies*. London: Sage.

Hedrick, T.E., Bickmann, L. and Rog, D.J. (1993) *Applied Research Design*. Newbury Park, CA: Sage.

Hodgkinson, G.P., Herriot, P. and Anderson, N. (2001) 'Re-aligning the stakeholders in management research: Lessons from industrial, work and organizational psychology', *British Journal of Management,* Vol. 12, Special Issue, pp. 41–8.

Huff, A.S. and Huff, J.O. (2001) 'Re-focusing the business school agenda', *British Journal of Management*, Vol. 12, Special Issue, pp. 49–54.

Huff, A., Tranfield, D. and van Aken, J. (2006) 'Management as a design science mindful of art and surprise. A conversation between Anne Huff, David Tranfield, and Joan Ernst van Aken', *Journal of Management Inquiry*, Vol. 15. No. 4, pp. 413–24.

Lemelson-MIT Program (2007) 'Art Fry and Spencer Silver'. Available at: http://web.mit.edu/invent/iow/frysilver.html [Accessed 19 December 2007.]

Rousseau, D. (2006) 'Is there such a thing as "evidence-based management?"', *Academy of Management Review*, Vol. 31, No. 2, pp. 256–69.

Saunders, M.N.K. and Lewis, P. (1997) 'Great ideas and blind alleys? A review of the literature on starting research', *Management Learning*, Vol. 28, No. 3, pp. 283–99.

Shapiro, D., Kirkman, B. and Courtney, H. (2007) 'Perceived causes and solutions of the translation problem in management research', *Academy of Management Journal*, Vol. 50, No. 2, pp. 249–66.

Starkey, K. and Madan, P. (2001) 'Bridging the relevance gap: aligning stakeholders in the future of management research', *British Journal of Management*, Vol. 12, Special Issue, pp. 3–26.

Tranfield, D. and Starkey, K. (1998) 'The nature, social organization and promotion of management research: towards policy', *British Journal of Management*, Vol. 9, pp. 341–53.

Tranfield, D. and Denyer, D. (2004) 'Linking theory to practice: a grand challenge for management research in the 21st century?', *Organization Management Journal*, Vol. 1, No. 1, pp. 10–14.

Van De Ven, A. and Johnson, P. (2006) 'Knowledge for Theory and Practice', *Academy of Management Review,* Vol. 31, No. 4, pp. 802–21.

Walliman, N. (2005) *Your Research Project: A Step by Step Guide for the First-Time Researcher* (2nd edn). London: Sage.

Further reading

Easterby-Smith, M., Thorpe, R. Jackson, P. and Lowe, A. (2008). ***Management Research.*** **(3rd edn). London: Sage. Chapter 1** provides a very clear and readable introduction to management research and how it is distinct from other forms of research.

Starkey, K. and Madan, P. (2001) 'Bridging the relevance gap: aligning stakeholders in the future of management research', ***British Journal of Management*****, Vol. 12, Special Issue, pp. 3–26.** This paper argues the need for relevant management research within a Mode 2 framework, emphasising a need for research partnership.

Case 1
Isabelle's research dilemma

Source: Baron Bratby/Alamy

Isabelle was very thoughtful. She had a puzzled look on her face. The dilemma she had was one experienced by many students in conducting research for a dissertation. Her research was concerned with managers and how they coped with pressure in the workplace. She particularly wanted to find out the coping strategies they used. This required consideration of theory and method and whether the research would have practical relevance. After her preliminary reading around the topic she decided that it was necessary to engage in both the world of theory and the world of practice and that the problems addressed would develop out of the interaction between these two worlds.

Theory in management could be seen as problematic, because for some researchers management is not a discipline. It is perceived as multi-disciplinary with many of its early practitioners receiving their training in the social sciences (Pettigrew 2001). Isabelle thought this could be advantageous in that it enables management research to gain new insights that may not be obtained through a number of disciplines separately. She also considered that a topic on pressure and coping could be understood at a number of levels of analysis from an individual to a structural level. In doing this she would be considering theoretical ideas and attempting to perceive them in a pragmatic way. It also meant looking at them anew which would provide some imaginative and original insights for her dissertation.

Isabelle found that more traditional research on managing pressure focused on positivistic approaches with an emphasis on being scientific and rigorous. This approach often uses quantitative methods with an emphasis on measuring and the use of factor analysis. Researchers hope this allows them to find statistical correlations between two variables and demonstrate some relationship between sources of pressure and possible physical, psychological or even physiological outcomes, if coping strategies were not successful. Research of this kind can be found in the work of Sadri and Marcoulides (1997) and Wheatley (2000).

Isabelle decided she would not use this approach. She felt that a number of students' dissertations had already used this approach and she wanted to get away from statistical analysis and examining pressure on managers using a positivistic approach. She also thought that this traditional research ignored the managers' biography which could prove to be important in understanding how the manager coped with pressure. The more traditional approach seems to perceive the individual as passive and playing little part in making and constructing his/her reality. It was as if the researcher with questions asked in the questionnaire had already structured the reality. However, people working in organisations do have histories, futures and expectations and pursue their individual goals. For example, long-term sources of a person's distress may be traced back to experiences at work many years before. To study this would require Isabelle to use a different method. She decided to adopt in-depth interviews as primary sources so that she could study the turning-points in the lives of her participants over a period of time. This may indicate why they took particular decisions and the consequences of making those decisions.

In terms of method Isabelle decided that the approach she would adopt would be qualitative rather than quantitative. This would involve using in-depth interviews. She would also use life stories and family histories because this kind of biographical approach was more holistic

(Miller 2007). This holistic viewpoint manifested itself in two ways. Firstly, biographical data range across time. Hence, 'a biographical approach is indicated where the area of interest is either the effect of change across time, historical events as these events have impinged upon the individual, or his or her movement along their life course' (Miller 2007:74). Secondly, the biographical approach is a bridge between social structure and the individual. Social structure is a complex concept in which there was some disagreement among social scientists. But it can be understood to mean a relative enduring pattern of social arrangements within a particular society, group or social organisation. Thus, social structures may constrain the individual's behaviour and expectations. Discussing your biography means telling about the constraints and opportunities, and turning-points that were available in the past and how one dealt with them. The biographical approach is about the intersection between the individual and social structure.

In conducting such research Isabelle knew she had to deal with complex issues with the subject-matter and the method she wanted to adopt. The relationship between the interviewee and interviewer is central to this type of research. She felt she had the emotional maturity to manage the process. Most importantly she felt that the research was rigorous, systematic and relevant to managers in the workplace.

References

Miller, R.L. (2007) *Researching Life Stories and Family Histories*. London: Sage Publications.

Pettigrew, A.M. (2001) 'Management research after modernism', *British Journal of Management*, Vol. 12, pp. 61–70.

Sadri, G. and Marcoulides, G.A. (1997) 'An examination of academic and occupational stress in the USA', *International Journal of Educational Management*, Vol. 11, No. 1, pp. 32–43.

Wheatley, R. (2000) *Taking the Strain. A Survey of Managers and Workplace Stress*. London: Institute of Management.

Questions

1 How do you think Isabelle's understanding of theory and method changed in adopting the approach she chose?
2 What particular knowledge and skills did she develop in preparing this research?
3 What problems do you think she would have anticipated in conducting research into pressure and coping among managers that her literature review may not have identified?

Self-check answers

1.1 The features you outline are likely to include the:

- transdisciplinary nature of business and management research;
- development of ideas that are related to practice and in particular the requirement for the research to have some practical consequence;
- need for research to complete the virtuous circle of theory and practice;
- addressing of problems that grow out of the interaction between the worlds of theory and practice.

1.2 The key differences between basic and applied research relate to both the purpose and the context in which it is undertaken. They are summarised in Figure 1.1.

1.3 Figure 1.2 emphasises the importance of planning during your research project. Forward planning needs to occur at all stages up to submission. In addition, you will need to reflect on and to revise your work throughout the life of the research project. This reflection needs to have a wide focus. You should both consider the stage you have reached and revisit earlier stages and work through them again. Reflection may also lead you to amend your research plan. This should be expected, although large amendments in the later stages of your research project are unlikely.

Get ahead using resources on the Companion Website at:
www.pearsoned.co.uk/saunders

- Improve your SPSS and NVivo research analysis with practice tutorials.
- Save time researching on the Internet with the Smarter Online Searching Guide.
- Test your progress using self-assessment questions.
- Follow live links to useful websites.

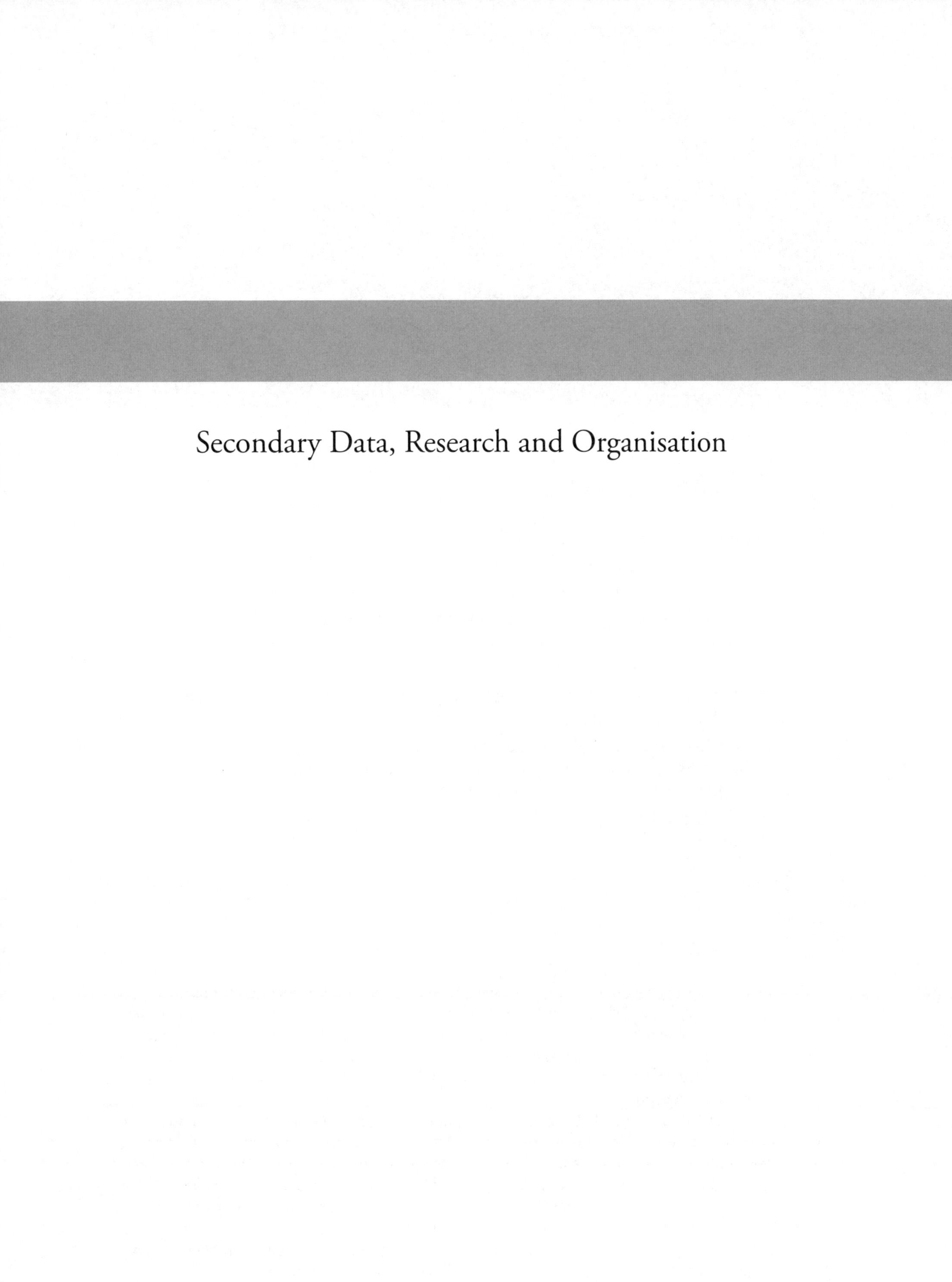

Secondary Data, Research and Organisation

Chapter 8

Using secondary data

Learning outcomes

By the end of this chapter you should be able to:

- identify the full variety of secondary data that are available;
- appreciate ways in which secondary data can be utilised to help to answer research question(s) and to meet objectives;
- understand the advantages and disadvantages of using secondary data in research projects;
- use a range of techniques, including published guides and the Internet, to locate secondary data;
- evaluate the suitability of secondary data for answering research question(s) and meeting objectives in terms of coverage, validity, reliability and measurement bias;
- apply the knowledge, skills and understanding gained to your own research project.

8.1 Introduction

When first considering how to answer their research question(s) or meet their objectives, few of our students consider initially the possibility of reanalysing data that have already been collected for some other purpose. Such data are known as **secondary data**. Most automatically think in terms of collecting new (**primary**) **data** specifically for that purpose. Yet, despite this, such secondary data can provide a useful source from which to answer, or partially to answer, your research question(s).

Secondary data include both raw data and published summaries. Most organisations collect and store a variety of data to support their operations: for example, payroll details, copies of letters, minutes of meetings and accounts of sales of goods or services. Quality daily newspapers contain a wealth of data, including reports about takeover bids and companies' share prices. Government departments undertake surveys and publish official statistics covering social, demographic and economic topics. Consumer research organisations collect data that are used subsequently by different clients. Trade organisations collect data from their members on topics such as sales that are subsequently aggregated and published.

Some of these data, in particular, documents such as company minutes, are available only from the organisations that produce them, and so access will need to be negotiated (Section 6.3). Others, including government surveys such as a census of population, are widely available in published form as well as via the Internet or on CD-ROM in university libraries. A growing variety have been deposited in, and are available from, data archives. In addition, the vast majority of companies and professional organisations have their own Internet sites from which data may be obtained. Online computer databases containing company information can be accessed via the Internet through information gateways, such as Biz/Ed (Table 3.5).

For certain types of research project, such as those requiring national or international comparisons, secondary data will probably provide the main source to answer your research question(s) and to address your objectives. However, if you are undertaking your research project as part of a course of study, we recommend that you check the assessment regulations before

These days, data about people's whereabouts, purchases, behaviour and personal lives are gathered, stored and shared on a scale that no repressive political dictator would ever have thought possible. Much of the time, there is nothing obviously sinister about this. Governments say they need to gather data to assist the fight against terrorism or protect public safety; commercial organisations argue that they do it to deliver goods and services more effectively. But the widespread use of electronic data-gathering and processing is remarkable compared with the situation even as recently as 10 years ago.

We can all think of examples of how the technology reveals information about what we have been doing. The Oyster payment card used on the London Underground system tells those who want to know where we have travelled and at what time; the mobile phone allows identification of where we are at a particular time and the credit card will show where and when we make purchases; many of our telephone calls to call centres are recorded and the search engine Google stores data on our web searches for 18 months.

Such data are obtained every time we interact directly or indirectly with these organisations' electronic systems. These data are often reused for purposes other than that for which they were originally collected.

Oyster card
Source: © Philip Lewis 2008.

They are aggregated to provide information about, for example, different geographical regions or social groups. They are merged with other data to form new data sets, the creation of these secondary data sets allowing new relationships to be explored. They are also made available or sold to other people and organisations for new purposes as secondary data.

deciding to rely entirely on secondary data. You may be required to collect primary data for your research project. Most research questions are answered using some combination of secondary and primary data. Where limited appropriate secondary data are available, you will have to rely mainly on data you collect yourself.

In this chapter we examine the different types of secondary data that are likely to be available to help you to answer your research question(s) and meet your objectives, how you might use them (Section 8.2), and a range of methods, including published guides, for locating these data (Section 8.3). We then consider the advantages and disadvantages of using secondary data (Section 8.4) and discuss ways of evaluating their validity and reliability (Section 8.5). We do not attempt to provide a comprehensive list of secondary data sources, as this would be an impossible task within the space available.

8.2 Types of secondary data and uses in research

Secondary data include both quantitative and qualitative data (Section 5.4), and they are used principally in both descriptive and explanatory research. The data you use may be **raw data**, where there has been little if any processing, or **compiled data** that have received some form of selection or summarising (Kervin 1999). Within business and management research such data are used most frequently as part of a case study or survey research strategy. However, there is no reason not to include secondary data in other research strategies, including archival research, action research and experimental research.

Different researchers (e.g. Bryman 1989; Dale *et al.* 1988; Hakim 1982, 2000; Robson 2002) have generated a variety of classifications for secondary data. These classifications do not, however, capture the full variety of data. We have therefore built on their ideas to create three main sub-groups of secondary data: documentary data, survey-based data, and those compiled from multiple sources (Figure 8.1).

Documentary secondary data

Documentary secondary data are often used in research projects that also use primary data collection methods. However, you can also use them on their own or with other sources of secondary data, for example for business history research within an archival research strategy. Documentary secondary data include written materials such as notices, correspondence (including emails), minutes of meetings, reports to shareholders, diaries, transcripts of speeches and administrative and public records (Box 8.1). Written documents can also include books, journal and magazine articles and newspapers. These can be important raw data sources in their own right, as well as a storage medium for compiled data. You could use written documents to provide qualitative data such as managers' espoused reasons for decisions. They could also be used to generate statistical measures such as data on absenteeism and profitability derived from company records (Bryman 1989).

Documentary secondary data also include non-written materials (Figure 8.2), such as voice and video recordings, pictures, drawings, films and television programmes (Robson 2002), DVDs and CD-ROMs as well as organisations' databases. These data can be analysed both quantitatively and qualitatively. In addition, they can be used to help to triangulate findings based on other data, such as written documents and primary data collected through observation, interviews or questionnaires (Chapters 9, 10 and 11).

For your research project, the documentary sources you have available will depend on whether you have been granted access to an organisation's records as well as on your

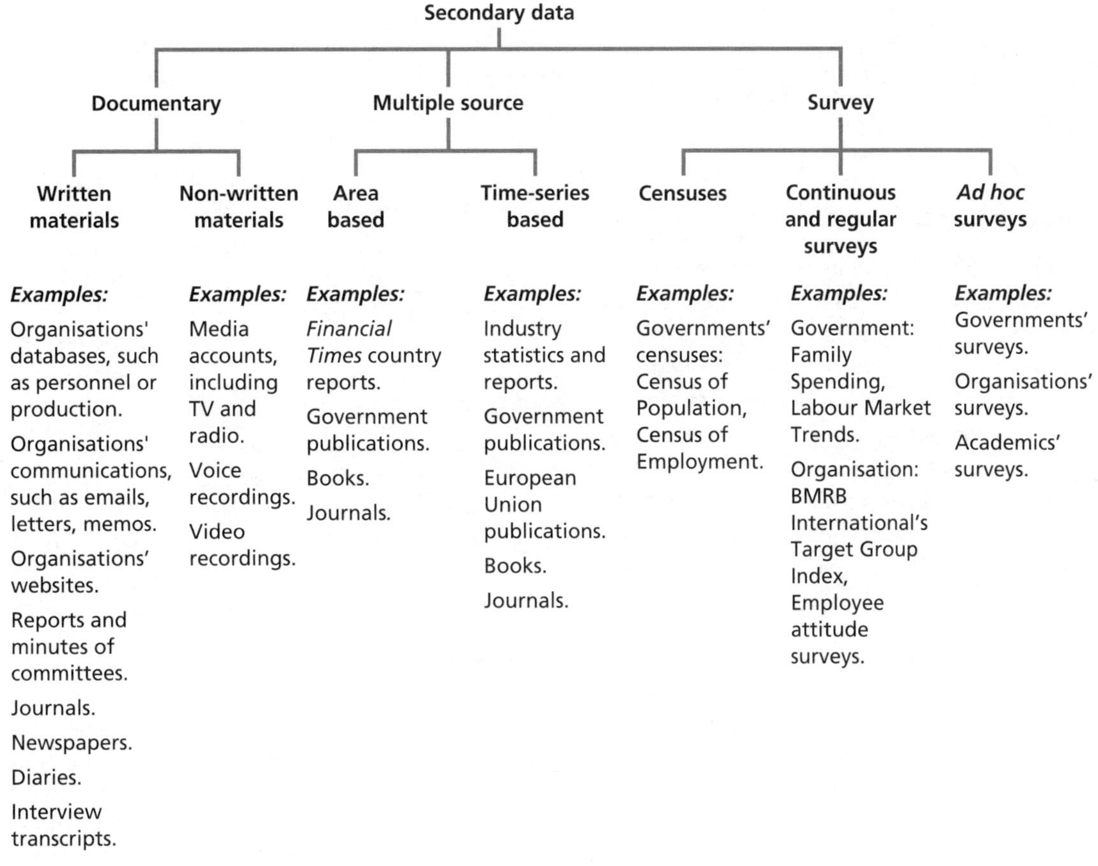

Figure 8.1 Types of secondary data
Source: © Mark Saunders, Philip Lewis and Adrian Thornhill, 2006.

success in locating library, data archive and commercial sources (Section 8.3). Access to an organisation's data will be dependent on gatekeepers within that organisation (Section 6.3). In our experience, those research projects that make use of documentary secondary data often do so as part of a within-company action research project or a case study of a particular organisation.

Survey-based secondary data

Survey-based secondary data refers to data collected using a survey strategy, usually by questionnaires (Chapter 11) that have already been analysed for their original purpose. Such data normally refer to organisations, people or households. They are made available as compiled data tables or, increasingly frequently, as a downloadable matrix of raw data (Section 12.2) for secondary analysis.

Survey-based secondary data will have been collected through one of three distinct sub-types of survey strategy: censuses, continuous/regular surveys or ad hoc surveys (Figure 8.1). Censuses are usually carried out by governments and are unique because, unlike surveys, participation is obligatory (Hakim 2000). Consequently, they provide very good coverage of the population surveyed. They include censuses of population, which have been carried out in many countries since the eighteenth century and in the UK

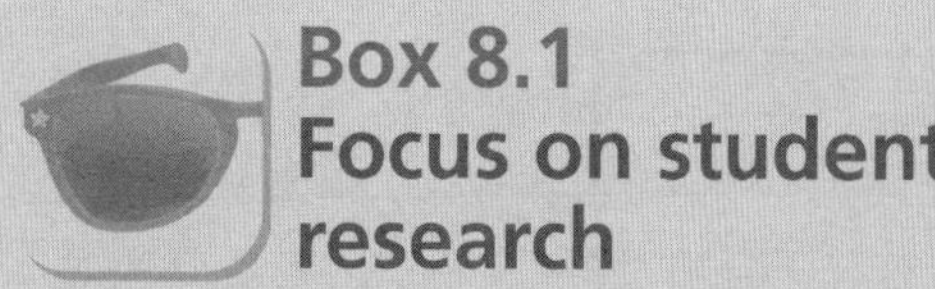

Box 8.1 Focus on student research

Using documentary secondary data

Sasha was interested in how her work placement organisation dealt with complaints by customers. Her mentor within the organisation arranged for her to have access to the paper-based files containing customers' letters of complaint and the replies sent by the organisation's customer-relations team (written documentary secondary data). Reading through the customer's letters, Sasha soon realised that many of these customers wrote to complain because they had not received a satisfactory response when they had complained earlier by telephone. She, therefore, asked her mentor if records were kept of complaints made by customers by telephone. Her mentor said that summary details of all telephone conversations by the customer-relations team, including complaints, were kept in their database (written documentary secondary data) and offered to find out precisely what data were held. Her mentor was, however, doubtful as to whether these data would be as detailed as the customers' letters.

On receiving details of the data held in the customer-relations database, Sasha realised that the next stage would be to match the complaints data from the paper-based files with telephone complaints data. The latter, she hoped, would enable her to to obtain a complete list of all complaints and set the written complaints in context of all complaints received by the organisation.

since 1801 (Office for National Statistics 2001), and other surveys, such as the UK Annual Survey of Hours and Earnings. Published tabulations are available via the Internet for more recent UK censuses, but it is now also possible to obtain the raw data 100 years after census via the Internet (see Table 8.3). In contrast, the UK Annual Survey of Hours and Earnings, which replaced the New Earnings Survey (1970–2003), provides information on the levels, make-up and distribution of earnings as well as details of hours worked and is only published online (Office for National Statistics 2007a). The data from censuses conducted by many governments are intended to meet the needs of government departments as well as of local government. As a consequence they are usually clearly defined, well documented and of a high quality. Such data are easily accessible in compiled form, and are widely used by other organisations and individual researchers.

Continuous and regular surveys are those surveys, excluding censuses, that are repeated over time (Hakim 1982). They include surveys where data are collected throughout the year, such as the UK's *Social Trends* (Office for National Statistics 2007d), and those repeated at regular intervals. The latter include the Labour Force Survey, which since 1998 has been undertaken quarterly using a core set of questions by Member States throughout the European Union. This means that some comparative data are available for Member States, although access to these data is limited by European and individual countries' legislation (Office for National Statistics 2007a). Non-governmental bodies also carry out regular surveys. These include general-purpose market research surveys such as BMRB International's Target Group Index. Because of the Target Group Index's commercial nature, the data are very expensive. However, BMRB International has provided copies of reports (usually over three years old) to between 20 and 30 UK university libraries. Many large organisations undertake regular surveys, a common example being the employee attitude survey. However, because of the sensitive nature of such information, it is often difficult to gain access to such survey data, especially in its raw form.

Census and continuous and regular survey data provide a useful resource with which to compare or set in context your own research findings. Aggregate data are often available via the Internet, on CD-ROMs or in published form in libraries (Section 8.3), in particular, for government surveys. When using these data you need to check when they were collected, as it often takes at least a year for publication to occur! If you are undertaking research in one UK organisation, you could use these data to place your case-study organisation within the context of its industry group or division using the Census of Employment. Aggregated results of the Census of Employment can be found in *Labour Market Trends* as well as via the UK government's official statistics information gateway *national statistics*. Alternatively, you might explore issues already highlighted by data from an organisation survey through in-depth interviews.

Survey secondary data may be available in sufficient detail to provide the main data set from which to answer your research question(s) and to meet your objectives. Alternatively, they may be the only way in which you can obtain the required data. If your research question is concerned with national variations in consumer spending it is unlikely that you will be able to collect sufficient data. You, therefore, will need to rely on secondary data such as those contained in *Family Spending* (formerly the Family Expenditure Survey; Office for National Statistics 2007b). This reports findings from the Expenditure and Foods Survey. For some research questions and objectives suitable data will be available in published form. For others, you may need more disaggregated data. This may be available via the Internet (Section 3.4), on CD-ROM, or from archives (Section 8.3). We have found that for most business and management research involving secondary data you are unlikely to find all the data you require from one source. Rather, your research project is likely to involve detective work in which you build your own multiple-source data set using different data items from a variety of secondary data sources and perhaps linking these to primary data you have collected yourself (Box 8.2). Like all detective work, finding data that help to answer a research question or meet an objective is immensely satisfying.

Box 8.2 Focus on management research

Comparing eating habits in 1975 and 2000

Since 1975 food preparation and consumption in the UK has seen further and more intense dependence on food being treated as a commercial commodity. Eating and drinking out, the growth of pre-prepared convenience foods and the diffusion of domestic technologies have all impacted on the way in which food is provisioned and consumed. By 2000 eating and drinking out had become a thoroughly established social norm and food preparation a less time consuming activity.

In an article published in the *British Journal of Sociology*, Cheng *et al.* (2007) explore the sociological dimension of food consumption in the UK in the past three decades, the conclusions of which are of great interest and commercial value to all those industries concerned with the food provision.

Cheng *et al.* used two sets of data on individuals' use of time. The first consisted of data on 1274 people in 1975 and the second, 8522 in 2000. Individuals were asked to keep diaries for seven days in 1975 and for one weekday and one weekend day in 2000. They were asked to record their activities in slots of 30 minutes in 1975 and 10 minutes in 2000. Cheng *et al.* used statistical techniques to take account of over-sampling of specific sub-groups and non-response and corrected for the distributions of sex and age and to bring the sample in line with the national population. Descriptive statistics of mean minutes spent in the components of the practice of eating, and rates of participation, were calculated in order to provide a broad overview of trends in food consumption. Multiple regression analysis was then employed to analyse the socio-demographic basis of the amount of time devoted to the various components of the practice of eating.

Cheng *et al.* found that there has been an overall decline in the amount of time devoted to the consumption of food in the UK. However they found that while time diary data provides strong confirmation of the greater pervasiveness of commercially prepared food provisioning, many aspects of the performance of eating are resilient to change. The researchers saw a substantial increase in the amount of time allocated to eating and drinking

Box 8.2 Focus on management research (continued)

away from home, and also greater variety in the duration of episodes. However, the duration of episodes for eating at home has remained stable since 1975. Cheng *et al.* found that eating out substitutes for eating at home to some extent, but does not cause a radical transformation in patterns of home-based eating and drinking. Thirdly the authors demonstrated that the shifting temporal organisation of daily life does not appear to transform eating events. They noted an increase in episodes of eating out that are of a short duration, but no apparent decline in longer episodes. Eating remains a sociable and collective practice, despite shifting temporal pressures which make the coordination of eating events within social networks more difficult.

Social differentiation on the basis of employment status, gender, age and household composition persist. Data analysis reveals that some social divisions have eroded; but others persist, with household structure becoming a more important source of differentiation.

Ad hoc surveys are usually one-off surveys and are far more specific in their subject matter. They include data from questionnaires that have been undertaken by independent researchers as well as interviews undertaken by organisations and governments. Because of their *ad hoc* nature, you will probably find it more difficult to discover relevant surveys. However, it may be that an organisation in which you are undertaking research has conducted its own questionnaire, on an issue related to your research. Some organisations will provide you with a report containing aggregated data; others may be willing to let you reanalyse the raw data from this *ad hoc* survey. Alternatively, you may be able to gain access to and use raw data from an *ad hoc* survey that has been deposited in an archive (Section 8.3).

Multiple-source secondary data

Multiple-source secondary data can be based entirely on documentary or on survey secondary data, or can be an amalgam of the two. The key factor is that different data sets have been combined to form another data set prior to your accessing the data. One of the more common types of multiple-source data that you are likely to come across in document form is various compilations of company information such as *Europe's 15,000 Largest Companies* (ELC International 2007). This contains comparable data on the top 15 000 European companies ranked by sales, profits and number of employees as well as alphabetical listings. Other multiple-source secondary data include the various shares price listings for different stock markets in the financial pages of quality newspapers. These are available in most university libraries, including back copies CD-ROM or microfilm. However, you need to beware of relying on CD-ROM copies for tabular data or diagrams as a few still contain only the text of articles.

The way in which a multiple-source data set has been compiled will dictate the sorts of research question(s) or objectives with which you can use it. One method of compilation is to extract and combine selected comparable variables from a number of surveys or from the same survey that has been repeated a number of times to provide a **time series** of data. For many research projects of undergraduate and taught Masters courses, this is one of the few ways in which you will be able to get data over a long period to undertake a longitudinal study. Other ways of obtaining time-series data are to use a series of company documents, such as appointment letters or public and administrative records, to create your own longitudinal secondary data set. Examples include the UK Employment Department's stoppages at work data held by the Data Archive based at the University of Essex and those derived by researchers from nineteenth-century population census returns, which, in the UK, are accessible to the public after 100 years.

Data can also be compiled for the same population over time using a series of 'snapshots' to form **cohort studies**. Such studies are relatively rare, owing to the difficulty of maintaining contact with members of the cohort from year to year. An example is the UK television series, 'Seven Up' (already mentioned in Section 5.5), which has followed a cohort since they were schoolchildren at seven-year intervals for over 50 years.

Secondary data from different sources can also be combined, if they have the same geographical basis, to form area-based data sets (Hakim 2000). Such data sets usually draw together quantifiable information and statistics, and are commonly produced by governments for their country. Area-based multiple-source data sets are usually available in published form for the countries and their component standard economic planning regions. Those more widely used by our students include the UK's *Annual Abstract of Statistics* (Office for National Statistics 2008), *Europe in figures: Eurostat Yearbook 2008* (Eurostat 2008a) and the journal, *Labour Market Trends*. Area-based multiple-source data sets are also available from data archives. These include data such as the Labour Force Survey (Office for National Statistics 2007c) and Eurostat's statistical data collections for member countries (Eurostat 2008b).

8.3 Locating secondary data

Unless you are approaching your research project with the intention of analysing one specific secondary data set that you already know well, your first step will be to ascertain whether the data you need are available. Your research question(s), objectives and the literature you have reviewed will guide this. For many research projects you are likely to be unsure as to whether the data you require are available as secondary data. Fortunately, there are a number of pointers to the sorts of data that are likely to be available.

The breadth of data discussed in the previous sections serves only to emphasise the variety of possible locations in which such data may be found. Finding relevant secondary data requires detective work, which has two interlinked stages:

1 establishing that the sort of data you require are likely to be available as secondary data;
2 locating the precise data you require.

The availability of secondary data

There are a number of clues to whether the secondary data you require are likely to be available. As part of your literature review you will have already read books and journal articles on your chosen topic. Where these have made use of secondary data, they will provide you with an idea of the sort of data that are available. In addition, these books and articles should contain full references to the sources of the data. Where these refer to published secondary data such as multiple-source or survey reports it is usually relatively easy to track down the original source. Quality national newspapers are also often a good source as they often report summary findings of recent government reports. Your tutors have probably already suggested that you read a quality national newspaper on a regular basis, advice we would fully endorse as it is an excellent way of keeping up to date with recent events in the business world. In addition, there are now many online news services, such as BBC News Online (see Box 8.3).

References for unpublished and documentary secondary data are often less specific, referring to 'unpublished survey results' or an 'in-house company survey'. Although these may be insufficient to locate or access the actual secondary data, they still provide useful clues about the sort of data that might be found within organisations and which might prove useful. Subject-specific textbooks such as Curran and Blackburn's (2001) *Researching the Small Enterprise* can provide a clear indication of the secondary sources available in

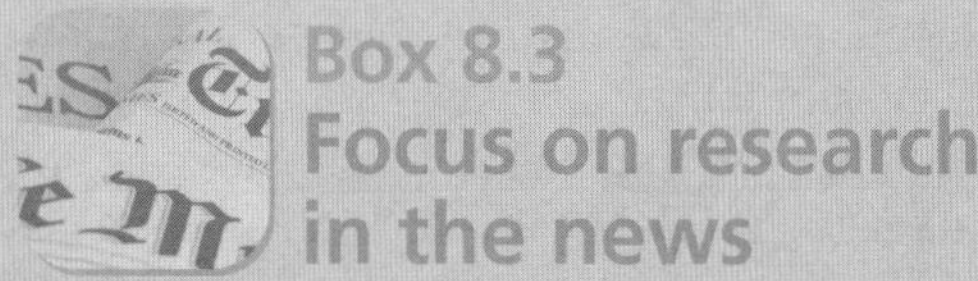

Britain's favourite fakes: public attitudes to counterfeiting

A 2008 episode of the BBC TV business programme, 'The Money Programme' revealed that counterfeiting cost Britain around £11 bn last year. The programme compared 2008 with the situation 20 years ago when the counterfeiting business was 1 per cent of the its 2008 size. The programme advanced the view that counterfeiting is a serious problem for businesses. A contributor to the programme felt that if businesses had a line in their annual report detailing sales lost due to counterfeits, then more would be done to solve the problem.

The British Video Association believes that nearly 80 million fake DVDs are bought each year in Britain, and it appears to be a growing problem. In 2007, 2.8 million fake DVDs were seized by the authorities, a 74 per cent increase on the previous year. Electrical goods giant Canon has seen its video cameras, and printer cartridges counterfeited. The whole electronics industry is affected. In Europe the printer cartridge market is worth some €30 bn ($44 bn; £22 bn) a year and it's estimated that 7 per cent of it is counterfeit. More worryingly, Canon and other electronics manufacturers are concerned about the rise in counterfeiting of products including batteries and chargers. These fakes have the potential to kill.

A 2007 MORI survey (IPSOS MORI 2007) of 996 adults aged 15+ in the UK shows that perfume/fragrance (67%), watches (64%) and clothing/footwear (63%) are among the most widely known goods to be counterfeited. 40% of respondents said that they would knowingly purchase a counterfeit product if the price and quality of the goods were acceptable. Among these people, the most popular counterfeit goods to purchase were clothing/footwear (76%), watches (43%) and perfume/fragrance (38%).

Around a third of respondents said that they would contact the local trading standards office if they had unknowingly purchased a counterfeit product. However, 29 per cent said that they would not do anything and that they would put it down to experience. Sixty-five per cent agreed that they were against any form of product counterfeiting, and 69 per cent said that the government should do more to tackle the problem of product counterfeiting.

The survey tested the level of the problems that counterfeiting causes: 61 per cent of respondents believed that the government loses millions of pounds in VAT and other taxes because of counterfeiting; 57 per cent thought that counterfeiting can damage the economic well-being of businesses; 56 per cent felt that some fake or counterfeit products can put the purchaser at risk of personal injury or death, and 39 per cent thought that counterfeiting is very often one of the most profitable (and virtually risk-free) illegal activities of organised criminals and terrorists and helps to fund drug dealing.

Source: derived from an article by Harcourt-Webster, Adam (2008) 'BBC Business', 14 Feb. Available at: http://news.bbc.co.uk/1/hi/business/7245040.stm

your research area, in this instance small enterprises. Other textbooks, such as Kingsbury's (1997) *IT Answers to HR Questions*, can provide you with valuable clues about the sort of documentary secondary data that are likely to exist within organisations' management information systems.

Tertiary literature such as indexes and catalogues can also help you to locate secondary data (Sections 3.2–3.4). Data archive catalogues, such as for the UK Data Archive at the University of Essex, may prove a useful source of the sorts of secondary data available.[1] This archive holds the UK's largest collection of qualitative and quantitative digital social science and humanities data sets for use by the research community (UK Data

[1]There are numerous other data archives in Europe and the USA. The UK Data Archive can provide access to international data through cooperative agreements and memberships of data archives throughout the world. It also provides a useful gateway to other data archives' websites, such as the Danish Data Archive, DDA and the Dutch Data Archive, Steinmetz (UK Data Archive 2008).

Archive, 2008). These data have been acquired from academic, commercial and government sources, and relate mainly to post-war Britain. The complete catalogue of these can be accessed and searched via the Internet (Section 3.5) through the Archive's home page (see Table 8.2). However, it should be remembered that the supply of data and documentation for all of the UK Data Archive's data sets is charged at cost, and there may be additional administrative and royalty charges.

More recently, online indexes and catalogues have become available with direct linkages to downloadable files, often in spreadsheet format. Government websites such as the UK government's *Directgov* and the European Union's *Europa* provide useful gateways to a wide range of statistical data, reports and legislative documents. However, although data from such government sources are usually of good quality, those from other sources may be neither valid nor reliable. It is important, therefore, that you evaluate the suitability of such secondary data for your research (Section 8.5).

Informal discussions are also often a useful source. Acknowledged experts, colleagues, librarians or your project tutor may well have knowledge of the sorts of data that might be available. In addition, there is a range of published guides to secondary data sources. Those business and management guides that we, and our students, have found most useful are outlined in Table 8.1. However, there are also guides that provide more detail on sources for specific subject areas such as marketing and finance.

Finding secondary data

Once you have ascertained that secondary data are likely to exist, you need to find their precise location. For secondary data published by governments this will be quite easy. Precise references are often given in published guides (Table 8.1) and, where other researchers have made use of them, a full reference should exist. Locating published secondary data that are likely to be held by libraries or secondary data held in archives is relatively

Table 8.1 Published guides to possible secondary data sources

Guide	Coverage
Corris, A., Yin, B. and Ricketts, C. (2000) *Guide to Official Statistics*. London: Office for National Statistics. Available at: http://www.statistics.gov.uk/downloads/theme_compendia/GOS2000_v5.pdf	Official statistics produced by UK government
Mort, D. (2002) *Business Information Handbook*. Headland: Headland Press	Company and market information, online business information and a who's who in business information
Mort, D. and Wilkins, W. (2000) *Sources of Unofficial United Kingdom Statistics* (4th edn). Aldershot: Gower	Unofficial UK statistics collected by major survey organisations; lists of who produces these data
Library Association (2005) *Libraries in the United Kingdom and Republic of Ireland*. London: Library Association	Lists of 3000 libraries in the UK and Eire
Dale, P. (2004) *Guide to Libraries and Information Units in Government Departments and Other Organisations* (34th edn). London: British Library Publishing	Lists libraries and information services in UK government departments and related agencies
McKenzie, E. (2003) *Guide to Libraries in Key UK Companies*. London: British Library	Lists libraries in UK companies that are prepared to accept serious enquiries from outside

Box 8.4 Focus on management research

Using content analysis of the literature to study cross-cultural advertising research

An article in *International Marketing Review* (Okazaki and Mueller 2007) reports a study of the recent history of cross-cultural advertising research and suggests new directions in exploring the role that culture plays in cross-national commercial communications.

To assess the research to date, the authors studied previously conducted content analyses of the literature, and updated these by performing an expanded longitudinal citation analysis of cross-cultural advertising investigations. They used only studies which examined two or more countries in the analysis. Articles were selected from seven journals considered representative in terms of international marketing and advertising research. The publications were analysed by topic areas addressed, research methods employed, and countries examined.

Okazaki and Mueller's analysis revealed that cultural values were the most studied topic area. In terms of methodology, content analysis was the most widely employed approach, followed by surveys. North America and the 'original' EU member countries were most frequently investigated. In contrast, they found that research focusing on newer EU member countries was limited Moreover, there was notable lack of research on Latin America, the Middle East and, in particular, Africa.

Okazaki and Mueller summarised the major cultural theories that have dominated cross-cultural advertising research to date, including Hofstede's (1980) cultural dimensions, albeit they notcd that researchers are turning to other disciplines for new insights.

straightforward (Box 8.4). Specialist libraries with specific subject collections such as market research reports can usually be located using the Library Association's (2005) publication or guides by Dale (2004) and McKenzie (2003) (Table 8.1). If you are unsure where to start, confess your ignorance and ask a librarian. This will usually result in a great deal of helpful advice, as well as saving you time. Once the appropriate abstracting tool or catalogue has been located and its use demonstrated, it can be searched using similar techniques to those employed in your literature search (Section 3.5).

Data that are held by organisations are more difficult to locate. For within-organisation data we have found that the information or data manager within the appropriate department is most likely to know the precise secondary data that are held. This is the person who will also help or hinder your eventual access to the data and can be thought of as the gatekeeper to the information (Section 6.3).

Data on the Internet can be located using information gateways such as the University of Michigan's Documents Center (Table 8.2), and search tools where you search for all possible locations that match key words associated with your research question(s) or objectives (Section 3.5). In some cases data will be located at sites hosted by companies and professional organisations and trade associationsu. A good way of finding an organisation's home page is to use a general search engine (Table 3.5) or, in the case of UK-based companies, the links provided by the Yellow Pages UK subject directory (Table 3.5). Additional guidance regarding how to use general search engines such as Google is given in Marketing Insights' *Smarter Internet Searching Guide*, which is available via this book's web page. However, searching for relevant data is often very time consuming. In addition, although the amount of data on the Internet is increasing rapidly, some of it is, in our experience, of dubious quality. The evaluation of secondary data sources, including those available via the Internet, is discussed in Section 8.5.

Once you have located a possible secondary data set, you need to be certain that it will meet your needs. For documentary data or data in a published form the easiest way is to

Table 8.2 Selected information gateways to secondary data on the Internet

Name	Internet address	Comment
Biz/ed	http://www.bized.co.uk/	Gateway for primary and secondary business and management information. UK focus
Directgov	http://www.direct.gov.uk/	UK government information service with links to government departments, official statistics, etc.
Europa	http://europa.eu.int	Information (including press releases, legislation, fact sheets) published by European Union. Links include Eurostat statistics information gateway
RBA Information Services	http://www.rba.co.uk/	Business information gateway with links to business, statistical, government and country sites
SOSIG	http://www.sosig.ac.uk	Evaluates and describes social science sites including those with statistical data. UK focus
UK Data Archive	http://www.data-archive.ac.uk	Collection of UK digital data in the social science and humanities fields. Links to data archives worldwide
University of Michigan	http://www.lib.umich.edu/govdocs/	Although predominantly American in focus, has excellent annotated links to international agencies, non-American governmental websites and their statistical agencies

obtain and evaluate a sample copy of the data and a detailed description of how it was collected. For survey data that are available in computer-readable form, this is likely to involve some cost. One alternative is to obtain and evaluate detailed definitions for the data set variables (which include how they are coded; Section 12.2) and the documentation that describes how the data were collected. This evaluation process is discussed in Section 8.5.

Table 8.3 Selected secondary data sites on the Internet

Name	Internet address	Comment
Economic and Social Data Service (ESDS)	http://www.esds.ac.uk	Access to and support for economic and social data, both quantitative and qualitative for both the UK and other countries
FT Info	http://news.ft.com/	Company information on 11 000 companies, including financial performance
Global Market Information Database	http://www.gmid.euromonitor.com	Produced by Euromonitor. Key business intelligence on countries, companies, markets, and consumers
Hemscott	http://www.hemscott.net	Hemmington Scott's guide to companies and investment trusts, report service and market activity analysis
Hoover's Online	http://www.hoovers.com	Company information on 12 000 US and international companies
MIMAS	http://www.mimas.ac.uk	National data centre for UK higher education institutions providing access to key data such as UK census. NB: for some data sets you will need to register through your university

Table 8.3 *(continued)*

Countries	Internet address	Comment
European Union	http://europa.eu.int/comm/eurostat/	Site of European Union's statistical information service. This site is available in English as well as other languages
France	http://www.insee.fr	Site of France's National Institute for Statistics including both statistics and government publications. Much of this website is available in English
Germany	http://www.destatis.de	Site of Germany's Federal Statistical Office with a number of useful links. Much of this website is available in English
Ireland (Eire)	http://www.cso.ie	Site of the Irish Central Statistical Office (CSO), the government body responsible for compiling Irish official statistics
Netherlands	http://www.cbs.nl	Site of the Netherland's Central Bureau of Statistics (CBS). Much of this website is available in English. Provides access to StatLine, which contains statistical data that can be downloaded free of charge
United Kingdom	http://www.statistics.gov.uk	The official UK statistics site containing official UK statistics and information about statistics, which can be accessed and downloaded free of charge

8.4 Advantages and disadvantages of secondary data

Advantages

May have fewer resource requirements

For many research questions and objectives the main advantage of using secondary data is the enormous saving in resources, in particular your time and money (Ghauri and Grønhaug 2005). In general, it is much less expensive to use secondary data than to collect the data yourself. Consequently, you may be able to analyse far larger data sets such as those collected by government surveys. You will also have more time to think about theoretical aims and substantive issues, as your data will already be collected, and subsequently you will be able to spend more time and effort analysing and interpreting the data.

Unobtrusive

If you need your data quickly, secondary data may be the only viable alternative. In addition, they are likely to be higher-quality data than could be obtained by collecting your own (Stewart and Kamins 1993). Using secondary data within organisations may also have the advantage that, because they have already been collected, they provide an unobtrusive measure. Cowton (1998) refers to this advantage as eavesdropping, emphasising its benefits for sensitive situations.

Longitudinal studies may be feasible

For many research projects time constraints mean that secondary data provide the only possibility of undertaking longitudinal studies. This is possible either by creating your own or by using an existing multiple-source data set (Section 8.2). Comparative research may also be possible if comparable data are available. You may find this to be of particular use for research questions and objectives that require regional or international comparisons. However, you need to ensure that the data you are comparing were collected and recorded using methods that are comparable. Comparisons relying on unpublished data or data that are currently unavailable in that format, such as the creation of new tables from existing census data, are likely to be expensive, as such tabulations will have to be specially prepared. In addition, your research is dependent on access being granted by the owners of the data, principally governments (Dale *et al.* 1988), although this is becoming easier as more data is made available via the Internet. In addition, many countries are enshrining increased rights of access to information held by public authorities through freedom of information legislation such as the UK's Freedom of Information Act 2005. This gives you a general right to access to recorded information held by public authorities, although a charge may be payable (Information Commissioner's Office 2008). However, this is dependent upon your request not being contrary to relevant data protection legislation or agreements (Chapter 6.5).

Can provide comparative and contextual data

Often it can be useful to compare data that you have collected with secondary data. This means that you can place your own findings within a more general context or, alternatively, triangulate your findings (Section 5.3). If you have undertaken a sample survey, perhaps of potential customers, secondary data such as the Census can be used to assess the generalisability of findings, in other words how representative these data are of the total population (Section 7.2).

Can result in unforeseen discoveries

Re-analysing secondary data can also lead to unforeseen or unexpected new discoveries. Dale *et al.* (1988) cite establishing the link between smoking and lung cancer as an example of such a serendipitous discovery. In this example the link was established through secondary analysis of medical records that had not been collected with the intention of exploring any such relationship.

Permanence of data

Unlike data that you collect yourself, secondary data generally provide a source of data that is both permanent and available in a form that may be checked relatively easily by others (Denscombe 2007). This means that the data and your research findings are more open to public scrutiny.

Disadvantages

May be collected for a purpose that does not match your need

Data that you collect yourself will be collected with a specific purpose in mind: to answer your research question(s) and to meet your objectives. Unfortunately, secondary data will

Box 8.5 Focus on management research

The pitfalls of secondary data

Alison Wolf is the Sir Roy Griffiths Professor of public-sector management at King's College, London. In a 2007 article in *The Times Higher Education Supplement* (Wolf 2007), she issues some warnings to students using secondary data in their research, particularly in an era when such data are readily available on the Internet. Her main concern is the lack of questioning that many of us adopt when approaching secondary data. In her view many of us 'have a tendency to assume that quantitative data must be out there waiting to be found: on the web, organised and collated. How the figures get there and who collected the data and analysed them are not questions they seem to ask. Nor do they probe definitions (let alone response rates) – or not unless and until they start trying to locate, manipulate and integrate a variety of data on a specific subject' (Wolf 2007).

According to Wolf, some of the major pitfalls are assuming that samples are representative; and that the people who filled in questionnaires all did so in such a way that we can put faith in the results. They may not have been truthful in their responses, have taken the questions seriously or, indeed, have understood fully the questions. Moreover, Wolf notes that it should not be assumed that whoever coded and entered the data knew what they were doing; and that it was clear what all the observations meant.

Wolf gives the exampe of one of her recent students who wanted to track how many history graduates from a given university enter teaching over a 20-year period. She points out that 'teaching' as a recorded student destination sometimes includes further education as well as schools, sometimes includes higher education as well, sometimes neither. Also, what counts as a 'history' graduate, may not be clear.

Wolf sounds other warning using the example of official UK governemnt statistics. First, statistics that were routinely calculated can suddenly disappear. She gives the example of the decision, by the Office for National Statistics, suddenly to stop calculating average non-manual earnings. This caused major problems for one of her students. In addition, and more frequently, definitions change constantly in ways that seem to be dictated by changing government priorities which makes it difficult to track changes over time. Wolf cites the example of education, where statistics are reported in terms of performance targets that keep changing. She concludes that this is as serious matter as good statistics are at the heart of governmental accountability, as well as good policymaking.

have been collected for a specific purpose that differs from your research question(s) or objectives (Denscombe 2007). Consequently, the data you are considering may be inappropriate to your research question. If this is the case then you need to find an alternative source, or collect the data yourself! More probably, you will be able to answer your research question or address your objective only partially. Common reasons for this include the data being collected a few years earlier and so not being current, or the methods of collection differing between the original data sources which have been amalgamated subsequently to form the secondary data set you intend to use (Box 8.5). Where the data are non-current and you have access to primary data, such as in a research project that is examining an issue within an organisation, you are likely to have to combine secondary and primary data.

Access may be difficult or costly

Where data have been collected for commercial reasons, gaining access may be difficult or costly. Market research reports, such as those produced by Mintel or KeyNote, may cost a great deal. If the report(s) that you require are not available in your library, they can rarely be accessed free of charge via the Internet or borrowed on inter-library loan and you will need to identify (Section 8.3) and visit the library that holds that collection.

Aggregations and definitions may be unsuitable

The fact that secondary data were collected for a particular purpose may result in other, including ethical (Section 6.4), problems. Much of the secondary data you use is likely to be in published reports. As part of the compilation, process data will have been aggregated in some way. These aggregations, while meeting the requirements of the original research, may not be quite so suitable for your research (Box 8.6). The definitions of data variables may not be the most appropriate for your research question(s) or objectives. In addition, where you are intending to combine data sets, definitions may differ markedly or have been revised over time. Alternatively, the documents you are using may represent the interpretations of those who produced them, rather than offer an objective picture of reality.

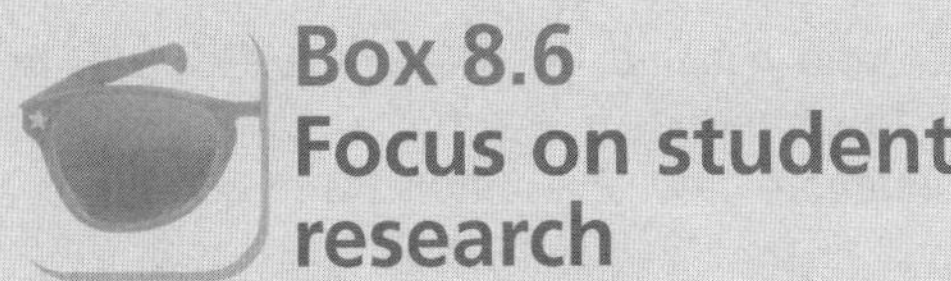

Box 8.6 Focus on student research

Changing definitions

As part of his research, Jeremy wished to use longitudinal data on the numbers of males and females disaggregated by some form of social grouping. Using the UK government's national statistics website (Table 8.3), he quickly found and downloaded data which classified males and females using the National Statistics Socio-economic Classification (NS-SEC). However, this classification appeared to have been used only from 2001. Prior to this date, two separate classifications had been used: social class (SC) and socio-economic group (SEG), for which much longer time series of data were available. Before arranging an appointment with his project tutor to discuss this potential problem, Jeremy made a note of the two classifications:

NS-SEC		SC	
1	Higher managerial and professional occupations	I	Professional
2	Lower managerial and professional occupations	II	Managerial and technical
3	Intermediate occupations	IIIa	Skilled non-manual
4	Small employers and own account workers	IIIb	Skilled manual
5	Lower supervisory and technical occupations	IV	Semi-skilled
6	Semi-routine occupations	V	Unskilled
7	Routine occupations		

During their meeting later that week, Jeremy's tutor referred him to research on the NS-SEC which compared this with the old measures of SC and SEG and made suggestions regarding the continuity of the measures. Jeremy noted down the reference:

Heath, A., Martin, J. and Beerten, R. (2003) 'Old and new social class measures – a comparison', in Rose, D. and Pevalin, D.J. (eds), *A Researcher's Guide to the National Statistics Socio-economic Classification,* London, Sage, pp. 226–42.

No real control over data quality

Although many of the secondary data sets available from governments and data archives are of higher quality than you could ever collect yourself, this is not always the case. For this reason care must be taken and data sources must be evaluated carefully, as outlined in Section 8.5.

Initial purpose may affect how data are presented

When using data that are presented as part of a report you also need to be aware of the purpose of that report and the impact that this will have on the way the data are presented. This is especially so for internal organisational documents and external documents such as published company reports and newspaper reports. Reichman (1962; cited by Stewart and Kamins 1993) emphasises this point referring to newspapers, although the sentiments apply to many documents. He argues that newspapers select what they consider to be the most significant points and emphasise these at the expense of supporting data. This, Reichman states, is not a criticism as the purpose of the reporting is to bring these points to the attention of readers rather than to provide a full and detailed account. However, if we generalise from these ideas, we can see that the culture, predispositions and ideals of those who originally collected and collated the secondary data will have influenced the nature of these data at least to some extent. For these reasons you must evaluate carefully any secondary data you intend to use. Possible ways of doing this are discussed in the next section.

8.5 Evaluating secondary data sources

Secondary data must be viewed with the same caution as any primary data that you collect. You need to be sure that:

- they will enable you to answer your research question(s) and to meet your objectives;
- the benefits associated with their use will be greater than the costs;
- you will be allowed access to the data (Section 6.3).

Secondary sources that appear relevant at first may not on closer examination be appropriate to your research question(s) or objectives. It is therefore important to evaluate the suitability of secondary data sources for your research.

Stewart and Kamins (1993) argue that, if you are using secondary data, you are at an advantage compared with researchers using primary data. Because the data already exist you can evaluate them prior to use. The time you spend evaluating any potential secondary data source is time well spent, as rejecting unsuitable data earlier can save much wasted time later! Such investigations are even more important when you have a number of possible secondary data sources you could use. Most authors suggest a range of validity and reliability (Section 5.6) criteria against which you can evaluate potential secondary data. These, we believe, can be incorporated into a three-stage process (Figure 8.2).

Alongside this process you need also to consider the accessibility of the secondary data. For some secondary data sources, in particular those available via the Internet or in your library, this will not be a problem. It may, however, still necessitate long hours working in the library if the sources are 'for reference only'. For other data sources, such as those within organisations, you need to obtain permission prior to gaining access. This will be necessary even if you are working for the organisation. These issues

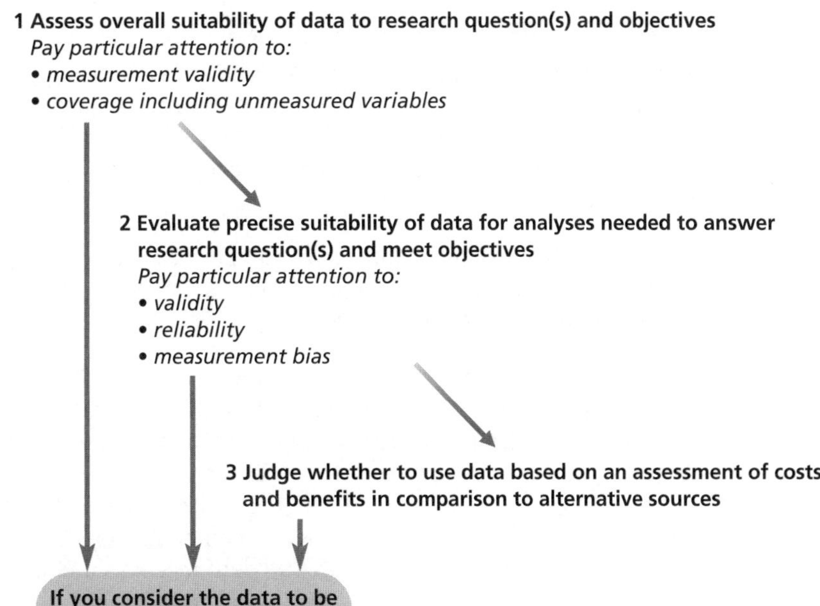

Figure 8.2 Evaluating potential secondary data sources

are discussed in Section 6.3, so we can now consider the evaluation process in more detail.

Overall suitability

Measurement validity

One of the most important criteria for the suitability of any data set is **measurement validity**. Secondary data that fail to provide you with the information that you need to answer your research question(s) or meet your objectives will result in invalid answers (Kervin 1999). Often when you are using secondary survey data you will find that the measures used do not quite match those that you need (Jacob 1994). For example, a manufacturing organisation may record monthly sales whereas you are interested in monthly orders. This may cause you a problem when you undertake your analyses believing that you have found a relationship with sales whereas in fact your relationship is with the number of orders. Alternatively, you may be using minutes of company meetings as a proxy for what actually happened in those meetings. These are likely to reflect a particular interpretation of what happened, the events being recorded from a particular viewpoint, often the chairperson's. You, therefore, need to be cautious before accepting such records at face value (Denscombe 2007).

Unfortunately, there are no clear solutions to problems of measurement invalidity. All you can do is try to evaluate the extent of the data's validity and make your own decision. A common way of doing this is to examine how other researchers have coped with this problem for a similar secondary data set in a similar context. If they found that the measures, while not exact, were suitable, then you can be more certain that they will be suitable for your research question(s) and objectives. If they had problems, then you may be able to incorporate their suggestions as to how to overcome them. Your literature search (Sections 3.4 and 3.5) will probably have identified other such studies already.

Coverage and unmeasured variables

The other important suitability criterion is **coverage**. You need to be sure that the secondary data cover the population about which you need data, for the time period you need, and contain data variables that will enable you to answer your research question(s) and to meet your objectives. For all secondary data sets coverage will be concerned with two issues:

- ensuring that unwanted data are or can be excluded;
- ensuring that sufficient data remain for analyses to be undertaken once unwanted data have been excluded (Hakim 2000).

When analysing secondary survey data, you will need to exclude those data that are not relevant to your research question(s) or objectives. Service companies, for example, need to be excluded if you are concerned only with manufacturing companies. However, in doing this it may be that insufficient data remain for you to undertake the quantitative analyses you require (Sections 12.4 and 12.5). For documentary sources, you will need to ensure that the data contained relate to the population identified in your research. For example, check that the minutes are of board meetings and that they cover the required time period. Where you are intending to undertake a longitudinal study, you also need to ensure that the data are available for the entire period in which you are interested.

Some secondary data sets, in particular those collected using a survey strategy, may not include variables you have identified as necessary for your analysis. These are termed unmeasured variables. Their absence may not be particularly important if you are undertaking descriptive research. However, it could drastically affect the outcome of explanatory research as a potentially important variable has been excluded.

Precise suitability

Reliability and validity

The reliability and validity (Section 5.6) you ascribe to secondary data are functions of the method by which the data were collected and the source. You can make a quick assessment of these by looking at the source of the data. Dochartaigh (2002) and others refer to this as assessing the *authority* or reputation of the source. Survey data from large, well-known organisations such as those found in Mintel and Key Note market research reports are likely to be reliable and trustworthy. The continued existence of such organisations is dependent on the credibility of their data. Consequently, their procedures for collecting and compiling the data are likely to be well thought through and accurate. Survey data from government organisations are also likely to be reliable, although they may not always be perceived as such (Box 8.7). However, you will probably find the validity of documentary data such as organisations' records more difficult to assess. While organisations may argue that their records are reliable, there are often inconsistencies and inaccuracies. You, therefore, need also to examine the method by which the data were collected and try to ascertain the precision needed by the original (primary) user.

Dochartaigh (2002) suggests a number of areas for initial assessment of the authority of documents available via the Internet. These, we believe, can be adapted to assess the authority of all types of secondary data. First, as suggested in the previous paragraph, it is important to discover the person or organisation responsible for the data and to be able to obtain additional information through which you can assess the reliability of the source. For data in printed publications this is usually reasonably straightforward (Section 3.6). However, for secondary data obtained via the Internet it may be more difficult. Although

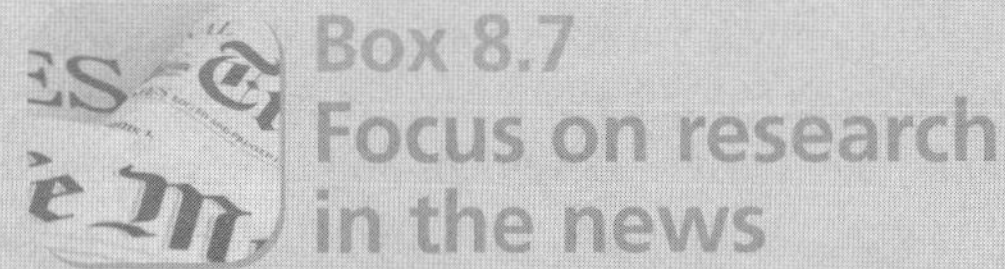

Box 8.7
Focus on research in the news

The validity of politically sensitive data: binge-drinking in Australia

There has been much publicity in the UK in recent years about the problem of so-called 'binge drinking' – a term usually used to refer to heavy drinking over an evening or similar time span – and often associated with drinking with the intention of becoming intoxicated and, usually, in large groups. But it is not a phenomenon that is to be found in only the UK. A report in the *Sydney Morning Herald* (2008) indicates that it is also a problem in Australia. What this report also indicates is the sensitive political nature of subjects such as this which raise questions about the availability and validity of data on the subject.

The *Sydney Morning Herald* reports that two Sydney pubs named hotels of the year over the past three years have also topped a police list of the 100 most violent pubs and clubs in the state. The Mean Fiddler Hotel at Rouse Hill and The Coogee Bay Hotel are ranked one and two on a list of assaults on licensed premises for 2007. The *Herald* has obtained the figures of assaults in pubs and clubs after a year-long freedom-of-information battle to obtain more comprehensive data held by police that include offences committed on the street after drinkers have left licensed premises. While the battle for this detail continues, the assault data provides the best guide yet to where alcohol-related violence is happening. They rank the Mean Fiddler with 51 assaults at the top, followed by the Coogee Bay with 41.

The list of assaults in the top 100 licensed premises, obtained from the New South Wales (NSW) Bureau of Crime Statistics and Research, is based on police records compiled for the first nine months of last year. The figures only record assaults inside the hotel and were certain to grossly understate the real level of assaults, said the director of the NSW Bureau of Crime Statistics and Research, Don Weatherburn. 'We know from national surveys generally that the vast bulk of assaults are not reported,' he said. 'These would be the most serious assaults and probably the tip of the iceberg.' He said that the Bureau of Statistics carried out a national study on violence in 2005 which found that 33.8 per cent of all assaults for males occurred on licensed premises while the figures for all people were 25 per cent. 'That's why I think the police figures grossly underestimate the number of assaults on licensed premises,' said Dr Weatherburn.

The release of the list of the most violent hotels comes a fortnight after the Prime Minister, Kevin Rudd, said binge drinking among young people had reached epidemic proportions, and that police had told him alcohol abuse 'lies at the core of increasing spates of urban violence around the country'. Just before he made his remarks, the Alcohol Education and Rehabilitation Foundation produced a report on violence and alcohol that found one in 10 Australians were frightened by a drunk during the festive season.

Despite growing pressure for new strategies to curb the level of alcohol-fuelled violence, such as curbing the trading hours of late-opening hotels like the Coogee Bay and the Mean Fiddler, NSW Police and the Australian Hotels Association are fighting to stop the release under freedom-of-information laws of data linking alcohol-related incidents to hotels or clubs, including incidents which take place off the premises. The *Herald* has been trying for more than a year to see the data, which have been gathered by police for nearly a decade. Police have been asking people who were victims or perpetrators of an offence where they were last drinking. As well as assaults, the data include other offences, such as driving and malicious damage.

Police say it would cause 'an unreasonable adverse effect' on the hotels to release the data and would undermine the programme that is designed to reduce the number of alcohol-related incidents by discussing the data with the licensees. But many community groups and local-government officials say the data should be released as they would provide people with evidence about problems associated with hotels. The Mayor of Manly, Dr Peter Macdonald, said that there was not enough information available to consumers about problems linked to alcohol. 'The release of the data would allow patrons and potential patrons to know where a large number of incidents are regularly linked to a particular hotel and to include that information when deciding where to go, especially at night.'

organisation names, such as the 'Center for Research into . . .' or 'Institute for the Study of . . .', may appear initially to be credible, publication via the Internet is not controlled, and such names are sometimes used to suggest pseudo-academic credibility. Dochartaigh (2002) therefore suggests that you look also for a copyright statement and the existence of published documents relating to the data to help validation. The former of these, when it exists, can provide an indication of who is responsible for the data. The latter, he argues, reinforces the data's authority, as printed publications are regarded as more reliable. In addition, Internet sources often contain an email address or other means of contacting the author for comments and questions about the Internet site and its contents (Dees 2000). However, beware of applying these criteria too rigidly as sometimes the most authoritative web pages do not include the information outlined above. Dochartaigh (2002) suggests that this is because those with most authority often feel the least need to proclaim it!

For all secondary data, a detailed assessment of the validity and reliability will involve you in an assessment of the method or methods used to collect the data (Dale *et al.* 1988). These may be provided by hyperlinks for Internet-based data sets. Alternatively, they may be discussed in the methodology section of an associated report. Your assessment will involve looking at who were responsible for collecting or recording the information and examining the context in which the data were collected. From this you should gain some feeling regarding the likelihood of potential errors or biases. In addition, you need to look at the process by which the data were selected and collected or recorded. Where sampling has been used to select cases (usually as part of a survey strategy), the sampling procedure adopted and the associated sampling error and response rates (Section 7.2) will give clues to validity. Secondary data collected through a survey with a high response rate are also likely to be more reliable than from that with a low response rate. However, commercial providers of high-quality, reliable data sets may be unwilling to disclose details about how data were collected. This is particularly the case where these organisations see the methodology as important to their competitive advantage.

For some documentary sources, such as diaries, transcripts of interviews or meetings, it is unlikely that there will be a formal methodology describing how the data were collected. The reliability of these data will therefore be difficult to assess, although you may be able to discover the context in which the data were collected. For example, letters, emails and memos contain no formal obligation for the writer to give a full and accurate portrayal of events. Rather they are written from a personal point of view and expect the recipient to be aware of the context (Denscombe 2007). This means that these data are more likely to be useful as a source of the writer's perceptions and views than as an objective account of reality. The fact that you did not collect and were not present when these data were collected will also affect your analyses. Dale *et al.* (1988) argue that full analyses of in-depth interview data require an understanding derived from participating in social interactions that cannot be fully recorded on tape or by transcript.

The validity and reliability of collection methods for survey data will be easier to assess where you have a clear explanation of the techniques used to collect the data. This needs to include a clear explanation of any sampling techniques used and response rates (discussed earlier) as well as a copy of the survey instrument, which will usually be a questionnaire. By examining the questions by which data were collected, you will gain a further indication of the validity.

Where data have been compiled, as in a report, you need to pay careful attention to how these data were analysed and how the results are reported. Where percentages (or proportions) are used without actually giving the totals on which these figures are based, you need to examine the data very carefully. For example, a 50 per cent increase in the number of clients from two to three for a small company may be of less relevance than the 20 per cent increase in the number of clients from 1000 to 1200 for a larger company in the same market! Similarly, where quotations appear to be used selectively without other supporting evidence you should beware, as the data may be unreliable. Remember, the further away you are from the original data, the more difficult it will be to judge their quality (Patzer 1996).

Measurement bias

Measurement bias can occur for two reasons (Kervin 1999):

- deliberate or intentional distortion of data;
- changes in the way data are collected.

Deliberate distortion occurs when data are recorded inaccurately on purpose, and is most common for secondary data sources such as organisational records. Managers may deliberately fail to record minor accidents to improve safety reports for their departments. Data that have been collected to further a particular cause or the interests of a particular group are more likely to be suspect as the purpose of the study may be to reach a predetermined conclusion (Jacob 1994). Reports of consumer satisfaction surveys may deliberately play down negative comments to make the service appear better to their target audience of senior managers and shareholders, and graphs may deliberately be distorted to show an organisation in a more favourable light.

Other distortions may be deliberate but not intended for any advantage. Employees keeping time diaries might record only the approximate time spent on their main duties rather than accounting precisely for every minute. People responding to a structured interview (questionnaire) might adjust their responses to please the interviewer (Section 11.2).

Unfortunately, measurement bias resulting from deliberate distortion is difficult to detect. While we believe that you should adopt a neutral stance about the possibility of bias, you still need to look for pressures on the original source that might have biased the data. For written documents such as minutes, reports and memos the intended target audience may suggest possible bias, as indicated earlier in this section. Therefore, where possible you will need to triangulate the findings with other independent data sources. This is sometimes referred to as a *cross-check verification* (Patzer 1996). Where data from two or more independent sources suggest similar conclusions, you can have more confidence that the data on which they are based are not distorted. Conversely, where data suggest different conclusions you need to be more wary of the results.

Box 8.8 Focus on student research

Assessing the suitability of data available via the Internet

As part of a research project on changing consumer spending patterns in Europe, Jocelyn wished to establish how the cost of living had altered in the European Union since the accession of the 10 new Member States in 2004. Other research that she had read as part of her literature review had utilised the European Union's Harmonized Index of Consumer Prices (HICPs). She, therefore, decided to see whether this information was available via the Internet from the European Union's *Europa* information gateway. On accessing the *Eurostat* home page, she noticed that there was a link to a report on 'Harmonized Indices of Consumer Prices'.

Jocelyn clicked on this link and downloaded the report (Eurostat 2008c), saving it onto her MP3 player. A brief look at the data suggested that it would be suitable in terms of coverage for her research. It also contained a link to the most recent (April 2008) HICPs which she downloaded.

Jocelyn was happy with the data's overall suitability and the credibility of the source, the data having been compiled for the European Union using data collected in each of the Member States. She also discovered that the actual data collected were governed by a series of European Union regulations.

Box 8.8
Focus on student research *(continued)*

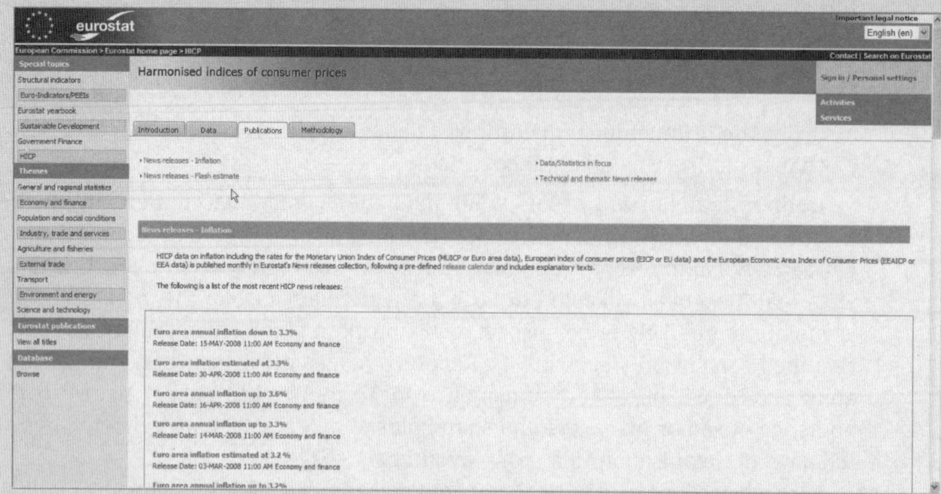

Source: © European Communities, 2008. Reproduced with permission.

In order to be certain about the precise suitability of the HICPs, Jocelyn needed to find out exactly how the index had been calculated and how the data on which it was based had been collected. The *Eurostat* publication provided an overview of how the index was calculated, summarising the nature of goods and services that were included. The data for the HICPs were collected in each Member State using a combination of visits to local retailers and service providers and central collection (via mail, telephone, email and the Internet), over 1 million price observations being used each month! One potential problem was also highlighted: there was no uniform basket of goods and services applying to all member states. Rather, the precise nature of some goods and services included in the HICPs varied from country to country, reflecting the reality of expenditure in each of the countries. Jocelyn decided that this would not present too great a problem as she was going to use these data only to contextualise her research.

The Eurostat publication emphasised that the HICP was a price rather than a cost of living index. However, it also emphasised that, despite conceptual differences between price and the cost of living, there were unlikely to be substantial differences in practice. Jocelyn therefore decided to use the HICPs as a surrogate for the cost of living.

Changes in the way in which data were collected can also introduce changes in measurement bias. Provided that the method of collecting data remains constant in terms of the people collecting it and the procedures used, the measurement biases should remain constant. Once the method is altered, perhaps through a new procedure of taking minutes or a new data collection form, then the bias also changes. This is very important for longitudinal data sets such as the UK's Retail Price Index where you are interested in trends rather than actual numbers. Your detection of biases is dependent on discovering that the way data are recorded has changed. Within-company sources are less likely to have documented these changes than government-sponsored sources.

Costs and benefits

Kervin (1999) argues that the final criterion for assessing secondary data is a comparison of the costs of acquiring them with the benefits they will bring. Costs include both time and financial resources that you will need to devote to obtaining the data. Some data will be available in your local library and so will be free, although you will have to pay for any photocopying you need. Other data will require lengthy negotiations before access is granted (Section 6.3). Even then, the granting of access may not be certain (Stewart and Kamins 1993). Data from market research companies or special tabulations from government surveys will have to be ordered specially and will normally be charged for: consequently, these will be relatively costly.

Benefits from data can be assessed in terms of the extent to which they will enable you to answer your research question(s) and meet your objectives. You will be able to form a judgement on the benefits from your assessment of the data set's overall and precise suitability (discussed earlier in this section). This assessment is summarised as a checklist of questions in Box 8.9. An important additional benefit is the form in which you receive the data. If the data are already in computer-readable form this will save you considerable time as you will not need to re-enter the data prior to analysis (Sections 12.2 and 13.3). However, when assessing the costs and benefits you must remember that data that are not completely reliable and contain some bias are better than no data at all, if they enable you to start to answer your research question(s) and achieve your objectives.

Box 8.9 Checklist

Evaluating your secondary data sources

Overall suitability

- ✔ Does the data set contain the information you require to answer your research question(s) and meet your objectives?
- ✔ Do the measures used match those you require?
- ✔ Is the data set a proxy for the data you really need?
- ✔ Does the data set cover the population that is the subject of your research?
- ✔ Does the data set cover the geographical area that is the subject of your research?
- ✔ Can data about the population that is the subject of your research be separated from unwanted data?
- ✔ Are the data for the right time period or sufficiently up to date?
- ✔ Are data available for all the variables you require to answer your research question(s) and meet your objectives?

Precise suitability

- ✔ How reliable is the data set you are thinking of using?
- ✔ How credible is the data source?
- ✔ Is it clear what the source of the data is?
- ✔ Do the credentials of the source of the data (author, institution or organisation sponsoring the data) suggest it is likely to be reliable?
- ✔ Do the data have an associated copyright statement?
- ✔ Do associated published documents exist?
- ✔ Does the source contain contact details for obtaining further information about the data?
- ✔ Is the method clearly described?
- ✔ If sampling was used, what was the procedure and what were the associated sampling errors and response rates?
- ✔ Who was responsible for collecting or recording the data?
- ✔ (For surveys) Is a copy of the questionnaire or interview checklist included?
- ✔ (For compiled data) Are you clear how the data were analysed and compiled?
- ✔ Are the data likely to contain measurement bias?
- ✔ What was the original purpose for which the data were collected?
- ✔ Who was the target audience and what was its relationship to the data collector or compiler (were there any vested interests)?

Box 8.9
Checklist *(continued)*

- ✔ Have there been any documented changes in the way the data are measured or recorded including definition changes?
- ✔ How consistent are the data obtained from this source when compared with data from other sources?
- ✔ Are you happy that the data have been recorded accurately?

Costs and benefits

- ✔ What are the financial and time costs of obtaining these data?
- ✔ Can the data be downloaded into a spreadsheet, statistical analysis software or word processor?
- ✔ Do the overall benefits of using these secondary data sources outweigh the associated costs?

Source: authors' experience; Blumberg *et al.* (2008); Dale *et al.* (1988); Dochartaigh (2002); Jacob (1994); Kervin (1999); Stewart and Kamins (1993).

8.6 Summary

- Data that have already been collected for some other purpose, perhaps processed and subsequently stored, are termed secondary data. There are three main types of secondary data: documentary, survey and those from multiple sources.
- Most research projects require some combination of secondary and primary data to answer your research question(s) and to meet your objectives. You can use secondary data in a variety of ways. These include:
  - to provide your main data set;
  - to provide longitudinal (time-series) data;
  - to provide area-based data;
  - to compare with, or set in context, your own research findings.
- Any secondary data you use will have been collected for a specific purpose. This purpose may not match that of your research. In addition, the secondary data are likely to be less current than any data you collect yourself.
- Finding the secondary data you require is a matter of detective work. This will involve you in:
  - establishing whether the sort of data that you require are likely to be available;
  - locating the precise data.
- Once located, you must assess secondary data sources to ensure their overall suitability for your research question(s) and objectives. In particular, you need to pay attention to the measurement validity and coverage of the data.
- You must also evaluate the precise suitability of the secondary data. Your evaluation should include both reliability and any likely measurement bias. You can then make a judgement on the basis of the costs and benefits of using the data in comparison with alternative sources.
- When assessing costs and benefits, you need to be mindful that secondary data that are not completely reliable and contain some bias are better than no data at all if they enable you partially to answer your research question(s) and to meet your objectives.

Self-check questions

Help with these questions is available at the end of the chapter.

8.1 Give three examples of different situations where you might use secondary data as part of your research.

8.2 You are undertaking a research project as part of your course. Your initial research question is 'How has the UK's import and export trade with other countries altered since its entry into the European Union?' List the arguments that you would use to convince someone of the suitability of using secondary data to answer this research question.

8.3 Suggest possible secondary data that would help you answer the following research questions. How would you locate these secondary data?

a To what extent do organisations' employee-relocation policies meet the needs of employees?

b How have consumer-spending patterns in your home country changed in the last 10 years?

c How have governments' attitudes to the public sector altered since 1979?

8.4 As part of case-study research based in a manufacturing company with over 500 customers, you have been given access to an internal market research report. This was undertaken by the company's marketing department. The report presents the results of a recent customer survey as percentages. The section in the report that describes how the data were collected and analysed is reproduced below:

> Data were collected from a sample of current customers selected from our customer database. The data were collected using an Internet-mediated questionnaire designed and administered via the online software tool SurveyMonkey™. Twenty-five customers responded, resulting in a 12.5 per cent response rate. These data were analysed using the SNAP™ computer software. Additional qualitative data based on in-depth interviews with customers were also included.

a Do you consider these data are likely to be reliable?

b Give reasons for your answer.

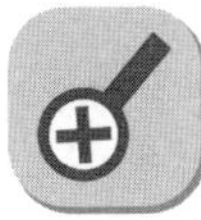

Review and discussion questions

8.5 With a friend revisit Figure 8.1, types of secondary data, and reread the accompanying text in Section 8.2. Agree to find and, where possible, make copies (either electronic or photocopy) of at least two examples of secondary data for each of the seven sub-headings:

a written materials;

b non-written materials;

c area based;

d time-series based;

e censuses;

f continuous and regular surveys;

g *ad hoc* surveys.

Compare and contrast the different examples of secondary data you have found.

8.6 Choose an appropriate information gateway from Table 8.2 to search the Internet for secondary data on a topic which you are currently studying as part of your course.

a 'Add to favourites' (bookmark) those sites which you think appear most relevant.

b Make notes regarding any secondary data that are likely to prove useful to either seminars for which you have to prepare or coursework you have still to undertake.

8.7 Agree with a friend to each evaluate the same secondary data set obtained via the Internet. This could be one of the data sets you found when undertaking question 8.6. Evaluate independently your secondary data set with regard to its overall and precise suitability using the checklist in Box 8.9. Do not forget to make notes regarding your answers to each of the points raised in the checklist. Discuss your answers with your friend.

Progressing your research project

Assessing the suitability of secondary data for your research

- Consider your research question(s) and objectives. Decide whether you need to use secondary data or a combination of primary and secondary data to answer your research question. (If you decide that you need only use secondary data and you are undertaking this research as part of a course of study, check your course's assessment regulations to ensure that this is permissible.)
- If you decide that you need to use secondary data, make sure that you are clear why and how you intend to use these data.
- Locate the secondary data that you require and make sure that permission for them to be used for your research is likely to be granted. Evaluate the suitability of the data for answering your research question and make your judgement based on assessment of its suitability, other benefits and the associated costs.
- Note down the reasons for your choices, including the possibilities and limitations of the data. You will need to justify your choices when you write about your research methods

References

Blumberg, B., Cooper, D.R. and Schindler, P.S. (2008) *Business Research Methods*. (International student edn). Maidenhead: McGraw-Hill Education.

Bryman, A. (1989) *Research Methods and Organisation Studies*. London: Unwin Hyman.

Cheng Shu-Li, Olsen, W., Southerton, D. and Warde, A. (2007) 'The changing practice of eating: Evidence from UK time diaries: 1975 and 2000', *British Journal of Sociology*, Vol. 58, No. 1, pp. 39–61.

Cowton, C.J. (1998) 'The use of secondary data in business ethics research', *Journal of Business Ethics*, Vol. 17, No. 4, pp. 423–34.

Curran, J. and Blackburn, R.A. (2001) *Researching the Small Enterprise*. London: Sage.

Dale, A., Arber, S. and Proctor, M. (1988) *Doing Secondary Analysis*. London: Unwin Hyman.

Dale, P. (2004) *Guide to Libraries and Information Units in Government Departments and Other Organisations* (4th edn). London: British Library Publishing.

Davies, J. (2001) 'International comparisons of labour disputes in 1999', *Labour Market Trends*, Vol. 109, No. 4, pp. 195–201.

Dees, R. (2000) *Writing the Modern Research Paper*. Boston, MA: Allyn and Bacon.

Denscombe, M. (2007) *The Good Research Guide* (3rd edn). Buckingham: Open University Press.

Dochartaigh, N.O. (2002) *The Internet Research Handbook: A Practical Guide for Students and Researchers in the Social Sciences*. London: Sage.

ELC International (2007) *Europe's 15 000 Largest Companies* (31st edn). Oxford: ELC International.

Eurostat (2008a) *Europe in Figures: Eurostat Yearbook 2008*. Luxembourg: Office for Official Publications of the European Communities.

Eurostat (2008b) Eurostat home page. Available at: http://epp.eurostat.ec.europa.eu/portal/page?_pageid=1090.30070682.1090_33076576&_dad=portal&_schema=PORTAL [Accessed 23 May 2008.]

Eurostat (2008c) 'Harmonized Indices of Consumer Prices'. Available at: http://epp.eurostat.ec.europa.eu/portal/page?_pageid=1073,46587259&_dad=portal&_schema=PORTAL&p_product_code=KS-QA-08-024 [Accessed 29 June 2008.]

Ghauri, P. and Grønhaug, K. (2005) *Research Methods in Business Studies: A Practical Guide* (3rd edn). Harlow: Financial Times Prentice Hall.

Hakim, C. (1982) *Secondary Analysis in Social Research*. London: Allen & Unwin.

Hakim, C. (2000) *Research Design: Successful Designs for Social and Economic Research* (2nd edn). London: Routledge.

Information Commissioners Office (2008) Freedom of Information Act. Available at: http://www.ico.gov.uk/what_we_cover/freedom_of_information.aspx [Accessed 23 May 2008.]

IPSOS MORI (2007) 'What do we really think about counterfeiting?' Available at: http://www.ipsos-mori.com/content/what-do-we-really-think-about-counterfeiting.ashx [Accessed 9 June 2008.]

Jacob, H. (1994) 'Using published data: errors and remedies', in M.S. Lewis-Beck. (ed.) *Research Practice*. London: Sage and Toppan, pp. 339–89.

Kervin, J.B. (1999) *Methods for Business Research* (2nd edn). New York: HarperCollins.

Kingsbury, P. (1997) *IT Answers to HR Questions*. London: Institute of Personnel and Development.

Library Association (2005) *Libraries in the United Kingdom and Republic of Ireland*. London: Library Assocation.

McKenzie, E. (2003) *Guide to Libraries in Key UK Companies*. London: British Library.

Office for National Statistics (2001) '200 years of the Census'. Available at: http://www.statistics.gov.uk/census2001/bicentenary/pdfs/200years.pdf [Accessed 23 May 2008.]

Office for National Statistics (2007a) 'Annual Survey of Hours and Earnings (ASHE) 2007 Results'. Available at: http://www.statistics.gov.uk/statBase/product.asp?vlnk=13101. [Accessed 21 May 2008.]

Office for National Statistics (2007b) 'Family Spending – A Report on the Expenditure and Food Survey'. Available at: http://www.statistics.gov.uk/StatBase/Product.asp?vlnk=361 [Accessed 23 May 2008.]

Office for National Statistics (2007c) 'Labour Force Survey'. Available at: http://www.statistics.gov.uk/StatBase/Source.asp?vlnk=358&More=Y [Accessed 23 May 2008.]

Office for National Statistics (2007d) 'Social Trends'. Available at: http://www.statistics.gov.uk/statbase/Product.asp?vlnk=5748&More=Y [Accessed 21 May 2008.]

Office for National Statistics (2008) 'Annual Abstract of Statistics'. Available at: http://www.statistics.gov.uk/statbase/Product.asp?vlnk=94&More=Y [Accessed 23 May 2008.]

Okazaki, S. and Mueller, B. (2007) 'Cross-cultural advertising research: where we have been and where we need to go', *International Marketing Review*, Vol. 25, No. 5, pp. 499–518.

Patzer, G.L. (1996) *Using Secondary Data in Market Research: United States and World-wide*. Westport, CT: Quorum Books.

Reichman, C.S. (1962) *Use and Abuse of Statistics*. New York: Oxford University Press.

Robson, C. (2002) *Real World Research* (2nd edn). Oxford: Blackwell.

Stewart, D.W. and Kamins, M.A. (1993) *Secondary Research: Information Sources and Methods* (2nd edn). Newbury Park, CA: Sage.

Sydney Morning Herald (2008) 'Revealed: the most violent pubs and clubs', 11 Mar.

UK Data Archive (2008) UK Data Archive. Available at: http://www.data-archive.ac.uk/ [Accessed 23 May 2008.]

Walker, A. (2002) *Living in Britain: Results from the 2000 General Household Survey*. London: Stationery Office.

Wolf, A. (2007) 'People have a tendency to assume that quantitative data must be out there on the web waiting to be found', *The Times Higher Education Supplement*, 12 Oct. Available at: http://www.timeshighereducation.co.uk/story.asp?sectioncode=26&storycode=310797 [Accessed 23 May 2008.]

Further reading

Hakim, C. (2000) *Research Design: Successful Designs for Social and Economic Research* (2nd edn). London: Routledge. Chapter 4 contains a good discussion with a series of examples from the social sciences regarding using administrative records and documents as secondary data.

Levitas, R. and Guy, W. (eds) (1996) *Interpreting Official Statistics.* London: Routledge. Although published more than a decade ago, this book provides a fascinating insight into UK published statistics. Of particular interest are Chapter 1, which outlines the changes in UK statistics since the 1980 Raynor review, Chapter 3, which looks at the measurement of unemployment, the discussion in Chapter 6 of the measurement of industrial injuries and their limitations, and Chapter 7, which examines gender segregation in the labour force, utilising data from the Labour Force Survey.

Stewart, D.W. and Kamins, M.A. (1993) *Secondary Research: Information Sources and Methods* (2nd edn). Newbury Park, CA: Sage. This provides a good discussion on the evaluation of secondary data (Chapter 2). It also provides a wealth of information on American government and non-government data sets and their acquisition.

Case 8
Patent grants and the implications for business

Source: E Streichan/Zefa/Corbis.

Chris was an MA student in international business and management. After taking a module entitled Intellectual Property (IP) in International Business (IB), he had taken great interest in this subject and had been determined to do a good-quality research project. However, in the first meeting with his supervisor, while feeling motivated, he realised that it was not enough to be determined and he needed to make greater effort on his project. His supervisor pointed out, based on his project proposal, that he needed to be more focused and precise. The supervisor had advised that the proposed focus of his research project – examining how Western corporate managers view the development of IP in the Eastern European countries using primary data – was too wide. He suggested narrowing it to assessing how IP systems differ between Western and Eastern European countries and what these differences imply for cross-border business activities, and only to use secondary data. The supervisor had particularly mentioned that it would be sensible for Chris to use his statistical skills to draw conclusions based on reliable secondary data commenting: 'Western corporate managers' views will involve primary data collection. It would be brilliant to do so, but given that you have only three months to do the project, including writing up, it would be difficult to produce a quality piece of work. There might be difficulties in collecting representative data due to access issues, time constraints and financial support.' At the end of the first meeting, Chris and his supervisor agreed that Chris would undertake a project to assess the differences between Western and Eastern European countries in terms of patent grants and the implications for businesses.

Before the second meeting, Chris conducted a search of the literature regarding IP system development particularly with the empirical focus on the EU countries. To his surprise, there were only three articles that specifically examined the patent grant issues in a comparative manner (Kotabe 1992a, 1992b; Yang 2008). Both authors had used raw data from the World IP Organisation (WIPO) database and conducted regression analyses on which they based their conclusions. When reading the articles referenced in these three papers, Chris found that they were suggesting theoretical reasons as to why France, Germany and the United Kingdom (UK) had higher grant ratios for domestic than for foreign applications to issue patent rights. These, he felt, could provide the justifications for questions for his research project. At this stage, Chris was very eager to see his supervisor to report his achievements. In the meeting, while the supervisor commended Chris's progress on identifying the appropriate literature, she also pointed out: 'The most important work to do at the literature review stage is to be able to critique on the existing work so that you can identify research gaps for your own study.' At the end of the meeting, Chris's supervisor asked him to establish precisely what secondary data he needed to obtain about patent applications and grants for the countries he wanted to focus on.

Following this advice, Chris designed a table to highlight the key information. This indicates the authors, research focus, empirical focus in relation to countries, data source and analytical methods. Upon completion, his findings were clear. The existing literature had not conducted grant ratio (grant lags) analysis with an empirical focus on any Eastern European countries. Meanwhile, although Britain, France and Germany were compared and contrasted with the United States by Kotabe (1992b), the conclusions were dated because they were based on data from the 1980s. A new study would enrich existing empirical findings by not only adding new countries (Eastern Europe) but also revealing the changes in Western Europe over the years in terms of grant ratios. In addition, through the studies, similarities and differences between Eastern and Western Europe could be identified. This, Chris felt, would allow him to make some recommendations relating to policy and business implications. To collect his data, he logged on http:\\www.wipo.org statistics, and downloaded all the annual patent statistics available for all the EU countries.

Author	Focus	Empirical focus	Data and methods
Kotabe (1992a)	Patent grant lags and ratios	US and Japan	WIPO data 1980s Lagged regression
Kotabe (1992b)	The same as above	US, Germany, UK and France	The same as above
Yang (2008)	The same as above	US and China	WIPO data (1985–2002)

With excitement, Chris presented his achievements proudly to his supervisor who was pleased with his enthusiasm and his hard work. In the meantime, the supervisor also pointed out that it was not enough to collect the data only. Chris also needed to justify why the secondary data collected from WIPO were appropriate and what issues arose from the data. Chris was surprised as he thought that data from a United Nations agency source like WIPO would be 'perfect'. The supervisor hinted to Chris that he had to look into the actual source of the WIPO data, the standardisation process to compile the data, and how the data had been categorised. He was advised to discuss possible weaknesses in the data in the 'Methodology' section of his project report. At the end of the meeting, Chris went home with an important task: analyse the data and come to see the supervisor again with some preliminary findings and understanding regarding how it had been collected.

Upon returning home, Chris sat at his computer for half an hour staring at the monitor. There were 27 countries, and each country had at least 90 years' worth of aggregate data. The data for Germany were extremely complex due to it being sub-divided into East and West Germany prior to reunification. He spent another hour trying to understand the data before he picked up the phone to call his supervisor for help. Chris was overwhelmed with the richness of the data and did not know where to start. After discussion, the supervisor suggested that he focus on a few countries instead of all EU countries, for example three countries from Western Europe and three from Eastern Europe, and also only focus on the data for West Germany.

Chris eventually finished his data analysis and submitted his project report. His great effort did not disappoint his supervisor; the project was awarded a distinction. However, the supervisor still commented that the discussion about the weakness of the data could have been more thoroughly presented.

References

Kotabe, M. (1992a) 'A Comparative Study of U.S. and Japanese Patent Systems', *Journal of International Business Studies*, Vol. 23, No. 1, pp. 147–68.

Kotabe, M. (1992b) 'The Impact of Foreign Patents on National Economy: A Case of the US, Japan, Germany and Britain', *Applied Economics*, Vol. 24, pp.1335–43.

Yang, D. (2008) 'Pendency and grant ratios on invention patents: A comparative study of the US and China', *Research Policy*. Available at: http://dx.doi.org/10.1016/j.respol.2008.03.008 [Accessed 14 May 2008.]

Questions

1 Why does the supervisor advise that Chris do a project using secondary data rather than collecting primary data?
2 What sources of information has Chris discovered through his search?
3 Do you find Chris's justification for his research project convincing? Give reasons for your answer?
4 Despite obtaining a distinction for the project, the supervisor commented that Chris should have discussed the limitations of his data sources more thoroughly. Visit the WIPO's website [http://www.wipo.org] and make a note of precisely how the data Chris used were compiled. Based upon this, how would you suggest that Chris present more thorough a discussion?

Additional case studies relating to material covered in this chapter are available via the book's Companion Website, **www.pearsoned.co.uk/saunders**. They are:

- The involvement of auditors in preliminary profit announcements
- Research and development in the UK pharmaceutical industry
- Small firms' internationalisation.

Self-check answers

8.1 Although it would be impossible to list all possible situations, the key features that should appear in your examples are listed below:
- to compare findings from your primary data;
- to place findings from your primary data in a wider context;
- to triangulate findings from other data sources;
- to provide the main data set where you wish to undertake research over a long period, to undertake historical research or to undertake comparative research on a national or international scale with limited resources.

8.2 The arguments you have listed should focus on the following issues:
- The study suggested by the research question requires historical data so that changes that have already happened can be explored. These data will, by definition, have already been collected.

- The timescale of the research (if part of a course) will be relatively short term. One solution for longitudinal studies in a short time frame is to use secondary data.
- The research question suggests an international comparative study. Given your likely limited resources, secondary data will provide the only feasible data sources.

8.3 **a** The secondary data required for this research question relate to organisations' employee relocation policies. The research question assumes that these sorts of data are likely to be available from organisations. Textbooks, research papers and informal discussions would enable you to confirm that these data were likely to be available. Informal discussions with individuals responsible for the personnel function in organisations would also confirm the existence and availability for research of such data.

b The secondary data required for this research question relate to consumer spending patterns in your home country. As these appear to be the sort of data in which the government would be interested, they may well be available via the Internet or in published form. For the UK, examination of various published guides (both governmental and non-governmental sources) would reveal that these data were collected by the annual Family Expenditure Survey, summary results of which are published (e.g. Office for National Statistics 2007). Summary data could then be downloaded via the UK government's statistics information gateway (Table 8.2). In addition, reports could be borrowed either from your university library or by using inter-library loan.

c The secondary data required for this research question are less clear. What you require is some source from which you can infer past and present government attitudes. Transcripts of ministers' speeches and newspaper reports might prove useful. However, to establish suitable secondary sources for this research question you would need to pay careful attention to those used by other researchers. These would be outlined in research papers and textbooks. Informal discussions could also prove useful.

8.4 **a** The data are unlikely to be reliable.

b Your judgement should be based on a combination of the following reasons:

- Initial examination of the report reveals that it is an internally conducted survey. As this has been undertaken by the marketing department of a large manufacturing company, you might assume that those undertaking the research had considerable expertise. Consequently, you might conclude the report contains credible data. However:
- The methodology is not clearly described. In particular:
  - The sampling procedure and associated sampling errors are not given.
  - It does not appear to contain a copy of the questionnaire. This means that it is impossible to check for bias in the way that questions were worded.
  - The methodology for the qualitative in-depth interviews is not described.
- In addition, the information provided in the methodology suggests that the data may be unreliable:
  - The reported response rate of 12.5 per cent is very low for a telephone survey (Section 7.2).
  - Responses from 25 people means that all tables and statistical analyses in the report are based on a maximum of 25 people. This may be too few for reliable results (Sections 7.2 and 12.5).

Get ahead using resources on the Companion Website at:
www.pearsoned.co.uk/saunders

- Improve your SPSS and NVivo research analysis with practice tutorials.
- Save time researching on the Internet with the Smarter Online Searching Guide.
- Test your progress using self-assessment questions.
- Follow live links to useful websites.

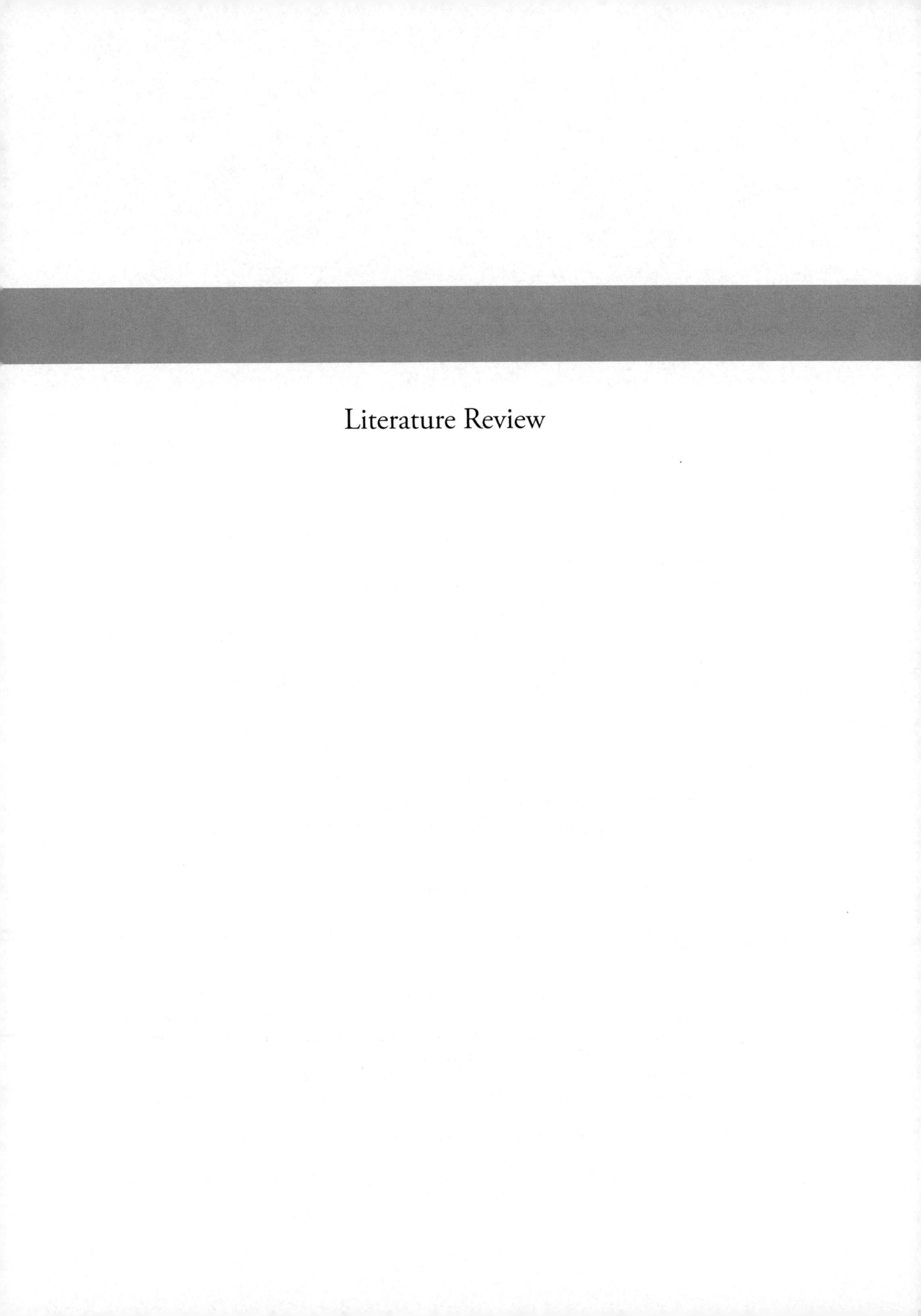

Literature Review

Chapter 3

Critically reviewing the literature

Learning outcomes

By the end of this chapter you should:

- understand the importance and purpose of the critical literature review to your research project;
- be able to adopt a critical perspective in your reading;
- know what you need to include when writing your critical review;
- be aware of the range of primary, secondary and tertiary literature sources available;
- be able to identify key words and to undertake a literature search using a range of methods;
- be able to evaluate the relevance, value and sufficiency of the literature found;
- be able to reference the literature found accurately;
- understand what is meant by plagiarism;
- be able to apply the knowledge, skills and understanding gained to your own research project.

3.1 Introduction

As part of your studies, you have almost certainly already been asked by your tutors to 'review the literature', 'write a literature review' or 'critically review the literature' on topics they have specified. Indeed, you may be like many students and have grown to fear the literature review, not because of the associated reading but because of the requirement both to make judgements as to the value of each piece of work and to organise those ideas and findings that are of value into a review. It is these two processes in particular that people find both difficult and time consuming.

Two major reasons exist for reviewing the literature (Sharp *et al.* 2002). The first, the preliminary search that helps you to generate and refine your research ideas, has already been discussed in Section 2.3. The second, often referred to as the **critical review** or **critical literature review**, is part of your research project proper. Most research textbooks, as well as your project tutor, will argue that this critical review of the literature is necessary. Although you may feel that you already have a good knowledge of your research area, we believe that reviewing the literature is essential. Project assessment criteria usually require you to demonstrate awareness of the current state of knowledge in your subject, its limitations, and how your research fits in this wider context (Gill and Johnson 2002). In Jankowicz's (2005:161) words:

> There is little point in reinventing the wheel . . . the work that you do is not done in a vacuum, but builds on the ideas of other people who have studied the field before you. This requires you describe what has been published, and to marshal the information in a relevant and critical way.

Recently, we were discussing the difficulties students have when writing their literature reviews for their research projects. Mark summarised what he felt we and fellow project tutors were saying:

'So what happens sometimes is . . . a student comes to see their project tutor having obviously done a great deal of work. The student presents the tutor with what they say is the finished literature review. Yet, the purpose of their review is unclear. It is little more than a summary of the articles and books read, each article or book being given one paragraph. Some students have arranged these paragraphs alphabetically in author order, others have arranged them in chronological order. None have linked or juxtaposed the ideas. Their literature reviews look more like adjacent pages from a catalogue rather than a critical review. Just like the items on these pages, each article or book has some similarities in terms of subject matter and so are grouped together. As in the catalogue, the reasons for these groupings are not made explicit. In addition, like the summary descriptions of items on the pages of a home shopping catalogue, each book or article is accorded equal status rather than the amount written reflecting its value to the student's research project.'

He concluded:

'Whilst such an approach obviously makes good sense for a shopping catalogue, it does not work for the critical review of the literature. We obviously need to explain better what we mean by a critical review of the literature to our students.'

A page from a book catalogue
Source: Pearson Education Ltd

The significance of your research and what you find out will inevitably be judged in relation to other people's research and their findings. You, therefore, need both to 'map and assess the existing intellectual territory' (Tranfield *et al.* 2003:208), establishing what research has been published in your chosen area, and, if possible, to try to identify any other research that might currently be in progress. Consequently, the items you read and write about will enhance your subject knowledge and help you to clarify your research question(s) further. This process is called 'critically reviewing the literature'.

For most research projects, your literature search will be an early activity. Despite this early start, it is usually necessary to continue searching throughout your project's life. The process can be likened to an upward spiral, culminating in the final draft of a written critical literature review (Figure 3.1). In the initial stage of your literature review, you will start to define the parameters to your research question(s) and objectives (Section 3.4). After generating key words and conducting your first search (Section 3.5), you will have a list of references to authors who have published on these subjects. Once these have been obtained, you can read and evaluate them (Section 3.6), record the ideas (Section 3.7) and start drafting your review. After the initial search, you will be able to redefine your parameters more

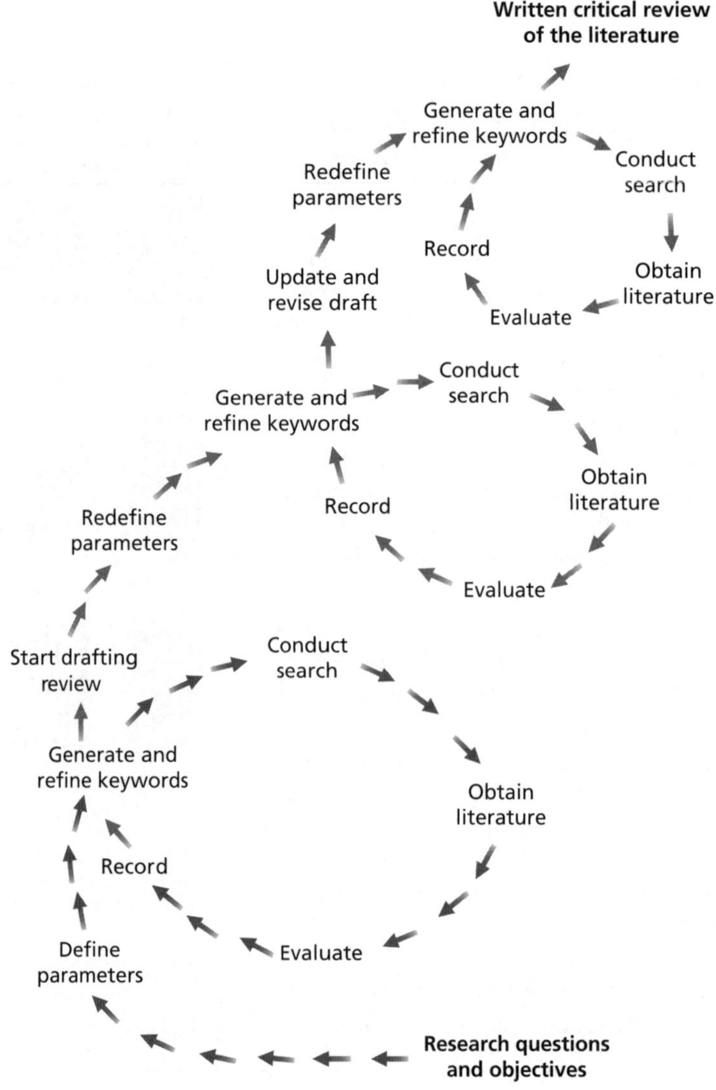

Figure 3.1 The literature review process
Source: © Mark Saunders, Philip Lewis, Adrian, Thornhill and Martin Jenkins 2003

precisely and undertake further searches, keeping in mind your research question(s) and objectives. As your thoughts develop, each subsequent search will be focused more precisely on material that is likely to be relevant. At the same time, you will probably be refining your research question(s) and objectives in the light of your reading (Section 2.4).

Unlike some academic disciplines, business and management research makes use of a wide range of literature. While your review is likely to include specific business disciplines such as finance, marketing and human resource management, it is also likely to include other disciplines. Those most frequently consulted by our students include economics, psychology, sociology and geography. Given this, and the importance of the review to your research, it is vital for you to be aware of what a critical literature review is and the range of literature available before you start the reviewing process. For these reasons, we start this chapter by outlining the purpose of your critical review of the literature, its content and what we mean by 'critical' (Section 3.2) and then discussing those literature resources available (Section 3.3).

3.2 The critical review

The purpose of the critical review

Reviewing the literature critically will provide the foundation on which your research is built. As you will have gathered from the introduction, its main purpose is to help you to develop a good understanding and insight into relevant previous research and the trends that have emerged. You would not expect a scientific researcher inquiring into the causes of cot death to start his or her research without first reading about the findings of other cot death research. Likewise, you should not expect to start your research without first reading what other researchers in your area have already found out.

The precise purpose of your reading of the literature will depend on the approach you are intending to use in your research. For some research projects you will use the literature to help you to identify theories and ideas that you will test using data. This is known as a **deductive approach** (Section 4.3) in which you develop a theoretical or conceptual framework, which you subsequently test using data. For other research projects you will be planning to explore your data and to develop theories from them that you will subsequently relate to the literature. This is known as an **inductive approach** (Section 4.3) and, although your research still has a clearly defined purpose with research question(s) and objectives, you do not start with any predetermined theories or conceptual frameworks. We believe such an approach cannot be taken without a competent knowledge of your subject area. It is, however, impossible to review every single piece of the literature before collecting your data. The purpose of your literature review is not to provide a summary of everything that has been written on your research topic, but to review the most relevant and significant research on your topic. If your analysis is effective, new findings and theories will emerge that neither you nor anyone else has thought about (Strauss and Corbin 1998). Despite this, when you write your critical review, you will need to show how your findings and the theories you have developed or are using relate to the research that has gone before, thereby demonstrating that you are familiar with what is already known about your research topic.

Your review also has a number of other purposes. Many of these have been highlighted by Gall *et al.* (2006) in their book for students undertaking educational research and are, we believe, of equal relevance to business and management researchers:

- to help you to refine further your research question(s) and objectives;
- to highlight research possibilities that have been overlooked implicitly in research to date;

- to discover explicit recommendations for further research. These can provide you with a superb justification for your own research question(s) and objectives;
- to help you to avoid simply repeating work that has been done already;
- to sample current opinions in newspapers, professional and trade journals, thereby gaining insights into the aspects of your research question(s) and objectives that are considered newsworthy;
- to discover and provide an insight into research approaches, strategies (Section 4.3) and techniques that may be appropriate to your own research question(s) and objectives.

Adopting critical perspective in your reading

Harvard College Library (2006) provides for its students a useful check list of skills to be practised for effective reading. These skills include:

> *Previewing*, which is looking around the text before you start reading in order to establish precisely its purpose and how it may inform your literature search;
> *Annotating*; that is conducting a dialogue with yourself, the author, and the issues and ideas at stake.

Here the Harvard advice, we think, is very useful. It urges readers to be 'thinking-intensive' (see Box 3.1).

> *Summarising*. The best way to determine that you've really got the point is to be able to state it in your own words. Outlining the argument of a text is a version of annotating, and can be done quite informally in the margins of the text.

Box 3.1 Checklist

Annotating your critical reading. Advice on how to read in a 'thinking-intensive' way

- ✔ First of all: throw away the highlighter in favour of a pen or pencil. Highlighting can actually distract from the business of learning and dilute your comprehension. It only seems like an active reading strategy; in actual fact, it can lull you into a dangerous passivity.
- ✔ Mark up the margins of your text with words: ideas that occur to you, notes about things that seem important to you, reminders of how issues in a text may connect with your research questions and objectives. This kind of interaction keeps you conscious of the reason you are reading. Throughout your research these annotations will be useful memory triggers.
- ✔ Develop your own symbol system: asterisk a key idea, for example, or use an exclamation point for the surprising, absurd, bizarre . . . Like your margin words, your hieroglyphs can help you reconstruct the important observations that you made at an earlier time. And they will be indispensable when you return to a text later in the term, in search of a particular passage that you may want to include in your project report.
- ✔ Get in the habit of hearing yourself ask questions – 'what does this mean?' 'why is he or she drawing that conclusion?' Write the questions down (in your margins, at the beginning or end of the reading, in a notebook, or elsewhere). They are reminders of the unfinished business you still have with a text: to come to terms with on your own, once you've had a chance to digest the material further, or have done further reading.

Comparing and Contrasting. Ask yourself how your thinking been altered by this reading or how has it affected your response to the issues and themes your research?

The Harvard College Library advice above suggests that you should get in the habit of hearing yourself ask questions of your reading. Wallace and Wray (2006) recommend the use of **review questions**. These are specific questions you ask of the reading, which will be linked either directly or, at least, indirectly, to your research question. So you may, for example, address a piece of reading with the view to it answering the question: 'what does research suggest are the main reasons why customers are likely to change car insurance provider?'

The word 'critical' has appeared in this chapter a number of times so far. It is vital in your reading of the literature that a critical stance should be taken. So what is meant by critical reading? Wallace and Wray (2006) sum this up rather succinctly by saying that 'the lengthy list if critical skills (required for critical reading) boil down to just two: the capacity to evaluate what you read and the capacity to relate what you read to other information'.

More specifically Wallace and Wray advocate the use of five critical questions to employ in critical reading. These are:

1 Why am I reading this? (The authors argue that this is where the review question in particularly valuable. It acts as a focusing device and ensures that you stick to the purpose of the reading and not get sidetracked too much by the author's agenda.)
2 What is the author trying to do in writing this? (The answer to this may assist you in deciding how valuable the writing may be for your purposes.)
3 What is the writer saying that is relevant to what I want to find out?
4 How convincing is what the author is saying? (In particular, is the argument based on a conclusion which is justified by the evidence?)
5 What use can I make of the reading?

The content of the critical review

As you begin to find, read and evaluate the literature, you will need to think how to combine the academic theories and ideas about which you are reading to form the critical review that will appear in your project report. Your review will need to evaluate the research that has already been undertaken in the area of your research project, show and explain the relationships between published research findings and reference the literature in which they were reported (Appendix 1). It will draw out the key points and trends (recognising any omissions and bias) and present them in a logical way which also shows the relationship to your own research. In doing this you will provide readers of your project report with the necessary background knowledge to your research question(s) and objectives and establish the boundaries of your own research. Your review will also enable the readers to see your ideas against the background of previous published research in the area. This does not necessarily mean that your ideas must extend, follow or approve those set out in the literature. You may be highly critical of the earlier research reported in the literature and seek to discredit it. However, if you wish to do this you must still review this literature, explain clearly why it is problematic, and then justify your own ideas.

In considering the content of your critical review, you will therefore need:

- to include the key academic theories within your chosen area of research;
- to demonstrate that your knowledge of your chosen area is up to date;
- through clear referencing, enable those reading your project report to find the original publications which you cite.

Box 3.2 Checklist

Evaluating the content of your critical literature review

✔ Have you ensured that the literature covered relates clearly to your research question and objectives?

✔ Have you covered the most relevant and significant theories of recognised experts in the area?

✔ Have you covered the most relevant and significant literature or at least a representative sample?

✔ Have you included up-to-date literature?

✔ Have you referenced all the literature used in the format prescribed in the assessment criteria?

In addition, by fully acknowledging the research of others you will avoid charges of plagiarism and the associated penalties (Section 3.8). The content of your critical review can be evaluated using the checklist in Box 3.2.

What is really meant by being 'critical' about the content

Within the context of your course you have probably already been asked to take a critical approach for previous assignments. However, it is worth considering what we mean by critical within the context of your literature review. Mingers (2000:225–6) argues that there are four aspects of a critical approach that should be fostered by management education:

- critique of rhetoric;
- critique of tradition;
- critique of authority;
- critique of objectivity.

The first of these, the 'critique of rhetoric', means appraising or evaluating a problem with effective use of language. In the context of your critical literature review, this emphasises the need for you, as the reviewer, to use your skills both of making reasoned judgements and of arguing effectively in writing. The other three aspects Mingers identifies also have implications for being critical when reading and writing about the work of others. This includes you questioning, where justification exists to do so, the conventional wisdom, the 'critique of tradition' and the dominant view portrayed in the literature you are reading, the 'critique of authority'. Finally, it is likely also to include recognising in your review that the knowledge and information you are discussing are not value free, the 'critique of objectivity'.

Being critical in reviewing the literature is, therefore, a combination of your skills and the attitude with which you read. In critically reviewing the literature, you need to read the literature about your research topic with some scepticism and be willing to question what you read. This means you need to be constantly considering and justifying with clear arguments your own critical stance. You, therefore, will have to read widely on your research topic and have a good understanding of the literature. Critically reviewing the literature for your research project, therefore, requires you to have gained topic-based

Box 3.3 Checklist

Evaluating whether your literature review is critical

- ✔ Have you shown how your research question relates to previous research reviewed?
- ✔ Have you assessed the strengths and weaknesses of the previous research reviewed?
- ✔ Have you been objective in your discussion and assessment of other people's research?
- ✔ Have you included references to research that is counter to your own opinion?
- ✔ Have you distinguished clearly between facts and opinions?
- ✔ Have you made reasoned judgements about the value and relevance of others' research to your own?
- ✔ Have you justified clearly your own ideas?
- ✔ Have you highlighted those areas where new research (yours!) is needed to provide fresh insights and taken these into account in your arguments? In particular:
  - ✔ where there are inconsistencies in current knowledge and understanding?
  - ✔ where there are omissions or bias in published research?
  - ✔ where research findings need to be tested further?
  - ✔ where evidence is lacking, inconclusive, contradictory or limited?
- ✔ Have you justified your arguments by referencing correctly published research?

background knowledge, understanding, the ability to reflect upon and to analyse the literature and, based on this, to make reasoned judgements that are argued effectively. When you use these skills to review the literature, the term 'critical' refers to the judgement you exercise. It, therefore, describes the process of providing a detailed and justified analysis of, and commentary on, the merits and faults of the key literature within your chosen area. This means that, for your review to be critical, you will need to have shown critical judgement.

Part of this judgement will inevitably mean being able to identify the most relevant and significant theories and recognised experts highlighted in Box 3.3. In addition, Dees (2003) suggests that this means you should:

- refer to and assess research by recognised experts in your chosen area;
- consider and discuss research that supports and research that opposes your ideas;
- make reasoned judgements regarding the value of others' research, showing clearly how it relates to your research;
- justify your arguments with valid evidence in a logical manner;
- distinguish clearly between fact and opinion.

These points are developed in Box 3.3, which contains a checklist to evaluate the extent to which your literature review is critical. The more questions to which you can answer 'yes', the more likely your review will be critical!

The structure of the critical review

The **literature review** that you write for your project report should therefore be a description and critical analysis of what other authors have written (Jankowicz 2005). When drafting your review you, therefore, need to focus on your research question(s) and objectives. One way of helping you to focus is to think of your literature review as discussing how far existing published research goes in answering your research question(s). The shortfall in the literature will be addressed, at least partially, in the remainder of your project report. Another way of helping you to focus is to ask yourself how your review relates to your objectives. If it does not, or does only partially, there is a need for a clearer focus on your objectives. The precise structure of the critical review is usually your choice, although you should check, as it may be specified in the assessment criteria. Three common structures are:

- a single chapter;
- a series of chapters;
- throughout the project report as you tackle various issues.

In all project reports, you should return to the key issues from the literature in your discussion and conclusions (Section 14.3).

Within your critical review, you will need to juxtapose different authors' ideas and form your own opinions and conclusions based on these. Although you will not be able to start writing until you have undertaken some reading, we recommend that you start drafting your review early (Figure 3.1). What you write can then be updated and revised as you read more.

A common mistake with critical literature reviews, highlighted at the start of this chapter, is that they become uncritical listings of previous research. Often they are little more than annotated bibliographies (Hart 1998), individual items being selected because they fit with what the researcher is proposing (Greenhalgh 1997). Although there is no single structure that your critical review should take, our students have found it useful to think of the review as a funnel in which you:

1 start at a more general level before narrowing down to your specific research question(s) and objectives;
2 provide a brief overview of key ideas and themes;
3 summarise, compare and contrast the research of the key writers;
4 narrow down to highlight previous research work most relevant to your own research;
5 provide a detailed account of the findings of this research and show how they are related;
6 highlight those aspects where your own research will provide fresh insights;
7 lead the reader into subsequent sections of your project report, which explore these issues.

In addition, some writers argue that, in order to improve the transparency of your review process, you should explain precisely how you searched for selected the literature you have included in your review, outlining your choice of key words and of databases used (Tranfield *et al.* 2003). Within the 'funnel' we have just proposed, this can be thought of as step 0! This is discussed in more detail in Sections 3.4 and 3.5.

Whichever way you structure your review you must demonstrate that you have read, understood and evaluated the items you have located. The key to writing a critical literature review is therefore to link the different ideas you find in the literature to form a coherent and cohesive argument, which sets in context and justifies your research. Obviously, it should relate to your research question and objectives. It should show a clear link from these as well as a clear link to the empirical work that will follow. Box 3.4 provides a checklist to help you ensure that the structure of your literature review supports this. Subsequent parts of your project report (Section 14.3) must follow on from this.

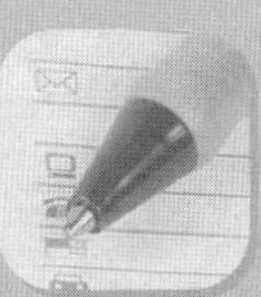

Box 3.4 Checklist

Evaluating the structure of your literature review

✔ Does your literature review have a clear title which describes the focus of your research rather than just saying 'literature review'?

✔ Have you explained precisely how you searched the literature, and the criteria used to select those studies included?

✔ Does your review start at a more general level before narrowing down?

✔ Is your literature review organised thematically around the ideas contained in the research being reviewed rather than the researchers?

✔ Are your arguments coherent and cohesive – do your ideas link in a way that will be logical to your reader?

✔ Have you used sub-headings within the literature review to help guide your reader?

✔ Does the way you have structured your literature review draw your reader's attention to those issues which are going to be the focus of your research?

✔ Does your literature review lead your reader into subsequent sections of your project report?

Box 3.5 Focus on management research

Structure of the literature review

An article published by Christine Williams and Mark Saunders in the *Service Industries Journal* (Williams and Saunders 2006:582–3) includes a review of the literature on problems associated with traditional approaches to measuring service quality. The following extract is taken from this review. Although your literature review will be longer than this, the extract illustrates:

- the overall structure of starting at a more general level before narrowing down;
- the provision of a brief overview of the key ideas;
- the linking of ideas;
- narrowing down to highlight that work which is most relevant to the research reported.

In their paper, Williams and Saunders subsequently review, in more detail, research involving the development of an alternative approach, the Service Template Process.

Traditional Approaches to measuring service quality

Traditional survey-based approaches to measuring service quality or customer satisfaction such as SERVQUAL (Parasuraman *et al.* 1985) measure the gap between service users' perceptions and expectations across a series of standardised dimensions characterising the service. Notwithstanding shortcomings of conceptualising service quality in this manner, recognised for example in the SERVQUAL debates (Carman 1990; Cronin and Taylor 1992), the use of the disconfirmation approach is reported widely in the literature (Parasuraman 1995; Robinson 1999).

Carman (1990) argues that constructs representing service quality are a function of a particular service and the industry within which it is located. Carman (2000) also confirms that different users of a service may assign different levels of importance to the same quality dimension. Furthermore, the use of generic constructs to measure a particular service's quality may not provide the details necessary to define the specific causes of a problem rather than its symptoms (Kilmann 1986). Generic constructs, therefore,

Box 3.5
Focus on management research (continued)

may fail to account for the uniqueness and realities of specific services, and how these are expressed and interpreted by the parties involved. Furthermore, where these measures are used only from the perspective of service user or deliverer, any problems identified are unlikely to reflect fully the dyadic nature of service encounters (Svensson 2001).

If the measurement of service quality is to lead to improvement, data collected must be useful. In this context, usefulness can be viewed from three interrelated perspectives. The first emphasises the suitability of the constructs used to capture perceptions of reality considered important by each party involved within the specific service (Chi Cui *et al.* 2003), in other words, construct validity. The second perspective relates to the implications of the sufficiency of detail in respect of a clear understanding of the particular service situation. Kilmann (1986:131) summarises this as the need to 'define problem causes rather than just symptoms'. The third is concerned with the extent to which these data enable meanings to be understood and explored and quality improvement agendas derived.

Problems of second order interpretation (Yin 2003) can occur when data collected using measures of service quality are subject to interpretation by third parties, such as consultants or managers. The meanings ascribed to the data by the interpreter may differ from those given by service users or deliverers, leading to inconsistency in interpretation. A person undertaking an inquiry may have filtered and added her or his own understanding to the language used and emphases placed by respondents, rather than it being understood and interpreted as intended (Foddy 1994). Consequently, meanings in the data may be lost, or at best, mis-reported. Furthermore, traditional approaches do not normally require respondents to indicate the relative importance of quality constructs (Pitt *et al.* 1995). Such analyses usually involve the person undertaking the inquiry judging what is important, concentrating attention on those areas that she or he believes are of critical concern (Foddy 1994; Krueger 1994). Consequently, her or his judgement about which characteristics are key to the quality of service forms the basis for analysis and future action.

Source: Williams, C.S. and Saunders, M.N.K. (2006).

3.3 Literature sources available

An overview

The literature sources available to help you to develop a good understanding of, and insight into, previous research can be divided into three categories: primary (published and unpublished), secondary, and tertiary (Figure 3.2). In reality these categories often overlap: for example, primary literature sources, including conference proceedings, can appear in journals, and some books contain indexes to primary and secondary literature.

The different categories of literature resources represent the flow of information from the original source. Often as information flows from primary to secondary to tertiary sources it becomes less detailed and authoritative but more easily accessible. Recognising this information flow helps you to identify the most appropriate sources of literature for your needs. Some research projects may access only secondary literature sources whereas others will necessitate the use of primary sources.

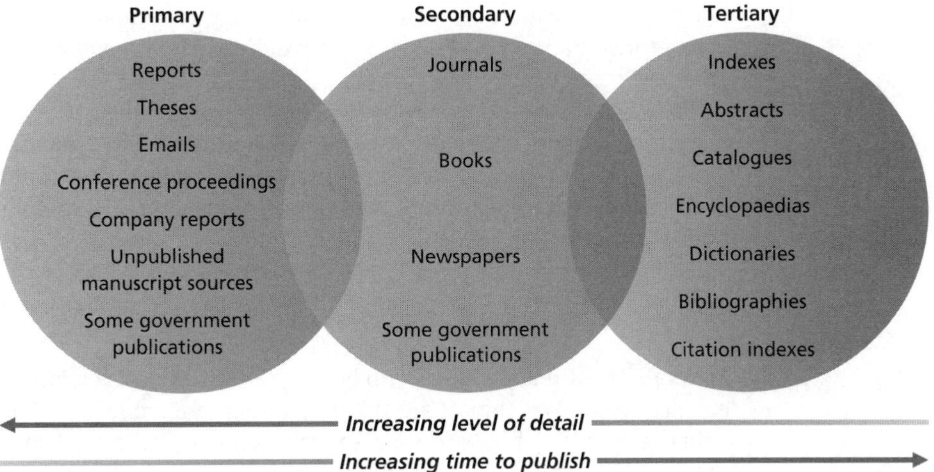

Figure 3.2 Literature sources available

The nature of this information flow is typical of traditional printed publications. However, the Internet is changing this situation, providing a more direct means of both publishing and accessing information. Alongside this, moves toward 'freedom of information' mean that what were traditionally 'grey literature', such as some government publications, are increasingly being made available, usually via the Internet. The majority of academic publications still exhibit this information flow, although the final place of publication is increasingly the Internet.

Figure 3.2 also illustrates the reduced currency of secondary literature sources, which are utilising information already published in primary sources. Because of the time taken to publish, the information in these sources can be dated. Your literature review should reflect current thinking as far as possible, so the limitations of such sources must be recognised.

Primary literature sources are the first occurrence of a piece of work. They include published sources such as reports and some central and local government publications such as White Papers and planning documents. They also include unpublished manuscript sources such as letters, memos and committee minutes that may be analysed as data in their own right (Section 8.2). It is because primary literature sources can be difficult to trace that they are sometimes referred to as **grey literature**.

Secondary literature sources such as books and journals are the subsequent publication of primary literature. These publications are aimed at a wider audience. They are easier to locate than primary literature as they are better covered by the tertiary literature.

Tertiary literature sources, also called 'search tools', are designed either to help to locate primary and secondary literature or to introduce a topic. They, therefore, include indexes and abstracts as well as encyclopaedias and bibliographies.

Your use of these literature sources will depend on your research question(s) and objectives, the need for secondary data to answer them (Section 8.3) and the time available. For some research projects you may use only tertiary and secondary literature; for others you may need to locate primary literature as well. Most research projects will make the greatest use of secondary literature, and so it is this we consider first, followed by the primary literature. Tertiary literature sources are not discussed until Section 3.5, as their major use is in conducting a literature search.

Secondary literature sources

The number of secondary literature sources available to you is expanding rapidly, especially as new resources are developed or made available via the Internet. Your university's librarians are likely to be aware of a wide range of secondary literature in business and management that can be accessed from your library, and will keep themselves up to date with new resources.

The main secondary literature sources that you are likely to use, along with those primary sources most frequently used for a literature review, are outlined in Table 3.1. The most important when placing your ideas in the context of earlier research are refereed academic journals. Books are, however, likely to be more important than professional and trade journals in this context.

Journals

Journals are also known as 'periodicals', 'serials' and 'magazines', and are published on a regular basis. While most are still produced in printed form, many additionally provide online access, via a subscription service. Journals are a vital literature source for any research. The articles are easily accessible. They are well covered by tertiary literature, and a good selection can be accessed from most university libraries either in print, for reference purposes, or via their online services. This online access is usually restricted to members of the university (Table 3.1). Trade and some professional journals may be covered only partially by the tertiary literature (Table 3.2). You, therefore, need to browse these journals regularly to be sure of finding useful items. Many journals' content pages can also be browsed via the Internet (Section 3.5).

Articles in **refereed academic journals** (such as the *Journal of Management Studies*) are evaluated by academic peers prior to publication, to assess their quality and suitability. They are usually written by recognised experts in the field. There will be usually be detailed footnotes; an extensive bibliography; rigorous attention to detail; and verification of information. Such articles are written for a more narrow audience of scholars with a particular interest in the field. The language used may be technical or highly specialised as a prior knowledge of the topic will be assumed. Often, an accepted article will still need to undergo several serious revisions, based on the referees' comments, before it actually appears in print.

These are usually the most useful for research projects as they will contain detailed reports of relevant earlier research. Not all academic journals are refereed. Most *non-refereed academic journals* will have an editor and possibly an editorial board with subject knowledge to select articles. The relevance and usefulness of such journals varies considerably, and occasionally you may need to be wary of possible bias (Section 3.6).

Professional journals (such as *People Management*) are produced for their members by organisations such as the Chartered Institute of Personnel and Development (CIPD), the Association of Chartered Certified Accountants (ACCA) and the American Marketing Association (AMA). They contain a mix of news-related items and articles that are more detailed. However, you need to exercise caution, as articles can be biased towards their author's or the organisation's views. Articles are often of a more practical nature and more closely related to professional needs than those in academic journals. Some organisations will also produce newsletters or current awareness publications that you may find useful for up-to-date information. Some professional organisations now give access to selected articles in their journals via their web pages, though these may be only accessible to members (see Table 8.2 and Section 3.5). Trade journals fulfil a similar function to professional journals. They are published by trade organisations or aimed at particular industries or trades such as catering or mining. Often they focus on new products or services and news items. They rarely contain articles based on empirical research, although some provide summaries of research. You should therefore use these with considerable caution for your research project.

Table 3.1 Main secondary and primary literature sources

<table>
<tr><th>Source</th><th>Frequency of publication</th><th>Format of publication</th><th>Coverage by abstracts and indexes (tertiary sources)</th><th>Likely availability</th></tr>
<tr><td>Refereed academic journal, non-refereed academic journal</td><td>Mainly monthly or quarterly</td><td rowspan="3">Mainly printed, vast majority now available via the Internet. Can be also available on CD-ROM</td><td>Well covered. In addition, content pages often available for searching via publishers' websites</td><td rowspan="2">Kept as reference in most university libraries; with many accessible via the Internet through various subscription services. Those not available locally can usually be obtained using inter-library loans. Professional organisations may also provide access to their journals via their own web pages</td></tr>
<tr><td>Professional journal</td><td rowspan="2">Mainly weekly or monthly</td><td rowspan="2">Increasingly well covered by services such as ABI/Inform and Business Source Premier. In addition, content pages often available for searching via publishers' websites</td></tr>
<tr><td>Trade journal</td><td>Not as widely available in university libraries as academic and refereed journals. Can be obtained using inter-library loans. Most trade associations will have an associated website</td></tr>
<tr><td>Books</td><td>Once; subsequent editions may be published</td><td>Mainly printed, increasingly available via the Internet including some text reproduced on line. Can also be available on CD-ROM</td><td>Well covered by abstracts and indexes. Searches can be undertaken on remote university OPACs* via the Internet</td><td>Widely available. Those not available locally can be obtained using interlibrary loans</td></tr>
<tr><td>Newspapers</td><td>Mainly daily or weekly</td><td>'Quality' newspapers now available on the Internet or through subscription online databases. Also available on CD-ROM and microfilm (for older back-runs)</td><td>Specialised indexes available. CD-ROM and Internet format easy to search using key words</td><td>Home nation 'quality' newspapers kept as reference in most university libraries. Internet access to stories, often with additional information on the websites, for most national and international 'quality' newspapers</td></tr>
<tr><td>Conference proceedings</td><td>Dependent on the conference, sometimes as part of journal</td><td>As for refereed academic journals. May be published in book form (e.g. Index to Conference Proceedings). Some conference proceedings or abstracts are published on the Internet</td><td>Depends on conference, although often limited. Specialist indexes sometimes available</td><td rowspan="2">Not widely held by university libraries. May be possible to obtain using inter-library loans</td></tr>
<tr><td>Reports</td><td>Once</td><td>As for refereed academic journals. Government reports increasingly accessible via the Internet</td><td>Poor compared with most secondary sources, although some specialised indexes exist</td></tr>
<tr><td>Theses</td><td>On the awarding of the research degree</td><td>Mainly printed</td><td>Good for PhD and MPhil research degrees, otherwise poor</td><td>Usually obtained using inter-library loans. Often only one copy</td></tr>
</table>

*OPAC, Online Public Access Catalogue.

Source: © Mark Saunders, Philip Lewis and Adrian Thornhill 2008.

Table 3.2 Tertiary literature sources and their coverage

Name	Format	Coverage
ABI Inform	Internet, CD-ROM	Indexes approximately 100 international business and management journals. Also contains a wide range of trade and professional titles. Covers additional subjects such as engineering, law and medicine. Full text of selected articles from 500 journals may be available depending on subscription (CD-ROM updated monthly)
British National Bibliography (BNB)	CD-ROM, print	Bibliographic information for books and serials (journals) deposited at the British Library by UK and Irish publishers since 1950
British Library Integrated Catalogue	Internet	Gives access to British Library catalogues including reference collections and document supply collections (books, journals, reports, conferences, theses)
Wilson Business Periodicals Index	Internet	Indexes English language business periodicals (articles and book reviews). North American focus. Selection for indexing is by subscriber preference and has altered over time (since 1959)
EBSCO Business Source Premier	Internet	Full-text articles from over 2000 management, business, economics and information technology journals, over 600 of which are refereed. Also containes a wide range of trade and professional titles
EMERALD Fulltext	Internet	801 full-text journals from MCB University Press
Emerald Management Xtra	Internet	Provides access to 160 full text journals and reviews from 300 management journals.
Global Books in Print	Internet	English language bibliographic information for books in print from most of the world
Helecon	Internet	Combined indexes from seven European databases on business and management. European focus
Index to Conference Proceedings	Internet	Proceedings of all significant conferences held worldwide. Annual cumulation available via the website as part of the Document Supply Conference File from the British Library Integrated Catalogue
Index to Theses	Internet	A comprehensive listing of theses with abstracts accepted for higher degrees by universities in Great Britain and Ireland since 1716
Ingenta	Internet	Journals contents page service, updated daily
ISI Web of Science	Internet	Includes access to a wide range of services, including citation indexes
Key Note Reports	Internet	Key Note market information reports
Lexis Nexis Executive	Internet	News coverage from approximately 12 000 publications, national and local newspapers, press releases, transcripts of TV broadcasts, newswires, statistical bulletins, magazines and trade journals
MINTEL	Internet, CD-ROM	Mintel reports plus short business press articles used in the compilation of the reports
Research Index	Internet, print	Indexes articles and news items of financial interest that appear in the UK national newspapers, professional and trade journals (updated frequently)
Sage Publications/ SRM Database of Social Research Methodology	Internet CD-ROM	Abstracts of methodological literature published in English, German, French and Dutch since 1970
Social Science Citation Index	Internet	Access to current and retrospective bibliographic information, author abstracts, and cited references found in over 1700 social sciences journals covering more than 50 disciplines. Also covers items from approximately 3300 of the world's leading science and technology journals
UK Official Publications (UKOP)	Internet	UKOP is the official catalogue of UK official publications since 1980. Containing 450 000 records from over 2000 public bodies

Books

Books and monographs are written for specific audiences. Some are aimed at the academic market, with a theoretical slant. Others, aimed at practising professionals, may be more applied in their content. The material in books is usually presented in a more ordered and accessible manner than in journals, pulling together a wider range of topics. They are, therefore, particularly useful as introductory sources to help clarify your research question(s) and objectives or the research methods you intend to use. Some academic text-books, such as this one, are now supported by web pages providing additional information. However, books may contain out-of-date material even by the time they are published.

Newspapers

Newspapers are a good source of topical events, developments within business and government, as well as recent statistical information such as share prices. They also sometimes review recent research reports (Box 3.6). The main 'quality' newspapers have websites

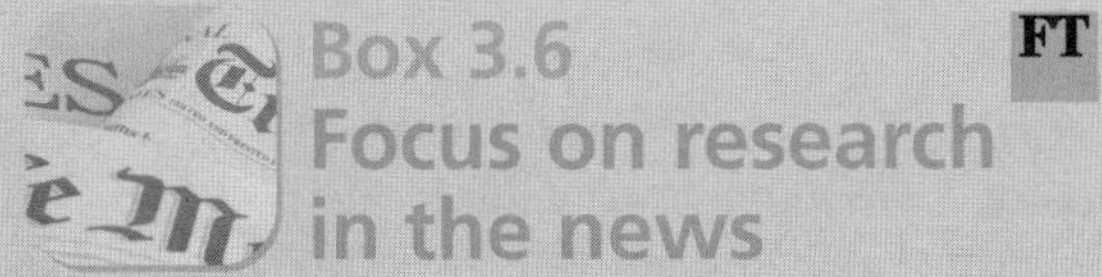

Box 3.6 Focus on research in the news FT

Biofuel targets in EU 'will outweigh benefits'

A plan to increase the use of biofuels in Europe may do nothing to help fight climate change and incur costs that outweigh the benefits, says an internal European Union report. The unpublished study by the Joint Research Centre, the European Commission's in-house scientific institute, may complicate the Commission's plans to set a new biofuels target so that by 2020 they account for 10 per cent of transport fuels in the 27-member EU.

'The costs will almost certainly outweigh the benefits', says the report, a copy of which has been obtained by the *Financial Times*. 'The decrease in welfare caused by imposing a biofuels target' is between €33 bn ($48 bn, £25 bn) and €65 bn, the study says. 'The uncertainty is too great to say whether the EU 10 per cent biofuel target will save greenhouse gas or not', it adds.

EU leaders called for the target last year as part of a move to cut greenhouse gas emissions by 20 per cent of 1990 levels by 2020.

However, some commissioners have expressed concern about the knock-on effects of using plants for fuel. Indonesia has seen mass street protests this week over record soyabean prices triggered by US farmers opting to grow corn to supply the biofuel industry. Green groups are also concerned that forests could be cleared for food crops that have been displaced by biofuel plantations. Corn and palm oil are among the most popular biofuel sources, though only sugar from Brazil is considered sufficiently 'green' by the Joint Research Centre as it grows quickly and produces a lot of energy.

A Commission spokeswoman said the centre's report had not been peer reviewed. She said: 'It is a contribution to the debate. We are looking at the whole picture and we will have sustainability criteria'.

In the draft directive, only those biofuel sources grown on land that was not forest or peat bog can be counted. There would also be a minimum level of greenhouse-gas saving, as some require more carbon to make than fossil fuels burn. Countries would have to monitor imports to check their origin. However, since the World Trade Organisation governs trade in biofuels, it is not possible to block them on environmental grounds.

The Joint Research Centre suggests that it would be more efficient to use biomass to generate power and that the separate transport target be scrapped. It is even doubtful of the merits of using waste products, such as straw, since transporting large quantities to biofuel factories itself requires fuel.

Adrian Bebb, of Friends of the Earth, said: 'The report has a damning verdict on the EU policy. It should be abandoned in favour of real solutions to climate change.'

Source: article by Bounds, Andrew (2008) *Financial Times*, 18 Jan.

carrying the main stories and supporting information. Back copies starting in the early 1990s are available on CD-ROM or online via a full-text subscription service, such as *Proquest Newspapers* (Table 3.1). Current editions of newspapers can usually be found via the Internet. Most newspapers have a dedicated website and provide access to a limited full-text service free of charge. Items in earlier issues are more difficult to access, as they are usually stored on microfilm and need to be located using printed indexes. However, you need to be careful, as newspapers may contain bias in their coverage, be it political, geographical or personal. Reporting can also be inaccurate, and you may not pick up any subsequent amendments. In addition, the news presented is filtered depending on events at the time, with priority given to more headline-grabbing stories (Stewart and Kamins, 1993).

Primary literature sources

Primary literature sources are more difficult to locate, although an increasing number are now being made available via the Internet (Table 3.1). The most accessible, and those most likely to be of use in showing how your research relates to that of other people, are reports, conference proceedings and theses.

Reports

Reports include market research reports such as those produced by Mintel and Keynote, government reports and academic reports. Even if you are able to locate these, you may find it difficult to gain access to them because they are not as widely available as books (Section 8.4). Reports are not well indexed in the tertiary literature, and you will need to rely on specific search tools such as the *British National Bibliography for Report Literature* and the British Library Public Catalogue (see Table 3.2).

The move toward 'freedom for information' by many Western governments has resulted in more information being made available via the web, for example the European Union's (EU) European Commission website and the Commission's Statistics website Eurostat. These and other governmental websites are listed in Table 8.3. European 'grey literature', including reports, conference proceedings, and discussion and policy papers, has been covered since 1980 by SIGLE (System for Information on Grey Literature in Europe) and is available from the publisher OVID.

Individual academics are also increasingly publishing reports and their research on the Internet. These can be a useful source of information. However, they may not have gone through the same review and evaluation process as journal articles and books. It is therefore important to try to assess the authority of the author, and to beware of personal bias.

Conference proceedings

Conference proceedings, sometimes referred to as symposia, are often published as unique titles within journals or as books. Most conferences will have a theme that is very specific, but some have a wide-ranging overview. Proceedings are not well indexed by tertiary literature so, as with reports, you may have to rely on specific search tools such as *Index to Conference Proceedings* and the British Library Public Catalogue (Table 3.2) as well as more general search engines such as Google. If you do locate and are able to obtain the proceedings for a conference on the theme of your research, you will have a wealth of relevant information. Many conferences have associated web pages providing abstracts and occasionally the full papers presented at the conference.

Theses

Theses are unique and so for a major research project can be a good source of detailed information; they will also be a good source of further references. Unfortunately, they can be difficult to locate and, when found, difficult to access as there may be only one copy at the awarding institution. Specific search tools are available, such as *Index to Theses* (see Table 3.2). Only research degrees such as PhD and MPhil are covered well by these tertiary resources. Research undertaken as part of a taught masters degree is not covered as systematically.

3.4 Planning your literature search strategy

It is important that you plan this search carefully to ensure that you locate relevant and up-to-date literature. This will enable you to establish what research has been previously published in your area and to relate your own research to it. All our students have found their literature search a time-consuming process, which takes far longer than expected. Fortunately, time spent planning will be repaid in time saved when searching the literature. As you start to plan your search, you need to beware of information overload! One of the easiest ways to avoid this is to start the main search for your critical review with a clearly defined research question(s), objectives and outline proposal (Sections 2.4 and 2.5). Before commencing your literature search, we suggest that you undertake further planning by writing down your search strategy and, if possible, discussing it with your project tutor. This should include:

- the parameters of your search;
- the key words and search terms you intend to use;
- the databases and search engines you intend to use;
- the criteria you intend to use to select the relevant and useful studies from all the items you find.

Whilst it is inevitable that your search strategy will be refined as your literature search progresses, we believe that such a planned approach is important as it forces you to think carefully about your research strategy and justify, at least to yourself, why you are doing what you are doing.

Defining the parameters of your search

For most research questions and objectives you will have a good idea of which subject matter is going to be relevant. You will, however, be less clear about the parameters within which you need to search. In particular, you need to be clear about the following (Bell 2005):

- language of publication (e.g. English);
- subject area (e.g. accountancy);
- business sector (e.g. manufacturing);
- geographical area (e.g. Europe);
- publication period (e.g. the last 10 years);
- literature type (e.g. refereed journals and books).

One way of starting to firm up these parameters is to re-examine your lecture notes and course textbooks in the area of your research question. While re-examining these, we suggest you make a note of subjects that appear most relevant to your research question and the names of relevant authors. These will be helpful when generating possible key words later.

For example, if your research was on the marketing benefits of arts sponsorship to UK banking organisations you might identify the subject area as marketing and sponsorship. Implicit in this is the need to think broadly. A common comment we hear from students

Box 3.7 Focus on student research

Defining parameters for a research question

Simon's research question was 'How have green issues influenced the way in which manufacturers advertise cars?' To be certain of finding material, he defined each parameter in narrow and, in most instances, broader terms:

Parameter	Narrow	Broader
Language	UK (e.g. car)	UK and USA (e.g. car and automobile)
Subject area	Green issues	Environmental issues
	Motor industry	Manufacturing
	Advertising	Marketing
Business sector	Motor industry	Manufacturing
Geographical area	UK	Europe and North America
Publication period	Last 5 years	Last 15 years
Literature type	Refereed journals and books	Journals and books

who have attempted a literature search is 'there's nothing written on my research topic'. This is usually because they have identified one or more of their parameters too narrowly (or chosen key words that do not match the control language, Section 3.5). We, therefore, recommend that if you encounter this problem you broaden one or more of your parameters to include material that your narrower search would not have located (Box 3.7).

Generating your key words

It is important at this stage to read both articles by key authors and recent review articles in the area of your research. This will help you to define your subject matter and to suggest appropriate key words. Recent review articles in your research area are often helpful here as they discuss the current state of research for a particular topic and can help you to refine your key words. In addition, they will probably contain references to other work that is pertinent to your research question(s) and objectives (Box 3.8). If you are unsure about review articles, your project tutor should be able to point you in the right direction. Another potentially useful source of references is dissertations and theses in your university's library.

After re-reading your lecture notes and textbooks and undertaking this limited reading you will have a list of subjects that appear relevant to your research project. You now need to define precisely what is relevant to your research in terms of key words.

The identification of **key words** or 'search' terms is the most important part of planning your search for relevant literature (Bell 2005). Key words are the basic terms that describe your research question(s) and objectives, and will be used to search the tertiary literature. Key words (which can include authors' surnames identified in the examination of your lecture notes and course textbooks) can be identified using one or a number

Box 3.8 Focus on management research

Using an archival research method in the framework for conducting and evaluating research

In one of the most recently read articles from the *International Journal of Management Reviews*, Srivastava (2007) uses a sophisticated method of literature review in a review of supply chain management. The article argues that there is a growing need for integrating environmentally sound choices into supply-chain management research and practice. The author peruses the literature and concludes that a broad frame of reference for green supply-chain management (GrSCM) is not adequately developed and that a succinct classification to help academicians, researchers and practitioners in understanding integrated GrSCM from a wider perspective is needed.

Srivastava covers the literature on GrSCM exhaustively from its conceptualisation, primarily taking a 'reverse logistics angle'. Using the rich body of available literature, including earlier reviews that had relatively limited perspectives, the literature on GrSCM is classified on the basis of the problem context in supply chain's major influential areas. It is also classified on the basis of methodology and approach adopted. Various mathematical tools/techniques used in literature *vis-à-vis* the contexts of GrSCM are mapped. A timeline indicating relevant papers is also provided as a ready reference.

The literature research is driven by theoretical preconsiderations and may be classified as an archival research method in the framework for conducting and evaluating research suggested by Searcy and Mentzer (2003). The process of analysis comprises the following steps:

- *Defining unit of analysis:* the unit of analysis was defined as a single research paper/book.
- *Classification context:* the classification context to be applied in the literature review to structure and classify the material was selected and defined. There were two contexts: the problem context and methodology/approach context.
- *Material evaluation:* the material was analysed and sorted according to the classification context. This allowed identification of relevant issues and interpretation of the results. Problem context and related methodology/approaches allowed classification of the reviewed literature. Srivastava argues that this can be derived deductively or inductively.
- *Collecting publications and delimiting the field:* Srivastava's literature review focuses upon books, edited volumes and journal articles only, from 1990. Library databases were used where a keyword search using some important keywords such as 'green supply chain', remanufacturing', 'green purchasing', 'green design', 'industrial ecology', 'industrial ecosystems', 'RL', 'remanufacturing' and 'waste management' were conducted.

To delimit the number of publications, empirical papers mainly addressing firm-level or specific operational issues were excluded from the review. Similarly, highly technical work on topics such as life-cycle assessment, inventory, pollution prevention and disassembly were also excluded from the review. Research with a highly ecological rather than supply chain perspective (green purchasing, industrial ecology and industrial ecosystems) was also excluded. Srivastava used the published literature from 1990 onwards to go back to other papers by cross-referencing. As the published literature is interlinked to a considerable degree, one paper (stem) leads to others (branches). So, one thread, leads to others. As references accumulated, it was found that some of them were more central and useful than others. Srivastava considered such references as seminal papers. These were also found to be generally referenced a number of times in subsequent literature. Thus, within the defined objective, this work integrates and takes forward the literature on GrSCM since its conceptualisation. About 1500 books, articles from journals and edited volumes were covered and generated a list of 227 cited references which are given at the end of the article.

References

Searcy, D.L. and Mentzer, J.T. (2003) 'A framework for conducting and evaluating research', *Journal of Accounting Literature*, 22, pp. 130–67.

Srivastava, S. (2007) 'Green supply-chain management: A state-of-the-art literature review', *International Journal of Management Reviews*, 9(1), pp. 53–80.

of different techniques in combination. Those found most useful by our students include:

Discussion

We believe you should be taking every opportunity to discuss your research. In discussing your work with others, whether face to face, by email or by letter, you will be sharing your ideas, getting feedback and obtaining new ideas and approaches. This process will help you to refine and clarify your topic.

Initial reading, dictionaries, encyclopaedias, handbooks and thesauruses

To produce the most relevant key words you may need to build on your brainstorming session with support materials such as dictionaries, encyclopedias, handbooks and thesauruses, both general and subject specific. These are also good starting points for new topics with which you may be unfamiliar and for related subject areas. Initial reading, particularly of recent review articles, may also be of help here. Project tutors, colleagues and librarians can also be useful sources of ideas.

It is also possible to obtain definitions via the Internet. The online search engine Google offers a 'define' search option (by typing 'Define:[enter term]') that provides links to websites providing definitions. Definitions are also offered in free online encyclopaedias such as Wikipedia (see Box 3.9).[1] These are often available in multiple languages and, although

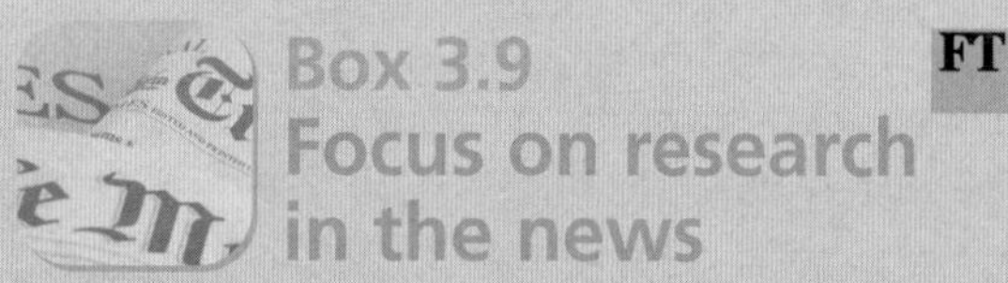

FT

Google has taken direct aim at Wikipedia with a project designed to supplant the collectively produced encyclopedia as the primary source for basic information on the web. Known as 'Knol', and currently restricted to a limited test, the service is a highly ambitious attempt to collect and organise 'user-generated information' in all fields of knowledge.

The move echoes other Google efforts to transform online behaviour. With Google's service, anyone will eventually be able to write a web page about any topic they want, and have it indexed by Google and other search engines. Authors will also be able to benefit from any advertising placed on the page. Google has given few details about how it would rank submissions to highlight the most accurate or useful, but said user ratings would be important.

'A Knol on a particular topic is meant to be the first thing someone who searches for this topic for the first time will want to read', Udi Manber, a Google engineer, wrote on a blog post that announced the project. That role is often taken by Wikipedia entries, which frequently appear high on Google's and other search engines' results, making the collective encyclopedia one of the 10 most visited sites.

The design of the Google project seeks to address some of the fundamental issues that have hampered the controversial Wikipedia. Entries in the encyclopedia are anonymous and often lead to heated 'edit wars', as people with rival opinions compete to change items. By contrast, Google plans to identify its writers and avoid the collective editing process altogether. 'The key idea behind the Knol project is to highlight authors', Mr Manber said. He added Google expected rival notes to appear on many topics: 'Competition of ideas is a good thing'. That approach will avoid the 'problems of governance that come from trying to run a collaborative community' like Wikipedia, said Larry Sanger, a founder of the website who split with that project over its failure to apply stricter editing policies.

Source: article by Waters, Richard (2007) *Financial Times*, 15 Dec.

[1]The Internet address for Wikipedia is http://www.wikipedia.org/.

anyone is allowed to edit the entries, inappropriate changes are usually removed quickly (Wikipedia 2008). However, whilst these websites may be useful for a quick reference or in helping to define keywords, your university will almost certainly expect you to justify the definitions in your research project using refereed journal articles or textbooks.

Brainstorming

Brainstorming has already been outlined as a technique for helping you to develop your research question (Section 2.3). However, it is also helpful for generating key words. Either individually or as part of a group, you write down all the words and short phrases that come to mind on your research topic (Box 3.10). These are then evaluated and key words (and phrases) selected.

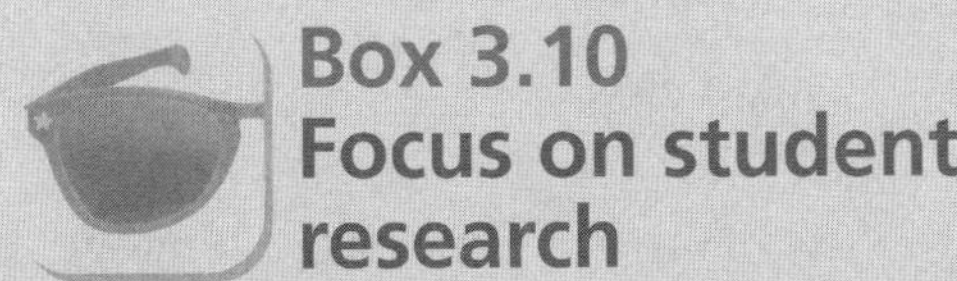

Box 3.10 Focus on student research

Generating key words

Han's research question was 'How do the actual management requirements of a school pupil record administration system differ from those suggested by the literature?' She brainstormed this question with her peer group, all of whom were teachers in Hong Kong. The resulting list included the following key words and phrases:

schools, pupil records, administration, user requirements, computer, management information system, access, legislation, information, database, security, UK, Hong Kong, theories

The group evaluated these and others. As a result, the following key words (and phrases) were selected:

pupil records, management information system, computer, database, user requirement

Dictionaries and encyclopaedias were used subsequently to add to the choice of key words:

student record, MIS, security

Han made a note of these prior to using them in combination to search the tertiary literature sources.

Relevance trees

Relevance trees provide a useful method of bringing some form of structure to your literature search and of guiding your search process (Sharp *et al.* 2002). They look similar to an organisation chart and are a hierarchical 'graph-like' arrangement of headings and subheadings (Box 3.11). These headings and subheadings describe your research question(s) and objectives and may be key words (including authors' names) with which you can search. Relevance trees are often constructed after brainstorming. They enable you to decide either with help or on your own (Jankowicz 2005):

- which key words are directly relevant to your research question(s) and objectives;
- which areas you will search first and which your search will use later;
- which areas are more important – these tend to have more branches.

To construct a relevance tree:

1. Start with your research question or objective at the top level.
2. Identify two or more subject areas that you think are important.
3. Further subdivide each major subject area into sub-areas that you think are of relevance.
4. Further divide the sub-areas into more precise sub-areas that you think are of relevance.

5 Identify those areas that you need to search immediately and those that you particularly need to focus on. Your project tutor will be of particular help here.
6 As your reading and reviewing progress, add new areas to your relevance tree.

Computer software to help generate relevance trees, such as Inspiration (2008) and MindGenius (2008), is also increasingly available in universities. Using this software also allows you to attach notes to your relevance tree and can help generate an initial structure for your literature review.

3.5 Conducting your literature search

Your literature search will probably be conducted using a variety of approaches:

- searching using tertiary literature sources;
- obtaining relevant literature (Section 3.6) referenced in books and journal articles you have already read;
- scanning and browsing secondary literature in your library;
- searching using the Internet.

Eventually it is likely you will be using a variety of these in combination. However, we suggest that you start your search by obtaining relevant literature that has been referenced in books and articles you have already read. Although books are unlikely to give adequate up-to-date coverage of your research question, they provide a useful starting point and usually contain some references to further reading. Reading these will enable you to refine your research question(s), objectives and the associated key words prior to

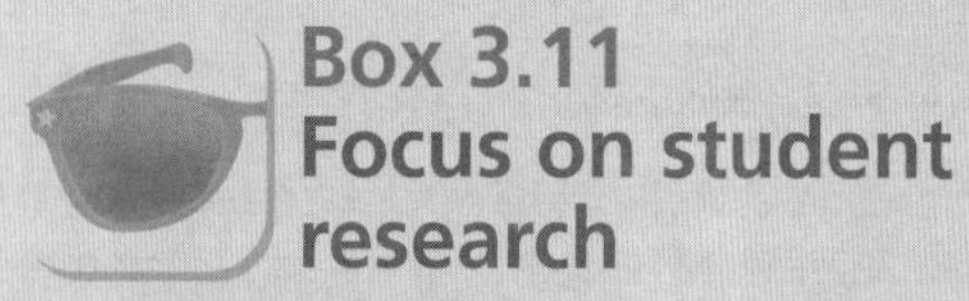

Box 3.11 Focus on student research

Using a relevance tree

Sadie's research question was 'Is there a link between benchmarking and Total Quality Management?' After brainstorming her question, she decided to construct a relevance tree using the key words and phrases that had been generated.

Using her relevance tree Sadie identified those areas that she needed to search immediately (underlined) and those that she particularly needed to focus on (starred*):

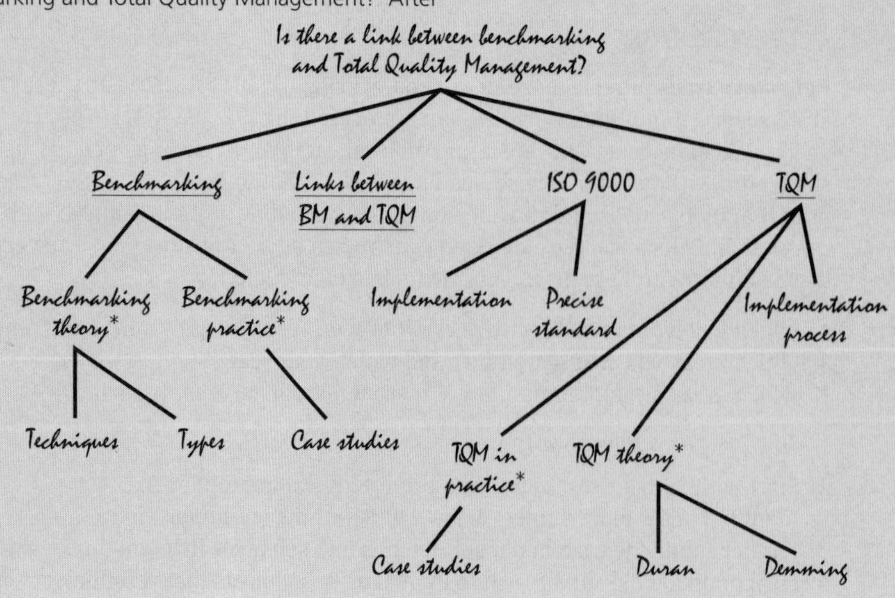

searching using tertiary literature sources. It will also help you to see more clearly how your research relates to previous research, and will provide fresh insights.

Tertiary literature sources

A variety of tertiary literature is available to help you in your search. Most of these publications are called indexes and abstracts, and a selection will be accessible via the Internet or held by your university library. It is very tempting with easy access to the Internet to start your literature search with an Internet search engine. Whilst this can retrieve some useful information it must be treated with care. Your project report is expected to be an academic piece of work and hence must use academic sources. Therefore it is essential that you use tertiary sources that provide access to academic literature. Many of these can now be easily accessed via the Internet anyway. An index will, as its name suggests, index articles from a range of journals and sometimes books, chapters from books, reports, theses, conferences and research. The information provided will be sufficient to locate the item – for example, for journal articles:

- author or authors of the article;
- date of publication;
- title of the article;
- title of the journal;
- volume and part number of the journal issue;
- page numbers of the article.

Most index searches will be undertaken to find articles using key words, including the author's name. Occasionally you may wish to search by finding those authors who have referenced (cited) a key article after it has been published. A citation index enables you to do this as it lists by author the other authors who have cited that author's publications subsequent to their publication.

An **abstract** provides the same information as an index but also includes a summary of the article, hence the term abstract. This abstract can be useful in helping you to assess the content and relevance of an article to your research before obtaining a copy. You should beware of using abstracts, as a substitute for the full article, as a source of information for your research. They contain only a summary of the article and are likely to exclude much of relevance.

Indexes and abstracts are produced in printed and electronic (computerised) formats, the latter often being referred to as online databases. This is the term we shall use to refer to all electronic information sources. With the increasing amount of information available electronically, printed indexes and abstracts are often overlooked. Yet, they can still provide a valuable resource, providing a varied and sometimes more specific range of information. An increasing number of online databases contain full-text articles. This has helped both to simplify literature searching and to make it a more seamless process, with the searching and retrieval of the full text available from the same source. Most of these online databases will allow you to print, save or email your results. The latter two options will obviously help save you printing costs.

Access to the majority of databases that you will use via the Internet will be paid for by a subscription from your university. There are, however, some pay-as-you-use databases, where the cost of the search is passed on to the user. Online databases provide a wealth of information. Whilst many online databases are intuitive to use, it is still advisable to obtain a librarian's help or to attend a training session prior to your search to find out about the specific features available. It is also vital that you plan and prepare your search in advance so your time is not wasted. For many databases, password protected access is now possible from remote sites such as home or work as well as from your university. Your librarian should have more information on this. An additional source of information via the Internet, which our students have found useful, is publishers' web pages. These often include journals' content pages (see Table 3.4).

Most university library OPACs (online public access catalogues) are now accessible via the Internet (see Table 3.5 on p. 87). These provide a very useful means of locating resources. If you identify useful collections of books and journals, it is possible to make use of other university libraries in the vacations. Within the UK, the SCONUL Vacation Access Scheme gives details of access policies of the libraries in UK higher-education institutions.[2]

To ensure maximum coverage in your search you need to use all appropriate abstracts and indexes. One mistake many people make is to restrict their searches to one or two business and management tertiary sources rather than to use a variety. The coverage of each abstract and index differs in both geographical coverage and type of journal (Section 3.3). In addition, an abstract or index may state that it indexes a particular journal yet may do so only selectively. This emphasises the importance of using a range of databases to ensure a wide coverage of available literature. Some of those more frequently used are outlined in Table 3.2. However, new databases are being developed all the time so it is worth asking a librarian for advice.

Searching using tertiary literature

Once your key words have been identified, searching using tertiary literature is a relatively straightforward process. You need to:

1. ensure that your key words match the controlled index language (unless you can use free text searching);
2. search appropriate printed and database sources;
3. note precise details, including the search strings used, of the actual searches you have undertaken for each database;
4. note the full reference of each item found; this can normally be done by cutting and pasting the references.

Tranfield *et al.* (2003), in their article on **systematic review**, emphasise the importance of reporting your literature search strategy in sufficient detail to ensure that your search could be replicated (Boxes 3.12, 3.13). Your review will be based on the subset of those items found which you consider are relevant.

Printed sources

Although they are increasingly rare, printed indexes and abstracts require a different searching technique from electronic databases. The coverage of printed indexes tends to be smaller and possibly more specialised than that of databases. Unlike databases, it is normally only possible to search by author or one broad subject heading, although some cross-references may be included. Because they are paper based, each issue or annual accumulation must be searched individually, which can be time consuming.

Databases

Most databases, in contrast, allow more precise searches using combinations of search terms. These can include indexed key words, which will need to match the database's **controlled index language** of pre-selected terms and phrases or 'descriptors'. These can include specified subject words, author names, and journal titles. If your key words do

---

[2]Details of these can be found on the Internet at: http://www.sconul.ac.uk/use_lib/vacation.html.

Box 3.12 Focus on management research

Conducting a review of the literature through the process of systematic review

Tranfield *et al.* (2003) emphasise that undertaking a review of the literature is an important part of any research project. The researcher maps and assesses the relevant intellectual territory in order to specify a research question which will develop knowledge of the topic. In their view, however, traditional 'narrative' reviews frequently lack thoroughness, and in many cases are not undertaken as genuine pieces of investigatory science. Consequently, they can lack a means for making sense of what the collection of studies is saying. These reviews can suffer from researcher bias and a lack of rigour. In addition, Tranfield *et al.* assert that the use of reviews of the available evidence to provide insights and guidance for intervention into operational needs of practitioners and policymakers has largely been of secondary importance. For practitioners, making sense of a mass of often-contradictory evidence has become more difficult. Inadequate or incomplete evidence seriously impedes policy formulation and implementation.

In their article Tranfield *et al.* explore ways in which evidence-informed management reviews might be achieved through the process of systematic review used in the medical sciences. Over the last 15 years, medical science has attempted to improve the review process by synthesising research in a systematic, transparent, and reproducible manner with the twin aims of enhancing the knowledge base and informing policymaking and practice.

According to Tranfield *et al.* and Denyer and Neely (2004) systematic review includes:

- the development of clear and precise aims and objectives for the literature review;
- pre-planned search methods;
- a comprehensive search of all potentially relevant articles;
- the use of clear assessment criteria in the selection of articles for review;
- assessment of the quality of the research in each article and of the strength of the findings;
- synthesising the individual studies using a clear framework;
- presenting the results in a balanced, impartial and comprehensive manner.

Both Tranfield *et al.* and Denyer and Neely (2004) outline how the review was undertaken. This includes how the key words used in the search were identified, and what they were; how the key words were combined into search strings using Boolean operators; the databases searched and the total numbers of articles found; and appendices that list the relevance criteria used to exclude and include articles in the review. Denyer and Neely argue that this should enable readers to determine the reasonableness of the decisions taken by the reviewers when writing their reviews as well as the appropriateness of the conclusions in each review.

not match those in the controlled index language, your search will be unsuccessful. You, therefore, need to check your key words with the 'index' or 'browse' option prior to searching. This is especially useful to establish how an author is indexed or whether hyphens should be used when entering specific terms. Some databases will also have a 'thesaurus' which links words in the controlled index language to other terms. Some thesauruses will provide a definition of the term used as well as indicating other broader subject areas, more specific subject areas or subjects related to the original term. Despite using these tools, your searches may still be unsuccessful. The most frequent causes of failure are summarised in Box 3.13 as a checklist.

Once individual key words have been checked, subsequent searches normally use a combination of key words linked using **Boolean logic**. These are known as **search strings** and enable you to combine, limit or widen the variety of items found using 'link terms' (Table 3.3). Boolean logic can also be used to construct search strings using dates, journal

Box 3.13 Checklist

Minimising problems with your key words

- ✔ Is the spelling incorrect? Behaviour is spelt with a 'u' in the UK but without in the USA.
- ✔ Is the language incorrect? Chemists in the UK but drug stores in the USA.
- ✔ Are you using incorrect terminology? In recent years some terms have been replaced by others, such as 'redundancy' being replaced by 'downsizing'.
- ✔ Are you using recognised acronyms and abbreviations? For example, UK for United Kingdom or ICI instead of Imperial Chemical Industries.
- ✔ Are you avoiding jargon and using accepted terminology? For example, downsizing rather than redundancy.
- ✔ Are you avoiding words that are not in the controlled index language?

Table 3.3 Common link terms that use Boolean logic

Link term	Purpose	Example	Outcome
AND	Narrows search	Recruitment AND interviewing AND skills	Only articles containing all three key words selected
OR	Widens search	Recruitment OR selection	Articles with at least one key word selected
NOT	Excludes terms from search	Recruitment NOT selection	Selects articles containing the key word 'recruitment' that do not contain the key word 'selection'
***(truncation)**	Uses word stems to pick up different	Motivat*	Selects articles with: Motivate Motivation Motivating
? (wild card)	Picks up different spellings	behavio?r	Selects articles with: Behavior Behaviour

titles and names of organisations or people. Initially it may be useful to limit your search to journal titles to which your university subscribes. It may also be valuable to narrow your search to specific years, especially if you are finding a wealth of items and need to concentrate on the most up to date. By contrast, searching by author allows you to broaden your search to find other work by known researchers in your area.

You can also search just one or more specified fields in the database such as the author, title or abstract. This may be useful if you wish to find articles by a key author in your subject area. Alternatively, many databases allow you to search the entire database rather than just the controlled vocabulary using **free text searching**. Free text searching is increasingly common for electronic publications both on CD-ROM and accessed via the Internet, in particular quality newspapers and journals. These may not have a controlled index language. There are, however, problems with using a free text search. In particular, the context of a key word may be inappropriate, leading to retrieval of numerous irrelevant articles and information overload.

Scanning and browsing

Any search will find only some of the relevant literature. You will therefore also need to scan and browse the literature. New publications such as journals are unlikely to be indexed immediately in tertiary literature, so you will need to browse these publications to gain an idea of their content. In contrast, scanning will involve you going through individual items such as a journal article to pick out points that relate to your own research. It is particularly important that you browse and scan trade and professional journals, as these are less likely to be covered by the tertiary literature.

To make browsing and scanning easier you should:

- identify when those journals that are the most relevant are published and regularly browse them;
- browse new book displays in libraries;
- scan new book reviews in journals and newspapers;
- scan publishers' new book catalogues where available;
- discuss your research with your project tutor and librarians, who may be aware of other relevant literature.

Internet access to resources now allows you to browse journals that may not be held in, or accessible from, your university library. Many publishers make the contents pages of their journals available without charge on the web (Table 3.4) and may offer an article alert service where they will provide a regular email update of articles in your area of interest. Alternatively, databases such as Ingenta provide access to thousands of journals' contents pages (Table 3.2). Professional journals may also be accessible through the web page of the professional organisation (Table 8.2). Many publishers make their current book catalogues available on the Internet, and these can be accessed either directly (Table 3.4) or through the publishers' catalogues' home page (see Table 3.5). In addition, websites of bookshops such as Amazon, Blackwell and the Internet Book Shop provide access to catalogues of books in print. These can usually be searched by author, title and subject, and may have reviews attached (Table 3.4). In addition, some bookseller websites (and Google Books) have a facility whereby you can view selected pages from the book. However, as when using electronic indexes and abstracts, it is important that you keep full details of the literature you have scanned and browsed (Box 3.14). As well as enabling you to outline the method you used for your literature review, it will also help prevent you repeating searches you have already undertaken.

Searching the Internet

The development of the Internet has revolutionised information gathering, including searching for literature. It will provide you with access to resources that may be of use either for your literature review or as secondary data (Chapter 8). However, you should beware, as these resources may be difficult to locate and the quality of the material is highly variable. This is emphasised by Clausen (1996:4), who likens the Internet to:

> . . . a huge vandalized library where someone has destroyed the catalogue and removed the front matter and indexes from most of the books. In addition thousands of unorganized fragments are added daily by a myriad of cranks, sages and persons with time on their hands who launch their unfiltered messages into cyberspace.

Table 3.4 Selected publishers' and bookshops' Internet addresses

Name	Internet address	Contents
Publishers		
Blackwell Publishers	http://www.blackwellpublishing.com	Books and journals
Cambridge University Press	http://www.cup.cam.ac.uk	Books and journals; links to other university presses and publishing-related services
Pearson Education Limited	http://www.pearsoned.co.uk	Business and management books for practitioners and students. Links to book-specific web pages
Office of Public Sector Information	http://www.opsi.gov.uk	OPSI publications, including full text of Statutory Instruments and Public Acts
Emerald	http://www.emeraldinsight.com	Over 100 professional and academic management journals
Open University Press	http://www.openup.co.uk	Books and journals
Oxford University Press	http://www.oup.co.uk	Books and journals, including full-text online journals, a database of abstracts
Prentice Hall	http://www.pearsoned.co.uk	Books and other study materials
Routledge	http://www.routledge.com	Books
Sage	http://www.sagepub.co.uk	Books, journals, software, CD-ROMs
Cengage (previously Thomson)	http://www.cengagelearning.co.uk	Books, and other study materials
Bookshops		
Amazon	http://www.amazon.co.uk	Searchable database principally of books (UK site)
	http://www.amazon.com	Searchable database principally of books (USA site)
Blackwell	http://www.blackwell.co.uk	Searchable database principally of books
Internet Book Shop UK	http://www.ibuk.com	Searchable database principally of books
Abe Books	http://www.abebooks.co.uk	New, second-hand, rare, or out-of-print, through 13 500 independent booksellers.
The Book Depository	http://www.bookdepository.co.uk/	
The Book Place	http://www.thebookplace.co.uk	Searchable database principally of books
TSO (The Stationery Office)	http://www.tsoshop.co.uk	Searchable database of UK books in print. Especially useful for UK government reports

NB: All services in this table were free at the time of writing.

Table 3.5 Selected Internet search tools and their coverage

Name	Internet address	Comment
General search engines		
Alta Vista Search	http://www.altavista.com	Searches web and Usenet newsgroups
Google	http://www.google.com	Access to over 3 billion documents
Google UK	http://www.google.co.uk	
Google Scholar	http://scholar.google.com/	Access to academic journals, theses, books, journals and abstracts from a limited number of academic and professional organisations. Access to the full text is often dependent on an institution's subscription to a journal or service
HotBot	http://www.hotbot.co.uk/	Searches web; useful features include sorting by date and media type
Lycos	http://www.lycos.com	Searches web, gopher and ftp sites; offers both key word and subject searching
Specialised search engines		
UK government	http://www.direct.gov.uk	Searches central and local government websites and government agencies
Information gateways		
Biz/Ed	http://www.bized.co.uk	Information service, links economics and business students and teachers and information providers
BUBL subject tree	http://bubl.ac.uk	Links to a vast range of Internet resources by alphabetical subject list or by class (subject) number order
Human Resource Management Resources on the Internet	http://www.nbs.ntu.ac.uk/research//depts/hrm/links.php	Annotated list of links. List split into sub-categories, and provides short description of content
HERO (UK Universities and Colleges OPACs)	http://www.hero.ac.uk	Links to UK university and college online public access (library) catalogues (OPACs)
Pinakes	http://www.hw.ac.uk/libWWW/irn/pinakes/pinakes.html	Links to major information gateways to Internet resources (especially UK based)
Publishers' catalogues homepage	http://www.lights.ca/publisher/	Links to major publishers' websites, listed alphabetically by country
Resource Discovery Network	http://www.rdn.ac.uk/	Subject-based information and Internet tutorials
SOSIG UK Business and Industrial Management Resource	http://www.sosig.ac.uk/roads/subject-listing/roads/subject-listing/	Detailed descriptions and links to UK business and industrial and industrial management sites
Subject directories		
Yahoo	http://dir.yahoo.com/	Subject-based directory
Yahoo UK	http://uk.yahoo.com	Optionally limits searches to just UK and Ireland
	http://uk.dir.yahoo.com/news_and_media/newspapers	Comprehensive listing of newspapers available on the Internet, worldwide
Yellow Pages UK	http://www.yell.co.uk	Telephone yellow pages with useful links to UK companies' home pages

There is a variety of approaches you can use for searching the Internet. These are summarised in Figure 3.3. Printed guides are available and can be a useful starting point for information. However, because of the rate at which the Internet is growing and the fact that material can literally disappear overnight, these guidebooks are likely to

Box 3.14 Focus on student research

Searching electronic indexes and abstracts

Matthew described his research project using the key words 'small business' and 'finance'. Unfortunately, he encountered problems when carrying out his search using one of the online databases of full text and abstracts for business, management and economics journals to which his university subscribed:

- When he entered the key word 'small business', he retrieved references to over 162 000 items many of which were in trade magazines.
- He was unsure how to combine his key words into search strings to make his search more specific.
- Full-text versions were not available for the many of the most recent items retrieved.

After discussing the problem, the librarian showed Matthew how to use the advanced search option of the online database. Using this, Matthew first searched using the terms 'small business' and 'finance' combined as a search string. This still resulted in over 500 items being highlighted.

He then refined his search further by limiting it to the collection of scholarly (peer reviewed) journals. This resulted in just over 200 items being retrieved. Matthew made a note of the details of his search:

Database:	Business Source Complete
Collection:	Scholarly (peer reviewed) journals
Dates:	1980 to 2008
Search:	small business AND finance
Fields searched:	Abstract
Date of search:	38 June 2008
Total items retrieved:	219

He then copied the references for these items (articles) onto his MP3 player. As Matthew scrolled through these, he noted that some of them had direct links to copies of the full text stored as a .pdf file. For many of the others, the librarian informed him that he could access the full text using different online databases. However, he still needed to assess each article's relevance to his research before obtaining full copies.

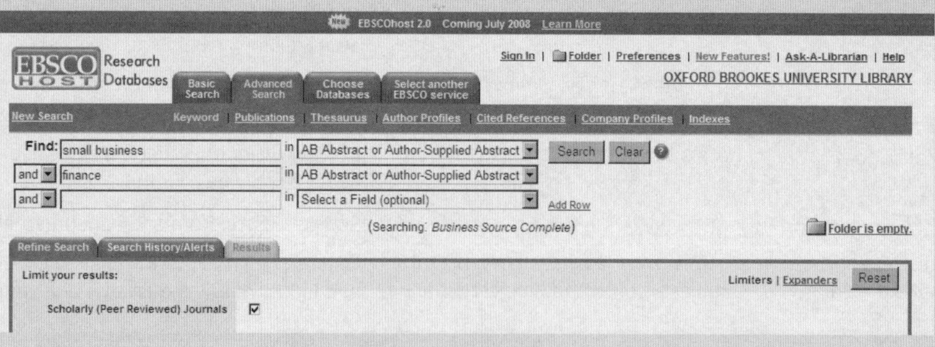

Source: EBSCO Information Services, reproduced with permission.

become out of date extremely quickly. Alternatively, you can use websites dedicated to providing support information on searching the Internet. One such example that our students have found useful is that provided by Phil Bradley, an information expert.[3] This contains information on different search engines, articles on Internet searching and web page and website design and is regularly updated. Another useful site is hosted by RBA Information Services.[4] This contains an excellent directory of business-related websites

[3]The Internet address of the home page of this site is http://www.philb.com/.

[4]The Internet address of the home page of this site is http://www.rba.co.uk.

as well as a wealth of more generic information on searching the Internet. Once again, we recommend that you keep full details of the Internet searches you have undertaken, making a note of:

- the search engine used;
- the precise search undertaken;
- the date when the search was undertaken;
- the total number of items retrieved.

Home pages

Addresses of Internet sites or home pages (such as http://www.surrey.ac.uk) can be the quickest and most direct method of accessing these resources. Addresses can be obtained from many sources, the most frequently used of which are guidebooks (e.g. Hahn 2008), newspaper reviews, articles in journals, librarians and lecturers. Home pages, which can have multiple linked pages and hypertext links whereby pointing and clicking on the screen takes you to another website, are similar to a title or contents page. Although home pages often contain publicity for a company or institution, they are an excellent way of navigating around the Internet, as they bring a selection of Internet site addresses and search tools together (Table 3.5). A problem with going directly to one address is that your search is constrained by other people's ideas. Similarly, hypertext links are limited by other people's ideas and the way they have linked pages.

Search tools

Search tools, often referred to as **search engines**, are probably the most important method of Internet searching for your literature review as they will enable you to locate most current and up-to-date items. Although normally accessed through home pages, each search tool will have its own address (Table 3.5).

Most search tools search by key words or subject trees. A *subject tree* is similar to a contents page or index. Some are in the form of alphabetical subject lists, whereas others are in hierarchical groups of subjects that are then further subdivided with links to more narrowly focused subject groups. It is vital that you do not rely on one search tool but use a variety, noting and evaluating each as you use them. Each search tool will have different interfaces, ways of searching and methods of displaying information. They will search different areas of the Internet and are likely to display different results.

Search tools can be divided into four distinct categories (Figure 3.3, Table 3.5):

- general search engines;
- meta search engines;
- specialised search engines and information gateways;
- subject directories.

Most search engines index every separate document. In contrast, subject directories index only the 'most important' Internet documents. Therefore, if you are using a clear term to search for an unknown vaguely described document, use a search engine. If you are looking for a document about a particular topic, use a subject directory (Habrakan *et al.* 2008).

General search engines such as Google and Google Scholar (Box 3.15) normally search parts of the Internet using key words and Boolean logic (Table 3.3) or a phrase. Each search engine uses an automated computer process to index and search, often resulting in a very large number of sites being found. As people have not evaluated these sites, many are usually inappropriate or unreliable. As no two general search engines search in precisely the same way it is advisable (and often necessary) to use more than one. In contrast, meta

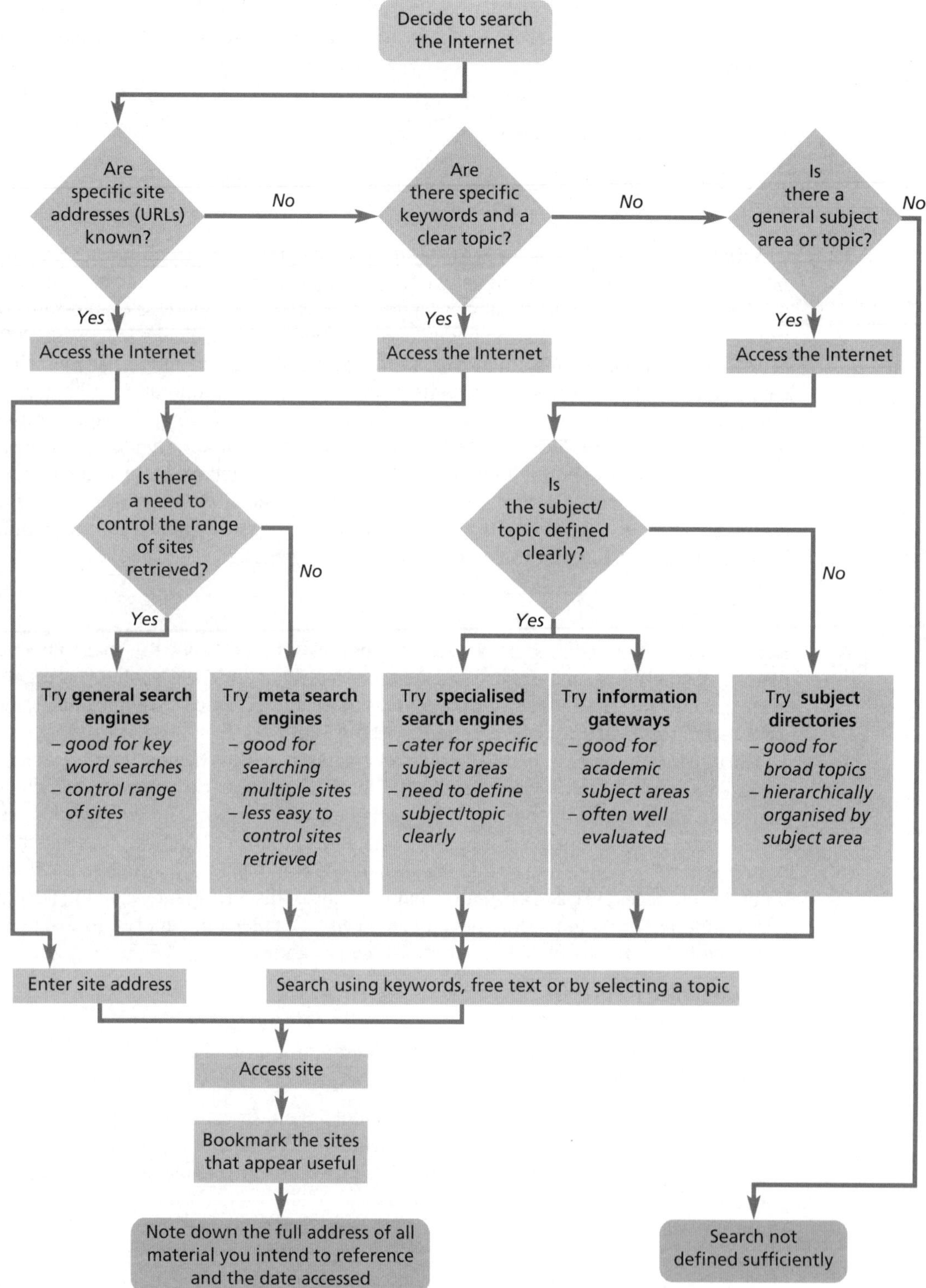

Figure 3.3 Searching the Internet
Source: © Mark Saunders, Philip Lewis, Adrain Thornhill and Martin Jenkins 2003.

search engines allow you to search using a selection of search engines at the same time, using the same interface. This makes searching easier, and the search can be faster. Unfortunately, it is less easy to control the sites that are retrieved. Consequently, meta search engines often generate more inappropriate or unreliable sites than general search engines.

Specialised search engines cater for specific subject areas. To use these it is necessary to define your general subject area prior to your search. Information gateways also require you to define your subject area. Information gateways are often compiled by staff from departments in academic institutions. Although the number of websites obtained is fewer, they can be far more relevant, as each site is evaluated prior to being added to the gateway.

Subject directories are hierarchically organised indexes categorised into subject areas, and are useful for searching for broad topics. As people normally compile them, their content has been partly censored and evaluated. Consequently, the number of sites retrieved is fewer but they usually provide material that is more appropriate. Most of the subject directories now offer some form of key word search and links to other search tools.

Search tools are becoming more prolific and sophisticated all the time. Be careful: their use can be extremely time consuming. Your search will probably locate a mass of resources, many of which will be irrelevant to you. It is also easy to become sidetracked to more interesting and glossy websites not relevant to your research needs! There are an increasing number of web-based tutorials to help you learn to search the web. One of these, Marketing Insights' *Smarter Online Searching Guide*, is available via this book's web page. This highlights using search tools, including Advanced search in Google and online e-business resources.

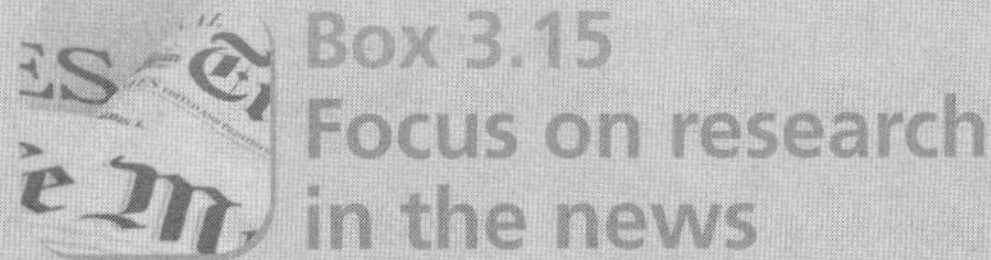

Box 3.15 Focus on research in the news

Microsoft reveals answer to Google Scholar

Microsoft has announced the release of an English-language beta version of Windows Live Academic Search, a service for searching academic journals. The release is available in Australia, Germany, Italy, Japan, Spain and the United Kingdom, as well as in the United States, and is marketed as an alternative to Google Scholar or SciFinder Scholar.

Academic Search indexes library-subscribed content and supports OpenURL, the library standard currently used for linking to subscription-based content. To operate Academic Search, libraries or research facilities must provide Microsoft with information on their OpenURL link resolver, a vendor that creates and manages the customized links to content. Academic search can then provide direct access links to the full text materials, based on their institutions' subscriptions.

Academic Search includes the expected sorting and citation-compiling features common to academic-journal searching. Researchers can control the amount of immediate information that comes up in search results in a variety of ways. Search results link directly to full articles from the publisher, if the user is researching from an institution that subscribes to that publishers' content.

Material that is not subscribed to by the searching institution still comes up in a search, with abstract and all relevant publication information available.

Microsoft announced that Academic Search currently covers only physics, electrical engineering and computer science, but it is working with publishers to expand content access. Upon testing, however, the system does seem to link to humanities journal portals such as the Oxford Journals' Forum for Modern Languages Studies.

In addition to academic returns, the current version of Academic Search provides search results for portals named 'Web', 'News', 'Local' and 'Feeds'. The service is undoubtedly a direct attempt to compete with Google Scholar. Academic Search can also be integrated into Windows Live, the new online Microsoft desktop service.

Source: article by Lombardi, Candace (2006) ZDNet News, 12 Apr. (http://news.zdnet.com/2100-9588_22-6060314.html). Used with permission of

Bookmarking

Once you have found a useful Internet site, you can note its address electronically. This process is termed 'bookmarking' or 'add to favourites' depending on the Internet browser you use. It uses the software to note the Internet address, and means that you will be able to access it again directly. The vast amount of resources available, and the fact that resources, home pages and sites can be added and deleted by their producers, means it is vital to keep a record of the addresses and a note of the date you accessed it (Section 3.7). These will be needed to reference your sources when you write your critical review (Section 3.2). When sufficient sites have been bookmarked, it is possible to arrange them in whatever hierarchical way you wish.

3.6 Obtaining and evaluating the literature

Obtaining the literature

After your initial search of books and journal articles, tertiary literature will provide you with details of what literature is available and where to locate it. The next stage (Figure 3.1) is to obtain these items. To do this you need to:

1. Check your library catalogue to find out whether your library holds the appropriate publication. Remember many libraries now, rather than holding publications such as journals and newspapers in paper form or CD-ROM, provide access via the Internet;
2. (For those publications that are held by your library or available via the Internet) note their location; and
   - **a** Find the publication and scan it to discover whether it is likely to be worth reading thoroughly – for articles it is often possible to make a reasonable assessment of relevance using the abstract; or
   - **b** Browse other books and journals with similar class marks to see whether they may also be of use;
3. (For those items that are not held by your library or available via the Internet) order the item from another library on **inter-library loan**. This is not a free service so make sure you really need it first. Our students have found that, in general, it is only worthwhile to use inter-library loan for articles from refereed journals and books.

Evaluating the literature

Two questions frequently asked by our students are 'How do I know what I'm reading is relevant?' and 'How do I know when I've read enough?' Both of these are concerned with the process of evaluation. They involve defining the scope of your review and assessing the value of the items that you have obtained in helping you to answer your research question(s). Although there are no set ways of approaching these questions, our students have found the following advice helpful.

You should, of course, read all the literature that is closely related to your research question(s) and objectives. The literature that is most likely to cause problems is that which is less closely related (Gall *et al.* 2006). For some research questions, particularly for new research areas, there is unlikely to be much closely related literature and so you will have to review more broadly. For research questions where research has been going on for some years you may be able to focus on more closely related literature.

Assessing relevance and value

Assessing the relevance of the literature you have collected to your research depends on your research question(s) and objectives. Remember that you are looking for relevance, not critically assessing the ideas contained within. When doing this, it helps to have thought about and made a note of the criteria for inclusion and exclusion prior to assessing each item of literature. In contrast, assessing the value of the literature you have collected is concerned with the quality of the research that has been undertaken. As such it is concerned with issues such as methodological rigour and theory robustness as well as the quality of the arguments. For example, you need to beware of managerial autobiographies, where a successful entrepreneur's or managing director's work experiences are presented as the way to achieve business success (Fisher 2007) and articles in trade magazines. The knowledge presented in such books and articles may well be subjective rather than based upon systematic research.

Box 3.16 provides a checklist to help you in this process.

Remember to make notes about the relevance of each item as you read it and the reasons why you came to your conclusion. You may need to include your evaluation as part of your critical review.

Assessing sufficiency

Your assessment of whether you have read a sufficient amount is even more complex. It is impossible to read everything, as you would never start to write your critical review, let alone your project report. Yet you need to be sure that your critical review discusses what research has already been undertaken and that you have positioned your research project in the wider context, citing the main writers in the field (Section 3.2). One clue that you have achieved this is when further searches provide mainly references to items you have already read. You also need to check what constitutes an acceptable amount of reading, in terms of both quality and quantity, with your project tutor.

Box 3.16 Checklist

Evaluating the relevance and value of literature to your research

Relevance

- ✔ How recent is the item?
- ✔ Is the item likely to have been superseded?
- ✔ Are the research questions or objectives sufficiently close to your own to make it relevant to your own research (in other words, does the item meet your relevance criteria for inclusion)?
- ✔ Is the context sufficiently different to make it marginal to your research question(s) and objectives (in other words, is the item excluded by your relevance criteria)?
- ✔ Have you seen references to this item (or its author) in other items that were useful?
- ✔ Does the item support or contradict your arguments? For either it will probably be worth reading!

Value

- ✔ Does the item appear to be biased? For example, does it use an illogical argument, emotionally toned words or appear to choose only those cases that support the point being made? Even if it is, it may still be relevant to your critical review!
- ✔ What are the methodological omissions within the work (e.g. sample selection, data collection, data analysis)? Even if there are many it still may be of relevance!
- ✔ Is the precision sufficient? Even if it is imprecise it may be the only item you can find and so still of relevance!
- ✔ Does the item provide guidance for future research?

Sources: authors' experience; Bell (2005); Fisher (2007); Jankowicz (2005); McNeill (2005).

3.7 Recording the literature

The literature search, as you will now be aware, is a vital part of your research project, in which you will invest a great deal of time and effort. As you read each item, you need to ask yourself how it contributes to your research question(s) and objectives and to make *notes* with this focus (Bell 2005). When doing this, many students download and print copies of articles or photocopy articles and pages from books to ensure that they have all the material. We believe that, even if you print or photocopy, you still need to make notes. The process of note making will help you to think through the ideas in the literature in relation to your research.

In addition to making notes, Sharp *et al.* (2002) identify three sets of information you need to record. These are:

- bibliographic details;
- brief summary of content;
- supplementary information.

Until the advent of inexpensive microcomputers it was usual to write this information on *index cards*. Database software such as Microsoft's Access™ or specialist bibliographic software such as Reference Manager for Windows™ or EndNote™ provide a powerful and flexible alternative method for recording the literature, although they will probably mean noting it down and transferring it to your database later. Recording can seem very tedious, but it must be done. We have seen many students frantically repeating searches for items that are crucial to their research because they failed to record all the necessary details in their database of references.

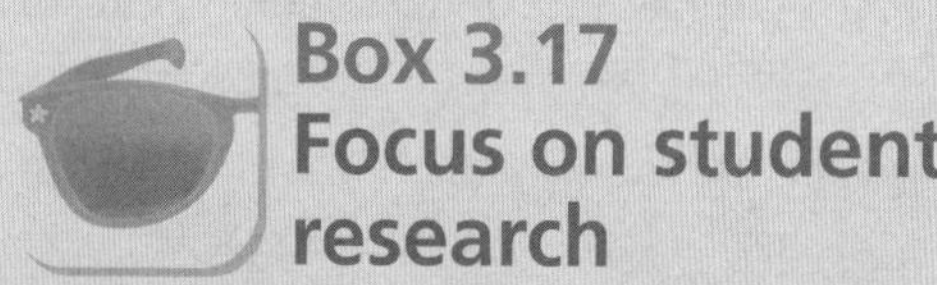

Box 3.17 Focus on student research

Undertaking an Internet search

Ceinwen's research question was reasonably defined, if somewhat broad. She wanted to assess the impact of European enlargement on small to medium-sized organisations. As part of her search strategy she decided, in addition to the academic databases of business and management journals, also to search the Internet using a general search engine. Her first key word 'European enlargement' revealed that there were over 505 000 sites and displayed the first 10. Of these, although in the broad topic area, none appeared to be relevant as they were not related specifically to small to medium-sized enterprises (SMEs):

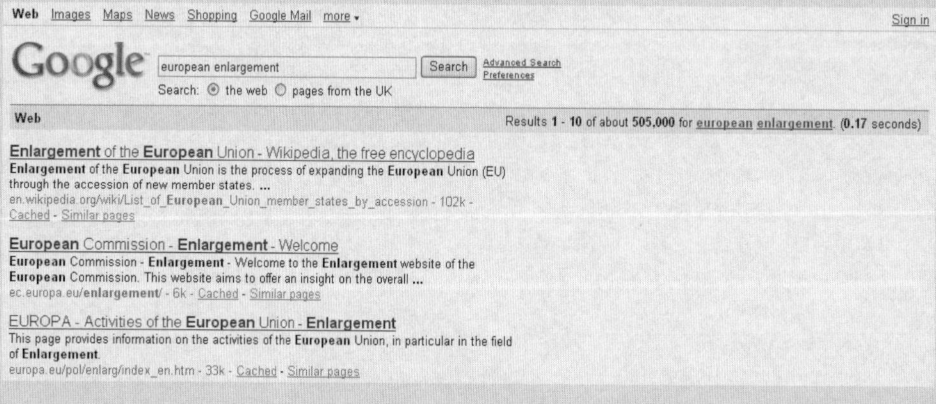

Box 3.17 Focus on student research

She decided to refine her search using the advanced search features of the search engine. Although the search engine still found over 1200 sites, the content of the first 10 appeared more relevant to her research question:

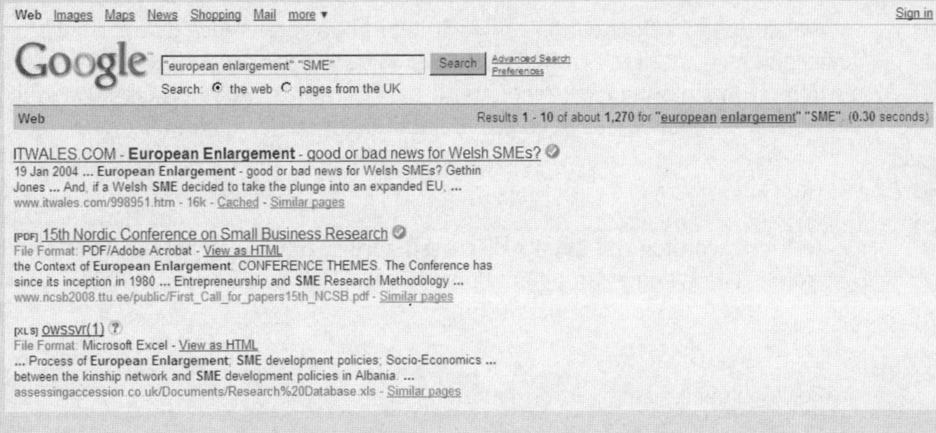

Ceinwen looked at the second site and found that it contained details of a conference entitled 'Challenges for Entrepreneurship and Small Business Development in the Context of European Enlargement' hosted by a University School of Management. She made a note of the keynote speakers so that she could search for academic articles written by them using her university's online databases. She then proceeded to look at the next site in her list.

Bibliographic details

For some project reports you will be required to include a **bibliography**. Convention dictates that this should include all the relevant items you consulted for your project, including those not referred to directly in the text. For others, you will be asked to include only a list of **references** for those items referred to directly in the text. The **bibliographic details** contained in both need to be sufficient to enable readers to find the original items. These details are summarised in Table 3.6.

Table 3.6 Bibliographic details required

Journal	Book	Chapter in an edited book
• Author(s) – surname, first name initials • Year of publication (in parentheses) • Title of article • Title of journal (underlined) • Volume • Part/issue • Page numbers (preceded by 'p.' for page or 'pp.'for pages)	• Author(s) – surname, first name initials • Year of publication (in parentheses) • Title and subtitle of book (underlined) • Edition • Place of publication • Publisher	• Author(s) – surname, first name initials • Year of publication (in parentheses) • Title of chapter • Author(s) of book – surname, first name initials • Title and subtitle of book (underlined) • Edition • Place of publication • Publisher • Page numbers of chapter

If an item has been taken from an electronic source you need to record as much of the information in Table 3.6 as is available along with details of format (e.g. CD-ROM). If you located the item via the Internet, you need to record the full address of the resource and the date you accessed the information as well (Appendix 1). This address is often referred to as the URL, the unique resource location or universal/uniform resource locator.

Most universities have a preferred referencing style that you must use in your project report. This will normally be prescribed in your assessment criteria. Three of the most common styles are the Harvard system (a version of which we have used in this book), the American Psychological Association (APA) System and the Vancouver or footnotes system. Guidelines on using each of these are given in Appendix 1.

Brief summary

A brief summary of the content of each item in your reference database will help you to locate the relevant items and facilitate reference to your notes and photocopies. This can be done by annotating each record with the key words used, to help locate the item and the abstract. It will also help you to maintain consistency in your searches.

Supplementary information

As well as recording the details discussed earlier, other information may also be worth recording. These items can be anything you feel will be of value. In Table 3.7 we outline those that we have found most useful.

Table 3.7 Supplementary information

Information	Reason
ISBN	The identifier for any book, and useful if the book has to be requested on inter-library loan
Class number (e.g. Dewey decimal)	Useful to locate books in your university's library and as a pointer to finding other books on the same subject
Quotations	Always note useful quotations in full and with the page number of the quote; if possible also take a photocopy or save entire document as a PDF file.
Where it was found	Noting where you found the item is useful, especially if it is not in your university library and you could only take notes
The tertiary resource used and the key words used to locate it	Useful to help identify resources for follow-up searches
Evaluative comments	Your personal notes on the value of the item to your research in relation to your relevance and value criteria
When the item was consulted	Especially important for items found via the Internet as these may disappear without trace
Filename	Useful if you have saved the document as a PDF file.

3.8 Plagiarism

There is no doubt that plagiarism has become an enormously important topic in academic institutions in recent years, largely as a result of the ease with which material can be copied from the Internet and passed of as the work of the individual student. It is a serious topic as the consequences of being found guilty of plagiarism can be severe as the example in Box 3.18 from a UK university shows.

Neville (2007) argues that plagiarism is an issue that runs parallel to a debate with recurring questions about the purpose of higher education in the twenty-first century. He notes that, on the one hand, there is the argument that an insistence on 'correct' referencing is supporting a system and a process of learning that is a legacy of a different time and society. This argument holds that universities are enforcing upon you an arcane practice of referencing that you will probably never use again outside higher education. On the other hand, there is the argument that plagiarism is an attack upon values of ethical, proper, decent behaviour: values consistent with a respect for others. These are ageless societal values that universities should try to maintain.

So what precisely is plagiarism? Easterby-Smith *et al.* (2008:50) define it is 'presenting the work and ideas of other people and passing them off as your own, without acknowledging the original source of the ideas used'. The same authors cite Park's (2003) list of four common forms of plagiarism which are commonly found in universities. These are listed below.

1 Stealing material from another source and passing it off as your own, for example:
   - buying a paper from a research service, essay bank or term-paper mill (either specially written for the individual or pre-written);
   - copying a whole paper from a source text without proper acknowledgement;
   - submitting another student's work with or without that student's knowledge (e.g. by copying a computer disk);

2 submitting a paper written by someone else (e.g. a peer or relative) and passing it off as your own;

Box 3.18 Focus on student research

Penalties for being found guilty of plagiarism

Overview of the penalties

There is a range of penalties that can be applied in cases of plagiarism. The penalty is chosen either by the School or the Committee on Applications and will depend on the seriousness of the offence and on whether there are any mitigating circumstances. Example penalties are:

1 only the sections of the assignment determined not to be plagiarised are marked;
2 academic year is failed and must be retaken;
3 student is excluded from the University.

The seriousness of the offence is related to issues such as:

- whether the student has committed offences previously;
- the magnitude of the plagiarism;
- the number of marks and the level of the assignment involved.

Source: University of Leeds. Available online at: http://www.lts.leeds.ac.uk/plagiarism/penalties.php?PHPSESSID=4582f0d02aa8927c671b34ddb8c4f459

3 copying sections of material from one or more source texts, supplying proper documentation (including the full reference) but leaving out quotation marks, thus giving the impression that the material has been paraphrased rather than directly quoted;
4 paraphrasing material from one or more source texts without supplying appropriate documentation;

It is tempting to think that all cases of plagiarism are a consequence of students either being too idle to pursue their research and writing diligently, or wishing to appear cleverer that they really are. But the fact is that plagiarism is an extremely complex issue and the reasons for it may owe as much to student confusion as willful negligence. That said, there is little excuse for confusion. All universities have ample guidance for students on the topic of plagiarism and will emphasise that it the responsibility of the individual student to become aware of the university's regulations surrounding its conduct. In addition, there is no shortage of excellent websites with guidance for students (e.g. the University of Alberta Libraries site at: http://www.library.ualberta.ca/guides/plagiarism/index.cfm).

In addition, an increasing number of universities ask students to check their own work using plagiarism detection software.

3.9 Summary

- A critical review of the literature is necessary to help you to develop a thorough understanding of, and insight into, previous research that relates to your research question(s) and objectives. Your review will set your research in context by critically discussing and referencing work that has already been undertaken, drawing out key points and presenting them in a logically argued way, and highlighting those areas where you will provide fresh insights. It will lead the reader into subsequent sections of your project report.
- There is no one correct structure for a critical review, although it is helpful to think of it as a funnel in which you start at a more general level prior to narrowing down to your specific research question(s) and objectives.
- Literature sources can be divided into three categories: primary, secondary and tertiary. In reality, these categories often overlap. Your use of these resources will depend on your research question(s) and objectives. Some may use only tertiary and secondary literature. For others, you may need to locate primary literature as well.
- When planning your literature search you need to:
  - have clearly defined research question(s) and objectives;
  - define the parameters of your search;
  - generate key words and search terms;
  - discuss your ideas as widely as possible.

  Techniques to help you in this include brainstorming and relevance trees.
- Your literature search is likely to be undertaken using a variety of approaches in tandem. These will include:
  - searching using tertiary sources and the Internet;
  - following up references in articles you have already read;
  - scanning and browsing secondary literature in your library.

  Don't forget to make precise notes of the search processes you have used and their results.
- Once obtained, the literature must be evaluated for its relevance to your research question(s) and objectives using clearly defined criteria. This must include a consideration of each item's currency. Each item must be read and noted. Bibliographic details, a brief description of the content and appropriate supplementary information should also be recorded.
- Care should be taken when writing your literature review not to plagiarise the work of others.

Self-check questions

Help with these questions is available at the end of the chapter.

3.1 The following extract and associated references are taken from the first draft of a critical literature review. The research project was concerned with the impact of direct insurers on the traditional motor insurer.
List the problems with this extract in terms of its:
a content;
b structure.
Jackson (1995) suggests that businesses must be developed from a customer rather than a product perspective. Lindesfarne (1994) demonstrates that direct selling gives the consumer increased control as it is up to them when and if they wish to respond to adverts or direct mail. MacKenzie (1995) comments that free gifts are useful for getting responses to adverts, which is ultimately what all direct insurers need. Bowen (1995) suggests that this type of company can be split into three equally important parts: marketing, insurance and information technology. Motor insurance is particularly price sensitive because of its compulsory nature and its perception by many to have no real 'value' to themselves.

Bowen, I. (1994) 'Short cut to success', *Post Magazine* 2, 26 July.
Jackson, D.R. (1995) 'Prudential's prudent parochialism', *Direct Marketing*, 26–29 April.
Lindisfarne, I. (1995) 'Death of a salesman', *Post Magazine* 15, 30–31 June.
MacKenzie, G. (1995) 'Rise of the freebie', *Post Magazine* 2, 5–6 February.

3.2 Outline the advice you would give a colleague on:
a how to plan her search;
b which literature to search first.

3.3 Brainstorm at least one of the following research questions, either on your own or with a colleague, and list the key words that you have generated.
a How effective is profit-related pay as a motivator?
b How do the opportunities available to a first-time house buyer through interpersonal discussion influence the process of selecting a financial institution for the purposes of applying for a house purchase loan?
c To what extent do new methods of direct selling of financial services pose a threat to existing providers?

3.4 You are having considerable problems with finding relevant material for your research when searching online databases. Suggest possible reasons why this might be so.

3.5 Rewrite the following passage as part of a critical literature review using the Harvard system of referencing:

From what I've read, the English Language Teaching market, which this company serves, remains attractive for publishers despite a decline in growth as this quote shows: 'Overall, the ELT materials market has continued to show growth, because, globally, the demand for English learning persists, albeit on a lower growth track than in the 1980s'.[1] The latest published statistics that I've been able to find (1999) tell us that there are 1,300 million ELT learners worldwide.[2] I therefore think that the need for good ELT authors is growing and, as Francis says: 'the name of the author remains a critical success factor, and an important sub-brand in many cases'.[3]

[1]R. Francis, 'Youngsters drive ELT growth', Bookseller, 23 May 2003, p. 26.
[2]Gasson, C. (ed.), Book Publishing in Britain (London: Bookseller Publications, 1999).
[3]R. Francis 'ELT Publishing', p. 93 in C. Gasson (ed.), Book Publishing in Britain (London: Bookseller Publications, 1999) pp. 86–104.

Review and discussion questions

3.6 Go to the website of the general search engine Google (http://www.google.com). Use the different Google services such as 'Google Search', 'Google Scholar' and 'University Search' to search for articles on a topic which you are currently studying as part of your course.
   a Make notes regarding the types of items that each of these services finds.
   b How do these services differ?
   c Which service do you think is likely to prove most useful to your research project?

3.7 Agree with a friend to each review the same article from a refereed academic journal, which contains a clear literature review section. Evaluate independently the literature review in your chosen article with regard to its content, critical nature and structure using the checklists in Boxes 3.2, 3.3 and 3.4 respectively. Do not forget to make notes regarding your answers to each of the points raised in the checklists. Discuss your answers with your friend.

3.8 Visit an online database or your university library and obtain a copy of an article that you think will be of use to an assignment you are both currently working on. Use the checklist in Box 3.16 to assess the relevance and value of the article to your assignment.

Progressing your research project

Critically reviewing the literature

- Consider your research questions and objectives. Use your lecture notes, course textbooks and relevant review articles to define both narrow and broader parameters of your literature search, considering language, subject area, business sector, geographical area, publication period and literature type.
- Generate key words and search terms using one or a variety of techniques such as reading, brainstorming and relevance trees. Discuss your ideas widely, including with your project tutor and colleagues.
- Start your search using both database and printed tertiary sources to identify relevant secondary literature. Begin with those tertiary sources that abstract and index academic journal articles and books. At the same time, obtain relevant literature that has been referenced in articles you have already read. Do not forget to record your searches systematically and in detail.
- Expand your search via other sources such as the Internet and by browsing and scanning.
- Obtain copies of items, evaluate them systematically and make notes. Remember also to record bibliographic details, a brief description of the content and supplementary information on an index card or in your reference database.
- Start drafting your critical review as early as possible, keeping in mind its purpose and taking care to reference properly and avoid plagiarism.
- Continue to search the literature throughout your research project to ensure that your review remains up to date.

References

Bell, J. (2005) *Doing Your Research Project* (4th edn). Maidenhead: Open University Press.

Clausen, H. (1996) 'Web information quality as seen from libraries', *New Library World* 97: 1130, pp. 4–8.

Dees, R. (2003) *Writing the Modern Research Paper* (4th edn). Boston, MA: Allyn and Bacon.

Denyer, D. and Neely, A. (2004) 'Introduction to special issue: innovation and productivity performance in the UK', *International Journal of Management Reviews,* Vol. 5/6, Nos. 3 and 4, pp. 131–5.

Easterby-Smith, M., Thorpe, R. Jackson, P. and Lowe, A. (2008) *Management Research* (3rd edn). Sage: London.

Fisher, C. (2007) *Researching and Writing a Dissertation for Business Students* (2nd edn). Harlow: Financial Times Prentice Hall.

Gall, M.D., Gall, J.P. and Borg, W. (2006) *Educational Research: An Introduction* (8th edn). New York: Longman.

Gill, J. and Johnson, P. (2002) *Research Methods for Managers.* (3rd edn). London: Paul Chapman.

Greenhalgh, T. (1997) 'Papers that summarize other papers (systematic reviews and meta-analyses)', *British Medical Journal,* Vol. 315, pp. 672–5.

Habrakan, A., Schmitz, R. and van Tilberg, P. (2008) 'Searching the World Wide Web: a basic tutorial', available at: http://www.tilburguniversity.nl/services/library/instruction/www/onlinecourse [Accessed 21 May 2008.]

Hahn, H. (2008) 'Harley Hahns Internet Yellow Pages', available at: http://www.harley.com/yp/home.html [Accessed 20 May 2008.]

Hart, C. (1998) *Doing a Literature Review.* London: Sage.

Harvard College Library (2006) 'Interrogating texts: 6 reading habits to develop in your first year at Harvard'. Available at: http://hcl.harvard.edu/research/guides/lamont_handouts/interrogatingtexts.html [Accessed 20 May 2008.]

Inspiration (2008) Inspiration homepage. Available at: http://www.inspiration.com [Accessed 21 May 2008.]

Jankowicz, A.D. (2005) *Business Research Projects* (4th edn). London: Thomson Learning.

McNeill, P. (2005). *Research Methods.* (3rd edn). London: Routledge.

MindGenius (2008) MindGenius homepage. Available at: http://www.mindgenius.com/website/presenter.aspx?type=doc&uri=/home.htm#topofpage [Accessed 21 May 2008.]

Mingers, J. (2000) 'What is it to be critical? Teaching a critical approach to management undergraduates', *Management Learning,* Vol. 31, No. 2, pp. 219–37.

Neville, C. (2007) *The complete guide to referencing and plagiarism*. Maidenhead: Open University Press.

Park, C. (2003) 'In other (people's) words: plagiarism by university students – literature and lessons', *Assessment & Evaluation in Higher Education*, Vol. 28, No. 5, pp. 471–88.

Searcy, D.L. and Mentzer, J.T. (2003) 'A framework for conducting and evaluating research', *Journal of Accounting Literature*, Vol. 22, pp. 130–67.

Sharp, J.A., Peters, J. and Howard, K. (2002) *The Management of a Student Research Project* (3rd edn). Aldershot: Gower.

Srivastava, S. (2007) 'Green supply-chain management: A state-of-the-art literature review', *International Journal of Management Review,* Vol. 9, No. 1, pp. 53–80.

Stewart, D.W. and Kamins, M.A. (1993) *Secondary Research: Information Sources and Methods* (2nd edn). Newbury Park: CA, Sage.

Strauss, A. and Corbin, J. (1998) *Basics of Qualitative Research* (2nd edn). Newbury Park, CA: Sage.

Tranfield, D., Denyer, D. and Smart, P. (2003) 'Towards a methodology for developing evidence-informed management knowledge by means of systematic review', *British Journal of Management*, Vol. 14, No. 3, pp. 207–22.

Wallace, M. and Wray, A. (2006) *Critical Reading and Writing for Postgraduates.* London: Sage.

Wikipedia (2008) Wikipedia home page. Available at: http://www.wikipedia.org [Accessed 21 May 2008.]

Williams C.S. and Saunders M.N.K. (2006) 'Developing the service template: From measurement to agendas for improvement', *Service Industries Journal*, Vol. 26, No. 5, pp. 1–15.

Further reading

Bell, J. (2005). *Doing Your Research Project.* (4th edn). Maidenhead: Open University Press. **Chapter 6** provides a good introduction to the process of reviewing the literature. The section on the critical review of the literature is especially helpful.

Habrakan, A., Schmitz, R. and van Tilberg, P. (2008) 'Searching the World Wide Web: a basic tutorial'. Available at: http://www.tilburguniversity.nl/services/library/instruction/www/onlinecourse [Accessed 21 May 2008.] This website provides an introduction to, and history of, the Internet and WWW along with an interactive tutorial. The tutorial offers an explanation of different types of information that you can find on the Internet and how to access them. It also contains a common-sense guide to searching for particular websites.

Neville, C. (2007). *The Complete Guide to Referencing and Plagiarism.* Maidenhead: Open University Press. **Chapter 4** is a very helpful guide on what constitutes plagiarism and how it can be avoided. The chapter ends with some useful exercises designed to ensure that the reader does not fall into some common traps.

Sharp, J.A., Peters, J. and Howard, K. (2002) *The Management of a Student Research Project.* (3rd edn). Aldershot: Gower. **Chapter 4** contains a useful in-depth discussion of the use of relevance trees in your literature search.

Tranfield, D., Denyer, D. and Smart, P. (2003) 'Towards a methodology for developing evidence-informed management knowledge by means of systematic review', *British Journal of Management,* Vol. 14, No. 3, pp. 207–22. This paper provides an excellent introduction to the process of systematic review. Although a full systematic review as outlined in this paper may be too time consuming for your research project, there are many useful points made regarding how to plan your search strategy and explain in your project report how your review was undertaken.

Case 3
Complexity theory and emergent change

Source: Rob Judges/Oxford/Alamy

Sarah was in the final year of her undergraduate business studies degree course. She was starting on her research project, and had been thinking about what to investigate. The module 'Organisational Change' that she had taken in her second year particularly interested her. Some of the ideas she had learned about related very clearly to an aspect of her university experience. At the beginning of her first year she had joined the university drama society, and since then she had been very actively involved. Sarah had noticed how different groups would form spontaneously among drama-society members from time to time. Those who became enthusiastic about a particular activity would work together to run workshops or put on plays. Meanwhile, other groups would get themselves organised to lobby forcefully for changes in the way the society was run. As a result, the drama society had gone from strength to strength. Membership was increasing and more adventurous productions were being staged, to great acclaim from other students.

Of the theories she had come across in the 'Organisational Change' module, complexity theory was the one that seemed intuitively to explain this success. Sarah was especially fascinated by the idea of 'self-organisation', where members collaborate spontaneously in responding to environmental demands and bring about desired change. It applied perfectly to her drama club experience – encouraging self-organisation must be a key to successful management of change anywhere. Sarah had a hunch that what she'd observed would happen in other societies and clubs in the university. She hit on the idea of using complexity theory as the conceptual framework for her research project, which would be an investigation of how members in other university societies and clubs worked together to run their activities and make change happen.

Her project tutor approved of what she proposed and invited her to begin by carrying out a review of literature on complexity theory and organisational change. The aim was to inform her research design and data collection methods. The question she chose to frame her review was: 'How does complexity theory suggest that organisational change should be managed?' Her literature search had soon produced plenty of texts. She started with the book by McMillan (2004), *Complexity, Organizations and Change*. This and each text she read afterwards reinforced her hunch that complexity theory showed how change could be managed effectively in any organisation. She did stumble on one text arguing against the application of complexity theory to organisational change, but she couldn't see much point in including it. The authors of the texts she did use explained what complexity theory was, showed how it applied to organizational change – occasionally reporting their own research – and offered prescriptions for managing change. It was easy to write her draft review because she agreed with so much of what the authors were saying.

But when she presented the draft review to her project tutor, she got a shock. The feedback was: 'This is a good summary of what you've read, but not critical enough. Your review question shows how you've assumed that complexity can be used to prescribe practice. How can you be sure? You've simply confirmed the prejudices you had before you started the review! You need to challenge what authors are saying, not just accept every claim they make. You've ignored the literature by authors who don't like the application of complexity theory for prescribing practice, when you could learn something from their criticisms. They might lead you to question your assumptions.'

Sarah was confused. What did the project tutor mean? Challenging authors sounded like being negative about everything she had just interpreted so positively. Her project tutor also recommended that she read the textbook by Wallace and Wray (2006), *Critical Reading and Writing for Postgraduates*, to help her become a more critical reader. She had a flick through the book, dubious because it was aimed at postgraduates, but quickly seized on the 'critical analysis' ideas about evaluating authors' claims. She realised she had never thought to check, say, whether authors had enough evidence to make their generalised claims convincing. Or whether they all meant the same thing by terms such as 'self-organisation'. Or whether their values as researchers coloured their claims in ways that others might find contentious. Sarah could now see that she had selected for inclusion in her review only those texts which supported her hunch – where authors were positive about applying complexity theory to organisational change. She had accepted all their claims without question and had ignored the one text that challenged them. Further, she had never thought to search for a published review on the topic. Could she learn from an expert reviewer, who might have examined more texts than she had? Why not include such a review article in her own effort?

So Sarah searched for reviews, locating one by Burnes (2005). He had included various texts whose authors were more sceptical about complexity theory. He had not just described the claims of complexity theory enthusiasts. Rather, he had described and evaluated all the claims – positive and negative – in a manner consistent with the advice offered by Wallace and Wray. Amongst the limitations he pointed to was the lack of empirical studies on organisational change using complexity theory. Yet, such research evidence would help to justify prescriptions about good practice in managing change. Without evidence, how could anyone know that prescriptions really worked? Sarah went back to the texts she had reviewed previously, looking for what was wrong with claims she had previously accepted. She completely changed her mind about the usefulness of complexity theory. Sarah promised herself that there would be no doubt about the second draft of her literature review being critical enough. She set herself a new review question: 'What are the weaknesses of using complexity theory to prescribe how change should be managed?' She would demonstrate how the complexity theory enthusiasts had simply confirmed their pre-existing prejudices, failing to acknowledge the limitations of their work and building their prescriptions more on wishful thinking than on hard research evidence.

When she handed in the second draft of her literature review to her project tutor she received another shock. The feedback this time was: 'A great improvement over your under- critical first draft. But it's now over-critical. Your new review question shows how you've now assumed that complexity theory can't be used to prescribe practice. How can you be sure? Try to adopt a more balanced approach to your critical review.' Sarah was now even more confused. What did the project tutor mean by 'balance'? And what were the implications for writing the third draft of her literature review?

References

Burnes, B. (2005) 'Complexity theories and organizational change', *International Journal of Management Reviews*, Vol. 7, No. 2, pp. 73–90.

McMillan, E. (2004) *Complexity, Organizations and Change*. London: Routledge.

Wallace, M. and Wray, A. (2006) *Critical Reading and Writing for Postgraduates*. London: Sage.

Questions

1 Why is it important for your research investigation that you be critical when reviewing the literature?
2 What might Sarah's project tutor mean by suggesting that a critical literature review should be 'balanced'?
3 What does Sarah need to do to develop a literature review which is sufficiently critical, yet also sufficiently balanced?

Additional case studies relating to material covered in this chapter are available via the book's Companion Website, **www.pearsoned.co.uk/saunders**. They are:

- The development of discount warehouse clubs;
- The problems of valuing intellectual capital;
- National cultures and management styles.

Self-check answers

3.1 There are numerous problems with the content and structure of this extract. Some of the more obvious include:

a The content consists of predominantly trade magazines, in particular *Post Magazine*, and there are no references of academic substance. Some of the references to individual authors have discrepancies: for example, was the article by Lindisfarne (or is it Lindesfarne?) published in 1994 or 1995?

b The items referenced are from 1994 and 1995. It is certain that more recent items are available.

c There is no real structure or argument in the extract. The extract is a list of what people have written, with no attempt to critically evaluate or juxtapose the ideas.

3.2 This is a difficult one without knowing her research question! However, you could still advise her on the general principles. Your advice will probably include:

a Define the parameters of the research, considering language, subject area, business sector, geographical area, publication period and literature type. Generate key words and search terms using one or a variety of techniques such as reading, brainstorming or relevance trees. Discuss her ideas as widely as possible, including with her tutor, librarians and you.

b Start the search using tertiary sources to identify relevant secondary literature. She should commence with those tertiary sources that abstract and index academic journal articles and books. At the same time she should obtain relevant literature that has been referenced in articles that she has already read.

3.3 There are no incorrect answers with brainstorming! However, you might like to check your key words for suitability prior to using them to search an appropriate database. We suggest that you follow the approach outlined in Section 3.5 under 'searching using the tertiary literature'.

3.4 There is a variety of possible reasons, including:

- One or more of the parameters of your search are defined too narrowly.
- The key words you have chosen do not appear in the controlled index language.
- Your spelling of the key word is incorrect.
- The terminology you are using is incorrect.
- The acronyms you have chosen are not used by databases.
- You are using jargon rather than accepted terminology.

3.5 There are two parts to this answer: rewriting the text and using the Harvard system of referencing. Your text will inevitably differ from the answer given below owing to your personal writing style. Don't worry about this too much as it is discussed in far more detail in Section 14.5. The references should follow the same format.

> Writing in the trade literature, Francis (2003:26) emphasises that the English Language Teaching (ELT) market remains attractive for publishers. He states: 'Overall, the ELT materials market has continued to show growth, because, globally, the demand for English learning persists, albeit on a lower growth track than in the 1980s'. This assertion is supported by published statistics (Gasson 1999), which indicate that there are 1,300 million ELT learners worldwide. Alongside this, the need for good ELT authors is growing, Francis (1999:93) asserting: 'the name of the author remains a critical success factor, and an important sub-brand in many cases'.

Gasson, C. (ed.) (1999) *Book Publishing in Britain*, London, Bookseller Publications.

Francis, R. (1999) 'ELT Publishing', in Gasson C. (ed.), *Book Publishing in Britain*, London, Bookseller Publications, 86–104.

Francis, R. (2003) 'Youngsters drive ELT growth', *Bookseller*, 23 May, p. 26.

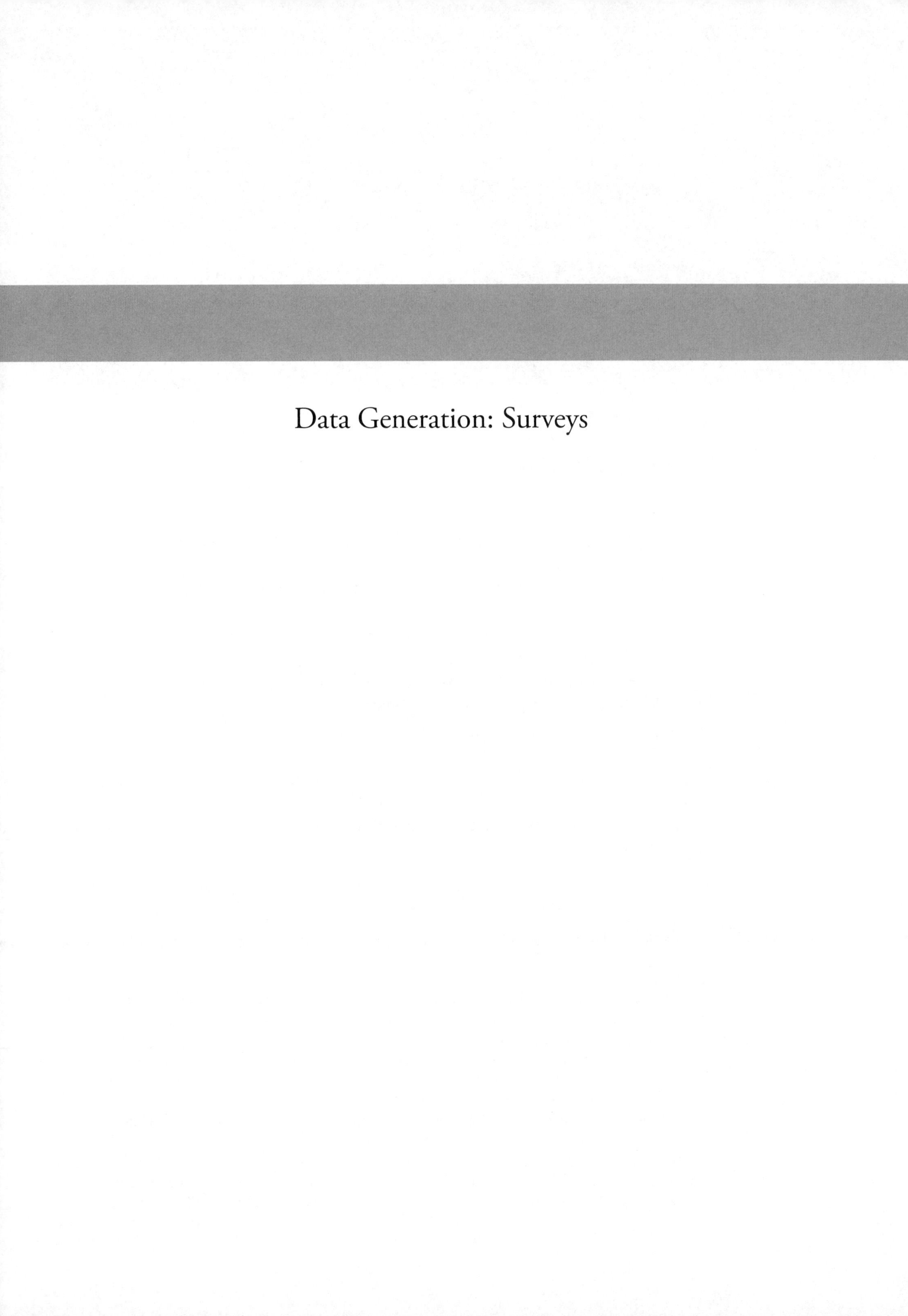

Data Generation: Surveys

Chapter 11

Collecting primary data using questionnaires

Learning outcomes

By the end of this chapter you should:

- understand the advantages and disadvantages of questionnaires as a data collection method;
- be aware of a range of self-administered and interviewer-administered questionnaires;
- be aware of the possible need to combine techniques within a research project;
- be able to select and justify the use of appropriate questionnaire techniques for a variety of research scenarios;
- be able to design, pilot and administer a questionnaire to answer research questions and to meet objectives;
- be able to take appropriate action to enhance response rates and to ensure the validity and reliability of the data collected;
- be able to apply the knowledge, skills and understanding gained to your own research project.

11.1 Introduction

Within business and management research, the greatest use of questionnaires is made within the survey strategy (Section 5.3). However, both experiment and case study research strategies can make use of these techniques. Although you probably have your own understanding of the term 'questionnaire', it is worth noting that there are a variety of definitions in common usage (Oppenheim 2000). Some people reserve it exclusively for questionnaires where the person answering the question actually records their own answers. Others use it as a more general term to also include interviews that are administered either face to face or by telephone.

In this book we use **questionnaire** as a general term to include all techniques of data collection in which each person is asked to respond to the same set of questions in a predetermined order (deVaus 2002). It, therefore, includes both structured interviews and telephone questionnaires as well as those in which the questions are answered without an interviewer being present, such as the Nando's online questionnaire. The range of techniques that fall under this broad heading are outlined in the next Section (11.2), along with their relative advantages and disadvantages.

The use of questionnaires is discussed in many research methods texts. These range from those that devote a few pages to it to those that specify precisely how you should construct and use them, such as Dillman's (2007) **tailored design method**. Perhaps not surprisingly, the questionnaire is one of the most widely used data collection techniques within the survey strategy. Because each person (respondent) is asked to respond to the same set of questions, it provides an efficient way of collecting responses from a large sample prior to quantitative analysis (Chapter 12). However, before you decide to use a questionnaire we should like to include a note of caution. Many authors (for example, Bell 2005; Oppenheim 2000) argue that it is far harder to produce a good questionnaire than you might think. You need to ensure that it will collect the precise data that you require to answer your research question(s) and achieve your objectives. This is of paramount importance because, like Nando's, you are unlikely to have more than one opportunity to collect the data. In particular, you will be unable to go back to

Questionnaires are a part of our everyday lives. For modules in your course, your lecturers have probably asked you and your fellow students to complete module-evaluation questionnaires, thereby collecting data on students' views. Similarly, when we visit a tourist attraction or have a meal in a restaurant, there is often the opportunity to complete a comment card. Some restaurants, such as Nando's, also use online questionnaires administered via their website as a way of collecting data from, and keeping in contact with, customers. As can be seen from the illustration, Nando's online questionnaire begins by emphasising the importance of feedback to them. A drop-down menu of choices is used to establish the category of feedback and details about the respondents including their name and contact details. The Nando's questionnaire provides space for general comments. David Manly from Nando's Marketing says, 'By asking the user to select the reason for their comment Nando's are able to respond to them as quickly as possible. The "category" acts as a filter for the messages to be distributed into the appropriate inboxes of the Customer Care team at Nando's.' These data help Nando's to maintain high levels of customer satisfaction.

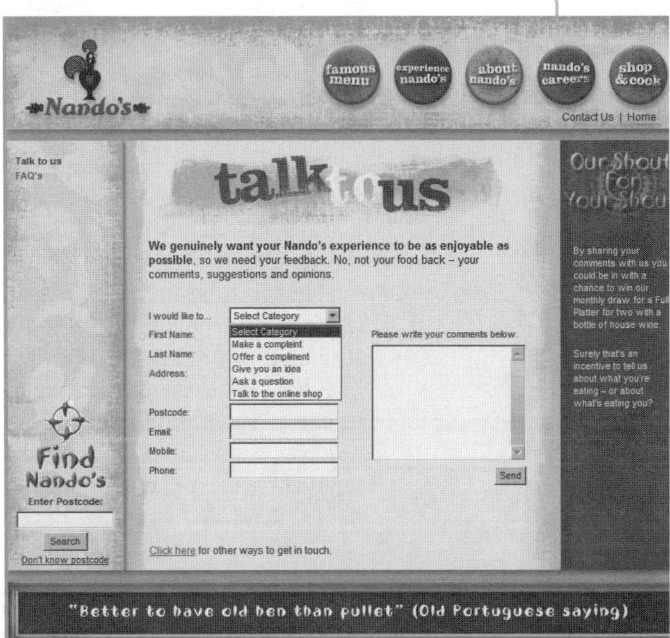

Extract from Nando's online questionnaire
Source: Nando's (2008), reproduced with permission.

those individuals who choose to remain anonymous and collect additional data using another questionnaire. These issues are discussed in Section 11.3.

The design of your questionnaire will affect the response rate and the reliability and validity of the data you collect. Response rates, validity and reliability can be maximised by:

- careful design of individual questions;
- clear and pleasing layout of the questionnaire;
- lucid explanation of the purpose of the questionnaire;
- pilot testing;
- carefully planned and executed administration.

Together these form Sections 11.4 and 11.5. In Section 11.4 we discuss designing your questionnaire. Administering the actual questionnaire is considered in Section 11.5 along with actions to help ensure high response rates.

11.2 An overview of questionnaire techniques

When to use questionnaires

We have found that many people use a questionnaire to collect data without considering other methods such as examination of secondary sources (Chapter 8), observation (Chapter 9), and semi-structured or unstructured interviews (Chapter 10). Our advice is to evaluate all possible data collection methods and to choose those most appropriate to your research question(s) and objectives. Questionnaires are usually not particularly good for exploratory or other research that requires large numbers of open-ended questions (Sections 10.2 and 10.3). They work best with standardised questions that you can be confident will be interpreted the same way by all respondents (Robson 2002).

Questionnaires therefore tend to be used for descriptive or explanatory research. Descriptive research, such as that undertaken using attitude and opinion questionnaires and questionnaires of organisational practices, will enable you to identify and describe the variability in different phenomena. In contrast, explanatory or analytical research will enable you to examine and explain relationships between variables, in particular cause-and-effect relationships. These two purposes have different research design requirements (Gill and Johnson 2002), which we shall discuss later (Section 11.3).

Although questionnaires may be used as the only data collection method, it may be better to link them with other methods in a multiple-methods research design (Section 5.4). For example, a questionnaire to discover customers' attitudes can be complemented by in-depth interviews to explore and understand these attitudes (Section 10.3). In addition, questionnaires, if worded correctly, normally require less skill and sensitivity to administer than semi-structured or in-depth interviews (Jankowicz 2005).

Types of questionnaire

The design of a questionnaire differs according to how it is administered and, in particular, the amount of contact you have with the respondents (Figure 11.1). **Self-administered questionnaires** are usually completed by the respondents. Such questionnaires are administered electronically using the Internet (**Internet-mediated questionnaires**) or intranet (**intranet-mediated questionnaires**), posted to respondents who return them by post after completion (**postal** or mail **questionnaires**), or delivered by hand to each

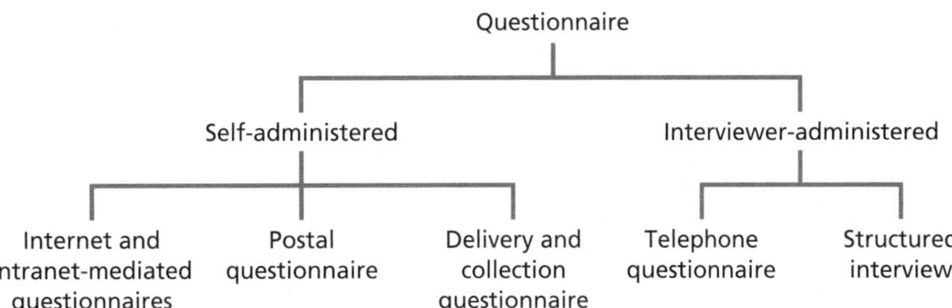

Figure 11.1 Types of questionnaire

respondent and collected later (**delivery and collection questionnaires**). Responses to **interviewer-administered questionnaires** are recorded by the interviewer on the basis of each respondent's answers. Questionnaires administered using the telephone are known as **telephone questionnaires**. The final category, **structured interviews** (sometimes known as **interview schedules**), refers to those questionnaires where interviewers physically meet respondents and ask the questions face to face. These differ from semi-structured and unstructured (in-depth) interviews (Section 10.2), as there is a defined schedule of questions, from which interviewers should not deviate.

The choice of questionnaire

Your choice of questionnaire will be influenced by a variety of factors related to your research question(s) and objectives (Table 11.1), and in particular the:

- characteristics of the respondents from whom you wish to collect data;
- importance of reaching a particular person as respondent;
- importance of respondents' answers not being contaminated or distorted;
- size of sample you require for your analysis, taking into account the likely response rate;
- types of question you need to ask to collect your data;
- number of questions you need to ask to collect your data.

These factors will not apply equally to your choice of questionnaire, and for some research questions or objectives may not apply at all. The type of questionnaire you choose will dictate how sure you can be that the respondent is the person whom you wish to answer the questions and thus the reliability of responses (Table 11.1). Even if you address a postal questionnaire to a company manager by name, you have no way of ensuring that the manager will be the respondent. The manager's assistant or someone else could complete it! Internet- and intranet-mediated questionnaires, and in particular those administered in conjunction with email, offer greater control because most users read and respond to their own mail at their personal computer (Witmer *et al.* 1999). With delivery and collection questionnaires, you can sometimes check who has answered the questions at collection. By contrast, interviewer-administered questionnaires enable you to ensure that the respondent is whom you want. This improves the reliability of your data. In addition, you can record who were non-respondents, allowing you to give some assessment of the impact of bias caused by refusals.

Any contamination of respondents' answers will reduce your data's reliability (Table 11.1). Sometimes, if they have insufficient knowledge or experience they may deliberately guess at the answer, a tendency known as **uninformed response.** This is particularly likely when the questionnaire has been incentivised (Section 11.5). Respondents to self-administered questionnaires are relatively unlikely to answer to please you

Table 11.1 Main attributes of questionnaires

Attribute	*Internet- and intranet-mediated*	*Postal*	*Delivery and collection*	*Telephone*	*Structured interview*
Population's characteristics for which suitable	Computer-literate individuals who can be contacted by email, Internet or intranet	Literate individuals who can be contacted by post; selected by name, household, organisation, etc.		Individuals who can be telephoned; selected by name, household, organisation, etc.	Any; selected by name, household, organisation, in the street etc.
Confidence that right person has responded	High if using email	Low	Low but can be checked at collection	High	
Likelihood of contamination or distortion of respondent's answer	Low	May be contaminated by consultation with others		Occasionally distorted or invented by interviewer	Occasionally contaminated by consultation or distorted/invented by interviewer
Size of sample	Large, can be geographically dispersed		Dependent on number of field workers	Dependent on number of interviewers	
Likely response rate[a]	Variable, 30% reasonable within organisations/via intranet, 11% or lower using Internet	Variable, 30% reasonable		High, 50–70% reasonable	
Feasible length of questionnaire	Conflicting advice; however, fewer 'screens' probably better	6–8 A4 pages		Up to half an hour	Variable depending on location
Suitable types of question	Closed questions but not too complex, complicated sequencing fine if uses IT, must be of interest to respondent	Closed questions but not too complex, simple sequencing only, must be of interest to respondent		Open and closed questions, including complicated questions, complicated sequencing fine	
Time taken to complete collection	2–6 weeks from distribution (dependent on number of follow-ups)	4–8 weeks from posting (dependent on number of follow-ups)	Dependent on sample size, number of field workers, etc.	Dependent on sample size, number of interviewers, etc., but slower than self-administered for same sample size	
Main financial resource implications	Web page design, although automated expert systems providers are reducing this dramatically	Outward and return postage, photocopying, clerical support, data entry	Field workers, travel, photocopying, clerical support, data entry	Interviewers, telephone calls, clerical support. Photocopying and data entry if not using CATI.[c] Programming, software and computers if using CATI	Interviewers, travel, clerical support. Photocopying and data entry if not using CAPI.[d] Programming, software and computers if using CAPI
Role of the interviewer/ field worker	None		Delivery and collection of questionnaires, enhancing respondent participation	Enhancing respondent participation, guiding the respondent through the questionnaire, answering respondents' questions	
Data input[b]	Usually automated	Closed questions can be designed so that responses may be entered using optical mark readers after questionnaire has been returned		Response to all questions entered at time of collection using CATI[c]	Response to all questions can be entered at time of collection using CAPI[d]

[a]Discussed in Chapter 7. [b]Discussed in Section 12.2. [c]Computer-aided telephone interviewing. [d]Computer-aided personal interviewing.

Sources: authors' experience; Dillman (2007); Hewson *et al.* (2003); Oppenheim (2000); deVaus (2002); Witmer *et al.* (1999).

or because they believe certain responses are more **socially desirable** (Dillman 2007). They may, however, discuss their answers with others, thereby contaminating their response. Respondents to telephone questionnaires and structured interviews are more likely to answer to please due to their contact with you, although the impact of this can be minimised by good interviewing technique (Section 10.5). Responses can also be contaminated or distorted when recorded. In extreme instances, interviewers may invent responses. For this reason, random checks of interviewers are often made by survey organisations. When writing your project report you will be expected to state your response rate. When doing this you need to be careful not to make unsubstantiated claims if comparing with other surveys' response rates. Whilst such comparisons place your survey's response rate in context, a higher than normal response rate does not prove that your findings are unbiased (Rogelberg and Stanton 2007). Similarly, a lower than normal response rate does not necessarily mean that responses are biased.

The type of questionnaire you choose will affect the number of people who respond (Section 7.2). Interviewer-administered questionnaires will usually have a higher response rate than self-administered questionnaires (Table 11.1). The size of your sample and the way in which it is selected will have implications for the confidence you can have in your data and the extent to which you can generalise (Section 7.2).

Longer questionnaires are best presented as a structured interview. In addition, they can include more complicated questions than telephone questionnaires or self-administered questionnaires (Oppenheim 2000). The presence of an interviewer (or the use of questionnaire software) means that it is also easier to route different subgroups of respondents to answer different questions using a filter question (Section 11.4). The suitability of different types of question also differs between techniques.

Your choice of questionnaire will also be affected by the resources you have available (Table 11.1), and in particular the:

- time available to complete the data collection;
- financial implications of data collection and entry;
- availability of interviewers and field workers to assist;
- ease of automating data entry.

The time needed for data collection increases markedly for delivery and collection questionnaires and structured interviews where the samples are geographically dispersed (Table 11.1). One way you can overcome this constraint is to select your sample using cluster sampling (Section 7.2). Unless your questionnaire is Internet or intranet-mediated, or **computer-aided personal interviewing (CAPI)** or **computer-aided telephone interviewing (CATI)** is used, you will need to consider the costs of reproducing the questionnaire, clerical support and entering the data for computer analysis. For postal and telephone questionnaires, cost estimates for postage and telephone calls will need to be included. If you are working for an organisation, postage costs may be reduced by using *Freepost* for questionnaire return. This means that you pay only postage and a small handling charge for those questionnaires that are returned by post. However, the use of Freepost rather than a stamp may adversely affect your response rates (see Table 11.4).

Virtually all data collected by questionnaires will be analysed by computer. Some packages (e.g. Snap Surveys™, Sphinx Development™ and SurveyMonkey.com™) allow you both to design your questionnaire, collect, enter and analyse the data within the same software. Once your data have been coded and entered into the computer you will be able to explore and analyse them far more quickly and thoroughly than by hand (Section 12.2). As a rough rule, you should analyse questionnaire data by computer if they have been collected from 30 or more respondents. For larger surveys, you may wish to automate the capture and input of data. For Internet- and intranet-mediated questionnaires (electronic

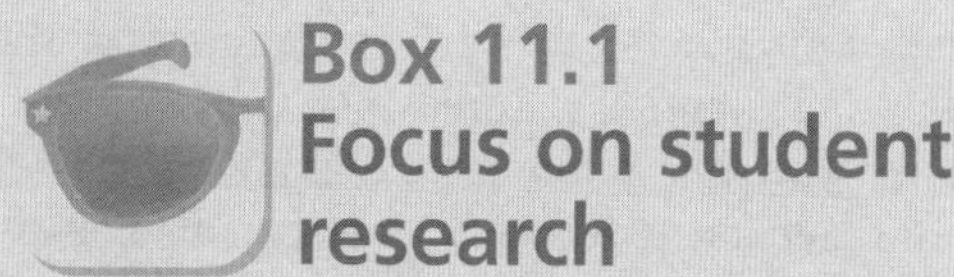

Box 11.1 Focus on student research

Closed question designed for an optical mark reader

Ben's research project involved sending out a questionnaire to a large number of people. Because of this he obtained permission to use his university's optical mark reader to input the data from his questionnaire. In his questionnaire, respondents are given clear instructions on how to mark their responses:

> Please use a pencil to mark your answer as a solid box like this: [—]
>
> If you make a mistake use an eraser to rub out your answer.
>
> 1 Please mark all the types of music that you regularly listen to:
>
> | | |
> |---|---|
> | Rock and Pop | [ ] |
> | Dance and Urban | [ ] |
> | Soundtracks | [ ] |
> | Jazz and Blues | [ ] |
> | Country | [ ] |
> | Easy listening | [ ] |
> | Folk | [ ] |
> | World | [ ] |
> | Classical | [ ] |
> | Other (please describe): .... | [ ] |

questionnaires), this is normally undertaken at the questionnaire design stage and, where the software is automated, costs are minimal. For example, SurveyMonkey.com™, an online software tool for creating and administering web-based questionnaires, at the time of writing charged $19.95 for up to 1000 responses a month, whilst a survey of 10 or fewer questionnaires and with 100 or fewer responses is free (SurveyMonkey.com 2008). For self-administered questionnaires, data capture and input is most straightforward for closed questions where respondents select and mark their answer from a prescribed list (Box 11.1).

The mark is read using an **optical mark reader**, which recognises and converts marks into data at rates often exceeding 200 pages a minute. Data for interviewer-administered questionnaires can be entered directly into the computer at the time of interview using CATI or CAPI software. With both types of software you read the questions to the respondent from the screen and enter their answers directly into the computer. Because of the costs of high-speed and high-capacity scanning equipment, software and pre-survey programming, CATI and CAPI are financially viable only for very large surveys or where repeated use of the hardware and software will be made.

In reality, you are almost certain to have to make compromises in your choice of questionnaire. These will be unique to your research as the decision about which questionnaire is most suitable cannot be answered in isolation from your research question(s) and objectives and the population or sample from whom you are collecting data.

11.3 Deciding what data need to be collected

Research design requirements

Unlike in-depth and semi-structured interviews (Chapter 10), the questions you ask in questionnaires need to be defined precisely prior to data collection. Whereas you can prompt and explore issues further with in-depth and semi-structured interviews, this will not be possible for questionnaires. In addition, the questionnaire offers only one chance to collect the data, as it is often difficult to identify respondents or to return to collect additional information. This means that the time you spend planning precisely what data you need to collect, how you intend to analyse them (Chapter 12) and designing your questionnaire to meet these requirements is crucial if you are to answer your research question(s) and meet your objectives.

For most management and business research the data you collect using questionnaires will be used for either descriptive or explanatory purposes. For questions where the main purpose is to describe the population's characteristics either at a fixed time or at a series of points over time to enable comparisons, you will normally need to administer your questionnaire to a sample. The sample needs to be as representative and accurate as possible where it will be used to generalise about the total population (Sections 7.1–7.3). You will also probably need to relate your findings to earlier research. It is therefore important that you select the appropriate characteristics to answer your research question(s) and to address your objectives. You, therefore, will need to have:

- reviewed the literature carefully;
- discussed your ideas with colleagues, your project tutor and other interested parties.

For research involving organisations, we have found it essential to understand the organisations in which we are undertaking the research. Similarly, for international or cross-cultural research it is important to have an understanding of the countries or cultures in which you are undertaking the research. Without this it is easy to make mistakes, such as using the wrong terminology or language, and to collect useless data. For many research projects an understanding of relevant organisations can be achieved through browsing company publications or their Internet sites (Section 8.3), observation (Chapter 9) and in-depth and semi-structured interviews (Chapter 10).

Explanatory research requires data to test a theory or theories. This means that, in addition to those issues raised for descriptive research, you need to define the theories you wish to test as relationships between variables prior to designing your questionnaire. You, therefore, will need to have reviewed the literature carefully, discussed your ideas widely, and conceptualised your own research clearly prior to designing your questionnaire (Ghauri and Grønhaug 2005). In particular, you need to be clear about which relationships you think are likely to exist between variables:

- a **dependent variable** changes in response to changes in other variables;
- an **independent variable** causes changes in a dependent variable;
- an **extraneous variable** might also cause changes in a dependent variable, thereby providing an alternative explanation to your independent variable or variables (Box 11.2).

Box 11.2 Focus on student research

Defining theories in terms of relationships between variables

As part of her research, Marie-Claude wished to test the theory that the incidence of repetitive strain injury (RSI) was linked to the number of rest periods that keyboard operators took each working day.

The relationship that was thought to exist between the variables was that the incidence of RSI was higher when fewer or no rest periods were taken each day. The dependent variable was the incidence of RSI and the independent variable was the number of rest periods taken each day. Marie-Claude thought that extraneous variables, such as the use of proper seating and wrist rests, might also influence the incidence of RSI. Data were collected, therefore, on these variables as well.

As these relationships are likely to be tested through statistical analysis (Section 12.5) of the data collected by your questionnaire, you need to be clear about the detail in which they will be measured at the design stage. Where possible, you should ensure that measures are compatible with those used in other relevant research so that comparisons can be made (Section 12.2).

Types of variable

Dillman (2007) distinguishes between three types of data variable that can be collected through questionnaires:

- opinion;
- behaviour;
- attribute.

These distinctions are important, as they will influence the way your questions are worded (Box 11.3). **Opinion variables** record how respondents feel about something or what they think or believe is true or false. In contrast, data on behaviours and attributes record what respondents do and are. When recording what respondents do, you are recording their behaviour. This differs from respondents' opinions because you are recording a concrete experience. **Behavioural variables** contain data on what people (or their organisations) did in the past, do now or will do in the future. By contrast, **attribute variables** contain data about the respondents' characteristics. Attributes are best thought of as things a respondent possesses, rather than things a respondent does (Dillman 2007). They are used to explore how opinions and behaviour differ between respondents as well as to check that the data collected are representative of the total population (Section 7.2). Attributes include characteristics such as age, gender, marital status, education, occupation and income.

Ensuring that essential data are collected

A problem experienced by many students and organisations we work with is how to ensure that the data collected will enable the research question(s) to be answered and the objectives achieved. Although no method is infallible, one way is to create a **data requirements table** (Table 11.2). This summarises the outcome of a six-step process:

1 Decide whether the main outcome of your research is descriptive or explanatory.
2 Sub-divide each research question or objective into more specific investigative questions about which you need to gather data.
3 Repeat the second stage if you feel that the investigative questions are not sufficiently precise.
4 Identify the variables about which you will need to collect data to answer each investigative question.
5 Establish the level of detail required from the data for each variable.
6 Develop measurement questions to capture the data at the level of data required for each variable.

Table 11.2 Data requirements table

Research question/objective:			
Type of research:			
Investigative questions	**Variable(s) required**	**Detail in which data measured**	**Check measurement question included in questionnaire ✓**

Box 11.3 Focus on student research

Opinion, behaviour and attribute questions

Sally was asked by her employer to undertake an anonymous survey of financial advisers' ethical values. In particular, her employer was interested in the advice given to clients. After some deliberation she came up with three questions that addressed the issue of putting clients' interests before their own:

2 How do you feel about the following statement? 'Financial advisers should place their clients' interest before their own'.

	Strongly agree	❑
	Mildly agree	❑
(Please tick the appropriate box)	Neither agree or disagree	❑
	Mildly disagree	❑
	Strongly disagree	❑

3 In general, do financial advisers place their clients' interests before their own?

	Always yes	❑
	Usually yes	❑
(Please tick the appropriate box)	Sometimes yes	❑
	Seldom yes	❑
	Never yes	❑

4 How often do you place your clients' interests before your own?

	81–100% of my time	❑
	61–80% of my time	❑
(Please tick the appropriate box)	41–60% of my time	❑
	21–40% of my time	❑
	0–20% of my time	❑

Sally's choice of question or questions to include in her questionnaire was dependent on whether she needed to collect data on financial advisers' opinions or behaviours. She designed question 2 to collect data on respondents' opinions about financial advisers placing their clients' interest before their own. This question asks respondents how they feel. In contrast, question 3 asks respondents whether financial advisers in general place their clients' interests before their own. It is, therefore, concerned with their opinions in terms of their individual beliefs regarding how financial advisers act. Question 4 focuses on how often the respondents actually place their clients' interests before their own. Unlike the previous questions, it is concerned with their actual behaviour rather than their opinion.

To answer her research questions and to meet her objectives, Sally also needed to collect data to explore how ethical values differed between sub-groupings of financial advisors. One theory she had was that ethical values were related to age. To test this she needed to collect data on the attribute age. After some deliberation she come up with question 5:

5 How old are you?

	Less than 30 years	❑
	30 to less than 40 years	❑
(Please tick the appropriate box)	40 to less than 50 years	❑
	50 to less than 60 years	❑
	60 years or over	❑

Investigative questions are the questions that you need to answer in order to address satisfactorily each research question and to meet each objective (Cooper and Schindler 2008). They need to be generated with regard to your research question(s) and objectives. For some investigative questions you will need to subdivide your first attempt into more detailed investigative questions. For each you need to be clear whether you are interested in respondents' opinions, behaviours or attributes (discussed earlier), as what appears to be a need to collect one sort of variable frequently turns out to be a need for another. We have found the literature review, discussions with interested parties and pilot studies to be of help here.

You then need to identify the variables about which you need to collect data to answer each investigative question and to decide the level of detail at which these are measured. Again, the review of the literature and associated research can suggest possibilities. However, if you are unsure about the detail needed you should measure at the more precise level. Although this is more time consuming, it will give you flexibility in your analyses. In these you will be able to use computer software to group or combine data (Section 12.2).

Once your table is complete (Box 11.4), it must be checked to make sure that all data necessary to answer your investigative questions are included. When checking, you need to be disciplined and to ensure that only data that are essential to answering your research question(s) and meeting your objectives are included. The final column is to remind you to check that your questionnaire actually includes a measurement question that collects the precise data required!

Box 11.4 Focus on student research

Data requirements table

As part of his work placement, Greg was asked to discover customer attitudes to the outside smoking area at restaurants and bars. Discussion with senior management and colleagues and reading relevant literature helped him to firm up his objective and investigative questions. A selection of these is included in the extract from his table of data requirements:

Research question/objective: To establish customers' attitudes to the outside smoking area at restaurants and bars			
Type of research: Predominantly descriptive, although wish to examine differences between restaurants and bars, and between different groups of customers			
Investigative questions	**Variable(s) required**	**Detail in which data measured**	**Check included in questionnaire ✓**
Do customers feel that they should have an outside smoking area at restaurants and bars as a right? (opinion)	*Opinion of customer on restaurants and bars providing an outside smoking area as a right*	*Feel . . . should be a right, should not be a right, no strong feelings [N.B. will need separate questions for restaurants and for bars]*	

Investigative questions	Variable(s) required	Detail in which data measured	Check included in questionnaire ✓
Do customers feel that restaurants and bars should provide an outside smoking area for smokers? (opinion)	*Opinion of customer to the provision of an outside smoking area for smokers*	*Feel . . . very strongly that it should, quite strongly that it should, no strong opinions, quite strongly that it should not, very strongly that it should not [N.B. will need separate questions for restaurants and for bars]*	
Do customers' opinions differ depending on	*(Opinion of employee – outlined above)*	*(Included above)*	
Age? (attribute)	*Age of employee*	*To nearest 5-year band (youngest 16, oldest 65+)*	
Whether or not a smoker? (behaviour)	*Smoker*	*Non-smoker, smokes but not in own home, smokes in own home*	
How representative are the responses of customers? (attributes)	*Age of customer* *Gender of customer* *Job [Note: must be able to compare with National Statistics Socio-Economic Classification (Rose and Pevalin 2003)]*	*(Included above)* *Male, female* *Higher managerial and professional occupations, Lower managerial and professional occupations, Intermediate occupations, Small employers and own-account workers, Lower supervisory and technical occupations, Semi-routine occupations, Routine occupations, Never worked and long-term unemployed*	

11.4 Designing the questionnaire

The internal validity and reliability of the data you collect and the response rate you achieve depend, to a large extent, on the design of your questions, the structure of your questionnaire, and the rigour of your pilot testing (all discussed in this section). A valid questionnaire will enable accurate data to be collected, and one that is reliable will mean that these data are collected consistently. Foddy (1994:17) discusses validity and reliability in terms of the questions and answers making sense. In particular, he emphasises that 'the question must be understood by the respondent in the way intended by the researcher and the answer given by the respondent must be understood by the researcher in the way intended by the respondent'. This means that there are at least four stages that must occur if the question is to be valid and reliable (Figure 11.2, Box 11.5). It also means that the

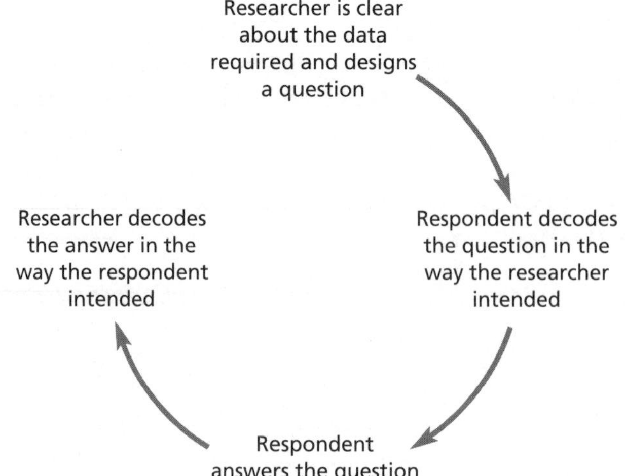

Figure 11.2 Stages that must occur if a question is to be valid and reliable
Source: developed from Foddy (1994) *Constructing Questions for Interviews and Questionnaires.* Reproduced with permission of Cambrige University Press.

design stage is likely to involve you in substantial rewriting in order to ensure that the respondent decodes the question in the way you intended. We, therefore, recommend that you use a word processor or survey design software such as SurveyMonkey.com™, Snap Surveys™ or Sphinx Development™.

Assessing validity

Internal validity in relation to questionnaires refers to the ability of your questionnaire to measure what you intend it to measure. This means you are concerned that what you find with your questionnaire actually represents the reality of what you are measuring. This presents you with a problem as, if you actually knew the reality of what you were measuring,

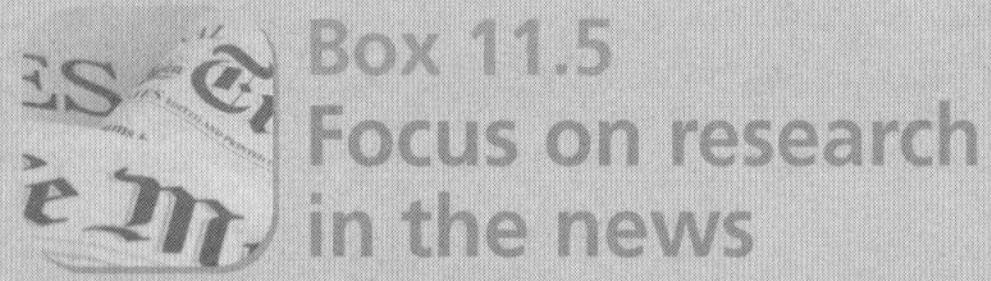

Box 11.5 Focus on research in the news

More poll questions than answers

A series of opinon polls conducted by different polling organisations to coincide with the 300th anniversary of Scotland's union with England produced very different results (Taylor 2007).

The poll conducted by Opinion Research Business on behalf of the BBC included the question:

'Would you like the Union to continue as it is or would you like to see it come to an end? If it were to end this would mean that Scotland became an independent country.'

In answering this question, 56 per cent of Scottish respondents said they would prefer the Union to continue as it is; 32 per cent responding they would prefer the Union to end.

In contrast, an earlier poll conducted by YouGov and reported in the *Sunday Times* asked:

'If there was a referendum tomorrow on whether Scotland should become independent, how would you vote?' When answering this question, 42 per cent of Scottish respondents voted against independence and 44 per cent of Scottish respondents voted for independence.

A separate poll conducted by ICM for the *Sunday Telegraph* found that 28 per cent of Scottish respondents did not approve of 'Scotland becoming an independent country', whilst 59 per cent did approve.

there would be no point in designing your questionnaire and using it to collect data! Researchers get round this problem by looking for other relevant evidence that supports the answers found using the questionnaire, relevance being determined by the nature of their research question and their own judgement.

Often, when discussing the validity of a questionnaire, researchers refer to content validity, criterion-related validity and construct validity (Cooper and Schindler 2008). **Content validity** refers to the extent to which the measurement device, in our case the measurement questions in the questionnaire, provides adequate coverage of the investigative questions. Judgement of what is 'adequate coverage' can be made in a number of ways. One is through careful definition of the research through the literature reviewed and, where appropriate, prior discussion with others. Another is to use a panel of individuals to assess whether each measurement question in the questionnaire is 'essential', 'useful but not essential', or 'not necessary'.

Criterion-related validity, sometimes known as **predictive validity**, is concerned with the ability of the measures (questions) to make accurate predictions. This means that if you are using the measurement questions within your questionnaire to predict customers' future buying behaviours, then a test of these measurement questions' criterion-related validity will be the extent to which they actually predict these customers' buying behaviours. In assessing criterion-related validity, you will be comparing the data from your questionnaire with that specified in the criterion in some way. Often this is undertaken using statistical analysis such as correlation (Section 12.5).

Construct validity refers to the extent to which your measurement questions actually measure the presence of those constructs you intended them to measure. This term is normally used when referring to constructs such as attitude scales, aptitude and personality tests and the like (Section 11.4) and can be thought of as answering the question: 'How well can you generalise from you measurement questions to your construct?' Because validation of such constructs against existing data is difficult, other methods are used. These are discussed in more detail in a range of texts, including Cooper and Schindler (2008).

Testing for reliability

As we outlined earlier, reliability refers to consistency. Although for a questionnaire to be valid it must be reliable, this is not sufficient on its own. Respondents may consistently interpret a question in your questionnaire in one way, when you mean something else! As a consequence, although the question is reliable, it does not really matter as it has no internal validity and so will not enable your research question to be answered. Reliability is therefore concerned with the robustness of your questionnaire and, in particular, whether or not it will produce consistent findings at different times and under different conditions, such as with different samples or, in the case of an interviewer-administered questionnaire, with different interviewers.

Mitchell (1996) outlines three common approaches to assessing reliability, in addition to comparing the data collected with other data from a variety of sources. Although the analysis for each of these is undertaken after data collection, they need to be considered at the questionnaire design stage. They are:

- test re-test;
- internal consistency;
- alternative form.

Test re-test estimates of reliability are obtained by correlating data collected with those from the same questionnaire collected under as near equivalent conditions as possible. The questionnaire therefore needs to be administered twice to respondents. This may create difficulties, as it is often difficult to persuade respondents to answer the same questionnaire twice. In addition, the longer the time interval between the two questionnaires, the lower the likelihood that respondents will answer the same way. We, therefore, recommend that you use this method only as a supplement to other methods.

Internal consistency involves correlating the responses to each question in the questionnaire with those to other questions in the questionnaire. It therefore measures the consistency of responses across either all the questions or a sub-group of the questions from your questionnaire. There are a variety of methods for calculating internal consistency, of which one of the most frequently used is Cronbach's alpha. Further details of this and other approaches can be found in Mitchell (1996) and in books discussing more advanced statistical analysis software such as Field (2005).

The final approach to testing for reliability outlined by Mitchell (1996) is 'alternative form'. This offers some sense of the reliability within your questionnaire through comparing responses to alternative forms of the same question or groups of questions. Where questions are included for this purpose, usually in longer questionnaires, they are often called 'check questions'. However, it is often difficult to ensure that these questions are substantially equivalent. Respondents may suffer from fatigue owing to the need to increase the length of the questionnaire, and they may spot the similar question and just refer back to their previous answer! It is therefore advisable to use check questions sparingly.

Designing individual questions

The design of each question should be determined by the data you need to collect (Section 11.3). When designing individual questions researchers do one of three things (Bourque and Clark 1994):

- adopt questions used in other questionnaires;
- adapt questions used in other questionnaires;
- develop their own questions.

Adopting or adapting questions may be necessary if you wish to replicate, or to compare your findings with, another study. This can allow reliability to be assessed. It is also more efficient than developing your own questions, provided that you can still collect the data you need to answer your research question(s) and to meet your objectives. Some survey design software includes questions that you may use. Alternatively, you may find questions and coding schemes that you feel will meet your needs in existing questionnaires, journal articles or in Internet-based question banks, such as the ESRC Question Bank. This consists of a database of questions and question methodology of UK social surveys going back to 1991 and is available from http://qb.soc.surrey.ac.uk.

However, before you adopt questions, beware! There are a vast number of poor questions in circulation, so always assess each question carefully. In addition, you need to check whether they are under copyright. If they are, you need to obtain the author's permission to use them. Even where there is no formal copyright you should, where possible, contact the author and obtain permission. In your project report you should state where you obtained the questions and give credit to their author.

Initially, you need only consider the type and wording of individual questions rather than the order in which they will appear on the form. Clear wording of questions using terms that are likely to be familiar to, and understood by, respondents can improve the validity of the questionnaire. Most types of questionnaire include a combination of open and closed questions. **Open questions**, sometimes referred to as open-ended questions (Dillman 2007), allow respondents to give answers in their own way (Fink 2003a). **Closed questions**, sometimes referred to as closed-ended questions (Dillman 2007) or **forced-choice questions** (deVaus 2002), provide a number of alternative answers from which the respondent is instructed to choose. The latter type of question is usually quicker and easier to answer, as they require minimal writing. Responses are also easier to compare as they have been predetermined. However, if these responses cannot be easily interpreted then these benefits are, to say the least, marginal (Foddy 1994). Within this chapter we highlight six types of closed question that we discuss later:

- list, where the respondent is offered a list of items, any of which may be selected;
- category, where only one response can be selected from a given set of categories;
- ranking, where the respondent is asked to place something in order;
- rating, in which a rating device is used to record responses;
- quantity, to which the response is a number giving the amount;
- matrix, where responses to two or more questions can be recorded using the same grid.

Prior to data analysis, you will need to group and code responses to each question. Detailed coding guidance is given in Section 12.2. You are strongly advised also to read this chapter prior to designing your questions.

Open questions

Open questions are used widely in in-depth and semi-structured interviews (Section 10.5). In questionnaires they are useful if you are unsure of the response, such as in exploratory research, when you require a detailed answer or when you want to find out what is uppermost in the respondent's mind. An example of an open question (from a self-administered questionnaire) is:

6 Please list up to three things you like about your job:

1 ....

2 ....

3 ....

With open questions, the precise wording of the question and the amount of space partially determine the length and fullness of response. However, if you leave too much space the question becomes off-putting. Question 6 collects data about what each respondent believes they like about their job. Thus if salary had been the reason uppermost in their mind this would probably have been recorded first. Unfortunately, when questionnaires are administered to large numbers of respondents, responses to open questions are extremely time consuming to code (Section 12.2). For this reason, it is usually advisable keep their use to a minimum.

List questions

List questions offer the respondent a list of responses, any of which they can choose. Such questions are useful when you need to be sure that the respondent has considered all possible responses. However, the list of responses must be defined clearly and meaningfully to the respondent. For structured interviews, it is often helpful to present the respondent with a prompt card listing all responses. The response categories you can use vary widely and include 'yes/no', 'agree/disagree' and 'applies/does not apply' along with 'don't know' or 'not sure'. If you intend to use what you hope is a complete list, you may wish to add a catch-all category of 'other'. This has been included in question 7, which collects data on respondents' religion. However, as you can read in Box 11.6, the use of 'other' can result in unforeseen responses!

FT

George Lucas is a god in Britain. Literally

According to official census figures, 390 000 Brits said their religious faith was 'Jedi'. Had this been an official category, it would have been the fourth largest religion in the UK, ahead of Sikhism.

Instead, the *Star Wars* fans were registered as atheists. 'We have put them among the 7.7 m people who said they had no religion,' a census official said. 'I suspect this was a decision which will not be challenged greatly.'

Evidently, aspirant Jedi masters were inspired by an email that asked them to record the unrecognised faith in the hope that their support would force the government to put Lucas on the same level as Moses, Christ and Mohammed.

'Imagine the official statistics of your country claiming a percentage of the population as practising "Jedi Knights"!!!' says the website *jedicensus.com*. Yes, imagine that.

Source: Financial Times (2003) 14 Feb.

7 What is your religion?

Please tick ✓ the appropriate box.

Buddhist	❑	None	❑
Christian	❑	Other	❑
Hindu	❑		
Jewish	❑	(Please say:).................................	
Muslim	❑		
Sikh	❑		

Question 7 collects data on the religion of the respondent. In this list question, the common practice of omitting negative response boxes has been adopted. Consequently, negative responses in this question not being, for example, a Christian, are inferred from each unmarked response. If you choose to do this, beware: non-response could also indicate uncertainty or, for some questions, that an item does not apply!

Category questions

In contrast, **category questions** are designed so that each respondent's answer can fit only one category. Such questions are particularly useful if you need to collect data about behaviour or attributes. The number of categories that you can include without affecting the accuracy of responses is dependent on the type of questionnaire. Self-administered questionnaires and telephone questionnaires should usually have no more than five response categories (Fink 2003a). Structured interviews can have more categories provided that a *prompt card* is used (Box 11.7) or, as in question 8, the interviewer categorises the responses.

8 How often do you visit this shopping centre?

Interviewer: listen to the respondent's answer and tick ✓ as appropriate.

❑ First visit	2 or more times a week	❑
❑ Once a week	Less than once a week to fortnightly	❑
❑ Less than fortnightly to once a month	Less often	❑

Box 11.7 Focus on student research

Use of a prompt card as part of a structured interview

As part of his interview schedule, Peter asked the following question:

> Which of the following daily newspapers have you read during the past month?
>
> *Show respondent card 3 with the names of the newspapers. Read out names of the newspapers one at a time. Record their response with a ✓ in the appropriate box.*

	Read	Not read	Don't know
The Daily Express	❑	❑	❑
Daily Mail	❑	❑	❑
The Daily Mirror	❑	❑	❑
Daily Star	❑	❑	❑
Financial Times	❑	❑	❑
The Guardian	❑	❑	❑
The Daily Telegraph	❑	❑	❑
The Independent	❑	❑	❑
The Sun	❑	❑	❑
The Times	❑	❑	❑

Peter gave card 3 to each respondent prior to reading out newspaper names and collected the card after the question had been completed.

3

THE DAILY EXPRESS

Daily Mail

The Daily Mirror

Daily Star

FINANCIAL TIMES

The **Guardian**

The Daily Telegraph

THE INDEPENDENT

The Sun

THE TIMES

You should arrange responses in a logical order so that it is easy to locate the response category that corresponds to each respondent's answer. Your categories should be mutually exclusive (should not overlap), and should cover all possible responses. The layout of your questionnaire should make it clear which boxes refer to which response category by placing them close to the appropriate text.

Ranking questions

A **ranking question** asks the respondent to place things in rank order. This means that you can discover their relative importance to the respondent. In question 9, taken from a postal questionnaire, the respondents are asked their beliefs about the relative importance of a series of features when choosing a new car. The catch-all feature of 'other' is included to allow respondents to add one other feature.

9 Please number each of the factors listed below in order of importance to you in your choice of a new car. Number the most important 1, the next 2 and so on. If a factor has no importance at all, please leave blank.

Factor	*Importance*
Carbon dioxide emissions	[ ]
Boot size	[ ]
Depreciation	[ ]
Safety features	[ ]
Fuel economy	[ ]
Price	[ ]
Driving enjoyment	[ ]
Other	[ ]
....	(⇐ Please describe)

With such questions, you need to ensure that the instructions are clear and will be understood by the respondent. In general, respondents find that ranking more than seven items takes too much effort reducing their motivation to complete the questionnaire, so you should keep your list to this length or shorter (Cooper and Schindler 2008). Respondents can rank accurately only when they can see or remember all items. This can be overcome with face-to-face questionnaires by using prompt cards on which you list all of the features to be ranked. However, telephone questionnaires should ask respondents to rank fewer items, as the respondent will need to rely on their memory.

Rating questions

Rating questions are often used to collect opinion data. They should not be confused with **scales** (discussed later in this section), which are a coherent set of questions or items that are regarded as indicators of a construct or concept (Corbetta 2003). Rating questions most frequently use the **Likert-style rating scale** in which the respondent is asked how strongly she or he agrees or disagrees with a statement or series of statements, usually on a four-, five-, six- or seven-point rating scale. Possible responses to rating questions should be presented in a straight line (such as in question 10) rather than in multiple lines or columns as this is how respondents are most likely to process the data (Dillman 2007). If you intend to use a series of statements, you should keep the same order of response categories to avoid confusing respondents (Dillman 2007). You should include, however, both positive and negative statements so as to ensure that the respondent reads each one carefully and thinks about which box to tick.

10 For the following statement please tick ✓ the box that matches your view most closely.

	Agree	Tend to agree	Tend to agree	Disagree
I feel employees' views have influenced the decisions taken by management.	❑	❑	❑	❑

Question 10 has been taken from a delivery and collection questionnaire to employees in an organisation and is designed to collect opinion data. In this rating question, an even number of points (four) has been used to force the respondent to express their feelings towards an implicitly positive statement. By contrast, question 11, also from a delivery and collection questionnaire, contains an odd number (five) of points on the rating scale. This rating scale allows the respondent to 'sit on the fence' by ticking the middle 'not sure' category when considering an implicitly negative statement. The phrase 'not sure' is used here as it is less threatening to the respondent than admitting they do not know. This rating question is designed to collect data on employees' opinions of the situation now.

11 For the following statement please tick ✓ the box that matches your view most closely.

	Agree	Tend to agree	Not sure	Tend to disagree	Disagree
I believe there are 'them and us' barriers to communication in the company now.	❑	❑	❑	❑	❑

You can expand this form of rating question further to record finer shades of opinion, a variety of which are outlined in Table 11.3. However, respondents to telephone questionnaires find it difficult to distinguish between values on rating scales of more than five points plus 'don't know'. In addition, there is little point in collecting data for seven or nine response categories, if these are subsequently combined in your analysis (Chapter 12). Colleagues and students often ask us how many points they should have on their rating scale. This is related to the likely measurement error. If you know that your respondents can only respond accurately to a three-point rating, then it is pointless to have a finer rating scale with more points!

In question 12 the respondent's attitude is captured on a 10-point **numeric rating scale**. In such rating questions it is important that the numbers reflect the feeling of the respondent. Thus, 1 reflects poor value for money, and 10 good value for money. Only these end categories (and sometimes the middle) are labelled and are known as self-anchoring rating scales. As in this question, graphics may also be used to reflect the rating scale visually, thereby aiding the respondent's interpretation. An additional category of 'not sure' or 'don't know' can be added and should be separated slightly from the rating scale.

Table 11.3 Response categories for different types of rating questions

Type of rating	Five categories	Seven categories
Agreement	Strongly agree Agree Neither agree nor disagree/not sure/uncertain* Disagree Strongly disagree	Strongly agree Agree/moderately agree/mostly agree* Slightly agree Neither agree nor disagree/not sure/uncertain* Slightly disagree Disagree/moderately disagree/mostly disagree* Strongly disagree
Amount	Far too much/nearly all/very large* Too much/more than half/large* About right/about half/some* Too little/less than half/small* Far too little/almost none/not at all*	Far too much/nearly all/very large* Too much/more than half/large* Slightly too much/quite large* About right/about half/some* Slightly too little/quite small* Too little/less than half/small* Far too little/almost none/not at all*
Frequency	All the time/always* Frequently/very often/most of the time* Sometimes/about as often as not/about half the time* Rarely/seldom/less than half the time* Never/practically never*	All the time/always* Almost all the time/almost always* Frequently/very often/most of the time* Sometimes/about as often as not/about half the time* Seldom Almost never/practically never* Never/not at all*
Likelihood	Very Good Reasonable Slight/bit* None/not at all*	Extremely Very Moderately Quite/reasonable* Somewhat Slight/bit* None/not at all*

*Response dependent on investigative question.
Source: developed from Tharenou *et al.* (2007) and authors' experience.

12 For the following statement please circle O the number that matches your view most closely.

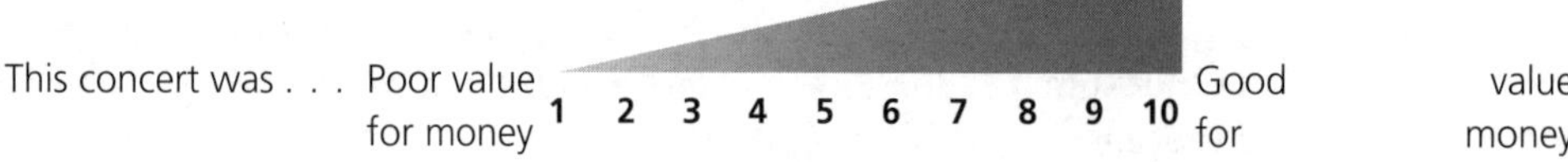

Box 11.8 Focus on management research

Semantic differential rating scales

In their study of the perception of messages conveyed by review and audit reports published in the *Accounting, Auditing and Accountability Journal*, Gay *et al.* (1998) reviewed the academic literature to identify the messages that these two types of report were intended to convey. Based upon this they developed a semantic differential scale consisting of 35 bipolar adjectival statements separated by a seven-point scale.

These adjectival statements were worded as polar opposites and included the following (Gay *et al.* 1998: 480):

	1 2 3 4 5 6 7	
The financial statements give a true and fair view	|_|_|_|_|_|_|	The financial statements do not give a true and fair view
The entity is free from fraud	|_|_|_|_|_|_|	The entity is not free from fraud

By using the semantic differential scale, Gay *et al.* (1998) were able to measure perceived messages in relation to the reliability of financial statements, auditor/management responsibility and the usefulness of such financial statements for decision making.

Another variation is the **semantic differential rating scale**. These are often used in consumer research to determine underlying attitudes. The respondent is asked to rate a single object or idea on a series of bipolar rating scales (Box 11.8). Each bipolar scale is described by a pair of opposite adjectives (question 13) designed to anchor respondents' attitudes towards service. For these rating scales, you should vary the position of positive and negative adjectives from left to right to reduce the tendency to read only the adjective on the left (Cooper and Schindler 2008).

13 On each of the lines below, place a x to show how you feel about the service you received at our restaurant.

Fast	_|_|_|_|_|_|_|_|_|_|_	Slow
Unfriendly	_|_|_|_|_|_|_|_|_|_|_	Friendly
Value for money	_|_|_|_|_|_|_|_|_|_|_	Over-priced

Rating questions have been combined to measure a wide variety of concepts such as customer loyalty, service quality and job satisfaction. For each concept the resultant measure or **scale** is represented by a scale score created by combining the scores for each of the rating questions. Each question is often referred to as a **scale item**. In the case of a simple Likert scale, for example, the scale score for each case would be calculated by adding together the scores of each of the questions (items) selected (deVaus 2002). A detailed discussion of creating scales, including those by Likert and Guttman, can be found in Corbetta (2003). However, rather than developing your own scales, it often makes sense to use or adapt existing scales (Schrauf and Navarro 2005). Since scaling techniques were first used in the 1930s, literally thousands of scales have been developed to measure attitudes and personality dimensions and to assess skills and abilities. Details

Box 11.9 Focus on student research

Using existing scales from the literature

When planning his questionnaire David, like most students, presumed he would need to design and develop his own measurement scale. However, after reading Schrauf and Navarro's (2005) paper on using existing scales, he realised that it would probably be possible to adopt an existing scale which had been reported in the academic literature. As he pointed out to his project tutor, this was particularly fortunate because the process of scale development was hugely time-consuming and could detract his attention from answering the actual research question.

In looking for a suitable published scale David asked himself a number of questions:

- Does the scale measure what I am interested in?
- Has the scale been empirically tested and validated?
- Was the scale designed for a similar group of respondents as my target population?

Fortunately, the answer to all these questions was 'yes'. David, therefore, emailed the scale's author to ask for formal permission.

of an individual scale can often be found by following up references in an article reporting research that uses that scale. In addition, there are a wide variety of handbooks that list these scales (e.g. Miller and Salkind 2002). These scales can, as highlighted in Box 11.9, be used in your own research providing they:

- measure what you interested in;
- have been empirically tested and validated;
- were designed for a reasonably similar group of respondents.

It is worth remembering that you should only make amendments to the scale where absolutely necessary as significant changes could impact upon both the validity of the scale and, subsequently, your results! You also need to beware that existing scales may be subject to copyright constraints. Even where there is no formal copyright, you should, where possible, contact the author and ask for permission. In your project report you should note where you obtained the scale and give credit to the author.

Quantity questions

The response to a **quantity question** is a number, which gives the amount of a characteristic. For this reason, such questions tend to be used to collect behaviour or attribute data. A common quantity question, which collects attribute data, is:

14 What is your year of birth? | 1 | 9 | | |

(For example, for 1988 write:) | 1 | 9 | 8 | 8 |

Because the data collected by this question could be entered into the computer without coding, the question can also be termed a **self-coded** question, that is one which each respondent codes her or himself.

Matrix questions

A **matrix** or grid of questions enables you to record the responses to two or more similar questions at the same time. As can be seen from question 15, created in SurveyMonkey.com™, questions are listed down the left-hand side of the page, and responses listed across the top.

The appropriate response to each question is then recorded in the cell where the row and column met. Although using a matrix saves space, Dillman (2007) suggests that respondents may have difficulties comprehending these designs and that they are a barrier to response.

15. The following items refer to your treatment by managers in general, who are responsible for making decisions in Anytown Manufacturing Company that affects your work. To what extent:

	to a large extent	to a quite large extent	to some extent	to a quite small extent	to a small extent	not at all
a. do they treat you with dignity?	○	○	○	○	○	○
b. do they treat you with respect?	○	○	○	○	○	○
c. are they at least as honest with bad news as good news in their communications with you?	○	○	○	○	○	○

Source: question layout created by SurveyMonkey.com (2008), Portland, Oregon, USA; author/owner: Ryan Finley. Reproduced with permission.

Question wording

The wording of each question will need careful consideration to ensure that the responses are valid – that is, measure what you think they do. Your questions will need to be checked within the context for which they were written rather than in abstract to ensure they are not misread (Box 11.10). Given this, the checklist in Box 11.11 should help you to avoid the most obvious problems associated with wording that threaten the validity of responses.

Box 11.10 Focus on student research

Misreading questions

Before becoming a student, Tracey worked for a UK-based market research agency and was responsible for much of their questionnaire design and analysis work. During her time at the agency she noted that certain words in questions were likely to be misread by respondents. The question 'In which county do you live?' was often answered as if the question had been 'In which country do you live?' This meant that rather than answering 'Worcestershire', the respondent would answer either 'England' or 'UK'. Later questionnaires for which Tracey was responsible used the question 'In which town do you live?', the response being used to establish and code the county in which the respondent lived.

Translating questions into other languages

Translating questions and associated instructions into another language requires care if your translated or target questionnaire is to be decoded and answered by respondents in the way you intended. For international research this is extremely important if the questions are to have the same meaning to all respondents. For this reason Usunier (1998) suggests that when translating the source questionnaire attention should be paid to:

- **lexical meaning** – the precise meaning of individual words (e.g. the French word *chaud* can be translated into two concepts in English and German, 'warm' and 'hot');
- **idiomatic meaning** – the meanings of a group of words that are natural to a native speaker and not deducible from those of the individual words (e.g. the English expression for informal communication, 'grapevine', has a similar idiomatic meaning as the

Box 11.11 Checklist

Your question wording

- ✓ Does your question collect data at the right level of detail to answer your investigative question as specified in your data requirements table?
- ✓ Will respondents have the necessary knowledge to answer your question? A question on the implications of a piece of European Union legislation would yield meaningless answers from those who were unaware of that legislation.
- ✓ Does your question talk down to respondents? It should not!
- ✓ Are the words used in your question familiar, and will all respondents understand them in the same way? In particular, you should use simple words and avoid jargon, abbreviations and colloquialisms.
- ✓ Are there any words that sound similar and might be confused with those used in your question? This is a particular problem with interviewer-administered questionnaires.
- ✓ Are there any words that look similar and might be confused if your question is read quickly? This is particularly important for self-administered questionnaires.
- ✓ Are there any words in your question that might cause offence? These might result in biased responses or a lower response rate.
- ✓ Can your question be shortened? Long questions are often difficult to understand, especially in interviewer-administered questionnaires, as the respondent needs to remember the whole question. Consequently, they often result in no response at all.
- ✓ Are you asking more than one question at the same time? The question 'How often do you visit your mother and father?' contains two separate questions, one about each parent, so responses would probably be impossible to interpret.
- ✓ Does your question include a negative or double negative? Questions that include the word 'not' are sometimes difficult to understand. The question 'Would you rather not use a non-medicated shampoo?' is far easier to understand when rephrased as: 'Would you rather use a medicated shampoo?'
- ✓ Is your question unambiguous? This can arise from poor sentence structure, using words with several different meanings or having an unclear investigative question. If you ask 'When did you leave school?' some respondents might state the year, others might give their age, while those still in education might give the time of day! Ambiguity can also occur in category questions. If you ask employers how many employees they have on their payroll and categorise their answers into three groups (up to 100, 100–250, 250 plus), they will not be clear which group to choose if they have 100 or 250 employees.
- ✓ Does your question imply that a certain answer is correct? If it does, the question is biased and will need to be reworded, such as with the question 'Many people believe that too little money is spent on our public Health Service. Do you believe this to be the case?' For this question, respondents are more likely to answer 'yes' to agree with and please the interviewer.
- ✓ Does your question prevent certain answers from being given? If it does, the question is biased and will need to be reworded. The question 'Is this the first time you have pretended to be sick?' implies that the respondent has pretended to be sick whether they answer yes or no!
- ✓ Is your question likely to embarrass the respondent? If it is, then you need either to reword it or to place it towards the end of the survey when you will, it is to be hoped, have gained the respondent's confidence. Questions on income can be asked as either precise amounts (more embarrassing), using a quantity question, or income bands (less embarrassing), using a category question.
- ✓ Have you incorporated advice appropriate for your type of questionnaire (such as the maximum number of categories) outlined in the earlier discussion of question types?
- ✓ Are answers to closed questions written so that at least one will apply to every respondent and so each of the list of responses is mutually exclusive ?
- ✓ Are the instructions on how to record each answer clear?

French expression *téléphone arabe,* meaning literally 'arab telephone' and the German expression *Mundpropaganda,* meaning literally 'mouth propaganda');

- **experiential meaning** – the equivalence of meanings of words and sentences for people in their everyday experiences (e.g. terms that are familiar in the source questionnaire's context such as 'dual career household' may be unfamiliar in the target questionnaire's context);
- grammar and syntax – the correct use of language, including the ordering of words and phrases to create well-formed sentences (e.g. in Japanese the ordering is quite different from English or Dutch, as verbs are at the end of sentences).

Usunier (1998) outlines a number of techniques for translating your source questionnaire. These, along with their advantages and disadvantages, are summarised in Table 11.4. In this table, the **source questionnaire** is the questionnaire that is to be translated, and the **target questionnaire** is the translated questionnaire. When writing your final project report, remember to include a copy of both the source and the target questionnaire as appendices. This will allow readers familiar with both languages to check that equivalent questions in both questionnaires have the same meaning.

Table 11.4 Translation techniques for questionnaires

	Direct translation	Back-translation	Parallel translation	Mixed techniques
Approach	Source questionnaire to target questionnaire	Source questionnaire to target questionnaire to source questionnaire; comparison of two new source questionnaires; creation of final version	Source questionnaire to target questionnaire by two or more independent translators; comparison of two target questionnaires; creation of final version	Back-translation undertaken by two or more independent translators; comparison of two new source questionnaires; creation of final version
Advantages	Easy to implement, relatively inexpensive	Likely to discover most problems	Leads to good wording of target questionnaire	Ensures best match between source and target questionnaires
Disadvantages	Can lead to many discrepancies (including those relating to meaning) between source and target questionnaire	Requires two translators, one a native speaker of the source language, the other a native speaker of the target language	Cannot ensure that lexical, idiomatic and experiential meanings are kept in target questionnaire	Costly, requires two or more independent translators. Implies that the source questionnaire can also be changed.

Source: developed from Usunier (1998) 'Translation techniques for questionnaires' in *International and Cross-Cultural Management Research*.

Question coding

If you are planning to analyse your data by computer, they will need to be coded prior to entry. For quantity questions, actual numbers can be used as codes. For other questions, you will need to design a coding scheme. Whenever possible, you should establish the coding scheme prior to collecting data and incorporate it into your questionnaire. This should take account of relevant existing coding schemes to enable comparisons with other data sets (Section 12.2).

For most closed questions you should be able to add codes to response categories. These can be printed on the questionnaire, thereby **pre-coding** the question and removing the need to code after data collection. Two ways of doing this are illustrated by questions 16 and 17, which collect data on the respondents' opinions.

		Excellent	Good	Reasonable	Poor	Awful
16	Is the service you receive? (Please circle O the number)	5	4	3	2	1
17	Is the service you receive? (Please tick ✓ the box)	❑5	❑1	❑3	❑2	❑4

The codes allocated to response categories will affect your analyses. In question 16 an ordered scale of numbers has been allocated to adjacent responses. This will make it far easier to aggregate responses using a computer (Section 12.2) to 'satisfactory' (5, 4 or 3) and 'unsatisfactory' (2 or 1) compared with the codes in question 17. We therefore recommend that you do not allocate codes as in question 17.

In contrast, if you are considering using an Internet- or intranet-mediated questionnaire you can create an **online form (questionnaire)** containing text boxes where the respondent enters information, check boxes that list the choices available to the respondent allowing them to 'check' or 'tick' one or more of them, and drop-down list boxes that restrict the respondent to selecting only one of the answers you specify (as in the Nando's questionnaire). Online forms are often included as part of word-processing software such as Microsoft Word™. Alternatively, as for question 18, you can use online software tools such as SurveyMonkey.com™ to create your online form. Both allow you to create a professional questionnaire and the respondent to complete the questionnaire online and return the data electronically in a variety of formats such as Excel™, SPSS™ compatible or a comma-delimited file.

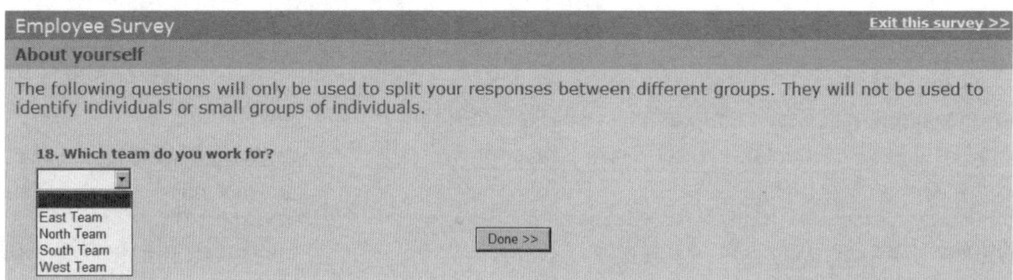

Source: question layout created by SurveyMonkey.com (2008), Portland, Oregon, USA; author/owner: Ryan Finley. Reproduced with permission.

For open questions you will need to reserve space on your data collection form to code responses after data collection. Question 19 has been designed to collect attribute data in a sample survey of 5000 people. Theoretically there could be hundreds of possible responses, and so sufficient spaces are left in the 'For office use only' box.

19 What is your full job title?

....

For Office use only
❑ ❑ ❑

Open questions, which generate lists of responses, are likely to require more complex coding using either the multiple-response or the multiple-dichotomy method. These are discussed in Section 12.2, and we recommend that you read this prior to designing your questions.

Constructing the questionnaire

The order and flow of questions

When constructing your questionnaire it is a good idea to spend time considering the order and flow of your questions. These should be logical to the respondent (and interviewer) rather than follow the order in your data requirements table (Table 11.2). To assist the flow of the survey it may be necessary to include **filter questions**. These identify those respondents for whom the following question or questions are not applicable, so they can skip those questions. You should beware of using more than two or three filter questions in self-administered questionnaires, as respondents tend to find having to skip questions annoying. More complex filter questions can be programmed using Internet- and intranet-mediated questionnaires and CAPI and CATI software so that skipped questions are never displayed on the screen and as a consequence never asked (Dillman 2007). In such situations the respondent is unlikely to be aware of the questions that have been skipped. The following example uses the answer to question 20 to determine whether questions 21 to 24 will be answered. (Questions 20 and 21 both collect data on attributes.)

20 Are you currently registered as unemployed? Yes ❑1

If 'no' go to question 25 No ❑2

21 How long have you been registered as unemployed? ☐☐ years ☐☐ months

(For example, for no years and six months write: ☐0 years ☐6 months)

Where you need to introduce new topics, phrases such as 'the following questions refer to . . .' or 'I am now going to ask you about . . .' are useful. And when wording your questions, you should remember the particular population for whom your questionnaire is designed. For interviewer-administered questionnaires, you will have to include instructions for the interviewer (Box 11.12). The checklist in Box 11.13 should help you to avoid the most obvious problems associated with question order and flow. For some questionnaires the advice contained may be contradictory. Where this is the case, you need to decide what is most important for your particular population.

The layout of the questionnaire

Layout is important for both self-administered and interviewer-administered questionnaires. Interviewer-administered questionnaires should be designed to make reading questions and filling in responses easy. The layout of self-administered questionnaires should, in addition, be attractive to encourage the respondent to fill it in and to return it, while not appearing too long. However, where the choice is between an extra page and a cramped questionnaire the former is likely to be more acceptable to respondents (Dillman 2007). Survey design and analysis software such as Snap™, Sphinx Development™ andSurveyMonkey.com™ contain a series of style templates for typefaces, colours and page layout, which are helpful in producing a professional-looking questionnaire more quickly (Snap Surveys 2008; Sphinx Development 2008; SurveyMonkey.com 2008). For paper-based surveys, the use of colour will increase the printing costs. However, it is worth noting that the best way of obtaining valid responses to questions is to keep both the visual appearance of the questionnaire and the wording of each question simple (Dillman 2007).

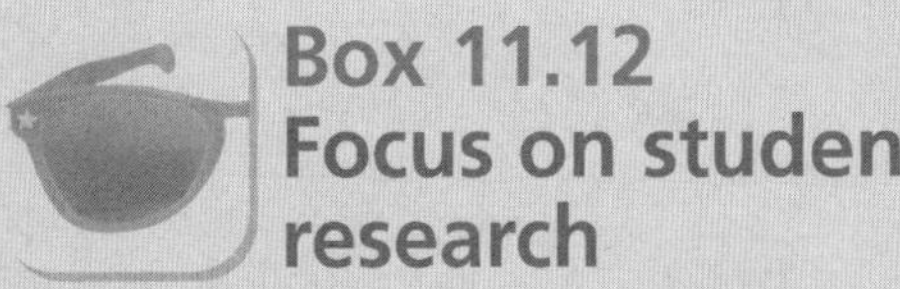

Box 11.12 Focus on student research

Introducing a series of rating questions in a telephone questionnaire

As part of a telephone questionnaire, Stefan needed to collect data on respondents' attitudes to motorway service stations. To do this he asked respondents to rate a series of statements using a Likert-type rating scale. These were recorded as a matrix. Because his survey was conducted by telephone the rating scale was restricted to four categories: strongly agree, agree, disagree, strongly disagree.

In order to make the questionnaire easy for the interviewer to follow, Stefan used italic script to highlight the interviewer's instructions and the words that the interviewer needed to read in bold. An extract is given below:

Now I'm going to read you several statements. Please tell me whether you strongly agree, agree, disagree or strongly disagree with each.

Interviewer: read out statements 22 to 30 one at a time and after each ask ...

Do you strongly agree, agree, disagree or strongly disagree?

Record respondent's response with a tick ✓

---

	strongly agree	agree	disagree	strongly disagree
22 I wish there were a greater number of service stations on motorways	☐4	☐3	☐2	☐1

Box 11.13 Checklist

Your question order

- ✔ Are questions at the beginning of your questionnaire more straightforward and ones the respondent will enjoy answering? Questions about attributes and behaviours are usually more straightforward to answer than those collecting data on opinions.
- ✔ Are questions at the beginning of your questionnaire obviously relevant to the stated purpose of your questionnaire? For example, questions requesting contextual information may appear irrelevant.
- ✔ Are questions and topics that are more complex placed towards the middle of your questionnaire? By this stage most respondents should be completing the survey with confidence but should not yet be bored or tired.
- ✔ Are personal and sensitive questions towards the end of your questionnaire, and is their purpose clearly explained? On being asked these a respondent may refuse to answer; however, if they are at the end of an interviewer-administered questionnaire you will still have the rest of the data!
- ✔ Are filter questions and routing instructions easy to follow so that there is a clear route through the questionnaire?
- ✔ (For interviewer-administered questionnaires) Are instructions to the interviewer easy to follow?
- ✔ Are questions grouped into obvious sections that will make sense to the respondent?
- ✔ Have you re-examined the wording of each question and ensured it is consistent with its position in the questionnaire as well as with the data you require?

Research findings on the extent to which the length of your questionnaire will affect your response rate are mixed (deVaus 2002). There is a widespread view that longer questionnaires will reduce response rates relative to shorter questionnaires (Edwards *et al.* 2002). However, a very short questionnaire may suggest that your research is insignificant and hence not worth bothering with. Conversely, a questionnaire that takes over two hours to complete might just be thrown away by the intended respondent. In general, we have found that a length of between four and eight A4 pages has been acceptable for within-organisation self-administered questionnaires. Telephone questionnaires of up to half an hour have caused few problems, whereas the acceptable length for structured interviews can vary from only a few minutes in the street to over two hours in a more comfortable environment (Section 10.6). Based on these experiences, we recommend you follow deVaus' (2002) advice:

- Do not make the questionnaire longer than is really necessary to meet your research questions and objectives.
- Do not be too obsessed with the length of your questionnaire.

Remember you can reduce apparent length without reducing legibility by using matrix questions (discussed earlier). Box 11.14 (overleaf)discusses the impact of administering a questionnaire online on response rates and Box 11.15 summarises the most important layout issues as a checklist.

Explaining the purpose of the questionnaire

The covering letter

Most self-administered questionnaires are accompanied by a **covering letter** or email, which explains the purpose of the survey. This is the first part of the questionnaire that a respondent should look at. Unfortunately, some of your sample will ignore it, while others use it to decide whether to answer the accompanying questionnaire.

Research by Dillman (2007) and others has shown that the messages contained in a self-administered questionnaire's covering letter will affect the response rate. The results of this research are summarised in the annotated letter (Figure 11.3).

For some research projects you may also send a letter prior to administering your questionnaire. This will be used by the respondent to decide whether to grant you access. Consequently, it is often the only opportunity you have to convince the respondent to participate in your research. Ways of ensuring this are discussed in Section 6.3.

Introducing the questionnaire

At the start of your questionnaire you need to explain clearly and concisely why you want the respondent to complete the survey. Dillman (2007) argues that, to achieve as high a response rate as possible, this should be done on the first page of the questionnaire in addition to the covering letter. He suggests that in addition to a summary of the main messages in the covering letter (Figure 11.3 on page 392) you include:

- a clear unbiased banner or title, which conveys the topic of the questionnaire and makes it sound interesting;
- a subtitle, which conveys the research nature of the topic (optional);
- a neutral graphic illustration or logo to add interest and to set the questionnaire apart (self-administered questionnaires).

This advice also applies to Internet and intranet-mediated questionnaires and is discussed later in this section.

Box 11.14 Focus on management research

Non-response and Internet- and intranet-mediated questionnaires

Thompson and Surface's (2007) paper, 'Employee Surveys Adminstered Online – Attitudes to the medium, non-response, and data representativeness' in the journal, *Organizational Research Methods*, notes a negative trend in response to web-based questionnaires and addresses research questions associated with how employees feel about completing questionnaires online. In addition, it asks whether web-based questionnaire media discourage response.

Data were collected from employees working at the headquarters of a military organisation using a combination of two web based questionnaires and focus groups. Their first research question 'To what degree do people dislike taking employee surveys online?' (Thompson and Surface 2007:242) was addressed, in part using data collected as responses to questions in the organisation's 'staff climate survey' and a paper based questionnaire administered as part of a focus group. This included questions such as (Thompson and Surface 2007:250):

	Strongly disagree	*Disagree*	*Neutral*	*Agree*	*Strongly agree*
I like taking the Command Climate Survey via the Web	❑	❑	❑	❑	❑

Their second research question 'Do reactions to the online medium deter survey participation?' (Thompson and Surface 2007:244) was addressed by a brief online follow-up questionnaire and focus groups within the organisation. Within the online questionnaire, participants were asked whether or not they had worked for the organisation at the time the first questionnaire had been administered and whether they had completed the staff climate survey. Those who worked for the organisation at the time of the first questionnaire and had not completed the staff climate survey were asked to select all the reasons that applied from the following list (Thompson and Surface 2007:246):

- *Waste of time because nothing is done with the results.*
- *Was concerned the response would be traced back to me.*
- *The survey didn't ask the right questions.*
- *Satisfied with the way things are and therefore didn't see the need to respond.*
- *Too busy to complete.*
- *Travelling for work/off sick/on leave/away from office.*
- *Not aware/never received it.*
- *Probably thought it was organisational spam and deleted it.*
- *Accidentally forgot to finish it.*
- *Computer problems.*

With regard to their first research question, Thompson and Surface found that whilst only 8 per cent of respondents to the online questionnaire disapproved of the web based format, 37 per cent of those responding to the same question in the paper based questionnaire disapproved. Based on this and other evidence they argued that web based questionnaires attract respondents whose attitudes to web based questionnaires are not representative of the broader population.

In considering their second research question, Thompson and Surface were particularly concerned as to whether administering a questionnaire using the web discouraged participation. They found that three adverse reactions to the medium had negative implications for web-based questionnaire response rates. These related to concerns about anonymity, computer problems and a failure to distinguish the email relating to the questionnaire from organisational spam.

Box 11.15 Checklist

Your questionnaire layout

- ✔ (For self-administered questionnaires) Do questions appear squashed on the page or screen? This will put the respondent off reading it and reduce the response rate. Unfortunately, a thick questionnaire is equally off-putting!
- ✔ (For paper based self-administered questionnaires) Is the questionnaire going to be printed on good-quality paper? This will imply that the survey is important.
- ✔ (For self-administered questionnaires) Is the questionnaire going to be printed or displayed on a warm-pastel colour? Warm pastel shades, such as yellow and pink, generate slightly more responses than white (Edwards *et al.* 2002) or cool colours, such as green or blue. White is a good neutral colour but bright or fluorescent colours should be avoided.
- ✔ (For structured interviews) Will the questions and instructions be printed on one side of the paper only? You will find it difficult to read the questions on back pages if you are using a questionnaire attached to a clipboard!
- ✔ Is your questionnaire easy to read? Questionnaires should be typed in 12 point or 10 point using a plain font. Excessively long and excessively short lines reduce legibility. Similarly, respondents find CAPITALS, *italics* and shaded backgrounds more difficult to read. However, if used consistently, they can make completing the questionnaire easier.
- ✔ Have you ensured that the use of shading, colour, font sizes, spacing and the formatting of questions is consistent throughout the questionnaire?
- ✔ Is your questionnaire laid out in a format that respondents are accustomed to reading? Research has shown that many people skim-read questionnaires (Dillman 2007). Instructions that can be read one line at a time from left to right moving down the page are, therefore, more likely to be followed correctly.

Interviewer-administered questionnaires will require this information to be phrased as a short introduction, which the interviewer can read to each respondent. A template for this (developed from deVaus 2002) is given in the next paragraph, while Box 11.16 on page 393 provides an example from a self-administered questionnaire.

> **Good morning / afternoon / evening. My name is (your name) from (your organisation). I am doing a research project to find out (brief description of purpose of the research). Your telephone number was drawn from a random sample of (brief description of the total population). The questions I should like to ask will take about (number) minutes. If you have any queries, I shall be happy to answer them. (Pause). Before I continue please can you confirm that this is (read out the telephone number) and that I am talking to (read out name/occupation/position in organisation to check that you have the right person). Please can I ask you the questions now?**

You will also need to have prepared answers to the more obvious questions that the respondent might ask you. These include the purpose of the survey, how you obtained the respondent's telephone number, who is conducting or sponsoring the survey, and why someone else cannot answer the questions instead (Lavrakas 1993).

Closing the questionnaire

At the end of your questionnaire you need to explain clearly what you want the respondent to do with their completed questionnaire. It is usual to start this section by thanking the respondent for completing the questionnaire, and by providing a contact name and telephone number for any queries they may have (Figure 11.3). You should then give

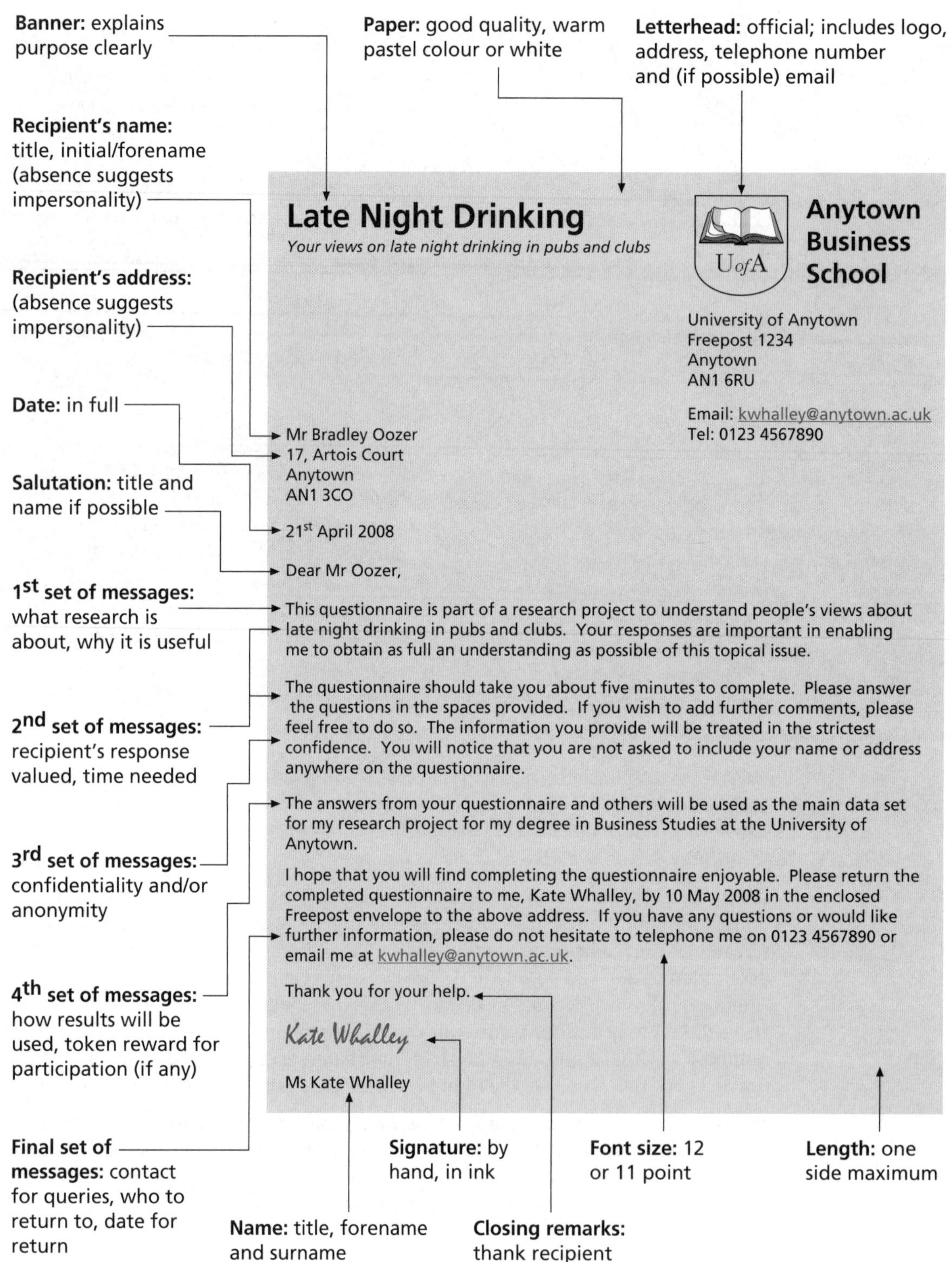

Late Night Drinking

Your views on late night drinking in pubs and clubs

Anytown Business School

UofA

University of Anytown
Freepost 1234
Anytown
AN1 6RU

Email: kwhalley@anytown.ac.uk
Tel: 0123 4567890

Mr Bradley Oozer
17, Artois Court
Anytown
AN1 3CO

21st April 2008

Dear Mr Oozer,

This questionnaire is part of a research project to understand people's views about late night drinking in pubs and clubs. Your responses are important in enabling me to obtain as full an understanding as possible of this topical issue.

The questionnaire should take you about five minutes to complete. Please answer the questions in the spaces provided. If you wish to add further comments, please feel free to do so. The information you provide will be treated in the strictest confidence. You will notice that you are not asked to include your name or address anywhere on the questionnaire.

The answers from your questionnaire and others will be used as the main data set for my research project for my degree in Business Studies at the University of Anytown.

I hope that you will find completing the questionnaire enjoyable. Please return the completed questionnaire to me, Kate Whalley, by 10 May 2008 in the enclosed Freepost envelope to the above address. If you have any questions or would like further information, please do not hesitate to telephone me on 0123 4567890 or email me at kwhalley@anytown.ac.uk.

Thank you for your help.

Kate Whalley

Ms Kate Whalley

Figure 11.3 Structure of a covering letter

Box 11.16
Focus on student research
Introducing a self-administered questionnaire

Liz asked her project tutor to comment on what she hoped was the final draft of her questionnaire. This included the following introduction:

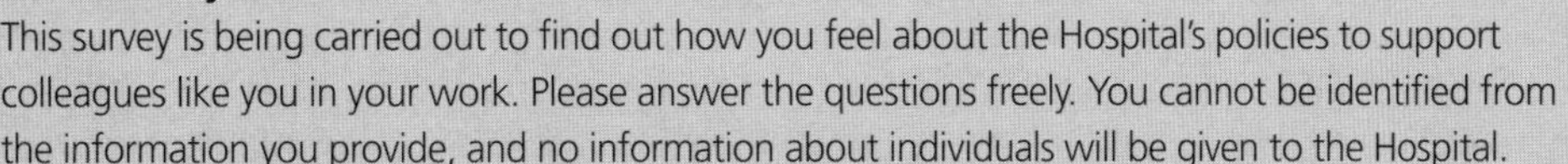

ANYTOWN PRIVATE HOSPITAL STAFF SURVEY

All your responses will be treated in the strictest of confidence and only aggregated data will be available to the Hospital. All questionnaires will be shredded once the data have been extracted. The Hospital will publish a summary of the results.

Not surprisingly, her project tutor suggested that she redraft her introduction. Her revised introduction follows:

Anytown Private Hospital

Staff Survey 2009

This survey is being carried out to find out how you feel about the Hospital's policies to support colleagues like you in your work. Please answer the questions freely. You cannot be identified from the information you provide, and no information about individuals will be given to the Hospital.

ALL THE INFORMATION YOU PROVIDE WILL BE TREATED IN THE STRICTEST CONFIDENCE

The questionnaire should take you about five minutes to complete. Please answer the questions in the space provided. Try to complete the questions at a time when you are unlikely to be disturbed. Also, do not spend too long on any one question. Your first thoughts are usually your best! Even if you feel the items covered may not apply directly to your working life, please do not ignore them. Your answers are essential in building an accurate picture of the issues that are important to improving our support for people working for this Hospital.

WHEN YOU HAVE COMPLETED THE QUESTIONNAIRE, PLEASE RETURN IT TO US IN THE ENCLOSED FREEPOST ENVELOPE NO LATER THAN 6 APRIL.

I hope you find completing the questionnaire enjoyable, and thank you for taking the time to help us. A summary of the findings will be published on the Hospital intranet. If you have any queries or would like further information about this project, please telephone me on 01234-5678910 or email me on epetrie@anytownhealthcare.com.

Thank you for your help.

Elizabeth Petrie

Elizabeth Petrie
Human Resources Department
Anytown Private Hospital
Anytown AN99 9HS

details of the date by which you would like the questionnaire returned and how and where to return it. A template for this is given in the next paragraph:

> Thank you for taking the time to complete this questionnaire. If you have any queries please do not hesitate to contact (your name) by telephoning (contact telephone number with answer machine/voice mail) or emailing (email address).
> Please return the completed questionnaire by (date) in the envelope provided to:
>
> (your name)
>
> (your address)

Pilot testing and assessing validity

Prior to using your questionnaire to collect data it should be pilot tested. The purpose of the **pilot test** is to refine the questionnaire so that respondents will have no problems in answering the questions and there will be no problems in recording the data. In addition, it will enable you to obtain some assessment of the questions' validity and the likely reliability of the data that will be collected. Preliminary analysis using the pilot test data can be undertaken to ensure that the data collected will enable your investigative questions to be answered.

Initially you should ask an expert or group of experts to comment on the representativeness and suitability of your questions. As well as allowing suggestions to be made on the structure of your questionnaire, this will help establish content validity and enable you to make necessary amendments prior to pilot testing with a group as similar as possible to the final population in your sample. For any research project there is a temptation to skip the pilot testing. We would endorse Bell's (2005:147) advice, 'however pressed for time you are, do your best to give the questionnaire a trial run', as, without a trial run, you have no way of knowing whether your questionnaire will succeed.

The number of people with whom you pilot your questionnaire and the number of pilot tests you conduct are dependent on your research question(s), your objectives, the size of your research project, the time and money resources you have available, and how well you have initially designed your questionnaire. Very large questionnaire surveys such as national censuses will have numerous field trials, starting with individual questions and working up to larger and more rigorous pilots of later drafts.

For smaller-scale questionnaires you are unlikely to have sufficient financial or time resources for large-scale field trials. However, it is still important that you pilot test your questionnaire. The number of people you choose should be sufficient to include any major variations in your population that you feel are likely to affect responses. For most student questionnaires this means that the minimum number for a pilot is 10 (Fink 2003b), although for large surveys between 100 and 200 responses is usual (Dillman 2007). Occasionally you may be extremely pushed for time. In such instances it is better to pilot test the questionnaire using friends or family than not at all! This will provide you with at least some idea of your questionnaire's **face validity**: that is, whether the questionnaire appears to make sense.

As part of your pilot you should check each completed pilot questionnaire to ensure that respondents have had no problems understanding or answering questions and have followed all instructions correctly (Fink 2003b). Their responses will provide you with an idea of the reliability and suitability of the questions. For self-administered questionnaires additional information about problems can be obtained by giving respondents a further short questionnaire. Bell (2005) suggests you should use this to find out:

- how long the questionnaire took to complete;
- the clarity of instructions;
- which, if any, questions were unclear or ambiguous;
- which, if any, questions the respondent felt uneasy about answering;
- whether in their opinion there were any major topic omissions;
- whether the layout was clear and attractive;
- any other comments.

Interviewer-administered questionnaires need to be tested with the respondents for all these points other than layout. One way of doing this is to form an assessment as each questionnaire progresses. Another is to interview any interviewers you are employing. However, you can also check by asking the respondent additional questions at the end of their interview. In addition, you will need to pilot test the questionnaire with interviewers to discover whether:

- there are any questions for which visual aids should have been provided;
- they have difficulty in finding their way through the questionnaire;
- they are recording answers correctly.

Once you have completed pilot testing you should write to your respondents thanking them for their help.

11.5 Administering the questionnaire

Once your questionnaire is designed, pilot tested and amended and your sample selected, the questionnaire can be used to collect data. This final stage is called administering the questionnaire. In administering your questionnaire it is important that you abide by your university's or professional body's code of ethics (Sections 6.4 and 6.5). When a respondent ticks a box they are giving their implied consent and have rights just like all research participants.

Inevitably you will need to gain access to your sample (Sections 6.2 and 6.3) and attempt to maximise the response rate. Edwards *et al.* (2002) identify 292 studies that have assessed between them the impact of 75 different strategies for increasing the response to postal questionnaires. These trials were published predominantly in marketing, business and statistical journals (42 per cent), medical and health-related journals (32 per cent) and psychological, educational and sociological journals (23 per cent). The findings of those studies that had more than 1000 participants are summarised in Table 11.5. Such increases in response rates are dependent upon your questionnaire being clearly worded and well laid out. In addition, it must be remembered that organisations and individuals are increasingly being bombarded with requests to respond to questionnaires and so may be unwilling to answer your questionnaire.

Which of these techniques you use to help to maximise responses will inevitably be dependent on the way in which your questionnaire is administered. It is the processes associated with administering each of the five types of questionnaire that we now consider.

Internet- and intranet-mediated questionnaires

For Internet- and intranet-mediated questionnaires, it is important to have a clear timetable that identifies the tasks that need to be done and the resources that will be needed. A good response is dependent on the recipient being motivated to answer the questionnaire and to send it back. Although the covering email (Section 11.4) and good design will help to ensure a high level of response, it must be remembered that, unlike paper questionnaires, the designer and respondent may see different images displayed on their monitors. Alternative computer operating systems, Internet browsers and display screens can all result in the image being displayed differently, emphasising the need to ensure the questionnaire design is clear (Dillman 2007).

Internet- and intranet-mediated questionnaires are usually administered in one of two ways: via email or via a website (Hewson *et al.* 2003). The first of these uses email to 'post' and receive questionnaires or the web link to the questionnaire and is dependent on having a list of addresses. Although it is possible to obtain such lists from an Internet-based employment directory or via a search engine (Section 3.5), we would not recommend you

Table 11.5 Relative impact of strategies for raising postal questionnaire response rates

Strategy	Relative impact
Incentives	
Monetary incentive v. no incentive	Very high
Incentive sent with questionnaire v. incentive on questionnaire return	High
Non-monetary incentive v. no incentive	Low
Length	
Shorter questionnaire v. longer questionnaire	Very high
Appearance	
Brown envelope v. white envelope	High but variable
Coloured ink v. standard	Medium
*Folder or booklet.*v. stapled pages	Low
More personalised v. less personalised	Low
Coloured *questionnaire* v. white questionnaire	Very low
Identifying feature on the return v. none	Very low but variable
Delivery	
Recorded delivery v. standard delivery	Very high
Stamped return envelope v. business reply or franked	Medium
First class post outwards v. other class	Low
Sent to work address v. sent to home address	Low but variable
Pre-paid return v. not pre-paid	Low but variable
Commemorative stamp v. *ordinary stamp*	Low but variable
Stamped outward envelope v. franked	Negligible
Contact	
Pre-contact v. no pre-contact	Medium
Follow-up v. no follow-up	Medium
Postal follow-up including questionnaire v. postal follow-up excluding questionnaire	Medium
Pre-contact by telephone v. *pre-contact by post*	Low
Mention of follow-up contact v. none	Negligible
Content	
More interesting v. less interesting questionnaire	Very high
User friendly questionnaire v. standard	Medium
Attribute and behaviour questions only v. attribute, behaviour and attitude questions	Medium
More relevant questions first v. other questions first	Low
Most general question first v. last	Low
Sensitive questions included v. *sensitive questions not included*	Very low
Demographic questions first v. other questions first	Negligible
'Don't know' boxes included v. not included	Negligible
Origin	
University sponsorship as a source v. *other organisation*	Medium
Sent by more senior or well-known person v. less senior or less well-known	Low but variable
Ethnically unidentifiable/white name v. other name	Low but variable
Communication	
Explanation for not participating requested v. not requested	Medium
Choice to opt out from study offered v. not given	Low
Instructions given v. *not given*	Low but variable
Benefits to respondent stressed v. other benefits	Very low
Benefits to sponsor stressed v. other benefits	Negligible
Benefits to society stressed v. other benefits	Negligible
Response deadline given v. no deadline	Negligible

Note: strategies in italics increase response rates relative to those in normal font.
Source: developed from Edwards *et al.* 2002.

obtain them this way. If you are considering using the Internet for research, you should abide by the general operating guidelines or **netiquette**. This includes (Hewson *et al.* 2003):

- ensuring emails and postings to user groups are relevant and that you do not send junk emails (spam);
- remembering that invitations to participate sent to over 20 user groups at once are deemed as unacceptable by many net vigilantes and so you should not exceed this threshold;
- avoiding sending your email to multiple mailing lists as this is likely to result in individuals receiving multiple copies of your email (this is known as **cross-posting**);
- avoiding the use of email attachments as these can contain viruses.

Failure to do this is likely to result in 'few responses and a barrage of emails informing the researcher of their non-compliance' (Coomber 1997:10). Despite this, questionnaires can be successfully administered by email within organisations provided that all of the sample have access to it and use it (Box 11.17). However, unless an anonymous server or mailbox that removes email addresses is used for returning questionnaires, respondents will be identifiable by their email addresses (Witmer *et al.* 1999). If you choose to use email, we suggest that you:

1 contact recipients by email and advise them to expect a questionnaire – a **pre-survey contact** (Section 6.3);
2 email the questionnaire or a direct web link (hyperlink) with a covering email. Where possible, the letter and questionnaire or hyperlink should be part of the email message rather than an attached file to avoid viruses. You should make sure that this will arrive when recipients are likely to be receptive. For most organisations Fridays and days surrounding major public holidays have been shown to be a poor time;

Box 11.17 Research in the news FT

TNS warns over reliability of data collected online

Businesses are challenging the reliability of some data collected online – the fastest-growing method in the market research industry.

Taylor Nelson Sofres, the global market research group, said companies were concerned that the emergence of 'professional' web respondents simultaneously signed up to several online research panels could skew results from the web.

Over-questioning of panellists, who can be interviewed quicker and cheaper online than by telephone or in person, is also seen as a danger, while maintaining the credibility of web data will be vital if the medium is to continue its recent growth as a research tool, according to TNS.

David Lowden, Chief Executive of TNS, said: 'We have strict rules on how we use online respondents. That is not the case with all suppliers. Our response rates to online questionnaires tend to be 40–50 per cent. But there are companies where it is less than 5 per cent, because they simply send too many questions'.

The amount of TNS business based on data from its Internet panels rose 22 per cent during the first half of 2007, compared with a forecast 5.9 per cent rise in underlying group revenues. Overall, in the six months to June 30, pre-tax profits rose 13 per cent from £30 m to £33.9 m on revenues of £497.4 m (£480.5 m). Earnings per share increased 33 per cent to 5.9p (3.9p) and the interim dividend is 1.6p (1.4p). The shares fell ½p to 228p.

Source: article by Grande, Carlos (2007) *Financial Times*, 4 Sept.

3 email the first **follow-up** one week after emailing out the questionnaire to all recipients. This should thank early respondents and remind non-respondents to answer (a copy of the questionnaire or hyperlink should be included);
4 email the second follow-up to people who have not responded after three weeks. This should include another covering letter and a copy of the questionnaire or hyperlink. The covering letter should be reworded to further emphasise the importance of completing the questionnaire;
5 also use a third follow-up if time allows or your response rate is low.

Alternatively, the questionnaire can be advertised on the Internet or on the intranet and respondents invited to access the questionnaire via a hyperlink and to fill it in. Adopting this web-based approach observes netiquette and means that respondents can remain anonymous and, of equal importance, are unable to modify the questionnaire (Witmer *et al.* 1999). The stages involved are:

1 Ensure that a website has been set up that explains the purpose of the research and how to complete the questionnaire (this takes the place of the covering letter).
2 Ensure that the questionnaire has been set up on the web and has a hyperlink from the website.
3 Advertise the website widely using a range of media (for example, an email pre-survey contact or a banner advertisement on a page that is likely to be looked at by the target population), using a hyperlink to the questionnaire and highlighting the closing date.
4 When the respondent completes the questionnaire, ensure that the data file is generated and saved automatically and that the web-based software prevents multiple responses from one respondent.
5 For web-based questionnaires advertised using an email pre-survey contact, email all recipients one week after the initial email thanking early respondents and reminding others to respond. The hyperlink should be embedded in the email.
6 For web-based questionnaires advertised using an email pre-survey contact, email a second follow-up to people who have not responded after three weeks. The email should be reworded to emphasise further the importance of completing the questionnaire. For anonymous questionnaires, a second follow-up will not be possible, as you should not be able to tell who has responded!

Response rates from web advertisements are likely to be very low, and there are considerable problems of non-response bias as the respondent has to take extra steps to locate and complete the questionnaire (Coomber 1997). Consequently, it is likely to be very difficult to obtain a representative sample from which you might generalise. This is not to say that this approach should not be used as it can, for example, enable you to contact difficult-to-access groups. It all depends, as you would expect us to say, on your research question and objectives!

Postal questionnaires

For postal questionnaires, it is also important to have a well-written covering letter and good design to help to ensure a high level of response. As with online questionnaires, a clear timetable and well-executed administration process are important (Box 11.18).

Our advice for postal questionnaires (developed from deVaus 2002) can be split into six stages:

1 Ensure that questionnaires and letters are printed, and envelopes addressed.
2 Contact recipients by post, telephone or email and advise them to expect a questionnaire – a pre-survey contact (Section 6.3). This stage is often omitted for cost reasons.

Box 11.18 Focus on management research

Questionnaire administration

Mark and Adrian undertook an attitude survey of parents of pupils at a school using a questionnaire. Prior to the survey, a pre-survey contact letter was sent to all parents, using their children to deliver the letter. The questionnaire, covering letter and postage-paid reply envelope were delivered in the same manner a week later. By the end of the first week after the questionnaire had been delivered, 52 questionnaires had been returned. This represented 16 per cent of families whose children attended the school. At the start of the next week a follow-up letter was delivered by hand to all parents. This thanked those who had already responded and encouraged those parents who had yet to return their completed questionnaire to do so. After this, the rate at which questionnaires were returned increased. By the end of the second week 126 questionnaires had been returned, representing a 38 per cent response rate. By the last day for receipt of questionnaires specified in the covering letter, 161 had been returned, increasing the response rate to 48 per cent. However, an additional 41 questionnaires were received after this deadline, resulting in an overall response rate of 60 per cent. The administration of the questionnaire had taken over four weeks from the pre-survey contact letter to the receipt of the last completed questionnaire.

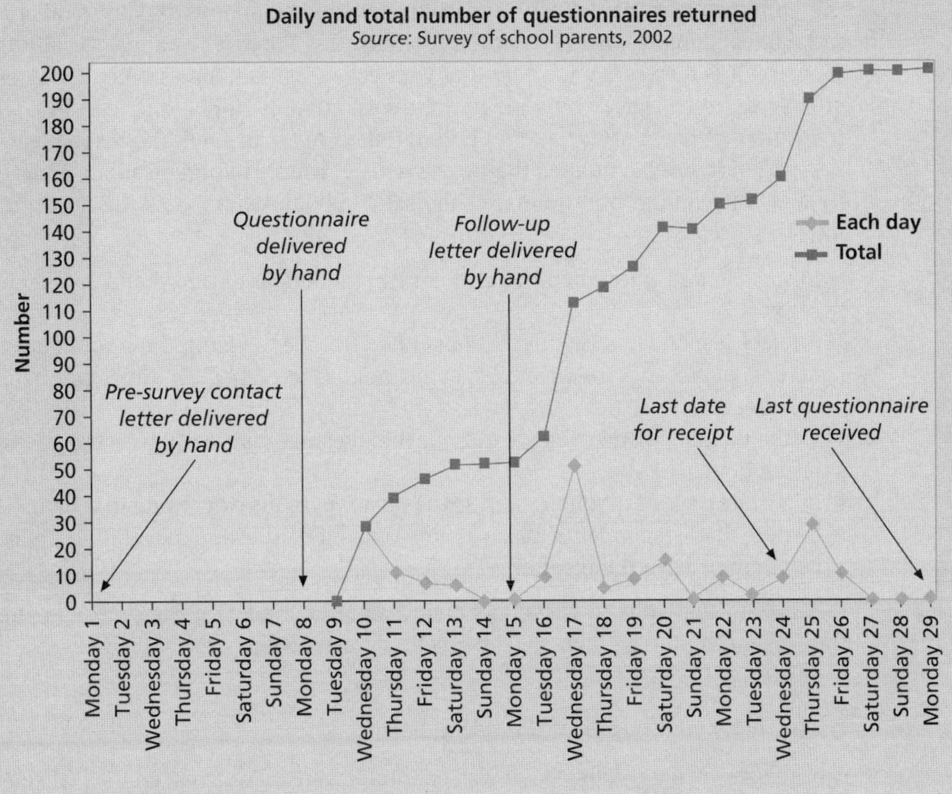

3 Post the survey with a covering letter and a return envelope (and fax cover sheet). You should make sure that this will arrive when recipients are likely to be receptive. For most organisations Fridays and days surrounding major public holidays have been shown to be a poor time.

4 Post (or email) the first follow-up one week after posting out the survey to all recipients. For posted questionnaires this should take the form of a postcard designed to thank early respondents and to remind rather than to persuade non-respondents.
5 Post the second follow-up to people who have not responded after three weeks. This should contain another copy of the questionnaire, a new return envelope and a new covering letter. The covering letter should be reworded to emphasise further the importance of completing the questionnaire. For anonymous questionnaires a second follow-up will not be possible, as you should not be able to tell who has responded!
6 Also use a third follow-up if time allows or your response rate is low. For this it may be possible to use recorded delivery (post), telephone calls or even call in person to emphasise the importance of responding.

Additionally, deVaus (2002) advises placing a unique identification number on each questionnaire, which is recorded on your list of recipients. This makes it easy to check and follow up non-respondents and, according to Dillman (2007) and Edwards *et al.* (2002), has little, if any, effect on response rates. However, identification numbers should not be used if you have assured respondents that their replies will be anonymous!

Delivery and collection questionnaires

The administration of delivery and collection questionnaires is very similar to that of postal questionnaires. However, you or field staff will deliver and call to collect the questionnaire. It is therefore important that your covering letter states when the questionnaire is likely to be collected. As with postal questionnaires, follow-ups can be used, calling at a variety of times of day and on different days to try to catch the respondent.

A variation on this process that we have used widely in organisations allows for delivery and collection of questionnaires the same day and eliminates the need for a follow-up. The stages are:

1 Ensure that all questionnaires and covering letters are printed and a collection box is ready.
2 Contact respondents by internal post or telephone advising them to attend a meeting or one of a series of meetings to be held (preferably) in the organisation's time (Section 6.3).
3 At the meeting or meetings, hand out the questionnaire with a covering letter to each respondent.
4 Introduce the questionnaire and stress its anonymous or confidential nature.
5 Ensure that respondents place their completed questionnaires in a collection box before they leave the meeting.

Although this adds to costs, as employees are completing the questionnaire in work time, response rates as high as 98 per cent are achievable!

Telephone questionnaires

The quality of data collected using telephone questionnaires will be affected by the researcher's competence to conduct interviews. This is discussed in Section 10.5. Once your sample has been selected, you need to:

1 ensure that all questionnaires are printed or, for CATI, that the software has been programmed and tested;
2 where possible and resources allow, contact respondents by post, email or telephone advising them to expect a telephone call (Section 6.3);

3 telephone each respondent, recording the date and time of call and whether or not the questionnaire was completed. You should note any specific times that have been arranged for call-backs. For calls that were not successful you should note the reason, such as no reply or telephone disconnected;
4 for unsuccessful calls where there was no reply, try three more times, each at a different time and on a different day, and note the same information;
5 make call-back calls at the time arranged.

Structured interviews

Conducting structured interviews uses many of the skills required for in-depth and semi-structured interviews (Section 10.5). Issues such as interviewer appearance and preparedness are important and will affect the response rate (Section 10.4). However, once your sample has been selected you need to:

1 ensure that all questionnaires are printed or, for CAPI, that the software has been programmed and tested;
2 contact respondents by post, email or telephone advising them to expect an interviewer to call within the next week. This stage is often omitted for cost reasons;
3 (for large-scale surveys) divide the sample into assignments that are of a manageable size (50–100) for one interviewer;
4 contact each respondent or potential respondent in person, recording the date and time of contact and whether or not the interview was completed. You should note down any specific times that have been arranged for return visits. For contacts that were not successful, you should note down the reason;
5 try unsuccessful contacts at least twice more, each at a different time and on a different day, and note down the same information;
6 visit respondents at the times arranged for return visits.

11.6 Summary

- Questionnaires collect data by asking people to respond to exactly the same set of questions. They are often used as part of a survey strategy to collect descriptive and explanatory data about opinions, behaviours and attributes. Data collected are normally analysed by computer.
- Your choice of questionnaire will be influenced by your research question(s) and objectives and the resources that you have available. The five main types are Internet- or intranet-mediated, postal, delivery and collection, telephone and interview schedule.
- Prior to designing a questionnaire, you must know precisely what data you need to collect to answer your research question(s) and to meet your objectives. One way of helping to ensure that you collect these data is to use a data requirements table.
- The validity and reliability of the data you collect and the response rate you achieve depend largely on the design of your questions, the structure of your questionnaire, and the rigour of your pilot testing.
- When designing your questionnaire you should consider the wording of individual questions prior to the order in which they appear. Questions can be divided into open and closed. The six types of closed questions are list, category, ranking, rating, quantity and matrix.
- Wherever possible, closed questions should be pre-coded on your questionnaire to facilitate data input and subsequent analyses.
- The order and flow of questions in the questionnaire should be logical to the respondent. This can be assisted by filter questions and linking phrases.

- The questionnaire should be laid out so that it is easy to read and the responses are easy to fill in.
- Questionnaires must be introduced carefully to the respondent to ensure a high response rate. For self-administered questionnaires this should take the form of a covering letter; for interviewer-administered questions it will be done by the interviewer.
- All questionnaires should be pilot tested prior to their administration to assess the validity and likely reliability of the questions.
- Administration of questionnaires needs to be appropriate to the type of questionnaire.

Self-check questions

Help with these questions is available at the end of the chapter.

11.1 In what circumstances would you choose to use a delivery and collection questionnaire rather than a postal questionnaire? Give reasons for your answer.

11.2 The following questions have been taken from a questionnaire about flexibility of labour.

i Do you agree or disagree with the use of nil hours contracts by employers?

(Please tick appropriate box)

Strongly agree ❑$_4$
Agree ❑$_3$
Disagree ❑$_2$
Strongly disagree ❑$_1$

ii Have you ever been employed on a nil hours contract?

(Please tick appropriate box)

Yes ❑$_1$
No ❑$_2$
Not sure ❑$_3$

iii What is your marital status?

(Please tick appropriate box)

Single ❑$_1$
Married or living in long-term relationship ❑$_2$
Widowed ❑$_3$
Divorced ❑$_4$
Other ❑$_5$
.... (⇐ Please describe)

iv Please describe what you think would be the main impact on employees of a nil hours contract.

For each question identify:

a the type of data variable for which data are being collected;
b the type of question.

You should give reasons for your answers.

11.3 You are undertaking research on the use of children's book clubs by householders within mainland Europe. As part of this, you have already undertaken in-depth interviews with households who belong and do not belong to children's book clubs. This, along with a literature review, has suggested a number of investigative questions from which you start to construct a table of data requirements.

a For each investigative question listed, decide whether you will need to collect data on opinions, behaviours or attributes.

Research question/objective: *To establish mainland Europe's householders' opinions about children's book clubs*			
Type of research: *Predominantly descriptive, although wish to explain differences between householders*			
Investigative questions	**Variable(s) required**	**Detail in which data measured**	**Check measurement question included in questionnaire ✓**
a Do householders think that children's book clubs are a good or a bad idea?			
b What things do householders like most about children's book clubs?			
c Would householders be interested in an all-ages book club?			
d How much per year do households spend on children's books?			
e Do households' responses differ depending on: (i) number of children? (ii) whether already members of a children's book club?			

b Complete the table of data requirements for each of the investigative questions already listed. (You may embellish the scenario to help in your choice of variables required and how the data will be measured as you feel necessary.)

11.4 Design pre-coded or self-coded questions to collect data for each of the investigative questions in self-check question 11.3. Note that you will need to answer self-check question 11.3 first (or use the answer at the end of this chapter).

11.5 What issues will you need to consider when translating your questionnaire?

11.6 You work for a major consumer research bureau that has been commissioned by 11 major UK companies to design and administer a telephone questionnaire. The purpose of this questionnaire is to describe and explain relationships between adult consumers' lifestyles, opinions and purchasing intentions. Write the introduction to this telephone questionnaire, to be read by an interviewer to each respondent. You may embellish the scenario and include any other relevant information you wish.

11.7 You have been asked by a well-known national charity 'Work for All' to carry out research into the effects of long-term unemployment throughout the UK. The charity intends to use the findings of this research as part of a major campaign to highlight public awareness about the effects of long-term unemployment. The charity has drawn up a list of names and addresses of people who are or were long-term unemployed with whom they have had contact over the past six months. Write a covering letter to accompany the postal questionnaire. You may embellish the scenario and include any other relevant information you wish.

11.8 You have been asked to give a presentation to a group of managers at an oil exploration company to gain access to undertake your research. As part of the presentation you outline your methodology, which includes piloting the questionnaire. In the ensuing question and answer session one of the managers asks you to justify the need for a pilot study, arguing that 'given the time constraints the pilot can be left out'. List the arguments that you would use to convince him that pilot testing is essential to your methodology'.

Review and discussion questions

11.9 If you wish for more help with designing questionnaires, visit the website http:www.statpac.com/surveys/ and download and work through the tutorial 'Designing Surveys and Questionnaires'.

11.10 Obtain a copy of a 'customer questionnaire' from a department store or restaurant. For each question on the questionnaire establish whether it is collecting data about opinions, behaviours or attributes. Do you consider any of the questions are potentially misleading? If yes, how do you think the question could be improved? Discuss the answer to these questions in relation to your questionnaire with a friend.

11.11 Visit the website of an online questionnaire provider. A selection of possible providers can be found by typing 'online questionnaire provider' or 'online survey provider' into the Google search engine. Use the online software to design a simple questionnaire. To what extent does the questionnaire you have designed meet the requirements of the checklists in Boxes 11.11, 11.13 and 11.15?

11.12 Visit your university library or use the Internet to view a copy of a report for a recent national government survey in which you are interested. If you are using the Internet, the national government websites listed in Table 8.3 are a good place to start. Check the appendices in the report to see if a copy of the questionnaire used to collect the data is included. Of the types of question – open, list, category, ranking, rating, quantity and grid – which is most used and which is least frequently used? Note down any that may be of use to you in your research project.

Progressing your research project

Using questionnaires in your research

- Return to your research question(s) and objectives. Decide on how appropriate it would be to use questionnaires as part of your research strategy. If you do decide that this is appropriate, note down the reasons why you think it will be sensible to collect at least some of your data in this way. If you decide that using a questionnaire is not appropriate, justify your decision.
- If you decide that using a questionnaire is appropriate, re-read Chapter 7 on sampling and, in conjunction with this chapter, decide which of the five types of questionnaire will be most appropriate. Note down your choice of questionnaire and the reasons for this choice.
- Construct a data requirements table and work out precisely what data you need to answer your investigative questions. Remember that you will need to relate your investigative questions and data requirements back to the literature you have reviewed and any preliminary research you have already undertaken.

- Design the separate questions to collect the data specified in your data requirements table. Wherever possible, try to use closed questions and to adhere to the suggestions in the question wording checklist. If you are intending to analyse your questionnaire by computer, read Section 12.2 and pre-code questions on the questionnaire whenever possible.
- Order your questions to make reading the questions and filling in the responses as logical as possible to the respondent. Wherever possible, try to adhere to the checklist for layout. Remember that interviewer-administered questionnaires will need instructions for the interviewer.
- Write the introduction to your questionnaire and, where appropriate, a covering letter.
- Pilot test your questionnaire with as similar a group as possible to the final group in your sample. Pay special attention to issues of validity and reliability.
- Administer your questionnaire and remember to send out a follow-up survey to non-respondents whenever possible.

References

Bell, J. (2005) *Doing Your Research Project* (4th edn). Buckingham: Open University Press.

Bourque, L.B. and Clark, V.A. (1994) 'Processing data: the survey example', in M.S. Lewis-Beck *Research Practice*. London: Sage, pp. 1–88.

Coomber, R. (1997) 'Using the Internet for survey research', *Sociological Research Online*, Vol. 2, No. 2. Available at: http://www.socresonline.org.uk/socresonline/2/2/2.html [Accessed 20 April 2008.]

Cooper, D.R. and Schindler, P.S. (2008) *Business Research Methods*, (10th edn). Boston, MA and Burr Ridge, IL: McGraw-Hill.

Corbetta, P. (2003) *Social Research: Theory, Methods and Techniques*. London: Sage.

deVaus, D.A. (2002) *Surveys in Social Research*. (5th edn). London: Routledge.

Dillman, D.A. (2007) *Mail and Internet Surveys: The Tailored Design Method* (2nd edn). Hoboken, NJ: Wiley.

Edwards, P., Roberts, I., Clarke, M., Di Giuseppe, C., Pratap, S., Wentz, R., and Kwan, I. (2002) 'Increasing response rates to postal questionnaires: systematic review', *British Medical Journal*, No. 324, May, pp. 1183–91.

Field, A. (2005) *Discovering Statistics Using SPSS* (2nd edn). London: Sage.

Fink, A. (2003a) *How to Ask Survey Questions*. (2nd edn). Thousand Oaks, CA: Sage.

Fink, A. (2003b) *The Survey Handbook*. (2nd edn). Thousand Oaks, CA: Sage.

Foddy, W. (1994) *Constructing Questions for Interviews and Questionnaires*. Cambridge: Cambridge University Press.

Gay, G., Schelluch, P. and Baines, A. (1998) 'Perceptions of messages conveyed by review and audit reports', *Accounting, Auditing and Accountability Journal*, Vol. 11, No. 4, pp. 472–94.

Ghauri, P. and Grønhaug, K. (2005) *Research Methods in Business Studies: A Practical Guide* (3rd edn). Harlow: Financial Times Prentice Hall.

Gill, J. and Johnson, P. (2002) *Research Methods for Managers* (3rd edn). London: Paul Chapman.

Hewson, C., Yule, P., Laurent, D. and Vogel, C. (2003) *Internet Research Methods: A Practical Guide for the Social and Behavioural Sciences*. London: Sage.

Jankowicz, A.D. (2005) *Business Research Projects* (4th edn). London: Thomson Learning.

Lavrakas, P.J. (1993) *Telephone Survey Methods: Sampling, Selection and Supervision.* Newbury Park, CA: Sage.

Miller, D.C. and Salkind, N.J. (eds) (2002) *Handbook of Research Design and Social Measurement* (6th edn). Thousand Oaks, CA: Sage.

Mitchell, V. (1996) 'Assessing the reliability and validity of questionnaires: an empirical example', *Journal of Applied Management Studies,* Vol. 5, No. 2, pp. 199–207.

Nando's (2008) 'Talk to us'. Available at: http://www.nandos.co.uk/faq/CU/Contact_Us.html# [Accessed 27 April 2008.]

Oppenheim, A.N. (2000) *Questionnaire Design, Interviewing and Attitude Measurement* (new edn). London: Continuum International.

Robson, C. (2002) *Real World Research* (2nd edn). Oxford: Blackwell.

Rogelberg, S.G. and Stanton, J.M. (2007) 'Understanding and dealing with organizational survey nonresponse', *Organizational Research Methods*, Vol. 10. pp. 195–208.

Rose, D. and Pevalin, D.J. (2003) 'The NS-SEC explained', in D. Rose and D.J. Pevalin (eds) *A Researcher's Guide to the National Statistics Socio-economic Classification*. London: Sage, pp. 28–43.

Schrauf, R.W. and Navarro, E. (2005) 'Using existing tests and scales in the field', *Field Methods,* Vol. 17, No. 4, pp. 373–93.

Snap Surveys (2008) 'Snap Surveys: The complete survey solution'. Available at: http://www.snapsurveys.com [Accessed 20 April 2008.]

Sphinx Development (2008) 'Sphinx Development'. Available at: http://www.sphinxdevelopment.co.uk/ [Accessed 20 April 2008.]

SurveyMonkey.com (2008) SurveyMonkey.com. Available at: http://www.surveymonkey.com [Accessed 20 April 2008.]

Taylor, B. (2007) 'More poll questions than answers'. Available at: http://news.bbc.co.uk/1/hi/scotland/6264483.stm [Accessed 14 April 2008.]

Tharenou, P., Donohue, R. and Cooper, B. (2007) *Management Research Methods.* Melbourne: Cambridge University Press.

Thompson and Surface (2007) 'Employee surveys administered online – attitudes to the medium, non-response, and data representativeness', *Organizational Research Methods*, Vol. 10, No. 2, pp. 241–61.

Usunier, J.-C. (1998) *International and Cross-Cultural Management Research*. London: Sage.

Witmer, D.F., Colman, R.W. and Katzman, S.L. (1999) 'From paper and pen to screen and keyboard: Towards a methodology for survey research on the Internet', in S. Jones (ed.) *Doing Internet Research.* Thousand Oaks, CA: Sage, pp. 145–62.

Further reading

deVaus, D.A. (2002) *Surveys in Social Research* (5th edn). London: Routledge. Chapters 7 and 8 provide a detailed guide to constructing and administering questionnaires, respectively.

Dillman, D.A. (2007) *Mail and Internet Surveys: The Tailored Design Method* (2nd edn). Hoboken, NJ: Wiley. The updated second edition of this classic text contains an extremely detailed and well-researched discussion of how to design postal and Internet-based questionnaires to maximise response rates. The new appendix is particularly helpful regarding recent developments.

Foddy, W. (1994) *Constructing Questions for Interviews and Questionnaires.* Cambridge: Cambridge University Press. This contains a wealth of information on framing questions, including the use of scaling techniques.

Hewson, C., Yule, P., Laurent, D. and Vogel, C. (2003) *Internet Research Methods: A Practical Guide for the Social and Behavioural Sciences*. London: Sage. Chapter 3 offers a useful overview of Internet-mediated research, including a discussion of questionnaires, whilst Chapter 5 discusses design issues concerned with Internet-mediated questionnaires.

Case 11
Downsizing in the Middle East

Amman, Jordan
Source: ©2008 Mohammad Al Kilani

As an overseas student, Zaid Kilani chose to research downsizing in his home country in the Middle East. He was encouraged by his tutor to research downsizing in a non-Western context. Zaid decided to investigate how employees perceive the downsizing process. To delimit his research project, he decided to focus on one downsizing method that is used in downsizing the civil service in his home country. Further, he focused on one aspect of employees' perception, which was fairness of the downsizing process.

Zaid undertook his research from a positivistic philosophical stance. He conducted a thorough review of the literature, stated his research aims, and formed hypotheses that could be tested statistically. The required data were to be collected via self-administered postal questionnaire, which he wished to send to a sample of the total population of the of 2800 ex-civil servants.

A list of these ex-civil servants that included their names, ex-employers, and other details were provided by the Civil Service Bureau in his home country. Unfortunately, no contact details were available. One possible way to overcome this obstacle could have been to contact their previous employers and ask them for the contact details. However, this was deemed unethical as he would be requesting personal details. The alternative, which Zaid adopted, was to search for the ex-employees' names in the general telephone book, contact them by telephone, ask for their informed consent to participate, and, if they accepted, ask for their convenient postal address. Zaid realised that a further obstacle was that as an unknown male, even though he was a researcher, it would not be tolerable for him to contact female respondents and ask for such information. He, therefore, assigned a female assistant to contact female respondents. To facilitate the process of searching for telephone numbers, Zaid purchased an electronic copy of the general telephone book, enabling him to search using a computer.

As Arabic is the first language in Zaid's home country, it was prudent to translate the questionnaire into Arabic to minimise the possibility of non-response due to language difficulties. To fulfil this object, he decided to follow Usunier's (1998) suggestion and used parallel translation. This involved having several independent translations from English to Arabic, comparing the translated versions, and subsequently arriving at a final version in Arabic. As Zaid is an Arabic native, he felt this would help to ensure that the specific meanings included in his questionnaire were fully rendered in the Arabic version.

To translate the questionnaire by using the parallel-translation technique, two Arabic native translators were appointed. One of the translators had an MBA degree while the other had a Bachelor degree in business administration. Each of them had experience in translation from English to Arabic and back while working with his home country's civil service. Zaid provided each of the translators with a copy of the English version of the questionnaire and its covering letter to translate independently into Arabic. Subsequently, the translators and Zaid had a meeting to discuss the translated versions question by question. The Arabic version was prepared after minor differences between the two translated questionnaires were found and then reconciled. The differences pertained to the expressions 'job' and 'civil servant'. The word 'job' has several equivalents, so the translators and the author agreed on the most appropriate word. In addition, the expression 'civil servant' may imply inferiority in Arabic. For this reason, the term 'civil employee' was used. For language-gender considerations, two versions of the covering letters were prepared: one to address female respondents and the other to address male respondents. Afterwards, the Arabic version of the questionnaire and its covering letter were piloted.

Date

Title and name of respondent

Address of respondent

Dear respondent name,

Participating in a survey

I am a student in the UK. The topic I am researching is the attitudes of civil servants who were downsized. I enclose a questionnaire, which asks for your views about the topic.

You are one of a sample of 843 civil servants who were downsized. You were selected randomly from a list of all the civil servants' names who were downsized. This list was obtained from the Civil Service Bureau.

The questionnaire forms a major part of my research, and I would value it highly if you would agree to participate by filling it in. In giving your views, you will also help to further my understanding about the downsizing process.

I must emphasise that your participation is entirely voluntary, and it is up to you to decide whether or not you wish to take part.

Let me assure you that all the information that you provide will be dealt with anonymously and confidentially, and will only be used for purpose of this study. I will ensure that the data collected from you and others are stored electronically at the University and are password protected. It will be kept for a minimum of five years.

Please complete the questionnaire and return it in the enclosed stamped, addressed envelope by [a date, give them about a week or 10 days].

Should you have any query, please contact me on my mobile 0712 345 678 910, or the daytime landline 0987 654 321 000.

This research has been reviewed by the University Research Ethics Committee at the University of Anytown. If you have any concerns about the conduct of this research, please contact the Chair of the committee on ethics@anytown.ac.uk or telephone the Secretary to the committee on 012345555555.

I am grateful for your kindness, and thank you for your generous help in completing this questionnaire to help me with my postgraduate research.

Yours faithfully

Zaid

Student at the University of Anytown

Questions

1 What are the possible disadvantages of the way that Zaid used to contact respondent?
2 Outline the possible disadvantages of using a parallel translation technique?
3 You have been asked to comment on the covering letter that Zaid prepared. What are your suggestions to improve this covering letter?

Additional case studies relating to material covered in this chapter are available via the book's Companion Website, **www.pearsoned.co.uk/saunders**. They are:

- The provision of leisure activities for younger people in rural areas
- Job satisfaction in an Australian organisation
- Service quality in health-care supply chains.

Self-check answers

11.1 When you:

- wanted to check that the person whom you wished to answer the questions had actually answered the questions;
- have sufficient resources to devote to delivery and collection and the geographical area over which the questionnaire is administered is small;
- can use field workers to enhance response rates. Delivery and collection questionnaires have a moderately high response rate of between 30 and 50 per cent compared with 30 per cent offered on average by a postal questionnaire;
- are administering a questionnaire to an organisation's employees and require a very high response rate. By administering the questionnaire to groups of employees in work time and collecting it on completion, response rates of up to 98 per cent can be achieved.

11.2 **a** **i** Opinion data: the question is asking how the respondent *feels* about the use of nil hours contracts by employees.
ii Behaviour data: the question is asking about the *concrete experience* of being employed on a nil hours contract.
iii Attribute data: the question is asking about the respondent's *characteristics*.
iv Opinion data: the question is asking the respondent what they *think* or *believe* would be the impact on employees.
b **i** Rating question using a Likert-type scale in which the respondent is asked how strongly they agree or disagree with the statement.
ii Category question in which the respondent's answer can fit only one answer.
iii Category question as before.
iv Open question in which the respondent can answer in their own way.

11.3 Although your answer is unlikely to be precisely the same, the completed table of data requirements below should enable you to check you are on the right lines.

Research question/objective: To establish householders' opinions about children's book clubs			
Type of research: Predominantly descriptive, although wish to explain differences between householders			
Investigative questions	**Variable(s) required**	**Detail in which data measured**	**Check measurement question included in questionnaire ✓**
Do householders think that children's book clubs are a good or a bad idea? (opinion – this is because you are really asking how householders feel)	Opinion about children's book clubs	Very good idea, good idea, neither a good nor a bad idea, bad idea, very bad idea	
What things do householders like most about children's book clubs? (opinion)	What householders like about children's book clubs	Get them to rank the following things (generated from earlier in-depth interviews): monthly magazine, lower prices, credit, choice, special offers, shopping at home	
Would householders be interested in an all-ages book club? (behaviour)	Interest in a book club which was for both adults and children	Interested, not interested, may be interested	
How much per year do households spend on children's books? (behaviour)	Amount spent on children's books by adults and children per year by household	(Answers to the nearest €) €0 to €10, €11 to €20, €21 to €30, €31 to €50, €51 to €100, over €100	
Do households' responses differ depending on: • *Number of children?* (attribute) • *Whether already members of a children's book club?* (behaviour)	Number of children aged under 16 Children's book club member	Actual number Yes, no	

11.4 a Please complete the following statement by ticking the phrase that matches your feelings most closely . . .

I feel children's book clubs are . . . . a very good idea ❑ 5

. . . a good idea ❑ 4

. . . neither a good nor a bad idea ❑ 3

. . . a bad idea ❑ 2

. . . a very bad idea ❑ 1

b Please number each of the features of children's book clubs listed below in order of how much you like them. Number the most important 1, the next 2 and so on. The feature you like the least should be given the highest number.

Feature	**How much liked**
Monthly magazine	☐
Lower prices	☐
Credit	☐
Choice	☐
Special offers	☐
Shopping at home	☐

c Would you be interested in a book club that was for both adults and children?
(Please tick the appropriate box) Yes ☐ 1
No ☐ 2
Not sure ☐ 3

d How much money is spent in total each year on children's books by all the adults and children living in your household?
(Please tick the appropriate box) €0 to €10 ☐ 1
€11 to €20 ☐ 2
€21 to €30 ☐ 3
€31 to €50 ☐ 4
€51 to €100 ☐ 5
Over €100 ☐ 6

e i. How many children aged under 16 are living in your household?
☐ children
(For example, for 3 write:) [3] children

ii. Is any person living in your household a member of a children's book club?
(Please tick the appropriate box) Yes ☐ 1
No ☐ 2

11.5 When translating your questionnaire you will need to ensure that:

- the precise meaning of individual words is kept (lexical equivalence);
- the meanings of groups of words and phrases that are natural to a native speaker but cannot be translated literally are kept (idiomatic equivalence);
- the correct grammar and syntax are used.

In addition, you should, if possible, use back translation, parallel translation or mixed translation techniques to ensure that there are no differences between the source and the target questionnaire.

11.6 Although the precise wording of your answer is likely to differ, it would probably be something like this:

Good morning/afternoon/evening. My name is ____ from JJ Consumer Research. We are doing an important national survey covering lifestyles, opinions and likely future purchases of adult consumers. Your telephone number has been selected at random. The questions I need to ask you will take about 15 minutes. If you have any queries I shall be happy to answer them (*pause*). Before I continue please can you confirm that this is (*read out telephone number including dialling code*) and that I am talking to a person aged 18 or over. Please can I ask you the first question now?

11.7 Although the precise wording of your answer is likely to differ, it would probably be something like the letter below.

Work for All

Registered charity No: 123456789

B&J Market Research Ltd
St Richard's House
Malvern
Worcestershire WR14 12Z
Phone 01684–56789101
Fax 01684–56789102

Email andy@b&jmarketresearch.co.uk

Respondent's name

Respondent's address

Today's date

Dear *title name*

Work for All is conducting research into the effects of long-term unemployment. This is an issue of great importance within the UK and yet little is currently known about the consequences.

You are one of a small number of people who are being asked to give your opinion on this issue. You were selected at random from Work for All's list of contacts. In order that the results will truly represent people who have experienced long-term unemployment, it is important that your questionnaire is completed and returned.

All the information you give us will be totally confidential. You will notice that your name and address do not appear on the questionnaire and that there is no identification number. The results of this research will be passed to Work for All, who will be mounting a major campaign in the New Year to highlight public awareness about the effects of long-term unemployment.

If you have any questions you wish to ask or there is anything you wish to discuss please do not hesitate to telephone me, or my assistant Benjamin Marks, on 01684–56789101 during the day. You can call me at home on 01234–123456789 evenings and weekends. Thank you for your help.

Yours sincerely

Andy Nother

Mr Andy Nother

Project Manager

11.8 Despite the time constraints, pilot testing is essential to your methodology for the following reasons:

- to find out how long the questionnaire takes to complete;
- to check that respondents understand and can follow the instructions on the questionnaire (including filter questions);
- to ensure that all respondents understand the wording of individual questions in the same way and that there are no unclear or ambiguous questions;
- to ensure that you have the same understanding of the wording of individual questions as the respondents;
- to check that respondents have no problems in answering questions; for example:
  - all possible answers are covered in list questions;
  - whether there are any questions that respondents feel uneasy about answering;
- to discover whether there are any major topic omissions;
- to provide an idea of the validity of the questions that are being asked;

- to provide an idea of the reliability of the questions by checking responses from individual respondents to similar questions;
- to check that the layout appears clear and attractive;
- to provide limited test data so you can check that the proposed analyses will work.

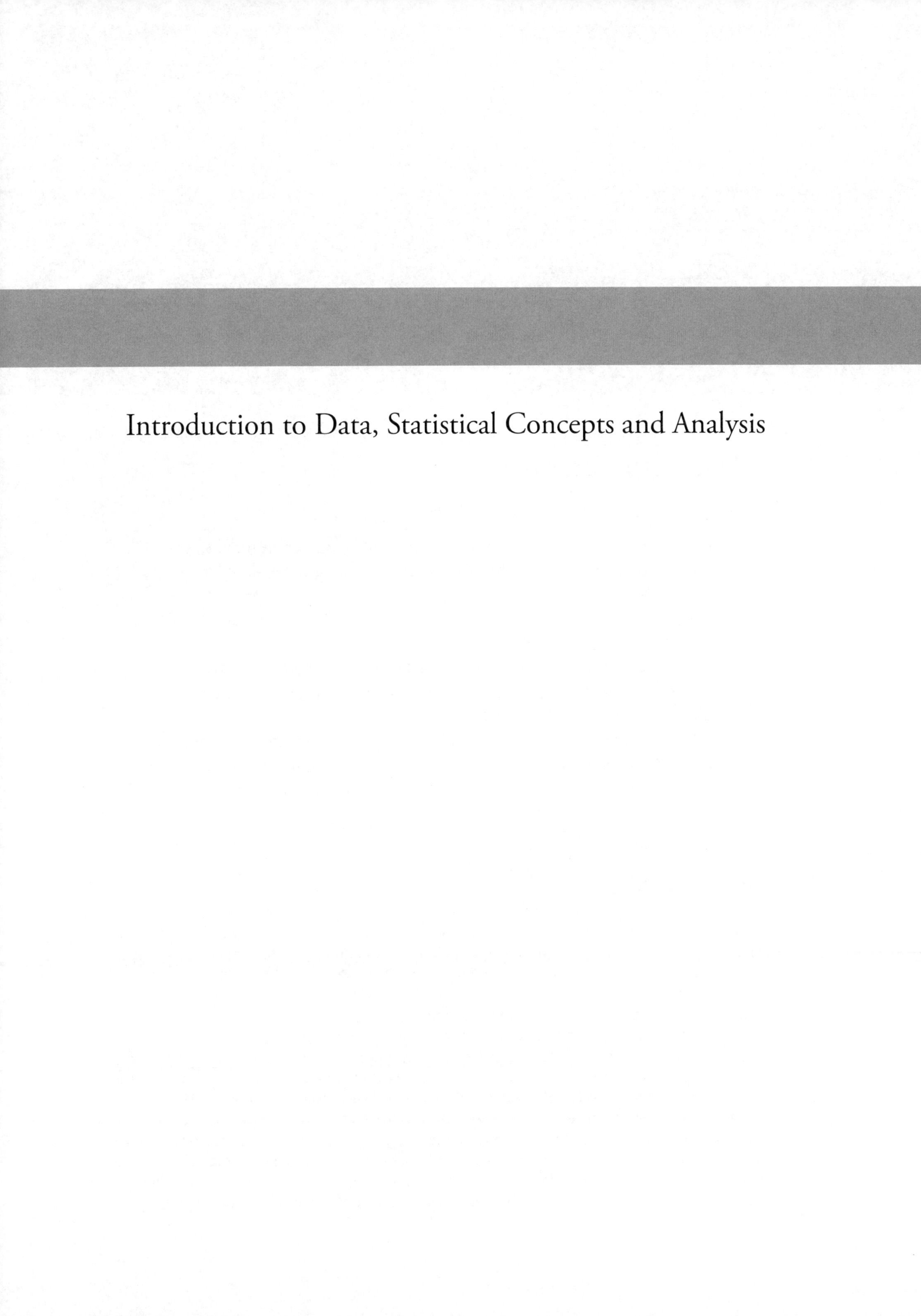

Introduction to Data, Statistical Concepts and Analysis

Chapter 12

Analysing quantitative data

Learning outcomes

By the end of this chapter, you should be able to:

- identify the main issues that you need to consider when preparing quantitative data for analysis and when analysing these data by computer;
- recognise different types of data and understand the implications of data type for subsequent analyses;
- create a data matrix and to code data for analysis by computer;
- select the most appropriate tables and diagrams to explore and illustrate different aspects of your data;
- select the most appropriate statistics to describe individual variables and to examine relationships between variables and trends in your data;
- interpret the tables, diagrams and statistics that you use correctly.

12.1 Introduction

Quantitative data in a raw form, that is, before these data have been processed and analysed, convey very little meaning to most people. These data, therefore, need to be processed to make them useful, that is, to turn them into information. Quantitative analysis techniques such as graphs, charts and statistics allow us to do this; helping us to explore, present, describe and examine relationships and trends within our data.

Virtually any business and management research you undertake is likely to involve some numerical data or contain data that could usefully be quantified to help you answer your research question(s) and to meet your objectives. **Quantitative data** refer to all such data and can be a product of all research strategies (Section 5.3). It can range from simple counts such as the frequency of occurrences to more complex data such as test scores, prices or rental costs. To be useful these data need to be analysed and interpreted. Quantitative analysis techniques assist you in this process. They range from creating simple tables or diagrams that show the frequency of occurrence and using statistics such as indices to enable comparisons, through establishing statistical relationships between variables to complex statistical modelling.

Until the advent of powerful personal computers, data were analysed either by hand or by using mainframe computers. The former of these was extremely time consuming and prone to error, the latter expensive. Fortunately, the by-hand or calculator 'number-crunching' and 'charting' elements of quantitative analysis have been incorporated into relatively inexpensive personal-computer-based analysis software. These range from spreadsheets such as Excel™ to more advanced data management and statistical analysis software packages such as Minitab™, SAS™, SPSS for Windows™ and Statview™. They also include more specialised survey design and analysis packages such as SNAP™ and SphinxSurvey™. Consequently, it is no longer necessary for you to be able to draw presentation-quality diagrams or to calculate statistics by hand as these can be done using a computer. However, if your analyses are to be straightforward and of any value you need to:

- have prepared your data with quantitative analyses in mind;
- be aware of and know when to use different charting and statistical techniques.

For prospective students, the cost of living is an important aspect in their choice of where to study, these costs varying markedly between different university towns and cities. Quantitative analysis techniques can help make sense of the thousands of pieces of data needed to work out a typical student's living costs. One such analysis conducted by the organisation Push (2007) in conjunction with Costcutter is the student living costs index. This uses data relating to 136 UK universities and colleges about student housing costs (collected by questionnaires and 'visits'), grocery costs (collected for a specified basket of goods as purchased from the branch of Costcutter nearest to the university's main address) and drink costs (collected by 'visits' to the student bar and a local public house). The index gave the average weekly student living cost at each of the UK's universities and colleges (£119.52 in 2007) the value of 100. Those universities and colleges with a weekly student living cost closest to this average in 2007 were the University of Chester (index = 99.6) and the University College for the Creative Arts (index = 100.4). The university with the lowest student living cost index was Bradford (index = 73.0), where costs were 73 per cent of the average. In contrast, the index for the Royal Academy of Music, which had the highest weekly student living cost was 168.2, 68 per cent higher than the average. Push's index allows easy comparisons between the UK's universities and colleges.

Student accommodation in Birmingham
Source: © Mark Saunders 2008

Robson (2002:393) summarises this, arguing that quantitative data analysis is:

> . . . a field where it is not at all difficult to carry out an analysis which is simply wrong, or inappropriate for your purposes. And the negative side of readily available analysis software is that it becomes that much easier to generate elegantly presented rubbish.

He also emphasises the need to seek advice regarding statistical analyses, a sentiment that we support strongly.

This chapter builds on the ideas outlined in earlier chapters about data collection. It assumes that you will use a personal computer (with at least a spreadsheet) to undertake all but the most simple quantitative analyses. Although it does not focus on one particular piece of analysis software, you will notice in the Focus on Student Research boxes that many of the analyses were undertaken using widely available software such as Excel and SPSS. If you wish to develop your skills in either of these software packages, self-teach packages are available via our companion website. In addition, there are numerous statistics books already published that concentrate on specific software packages. These include Dancey and Reidy (2008), Field (2005) or Kinnear and Gray (2007) on SPSS, and Morris (2003) or Curwin and Slater (2007) on Excel. Likewise, this chapter does not attempt to provide an in-depth discussion of the wide range of graphical and statistical techniques available or to cover more complex statistical modelling, as these are already covered elsewhere (e.g. Dancey and Reidy 2008; Hair *et al.* 2006; Everitt and Dunn 2001; Hays 1994; Henry 1995). Rather it discusses issues that need to be considered at the planning and analysis stages of your research project, and outlines analytical techniques that our students have found to be of most use. In particular, the chapter is concerned with:

- preparing, inputting into a computer and checking your data (Section 12.2);
- choosing the most appropriate tables and diagrams to explore and present your data (Section 12.3);
- choosing the most appropriate statistics to describe your data (Section 12.4);
- choosing the most appropriate statistics to examine relationships and trends in your data (Section 12.5).

12.2 Preparing, inputting and checking data

If you intend to undertake quantitative analysis we recommend that you consider the:

- type of data (scale of measurement);
- format in which your data will be input to the analysis software;
- impact of data coding on subsequent analyses (for different data types);
- need to weight cases;
- methods you intend to use to check data for errors.

Ideally, all of these should be considered before obtaining your data. This is equally important for both primary and secondary data analysis, although you obviously have far greater control over the type, format and coding of primary data. We shall now consider each of these.

Data types

Many business statistics textbooks classify quantitative data into *data types* using a hierarchy of measurement, often in ascending order of numerical precision (Berman Brown and

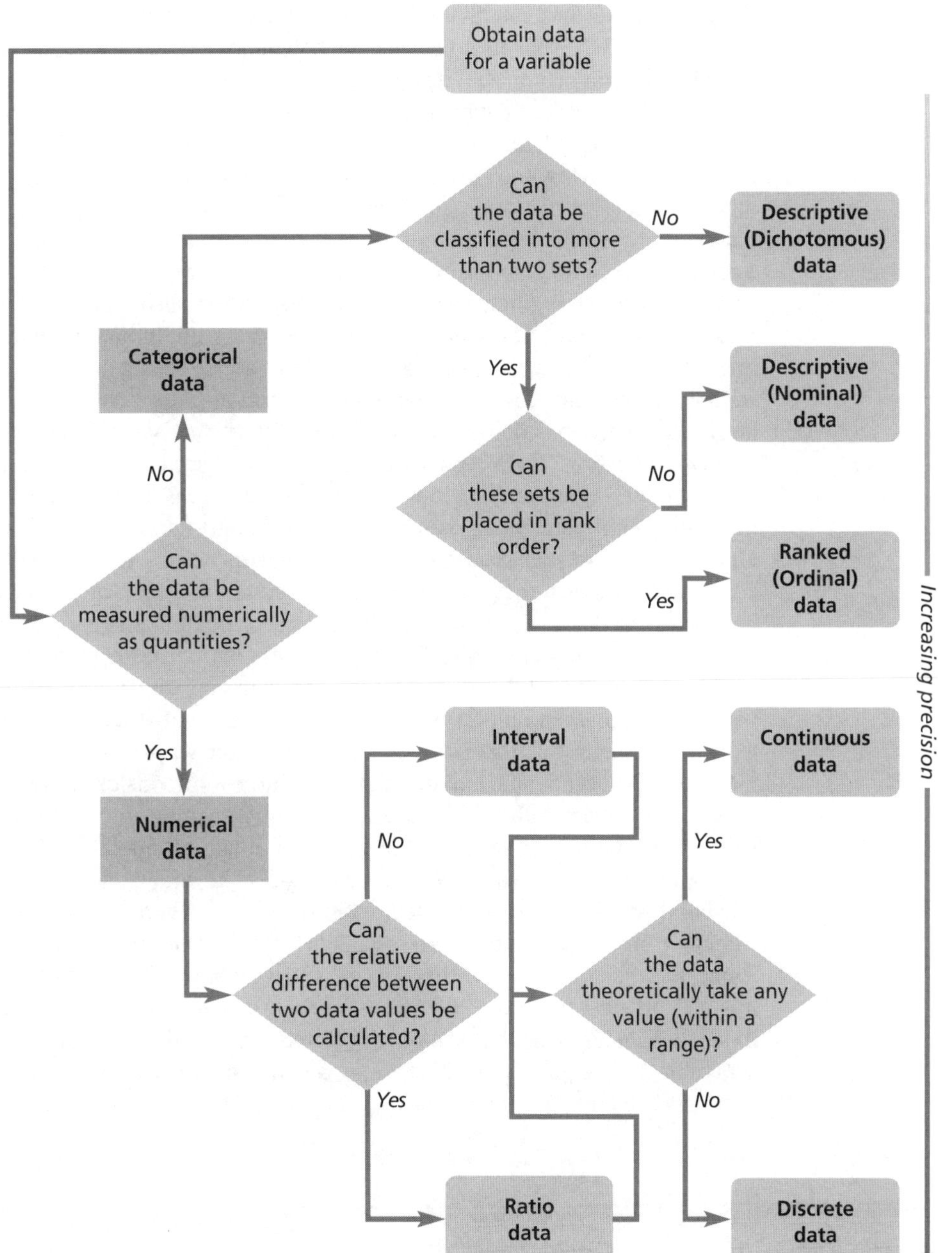

Figure 12.1 Defining the data type

Saunders 2008; Dancey and Reidy 2008). These different levels of numerical measurement dictate the range of techniques available to you for the presentation, summary and analysis of your data. They are discussed in more detail in subsequent sections of this chapter.

Quantitative data can be divided into two distinct groups: categorical and numerical (Figure 12.1). **Categorical data** refer to data whose values cannot be measured numerically but can be either classified into sets (categories) according to the characteristics that identify or describe the variable or placed in rank order (Berman Brown and Saunders 2008).

They can be further sub-divided into descriptive and ranked. A car manufacturer might categorise the types of cars it produces as hatchback, saloon and estate. These are known as **descriptive data** or **nominal data** as it is impossible to define the category numerically or to rank it. Rather these data simply count the number of occurrences in each category of a variable. For virtually all analyses the categories should be unambiguous and discrete; in other words, having one particular feature, such as a car being a hatchback, excludes all other features for that variable. This prevents questions arising as to which category an individual case belongs. Although these data are purely descriptive, you can count them to establish which category has the most and whether cases are spread evenly between categories (Morris 2003). Some statisticians (and statistics) also separate descriptive data where there are only two categories. These are known as **dichotomous data**, as the variable is divided into two categories, such as the variable gender being divided into female and male. **Ranked** (or **ordinal**) **data** are a more precise form of categorical data. In such instances you know the relative position of each case within your data set, although the actual numerical measures (such as scores) on which the position is based are not recorded (Box 12.1). Rating or scale questions, such as where a respondent is asked to rate how strongly she or he agrees with a statement, collect ranked (ordinal) data. Despite this, some researchers argue that, where such data are likely to have similar size gaps between data values, they can be analysed as if they were numerical interval data (Blumberg *et al.* 2008).

Numerical data, which are sometimes termed 'quantifiable', are those whose values are measured or counted numerically as quantities (Berman Brown and Saunders 2008). This means that numerical data are more precise than categorical as you can assign each data value a position on a numerical scale. It also means that you can analyse these data using a far wider range of statistics. There are two possible ways of sub-dividing numerical data: into interval or ratio data and, alternatively, into continuous or discrete data (Figure 12.1). If you have **interval data** you can state the difference or 'interval' between any two data values for a particular variable, but you cannot state the relative difference. This means that values on an interval scale can meaningfully be added and subtracted, but not multiplied and divided. The Celsius temperature scale is a good example of an interval scale. Although the difference between, say, 20°C and 30°C is 10°C it does not mean that 30°C is one and a half times as warm. This is because 0°C does not represent a true zero. When it is 0°C outside, there is still some warmth, rather than none at all! In contrast, for **ratio data**, you can also calculate the relative difference or ratio between any two data values for a variable. Consequently, if a multinational company makes a profit of $300 000 000 in one year and $600 000 000 the following year, we can say that profits have doubled.

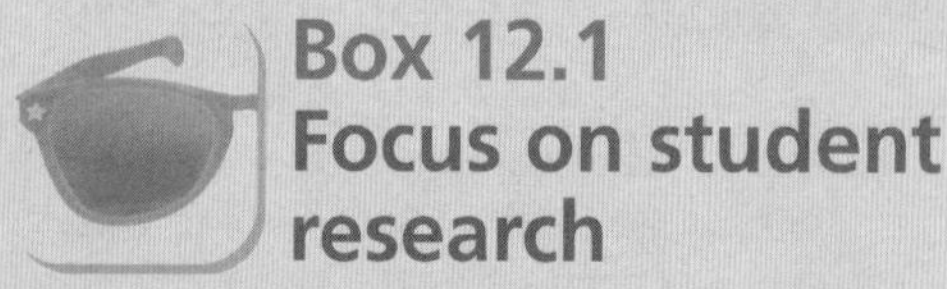

Box 12.1 Focus on student research

Scales of measurement

As part of a marketing questionnaire, Rashid asked individual customers to rank up to five features of a new product in order of importance to them. Data collected were, therefore, categorical and ranked (ordinal). Initial analyses made use of these ranked data. Unfortunately, a substantial minority of customers had ticked, rather than ranked, those features of importance to them.

All responses that had been ranked originally were therefore recoded to 'of some importance'. This reduced the precision of measurement from ranked (ordinal) to descriptive (nominal) but enabled Rashid to use all responses in the subsequent analyses.

Continuous data are those whose values can theoretically take any value (sometimes within a restricted range) provided that you can measure them accurately enough (Dancey and Reidy 2008). Data such as furnace temperature, delivery distance and length of service are therefore continuous data. **Discrete data** can, by contrast, be measured precisely. Each case takes one of a finite number of values from a scale that measures changes in discrete units. These data are often whole numbers (**integers**) such as the number of mobile telephones manufactured or customers served. However, in some instances (e.g. UK shoe size) discrete data will include non-integer values. Definitions of discrete and continuous data are, in reality, dependent on how your data values are measured. The number of customers served by a large organisation is strictly a discrete datum as you are unlikely to get a part customer! However, for a large organisation with many customers you might treat this as a continuous datum, as the discrete measuring units are exceedingly small compared with the total number being measured.

Understanding differences between types of data is extremely important when analysing your data quantitatively, for two reasons. Firstly, it is extremely easy with analysis software to generate statistics from your data that are inappropriate for the data type and are consequently of little value (Box 12.2, overleaf). Secondly, the more precise the scale of measurement, the greater the range of analytical techniques available to you. Data that have been collected and coded using a precise numerical scale of measurement can also be regrouped to a less precise level where they can also be analysed (Box 12.1). For example, a student's score in a test could be recorded as the actual mark (discrete data) or as the position in their class (ranked data). By contrast, less precise data cannot be made more precise. Therefore, if you are not sure about the scale of measurement you require, it is usually better to collect data at the highest level of precision possible and to regroup them if necessary.

Data layout

Some primary data collection methods, such as computer-aided personal interviewing (CAPI), computer-aided telephone interviewing (CATI) and online questionnaires automatically enter and save data to a computer file at the time of collection, often using predefined codes. These data can subsequently be exported in a range of formats to ensure they are compatible with different analysis software. Survey design and analysis software such as SNAP and SphinxSurvey goes one stage further and integrates the analysis software in the same package as the questionnaire design/data input software (Snap Surveys, 2008; Sphinx, 2008). Alternatively, secondary data (Section 8.3) accessed from CD-ROMs or via the Internet can be saved to a file, removing the need for re-entering. For such data, it is often possible to specify a data layout compatible with your analysis software. For other data collection methods, you will have to prepare and enter your data for computer analysis. You therefore need to be clear about the precise data layout requirements of your analysis software.

Virtually all analysis software will accept your data if they are entered in table format. This table is called a **data matrix** (Table 12.1). Once data have been entered into your

Table 12.1 A simple data matrix

	Id	Variable 1	Variable 2	Variable 3	Variable 4
Case 1	1	27	1	2	1
Case 2	2	19	2	1	2
Case 3	3	24	2	3	1

Box 12.2 Focus on management research

Ownership structure and operating performance of acquiring firms

The relationship between ownership structures and the long-term operating profit of acquiring firms has been the subject of much work on mergers and acquisitions. Research by Yen and André (2007) published in the *Journal of Economics and Business* explores the role of governance mechanisms and deal characteristics on value creation subsequent to such mergers and acquisitions revealing that, once such factors are taken into account, the relationship between ownership and value creation is non-linear. Higher levels of ownership are associated with positive post-acquisition performance; companies with large shareholders but only between 10 per cent and 20 per cent of the voting shares, significantly underperforming compared to their peers. Based upon data relating to 287 takeovers in English origin countries excluding the United States they reveal a number of insights as to why this might be the case.

In their paper, Yen and André outline clearly the variables used in their analysis, and the level of numerical measurement recorded. The variables include:

Variable	Numerical measurement recorded
Concentration of ownership	Ranked data – more than 10% to 20%, more than 20% to 50%, more than 50%
Percentage of voting shares	Continuous data – actual percentage held by largest shareholder
Separation of ownership and cash flow rights in acquiring firm	Dichotomous data – separated, not separated
Relationship of chief executive officer to largest shareholder	Dichotomous data – related, not related
Number of directors on the board	Discrete data – actual number on the board
Legal origin of the target firm	Dichotomous data – English, not English
Initial opposition of management or the board of target firm to the deal	Dichotomous data – opposed, not opposed

analysis software, it is usually possible to save them in a format that can be read by other software. Within a data matrix, each column usually represents a separate **variable** for which you have obtained data. Each matrix row contains the variables for an individual **case**, that is, an individual unit for which data have been obtained. If your data have been collected using a survey, each row will contain the data from one survey form. Alternatively, for longitudinal data such as a company's share price over time, each row (case) might be a different time period. Secondary data that have already been stored in computer-readable form will almost always be held as a large data matrix. For such data sets you usually select the subset of variables and cases you require and save these as a separate matrix. If you are entering your own data, they are typed directly into your chosen analysis software one case (row) at a time using codes to record the data (Box 12.4). Larger data sets with more data variables and cases are recorded using larger data matrices. Although data matrices store data using one column for each variable, this may not be the same as one column for each question for data collected using surveys.

Box 12.3 Focus on student research

The implications of data types for analysis

Pierre's research was concerned with customers' satisfaction for a small hotel group of six hotels. In collecting the data he had asked 1044 customers to indicate the hotel at which they were staying when they completed their questionnaires. Each hotel was subsequently allocated a numerical code and this data entered into the computer in the variable 'Hotel':

Hotel	Code
Amsterdam	1
Antwerp	2
Eindhoven	3
Nijmegen	4
Rotterdam	5
Tilburg	6

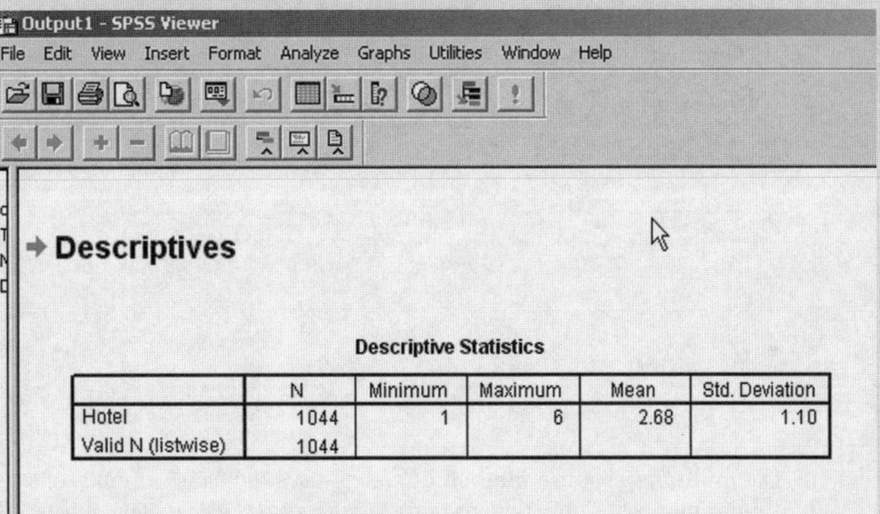

	N	Minimum	Maximum	Mean	Std. Deviation
Hotel	1044	1	6	2.68	1.10
Valid N (listwise)	1044				

In his initial analysis, Pierre used the computer to calculate descriptive statistics for every data variable including the variable 'Hotel'. These included the minimum value (the code for Amsterdam), the maximum value (the code for Tilburg), the mean and the standard deviation. Looking at his computer screen, Pierre noted that the mean (average) was 2.68 and the standard deviation was 1.10. He had forgotten that the data for this variable were categorical and, consequently, the descriptive statistics he had chosen were inappropriate.

We strongly recommend that you save your data regularly as you are entering it, to minimise the chances of deleting it all by accident! In addition, you should save a back-up or security copy on your MP3 player or other mass storage device, or burn it onto a CD.

If you intend to enter data into a spreadsheet, the first variable is in column A, the second in column B and so on. Each cell in the first row (1) should contain a short variable name to enable you to identify each variable. Subsequent rows (2 onwards) will each contain the data for one case (Box 12.4). Statistical analysis software follows the same logic, although the variable names are usually displayed 'above' the first row (Box 12.5).

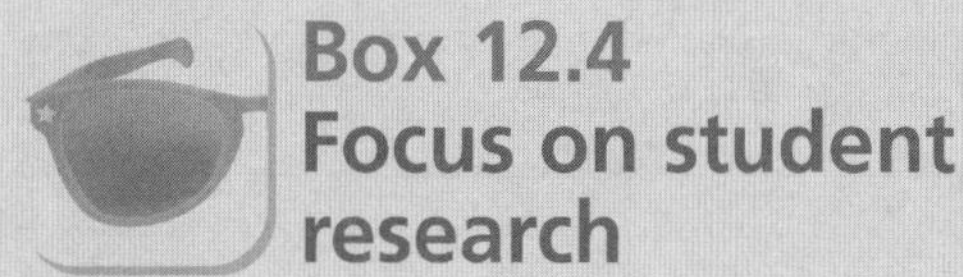

Box 12.4 Focus on student research

An Excel data matrix

Lucy's data related to employees who were working or had worked for a large public sector organisation. In her Excel spreadsheet, the first variable (id) was the *survey form identifier*. This meant that she could link data for each case (row) in her matrix to the survey form when checking for errors (discussed later). The second variable (age) contained numerical data, the age of each respondent (case) at the time her questionnaire was administered. Subsequent variables contained the remaining data: the third (gender) recorded this dichotomous data using code 1 for male and 2 for female; the fourth (service) recorded numerical data about each case's length of service to the nearest year in the organisation. The final dichotomous variable (employed) recorded whether each respondent was (code 1) or was not (code 2) employed by the organisation at the time the data were collected. The codes used by Lucy, therefore, had different meanings for different variables.

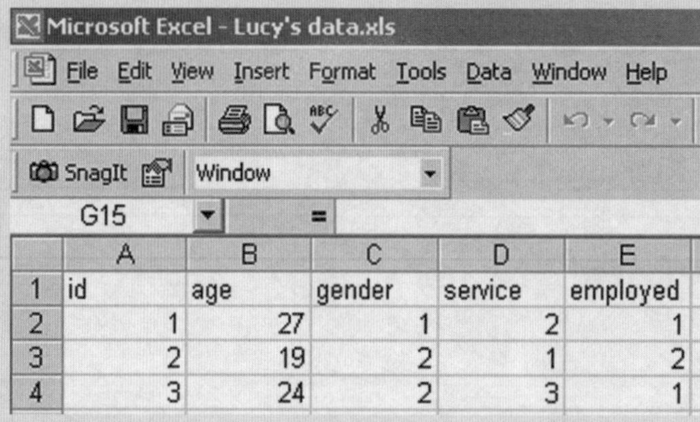

	A	B	C	D	E
1	id	age	gender	service	employed
2	1	27	1	2	1
3	2	19	2	1	2
4	3	24	2	3	1

The **multiple-response method** of coding uses the same number of variables as the maximum number of different responses from any one case. For question 2 these were named 'like1', 'like2', 'like3', 'like4' and 'like5' (Box 12.5). Each of these variables would use the same codes and could include any of the responses as a category. Statistical analysis software often contains special multiple-response procedures to analyse such data. The alternative, the **multiple-dichotomy method** of coding, uses a separate variable for each different answer (Box 12.5). For question 2 (Box 12.5) a separate variable could have been used for each 'thing' listed: for example, salary, location, colleagues, hours, holidays, car and so on. You subsequently would code each variable as 'listed' or 'not listed' for each case. This makes it easy to calculate the number of responses for each 'thing' (deVaus 2002).

Coding

All data types should, with few exceptions, be recorded using numerical codes. This enables you to enter the data quickly using the numeric keypad on your keyboard and with fewer errors. It also makes subsequent analyses, in particular those that require re-coding of data to create new variables, more straightforward. Unfortunately, analyses of limited meaning are also easier, such as calculating a mean (average) gender from codes 1 and 2, or the average hotel location (Box 12.3)! A common exception to using a numerical

Box 12.5 Focus on student research

Data coding

As part of a market-research interview survey, Zack needed to discover which of four products (tomato ketchup, brown sauce, soy sauce, vinegar) had been purchased within the last month by consumers. He, therefore, needed to collect four data items from each respondent:

- Tomato ketchup purchased within the last month? Yes/No
- Brown sauce purchased within the last month? Yes/No
- Soy sauce purchased within the last month? Yes/No
- Salad dressing purchased within the last month? Yes/No

Each of these data items is a separate variable. However, the data were collected using one question:

1 Which of the following items have you purchased within the last month?

Item	**Purchased**	**Not purchased**	**Not sure**
Tomato ketchup	☐1	☐2	☐3
Brown sauce	☐1	☐2	☐3
Soy sauce	☐1	☐2	☐3
Salad dressing	☐1	☐2	☐3

The data Zack collected from each respondent formed four separate variables in the data matrix using numerical codes (1 = purchased, 2 = not purchased, 3 = not sure). This is known as multiple-dichotomy coding:

zakdata.sav - SPSS Data Editor

File Edit View Data Transform Analyze Graphs Utilities Window Help

1 : tomato 1

	tomato	brown	soy	saladdre	like1	like2
1	1	1	1	2	23	31
2	2	2	2	3	12	15
3	1	2	3	1	23	12

Zack also included a question (Question 2 below) that could theoretically have millions of possible responses for each of the 'things'. For such questions, the number that each respondent mentions may also vary. Our experience suggests that virtually all respondents will select five or fewer. Zack, therefore, left space to code up to five responses after data had been collected.

For office use only

2 List up to five things you like about tomato ketchup

.... ❑ ❑ ❑ ❑
.... ❑ ❑ ❑ ❑
.... ❑ ❑ ❑ ❑
.... ❑ ❑ ❑ ❑
.... ❑ ❑ ❑ ❑

code for categorical data is where a postcode is used as the code for a geographical reference. If you are using a spreadsheet, you will need to keep a list of codes for each variable. Statistical analysis software can store these so that each code is automatically labelled.

Coding numerical data

Actual numbers are often used as codes for numerical data, even though this level of precision may not be required. Once you have entered your data as a matrix, you can use analysis software to group or combine data to form additional variables with less detailed categories. This process is referred to as **re-coding**. For example, a Republic of Ireland's employee's salary could be coded to the nearest euro and entered into the matrix as 43543 (numerical discrete data). Later, re-coding could be used to place it in a group of similar salaries, from €40 000 to €49 999 (categorical ranked data).

Coding categorical data

Codes are often applied to categorical data with little thought, although you can design a coding scheme that will make subsequent analyses far simpler. For many secondary data sources (such as government surveys), a suitable coding scheme will have already been devised when the data were first collected. However, for some secondary and all primary data you will need to decide on a coding scheme. Prior to this, you need to establish the highest level of precision required by your analyses (Box 12.2).

Existing coding schemes can be used for many variables. These include industrial classification (Great Britain Office for National Statistics 2002), occupation (Great Britain Office for National Statistics 2000a, 2000b), social class (Heath *et al.* 2003), socioeconomic classification (Rose and Pevalin 2003) and ethnic group (Smith 2002) as well as social attitude variables (Park *et al.* 2007). Wherever possible, we recommend you use these as they:

- save time;
- are normally well tested;
- allow comparisons of your results with other (often larger) surveys.

These codes should be included on your data collection form as **pre-set codes** provided that there are a limited number of categories (Section 11.4), and they will be understood by the person filling in the form. Even if you decide not to use an existing coding scheme, perhaps because of a lack of detail, you should ensure that your codes are still compatible. This means that you will be able to compare your data with those already collected.

Coding at data collection occurs when there is a limited range of well-established categories into which the data can be placed. These are included on your data collection form, and the person filling in the form selects the correct category.

Coding after data collection is necessary when you are unclear of the likely responses or there are a large number of possible responses in the coding scheme. To ensure that the coding scheme captures the variety in responses (and will work!) it is better to wait until data from the first 50 to 100 cases are available and then develop the coding scheme. This is called the **codebook** (Box 12.6). As when designing your data collection method(s) (Chapters 8, 9, 10, and 11), it is essential to be clear about the intended analyses, in particular:

- the level of precision required;
- the coding schemes used by surveys with which comparisons are to be made.

To create your codebook for each variable you:

1 examine the data and establish broad groupings;
2 sub-divide the broad groupings into increasingly specific sub-groups dependent on your intended analyses;

3 allocate codes to all categories at the most precise level of detail required;
4 note the actual responses that are allocated to each category and produce a codebook;
5 ensure that those categories that may need to be aggregated are given adjacent codes to facilitate re-coding.

Coding missing data

Each variable for each case in your data set should have a code, even if no data have been collected. The choice of code is up to you, although some statistical analysis software have a code that is used by default. A missing data code is used to indicate why data are missing. Four main reasons for missing data are identified by deVaus (2002):

- The data were not required from the respondent, perhaps because of a skip generated by a filter question in a survey.
- The respondent refused to answer the question (a **non-response**).
- The respondent did not know the answer or did not have an opinion. Sometimes this is treated as implying an answer; on other occasions it is treated as missing data.
- The respondent may have missed a question by mistake, or the respondent's answer may be unclear.

In addition, it may be that:

- leaving part of a question in a survey blank implies an answer; in such cases the data are not classified as missing (Section 11.4).

Statistical analysis software often reserves a special code for missing data. Cases with missing data can then be excluded from subsequent analyses when necessary (Box 12.6, overleaf). For some analyses it may be necessary to distinguish between reasons for missing data using different codes.

Entering data

Once your data have been coded, you can enter them into the computer. Increasingly, data analysis software contains algorithms that check the data for obvious errors as it is entered. Despite this, it is essential that you take considerable care to ensure that your data are entered correctly. When entering data the well-known maxim 'rubbish in, rubbish out' certainly applies! More sophisticated analysis software allows you to attach individual labels to each variable and the codes associated with each of them. If this is feasible, we strongly recommend that you do this. By ensuring the labels replicate the exact words used in the data collection, you will reduce the number of opportunities for misinterpretation when analysing your data. Taking this advice for the variable 'like1' in Box 12.6 would result in the variable label 'List up to three things you like about this restaurant', each value being labelled with the actual response in the coding scheme.

Checking for errors

No matter how carefully you code and subsequently enter data there will always be some errors. The main methods to check data for errors are as follows:

- Look for illegitimate codes. In any coding scheme, only certain numbers are allocated. Other numbers are, therefore, errors. Common errors are the inclusion of letters O and o instead of zero, letters l or I instead of 1, and number 7 instead of 1.

Box 12.6 Focus on student research

Creating a codebook, coding multiple responses and entering data

As part of his research project, Amil used a questionnaire to collect data from the customers of a local themed restaurant. The questionnaire included an open question which asked 'List up to three things you like about this restaurant.' The data included over 50 different 'things' that the 186 customers responding liked about the restaurant, although the maximum number mentioned by any one customer was three.

Once data had been collected, Amil devised a hierarchical coding scheme based on what the customers liked about the restaurant. Codes were allocated to each 'thing' a customer liked, as shown in the extract below.

Codes were entered into three (the maximum number customers were asked to list) variables, like1, like2 and like3 in the data matrix using the multiple-response method for coding. This meant that any response could appear in any of the three variables. When there were fewer than three responses given, the code '.' was entered in the remaining outlet variables, signifying missing data. The first customer in the extract below listed 'things' coded 11, 21 and 42, the next 3 and 21 and so on. No significance was attached to the order of variables to which responses were coded.

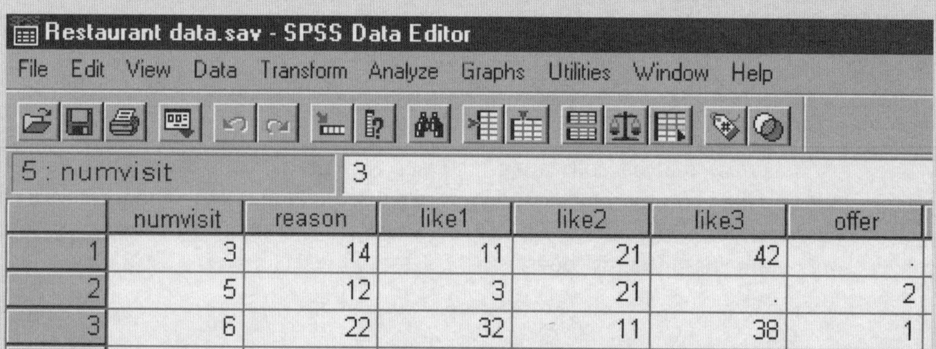

	numvisit	reason	like1	like2	like3	offer
1	3	14	11	21	42	.
2	5	12	3	21	.	2
3	6	22	32	11	38	1

Extract from coding scheme used to classify responses

Grouping	Sub-grouping	Response	Code
Physical surroundings			1–9
		Decoration	1
		Use of colour	2
		Comfort of seating	3
Dining experience	*Menu*		10–19
		Choice	11
		Regularly changed	12
	Food		20–29
		Freshly prepared	21
		Organic	22
		Served at correct temperature	23

Grouping	Sub-grouping	Response	Code
	Staff attitude		30–39
		Knowledgeable	31
		Greet by name	32
		Know what diners prefer	33
		Discreet	34
		Do not hassle	35
		Good service	36
		Friendly	37
		Have a sense of humour	38
	Drinks		40–49
		Value for money	41
		Good selection of wines	42
		Good selection of beers	43
		Served at correct temperature	44

The hierarchical coding scheme meant that individual responses could subsequently be re-coded into sub-groupings and groupings such as those indicated earlier to facilitate a range of different analyses. These were undertaken using statistical analysis software.

- Look for illogical relationships. For example, if a person is coded to the 'higher managerial occupations' socioeconomic classification category and she describes her work as 'manual' it is likely an error has occurred.
- Check that rules in filter questions are followed. Certain responses to filter questions (Section 11.4) mean that other variables should be coded as missing values. If this has not happened there has been an error.

For each possible error, you need to discover whether it occurred at coding or data entry and then correct it. By giving each case a unique identifier (normally a number), it is possible to link the matrix to the original data. You must remember to write the identifier on the data collection form and enter it along with the other data into the matrix.

Data checking is very time consuming and so is often not undertaken. Beware: not doing it is very dangerous and can result in incorrect results from which false conclusions are drawn!

Weighting cases

Most data you use will be a sample. For some forms of probability sampling, such as stratified random sampling (Section 7.2), you may have used a different sampling fraction for each stratum. Alternatively, you may have obtained a different response rate for each of the strata. To obtain an accurate overall picture you will need to take account of these differences in response rates between strata. A common method of achieving this is to use cases from those strata that have lower proportions of responses to represent more

Box 12.7 Focus on student research

Weighting cases

Doris had used stratified random sampling to select her sample. The percentage of each stratum's population that responded is given below:

- Upper stratum: 90%
- Lower stratum: 65%

To account for the differences in the response rates between strata she decided to weight the cases prior to analysis.

The weight for the upper stratum was: $\frac{90}{90} = 1$

This meant that each case in the upper stratum counted as 1 case in her analysis.

The weight for the lower stratum was: $\frac{90}{65} = 1.38$

This meant that each case in the lower stratum counted for 1.38 cases in her analysis.

Doris entered these as a separate variable in her data set and used the statistical analysis software to apply the weights.

than one case in your analysis (Box 12.7). Most statistical analysis software allows you to do this by **weighting** cases. To weight the cases you:

1 Calculate the percentage of the population responding for each stratum.
2 Establish which stratum had the highest percentage of the population responding.
3 Calculate the weight for each stratum using the following formula:

$$\text{weight} = \frac{\text{highest proportion of population responding for any stratum}}{\text{proportion of population responding in stratum for which calculating weight}}$$

(Note: if your calculations are correct this will always result in the weight for the stratum with the highest proportion of the population responding being 1.)

4 Apply the appropriate weight to each case.

Beware: many authors (for example, Hays 1994) question the validity of using statistics to make inferences from your sample if you have weighted cases.

12.3 Exploring and presenting data

Once your data have been entered and checked for errors, you are ready to start your analysis. We have found Tukey's (1977) **exploratory data analysis (EDA)** approach useful in these initial stages. This approach emphasises the use of diagrams to explore and understand your data, emphasising the importance of using your data to guide your choices of analysis techniques. As you would expect, we believe that it is important to keep your research question(s) and objectives in mind when exploring your data. However, the exploratory data analysis approach allows you flexibility to introduce previously unplanned analyses to respond to new findings. It therefore formalises the common practice of looking for other relationships in data, which your research was not initially designed to test. This should not be discounted, as it may suggest other fruitful avenues for analysis. In addition, computers make this relatively easy and quick.

Even at this stage it is important that you structure and label clearly each diagram and table to avoid possible misinterpretation. Box 12.8 provides a summary checklist of the points to remember when designing a diagram or table.

Box 12.8
Checklist

Designing your diagrams and tables

For both diagrams and tables

✔ Does it have a brief but clear and descriptive title?
✔ Are the units of measurement used stated clearly?
✔ Are the sources of data used stated clearly?
✔ Are there notes to explain abbreviations and unusual terminology?
✔ Does it state the size of the sample on which the values in the table are based?

For diagrams

✔ Does it have clear axis labels?
✔ Are bars and their components in the same logical sequence?
✔ Is more dense shading used for smaller areas?
✔ Have you avoided misrepresenting or distorting the data
✔ Is a key or legend included (where necessary)?

For tables

✔ Does it have clear column and row headings?
✔ Are columns and rows in a logical sequence?

We have found it best to begin exploratory analysis by looking at individual variables and their components. The key aspects you may need to consider will be guided by your research question(s) and objectives, and are likely to include (Sparrow 1989):

- specific values;
- highest and lowest values;
- trends over time;
- proportions;
- distributions.

Once you have explored these, you can then begin to compare and look for relationships between variables, considering in addition (Sparrow 1989):

- conjunctions (the point where values for two or more variables intersect);
- totals;
- interdependence and relationships.

These are summarised in Table 12.2. Most analysis software contains procedures to create tables and diagrams. Your choice will depend on those aspects of the data that you wish to emphasise and the scale of measurement at which the data were recorded. This section is concerned only with tables and two-dimensional diagrams, including pictograms, available on most spreadsheets (Table 12.2). Three-dimensional diagrams are not discussed, as these often can hinder interpretation. Those tables and diagrams most pertinent to your research question(s) and objectives will eventually appear in your research report to support your arguments. You, therefore, should save an electronic copy of all tables and diagrams which you create.

Exploring and presenting individual variables

To show specific values

The simplest way of summarising data for individual variables so that specific values can be read is to use a **table** (**frequency distribution**). For categorical data, the table summarises the number of cases (frequency) in each category. For variables where there are likely to be a large number of categories (or values for numerical data), you will need to group the data into categories that reflect your research question(s) and objectives.

Table 12.2 Data presentation by data type: a summary

	Categorical		Numerical	
	Descriptive	**Ranked**	**Continuous**	**Discrete**
To show one variable so that any specific value can be read easily	Table/frequency distribution (data often grouped)			
To show the frequency of occurrences of categories or values for one variable so that highest and lowest are clear	Bar chart or pictogram (data may need grouping)		Histogram or frequency polygon (data must be grouped)	Bar chart or pictogram (data may need grouping)
To show the trend for a variable		Line graph or bar chart	Line graph or histogram	Line graph or bar chart
To show the proportion of occurrences of categories or values for one variable	Pie chart or bar chart (data may need grouping)		Histogram or pie chart (data must be grouped)	Pie chart or bar chart (data may need grouping)
To show the distribution of values for one variable			Frequency polygon, histogram (data must be grouped) or box plot	Frequency polygon, bar chart (data may need grouping) or box plot
To show the *interdependence* between two or more variables so that any *specific* value can be read easily	Contingency table/cross-tabulation (data often grouped)			
To compare the frequency of occurrences of categories or values for two or more variables so that *highest* and *lowest* are clear	Multiple bar chart (continuous data must be grouped, other data may need grouping)			
To compare the *trends* for two or more variables so that *conjunctions* are clear		Multiple line graph or multiple bar chart		
To compare the *proportions* of occurrences of categories or values for two or more variables	Comparative pie charts or percentage component bar chart (continuous data must be grouped, other data may need grouping)			
To compare the *distribution* of values for two or more variables			Multiple box plot	
To compare the frequency of occurrences of categories or values for two or more variables so that *totals* are clear	Stacked bar chart (continuous data must be grouped, other data may need grouping)			
To compare the *proportions* and *totals* of occurrences of categories or values for two or more variables	Comparative proportional pie charts (continuous data must be grouped, other data may need grouping)			
To show the *relationship* between cases for two variables		Scatter graph/scatter plot		

Source: © Mark Saunders, Philip Lewis and Adrian Thornhill 2008.

To show highest and lowest values

Tables attach no visual significance to highest or lowest values unless emphasised by alternative fonts. Diagrams can provide visual clues, although both categorical and numerical data may need grouping. For categorical and discrete data, bar charts and pictograms are both suitable. Generally, bar charts provide a more accurate representation and should be used for research reports, whereas pictograms convey a general impression and can be used to gain an audience's attention. In a **bar chart**, the height or length of each bar represents the frequency of occurrence. Bars are separated by gaps, usually half the width of the bars. Bar charts where the bars are vertical (as in Figure 12.2) are sometimes called column charts. This bar chart emphasises that the European Union Member State with the highest total carbon dioxide emissions in 2005 was Germany, whilst Malta had the lowest total carbon dioxide emissions.

To emphasise the relative values represented by each of the bars in a bar chart, the bars may be reordered in either descending or ascending order of the frequency of occurrence represented by each bar (Figure 12.3).

Most researchers use a histogram to show highest and lowest values for continuous data. Prior to being drawn, data will often need to be grouped into class intervals. In a **histogram**, the area of each bar represents the frequency of occurrence and the continuous nature of the data is emphasised by the absence of gaps between the bars. For equal width class intervals, the height of your bar still represents the frequency of occurrences (Figures 12.4 and 12.5) and so the highest and lowest values are easy to distinguish. For histograms with unequal class interval widths, this is not the case. In Figure 12.4 the

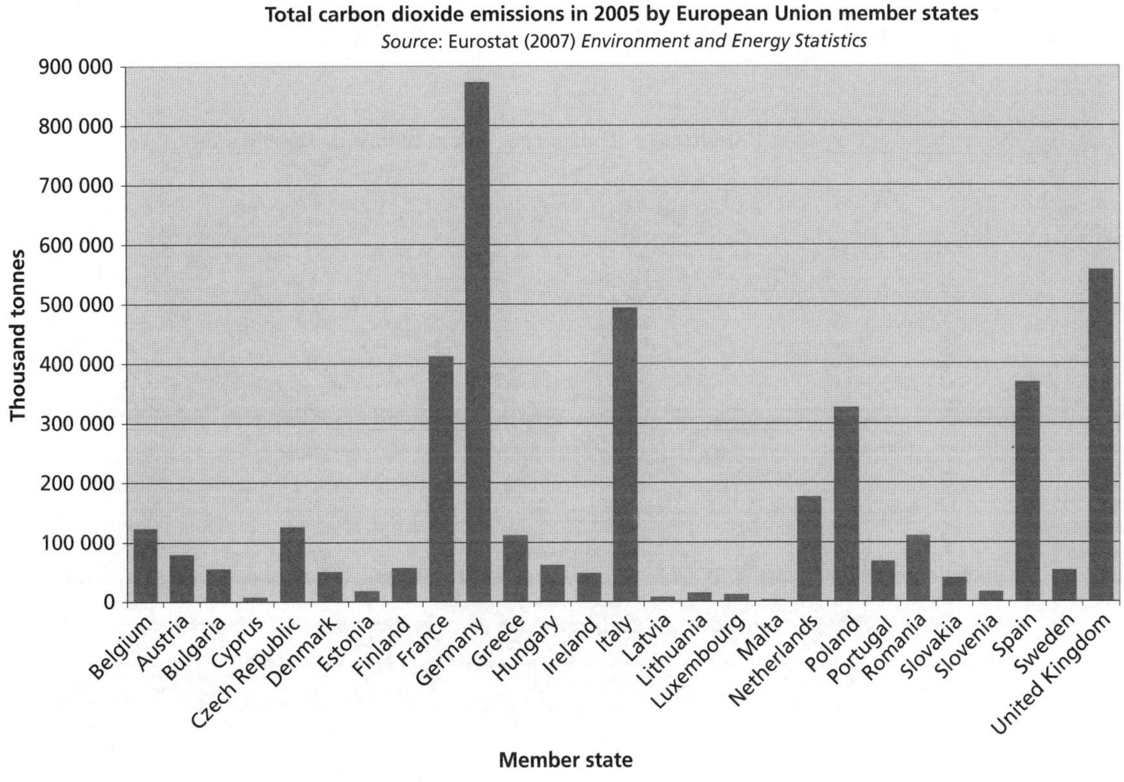

Figure 12.2 Bar chart

Source: adapted from Eurostat (2007) © European Communities, 2007. Reproduced with permission.

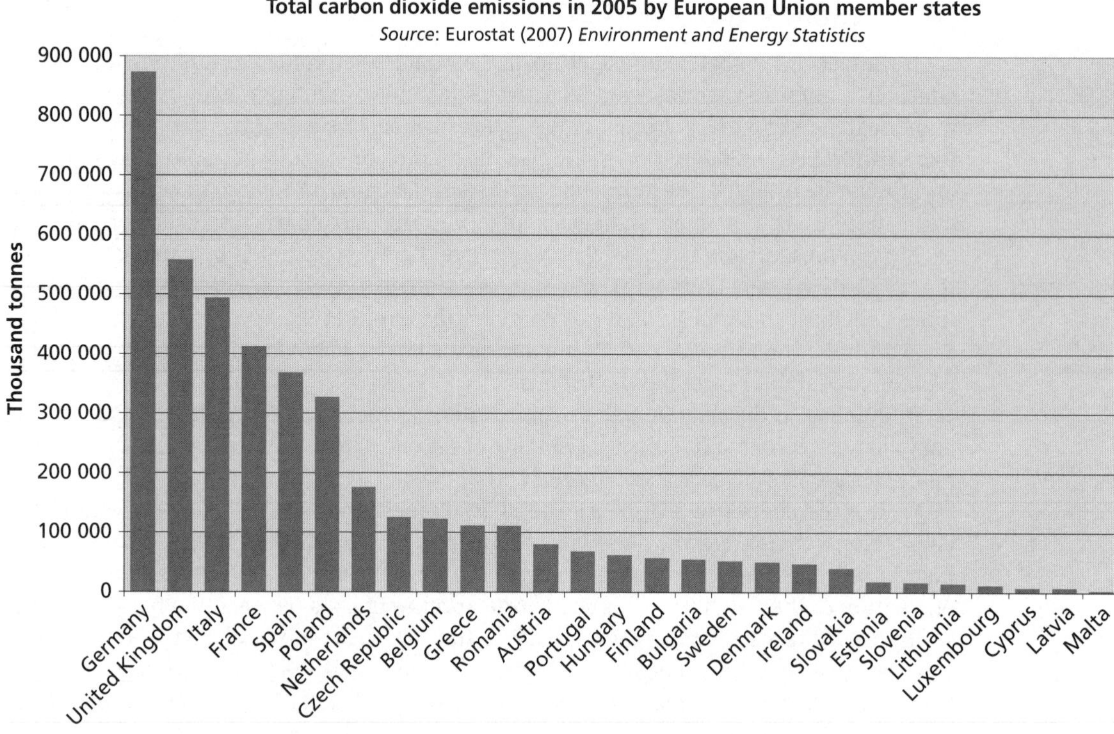

Figure 12.3 Bar chart (data reordered)

Source: adapted from Eurostat (2007) © European Communities, 2007. Reproduced with permission.

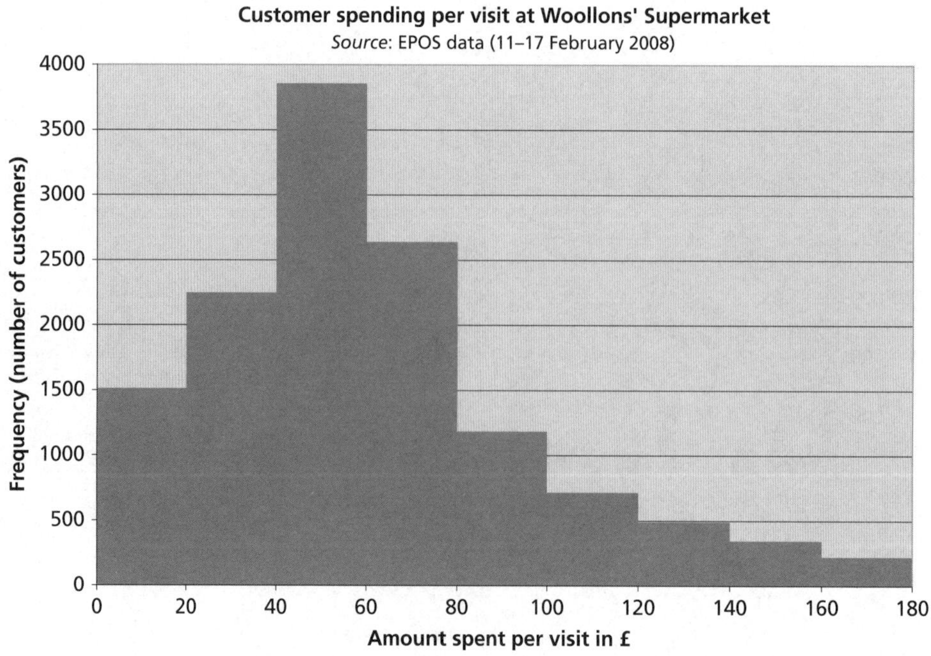

Figure 12.4 Histogram

histogram emphasises that the most frequent amount spent is £40 to £60, whilst the least frequent amount spent is £160 to £180. In Figure 12.5 the histogram emphasises that the highest number of Harley-Davidson motorcycles shipped worldwide was in 2006, and the lowest number in 1996.

Analysis software treats histograms for data of equal width class intervals as a variation of a bar chart. Unfortunately, few spreadsheets will cope automatically with the calculations required to draw histograms for unequal class intervals. Consequently, you may have to use a bar chart owing to the limitations of your analysis software.

In a **pictogram**, each bar is replaced by a picture or series of pictures chosen to represent the data. To illustrate the impact of doing this, we have used data of worldwide Harley-Davidson motorcycle shipments to generate both a histogram (Figure 12.5) and a pictogram (Figure 12.6). In the pictogram each picture represents 20 000 motorcycles. Pictures in pictograms can, like bars in bar charts and histograms, be shown in columns or horizontally. The height of the column or length of the bar made up by the pictures represents the frequency of occurrence. In this case we felt it was more logical to group the pictures as a horizontal bar rather than vertically on top of each other. You will have probably also noticed that, in the pictogram, there are gaps between the bars. Whilst this normally signifies discrete categories of data, it is also acceptable to do this for continuous data (such as years) when drawing a pictogram to aid clarity. Although analysis software allows you to convert a bar chart or histogram to a pictogram both easily and accurately, it is more difficult to establish the actual data values from a pictogram. This is because the number of units part of a picture represents is not immediately clear. For example, in Figure 12.6, how many motorcycles shipped would a rear wheel represent?

Pictograms have a further drawback, namely that it is very easy to misrepresent the data. Both Figure 12.5 and Figure 12.6 show that shipments of Harley-Davidson

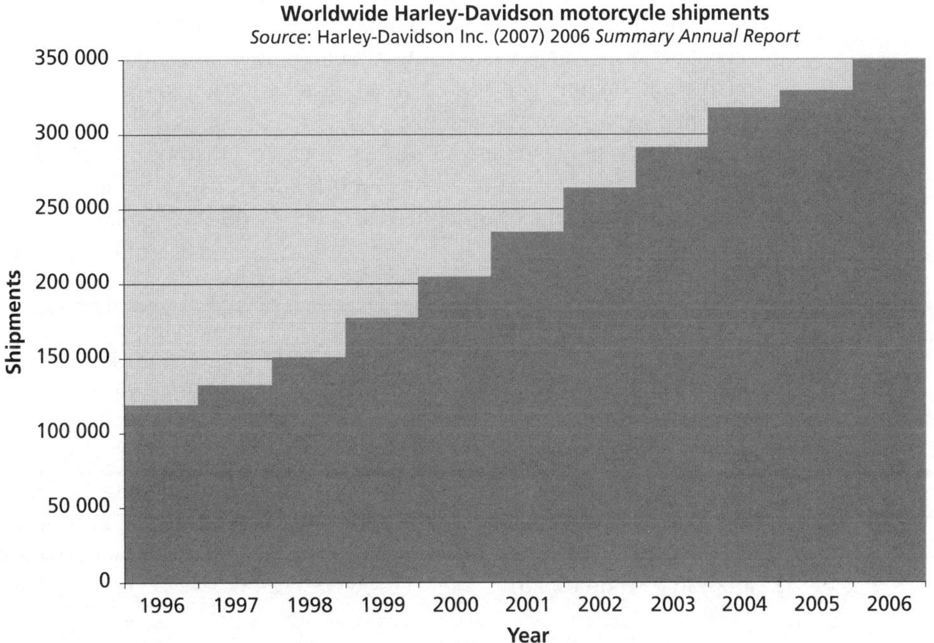

Figure 12.5 Histogram

Source: Harley-Davidson Inc. (2007) 2006 Summary Annual Report. Reproduced with permission.

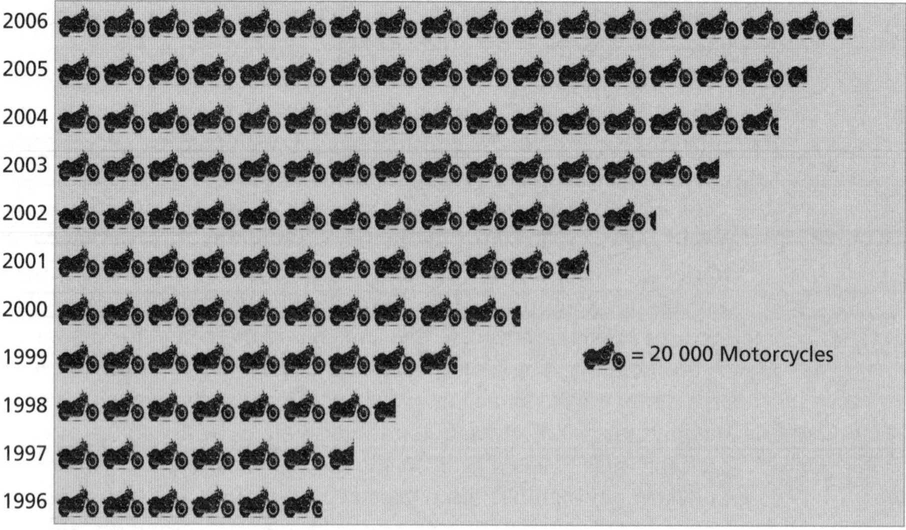

Figure 12.6 Pictogram
Source: Harley-Davidson Inc. (2007) 2006 Summary Annual Report. Reproduced with permission.

motorcycles doubled between 1999 and 2006. Using our analysis software, this could have been represented using a picture of a motorcycle in 2006 that was nearly twice as long as the picture in 1999. However, in order to keep the proportions of the motorcycle accurate, the picture would have needed to be nearly twice as tall. Consequently, the actual area of the picture would have been nearly four times as great and would have been interpreted as motorcycle shipments almost quadrupling. Because of this we would recommend that, if you are using a pictogram, you decide on a standard value for each picture and do not alter its size. In addition, you should include a key or note to indicate the value each picture represents.

Frequency polygons are used less often to illustrate limits. Most analysis software treats them as a version of a line graph (Figure 12.7) in which the lines are extended to meet the horizontal axis, provided that class widths are equal.

To show a trend

Trends can only be presented for variables containing numerical (and occasionally ranked) longitudinal data. The most suitable diagram for exploring the trend is a **line graph** (Anderson *et al.* 1999) in which your data values for each time period are joined with a line to represent the trend (Figure 12.7). In Figure 12.7 the line graph emphasises the upward trend in the number of Harley-Davidson motorcycles shipped worldwide between 1996 and 2006. You can also use histograms (Figure 12.5) to show trends over continuous time periods and bar charts (Figure 12.2) to show trends between discrete time periods. The trend can also be calculated using time series-analysis (Section 12.5).

To show proportions

Research has shown that the most frequently used diagram to emphasise the proportion or share of occurrences is the pie chart, although bar charts have been shown to give

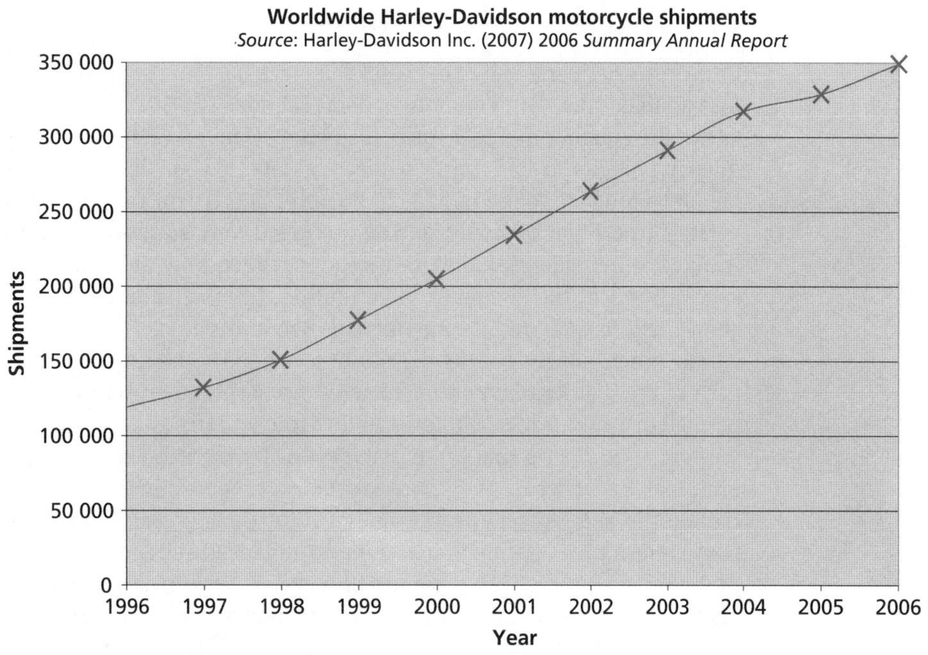

Figure 12.7 Line graph
Source: Harley-Davidson Inc. (2007) 2006 Summary Annual Report. Reproduced with permission.

equally good results (Anderson *et al.* 1999). A **pie chart** is divided into proportional segments according to the share each has of the total value (Figure 12.8). For numerical and some categorical data you will need to group data prior to drawing the pie chart, as it is difficult to interpret pie charts with more than six segments (Morris 2003).

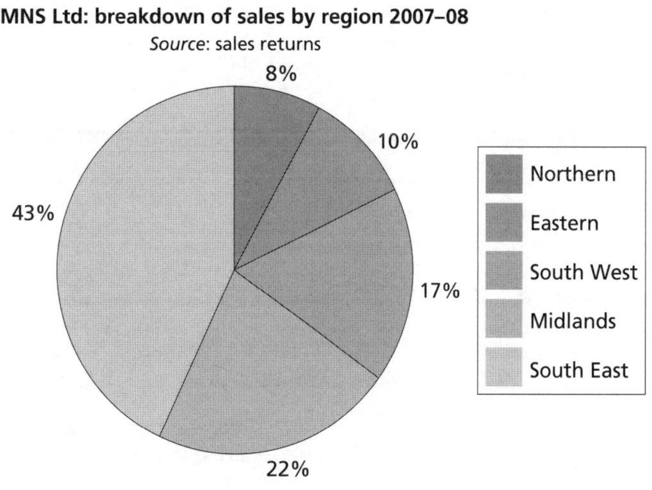

Figure 12.8 Pie chart

To show the distribution of values

Prior to using many statistical tests it is necessary to establish the distribution of values for variables containing numerical data (Sections 12.4, 12.5). This can be seen by plotting either a frequency polygon or a histogram (Figure 12.4) for continuous data or a frequency polygon or bar chart for discrete data. If your diagram shows a bunching to the left and a long tail to the right as in Figure 12.4 the data are **positively skewed**. If the converse is true (Figure 12.5), the data are **negatively skewed**. If your data are equally distributed either side of the highest frequency then they are **symmetrically distributed**. A special form of the symmetric distribution, in which the data can be plotted as a bell-shaped curve, is known as the **normal distribution**.

The other indicator of the distribution's shape is the **kurtosis** – the pointedness or flatness of the distribution compared with the normal distribution. If a distribution is more pointed or peaked, it is said to be leptokurtic and the kurtosis value is positive. If a distribution is flatter, it is said to be platykurtic and the kurtosis value is negative. A distribution that is between the more extremes of peakedness and flatness is said to be mesokurtic and has a kurtosis value of zero (Dancey and Reidy 2008).

An alternative often included in more advanced statistical analysis software is the **box plot** (Figure 12.9). This diagram provides you with a pictorial representation of the distribution of the data for a variable. The plot shows where the middle value or median is, how this relates to the middle 50 per cent of the data or inter-quartile range, and highest and lowest values or *extremes* (Section 12.4). It also highlights outliers, those values that are very different from the data. In Figure 12.9 the two outliers might be due to mistakes in data entry. Alternatively, they may be correct and emphasise that sales for these two cases (93 and 88) are far higher. In this example we can see that the data values for the variable are positively skewed as there is a long tail to the right.

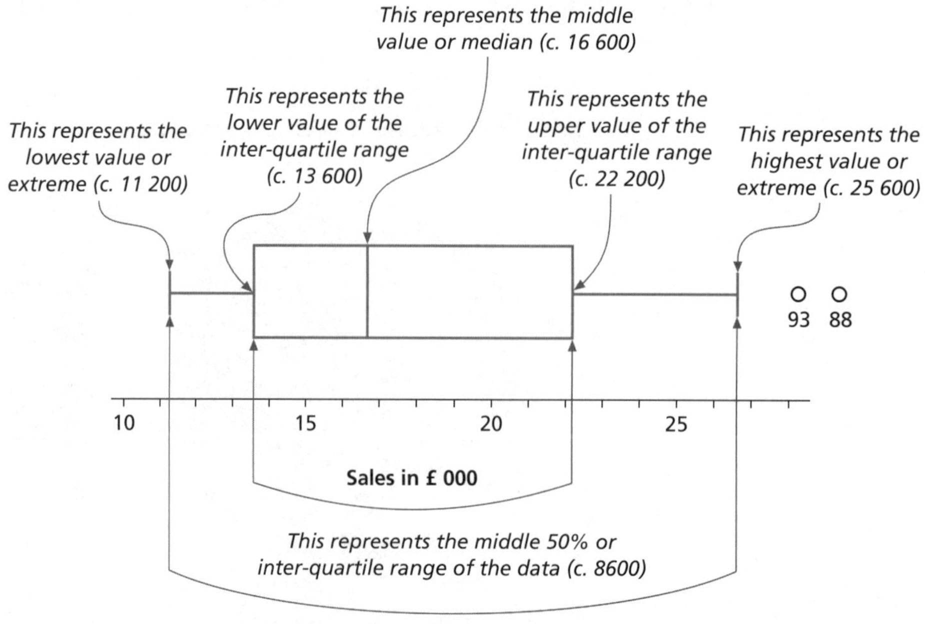

Figure 12.9 Annotated box plot

Box 12.9 Focus on student research

Exploring and presenting data for individual variables

As part of audience research for his dissertation, Valentin asked people attending a play at a provincial theatre to complete a short questionnaire. This collected responses to 25 questions including:

3 How many plays (including this one) have you seen at this theatre in the past year?

___ ___

11 This play is good value for money

strongly disagree ❑1 disagree ❑2

agree ❑3 strongly agree ❑4

24 How old are you?

Under 18 ❑1 18 to 34 ❑2

35 to 64 ❑3 65 and over ❑4

Exploratory analyses were undertaken using analysis software and diagrams and tables generated. For question 3, which collected discrete data, the aspects that were most important were the distribution of values and the highest and lowest numbers of plays seen. A bar chart, therefore, was drawn:

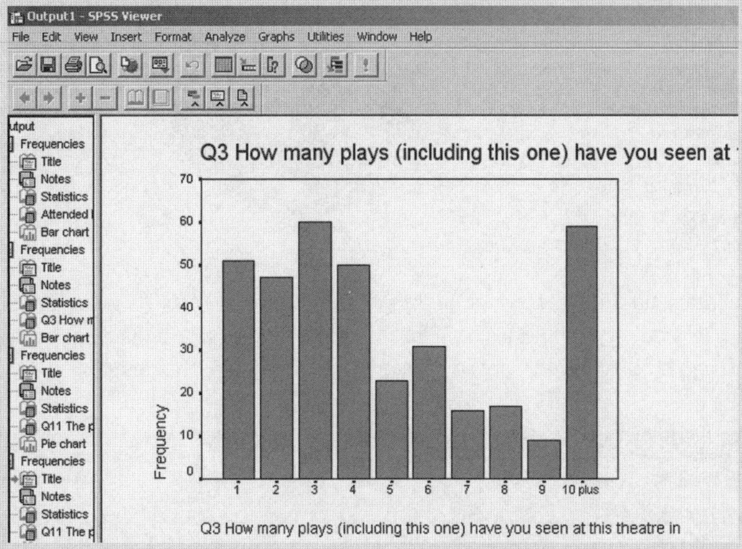

This emphasised that the most frequent number of plays seen by respondents was three and the least frequent number of plays seen by the respondents was either nine or probably some larger number. It also suggested that the distribution was positively skewed towards lower numbers of plays seen.

For question 11 (categorical data), the most important aspect was the proportions of people agreeing and disagreeing with the statement. A pie chart (see overleaf) was therefore drawn using similar shadings for the two agree categories and for the two disagree categories.

This emphasised that the vast majority of respondents (95 per cent) agreed that the play was good value for money.

Box 12.9 Focus on student research *(continued)*

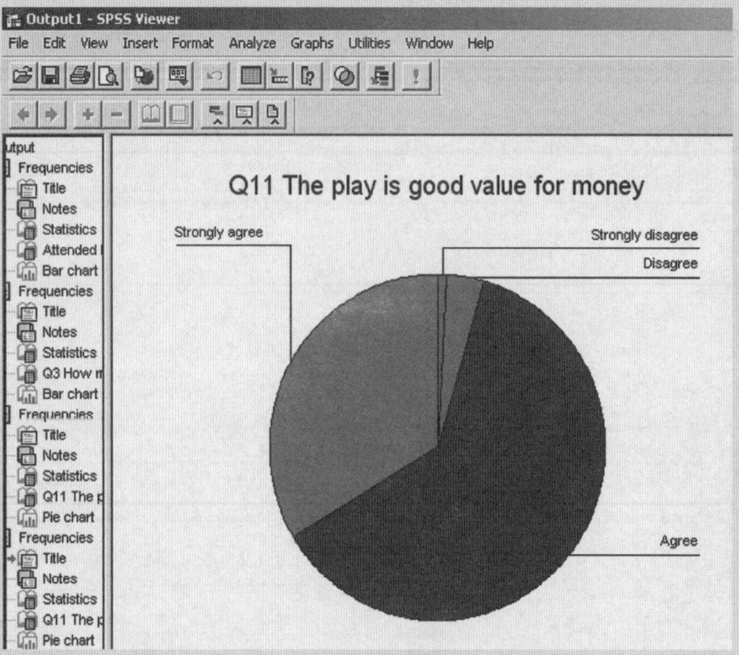

Question 24 collected data on each respondent's age. This question had grouped continuous data into four unequal-width age groups. For this analysis, the most important aspects were the specific number and percentage of respondents in each age category and so a table was constructed.

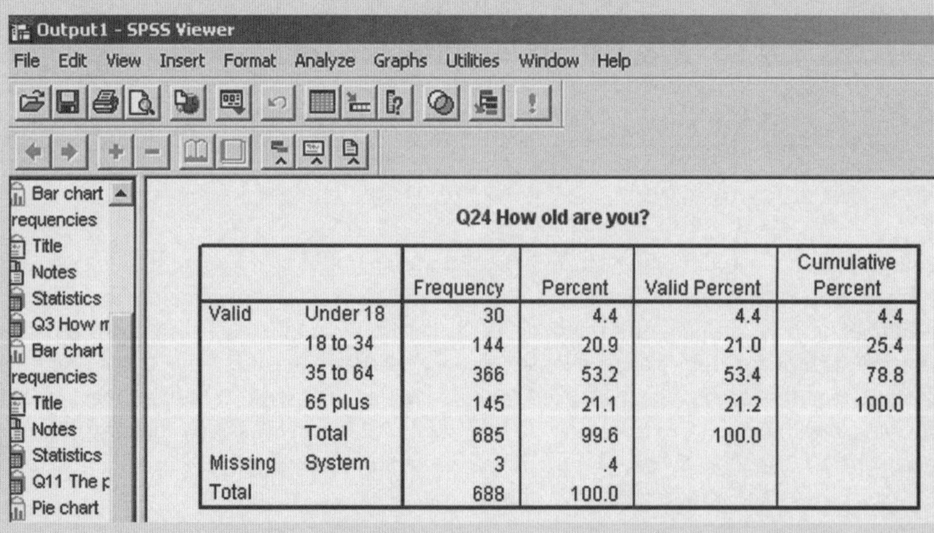

Q24 How old are you?

		Frequency	Percent	Valid Percent	Cumulative Percent
Valid	Under 18	30	4.4	4.4	4.4
	18 to 34	144	20.9	21.0	25.4
	35 to 64	366	53.2	53.4	78.8
	65 plus	145	21.1	21.2	100.0
	Total	685	99.6	100.0	
Missing	System	3	.4		
Total		688	100.0		

Comparing variables

To show specific values and interdependence

As with individual variables the best method of finding specific data values is a table. This is known as a **contingency table** or **cross-tabulation** (Table 12.3), and it also enables you to examine interdependence between the variables. For variables where there are likely to be a large number of categories (or values for numerical data), you may need to group the data to prevent the table from becoming too large.

Most statistical analysis software allows you to add totals, and row and column percentages when designing your table. Statistical analyses such as chi square can also be undertaken at the same time (Section 12.5).

Table 12.3 Contingency table: number of insurance claims by gender, 2008

Number of claims*	Male	Female	Total
0	10032	13478	23510
1	2156	1430	3586
2	120	25	145
3	13	4	17
Total	12321	14937	27258

*No clients had more than three claims.
Source: PJ Insurance Services.

To compare highest and lowest values

Comparisons of variables that emphasise the highest and lowest rather than precise values are best explored using a **multiple bar chart** (Anderson *et al.* 1999), also known as a *compound bar chart*. As for a bar chart, continuous data – or data where there are many values or categories – need to be grouped. Within any multiple bar chart you are likely to find it easiest to compare between adjacent bars. The multiple bar chart (Box 12.10, overleaf) has therefore been drawn to emphasise comparisons between new fund launches, mergers and closures and the net increase in funds rather than between years.

To compare proportions

Comparison of proportions between variables uses either a **percentage component bar chart** or two or more pie charts. Either type of diagram can be used for all data types, provided that continuous data, and data where there are more than six values or categories, are grouped. Percentage component bar charts are more straightforward to draw than comparative pie charts when using most spreadsheets. Within your percentage component bar chart, comparisons will be easiest between adjacent bars. The chart in Figure 12.10 (see overleaf) has been drawn to compare proportions of each type of response between products. Consumers' responses for each product, therefore, form a single bar.

To compare trends and conjunctions

The most suitable diagram to compare trends for two or more numerical (or occasionally ranked) variables is a **multiple line graph** where one line represents each variable

Box 12.10
Focus on research in the news

FT

FSA warns on derivatives dangers

Source: from an article by Johnson, Steve (2008) 'FSA warns on derivatives dangers', *Financial Times*, 11 Feb.

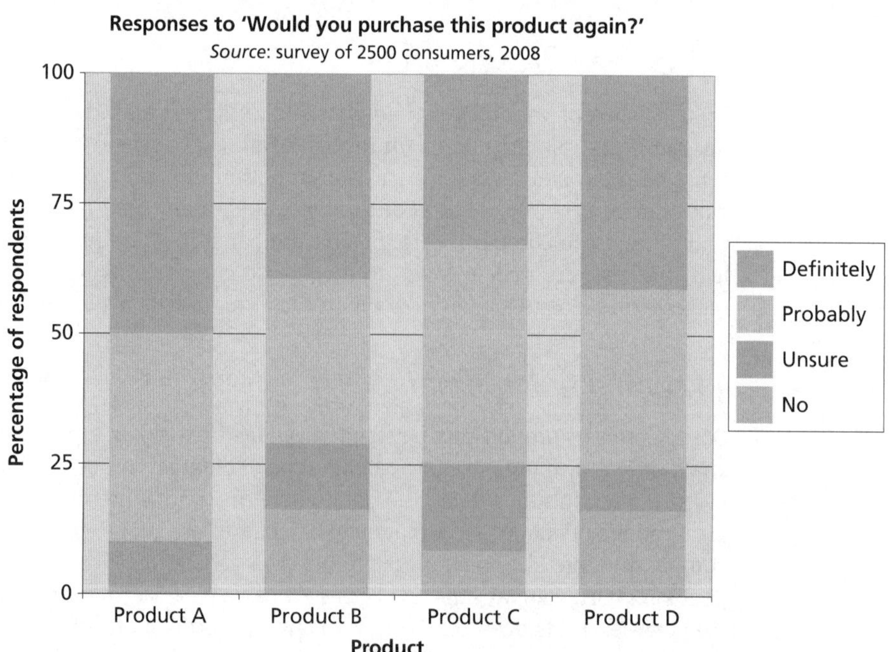

Figure 12.10 Percentage component bar chart

(Henry 1995). You can also use multiple bar charts (Box 12.10) in which bars for the same time period are placed adjacent.

If you need to look for conjunctions in the trends – that is, where values for two or more variables intersect – this is where the lines on a multiple line graph cross.

To compare totals

Comparison of totals between variables uses a variation of the bar chart. A **stacked bar chart** can be used for all data types provided that continuous data and data where there are more than six possible values or categories are grouped. As with percentage component bar charts, the design of the stacked bar chart is dictated by the totals you want to compare. For this reason, in Figure 12.11 sales for each quarter have been stacked to give totals which can be compared between companies.

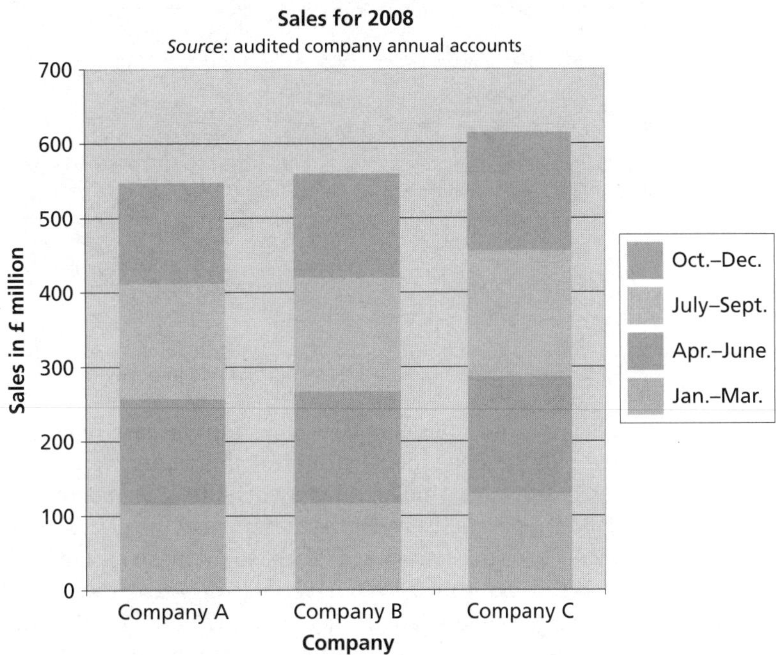

Figure 12.11 Stacked bar chart

To compare proportions and totals

To compare both proportions of each category or value and the totals for two or more variables it is best to use **comparative proportional pie charts** for all data types. For each comparative proportional pie chart the total area of the pie chart represents the total for that variable. By contrast, the angle of each segment represents the relative proportion of a category within the variable (Figure 12.8). Because of the complexity of drawing comparative proportional pie charts, they are rarely used for exploratory data analysis, although they can be used to good effect in research reports.

To compare the distribution of values

Often it is useful to compare the distribution of values for two or more variables. Plotting multiple frequency polygons or bar charts (Box 12.10) will enable you to compare distributions for up to three or four variables. After this your diagram is likely just to look a mess! An alternative is to use a diagram of multiple box plots, similar to the one in Figure 12.9. This provides a pictorial representation of the distribution of the data for the variables in which you are interested. These plots can be compared and are interpreted in the same way as the single box plot.

To show the relationship between cases for variables

You can explore possible relationships between ranked and numerical data variables by plotting one variable against another. This is called a **scatter graph** or **scatter plot**, and

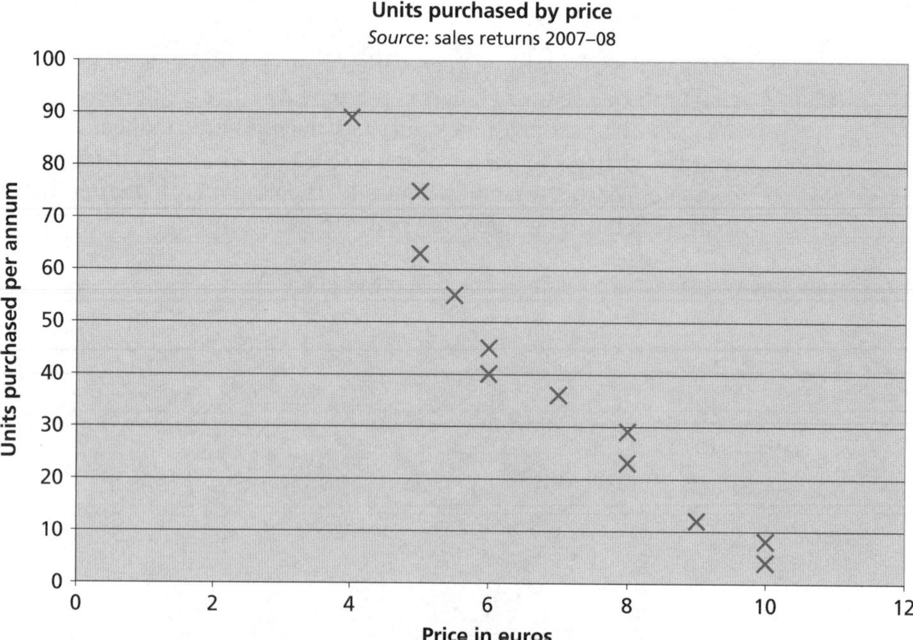

Figure 12.12
Scatter graph

each cross (point) represents the values for one case (Figure 12.12). Convention dictates that you plot the **dependent variable** – that is, the variable that changes in response to changes in the other **(independent) variable** – against the vertical axis. The strength of the relationship is indicated by the closeness of the points to an imaginary straight line. If, as the values for one variable increase, so do those for the other, you have a positive relationship. If, as the values for one variable decrease, those for the other variable increase, you have a negative relationship. Thus in Figure 12.12 there is a negative relationship between the two variables. The strength of this relationship can be assessed statistically using techniques such as correlation or regression (Section 12.5).

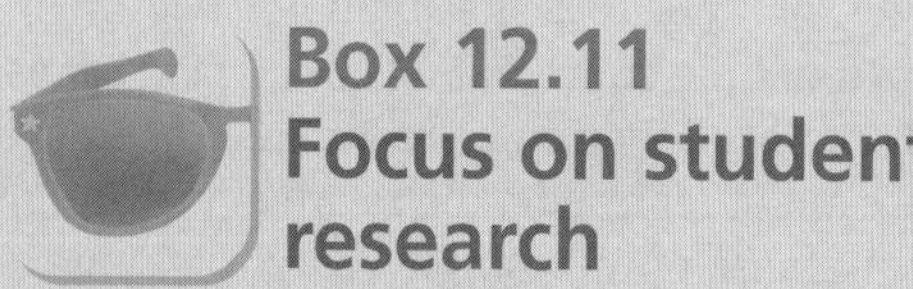

Box 12.11 Focus on student research

Comparing variables

Francis was asked by his uncle, an independent ice cream manufacturer, to examine the records of monthly sales of ice cream for 2007 and 2008. In addition, his uncle had obtained longitudinal data on average (mean) daily hours of sunshine for each month for the same time period from their local weather station. Francis decided to explore data on sales of the three best-selling flavours (vanilla, strawberry and chocolate), paying particular attention to:

- comparative trends in sales;
- the relationship between sales and amount of sunshine.

To compare trends in sales between the three flavours he plotted a multiple line graph using a spreadsheet.

This indicated that sales for all flavours of ice cream were following a seasonal pattern but with an overall upward trend. It also showed that sales of vanilla ice cream were highest, and that those of chocolate had overtaken strawberry. The multiple line graph highlighted the conjunction when sales of chocolate first exceeded strawberry, September 2008.

To show relationships between sales and amount of sunshine Francis plotted scatter graphs for sales

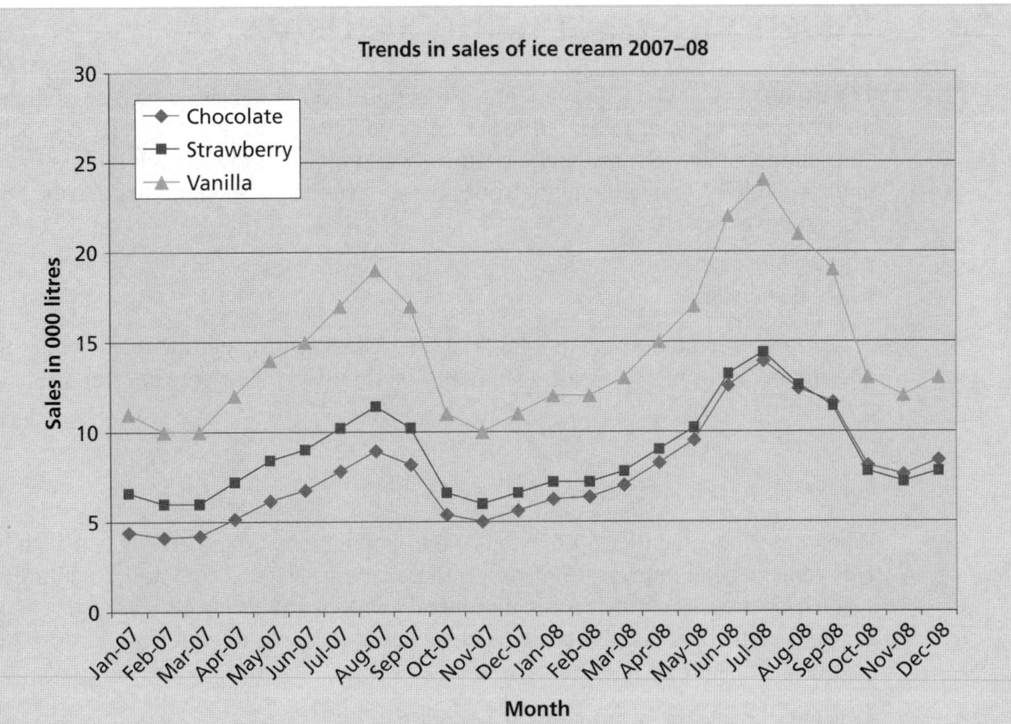

of each ice cream flavour against average (mean) daily hours of sunshine for each month. He plotted sales on the vertical axis, as he presumed that these were dependent on the amount of sunshine, for example:

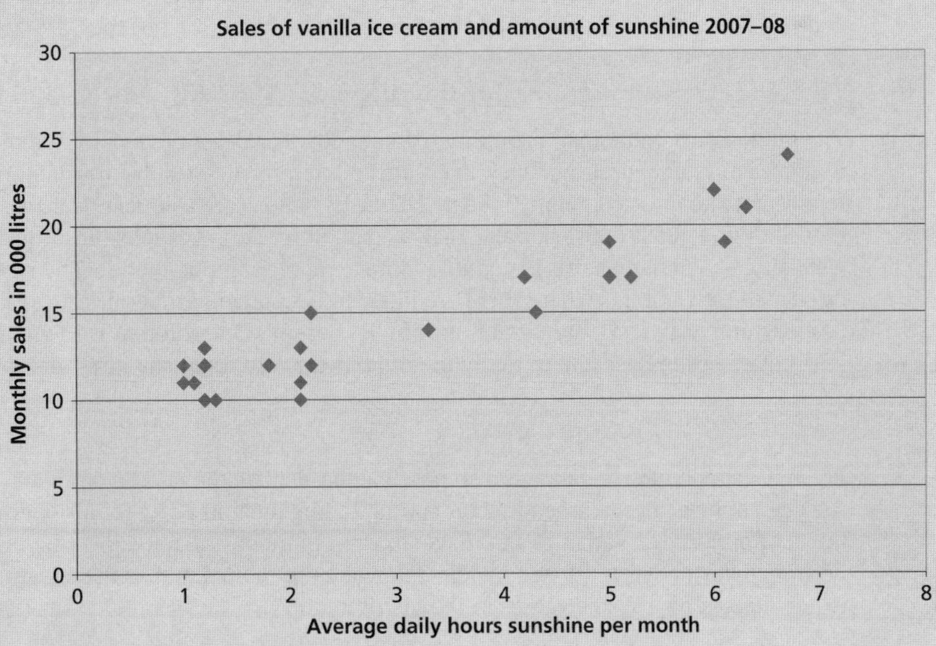

The scatter graph showed that there was a positive relationship between the amount of sunshine and sales of vanilla flavour ice cream. Subsequent scatter plots revealed similar relationships for strawberry and chocolate flavours.

12.4 Describing data using statistics

The exploratory data analysis approach (Section 12.3) emphasised the use of diagrams to understand your data. **Descriptive statistics** enable you to describe (and compare) variables numerically. Your research question(s) and objectives, although limited by the type of data (Table 12.4), should guide your choice of statistics. Statistics to describe a variable focus on two aspects:

- the central tendency;
- the dispersion.

These are summarised in Table 12.4. Those most pertinent to your research question(s) and objectives will eventually be quoted in your research report as support for your arguments.

Describing the central tendency

When describing data for both samples and populations quantitatively it is usual to provide some general impression of values that could be seen as common, middling or average. These are termed measures of **central tendency** and are discussed in virtually all statistics textbooks. The three ways of measuring the central tendency most used in business research are the:

- value that occurs most frequently (mode);
- middle value or mid-point after the data have been ranked (median);
- value, often known as the average, that includes all data values in its calculation (mean).

However, as we saw in Box 12.3, beware: if you have used numerical codes, most analysis software can calculate all three measures whether or not they are appropriate!

To represent the value that occurs most frequently

The **mode** is the value that occurs most frequently. For descriptive data, the mode is the only measure of central tendency that can be interpreted sensibly. You might read in a report that the most common (modal) colour of motor cars sold last year was silver, or that the two equally most popular makes of motorcycle in response to a questionnaire were Honda and Yamaha (it is possible to have more than one mode). The mode can be calculated for variables where there are likely to be a large number of categories (or values for numerical data), although it may be less useful. One solution is to group the data into suitable categories and to quote the most frequently occurring or **modal group**.

To represent the middle value

If you have quantitative data it is also possible to calculate the middle or **median** value by ranking all the values in ascending order and finding the mid-point (or **50th percentile**) in the distribution. For variables that have an even number of data values the median will occur halfway between the two middle data values. The median has the advantage that it is not affected by extreme values in the distribution.

To include all data values

The most frequently used measure of central tendency is the **mean** (average in everyday language), which includes all data values in its calculation. However, it is usually only possible to calculate a meaningful mean using numerical data.

Table 12.4 Descriptive statistics by data type: a summary

To calculate a measure of:		Categorical		Numerical	
		Descriptive	**Ranked**	**Continuous**	**Discrete**
Central tendency that . . .	. . . represents the value that occurs most frequently	Mode			
	. . . represents the middle value			Median	
	. . . includes all data values (average)			Mean	
Dispersion that . . .	. . . states the difference between the highest and lowest values			Range (data need not be normally distributed but must be placed in rank order)	
	. . . states the difference within the middle 50% of values			Inter-quartile range (data need not be normally distributed but must be placed in rank order)	
	. . . states the difference within another fraction of the values			Deciles or percentiles (data need not be normally distributed but must be placed in rank order)	
	. . . describes the extent to which data values differ from the mean			Variance, or more usually, the standard deviation (data should be normally distributed)	
	. . . compares the extent to which data values differ from the mean between variables			Coefficient of variation (data should be normally distributed)	
	. . . allows the relative extent that different data values differ to be compared			Index numbers	

Source: © Mark Saunders, Philip Lewis and Adrian Thornhill 2008.

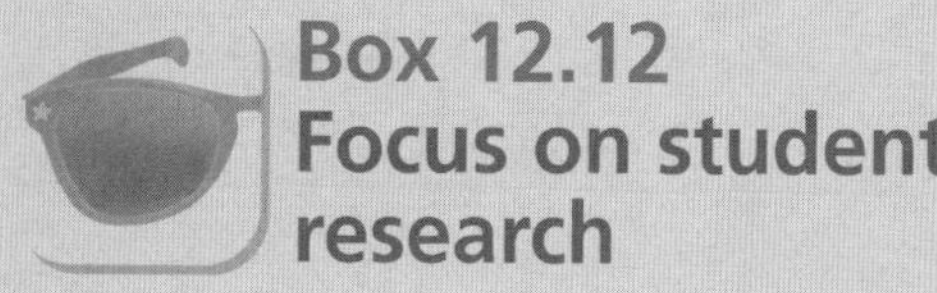

Box 12.12 Focus on student research

Measuring the central tendency

As part of her research project, Kylie had obtained secondary data from the service department of her organisation on the length of time for which their customers had held service contracts:

Length of time held contract	Number of customers
<3 months	50
3 to <6 months	44
6 months to <1 year	71
1 to <2 years	105
2 to <3 years	74
3 to <4 years	35
4 to <5 years	27
5+ years	11

Her exploratory analysis revealed a positively skewed distribution (long tail to the right).

From the table, the largest single group of customers were those who had contracts for 1 to 2 years. This was the modal time period (most commonly occurring). However, the usefulness of this statistic is limited owing to the variety of class widths. By definition, half of the organisation's customers will have held contracts below the median time period (approximately 1 year 5 months) and half above it. As there are 11 customers who have held service contracts for over 5 years, the mean time period (approximately 1 year 9 months) is pulled towards longer times. This is represented by the skewed shape of the distribution.

Kylie needed to decide which of these measures of central tendency to include in her research report. As the mode made little sense she quoted the median and mean when interpreting her data:

> The length of time for which customers have held service contracts is positively skewed. Although mean length of time is approximately 1 year 9 months, half of customers have held service contracts for less than 1 year 5 months (median). Grouping of these data means that it is not possible to calculate a meaningful mode.

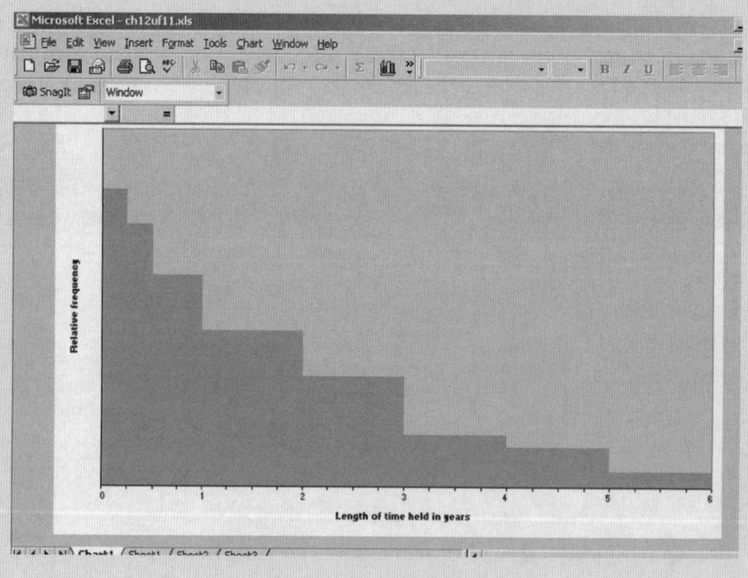

The value of your mean is unduly influenced by extreme data values in skewed distributions (Section 12.3). In such distributions the mean tends to get drawn towards the long tail of extreme data values and may be less representative of the central tendency. For this and other reasons Anderson *et al.* (1999) suggests that the median may be a more useful descriptive statistic. However, because the mean is the building block for many of the statistical tests used to explore relationships (Section 12.5), it is usual to include it as at least one of the measures of central tendency for numerical data in your report. This is, of course, provided that it makes sense!

Describing the dispersion

As well as describing the central tendency for a variable, it is important to describe how the data values are dispersed around the central tendency. As you can see from Table 12.4, this is only possible for numerical data. Two of the most frequently used ways of describing the dispersion are the:

- difference within the middle 50 per cent of values (inter-quartile range);
- extent to which values differ from the mean (standard deviation).

Although these **dispersion measures** are suitable only for numerical data, most statistical analysis software will also calculate them for categorical data if you have used numerical codes!

To state the difference between values

In order to get a quick impression of the distribution of data values for a variable you could simply calculate the difference between the lowest and the highest values – that is, the **range**. However, this statistic is rarely used in research reports as it represents only the extreme values.

A more frequently used statistic is the **inter-quartile range**. As we discussed earlier, the median divides the range into two. The range can be further divided into four equal sections called **quartiles**. The **lower quartile** is the value below which a quarter of your data values will fall; the **upper quartile** is the value above which a quarter of your data values will fall. As you would expect, the remaining half of your data values will fall between the lower and upper quartiles. The difference between the upper and lower quartiles is the inter-quartile range (Morris 2003). As a consequence, it is concerned only with the middle 50 per cent of data values and ignores extreme values.

You can also calculate the range for other fractions of a variable's distribution. One alternative is to divide your distribution using **percentiles**. These split your distribution into 100 equal parts. Obviously the lower quartile is the 25th percentile and the upper quartile the 75th percentile. However, you could calculate a range between the 10th and 90th percentiles so as to include 80 per cent of your data values. Another alternative is to divide the range into 10 equal parts called **deciles**.

To describe and compare the extent by which values differ from the mean

Conceptually and statistically in research it is important to look at the extent to which the data values for a variable are spread around their mean, as this is what you need to know to assess its usefulness as a typical value for the distribution. If your data values are all close to the mean, then the mean is more typical than if they vary widely. To describe the extent of spread of numerical data you use the **standard deviation**. If your data are a sample (Section 7.1) this is calculated using a slightly different formula than if your data are a population, although if your sample is larger than about 30 cases there is little difference in the two statistics (Morris 2003).

You may need to compare the relative spread of data between distributions of different magnitudes (e.g. one may be measured in hundreds of tonnes, the other in billions of tonnes). To make a meaningful comparison you will need to take account of these different magnitudes. A common way of doing this is:

1 to divide the standard deviation by the mean;
2 then to multiply your answer by 100.

This results in a statistic called the **coefficient of variation** (Diamantopoulos and Schlegelmilch 1997). The values of this statistic can then be compared. The distribution with the largest coefficient of variation has the largest relative spread of data (Box 12.13).

Alternatively, as discussed in the introduction in relation to the cost of living at different universities and colleges, you may wish to compare the relative extent to which data values differ. One way of doing this is to use **index numbers** and consider the relative differences rather than actual data values. Such indices compare each data value against a base value that is normally given the value of 100, differences being calculated relative to this value. An index number greater than 100 would represent a larger or higher data value relative to the base value and an index less than 100, a smaller or lower data value.

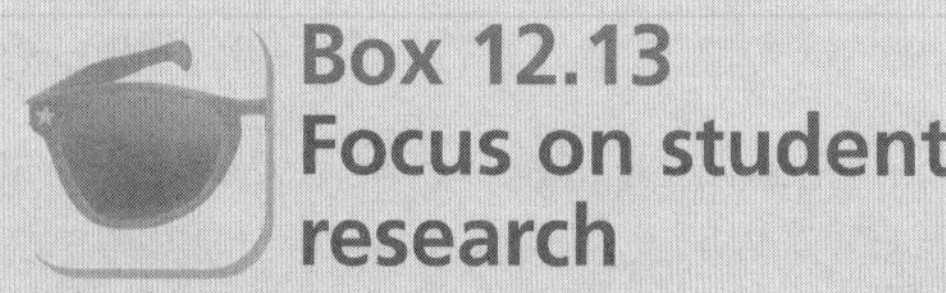

Box 12.13 Focus on student research

Describing variables and comparing their dispersion

Cathy was interested in the total value of transactions at the main and sub-branches of a major bank. The mean value of total transactions at the main branches was approximately five times as high as that for the sub-branches. This made it difficult to compare the relative spread in total value of transactions between the two types of branches. By calculating the coefficients of variation Cathy found that there was relatively more variation in the total value of transactions at the main branches than at the sub-branches. This is because the coefficient of variation for the main branches was larger (23.62) than the coefficient for the sub-branches (18.08).

Microsoft Excel - ch12uf12.xls

	A	B	C	D
23	Branch type	Mean total transaction value	Standard deviation	Coefficient of variation
24	Main	£ 6,000,000	£1,417,000	23.62
25	Sub	£ 1,200,000	£ 217,000	18.08

To calculate an index number for each case for a data variable you use the following formula:

$$\text{index number for case} = \frac{\text{data value for case}}{\text{base data value}} \times 100$$

For our introductory example, the data value for each case (university or college) was calculated by creating a weighted total cost of three different indicators: the weighted mean cost of a range of accommodation options, the weighted mean cost of a tray of drinks (beer, wine and orange juice) and the cost of the student 'basket of goods' of specified foodstuffs and drinks (Push 2007). The base data value was the mean weighted total cost for all the universities and colleges in the UK.

12.5 Examining relationships, differences and trends using statistics

One of the questions you are most likely to ask in your analysis is: 'How does a variable relate to another variable?' In statistical analysis you answer this question by testing the likelihood of the relationship (or one more extreme) occurring by chance alone, if there really was no difference in the population from which the sample was drawn (Robson 2002). This process is known as significance or hypothesis testing as, in effect, you are comparing the data you have collected with what you would theoretically expect to happen. Significance testing can therefore be thought of as helping to rule out the possibility that your result could be due to random variation in your sample.

There are two main groups of statistical significance tests: non-parametric and parametric. **Non-parametric statistics** are designed to be used when your data are not normally distributed. Not surprisingly, this most often means they are used with categorical data. In contrast, **parametric statistics** are used with numerical data. Although parametric statistics are considered more powerful because they use numerical data, a number of assumptions about the actual data being used need to be satisfied if they are not to produce spurious results (Blumberg *et al.* 2008). These include:

- the data cases selected for the sample should be independent, in other words the selection of any one case for your sample should not affect the probability of any other case being included in the same sample;
- the data cases should be drawn from normally distributed populations (Section 12.3);
- the populations from which the data cases are drawn should have equal variances (don't worry, the term variance is explained later in Section 12.5);
- the data used should be numerical.

If these assumptions are not satisfied, it is often still possible to use non-parametric statistics.

The way in which this significance is tested using both non-parametric and parametric statistics can be thought of as answering one from a series of questions, dependent on the data type:

- Is the association statistically significant?
- Are the differences statistically significant?

- What is the strength of the relationship, and is it statistically significant?
- Are the predicted values statistically significant?

These are summarised in Table 12.5 along with statistics used to help examine trends.

Testing for significant relationships and differences

Testing the probability of a pattern such as a relationship between variables occurring by chance alone is known as **significance testing** (Berman Brown and Saunders 2008). As part of your research project, you might have collected sample data to examine the relationship between two variables. Once you have entered data into the analysis software, chosen the statistic and clicked on the appropriate icon, an answer will appear as if by magic! With most statistical analysis software this will consist of a test statistic, the degrees of freedom (*df*) and, based on these, the probability (*p-value*) of your test result or one more extreme occurring by chance alone. If the probability of your test statistic or one more extreme having occurred by chance alone is very low (usually $p < 0.05$ or lower[1]), then you have a statistically significant relationship. Statisticians refer to this as rejecting the null hypothesis and accepting the hypothesis, often abbreviating the terms null hypothesis to H_0 and hypothesis to H_1. Consequently, rejecting a null hypothesis will mean rejecting a testable statement something like 'there is no significant difference between . . .' and accepting a testable statement something like 'there is a significant difference between . . .'. If the probability of obtaining the test statistic or one more extreme by chance alone is higher than 0.05, then you conclude that the relationship is not statistically significant. Statisticians refer to this as accepting the **null hypothesis**. There may still be a relationship between the variables under such circumstances, but you cannot make the conclusion with any certainty.

Despite our discussion of hypothesis testing, albeit briefly, it is worth mentioning that a great deal of quantitative analysis, when written up, does not specify actual hypotheses. Rather, the theoretical underpinnings of the research and the research questions provide the context within which the probability of relationships between variables occurring by chance alone is tested. Thus although hypothesis testing has taken place, it is often only discussed in terms of statistical significance.

The statistical significance of the relationship indicated by a test statistic is determined in part by your sample size (Section 7.2). One consequence of this is that it is very difficult to obtain a significant test statistic with a small sample. Conversely, by increasing your sample size, less obvious relationships and differences will be found to be statistically significant until, with extremely large samples, almost any relationship or difference will be significant (Anderson 2003). This is inevitable as your sample is becoming closer in size to the population from which it was selected. You, therefore, need to remember that small populations can make statistical tests insensitive, while very large samples can make statistical tests overly sensitive. One consequence of this is that, if you expect a difference or relationship will be small, you need to have a larger sample size.

---

[1]A probability of 0.05 means that the probability of your test result or one more extreme occurring by chance alone, if there really was no difference in the population from which the sample was drawn, is 5 in 100, that is 1 in 20.

Table 12.5 Statistics to examine relationships, differences and trends by data type: a summary

	Categorical		Numerical	
	Descriptive	**Ranked**	**Continuous**	**Discrete**
To test whether two variables are associated	Chi square (data may need grouping)		Chi square if variable grouped into discrete classes	
	Cramer's V Phi (both variables must be dichotomous)			
To test whether two groups (categories) are different		Kolmogorov-Smirnov (data may need grouping) or Mann-Whitney *U* test	Independent ***t***-test or paired ***t***-test (often used to test for changes over time) or Mann-Whitney *U* test (where data skewed or a small sample)	
To test whether three or more groups (categories) are different			Analysis of variance (ANOVA)	
To assess the strength of relationship between two variables		Spearman's rank correlation coefficient (Spearman's rho) or Kendall's rank order correlation coefficient (Kendall's tau)	Pearson's product moment correlation coefficient (PMCC)	
To assess the strength of a relationship between one dependent and one independent variable			Coefficient of determination (regression coefficient)	
To assess the strength of a relationship between one dependent and two or more independent variables			Coefficient of multiple determination (multiple regression coefficient)	
To predict the value of a dependent variable from one or more independent variables			Regression equation (regression analysis)	
To examine relative change (trend) over time			Index numbers	
To compare relative changes (trends)over time			Index numbers	
To determine the trend over time of a series of data			Time series: moving averages or Regression equation (regression analysis)	

Source: © Mark Saunders, Philip Lewis and Adrian Thornhill 2008.

Type I and Type II errors

Inevitably, errors can occur when making inferences from samples. Statisticians refer to these as Type I and Type II errors. Blumberg *et al.* (2008) use the analogy of legal decisions to explain Type I and Type II errors. In their analogy they equate a Type I error to a person who is innocent being unjustly convicted and a Type II error to a person who is guilty of a crime being unjustly acquitted. In business and management research we would say that an error made by wrongly coming to a decision that something is true when in reality it is not is a **Type I error**. Type I errors might involve your concluding that two variables are related when they are not, or incorrectly concluding that a sample statistic exceeds the value that would be expected by chance alone. This means you are rejecting your null hypothesis when you should not. The term '**statistical significance**' discussed earlier therefore refers to the probability of making a Type I error. A **Type II error** involves the opposite occurring. In other words, you conclude that something is not true, when in reality it is, and accept your null hypothesis. This means that Type II errors might involve you in concluding that two variables are not related when they are, or that a sample statistic does not exceed the value that would be expected by chance alone.

Given that a Type II error is the inverse of a Type I error, it follows that if we reduce our chances of making a Type I error by setting the significance level to 0.01 rather than 0.05, we increase our chances of making a Type II error by a corresponding amount. This is not an insurmountable problem, as researchers usually consider Type I errors more serious and prefer to take a small chance of saying something is true when it is not (Figure 12.13). It is, therefore, generally more important to minimise Type I than Type II errors.

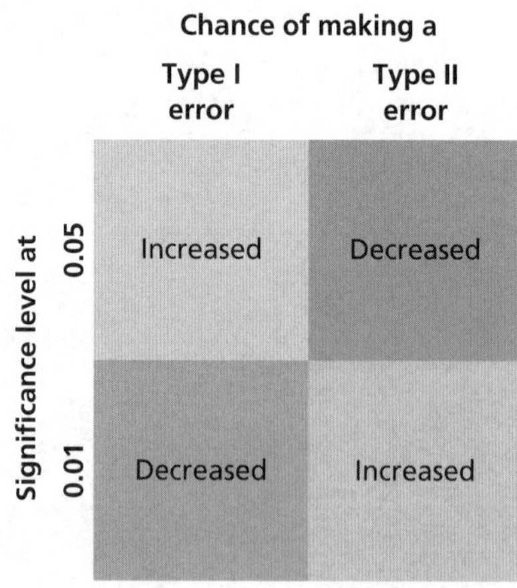

Figure 12.13 Type I and Type II errors

To test whether two variables are associated

Often descriptive or numerical data will be summarised as a two-way contingency table (such as Table 12.3). The **chi square test** enables you to find out how likely it is that the two variables are associated. It is based on a comparison of the observed values in the table with what might be expected if the two distributions were entirely independent. Therefore you are assessing the likelihood of the data in your table, or data more extreme, occurring by chance alone by comparing it with what you would expect if the two variables were independent of each other. This could be phrased as the null hypothesis: 'there is no significant difference . . .'.

The test relies on:

- the categories used in the contingency table being mutually exclusive, so that each observation falls into only one category or class interval;
- no more than 25 per cent of the cells in the table having expected values of less than 5. For contingency tables of two rows and two columns, no expected values of less than 10 are preferable (Dancey and Reidy 2008).

If the latter assumption is not met, the accepted solution is to combine rows and columns where this produces meaningful data.

The chi square (χ^2) test calculates the probability that the data in your table, or data more extreme, could occur by chance alone. Most statistical analysis software does this automatically. However, if you are using a spreadsheet you will usually need to look up the probability in a 'critical values of chi square' table using your calculated chi square value and the degrees of freedom.[2] This table is included in most statistics textbooks. A probability of 0.05 means that there is only a 5 per cent chance of the data in your table occurring by chance alone, and is termed statistically significant. Therefore, a probability of 0.05 or smaller means you can be at least 95 per cent certain that the relationship between your two variables could not have occurred by chance factors alone. When interpreting probabilities from software packages, beware: owing to statistical rounding of numbers a probability of 0.000 does not mean zero, but that it is less than 0.001 (Box 12.14).

Some software packages, such as SPSS, calculate the statistic **Cramer's V** alongside the chi square statistic (Box 12.14). If you include the value of Cramer's V in your research report, it is usual to do so in addition to the chi square statistic. Whereas the chi square statistic gives the probability that data in a table, or data more extreme, could occur by chance alone; Cramer's V measures the association between the two variables within the table on a scale where 0 represents no association and 1 represents perfect association. Because the value of Cramer's V is always between 0 and 1, the relative strengths of significant associations between different pairs of variables can be compared.

An alternative statistic used to measure the association between two variables is **Phi**. This statistic measures the association on a scale between -1 (perfect negative association), through 0 (no association) to 1 (perfect association). However, unlike Cramer's V, using Phi to compare the relative strengths of significant associations between pairs of variables can be problematic. This is because, although values of Phi will only range between -1 and 1 when measuring the association between two dichotomous variables, they may exceed these extremes when measuring the association for categorical variables where at least one of these variables has more than two categories. For this reason, we recommend that you use Phi only when comparing pairs of dichotomous variables.

To test whether two groups are different

Ranked data Sometimes it is necessary to see whether the distribution of an observed set of values for each category of a variable differs from a specified distribution, for example whether your sample differs from the population from which it was selected. The **Kolmogorov–Smirnov test** enables you to establish this for ranked data (Kanji 2006). It is based on a comparison of the cumulative proportions of the observed values in each category with the cumulative proportions in the same categories for the specified population. Therefore you are testing the likelihood of the distribution of your observed data differing from that of the specified population by chance alone.

---

[2]Degrees of freedom are the number of values free to vary when computing a statistic. The number of degrees of freedom for a contingency table of at least 2 rows and 2 columns of data is calculated from (number of rows in the table −1) × (number of columns in the table −1).

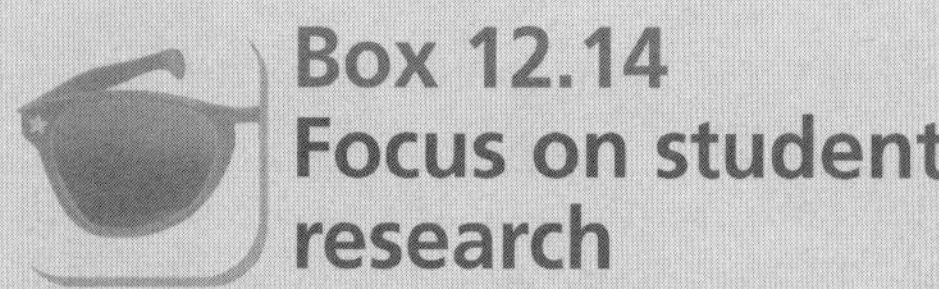

Box 12.14 Focus on student research

Testing whether two variables are associated

As part of his research project, John wanted to find out whether there was a significant association between grade of respondent and gender. Earlier analysis using SPSS had indicated that there were 385 respondents in his sample with no missing data for either variable. However, it had also highlighted the small numbers of respondents in the highest grade (GC01 to GC05) categories:

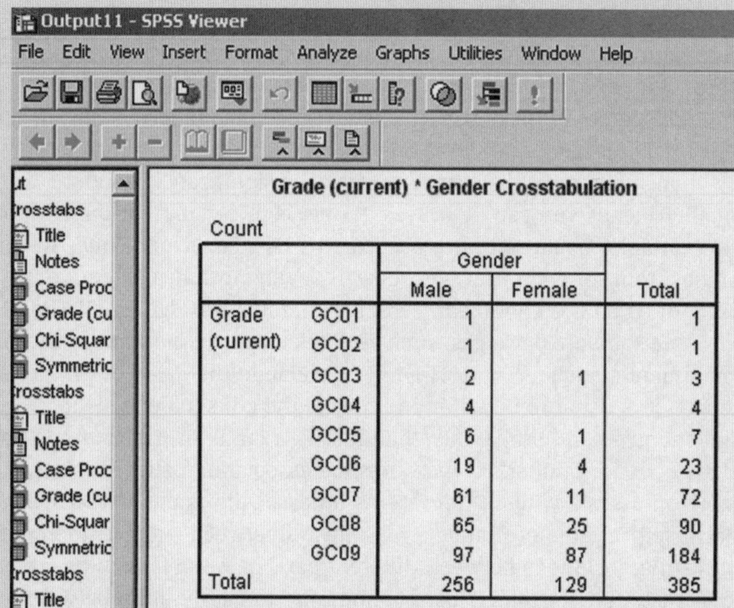

Grade (current) * Gender Crosstabulation

Count

		Gender		
		Male	Female	Total
Grade (current)	GC01	1		1
	GC02	1		1
	GC03	2	1	3
	GC04	4		4
	GC05	6	1	7
	GC06	19	4	23
	GC07	61	11	72
	GC08	65	25	90
	GC09	97	87	184
Total		256	129	385

Bearing in mind the assumptions of the chi square test, John decided to combine categories GC01 through GC05 to create a new grade GC01-5 using SPSS:

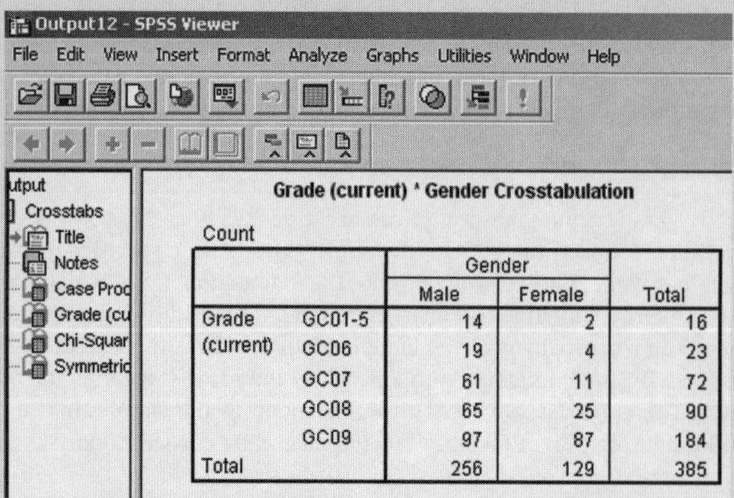

Grade (current) * Gender Crosstabulation

Count

		Gender		
		Male	Female	Total
Grade (current)	GC01-5	14	2	16
	GC06	19	4	23
	GC07	61	11	72
	GC08	65	25	90
	GC09	97	87	184
Total		256	129	385

He then used his analysis software to undertake a chi square test and calculate Cramer's V:

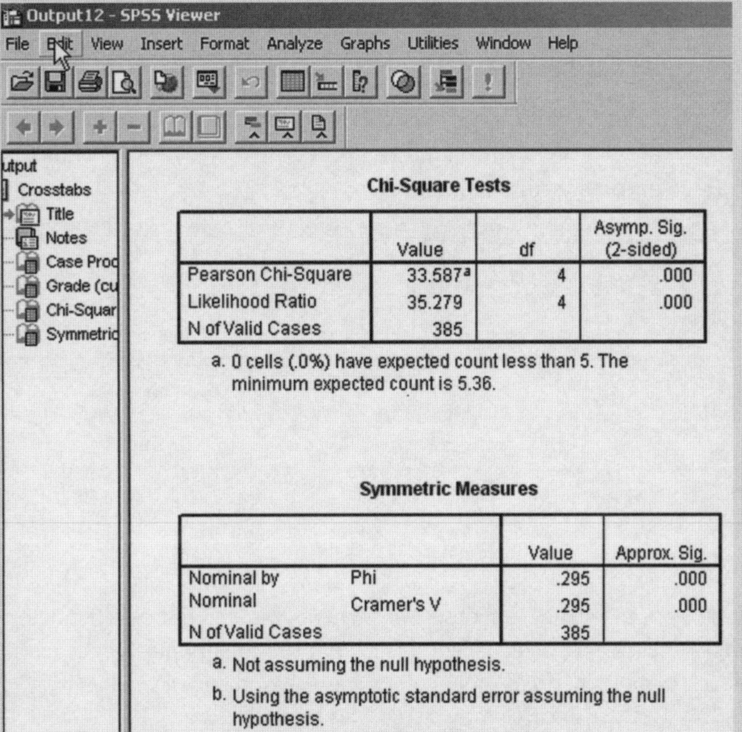

Chi-Square Tests

	Value	df	Asymp. Sig. (2-sided)
Pearson Chi-Square	33.587[a]	4	.000
Likelihood Ratio	35.279	4	.000
N of Valid Cases	385		

a. 0 cells (.0%) have expected count less than 5. The minimum expected count is 5.36.

Symmetric Measures

		Value	Approx. Sig.
Nominal by Nominal	Phi	.295	.000
	Cramer's V	.295	.000
N of Valid Cases		385	

a. Not assuming the null hypothesis.

b. Using the asymptotic standard error assuming the null hypothesis.

As can be seen, this resulted in an overall chi square value of 33.59 with 4 degrees of freedom (df). The significance of .000 (Asymp. Sig.) meant that the probability of the values in his table occurring by chance alone was less than 0.001. He therefore concluded that the relationship between gender and grade was extremely unlikely to be explained by chance factors alone and quoted the statistic in his project report:

$$[\chi^2 = 33.59, df = 4, p < 0.001]^*$$

The Cramer's V value of .295, significant at the .000 level (Approx. Sig.), showed that the association between gender and grade, although weak, was positive. This meant that men (coded 1 whereas females were coded 2) were more likely to be employed at higher grades GC01–5 (coded using lower numbers). John also quoted this statistic in his project report:

$$[V_c = 0.295, p < 0.001]$$

To explore this association further, John examined the cell values in relation to the row and column totals. Of males, 5 per cent were in higher grades (GC01–5) compared to less than 2 per cent of females. In contrast, only 38 per cent of males were in the lowest grade (GC09) compared with 67 per cent of females.

*You will have noticed that the computer printout in this box does not have a zero before the decimal point. This is because most software packages follow the North American convention, in contrast to the UK convention of placing a zero before the decimal point.

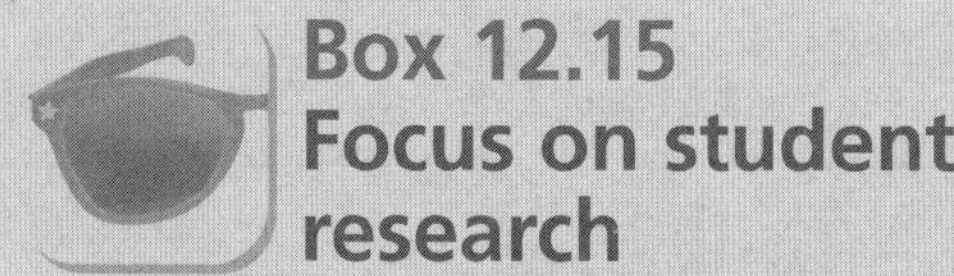

Box 12.15 Focus on student research

Testing the representativeness of a sample

Benson's research question was, 'To what extent do the espoused values of an organisation match the underlying cultural assumptions?' As part of his research, he sent a questionnaire to the 150 employees in the organisation where he worked and 97 of these responded. The responses from each category of employee in terms of their seniority within the organisation's hierarchy were as shown in the spreadsheet:

Microsoft Excel - benson's data.xls

	A	B	C	D	E	F	G	H
1			Shop floor workers	Technicians	Supervisors	Quality managers	Management team	Total
2	Respondents	Number	49	15	21	8	4	97
3		Cumulative proportion	0.505	0.660	0.876	0.959	1.000	
4	Total Employees	Number	73	31	24	17	5	150
5		Cumulative proportion	0.487	0.693	0.853	0.967	1.000	
6	*Difference*		0.018	0.034	0.023	0.008	0.000	

The maximum difference between his observed cumulative proportion (that for respondents) and his specified cumulative proportion (that for total employees) was 0.034. This was the value of his *D* statistic. Consulting a 'critical values of *D* for the Kolmogorov–Smirnov test' table for a sample size of 97 revealed the probability that the two distributions differed by chance alone was less than 0.01, in other words, less than 1 per cent. He concluded that those employees who responded did not differ significantly from the total population in terms of their seniority with the organisation's hierarchy. This was stated in his research report:

> Statistical analysis showed the sample selected did not differ significantly from all employees in terms of their seniority within the organisation's hierarchy [$D = .034, p < .01$].

The Kolmogorov–Smirnov test calculates a *D* statistic that is then used to work out the probability of the two distributions differing by chance alone. Although the test and statistic are not often found in analysis software, they are relatively straightforward to calculate using a spreadsheet (Box 12.15). A reasonably clear description of this can be found in Cohen and Holliday (1996). Once calculated, you will need to look up the significance of your *D* value in a 'critical values of *D* for the Kolmogorov–Smirnov test' table. A probability of 0.05 means that there is only a 5 per cent chance that the two distributions differ by chance alone, and is termed statistically significant. Therefore a probability of 0.05 or smaller means you can be at least 95 per cent certain that the difference between your two distributions cannot be explained by chance factors alone.

Numerical data If a numerical variable can be divided into two distinct groups using a descriptive variable you can assess the likelihood of these groups being different using an **independent groups *t*-test**. This compares the difference in the means of the two groups using a measure of the spread of the scores. If the likelihood of any difference between these two groups occurring by chance alone is low, this will be represented by a large *t* statistic with a probability less than 0.05. This is termed statistically significant.

Alternatively, you might have numerical data for two variables that measure the same feature but under different conditions. Your research could focus on the effects of an intervention such as employee counselling. As a consequence, you would have pairs of data that measure work performance before and after counselling for each case. To assess the likelihood of any difference between your two variables (each half of the pair) occurring by chance alone you would use a **paired *t*-test** (Box 12.16). Although the calculation of this is slightly different, your interpretation would be the same as for the independent groups *t*-test.

Although the ***t*-test** assumes that the data are normally distributed (Section 12.3), this can be ignored without too many problems even with sample sizes of less than 30 (Hays 1994). The assumption that the data for the two groups have the same variance (standard deviation

Testing whether two groups are different

Schneider and Cornwell's (2005) paper in the *International Journal of Advertising* is concerned with the practice of placing brand names, logos and products in computer games. In particular, it is concerned with the impact of different placement practices on game players' recall of brand name, logo and product. This, they highlight, is of increasing importance owing to the rapid increase in the cost of producing a top-quality computer game and the need to seek out methods to subsidise these costs, such as through shared marketing and cross-promotional campaigns. In their paper they propose a number of hypotheses regarding the placement of brands using 'banners', the computer game equivalent of displaying a banner at a sporting event. Four of these hypotheses are listed in the subsequent table.

Having collected data by questionnaire from 46 participants on the brands and products they could remember after playing a particular game for a specified period, the hypotheses were tested using paired samples *t*-tests. The results for the first four hypotheses were as follows:

Hypothesis	***t* value**	**Df**	**Significance (2-tailed)**
Prominent placements will elicit greater recall than subtle placements	5.627	45	<0.001
Prominent placements will elicit greater recognition than subtle placements	9.833	45	<0.001
Experienced players will show greater recall of brand placement than novice players	2.383	44	<0.02
Experienced players will show greater recognition of brand placement than novice players	3.734	44	<0.001

Based on these results, Schneider and Cornwell argued that the banners which had been placed prominently were siginificantly better recalled than those placed subtly. In addition, prominent placements of banners were siginificantly better recognised than subtle placements. This, along with other aspects of their research, was used to provide guidance regarding the characteristics of successful banner placement in computer games.

squared) can also be ignored provided that the two samples are of similar size (Hays 1994). If the data are skewed or the sample size is small, the most appropriate statistical test is the Mann-Whitney *U* Test. This test is the non-parametric equivalent of the independent groups *t*-test (Dancey and Reidy 2008). Consequently, if the likelihood of any difference between these two groups occurring by chance alone is low, this will be represented by a large *U* statistic with a probability less than 0.05. This is termed statistically significant.

To test whether three or more groups are different

If a numerical variable is divided into three or more distinct groups using a descriptive variable, you can assess the likelihood of these groups being different occurring by chance alone by using **one-way analysis of variance** or one-way **ANOVA** (Table 12.5). As you can gather from its name, ANOVA analyses the **variance**, that is, the spread of data values, within and between groups of data by comparing means. The *F* ratio or *F* statistic represents these differences. If the likelihood of any difference between groups occurring by chance alone is low, this will be represented by a large *F* ratio with a probability of less than 0.05. This is termed statistically significant (Box 12.17).

Box 12.17 Focus on student research

Testing whether three (or more) groups are different

Andy was interested to discover whether there were differences in job satisfaction across three groups of employees (managers, administrators, shop floor workers) within a manufacturing organisation. He decided to measure job satisfaction using a tried-and-tested scale based on five questions that resulted in a job satisfaction score (numerical data) for each employee. He labelled this scale 'broad view of job satisfaction'.

After ensuring that the assumptions of one-way ANOVA were satisfied, he analysed his data using statistical analysis software. His output included the following:

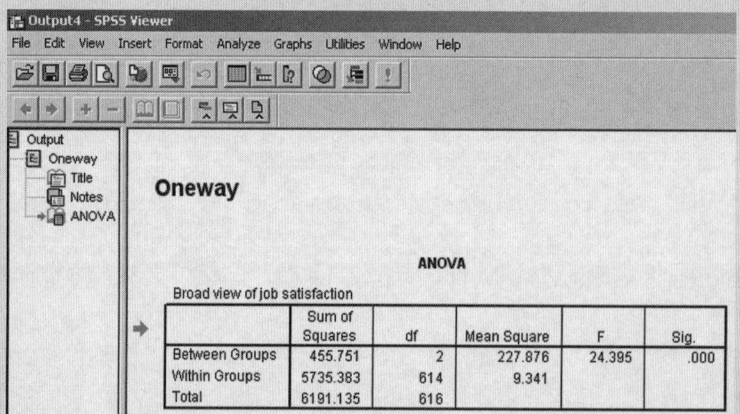

Output4 - SPSS Viewer

File Edit View Insert Format Analyze Graphs Utilities Window Help

Output
Oneway
Title
Notes
ANOVA

Oneway

ANOVA

Broad view of job satisfaction

	Sum of Squares	df	Mean Square	F	Sig.
Between Groups	455.751	2	227.876	24.395	.000
Within Groups	5735.383	614	9.341		
Total	6191.135	616			

This output shows that the *F* ratio value of 24.395 with 2 and 614 degrees of freedom (df) has a probability of occurrence by chance alone of less than 0.001 if there is no significant difference between the three groups. In his research report Andy concluded that there was:

> a statistically significant [$F = 24.39, p < .001$] difference in job satisfaction between managers, administrators, and shop floor workers.

The following assumptions need to be met before using one-way ANOVA. More detailed discussion is available in Hays (1994) and Dancey and Reidy (2008).

- Each data value is independent and does not relate to any of the other data values. This means that you should not use one-way ANOVA where data values are related in some way, such as the same case being tested repeatedly.
- The data for each group are normally distributed (Section 12.3). This assumption is not particularly important provided that the number of cases in each group is large (30 or more).
- The data for each group have the same variance (standard deviation squared). However, provided that the number of cases in the largest group is not more than 1.5 times that of the smallest group, this appears to have very little effect on the test results.

Assessing the strength of relationship

If your data set contains ranked or numerical data, it is likely that, as part of your exploratory data analysis, you will already have plotted the relationship between cases for these ranked or numerical variables using a scatter graph (Figure 12.12). Such relationships might include those between weekly sales of a new product and those of a similar established product, or age of employees and their length of service with the company. These examples emphasise the fact that your data can contain two sorts of relationship:

- those where a change in one variable is accompanied by a change in another variable but it is not clear which variable caused the other to change, a **correlation**;
- those where a change in one or more (independent) variables causes a change in another (dependent) variable, a cause-and-effect relationship.

To assess the strength of relationship between pairs of variables

A **correlation coefficient** enables you to quantify the strength of the linear relationship between two ranked or numerical variables. This coefficient (usually represented by the letter *r*) can take on any value between -1 and $+1$ (Figure 12.14). A value of $+1$ represents a perfect **positive correlation**. This means that the two variables are precisely related and that, as values of one variable increase, values of the other variable will increase. By contrast, a value of -1 represents a perfect **negative correlation**. Again, this means that the two variables are precisely related; however, as the values of one variable increase those of the other decrease. Correlation coefficients between -1 and $+1$ represent weaker positive and negative correlations, a value of 0 meaning the variables are perfectly independent. Within business research it is extremely unusual to obtain perfect correlations.

For data collected from a sample you will need to know the probability of your correlation coefficient having occurred by chance alone. Most analysis software calculates this probability automatically (Box 12.18). As outlined earlier, if this probability is very low (usually less than 0.05) then it is considered statistically significant. If the probability is greater than 0.05 then your relationship is not statistically significant.

Figure 12.14 Values of the correlation coefficient

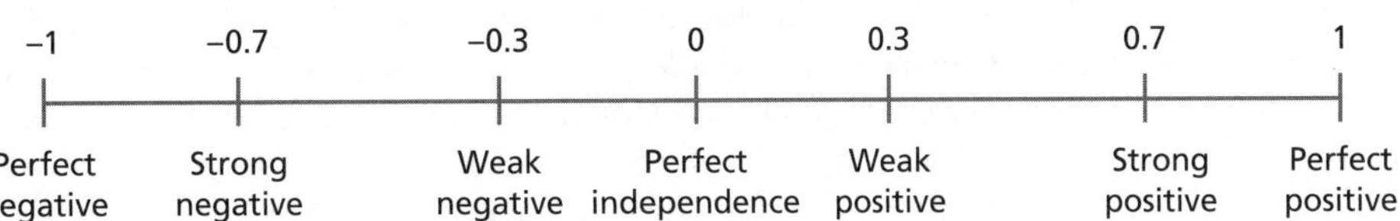

Box 12.18 Focus on student research

Assessing the strength of relationship between pairs of variables

As part of his research project, Hassan obtained data from a company on the number of television advertisements, number of enquiries and number of sales of their product. These data were entered into the statistical analysis software. He wished to discover whether there were any relationships between the following pairs of these variables:

- number of television advertisements and number of enquiries;
- number of television advertisements and number of sales;
- number of enquiries and number of sales.

As the data were numerical, he used the statistical analysis software to calculate Pearson's product moment correlation coefficients for all pairs of variables. The output was a correlation matrix:

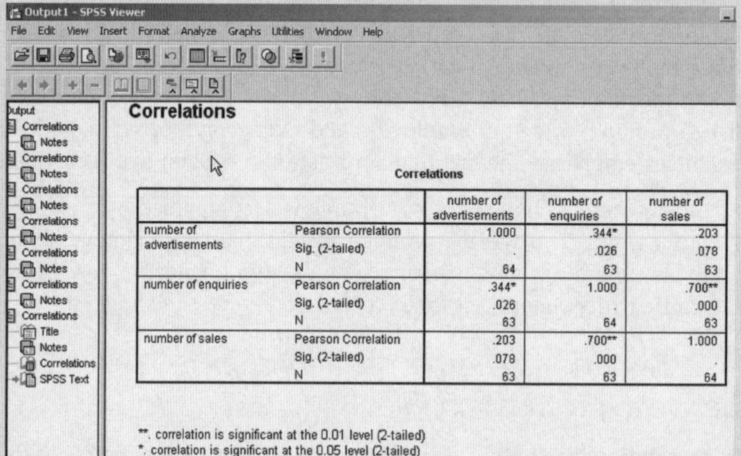

Output1 - SPSS Viewer

Correlations

Correlations

		number of advertisements	number of enquiries	number of sales
number of advertisements	Pearson Correlation	1.000	.344*	.203
	Sig. (2-tailed)	.	.026	.078
	N	64	63	63
number of enquiries	Pearson Correlation	.344*	1.000	.700**
	Sig. (2-tailed)	.026	.	.000
	N	63	64	63
number of sales	Pearson Correlation	.203	.700**	1.000
	Sig. (2-tailed)	.078	.000	.
	N	63	63	64

**. correlation is significant at the 0.01 level (2-tailed)
*. correlation is significant at the 0.05 level (2-tailed)

Hassan's matrix is symmetrical because correlation implies only a relationship rather than a cause-and-effect relationship. The value in each cell of the matrix is the correlation coefficient. Thus, the correlation between the number of advertisements and the number of enquiries is 0.344. This coefficient shows that there is a fairly weak but positive relationship between the number of television advertisements and the number of enquiries. The (*) highlights that the probability of this correlation coefficient occurring by chance alone is less than 0.05 (5 per cent). This correlation coefficient is therefore statistically significant.

Using the data in this matrix Hassan concluded that:

> There is a statistically significant strong positive relationship between the number of enquiries and the number of sales ($r = .700, p < .01$) and a statistically significant but weaker relationship between the number of television advertisements and the number of enquiries ($r = .344, p < .05$). However, there is no statistically significant relationship between the number of television advertisements and the number of sales ($r = .203, p > .05$).

If both your variables contain numerical data you should use **Pearson's product moment correlation coefficient** (PMCC) to assess the strength of relationship (Table 12.5). Where these data are from a sample then the sample should have been selected at random. However, if one or both of your variables contain rank data you cannot use PMCC, but will need to use a correlation coefficient that is calculated using ranked data. Such rank correlation coefficients represent the degree of agreement between the two sets of rankings. Before calculating the rank correlation coefficient, you will need to ensure that the data for both variables are ranked. Where one of the variables is numerical this will necessitate converting these data to ranked data. Subsequently, you have a choice of rank correlation coefficients. The two used most widely in business and management research are **Spearman's rank correlation coefficient** (Spearman's rho) and **Kendall's rank correlation coefficient** (Kendall's tau). Where data is being used from a sample, both these rank correlation coefficients assume that the sample is selected at random and the data are ranked (ordinal). Given this, it is not surprising that, whenever you can use Spearman's rank correlation coefficient, you can also use Kendall's rank correlation coefficient. However, if your data for a variable contain tied ranks, Kendall's rank correlation coefficient is generally considered to be the more appropriate of these coefficients to use. Although each of the correlation coefficients discussed uses a different formula in its calculation, the resulting coefficient is interpreted in the same way as PMCC.

To assess the strength of a cause-and-effect relationship between variables

In contrast to the correlation coefficient, the **coefficient of determination** (sometimes known as the **regression coefficient**) enables you to assess the strength of relationship between a numerical dependent variable and one or more numerical independent variables. Once again, where these data have been selected from a sample, the sample must have been selected at random. For a dependent variable and one (or perhaps two) independent variables you will have probably already plotted this relationship on a scatter graph. If you have more than two independent variables this is unlikely as it is very difficult to represent four or more scatter graph axes visually!

The coefficient of determination (represented by r^2) can take on any value between 0 and +1. It measures the proportion of the variation in a dependent variable (amount of sales) that can be explained statistically by the independent variable (marketing expenditure) or variables (marketing expenditure, number of sales staff, etc.). This means that if all the variation in amount of sales can be explained by the marketing expenditure and the number of sales staff, the coefficient of determination will be 1. If 50 per cent of the variation can be explained, the coefficient of determination will be 0.5, and if none of the variation can be explained, the coefficient will be 0 (Box 12.19). Within our research we have rarely obtained a coefficient above 0.8.

Box 12.19 Focus on student research

Assessing a cause-and-effect relationship

As part of her research project, Arethea wanted to assess the relationship between all the employees' annual salaries and the number of years each had been employed by an organisation. She believed that an employee's annual salary would be dependent on the number of years for which she or he had been employed (the independent variable). Arethea entered these data into her analysis software and calculated a coefficient of determination (r^2) of 0.37.

As she was using data for all employees of the firm (the total population) rather than a sample, the probability of her coefficient occurring by chance alone was 0. She therefore concluded that 37 per cent of the variation in current employees' salary could be explained by the number of years they had been employed by the organisation.

The process of calculating coefficient of determination and regression equation using one independent variable is normally termed **regression analysis**. Calculating a **coefficient of multiple determination** (or **multiple regression coefficient**) and regression equation using two or more independent variables is termed **multiple regression analysis**. The calculations and interpretation required by multiple regression are relatively complicated, and we advise you to use statistical analysis software and consult a detailed statistics textbook or computer manual such as Norusis (2007). Most statistical analysis software will calculate the significance of the coefficient of multiple determination for sample data automatically. A very low significance value (usually less than 0.05) means that your coefficient is unlikely to have occurred by chance alone. A value greater than 0.05 means you can conclude that your coefficient of multiple determination could have occurred by chance alone.

To predict the value of a variable from one or more other variables

Regression analysis can also be used to predict the values of a dependent variable given the values of one or more independent variables by calculating a **regression equation**. You may wish to predict the amount of sales for a specified marketing expenditure and number of sales staff. You would represent this as a regression equation:

$$AoS_i = \alpha + \beta_1 ME_i + \beta_2 NSS_i$$

where:

AoS is the Amount of Sales
ME is the Marketing Expenditure
NSS is the Number of Sales Staff
α is the regression constant
β_1 and β_2 are the beta coefficients

This equation can be translated as stating:

$$Amount\ of\ Sales_i = value + (\beta_1 \times Marketing\ Expenditure_i) + (\beta_2 \times Number\ of\ Sales\ Staff_i)$$

Using regression analysis you would calculate the values of the constant coefficient α and the slope coefficients β_1 and β_2 from data you had already collected on amount of sales, marketing expenditure and number of sales staff. A specified marketing expenditure and number of sales staff could then be substituted into the regression equation to predict the amount of sales that would be generated. When calculating a regression equation you need to ensure the following assumptions are met:

- The relationship between dependent and independent variables is linear. **Linearity** refers to the degree to which the change in the dependent variable is related to the change in the independent variables. Linearity can easily be examined through residual plots (these are usually drawn by the analysis software). Two things may influence the linearity. First, individual cases with extreme values on one or more variables (outliers) may violate the assumption of linearity. It is, therefore, important to identify these outliers and, if appropriate, exclude them from the regression analysis. Second, the values for one or more variables may violate the assumption of linearity. For these variables the data values may need to be transformed. Techniques for this can be found in other, more specialised books on multivariate data analysis, for example Anderson (2003).
- The extent to which the data values for the dependent and independent variables have equal variances (this term was explained earlier in Section 12.4), also known as **homoscedasticity**. Again, analysis software usually contains statistical tests for equal

variance. For example, the Levene test for homogeneity of variance measures the equality of variances for a single pair of variables. If **heteroscedasticity** (that is, unequal variances) exists, it may still be possible to carry out your analysis. Further details of this can again be found in more specialised books on multivariate analysis such as Anderson (2003).

- Absence of correlation between two or more independent variables (**collinearity** or **multicollinearity**), as this makes it difficult to determine the separate effects of individual variables. The simplest diagnostic is to use the correlation coefficients, extreme collinearity being represented by a correlation coefficient of 1. The rule of thumb is that the presence of high correlations (generally 0.90 and above) indicates substantial collinearity (Hair *et al.* 2006). Other common measures include the tolerance value and its inverse – the **variance inflation factor** (VIF). Hair *et al.* (2006) recommend that a very small tolerance value (0.10 or below) or a large VIF value (10 or above) indicates high collinearity.
- The data for the independent variables and dependent variable are normally distributed (Section 12.3).

The coefficient of determination, r^2 (discussed earlier), can be used as a measure of how good a predictor your regression equation is likely to be. If your equation is a perfect predictor then the coefficient of determination will be 1. If the equation can predict only 50 per cent of the variation, then the coefficient of determination will be 0.5, and if the equation predicts none of the variation, the coefficient will be 0. The coefficient of multiple determination (R^2) indicates the degree of the goodness of fit for your estimated multiple regression equation. It can be interpreted as how good a predictor your multiple regression equation is likely to be. It represents the proportion of the variability in the dependent variable that can be explained by your multiple regression equation. This means that when multiplied by 100, the coefficient of multiple determination can be interpreted as the percentage of variation in the dependent variable that can be explained by the estimated regression equation. The adjusted R^2 statistic (which takes into account the number of independent variables in your regression equation) is preferred by some researchers as it helps avoid overestimating the impact of adding an independent variable on the amount of variability explained by the estimated regression equation.

The *t*-test and *F*-test are used to work out the probability of the relationship represented by your regression analysis having occurred by chance. In simple linear regression (with one independent and one dependent variable), the *t*-test and *F*-test will give you the same answer. However, in multiple regression, the *t*-test is used to find out the probability of the relationship between each of the individual independent variables and the dependent variable occurring by chance. In contrast, the *F*-test is used to find out the overall probability of the relationship between the dependent variable and all the independent variables occurring by chance. The *t* distribution table and the *F* distribution table are used to determine whether a *t*-test or an *F*-test is significant by comparing the results with the *t* distribution and *F* distribution respectively, given the degrees of freedom and the pre-defined significance level.

Examining trends

When examining longitudinal data the first thing we recommend you do is to draw a line graph to obtain a visual representation of the trend (Figure 12.7). Subsequent to this, statistical analyses can be undertaken. Three of the more common uses of such analyses are:

- to examine the trend or relative change for a single variable over time;
- to compare trends or the relative change for variables measured in different units or of different magnitudes;
- to determine the long-term trend and forecast future values for a variable.

These have been summarised earlier in Table 12.5.

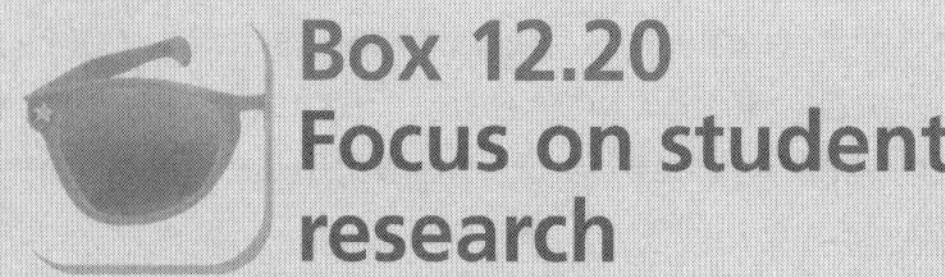

Box 12.20 Focus on student research

Forecasting number of road injury accidents

As part of her research project, Nimmi had obtained data on the number of road injury accidents and the number of drivers breath tested for alcohol in 39 police force areas. In addition, she obtained data on the total population (in thousands) for each of these areas from the most recent census. Nimmi wished to find out if it was possible to predict the number of road injury accidents (*RIA*) in each police area (her dependent variable) using the number of drivers breath tested (*BT*) and the total population in thousands (*POP*) for each of the police force areas (independent variables). This she represented as an equation:

$$RIA_i = \alpha + \beta_1 BT_i + \beta_2 POP_i$$

Nimmi entered her data into the analysis software and undertook a multiple regression. She scrolled down the output file and found the table headed 'Coefficients':

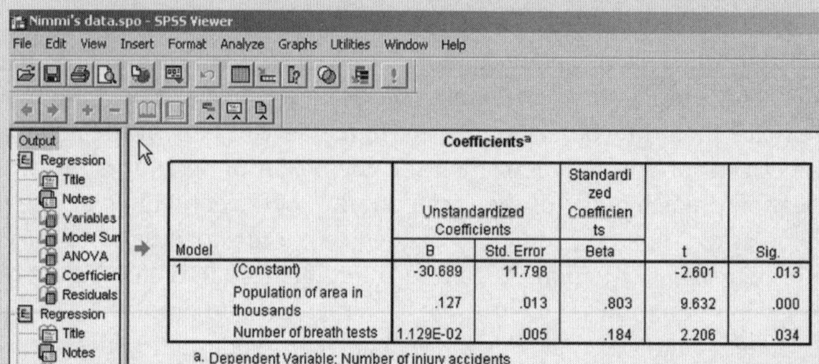

Coefficients[a]

Model		Unstandardized Coefficients B	Std. Error	Standardized Coefficients Beta	t	Sig.
1	(Constant)	-30.689	11.798		-2.601	.013
	Population of area in thousands	.127	.013	.803	9.632	.000
	Number of breath tests	1.129E-02	.005	.184	2.206	.034

a. Dependent Variable: Number of injury accidents

Nimmi substituted the 'unstandardized coefficients' into her regression equation (after rounding the values):

$$RIA_i = -30.7 + 0.01BT_i + 0.13POP_i$$

This meant she could now predict the number of road injury accidents for a police area of different populations for different numbers of drivers breath tested for alcohol. For example, the number of road injury accidents for an area of 500 000 population in which 10 000 drivers were breath tested for alcohol can now be estimated:

$$-30.7 + (0.01 \times 10000) + (0.13 \times 500)$$
$$= -30.5 + 100 + 65$$
$$= 135$$

In order to check the usefulness of these estimates, Nimmi scrolled back up her output and looked at the results of R^2, *t*-test and *F*-test:

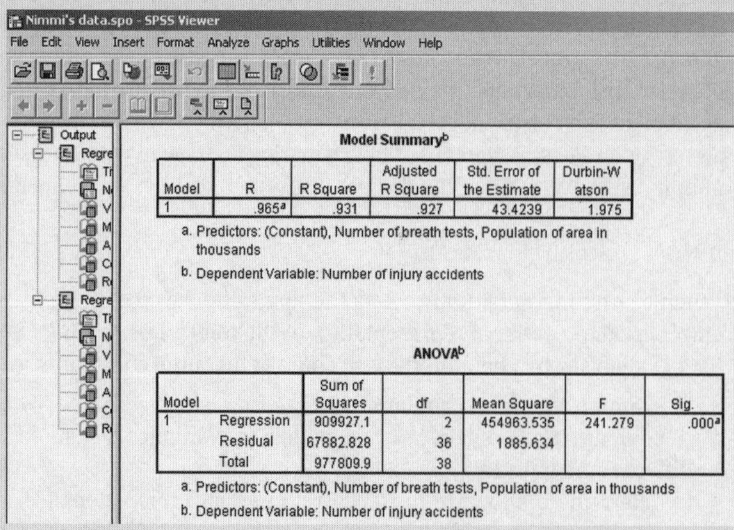

Model Summary[b]

Model	R	R Square	Adjusted R Square	Std. Error of the Estimate	Durbin-Watson
1	.965[a]	.931	.927	43.4239	1.975

a. Predictors: (Constant), Number of breath tests, Population of area in thousands

b. Dependent Variable: Number of injury accidents

ANOVA[b]

Model		Sum of Squares	df	Mean Square	F	Sig.
1	Regression	909927.1	2	454963.535	241.279	.000[a]
	Residual	67882.828	36	1885.634		
	Total	977809.9	38			

a. Predictors: (Constant), Number of breath tests, Population of area in thousands

b. Dependent Variable: Number of injury accidents

The R^2 and adjusted R^2 values of 0.965 and 0.931 respectively both indicated that there was a high degree of goodness of fit of her regression model. It also means that over 90 per cent of variance in the dependent variable (the number of road injury accidents) can be explained by the regression model. The *F*-test result was 241.279 with a significance ('Sig.') of .000. This meant that the probability of these results occurring by chance was less than 0.0005. Therefore, a significant relationship was present between the number of road injury accidents in an area and the population of the area, and the number of drivers breath tested for alcohol.

The *t*-test results for the individual regression coefficients (shown in the first extract) for the two independent variables were 9.632 and 2.206. Once again, the probability of both these results occurring by chance was less than 0.05, being less than 0.001 for the independent variable population of area in thousands and 0.034 for the independent variable number of breath tests. This means that the regression coefficients for these variables were both statistically significant at the $p < 0.05$ level.

To examine the trend

To answer some research question(s) and meet some objectives you may need to examine the trend for one variable. One way of doing this is to use **index numbers** to compare the relative magnitude for each data value (case) over time rather than using the actual data value. Index numbers are also widely used in business publications and by organisations. The *Financial Times* share indices such as the FTSE 100 (Box 12.21, overleaf) and the Retail Price Index are well-known examples.

Although such indices can involve quite complex calculations, they all compare change over time against a base period. The **base period** is normally given the value of 100 (or 1000 in the case of many share indices, including the FTSE 100), and change is calculated relative to this. Thus a value greater than 100 would represent an increase relative to the base period, and a value less than 100 a decrease.

To calculate simple index numbers for each case of a longitudinal variable you use the following formula:

$$\text{index number of case} = \frac{\text{data value for case}}{\text{data value for base period}} \times 100$$

Thus, if a company's sales were 125 000 units in 2007 (base period) and 150 000 units in 2008, the index number for 2007 would be 100 and for 2008 it would be 120.

To compare trends

To answer some other research question(s) and to meet the associated objectives you may need to compare trends between two or more variables measured in different units or at different magnitudes. For example, to compare changes in prices of fuel oil and coal over time is difficult as the prices are recorded for different units (litres and tonnes). One way of overcoming this is to use index numbers (Section 12.4) and compare the relative changes in the value of the index rather than actual figures. The index numbers for each variable are calculated in the same way as outlined earlier.

To determine the trend and forecasting

The trend can be estimated by drawing a freehand line through the data on a line graph. However, these data are often subject to variations such as seasonal variations, and so this method is not very accurate. A straightforward way of overcoming this is to calculate

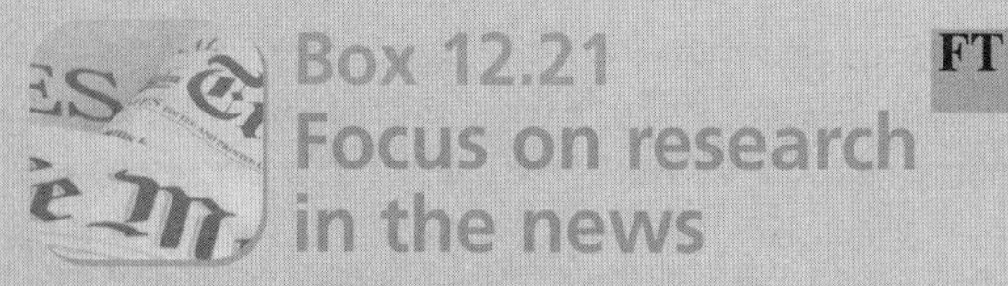

FT

Rock faces FTSE 100 exit

The most comprehensive reshuffle of the FTSE 100 index since the aftermath of the dotcom bubble is expected to be announced by index compiler FTSE today.

Seven blue-chip companies, including Northern Rock, the stricken mortgage lender, and Barratt Developments, the housebuilder, could be ejected from the index when the results of the latest quarterly reshuffle are revealed. Punch Taverns and Mitchells & Butlers, the pub operators, Daily Mail & General Trust, the newspaper publisher, DSG International, the high street retailer and Tate & Lyle, the sugar and sweeteners group that has issued several profit warnings, are also likely to lose their places.

The changes broadly reflect the impact of the credit squeeze and the expectation that the UK economy will slow sharply next year, according to analysts. In the past three months, M&B and DSG have both lost almost a quarter of their respective values as investors have fretted about waning consumer confidence, while Barratt shares have tumbled 45 per cent. The last time the FTSE 100 saw such wide-ranging changes was in September 2001 when eight companies left the index. They included IT companies Misys and CMG and telecom companies Energis, Telewest, Colt Telecom and Marconi.

Mike Lenhoff, chief strategist at Brewin Dolphin, said that although consumer-facing stocks were out of favour, further interest rate cuts would help companies such as Barratt. 'If we get the sort of rate cuts that the markets are expecting then the consumer stocks could do really well. This is also where the value lies, given how far some of these stocks have fallen,' he said.

New entrants to the FTSE 100 are expected to include Kelda Group, the water company, FirstGroup, which operates 40000 yellow school buses in the US, and TUI Group and Thomas Cook, the recently enlarged package tour operators. Cairn Energy, which was demoted from the main index this year, should also join the FTSE 100, along with Admiral, the insurer, and G4S, the security group. Meanwhile, Paragon, the specialist mortgage lender, Pendragon, the UK's largest car dealership, and Luminar, the bar and nightclub operator, are all likely to be demoted from the FTSE 250 mid cap index. Likely replacements include mining group Aricom, which recently switched its listing from Aim, Dignity, the funerals services group, and 888.com, the online gaming company.

Calculated using last night's closing prices, changes to the FTSE indices take effect after the close of business on December 21. An FTSE 100 stock is ejected if it falls to position 111 or below, while a stock must fall below position 376 for demotion from the FTSE 250 index. The changes to the index are subject to ratification by FTSE's review committee.

Source: article by Orr, Robert and Hume, Neil (2007) *Financial Times*, 12 Dec.

a moving average for the time series of data values. Calculating a **moving average** involves replacing each value in the time series with the mean of that value and those values directly preceding and following it (Morris 2003). This smoothes out the variation in the data so that you can see the trend more clearly. The calculation of a moving average is relatively straightforward using either a spreadsheet or statistical analysis software.

Once the trend has been established, it is possible to forecast future values by continuing the trend forward for time periods for which data have not been collected. This involves calculating the **long-term trend** – that is, the amount by which values are changing each time period after variations have been smoothed out. Once again, this is relatively straightforward to calculate using analysis software. Forecasting can also be undertaken using other statistical methods, including regression analysis.

If you are using regression for your time series analysis, the **Durbin-Watson statistic** can be used to discover whether the value of your dependent variable at time t is related to its value at the previous time period, commonly referred to as $t - 1$. This situation, known as **autocorrelation** or **serial correlation**, is important as it means that the results of your regression analysis are less likely to be reliable. The Durbin-Watson statistic ranges in value from zero to four. A value of two indicates no autocorrelation. A value towards zero indicates positive autocorrelation. Conversely, a value towards four indicates negative autocorrelation. More detailed discussion of the Durbin-Watson test can be found in other, more specialised books on multivariate data analysis, for example Anderson (2003).

12.6 Summary

- Data for quantitative analysis can be collected and subsequently coded at different scales of measurement. The data type (precision of measurement) will constrain the data presentation, summary and analysis techniques you can use.
- Data are entered for computer analysis as a data matrix in which each column usually represents a variable and each row a case. Your first variable should be a unique identifier to facilitate error checking.
- All data should, with few exceptions, be recorded using numerical codes to facilitate analyses.
- Where possible, you should use existing coding schemes to enable comparisons.
- For primary data you should include pre-set codes on the data collection form to minimise coding after collection. For variables where responses are not known, you will need to develop a codebook after data have been collected for the first 50 to 100 cases.
- You should enter codes for all data values, including missing data.
- Your data matrix must be checked for errors.
- Your initial analysis should explore data using both tables and diagrams. Your choice of table or diagram will be influenced by your research question(s) and objectives, the aspects of the data you wish to emphasise, and the scale of measurement at which the data were recorded. This may involve using:
  - tables to show specific values;
  - bar charts, multiple bar charts, histograms and, occasionally, pictograms to show highest and lowest values;
  - line graphs to show trends;
  - pie charts and percentage component bar charts to show proportions;
  - box plots to show distributions;
  - scatter graphs to show relationships between variables.
- Subsequent analyses will involve describing your data and exploring relationships using statistics. As before, your choice of statistics will be influenced by your research question(s) and objectives and the scale of measurement at which the data were recorded. Your analysis may involve using statistics such as:
  - the mean, median and mode to describe the central tendency;
  - the inter-quartile range and the standard deviation to describe the dispersion;
  - chi square, Cramer's V and phi to test whether two variables are significantly associated;
  - Kolmogorov-Smirnov to test whether the values differ significantly from a specified population;
  - *t*-tests and ANOVA to test whether groups are significantly different;
  - correlation and regression to assess the strength of relationships between variables;
  - regression analysis to predict values.
- Longitudinal data may necessitate selecting different statistical techniques such as:
  - index numbers to establish a trend or to compare trends between two or more variables measured in different units or at different magnitudes;
  - moving averages and regression analysis to determine the trend and forecast.

Self-check questions

Help with these questions is available at the end of the chapter.

12.1 The following secondary data have been obtained from the Park Trading Company's audited annual accounts:

Year end	Income	Expenditure
2000	11000000	9500000
2001	15200000	12900000
2002	17050000	14000000
2003	17900000	14900000
2004	19000000	16100000
2005	18700000	17200000
2006	17100000	18100000
2007	17700000	19500000
2008	19900000	20000000

a Which are the variables and which are the cases?
b Sketch a possible data matrix for these data for entering into a spreadsheet.

12.2 a How many variables will be generated from the following request?

Please tell me up to five things you like about this film. For office use

.... ❑❑❑
.... ❑❑❑
.... ❑❑❑
.... ❑❑❑
.... ❑❑❑

b How would you go about devising a coding scheme for these variables from a survey of 500 cinema patrons?

12.3 a Illustrate the data from the Park Trading Company's audited annual accounts (self-check question 12.1) to show trends in income and expenditure.
b What does your diagram emphasise?
c What diagram would you use to emphasise the years with the lowest and highest income?

12.4 As part of research into the impact of television advertising on donations by credit card to a major disaster appeal, data have been collected on the number of viewers reached and the number of donations each day for the past two weeks.
a Which diagram or diagrams would you use to explore these data?
b Give reasons for your choice.

12.5 a Which measures of central tendency and dispersion would you choose to describe the Park Trading Company's income (self-check question 12.1) over the period 2000–2008?
b Give reasons for your choice.

12.6 A colleague has collected data from a sample of 80 students. He presents you with the following output from the statistical analysis software:

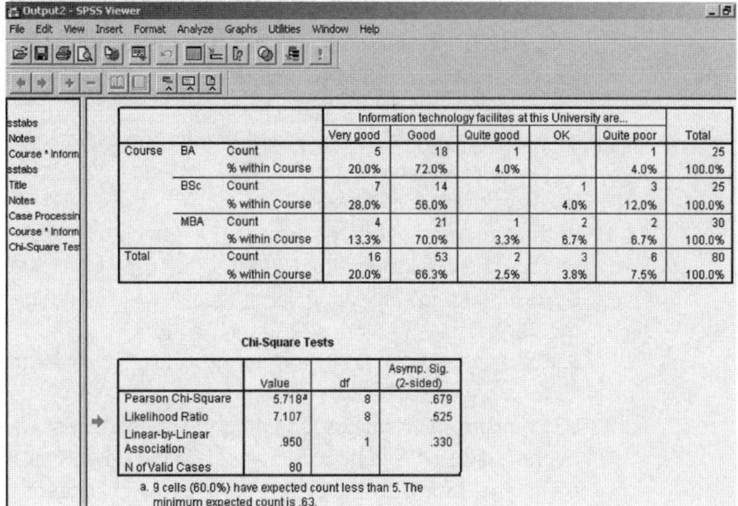

			Information technology facilites at this University are...					
			Very good	Good	Quite good	OK	Quite poor	Total
Course	BA	Count	5	18	1		1	25
		% within Course	20.0%	72.0%	4.0%		4.0%	100.0%
	BSc	Count	7	14		1	3	25
		% within Course	28.0%	56.0%		4.0%	12.0%	100.0%
	MBA	Count	4	21	1	2	2	30
		% within Course	13.3%	70.0%	3.3%	6.7%	6.7%	100.0%
Total		Count	16	53	2	3	6	80
		% within Course	20.0%	66.3%	2.5%	3.8%	7.5%	100.0%

Chi-Square Tests

	Value	df	Asymp. Sig. (2-sided)
Pearson Chi-Square	5.718[a]	8	.679
Likelihood Ratio	7.107	8	.525
Linear-by-Linear Association	.950	1	.330
N of Valid Cases	80		

a. 9 cells (60.0%) have expected count less than 5. The minimum expected count is .63.

Explain what this tells you about undergraduate and postgraduate students' opinion of the information technology facilities.

12.7 Briefly describe when you would use regression analysis and correlation analysis, using examples to illustrate your answer.

12.8 **a** Use an appropriate technique to compare the following data on share prices for two financial service companies over the past six months, using the period six months ago as the base period:

	EJ Investment Holdings	AE Financial Services
Price 6 months ago	€10	€587
Price 4 months ago	€12	€613
Price 2 months ago	€13	€658
Current price	€14	€690

b Which company's share prices have increased most in the last six months? (Note: you should quote relevant statistics to justify your answer.)

Review and discussion questions

12.9 Use a search engine to discover coding schemes that already exist for ethnic group, family expenditure, industry group, socio-economic class and the like. To do this you will probably find it best to type the phrase "coding ethnic group" into the search box.

a Discuss how credible you think each coding scheme is with a friend. To come to an agreed answer pay particular attention to:
- the organisation (or person) that is responsible for the coding scheme;
- any explanations regarding the coding scheme's design;
- use of the coding scheme to date.

b Widen your search to include coding schemes that may be of use for your research project. Make a note of the web address of any that are of interest.

12.10 With a friend, choose a large company in which you are interested. Obtain a copy of the annual report for this company. If it is not readily available via the Internet, hard copy can often be obtained from your university library. Examine the use of tables, graphs and charts in your chosen company's report.

- **a** To what extent does the use of graphs and charts in your chosen report follow the guidance summarised in Box 12.8 and Table 12.2?
- **b** Why do you think this is?

12.11 With a group of friends, each choose a different share price index. Well-known indices you could chose include the Nasdaq Composite Index, France's CAC 40, Germany's Xetra Dax, Hong Kong's HIS-Hang Seng, Japan's Nikkei Average Index, the UK's FTSE 100 and the USA's Dow Jones Industrial Average Index.

- **a** For each of the indices, find out how it is calculated and note down its daily values for a one-week period.
- **b** Compare your findings regarding the calculation of your chosen index with those for the indices chosen by your friends, noting down similarities and differences.
- **c** To what extent do the indices differ in the changes in share prices they show? Why do you think this is?

12.12 Find out whether your university provides you with access to SPSS. If it does, visit this book's companion website and download the self-teach package and associated data sets. Work through this to explore the features of SPSS.

Progressing your research project

Analysing your data quantitatively

- Examine the technique(s) you are proposing to use to collect data to answer your research question. You need to decide whether you are collecting any data that could usefully be analysed quantitatively.
- If you decide that your data should be analysed quantitatively, you must ensure that the data collection methods you intend to use have been designed to make analysis by computer as straightforward as possible. In particular, you need to pay attention to the coding scheme for each variable and the layout of your data matrix.
- Once your data have been entered into a computer and the dataset opened in your analysis software, you will need to explore and present them. Bearing your research question in mind, you should select the most appropriate diagrams and tables after considering the suitability of all possible techniques. Remember to label your diagrams clearly and to keep an electronic copy, as they may form part of your research report.
- Once you are familiar with your data, describe and explore relationships using those statistical techniques that best help you to answer your research questions and are suitable for the data type. Remember to keep an annotated copy of your analyses, as you will need to quote statistics to justify statements you make in the findings section of your research report.

References

Anderson, T.W. (2003) *An Introduction to Multivariate Statistical Analysis.* New York: John Wiley.

Anderson, D.R., Sweeney, D.J. and Williams, T.A. (1999) *Statistics for Business and Economics* (7th edn). Cincinnati, OH: South-Western College Publishing.

Berman Brown, R. and Saunders, M. (2008) *Dealing with statistics: What You Need to Know.* Maidenhead: McGraw-Hill Open University Press.

Blumberg, B., Cooper, D.R. and Schindler, D.S. (2008) *Business Research Methods.* Maidenhead: McGraw-Hill.

Cohen, L. and Holliday, M. (1996) *Practical Statistics for Students.* London: Paul Chapman.

Curwin, J. and Slater, R. (2007) *Quantitative Methods: A Short Course*. London: Thomson Learning EMEA.

Dancey, C.P. and Reidy, J. (2008) *Statistics Without Maths for Psychology: Using SPSS for Windows* (4th edn). Harlow: Prentice Hall.

deVaus, D.A. (2002) *Surveys in Social Research* (5th edn). London: Routledge.

Diamantopoulos, A. and Schlegelmilch, B.B. (1997) *Taking the Fear Out of Data Analysis.* London: Dryden Press.

Eurostat (2007) 'Environment and energy statistics – data air emissions'. Available at: http://epp.eurostat.cec.eu.int/portal/page?_pageid=1090,30070682,1090_30298591&_dad=portal&_schema=PORTAL [Accessed 16 December 2007.]

Everitt, B.S. and Dunn, G. (2001) *Applied Multivariate Data Analysis* (2nd edn). London: Arnold.

Field, A. (2005) *Discovering Statistics Using SPSS* (2nd edn). London: Sage.

Great Britain Office for National Statistics (2000a) *Standard Occupation Classification Volume 1: Structure and Description of Unit Groups.* London: Stationery Office.

Great Britain Office for National Statistics (2000b) *Standard Occupation Classification Volume 2: The Coding Index.* London: Stationery Office.

Great Britain Office for National Statistics (2002) *Index to the UK Standard Industrial Classification of Economic Activities 2003, UK SIC (2003).* London: Stationery Office.

Hair, J.F., Black, B., Babin, B., Anderson, R.E. and Tatham, R.L. (2006) *Multivariate Data Analysis* (6th edn). Harlow: Pearson Education.

Harley-Davidson (2007) *Harley-Davidson Inc. 2006 Summary Annual Report.* Available at: http://www.harley-davidson.com/wcm/Content/Pages/Investor_Relations/2006_annual_report_launch.jsp?HDCWPSession=9Sv1LnXZHD7LNcXLTPZ4r2kHNryQn1cjl5hbyQjGtJ8SrswTgltt!1509673641!1097132701&locale=en_US [Accessed 16 December 2007.]

Hays, W.L. (1994) *Statistics* (4th edn). London: Holt-Saunders.

Heath, A., Martin, J. and Beerton, R. (2003) 'Old and new social class measures', in D. Rose and D.J. Pevalin (eds) *A Researcher's Guide to the National Statistics Socio-economic Classification.* London: Sage, pp. 226–43.

Henry, G.T. (1995) *Graphing Data: Techniques for Display and Analysis.* Thousand Oaks, CA: Sage.

Kanji, G.K. (2006) *100 Statistical Tests* (3rd edn). London: Sage.

Kinnear, P.R. and Gray, C.D. (2007) *SPSS 15 Made Simple*. Hove: Psychology Press.

Morris, C. (2003) *Quantitative Approaches in Business Studies* (6th edn). Harlow: Financial Times Prentice Hall.

Norusis, M.J. (2007) *SPSS 15 Guide to Data Analysis*. London: Prentice Hall.

Park, A., Curtice, J., Thomson, K., Phillips, M., Johnson M. and Clery, E. (2007) *British Social Attitudes: 24th Report.* London: Sage.

Push. (2007) 'Push reveals the real costs of higher education'. Available at: http://www.push.co.uk/Document.aspx?id=9E3FCB0D-7275-4BF3-BFA4-8AEEF1D847D1§ion=&l2section [Accessed 16 December 2007.]

Robson, C. (2002) *Real World Research* (2nd edn). Oxford: Blackwell.

Rose, D. and Pevalin, D.J. (2003) 'The NS-SEC explained', in D. Rose and D.J. Pevalin (eds) *A Researcher's Guide to the National Statistics Socio-economic Classification*. London: Sage, pp. 28–43.

Schneider, L.-P. and Cornwell, T.B. (2005) 'Cashing in on crashes via brand placement in computer games', *International Journal of Advertising*, Vol. 24, No. 3, pp. 321–43.

Smith, A. (2002) 'The new ethnicity classification in the Labour Force Survey', *Labour Market Trends*, Dec., pp. 657–66.

Snap Surveys (2008) Snap Surveys home page. Available at: http://www.snapsurveys.com [Accessed 1 January 2008.]

Sparrow, J. (1989) 'Graphic displays in information systems: some data properties influencing the effectiveness of alternate forms', *Behaviour and Information Technology*, Vol. 8, No. 1, pp. 43–56.

Sphinx (2008) Sphinx data analysis and survey softwares. Available at: http://www.lesphinx-developpement.fr/en/home/home_sphinx.php [Accessed 1 January 2008.]

Tukey, J.W. (1977) *Exploratory Data Analysis.* Reading, MA: Addison-Wesley.

Yen. T.-Y. and André, P. (2007) 'Ownership structure and operating performance of acquiring firms: the case of English-origin countries', *Journal of Economics and Business*, Vol. 59, No. 5, pp. 380–405.

Further Reading

Berman Brown, R. and Saunders, M. (2008) ***Dealing with statistics: What you need to know.*** **Maidenhead: McGraw Hill Open University Press.** This is a statistics book that assumes virtually no statistical knowledge focusing upon which test or graph, when to use it and why. It is written for people who are fearful and anxious about statistics and do not think they can understand numbers!

Blastland, M. and Dilnot, A. (2007) ***The Tiger than Isn't.*** **London: Profile Books.** This is a very different type of book on statistics. Rather than explaining how to calculate different statistics it explains how to make sense of the numbers and statistics which we are confronted with in the news media and other publications. It is well worth reading and will almost certainly help you to better understand and interpret numbers and statistics.

Dancey, C.P. and Reidy, J. (2008) ***Statistics Without Maths for Psychology: Using SPSS for Windows*** **(4th edn). Harlow: Prentice Hall.** This book introduces key statistical concepts and techniques, avoiding as much maths as possible. It also provides clear descriptions of how to perform statistical tests using SPSS and how to report your results both graphically and in texts.

deVaus, D.A. (2002) ***Surveys in Social Research*** **(5th edn). London: Routledge.** Chapters 9 and 10 contain an excellent discussion about coding data and preparing data for analysis. Part IV (Chapters 12–18) provides a detailed discussion of how to analyse survey data.

Field, A. (2005). ***Discovering Statistics Using SPSS*** **(2nd edn). London: Sage.** This book offers a clearly explained guide to statistics and using SPSS for Windows. It is divided into four levels, the lowest of which assumes no familiarity with the data analysis software and very little with statistics. It covers inputting data and how to generate and interpret a wide range of tables, diagrams and statistics using SPSS version 13. If you are using an earlier version of SPSS, particularly pre-version 9, be sure to use a book written specifically for that version as there are a number of changes between versions.

Hair, J.F., Black, B., Babin, B., Anderson, R.E. and Tatham, R.L. (2006) ***Multivariate Data Analysis.*** **(6th edn). Harlow: Pearson Education.** This book provides detailed information on statistical concepts and techniques. Issues pertinent to design, assumptions, estimation and interpretation are systematically explained for users of more advanced statistical techniques.

Morris, C. (2003) ***Quantitative Approaches in Business Studies.*** **(6th edn). Harlow, Financial Times Prentice Hall.** This gives a clear introduction to the use of mathematical and statistical techniques and diagrams in business. Guidance is given on using the Excel spreadsheet.

Case 12
Small business owner managers' skill sets

Since arriving at university, Ishmael had become increasingly interested in small businesses. He had taken all the modules concerned with Small Businesses and Entrepreneurship and chosen to answer a question about small business owner managers for his research project:

'How important do small business owner managers consider the different skill sets needed to run a small business and why?'

Although the project tutor had felt Ishmael's question needed more refinement and suggested that he needed to read widely before collecting any data, Ishmael was pleased with his research question and his method. During his reading to prepare his research proposal he had come across a paper by Brown *et al.* (2006) in the journal *Accounting Forum*. This included, as an appendix, the questions Brown and colleagues had asked small business managers in their questionnaire. He had decided to adapt some of these questions for his own Internet-mediated questionnaire that he administered to small business managers including:

Entrepreneurial Skills — Exit this survey

3. How confident are you in your skills in the following areas?

	5 - very confident	4	3	2	1 - not at all confident
Marketing and sales					
Interpersonal					
Financial/accounts					
Managerial					
Business planning					
IT					
Time management					
Technical (e.g. plumbing skills for plumber)					

4. How important do you think each of the following skills is in running your business at the moment?

	5 - very confident	4	3	2	1 - not at all confident
Marketing and sales					
Interpersonal					
Financial/accounts					
Managerial					
Business planning					
IT					
Time management					
Technical (e.g. plumbing skills for plumber)					

Source: question layout created by SurveyMonkey.com (2008), Portland, Oregon, USA; author/owner: Ryan Finley. Reproduced with permission.

In his initial analysis, Ishmael used SPSS to produce a set of descriptive statistics for each of his questions. For questions three and four these were:

Descriptive Statistics

	N	Minimum	Maximum	Mean	Std. Deviation
3 Confidence in own skills in marketing and sales	96	1	5	3.44	1.074
3 Confidence in own skills in interpersonal	96	2	5	4.06	.723
3 Confidence in own skills in financial/accounts	96	1	5	3.10	.989
3 Confidence in own skills in managerial	96	0	5	3.60	.864
3 Confidence in own skills in business planning	96	1	5	3.17	.959
3 Confidence in own skills in IT	96	1	5	3.39	1.137
3 Confidence in own skills in technical (e.g plumbing skills for plumber)	96	0	5	4.02	1.095
3 Confidence in own skills in time management	96	1	5	3.28	.879
4 Importance of skills in running business-marketing/selling	96	1	5	4.49	.951
4 Importance of skills in running business-interpersonal	96	0	5	4.06	1.177
4 Importance of skills in running business-financial/accounts	96	2	5	3.83	1.002
4 Importance of skills in running business-managerial	96	0	5	3.55	1.141
4 Importance of skills in running business-business planning	96	0	5	4.18	.962
4 Importance of skills in running business-IT	96	0	5	3.35	1.222
4 Importance of skills in running business-technical (e.g. plumbing for plumber)	96	0	5	4.15	1.026
4 Importance of skills in running business-time management	96	1	5	4.05	.863
Valid N (listwise)	96				

He then decided to see if his respondents' perceived confidence in their own skills was related to their perceived importance for each of these skills. Because Ishmael was uncertain as to which statistics to use to examine possible relationships, he used SPSS to both calculate correlation coefficients and to undertake a series of chi square tests:

Correlations

Correlations

		3 Confidence in own skills in marketing and sales	3 Confidence in own skills in interpersonal	3 Confidence in own skills in financial /accounts	4 Importance of skills in running business -marketing /selling	4 Importance of skills in running business -interpersonal	4 Importance of skills in running business -financial /accounts
3 Confidence in own skills in marketing and sales	Pearson Correlation	1	.303**	.056	.241*	−.030	.049
	Sig. (2-tailed)		.003	.590	.018	.770	.636
	N	96	96	96	96	96	96
3 Confidence in own skills in interpersonal	Pearson Correlation	.303**	1	−.068	.047	.119	−.029
	Sig. (2-tailed)	.003		.510	.650	.248	.779
	N	96	96	96	96	96	96
3 Confidence in own skills in financial/accounts	Pearson Correlation	.056	−.068	1	.225*	−.177	−.014
	Sig. (2-tailed)	.590	.510		.028	.084	.891
	N	96	96	96	96	96	96
4 Importance of skills in running business -marketing/selling	Pearson Correlation	.241*	.047	.225*	1	.076	.109
	Sig. (2-tailed)	.018	.650	.028		.463	.292
	N	96	96	96	96	96	96
4 Importance of skills in running business -interpersonal	Pearson Correlation	−.030	.119	−.177	.076	1	.321**
	Sig. (2-tailed)	.770	.248	.084	.463		.001
	N	96	96	96	96	96	96
4 Importance of skills in running business -financial/accounts	Pearson Correlation	.049	−.029	−.014	.109	.321**	1
	Sig. (2-tailed)	.636	.779	.891	.292	.001	
	N	96	96	96	96	96	96

**. Correlation is significant at the 0.01 level (2-tailed).

*. Correlation is significant at the 0.05 level (2-tailed).

Ishmael showed a friend his questionnaire and the SPSS output from his preliminary analysis relating to questions three and four. Over a cup of coffee he asked for advice regarding the analysis of his data. In the subsequent discussion Ishmael emphasised that, as part of the assessment criteria for his research project, he would need to explain why he had chosen to use particular statistics and diagrams.

3 Confidence in own skills in marketing and sales * 4 Importance of skills in running business–marketing/selling

Chi-Square Tests

	Value	df	Asymp. Sig. (2-sided)
Pearson Chi-Square	32.603[a]	16	.008
Likelihood Ratio	22.958	16	.115
Linear-by-Linear Association	5.536	1	.019
N of Valid Cases	96		

a. 20 cells (80.0%) have expected count less than 5. The minimum expected count is .08.

3 Confidence in own skills in marketing and sales * 4 Importance of skills in running business–interpersonal

Chi-Square Tests

	Value	df	Asymp. Sig. (2-sided)
Pearson Chi-Square	16.662[a]	20	.675
Likelihood Ratio	16.736	20	.670
Linear-by-Linear Association	.087	1	.769
N of Valid Cases	96		

a. 23 cells (76.7%) have expected count less than 5. The minimum expected count is .04.

References

Brown, R.B., Saunders, M.N.K., and Beresford, R. (2006) 'You owe it to yourselves: the financially literate manager', *Accounting Forum*, Vol. 30, No. 2, pp. 179–91.

SurveyMonkey.com (2008) SurveyMonkey.com. Available at: http://www.surveymonkey.com [Accessed 29 June 2008.]

Questions

1 Ishmael appears uncertain regarding his choice of statistics (the mean and standard deviation) in the first table to describe the responses to questions 3 and 4.
   a How would you advise him?
   b What diagrams would you suggest Ishmael uses to present the data from these questions?
2 Examine the remaining two extracts reporting correlation coefficients and chi square tests. Should Ishmael use either the Pearson's product moment correlation coefficients or the chi square tests as reported in these extracts?
3 Ishmael has decided to undertake further statistical analyses to see if there is any relationship between his respondents' perceived confidence in their own skills and their perceived importance for the same set of skills. Outline the analysis process you would recommend including, if necessary, any further work that might be needed to satisfy your chosen test's assumptions.

Additional case studies relating to material covered in this chapter are available via the book's Companion Website, **www.pearsoned.co.uk/saunders**. They are:

- The marketing of arts festivals
- Marketing a golf course
- The impact of family ownership on financial performance.

Self-check answers

12.1 a The variables are 'income', 'expenditure' and 'year'. There is no real need for a separate case identifier as the variable 'year' can also fulfil this function. Each case (year) is represented by one row of data.

b When the data are entered into a spreadsheet the first column will be the case identifier, for these data the year. Income and expenditure should not be entered with the £ sign as this can be formatted subsequently using the spreadsheet:

	A	B	C
1	*Year*	*Income (£)*	*Expenditure (£)*
2	2000	11000000	9500000
3	2001	15200000	12900000
4	2002	17050000	14000000
5	2003	17900000	14900000
6	2004	19000000	16100000
7	2005	18700000	17200000
8	2006	17100000	18100000
9	2007	17700000	19500000
10	2008	19900000	20000000

12.2 a There is no one correct answer to this question as the number of variables will depend on the method used to code these descriptive data. If you choose the multiple response method, five variables will be generated. If the multiple dichotomy method is used the number of variables will depend on the number of different responses.

b Your first priority is to decide on the level of detail of your intended analyses. Your coding scheme should, if possible, be based on an existing coding scheme. If this is of insufficient detail then it should be designed to be compatible to allow comparisons. To design the coding scheme you need to take the responses from the first 50–100 cases and establish broad groupings. These can be subdivided into increasingly specific subgroups until the detail is sufficient for the intended analysis. Codes can then be allocated to these sub-groups. If you ensure that similar responses receive adjacent codes, this will make any subsequent grouping easier. The actual responses that correspond to each code should be noted in a codebook. Codes should be allocated to data on the data collection form in the 'For office use' box. These codes need to include missing data, such as when four or fewer 'things' have been mentioned.

12.3 a Park Trading Company – Income and Expenditure 2000–08

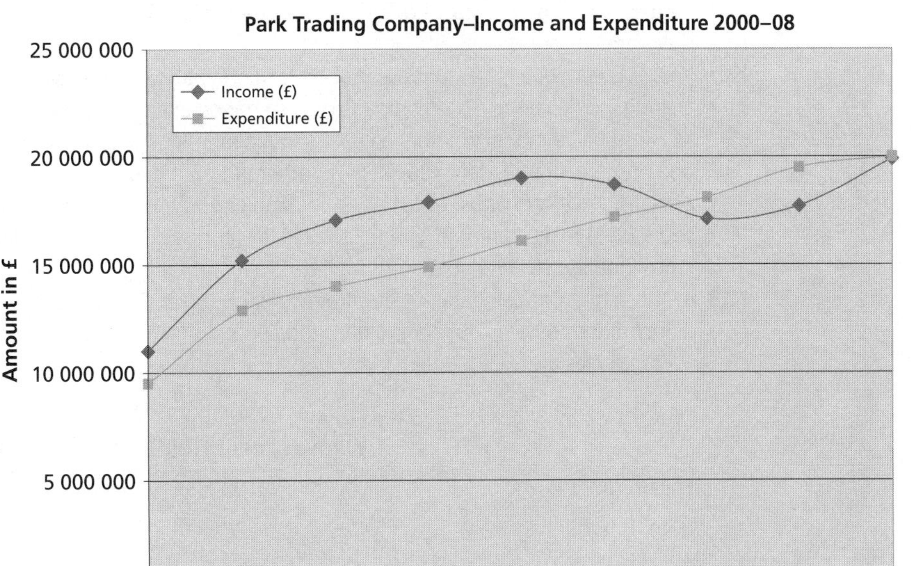

b Your diagram (it is hoped) emphasises the upward trends of expenditure and (to a lesser extent) income. It also highlights the conjunction where income falls below expenditure in 2006.

c To emphasise the years with the lowest and highest income, you would probably use a histogram because the data are continuous. A frequency polygon would also be suitable.

12.4 a You would probably use a scatter graph in which number of donations would be the dependent variable and number of viewers reached by the advertisement the independent variable.

b This would enable you to see whether there was any relationship between number of viewers reached and number of donations.

12.5 a The first thing you need to do is to establish the data type. As it is numerical, you could theoretically use all three measures of central tendency and both the standard deviation and inter-quartile range. However, you would probably calculate the mean and perhaps the median as measures of central tendency and the standard deviation and perhaps the inter-quartile range as measures of dispersion.

b The mean would be chosen because it includes all data values. The median might be chosen to represent the middle income over the 2000–08 period. The mode would be of little use for these data as each year has different income values.

If you had chosen the mean you would probably choose the standard deviation, as this describes the dispersion of data values around the mean. The inter-quartile range is normally chosen where there are extreme data values that need to be ignored. This is not the case for these data.

12.6 The probability of a chi square value of 5.718 with 8 degrees of freedom occurring by chance alone for these data is 0.679. This means that statistically the association between type of student and their opinion of the information technology facilities is extremely likely to be explained by chance alone. In addition, the assumption of the chi square test that no more than 20 per cent of expected values should be less than 5 has not been satisfied.

To explore this lack of association further, you examine the cell values in relation to the row and column totals. For all courses, over 80 per cent of respondents thought the information technology facilities were good or very good. The only course where respondents felt information technology facilities were poor was the BSc, but this represented only three respondents.

12.7 Your answer needs to emphasise that correlation analysis is used to establish whether a change in one variable is accompanied by a change in another. In contrast, regression analysis is used to establish whether a change in a dependent variable is caused by changes in one or more independent variables – in other words, a cause-and-effect relationship. Although it is impossible to list all the examples you might use to illustrate your answer, you should make sure that your examples for regression illustrate a dependent and one or more independent variables.

12.8 **a** These quantitative data are of different magnitudes. Therefore, the most appropriate technique to compare these data is index numbers. The index numbers for the two companies are:

	EJ Investment Holdings	**AE Financial Services**
Price 6 months ago	100	100.0
Price 4 months ago	120	104.4
Price 2 months ago	130	112.1
Current price	140	117.5

b The price of AE Financial Services' shares has increased by €103 compared with an increase of €4 for EJ Investment Holdings' share price. However, the proportional increase in prices has been greatest for EJ Investment Holdings. Using six months ago as the base period (with a base index number of 100), the index for EJ Investment Holdings' share price is now 140 while the index for AE Financial Services' share price is 117.5.

Get ahead using resources on the Companion Website at:
www.pearsoned.co.uk/saunders

- Improve your SPSS and NVivo research analysis with practice tutorials.
- Save time researching on the Internet with the Smarter Online Searching Guide.
- Test your progress using self-assessment questions.
- Follow live links to useful websites.

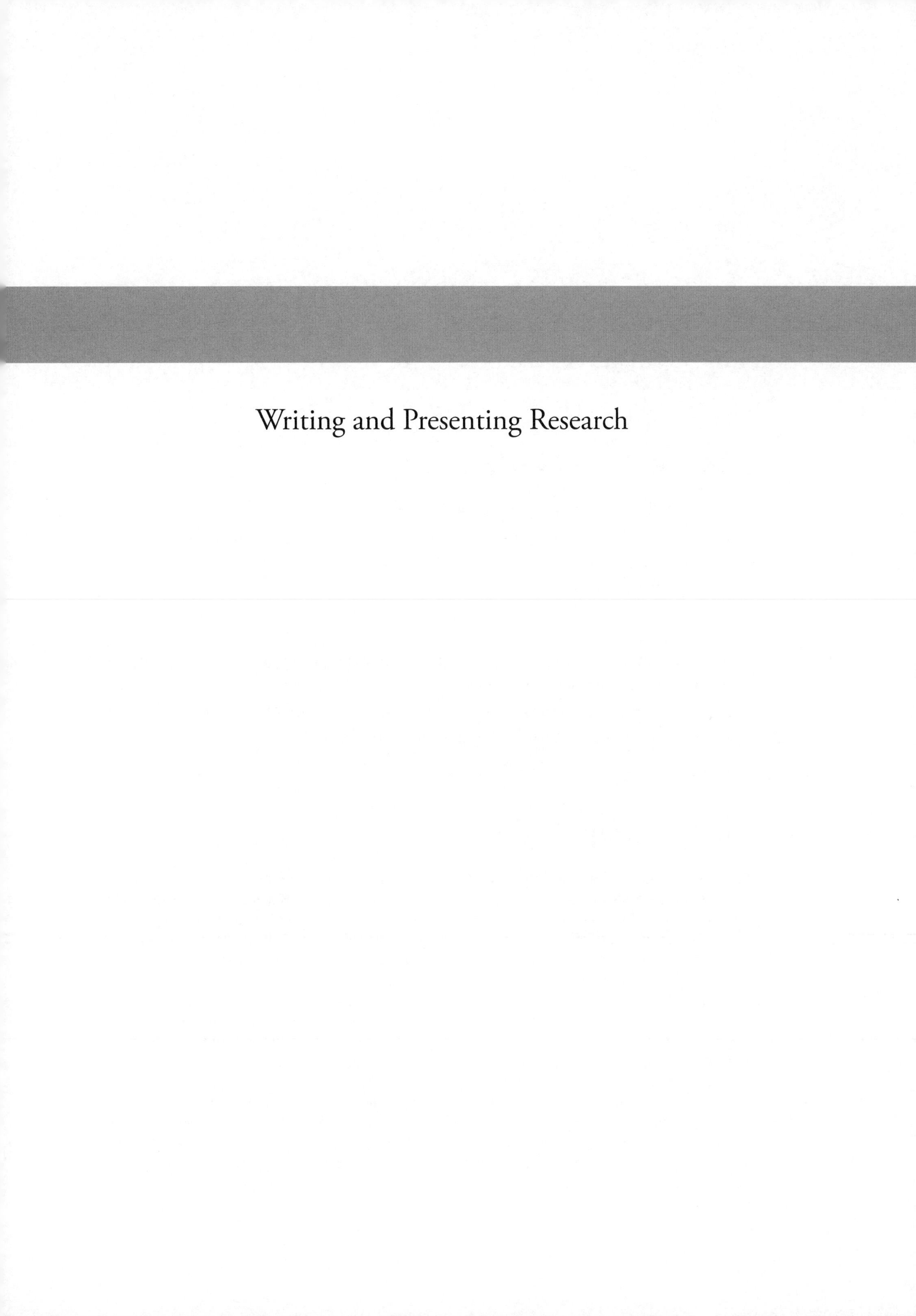

Writing and Presenting Research

Chapter 14

Writing and presenting your project report

Learning outcomes

By the end of this chapter you should be able to:

- view the writing of the final project report as an exciting prospect;
- write in such a way that you can reflect on all you have learned while conducting the research;
- write a final project report that presents an authoritative account of your research;
- adopt an appropriate format, structure and style for the final project report;
- differentiate between a project report and a consultancy report;
- ensure that your report meets the necessary assessment criteria;
- plan and design an oral presentation of your report.

14.1 Introduction

Some of you may view the process of writing your **project report** and presenting it orally as an exciting prospect. However, it is more likely that you will approach this stage of your research with a mixture of resignation and trepidation. This is a great pity. We believe that writing about your work is the most effective way of clarifying your thoughts. This suggests that writing should not be seen as the last stage of your research but thought of as something that is continuous throughout the research process.

Writing is a powerful way of learning (Griffiths 1993). Most teachers will tell you that the best way to learn is to teach. This is because of the necessity to understand something thoroughly yourself before you can begin to explain it to others. This is the position you are in as the writer of your project report. You have to explain a highly complex set of ideas and facts to an audience that you must assume has little or no knowledge of your subject. There is another problem here, which has a parallel with teaching. Often, the more familiar you are with a subject, the more difficult it is to explain it to others with no knowledge of that subject. You will be so familiar with your subject that, like the teacher, you will find it difficult to put yourself in the place of the reader. The result of this is that you may fail to explain something that you assume the reader will know. Even worse, you may leave out important material that should be included.

However, why do most of us view writing with such concern? Veroff (2001) argues that much of this is rooted in the experience we have of writing. Many of us are afraid of exposing our efforts to an audience that we feel will be more likely to criticise than encourage. In our education much of our writing has been little more than rehashing the ideas of others. This has taught us to think of writing as a boring, repetitive process. Some of us are impatient. We are unwilling to devote the time and energy (and inevitable frustration) that is needed for writing.

This fear of criticism is captured perfectly by Richards (1986), who recites the story of being asked by the distinguished sociologist Howard Becker to adopt his method of sitting down and writing what came into her head about the research she had done without even consulting her notes. Her fears of producing poor-quality material, which would be derided by colleagues who saw her work, are described vividly. It is a fear most of us experience.

We agree with Phillips and Pugh (2005), who note that writing is the only time when we really think. This suggests that writing your project report is something that should not be left until every other part of your research has been completed. However, there will be more on that in the next section.

We all write a lot more than we think. We email; send endless numbers of text messages on our mobile phones; add comments to conversations on web pages. Now many of us are becoming 'bloggers'. A **blog**, or **web log**, is a written account of a mixture of what is happening in a person's life and what is happening on the Internet, published on the Internet. It's a kind of hybrid diary/guide website, although there are as many unique types of blogs as there are people.

Blogging is an exciting way to publish on the Internet. You can share pictures, video, links, documents, newsletters, opinions and more, with family and friends. You can have a website without being a webmaster. There is no HTML to learn and no new software to download and install. Unlike traditional websites, web logs give you the opportunity to connect with others because they are a conversation rather than a billboard. You post content – others can post their responses. Moreover, privacy is not an issue. You control who is authorised to view personal photos or confidential documents by placing them in a private viewing area. Blogging will even allow you to ban undesirable users.

An everyday scene in New York, which could be the content of a photo blog
Source: © Ben Saunders 2008.

You can compose blogs on any topic you choose: travel (see photo), your hobby, photography, your family or even your research project! Above all, it's a great way to get writing!

For many of us the fear of making an oral presentation is even more daunting. As we note in Section 14.7, some of this apprehension can be overcome by thorough preparation. But at least you have the consolation of knowing that you will be an expert in your topic.

In this chapter we begin (Section 14.2) by looking at issues concerned with getting started in the writing process including the importance of generating a plan. Sections 14.3 and 14.4 are devoted to the core issues of writing your project report – structure and content and explain the differences between a project report and a consultancy report. We then consider the topic of writing style (Section 14.5) before examining how to meet the assessment criteria (Section 14.6). The chapter ends (Section 14.7) with a look at the preparation and delivery of the oral presentation.

14.2 Getting started with writing

If writing is synonymous with thinking, it follows that writing is something you should do throughout the whole research process. Chapter 2 emphasises the need for clear ideas in writing about research questions and objectives. If you have done this already you will know the difficulty of committing your vague ideas to paper and amending them continually until they express your ideas with brevity, clarity and accuracy. However, there is no reason why your research proposal and plan should be the last writing you do before you finally write up your research in the project report. We encourage you to write as a continual process throughout the research.

Many researchers find it helpful to write the literature review early on in their research. This has clear benefits. It gets you writing on a part of the research process that necessarily comes early in that process. Also, it focuses your thinking on the way in which the literature will inform the research strategy you adopt. You will be pleased you wrote this part of the report when the time pressure is on as the submission deadline for your report approaches. Do not worry that early writing of the literature review means that subsequently published relevant literature is ignored in your review. It can always be incorporated at a later date. This is one of the advantages of using word processing, a topic that we shall cover later in this section.

Having discouraged you from thinking of writing as a process you leave until the end of your research, this section goes on to consider a number of practical hints to assist you to get started.

Create time for your writing

Writing is not an activity that can be allocated an odd half-hour whenever it is convenient. It requires sustained concentration. The amount of time needed to make real progress in your writing is dependent on the way in which you prefer to work. Most people find that it takes at least a day to write about 2000 words, but we all work in different ways. Once some people have started, they prefer to continue until they drop from exhaustion! Others like to set a strict timetable where three or four hours a day are devoted to writing. Whichever category you are in, make sure that you have time for writing allocated in your diary. We have found that it is helpful to have blocks of time where writing can take place on successive days. This ensures a degree of continuity of ideas, which is not as easy if you keep having to 'think your way back' into your research.

Write when your mind is fresh

We have emphasised so far in this chapter that writing should be a highly creative process. It is important, therefore, that you write at the time of day when your mind is at its freshest. All of us have jobs to do during the day that require little or no creativity. Arrange your day so that the uncreative jobs are done in the time when you are at your least mentally alert.

Find a regular writing place

Most of us have one place where we do our writing. It is so important that we often cannot write in unfamiliar surroundings. If this is the case with you it is essential that you combine this psychological comfort with a few practical features of your writing place that will enhance your productivity. One of the most important of these is to ensure that you are not interrupted. A simple 'do not disturb' sign on the door usually works wonders. You may, like Phil, find a telephone-answering service useful. Remove all distractions, such as television, magazines and computer games, from the room. It may be that you need background noise, even your MP3 player, to help you concentrate. One person's distractions are another person's necessities. What is important is to know what distracts you and to remove those distractions.

Set goals and achieve them

This is the height of self-discipline. Most writers set themselves targets for the period of writing. Usually this is a set number of words. It is better to be realistic about these goals. If you are too ambitious the quality of your work may suffer as you rush to meet the goal. You may be as self-disciplined as Mark, who sets himself sub-goals during the day and rewards the achievement of these goals with coffee breaks. What is important is that you see this as entering into a contract with yourself. If you break this contract by not meeting your goal, you are the one who should feel guilty. You may like to enter into a similar arrangement with a close friend on the understanding that each of you will insist on the other meeting your goals.

Use word processing

Word processing has revolutionised writing (Box 14.1). There are still some who prefer to write longhand before word-processing the final report. However, for those of us who 'think onto the screen' the main advantage of word processing is that it enables us to keep

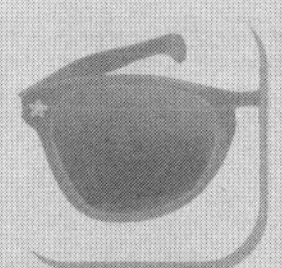

Box 14.1
Focus on student research

Using word processing to transcribe field notes to the final project report

Phil made interview notes in longhand during the interviews that he conducted with managers about the pay system in their organisations. He was particularly careful to note verbatim especially relevant comments from the managers.

Phil ensured that he word-processed these notes, either on his laptop on the return train journey at the end of the day, or at home in the evening.

When writing the project report, Phil found the word-processed notes invaluable. He wanted to use some of the verbatim quotes to illustrate key arguments that he was developing from the data. He was able to insert many of these into the report, thus saving time and ensuring accuracy of transcription.

amending copy without having to fill the waste paper basket with numerous unsatisfactory attempts. In addition, word processing enables you to keep updating your project report as you develop new ideas or become dissatisfied with old ones. There is, however, a potential problem here. The ease with which you can keep inserting and deleting text means that relevant 'flagging' material will need to be changed. At its simplest, this may be the contents page or the announcement at the beginning of a chapter that the chapter will cover certain ground. However, it is just as likely to be an obscure reference buried in the text to a table that you have deleted, thus making the reference redundant.

Two other advantages of word processing may have occurred to you. First, most packages have a word count facility. You can use this to check your progress towards the word goal you have set yourself for the writing session. The second advantage is the readability statistics that are a feature of Microsoft Word. This allows you to check not only spelling, but also the average number of sentences per paragraph and words per sentence. To do this click on the 'Tools' menu, click 'Options...', and then click the 'Spelling & Grammar' tab. Select the 'Check grammar with spelling' and the 'Show readability statistics' check boxes and click on 'OK'. Next time you click on 'Spelling & Grammar' Word will display readability statistics.

The necessity of keeping back-up copies of your work should go without saying. However, do learn from the experience of one of our students, who lost all his research material as a consequence of not keeping adequate back-up copies. This led to him having to abandon his research project completely.

Generate a plan

Few of us can sit down and write without a lot of thought and planning. We all have our own systems for doing this. However, most people find it essential to construct a plan before they start writing. Veroff (2001) describes the 'clustering' method. This may be familiar to you. The method's stages are:

1 Write the main topic in the middle of a sheet of paper.
2 Jot down the other ideas that occur to you at other points on the page.
3 As the page begins to fill, relationships between the ideas suggest themselves and lines between the ideas may be drawn.
4 This allows you to group the ideas into discrete but related 'chunks', which enables you to devise an outline structure for a section, or chapter.

This chapter started out as just such a pencilled plan written on four pieces of A4 held together with sticky tape. It is essential to get your ideas into some form of order at the outset. This will give you encouragement to start writing.

Finish the writing session on a high point

Many writers prefer to finish their writing session while they are in the middle of a section to which they will look forward to returning. This eases the way in next time. The worst thing you can do is to leave a complex section half completed. It will be difficult to pick up the threads.

Get friends to read your work

Writing is creative and exciting, but checking our work is not. The importance of getting someone else to read through your material cannot be over-emphasised. Your project tutor should not be the first person who reads your report, even in its draft form.

Ask your friend to be constructively critical. Your friend must be prepared to tell you about things in the text that are not easy to understand – to point out omissions, spelling, punctuation and grammatical errors. Overall, your friend must tell you whether the piece of writing makes sense and achieves its purpose.

This is not an easy process for you or your critical friend. Most of us are sensitive to criticism, particularly when the consequence of it is the necessity to do a lot more work. Many of us are also hesitant about giving criticism. However, if your project report does not communicate to the reader in the way it should, you will get it back for revision work in the long run. It is much better to try to ensure that this does not happen.

14.3 Structuring your project report

Suggested structure

Most writers agree with Robson (2002) on the general structure to adopt for a project report that is the end product of your research. This is:

- Abstract
- Introduction
- Literature review
- Method
- Results
- Discussion
- Conclusions
- References
- Appendices.

However, this suggested structure should not inhibit you from adopting something different. The structure outlined above fits the deductive approach particularly closely. It assumes that the literature was reviewed to establish the current state of knowledge on the topic and this informed the method adopted. Reporting the findings in a factual manner gives rise to a detailed consideration of what these findings mean to the specific piece of research that has been conducted and to the current state of knowledge on the topic. However, if your research is essentially inductive, it may be that you prefer to structure the report in a different way. You may prefer to tell your story (that is, to explain your conclusions) in the early part of the report. This may include a clear explanation of how this story relates to the existing literature on the topic. This could be followed by a detailed explanation of how you arrived at these conclusions (a combination of an explanation of method adopted and findings established). The precise structure you adopt is less important than the necessity for your reader to be absolutely clear about what you are saying and for you to meet the assessment criteria.

Phillips and Pugh (2005) note that these general sections can be sub-divided into one or more relevant chapters depending on the topic and the way in which you want to present your particular **storyline**. This is a vital point. Your structure should have a logical flow. Your readers should know the journey on which they are being taken, and should know at all times the point in the journey that has been reached. Above all, the structure you adopt should enable your reader, having read the report, to identify the storyline clearly.

We shall now explain how to distinguish between these broad sections by outlining their purpose and content.

The abstract

The **abstract** is probably the most important part of your report because it may be the only part that some will read. It is a short summary of the complete content of the project report. This enables those who are not sure whether they wish to read the complete report to make an informed decision. For those who intend to read the whole report the abstract prepares them for what is to come. It should contain four short paragraphs with the answers to the following questions:

1 What were my research questions, and why were these important?
2 How did I go about answering the research questions?
3 What did I find out in response to my research questions?
4 What conclusions do I draw regarding my research questions?

The academic publisher, Emerald, gives advice to potential academic authors on how to compile an abstract. This is shown in Box 14.2. Although referring to academic journal articles (papers), it is useful to consider in terms of preparation of your research report and any subsequent publication.

Smith (1991) lists five principles for the writing of a good abstract. He argues that:

1 It should be short. Try to keep it to a maximum of two sides of A4. (Some universities stipulate a maximum length, often 300–500 words.)
2 It must be self-contained. Since it may be the only part of your project report that some people see, it follows that it must summarise the complete content of your report.
3 It must satisfy your reader's needs. Your reader must be told about the problem, or central issue, that the research addressed and the method adopted to pursue the issue. It must also contain a brief statement of the main results and conclusions.

Box 14.2 Focus on management research

Advice on the preparation of an abstract for publication

Abstracts should contain no more than 250 words. Write concisely and clearly. The abstract should reflect only what appears in the original paper.

Purpose of this paper
What are the reason(s) for writing the paper or the aims of the research?

Design/methodology/approach
How are the objectives achieved? Include the main method(s) used for the research. What is the approach to the topic and what is the theoretical or subject scope of the paper?

Findings
What was found in the course of the work? This will refer to analysis, discussion, or results.

Research limitations/implications (if applicable)
If research is reported on in the paper, this section must be completed and should include suggestions for future research and any identified limitations in the research process.

Practical implications (if applicable)
What outcomes and implications for practice, applications and consequences are identified? Not all papers will have practical implications but most will. What changes to practice should be made as a result of this research/paper?

What is original/value of paper
What is new in the paper? State the value of the paper and to whom.

Source: From Emerald Group Publishing (2008) 'How to . . . write an abstract'. From The Emerald website, http://info.emeraldinsight.com/authors/guides/abstracts.htm. Reproduced with permission.

4 It must convey the same emphasis as the project report, with the consequence that the reader should get an accurate impression of the report's contents from the abstract.
5 It should be objective, precise and easy to read. The project report contents page should give you the outline structure for the abstract. Summarising each section should give you an accurate résumé of the content of the report. Do ensure that you stick to what you have written in the report. The abstract is not the place for elaborating any of your main themes. Be objective. You will need to write several drafts before you eliminate every word that is not absolutely necessary. The purpose is to convey the content of your report in as clear and brief a way as possible.

Writing a good abstract is difficult. The obvious thing to do is to write it after you have finished the report. We suggest that you draft it at the start of your writing so that you have got your storyline abundantly clear in your mind. You can then amend the draft when you have finished the report so that it conforms to the five principles above. Box 14.3 is a good example of an abstract that meets most of the criteria for an effective abstract that we list above.

Box 14.3 Focus on management research

Abstract from a refereed journal article on the changing travel behaviour of Austria's ageing population and its impact on tourism

As the population of the Western world is ageing, the importance of seniors for the tourism economy is growing. Seniors are expected to be an important future market. Thus, overall leisure behaviour in general, and travel and tourism behaviour in particular, are analysed for the example of the Austrian market.

A focus group was conducted with participants aged 55+, where their leisure and travel habits as well as preferences were investigated.

The results showed that leisure and travelling played a major role in the participants' lives. Additionally, the participants did not change their travel behaviour considerably when entering retirement status. While they changed their preferences to longer stays and to travelling off-season, their preferences considering holiday destinations, mode of transport or distance of travel did not change significantly. The assumption that travel behaviour and travel preferences are acquired over a longer time span during the life of tourists and, therefore, will not change considerably when retiring can be confirmed for the participants of the focus group.

It can be concluded that future senior tourists will differ from today's travelling seniors in their travel behaviour and their preferences. A larger sample and more detailed research concerning the actual motivation and preferences of Austrian holiday travellers, as well as the factors influencing them, are necessary in order to be able to react adequately to future demands of senior tourists.

The paper contributes to a better understanding of the importance of and attitude towards leisure and tourism in the growing senior market. Based on the results of a focus group, it serves as a basis for further research in the field.

Source: Möller, C., Weiermair, K. and Wintersberger, E. (2007) 'The changing travel behaviour of Austria's ageing population and its impact on tourism', *Tourism Review*, 62 (3/4), pp. 15–20.

The introductory chapter

The **introduction** should give the reader a clear idea about the central issue of concern in your research and why you thought that this was worth studying. It should also include a full statement of your research question(s) and research objectives. If your research is based in an organisation, we think that it is a good idea to include in this chapter some details of the organisation, such as its history, size, products and services. This may be a general background to the more specific detail on the research setting you include in the method chapter. It is also important to include in this chapter a 'route map' to guide the reader through the rest of the report. This will give brief details of the content of each chapter and present an overview of how your storyline unfolds.

This will usually be a fairly brief chapter, but it is vitally important.

The literature review

Chapter 3 deals in detail with the writing of a literature review. All that it is necessary to comment on here is the position of this chapter in the project report. We suggest that this is placed before the methodology chapter.

The main purposes of your literature review are to set your study within its wider context and to show the reader how your study supplements the work that has already been done on your topic. The literature review, therefore, may inform directly your research questions (see Box 14.4) and any specific hypotheses that your research is designed to test. These hypotheses will also suggest a particular research approach, strategy and data collection techniques. If, on the other hand, you are working inductively (that is, from data to theory) your literature review may serve the purpose of illuminating and enriching your conclusions.

The title of your literature review chapter should reflect the content of the chapter. It may draw on one of the main themes in the review. We recommend that you do not call it simply 'literature review'. It may be that your literature is reviewed in more than one chapter. This would be the case, for example, where you were using more than one body of literature in your research.

Box 14.4 Focus on student research

Using the literature review to inform the research questions

Guiyan was a Chinese student studying for an MA in a UK university. In her research dissertation she was interested to know whether Chinese managers would be able to conduct performance appraisal schemes effectively in China with Chinese employees. She was aware that there were certain aspects of Chinese culture that would make this difficult. Guiyan studied two bodies of literature: that relating to the managerial skills of performance appraisal, and a second concerned with the effects of Chinese culture on the ways in which Chinese managers manage their employees. She presented both in a literature review chapter. She structured her chapter around three questions:

1 What are the key skills needed by managers to conduct performance appraisal effectively?
2 What are the most important aspects of Chinese culture which impact upon on the ways in which Chinese managers manage their employees?
3 To what extent will the aspects of Chinese culture, explained in the answer to question 2, affect the ability of Chinese managers to conduct performance appraisal effectively?

From this, Guiyan developed a theoretical proposition that supported her initial idea that certain aspects of Chinese culture would make the conduct of performance appraisal by Chinese managers with Chinese employees difficult. She was then ready to move on to her method chapter, which was an explanation of the way in which she would test her theoretical proposition.

The method chapter

This should be a detailed chapter giving the reader sufficient information to make an estimate of the reliability and validity of your methods. Box 14.5 provides a useful checklist of the points that you should include in the method chapter.

Box 14.5 Checklist

Points to include in your method chapter

Setting

- ✔ What was the research setting?
- ✔ Why did you choose that particular setting?
- ✔ What ethical issues were raised by the study, and how were these addressed?

Participants

- ✔ How many?
- ✔ How were they selected?
- ✔ What were their characteristics?
- ✔ How were refusals/non-returns handled?

Materials

- ✔ What tests/scales/interview or observation schedules/questionnaires were used?
- ✔ How were purpose-made instruments developed?
- ✔ How were the resulting data analysed?

Procedures

- ✔ What were the characteristics of the interviewers and observers, and how were they trained?
- ✔ How valid and reliable do you think the procedures were?
- ✔ What instructions were given to participants?
- ✔ How many interviews/observations/questionnaires were there; how long did they last; where did they take place?
- ✔ When was the research carried out?

Source: developed from Robson (2002) *Real World Research* (2nd edn). Oxford: Blackwell. Reproduced with permission.

The results chapter(s)

It may well be that your report will contain more than one results chapter. The question you should ask yourself is: 'Is more than one results chapter necessary to communicate my findings clearly?'

The results chapter or chapters are probably the most straightforward to write. It is your opportunity to report the facts that your research discovered. This is where you will include such tables and graphs that will illustrate your findings (do not put these in the appendices). The chapter may also contain verbatim quotes from interviewees, or sections of narrative account that illustrate periods of unstructured observation. This is a particularly powerful way in which you can convey the richness of your data. It is the qualitative equivalent of tables and graphs. Often, a short verbatim quote can convey with penetrating simplicity a particularly difficult concept that you are trying to explain. Do not be afraid to capture precisely what the interviewee said. Slang and swear words are often the most revealing, and provide amusement for the reader!

There are two important points to bear in mind when writing your results. The first is to stress that the purpose is to present facts. It is normally not appropriate in this chapter to begin to offer opinions on the facts. This is for the following chapter(s). Many of us become confused about the difference between findings and the conclusions drawn from these which form the basis of the discussion and conclusions chapters. One way of overcoming the confusion is to draw up a table with two columns. The first should be headed 'What I found out' and the second 'What judgements I have formed as a result of what I found out'. The first list is entirely factual (e.g. 66 per cent of respondents indicated they preferred to receive email messages rather than paper memos) and therefore the content of your findings chapter. The second list will be your judgements based on what you found out (e.g. it appears that electronic forms of communication are preferred to traditional) and therefore the content of your conclusions section.

The second point links to the first. Drawing up a table will lead you to a consideration of the way in which you present your findings. The purpose of your project report is to communicate the answer to your research question to your audience in as clear a manner as possible. Therefore you should structure your findings in a clear, logical and easily understood manner. There are many ways of doing this. One of the simplest is to return to the research objectives and let these dictate the order in which you present your findings. Alternatively, you may prefer to report your findings thematically. You could present the themes in descending order of importance. Whichever method you choose should be obvious to the reader. As with the literature review, the chapter(s) devoted to research should be titled in an interesting way that reflects the content of findings.

The clarity of your findings should be such that they may find their way into a news report similar to that in Box 14.6.

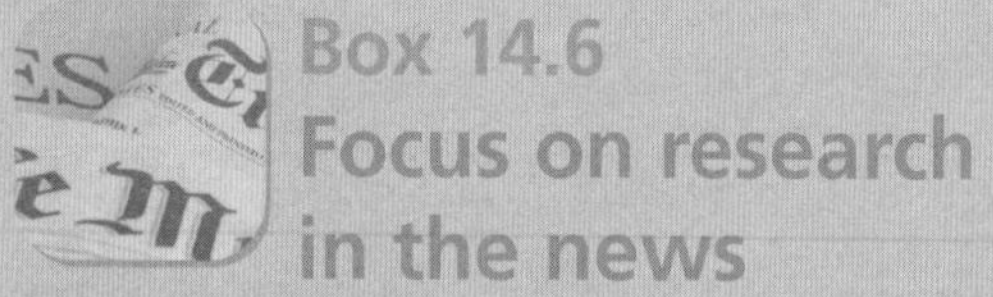

Report concludes that privacy rights 'fragile' in 2007

Threats to personal privacy got more severe in 2007, a report has claimed. Compiled by Privacy International and the Electronic Privacy Information Center the report details global trends in privacy protection and surveillance.

It found that in 2007 more nations than ever ranked as places where surveillance had become 'endemic'. The move toward greater surveillance had left the fundamental right to a private life 'fragile and exposed', the report said.

The 1000 page report from the two campaigning groups details what governments, companies and lobby groups have done in the past 12 months to defend or dismantle privacy online or offline. Overall, wrote the report's authors, privacy protection 'worsened' during 2007. As in previous years, the report found no nation which consistently tried to uphold privacy or gave substantial help, legislative or otherwise, to protect personal data.

Greece topped the table of 47 countries ranked in the report and was the only one that was identified as having 'adequate safeguards against abuse'. Most countries surveyed were classed as having 'some safeguards but weakened protections' or a 'systemic failure' to defend citizens' private lives. In 2007 the survey found surveillance 'endemic' in nine countries – compared to five in 2006. The nine were – England, Wales, Malaysia, China, Russia, Singapore, Taiwan, Thailand and the USA.

The report said that greater scrutiny of citizens grew out of two trends – government efforts to beef up national security and a burgeoning industry built around surveillance or the data it collects. It noted that action by lobby groups or campaigners to protect privacy were 'marginal' and added that any substantive effort to fight back could struggle against the complex and diverse threats ranged against privacy.

Source: derived from BBC News Online, 31 Dec. 2007.

The discussion chapter

Findings presented without reflective thought run the risk of your reader asking 'so what?': what meaning do these findings have for me?; for my organisation?; for professional practice?; for the development of theory? So the main focus of the discussion chapter is on the interpretation of the results that you presented in the previous chapter. You should state the relation of the findings to the goals, questions and hypotheses that you stated in the introductory chapter. In addition, the discussion chapter will benefit from a consideration of the implications of your research for the relevant theories which you detailed in your literature review. It is usual to discuss the strengths, weaknesses and limitations of your study. However, it is not a good idea to be too modest here and draw attention to aspects of your research which you may consider to be a limitation but that the reader has not noticed!

The discussion chapter is where you have the opportunity to shine. It will show the degree of insight that you exhibit in reaching your conclusions. However, it is the part of the report that most of us find difficult. It is the second major opportunity in the research process to demonstrate real originality of thought (the first time being at the stage where you choose the research topic). Because of that, we urge you to pay due attention to the discussion chapter. In our view it should normally be at least as long as your results chapter(s). Crucially, here you are making judgements rather than reporting facts, so this is where your maturity of understanding can shine through.

The conclusion chapter

This should be a conclusion to the whole project (and not just the research findings). Check that your work answers the questions in Box 14.7.

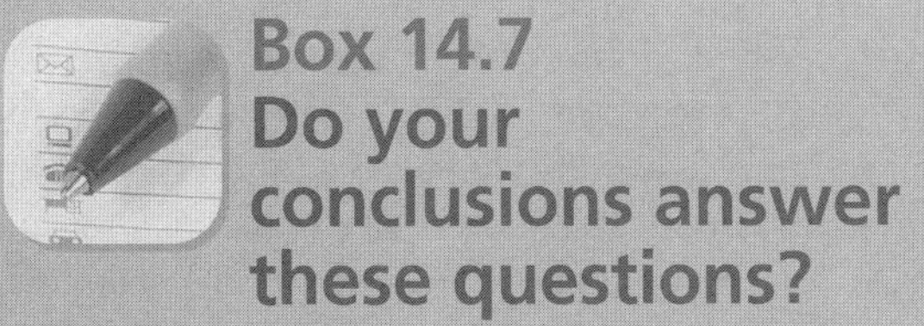

Box 14.7 Do your conclusions answer these questions?

- ✔ Did the research project meet your research objectives?
- ✔ Did the research project answer your research questions?
- ✔ What are the main findings of the research?
- ✔ Are there any recommendations for future action based on the conclusions you have drawn?
- ✔ Do you have any overall conclusions on the research process itself?
- ✔ Where should further research be focused? (Typically this will consider two points: firstly, new areas of investigation implied by developments in your project, and secondly parts of your work which were not completed due to time constraints and/or problems encountered.)

You may find that the clearest way to present your conclusions is to follow a similar structure to the one used in your findings section. If that structure reflects the research objectives then it should make certain that your conclusions would address them. Drawing up a matrix similar to that in Figure 14.1 may help you in structuring your

Research questions	**Results** *(what factual information did I discover in relation to the specific research questions?)*	**Conclusions** *(what judgements can I make about the results in relation to the specific research questions?)*
What are the operational differences between different shifts in the production plant?	Cases of indiscipline in the last six months have been twice as frequent on the night shift as on the day shift	The night shift indiscipline problems may be due to the reluctance of operators to work on this shift

Figure 14.1 Using a matrix in the planning of the content for the results and conclusions chapters

findings and conclusions. The result should be a clear statement of conclusions drawn similar to that shown in Box 14.8 (opposite).

You may also have a final section in your conclusion chapter(s) called '**discussion**'. Alternatively, you may make this a separate chapter with this general heading. Here you would turn to your conclusions and ask such questions as: 'What does this mean?' 'What are the implications for organisations?' 'What are the implications for the current state of knowledge of the topic?' 'How does it add to the literature?' 'What are the implications for future research?' The conclusions chapter should not include new material but the discussion may do so, as long as it is germane to the point you are making about your conclusions.

An alternative approach to the matrix is to draw a 'mind map' (see Section 2.3), which places the findings randomly on a blank page and links conclusions to these findings by way of lines and arrows. For some of you this may be a more creative approach, which enables you to associate groups of findings with conclusions and vice versa.

Answering the research question(s), meeting the objectives and, if appropriate, supporting or otherwise the research hypotheses is the main purpose of the conclusions chapter. This is where you will consider the findings presented in the previous chapter. You should also return to your literature review and ask yourself 'What do my conclusions add to the understanding of the topic displayed in the literature?'

It may be that there are practical implications of your findings. In a management report this would normally form the content of a chapter specifically devoted to recommendations. We suggest that you check with your project tutor whether this is expected. In the reports that students are required to prepare on some professional courses this is an important requirement. For academic degree programmes it is often unnecessary.

Even if you do not specify any practical implications of your research you may comment in the conclusions chapter on what your research implies for any future research. This is a logical extension of a section in the conclusions chapter that should be devoted to the limitations of your research. These limitations may be the size of sample, the snapshot nature of the research, or the restriction to one geographical area of an organisation. Virtually all research has its limitations. This section should not be seen as a confession of your weaknesses, but as a mature reflection on the degree to which your findings and conclusions can be said to be the 'truth'.

References

A range of conventions are used to reference the material of other writers' material that you have cited in your text. Appendix 1 illustrates three of the most popular of these, the Harvard, footnotes and American Psychological Association (APA) systems. However, we suggest that you consult your project tutor about the system that is appropriate for your project report, as many universities require their own variation of these systems.

It is a good idea to start your references section at the beginning of the writing process and add to it as you go along. It will be a tedious and time-consuming task if left until you have completed the main body of the text. If you do leave it until the end, the time spent on compiling the reference section is time that would have been better spent on checking and amending your report.

At the start of your report you must acknowledge all those who have contributed to your research (including your project tutor!). In addition, you should ensure that you have cited in your reference section all those sources to which you have referred in the text. In order to avoid charges of plagiarism you should ensure that all data and material taken verbatim from another person's published or unpublished written or electronic

Box 14.8 Focus on management research

Psychological and behavioural drivers of online clothes purchasing

Goldsmith and Flynn (2006) studied selected demographic and psychological characteristics that lead consumers to buy clothing online. They surveyed 805 consumers who described their online clothing buying as well as how innovative and involved they were for clothing and fashion, how innovative they were with regard to buying on the Internet, and how much they purchased clothing through catalogues.

The resulting article is structured along the classic lines of introduction, literature review, hypotheses, research method, results and discussion. We summarise here their discussion section to give you an understanding of the character of their conclusions.

The purpose of Goldsmith and Flynn's study was to assess the relative influence of several key variables on the amount of online clothing buying. The data analysis revealed that three demographic variables (age, sex and income) played a relatively minor role in explaining online clothing buying. Better predictors were an enthusiasm and venturesomeness for online buying in general and a history of buying clothes from catalogues. Fashion innovativeness was weakly related to online buying, but fashion involvement was not. It appears that being an Internet innovator and an experienced catalogue shopper are more predictive of online clothing shopping than an interest in fashion.

Goldsmith and Flynn's discussion section is based on the implications of their findings. These are summarised below.

First, being a catalogue shopper, a consumer with a previous history of shopping from home, is a significant predictor of shopping online. This is probably due to a general propensity or affinity for direct buying, but might also be due to the presence of many catalogue retailers on the web. If a shopper has experience with a direct merchant it is a smaller leap of faith to move from catalogue to online shopping with the same retailer. So the Land's End catalogue buyer might be easily encouraged to buy from Land's End online. It is also possible that circumstances leading one to buy via catalogues, such as time pressure or limited access to stores, would also lead to online purchasing.

Second, because innovativeness for online shopping predicts online clothing purchase, Goldsmith and Flynn conclude that shopping via the Internet is in its earlier stages of the diffusion process. If online shopping were more broadly diffused, innovators would not be so heavily represented among such shoppers. They conclude that as innovators are an important buying group, this implies that the phenomenon will grow in the future.

Third, the enduring involvement in a product category does not necessarily predict more buying of that category through a new medium. While personal importance of fashion is linked to more buying in that category, being a 'clotheshorse' was not a good indicator of shopping for clothing online. Increased shopping via the Internet appears to be better predicted by the tendency to be a home shopper than by strong interest in the product category. E-commerce clothing managers would do well to focus more effort on wooing Internet innovators than fashion innovators.

Fourth, the likelihood of a consumer shopping from home and their venturesomeness with regard to new shopping media seem to be the most prominent factors predicting online shopping. This is important because individual differences in these areas trump product-category-related differences in predicting medium choice. The implications are straightforward. Catalogue shoppers are likely to be the same as online shoppers. Catalogue managers should work to encourage their customers to migrate to the web.

Goldsmith and Flynn point out that their findings are limited by the sample and measures used. Studies of other populations of consumers using other measures should be done to confirm and expand these results. Another limitation lies in the self-report nature of the shopping variables that might introduce measurement error into the data. However, they claim that their findings do contribute to our understanding of online clothing shopping, and future studies can build on these results to complete this picture.

work is explicitly identified and referenced to its author. This also extends to work which is referred to in the written work of others. Even if this work is not quoted verbatim, the originator should be cited in your references. If you are in any doubt about this it is important that you consult your tutor. The proliferation of online material now is such that all academic institutions are very mindful of plagiarism.

Appendices

In general, **appendices** should be kept to the minimum. If they are so important that your reader's understanding of the points you are making in the text makes their inclusion in the report necessary, then they should be in the main body of the text. If, on the other hand, the material is 'interesting to know' rather than 'essential to know' then it should be in the appendices. Often students feel tempted to include appendices to 'pad out' a project report. Resist this temptation. Your readers will not be reading your report for leisure reading. They will be pressed for time and will probably not look at your appendices. Your project report will stand or fall on the quality of the main text. However, your appendices should include a blank copy of your questionnaire, interview or observation schedule. Where these have been conducted in a language different from that in which you write your submitted project report you will need to submit both this version and the translation.

The management report

You may have wondered why we made no reference to recommendations in the report structure. In the typical **management report** or consultancy report (discussed later) this may be the most important section. The hard-pressed executive reading your report may turn to your recommendations first to see what action needs to be taken to tackle the issue.

Whether you include a recommendation section depends on the objectives of your research. If you are doing exploratory research you may well write recommendations, among which will be suggestions for the pursuit of further research. However, if your research is designed to explain or describe, recommendations are less likely. For example, the research question 'Why do small engineering companies in the UK reinvest less of their profits in their businesses than their German counterparts?' may imply clear points for action. However, strictly speaking, recommendations are outside the scope of the research question, which is to discover 'Why?' not 'What can be done about it?' The message is clear. If you want your research to change the situation that you are researching, then include the need to develop recommendations in your research objectives.

Length of the project report

You will probably have guidelines on the number of words your project report should contain. Do stick to these. However interesting your report, your tutors will have others to read, so they will not thank you for exceeding the limit. Indeed, if you can meet your research objectives fully in a clear and absorbing report that is significantly shorter than the word limit, the good mood in which you put your tutors may be reflected in a higher grade. Reports that exceed the word limit are usually excessively verbose. It is more difficult to be succinct. Do not fall into the trap of writing a long report because you did not have the time to write a shorter one.

14.4 Organising the project report's content

Choosing a title

This is the part of the project report on which most of us spend the least time. Yet it is the only knowledge that many people have of the project. Day and Gastel (2006) comment that a good title is one that has the minimum possible number of words that describe accurately the content of the paper. Try choosing a title and then ask a colleague who knows your subject what they think the title describes. If their description matches your content then stick with your title.

Tell a clear story

Be prepared for your project tutor to ask you 'What's your main storyline?' Your storyline (your central argument or thesis) should be clear, simple and straightforward. It should be so clear that you can stop the next person you see walking towards you and tell that person what your project report's storyline is and he or she will say 'Yes, I understand that'. This is where writing the abstract helps. It forces you to think clearly about the storyline because you have to summarise it in so few words.

A simple format for developing the storyline is shown in Figure 14.2.

Another way of checking to see whether your storyline is clear is to 'reason backwards'. An example of this may be a report that ends in clear recommendations for action. Start by explaining your recommendations to the manager who, for example, may have to spend money on their implementation. This invites the question from that manager: 'What makes you recommend this action?' Your answer should be: 'I came to the conclusion in my report that they are necessary.' The follow-up question from the manager here could be: 'On what basis do you draw these conclusions?' Here your answer is, of course, on the findings that you established. The next question asked by the manager is: 'How did you arrive at these findings?' in response to which you explain your method. The

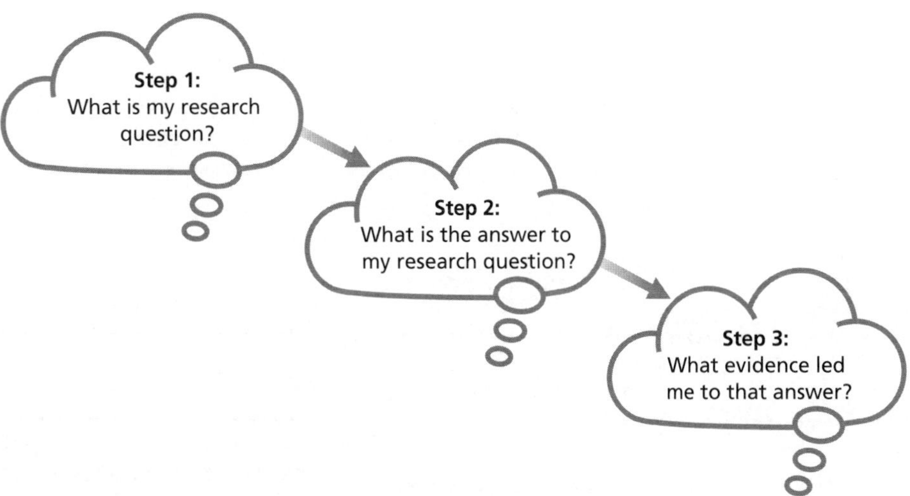

Figure 14.2 A format for developing the storyline

Souce: developed from Raimond (1993:175) *Management Project: Design, Research and Presentation.* Reproduced with permission of Thompson Publishing Services.

manager may counter by asking you why she should take any notice of your findings. The response to this is that you took care to design a research strategy that would lead to valid and reliable findings. Moreover, that research strategy is based on clear research objectives and a detailed review of the relevant literature.

Such 'reasoning backwards' is a useful check to see not only whether your storyline is clear but also that it stands up to logical analysis.

Helping the reader to get all the information out

Dividing your work

One of us once received the first draft of a twenty-thousand-word project report that had virtually no divisions except the chapters. It was like looking at a road map that did not include any road numbers or towns. It was just as difficult to find your way around that report as it would be to journey between two cities using a townless road map. The content of the project report seemed fine. However, it was hard to be sure about this because it was so difficult to spot any gaps in the ground it covered. What was needed were some signposts and some town names. Do not think about how you can put in all your information. Instead, concentrate on helping the reader to get all the information out (Box 14.9).

The message is simple. Divide your work in such a way that it is easy for readers to find their way round it and for them always to be clear where they are, where they have come from, and where they are going.

To do this you may find it helpful to return to the matrix idea in Figure 14.1. You will see that each column of the matrix represents the broad content of a chapter. The cells indicate the way in which the chapters may be divided. Each division may have a sub-division.

We hope that you have noticed that we have employed a similar system in this book. However, this book is printed in more than one colour. The equivalent would be that each chapter section is identified by bold upper-case letters. The sub-headings are bold lower-case, and further divisions of the subsection content are denoted by bold, lower-case italics. Smith (1991) explains various ways of organising and signposting text. It is not important which way you do this as long as your approach is consistent and it helps the reader around the report and matches the ways specified by your examining institution.

Previewing and summarising chapters

A further way in which you can signpost your work is to 'top and tail' each chapter. This is to include a few words at the beginning of the chapter (Smith 1991) that provide a

Box 14.9
Focus on student research

Developing a storyline

Step 1
I wanted to know whether, as the literature suggested, organisational structures are determined by their strategies.

Step 2
The answer is that organisation structures are in part determined by strategies and in part by *ad hoc* factors that owe little to strategy considerations.

Step 3
I based this answer on interviews with senior managers in three large UK organisations and examination of the minutes of meetings at which structural issues were discussed. The particular focus was on the removal of management positions.

description of how the chapter is to contribute to answering the research question, the methods used in this part of the study, and the points that are covered. At the end of each chapter it is useful if the reader has a brief summary of the content of the chapter and a very brief indication of how this content links to the following chapter. This may seem like repetition. However, it helps the reader on her or his journey through your report and ensures that you, the writer, are on the correct road.

Tables and graphics

Your reader will find your project report more accessible and easier to read if you present some of your data and ideas in tables and graphics. It is not only numerical data that can be presented in tables. You can also present ideas that can be easily compared. Table 13.1 is an example of this.

Do not be tempted to put your numerical tables in the appendices. They will probably be some of your most important data. Include them and comment on them in the text. Your commentary should note the significance of the data in the tables. It should not simply describe the table's contents.

Section 12.3 has detail on the presentation of tables and diagrams.

A final note of caution should be sounded. To avoid confusing your reader, do make sure that, wherever possible, you have introduced the table or diagram before it appears in the text.

One report?

Many researchers of management topics face the dilemma of having to write for more than one audience. In addition to the academic audience, who possibly will mark and grade the report for a degree or a diploma, it may be necessary to prepare a report for the management of the employing organisation, or, indeed, a non-employing organisation both of whom who will be interested in the practical benefit that the report promises. This raises the thorny question, 'For whom should the report be written?'

Many people have resolved this dilemma by writing two reports: one for each audience. The academic report will usually be much longer and contain contextual description that the organisational audience does not require. Similarly, those managers reading the report will probably be less interested in the literature review and the development of theory than the academic audience. If the research question did not imply the necessity for recommendations for future action, these may need to be written for the organisational version. The content of this chapter concentrates on the academic report. However, in the sub-section below we include a brief discussion on consultancy reports.

Fortunately, the advent of word processing makes the job of compiling more than one report quite easy. Some careful cutting and pasting will be necessary. However, what should always be kept in mind is the audience that each specific report is addressing. Take care not to fall between two stools. Write each report for its audience in style and content.

The consultancy report

Here we assume that the report that you write for the management of the employing organisation, or a non-employing organisation, follow the same format. For this reason we refer to both as **consultancy reports**.

Advice from the Institute of Management Consultancy (now the Institute of Business Consulting) suggests that a number of key questions need to be asked before the consultancy report is planned. Among these are: what information does management expect?; with what level of detail?; how much knowledge does management already have?; for what purpose will the report be used?; who will read it? Another fundamental question is: what key messages and recommendations do you want to impart? To be consistent with the main thrust of this chapter a report structure such as:

- Executive summary
- Introduction
- Results
- Conclusions
- Recommendations

is the most straightforward.

There is, however, an alternative structure which, arguably, is simpler and delivers the message more forcibly. In this you start with your main message and then provide the information that supports it. This second structure, will, however, involve you in more alteration of the academic report you have written.

Decisions about what to include in (and, just as importantly, to exclude from) the report requires ruthlessness. Only information that is essential to management should go in the main body of the report; any information that is 'important' or 'of interest' should be relegated to appendices. Additional detail, for example figures, references or diagrams are all examples of 'important' information. The Institute of Management Consultancy suggests that you should put yourself in the reader's shoes. The management reader will be short of time and want only essential detail. That said, the management reader will be interested in the background to the project and in how you carried out the research. But the main purpose of the report will be to tell management your recommendations. Recommendations equate with action, and managers are paid to act! As with the academic report, division of the report content into logical sections with clear sub-headings will lead management through the report and show them where to find specific topics.

The executive summary is likely to be the part of the report on which managers will concentrate. It is important that it can stand alone and that it contains real information, including hard facts and figures. If your report includes recommendations, the executive summary should make it clear what these are and include their implications, values and costs. As with the abstract, the executive summary should be short (no more than two pages) and designed to get your main message across.

Two final points about the writing style of the consultancy report. The reader will not appreciate long words, complicated language, 'management speak' or a multitude of acronyms and abbreviations. If it is necessary to use complex technical terms, make sure you provide a glossary in the appendix.

Finally, it is more appropriate to use the first person in the consultancy report. Language like 'it was found', 'it is estimated', 'it is recommended' does not sound more professional; it simply depersonalises your report and makes it less accessible. Be bold and put yourself at the heart of your writing!

As well as presenting two written reports you may have to present your report orally. In the next two sections we address the writing of reports, and in the final section (14.7), we turn our attention to their oral presentation.

14.5 Developing an appropriate writing style

Much of your concern in writing your project report will be about what you write. In this section of the chapter we ask you to think about the way you write. Your writing style is just as important as the content, structure and layout of your report. That said, it is often observed that good writing cannot substitute for flawed thinking (Phillips and Pugh 2005). In fact, the clearer the writing the more flawed thinking is exposed. However, poor writing can spoil the effect of good-quality thought.

Clarity and simplicity

> **The . . . lack of ready intelligibility [in scholarly writing], I believe, usually has little or nothing to do with the complexity of the subject matter, and nothing at all to do with profundity of thought. It has to do almost entirely with certain confusions of the academic writer about his own status . . . To overcome the academic prose you first of all have to overcome the academic pose . . .**
>
> Wright Mills (1970:239–40)

Each Christmas, Mark accompanies his Christmas cards with a family newsletter. It is written in a simple, direct and friendly manner that is easy and enjoyable to read. Few of the project reports we read are written in such a simple, direct manner. They are more elaborate in their explanation: they use difficult words where Mark's family newsletter would use simple ones. They adopt the academic pose.

Phil tells a story that reinforces the point made by Wright Mills in the above quotation. He was asked by a student to comment on her thesis in progress, which was about the impact of a particular job advertising strategy. He thought that it was written in an over-elaborate and 'academic' way. After many suggestions for amendments Phil came across a sentence that explained that the strategy his student was studying 'was characterised by factors congruent with the results of a lifestyle analysis of the target market'. Phil thought that this was too wordy. He suggested making it simpler. His student examined the sentence at length and declared she could see no way of improving it. Phil thought that it could say 'it was a strategy that matched the lifestyles of those at whom it was aimed'. His student protested. She agreed it was shorter and clearer but protested that it was less 'academic'. We think that clarity and simplicity are more important than wishing to appear academic. Your project report is a piece of communication in the same way as Mark's Christmas newsletter.

Phillips and Pugh (2005) advise that you should aim to provide readers with a report that they cannot put down until 2.00 a.m. or later for fear of spoiling the flow. (If you are reading this chapter at 2.30 a.m. we have succeeded!)

Write simple sentences

A common source of lack of clarity is the confusing sentence (see Box 14.10). This is often because it is too long. A simple rule to adopt is: one idea – one sentence. Mark reads his work out loud. If the sentences are too long, he runs out of breath! This is another useful guide to sentence length.

Avoid jargon

Jargon should not be confused with technical terminology. Some technical terms are unavoidable. To assist your reader, it is best to put a glossary of such terms in the appendices. However, do not assume that your reader will have such a full knowledge as you of the subject and, in particular, the context. Here, and in all cases, try to put yourself in the position of the reader. Phil makes this point to students who use organisations as vehicles to write assignments. He asks them to 'mark' past (anonymous) assignments. They are usually horrified at the assumptions that their fellow students make about the tutor's prior knowledge.

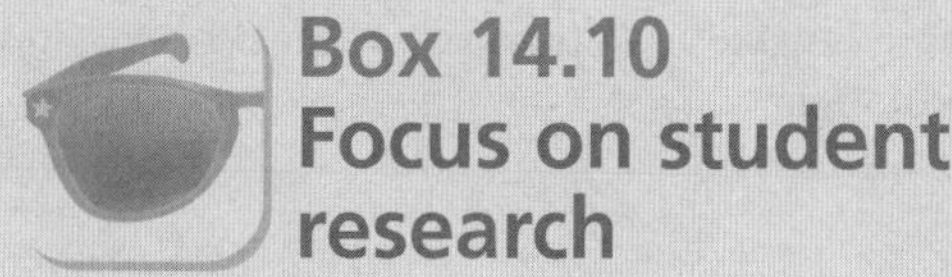

Box 14.10 Focus on student research

Writing clearer sentences

Consider the following sentence.

While it is true to say that researchers have illusions of academic grandeur when they sit down to write their project report, and who can blame them because they have had to demonstrate skill and resilience to get to this point in their studies, they nonetheless must consider that writing a project report is an exercise in communication, and nobody likes reading a lot of ideas that are expressed in such a confusing and pretentious way that nobody can understand them, let alone the poor tutor who has to plough through it all to try and make some sense of it.

There appear to be at least six separate ideas in this sentence. It contains 101 words (when marking, we sometimes come across sentences with over 150!). In addition, it contains a common way of introducing multiple ideas into a sentence: the embedded clause. In the sentence above the embedded clause is '. . . and who can blame them because they have had to demonstrate skill and resilience to get to this point in their studies,...' The give-away is the first word in the sentence: 'While'. This invites an embedded clause. The point here is that potentially rich ideas get buried away in the literary undergrowth. Dig them up and replant them. Let them flourish in a sentence of their own.

The sentence needs to be clearer and simpler. However, it should not lose any of its meaning. Halving the number of words and dividing up the sentence into smaller clearer sentences results in the following:

> Researchers have illusions of academic grandeur when they write their project report. This is understandable. They have demonstrated skill and resilience to reach this point in their studies. However, writing a project report is an exercise in communication. Nobody likes confusing and pretentious writing that is difficult to understand. Pity the tutor who has to make sense of it.

What can be avoided is the sort of jargon that *The New Oxford English Dictionary* (1998) defines as 'gibberish' and 'debased language'. You will know the sort of phrases: 'ongoing situation'; 'going down the route of'; 'at the end of the day'; 'the bottom line'; 'at this moment in time'. It is not just that they are ugly but they are not clear and simple. For example, 'now' is much clearer and simpler than 'at this moment in time'.

Beware of using large numbers of quotations from the literature

We believe that quotations from the literature should be used infrequently in your project report. Occasionally we receive draft projects that consist of little more than a series of quotations from books and journal articles that a student has linked together with a few sentences of her or his own. This tells us very little about the student's understanding of the concepts within the quotations. All it shows is that he or she has looked at the book or journal article and, it is hoped, can acknowledge sources correctly! In addition, by using quotations in this way the student's line of argument tends to become disjointed and less easy to follow. It is therefore usually better to explain other people's ideas in your own words.

That is not to say that you should never use quotations. As you have seen, we have used direct quotations from other people's work in this book. Rather we would advise you to use them sparingly to create maximum impact in supporting your storyline.

Check your spelling and grammar

Spelling is still a problem for many of us, in spite of the word processing software's spelling check facility. It will not correct your 'moral' when you wished to say 'morale' or sort out when you should write 'practise' rather than 'practice'. This is where the friend who is reading your draft can help, provided that friend is a competent speller. Tutors tend to be more patient with errors of this kind than those that reflect carelessness. However, the point remains that spelling errors detract from the quality of your presentation and the authority of your ideas.

Avoiding common grammatical errors

Grammatical errors threaten the credibility of our writing. In Table 14.1. we outline 10 of the most common errors, most of which, with some careful checking, can be avoided.

It is not our intention here to conduct an English grammar lesson. Some of the common errors in Table 14.1 are self-explanatory.

You may argue that the **split infinitive** is not often thought of as an error these days. However, 'to boldly go' ahead with your project report ignoring this rule risks irritating your reader – something you can ill afford to do. You want the reader to concentrate on your ideas.

Day's 'dangling participle' warning is amusingly illustrated by the draft questionnaire shown to us by a student. This asked for 'the amount of people you employ in your organisation, broken down by sex'. We wrote on our copy: 'We haven't got people in that category: they've not got the energy when they work here!' (Remember that when writing your questionnaire!)

Some of the more obvious grammatical errors you can spot by reading your text aloud to yourself. You need not know the grammatical rules; they often just sound wrong.

Table 14.1 Ten common grammatical errors

Often we write	The correct way is
1 Each pronoun should agree with **their** antecedent.	Each pronoun should agree with **its** antecedent.
2 Just between you and **I**, case is important.	Just between you and **me**, case is important.
3 A preposition is a poor word to end a sentence **with**	A preposition is a poor word **with which** to end a sentence.
4 Verbs **has** to agree with their subject.	Verbs **have** to agree with their subject.
5 Do not use **no** double negatives	Do not use double negatives.
6 Remember **to never split** an infinitive.	Remember **never to split** an infinitive.
7 When dangling, do not use participles.	Do not use dangling participles.
8 Avoid clichés like the plague.	To avoid clichés like the plague!
9 Do not write a run-on sentence it is difficult when you got to punctuate it so it makes sense when the reader reads what you wrote.	Do not write a run-on sentence. It is difficult to punctuate it so that it makes sense to the reader.
10 The data **is** included in this section.	The data **are** included in this section.

Source: developed from Day (1998:160).

Person, tense and gender

Traditionally, academic writing has been dry and unexciting. This is partly because the convention has been to write impersonally, in the past **tense** and in the **passive voice** (e.g. 'interviews were conducted following the administration of questionnaires').

The writer was expected to be distanced from the text. This convention is no longer as strong. It is a matter of preferred style rather than rules. The research approach that dominates your methods may dictate your choice of **personal pronoun**. Section 4.2 notes that one feature of positivism is that 'the researcher is independent of, and neither affects nor is affected by, the subject of the research'. It follows from this that an impersonal style is more appropriate. By contrast, Section 9.2 notes that the participant observer 'participates in the daily life of people under study'. The researcher is an intrinsic part of the research process. Use of the first person seems more logical here. However, style is important. Use of the term 'the author' sounds too impersonal and stilted. In contrast, excessive use of 'I' and 'we' may raise questions in your readers' minds about your ability to stand outside your data and to be objective.

Day (1998) identifies rules for the use correct use of tense. He suggests that you should normally use the present tense when referring to previously published work (e.g. Day identifies) and the past tense when referring to your present results (e.g. I found that . . .)'. Although he notes exceptions to this rule, it serves as a useful guide.

Day and Gastel (2006) and Becker (2008) both stridently attack the passive voice (it was found that) and champion the use of the **active voice** (I found that). Certainly, it is clearer, shorter and unambiguous. It is a good idea to check with your project tutor here which is most likely to be acceptable.

Finally, a note about the use of language that assumes the gender of a classification of people. The most obvious example of these is the constant reference to managers as 'he'. Not only is this inaccurate in many organisations, it also gives offence to many people of both sexes. Those offended will probably include your readers! It is simple enough to avoid (e.g. 'I propose to interview each executive unless he refuses' becomes 'I propose to interview each executive unless I receive a refusal') but often less easy to spot. The further reading section in the first draft of this chapter referred to Becker as a 'master craftsman'. These notes on language and gender prompted us to change it to 'an expert in the field'. Appendix 4 gives more detailed guidance on the use of non-discriminatory language.

It is a good idea to be aware of any specific discriminatory or potentially insulting concepts, terms and expressions which may be used in your research due to the particular context of the research (e.g. the industry or organisation in which you work). If your work has an international dimension, it is also a good idea to be aware of any country-specific or national guidelines on the non-discriminatory use of language.

Preserving anonymity

You may have given the participants (and the organisations) from whom you collected data an undertaking that you would not disclose their identity in anything you write. In this case you will need to conceal their identity in your project report. The usual way of doing this is to invent pseudonyms for organisations and not to name individual participants. This should not detract from the impact of your report.

Similarly, your sponsoring organisation(s) may have requested sight of your report before it is submitted. Should there be misgivings about the content of the report you should be able to alleviate these by the use of pseudonyms. This is usually a better option than significant text changes.

The need for continual revision

Adrian asked a group of undergraduate students how many of them did more than one draft of their assignment papers. He did not expect that many would reply that they did.

What he did not predict was that many of them had not even thought that this was necessary.

Submitting the first attempt is due partly to the heavy assessment loads on many courses, which means that students are constantly having to 'keep up with the clock'. On part-time courses, students these days have so many demands in their daily work that writing an assignment just once is all that is possible. This is the way most of us learned to write at school. The paper is usually seen only by the teacher. The arrangement is a private one.

However, project reports are different. They will be seen by an audience much wider than one tutor. They will usually be lodged in the library to be read by succeeding students. You will be judged on the quality of your work. For that reason we urge you most strongly to polish your work with successive drafts until you are happy that you can do no better.

The final version of this chapter (which, incidentally, even for the first edition of this book, was read by five people and was the last of seven or eight drafts) contains guidelines that you can use to evaluate your first draft. These are summarised in the checklist in Box 14.11.

Having been through this checklist you may decide to make minor alterations to your text. On the other hand you may rewrite sections or move sections within chapters to other chapters. Keep asking yourself 'How can I make the reader's task easier?'

After each successive draft do leave a space of time for your thoughts to mature. It is amazing how something you wrote a few days before will now make no sense to you. However, you will also be impressed with the clarity and insight of some passages.

Having completed a second draft you may now feel confident enough to give it to your colleague or friend to read. Ask your reader to use the checklist above, to which you can add specific points that you feel are important (e.g. are my arguments well reasoned?).

Box 14.11 Checklist

Evaluating your first draft

- ✔ Is there a clear structure?
- ✔ Is there a clear storyline?
- ✔ Does your abstract reflect accurately the whole content of the report?
- ✔ Does your introduction state clearly the research question(s) and objectives?
- ✔ Does your literature review inform the later content of the report?
- ✔ Are your methods clearly explained?
- ✔ Have you made a clear distinction between findings and conclusions in the two relevant chapters?
- ✔ Have you checked all your references and presented these in the required manner?
- ✔ Is there any text material that should be in the appendices or vice versa?
- ✔ Does your title reflect accurately your content?
- ✔ Have you divided up your text throughout with suitable headings?
- ✔ Does each chapter have a preview and a summary?
- ✔ Are you happy that your writing is clear, simple and direct?
- ✔ Have you eliminated all jargon?
- ✔ Have you eliminated all unnecessary quotations?
- ✔ Have you checked spelling and grammar?
- ✔ Have you checked for assumptions about gender?
- ✔ Is your report in a format that will be acceptable to the assessing body?

14.6 Meeting the assessment criteria

Your readers will be assessing your work against the assessment criteria that apply to your research programme. Therefore, it is essential that you familiarise yourself with these criteria. Easterby-Smith *et al.* (2008) cite Bloom's (1971) well-known taxonomy of educational objectives to illustrate the level that project reports should meet. At the lower levels project reports should show knowledge and comprehension of the topic covered. At the intermediate levels they should contain evidence of application and analysis. Application is thought of as the ability to apply certain principles and rules in particular situations. Your method section should be the principal vehicle for demonstrating application. Analysis may be illustrated by your ability to break down your data and to clarify the nature of the component parts and the relationship between them. Whatever your assessment criteria, it is certain that you will be expected to demonstrate your ability at these lower and intermediate levels.

The higher levels are **synthesis** and **evaluation**. Rowntree (1987:103) defines synthesis as 'the ability to arrange and assemble various elements so as to make a new statement or plan or conclusion – a unique communication'. The emphasis put on conclusions and, in particular, on the development of a storyline in your project report suggests that we feel that you should be showing evidence of synthesis. Evaluation refers to 'the ability to judge materials or methods in terms of internal accuracy and consistency or by comparison with external criteria' (Rowntree 1987:103). You have the chance to show this ability in the literature review and in the awareness of the limitations of your own research (see Section 14.3).

In summary, we think that each of the levels of educational objectives should be demonstrated in your project report.

14.7 Oral presentation of the report

Many students, particularly on professional courses, have to present their project report orally as part of the assessment process. The skills required here are quite different from those involved with writing. We discuss them here under three headings: planning and preparation; the use of visual aids; and presenting.

Planning and preparing

We make no apology for starting this section with the trainer's old adage 'Failing to prepare is preparing to fail'. Your assessors will forgive any inadequacies that stem from inexperience, but they will be much less forgiving of students who have paid little attention to preparation. You can be sure of one thing about insufficient preparation: it shows, particularly to the experienced tutor.

All presentations should have clear aims and objectives. This is not the place to analyse the difference between these. Suffice to say that your aim should be to give the audience members an overview of your report in such a way that it will capture their interest. Keep it clear and simple. By doing so you will meet the most basic assessment criterion: that some time later the tutor in the audience can remember clearly your main project storyline. Your objectives are more specific. They should start you thinking about the interests of your audience. These should be phrased in terms of what it is you want your audience members to be able to do after your presentation. Since your presentation will usually be confined to the imparting of knowledge, it is sufficient to phrase your objectives in terms of the audience members being able, for example, to define, describe, explain or clarify. It is a good idea to share the objectives with your audience members so they know about the journey on which they are being taken (Box 14.12).

Setting clear objectives for your presentation leads you neatly to deciding the content. This should be straightforward because your abstract should serve as your guide to the content. After all, the purpose of the abstract is to give the reader a brief overview of the report, which is precisely the same purpose as the presentation. How much detail you go into on each point will be determined largely by the time at your disposal. But the audience member who wants more detail can always ask you to elaborate, or read it in the report.

The final point to note here is to think about the general approach you will adopt in delivering your presentation. It is a good idea to involve the audience members rather than simply tell them what it is you want them to know. Thirty minutes of you talking at the audience members can seem like an age, for you and sometimes for them! Asking them to ask questions throughout the presentation is a good way of ensuring that the talk is not all in one direction. Rarely will tutors miss the opportunity of asking you to 'dig a little deeper' to test your understanding, so don't worry that no questions will arise. However, you must be careful to ensure that you do not let questions and answers run away with time. The more you open up your presentation to debate, the less control you have of time. In general we do not think it is a good idea to attempt to emulate tutors and turn your presentation into a teaching session. We have seen students set the audience mini-exercises to get them involved, but often these tend to fall flat. Play to your strengths and enjoy the opportunity to share your detailed knowledge with an interested audience.

Using visual aids

Now another old adage: 'I hear and I forget, I see and I remember' (Rawlins 1999:37). The use of **visual aids** will do more than enhance the understanding of your audience. It will help you to look better prepared and therefore more professional. It is unlikely that you will have the time to use elaborate media such as video or photographic slides, and often your subject matter will not lend itself to their use. So we shall confine our discussion here to the use of more prosaic media such as the overhead projector and the whiteboard.

A simple set of slides will perform the same function as a set of notes, in that it will ensure that you do not forget key points, and will help you to keep your presentation on track. You will know the material so well that a key point noted on the overhead will be enough to trigger your thought process and focus the attention of the audience. Key points will also ensure that you are not tempted to read a script for your presentation, something that will not sustain the attention of your audience for very long.

The use of Microsoft **PowerPoint**™ has revolutionised the preparation of overhead projector transparencies. It is now easy to produce a highly professional presentation, which can include simple illustrations to reinforce a point or add a little humour. You may have the facility to project the slides direct to a screen using a computer, which clearly adds to the degree of professionalism (Box 14.12). This allows you electronically to reveal each point as you talk about it while concealing forthcoming points. Alternatively, you may need to print the slides from PowerPoint and copy these to acetates and show them using an overhead projector. The latter method means that you must ensure that your slides are numbered and kept in a neat pile when shown, otherwise you will be searching for the correct slide to show at a particular time. PowerPoint also allows you to print miniature versions of your slides as handouts (Version 5, Box 14.12) which is a very useful *aide-mémoire* for the audience.

Box 14.12 Focus on student research

Presenting the objectives for a project

Phil created the following slides as part of a lecture on project presentation. To help give a professional appearance to his slides, he used the Microsoft PowerPoint™ program. This allows you to produce various designs of slide to meet your purpose, examples of which are shown in the following versions:

Version 1: Standard PowerPoint slide

Objectives for a presentation

- Describe the purpose of the research project.
- Explain the context in which the research project research was set.
- Identify the research strategy adopted and the reasons for its choice.
- List the main findings, conclusions and recommendations flowing from the research.
- *N.B. Detail related to the specific project may be added.*

Version 2: PowerPoint slide using design template

Objectives for a presentation

- Describe the purpose of the research project.
- Explain the context in which the research project research was set.
- Identify the research strategy adopted and the reasons for its choice.
- List the main findings, conclusions and recommendations flowing from the research.

N.B. Detail related to the specific project may be added.

Version 3: PowerPoint slide using more colour

Objectives for a presentation

- Describe the purpose of the research project.
- Explain the context in which the research project research was set.
- Identify the research strategy adopted and the reasons for its choice.
- List the main findings, conclusions and recommendations flowing from the research.

n.b. Detail related to the specific project may be added.

Version 4: PowerPoint slide with photograph inserted

Objectives for a presentation

- Describe the purpose of the research project.
- Explain the context in which the research project research was set.
- Identify the research strategy adopted and the reasons for its choice.
- List the main findings, conclusions and recommendations flowing from the research.
- *N.B. Detail related to the specific project may be added.*

Version 5: PowerPoint slide with space for audience to add notes

Objectives for a presentation

- Describe the purpose of the research project.
- Explain the context in which the research project research was set.
- Identify the research strategy adopted and the reasons for its choice.
- List the main findings, conclusions and recommendations flowing from the research.
- *N.B. Detail related to the specific project may be added.*

Box 14.13 Using powerpoint to your advantage

Let's face it, PowerPoint presentations can be dull and boring! But we all continue to rely on them to deliver information. Harvard University psychology professor Stephen Kosslyn (2007) in his new book, *Clear and to the Point* has some useful tips on keeping the audience awake.

Kosslyn's main points are:

Keep it simple. Don't include so much information that the audience loses the thread of your argument. Kosslyn thinks that telling them too much will leave them overwhelmed, disoriented and irritated. The rule of thumb: an effective presentation is organised around a central message, everything you include should reinforce that message. If in doubt, leave it out.

Tell them what they need to know. Don't assume too much knowledge on the part of the audience. Too many bullet points and too much industry jargon may confuse your message. Your audience will spend its time trying to decipher your "code" rather than listening. Be clear. Don't treat listeners like insiders unless they are.

Know the audience. Tailor the material to fit the audience's interests and concerns. A listener who feels personally connected with the material will be more likely to consider it and remember it. People will listen and remember only if you're telling them something they want to know.

Use visuals only to clarify. PowerPoint has so many clever features that we are all tempted to overdo the charts, graphs and other visual attractions. Less is more.

Give the audience time to digest. Build in breaks. Use relevant anecdotes (or even jokes) to lighten the content-heavy parts of your presentation. This will give your audience the opportunity to digest the details. The rule of thumb: make sure your interjections help illustrate your point, and don't run the risk of offending your audience.

Source: article by Loeb, Marshall (2007) *Colorado Spring Gazette*, 23 Sept. Available online at: http://www.gazette.com/articles/audience_27641 article.html/information_powerpoint.html.

You may want to supplement your pre-prepared slides with the use of the whiteboard. This may be useful for explaining points in relation to questions you receive. A word of warning here: ensure that you use dry markers that can be wiped from the board. A vain attempt to erase the results of a permanent pen in front of your audience will do nothing to enhance your confidence. Ensuring that you have dry wipe markers (use only black and blue pens – red and green are too faint), and checking computers and overhead projectors before the presentation, serve to emphasise the need for careful preparation.

Making the presentation

The first thing to say here is: don't worry about nerves. As Janner (1984:15) says: 'Confidence comes with preparation, practice and training.' Your audience will expect you to be a little nervous. Indeed, without some nervous tension before your presentation it is unlikely you will do yourself justice. Be positive about your presentation and your report. Trial your presentation on a friend to ensure that it flows logically and smoothly and that you can deliver it in the allotted time. In our experience most students put too much material in their presentations, although they worry beforehand that they have not got enough.

It is important that your presentation has a clear structure. We can do no better than repeat the words of a famous evangelist: when asked how he held the attention of his audience, he replied 'First I tell them what I'm going to say, then I say it, then I tell them what I've said' (Parry 1991:17). Parry (1991) notes that audiences like to know where they are going, they like to know how they are progressing on the journey, and they like to know when they have arrived.

Finally some practical points that will help.

- Think about whether you would prefer to sit or stand at the presentation. The former may be better to foster debate, the latter is likely to give you a sense of 'control' (Rawlins 1999). Which one you choose may depend upon the circumstances of the presentation, including the approach you wish to adopt, the room layout, the equipment you are using and your preferred style.
- Consider how you will deal with difficult questions. Rehearse these and your answers in your mind so that you can deal with them confidently during the presentation.
- Avoid jargon.
- Check the room before the presentation to ensure you have everything you need, you are happy and familiar with the layout, and all your equipment is working.

14.8 Summary

- Writing is a powerful way of clarifying your thinking.
- Writing is a creative process, which needs the right conditions if it is to produce successful results.
- Your project report should have a clear structure that enables you to develop a clear storyline.
- Your report should be laid out in such a way that your reader finds all the information readily accessible.
- You should try to develop a clear, simple writing style that will make reading the report an easy and enjoyable experience.
- Spelling and grammatical errors should be avoided.
- Do not think of your first draft as your last. Be prepared to rewrite your report several times until you think it is the best you can do.
- Failing to prepare for your presentation is preparing to fail.
- Visual aids will enhance the understanding of your audience and lend your presentation professionalism.
- Remember: tell them what you're going to say, say it, then tell them what you've said.

Self-check questions

Help with these questions is available at the end of the chapter.

14.1 Your project tutor has returned your draft project report with the suggestion that you make a clearer distinction between your results and your conclusions. How will you go about this?

14.2 Why is it considered good practice to acknowledge the limitations of your research in the project report?

14.3 Look again at the quote from Wright Mills cited early in Section 14.5. Rewrite this so that his idea is communicated to the reader in the clearest way possible.

14.4 There are other problems that must be avoided when repositioning sections of your report in the redrafting processes. What are they?

14.5 Look at the PowerPoint slide below and comment on any weaknesses.

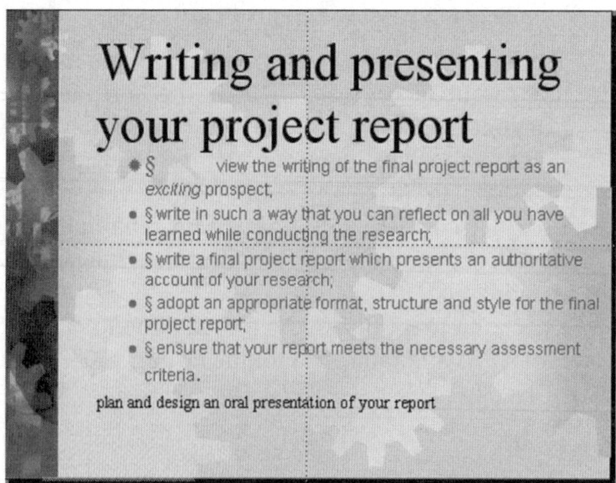

Review and discussion questions

14.6 Draft a plan for your dissertation, show it to your friends and compare your plan with those they have drafted. Explain the reason for any differences between your plan and those of your friends.

14.7 Look through several of the refereed academic journals that relate to your subject area. Choose an article that is based upon some primary research and note the structure of the article. Decide whether you agree with the way in which the author has structured the article and think of ways in which you may have done this differently.

14.8 Share pieces of your writing with a group of your friends. Look at the example in Box 14.10 and subject all the pieces to the 'write clearer sentences' test.

Progressing your research project

Writing your project report

- Design a clear structure for your report that broadly fits the structure suggested in Section 14.3. Ensure that the structure you design accommodates a clear storyline and meets the expectations of your audience.
- Write the report's abstract. Remember that you will need to rewrite this when you have finished your first draft.
- Compile the main body of the report. How will you ensure that the literature review relates to the following chapters? What method will you adopt to make the distinction between result and conclusions?
- Give your report the 'reader-friendly' test to ensure that the style is easy to read and free from avoidable errors.

References

BBC News Online (2007) 'Privacy rights 'fragile' in 2007', 31 Dec. Available at: http://news.bbc.co.uk/1/hi/technology/7165778.stm [Accessed 24 May 2008.]

Becker, H. (2008) *Writing for Social Scientists*. Chicago, IL.:University of Chicago Press.

Bloom, B. (ed.) (1971) *Taxonomy of Educational Objectives: Cognitive Domain*. New York: McKay.

Day, R. (1998) *How to Write and Publish a Scientific Paper* (5th edn). Phoenix, AZ: Oryx Press.

Day, R. and Gastel. B. (2006) *How to Write and Publish a Scientific Paper* (6th edn). Cambridge: Cambridge University Press.

Easterby-Smith, M., Thorpe, R. and Jackson, P. (2008) *Management Research* (3rd edn). London: Sage.

Emerald Group Publishing (2006) 'Writing for an Emerald publication: instructions for writing a structured abstract'. Available at: http://info.emeraldinsight.com/authors/guides/abstracts.htm [Accessed 25 May 2008.]

Goldsmith, R. and Flynn, L. (2006) 'Psychological and behavioral drivers of online clothing purchase', *Journal of Fashion Marketing and Management*, Vol. 8, No. 1, pp. 84–95.

Griffiths, M. (1993) 'Productive writing', *The New Academic*, Autumn, pp. 29–31.

Janner, G. (1984) *Janner on Presentations*. London: Business Books Ltd.

Kosslyn, S. (2007) *Clear and to the Point: 8 Psychological Principles for Compelling PowerPoint Presentations*. New York: Oxford University Press.

Möller, C., Weiermair, K. and Wintersberger, E. (2007) 'The changing travel behaviour of Austria's ageing population and its impact on tourism', *Tourism Review*, Vol. 62, Nos. 3/4, pp. 15–20.

Parry, H. (1991) *Successful Business Presentations*. Kingston-upon-Thames: Croner.

Pearsall, J. (ed.) (1998) *The New Oxford English Dictionary*. Oxford: Oxford University Press.

Phillips, E.M. and Pugh, D.S. (2005) *How to get a PhD* (3rd edn). Maidenhead: Open University Press.

Raimond, P. (1993) *Management Projects: Design. Research and Presentation*. London: Chapman & Hall.

Rawlins, K. (1999) *Presentation and Communication Skills: A Handbook for Practitioners*. London: Emap Healthcare Ltd.

Richards, P. (1986) 'Risk', in H. Becker, *Writing for Social Scientists*. Chicago, IL: University of Chicago Press, pp. 108–20.

Robson, C. (2002) *Real World Research* (2nd edn). Oxford: Blackwell.

Rowntree, D. (1987) *Assessing Students: How Shall We Know Them?* (revised edn). London: Harper & Row.

Smith, C.B. (1991) *A Guide to Business Research*. Chicago, IL: Nelson-Hall.

Veroff, J. (2001) 'Writing', in K. Rudestam and R. Newton. R. (eds), *Surviving your Dissertation* (2nd edn). Newbury Park, CA: Sage.

Wright Mills, C. (1970) 'On intellectual craftsmanship', in C. Wright Mills, *The Sociological Imagination*. London: Pelican.

Further reading

Becker, H. (2008) *Writing for Social Scientists*. Chicago, IL: University of Chicago Press. This is a highly readable book, full of anecdotes, from an expert in the field. It is rich in ideas about how writing may be improved. Most of these have been developed by Becker from his own writing and teaching. Such is the emphasis that Becker puts on rewriting that the title would more accurately be 'Rewriting for Social Scientists'.

Day, R. and Gastel, B. (2006) *How to Write and Publish a Scientific Paper* (6th edn). *Cambridge: Cambridge University Press.* This takes the reader through the whole process, with a host of useful advice. It is funny and irreverent but none the less valuable for that!

Fisher, C. (2004) *Researching and Writing a Dissertation*. Harlow: FT Prentice Hall. Chapter 6 has lots of useful tips for the writing-up process.

Rawlins, K. (1999) *Presentation and Communication Skills: A Handbook for Practitioners*. Basingstoke: Palgrave MacMillan. A very useful and practical guide for the inexperienced.

Smith, C.B. (1991) *A Guide to Business Research*. Chicago, IL: Nelson-Hall. Chapters 7–10 provide an excellent introduction to writing for business and management researchers.

Case 14
James' consultancy report on managers' financial information needs

Radisson Hotel, St Petersburg
Source: Alex Segre/Alamy

James, the Area Financial Controller (London) in the Europe, Middle East & Africa (EMEA) region of an international hotel group, is currently studying for a part-time Masters degree. As part of the programme, he is required to complete a consultancy project for an in-house client within his own organisation.

Aware of James' ongoing studies, the Regional Vice-President (Finance), who is based in Brussels, telephoned with the following proposition:

> *James, we've been set a new five-year bottom-line profit target of €300 m for the region. As part of the strategy to achieve the target we need to improve our financial management decision-making at the hotel property level – would you like to get involved with this in relation to your Masters consultancy project?*

From James' point of view, the Vice-President's request for the assignment was timely for two reasons. Firstly, it fitted conveniently with the need to develop a consultancy project for his studies. Secondly, he had already been stimulated by the work of Graham and Harris (1999) on *Developing a Profit Planning Framework* for another major international hotel chain to begin his own assessment and testing of the practicability of applying marginal analysis in one of his London hotels. Consequently, after discussion with his project tutor, James accepted the Regional Vice-President's short brief. This stated:

> *In the light of current best practice, assess the financial reporting for decision-making at the properties in the region and submit a report to me recommending the future financial information needs of managers, together with a training and development strategy to support the implementation of your recommendations.*

After discussing his ideas and agreeing a suitable consultancy proposal with his project tutor, James made a formal presentation to the Regional Vice-President's EMEA Financial Management Board in Brussels. Whilst the proposal included the purpose of the investigation and a method for determining the current and future financial information needs of managers, the core of the proposal was the implementation of marginal accounting techniques across the EMEA region, adapted from Graham and Harris' (1999) conceptual framework. The Board liked the presentation and asked James to commence the assignment.

With the guidance of his project tutor, James began work by spending time in the university library getting to grips with books and articles relating to the theory and application of marginal accounting techniques and searching the Internet for possible accounting firm and hospitality consulting firm reports on implementing the techniques in hotels. He also began reading Wickham and Wickham's (2008) *Management Consulting* and Thomas' (2003) *High-Performance Consulting Skills* in order to gain an understanding of what the consulting process entailed. Concurrently with the desk research, he arranged interview visits to a number of department managers across the EMEA region to discover their opinions as to the relevance of the financial information they were receiving for day-to-day decision-making purposes.

Analysis of James' interview responses revealed a mismatch between the information being produced by the hotel property financial controllers and the type of decisions being taken by managers; in effect, financial controllers were producing reports by departments whilst managers were making decisions by market segment. James realised this situation was primarily due to the accounting systems being used in the hotel industry. Most hotel companies use the *Uniform System of Accounts for the Lodging Industry* (2006), the industry standard based on the traditional departmental method of operating hotels, i.e. rooms (bedrooms), food (restaurants) and beverage (bars). Whilst *USALI* is a widely accepted hotel accounting system, its emphasis is on controlling and reporting (the past) to the corporate hierarchy rather than producing information for decision making (for the future), so was not conducive to achieving the VP's objective of improving decision-making at the properties. In fact, this was the very reason James had been investigating and assessing the case for marginal analysis in the company. Marginal analysis, he believed, could provide an important first step along the road to providing more relevant financial information for managers' routine, day-to-day, decision-making. Thus, it became clear to James that both the hotel property financial controllers and department managers should produce (financial controllers) and use (department managers) marginal accounting information in reports for routine decision-making.

Having completed the interviews, analysed the responses and read the relevant books, articles and consulting surveys, James felt that he was ready to begin the task of drafting his report for the VP's Financial Management Board in Brussels. To assist him in the design and preparation of a suitable report, James had made reference to Sally Garratt's (1991) *How to be a Consultant* and Calvert Markham's (1997) *Practical Management Consultancy*. He made an appointment with his project tutor to show him his primary and secondary findings and to ask his advice on the structure, content and layout of the report. Among other issues, James' tutor emphasised that a critical element of report writing was to address the 'brief' and reflect on the 'audience'.

References

Garratt, S. (1991) *How to Be a Consultant.* Aldershot: Gower.

Graham, I. and Harris, P. (1999) 'Development of a profit planning framework in an international hotel chain: A case study', *International Journal of Contemporary Hospitality Management*, Vol. 11, No. 5, pp. 198–208.

Hotel Association of New York City (2006) *Uniform System of Accounts for the Lodging industry.* East Lansing: American Hotel and Lodging Educational Institute.

Markham, C. (1997) *Practical Management Consultancy* (3rd edn). Milton Keynes: Accountancy Books (ICAE&W).

Thomas , M. (2003) *High-Performance Consulting Skills.* London: Thorgood.

Wickham, P. and Wickham, L. (2008) *Management Consulting: Delivering an Effective Project* (3rd edn). Harlow: Pearson Education.

Questions

1 Draft an outline structure of headings that would be broadly suitable for the main body of a consultancy report for James' client (including James' report) and explain the purpose of such a report.

2 Outline the content that you would expect James to include under each of the 'main headings' you have proposed for the report.
3 Outline the purpose and content of an 'executive summary' in a consultancy report.

Additional case studies relating to material covered in this chapter are available via the book's Companion Website, **www.pearsoned.co.uk/saunders**. They are:

- Writing Lata's project report
- Amina's story
- Akasma's draft disappointment.

Self-check answers

14.1 This is easier said than done. Start by going through your results chapter, continually asking yourself 'Did I find this out?' You will probably weed out a lot of things that you have thought about that are related to points you found out. These belong in the conclusions (or discussion) chapter.

Now turn to the conclusions chapter, asking yourself the question: 'Is this a reflection of what I found out?' If the points are a repeat of what you covered in your findings section, then cut them out and make sure you write reflections on the findings.

14.2 It shows that you have thought about your research design. It demonstrates that you have insight into the various ways of pursuing research. Remember that there is no perfect research design. Look again at Section 5.4. This asked the question, 'How do you know that the answer to the research question(s) is the correct one?' The answer, of course, is that in the literal sense of the question you cannot know. All you can do is reduce the possibility of getting the answer wrong.

14.3 Academic writing is often difficult to understand. This is not usually because the subject matter is complex or the thoughts profound. It is because the writer thinks it necessary to write in an 'academic' way.

14.4 The 'road map' you announced in the introduction may not now be correct. The previews and summaries at the beginning and end of the relevant chapters may need changing. A more serious potential problem is that the storyline may be altered. This should not be the case. Nonetheless, it is important to reread the whole report to ensure that the repositioning does not alter its sense of coherence.

14.5.1 Well, it looks a bit of a mess! The title is too big: it is out of proportion to the rest of the text. Not all the points are 'bulleted', and the spaces between the bullet and text are not consistent. There are three different fonts and, most importantly, there is too much text on the slide. All of these faults are easily rectifiable. It is worth playing around with it and making a few mistakes – it's a good way of learning!

Get ahead using resources on the Companion Website at:
www.pearsoned.co.uk/saunders

- Improve your SPSS and NVivo research analysis with practice tutorials.
- Save time researching on the Internet with the Smarter Online Searching Guide.
- Test your progress using self-assessment questions.
- Follow live links to useful websites.